ANNUAL REVIEW
of
OCEAN AFFAIRS:

LAW and POLICY,
MAIN DOCUMENTS
1985 - 1987

ANNUAL REVIEW

of

OCEAN AFFAIRS:

LAW and POLICY, MAIN DOCUMENTS 1985 - 1987

Volumes I & II

Compiled and Edited by the United Nations
Office for Ocean Affairs and the Law of the Sea

1989
UNIFO Publishers, Inc.
Sarasota, Florida

Published by UNIFO Publishers, Inc.
P.O. Box 3858   Sarasota, FL 34230

ISBN: 0-89111-025-9
ISSN: 1040-824X

Manufactured in the United States of America

The paper used in this publication meets the minimum requirements of American National Standard for
Information Sciences — Permanence of Paper for Printed Library Materials, ANSI Z39.48-1984.   ∞ ™

CONTENTS

VOLUME I

* - References aligned with "Document" are document citations.

2. INFRINGEMENT OF SAFETY ZONES

VI   SALVAGE AND RELATED ISSUES 343

1. PREPARATION OF A DRAFT CONVENTION

VII   SPECIAL ISSUES 353

1. ILLICIT DRUG TRAFFICKING

A. Preparation of a Draft Convention

B. Control Measures

2. UNLAWFUL ACTS AGAINST THE SAFETY OF NAVIGATION AND OFFSHORE PLATFORMS

A. Preventive Measures

B. Preparation of a Draft Convention

VOLUME II

3. POLLUTION FROM DUMPING

3. MARINE MAMMALS

XII MARINE SCIENTIFIC RESEARCH

1. INTERNATIONAL CO-OPERATION AND THE CONSENT RÉGIME

2. LEGAL STATUS OF OCEAN DATA ACQUISITION SYSTEMS (ODAS)

PUBLISHER'S NOTE

No body of international law is in such a dynamic state of growth as is the Law of the Sea. In producing the first two volumes of this major new series, we have become increasingly aware of the monumental task entrusted to the United Nations in creating hundreds -- if not thousands -- of new rules and regulations concerning every conceivable aspect of ocean affairs.

A sizeable corpus of legal instruments and other documents evolved from 1985 through 1987 which, in itself, represents remarkable progress in applying the collective will of 159 sovereign nation states to a territory extending over seventy percent of the earth's surface! This continuing momentum translates into a yearly compilation of important documentation which, we have been assured, can be contained in a single, annual volume, thus keeping subscribers up to date. Should it prove necessary, however, supplements will be issued as required.

Producing the first two volumes of this complex reference work has been a professional challenge. We gratefully acknowledge the tireless assistance and patience extended to us by the United Nations Office for Ocean Affairs and the Law of the Sea during the many months of production. Now, having launched this ongoing reference series, we can only hope it will justify the painstaking endeavour of all concerned by ably serving its discerning readership.

John Burn, Publisher
UNIFO
Sarasota, Florida
March, 1989

PREFACE

The United Nations Office for Ocean Affairs and the Law of the Sea each year prepares a summary report to the General Assembly on main developments in ocean affairs, particularly those relating to the 1982 United Nations Convention on the Law of the Sea.

The Convention deals with all aspects of ocean space and its uses; it therefore encompasses many distinct subject areas and thus, involves numerous international and regional organizations with legislative and policy-making functions. There are, moreover, important interrelationships and recurring themes in law of the sea subjects. The main purpose, consequently, of the annual reports on the Law of the Sea is to promote an overall understanding of the main developments and dominant themes in this important field of international law and policy.

In view of the great demand for ready access to the main international materials which record the developments in the many sectors involved, this new documentary series has been instituted by the United Nations to assist individuals and institutions interested in ocean affairs.

The Annual Reviews will thus present the annual reports on the Law of the Sea and selected extracts from reports, studies, working papers, etc. of the United Nations and other international organizations, together with additional references, in order to provide a comprehensive overview of the relevant developments on legal and policy matters at the intergovernmental level which are described in the annual reports. They do not include the documentation of the Preparatory Commission for the International Sea-Bed Authority and for the International Tribunal on the Law of the Sea, which will be published separately.

These first two volumes cover the years 1985-1987; subsequent volumes will be issued annually. The documentary materials have been organized according to the main subject areas involved and an index provides additional assistance in researching the many aspects of ocean affairs. The index will be cumulative so that it will be possible to trace the origins and prior history of developments.

It may be noted, that since the annual reports on the Law of the Sea to the General Assembly are prepared well before the end of a year, in some cases the volumes contain material not taken into account in the annual report for that year.

The preparation of this new documentary series has only been made possible with the close co-operation of the international organizations concerned.

I

MAIN DEVELOPMENTS
IN OCEAN AFFAIRS

1.   United Nations Reports and Resolutions

2.   Implications of the Law of the Sea
   Convention for Other Instruments

1

United Nations Reports and Resolutions

UN General Assembly   A/40/923
Fortieth Session   27 November 1985
                                                      Extract

Law of the Sea

Report of the Secretary-General

CONTENTS

INTRODUCTION

1.   The 1982 United Nations Convention on the Law of the Sea[1] continues to enjoy wide support among States, as evidenced by the unprecedented number of signatures appended to it and the growing number of ratifications. Even before its entry into force, the Convention is exerting a considerable influence on all aspects of the law of the sea, as well as on marine affairs in general. Some of the important developments are highlighted in the present report, which is submitted to the General Assembly in compliance with its resolution 39/73 of 13 December 1984 requesting the Secretary-General, *inter alia*, to report on the developments relating to the Convention and on the implementation of that resolution. The report is divided into two parts. Part One contains an overview of the impact of the Convention on State practice and on the mandates and activities of international organizations concerned with marine affairs, decisions of the International Court of Justice and other tribunals, and information on other developments relating to the law of the sea. Part Two outlines the activities of the Office of the Special Representative of the Secretary-General for the Law of the Sea in the discharge of its mandate under the medium-term plan. The present report is the second of such reports submitted to the General Assembly; the first report was submitted to the Assembly at its thirty-ninth session (A/39/647 and Corr.1).

PART ONE

DEVELOPMENTS RELATING TO THE UNITED NATIONS CONVENTION ON THE LAW OF THE SEA

I. STATUS OF THE CONVENTION

2.   The United Nations Convention on the Law of the Sea closed for signature on 9 December 1984, having received a total of 159 signatures.

3.   Upon signature, 36 States and one of the entities referred to in article 305, paragraph 1, made declarations under article 310 of the Convention. Among those, six States[2] made declarations in accordance with article 287 with respect to the choice of procedure for the

settlement of disputes concerning the interpretation or application of the Convention and one entity[3] made a declaration in accordance with annex IX, article 2 of the Convention. Declarations made upon signature were issued by the Legal Office and are also included in **The Law of the Sea - Status of the United Nations Convention on the Law of the Sea,**[4] prepared by the Office of the Special Representative of the Secretary-General for the Law of the Sea.

4. In accordance with article 308, paragraph 1, the Convention will enter into force 12 months after the date of the deposit of the sixtieth instrument of ratification or accession. As at 19 November 1985, 25 instruments of ratification have been deposited with the Secretary-General, as follows: Bahamas; Bahrain; Belize; Cameroon; Cuba; Egypt; Fiji; Gambia; Ghana; Guinea; Iceland; Iraq; Ivory Coast; Jamaica; Mali; Mexico; Philippines; Saint Lucia; Senegal; Sudan; Togo; Tunisia; United Republic of Tanzania; Zambia and the United Nations Council for Namibia.

5. Upon ratification, five States (Cuba, Egypt, Iceland, the Philippines and Tunisia) made declarations under article 310 of the Convention. Bulgaria, the Byelorussian Soviet Socialist Republic, Czechoslovakia and the Union of Soviet Socialist Republics have lodged objections to the declaration of the Philippines on the grounds that it is incompatible with article 310 of the Convention. It will be recalled that article 309 provides that no reservation or exceptions may be made to the Convention unless expressly permitted by other articles of the Convention. Under article 310, however, States are entitled to make declarations or statements. Article 310 reads as follows: "Article 309 does not preclude a State, when signing, ratifying or acceding to the Convention from making declarations or statements, however phrased or named, with a view, *inter alia*, to the harmonization of its laws and regulations with the provisions of the Convention, provided that said declarations or statements do not purport to exclude or to modify the legal effect of the provisions of the Convention in their application to that State." The texts of declarations made by these States were issued by the Legal Office and are also included in **The Law of the Sea - Status of the United Nations Convention on the Law of the Sea.**[4] This publication also contains other declarations, objections or notes with respect to declarations made upon ratification.

II. STATE PRACTICE AND NATIONAL POLICY

6. The provisions of the Convention have continued to exert an important influence on the development of national policy with respect to law of the sea matters. Since the submission of the report of the Secretary-General to the thirty-ninth session of the General Assembly (A/39/647 and Corr.1), further developments and trends in national policy regarding marine affairs are to be noted. From the information received or collected by the Office of the Special Representative of the Secretary-General for the Law of the Sea, it is seen that a number of States have adopted national legislation dealing with a variety of marine issues, which, in particular, relate to such matters as the determination of the baselines, the breadth and status of the territorial sea, the establishment of exclusive economic zones, the definition of the continental shelf and the delimitation of maritime boundaries between States with opposite or adjacent coasts.

7. The Convention has set clear limits for areas falling under national sovereignty and jurisdiction - a limit of 12 nautical miles for the territorial sea, 24 nautical miles for the contiguous zone and 200 miles for the exclusive economic zone. It was the historic failure to establish specific limits to the territorial sea which gave rise to uncertainty as to the validity of

claims to extended areas of territorial seas. The widespread agreement to a 12-mile territorial sea as reflected in the Convention has been increasingly confirmed by the practice of a large number of States.

8.   In his report (A/39/647 and Corr.1) the Secretary-General had noted that some 80 States have established territorial seas of 12 nautical miles. Since then several States have enacted legislation on the territorial sea. Among the latter group of States, five have adopted a 12-mile territorial sea[5] and three have adopted legislation setting out specific co-ordinates to establish the outer limits of the territorial sea within the 12-mile limit.[6] The legislation of two States expressly sets out the legal status of the territorial sea[7] consistent with the Convention on the Law of the Sea.

9.   At present a total of some 89 States have a territorial sea of 12 nautical miles in breadth[8] while 22 still have legislation establishing the limits of the territorial sea beyond 12 nautical miles.[9] It is noteworthy that the legislation of these States pre-dates the adoption of the 1982 Convention on the Law of the Sea while recent legislation on this issue has largely conformed to the relevant provisions of the Convention as States continue to harmonize their national legislation with the Convention.

10.   There are 79 States from all regions which have promulgated laws or decrees establishing exclusive economic zones or exclusive fishery zones of up to 200 nautical miles.[10] The new concept of the exclusive economic zone as embodied in the Convention on the Law of the Sea has continued to receive widespread support from the international community. The International Court of Justice itself has stated that this concept "may be regarded as part of modern international law".[11]

11.   As has been noted in the report of the Secretary-General (A/39/647 and Corr.1), an examination of the maritime legislation of States reveals that several of these legislative enactments diverge, sometimes in important respects, from the provisions on the exclusive economic zone as provided for in the Convention. Several of those laws were based on earlier versions of the text, particularly the Informal Single Negotiating Text.[12] The provisions of these informal negotiating texts were subject to change and indeed were changed over the years. Thus, the legislation of a number of coastal States does not fully reflect all those modifications made to the texts which are now embodied in the United Nations Convention on the Law of the Sea. Some of these modifications represented delicate compromises resulting from difficult and prolonged negotiations. However, some States have already modified their legislation to conform to the relevant provisions of the Convention and others are in the course of reviewing their legislation.

12.   With respect to the continental shelf, 17 States have enacted legislation incorporating the concept of natural prolongation as embodied in the Convention.[13] At least two of these States have enacted legislation incorporating some of the more detailed technical provisions of the Convention.[14]

III. SETTLEMENT OF CONFLICTS AND DISPUTES

13.   Expanded coastal States jurisdiction over adjacent maritime areas that has been such a distinctive feature of the new legal régime for the seas has inevitably created several potential conflicts and disputes among States. The Convention, by providing a legal order for the seas, has promoted the peaceful resolution of such conflicts. Moreover, the Convention itself

contains a mechanism for the peaceful settlement of disputes concerning its interpretation and application.

14.　Several disputes with respect to maritime delimitation have already been resolved either by the conclusion of delimitation agreements or by international adjudication or other forms of peaceful settlement. As an example of the latter, the dispute between Argentina and Chile in the Beagle Channel was submitted to the mediation of Pope John Paul II. Through this mediation Argentina and Chile were able to conclude on 18 October 1984 a Treaty of Peace and Friendship, which, *inter alia*, dealt with the maritime boundary in the Beagle Channel. Argentina ratified the Treaty on 14 March 1985 and Chile on 11 April. On 1 May, both States signed the Treaty at Rome in the Vatican. The Parties have begun implementing the provisions of the Treaty.

15.　Among the recent cases concerning maritime delimitation submitted to third party procedure for the settlement of disputes are the disputes between Guinea and Guinea-Bissau and between Malta and the Libyan Arab Jamahiriya. The first was submitted to an arbitral tribunal and the second to the International Court of Justice. The Court is also seized with an Application for Revision and Interpretation of the Judgment of 24 February 1982 in the case concerning the continental shelf (Tunisia/Libyan Arab Jamahiriya).[11]

Guinea - Guinea-Bissau

16.　On 14 February 1985, the Arbitral Award for the delimitation of Maritime Boundaries between Guinea and Guinea-Bissau was handed down.[15] The Tribunal was posed with the following questions: first, whether the Convention of 12 May 1886 between France and Portugal - the former metropolitan countries - had determined the maritime frontier between the two west African States; second, whether the protocols and annexes of that Convention were of any juridical value in its interpretation; and finally, in the light of the response to those questions, what was the boundary line which delimited the maritime areas appertaining respectively to Guinea-Bissau and to Guinea?

17.　The Award held that the 1886 Convention had not determined the maritime frontier between those two States and that the protocols and annexes played a significant role in the interpretation of the Treaty. The Tribunal noted that the Convention was essentially concerned with land territory.

18.　The Tribunal, as it was required, delineated a single boundary covering the territorial sea, the exclusive economic zone and the continental shelf. It is noteworthy that the Tribunal declared that the essential objective of its decision was to reach an equitable solution within the context of article 74, paragraph 1, and article 83, paragraph 1, of the United Nations Convention on the Law of the Sea.[16]

Libyan Arab Jamahiriya

19.　On 3 June 1985, the International Court of Justice handed down its judgement in the case concerning the continental shelf between Libyan Arab Jamahiriya and Malta. The Court was requested to decide what principles and rules of international law were applicable to the delimitation of the continental shelf between Malta and the Libyan Arab Republic, and how in practice such principles and rules can be applied by the two States.

20. In its judgement, the Court stated what principles and rules of international law were applicable to the delimitation of the continental shelf between the two States and the circumstances and factors to be taken into consideration in order to achieve an equitable delimitation. Accordingly, in this case, it declared that an equitable result should be obtained first by drawing between the 13° 50' and the 15° 10' meridians a median line, of which every point is equidistant from the low water mark of the relevant coasts of Malta, on the one hand, and of the Libyan Arab Jamahiriya, on the other, and by then transposing this line northward by 18' and as to intersect the 15° 10' E meridian at a latitude of approximately 34° 30' N.[17]

21. In its decision, the Court made some significant observations on the consequences for the delimitation of the continental shelf between States of the adoption of the concept of the exclusive economic zone as embodied in the United Nations Convention on the Law of the Sea. The following is a brief synopsis of these observations.

22. The Court noted that, although the case related only to the delimitation of the continental shelf and not to that of the exclusive economic zone, the principles and rules underlying the latter concept could not be left out of consideration. The Court stated that, as the 1982 Convention demonstrated, the two institutions - continental shelf and exclusive economic zone - were linked together in modern law. Since the rights enjoyed by a State over its continental shelf would also be possessed by it over the sea-bed and subsoil of any exclusive economic zone which it might proclaim, one of the relevant circumstances to be taken into account for the delimitation of the continental shelf of a State was the legally permissible extent of the exclusive economic zone pertaining to that State. It added that this did not mean that the concept of the continental shelf had been absorbed by that of the exclusive economic zone; it did, however, signify that greater importance was to be attributed "to elements, such as distance from the coast, which are common to both concepts".[18]

23. A further implication noted by the Court was that since the development of the law enabled a State to claim that its continental shelf extended up to as far as 200 miles from the coast, "whatever the geological characteristics of the corresponding sea-bed and subsoil", there was no reason to ascribe any role to geological or geophysical factors within that distance, either in verifying the legal title of the State concerned or in proceeding to a delimitation as between their claims.[19]

24. In this connection, the Court made some significant comments on the role of natural prolongation on the delimitation of maritime areas. It observed that:

> "the idea of natural prolongation was not superseded by distance. What it did mean was that where the continental margin did not extend as far as 200 miles from the shore, natural prolongation, which in spite of its physical origin has throughout its history become more and more a complex and juridical concept, is in part defined by distance from the shore, irrespective of the physical nature of the intervening sea-bed and subsoil."[20]

25. As the law now stands, each coastal State is entitled to exercise sovereign rights over the continental shelf off its coasts for the purpose of exploring and exploiting its natural resources up to a distance of 200 miles from the baselines subject of course to delimitation with neighbouring States - whatever the physical or geological features of the sea-bed within the area comprised between the coast and the 200-mile limit.[21]

26.   The Court, however, warned that the introduction of the criterion of distance did not have the effect of establishing a principle of "absolute proximities" or of conferring upon the equidistance method of delimitation the status of a general rule, or an obligatory method of delimitation, or of a priority method to be tested in every case. It further observed that the fact that, in the circumstances of the case, the drawing of a median line constituted an appropriate first step in the delimitation process did not mean that an equidistance line will be an appropriate beginning in all cases, or even in cases of delimitation with respect to States with opposite coasts.[22]

27.   The Court, as it has done before,[23] did not consider that "a delimitation should be influenced by the relative economic position of the two States in question, in such a way that the area of continental shelf regarded as appertaining to the less rich of the two States would be somewhat increased in order to compensate for the inferiority in economic resources".[24]

28.   The International Court of Justice has continued to endorse the relevant provisions of the 1982 Convention and to develop in particular the jurisprudence relating to the delimitation of maritime areas by investing the delimitation provisions of the Convention with a specific content.

IV. OTHER DEVELOPMENTS RELATING TO THE LAW OF THE SEA

A. Peaceful uses

29.   There has been a growing tendency in the international community to promote the peaceful uses of the oceans. Indeed the peaceful uses of the oceans is a fundamental objective of the Convention on the Law of the Sea. In addition to the Convention, there has been a number of multilateral treaties and instruments which have the same objective. Among them are the Antarctic Treaty (1959), the Treaty Banning Nuclear Weapon Tests in the Atmosphere, In Outer Space and Under Water (Partial Test Ban Treaty) (1963), Treaty for the Prohibition of Nuclear Weapons in Latin America (Treaty of Tlatelolco) (1967), the Treaty on the Prohibition of the Emplacement of Nuclear Weapons and Other Weapons of Mass Destruction on the Sea-Bed and the Ocean Floor and in the Subsoil Thereof (Sea-Bed Treaty) (1971) and the various proposals to establish nuclear-weapon-free zones and zones of peace. Most of these instruments cover land territories as well as large areas of oceans.

30.   **Naval arms race.**   More recently the General Assembly itself has requested a comprehensive study on the naval arms race, on naval forces and naval arms systems, including maritime nuclear-weapons systems, with a view to analysing their possible implications for international security, for the freedom of the high seas, for international shipping routes and for the exploitation of marine resources, thereby facilitating the identification of possible areas for disarmament and confidence-building measures. This study has been transmitted to the General Assembly at its fortieth session in the report of the Secretary-General (A/40/535, annex).

31.   The study accords great weight to the impact of the United Nations Convention on the Law of the Sea on the strategic uses of the seas and contains a comprehensive review of the provisions of the Convention which may affect maritime activities and naval operations. It observes that the use of naval forces in the exercise of sovereign rights is legitimate. However, there are sometimes conflicts of interest between naval activities and non-military uses of the sea, just as there are conflicts between latent security threats and the freedom of navigation. It

urges that naval activities should take account, *inter alia*, of the legitimate interests of coastal States and that it is important that such activities should be compatible with the provisions of the Convention.

32.   The study observes that, in the context of naval activities, the early entry into force of the Convention on the Law of the Sea will give strong additional support to the security régime at sea. It therefore encourages its early entry into force and its full implementation.

33.   The study notes that the new law of the sea increases the national responsibilities of coastal States and consequently increases the need of many of those States to develop naval capabilities; but it warns, however, that the widened national responsibilities should not be misused as a justification for the expansion and utilization of naval force.

34.   The **South Pacific Nuclear Free Zone Treaty**. A recent example of the continuing trend to promote the peaceful uses of the oceans is the South Pacific Nuclear Free Zone Treaty. This instrument was adopted by the South Pacific Forum at Raratonga, Cook Islands, on 6 August 1985 and will enter into force when eight instruments of ratification have been deposited. The nuclear-free zone established by the Treaty extends from the western shores of the Australian continent to the western coast of the Latin American continent. It stretches north to the equator and south to Antarctica. Thus it abuts on the nuclear-weapon-free zones of Latin America and Antarctica.

35.   The Treaty prohibits the use, testing or stationing of nuclear explosive devices in the South Pacific. It leaves to each signatory State the right to decide for itself such questions as access of foreign vessels or aircraft to its ports and airfields. The rights of States under international law with regard to freedom of the high seas remain unaffected by the Treaty. Finally, it prohibits ocean dumping of nuclear wastes in the region.

36.   There are three protocols to the Treaty: the first invites France, the United States of America and the United Kingdom of Great Britain and Northern Ireland to apply key provisions of the Treaty to their South Pacific territories; the other two invite the five nuclear-weapon States not to use or threaten to use nuclear weapons against Parties to the Treaty and not to test nuclear explosive devices within the zone. These protocols have not yet been adopted.

B.   Maritime law

1.   Maritime safety and navigation

37.   Work has continued in the International Maritime Organization (IMO) with a view to amending the 1974 International Convention for the Safety of Life at Sea and the 1966 Load Line Convention and adopting a new convention to replace the 1910 Convention on Salvage and Assistance at Sea. A conference is envisaged in 1988 for the first two of these projects. The IMO Legal Committee is continuing its preparation of a draft revision of the Salvage Convention. This involves matters of both private and public law. In this connection, it may be noted that, *inter alia*, a proposal to provide special compensation to a salvor who has carried out specific preventive measures to protect the environment is under consideration. The fourteenth session of the IMO Assembly has adopted a number of recommendations relating to maritime safety. These include guidelines for vessel traffic services. New and

amended routeing systems other than traffic separation schemes have been adopted, subject to confirmation by the Assembly.

2. Rescue at sea and piracy

38. On 22 June 1985, the 1979 International Convention on Maritime Search and Rescue entered into force. Its main purpose is to facilitate co-operation between search and rescue (SAR) organizations and between those participating in SAR operations at sea by establishing the legal and technical basis for an international SAR plan. An annex to the Convention contains the technical requirements for ensuring the provision of adequate maritime SAR services off the coasts of the States Parties. The delimitation of SAR regions is established by agreement among the Parties. The Convention states that Parties should authorize immediate entry into their territorial sea of rescue units from other Parties solely for the purpose of search and rescue. The Convention also provides that ship reporting systems should be established where necessary to facilitate SAR operations. It is envisaged that a global maritime distress and safety system will be developed to support the SAR plan prescribed in the Convention. In this area IMO works closely with International Telecommunication Union (ITU), World Meteorological Organization (WMO), and INMARSAT (International Maritime Satellite). IMO has also developed a format for a ship reporting system and two manuals on search and rescue, the provisions of which are co-ordinated with the International Civil Aviation Organization (ICAO).

39. The principle of the duty to render assistance to persons in distress at sea which is embodied in the Convention on the Law of the Sea (art. 98) has special importance in relation to the rescue of asylum-seekers. The number of rescues made has decreased significantly in the past two years, thus giving greater importance to Rescue at Sea Resettlement Offers (RASRO) scheme of the Office of the United Nations High Commissioner for Refugees (UNHCR). In addition to the efforts of UNHCR, IMO keeps under continuing review information and proposals relevant to the rescue of asylum-seekers in distress at sea. Most recently the IMO Council in June 1985 expressed full support for the objective of promoting appropriate humanitarian measures to assist or rescue persons in distress at sea and adopted a decision urging Governments, organizations and ship owners concerned to intensify their efforts in ensuring that the necessary assistance is provided to any person in distress at sea. The Secretary-General of IMO is directed to continue consultations with all appropriate bodies of the United Nations, including UNHCR, in order to further these objectives.

40. Piracy and armed robbery against ships is of particular concern in such areas as West Africa, the Malacca Straits and the South China Sea. While there has been an encouraging decline in the percentage of boats attacked in the South China Sea the level of violence associated with such attacks has remained high. Under the Anti-Piracy Arrangements established by the Royal Thai Government, which has now been extended for a third year through the co-operation of a number of donor Governments, continuing efforts are being made including preventive sea and air patrols, follow-up investigation and prosecution of suspects and nation-wide registration of fishing boats. IMO and UNHCR also maintain close contacts on these questions, and IMO continues to study both rescue at sea and anti-piracy problems.

3. Conditions for registration of ships

41. The United Nations Conference on Conditions for Registration of Ships (United Nations Conference on Trade and Development (UNCTAD)) held the third part of its session in July

1985. At the fourth part, scheduled for 20 January to 7 February 1986, the Conference can be expected to finalize and adopt an international agreement concerning the conditions under which vessels should be accepted on national shipping registers. The outcome of this Conference is of direct relevance to the implementation of articles 91, 92 and 94 of the United Nations Convention on the Law of the Sea.

42. The principle according to which there must exist a genuine link between a ship and the State whose flag it flies is embodied in article 91 of the Convention. This article states moreover that each State shall fix the conditions for the grant of its nationality to ships, for the registration of ships in its territory and for the right to fly its flag. Article 94 of the Convention deals with the duties of the flag State with regard to vessels flying its flag and, in this respect, the Convention establishes international norms for the exercise of jurisdiction and control by flag States.

43. Although article 91 gives certain flexibility to a State to establish the conditions, it does, however, leave unresolved the issue as to what exactly are the elements which constitute the genuine link between a State and a vessel for the State to exercise effectively its jurisdiction and control in compliance with article 94. The Conference is attempting to resolve the issue by giving content at the international level to the notion of a genuine link. Such an international agreement would be complementary to the Convention on the Law of the Sea by establishing the minimum conditions for registering of ships without affecting the right of individual States to actually fix these conditions.

44. The Conference made considerable progress at the third part of its session and arrived at an agreed text on the contentious issues of national participation and management, manning and ownership of ships. These had been some of the most difficult areas in the negotiations: firstly, in view of the widely divergent interpretations between different countries or groups of countries of the concept of the genuine link and, secondly, in view of the very different systems and legislative provisions in this regard which exist in different countries with different economic systems.

4. Maritime labour law

45. The International Labour Office (ILO) is preparing for a Preparatory Technical Maritime Conference in 1986 and a full Maritime Session of the International Labour Conference in 1987. It is expected that these meetings will result in the adoption of new or revised international labour Conventions and Recommendations in 1987 on the following subjects: health protection and medical care for seafarers; seafarers welfare at sea and in ports; repatriation of seafarers; and social security protection for seafarers, including those serving in ships flying flags other than those of their own country.

46. **Offshore industrial installations**. The ILO Committee of Experts on the Application of Conventions and Recommendations, is examining the application by States of ILO Conventions to fixed and mobile installations used in the exploration and exploitation of offshore mineral and petroleum resources.[25] The Committee observed that reports from 53 Governments and a number of employers' or workers' organizations have revealed a variety of situations and a differing legislative approach to the problems raised by such installations, particularly in respect of an overlap of maritime law and land-based law. As to the legal nature of offshore installations, some countries make a distinction in their legislation as between mobile and fixed installations, which as a result are subject to different regulations:

mobile installations where defined as ships are thus subject to maritime legislation; fixed installations where regarded as land-based installations are thus subject to legislation determined on a case-by-case basis. In addition, there is a divergent approach in respect of jurisdiction, notably in cases where mobile installations are regarded as ships: some countries regard their legislation as applicable to offshore installations operating in their maritime zones, regardless of their nationality; others consider that the primary jurisdiction, even in their own territory, is that of the flag State, so that the responsibility for the application of ILO Conventions rests with the State where the craft is registered.

47. The ILO Joint Maritime Commission in September 1984, as noted in the report of the Secretary-General (A/39/647 and Corr.1), had adopted a resolution requesting that a study be undertaken together with IMO to determine which mobile units would be classified as ships and suggesting that there be an expert review of occupational safety, health and working conditions on board maritime mobile offshore units. The ILO Governing Body, at its February-March session in 1985, has since requested that a preliminary study be undertaken with a view to determining the main problems which should be examined in this very complex field.

48. The Committee of Experts has stated that it considers problems concerning the legal status of offshore industrial installations, the legislation applicable to workers thereon, the type of jurisdiction exercised by States over these installations, and the possible obligations arising from the licensing of the installation for the purposes of exploration and exploitation, to be of far-reaching consequence. The legal uncertainties revealed and the resulting lack of uniformity in the legislative approach to the problem may have adverse effects on the application of international labour conventions. Consequently, the possible adoption of standards on the conditions of work in offshore industrial activities will still require detailed legal analysis of such problems as have been outlined above. The Committee has once again, therefore, invited Governments to continue sending information on all those matters that will help clarify the legal questions involved.

49. Considering the relationship of many of these questions to provisions of the Convention on the Law of the Sea particularly articles 60 and 80, the Office of the Special Representative of the Secretary-General for the Law of the Sea has offered its advice and assistance to the ILO.

50. The ILO Committee has also stated that extensive research is needed into the actual conditions prevailing in these offshore activities, and that information on safety and health protection measures will be particularly useful. In this respect, it may be noted that the tripartite ILO Petroleum Committee will meet in April 1986 and will be examining developments and problems in the offshore petroleum industry, in particular in the fields of occupational safety and health and manpower planning.

C. Environmental law

1. Prevention and control of marine pollution from ships

51. **MARPOL 73/78.** The International Convention for the Prevention of Pollution from Ships, 1973, as modified by the Protocol of 1978 (MARPOL 73/78), now covers more than 80 per cent of the world's merchant tonnage and is in force with 38 States parties. Amendments to the Convention, adopted in 1984, will enter into force on 7 January 1986.

52.   The IMO Council at its fifty-fourth session noted the views and suggestions made on the adequate provision of reception facilities in ports (see art. 211 (6) (a) of the Convention on the Law of the Sea). IMO is to draw the attention of Governments to the fact that the provision of necessary reception facilities for oil and chemical residues is essential for the successful implementation of MARPOL 73/78.

53.   **Civil liability and compensation.** The 1984 Protocols amending the International Convention on Civil Liability for Oil Pollution Damage, 1969, and the International Convention on the Establishment of an International Fund for Compensation for Oil Pollution Damage, 1971, remain open for signature and ratification, and each has been signed by nine States. The 1984 Protocols increase liability limits for oil spill damages contained in the original conventions, extend the application of the conventions to a limit of 200 miles, cover the costs of preventive measures and restoration, and add new categories of vessels.

54.   The IMO Legal Committee has under consideration a possible new convention on liability and compensation for damage in connection with the carriage of noxious and hazardous substances by sea.

2.   Prevention and control of marine pollution from dumping

55.   **London Dumping Convention.**[26] The Ninth Consultative Meeting of 60 Contracting Parties to the Convention on the Prevention of Marine Pollution by Dumping of Wastes and Other Matter (London Dumping Convention (LDC), 1972), held in September 1985, adopted revised criteria for the allocation of substances to the annexes of the Convention including the Guidelines which supersede the existing Guidelines (LDC V/12, annex 2).[27] The meeting also dealt with incineration at sea (see also para. 70), monitoring and relations with other organizations, especially the United Nations Environment Programme (UNEP) and the Intergovernmental Oceanographic Commission (IOC). It considered other matters, including environmental hazards caused by the disposal at sea of persistent substances such as plastics and other persistent synthetic materials (including fishing nets). It concluded that the deliberate disposal of ship-generated wastes, whether or not such deliberate disposal is covered by annex V of MARPOL 73/78[28] or constitutes dumping under the London Dumping Convention, is none the less against the purposes of the Convention.

56.   The Consultative Meeting also examined the problem of the import and export of hazardous wastes for disposal at sea[29] and means to establish further control and to provide information needed on such transfrontier shipments. While the subject of transfrontier shipment of wastes has much broader implications than dumping at sea, the Consultative Meeting considered it desirable to evaluate the overall question in order to identify those areas that have direct relevance to dumping.

57.   While the London Dumping Convention deals specifically with the deliberate disposal of wastes at sea, it is becoming increasingly necessary for States to find ways and means of providing for regular review of waste disposal options in general. The London Dumping Convention Task Team 2000, in its report to the Contracting Parties recommended the calling of special conferences or symposia to review periodically specific waste or waste treatment and disposal techniques.

58.   **Dumping of radioactive wastes at sea and into the sea-bed.** The Ninth Consultative Meeting examined the report of an Expert Scientific Panel set up to examine the dumping at

sea of radioactive wastes. After consideration of the report and detailed discussion as to whether its suspension on dumping should be continued,[30] the Consultative Meeting decided to maintain the suspension of all dumping at sea of radioactive wastes and other matter to permit time for further studies and assessments, including that of the option of land-based disposal, and called upon Contracting Parties, *inter alia*, to develop procedures for the assessment of liability regarding State responsibility for damage to the environment of other States or to any other area of the environment resulting from such dumping.

59.   With regard to disposal into the sea-bed of high-level radioactive wastes, the Consultative Meeting agreed to defer further consideration of this matter to its next meeting. The Nuclear Energy Agency of the Organization for Economic Co-operation and Development (OECD/ NEA) reported to the Contracting Parties that the first phase of research to assess the feasibility of disposal of high-level radioactive wastes beneath the ocean floor was scheduled for completion in 1988 and that there was no plan for the time being to carry out any experiment involving the emplacement of such wastes into the sea-bed.

60.   The International Atomic Energy Agency (IAEA) is entrusted by the London Dumping Convention with the elaboration of criteria for defining high-level radioactive waste unsuitable for dumping at sea; the Convention also requires IAEA to provide recommendations for the dumping of low-level radioactive waste. A new revised definition of high-level radioactive wastes or other high-level radioactive matter unsuitable for dumping at sea, with recommendations for the issue of special permits for the dumping of low-level radioactive wastes, was transmitted to the Ninth Consultative Meeting and will be considered at the Tenth Consultative Meeting in October 1986.

61.   The revised definition of radioactive material unsuitable for dumping at sea has been formulated, in part, in qualitative terms and, in part, in numerical terms, based on the principles of radiation protection and scientific modelling. They provide guidance on the nature and quantities of radioactive waste that may be dumped at any given dumping site, under the provisions of the London Dumping Convention, together with guidance on dumping procedures.

62.   **Implications of the Convention on the Law of the Sea for dumping instruments.** The Contracting Parties to the London Dumping Convention decided that at the Tenth Consultative Meeting they will examine the relationship between the requirements of that Convention and the Convention on the Law of the Sea. This work had been started in 1975 and again in 1981, but was set aside to be taken up following the adoption of the Convention on the Law of the Sea. It will be recalled that the 1972 London Dumping Convention did not specify, in view of the convening of the Third United Nations Conference on the Law of the Sea, the limits of the area in which a State has the right to apply the provision against foreign vessels. Article XIII of that Convention reads as follows: "Nothing in this Convention shall prejudice the codification and development of the law of the sea by the United Nations Conference on the Law of the Sea convened pursuant to resolution 2750 C (XXV) of the General Assembly of the United Nations nor the present or future claim and legal views of any State concerning the law of the sea and the nature and extent of coastal and flag State jurisdiction. The Contracting Parties agree to consult at a meeting to be convened by the organization after the Law of the Sea Conference, and in any case not later than 1976, with a view to defining the nature and extent of the right and responsibility of a coastal State to apply the Convention in a zone adjacent to its coast." The Contracting Parties will also be giving attention, *inter alia*, to article VII (3) by which they agree to co-operate in the development of

procedures for the effective application of the Convention on the high seas, including procedures for the reporting of vessels and aircraft observed dumping in contravention of the Convention. The Consultative Meeting has agreed that this matter should be considered in conjunction with article XIII of the Convention. The Office of the Special Representative of the Secretary-General for the Law of the Sea will be co-operating with IMO's LDC secretariat on this examination of the relationship between the London Dumping Convention and the United Nations Convention on the Law of the Sea.

63. The Oslo Commission has studied the possible implications of the provisions of the Convention on the Law of the Sea for the 1972 Convention for the Prevention of Marine Pollution by Dumping from Ships and Aircraft (Oslo Convention) which is a regional instrument.[31] The Commission considered that, for the most part, the two Conventions were compatible and that such minor differences as existed did not justify any amendment of the Oslo Convention. In considering the provisions of article 210 (5) of the Convention on the Law of the Sea the Commission pointed out that the Convention provides a legal framework which requires specific implementation by national legislation. The Parties to the Oslo Convention could therefore enact legislation applying the rules of that Convention to their respective exclusive economic zones. It was recognized that it might be desirable to amend the Oslo Convention in this respect at an appropriate future date: for example, an amendment to its article 15 (1) could be made to reflect the extension of the jurisdiction of coastal States to the exclusive economic zone and its article 2 might be amended to mention expressly the provisions relating to the exclusive economic zone.

64. The Oslo Commission has also studied article 60 of the United Nations Convention on the Law of the Sea which, *inter alia*, requires abandoned or discarded off-shore platforms to be removed in such a way as to ensure safety of navigation, taking into account any generally accepted international standards established in this regard by the competent international organization. It may be noted that the definition of dumping provided for in article 1 of the Convention on the Law of the Sea includes deliberate disposal of such platforms whereas the Oslo Convention does not expressly include such disposal. The Commission considered, however, that since the provisions of Annex II to the Oslo Convention concern the dumping of bulky wastes and that the practice is to issue permits for such dumping, it could be concluded that the dumping of platforms into the sea was within its competence. It thus agreed that all Parties should consult with their national legal experts as to whether the provisions of the Oslo Convention could be construed as controlling the dumping of platforms or whether a specific amendment is desirable. The Commission agreed that its concerns about future disposal of platforms should also be addressed to the appropriate IMO body. The Oslo Commission will take up the question of whether or not to prepare an explicit recommendation on the dismantling and removal of platforms at its twelfth meeting in 1986.

3. Prevention and control of marine pollution from land-based sources

65. While marine pollution from ships and from dumping at sea are regulated by global conventions and several regional instruments, marine pollution from land-based sources is regulated only on a regional basis (for example, the 1974 Paris Convention, the 1976 Barcelona Protocol and the 1981 Lima Protocol). Work at the global level was initiated by UNEP in 1981 within the framework of its programme for the development and periodic review of environmental law. Basic questions have been addressed concerning the challenge of identifying and selecting criteria for designating substances which are potentially harmful to the marine environment and criteria which should be used to decide on how such a substance

might be managed in the marine environment. The most favoured approach to date has been a black/grey list approach. With respect to land-based sources, concerns over how agreement can be reached on which substances belong to what list has prompted detailed consideration of possible alternative approaches such as water-quality criteria and assimilative capacity.

66. The *ad hoc* Working Group of government-nominated experts set up for the purpose completed its work on 19 April 1985 with the adoption of the "Montreal Guidelines for the Protection of the Marine Environment against Pollution from Land-Based Sources". These include three technical annexes: Strategies for protecting, preserving and enhancing the quality of the marine environment; Classification of substances; Monitoring and data management. The Guidelines were prepared on the basis of common elements and principles drawn from relevant existing agreements (including Part XII of the United Nations Convention on the Law of the Sea), and drawing upon experience gained in their preparation and implementation. The UNEP Governing Council, by decision 13/18/II, encouraged "States and international organizations to take the Montreal Guidelines into account in the process of developing bilateral, regional and, as appropriate, global agreements in this field".

4. Prevention and control of marine pollution from sea-bed activities subject to national jurisdiction

67. The Governing Council of UNEP, by decision 13/18/IV (1985), took note of the progress report prepared on the use that has been made of the conclusions and guidelines prepared by the UNEP Working Group of Experts on Environmental Law, and authorized the Executive Director to transmit the report (UNEP/GC.13/9/Add.1) together with any comments made by delegations thereon to the General Assembly at its fortieth session. The Council called on "Governments to make use of . . . the conclusions of the study of the legal aspects concerning the environment related to off-shore mining and drilling within the limits of national jurisdiction undertaken by the Working Group of Experts on Environmental Law, as guidelines and recommendations in the formulation of bilateral or multilateral conventions . . ."

5. Regional seas conventions and protocols

68. On 21 June 1985, the Convention for the Protection, Management and Development of Marine and Coastal Environment of the Eastern African Region was adopted at Nairobi, together with a Protocol concerning Protected Areas and Wild Fauna and Flora in the Eastern African Region, and a Protocol concerning Co-operation in Combating Marine Pollution in Cases of Emergency in the Eastern African Region. The Convention and Protocols will enter into force after six ratifications have been deposited with the Government of Kenya.

69. This new Convention and its Protocols bring the number of conventions and protocols adopted within the framework of the UNEP's Regional Seas Programme to a total of 20.[32] Further agreements are now in preparation for the South Pacific by the South Pacific Regional Environmental Protection (SPREP), which is under the auspices of UNEP, the Economic and Social Commission for Asia and the Pacific (ESCAP), the South Pacific Commission and the South Pacific Bureau for Economic Co-operation. In addition to the proposed convention relating to the protection of the natural resources and environment of the South Pacific region, there are also two proposed protocols for the prevention of pollution of the South Pacific region by dumping (see para. 35 above) and for combating emergencies from pollution by oil and hazardous substances.

70.   The Third Intergovernmental Meeting of the Action Plan for the Caribbean Environmental Programme (April 1985) adopted a resolution on "Dumping and incineration of hazardous wastes and toxic substances in the Wider Caribbean Region", which emphasized the Meeting's commitment to international agreements and its opposition to incineration of wastes which do not conform to international standards and urged countries to observe the provisions of international agreements on carriage, handling and disposal of hazardous wastes and toxic substances at sea.

D. Fisheries management and development

71.   The concept of the exclusive economic zone (EEZ) embodied in the 1982 United Nations Convention on the Law of the Sea has become an essential factor in fisheries management and development.   The 1984 FAO World Fisheries Conference created new awareness of the present and potential role of fisheries and of the contribution they make to national self-sufficiency in food production and to food security.   The work of the Conference has brought new attention to fisheries from national authorities at the highest level, including those of donor countries, and from international institutions including the financial institutions.

72.   **Follow-up to the 1984 World Conference on Fisheries Management and Development**. The Conference had endorsed a Strategy comprising well-considered guidelines and principles for fisheries management and development.   The Strategy recognizes that the applicability of the new law of the sea has been generally accepted with regard to the right of coastal States to manage fisheries within their jurisdiction.   The principles and guidelines in the Strategy take full account of national sovereignty, providing enough flexibility to meet the particular requirements of individual countries.   The Strategy does not intend to re-open issues already settled at the Third United Nations Conference on the Law of the Sea.   It is without prejudice to the provisions of the Convention on the Law of the Sea.

73.   The World Conference also adopted a comprehensive and integrated package of five programmes of action, complementing the EEZ Programme of the Food and Agriculture Organization of the United Nations (FAO).   These provide the framework for development assistance, not only for that provided by FAO but also by multilateral and bilateral agencies, by regional organizations and by FAO Member States themselves.   The programmes are to be implemented at interregional, regional and sub-regional levels in order to facilitate co-ordination of fisheries development.   The 1984 Conference also adopted a number of resolutions concerning specific aspects of fisheries management and development.

74.   The Strategy and programmes of action have been endorsed by the General Assembly at its thirty-ninth session, and by the FAO Regional Conferences for Africa and for Latin America and the Caribbean.   The FAO regional fisheries bodies have examined the practical implications of their implementation.   The first Plenary meeting of Fisheries Ministers to the Latin American Organization for Fisheries Development (OLDESPESCA, set up in November 1984) has also endorsed the results of the 1984 Conference.   Two major seminars (sponsored by India and Spain) have provided forums for further examination of selected issues.   The European Parliament has adopted (April 1985) a resolution requesting the European Economic Community (EEC)[33] to co-operate fully with FAO in implementing the Strategy and Programmes of Action and to integrate its own efforts to promote fisheries in developing countries with measures taken or proposed by FAO and other organizations.   The sixteenth session (April 1985) of the FAO Committee on Fisheries (COFI) has made various proposals on the implementation of the Strategy and Programmes which were endorsed by the

FAO Council in June 1985. These decisions primarily concern the preparation of periodic progress reports, by Governments and FAO, and also covering activities outside the framework of FAO. The first such progress report is scheduled for early 1987, for submission both to COFI and the governing bodies of FAO.

75. Other follow-up activities include:

(a) An Expert Consultation on Fishing Vessel Marking which was held under the auspices of Canada, in February 1985, recommended the use of the ITU Radio Call Signs (IRCS) without prejudice to international conventions or national practices or requirements. Further consultations will be held with a view to possible adoption of a standardized marking system;

(b) COFI has established a Sub-Committee on Fish Trade, open to all member States of FAO, which will provide the desired forum for consultations on the technical and economic aspects of international trade in fish and fishery products, including pertinent aspects of production and consumption. A related development is the Regional Fish Marketing Information Service for Africa (INFOPECHE) which has recently become operational. Also of note is the proposal to convene a Conference of Plenipotentiaries to adopt an agreement for the establishment of an intergovernmental organization for marketing information and advisory services for fisheries products in the Asia and Pacific Region (INFOFISH) which has been endorsed by Indo-Pacific Fisheries Committee (December 1984). These systems relate also to FAO's new computerized Fish Market Indicator System (GLOBEFISH) containing information concerning markets for important fishery commodities and trends in international trade.

76. There has been a net increase in the resources proposed for fisheries in the work of the Organization in 1986/87 which should strengthen FAO's technical capacity to implement the Strategy and the programmes. In that connection, COFI has emphasized, *inter alia*, the importance of strengthened activities in the assessment of stocks occurring within the EEZs of two or more States, of multi-species stocks and of tuna resources. The biennial programme continues to provide for assistance to countries on fisheries legislation, on access agreements, joint venture policies and agreements and on means of regional co-operation in fisheries.

Major emphases in regional fisheries bodies

77. The discussions in recent meetings of FAO and other regional fisheries bodies emphasize both the benefits to be derived by developing countries from a collective approach at regional and sub-regional levels, and the need for co-operation between developing coastal States and those developed distant-water fishing countries which possess appropriate technical experience and capabilities.

78. The Fishery Committee for the Eastern Central Atlantic (CECAF), for example, has recommended that member States of the region and other States, including those which are not members but which fish in the region, as well as regional organizations, such as EEC, contribute to the technical and financial support of its activities either directly or by harmonizing bilateral programmes with the regional programme.[34] The majority of coastal States in the West African region still require substantial assistance to enable them to derive maximum benefit from the fishery resources in their EEZs. They need to develop national capabilities to tackle effectively the problems of fisheries management and development in line

with the Strategy and programmes of the 1984 Conference.   FAO is thus developing a programme of training designed to upgrade national capabilities.

79.   A new Convention was adopted in 1984 establishing a Regional Fishery Commission for the Gulf of Guinea.   Under this Convention the Parties undertake to promote co-operation in fisheries matters among themselves and to co-ordinate conservation, management and exploitation of marine living resources with special reference to shared stocks within the area of the Convention.   Co-operation will address in particular the following matters: (a) determining a concerted attitude towards the activities of both national and foreign vessels (including a system of international control applicable throughout the area of the Convention); (b) harmonizing national fishery legislation in order to attain uniformity; (c) promoting harmonious development of fisheries, with particular emphasis on training, conduct of scientific research and the protection of the marine environment; (d) adopting a common fishery policy in selected sectors; and (e) considering the granting of reciprocal fishing rights in their respective exclusive economic zones.

80.   In the Western Central Atlantic, WECAFC has stressed harmonization and co-operation in matters relating to fisheries and has proposed various projects as a result, for example, development of national legislation on the control of marine pollution (under the UNEP Caribbean Environment Programme) and for training of fishery lawyers and administrators.

81.   In the Indian Ocean, there has been a rapid growth in the potential of fisheries, particularly as regards tuna (see paras. 85 to 87).   Since participation by coastal States in fisheries depends on local efforts as well as on the efforts and development policies of individual Governments, FAO is promoting the sharing of experience and seeking to accelerate its assistance to countries in the region in acquiring information on the most efficient techniques for expanding the resources.   The growth in activities in the Indian Ocean is reflected in the fact that the region is currently receiving the largest share of donor contributions for the implementation of the FAO 1984 programmes of action.

82.   In the South Pacific, the recommendations of the South Pacific Forum Fisheries Agency on harmonization and co-ordination of fisheries régimes and access agreements[35] are being implemented within national legislation and in the access agreements with distant-water fishing nations.   There is thus a growing collective strength in the region, and greater benefits have been secured from the activities of foreign fishing vessels.   The Agency has played a major role in helping its members maximize their economic returns from their exclusive economic zones, particularly from foreign licences, but also by providing market intelligence, assisting in access negotiations and by co-ordinating a regional approach in dealing with distant-water fishing nations.   As many of its member countries are small and have limited resources, the Agency maintains a comprehensive data base on international fisheries and has established a regional register of fishing vessels to assist with enforcement, which has been successful in obtaining compliance by vessels fishing illegally.   The Agency is also increasing the support it gives its members in the development of their national fishing operations, including training in all aspects of exclusive economic zone management.

83.   In the South Pacific, the Permanent Commission for the South Pacific (SPPC) has devoted particular attention to the question of increasing trans-oceanic co-operation among all Pacific Basin countries.   Areas of proposed co-operation include law of the sea and marine sciences, common policies on protection of the marine environment and conservation of living resources.

84. With regard to fishing in the Southern Ocean, the Convention on the Conservation of Antarctic Marine Living Resources (CCAMLR) was elaborated in 1980 by the parties to the Antarctic Treaty. This Convention establishes a Commission which is charged with the conservation of marine living resources south of the Antarctic convergence in accordance with a unique ecosystem approach. The Commission took its first conservation measures in 1984 by closing certain waters to fishing and establishing minimum mesh sizes, and has adopted further measures and recommended fishing practices this year. Several working groups are also involved in assessing data on various fish species within the Convention area.

Recent developments in respect of highly migratory species

85. In the Indian Ocean there has been a rapid growth in tuna fisheries. Co-operation for tuna management and conservation between all parties concerned is essential in view of the highly migratory nature of these species. Article 64 of the Convention on the Law of the Sea recognizes the need for co-operation "with a view to ensuring conservation and promoting the objective of optimum utilization of such highly migratory species throughout the region".

86. The Indian Ocean Fishery Commission (IOFC) is giving particular attention to co-operation on research and statistics. The UNDP/FAO Indo-Pacific Tuna Development and Management Programme is being strengthened and will centre its activities in the Indian Ocean and South-East Asia. This realignment has been justified by the rapid growth of the purse seine fishery in the Indian Ocean. Another important project has been the FAO/Japan project for Investigation of Indian Ocean and Western Pacific Small Tuna Resources. In both projects, co-operation of both coastal countries and distant-water fishing nations is considered essential for the collection and compilation of the detailed data required for stock assessment purposes. This requirement was emphasized by IOFC at its last session (July 1985).

87. The members of IOFC have recognized that the situation in the Indian Ocean is unique in that the Commission includes a large number of developing coastal countries, accounting for about 45 per cent of the total tuna catches. This special combination of interests and capabilities was recognized as requiring institutional arrangements appropriate to the region.

88. In the Atlantic, the International Commission for the Conservation of Atlantic Tunas (ICCAT) has been reviewing its tuna management measures, particularly as regards the problem of effective implementation in the eastern and central Atlantic.

89. The Permanent Commission for the South Pacific (SPPC) has been considering a draft convention on tuna for a large area of the east Pacific covering both waters under national jurisdiction and the adjacent high seas. The draft convention calls for the establishment of a new organization with the authority to determine the total allowable catch (TAC) for tuna in the area of the convention.[36] Licences for fishing on the high seas would be issued by the secretariat of the organization in accordance with conditions set by a council. The convention would be open to all coastal States of the eastern Pacific and to States from other areas whose vessels are fishing for tuna and tuna-like species in the area.

90. In the South-west Pacific, a major part of the work of the South Pacific Commission (SPC), under its Tuna and Bill Fish Assessment Programme, is devoted to the collection of information on the rapidly expanding international fisheries in the area for tuna and other highly migratory species - the major fisheries resources of the region. Its principal activities are the establishment of a regional fisheries statistics system, to which all licensed industrial

fishing vessels operating in SPC member countries are to provide catch and effort data, and assessment of interaction between fisheries, both between countries and between different fishing methods. A particularly important aspect of this work is the determination of the effects of the growing industrial fleet on the region's small-scale and subsistence fishermen. SPC has brought the coastal States and the distant-water fishing nations together to explore ways and means of improving data input to the SPC programme. Data for fisheries within the exclusive economic zones of SPC members from industrial-scale fishing vessels is generally complete; however, there is only limited data on fishing from a number of high seas areas in the SPC region. Furthermore, fisheries outside the SPC region interact with the regional fishery due to the highly migratory nature of the resource and data thereon is limited. There has thus been considerable discussion of the need for an organizational structure which would enable distant-water fishing nations to participate more actively in the SPC programme.

91.   The South Pacific Forum Fisheries Agency (SPFFA) is currently assisting its members in negotiations with the United States Government on a multilateral fisheries access agreement on tuna, which would cover the combined exclusive economic zones of participating countries. There has been detailed discussion of terms and conditions of access and on enforcement rights of the coastal States and the flag States.

92.   While tropical tuna in the South Pacific region appear to be harvested at sustainable levels, there has been serious concern about the depleted state of the southern bluefin tuna stock. Consistent with article 64 of the Convention on the Law of the Sea, trilateral negotiations have been taking place on a regular basis since 1983 between Australia, Japan and New Zealand on the future management of this endangered resource. The three countries have agreed that catch limits will have to be adhered to and each has voluntarily taken action to this end. Agreement has yet to be reached on a legally binding management régime, however, and the negotiations are to continue.

Anadromous species

93.   The new organization established by the 1983 Convention for the Conservation of the Salmon in the North Atlantic (NASCO) has undertaken as one of its first steps an analysis of catch statistics for salmon stock taken in rivers and areas of fishing jurisdiction of the six Parties. In the north Pacific, the United States-Canada West Coast Salmon Agreement, signed in January 1985, was ratified by both countries in March.

Marine mammals

94.   The International Whaling Commission (IWC) in July 1985 established a Working Group to produce recommendations for the 1986 meeting of the Commission on the issuance of permits that allow the taking of whales for scientific research purposes. It also encouraged Governments to ensure that such scientific research conforms with research guidelines established by the IWC Scientific Committee and that it does not assume the characteristics of commercial activities.

E.   Marine science, technology and ocean services

95.   **Marine science and technology development.** The increasing depletion of traditional land-based resources of energy, food, materials and, for some countries, space and increased requirements for transportation has resulted in a significantly increased use of the oceans in

the twentieth century. Technology designed to facilitate exploration and exploitation of the oceanic environment and resources of the coastal areas and beyond has correspondingly developed rapidly and continues to do so.

96. Some recent advances of note concern ocean floor mapping, underwater technology and improvements in navigation systems:

(a) More of the ocean floor can now be seen in greater detail. Ocean floor mapping has taken a tremendous leap forward with the use of seismic "swath-mapping" tools. These new side-scan sonar instruments can provide acoustic images of a broad swath of the sea-floor, extending up to a width of several kilometres from the survey vessels. These images are analogous to aerial photographs and are most useful in quickly mapping sea-floor surface features over large regions, for example, through the use of GLORIA (Geological Long Range Inclined Asdic) developed by the United Kingdom's Institute of Oceanographic Sciences, a plan view can be obtained of wide expanses of sea-floor of the exclusive economic zone - from 150 metres water depth to the deepest part in the trenches;

(b) Equally significant has been the development of greater mobility under water and for longer periods of time. For example, ROVs (remotely operated vehicles) can retrieve objects at depths of 6,500 m like the black box of the Air India jumbo jet that crashed in July 1985, assist in repairs of underwater cables and photograph the liner "Titanic" in 4,000 m of water. A new French submersible, the **Nautile**, is able to operate over 97 per cent of the ocean floor to a depth of 6,000 m. In July of 1984 in the waters off Brazil, the offshore record of drilling 838 m into the sea-bed in 25 hours was set by a French semi-submersible. Following in the footsteps of the recently retired **Glomar Challenger, Joides Resolution** is now capable of drilling to depths of 9,000 m, deeper than has ever previously been possible;

(c) Improved navigation systems enable more precise positioning of vessels. A new satellite navigation system (NAVSTAR-GPS) has been developed and is expected to be available and fully operational by 1986-1987. This system promises to improve present navigational capabilities dramatically, allowing continuous fixing of positions, anywhere, anytime, and to within a few metres.

97. Critical analysis and synthesis of available non-proprietary geological and geophysical data for the continental shelf and oceanographic areas as well as systematic compilation of ocean floor geological and geophysical and other thematic maps are necessary to provide a reliable basis for assessing marine mineral resources and providing exploration and development guidelines. The preparation of such maps is given high priority by the Committee for Co-ordination of Joint Prospecting for Mineral Resources in the Ocean Offshore Areas (CCOP) in the Indian Ocean region. CCOP has compiled a sedimentary basin map of the region on a scale of 1:5 million, co-operating with relevant national programmes and with the ongoing circum-Pacific map project.

98. Also of note is the recently established National Geophysical Data Centre (by the United States National Oceanic and Atmospheric Administration), which is developing, *inter alia*, a comprehensive data base and bibliography on marine mineral deposits of manganese nodules, phosphorites and polymetallic sulphites. It will provide current data on the formation, occurrence, grade and abundance of these deposits. The bibliography is a searchable on-line system containing reference to both published and unpublished works.

99.   **Conduct of marine scientific research**.   The International Council for Exploration of Seas (ICES), whose area of competence is the Atlantic and adjacent seas with particular reference to the north Atlantic, now has under consideration the question of facilitating the conduct of marine scientific research in the exclusive economic zones of its 18 member countries.

100.   **Scientific investigation of the marine environment**.   The Intergovernmental Oceanographic Commission's (IOC) environmental work is carried out through the GIPME programme (Global Investigation of Pollution in the Marine Environment), one of the aims of which is to obtain the means of assessing the global effects of marine pollution.   In this respect it may be noted that a new GESAMP Working Group has been established to prepare a new review of the health of the oceans.   That review will use the results and conclusions of specialized scientific bodies as well as data provided by relevant international and national programmes assessing the state of the oceans.   The new group will also assess global and regional trends arising from ongoing and planned human activities that may affect the productivity of the oceans (on all trophic levels), the quality of ocean resources for human use and the integrity of the role of the oceans in the energy balance of the earth.

101.   The Convention on the Law of the Sea, in article 204, provides the framework for monitoring the risk and effect of pollution.   In the case of GIPME, the monitoring work is done through two groups of experts on Methods, Standards and Intercalibration (GEMSI) and on Effects of Pollutants (GEEP).   A plan is under development by GEMSI for a baseline study of the levels of selected metals in parts of the Atlantic, to be carried out in 1986.   Such studies provide the data necessary for evaluating the health of the oceans.   The work of GEEP is associated with that of developing guidelines for determining the sensitivity of specific areas to marine pollution.   This activity is regulated by articles 194 (5) and 211 (6) dealing with special areas of the marine environment, and article 201 of the Convention on the Law of the Sea which calls for the establishment of appropriate scientific criteria for the formulation and elaboration of rules, standards and recommended practice and procedures.

102.   Monitoring is particularly important for the effective application of dumping instruments.   Indeed, the Ninth Consultative Meeting of Contracting Parties to the London Dumping Convention has recently agreed that it was important to clarify that the purpose of monitoring was to demonstrate that dumping activities were being carried out in compliance with the Convention.   The IOC and the London Dumping Convention Parties will intensify co-operation on matters such as pollution monitoring and its requirements, effects studies, development of internationally accepted methods for pollution analysis, assessment of the health of the oceans and of the vulnerability of marine areas.

103.   For the purposes of its new Revised Definition and Recommendations (see para. 61 above), and for its current consideration of the *de minimis* level of radioactivity below which substances can be regarded as non-radioactive for the purposes of the London Dumping Convention, IAEA has a particular interest in the coastal modelling work of GESAMP.   That work is to evaluate the state of the art of coastal (including continental shelf) modelling relevant to waste disposal in such waters; to determine what parameters are site-specific and what are generic to a number of coastal situations; and to make recommendations as to the types of models appropriate for specific coastal situations.

104.   **Hydrography**.   Hydrographic surveying and nautical charting play an important part in many development programmes as well as being crucial for the safety of navigation.   The

International Hydrographic Organization (IHO) has recently conducted, in co-operation with the United Nations Department of Technical Co-operation for Development, a survey of the status of hydrographic surveying and nautical charting world wide.[37] The survey includes details on some 60 out of 140 coastal States, as to whether or not national waters are adequately surveyed or require re-survey or are not surveyed. From the information obtained, it is apparent that an enormous amount of work is necessary to provide up-to-date nautical charts. Noted in particular was the low response rate to the IHO inquiry from Africa and the Pacific, where there are very large exclusive economic zones, where sea-borne trade is vital and where capability in hydrographic surveying and nautical charting is at best minimal. The IHO survey concludes that large areas of continental shelves and exclusive economic zone waters are inadequately surveyed or not surveyed at all and that the majority of coastal States have little or no capability for carrying out even vital port or port-approach surveys or for publishing charts ensuring safety of navigation in waters under their jurisdiction or for mapping the sea-bed of their exclusive economic zones.[38] There is little hope that States will be able quickly to remedy the situation given the high costs and time needed to create even an elementary hydrographic capability; IHO has consequently emphasized the need for a long-term plan to train personnel in basic skills and to utilize all possible applicable technology for hydrographic and charting operations.

105.   The IHO is actively pursuing the development of new co-operative relationships with IMO and IOC in order to strengthen the acquisition and dissemination of modern hydrographic data and technical assistance to developing countries. Thus IMO has lent its strong support to the establishment of regional hydrographic commissions and charting groups[39] since adequate hydrography surveying is particularly important in establishing traffic separation schemes. The joint IHO/IOC Committee for GEBCO (General Bathymetric Chart of the Oceans) has now proposed the establishment of an Ocean Mapping Unit, the objectives of which are to establish an international service for the provision of the best available maps of and related information on ocean floor morphology and other oceano-graphic parameters; to provide related educational and training facilities to meet the needs of the developing countries in the context of the Convention on the Law of the Sea; and to develop similar facilities for use on a national or regional basis. The Executive Council of IOC has also recently decided to create a consultative group on ocean mapping to keep under continuous review all ocean mapping activities of IOC.

106. **Meteorological operations.**   The World Meteorological Organization's (WMO) operational activities over the world ocean continue to progress, in particular: the global collection and exchange of marine meteorological observations under the World Weather Watch Programme; the co-ordinated provision of meteorological information under the Marine Meteorological Services Programme; and the world-wide collection and exchange of operational oceanographic data and the provision of relevant information under the Integrated Global Ocean Services System Programme. The major research project, "Tropical Ocean and Global Atmosphere (TOGA)", started in January 1985 to support the World Climate Research Programme, involves the deployment of multiple ocean observing systems such as drifting buoys, voluntary observing ships, research ships and satellites. WMO has advised the Special Representative of the Secretary-General for the Law of the Sea that all these activities are being carried out in an orderly manner and that no restrictive measures by any maritime State have been reported.

F. Resource development in the exclusive economic zone - general

107.   The developments of an economic and technological nature are an essential component of developments relating to the Convention on the Law of the Sea. To the extent that such developments significantly impact on developments relating to the Convention, they have been included in the review under section IV of the present report. The existing and potential importance of the ocean sector for development and planning has been growing significantly, particularly following the adoption of the United Nations Convention on the Law of the Sea. Economic and Social Council resolution 1985/75, adopted by the Council on 26 July 1985, acknowledged that the resources of the ocean represent an important existing and potential contribution to the developmental process of States. It further noted that an increasing number of Member States, especially those that are developing countries, have embarked on activities designed to make full, rational use of the resources of the ocean, in particular in the exclusive economic zone. The concept of the exclusive economic zone and its implementation flow from the Convention. The Council further requested the Secretary-General to submit to it in 1987 a report that identifies specific and practical needs and problems encountered by countries, in particular developing countries, in the management of the exclusive economic zone and the development of its resources, as well as the types of activities and approaches to their implementation required for countries, with the support of the United Nations, to respond most effectively to those needs and problems, and to transmit to the General Assembly at its forty-second session the conclusions and recommendations of the Council. The conclusions and recommendations of the Council, in respect of the 1987 report, will indicate the response of Governments to developments of an economic and technical nature flowing from the Convention and, as such, will be reflected in the report of the Secretary-General to the Assembly on the developments relating to the Convention on the Law of the Sea.

V.   THE PREPARATORY COMMISSION FOR THE INTERNATIONAL SEA-BED AUTHORITY AND FOR THE INTERNATIONAL TRIBUNAL FOR THE LAW OF THE SEA

108.   The Preparatory Commission met twice during 1985. It held its third session at Kingston, Jamaica, from 11 March to 4 April 1985, and a meeting at Geneva, from 12 August to 4 September. It has decided to hold its fourth regular session at Kingston, from 17 March to 11 April 1986, and to hold its summer meeting in 1986 at Geneva, Kingston or New York as it may decide. A three-day meeting of the Group of 77 will precede each meeting of the Commission.

109.   An important development during the Geneva meeting was the adoption on 30 August 1985 by the Preparatory Commission of a Declaration (document LOS/PCN/72). This Declaration recalled, *inter alia*, the Declaration of Principles in General Assembly resolution 2749 (XXV) of 17 December 1970 proclaiming that the deep sea-bed and its resources are the common heritage of mankind, and that article 137 of the Convention on the Law of the Sea proclaims that "no state or natural or juridical person shall claim, acquire or exercise rights with regard to the minerals recovered from the Area except in accordance with Part XI of the Convention". It also expressed its "deep concern that some States have undertaken certain actions which undermine the Convention and which are contrary to the mandate of the Preparatory Commission".

110.   The Declaration declared that:

"(a)   The only régime for exploration and exploitation of the Area and its resources is that established by the United Nations Convention on the Law of the Sea and related resolutions adopted by the Third United Nations Conference on the Law of the Sea;

"(b)   Any claim, agreement or action regarding the Area and its resources undertaken outside the Preparatory Commission which is incompatible with the United Nations Convention on the Law of the Sea and its related resolutions shall not be recognized."

111.   The Declaration rejected "such claim, agreement or action as a basis for creating legal rights and regards it as wholly illegal".

112.   The Declaration was adopted without a vote following an understanding between its sponsors, the Group of 77, and a number of other delegations on the text of the following statement which the Chairman read out at the time of the adoption:

"After consultation with delegations, it is my understanding that the draft declaration contained in document LOS/PCN/L.21 of 12 August 1985 commands a large majority in the Preparatory Commission. I, therefore, take it that consequently the draft declaration has been approved and has been adopted.

"I note that a number of delegations, while appreciating the preoccupation of that majority, could not give support to the declaration because of their concerns about some aspects of the substance and the effect of the declaration."

113.   In the light of the adoption of the Declaration, the Group of Eastern European Socialist Countries did not press for a decision on its own draft resolution on the same subject (LOS/PCN/L.7/Rev.2) which had been originally tabled the previous summer at Geneva.

114.   The plenary of the Commission and its four Special Commissions continued their work in accordance with their respective mandates as follows:

The plenary

(a)   **The implementation of resolution II**

115.   In order to complete the rules for the registration of pioneer investors, the plenary has still to address two issues. The first relates to the nature, composition and function of the group of technical experts to assist the Preparatory Commission in examining applications and the second concerns the confidentiality of data and information.

116.   In the mean time, the question of overlapping claims has been the subject of consultations undertaken informally by the Chairman, especially with the three applicants whose application areas in the North-east Pacific Ocean overlap, namely France, Japan and the Union of Soviet Socialist Republics. India, which is also an applicant and which claims a site in the Indian Ocean, has no such conflicts. While it was possible to resolve provisionally the conflict between Japan and the Soviet Union, the overlap between France and the Soviet

Union created particular problems for the two countries in that it was difficult to find a solution which would meet all the conditions set out in paragraph 3 of resolution II, which, *inter alia*, provides that each applicant must submit two areas of equal commercial value, one of which will be reserved for the Enterprise of the Authority.

117.   At the Geneva meeting, it was decided that these consultations would be pursued during the intersessional period, with a timetable for a meeting among the applicants themselves early in December and a meeting with the Chairman during the latter part of January 1986 before the fourth session of the Preparatory Commission. If an understanding has been achieved, the Commission will continue its examination of the rules for registration, adopt them and proceed to the next stage. If no agreement has been reached, the Chairman will request the Preparatory Commission to decide on the procedure to be followed thereafter.

(b)   **The preparation of the rules, regulations and procedures relating to the organs of the Authority**

118.   The plenary on the Commission completed the second reading of the draft rules of procedure of the Assembly and has provisionally adopted a considerable number of these rules. During the second reading, it did not consider the rules which concerned the status and extent of participation by States observers to the Authority and the question as to whether main committees should be institutionalized in the rules of the Assembly. Nor were rules which raised the issue of decision-making and financial and budgetary matters considered. The Chairman intended to continue consultations on these issues.

119.   The plenary also began consideration of the draft rules of procedure of the Council prepared by the secretariat and has completed its examination of more than two-thirds of these rules. A number of these rules have been provisionally adopted.

120.   The issues of decision-making and financial and budgetary matters were also at the heart of the discussions on the rules of the Council. In view of the close interrelationship between the rules of procedure on financial and budgetary matters being prepared for the various organs of the Authority, it is expected that these matters will be considered in their entirety at an appropriate stage.

Special Commission 1

121.   The Special Commission which is undertaking studies on the problems which would be encountered by developing land-based producer States from sea-bed mineral production continued its consideration of the data and information on the mineral market, the identification of developing land-based producer States most likely to be affected and possible measures that might be taken in the event of adverse effects. At the Geneva meeting, the Commission focused its attention more particularly on concrete formulation of the criteria for the developing States which would be affected; preparation of an outline for an in-depth study of possible effects of sea-bed production on such States and investigation of associated problems; and the formulation of certain guidelines that will need to be taken into account by the Authority in devising any remedial or assistance measures. In addition to the data and information provided by the secretariat, the Commission had before it responses from 19 international organizations on remedial measures, and programmes and activities undertaken by them in various economic fields. However, there is a realization within the Commission

that no concrete recommendation can be made until sea-bed mineral production actually begins and its impact experienced.

Special Commission 2

122.   The Special Commission which is preparing for the establishment of the Enterprise considered a project profile prepared by the secretariat for a deep sea-bed mining operation. This paper marked a new phase in the work of the Preparatory Commission, providing a concrete basis for discussion of mining operations and indicating the various steps involved in their establishment. The paper concentrated on a number of operational options open to the Enterprise, comparing them in terms of their financial and manpower requirements. The difficulties inherent in such exercises, including those arising from the nature of the assumptions that need to be made, received particular attention.

123.   The Commission decided that, at the next session, it will begin detailed examination of the operational options, taking first that of an integrated mining project by the Enterprise alone. At the same time, it is to be noted that there is a continued emphasis on the joint venture option in the belief that it is potentially the most practicable.

124.   The other important subject discussed was that of training in relation to the manpower requirements of the Enterprise. The essential part of the mandate of Special Commission 2 is reflected in paragraph 12 of resolution II which contains the obligations and responsibilities of registered pioneer investors and certifying States. It is thus accepted that Special Commission 2 can only effectively pursue its mandate in matters such as training in consultation with them and that its ability to proceed expeditiously with its work is therefore connected with the implementation of resolution II by the Preparatory Commission.

Special Commission 3

125.   The Special Commission which is preparing the rules, regulations and procedures for the exploration and exploitation of the deep sea-bed began consideration of the draft regulation on prospecting, exploration and exploitation of polymetallic nodules in the Area (LOS/PCN/SCN.3/WP.6). The Commission examined the rules concerning prospecting and applications for approval of plans of work.

126.   The Commission discussed in particular the question of notification of prospecting and the submission of reports by prospectors to the Authority, the right to apply, the time of submission of approval of plans of work, the submission of applications and the form of applications.

127.   The Commission also considered the provisions relating to the content of the application such as those dealing with financial and technical capabilities of the applicant, undertakings by the applicant, previous contracts with the Authority, certificate of compliance, applications for reserved areas, the total area covered by the application and data on estimated commercial value.

128.   The Commission left in abeyance its discussions as to whether the application should be submitted in one stage, i.e., containing two areas of equal commercial value together with a plan of work, or in two stages, which will first require the selection of a reserved site for the

Enterprise of the Authority and then the subsequent submission of a plan of work in respect of the site to be allocated to the applicant.

Special Commission 4

129.   The Special Commission which is dealing with the preparation of recommendations regarding practical arrangements for the establishment of the International Tribunal on the Law of the Sea continued its examination of the draft rules of procedure for the Tribunal. The Commission has already considered a number of issues such as who may represent parties before the Tribunal, and the privileges, immunities and facilities which should be accorded the representatives of parties, agents and counsels. At the Geneva meeting the Commission dealt in particular with proceedings in cases brought before the Tribunal. This included incidental proceedings which consist of preliminary objections, counter-claims, intervention by interested parties, special reference and discontinuance of proceedings. It also dealt with proceedings before chambers, the interpretation and revision of judgements and the modification of the rules in particular cases. On the subject of revision of judgements, although neither the Convention nor the Statute of the Tribunal expressly provides for it, agreement was reached that provision should be made in the draft rules of procedure by which judgements may be revised on the basis of the discovery of a new fact of a decisive nature which came to light after the judgement.

130.   The Commission also considered a draft set of rules prepared by the secretariat dealing with procedure for the prompt release of vessels and crew. The Convention on the Law of the Sea empowers the Tribunal to act if a detaining State fails to release vessels as required by the Convention upon posting of a reasonable bond or security. The procedures formulated in this connection are both unusual and exceptional and are of immediate concern to fishing States and maritime States.

. . .

Notes

1.   Official Records of the Third United Nations Conference on the Law of the Sea, vol. XVII (United Nations publication, Sales No. E.84.V.3), document A/CONF.62/122.
2.   Those States were Belgium, the Byelorussian Soviet Socialist Republic, the German Democratic Republic, the Ukrainian Soviet Socialist Republic, the Union of Soviet Socialist Republics and Uruguay.
3.   European Economic Community.
4.   United Nations publication, Sales No. E.85.V.5.
5.   Equatorial Guinea; the German Democratic Republic; Madagascar; the Netherlands and Senegal.
6.   The German Democratic Republic; Germany, Federal Republic of; and the Netherlands.
7.   Equatorial Guinea and France. It may be noted that the French Decree No. 85-185 of 6 February 1985 contains a detailed set of rules regulating the passage of foreign ships through French territorial seas.
8.   States with a 12-mile territorial sea are: Algeria; Antigua and Barbuda; Bangladesh; Barbados; Bulgaria; Burma; Canada; Cape Verde; China; Colombia; Comoros; Cook Islands; Costa Rica; Cuba; Cyprus; Democratic Kampuchea; Democratic Yemen; Djibouti; Dominica; Egypt; Equatorial Guinea; Ethiopia; Fiji; France; the Gambia; German Democratic Republic; Grenada; Guatemala; Guinea; Guinea-Bissau; Guyana; Haiti; Honduras; Iceland; India; Indonesia; Iran (Islamic Republic of); Iraq; Italy; the Ivory Coast (Côte d'Ivoire); Jamaica; Japan; Kenya; Kuwait; Libyan Arab Jamahiriya; Madagascar; Malaysia; Maldives; Malta; Mauritius; Mexico; Monaco; Morocco; Mozambique; Nauru; Netherlands; New Zealand; Niue; Oman; Pakistan; Papua New Guinea; Poland; Portugal; Republic of Korea; Romania; Samoa; Sao Tome and Principe; Saudi Arabia; Senegal; Seychelles; Solomon Islands; South Africa; Spain; Sri Lanka; Sudan; Suriname; Sweden; Thailand; Tonga; Trinidad and Tobago; Tunisia; Ukrainian Soviet Socialist Republic; Union of Soviet Socialist Republics; Vanuatu; Venezuela; Viet Nam; Yemen; Yugoslavia and Zaire.
9.   States with territorial seas greater than 12 nautical miles are: Albania; Angola; Argentina; Benin; Brazil; Cameroon; Congo; Ecuador; El Salvador; Gabon; Ghana; Liberia; Mauritania; Nicaragua; Nigeria; Panama; Sierra Leone; Somalia; Syrian Arab Republic; Togo; United Republic of Tanzania and Uruguay.
10.   The States with exclusive economic zones are: Angola; Antigua and Barbuda; Bangladesh; Barbados; Burma; Cape Verde; Colombia; Comoros; Cook Islands; Costa Rica; Cuba; Democratic Kampuchea; Democratic People's Republic of Korea; Democratic Yemen; Djibouti; Dominica; Dominican Republic; Equatorial Guinea; Fiji; France;

Grenada; Guatemala; Guinea; Guinea-Bissau; Guyana; Haiti; Honduras; Iceland; India; Indonesia; Ivory Coast (Côte d'Ivoire); Kenya; Kiribati; Madagascar; Maldives; Mauritania; Mauritius; Mexico; Morocco; Mozambique; New Zealand; Nigeria; Niue; Norway; Oman; Pakistan; Philippines; Portugal; Qatar; Samoa; Sao Tome and Principe; Senegal; Seychelles; Solomon Islands; Spain; Sri Lanka; Suriname; Togo; Tonga; Union of Soviet Socialist Republics; United Arab Emirates; United States of America; Vanuatu; Venezuela and Viet Nam. States with exclusive fishery zones include: Australia; Bahamas; Canada; Denmark; Gambia; German Democratic Republic; Germany, Federal Republic of; Iran (Islamic Republic of); Ireland; Japan; Nauru; Netherlands; Papua New Guinea; Tuvalu and United Kingdom of Great Britain and Northern Ireland.

11. International Court of Justice, Reports of Judgments, 1982, "Case concerning the continental shelf: Tunisia-Libyan Arab Jamahiriya", p. 74, para. 100.

12. Official Records of the Third United Nations Conference on the Law of the Sea, vol. IV, document A/CONF.62/WP.8, part II, p. 152.

13. These States are: Burma; Cook Islands; Chile; Democratic Kampuchea; Democratic Yemen; Guyana; Iceland; India; Madagascar; Mauritius; New Zealand, Pakistan; Senegal; Seychelles; Sri Lanka; Vanuatu and Viet Nam.

14. Madagascar and Chile.

15. Tribunal arbitral pour la delimitation de la frontière maritime Guinea-Guinea-Bissau, sentence of 14 February 1985, para. 56.

16. Ibid., para. 88.

17. International Court of Justice, Reports of Judgments, 1985; for the operative part of the judgement, see "Case concerning the continental shelf - Libyan Arab Jamahiriya-Malta", para. 79.

18. Ibid., para. 33.

19. Ibid., para. 39.

20. Ibid., para. 34.

21. Ibid., para. 77.

22. Ibid., para. 77.

23. Ibid., 1982, "Case concerning the continental shelf: Tunisia-Libyan Arab Jamahiriya", para. 107.

24. Ibid., 1985, "Case concerning the continental shelf - Libyan Arab Jamahiriya-Malta", para. 50.

25. For its reports, see the International Labour Conference, sixty-ninth session (1983), report III, part 4(A); seventieth session (1984), report III, part 4(A); seventy-first session, (1985), report III, part 4(A).

26. For a comprehensive account of the history of the London Dumping Convention (LDC), containing the provisions of the Convention and a complete listing of the decisions made by Consultative Meetings (1975 to 1984), see International Maritime Organization document LDC/9/INF.2, 28 May 1985.

27. The Oslo Commission has also adopted Guidelines for the allocation of substances to the annexes, similar to those adopted for the London Dumping Convention (LDC), and has decided to amend the annexes to the 1972 Convention for the Prevention of Marine Pollution by Dumping from Ships and Aircraft (Oslo Convention), which will have the effect of bringing them in some respects more into line with those of the LDC. The Oslo Commission has also adopted decisions concerning requirements for chemical analysis of different categories of dumped wastes and for prior notification of intentions to issue special permits. All the Parties to the Oslo Convention are also Contracting Parties to the LDC (with the 1985 ratification of the LDC by Belgium).

28. Discharge into the sea of plastics, in wastes generated on board a ship, is prohibited under MARPOL 73/78, annex V. This annex is not yet in force; however, 22 States representing some 41 per cent of the world merchant fleet have ratified it and further acceptances are required to cover the additional 9 per cent of the world fleet needed for its entry into force.

29. The United Nations Environment Programme (UNEP), the Organization for Economic Co-operation and Development (OECD), the European Economic Community (EEC) and the Oslo/Paris Commissions are also examining questions of transfrontier shipment of hazardous wastes. A decision and recommendations on transfrontier movement of hazardous wastes (C(83)(180)(Final)), adopted by the OECD Council in February 1984, will be the first binding international legal instrument aimed at improving control in this area. Current OECD work focuses on practical measures necessary to implement the decision of OECD member countries, e.g. preparation of Draft Guidelines on Transfrontier Movements of Hazardous Wastes Comprising a Sea Crossing. These Guidelines cite the United Nations Convention on the Law of the Sea, articles 192 and 194 (1). In 1984, the Council of the European Community adopted a "Directive on the Supervision and Control within the European Community of Transfrontier Shipment of Hazardous Wastes", which entered into force on 1 October 1985. The Guidelines under preparation by UNEP for the environmentally sound management of hazardous wastes (see UNEP/WG.95/4) are intended to include guidance on transfrontier movement of such wastes including notification and consent procedures. The problems involved are discussed in document UNEP/WG.95/2.

30. The Seventh Consultative Meeting (1983) had adopted a resolution prohibiting low-level dumping of radioactive wastes and other matter pending a scientific review of the risks of such dumping. The Eighth Consultative Meeting (1984) had formulated more specific terms of reference for the scientific review. It may be noted that the existing site for such dumping is in the north-east Atlantic, controlled by the Nuclear Energy Agency of the Organization for Economic Co-operation and Development (OECD/NEA), which has been reviewing the suitability of the site (see "Review of the continued suitability of the dumping site for radioactive waste in the north-east Atlantic, 1985", OECD). OECD/NEA's "Bilateral Convention Surveillance Mechanism for the Sea Dumping of Radioactive Wastes" is the mechanism, in which all member States of the European Community and Switzerland

participate, which assures that such dumping is carried out in accordance with the requirements of the London Dumping Convention.

31.   See the report of the Oslo Commission submitted to the Ninth Consultative Meeting of Contracting Parties to the London Dumping Convention (LDC 9/9/2), 16 August 1985.

32.   The other agreements adopted in this context concern the Mediterranean (Barcelona Convention and Protocols, 1976; Athens Protocol, 1980; Geneva Protocol, 1982), the Kuwait Action Plan Region (Kuwait Convention and Protocol, 1978), the Western and Central African Region (Abidjan Convention and Protocol, 1981), the Red Sea and Gulf of Aden (Jeddah Convention and Protocol, 1982), the South-East Pacific (Lima Convention and Protocol, 1981; Quito Protocol, 1983), and the Wider Caribbean (Cartagena Convention and Protocol, 1983). The first meeting of States Parties to the Abidjan Convention (in force August 1984) took place in April 1985 to consider follow-up measures and the establishment of a permanent secretariat.

33.   The European Economic Community (EEC) has exclusive competence for concluding bilateral fisheries agreements with third countries, through which different types of compensation can be given in exchange for access to fishing grounds, e.g., in the form of financial compensation to be used in project implementation, scientific programmes, services, fellowships, and the provision of data on fishing activities to improve knowledge of stocks. More than seven such agreements have now been signed. A special chapter of the Third Lomé Convention between the EEC and 66 African, Caribbean and Pacific States (ACP) is dedicated to fisheries. EEC co-operative projects will also be conducted with non-ACP countries, e.g., with the Association of South-East Asian Nations (ASEAN) on data collection. As a further consequence of EEC's increased attention to its co-ordination with regional fisheries bodies, it has participated for the first time in the Indian Ocean Fisheries Commission, July 1985. EEC membership in various regional agreements is under consideration: the ICCAT Convention (International Convention for the Conservation of Atlantic Tunas), for example, was amended in 1984 to make it possible for EEC and other organizations for economic integration to become members of that Commission; similar amendment to the International Convention for the South East Atlantic Fisheries has also been proposed.

34.   The Sub-Committee on Management of Resources Within Limits of National Jurisdiction of the Fishery Committee for the Eastern Central Atlantic (CECAF) provides the framework for co-operation among the coastal States of the region. It reviews matters such as harmonization of national policies and laws, the apportionment of quotas in the case of shared stocks and the co-ordination of the control and surveillance of ships operating in areas under national jurisdiction. It has not been considered necessary as yet to modify the statutory provisions of CECAF dealing with membership.

35.   The framework of minimum terms and conditions of access were adopted by all South Pacific Forum States at the 1982 Forum meeting.

36.   The draft Convention provides that this would be done taking into account the national TACs (total allowable catch) decided by each coastal State for the waters under its jurisdiction. For the areas under national jurisdiction, fishing licences would be issued by coastal States. Every year, each coastal State would communicate to the secretariat the proportion of the TAC which cannot be exploited by its own fishermen. The secretariat under the proposed convention would then disseminate such information among potentially interested fishermen and would facilitate arrangements for the granting of fishing licences.

37.   This was done for the Third United Nations Regional Cartographic Conference for the Americas, February-March 1985. See E/CONF.77/L.12.

38.   Even highly developed industrial coastal States face major problems, e.g., the United Kingdom quotes 66.8 per cent of its maritime zones as unsurveyed, 23.3 per cent as requiring re-survey and only 9.9 per cent as adequately surveyed. Developing island country States like Fiji face a situation where more than 99 per cent is unsurveyed.

39.   The hydrographic commissions and charting groups cover: Baltic Sea, United States of America/Canada, eastern Atlantic, Mediterranean and Black Seas, east Asia, North Sea, and the northern group of Scandinavian countries. A Commission or group has also been proposed for the south-west Pacific. The main purpose of these bodies is to scheme and allocate production responsibilities for large-scale and medium-scale international charts on a world-wide basis.

. . .

- - - - -

UN General Assembly   A/RES/40/63
Fortieth Session   25 February 1986

Resolution 40/63.   Law of the Sea

The General Assembly

Recalling its resolutions 37/66 of 3 December 1982, 38/59 A of 14 December 1983 and 39/73 of 13 December 1984, regarding the law of the sea,

Taking note of the increasing and overwhelming support for the United Nations Convention on the Law of the Sea,[1] as evidenced, *inter alia*, by the one hundred and fifty-nine signatures as of 9 December 1984, the closing date for signature, and twenty-four of the sixty ratifications or accessions required for entry into force of the Convention,

Considering that, in its resolution 2749 (XXV) of 17 December 1970, it proclaimed that the sea-bed and ocean floor, and the subsoil thereof, beyond the limits of national jurisdiction, as well as the resources of the area, are the common heritage of mankind,

Recalling that the Convention provides the régime to be applied to the Area and its resources,

Further recalling the Declaration adopted by the Preparatory Commission for the International Sea-Bed Authority and for the International Tribunal for the Law of the Sea on 30 August 1985,[2]

Seriously concerned at any attempt to undermine the Convention and the related resolutions of the Third United Nations Conference on the Law of the Sea,[3]

Recognizing that, as stated in the third preambular paragraph of the Convention the problems of ocean space are closely interrelated and need to be considered as a whole,

Convinced that it is important to safeguard the unified character of the Convention and related resolutions adopted therewith and to refrain from any action to apply their provisions selectively, in a manner inconsistent with their object and purpose,

Emphasizing the need for States to ensure consistent application of the Convention, as well as the need for harmonization of national legislation with the provisions of the Convention,

Recognizing also the need for co-operation in the early and effective implementation by the Preparatory Commission of resolution II of the Third United Nations Conference on the Law of the Sea,[3]

Noting the increasing needs of countries, especially developing countries, for information, advice and assistance in the implementation of the Convention and in their developmental process for the full realization of the benefits of the comprehensive legal régime established by the Convention,

Noting also that the Preparatory Commission has decided to hold its fourth regular session at Kingston from 17 March to 11 April 1986 and its summer meeting in 1986 at Geneva, Kingston or New York as it may decide,[4]

Taking note of activities carried out in 1985 under the major programme on marine affairs, set forth in chapter 25 of the medium-term plan for the period 1984-1989,[5] in accordance with the report of the Secretary-General[6] as approved in General Assembly resolution 38/59 A,

Recognizing that the United Nations Convention on the Law of the Sea encompasses all uses and resources of the oceans and that all related activities within the United Nations system need to be implemented in a manner consistent with it,

Recalling its approval of the financing of the expenses of the Preparatory Commission from the regular budget of the United Nations,

Taking special note of the report of the Secretary-General prepared in response to paragraph 10 of General Assembly resolution 39/73,[7]

1.   *Recalls* the historic significance of the United Nations Convention on the Law of the Sea as an important contribution to the maintenance of peace, justice and progress for all peoples of the world;

2.   *Expresses its satisfaction* at the increasing number of ratifications deposited with the Secretary-General;

3.   *Calls upon* all States that have not done so to consider ratifying or acceding to the Convention at the earliest possible date to allow the effective entry into force of the new legal régime for the uses of the sea and its resources;

4.   *Calls upon* all States to safeguard the unified character of the Convention and related resolutions adopted therewith;

5.   *Takes note* of the Declaration adopted by the Preparatory Commission for the International Sea-Bed Authority and for the International Tribunal for the Law of the Sea on 30 August 1985;[2]

6.   *Calls upon* States to desist from taking actions which undermine the Convention or defeat its object and purpose;

7.   *Calls upon* States to observe the provisions of the Convention when enacting their national legislation;

8.   *Calls* for an early adoption of the rules for registration of pioneer investors in order to ensure the effective implementation of resolution II of the Third United Nations Conference on the Law of the Sea, including the registration of pioneer investors;

9.   *Expresses its appreciation* for the effective execution by the Secretary-General of the central programme in law of the sea affairs under chapter 25 of the medium-term plan for the period 1984-1989

10.   *Further expresses its appreciation* for the report of the Secretary-General prepared in response to General Assembly resolution 39/73 and requests him to continue to carry out the activities outlined therein, as well as those aimed at the strengthening of the new legal régime of the sea, special emphasis being placed on the work of the Preparatory Commission for the International Sea-Bed Authority and for the International Tribunal for the Law of the Sea, including the implementation of resolution II of the Third United Nations Conference on the Law of the Sea;

11. *Approves* the programme of meetings of the Preparatory Commission for 1986;[4]

12. *Calls upon* the Secretary-General to continue to assist States in the implementation of the Convention and in the development of a consistent and uniform approach to the new legal régime thereunder, as well as in their national, subregional and regional efforts towards the full realization of the benefits therefrom and invites the organs and organizations of the United Nations system to co-operate and lend assistance in these endeavours;

13. *Requests* the Secretary-General to report to the General Assembly at its forty-first session on developments relating to the Convention and on the implementation of the present resolution;

14. *Decides* to include in the provisional agenda of its forty-first session the item entitled "Law of the sea".

110th plenary meeting
10 December 1985

Notes

1. <u>Official Records of the Third United Nations Conference on the Law of the Sea</u>, vol. XVII (United Nations publication, Sales No. E.84.V.3), document A/CONF.62/122.
2. LOS/PCN/72; see also A/40/923, paras. 109-112, on the Declaration and the Chairman's statement at its adoption.
3. <u>Official Records of the Third United Nations Conference on the Law of the Sea</u>, vol. XVII (United Nations publication, Sales No. E.84.V.3), document A/CONF.62/121, annex I.
4. See A/40/923, para. 108.
5. <u>Official Records of the General Assembly, Thirty-seventh Session, Supplement No. 6A</u> (A/37/6/Add.1). annex II.
6. A/38/570 and Corr.1 and Add.1 and Add.1/Corr.1.
7. A/40/923.

- - - - -

UN General Assembly   A/41/742
Forty-first Session   28 October 1986
           Extract

Law of the Sea

Report of the Secretary-General

CONTENTS

Paragraphs

PART ONE

DEVELOPMENTS RELATING TO THE UNITED NATIONS CONVENTION ON THE LAW OF THE SEA

INTRODUCTION

1.   This report is submitted to the General Assembly in response to its resolution 40/63 of 10 December 1985 requesting the Secretary-General, *inter alia*, to report on developments relating to the United Nations Convention on the Law of the Sea[1] and on the implementation of that resolution.   The present report is the third such report submitted to the General Assembly, the first of which was submitted to its thirty-ninth session (A/39/647 and Corr.1 and Add.1) and the second to the fortieth session (A/40/923).   It is divided into two parts. Part One contains an overview of the impact of the Convention on State practice and on the mandates and activities of international organizations concerned with marine affairs, decisions of the International Court of Justice and other tribunals, and information on other developments relating to the law of the sea.   Part Two outlines the activities of the Office of the Special Representative of the Secretary-General for the Law of the Sea in the discharge of its mandate under the medium-term plan.

2.   The United Nations Convention on the Law of the Sea continues to enjoy wide support among States, as evidenced by the unprecedented number of signatures appended to it and the growing number of ratifications.   Although the Convention is not yet in force its impact and considerable influence is already apparent in all aspects of law of the sea as well as marine affairs in general.   The broad support it enjoys is being reinforced by a growing volume of national legislation on maritime issues based on the Convention.   Its influence is also apparent in the work of global, regional and subregional organizations and institutions.   The report highlights some of the important developments that have taken place in law of the sea and related issues during the past year.

PART ONE

DEVELOPMENTS RELATING TO THE UNITED NATIONS CONVENTION ON THE LAW OF THE SEA

I. STATUS OF THE CONVENTION

3.   The United Nations Convention on the Law of the Sea closed for signature on 9 December 1984, having received a total of 159 signatures.   The text of the declarations made upon signature are included in **The Law of the Sea - Status of the United Nations Convention on the Law of the Sea**,[2] prepared by the Office of the Special Representative of the Secretary-General for the Law of the Sea.

4.   The Convention will enter into force 12 months after the date of deposit of the sixtieth instrument of ratification or accession. As at 20 October 1986, 32 instruments of ratification have been deposited with the Secretary-General, as follows: Bahamas, Bahrain, Belize, Cameroon, Cuba, Egypt, Fiji, Gambia, Ghana, Guinea, Guinea-Bissau, Iceland, Indonesia, Iraq, Ivory Coast, Jamaica, Kuwait, Mali, Mexico, Nigeria, Paraguay, Philippines, Saint Lucia,

Senegal, Sudan, Togo, Trinidad and Tobago, Tunisia, United Republic of Tanzania, Yugoslavia, Zambia and the United Nations Council for Namibia.

5.   Upon ratification, eight States made declarations.[3] Among those, three States made declarations under article 310.[4] Four States made declarations in accordance with article 287 with respect to the choice of procedure for the settlement of disputes concerning the interpretation or application of the Convention.[5] Two States made declarations under article 298 with respect to the categories of disputes excepted from the binding dispute-settlement procedures contained in section 2 of Part XV of the Convention.[6]

6.   In addition to specific national acts referred to above, there is continuing broad support for the Convention evidenced by several recent declarations in regional and other multilateral forums as illustrated, *inter alia*, by the appeal made by the Council of Ministers of the Organization of African Unity to its Member States to accelerate their constitutional processes for the ratification of the Convention, and the expression of satisfaction by the Co-ordinating Bureau of the Movement of Non-Aligned Countries for the increasing and overwhelming support for the Convention (A/41/654 and A/41/341-S/18065 and Corr.1).

II. STATE PRACTICE AND NATIONAL POLICY

7.   States have continued to base their national maritime policy, particularly with respect to their maritime legislation, on the norms contained in the Convention. Since the submission of the report of the Secretary-General to the fortieth session of the General Assembly (A/40/923) further developments have occurred regarding marine affairs.

8.   From the information received or collected by the Office of the Special Representative of the Secretary-General, States have been enacting national legislation and concluding agreements on several maritime issues, particularly with regard to maritime zones falling under their sovereignty and jurisdiction - the territorial sea, the exclusive economic zone and the continental shelf - and the delimitation of maritime boundaries between States with opposite or adjacent coasts.

9.   By virtue of the Convention, coastal States are entitled to extend their territorial seas up to a breath of 12 nautical miles. It is generally acknowledged that the 12-mile limit to the territorial sea has now become part of the general practice of States. In this respect the Convention has settled a long-standing controversy concerning the breadth of the territorial sea, claims for which vary from 3 to 200 miles. It may be noted that the number of States claiming a 12-mile territorial sea continues to increase. Some 100 States[7] now claim a 12-mile territorial sea as compared with 89 reported last year. It is of some importance to note that some States[8] that had made territorial sea claims exceeding the 12-mile limit have now modified their legislation to conform to the relevant provisions of the Convention, and others are reviewing their legislation in the light of the provisions of the Convention.

10.   In his report (A/40/923) the Secretary-General had noted that some 79 States from all regions had promulgated laws and decrees establishing exclusive economic zones and exclusive fishery zones of up to 200 nautical miles. This number has increased to 85[9] - a clear testimony that international law as reflected in the Convention and the practice of States have sanctioned a new international rule to the effect that a coastal State has sovereign rights to explore, exploit, conserve and manage the natural resources to be found in the exclusive economic zone.[10]

11. The Convention provides that the continental shelf comprises the sea-bed and subsoil of the submarine areas that extend beyond the limit of the territorial seas throughout the natural prolongation of its land territory or to a distance of 200 nautical miles from the baselines from which the breadth of territorial sea is measured. Some 18 States have adopted this formula in their legislation on the continental shelf.[11] The Convention has also established technical criteria for the delimitation of the outer limits of the continental shelf where the shelf extends beyond the 200-mile limit. A few States have commenced incorporating some of those criteria in their legislation.[12]

12. As may be seen from above, there is broad acceptance of the basic principles contained in the Convention relating to the rights of States over maritime zones. There is, however, a continuing need to encourage States towards uniform and consistent application of those principles in their national policy and practices.

13. Recent legislation enacted by Mexico (the Federal Act relating to the Sea of 8 January 1986) deserves special mention because of its comprehensiveness and its conformity with the provisions of the Convention. This legislation consists of 65 articles and is divided into 2 parts. The first consists of general provisions on the scope of the Act and the rules applicable to issues such as marine installations, conservation and utilization of living and non-living natural resources, the protection and preservation of the marine environment and marine scientific research. The second part refers to the more specific régimes applicable to national maritime zones. The norms of this legislation have been based on those embodied in the Convention.[13]

III. SETTLEMENT OF CONFLICTS AND DISPUTES

14. As States continue implementing the new law of the sea as embodied in the Convention, conflicts and disputes arise, especially from the adoption of the new concept of the exclusive economic zone. A large number of these disputes have already been resolved by agreements. However, as is well known, a considerable number of disputes concerning the delimitation of the new maritime zones still remains.

15. Among the recent cases concerning maritime issues submitted to third-party procedure for dispute settlement are the dispute between Tunisia and the Libyan Arab Jamahiriya concerning the revision and interpretation of the Judgment of 24 February 1982, and between Canada and France in respect of filleting within the Gulf of Saint Lawrence. The former was submitted to the International Court of Justice and the latter to an arbitral tribunal.

16. It should also be noted that Guinea-Bissau and Senegal have submitted the delimitation of their maritime frontier to an arbitral tribunal. The tribunal commenced its work on 6 June 1986. More recently Honduras and El Salvador have agreed to submit to the International Court of Justice their dispute relating to their land and maritime frontier (see A/41/PV.26, p. 23).

Tunisia - Libyan Arab Jamahiriya (revision and interpretation of the Judgment of 24 February 1982)

17. On 10 December 1985, the International Court of Justice handed down its decision in the Application for Revision and Interpretation of the Judgment of 24 February 1982 in the Case Concerning the Continental Shelf between Tunisia and the Libyan Arab Jamahiriya. The Tunisian application contained three distinct requests: an application for revision of the 1982

Judgment of the Court on the basis of article 61 of the Statute of the Court; an application for interpretation of the Judgment, on the basis of article 60 of the Statute; and a request to "correct an error" in that Judgment.[14]

18.   The Court held that the correct co-ordinates of Concession No. 137 were obtainable by Tunisia, and, this, together with the fact that it was in its own interest to ascertain them, signifies that the essential conditions of admissibility of a request for revision laid down in paragraph 1 of article 61 of the Statute, namely ignorance of a new fact, not due to negligence, were lacking.[15] Moreover the details of the correct co-ordinates did not constitute "a fact of such a nature as to be a decisive factor"[16] within the meaning of article 61 of the Statute. The Court found that the request for interpretation in the first sector was based upon a misreading of the purpose of the relevant passage of the operative clause of the 1982 Judgment and, though the request was admissible, the Court was unable to uphold Tunisia's submission as to the correct interpretation in this respect.[17] It stated that the request for the correction of an error was also based upon a misreading of the Judgment and was therefore unable to uphold the final submission of Tunisia that "the most westerly point of the Gulf of Gabes lies in latitude 34° 05' 20" (Carthage). The Court noted that it had expressly decided in 1982 that "the precise co-ordinates of this point will be for the experts to determine" and it would not be consistent with that decision for the Court to state that a specific co-ordinate constituted the most westerly point of the Gulf of Gabes.18

Canada - France

19.   On 17 July 1986 the Arbitral Award between Canada and France was handed down. The Tribunal was requested to adjudicate "in accordance with international law, the dispute between the Parties in respect of filleting within the Gulf of Saint Lawrence" by certain French trawlers registered in Saint Pierre and Miquelon.[19] The Tribunal decided by two votes to one that Canada was not entitled to forbid such French trawlers to fillet their catch in the Gulf of Saint Lawrence. The Tribunal based its decision primarily on its interpretation of the 1972 Agreement between Canada and France on their mutual fishing relations in its context, in the light of its object and purpose and having regard to the circumstances in which it was concluded. It may be noted that, with respect to the status of the exclusive economic zone, the Tribunal observed that the Third United Nations Conference on the Law of the Sea and the practice followed by States on the subject of sea fishing even while the Conference was in progress have crystallized and sanctioned a new international rule to the effect that in its exclusive economic zone a coastal State has sovereign rights in order to explore and exploit, conserve and manage natural resources.

20.   The Tribunal, as it was required to decide the dispute "in accordance with international law", took into account developments in international law of the sea since the conclusion of the 1972 Agreement. In this context it examined certain provisions of the United Nations Convention on the Law of the Sea dealing with the conservation and management of the living resources in the exclusive economic zone. The Tribunal noted in particular that when article 62, paragraph 4 (c), provided that coastal States regulations may relate to the types, sizes and amount of "gear" used by fishing vessels, it referred only to "fishing equipment", as indicated by paragraph 4 (a). It declared that the provision did not cover filleting equipment, since equipment used for fish processing cannot be assimilated to fishing equipment in the ordinary meaning of the term. In the Tribunal's view, the regulation of filleting at sea could not *a priori* be justified by coastal State Powers under the rules of the new law of the sea.

IV. OTHER DEVELOPMENTS RELATING TO THE LAW OF THE SEA

A. Peaceful uses

1. Naval arms race

21. The views of Member States on the question of the naval arms race, as reflected in comments on the study of the Secretary-General (A/40/535) and in subsequent discussions in the Disarmament Commission,[20] were notably consistent in their affirmation of the validity and importance of the Convention on the Law of the Sea for the peaceful uses of the seas and the development of their resources. Great significance was also attached to the entry into force and full implementation of the Convention for international peace and security, as well as for the future international conduct of maritime affairs.

22. The risk that conflicts of interest between naval activities and non-military uses of the sea could give rise to security threats or infringements on the freedom of navigation and the safety of maritime communication was stressed by the majority of States commenting on the study of the Secretary-General.

23. Certain principles were identified for the purpose of guiding the future work of the Commission, among them, that future arms limitation or disarmament measures relating to the oceans should not take the form of amendments to the Convention on the Law of the Sea but should be embodied in separate legal instruments in harmony with it.

2. South Pacific region

24. The South Pacific Nuclear Free Zone Treaty, opened for signature on 6 August 1985 at Raratonga, has been signed by 10 South Pacific Forum members and ratified by the Cook Islands, Tuvalu, Fiji and Niue. Eight ratifications are needed for its entry into force.

25. The Treaty explicitly preserves the rights of States in international law with regard to the freedom of the seas and upholds the régime of innocent passage, archipelagic sea lane passage and transit passage of straits (arts. 2 (2) and 5 (2)). The Treaty imposes obligations on the countries of the region to exclude nuclear weapons from their territories. The three Protocols subsequently adopted at the 17th South Pacific Forum meeting (August 1986) seek the agreement of the nuclear Powers also to apply the prohibition on manufacture, stationing and nuclear testing, as well as the verification system. The Protocols will open for signature when the Treaty comes into force, or on 1 December 1986, whichever comes first.

26. It was agreed that if the Forum should decide in the future to amend the Treaty in ways that might affect the obligations of States signatories to the Protocols, the Forum would consult with the States concerned. A special withdrawal clause has also been included in each of the three Protocols that would enable the signatories to withdraw should any "extraordinary events" jeopardize their "supreme interests".

3. South Atlantic region

27. Under a new item, entitled "Zone of peace and co-operation in the South Atlantic", the forty-first session of the General Assembly, *inter alia*, solemnly declared the Atlantic Ocean, in the region situated between Africa and South America, a "Zone of Peace and Co-operation of

the South Atlantic". It called upon all States of the zone of the South Atlantic to promote further regional co-operation, *inter alia*, for social and economic development, the protection of the environment, the conservation of living resources and the peace and security of the whole region. The Assembly further called upon all States of all other regions, in particular the militarily significant States, scrupulously to respect the region of the South Atlantic as a zone of peace and co-operation, especially through the reduction and eventual elimination of their military presence there, the non-introduction of nuclear weapons or other weapons of mass destruction and the non-extension into the region of rivalries and conflicts that are foreign to it (A/41/143 and resolution 41/11 of 27 October 1986).

B. Maritime law

1. Maritime safety and navigation

28. The Convention has had particularly notable effects on the work of the International Maritime Organization (IMO), as the principal competent international organization for maritime safety and navigation and the prevention and control of marine pollution from ships. Recently, the rate of acceptance of IMO conventions has greatly increased, as has the Organization's membership. At present, 21 out of 28 IMO conventions and protocols are in force. IMO, with the co-operation of the Office of the Special Representative, has recently taken up a study of the complex relationships between the Convention and IMO conventions, as well as the standard-setting and other functions of IMO. A paper is currently being prepared for publication.

(a) Status of conventions

29. On 1 July 1986, the 1983 Amendments to the 1974 International Convention on the Safety of Life at Sea entered into force. Work continues on the preparation of further amendments to the 1966 Load Line Convention and to the International Convention on the Safety of Life at Sea, which would be adopted at a diplomatic conference to be held in 1988. A number of draft amendments to international conventions and codes will be submitted to the 1987 IMO Assembly, including draft amendments to the 1972 Collision Regulations and the International Code of Signals.

(b) Safety of life at sea

30. The International Convention on the Safety of Life at Sea is one of the oldest and most important international conventions dealing with maritime safety. The sinking of the Titanic in 1912 led to the first International Convention on the Safety of Life at Sea in 1914. The present Convention covers all safety aspects of ship construction and equipment, life-saving appliances, radio communications, safety of navigation, carriage of grain, carriage of dangerous goods and nuclear ships. The 1983 Amendments extend the application of the International Convention on the Safety of Life at Sea to chemical tankers and liquefied gas carriers by reference to two new codes developed by IMO: the International Bulk Chemical Code and the International Gas Carrier Code. Under the new amendments these codes are now treated as mandatory; amendments to be adopted in 1988 will make key precautions on the carriage of cargoes mandatory.

(c) Search and rescue

31. A universal search and rescue plan is being prepared, which will be supported by a new global maritime distress and safety system, now under elaboration by IMO, in co-operation with the International Telecommunication Union (ITU), the World Meteorological Organization (WMO), the International Hydrographic Organization (IHO) and the International Maritime Satellite (INMARSAT). It is envisaged that this new system will be introduced into the International Convention on the Safety of Life of Sea in 1988 and will be implemented in the early 1990s. Under the future global maritime distress and safety system, search and rescue authorities ashore as well as shipping in the vicinity will be alerted to a distress incident so effective assistance can be provided with a minimum of delay. The new system will use both satellite and terrestrial techniques integrated to form an efficient communication network.

(d) Ship routing and related matters

32. A number of important resolutions relating to navigational safety, were adopted at the last session of the IMO Assembly: resolutions A.572(14) and A.573(14) on ship routing; resolution A.578(14) setting forth guidelines for vessel traffic services; and resolution A.580 (14) on regional hydrographic commissions and regional charting groups (see para. 82).

(e) Port State enforcement

33. Progress under the 1982 Memorandum of Understanding on Port State Control, signed by 14 European States, was reviewed this year. Under the terms of the Memorandum, signatory States are required to inspect vessels in port on all safety matters, particularly vessels carrying pollutants and hazardous and noxious cargoes. The review found that the established target had been reached: the inspections made corresponded to 25 per cent of the estimated annual number of foreign merchant ships entering the ports of signatory States.

(f) Offshore structures

34. There are now more than 6,000 offshore installations around the world, so several organizations are paying increasing attention to the various legal and technical issues they raise. Technological developments point to the use of offshore structures in more hostile environments, which raises additional questions about labour conditions. Concerns over a potential increase in violent incidents at sea have led to greater security precautions. Safety zone designations are not without significance for navigational freedoms and efforts are therefore being made to limit zones to the agreed minimum needed to protect the installations. Finally, there are a number of considerations concerning their dismantlement and removal: the navigational hazards posed if they are not removed; the costs of removal, which increase dramatically with size, distance and poor environmental conditions; and the question of achieving some international uniformity in the requirements imposed in the interests of world shipping.

35. The IMO Maritime Safety Committee has under consideration questions of infringement of safety zones around offshore structures and the removal of abandoned or disused offshore platforms, from the point of view of navigational safety. The Committee has seen no apparent need to amend the Collision Regulations or to increase the size of the safety zones authorized by the Convention on the Law of the Sea (art. 60). It endorsed the view that strict

enforcement of safety measures to protect offshore structures and prosecution by flag States of ships infringing safety zones would provide a better solution.

36.   The Consultative Parties to the London Dumping Convention are considering, as are Parties to the Oslo Dumping Convention, with reference to article 60 of the Convention on the Law of the Sea, whether there is a need to develop specific guidelines for the ultimate disposal at sea of offshore installations.   Account would be taken of any recommendations concerning safety of navigation being considered by the Maritime Safety Committee.

37.   Since 1981, the International Labour Organization (ILO) has studied working conditions on offshore industrial installations used in the exploration and exploitation of mineral and petroleum resources.[21]   The ILO Committee concerned has found that the law on offshore installations is at an early stage in terms of the development of new regulations.   It has once again invited Governments to submit information that would clarify certain problems, in particular the legal status of offshore industrial installations, the laws applicable to the workers concerned, the manner in which jurisdiction is exercised and the effect of these factors on the scope of application of ILO conventions.   A preparatory study is planned to determine the main problems that should be examined in this very complex field.

38.   The International Hydrographic Organization (IHO) is looking at the charting of offshore installations, especially abandoned ones, and has decided that IHO symbols will not be altered until further developments make revision necessary.   It has none the less expressed great concern about the incomplete dissemination of information on new offshore structures by some coastal States and private companies.

(g)   Salvage and related issues

39.   The IMO Legal Committee has made progress on its preparation of a new convention on salvage and assistance at sea to replace the 1910 Convention on the subject.   A diplomatic conference to adopt a new convention is expected to be held some time after 1987.   In its consideration of certain public law aspects of salvage, particular attention has been given to the question of notification requirements in respect of maritime incidents that pose the threat of marine pollution.   The Committee noted that amendments proposed in the IMO Marine Environment Protection Committee in respect of the Protocol of 1978 to the International Convention for the Prevention of Pollution from Ships, 1973 (MARPOL 73/78), had not been adopted, but that the Committee had agreed to include a reporting requirement in the Guidelines for Reporting Incidents Involving Harmful Substances.[22]   Further consideration will be given, however, to this and other questions that entail issues of environmental protection.   The Committee has agreed to exclude from the ambit of the Convention fixed platforms used for hydrocarbon production, storage and transportation systems.

2.   Other aspects of shipping

Convention on Conditions for Registration of Ships

40.   On 7 February 1986, after 10 years of negotiations, the United Nations Conference on Conditions for Registration of Ships adopted a Convention[23] that for the first time defines in an international instrument the elements of the "genuine link" that should exist between a ship and the State whose flag it flies.   The concept of a "genuine link" had been embodied in the

Convention on the Law of the Sea, but has never before been expressly defined in any international instrument.

41.   The central provisions of the 1986 Convention (arts. 8, 9 and 10) provide for participation by nationals of the flag State in the ownership, manning and management of ships on its register, thus establishing what are widely regarded as the key and necessary economic criteria that give meaning to the concept. A distinctive feature of the Convention is that it gives States a choice between complying with the provisions on ownership or with those on manning (art. 7).

42.   The Convention will enter into force 12 months after it has been ratified by 40 States, representing 25 per cent of gross registered tonnage of ships used in international seaborne trade of 500 gross registered tonnage and above.

43.   Considering that an important early objective of the exercise for the majority of countries was the phasing out of open registries (flags of convenience), it was emphasized that the Convention would, in time, bring about the abolition of certain abuses having their origin in inadequate links between a ship and its flag State.

3.   Violence at sea

44.   The General Assembly, by resolution 40/61 of 9 December 1985, called on IMO to address issues of violence at sea and to study the problem of terrorism aboard or against ships with a view to making recommendations on appropriate measures. The IMO Assembly subsequently adopted resolution A.584(14) on "Measures to prevent unlawful acts which threaten the safety of ships and the security of their passengers and crews", following which the Maritime Safety Committee prepared detailed guidelines intended to assist States when reviewing and where necessary strengthening port and on-board security measures.[24] They focus on controlling access to vessels whether at sea or in port.

45.   The Maritime Safety Committee discussed separately measures to prevent unlawful acts against passengers and crews on board ships, and piracy and armed robbery. Attention to the former issue is directly attributable to the **Achille Lauro** incident and the measures recommended by the Committee fall within this first topic. The first priority was understood to be the introduction of practical security measures, and since world-wide shipping is not centrally regulated in the way that international air traffic tends to be, the Committee was able to benefit from the standards and recommended practices adopted by the International Civil Aviation Organization (ICAO) on aviation security.

46.   IMO regularly reviews the situation worldwide with respect to acts of piracy and armed robbery committed against ships. The incidents occur in the equatorial areas of South-East Asia, West Africa and the Caribbean. Attacks are aimed primarily at Vietnamese refugees in the Gulf of Thailand, and at commercial shipping on the west coast of Africa (particularly the Port of Lagos) and in the South China Sea, especially in the Singapore/Phillip Channel, where in spite of a maritime patrol surveillance system, agreed to by Singapore, Indonesia and Malaysia, piratical activities have continued.   There have also been numerous largely unconfirmed reports of "yachtjacking" by drug smugglers in the Caribbean.

47.   The rate of pirate attacks on refugees and asylum seekers has diminished during the present period compared to 1983/1984, and it is encouraging to note that there has been a

considerable decline (from 62 per cent to 42 per cent) in the high risk area of the southern part of the Gulf of Thailand. The anti-piracy arrangement established by the Royal Thai Government with the co-operation of a number of donor Governments remains a very important deterrent and has therefore been extended for a further 12-month period until June 1987. It continues to provide preventive sea and air patrols, follow-up investigation and prosecution of suspects, and nation-wide registration of fishing boats.

48. Fears have been expressed in many quarters that violence at sea may increase because of numerous political, economic and military factors, so that more attention is now being paid to the problems relating to piracy and armed robbery, and other unlawful acts including terrorism. Piracy is clearly defined and universally recognized and condemned as a crime against nations (art. 101 of the 1982 Convention on the Law of the Sea). Terrorism, however, remains largely undefined and on previous occasions where a purported act of piracy has involved insurgents the international law against piracy has not been considered applicable.

49. Since the law of piracy also requires that pirates on the high seas be apprehended by a warship or similar state vessel, effective control becomes an expensive proposition and attention has been drawn to the need for co-operative measures, particularly at the regional level. Attention has been drawn by experts to a possible basis for co-operative measures to suppress unlawful acts, at least as far as straits are concerned, in articles 43 and 44 of the Convention. While they are intended to focus primarily on co-operation as regards marine pollution and hazards to navigation and overflight, they none the less establish a general principle, it is argued, for co-operative action on matters of common interest to both straits States and user States.

4. Rescue of refugees at sea

50. In addition to its efforts, with IMO, to ensure that refugees and asylum seekers are protected from pirate attacks, the Office of the United Nations High Commissioner for Refugees (UNHCR) has continuing concerns as to their rescue when in distress at sea. Fortunately, the situation has shown a substantial degree of improvement, in part because of the intensification of promotional activities undertaken by the relevant international organizations, Governments and shipowners. The main components of these activities are the Rescue at Sea and Disembarkation Resettlement Offers (RASRO and DISERO) and the funds for reimbursement of the costs involved in rescue.

5. Maritime labour law

51. The Preparatory Technical Maritime Conference of ILO, held in May 1986, has prepared drafts of new instruments and recommendations for adoption by the Maritime Session of the International Labour Conference in October 1987. The draft conventions deal with seafarers' welfare, social security, health protection and medical care, repatriation, and minimum standards in merchant shipping.

6. Illicit traffic in drugs and psychotropic substances

52. Article 27 (1) of the Convention on the Law of the Sea provides that a coastal State may exercise its criminal jurisdiction on board a foreign ship passing through the territorial sea to conduct an investigation or arrest a person if it is necessary for the suppression of illicit drug trafficking. Article 33 provides for a coastal State to exercise jurisdiction in the 24-mile

contiguous zone to prevent infringement of customs and sanitary laws and regulations and to punish the infringement of such laws and regulations. On the high seas, article 108 (1) of the Convention obliges States to co-operate in the suppression of illicit traffic in narcotic drugs and psychotropic substances. Any State "which has reasonable grounds for believing that a ship flying its flag is engaged in illicit traffic . . . may request the co-operation of other States to suppress such traffic".

53. At the 1986 session of the Commission on Narcotic Drugs it was decided to include "strengthening mutual co-operation among States in the suppression of illicit drug trafficking on the high seas" as an element of the new Convention to Combat Drug Trafficking.[25] The preliminary draft convention prepared by the Secretary-General will be considered at the next session of the Commission on Narcotic Drugs (February 1987).

54. Other organizations are also seized with the drug trafficking problem. The IMO Facilitation Committee has noted with great concern the alarming increase in the use of ships to smuggle drugs. It has agreed that IMO should co-operate with the Customs Co-operation Council (CCC) and the International Chamber of Shipping (ICS) to develop guidelines to combat drug trafficking. The IMO Committee will begin with guidelines for seafarers, and, as a longer-term project, will develop recommended measures directed to all organizations and authorities involved in combating drug trafficking.[26]

C. Environmental law

1. Prevention and control of marine pollution from ships

55. It should be noted that many aspects of maritime safety and navigation dealt with above concern equally the prevention and control of marine pollution from ships. In recent years, great strides have been made in the development of international law and standards that deal directly or indirectly with ship-source pollution. The real catalyst has been the entry into force in 1983 of MARPOL 73/78. Its construction standards make the problems associated with older vessels obsolete and its operating requirements have made deliberate pollution unnecessary. New amendments adopted in December 1985 and due to enter into force in April 1987 concern its Annex II (Regulations for the control of pollution by noxious liquid substances in bulk) and Protocol I (Provisions concerning reports on incidents involving harmful substances).

56. An important series of decisions made in the current period are indicative of the concerns of the Organization in respect of the prevention and control of marine pollution from ships. IMO Assembly resolutions A.585(14), 586(14) and 587(14) deal, respectively, with the provision of facilities in ports for the reception of oily wastes from ships; revised guidelines and specifications for oil discharge monitoring and control systems for oil tankers; and arrangements for combating major incidents or threats of marine pollution. Resolutions of the Marine Environment Protection Committee (MEPC 25(23), 26(23) and 27(23)) established Guidelines for surveys under Annex II of MARPOL 73/78; Procedures for the control of ships and discharges under Annex II; and a Categorization of liquid substances.

57. Considerable efforts are being made in the present period to update the requirements for the discharge of noxious liquid substances from chemical tankers. This has so far involved the hazard evaluation of about 2,000 chemicals, based on the hazard profiles prepared by

GESAMP (see paras. 71 to 75). Considerable progress has also been made on bringing marine pollutants within the ambit of the International Maritime Dangerous Goods Code.

Liability for maritime claims

58. The conditions for entry into force of the Convention on Limitation of Liability for Maritime Claims, 1976, were met on 1 November 1985. The Convention, which presently has 15 Contracting States, will enter into force on 1 December 1986.

2. Prevention and control of marine pollution from dumping

59. There are now 61 Contracting Parties to the 1972 London Dumping Convention. The Tenth Consultative Meeting, held in October 1986, has made recommendations on the following matters.

(a) Dumping of radioactive wastes at sea

60. In accordance with resolution LDC.21(9), the suspension of all dumping at sea of low-level radioactive wastes and other matter has been observed by Contracting Parties. The Tenth Meeting established a panel that will undertake studies and assessments of the political, legal, economic and social aspects of the question; the issue of comparative land-based options and the costs and risks associated with these options; and the question of whether it can be proven that any dumping of radioactive wastes and other radioactive matter will not harm human life and/or cause significant damage to the marine environment.[27]

(b) Incineration of wastes at sea and dumping of dredged material

61. A joint London Dumping Convention/Oslo Commission expert group on incineration at sea was established. The Consultative Meeting considered that the interpretation given Annex II of MARPOL 73/78 by the IMO Marine Environment Protection Committee concerning surveillance of cleaning operations at sea by incineration vessels had alleviated its concerns that guidelines adopted under the London Dumping Convention should be consistent with related international requirements. Considering that Annex II will enter into force in April 1987, the Contracting Parties agreed that MARPOL's requirements would take precedence over the provisions of the London Dumping Convention. Those Parties that had not ratified MARPOL 73/78 would continue to apply the Interim Guidelines of the London Dumping Convention.

62. The Scientific Group on Dumping[28] had prepared specific guidelines for the dumping at sea of dredged material in order to facilitate procedures for issuing such permits, taking into account the continuous need of many Contracting Parties to maintain shipping lanes and harbours. These were adopted, with some modifications, as Guidelines on the Application of the Annex to the Disposal of Dredged Material.

(c) Import/export of wastes for disposal at sea

63. A number of Contracting Parties had co-operated in the preparation of a study covering the relationship between the London Dumping Convention and the work of other international organizations, the division of responsibilities between exporting, transit and importing countries, the relationship between private entities and national authorities and the

need for additional measures under the London Dumping Convention. The Meeting took account of the activities of other organizations, such as the Organization for Economic Co-operation and Development (OECD),[29] the European Community, the Oslo Commission and the United Nations Development Programme (UNEP).[30]

64. The Meeting recommended that Contracting Parties not export wastes for sea disposal to States not Parties to the Convention or to an appropriate regional convention unless there are compelling reasons and clear evidence that wastes would be disposed of in compliance with LDC requirements, and suggested measures that exporting States may take to ensure proper disposal of wastes at sea, including advance notification of any intended movement of wastes.

(d) Implications of the Law of the Sea Convention for the London Dumping Convention

65. The Tenth Consultative Meeting for the first time took up this question in accordance with article XIII of the London Dumping Convention, which called on Parties to consider the right and responsibility of a coastal State to apply the London Dumping Convention in a zone adjacent to its coast. That discussion had been deferred until the outcome of the Conference on the Law of the Sea was sufficiently clear to provide a basis for definitive rights and responsibilities of States in the context of that Convention. The Parties were also called on under article VII (3) to develop procedures for the effective application of the London Dumping Convention, particularly on the high seas, including procedures for the reporting of vessels and aircraft observed dumping in contravention of the Convention. The two matters were to be considered together.

66. The meeting set up an intersessional *ad hoc* expert group, to report on these matters at the next Consultative Meeting (1988), for which the Office of the Special Representative will provide the relevant advice and assistance.[31] That Group will also consider procedures for the assessment of liability in accordance with the principles of international law regarding State responsibility for damage to the environment of other States or to any other area of the environment resulting from radioactive waste dumping. The legal aspects of the disposal of abandoned or disused offshore structures will await the outcome of work by the IMO Sub-Committee on Safety of Navigation. Contracting Parties were invited to provide the IMO secretariat with national legislation relevant to dumping, which would then be forwarded to the Office of the Special Representative for inclusion in its legislative data base and subsequent publication.

3. Regional conventions

67. Nine action plans have been adopted and are being implemented for the 11 regions that make up the United Nations Environment Programme (UNEP) Regional Seas Programme. Seven regional conventions (supplemented with 13 protocols) have now been adopted, which provide the legal framework for these action plans. Four of these conventions have entered into force.[32]

(a) South-East Pacific region

68. The Protocol for the Protection of the South-East Pacific against Pollution from Land-Based Sources entered into force on 23 September 1986. The Agreement for the region and the Protocol on combating pollution by oil and other harmful substances in cases of emergency were already in force, so that this region is now the third where all the legal instruments have entered into force.

(b) **South-West Pacific region**

69. A draft Convention for the Protection of the Natural Resources and Environment of the South Pacific Region and associated Protocols on dumping and oil pollution emergencies will be submitted to a plenipotentiary conference in November 1986. This work has been carried out under the auspices of the South Pacific Commission, and also the Economic and Social Commission for Asia and the Pacific (ESCAP), UNEP and the South Pacific Bureau for Economic Co-operation.

D. Marine scientific research and ocean services

70. Substantial developments have taken place in marine sciences and services, largely as a consequence of the new ocean régime. There are many major co-operative undertakings in the field of marine scientific research and ocean sciences, both at the international and, increasingly, at the regional level. The present report will focus on a few selected aspects.

1. Marine pollution and ecological research

71. Important scientific questions concerning marine pollution are considered by the Group of Experts on the Scientific Aspects of Marine Pollution (GESAMP), a scientific group, jointly sponsored by the International Maritime Organization (IMO), the Food and Agriculture Organization of the United Nations (FAO), the United Nations Educational, Scientific and Cultural Organization (UNESCO), the World Meteorological Organization (WMO), the World Health Organization (WHO), the International Atomic Energy Agency (IAEA), the United Nations and UNEP, which provides these organizations with advice and assistance. For example, it keeps under constant review a wide variety of potentially harmful substances, studying their sources, the amounts that enter the sea and their pathways and possible effects on the marine environment. Its work in evaluating the hazards of harmful substances carried by ship has been of great importance for a number of IMO conventions and rules and regulations.

72. Also under periodic review is the state of the marine environment for which work the Group concentrates on levels and distribution of pollutants in the marine environment; human activities contributing to the pollution load of the oceans; effects of human activities on both marine ecosystems and human health; and the trends in both levels and effects. It also studies climatic change effects; geographic areas and specific habitats; and international control strategies.

73. A new interest is evident in ocean disposal as a choice for dealing with bio-degradable, non-persistent wastes and other wastes that could be safely diluted. Scientific efforts to evaluate and re-evaluate the oceans' capacity to safely receive different types of wastes are commanding a new priority. Study of the "assimilative capacity" of the oceans, however, presents major scientific problems. GESAMP's work on methodology and guidelines for assessing the impact of pollutants has been focusing on the difficulties of quantifying some of the parameters involved.[33]

74. Under the Global Investigation of Pollution in the Marine Environment programme, the Intergovernmental Oceanographic Commission (IOC) is developing a Marine Pollution Monitoring System with emphasis on integrated global ocean monitoring, open-ocean baseline studies, marine data management and the development of regional components.

75. Under UNEP auspices, 33 globally applicable methodological guidelines have now been completed for assessing the levels, effects and trends of marine pollution. These are used to obtain reliable and globally comparable results from pollution research and monitoring programmes. A total of five "reference materials" are also now available for the intercalibration of sampling and analytical techniques. By this means the quality of data generated through various programmes can be controlled.

Protected areas[34]

76. In several forums, work has begun on the scientific and other aspects related to the identification of vulnerable or particularly sensitive sea areas, a concept that is incorporated within the Convention (art. 194, para. 5 and art. 211, para. 6). With regard to pollution from ships (and related maritime activities), the IMO Marine Environment Protection Committee established a new working group to look into the concept of "specifically protected areas" within the context of the MARPOL treaty, focusing on the usefulness of the concept and whether it should apply to very restricted areas with unique circumstances.

77. Studies of the effects of pollutants are an important first step towards establishing a solid scientific basis for defining and identifying such areas. The IOC/UNEP Group of Experts on the Effects of Pollutants recently established an *ad hoc* group to draft guidelines for ecological assessment and classification of vulnerable areas. The need for a common scientific definition has particular importance for contingency planning in response to oil and chemical spills.[35]

2. Oceanographic and meteorological research

(a) **Ocean data acquisition systems**

78. There has been a rapid increase in the use of drifting meteorological and oceanographic buoys and other ocean data acquisition systems to obtain data from the world's oceans. The number of buoys whose reports were inserted onto the global telecommunication system of WMO for global distribution increased from 73 in 1984 to 175 in 1986. These numbers, WMO notes, represent only about 30 per cent of the drifting buoys actually deployed, most of which make limited measurements for purely oceanographic research purposes and whose data by decision of their deployers are not made available for general distribution. It is anticipated that the number of buoys will continue to expand at about the same rate as indicated in the WMO figures. In order to ensure the appropriate co-ordination and maximum benefits from this continuing deployment, the WMO Executive Council in 1985 established a Drifting Buoy Co-operation Panel, which is now sponsored also by IOC. WMO, IOC and IMO are now consulting on the legal aspects of scientific installations and equipment deployed in the marine environment.[36]

(b) **World Climate Research Programme**

79. After a 10-year period of planning and development within the international scientific community, this programme has now entered its first implementation phase. An unprecedented long-term effort will be required to compile an adequate set of global observations. There are two major experimental projects under the World Climate Research Programme: the Study of the Tropical Oceans and Global Atmosphere and the World Ocean Circulation Experiment.

80.   The Study of the Tropical Oceans and Global Atmosphere started in 1985. Its design is based on the concept that air-sea interaction in the tropics can significantly affect climatic events on regional and broader scales. Tropical marine areas have been singled out for this close examination also because some of the world's most productive fisheries are supported on the eastern boundaries of the equatorial oceans. Negotiations to establish the network of international centres needed to collect, process and disseminate data from the study are under way with laboratories and data centres.

E. Hydrography and charting

81.   The advent of ships with exceptionally deep draughts, the recognition of the need to protect the marine environment, changing maritime trade patterns, the growing importance of marine mineral resources, as well as the new ocean régime, have all served to highlight the inadequacies of existing nautical charts and publications. Charts that served well just a few years ago now require recompilation to incorporate new data. The deficiency is not limited to sparsely surveyed waters of developing nations, but also exists in the coastal waters of major industrial States. Fortunately, technology has advanced to a point where new instruments and techniques greatly facilitate the conduct of the precise and extensive surveys required. International co-operation in hydrographic surveying and charting programmes to make good the inadequacies of existing charts has increased substantially in recent years.

82.   Final agreement at IHO was recently reached on the international specifications for an integrated scheme of International Charts at medium and small scales to meet the needs of international shipping. For areas where regional commissions do not exist, IHO promotes the establishment of regional charting groups for that purpose. IMO (see para. 32) has also called for the further development of regional hydrographic commissions and charting groups.[37]

83.   The World Series of Bathymetric Plotting Sheets requires the collection and dissemination of bathymetric data on a global basis. The bathymetric data are also used for the preparation of the General Bathymetric Chart of the Oceans, which covers the world oceans. The series, now comprising 18 separate sheets, is produced jointly by IHO and IOC. Four new bathymetric charting projects have been approved for the Caribbean and Pacific coast of Central America, the Central Eastern Atlantic, the Western Indian Ocean and the Red Sea and Gulf of Aden. Further work is also scheduled for the Mediterranean, and on the geological/geophysical atlases of the Atlantic and Pacific Oceans.

Hydrographic aspects of the Convention

84.   The XIIIth International Hydrographic Conference (May 1987) will examine the results of the IHO Working Group on the Technical Aspects of the Convention on the Law of the Sea. The aim is to produce a technical guide to the hydrographic aspects of the Convention, which would include a list of the relevant hydrographic terms and concepts, including illustrations of a general nature; practical applications in terms of field work, charting work and computations; and an annotated bibliography. The Group has identified more than 120 terms or concepts in the Convention having hydrographic implications.

F. Marine technology

85.   Marine technologies designed for surveying coastal areas, the exclusive economic zone and the deep ocean for both living and non-living resources as well as for purely scientific

purposes continue to be refined and modified. Coastal states desiring to make optimal use of available technologies are finding the assessment of new technologies more demanding. In addition, problems involved in sharing and exchange of data emanating from these technologies are of growing concern to States as well as to international and regional organizations.

(a) **Remote sensing and space technology**

86.   Applications to marine areas of remote sensing satellite data are continuing to evolve. A new source of high spatial resolution data became available in late 1985 with the launch by France of the SPOT-1 satellite. Uses of the data include support for coastal inventory and management, especially in areas such as salt marsh mapping, reef mapping and cartography of lagoons. An improved method of locating seamounts, which is of interest for both geological mapping and fisheries resource assessment, using SEASAT altimetric data analysis has been developed and tested by Institute Francais de Recherche Scientifique pour le Développement en Co-opération.

87.   While developments in space technology applications in marine affairs are continuing, as with marine science, regional co-operation is seen as a means by which developing countries can benefit from such applications. Of particular relevance in this context was the recent United Nations Regional Meeting of Experts on Space Technology Applications in the Indian Ocean Region.[38] The objective of the meeting was to analyse the role of space science and technology and its application in evaluating and managing the marine resources and environment of the region.

88.   The meeting recommended, *inter alia*, the need for a Standing Group of Regional Experts in Space Technology Applications for the countries of the region to prepare programmes of action and to make further recommendations for mechanisms for co-ordinating activities in remote sensing, meteorology and communication/navigation. The meeting also proposed that countries of the region should appoint national focal points to collect and exchange information on all national marine remote sensing and space technology applications. The Experts called for co-operation in the application of these technologies in exclusive economic zone exploration, in particular to the nearshore and coastal biological and geological parameters, such as synoptic measurements of water, wind, wave heights and current, upwelling areas, and surveys of alternate protein sources, surveys of wetlands and shallow water mapping of estuaries, lagoons and endangered beach areas.

89.   The need for co-operation within the region through relevant international organizations and in the implementation of prospective maritime distress and safety systems in providing navigational and meteorological warnings, forecasts and distress alerts was also noted.

(b) **Side-scan sonar**

90.   Systems designed to achieve detailed mapping of the seafloor using both long-range and short-range side-scan sonar are continuing to evolve and their availability is increasing. A new advanced SeaMARC system, SeaMARC-S, developed from the Hawaii Institute of Geophysics SeaMARC II, a high resolution system that is capable of being transported by air is currently undergoing testing in Hawaii. It can detect objects as small as a small airplane in its 1 km swath range and then zoom in on them in great detail in its narrower range. The system is expected to be fully operational by October 1986. GLORIA, the long-range system developed

at the Institute of Oceanographic Sciences in the United Kingdom, will soon be available commercially. A new manganese nodule exploration system used to estimate abundance (kg/m2) while the ship is under way has been developed and used by a Japanese company. The system is a Multi-Frequency Exploration System that uses a combination of technologies that can effectively reduce exploration time and costs.

(c) Submersibles

91. Submersibles have taken a dominant position in the exploration of the ocean. Manned submersibles occupy a special place among the tools of oceanography because they permit direct observation and imaging of ocean floors and also allow the direct gathering of undamaged samples and experiments to be performed on site. A major workshop was held in Suva, Fiji in September 1985, which focused on the technical possibilities of using several manned submersibles and several remote-controlled instrument units to carry out geological and geophysical research in the South Pacific. The workshop also sought to encourage international co-operation in the use of submersibles.

G. Fisheries management, development and control

1. Follow-up to the 1984 FAO World Conference on Fisheries

(a) Periodic reports on the Strategy adopted by the 1984 Conference

92. A preliminary report on the progress achieved in implementing the Strategy will be presented to the FAO Committee on Fisheries (May 1987), and a fuller report to the twenty-fourth session of the FAO Conference in November 1987. The forthcoming review will be based primarily upon national reports submitted by Governments, implemented by special studies undertaken by FAO.

(b) Marking of fishing vessels

93. A decision of the 1984 World Conference called on States to adopt standard specifications for identification and marking of fishing vessels, since existing international maritime laws, customs and practices for ship identification are not sufficient for fishing vessels, and up until recently at least, coastal States have required diverse methods for the marking and identification of foreign fishing vessels operating in their exclusive economic zones. A second expert consultation to prepare technical specifications was held in 1986. Those specifications are based on an established international system from which the identity and nationality of vessels can be readily determined, irrespective of size and tonnage, and for which an international register is already maintained.

(c) FAO activities

94. FAO activities are now being subsumed under Action Programme I approved by the Conference, entitled Planning, Management and Development of Fisheries. Its purpose is to provide countries, through direct technical advisory services, with immediate access to the full range of skills required for sound management and development, in such areas as biology, economics and law, and to assist them through training in the development of national capabilities. Support also is given to FAO and non-FAO regional fisheries bodies.

95. In the past year, some 25 interdisciplinary policy and planning missions have advised developing coastal States on the prospects for development of fishery resources within their exclusive economic zones, as well as on management requirements. FAO has also been recently called upon to undertake a preliminary technical study on the state of fish stocks in the south-west Atlantic region (see A/AC.109/878). FAO is also involved in promoting consultations on shrimp resources among Suriname, French Guiana, Guyana, Venezuela and Trinidad and Tobago.

2. Current trends in fisheries

96. Fisheries management and development plans are now concentrating on the state of knowledge of the fishery and the management objective. Where active management measures are called for, the plans detail any catch or effort limitation schemes, criteria for issuance of licenses, etc. FAO has been looking at the traditional methods of management through total allowable catches and particularly at economic and other effects of management systems based solely on the enforcement of unallocated total allowable catches. Such systems have tended to encourage over-capitalization and severe problems have been encountered in their administration and enforcement, particularly where there is a dearth of trained scientific staff to carry out the necessary stock assessment and inadequate machinery to ensure an accurate and timely flow of statistical information on catches. As a consequence more emphasis is now placed on the management functions of access agreements and licensing and on controls that are easier to administer.

97. Basic fisheries laws are now under active review in many countries and particular attention is being given not only to the formulation of more comprehensive legislative frameworks in which to manage fisheries and to the strengthening of controls over foreign fishing operations, but also to harmonizing key aspects of legislation, at regional and sub-regional levels, as appropriate to management goals and enforcement requirements.

(a) Regional harmonization of legislation and management systems

98. Harmonization efforts are well under way in many areas of the world at a regional level. In other areas at a subregional level where activities at a broader level are not warranted because of disparities of geography and resources. Subregional incentives for harmonization are strongest where stocks are shared or interrelated. The practice of States sharing the same stock or stocks of associated species shows an emerging norm of customary international law providing for States the obligation to co-ordinate and ensure conservation and development of such stocks in conformity with the Convention (art. 63). Emphasis is on the need to foster close co-operation between all countries that comprise a natural management area, whether that be at regional or subregional levels or whether or not it can be effected through an existing common organization.

(b) Surveillance, control and enforcement

99. The particular problems of surveillance and enforcement for developing countries are also being dealt with at subregional and regional levels. The dominant policy of most coastal States is the development of national fishing capabilities and the eventual phasing out of foreign access. Until then, the problem remains as to how to achieve cost-effective control over foreign fishing in the exclusive economic zone.

100.   The most modern legislative tendency is to require both an access agreement and individual licenses for foreign fishing operations based outside the coastal State. Given the current attention to enforcement, the actual system of granting access rights is more and more designed to facilitate that objective. Access is no longer granted exclusively in terms of fish quotas (which may necessitate expensive seaborne inspections) but in terms of the number and size of vessels and the time spent on fishing grounds, which can be verified by less costly aerial surveillance.

101.   The last few years have seen the development of a number of regional co-operative mechanisms to deal with the control of foreign fishing. These range from joint licensing schemes, as in the European Community (EEC) and South Pacific regions, to arrangements for harmonized conditions of access and co-operative enforcement mechanisms. On the latter, the South Pacific Forum Fisheries Agency (FFA) register and the proposal for an EEC inspectorate of member State enforcement administrations are leading examples.

3. South-west Pacific region

102.   Many of the countries of the South Pacific have already introduced new fisheries legislation, of a comprehensive nature, which recognizes the importance of regional co-operation, particularly with respect to the licensing and control of foreign fishing operations. FFA provides co-ordination and assistance with the objective of harmonizing the legal régimes and regulations of the individual States. Decisions taken by the South Pacific Forum in 1982 had called for the establishment of a regional register of fishing vessels; uniform vessel identification standards; exchange of information on illegal fishing activities; minimum reporting conditions for foreign fishing vessels; the maintenance of standard fishing logs; the concept of flag State responsibility; requirements concerning observers on board foreign vessels; and stowage of gear by transitting vessels. A subregional agreement, the 1981 Nauru Agreement, provides for even closer co-operation to harmonize the management of common stocks. (Comparable action has been taken by the Organization of Eastern Caribbean States.) Since 1982, developments have been rapid: the regional register is in operation; agreement has been reached on a number of minimum conditions for access, incorporated in both national legislation and access agreements in the region; a programme for promoting regional co-operation in surveillance and enforcement has been established; and a number of schemes for regional joint licensing of foreign fishing vessels are already in operation. An agreement on tuna fishing with the United States has also been concluded in October 1986.

(a)   Harmonization of penalties

103.   FFA is also concentrating on the adoption of similar enforcement procedures with respect to boarding inspection, collection of evidence and seizure, and the harmonization of penalty levels.   In another context, the Caribbean Community (CARICOM) has also recognized that gross disparities in penalty levels can produce effects similar to different fee levels by diverting or attracting fishing vessels from one area to another.

(b)   Scientific programme

104.   The South Pacific Commission's Tuna and Billfish Assessment Programme is devoted to the collection of information on the rapidly expanding international fisheries in the area for tuna and other pelagic species - the major industrial fisheries resource of the region. Its principal activities are the establishment of a regional fisheries statistics system, to which

foreign fishing vessels operating in the region provide catch and effort data, the assessment of interaction between fisheries, both between countries and between different fishing methods, and the evaluation of the rate of exploitation of major species. A particularly important aspect of this work is the determination of the effects of the growing commercial fleets on the region's small-scale and subsistence fishermen. Data for fisheries within the exclusive economic zones from industrial-scale fishing vessels are generally complete; however, there are only limited data on fishing from a number of high sea areas in the region.

4. Caribbean region

105.   Many of the recommendations of the WECAFC/CARICOM Workshop held in June 1986,[39] are indicative of the kind of activity being pursued in other regions also. States were called upon to take prompt measures to review their fisheries legislation to bring it into line with the Convention and to provide a legal basis for the management and the development of fisheries, embodied where possible in a single, comprehensive fisheries act.

106.   States sharing common or related stocks with neighbouring States, whether members of the same organization or not, were called on to harmonize their fisheries legislation, and to continue to co-operate on the formulation of common principles and guidelines for incorporation in new legislation. CARICOM has recognized that while differences in geography and resources did not make it appropriate to develop a common regional model for legislation, common approaches in certain areas were called for to deal with problems of implementation of the Convention, control of foreign fishing operations, delimitation of maritime boundaries and uniform measures where stocks and/or fleets are shared. Particular attention was paid to the Convention's provisions as they affect national legislation in respect of seizure and forfeiture of boats and catch.

107.   CARICOM noted that enforcement measures that have proven value include standardized markings for vessels, reports of entry and exit of vessels to and from the exclusive economic zone and use of log books to record catch, area and type of catch. It was further noted, as regards the methods of authorizing foreign fishing, that quotas are a difficult procedure and are costly to monitor. As in the South Pacific, it is generally held that more effective systems would be those permitting fishing by a fixed number of vessels and/or by establishing fishing days.

5. South-east Pacific region

108.   A draft agreement creating a tuna organization for the South-East Pacific has been approved (July 1986) and will be submitted to a plenipotentiary meeting next year. The agreement's area would be that necessary to encompass the species involved and thus would cover both areas of national jurisdiction as well as portions of the adjacent high seas (up to the 145 west meridian). The new organization would be known as the East-Pacific Tuna Organization and would be open to all coastal States of the region and other States whose vessels catch the species concerned within the agreement area.

6. Marine mammals

109.   Practice with regard to marine mammals conforms with the provisions of the Convention (art. 65 and 116). The most noteworthy actions to date at the international level are: the five-year moratorium by the International Whaling Commission (IWC) on commercial whaling beginning in 1986, and the recent IWC decision on the taking of whales

for scientific purposes; decisions of the First Meeting of States Parties to the 1979 Bonn Convention on Highly Migratory Species concerning small cetaceans and the development of regional agreements for their conservation in the Baltic and North Seas;[40] and the implementation of the 1984 FAO/UNEP Global Plan of Action for the Conservation, Management and Utilization of Marine Mammals.[41] IOC has also recently given attention to levels and effects of pollutants on marine mammals, particularly on their reproduction and their immunity systems.[42]

110.   Under the International Whaling Convention, special permits are required for the killing, taking and treating of whales for scientific purposes. In view of certain difficulties that had arisen on this matter, IWC at its meeting in June 1986 adopted a consensus resolution to cover the period until the comprehensive assessment is completed, which supplements and strengthens existing requirements. It essentially subjects decisions of Contracting Parties regarding permits to the advice of the IWC Scientific Committee. Some guidelines are incorporated in the resolution.

111.   The duration of any permits issued are to be strictly limited to the time needed to complete the proposed research work. In addition, great care is to be taken where whales from protected stock are involved. Under this resolution, Contracting Parties are asked to submit proposals (and research results obtained under previous permits) to the next annual meeting of the Scientific Committee.

H. Land-locked States

Land-locked States

112.   The 1986 Meeting of the Non-Aligned Countries called for the urgent implementation of earlier decisions in respect of land-locked developing countries, in order "to ensure their right of free access to and from the sea and freedom of transit, as provided for in article 125 of the Convention". They further recognized that these must be realized in compliance with paragraphs 2 and 3 of article 125 so that "any programme or action in respect of such transit facilities should be undertaken in consultation with, and with the approval of the transit country concerned".

113.   A recent report of the United Nations Conference on Trade and Development (UNCTAD)[43] points to the need for full commitment by land-locked countries and their transit neighbours to efforts to establish bilateral and subregional legal, institutional and administrative mechanisms that would regulate the smooth flow of transit cargo. These commitments are reflected in the activities of Southern African (SADCC) countries and in the Northern Corridor Agreement recently signed by Burundi, Kenya, Rwanda and Uganda.

114.   In the region of the Economic Commission for Latin America and the Caribbean (ECLAC), an agreement is being sought before the end of 1986 on a system for the transit of goods between Bolivia and Peru. Various studies on the subject have been done by Bolivian and Peruvian experts under the auspices of the Commission of the Cartagena Agreement, ECLAC and ILO.

V. THE PREPARATORY COMMISSION FOR THE INTERNATIONAL SEA-BED AUTHORITY AND FOR THE INTERNATIONAL TRIBUNAL FOR THE LAW OF THE SEA

115.   The Preparatory Commission met twice during 1986. It held its fourth session at Kingston from 17 March to 11 April 1986, and a meeting in New York from 11 August to 5 September 1986. It has decided to hold its fifth session at Kingston from 30 March to 24 April 1987. The Commission will decide the venue of its summer meeting, whether Geneva, Kingston or New York, at that session.

A. The plenary

1. The implementation of resolution II

116.   During the period preceding the fourth session of the Commission the four applicants for registration as pioneer investors - France, India, Japan and the Soviet Union - participated in intensive consultations. They held meetings at Geneva, Tokyo and, finally at Arusha, United Republic of Tanzania, in February 1986. At the Arusha meeting, the four applicants presented a set of proposals, which is incorporated in what has now come to be known as the Arusha Understanding. This Understanding provided a mechanism for resolving the overlaps that existed between France, Japan and the Union of Soviet Socialist Republics in their claims for mine sites in the north-east Pacific. It also established procedures for dealing with overlaps with potential applicants for pioneer investor status.

117.   At the fourth session the four applicants undertook intensive consultations on the Arusha Understanding with various interest groups and individual delegations. It was clear that the Arusha Understanding was a good basis for resolving conflicts arising from overlapping claims and for accommodating the interests of the Authority and those of the first group of applicants. Further consultations were, however, necessary.

118.   At the New York meeting of the Commission, these consultations continued. During these consultations, which were arduous and prolonged, all issues relating to a package of understanding were negotiated between the different interest groups. Finally it was possible to put together a more comprehensive understanding establishing mechanisms and procedures for the registration of applicants for pioneer status under resolution II (document LOS/PCN/L.41/Rev.1). The understanding was adopted unanimously on 5 September 1986.

119.   This decision marks a new stage in the developments of the law of the sea since the adoption of the Convention in 1982. It has paved the way for the Preparatory Commission to proceed with its mandate to implement resolution II. The understanding removes certain practical problems that were not envisaged at the Conference arising from the concentration of claims in a part of the ocean.

120.   This understanding takes into account the interests of all groups of States as well as those of the Enterprise. The procedures and mechanisms established in this understanding should lead to the registration of the first group of applicants, which had been delayed for almost two years. It would give practical effect to the new régime for deep sea-bed mining under the Convention since the rights and interests acquired as pioneer investors would be recognized under Part XI of the Convention on its entry into force. The consideration given to potential pioneer investors as reflected in this understanding emphasizes the fact that the Preparatory Commission has acted equitably to safeguard the interests of all.

121.   In addition to the substantive matters, the understanding sets out the procedures and time-frame for registration, starting from the submission to the Secretary-General by 25

March 1987 of revised applications by each of the first four pioneer applicants, following adjustments as a result of this understanding, of their respective application areas.

122. A review of the applications is to be undertaken by a 15-member group of technical experts drawn from a list compiled by the Secretary-General from nominations of States and appointed by the Chairman in consultation with regional groups. The technical experts will meet during the first week of the next session. The General Committee will meet during the second week of the session to consider and register applications, taking into account the report submitted by the group of technical experts.

123. In other developments the Preparatory Commission adopted a declaration on 11 April 1986 by 59 votes to 7, with 10 abstentions (LOS/PCN/78) reaffirming its declaration of 30 August 1985 (LOS/PCN/72; see also Report of the Secretary-General, A/40/923, paras. 110-112), reiterating its rejection of any claim, agreement or action that is incompatible with the Convention and related resolutions, and asserting that such actions were wholly illegal and devoid of any basis for creating legal rights.

124. The Commission adopted this declaration in response to the issuance of licenses for the exploration of parts of the International Sea-Bed Area by the United Kingdom and the Federal Republic of Germany.

2. The preparation of the rules, regulations and procedures relating to the organs of the Authority

125. The plenary of the Commission completed the first reading of the draft rules of procedure of the Council and those of the Legal and Technical Commission. At the New York meeting the plenary began consideration of the draft rules of procedure of the Economic Planning Commission.

126. A number of these rules were provisionally adopted by the plenary. However, rules that concerned issues such as the status of observers, decision-making, financial and budgetary matters and the issue of confidentiality of data and information relating to mine sites submitted to the Authority were left pending. The financial and budgetary matters would be considered as a whole at a later stage.

127. It may be noted that the issue of confidentiality of data and information is a general one and that it also concerns the Special Commissions. As a consequence it has been suggested that this issue should be dealt with as a package covering all aspects.

128. At the next session of the Commission, the plenary will continue the first reading of the draft rules of the Economic Planning Commission. It will then commence the second reading of the revised draft rules of procedure of the Council contained in document LOS/PCN/WP.26/Rev.1, having already completed the second reading of the draft rules of procedure of the Assembly.

B. Special Commission 1

129. The Special Commission is undertaking studies on the problems that would be encountered by developing land-based producer States from sea-bed mineral production. Having considered the likely list of States to be affected and the criteria for establishing dependency and the mineral exports likely to be affected by production of minerals from the

sea-bed, the Commission moved to consider remedial measures that may be undertaken. For this purpose it studied the various existing international mechanisms dealing with the same matter in respect of other commodities.

130.   Some of the specific measures considered by the Special Commission were the question of establishment of a compensation fund or other special fund and measures to reduce adverse effects through bilateral agreements between developing traditional exporters of the affected mineral and traditional importing States of such mineral that have become a producer of these minerals from the resources of the international sea-bed area.

131.   The proposals on these specific measures were the subject of extensive discussions. The debate focused in particular on the system of compensation and the compensation fund. Some delegations were of the view that it was mandatory for the Authority that a system of compensation and a compensation fund should be established. Others were of the opinion that such a system and fund were not needed. There was general agreement, however, that the Special Commission was mandated to undertake studies on the establishment of a compensation fund.

C. Special Commission 2

132.   Special Commission 2, which deals with the establishment of the Enterprise, considered the question of manpower requirements and training that it thought could be more effectively pursued once the registration of pioneer investors had been achieved. At the Kingston session the Special Commission considered a study prepared by the delegation of Australia on the economic viability of deep sea-bed mining (LOS/PCN/SCN.2/WP.10 and Add.1). While some delegations felt that the study was realistic, others questioned the assumptions made. In this connection, it has been noted that the present unfavourable prospects for sea-bed mining did not permit agreement on a single set of working parameters.

133.   The Commission has decided to turn also to those matters that are internal to the Enterprise and relatively unaffected by economic conditions. An attempt will be made at the fifth session of the Preparatory Commission to outline the main features of the internal administration and management of the Enterprise, with special attention to its unique and distinct status as a commercial entity operating at the international level.

D. Special Commission 3

134.   Special Commission 3, which is preparing the rules, regulations and procedures for the exploration and exploitation of the deep sea-bed, continued with its consideration of the draft regulations on prospecting, exploration and exploitation of polymetallic nodules in the Area (LOS/PCN/SCN.3/WP.6). More specifically it considered the rules relating to the content of a plan of work and the data and information required to be submitted by each applicant. The discussions were very detailed and technical. The Commission also dealt with the question of custody and confidentiality of data and information, the question of application fees, the processing of applications and the conclusion of contracts.

135.   At the New York meeting the Special Commission took up discussion of the financial terms of contracts contained in document LOS/PCN/SCN.3/Add.2 and Corr.1. The Commission made progress in the consideration of the financial terms of contracts, which has been acknowledged to be of crucial importance to successful undertakings in the field of deep sea-bed mining as well as for the benefit to be derived for the international community. After

completing the in-depth consideration of the financial terms of contracts, the Commission intends to look into the question of financial incentives at the next session of the Preparatory Commission.

E. Special Commission 4

136.   Special Commission 4 is dealing with the preparation of recommendations regarding practical arrangements for the establishment of the International Tribunal for the Law of the Sea. At the fourth session in Kingston the Special Commission completed its article-by-article examination of the draft rules of the Tribunal (LOS/PCN/SCN.4/WP.2). In the course of the examination the Commission discussed provisions covering cases where parties to a dispute are international organizations, in accordance with Annex IX of the Convention, consortia or other entities, whose components are of more than one nationality whether such components were other consortia or natural or juridical persons.

137.   The Special Commission also discussed guidelines for draft rules in cases where an international organization is an applicant before the Tribunal or its chambers and the Tribunal *proprio motu* needs to examine, or the respondent claims the right to raise the question of the *locus standi* of the international organization.

138.   At the New York meeting the Special Commission began consideration of the revised draft rules. The discussion focused on those rules that were new and had been formulated as a result of a general discussion on the subject.

139.   At its fourth session, the Special Commission decided that in order to facilitate discussions concerning the seat of the Tribunal, the Chairman should carry out informal consultations. At the New York meeting, the Chairman reported to the Special Commission that he had begun informal consultations on an informal proposal. However, regional and interest groups, as well as individual delegations, were not yet in a position to express a view. These informal consultations will continue during the fifth session. At this session the Special Commission would also examine the draft headquarters agreement prepared by the Secretariat following its consideration of the revised draft rules.

. . .

Notes

1.   Official Records of the Third United Nations Conference on the Law of the Sea, vol. XVII (United Nations publication, Sales No. E.84.V.3), document A/CONF.62/122.
2.   United Nations publication, Sales No. E.85.V.5.
3.   Cuba, Egypt, Guinea-Bissau, Iceland, Philippines, Tunisia, United Republic of Tanzania and Yugoslavia.
4.   Egypt, the Philippines and Yugoslavia.
5.   Cuba, Egypt, Guinea-Bissau and the United Republic of Tanzania.
6.   Iceland and Tunisia.
7.   Algeria; Antigua and Barbuda; Bangladesh; Barbados; Brunei Darussalam; Bulgaria; Burma; Canada; Cape Verde; China; Colombia; Comoros; Cook Islands; Costa Rica; Côte d'Ivoire; Cuba; Cyprus; Democratic Kampuchea; Democratic People's Republic of Korea; Democratic Yemen; Djibouti; Dominica; Egypt; Equatorial Guinea; Ethiopia; Fiji; France; Gambia; German Democratic Republic; Ghana; Grenada; Guatemala; Guinea; Guinea-Bissau; Guyana; Haiti; Honduras; Iceland; India; Indonesia; Iran (Islamic Republic of); Iraq; Italy; Jamaica; Japan; Kenya; Kiribati; Kuwait; Lebanon; Libyan Arab Jamahiriya; Madagascar; Malaysia; Maldives; Malta; Mauritius; Mexico; Monaco; Morocco; Mozambique; Nauru; Netherlands; New Zealand; Niue; Oman; Pakistan; Papua New Guinea; Poland; Portugal; Republic of Korea; Romania; Saint Christopher and Nevis; Saint Lucia; Saint Vincent and the Grenadines; Samoa; Sao Tome and Principe; Saudi Arabia; Senegal; Seychelles; Solomon Islands; South Africa; Spain; Sri Lanka; Sudan; Suriname; Sweden; Thailand; Tonga; Trinidad and Tobago; Tunisia; Turkey; Tuvalu; Ukrainian SSR; Union of Soviet Socialist Republics; United Arab Emirates; Vanuatu; Venezuela; Viet Nam; Yemen; Yugoslavia and Zaire.
8.   Senegal, 25 February 1985; Madagascar, 16 September 1985; Ghana, 2 August 1986.

9.   Antigua and Barbuda; Australia; Bahamas; Bangladesh; Barbados; Burma; Canada; Cape Verde; Chile; Colombia; Comoros; Cook Islands; Costa Rica; Côte d'Ivoire; Cuba; Democratic Kampuchea; Democratic People's Republic of Korea; Democratic Yemen; Denmark; Djibouti; Dominica; Dominican Republic; Equatorial Guinea; Fiji; France; Gambia; Ghana; Germany, Federal Republic of; Grenada; Guatemala; Guinea; Guinea-Bissau; Guyana; Haiti; Honduras; Iceland; India; Indonesia; Ireland; Japan; Kenya; Kiribati; Madagascar; Malaysia; Mauritania; Mauritius; Mexico; Morocco; Mozambique; Nauru; Netherlands; New Zealand; Nigeria; Niue; Norway; Oman; Pakistan; Papua New Guinea; Philippines; Portugal; Romania; Saint Christopher and Nevis; Saint Lucia; Saint Vincent and the Grenadines; Samoa; Sao Tome and Principe; Senegal; Seychelles; Solomon Islands; South Africa; Spain; Sri Lanka; Suriname; Sweden; Thailand; Togo; Tonga; Tuvalu; Ukrainian SSR; Union of Soviet Socialist Republics; United Kingdom of Great Britain and Northern Ireland; United States of America; Vanuatu; Venezuela and Viet Nam.

10.   Arbitral award of 17 July 1986 between Canada and France, para. 49.

11.   Burma; Cook Islands; Democratic Yemen; Dominican Republic; Ghana; Guyana; Iceland; India; Mauritania; Mauritius; Mexico; New Zealand; Pakistan; Senegal; Seychelles; Sri Lanka; Vanuatu and Viet Nam.

12.   Chile, Ecuador, Iceland and Madagascar.

13.   See Law of the Sea Bulletin, No. 7, April 1986, p. 53.

14.   Application for Revision and Interpretation of the Judgment of 24 February 1982 in the "Case concerning the continental shelf: Tunisia-Libyan Arab Jamahiriya", International Court of Justice, Report of Judgments, 1985, para. 7.

15.   Ibid., para. 28.

16.   Ibid., para. 39.

17.   Ibid., para. 50.

18.   Ibid., para. 62.

19.   See article 2 of the 1985 Arbitral Agreement and article 4 (b) of the 1972 Agreement between Canada and France on their Mutual Fishing Relations.

20.   See A/CN.10/73; A/CN.10/77 and Add.1-2; A/CN.10/78; A/CN.10/80; and A/CN.10/83, Chairman's Paper on Substantive Consideration of the Question of the Naval Arms Race and Disarmament.

21.   See Report III (Part 4A) of the ILO seventy-second session, 1986 [the Report of the Committee of Experts on the Application of Conventions and Recommendations).

22.   See IMO resolution MEPC 22(22).

23.   See Law of the Sea Bulletin, No. 7, April 1986, p. 87.

24.   IMO document MSC/Circ.443, 26 September 1986.

25.   The draft Convention is contained in document E/CN.7/1987/2. Comments and proposals requested of Governments for the purpose of preparing this draft Convention are summarized in documents E/CN.7/1986/2 and Add.1-3. The Commission on Narcotic Drugs had also established an expert group on counter measures to drug smuggling by air and sea. Its report is contained in E/CN.7/1986/11/Add.3.

26.   IMO's co-operation with CCC and ICS would cover the following points: measures to prevent drugs being smuggled on board; ways of improving the detection of drugs concealed on board; measures to discourage abuse of drugs by seafarers and their involvement in trafficking; information about types, nature and characteristics of drugs commonly smuggled; education and training; and action to be taken by ship operators and their employees when drugs are found.

27.   See report of the meeting, LDC 10/15, which also contains the statements made by the Parties expressing reservations concerning this decision.

28.   A standing Group was formed in view of the increasing needs of the Contracting Parties for scientific information, advice and guidance. The scientific elements of the current Action Plan of the Parties are: development of criteria for determining "harmlessness" and "trace contaminants" of LDC Annex I materials dumped at sea; protection of particularly sensitive sea areas; sub-sea-bed disposal of wastes; monitoring the conditions of the seas for the purpose of the Convention (development of programmes, guidelines, notification formats); surveillance of international waters in relation to activities liable to cause harm to the marine environment; consideration of questions related to disposal of wastes derived from deep-sea mining operations; and hazards caused by the loss or disposal of persistent plastics (including fishing nets).

29.   A Decision-Recommendation on Exports of Hazardous Wastes from the OECD-Area was adopted by the OECD Council on 5 June 1986.

30.   See the so-called Cairo Guidelines and Principles for the Environmentally Sound Management of Hazardous Wastes, particularly its paragraphs 26 and 28 on notification and consent procedure in respect of transfrontier movement of hazardous wastes, and co-operation in the management of hazardous wastes.

31.   LOS Publication, "Pollution by Dumping: Legislative History of Articles 1, paragraph 1(5), 210 and 216 of the United Nations Convention on the Law of the Sea" is part of the documentation of the Tenth Consultative Meeting.

32.   The four UNEP regional seas conventions in force are: the 1976 Barcelona Convention, the 1978 Kuwait Convention, the 1981 Abidjan Convention and the 1981 Lima Convention.

33.   See GESAMP Reports and Studies, No. 30, "Environmental Capacity - An Approach to Marine Pollution Prevention".

34.   Several regional Conventions (under the UNEP Regional Seas Programmes) include specific provisions concerning the establishment of protected areas, e.g. Protocol Concerning Mediterranean Specially Protected Areas, Protocol Concerning Protected Areas and Wild Fauna and Flora in the Eastern African Region.

35.   A first draft is contained in document IOC/GGE(EP) - II/3, annex IX.

36.   The 1986 IOC Executive Council called for an examination of the legal aspects of drifting buoys in consultation with IMO and WMO (resolution EC-XIX.7, part B). A 1972 IMO/UNESCO Preparatory Conference had drawn up a Preliminary Draft Convention on the Legal Status of Ocean Data Acquisition Systems (ODAS) and recommended the voluntary use of its technical annexes. It was agreed that a plenipotentiary conference should not be held until after the Third United Nations Conferences on the Law of the Sea had completed its work.

37.   There are now seven IHO Regional Hydrographic Commissions (Baltic, Scandinavia, the North Sea, the Mediterranean and Black Seas, East Asia, the Eastern Atlantic and United States/Canadian Waters). The Commissions meet regularly to discuss mutual hydrographic and chart production problems, to plan joint survey operations and provide for medium and large-scale International Chart coverage of their regions.

38.   Held at Colombo from 15-19 September 1986, at which experts from 20 States and several international organizations with activities in this field participated.

39.   See Report of the FAO/WECAFC/CARICOM Workshop on Fisheries Legislation in CARICOM Member States, May 1986, FAO document TCP/RLA/6652(T).

40.   See resolutions 1.6 and 1.7, Vol. I of the Proceedings of the First Meeting of States Parties to the Bonn Convention, UNEP.

41.   See, for example, the FAO/UNEP "Compendium of National Legislation on the Conservation of Marine Mammals", 1986.

42.   The IOC/UNEP Group of Experts on the Environmental Efforts of Marine Pollutants has considered that marine mammals may also be suitable monitoring organisms in which to detect changes over large scales of space and time. The use of marine mammals for such a purpose, however, would have to be confined, it was stressed, to those acquired on an opportunistic basis (occasional deaths, strandings, entanglements).

43.   "Progress in the implementation of specific action related to the particular needs and problems of land-locked developing countries", TD/B/1107.

. . .

- - - - -

UN General Assembly   A/RES/41/34
Forty-first Session   20 November 1986

Resolution 41/34. Law of the Sea

The General Assembly,

Reaffirming its resolutions 37/66 of 3 December 1982, 38/59 A of 14 December 1983, 39/73 of 13 December 1984 and 40/63 of 10 December 1985, regarding the law of the sea,

Recognizing that, as stated in the third preambular paragraph of the United Nations Convention on the Law of the Sea,[1] the problems of ocean space are closely interrelated and need to be considered as a whole,

Convinced that it is important to safeguard the unified character of the Convention and related resolutions adopted therewith and to refrain from any action to apply their provisions selectively, in a manner inconsistent with their object and purpose,

Emphasizing the need for States to ensure consistent application of the Convention, as well as the need for harmonization of national legislation with the provisions of the Convention,

Considering that, in its resolution 2749 (XXV) of 17 December 1970, it proclaimed that the sea-bed and ocean floor, and the subsoil thereof, beyond the limits of national jurisdiction, as well as the resources of the area, are the common heritage of mankind,

Recalling that the Convention provides the régime to be applied to the Area and its resources,

Seriously concerned at any attempt to undermine the Convention and the related resolutions of the Third United Nations Conference on the Law of the Sea,

Recognizing also the need for co-operation in the early and effective implementation by the Preparatory Commission for the International Sea-Bed Authority and for the International Tribunal for the Law of the Sea of resolution II of the Third United Nations Conference on the Law of the Sea,[2]

Noting the developments within the Preparatory Commission in 1985 and in 1986 and the significant progress made by the Preparatory Commission through its unanimous decision of 5 September 1986 to facilitate the registration of applicants as pioneer investors for deep sea-bed mining,[3]

Noting also that the Preparatory Commission has decided to hold its fifth regular session at Kingston from 30 March to 24 April 1987 and its summer meeting in 1987 at Geneva, Kingston or New York,[4]

Noting the increasing needs of countries, especially developing countries, for information, advice and assistance in the implementation of the Convention and in their developmental process for the full realization of the benefits of the comprehensive legal régime established by the Convention,

Recognizing that the United Nations Convention on the Law of the Sea encompasses all uses and resources of the sea and that all related activities within the United Nations system need to be implemented in a manner consistent with it,

Taking note of activities carried out in 1986 under the major programme on marine affairs, set forth in chapter 25 of the medium-term plan for the period 1984-1989,[5] in accordance with the report of the Secretary-General[6] as approved in General Assembly resolution 38/59 A,

Recalling its approval of the financing of the expenses of the Preparatory Commission from the regular budget of the United Nations,

Taking special note of the report of the Secretary-General prepared in pursuance of paragraph 13 of General Assembly resolution 40/63,[7]

1.   *Recalls* the historic significance of the United Nations Convention on the Law of the Sea as an important contribution to the maintenance of peace, justice and progress for all peoples of the world;

2.   *Expresses its satisfaction* at the increasing and overwhelming support for the Convention, as evidenced, *inter alia*, by the one hundred and fifty-nine signatures and thirty-two of the sixty ratifications or accessions required for entry into force of the Convention;

3.   *Calls upon* all States that have not done so to consider ratifying or acceding to the Convention at the earliest possible date to allow the effective entry into force of the new legal régime for the uses of the sea and its resources;

4.   *Calls upon* all States to safeguard the unified character of the Convention and related resolutions adopted therewith;

5.   *Also calls upon* States to observe the provisions of the Convention when enacting their national legislation;

6.   *Further calls upon* States to desist from taking actions which undermine the Convention or defeat its object and purpose;

7.   *Notes* the progress being made by the Preparatory Commission for the International Sea-Bed Authority and for the International Tribunal for the Law of the Sea in all areas of its work;

8.   *Expresses its satisfaction* at the important decision of the Preparatory Commission on 5 September 1986 that has created conditions for the early implementation of the régime for pioneer investors, contained in resolution II of the Third United Nations Conference on the Law of the Sea, thus facilitating the process of registration of applicants for pioneer investor status at the next session of the Preparatory Commission;

9.   *Expresses its appreciation* for the effective execution by the Secretary-General of the central programme in law of the sea affairs under chapter 25 of the medium-term plan for the period 1984-1989;

10.   *Further expresses its appreciation* for the report of the Secretary-General prepared in pursuance of General Assembly resolution 40/63 and requests him to continue to carry out the activities outlined therein, as well as those aimed at the strengthening of the new legal régime of the sea, special emphasis being placed on the work of the Preparatory Commission, including the implementation of resolution II of the Third United Nations Conference on the Law of the Sea;

11.   *Calls upon* the Secretary-General to continue to assist States in the implementation of the Convention and in the development of a consistent and uniform approach to the new legal régime thereunder, as well as in their national, subregional and regional efforts towards the full realization of the benefits therefrom and invites the organs and organizations of the United Nations system to co-operate and lend assistance in these endeavours;

12.   *Approves* the programme of meetings of the Preparatory Commission for 1987;[4]

13.   *Requests* the Secretary-General to report to the General Assembly at its forty-second session on developments relating to the Convention and on the implementation of the present resolution;

14.   *Decides* to include in the provisional agenda of its forty-second session the item entitled "Law of the sea".

58th plenary meeting
5 November 1986

Notes

1. <u>Official Records of the Third United Nations Conference on the Law of the Sea</u>, vol. XVII (United Nations publication, Sales No. E.84.V.3), document A/CONF.62/122.
2. <u>Ibid</u>., document A/CONF.62/121, annex I.
3. See LOS/PCN/L.41/Rev.1, annex.
4. See A/41/742, para. 115.
5. <u>Official Records of the General Assembly, Thirty-seventh Session, Supplement No. 6A</u> (A/37/6/Add.1), annex II.
6. A/38/570 and Corr.1 and Add.1 and Add.1/Corr.1.
7. A/41/742.

- - - - -

UN General Assembly
Forty-second Session

A/42/688
5 November 1987

Law of the Sea

Report of the Secretary-General

CONTENTS

PART TWO

ACTIVITIES OF THE OFFICE OF THE SPECIAL REPRESENTATIVE

INTRODUCTION

1.   General Assembly resolution 41/34 of 5 November 1986 requested the Secretary-General, *inter alia*, to report on developments relating to the United Nations Convention on the Law of the Sea[1] and on the implementation of the resolution. The present report is submitted in accordance with that request.[2] Following earlier practice, the present report is in two parts, the first of which reviews the impact of the Convention on state practice and related marine activities. It also reflects the activities of international organizations in these fields as well as those of the International Court of Justice and other tribunals dealing with the settlement of disputes concerning the law of the sea. The second part outlines the programmed activities of the Office of the Special Representative of the Secretary-General for the Law of the Sea under the medium-term plan.

2.   The United Nations Convention on the Law of the Sea continues to provide a focus for ocean-related activities and for marine affairs in general. It has attracted increasing support, with more than half of the ratifications or accessions required for its entry into force having been deposited, following the unprecedented number of signatures appended to it. It has exerted an immense influence on marine affairs in general. As States resort increasingly to the seas and oceans to supplement their developmental needs, there has been a marked trend

towards the establishment of maritime régimes consistent with the norms embodied in the Convention.

3.   While these developments in the uses of the seas in areas under national jurisdiction have continued to reinforce and strengthen the Convention, significant developments have also taken place in respect to the international régime for deep sea-bed mining. In this respect a historical step was taken when the Preparatory Commission for the International Sea-Bed Authority and the International Tribunal for the Law of the Sea decided to register India as a pioneer investor under resolution II. Before the end of 1987, the General Committee of the Preparatory Commission will consider the applications of France, Japan and the Union of Soviet Socialist Republics for registration as pioneer investors under resolution II. The allocation of mine sites to the pioneer investors is accompanied by the reservation of sea-bed areas of equal estimated commercial value for the International Sea-Bed Authority to be developed under the régime for the international sea-bed area.

4.   The increased impetus created by the maritime activities of States and their desire to benefit further from the uses of the seas and its resources have led to heightened activity in many international organizations. They have developed their programmes and activities to respond to these needs and to reflect the new régime for the oceans established by the Convention. Thus, many agencies and bodies of the United Nations, each within its sphere of competence, have responded to the enhanced activities of Member States.

5.   The activities at national and international levels relate to all aspects of the uses and resources of the seas and cover all fields of marine affairs. Consistent with these developments, the activities of the Secretariat in most aspects of marine affairs have been consolidated in order to rationalize and streamline the activities of the United Nations, thus avoiding overlaps and creating greater efficiency.

PART ONE

DEVELOPMENTS RELATING TO THE UNITED NATIONS CONVENTION
ON THE LAW OF THE SEA

I. STATUS OF THE CONVENTION

6.   The United Nations Convention on the Law of the Sea closed for signature on 9 December 1984, having received a total of 159 signatures. The Convention will enter into force 12 months after the date of deposit of the sixtieth instrument of ratification or accession. As at 3 November 1987, 35 instruments of ratification have been deposited with the Secretary-General, as follows: Bahamas, Bahrain, Belize, Cameroon, Cape Verde, Côte d'Ivoire, Cuba, Democratic Yemen, Egypt, Fiji, Gambia, Ghana, Guinea, Guinea-Bissau, Iceland, Indonesia, Iraq, Jamaica, Kuwait, Mali, Mexico, Nigeria, Paraguay, Philippines, Senegal, Saint Lucia, Sao Tome and Principe, Sudan, Togo, Trinidad and Tobago, Tunisia, United Republic of Tanzania, Yugoslavia, Zambia and the United Nations Council for Namibia.

7.   Upon ratification, 10 States made declarations.[3] Five States made declarations in accordance with article 287 with respect to the choice of procedure for the settlement of disputes concerning the interpretation or application of the Convention.[4] Three States made declarations under article 298 with respect to the categories of disputes excepted from the binding dispute-settlement procedures contained in Part XV, section 2, of the Convention.[5]

II. STATE PRACTICE AND NATIONAL POLICY

8.   The Convention remains the model on which States have based their maritime legislation with respect to maritime areas falling under their sovereignty and jurisdiction: the territorial sea, the contiguous zone, the exclusive economic zone, continental shelf and the régime of archipelagic States.

9.   It is generally accepted that the adoption by the Convention of a 12-mile territorial sea constitutes a major contribution to international maritime law. According to the latest information available, the number of States claiming a territorial sea of 12 miles is now 103.[6]

10.   States that are constituted by one or more mid-ocean archipelagos may, under certain conditions specified in the Convention, draw straight baselines joining the outermost islands and drying reefs of the archipelagos (archipelagic baselines). Under the Convention the waters enclosed within archipelagic baselines are known as "archipelagic waters" and the archipelagic State exercises sovereignty over such waters, its sea-bed, subsoil and the airspace above. The Convention has created a special régime for the passage of ships and aircraft through and above the archipelagic waters. The following States have incorporated the concept of "archipelagic States" in their legislation: Antigua and Barbuda, Cape Verde, Comoros, Fiji, Indonesia, Kiribati, Maldives, Mauritius, Philippines, Sao Tome and Principe, Solomon Islands, Trinidad and Tobago, Tuvalu and Vanuatu. It should be noted that on this matter the legislation of Indonesia and Philippines predates the Third United Nations Conference on the Law of the Sea.

11.   The Convention provides for a contiguous zone where a coastal State may exercise the control necessary to prevent and punish infringements of its custom, fiscal, immigration, health and safety laws or regulations committed within its territory or territorial sea. The Convention followed the 1958 Geneva Convention but has extended the contiguous zone from 12 to 24 nautical miles.

12.   Some 19 States have made express claims to a 24-mile contiguous zone as provided for in the Convention.[7]

13.   Of the 142 coastal States, some 72 have established exclusive economic zones and 19 exclusive fishery zones.

14.   The Convention provides that the continental shelf of a coastal State extends throughout the natural prolongation of its territory to the outer edge of the continental margin or to a distance of 200 miles from the baselines from which the breadth of the territorial sea is measured where the outer edge of the continental margin does not extend up to that distance. The Convention further provides technical criteria for the delimitation of the continental shelf where it extends beyond the 200 miles limit.

15.   While some States have enacted new legislation on the continental shelf, others have not yet updated their legislation, based as it is on the Geneva Convention on the Continental Shelf. Certain difficulties arise in the practical implementation of the technical criteria contained in the Convention, particularly with respect to acquisition of the geophysical and geological data concerning the continental margin. The acquisition of such data would require a scientific survey of continental margins. The delineation of the outer limit of the continental shelf of

States is also important in defining the international sea-bed area, which begins where areas under national jurisdiction end.

Maritime boundaries

16.   The political map of the world has been considerably altered by the extension of maritime jurisdiction of coastal States resulting from the 1982 Convention on the Law of the Sea.   The extended jurisdiction of States has necessitated the delimitation of boundaries between States with adjacent or opposite coastlines. Approximately 95 inter-State maritime boundary agreements have been concluded, representing about one third of the boundaries that need to be settled. Most of these boundary agreements were negotiated during the last 15 years, largely because of the surge of interest in offshore oil and gas in the early 1970s and the negotiations in the Third United Nations Conference on the Law of the Sea.

17.   It will be some years yet before the maritime political map of the world is complete. The North Sea and the Baltic Sea possess the most extensive delimitation system, although in the case of the latter there are still outstanding issues. In the Caribbean and Gulf of Mexico region boundary agreements have progressed well but further progress has been affected by the island geography of the region.   The Mediterranean, with its complex coastal configurations and islands of varying size producing numerous technical and legal problems, has long exemplified many maritime boundary problems. The complex political problems obtaining both in its western and eastern parts also help explain why only five agreements have been completed, four of these between Italy and its neighbours.[8]

18.   There are a number of boundaries in several regions that remain to be settled but that do not present any difficulties.   There are others, however, that may be subject to protracted disputes, the most difficult of which are those involving sovereignty over land territory, in particular, those involving sovereignty over islands.   The issue of sovereignty is the most common cause of conflict and until the question of ownership is settled, maritime boundary delimitation is not possible. The South China Sea and the Gulf of Thailand probably face the greatest difficulties, since islands are disputed and the maritime areas in question have hydrocarbon prospects or important fisheries and also carry strategic significance.

19.   States ultimately have every reason to seek prompt and lasting agreements in order not only to secure their areas of jurisdiction and pursue offshore mineral development and fisheries management but also for environmental management and national security.

20.   It should also be noted that in recent times joint development areas have become a useful method of resolving boundary disputes between neighbouring States and as a mechanism for co-operation in the exploration and development of offshore resources. This is exemplified in the following agreements: Bahrain/Saudi Arabia, 1958; Iran/Saudi Arabia, 1969; Sudan/ Saudi Arabia, 1973; Japan/Republic of Korea, 1974; Colombia/Dominican Republic, 1978; and Iceland/Norway, 1982.

Boundaries and management

21.   There is currently an active interest, particularly among marine geographers, in developing methodologies for integrating political boundaries with ocean management needs, which do not always correspond to them.[9]

22. Functional boundaries created for specific purposes, e.g. port operations, emergency measures and traffic separation lanes often reflect the pattern of the activity without any particular connection to political boundaries. All-important data bases for fisheries and ocean observing systems are based on geographical zones (by longitude and latitude). Many tasks associated with fisheries management are not best performed by reference only to jurisdictional boundaries. There has consequently been a trend towards harmonizing national policies to the needs of co-operative management and conservation of living resources transcending political boundaries. It is in the area of mineral resource development that political boundaries assume their true importance.

III. SETTLEMENT OF CONFLICTS AND DISPUTES

23. By a special agreement concluded at Esquipulas in Guatemala on 24 May 1986, El Salvador and Honduras submitted their land, island and maritime frontier dispute to the International Court of Justice for a decision. At the request of both Governments the Court has formed a special chamber of five judges to deal with the case.

24. The dispute concerns one third of the common frontier, about 469 square kilometres of territory, and also involves the determination of the juridical status of the maritime spaces of some islands in the Gulf of Fonseca.

IV. OTHER DEVELOPMENTS RELATING TO THE LAW OF THE SEA

A. Peaceful uses

1. Naval arms race

25. At its May session the Disarmament Commission[10] concurred with the view that, at the present stage, confidence-building measures, both in the global and the regional context, would be more amenable to further consideration and possible negotiation in the appropriate forums. It was recognized that a fundamental feature of the global maritime environment, both military and non-military, was freedom of navigation and that naval confidence-building measures should be in harmony with current law of the sea. Suggested initiatives included: extension of existing confidence-building measures to seas and oceans, especially to areas with the busiest sea lanes; prior notification of naval activities; the invitation of observers to naval exercises or manoeuvres; limitations on the number or scale of naval exercises in specific regions; exchange of information and greater openness on naval matters in general; and strict observance of existing maritime measures designed to build confidence. It was also felt that the possibility should be pursued of negotiating a multilateral agreement concerning the prevention of incidents at sea beyond the territorial sea in addition to existing bilateral agreements.[11]

2. The Gulf war and merchant shipping

26. The year 1980 saw the commencement of hostilities between Iran and Iraq. The so-called Gulf war has continued with intensifying hostilities. It has also assumed an increasingly maritime dimension, with frequent attacks being made on merchant ships in the Gulf. It has been estimated that since 1981 some 310 ships have been hit and either sunk or damaged.

27. The attacks on merchant shipping raise the issue of freedom of navigation on the high seas, and the right of passage through the territorial sea and international straits. It will be

recalled that the Security Council has, in resolution 598 (1987) (see also resolution 582 (1986)), reiterated its calls for a cease-fire and for, *inter alia*, discontinuance of all military activities on land, at sea and in the air. More recently a maritime session of the International Labour Conference attended by government, shipowner and seafarer delegations from 77 member countries of the International Labour Organization (ILO) adopted a resolution expressing serious concern that armed conflict endangered merchant shipping. It appealed to ILO member countries to exert their influence to persuade the warring States to refrain from attacking merchant shipping in international waters and to put an end to armed conflicts.

3. South Pacific region

28.   It may be noted that the South Pacific Nuclear Free Zone Treaty (described in the previous report, A/41/742) entered into force on 11 December 1986 with eight ratifications. The three associated Protocols were opened for signature on 1 December 1986. The first Protocol has not as yet been signed by any of the three nuclear-weapon States with territories in the region invited to apply key provisions of the Treaty to those territories. Protocols II and III, directed at all five nuclear-weapon States, have been signed by the Soviet Union and China.

B. Maritime law

1. Maritime law

(a) Implications of the Law of the Sea Convention for the International Maritime Organization and its conventions[12]

29.   The IMO Assembly decided that a careful and detailed examination of the provisions of the United Nations Convention on the Law of the Sea was necessary to assess the implications of the Convention for the conventions and work of IMO. It was particularly interested in determining the scope and areas of appropriate IMO assistance to member States and other agencies, and of the necessary collaboration with the Secretary-General on the provision of information, advice and assistance to developing countries on law of the sea matters within the competence of IMO. The study that was prepared in collaboration with the Office for Ocean Affairs and the Law of the Sea is now ready for issue and circulation.[13]

(b) Suppression of unlawful acts against the safety of navigation

30.   A new convention to fill a gap in international law will be adopted early in 1988. The first international actions on the problem, as demonstrated by the seizure of the SS **Achille Lauro**, were taken in late 1985 by the United Nations General Assembly and the IMO Assembly.[14] These were followed by the elaboration of preventive measures by the IMO Marine Safety Committee to protect ships, passengers and crews.[15] Shortly following the completion of this work, the question was then taken up in the IMO Council with a view to adopting an international instrument aimed at suppressing such terrorist acts. While three universal conventions[16] deal with the safety of air navigation in this respect, the safety of maritime navigation is not covered by any similar international instrument.[17]

31.   At the fifty-seventh session of the IMO Council, the Governments of Austria, Egypt and Italy proposed this step and presented a draft Convention to provide for a comprehensive suppression of unlawful acts committed against the safety of maritime navigation that endanger innocent human lives, jeopardize the safety of persons and property, seriously affect

the operation of maritime services and thus are of grave concern to the international community as a whole. The Council agreed unanimously that the matter was urgent and established an *ad hoc* Preparatory Committee with the mandate to prepare a draft convention on a priority basis.[18] That Committee considered the draft in March and again in May, as well as the possibility of extending the Convention to cover unlawful acts against fixed platforms, and submitted to the fifty-eighth session of the IMO Council a draft Convention for the Suppression of Unlawful Acts against the Safety of Maritime Navigation, as well as a draft Protocol for the Suppression of Unlawful Acts against the Safety of Fixed Platforms located on the Continental Shelf. The Council decided to convene a diplomatic conference to adopt the Convention, to be held at Rome from 1 to 10 March 1988.

32.   The draft IMO Convention is based on the absolute application of the principle either to prosecute or to extradite.[19] After defining the respective offences, it establishes each State party's obligation to extend its penal jurisdiction in order to pursue suspects in its territory or under its control, and either prosecute or extradite them to the country requesting their extradition that has jurisdiction to bring them to trial.

33.   The draft Convention closely follows in all essential elements and specific wording (definition of the "offence", severity of penalties, establishment of jurisdiction, inquiry into the offence, alternative between extradition or prosecution) the 1970 Hague Convention and the 1971 Montreal Convention.

(c)   **Offshore installations and structures**

34.   Article 60 of the Convention on the Law of the Sea requires that structures that are abandoned or disused shall be removed to ensure safety of navigation, taking into account any generally accepted international standards established by the competent international organization (IMO); it requires also that their removal shall have due regard to fishing, the protection of the marine environment and the rights and duties of other States. Where structures are not entirely removed, appropriate notification has to be provided of their depth, position and dimension.[20]

35.   As offshore petroleum resources are depleted, many more platforms and associated equipment will become redundant. It is important, therefore, to establish a policy on what is to be done with structures that have outlived their usefulness and may constitute dangers to navigation and other uses of the sea. As yet, few countries have experience with rig removal problems, although it has been found (in the Gulf of Mexico) that the use of explosive charges can be very destructive of marine life. Study of the technology required for total removal is indicated.

36.   Draft preliminary guidelines on safety questions related to the dismantling of disused or abandoned offshore structures have been prepared by the IMO Sub-Committee on Safety of Navigation;[21] a complete set of guidelines will not be finalized until other bodies, beginning with the IMO Marine Environmental Protection Committee, have examined the legal, environmental and technical aspects of the question.[22] FAO has already offered to co-operate.

37.   Safety issues of concern included determination of the depth to which rigs must be removed in order to safeguard surface and subsurface navigation; setting standards for maintenance of decommissioned rigs, including proper lighting and providing adequate notice to mariners of their location; and charting of those structures not completely removed.

Proposals ranged from removal only from locations traversed by shipping and only to the extent of ensuring a sufficient unobstructed water depth, to establishment of an international requirement for their total removal allowing only very limited exemptions, primarily for those structures which could be put to a *bona fide* new use, e.g. as an artificial reef to attract fish. Some coastal States were of the view that they should be allowed to decide on a case-by-case basis which platforms should be partially or completely removed, although total removal was considered advisable in shallow seas where the water depth is less than 300 metres. No clear decision has yet been reached on the question of complete or partial removal. The Sub-Committee will meet again in 1988 to study the advice and comments of the Marine Environmental Protection Committee. Subsequent considerations of environmental and fishery aspects can be expected to give final precision to the guidelines, which are the responsibility of the IMO Maritime Safety Committee.

38. At the same time, draft measures have been formulated on the prevention of infringement of safety zones around offshore structures (covering mobile offshore drilling units when on station,[23] production platforms, artificial islands, accommodation platforms, units and ancillary equipment), in view of the serious threats that any collision would pose for the safety of personnel, the environment and the structures themselves. The measures call for vessels to navigate carefully in the areas concerned, particularly where the installation or structure is also used as a navigational aid, to use any designated routing systems and to maintain a continuous listening watch in or near such areas. Coastal States should issue early notices to mariners advising of the locations of structures, the breadth of any safety zone and the rules applying therein, and any available fairways. They should also require operators to take adequate measures to prevent infringement of safety zones. Coastal States are called on to take appropriate action against those responsible for infringements or at least to notify the flag State, giving details of factual evidence sufficient to substantiate the infringement. The flag State should inform the coastal State of the follow-up action it takes. These measures thus recognize the competence of the coastal State to take action against and penalize violations of its rules concerning safety zones around offshore structures coming under its jurisdiction. These proposed measures now go to the fifteenth IMO Assembly for adoption.

2. Maritime labour law

Maritime labour

39. The drafts of the new instruments and recommendations, prepared by the Preparatory Technical Maritime Conference in May 1986, will go for adoption to the maritime session of the International Labour Conference in October 1987. The draft conventions deal with seafarers' welfare, social security, health protection and medical care, repatriation and minimum standards in merchant shipping and were described in the 1986 report (A/41/742).

3. Illicit traffic in drugs and psychotropic substances

40. The increasing difficulties encountered by law enforcement and other government agencies in coping with widespread and intensified illicit drug trafficking has led to preparation of a new convention to strengthen international co-operation and co-ordination among customs, police and judicial bodies, providing them with guidelines to intercept illegal drug traffic at all stages. The present draft, the product of an intergovernmental expert group, contains 14 articles.[24] Its provisions would seek to prevent illicit trafficking by sea (art. 12). In

addition, commercial carriers would be required to take reasonable precautions to prevent the use of their facilities and means of transport for illicit trafficking.[25]

41. Article 12 of the most recent draft of the Convention against Illicit Traffic in Narcotic Drugs and Psychotropic Substances[26] is of special interest to the law of the sea. It gives a State party the right to board, search and, if evidence of illicit traffic is discovered, seize a vessel flying the flag of another State beyond the external limits of the territorial sea of any State if there is reasonable grounds for believing that that vessel is engaged in illicit traffic. This right can be exercised if the State party has received prior permission from the flag State and is without prejudice to any rights provided for under general international law.

42. It may be noted that the Convention on the Law of the Sea provides that States shall co-operate in the suppression of illicit traffic in narcotic drugs and psychotropic substances engaged in by ships on the high seas (art. 108).

43. At the July meeting of the open-ended intergovernmental expert group, established by Economic and Social Council resolution 1987/27, on the preparation of a draft Convention against Illicit Traffic in Narcotic Drugs and Psychotropic Substances, article 12 gave rise to some important discussions. It was emphasized that any action against ships by States other than the flag States in cases where the evidence of illicit traffic was not clear and manifest could lead to abuses and might undermine important legal principles.

44. In the draft before the expert group, article 12 referred to the vessel engaged in illicit traffic as being on the high seas as defined in Part VII of the Convention on the Law of the Sea. The reference in the draft to the latter Convention was not considered appropriate by some delegations as that Convention, after its entry into force, might not be binding on all Parties to the future Convention on Illicit Traffic in Narcotic Drugs and Psychotropic Substances. The reference to the "high seas" was the object of divergent views. Instead of the term "high seas" the Group agreed to refer to the area "beyond the external limits of the territorial sea without prejudice to any rights enjoyed by the coastal State seaward of those limits". Some representatives expressed reservations with regard to this formulation, in view of the fact that, as signatories to the Convention on the Law of the Sea, they would construe the provisions of article 12 in a way compatible with their obligations under that instrument.

45. The Commission on Narcotic Drugs, by its resolution 3 (XXXII), endorsed the recommendation of the first Interregional Meeting of the Heads of National Drug Enforcement Agencies for co-operation in suppressing drug trafficking on the high seas, in free trade zones and where international commercial carriers are involved.[27]

46. The Comprehensive Outline[27] to combat drug abuse and trafficking adopted by the 1987 Vienna Drug Conference included, as Targets 26 and 28, "Surveillance of land, water and air approaches to the frontier" and "Controls over ships on the high seas and aircraft in international airspace". Under Target 26, Governments are called on to develop, implement and co-ordinate plans for maritime surveillance by national guard, coast guard and air control authorities; and to authorize coast guards and similar agencies to stop and search vessels and aircraft on reasonable grounds of suspicion of illicit carriage of drugs. Under Target 28, Governments are requested to permit law enforcement officials to board and seize a vessel unlawfully carrying drugs under certain conditions; to respond promptly when asked for permission to stop, board and search such a vessel if it is under its registry; and to conclude bilateral and regional agreements to strengthen co-operation in this area.

4. Other matters

Wrecks

47. With the 1985 discovery of the RMS **Titanic** about 700 kilometres south-east of Newfoundland, Canada, by a joint United States/French expedition, questions have arisen as to the status of this historical object and jurisdiction applicable to its use. The United States Congress adopted an act in 1986 to encourage the designation of the shipwreck as an "international maritime memorial" by means of an international agreement that would also protect its scientific, cultural and historical significance. The United States has pledged itself to co-operate with the United Kingdom, France, Canada and other interested parties to this end. Canada has claimed jurisdiction over the wreck, as lying on its continental slope. More recently a French expedition has been organized to salvage the RMS **Titanic**'s artifacts.

48. It will be recalled that the Convention imposes a general duty on States to protect archaeological and historical objects found at sea. A coastal State may prevent removal of such objects from the sea-bed of the contiguous zone without its approval (art. 303). Objects of an archaeological and historical nature found in the international sea-bed area are to be preserved or disposed of for the benefit of mankind as a whole, particular regard being paid to the preferential rights of the State or country of origin, or the State of cultural origin, or the State of historical and archaeological origin (art. 149).

C. Protection and preservation of the marine environment

1. General

49. All major reports on the environment published in 1987 express concern over the status of and trends in pollution of the seas, particularly in near shore areas, and call for the expansion of data bases for monitoring and assessment and the intensification of legal and institutional action.[28]

50. While considerable progress has been made on such global matters as the ozone layer and climatic changes due to increases in carbon dioxide and other greenhouse gases,[29] there are still considerable gaps and a particular lack of reliable information about the environment in developing countries, which also add to the difficulties of producing regional and global assessments of the state of the environment.[30] Most monitoring programmes are localized and true time series data for most areas are not available - a problem that affects all marine sciences.

51. The established priority for the United Nations Environment Programme (UNEP) Regional Seas Programme remains unchanged. However, it is recognized that action plans and related regulatory frameworks need now to be followed up with concrete implementation and greater financial commitment.

52. Recent developments on environmental impact assessment are notable.

2. Environmental impact assessment

53. Under the Convention on the Law of the Sea, States are required to co-operate directly or through competent international organizations undertaking programmes of scientific

research and encouraging exchange information and data acquired about pollution of the marine environment (art. 200). In particular they are obliged directly or through competent international organizations to provide appropriate assistance especially to developing States concerning the preparation of environmental assessments (art. 202). Concentrated attention has for some time been given to the methodology involved, primarily by UNEP, by the Organization for Economic Co-operation and Development (OECD), the Council for Mutual Economic Assistance (CMEA), the Economic Commission for Europe (ECE), and the Paris Commission.[31]

54. There are many ways of conducting environmental impact assessments and indeed a number of countries have developed legislation and machinery for their implementation. What was lacking was an acceptable global framework for conducting such assessments, not only for the benefit of States, but also for international development agencies.[32] Goals and principles have now been adopted by UNEP (decision 14/25). They seek to establish that before decisions are taken on activities that are likely to significantly affect the environment, the environmental effects of those activities should be taken fully into account (this goal is consistent with the provisions of article 206 of the Convention); to promote appropriate procedures in all countries consistent with national laws and decision-making processes; and to encourage procedures for information exchange, notification and consultation between States where significant transboundary effects may be likely. IMO has emphasized the importance of taking into account internationally accepted standards, including standards developed by competent international organizations, and of encouraging full use of existing international forums where States may consult and exchange information.

55. The goals and principles reflect a consensus view on such subjects as the early identification of potential environmental effects; the minimal requirements that an environmental impact assessment should include; the importance of impartiality and the opportunity for full comment during the assessment process; the need to include follow-up monitoring; and the minimal requirements that States should meet when their activities are likely to have significant effects on the environment of other States.

3. Regional Seas Programme

56. Nine of the 11 UNEP regional seas have adopted action plans and 5 out of the 7 regions with regulatory frameworks now have conventions in force. A total of 14 United Nations bodies and agencies and over 40 international and regional organizations now participate in the Regional Seas Programme. Recent developments of note concern the South Pacific, Wider Caribbean, Mediterranean and South and East Asian Seas Regions.

57. The following instruments were adopted for the South Pacific, in Noumea, on 25 November 1986: the Convention for the Protection and Development of the Natural Resources and Environment of the South Pacific Region, which requires the contracting parties to prevent, reduce and control pollution in the Convention area from any source, including that which might result from the testing of nuclear devices; the Protocol concerning Co-operation in Combating Marine Pollution Emergencies in the South Pacific Region; and the Protocol for the Prevention of Pollution of the South Pacific Region by Dumping, which reflects the provisions of both the London Dumping Convention and United Nations Law of the Sea Convention. The Convention is noteworthy for its linking of environmental management and resource development, and its recognition of the special ecological nature of the region.

58.   The Convention area is limited to the exclusive economic zones, to the territories of Parties, and to enclaves of high seas contained within the region; it stretches from Palau in the north-west to the Marshall Islands in the north, Kiribati in the north-east, Australia in the south-west, and New Zealand in the south-east. The acceptance of a prohibition on disposal of radioactive waste and other radioactive matter into the sea and sea-bed, without a demonstration that such disposal would or would be likely to cause harm to the marine environment, was conditional on limiting the Convention area, as described. A substantially larger Convention area had been sought earlier by some States of the region.

59.   There is now a draft action plan for the South Asian Seas Region. It envisages co-operation in implementing and enforcing relevant international agreements. Activities will concentrate on protected areas, state of the region's environment, contingency planning, land-based sources, environmentally sound waste management technology and associated policies, as well as environmental education and promotion of public awareness in countries of the region.

60.   For the East Asian Seas Region, an association of scientists is being formed to review projects and act as an advisory body. A new Centre for Specially Protected Areas has now been established for the Mediterranean at Tunis. The 1983 Cartagena Convention for the Wider Caribbean and its Protocol on pollution emergencies are now in force and the first meeting of States parties is scheduled for October 1987.

61.   The success of the Regional Seas Programme is attributed to its political strategy and to the requirement that management and financing be undertaken by the participating coastal States, but there is now a major challenge to be confronted in order to make the crucial move beyond general agreement on goals and co-operation on research. The need for greater focus on land-based sources of marine pollution in most regions has become more and more apparent, along with issues of waste management and requisite technology, matters that call for making solid investments.

4. Ocean dumping

62.   The decisions of the tenth Consultative Meeting of Contracting Parties to the London Dumping Convention were reported last year (A/41/742, paras. 59-66); the eleventh meeting will not be held until 1988. Important inter-sessional meetings, however, were planned on general scientific and legal aspects, and on the issues surrounding radioactive wastes.

63.   Wastes have become more and more complex in their nature, so that the London Dumping Convention Scientific Group on Dumping has had to make major changes and improvements in the allocation of substances to the annexes to the Convention and their position therein. The sheer magnitude of waste disposal problems in general, however, is a cause for special concern and the Group is also now actively considering alternative control strategies,[33] the results of which may be expected to have major impacts on the implementation of the global convention (the London Dumping Convention) and on the regional instruments (the Oslo Convention and UNEP regional instruments). Most regulatory systems at the moment are based on the black/grey list approach. While there would always be a need for a "prohibited" category of substances, or black list, the continuing dominance of the overall approach is now under serious evaluation. Under particularly close scrutiny is the concept of "environmental capacity",[34] which recognizes the ability of the environment as a whole to accommodate wastes, subject to proper assessment and control procedures.[35] It is

not a completely scientific concept; its application includes political and economic considerations.

64. The tenth Consultative Meeting agreed that the *Ad Hoc* Group of Legal Experts on Dumping should meet in October 1987 to consider the general implications of the Law of the Sea Convention for the London Dumping Convention and the nature and extent of the rights and responsibilities of a coastal State in a zone adjacent to its coast (London Dumping Convention articles VII (3) and XIII). It is also to study procedures for the assessment of liability for environmental damage resulting from dumping and incineration at sea.

5. Pollution from radioactive substances

65. The London Dumping Convention Panel of Experts on Radioactive Waste Disposal at Sea (October 1987) is called on to evaluate wider political, legal, economic and social aspects, and to consider the issue of comparative land-based options and associated costs and risks. It will also take up the difficult question of whether it can be proven that any dumping of these wastes will not harm human life and/or cause significant damage to the marine environment.

66. Attention is also drawn to the two 1986 Conventions adopted under the auspices of the International Atomic Energy Agency (IAEA) that are now in force: the Convention on Early Notification of a Nuclear Accident and the Convention on Assistance in the Case of a Nuclear Accident or Radiological Emergency. Certain of their provisions could be regarded as covering sea-related events since their application is not restricted to nuclear accidents occurring on land. The first Convention applies in the event of a nuclear accident having radiological transboundary significance for other States and involving specified facilities and activities, among them "any nuclear reactor wherever located" and the transport of nuclear fuels, radioactive wastes and radioisotopes (arts. 1 (1) and 1 (2) (a) (d) and (e)). Thus its States parties may well interpret such provisions as being applicable to offshore island nuclear installations, nuclear-powered ships and maritime carriage of nuclear or radioactive material. The second Convention on Emergency Assistance stipulates that a State party may request assistance, whether or not the accident or emergency originates within its territory, jurisdiction or control (art. 2 (1)). This suggests that this Convention also may be applicable in situations resulting from navigational accidents. Both Conventions assign IAEA a focal role in their implementation.

6. Pollution from ships

67. The International Convention for the Prevention of Pollution from Ships, 1973, and the Protocol of 1978 (MARPOL 73/78) now cover nearly 80 per cent of world shipping by virtue of the ratifications of 43 States. Optional annexes III (on harmful substances in packaged form) and V (on garbage) have been ratified by 27 States (41.85 per cent of world tonnage) and annex IV (on sewage) by 25 States (with 36.7 per cent of the tonnage). Ships and tankers carrying noxious liquid chemicals in bulk are now subject to international control by virtue of the 1985 amendments to MARPOL 73/78, annex II having entered into force on 6 April 1987, along with the amended Codes for ships carrying dangerous chemicals in bulk.

68. Annex II is primarily concerned with the way in which noxious liquid substances are handled, both as cargo into receiving tanks on shore and as wastes into the sea, following tank cleaning and other operations. Carriage requirements are covered by the bulk chemical Codes. Under the amended regulations, it is now possible to make reliable estimates of the size of reception facilities.[36]

7. Ice-covered areas

69.   The Convention on the Law of the Sea gives coastal States the right under certain conditions to adopt and enforce non-discriminatory laws and regulations for the prevention, reduction and control of vessel-source pollution in ice-covered areas within the limits of the exclusive economic zone (art. 234). The Helsinki Commission[37] has under urgent study various possible measures to be initiated with IMO to reduce the risk of accidents that could lead to pollution in ice-covered areas. They would cover safety of navigation, ship-board equipment and structural requirements for oil and chemical tankers and large ships.

8. Regional emergency co-operation

70.   There have been great advances in the development of regional anti-pollution arrangements and contingency planning activities at the regional, subregional and national levels. Eight regional protocols or agreements covering emergency co-operation have now been adopted, of which five (Mediterranean, Kuwait Action Plan Region, West and Central Africa, Red Sea and Gulf of Aden, and the South-East Pacific) are in force. The Association of South-East Asian Nations (ASEAN) has also drawn up a contingency plan with respect to offshore installations and coastal refineries. Now that almost all regions have arrangements, a necessary next step, as affirmed by several regional meetings, is development of operational manuals on regional or subregional contingency plans. IMO has in fact already done considerable work on the preparation of manuals on oil spills and spillages of hazardous substances other than oil.[38] Since in several regions there are many countries who receive no benefit from oil trading but experience a high level of risk from dense tanker traffic, the establishment of subregional stockpiles of pollution fighting equipment has been generally advanced as the best solution. Existing examples are for the Celebes Sea area, supported by the United Nations Development Programme (UNDP), and as planned by the oil industry, for the Strait of Malacca and Singapore.

71.   Regional arrangements should now see further development with the entry into force of Amended Protocol I of MARPOL (6 April 1987), which makes the reporting of incidents involving harmful substances compulsory.[39] These reports have to be made to IMO and to the interested parties. The nearest coastal State must be informed by the vessel involved as well as those ships assisting, including the salvor.

72.   Arrangements for international assistance for marine pollution emergencies have also seen major improvements. Submitted for the adoption of the IMO Assembly is a Marine Environment Protection Committee recommendation designed to overcome bureaucratic delays in implementing international assistance. It refers to the problem of timely clearance of material and equipment needed to respond to incidents and the need for Governments to make every effort to facilitate transportation movement of marine pollution response resources during an emergency situation. The European Parliament has created a new budgetary line for intervention in the case of environmental emergencies and has also decided that emergency aid following a serious marine pollution accident would be available to developing countries in accordance with the Lomé Convention and the budget of the Community.

D. Marine science and technology

73.   The present period is one of great significance for the future course of international co-operation in the marine sciences. Ever-increasing interest in ocean space and its resources,

new ocean-observing technologies and prospects for better understanding of major ocean phenomena and processes and their effects on resources, weather and climate have led to the emergence of long-term, large-scale and multidisciplinary co-operative investigations and ocean-observing systems. These require broad-scale integration and co-ordination of scientific effort, and the involvement of a greater number of States, particularly for regionally based activities.[40] At the same time, many regional scientific activities are needed to improve knowledge of more localized phenomena and processes. Co-operative activities must also serve the important purpose of expanding States' capabilities in science and technology.

74.   The main international ocean science programmes are those relating to living resources and non-living resources, ocean mapping, ocean dynamics and climate, and marine pollution research and monitoring.   The ocean service programmes are designed to yield the oceanographic and meteorological data and products necessary for scientific investigation and for the operations of ocean users. New ocean-observing technologies[41] and improved data collection, storage and exchange and computer modelling capabilities, as well as the general management of marine information are important issues for both the science and services programmes.

1.   Ocean science and non-living resources

75.   Planning for this jointly sponsored United Nations/Intergovernmental Oceanographic Commission (IOC) programme has made good progress. Highest priority has been given to the coastal zone and to study of sea-level changes due to climatic and/or tectonic processes, since these factors determine the occurrence of offshore minerals. This work will have a natural focus on the West Pacific region, where tectonics not only provide the framework for mineral occurrence but also for geological hazards, earthquakes, volcanic eruptions, tsunamis and landslips. The unravelling of the unusually complex processes in this region will help establish a general principle for the evolution of sedimentary sequences. The ocean science and non-living resources programme will thus have a close working relationship with the Committee for Co-ordination of Joint Prospecting for Mineral Resources in South Pacific Offshore Areas (CCOP/SOPAC). The research and training activities of that organization have also seen considerable development of late and an International Workshop on Geology, Geophysics and Mineral Resources in the South Pacific (planned for 1989) will review current programmes and draw up an eventual research plan for the region.

2.   Marine pollution research and monitoring

76.   There has been a marked increase in co-operative activities for environmental research and monitoring and in co-ordination as among IOC, IMO,[42] UNEP, the Food and Agriculture Organization (FAO), IAEA and the United Nations, much of it centring on the work of the various groups of experts under the IOC Global Investigation of Pollution in the Marine Environment (GIPME) and on the work of the Joint Group of Experts on the Scientific Aspects of Marine Pollution (GESAMP). Such developments are of considerable significance also for the planning and conduct of co-operative scientific investigations.

77.   "Vulnerable areas" are the focus of much attention, as noted in the 1986 report (A/41/742). The Marine Environmental Protection Committee is currently working towards the establishment of an inventory of sea areas beyond the territorial sea that are or will be protected; development, if necessary, of criteria for the selection of particularly sensitive areas; and initiation of protective action, where appropriate. IOC work in the field of biological effects measurements is of particular importance in this area.[43]

78.   GESAMP, jointly supported by eight United Nations organizations, advises them on a wide range of matters, including those of direct significance to the regulatory controls on marine pollution (e.g. for MARPOL 73/78).   Its current work deals with the review of potentially harmful substances; coastal modelling (concerning wastes discharged and dumped in coastal regions, including shelf areas); and consequences of low-level contamination of the marine environment.   This last work includes study of ecological changes due to low persistent concentrations or slow build-up of contaminants that may enter the sea from coastal discharges or come from atmospheric inputs, accidents and dumping; and consideration of what is involved in recovery of damaged ecosystems and habitats.   This work and that on coastal modelling is followed closely by the London Dumping Convention Consultative Meetings.

3.   Marine applications of space technology

79.   These have been developing steadily and the next decade promises to be particularly rich in satellite-derived maritime data and services - for oceanography and a variety of ocean studies,[44] marine resources surveys, maritime weather forecasting and disaster warning, and for global maritime communications for shipping.[45]

E.   The régime for marine scientific research

80.   Part XIII of the Convention, in its section 2, establishes the general principles of international co-operation for the promotion of marine scientific research for peaceful purposes and for the creation of favourable conditions for its conduct.   The coastal State's exclusive right to regulate marine scientific research conducted within its jurisdiction by foreign researching States and international organizations, and the conditions thereon, are set forth in the following provisions.

81.   A coastal State is entitled to require its consent for the carrying out of any maritime scientific research in its exclusive economic zone or on the continental shelf.   However, in normal circumstances coastal States shall grant their consent for marine scientific research projects.   This consent may be withheld in certain circumstances, e.g. if the research is of direct significance for the exploration and exploitation of natural resources, involves drilling into the continental shelf, the use of explosives or the introduction of harmful substances into the marine environment, or involves the construction, operation or use of artificial islands, installations and structures established for economic purposes.

82.   The researching State must comply with certain conditions.   For example, it must allow the coastal State to participate or be represented in the marine scientific research project, if requested, or it must provide the coastal State with the final results after the completion of the research.

83.   One overall effect of the consent régime is a much greater direct involvement by Governments in the conduct of marine scientific research, which consequently calls for more efficient communication mechanisms and channels.[46] Another is the rising costs of planning projects to ensure effective participation of developing country personnel and assisting with assessment and interpretation of research results.   A 1987 United Nations study (ST/ESA/191) has warned that national and international funding agencies must be prepared to support additional costs of international scientific co-operation.

84. Scientists and administrators from both developed and developing countries have reported some difficulties with the application of the consent rule and the modalities for granting consent. On the one hand some researching States report unreasonable refusal for projects, even where the oceanographic cruise has been officially announced by IOC, and refusal for ships to make ports of call for crew changes, equipment transfer and victualling. On the other hand, some coastal States have reported difficulties over access to full sets of data from approved projects.

85. The problems for multilateral co-operation were quite apparent at the fourteenth IOC Assembly this year. Concerns focused on the planning of major and complex ocean climate research, particularly on the World Ocean Circulation Experiment, where many more ships and more nations will be involved than in the Tropical Ocean component of the World Climate Research Programme (WCRP), requiring a higher degree of co-ordination of major resources and the ability for research vessels to operate in all parts of the ocean. Scientists look to IOC to ensure the necessary international co-operation and for the strengthening of co-ordination among the many intergovernmental component groups that make up large programmes like the World Climate Research Programme.

86. Researching States at the Assembly emphasized the need to strengthen the role of IOC in facilitating access to marine areas under national jurisdiction by research vessels participating in co-operative programmes, in facilitating transfrontier shipment of equipment, and in making data from those zones available. Various coastal States disagreed: it was not within the competence of IOC to facilitate access by research vessels and such activities remain subject to the Convention's consent régime.[47]

87. This basic question on the role of IOC has been central to the amendment of the relevant paragraph of the IOC statutes, for which a series of consultations was necessary to produce a compromise text. In that process stress was placed on the importance of not establishing two régimes - IOC and United Nations Convention on the Law of the Sea - for the conduct of marine scientific research in zones under national jurisdiction. The relevant provision requires IOC to "promote scientific investigation of the oceans and application of the results thereof for the benefit of all mankind and assist, on request, member States wishing to co-operate to these ends. Activities undertaken under this subparagraph shall be subject, in accordance with international law, to the régime for marine scientific research in zones under national jurisdiction".[48]

88. The large-scale research projects increasingly employ greatly advanced and expensive technologies, particularly satellite-based remote sensing and increasingly sophisticated data management systems, which have the effect of further widening the scientific gap between developed and developing countries. Without a working understanding of the modes and requirements of scientific investigation and analysis, effective implementation of the consent régime becomes more difficult, with implications also for training opportunities and for transfer of technology.

89. Developing country scientists have attributed some of the problems encountered to inadequate attention to the scientific and related technological aspects of marine development and lack of understanding as to the complexity of the marine environment and its resources. They have called for mechanisms promoting an appreciation of the economic value of the marine sciences, among officials and user communities. Certainly, a considerable part of any difficulty with the consent régime has to be attributed to inadequate resources in qualified

personnel, facilities and infrastructure. Solutions to such fundamental problems will only be possible with international and regional co-operation, augmented by assistance from developed countries and from the United Nations system.

90. There is need for a better understanding of the consent régime embodied in the Convention in order to promote harmonious application and to benefit both coastal States and the scientific community at large. The Office for Ocean Affairs and the Law of the Sea has already compiled national legislation and regulations on the subject for publication early next year. The next step is to determine actual practice and the true nature of the problems that exist and those that can be anticipated. The Office will be collaborating closely with IOC in this endeavour, the aim being to promote the necessary co-operation among States and more uniform and consistent application of the Convention through the publication of an explanation in practical terms of the régime for marine scientific research embodied in the Convention.

F. Fisheries management, development and control

91. FAO has in 1987 made its first review since 1977 of the world fisheries situation and outlook and its first examination of the implementation of the Strategy for Fisheries Management and Development adopted by the 1984 World Conference on Fisheries.[49] In view of the considerable value of these reviews, the Committee on Fisheries has decided that in future they will be done together at regular four-year intervals.[50]

1. World fisheries situation and outlook

92. The consistent growth recorded in recent years in total world catch is encouraging and there is every indication that the 1986 catch may have approached 89.2 million tons, 79 million tons of which comes from the oceans (56 per cent from the Pacific, 36 per cent from the Atlantic, 5 per cent from the Indian Ocean). Developing countries have expanded their share to 52 per cent of the total catch: South American and Asian developing countries reported higher catches; total African landings remain essentially unchanged. The catches in developed countries were back to 1984 levels, after low figures in 1985, due to higher catches by Japan and the USSR. European Economic Community (EEC) countries reported a slight decrease in 1986, while Canada and the United States reported increases. Significant changes have entered the world tuna fishery, where developing countries have increased their catches by more than 40 per cent since 1979 and quadrupled their share in the production of canned tuna. Other statistics of note are that 80 per cent of the catch is used for direct human consumption; 25 per cent is artisanal and 75 per cent industrial; and that one third of the total catch goes to international trade in fish and fishery products, with an increasing share to developing countries ($5 billion out of $16.9 billion).

93. Nevertheless, it should be observed that a great part of the recent increases in production comes almost entirely from catches of shoaling pelagic species (and mostly in the south-east Pacific), which are notoriously subject to fluctuations in abundance and have lower value since they are used for conversion to fish-meal rather than for direct human consumption.

94. The FAO review estimates that a further 20 million tons of fish a year will be needed by the year 2000 and it will be in the developing countries that the growth in demand for food fish will be greater. It concludes that there is little prospect for increasing the catch of demersal species and that better possibilities will lie with small (shoaling) pelagic species. However,

their abundance is known to fluctuate dramatically with evidence of interaction with other species so that more research directed at these species is indicated. It is assumed that for some time world fisheries will continue to be characterized by a strong demand for expensive products of preferred and often fully exploited species, and by continuing difficulties in marketing abundant, low-price fish. While the review concludes that a 20 million ton increase may be theoretically feasible, it emphasizes that only a part of that increase could come from more extensive or intensive fishing effort, and warns that the increases involved may have been largely achieved already. It was noted that the rest - at least half of the projected increase in supply - can be obtained only through management improvement, which must be concerned with the overall economic performance of the fisheries, improved utilization of resources (including the reduction of port-harvest losses); and effective development of aquaculture. Governments will need to strengthen institutions further to meet the complex tasks of fisheries management and deal with the economic and logistical problems of improving utilization.

95. At the meeting of the Committee on Fisheries much emphasis was placed on the critical information and data needs of fisheries management, and on evidence that data provided are not always of an acceptable quality. Fisheries research also needs greater attention, most particularly research on tropical fisheries, including provision of statistical services, which have been deteriorating over a long period.

96. Another important aspect of fishery policy will be to protect and enhance small-scale or artisanal fisheries. These produce over 20 million tons annually for direct consumption. They have the added benefits of being labour-intensive, requiring little capital investment and a low level of mechanization.

97. Over the past 20 years, a combination of expanding export markets for high-value products (notably shrimp and tuna) and national policies (supported by international donor agencies) have led to widespread use of new capital-intensive fishing technologies, which have profoundly affected the welfare of small-scale fishing communities around the world.

98. The key to progress in fisheries development in the developing countries is further promotion of the capabilities of these countries, through training and transfer of technology, and to this end sustained and co-ordinated effort is required on the part of donor agencies and development organizations. The recent UNDP review of fishery development projects is notable in this respect. The review, prompted by concerns with the low rate of success,[51] found that many failures were attributable to lack of available information and data and to inadequate analysis of resources available for exploitation before projects start and lack of monitoring of the reaction of stocks to increased exploitation. Many problems were also attributed to deterioration in the coverage of reported catch and other statistics. UNDP has concluded that fishery research is receiving less and less priority and that this trend must be reversed. The review also found that a series of co-ordinated special-purpose projects would be preferable to single multi-purpose projects, and that while regional and interregional projects can be most cost-effective, they must concentrate on problems best resolved by joint action.

2. 1984 Strategy for Fisheries Management and Development

99. The first progress report published under this title (COFI/87/3) provides ample evidence that the Strategy has generally proved to be a most persuasive tool for national fishery administrations seeking higher priority from government; a number have either taken direct action to strengthen their fishery administrations or have reformulated fishery plans on the

basis of its recommendations. The review also provides plentiful evidence of the serious attempts that are being made to improve management and utilization of resources, and the attention being given to the problem areas - lack of sufficient data for management purposes and problems with establishing effective control.

100.   The report makes it abundantly clear that collaboration between developed and developing countries, and among developing countries, is now a factor of very considerable importance in world fisheries. The number and scope of joint ventures and similar co-operative agreements are particularly numerous. While their value is undisputed, they must be negotiated carefully and equitably. There will be many more opportunities for such co-operation, especially among developing countries, on such matters as joint fishing enterprises, product development, resources research, intraregional trade, and particularly training and joint surveillance and fishing control systems. FAO is now acting with UNDP assistance on the Strategy's recommendation for co-operative use of fishery research, training and development vessels.

3. Marine mammals

101.   In view of the moratorium on whaling, the thirty-ninth annual meeting of the International Whaling Commission (IWC) again strengthened its limitations on the taking of whales for research purposes. Further criteria and guidelines have been set down for the IWC Scientific Committee to follow when reviewing research permit proposals, and a mechanism has been established whereby the Commission can recommend to member Governments that they revoke current permits and refrain from issuing new ones.

4. Regional fishery developments

102.   The seventeenth session of the Committee on Fisheries also provided an important opportunity to review the several problems FAO regional fishery bodies have faced in recent years on, for example, geographical coverage; participation of member States and other entities (e.g. EEC); management functions; scope of recommendations made; and co-operation with other organizations concerned with fisheries (COFI/87/9).

103.   Several of these problems are common to the concept and process of regionalism, most particularly that of appropriate geographic coverage and scope of functions and powers. Problems of geography vary from the necessity of having to belong to more than one regional fisheries body to overlapping among bodies, e.g. the Indian Ocean Fisheries Commission (IOFC) and the South Pacific Forum Fisheries Agency (SPFFA) overlap the original Indo-Pacific Fisheries Commission (IPFC). A different variant of the problem is that experienced by the Fishery Committee for the Eastern Central Atlantic (CECAF). This Committee first thought that it might be possible to introduce a more effective statistical system corresponding to exclusive economic zones in the region, but found too many difficulties with this approach. It has thus opted for a new and more detailed grid to be prepared on the basis of present knowledge of the distribution and migrations of fish stock.[52]

104.   Membership of regional bodies was dramatically affected by the Convention on the Law of the Sea: access by non-coastal States became more restrictive, but was often resolved through the creation of subsidiary bodies composed only of coastal States, specifically responsible for management questions in a subregion. FAO considers that broadly speaking the membership situation is satisfactory. No solution has been found, however, for upgrading EEC participation.

105. There are considerable differences in the degree of management competence among fishery bodies and FAO is suggesting that they be adjusted and strengthened, particularly in the IOFC and CECAF regions, where the status of certain stocks, particularly shared and straddling stocks, calls for the adoption of concerted management measures. The most interesting decision-making procedure is that of making potentially binding recommendations, subject to objections.[53] The General Fisheries Council for the Mediterranean is the only FAO body to use it (IPFC also has the ability), but the others would require reconstitution.

106. Improved co-operation with other organizations (and bilateral agencies) is of some concern to FAO. Not only have the number of international organizations concerned exclusively with fisheries increased, but many regional economic development organizations have also intensified efforts in the fisheries field (e.g. ASEAN and the Caribbean Community). FAO notes that while they do not provide an adequate geographical framework for co-operation in management, they can play an important role in the development process.

107. Several of the above issues are again illustrated in recent regional developments, along with persistent problems in obtaining the necessary information and data, in building fishery research capability and ensuring compliance. Also illustrated are the variations in management policy.

5. Eastern central Atlantic

108. The tenth session of CECAF, held in December 1986, was notable in several areas: on the question of appropriate geographical coverage, bilateral fishery agreements, and management measures and enforcement.

109. The Committee noted with concern that some coastal States were having considerable difficulties in obtaining statistics on foreign fishing and urged those having bilateral agreements to ensure compliance with clauses requiring timely declaration of reliable statistics. Others were requested to seek improved statistical data from partners and to intensify scientific co-operation with them. The Committee also called for a balance to be struck between the presence of foreign fleets and development of national capacity, as well as protection of artisanal fisheries from unfavourable competition with industrial fisheries.

110. CECAF has again endorsed the management approach recommended in 1985, when it advised that direct regulation of fishing efforts through a limitation of fishing capacity was more appropriate for rational management of national stocks than indirect limitation through total allowable catches; and that management of shared stocks called not only for the establishment of total allowable catches and catch allocation schemes among the countries concerned but a direct or concerted limitation of the fishing effort of each country.

111. The Sub-Regional Commission of CECAF, comprising Cape Verde, the Gambia, Guinea-Bissau, Mauritania and Senegal, is reviewing experience in other parts of the world on harmonization of legal controls and enforcement measures. For this, FAO has provided a subregional compendium of fisheries legislation, a review of co-operative measures in surveillance and enforcement in the south Pacific and the European Community and a paper on maritime hot pursuit as it affects fisheries.[54]

6. Western central Atlantic

112.   A review of articles 63 and 64 of the Convention on the Law of the Sea by a Western Central Atlantic Fisheries Commission Expert Consultation has concluded that the Convention on the Law of the Sea annex I list of highly migratory species did not include some species of importance to the Lesser Antilles region. For management purposes, these stocks were distinguished as follows: stocks occurring within a single exclusive economic zone; transboundary stocks; stocks migrating within the archipelago; stocks migrating only partially within the exclusive economic zone. The Committee has recognized that the distribution ranges and migration of resources exploited in common determine the number of States and territories that need to participate in any discussion on their rational management. Concrete management measures for shared resources will be defined on this basis.

7. South-west Atlantic

113.   Fishing efforts in the area have built up rapidly during the 1980s, as have the annual catch and the number of countries and vessels involved. The main fishing nations, by volume of their catches, are: Argentina, Poland, Japan, Uruguay, USSR, Spain, Bulgaria, German Democratic Republic, Republic of Korea and, since 1985, Cuba. With this rapid development came concerns as to potential over-exploitation and foreseeable difficulties over conservation and management. FAO therefore decided in 1985 to carry out an assessment of the state of the fish stocks in the area and that study is now available.[55]

114.   The main offshore fisheries include southern blue whiting, mostly fished by Poland and the Soviet Union, and the short finned squid, fished by most nations operating in the area.[56] The assessments of these depended primarily on the detailed information and data that were supplied by Poland and Japan. No detailed fishing effort data were provided by any of the other offshore fishing nations in the area. However, Argentina provided significant information on fisheries in the south-west Atlantic in general and the surveillance data provided by the United Kingdom gave good indications of the total fishing effort around the Falkland Islands (Malvinas). The study finds that southern blue whiting seem to be lightly to moderately exploited and do not call for management measures for the time being. In the case of the shortfin squid fishery, it is likely that the increased fishing effort in 1986 has created an overfishing situation. The study notes also that a variable proportion of the stock is distributed and exploited quite heavily (up to 50 per cent beyond the 200-mile limit). Adequate management clearly calls for good and reliable information on a continuous basis and for some kind of collaboration among the States operating in the area. The FAO study therefore calls attention to article 63 (2) of the Convention.

115.   Very little is currently known about the other main offshore fishery for the common squid, but, based on the results of past surveys and a comparison with estimated current catches and some other sparse information, there is a high probability for this stock to become over-exploited.

116.   The Committee on Fisheries has recognized the importance of the fisheries in the area (Statistical Area 41) and FAO's unique ability, under the present circumstances, to collate and analyse fisheries data (COFI report CL 91/7). FAO will therefore continue to monitor the situation, within its mandate as a specialized technical agency, and will update the study as appropriate. Countries fishing in the area were invited to co-operate with FAO particularly through the provision of all catch and effort data and biological information on the resources.

8. Indian Ocean

117. The main fishery issue is improvement of the present institutional framework for managing the tuna stocks.

118. It is to be noted that the Convention on the Law of the Sea has dramatically changed the nature of the responsibilities and powers of the existing fishery bodies involved with tuna (IOFC, IPFC, ICCAT, the Inter-America Tropical Tuna Commission (IATTC), the South Pacific Commission (SPC) and SPFFA).[57] FAO is concerned that relatively little attention is presently being given to new assessments of tuna stocks and called attention to the extreme difficulties in the last few years for tuna scientists to gain access to detailed catch and effort statistics for stock assessments (COFI 87/INF.4).

119. France, Japan, Seychelles, Sri Lanka and Thailand have begun a detailed review of the options available for long-term institutional arrangements for Indian Ocean tuna and have agreed that the future arrangement should cover two FAO Statistical Areas (51 and 57). No final agreement was reached on membership: some wished to restrict it to coastal States and States whose nationals fish for tuna in the region; others called additionally for the participation of countries that could contribute to scientific knowledge of the stocks. Most agreed that the new arrangements should provide for full management functions and the power to make potentially binding recommendations. The developing coastal States strongly emphasized the need for the new body to deal also with development aspects.

9. South-west Pacific

120. The negotiations that began in 1984 on a regional licensing agreement under which United States tuna fishermen could fish in the region were concluded with a Treaty between the United States and 16 South Pacific countries on 2 April 1987. It will enter into force when ratified by the United States and 10 States, three of which are specifically named (Papua New Guinea, Kiribati and Federal States of Micronesia). So far, Australia, Fiji, Papua New Guinea, New Zealand and Nauru have ratified. The Treaty sets out terms and conditions under which United States flag fishing vessels will be able to fish in some 10 million square miles of exclusive economic zones and high sea areas enclosed by the zones in the region. The tuna industry will pay annual licence fees and provide technical assistance; under a related agreement with SPFFA, the United States Government will provide economic support funds for five years to parties to the Treaty.

121. The Treaty is also of considerable interest in that it represents one of the first attempts to provide a practical working mechanism for the concept of flag State responsibility for compliance control. The United States Government would undertake to enforce the provisions of the agreement against its nationals and fishing vessels as a supplement to the enforcement measures taken by the coastal States themselves. Its penalty levels would be comparable to those in force for foreign vessels operating in the United States exclusive economic zone. The Treaty also contains specific provisions recognizing SPFFA's regional register of foreign fishing vessels.

122. Negotiations for this Treaty also brought a related matter into sharper focus: accurate charting of maritime boundaries. It has been emphasized that in any unilateral claim or bilateral boundary agreement enough technical information should be provided so that both claimant and user States will know where the limits are. Clear and unambiguous definitions for the various limits in the Treaty are given in an annex describing areas closed to United

States fishing off the coasts of the island States. Charts will be developed for use by the industry once the Treaty enters into force.

10. Eastern Pacific

123.   The new Eastern Pacific Tuna Fishing Agreement will establish a regional licensing régime. The Treaty has been ratified so far by Costa Rica, Honduras and the United States. Two additional coastal State ratifications are necessary for its entry into force. Also with a view to establishing a tuna fishing régime in the Eastern Pacific Ocean, a draft treaty was concluded in Guatemala in August 1987. This draft treaty is based on the new law of the sea and fully upholds the sovereign rights of coastal States over the living resources in the exclusive economic zones. The draft treaty will be considered at a conference to be held in Mexico in 1988 and will serve as an instrument in the establishment of a new institution concerning tuna fishing and conservation in the eastern Pacific. The following countries will participate in this conference: Chile, Colombia, Costa Rica, Ecuador, El Salvador, Guatemala, Mexico, Nicaragua, Panama and Peru.

11. South-East Asia

124.   The Indo-Pacific Fisheries Commission has concluded that severe over-fishing is prevalent throughout the region.[58] Catches of commercially valuable demersal fisheries have dropped sharply and some species have disappeared, and it is feared that the regional demand for fish will greatly exceed potential supplies, leading to increased prices and thus even greater pressures on fisheries. Efficient management measures become all the more critical. The Commission pinpointed the absence of property rights as the fundamental cause of waste and resulting conflicts and called for exclusive user rights, particularly for artisanal fishermen, and strong management authority.   Priority should be given to investment projects and programmes that facilitate better management.

G. Developments in regional co-operation

125.   The urgent concern of States to implement the Convention and to benefit from the resources under their jurisdiction is highlighted by the activities of the States not only at national levels but also at regional and subregional levels. They underscore the need for assistance to States at both national and regional levels. In this respect the following recent initiatives should be noted: a subregional Symposium, co-sponsored by Côte d'Ivoire and Cameroon; a subregional workshop under the auspices of the Organization of Eastern Caribbean States; the first Indian Ocean Marine Affairs Conference; and the Conference of the South-East Asian Project on Ocean Law and Policy.

126.   The Abidjan symposium held in June 1987 requested the Office for Ocean Affairs and the Law of the Sea to give priority assistance to the States of the West and Central African regions to implement the Convention on the Law of the Sea and to introduce the marine dimension in their developmental process. It also asked for United Nations assistance in organizing a training course on the development of offshore hard minerals in the region.

1. Organization of Eastern Caribbean States

127.   In September 1987, OECS held a workshop on certain maritime matters as they affected the region. The workshop considered the application to the OECS subregion of the relevant provisions of the Convention dealing with the determination of baselines, the status of

islands and insular formations, and the delimitation of maritime boundaries between States with adjacent and opposite coasts. The workshop discussed several issues relating to boundary-making in the Caribbean as a whole, and in particular, with reference to the subregion. It was noted that among the important factors affecting delimitation in the OECS region are the proximity of States and dependencies; the presence of islands, rocks, reefs and sandbanks; the presence of dependent territories of metropolitan Powers; and the distribution of the natural resource potential of the region.

2. Indian Ocean Marine Affairs Co-operation

128. The Indian Ocean Marine Affairs Co-operation Conference (IOMAC) held in January 1987 was a major undertaking involving some 34 countries. Its basic objective was to increase awareness of the potential for co-operation among States of the region and for co-operation with the United Nations system as well as the developed countries. The Conference set down the framework for co-operation and drew up a programme and plan of action that emphasizes pooling and sharing of scarce scientific and technical facilities and expertise, exchange and centralization of information and data and general improvement of communications at the regional level to optimize resources and avoid duplication of effort. It furthermore institutionalized co-operation in the establishment of an IOMAC secretariat and a 17-member Standing Committee. That group has already set some policy priorities: initiation and rapid development of a marine affairs information network (using national focal points); organization of inventories of national facilities and capabilities; and identification of training needs. International organizations are asked to liaise with IOMAC in building the necessary information network.

3. The South-East Asian Project on Ocean Law, Policy and Management[59]

129. SEAPOL has concentrated on the processes and problems associated with implementation of the Convention on the Law of the Sea in the region and particularly on boundary-making, conflict avoidance and dispute settlement, transit (in environmental and strategic terms), environmental protection and fishery management and conservation. The SEAPOL conference held in April 1987 also discussed the future for regional co-operation in ocean development and resource management and made a number of recommendations of considerable significance.

130. International organizations were called on to assist national legislative activity and other tasks of implementation of the Convention. The States themselves must seek out all opportunities for participation in international research, training, information and technical assistance programmes in the various ocean sectors, particularly where marine environmental, research and technological matters are concerned. Stress in general was placed on the general obligations of States to consult and give notice to neighbouring States, other interested States and competent international organizations, as prescribed in various provisions of the Convention, and seek out all opportunities for collaborative activities. Emphasis was also placed on the need to avoid unduly strict interpretation of coastal States' rights, particularly where conflicts with other States might ensue, and to seek bilateral and regional co-operative solutions wherever possible.

131. The general approach to regionalism was to begin with a focus on ASEAN. The conference readily accepted the notion that the need for bilateral treaty making in the region diminishes with the development of regional co-operation. The first step was considered to be

a consultative machinery to designate areas and issues under the Convention that lend themselves to regional co-operation.

V. THE PREPARATORY COMMISSION FOR THE INTERNATIONAL SEA-BED AUTHORITY AND FOR THE INTERNATIONAL TRIBUNAL FOR THE LAW OF THE SEA

132. The Preparatory Commission met twice during 1987. It held the fifth session at Kingston from 30 March to 16 April 1987, and a meeting in New York from 27 July to 21 August 1987. It has decided to hold its sixth session at Kingston from 14 March to 8 April 1988. Provision has been made for servicing a summer meeting of the Preparatory Commission in 1988 in New York.

A. The plenary

1. The implementation of resolution II

133. Following the Understanding of 5 September 1986 (LOS/PCN/L.41/Rev.1), it had been anticipated that the four applicants, namely France, India, Japan and the Soviet Union, would have submitted revised applications as pioneer investors, which would have been considered and registered during the fifth session of the Preparatory Commission. However, in the light of inter-sessional consultations that had taken place, the four applicants did not submit their revised applications and requested an extension of the deadline for their submission.

134. From the information provided to the Preparatory Commission by the first group of applicants and the potential applicants, the Commission was satisfied that substantial progress had been made and further time was necessary to complete the discussions that had begun during the inter-sessional period. Accordingly, the Preparatory Commission decided to extend the time for the submission of revised applications by the four applicants. These applications were to be submitted not later than one week prior to the summer meeting.

135. It was agreed that, unless the Preparatory Commission decided otherwise, the Group of Technical Experts, established in accordance with the Understanding of 5 September 1986, would convene at the beginning of the second week of the summer meeting in order to examine the applications submitted for registration and submit a report to the General Committee, which would also be convened during the summer meeting. The General Committee acts as the executive body on behalf of the Preparatory Commission for the purpose of registration. It was also agreed that India, which had no conflicts with respect to overlapping claims, could be registered separately, but that France, Japan and the Soviet Union were to be considered and registered simultaneously.

136. Following the Understanding of 10 April 1987 (LOS/PCN/L.43/Rev.1), the Group of Technical Experts was convened and began its meeting on 3 August 1987. However, in the light of certain developments, the Group was unable to examine the applications of all four applicants and in accordance with the Understanding of 10 April 1987, it began examining the revised application of India.

137. During the summer meeting the Preparatory Commission was informed that the negotiations aimed at resolving all pending practical problems, which had been in progress

since the last session of the Preparatory Commission, had been successfully concluded (LOS/PCN/L.49). The Secretary-General hailed this as the most important development since the adoption of the Convention in 1982. The first group of applicants and the potential applicants reported that a comprehensive settlement of practical problems had been achieved (LOS/PCN/90 and LOS/PCN/91). The outcome ensured that all applications submitted would now be considered by the Group and the General Committee with a view to their registration. However, because of the short lapse of time since the negotiations were concluded and the need for adjustment to certain applications, the date of consideration of the applications of France, Japan and the Soviet Union had to be postponed.

138. Accordingly, the next meeting of the Group of Technical Experts would be convened from 23 November to 4 December 1987. It would be followed by a meeting of the General Committee from 7 to 18 December 1987 in order to consider the revised applications of France, Japan and the Soviet Union as pioneer investors under resolution II.

Registration of India

139. The agreement on the resolution of conflicts with respect to overlapping claims was followed by a historic development in the Preparatory Commission when it decided to register India as the first pioneer investor in the international sea-bed area (LOS/PCN/94) on the basis of a report of the Group of Technical Experts (LOS/PCN/BUR/R.l). In accordance with resolution II of the Third United Nations Conference on the Law of the Sea, India has been allocated an area of 150,000 square kilometres in the south-central Indian Ocean basin. In this area India has the exclusive right to carry out activities leading up to the exploitation of polymetallic nodules. At the same time the Commission reserved from the Indian application an area of 150,000 square kilometres of equal estimated commercial value for future development by the International Sea-Bed Authority.

140. It was the general opinion that the registration of India as a pioneer investor represented a milestone in the evolution of the law of the sea. It was also the general view that the event not only marked the beginning of the implementation of the pioneer system established under resolution II, but in fact gave concrete meaning to the principle of the common heritage of mankind embodied in the 1982 Convention (LOS/PCN/L.54/Rev.1).

Other matters

141. At the 37th meeting of the Commission, the plenary elected by acclamation the nomination of the African Group, Mr. José Luis Jesus of the delegation of Cape Verde, as Chairman of the Preparatory Commission to succeed Mr. Joseph S. Warioba, Prime Minister of the United Republic of Tanzania.

142. At the 38th meeting of the plenary, the Commission commemorated the twentieth anniversary of the initiative of Malta relating to the reservation exclusively for peaceful purposes of the sea-bed beyond national jurisdiction and the use of its resources in the interest of mankind.

2. The preparation of the rules, regulations and procedures
relating to the organs of the Authority

143. The plenary continued the examination of the draft rules of procedure for the Economic Planning Commission and completed the first reading of these rules. It then took

up the examination of the revised rules of procedure of the Council and completed the second reading of these rules. On the second reading several of the draft rules were provisionally approved.

144. There was a lengthy debate on the proposals of the draft rules of procedure of the Council to establish a Finance Committee. There was general agreement on the advisory nature of the body and the qualifications of the members of this Committee. However, certain issues needed further discussion, such as whether the criteria for membership of the Committee should be based on the principle of equitable geographical distribution and special interests or only on the principle of equal geographical distribution, and whether the major contributors should constitute a special category.

145. Throughout its work on the draft rules of procedure of the various organs of the Authority, there were certain issues that were left pending. They concerned in particular financial and budgetary matters, decision-making, majorities required for elections, status of observers and subsidiary organs.

146. At the sixth session, the plenary will commence with a second reading of the draft rules of procedure of the Legal and Technical Commission and of the Economic Planning Commission. The plenary will then return to the pending draft rules of procedure of the Council.

B. Special Commission 1

147. The mandate of the Special Commission is to undertake studies on the problems that would be encountered by the developing land-based producer States likely to be most seriously affected by sea-bed mineral production. The Special Commission continued its discussion on possible remedial measures for such developing land-based producer States.

148. The view was expressed that there was no need for the Authority to devise any new remedial measures. The need for such measures may not arise since the very factors that would encourage commercial sea-bed mining in the future, for example high metal prices, would at the same time be helpful to land-based mining. Were the need to arise, existing economic measures of international, multilateral, regional and subregional organizations may be adequate to cope with the problem of developing land-based producers adversely affected by sea-bed mineral production. On the other hand, the view was maintained that it was necessary that the Authority adopt its own measures.

149. In the event that the Authority adopted its own measures, views diverged as to whether measures of economic adjustment assistance or a system of compensation would be the most effective way of dealing with the problems. Further, if a system of compensation was chosen it did not necessarily entail the establishment of a compensation fund. The questions were raised as to whether a system of compensation or compensation fund should be of a global, multilateral or bilateral nature. Divergent views were also expressed on the sources for financing of such a fund: whether part of the profit of the Enterprise would be the only source or whether the sea-bed miners should also contribute from their profits. There was general agreement, however, that developing land-based producers seriously affected by deep sea-bed mining should be provided with some form of assistance.

150. At its meeting in New York, the Special Commission concentrated mainly on the issue of subsidization in relation to deep sea-bed mining. Some delegations were of the opinion that

efficient land-based producers would be able to compete with sea-bed production as long as the latter was a commercial unsubsidized operation, and that the real threat to competitive land-based producers was subsidized sea-bed mining. These delegations suggested that an anti-subsidization recommendation should be an important element in the recommendations of the Special Commission to the Authority with regard to remedial measures for the problems of developing land-based producer States adversely affected by sea-bed production. Other delegations raised a number of questions about the applicability and effectiveness of the General Agreement on Tariffs and Trade (GATT)-type anti-subsidy provisions in relation to sea-bed mining. There were also questions as to whether any practical, realistic and effective anti-subsidy measures could be formulated at all. Some delegations were of the view that even if there was no subsidization of sea-bed mining, when sea-bed mining occurs, the very fact that there is a new source of supply of minerals would result in adverse effects on developing land-based producers; subsidization of sea-bed mining would merely aggravate the situation. These issues will continue to be deliberated by the Special Commission.

C. Special Commission 2

151. The Special Commission is charged with preparing for the establishment of the Enterprise, the operational arm of the Authority. It is also required under resolution II of the Conference to take the necessary measures to enable the Enterprise to keep pace with States and other entities that will be engaged in deep sea-bed mining. In particular, under the pioneer régime registered pioneer investors are required, *inter alia*, to provide training for the personnel of the Enterprise. At its session at Kingston, the Commission discussed in some detail the question of training, in particular, issues relating to timing, types of training and the costs of such training.

152. With regard to the question of when training should begin, views were expressed that the commencement of training should be limited to the viability of deep sea-bed mining. It was, however, argued that, in view of the importance of training for the participation of developing countries in all aspects of deep sea-bed mining, such a link should not be established, and that the earlier training could begin, the better it would be in order to keep pace with sea-bed mining development. Divergent views were held on the question of costs. On the one hand it was held that the costs of such training should be borne by the pioneer investors. The contrary view was that the costs should not be borne by the pioneer investors alone, but should be reimbursable by the Authority. It was agreed that an ad hoc working group on training would be established to formulate a training programme.

153. At its meeting in New York, the Special Commission discussed the administrative structure of the Enterprise, including the question of the establishment of an initial "nucleus" Enterprise. The description given in the Secretariat paper (LOS/PCN/SCN.2/WP.12) of the kind of monitoring, evaluating and continued preparatory functions that would need to be performed in the pre-feasibility period was generally accepted. There was general agreement on the necessity of keeping personnel and costs to a minimum.

154. With the registration of the first group of applicants the work of the Special Commission will now enter a more concrete phase. It would have to turn its attention to the implementation of paragraph 12 of resolution II. As a consequence, the programme of work for the sixth session will be the following: formulation and establishment of a training programme; structure and organization of the Enterprise; and the implementation of paragraph 12 of resolution II with respect to exploration and transfer of technology.

D. Special Commission 3

155.   The preparation of the rules, regulations and procedures for the exploration and exploitation of the deep sea-bed falls under the mandate of Special Commission 3. The Commission began a detailed consideration of draft articles dealing with the financial terms of a mining contract, which are viewed as being crucial to the successful undertaking of deep sea-bed mining. The articles considered deal with the annual fixed fee, the choice of system of financial contribution, production charges, the method of assessment of quantity of processed metals from nodules, the attribution of average price to such metals, notification of market value and payment of production charges, the Authority's share of attributable net proceeds and the determination of first and second periods of commercial production for graduated taxation.

156.   During its meeting in New York the Commission continued its discussion of the draft articles. In particular it examined the provisions relating to the issue of interest, the recovery of the contractor's development, the calculation and payment of the Authority's share of attributable net proceeds, accounting principles, payment to the Authority, the selection of accountants and the settlement of disputes.

157.   During the discussion of these draft articles and the various amendments, many comments were made, amendments submitted and suggestions offered.

158.   The Special Commission then had a general discussion on document LOS/PCN/SCN.3/WP.6/Add.3 (Draft Regulations on Financial Incentives) introduced by the Secretariat at the 60th meeting of the Special Commission.

159.   Views were expressed that financial incentives should be considered as a component of the financial rules. It was pointed out that the financial terms of contract created an unduly onerous burden for the contractor and that the provisions in articles 88 and 89 of document LOS/PCN/SCN.3/WP.6/Add.3 did not provide an adequate solution. What was required before detailed incentives were discussed were certain mechanisms and an institutional framework based on stable and clear criteria and non-discriminatory procedures under which uniform and predetermined incentives would be provided. It was suggested that the provision of such incentives should not be left to the discretion of the Authority but should be provided automatically under specific conditions clearly detailed in advance.

160.   Another view was that the provision of financial incentives could not be viewed as creating exceptions to the financial terms of contract. It was maintained that the provisions of article 13 of annex III of the Convention must prevail and that the availability of incentives should not become a general rule but only be awarded at the discretion of the Authority. It was also pointed out that it was important to consider the provision of financial incentives in terms of the revenues of the Authority.

161.   It was suggested that the provision of such incentives should not amount to subsidizing sea-bed mining especially to the detriment of land-based mining.

162.   It was further suggested that a higher degree of security for the contractor could be viewed as a financial incentive. Other additional incentives suggested were, *inter alia*, a partial or full refund of the annual fixed fee paid by the contractor where exploration did not lead to exploitation of a mine site and the right of the contractor to change his choice of making his

financial contribution to the Authority, i.e. by either paying a production charge only or paying a combination of the production charge and a share of net proceeds.

163.   Throughout the debate, a view was maintained that the provisions of the Convention should not be altered in the development of the rules and regulations for deep sea-bed mining. On the other hand, it was felt that the Commission should not be precluded from building on the provisions of the Convention. This raises the issue of the extent to which modifications can be made to the provisions of the Convention in the drafting of the mining code.

E.. Special Commission 4

164.   This Commission is preparing for the establishment of the International Tribunal for the Law of the Sea. The Special Commission has completed its second round of discussions on the draft Rules of the Tribunal, with the exception of one outstanding matter contained in an informal suggestion concerning procedures for the prompt release of vessels and crews, which should be completed early in the sixth session. The thrust of the discussions have been reflected in the revision of the Rules and the compromise proposals presented by the Secretariat at the request of the Special Commission. There has been widespread agreement within the Special Commission on virtually all issues relating to the Rules. The Secretariat has been requested to prepare a final revision of the draft Rules and it is expected that this revision would provide a broadly acceptable proposal for the Rules of the Tribunal.

165.   The Special Commission is now in the process of considering the requirements for a headquarters agreement between the Tribunal and the host country. The discussion is based on a draft headquarters agreement prepared by the Secretariat. On this subject as well, a most constructive spirit has prevailed and the discussions have progressed expeditiously to complete the first half of the draft. The second part of this draft will be presented by the Secretariat before the next session and it is anticipated that the Special Commission can conclude a first review of the subject by the end of the sixth session.

166.   There are several other items on the agenda of Special Commission 4, including the drafting of a protocol or agreement dealing with the subject of privileges and immunities of the Tribunal, its functionaries, officials and representatives of parties before it. For this purpose also, the Secretariat is expected to present a working paper for the sixth session.

167.   As mandated by the Special Commission, the Chairman's consultations on the matters relating to the seat of the Tribunal are proceeding, and it is hoped that a generally acceptable solution to this problem will be found. The problem arises from the fact that the host country identified in the Convention (Federal Republic of Germany) has not signed the Convention, nor has it acceded to it. An understanding was reached at the time when the host country was chosen that required it to be a party to the Convention.

PART TWO

ACTIVITIES OF THE OFFICE OF THE SPECIAL REPRESENTATIVE

I. INTRODUCTION

168.   The Office of the Special Representative of the Secretary-General for the Law of the Sea is presently entrusted with the responsibility of discharging the major programme on

marine affairs (chap. 25 of the medium-term plan for the period 1984-1989), comprising programme 1 (Law of the sea affairs) and programme 2 (Economic and technical aspects of marine affairs), with most aspects of the work carried out by the Secretariat in the field of marine affairs being consolidated in the Office of the Special Representative. The Office has been renamed the Office for Ocean Affairs and the Law of the Sea. The Office will thus implement a programme that combines the ongoing activities of the Office of the Special Representative of the Secretary-General for the Law of the Sea with most of those previously carried out by the former Ocean Economics and Technology Branch of the Department of International Economic and Social Affairs, as well as certain activities formerly carried out by the Sea and Ocean Affairs Section of the Department of Political and Security Council Affairs. This was one of the structural reforms effected by the Secretary-General[60] and reported to the Committee for Programme and Co-ordination, at its resumed twenty-seventh session in September 1987, which for this purpose has endorsed a consolidated programme budget for the Office (A/C.5/42/2/Rev.1).

169. In the field of marine affairs, the implications of the consolidation are that there will be a continuation of the ongoing responsibilities of the Office of the Special Representative of the Secretary-General for the Law of the Sea, which arise as a consequence of the adoption of the 1982 Convention establishing a comprehensive régime governing all uses of the oceans and their resources. These include such activities as reporting on developments relating to the Convention, the provision of information, advice and assistance to States, international and regional organizations, academic institutions, scholars and others on the legal, economic and political aspects of the Convention. It also involves the provision of advice and assistance to States, especially developing ones, on overall marine policy and management, the institutional implications thereof and the adaptation and adoption of national laws and regulations and the practical exercise of their rights and fulfillment of obligations in conformity with the Convention.

170. The Office also facilitates widespread acceptance of the new ocean régime, and monitors and reports on developments relating to the régime for the oceans at the international, regional and national levels. It also provides a focal point within the United Nations system for ocean-related activities. It fosters co-operation between offices and departments of the United Nations, its agencies and bodies in promoting a consistent approach towards the implementation of the Convention.

171. The Office also continues to provide secretariat services for the Commission for the International Sea-Bed Authority and for the International Tribunal for the Law of the Sea by providing the whole range of substantive and administrative support to the negotiations of this intergovernmental body (consisting of 159 members and 10 observers), which is preparing for the establishment of the International Sea-Bed Authority and the International Tribunal for the Law of the Sea. In its work programme the Office places special emphasis on the services of the Preparatory Commission and maintains an office at Kingston, Jamaica, to facilitate the servicing of the Commission.

172. The Office monitors developments relating to ocean affairs and law of the sea and, with the assistance of the material and data provided by the agencies and bodies of the United Nations, analyses these developments and submits the annual report of the Secretary-General on the developments to the General Assembly in accordance with its decision.

173.   These functions will be supplemented by the work previously carried out by the former Ocean Economics and Technology Branch of the Department of International Economic and Social Affairs (DIESA) in the areas of marine minerals (sea-bed and near-shore), coastal area and exclusive economic zone policy-making, planning and management, marine and coastal technology, marine information and data management and dissemination, and substantive support for technical co-operation will be carried out by the Office for Ocean Affairs and the Law of the Sea. This Office will thus also be responsible for the United Nations contribution to such joint inter-agency programmes and activities as Ocean Science in Relation to Non-Living Resources; the Aquatic Sciences and Fisheries Information System; the International Oceanographic Data Exchange; the Training, Education and Mutual Assistance in the Marine Sciences; the Group of Experts on Scientific Aspects of Marine Pollution; and the development of the Long-term and Expanded Programme of Oceanic Exploration and Research. The Office will also represent the Secretary-General at sessions of the Inter-Secretariat Committee on Scientific Programmes Relating to Oceanography. In addition, responsibility for factual reporting on developments in the sea and ocean affairs has been transferred to this Office from the Department for Political and Security Council Affairs.

II. ASSISTANCE AND SPECIAL STUDIES

174.   The process of ratification of the Convention has continued and currently 34 instruments of ratification have been deposited. During the period under review, the Office of the Special Representative has been requested to provide information, advice and assistance to facilitate the ratification process by providing clarification regarding provisions of the Convention and the interrelationship between such provisions as they affect the rights and duties of States. States, national agencies and institutions as well as intergovernmental and non-governmental organizations have also submitted numerous requests for different types of detailed information on matters relating to the régime for the oceans.

175.   The developmental process in many countries is witnessing the greater incorporation of the marine sector in their economies. This process is being undertaken at both the national and regional levels, thereby stimulating additional marine-related activities. The Office has been requested to participate in this process by preparing and presenting studies and reports on marine affairs as well as by participating in several meetings of intergovernmental and non-governmental organizations. Among such meetings were: the South Pacific Forum's Management Course for Government Officials (Kiribati); the Asian-African Legal Consultative Committee (Bangkok); the Indian Ocean Marine Affairs Conference (Colombo); the International Ocean Institute Management Course (Arusha, Tanzania); the Institute for Documentation on Marine Research and Studies (IDREM) (Abidjan); the Maritime Delimitation Workshop for Officials of the Organization of the Eastern Caribbean States (Saint Lucia); South-East Asian Project on Ocean Law, Policy and Management (Bangkok); Pacem in Maribus XV (Malta); the Seminar Relating to Exploration and Exploitation of Mineral Resources of the Sea-Bed: Legal, Technical and Environmental Aspects (Cartagena, Colombia); and the Committee for Co-ordination for Joint Prospecting for Mineral Resources in South Pacific Offshore Areas (Lae, Papua New Guinea).

176.   At the same time special emphasis was also placed on the preparation of studies dealing with sea-bed mining and preparations for the Authority and the Tribunal for the Preparatory Commission.

III. CO-OPERATION WITHIN THE UNITED NATIONS SYSTEM

177.   Previous resolutions on the law of the sea adopted by the General Assembly, including resolution 41/34, have recognized "that the United Nations Convention on the Law of the Sea encompasses all uses and resources of the sea and that all related activities within the United Nations system need to be implemented in a manner consistent with it". Consequently, the Office has continued to co-operate with and to assist in the work of United Nations agencies and bodies, other departments of the United Nations, and intergovernmental bodies involved in ocean-related matters. In particular the Office will continue to co-operate with the Department of International Economic and Social Affairs on matters of mutual interest, including the preparation of reports to the Economic and Social Council, as appropriate. A special effort has been made to undertake activities on global, regional and subregional bases, and to maintain and strengthen the established working relationship, including joint activities as appropriate, with organizations within the United Nations system, such as ICAO, IMO, UNESCO/IOC, FAO, ILO, the United Nations Conference on Trade and Development (UNCTAD) and UNEP. Concurrently, the Office has co-operated and assisted the regional commissions of the United Nations in their marine affairs activities and programmes. As in previous years, the regional commissions, especially those from the Asian, African and Latin American regions, have requested that assistance and information be provided by the Office of the Special Representative. The Office will continue to co-operate with regional commissions in the convening of regional groups of experts on marine survey and technology. The Office has also participated in the work of several specialized agencies and has been represented at meetings when appropriate. On the other hand, it continues to receive valuable assistance and co-operation from all the organizations within the United Nations system.

IV. SERVICING THE PREPARATORY COMMISSION

178.   The Preparatory Commission continued its deliberations on the establishment of the International Sea-Bed Authority and for the International Tribunal for the Law of the Sea. As in previous years, the General Assembly, by its resolution 41/34 requested the Secretary-General to place special emphasis on the work of the Preparatory Commission. The Office continued to provide the integrated servicing required by the Commission to enable it to undertake the activities it is mandated. In providing such service, the Secretariat continued to prepare studies and working papers dealing with various matters under consideration by the plenary of the Commission and its four Special Commissions. These working papers and studies included: revised rules of procedure of the Council; revised draft Rules of Procedure of the Legal and Technical Commission; revised draft Rules of Procedure of the Economic Planning Commission; system of compensation and/or a compensation fund; main elements of a training programme; a nucleus Enterprise; draft Regulations on Prospecting, Exploration and Exploitation of Polymetallic Nodules in the Area (Draft Regulations on Financial Incentives); draft Rules for the International Tribunal for the Law of the Sea; and draft headquarters agreement between the International Tribunal for the Law of the Sea and the Federal Republic of Germany.

V. LAW OF THE SEA INFORMATION SYSTEM

179.   During the past year, the Office has proceeded with the further development of its computerized Law of the Sea Information System (LOSIS). The system is composed of a group of data bases containing information relating to the law of the sea and related issues, which are updated on a continuing basis.

180.   One of these data bases, the Country Marine Profile Data Base, contains 98 categories of information for each of more than 160 countries and 80 additional entities (e.g. islands, dependent territories, etc.).   The information is of an economic or demographic nature (e.g. GNP, population, fishery import/export, shipping tonnage, etc.), geographical data (e.g. land area, length of coastline, area of the exclusive economic zone), limits of national jurisdiction (breadth of the territorial sea, contiguous zone, exclusive economic zone, fishery zone and the continental shelf), membership in regional or interest groups or in specialized agencies with ocean-related activities (e.g. IMO, FAO, IOC/UNESCO, the International Hydrographic Organization (IHO) and the International Maritime Satellite Organization), and United Nations regional commission membership. This data base also includes current information on the position of each State regarding the Convention on the Law of the Sea, such as signature of the Final Act, signature of the Convention, ratifications and declarations.   The data base has the ability to retrieve information by specific country, region, affiliate groups or relevant organizations and extract the pertinent data from a chosen subset of the 98 categories available.

181.   The National Marine Legislation Data Base (LEGISLAT) has been expanded since its inception last year from 1,060 to over 1,440 individual national laws and regulations entries.

182.   The development of the data base of Sea-Bed Committee documents referred to in the last report to the General Assembly is continuing and will allow, when completed, retrieval of references to that body of documentation by (a) subject-matter, listing sponsors and associated documents submitted, as well as statements, by country, made on the subjects; and (b) by country, listing their statements or proposals submitted by subject.

183.   LOSIS has been and is being developed as a dynamic tool.   Its future direction, expansion and emphasis will largely be determined by the nature of requests made by States and the research needs of the Office.   The co-operation of Member States is of particular importance in obtaining current and new legislation and other information relevant to State practice in matters pertaining to the Convention.

VI. ANALYTICAL STUDIES

184.   Analytical studies that are intended to trace the legislative history of the provisions of the Convention are being prepared as part of the established programme of the Office in order to illustrate and analyse, in the most accurate and objective manner, the negotiating process that resulted in the text of the Convention.

185.   These provisions relate to topics that need to be evaluated and assessed with regard to the positive development of the law of the sea: the series commenced with a publication dealing with an important subject in relation to the preservation of the marine environment, namely dumping.[61]

186.   The studies are designed to set out the history of the provisions, not only through an examination of the documents of the Third United Nations Conference on the Law of the Sea, but by utilizing, when appropriate, all relevant legal instruments such as the work of the International Law Commission, the First and Second United Nations Conferences on the Law of the Sea, provisions of the 1958 Geneva Conventions and the work of the Sea-Bed Committee. To complement the legal background, other multilateral instruments are referred to whenever relevant.

187.   Two new studies have been completed by the Office: the first, which concerns the legislative history of Part X of the Convention, i.e. the right of access of land-locked States to and from the sea and freedom of transit, has been published.[62] The second, which deals with the régime of islands (art. 121), has been submitted for publication. The anticipated publication programme has been affected by the financial constraints of the Organization and consequent measures that had to be taken. These studies continue to be in demand from Member States, United Nations organizations and other users. Requests for their publication in languages other than the two working languages have been made by the States.

188.   Six other studies dealing with archipelagic States (arts. 46 to 54); some aspects of the exclusive economic zone (art. 56, Rights, jurisdiction and duties of the coastal States in the exclusive economic zone, and art. 58, Rights and duties of other States in the exclusive economic zone); definition of the continental shelf (art. 76); navigation on the high seas (Part VII, sect. 1); régime of marine scientific research (Part XIII, sect. 3); and artificial islands, installations and structures are in varying stages of preparation and will be issued as they become available.

189.   The baseline provisions of the Convention are highly technical in nature and their application in different geographical and other circumstances are not always easily understood. There is a need to provide a simple explanation of the technical provisions. Accordingly, the Office is in the process of preparing a study as an aid to the practical application of the baseline provisions in the Convention specifically for the benefit of practitioners who are charged with the responsibility of implementing those provisions.[63] In the course of preparing this study, the Office has consulted on the technical aspects an informal group of experts in geography, hydrography and cartography, which was drawn from all regions. The observations and comments of the members of the group were most valuable and helpful. The group also recognized the usefulness of such a study to personnel in Member States who are implementing these provisions of the Convention. The study will be published early in 1988. The Office is grateful to the Government of Japan for providing some of the funds required for this project.

VII. STATE PRACTICE (NATIONAL LEGISLATION AND TREATIES)

190.   The Office continues to gather and process material reflecting State practice. The Convention continues to exert an important influence on the development of national policy with regard to law of the sea matters. In order to assist States in their efforts to implement the Convention and to promote a uniform and consistent application of the complex set of norms embodied in it, the Office has issued a publication entitled "Current Developments in State Practice".[64] This publication contains all available national maritime legislation enacted in the four years following the adoption of the Convention in 1982 as well as the texts of treaties relating to maritime matters concluded during this period.

191.   The preparation of studies incorporating comprehensive surveys of national legislation relating to subjects such as the continental shelf, the territorial sea, the contiguous zone and the conduct of marine scientific research in areas under coastal States' jurisdiction are in the process of being completed. Some difficulties have been encountered in obtaining the necessary legislation from certain States. The completion of these studies would be assisted if the States concerned could make available the relevant legislation. The Secretariat would like to renew its requests to them.

192.   The compilation of 74 bilateral agreements dealing with the delimitation of maritime boundaries concluded after 1970 will be finalized before the end of 1987. This publication reflects a very important aspect of the practice of States in relation to the delimitation of maritime boundaries between States with adjacent or opposite coasts in a period characterized by the extension of national jurisdiction. A collection of similar agreements concluded before 1970 will follow.

VIII.   LAW OF THE SEA REFERENCE COLLECTION LIBRARY AND PUBLICATION OF SELECTED BIBLIOGRAPHIES

193.   The Reference Collection Library of the Office for Ocean Affairs and the Law of the Sea continues to expand and is becoming one of the most complete reference libraries through a continuing collection of periodicals, legislative series, loose-leaf services, treaties and newly published books dealing with all aspects of the Law of the Sea Convention. The Reference Collection Library is designed to serve the needs of a multidisciplinary group of users such as members of accredited delegations and missions to the United Nations, secretariat staff and persons from academic institutions who are interested in the developing field of marine affairs. This specialized library continues to publish annually the "Law of the Sea: A Select Bibliography". The second bibliography in this series was published in early 1987 under the symbol LOS/LIB/2.[65] The third in this series will be submitted soon for publication under the symbol LOS/LIB/3. As in previous years the Reference Library works in close collaboration with the Dag Hammarskjöld Library and makes every attempt to obtain the most up-to-date information on current publications relating to the law of the sea and other activities in marine affairs.

IX.   THE LAW OF THE SEA BULLETIN

194.   Four issues of the **Law of the Sea Bulletin** have been published during the period under review (Nos. 8, 9, 10 and Special Issue No. 1). The **Law of the Sea Bulletin** continues to be a useful tool for States and intergovernmental bodies to be informed in a timely manner of current developments relating to the law of the sea and various activities in the field of marine affairs.   Many States use the **Bulletin** to give publicity to their new legislation or to declarations relating to the law of the sea.

195.   The **Bulletin** is entirely edited and distributed by the Office and is in considerable demand from a large number of Member States (including direct requests from government departments), international and non-governmental organizations, universities and scholars. (The mailing list, besides containing all the Member States of the Organization, includes about 400 names of individuals or institutions.) In order to improve the publication, a questionnaire soliciting reactions from readers and seeking suggestions on how to improve the **Bulletin** was prepared and incorporated in issue No. 9. A large number of very positive responses have been received.

X.   FELLOWSHIP PROGRAMME

196.   In carrying out its activities concerning the Hamilton Shirley Amerasinghe Fellowship on the Law of the Sea, the Office secured the participation of the fellow to whom the first award was made, Mr. Bala Bahadur Kunwar, at the educational institution with which he was associated, the University of Virginia. At its Center for Ocean Law and Policy, Mr. Kunwar carried out further research and studies on the subject of the rights of land-locked States

under the Convention, in particular the right of access to and from the sea and its resources. The subject was of particular relevance to the candidate, who is a national of a land-locked country, Nepal. He audited courses at the University of Virginia under the supervision of Professor John Norton Moore. Having completed his nine-month period with the University, he served an internship with the Office for Ocean Affairs and the Law of the Sea from February to May 1987. During the internship he was provided the opportunity to carry out further research on this subject in the context of the developments of the Third United Nations Conference on the Law of the Sea. As required by the terms of the fellowship, he has prepared a study, which, after review by the Office, will be incorporated in one of its publications.

197.   The arrangements for the second award of the fellowship in 1987 are proceeding. Application and nomination forms have been circulated globally through the United Nations information centres and offices of UNDP. The Advisory Panel for the second award, consisting of eminent persons in international relations, the law of the sea and related matters, comprises: T. T. B. Koh (Chairman), Elliot Richardson, Paul Bamela Engo, Felipe Paolillo, Tom Eric Vraalsen, Igor Ivanovich Yakovlev, Carl-August Fleischhauer and G. E. Chitty (Secretary to the Panel). The Panel is scheduled to meet on 20 November 1987 and based on its recommendations the Special Representative of the Secretary-General for the Law of the Sea will make the second award, which will be implemented in 1988.

198.   The period of specialized research/study under the fellowship programme will be made possible at one of the participating institutions, which are: the Center for Ocean Law and Policy, University of Virginia, United States; Dalhousie Law School, Halifax, Canada; the Graduate Institute of International Studies, Geneva; the Netherlands Institute for the Law of the Sea, University of Utrecht, the Netherlands; the Research Centre for International Law, University of Cambridge, United Kingdom; the School of Law, University of Georgia, United States; the School of Law, University of Miami, United States; the William S. Richardson School of Law, University of Hawaii, United States; and the Woods Hole Oceanographic Institution, Massachusetts, United States.

199.   Following earlier practice, after the conclusion of the research/study period with the educational institution, the fellow will serve a period of internship with the Office for Ocean Affairs and the Law of the Sea in New York.

200.   Depending upon the income available from the Hamilton Shirley Amerasinghe Fellowship Trust Fund, which at present is adequate for at least one fellowship, and based upon the costs involved for travel and subsistence while at the university and at United Nations Headquarters, there may be the possibility of awarding an additional fellowship.

201.   The investment of the fellowship fund has not yielded substantial returns, owing to prevailing interest rates and return on investments. Considering the growing interest in the fellowship and the prestigious educational institutions offering facilities free of charge for selected fellows, further contributions to the Fund would be welcome so as to expand the programme to accommodate more than one candidate each year.

Notes

1.   Official Records of the Third United Nations Conference on the Law of the Sea, vol. XVII (United Nations publication, Sales No. E.84.V.3), document A/CONF.62/122.

2.   The first report was submitted to the thirty-ninth session (A/39/647 and Corr.1 and Add.1); the second was submitted to the fortieth session (A/40/923); and the third annual report was submitted to the forty-first session (A/41/742).

3.   Cape Verde, Cuba, Democratic Yemen, Egypt, Guinea-Bissau, Iceland, Philippines, Tunisia, United Republic of Tanzania, and Yugoslavia.

4.   Cape Verde, Cuba, Egypt, Guinea-Bissau, and United Republic of Tanzania.

5.   Cape Verde, Iceland, and Tunisia.

6.   The most recent State to extend its territorial sea is the United Kingdom, which has enacted the Territorial Sea Act (1987). Those States with a territorial sea of 12 miles are as follows: Algeria; Antigua and Barbuda; Bangladesh; Barbados; Brunei Darussalam; Bulgaria; Burma; Canada; Cape Verde; Chile; China; Colombia; Comoros; Cook Islands; Costa Rica; Côte d'Ivoire; Cuba; Cyprus; Democratic Kampuchea; Democratic People's Republic of Korea; Democratic Yemen; Djibouti; Dominica; Egypt; Equatorial Guinea; Ethiopia; Fiji; France; Gabon; Gambia; German Democratic Republic; Ghana; Grenada; Guatemala; Guinea; Guinea-Bissau; Guyana; Haiti; Honduras; Iceland; India; Indonesia; Iran (Islamic Republic of); Iraq; Italy; Jamaica; Japan; Kenya; Kiribati; Kuwait; Lebanon; Libyan Arab Jamahiriya; Madagascar; Malaysia; Maldives; Malta; Mauritius; Mexico; Monaco; Morocco; Mozambique; Nauru; Netherlands; New Zealand; Niue; Oman; Pakistan; Papua New Guinea; Poland; Portugal; Republic of Korea; Romania; Samoa; Sao Tome and Principe; Saudi Arabia; Senegal; Seychelles; Solomon Islands; South Africa; Spain; Sri Lanka; Saint Kitts and Nevis; Saint Lucia; Saint Vincent and the Grenadines; Sudan; Suriname; Sweden; Thailand; Tonga; Trinidad and Tobago; Tunisia; Turkey; Tuvalu; Ukrainian SSR; United Arab Emirates; United Kingdom of Great Britain and Northern Ireland; Union of Soviet Socialist Republics; Vanuatu; Venezuela; Viet Nam; Yemen; Yugoslavia and Zaire.

7.   Antigua and Barbuda, Burma, Chile, Democratic Kampuchea, Democratic Yemen, Dominica, Dominican Republic, Gabon, Ghana, India, Madagascar, Malta, Morocco, Pakistan, Saint Lucia, Senegal, Sri Lanka, Vanuatu and Viet Nam.

8.   It is estimated that there are 36 more potential boundaries in the Mediterranean Sea to be settled. See also Blake, World Maritime Boundary Delimitation.

9.   For instance, the International Geographic Union has created a Study Group on Marine Geography with emphasis on management patterns in both coastal and offshore areas. Its first meeting was held in July 1987 at the Institute of Science and Technology, University of Wales (United Kingdom).

10.   See A/CN.10/90, 92, 101 and 102. It should be noted that the United States does not participate in the consultations on this issue in the Commission.

11.   At present two such agreements are known to exist: between the United States and the Soviet Union (Prevention of Incidents On and Over the High Seas, 1972) and between the United Kingdom and the Soviet Union (Agreement concerning the Prevention of Incidents at Sea beyond the Territorial Sea, 1986).

12.   Parties to the London Dumping Convention (LDC) have begun to look at the relationship between the Convention and the Convention on the Law of the Sea. ICAO has also undertaken a similar exercise to that of IMO. However, the work is not expected to be completed before mid-1989, in view of its Legal Committee's priority work on the draft instrument for the suppression of unlawful acts of violence at airports serving international civil aviation.

13.   Copies are available from IMO and the Office for Ocean Affairs and the Law of the Sea.

14.   General Assembly resolution 40/61; IMO Assembly resolution A/584(14).

15.   See IMO document MSC/Circ.443, 26 September 1986.

16.   The 1963 Tokyo Convention on Offences and Certain Other Acts Committed on Board Aircraft; the 1970 Hague Convention for the Suppression of Unlawful Seizure of Aircraft; and the 1971 Montreal Convention for the Suppression of Unlawful Acts against the Safety of Civil Aviation. A new draft Convention for the Suppression of Unlawful Acts at Airports serving International Civil Aviation is now being elaborated by ICAO.

17.   Acts of terrorism would seldom fall under the definition of piracy provided for in article 101 of the Convention on the Law of the Sea.

18.   IMO document C 57/D. See also document A/42/519.

19.   The Statement on Terrorism issued at the Venice Economic Summit on 9 June 1987, reaffirmed "the principle established by relevant international organizations of trying or extraditing according to national laws and international conventions those who have perpetrated acts of terrorism". The Summit welcomed the improvements in airport and maritime security and encouraged ICAO and IMO work in this regard.

20.   The 1958 Geneva Convention on the Continental Shelf had required total removal. Article 60 was the only provision to be amended when the draft Convention was submitted for adoption in April 1982. It was understood at the time that this modification of the previous obligation for total removal would be followed expeditiously by the adoption of binding international standards.

21.   See MSC report MSC/54/23. Draft guidelines are contained in NAV 33/15, annex VI.

22.   Ultimate disposal of scrapped rig structures will be on the agenda of the tenth Consultative Meeting of LDC, in 1988.

23.   When not engaged in a drilling operation, they are considered to be vessels. See draft IMO Assembly resolution on measures to prevent infringement of safety zones around offshore installations or structures (NAV 33/15, annex 7).

24.   E/CN.7/1987/2 and DND/DCIT/WP.12. For comments from Governments, see E/CN.7/1987/18.

25.   IMO has compiled guidelines on the prevention of drug smuggling on ships engaged in international traffic. ICAO is presently studying measures to ensure that commercial carriers are not used for this purpose and is developing a system of sanctions.

26.   See interim report of the Open-Ended Intergovernmental Expert Group Meeting on the Preparation of a Draft Convention against Illicit Traffic in Narcotic Drugs and Psychotropic Substances (DND/DCIT/WP.12).

27.   See also A/CONF.133/4.

28.   For example, the UNEP report (United Nations publication, Sales No. E.87.III.D.1). See also documentation on the environmental perspective to the year 2000 and beyond (UNEP/GC.14/16 and A/42/427).

29.   The Montreal Protocol on Substances that Deplete the Ozone Layer was adopted on 16 September 1987. A WMO world conference (late 1989) will assess scientific developments on greenhouse gases and climatic change.

30.   The OECD Environmental Committee has established a new project to improve environmental management and monitoring capabilities in developing countries.

31.   An OECD seminar (1987), as part of its environmental impact assessment activities, was held on environmental assessment and development assistance. The CMEA Board for Environmental Protection is also concentrating on the environmental impact assessment of major development programmes, as well as on waste technology for treatment and disposal.

32.   The Committee of International Development Institutions on the Environment consisting of the regional development banks, the Commission for the European Communities, IFAD, the Organization of American States, UNDP, the World Bank and UNEP, is intended to be the forum for ensuring integration of environmental considerations with the policies and operational activities not only of the multilateral agencies themselves but also of bilateral aid agencies.

33.   See IMO document LDC/SG.10/11.

34.   See GESAMP report No. 30. The experience of UNEP and the International Council for Exploration of the Sea (ICES) is recounted in IMO documents LDC/SG.10/2/4 and 5. The International Conference on Environmental Protection of the North Sea held in March 1987 also examined this concept and other aspects of achieving an integrated approach to marine environmental management.

35.   The concept is used in the 1985 Montreal guidelines on marine pollution from land-based sources.

36.   An international symposium on reception facilities held by IMO in May 1987 provided much useful information on Annex II for administrators, the shipping industry and port authorities.

37.   Eighth meeting, February 1987.

38.   Most recently, IMO Sales Document 630 87.07.E (Manual on Chemical Pollution Section 1 - Problem Assessment and Response Arrangements).

39.   Common pollution reporting systems have been adopted by the Bonn Agreement, the Copenhagen Agreement and the Helsinki Commission.

40.   IOC's relations with regional organizations, e.g. ICES (North Atlantic), the International Commission for the Scientific Exploration of the Mediterranean Sea (ICSEM) (Mediterranean), CPPS (South-east Pacific), have now been supplemented by co-operation with the two Co-ordinating Committees for Offshore Prospecting for East Asia and South Pacific.

41.   Acoustic Doppler current profiling, acoustic tomography, and other innovations in hydrographic and hydrochemical measurements; satellite altimetry, satellite scatterometry, passive/micro-wave radiometry and ocean spectrometry. A report is to be prepared by IOC on new technologies for ocean observation.

42.   The MARPOL and London Dumping Conventions are based upon scientific and technical considerations, so that IMO/IOC co-operation on marine science questions is important. Recent consultations have produced a greatly strengthened co-operation and IMO will now join UNEP in co-sponsoring GIPME/Group of Experts on Effects of Pollutants.

43.   See the report of the Third Session of the IOC Group of Experts on Effects of Pollutants, September 1986, in the IOC series, Reports of Meetings of Experts and Equivalent Bodies.

44.   See "Opportunities and Problems in Satellite Measurement of the Sea", UNESCO Technical Paper in Marine Sciences No. 46.

45.   Major progress in the establishment of a global maritime search and rescue plan may be made only with the help of satellite communications. The provisions of the Global Maritime Distress and Safety System incorporate the International Maritime Satellite System which now gives priority to distress communications and those with synthetic aperture reades forces and operations. Distress communications are provided free of charge; under discussion are favourable terms for meteorological and navigational notifications.

46.   Article 250 requires that consent be obtained through official channels.

47.   IOC is not the only organization to be called on to facilitate the conduct of co-operative projects undertaken in national jurisdiction; increasingly organizations such as CCOP/SOPAC are becoming more directly involved in the consent process.

48.   See article 2, paragraph 1 (j) of IOC Assembly resolution XIV-19. The unamended provision had read: "promote freedom of scientific investigation of the oceans for the benefit of all mankind, taking into account all interests and rights of coastal countries concerning scientific research in the zones under their jurisdiction".

49.   See FAO documents COFI/87/2 and 3; see also COFI/87/INF.4, "Review of the State of World Fishery Resources".

50.   See the report of the seventeenth session of the Committee on Fisheries (CL 91/7).

51.   See "Review of UNDP Support for Fisheries Developments", April 1986.

52.   See the report of tenth session of CECAF, December 1986.

53.   The procedure is used by the Commission for the Conservation of Antarctic Marine Living Resources (CCAMLR), IWC, the International Commission for the Conservation of Atlantic Tunas (ICCAT) and the Northwest Atlantic Fisheries Organization (NAFO).

54.   See FAO documents FL/COPACE/87/19(1987); Fisheries Law Advisory Programme circulars No. 6 (1986) and No. 8 (1987).

55.   FAO Fisheries Technical Paper (286), "The Patagonian Fishery Resources and the Offshore Fisheries in the South-West Atlantic" by J. Csirke, 1987. The study covers the area lying between 38° S to the north and 50° W to the east. See also A/AC.109/920, which presents the latest developments on Falkland Islands (Malvinas) fisheries and related problems, as reported by the Argentine and United Kingdom Governments. The United Kingdom "Declaration on South West Atlantic Fisheries" of 29 October 1986 is contained in A/41/777. (See also A/41/636, A/41/669-S/18378 and A/41/708-S/18399.)

56.   The important hake fishery is mostly coastal and fished by Argentina and Uruguay, who are actively involved in joint research programmes and management negotiations, as contemplated under the 1973 bilateral treaty.

57.   The new Eastern Pacific Tuna Fishing Agreement will establish a regional licensing régime, when in force.

58.   Symposium on the Exploitation and Management of Marine Fishery Resources in South-East Asia, April 1987, Darwin, Australia.

59.   Initiated in 1984, SEAPOL is administered by the Institute of Asian Studies at Chulalongkorn University, Bangkok, in co-operation with Dalhousie University, Canada.

60.   Press release SG/SM/3970.

61.   See United Nations publication, Sales No. E.85.V.12.

62.   See United Nations publication, Sales No. E.87.V.5.

63.   It should be noted that a regional training course on boundary-making baselines and other related matters was held in Singapore in 1987 under SEAPOL auspices, and that a workshop dealing with the same issues was also held in 1987 under the auspices of OECS.

64.   See United Nations publication, Sales No. E.87.V.3.

65.   See United Nations publication, Sales No. E.87.V.2.

- - - - -

UN General Assembly   A/RES/42/20
Forty-second Session   7 January 1988

Resolution 42/20.   Law of the Sea

The General Assembly,

Reaffirming its resolutions 37/66 of 3 December 1982, 38/59 A of 14 December 1983, 39/73 of 13 December 1984, 40/63 of 10 December 1985 and 41/34 of 5 November 1986, regarding the law of the sea,

Recognizing that, as stated in the third preambular paragraph of the United Nations Convention on the Law of the Sea,[1] the problems of ocean space are closely interrelated and need to be considered as a whole,

Convinced that it is important to safeguard the unified character of the Convention and related resolutions adopted therewith and to refrain from any action to apply their provisions selectively, in a manner inconsistent with their object and purpose,

Emphasizing the need for States to ensure consistent application of the Convention, as well as the need for harmonization of national legislation with the provisions of the Convention,

Considering that, in its resolution 2749 (XXV) of 17 December 1970, it proclaimed that the sea-bed and ocean floor, and the subsoil thereof, beyond the limits of national jurisdiction, as well as the resources of the area, are the common heritage of mankind,

Recalling that the Convention provides the régime to be applied to the Area and its resources,

Emphasizing that no State should undermine the Convention and related resolutions of the Third United Nations Conference on the Law of the Sea,

Recognizing also the need for co-operation in the early and effective implementation by the Preparatory Commission for the International Sea-Bed Authority and for the International Tribunal for the Law of the Sea of resolution II of the Third United Nations Conference on the Law of the Sea,[2]

Noting with satisfaction the progress made in the work of the Preparatory Commission since its inception, including the registration of India as a pioneer investor in the mining of the sea-bed and ocean floor and subsoil thereof, beyond the limits of national jurisdiction,

Noting the decision of the Preparatory Commission to convene its General Committee from 7 to 18 December 1987 for the purpose of considering the applications of France, Japan and the Union of Soviet Socialist Republics for registration as pioneer investors,

Noting also that the Preparatory Commission has decided to hold its sixth regular session at Kingston from 14 March to 8 April 1988 and that it will decide upon the summer meeting for 1988 during its next session,[3]

Noting further the increasing needs of countries, especially developing countries, for information, advice and assistance in the implementation of the Convention and in their developmental process for the full realization of the benefits of the comprehensive legal régime established by the Convention,

Recognizing that the Convention encompasses all uses and resources of the sea and that all related activities within the United Nations system need to be implemented in a manner consistent with it,

Taking note of activities carried out in 1987 under the major programme on marine affairs, set forth in chapter 25 of the medium-term plan for the period 1984-1989, in accordance with the report of the Secretary-General,[4] as approved in General Assembly resolution 38/59 A, and the report of the Secretary-General,[5]

Recalling its approval of the financing of the expenses of the Preparatory Commission from the regular budget of the United Nations,

Taking special note of the report of the Secretary-General prepared in pursuance of paragraph 13 of General Assembly resolution 41/34,[6]

1.   *Recalls* the historic significance of the United Nations Convention on the Law of the Sea as an important contribution to the maintenance of peace, justice and progress for all peoples of the world;

2.   *Expresses its satisfaction* at the increasing and overwhelming support for the Convention, as evidenced, *inter alia*, by the one hundred and fifty-nine signatures and thirty-five of the sixty ratifications or accessions required for entry into force of the Convention;

3.   *Calls upon* all States that have not done so to consider ratifying or acceding to the Convention at the earliest possible date to allow the effective entry into force of the new legal régime for the uses of the sea and its resources;

4.   *Calls upon* all States to safeguard the unified character of the Convention and related resolutions adopted therewith;

5.   *Also calls upon* States to observe the provisions of the Convention when enacting their national legislation;

6.   *Further calls upon* States to desist from taking actions which undermine the Convention or defeat its object and purpose;

7.   *Notes* the progress being made by the Preparatory Commission for the International Sea-Bed Authority and for the International Tribunal for the Law of the Sea in all areas of its work;

8.   *Expresses its satisfaction* at the successful resolution of conflicts of overlaps that had arisen in the claims of applicants for registration as pioneer investors and with those of certain potential applicants under resolution II of the Third United Nations Conference on the Law of the Sea;

9.   *Further expresses its satisfaction* at the historic decision of the Preparatory Commission of 17 August 1987 to register the first pioneer investor, namely India, and at the decision of the Preparatory Commission to convene its General Committee from 7 to 18 December 1987 for the purpose of considering the applications of France, Japan and the Union of Soviet Socialist Republics for registration as pioneer investors;

10.   *Expresses its appreciation* to the Secretary-General for his efforts in support of the Convention and for the effective execution of the major programme on marine affairs set forth in chapter 25 of the medium-term plan for the period 1984-1989;

11.   *Further expresses its appreciation* for the report of the Secretary-General prepared in pursuance of General Assembly resolution 41/34 and requests him to continue to carry out the activities outlined therein, as well as those aimed at the strengthening of the legal régime of the sea, special emphasis being placed on the work of the Preparatory Commission, including the implementation of resolution II of the Third United Nations Conference on the Law of the Sea;

12.   *Calls upon* the Secretary-General to continue to assist States in the implementation of the Convention and in the development of a consistent and uniform approach to the legal régime thereunder, as well as in their national, subregional and regional efforts towards the full realization of the benefits therefrom and invites the organs and organizations of the United Nations system to co-operate and lend assistance in these endeavours;

13. *Approves* the decision of the Preparatory Commission to hold its sixth regular session at Kingston from 14 March to 8 April 1988 and notes that the Preparatory Commission will decide upon the summer meeting for 1988 during its next session;[3]

14. *Requests* the Secretary-General to report to the General Assembly at its forty-third session on developments pertaining to the Convention and all related activities and on the implementation of the present resolution;

15. *Decides* to include in the provisional agenda of its forty-third session the item entitled "Law of the sea".

73rd plenary meeting
18 November 1987

Notes

1. Official Records of the Third United Nations Conference on the Law of the Sea, vol. XVII (United Nations publication, Sales No. E.84.V.3), document A/CONF.62/122.
2. Ibid., document A/CONF.62/121, annex I.
3. A/42/688, para. 132.
4. A/38/570 and Corr.1 and Add.1 and Add.1/Corr.1.
5. A/42/688.
6. Ibid.

- - - - -

Additional References

Law of the Sea and Ocean Affairs

Report of the Secretary-General on the work of the Organization. UN doc. A/42/1.

Law of the Sea and Environment. In Final Document of the Eighth Conference of Heads of State or Government of Non-Aligned Countries. In UN doc. A/41/697, Annex.

Law of the Sea. In Final Communiqué of the Special Ministerial Meeting of the Co-ordinating Bureau of the Movement of Non-Aligned Countries on Latin America and the Caribbean. UN doc. A/42/357.

Ocean Management: A Regional Perspective. The Prospects for Commonwealth Maritime Cooperation in Asia and the Pacific. Report by a Commonwealth Group of Experts. Publication of the Commonwealth Secretariat, Marlborough House, Pall Mall, London SW1Y 5HX.

Law of the Sea Publications of the United Nations

Official Text of the United Nations Convention on the Law of the Sea, with Annexes and Index; Final Act of the Third United Nations Conference on the Law of the Sea; Introductory Material on the Convention and the Conference. Sales No. E.83.V.5. (English, French and Spanish).

A Select Bibliography. 1985. Sales No. E.85.V.2. (English only).

A Select Bibliography, 1987. Sales No. E.87.V.2. (English only).

Status of the United Nations Convention on the Law of the Sea. Sales No. E.85.V.5. (Arabic, Chinese, English, French, Russian, Spanish).

Master File containing References to Official Documents of the Third United Nations Conference on the Law of the Sea. Sales No. E.85.V.9. (English, French, Spanish).

National Legislation on the Exclusive Economic Zone, the Economic Zone and the Exclusive Fishery Zone. Sales No. E.85.V.10. (English only).

Multilateral Treaties Relevant to the United Nations Convention on the Law of the Sea. Sales No. E.85.V.11. (English, French, Spanish).

Pollution by Dumping - Legislative History of Articles 1, paragraph 1(5), 210 and 216 of the United Nations Convention on the Law of the Sea. Sales No. E.85.V.12. (English, French, Spanish).

A Select Bibliography, 1987. Sales No. E.87.V.3. (English only).

Current Developments in State Practice. Sales No. E.87.V.3. (English, French, Spanish).

Rights of Access of Land-locked States to and from the Sea and Freedom of Transit - Legislative History of Part X, articles 124 to 132 of the United Nations Convention on the Law of the Sea. Sales No. E.87.V.5. (English only).

Maritime Boundary Agreements (1970-1984). Sales No. E.87.V.12. (English only).

Economic and Technical Aspects of Marine Affairs

Economic and Social Council resolution 1985/75. In UN doc. E/1985/INF/6.

Economic and Social Council resolution 1987/84. In UN doc. E/1987/87/Add.1.

Development of marine areas under national jurisdiction. Economic and Social Council decision E/DEC/1987/181. UN doc. E/1987/87/Add.1.

International cooperation and coordination within the United Nations System. UN doc. E/1987/128.

Economic Cooperation among Developing Countries in Marine Affairs. UN Sales No. E.87.II.A.12.

- - - - -

2

Implications of the Law of the Sea
Convention for Other Instruments

ICAO Air Law Instruments

ICAO Council   C-WP/8077
116th Session   1 October 1985

"United Nations Convention on the Law of the Sea - Implications,
If Any, for the Application of the Chicago Convention,
Its Annexes and Other International Air Law Instruments"
Report by the Rapporteur

References: Doc. 9397-LC/185, pages 4-8; C-Min. 109/6, C-WP/7777; C.Mins. 111/7 and
                8; State letter LE 4/41-84/33 of 16 April 1984; C-WP/7901; C-Min. 113/9.

1.   To implement the Decision 4/2 of the 25th Session of the Legal Committee (Doc. 9397-LC/185) and the decision of the 24th Session of the Assembly, the Council requested the Secretary-General to undertake a study of the item "United Nations Convention on the Law of the Sea - Implications, if any, for the application of the Chicago Convention, its Annexes and other international air law instruments" (C-Min. 109/6). The study prepared by the Secretary-General was presented to the Council in C-WP/7777; the Council decided to send the study to States and international organizations for comments (C.Mins. 111/7 and 8). States were invited, *inter alia*, to express opinions on the future work of the Legal Committee on this subject.

2.   At its 113th Session, on 28 November 1984 (C-Min. 113/9), the Council had for consideration the replies from States and international organizations on the study together with the determination by the Chairman of the Legal Committee concerning the ways and means to proceed in the study of the subject. The Council noted the determination of the Chairman of the Legal Committee to appoint a Rapporteur and agreed to it.

3.   The Chairman of the Legal Committee appointed as Rapporteur Mr. Arnold W.G. Kean, CBE (United Kingdom) whose report is reproduced in the Attachment hereto. The report presents an indepth analysis of all problems which can be identified and which appear relevant at the present time. The next logical step now is for the Legal Committee to decide on the future course of action on this subject.

Action by the Council

4.   The Council is invited:
     (a) to note the Rapporteur's Report; and

(b)   to request the Legal Committee of ICAO, at its 26th Session, to consider the Rapporteur's Report on the item "United Nations Convention on the Law of the Sea - implications, if any, for the application of the Chicago Convention, its Annexes and other international air law instruments" and to decide on the future work to be undertaken on this subject.

ATTACHMENT

United Nations Convention on the Law of the Sea - Implications, if any, for the application of the Chicago Convention, its Annexes and other international air law instruments

Report by the Rapporteur
(Mr. A.W.G. Kean, CBE)

1.   Your Rapporteur has derived much help from the study made by the Secretariat, for which his thanks are due.

2.   In response to an invitation from the Secretary General, 38 member States have sent in observations and 118 have not replied at the time of writing. Of those replying, five have written that they have no comments and five others have said that the subject should be removed from the Work Programme of the Legal Committee.[1] Another State considered further study "not absolutely necessary"[2], and another wished to keep the subject on the Work Programme for further study "in case of future need"[3]. One State thought the subject could best be considered if problems were actually encountered.[4]

3.   At the time of writing, the United Nations Convention on the Law of the Sea ("UNCLOS") has been ratified by 22 States, 60 ratifications being required for it to come into force. Some major coastal and aviation States are not expected to become parties. This raises the question whether and to what extent UNCLOS must be considered as a codification of existing international law, binding upon States whether or not they have become parties. This question has been taken up by the Secretariat's study at various points, and, your Rapporteur notes that in its Preamble, UNCLOS is stated to achieve "codification and progressive development of the law of the sea". The observations received from States express differing views, ranging from that of Mexico ["with the exception of some provisions of a technical nature relative to the international sea-bed area (UNCLOS) already constitutes customary law"] to that of Turkey ["it would be erroneous to state that the Convention represents *opinio juris ac necessitatis*" (paragraph 5.4 of the Secretariat's study)"]. The opinion expressed by the observations of most States which have touched on the question appears to be that there are a number of rules in UNCLOS which express existing law and on which there is a pre-existing consensus, but there are also rules of importance which are innovative and constitute "progressive development" rather than codification of existing law, and which cannot bind a State unless it becomes a party to the Convention.

4.   Your Rapporteur is of the opinion that this is a general question of international law which cannot be decided in the context of civil aviation alone, but which, if practical problems arise, will have to be decided by other means, perhaps by the general practice of States in relation to the Convention as a whole or by a decision of a competent court or tribunal to which it may be referred. It would not serve any useful purpose for the Sub-Committee or for the Legal Committee to attempt to determine this general question for itself without regard to

matters other than civil aviation. For this reason, if the Legal Committee is to continue to examine UNCLOS, it might be advisable for it to consider the text of UNCLOS and, without taking a position on the difficult question how far it is or may become binding customary law, to examine the implications of those provisions for the Chicago Convention. The observations of the Federal Republic of Germany express this view with clarity:

> "... at least at the present time the Legal Committee could restrict its activities to an exact indication of the present implications of the Convention on the Law of the Sea relative to air law, adding the legal opinion of the Committee in the few cases where this is necessary".

5.   The Secretariat's study has already dealt with these matters in some detail, and your Rapporteur has no wish merely to repeat what they have written. However, he hopes it will be helpful if he reexamines the general principles briefly and adds some comments of his own.

THE TERRITORIAL SEA

6.   Article 2 of the Chicago Convention provides that, for the purposes of that Convention, the territory of a State includes its territorial waters. The Convention does not specify the extent of those waters but leaves it to be determined by general international law. The resulting flexibility is such that an amendment of the Chicago Convention will not be necessary in order to take account of the provisions of UNCLOS as to the extent of the territorial sea. "Territorial sea", the expression used by UNCLOS, is thought to be identical in meaning with "territorial waters" used in the Chicago Convention.

7.   Article 2 of UNCLOS provides that the sovereignty of the coastal State extends to its territorial sea and must "be exercised subject to this Convention and other rules of international law". In consequence, that sovereignty must be exercised subject to such traffic rights as are granted for non-scheduled services by Article 5 of the Chicago Convention, or in respect of scheduled services by a relevant bilateral air services agreement or, as between parties to the International Air Services Transit Agreement of 1944, by that Agreement. Aircraft otherwise do not enjoy a right of innocent passage over the territorial sea, subject however to the right of transit passage through straits and archipelagic waters as specified in UNCLOS.

8.   There are other international instruments which are equally flexible and, without need for amendment, can accommodate the provisions of UNCLOS as to the territorial sea. Article V of the International Air Services Transit Agreement defines "territory" by reference to Article 2 of the Chicago Convention, as do many bilateral air services agreements. Other air services agreements achieve the same result by reproducing the provision of Article 2.

9.   The three Conventions dealing with criminal matters (Tokyo, 1963; The Hague, 1970; and Montreal, 1971) appear, however , to have been drafted without this point in mind, and it is therefore arguable that, for the purposes of those Conventions "territory" does not include the territorial sea, although that sea is subject to the sovereignty of the coastal State. The Rome Convention of 1952 also appears to be deficient in this respect, and in Article 30 defines "territory of a State" without taking this point into account.

THE CONTIGUOUS ZONE

10.   Article 33 of UNCLOS deals with the contiguous zone, adopting principles which are not an innovation but are set out in the Law of the Sea Convention of 1958. It is the subject of paragraph 8 of the Secretariat's study, which states that neither in 1958 nor subsequently was attention paid to the practical meaning of this provision for international civil aviation, either in theory or in practice. Your Rapporteur agrees with the Secretariat's observations, but would add two of his own:

1.   The contiguous zone must not exceed 24 nautical miles, measured from the same baselines as the territorial sea. It therefore coincides with part of the Exclusive Economic Zone ("EEZ"), which extends for a maximum of 200 nautical miles measured from the same baselines (Article 57). Article 33 would be otiose and meaningless as regards international civil aviation if as seems to be suggested in the comments of some States[5], the coastal State has the right to regulate by its national legislation all aeronautical activities in its EEZ, without relying on Article 33.

2.   The "control" allowed by Article 33 of UNCLOS must be exercised in a manner consistent with Article 3 *bis* of the Chicago Convention which states that (self-defence apart) weapons must not be used against civil aircraft in flight. In your Rapporteur's view, there can be no doubt that Article 3 *bis* prohibits the use of weapons against aircraft for any of the purposes specified in Article 33 of UNCLOS, i.e. for preventing or punishing the infringement, in its territory or territorial sea, of its customs, immigration or sanitary laws or regulations, none of which has to do with self-defence. In view of its wording and its unanimous adoption by the General Assembly of ICAO, Article 3 *bis* is clearly declaratory of existing law and the rules contained in it are therefore binding on States whether or not they have ratified it.

STRAITS USED FOR INTERNATIONAL NAVIGATION

11.   Part III of UNCLOS deals with those straits which are not specifically regulated by long-standing international conventions. It sets out for the first time a régime for straits used for international navigation between one part of the high seas or an EEZ and another part of the high seas or an EEZ. It is not clear how far in this context "navigation" includes air navigation. Article 37 is designed to identify certain straits, and it is sufficient for this purpose if there is international surface navigation.

12.   Because, in the case of a number of straits (such as Gibraltar, Dover and Hormuz) the 12-mile limit of the territorial sea under UNCLOS will mean that passage through the straits can no longer be made by or over the high seas, UNCLOS provides for a right of transit passage which, in the case of aircraft, would otherwise have required the permission of the coastal State for passage through the airspace above its territorial sea. The right applies to "all ships and aircraft", an expression which appears to include aircraft registered in States which are not parties to UNCLOS.

13.   The right of transit passage has certain consequences for foreign civil aircraft:

(a)   In the case of non-scheduled flight, such aircraft will enjoy the right of transit passage through territorial airspace independently of Article 5 of the Chicago Convention, and consequently the coastal State will be unable to require landing, to prescribe routes or to insist on special permission, as it otherwise could do under Article 5.

(b)   Similarly, in the case of scheduled air services such aircraft will be able to exercise the right of transit without the special permission or authorization required by Article 6 of the Chicago Convention. In such cases it will be irrelevant whether the coastal State has given permission under an air services agreement or under the International Air Services Transit Agreement (IASTA) or otherwise.

(c)   Because Article 44 of UNCLOS provides that the right of transit passage cannot be suspended, and because it exists independently of other conventions or agreements, it cannot be affected by their provisions for suspension, such as Article 89 of the Chicago Convention ("War and emergency conditions"), Article 1.1 of IASTA, and similar provisions of air services agreements.

(d)   The right of the coastal State under Article 9 of the Chicago Convention to create restricted or prohibited areas over its territory (including its territorial sea) for reasons of military necessity or public safety will not be exercisable so as to restrict or prohibit transit passage allowed by UNCLOS, nor will the right temporarily to restrict or prohibit flying over the whole or part of its territory in exceptional circumstances or during an emergency or in the interest of public safety.

14.   The duties of aircraft in transit passage are set out in Article 39 of UNCLOS, paragraphs 1 and 3 of which are relevant (paragraph 2 relates only to ships). Paragraph 3 in particular requires close study.

15.   Paragraph 3(a) of Article 39 of UNCLOS requires aircraft in transit passage to "observe the Rules of the Air established by ICAO as they apply to civil aircraft". Our Rapporteur agrees with paragraph 9.7 of the Secretariat's study that the reference is to Annex 2 as adopted and amended by the ICAO Council, without taking account of differences filed by contracting States under Article 38 of the Chicago Convention. The inability to rely on differences filed against Annex 2 is a new departure, bearing in mind that coastal States previously had the right to rely on such differences in respect of flight over their territorial waters. This new departure may perhaps be welcomed, as increasing the area in which the Rules of the Air established by ICAO are uniformly applied, which can be conducive to safety. The comments received from the International Federation of Airline Pilots' Associations (IFALPA) express support for international standardization of safety standards. See also paragraph 32 of this report.

16.   The comments of IATA have, however, raised an interesting point of legal interpretation which requires to be studied. Rule 2.1.1 of Annex 2 reads as follows:

"The rules of the air shall apply to aircraft bearing the nationality and registration marks of a contracting State, wherever they may be, **to the extent that they do not conflict with the rules published by the State having jurisdiction over the territory overflown**".   (emphasis added)

The question arises whether (bearing in mind that "territory" includes the territorial sea by virtue of Article 2 of the Chicago Convention) this imports *renvoi*, in the sense that Article 39.3(a) of UNCLOS requires aircraft in transit passage through straits to conform to the Rules of the Air in Annex 2, but those Rules themselves refer back to, and give priority to, the rules published by the State whose territorial sea is being overflown. This interpretation could lead to diversity of rules applying to transit over straits, to the detriment of safety. It was evidently not the interpretation favoured by the Council in adopting its Note to paragraph 2.1.1 of the Annex, where it is stated that "over the high seas these rules apply without exception", a statement that would have been incorrect if paragraph 2.1.1 of the Rules had produced a *renvoi* to national rules. In the present case, such an interpretation would defeat the apparent purpose of Article 39.3(a) to produce uniformity over straits.

17. There is, however, another problem which may arise. Aircraft in transit through straits will be required to comply with the Rules of the Air in Annex 2, without taking account of any differences which may have been filed by the coastal States; aircraft in flight from one side of the straits to the other will, on the contrary, be obliged to take account of such differences. In consequence, diversity of rules, and with it a risk of collision, may arise. Your Rapporteur understands that some 300 differences have been filed by 29 member States against the standards in Annex 2, but he is not competent to assess how far, if at all, the differences filed by coastal States are likely to give rise to risk of collisions or other hazards affecting aircraft in transit through straits and aircraft in flight across them. This may be a matter for initial study by the Air Navigation Commission rather than the Legal Committee, and it is possible that any problems can be solved by regional or bilateral agreements.

18. In paragraph 9.7 of their study the Secretariat have commented that Article 39.3(a) of UNCLOS "would lead to an extension of the ultimate legislative jurisdiction of the Council". Indeed, the Rules of the Air formulated by the Council will apply to flight in transit through straits, without the coastal State or States being able to file differences; whereas previously, the flight being through airspace above their territorial sea or seas, they had the right to file differences. Your Rapporteur agrees with the Secretariat's view that this *de facto* extension of the Council's "ultimate legislative jurisdiction" will have to be kept in mind by the Council when making decisions as to the Rules of the Air, but it will not require any amendment of the Chicago Convention or of Annex 2 as now written. However, the present Note to Rule 2.1.1 gives the impression that the Rules set out in the Annex apply without exception only to flight over the high seas, whereas under Article 39.3(a) of UNCLOS they will apply without exception to flight in transit passage over straits, and, under Article 54 of UNCLOS, over archipelagic air routes (see paragraph 24 of this report).

19. Paragraph 9.9 *et seq.* of the Secretariat's study deals with article 39.3(b) of UNCLOS, which imposes a duty on aircraft in transit over straits to monitor certain radio frequencies. Your Rapporteur is not qualified to consider such a technical matter, which is perhaps better dealt with by the Air Navigation Commission. He does, however, draw attention to the comments of the Netherlands, which do not agree with the Secretariat's belief that UNCLOS is in error, or that "it is a firmly established practice that the aircraft must monitor the international emergency frequency".

20. Article 40 of UNCLOS calls for comment. It specifically prohibits foreign ships, but not foreign aircraft, from carrying out research or survey activities in the course of transit passage through straits, without the prior authorization of the coastal State. Article 40 is extended to passage through archipelagic waters (Article 54). On the other hand Article 39.1(c) applies to

both ships and aircraft; it prohibits them, when in transit passage, from engaging in "any activities other than those incident to their normal modes of continuous and expeditious transit", which would appear to prohibit research and survey. If so, why then does Article 40 do so specifically in the case of ships but not aircraft? This apparent drafting error is probably of little practical importance. Article 36 of the Chicago Convention provides that a State may prohibit the use of photographic equipment over its territory, which includes its territorial sea, but this does not exclude all possible forms of surveillance or survey.

21. Article 42 of UNCLOS, which bears the heading "Laws and regulations of States bordering straits relating to transit passage", is a possible source of difficulty. Under Article 54 it extends to transit through archipelagic sea lanes. Evidently, paragraphs 1(a) and (c), 2 and 4 apply to ships but not to aircraft, which are under no obligation to comply with the laws of the coastal State referred to in those paragraphs, so far as Article 42 is concerned. These have to do with pollution and the loading and unloading of commodities, currency or persons. Perhaps the authors of UNCLOS did not realize that aircraft sometimes dump their fuel in an emergency, or that helicopters and airships in flight are capable of loading and unloading cargo and persons. Other aircraft, while in flight, can unload pamphlets or the like, or goods attached to parachutes. However that may be, paragraph 5 of Article 42 appears to contemplate that an aircraft entitled to sovereign immunity may contravene such laws as much as a ship. Your Rapporteur has been unable to find a wholly satisfactory explanation of Article 42, but he observes that Article 39.1(c) requires aircraft in transit through straits or archipelagic sea lanes to refrain from activities not incident to their normal modes of continuous and expeditious transit, except if rendered necessary by *force majeure* or distress.

ARCHIPELAGIC STATES

22. The territorial sea of archipelagic States will, under Article 48 of UNCLOS, be measured from archipelagic baselines drawn in accordance with Article 47. Under Article 49, recognition is given to the sovereignty of the archipelagic State over the waters within those baselines and the airspace over them. Articles 1 and 2 already recognize the sovereignty of States over the airspace above their territorial sea. These provisions of UNCLOS can be accommodated by the Chicago Convention as it stands, without need for it to be amended (cf. paragraph 6 of this report).

23. Under Article 53 of UNCLOS all ships and aircraft (an expression which evidently includes those of States not parties to UNCLOS) enjoy the right of passage through sea lanes and the airspace over them, designated by the archipelagic State, and passing through or over its archipelagic waters and the territorial sea adjacent thereto. If that State does not designate sea lanes or air routes, the right of passage may be exercised by the routes normally used for international navigation. This is provided for in Article 53.12.

24. In this connection it is important to note that Article 54 of UNCLOS applies, *mutatis mutandis*, to archipelagic passage the provisions of Articles 39, 40, 42 and 44 (which govern transit passage over straits). The comments in paragraphs 13 to 20 of this report are therefore applicable also to archipelagic passage.

25. Article 53.5 of UNCLOS prescribes requirements for the location of and departure from air routes for archipelagic passage. These will presumably require to be examined by the Air Navigation Commission. It will be observed that paragraphs 6 to 11 of Article 53 relate to traffic separation schemes for ships but not for aircraft, presumably because aircraft exercising

the right of passage over archipelagic waters and the adjacent territorial sea, will follow the Rules of the Air established by ICAO, as provided by Article 39.3(a) of UNCLOS, extended to archipelagic passage by Article 54.

THE EXCLUSIVE ECONOMIC ZONE

26.   Article 56.1 of UNCLOS states that the coastal State has, in the EEZ to which it is entitled under the Convention,

> "sovereign rights for the purpose of exploring and exploiting, conserving and managing the natural resources, whether living or non-living, of the waters superjacent to the sea-bed and of the sea-bed and its subsoil, and with regard to other activities for the economic exploitation and exploration of the zone, such as the production of energy from the water, currents and winds".

It is clear that the rights of the coastal State in the EEZ extend to economic exploitation, etc., of the sea-bed and water, but do not extend to the airspace above it. The examples given in Article 56.1 indicate the nature of the rights conferred.

27.   Article 58, however, makes specific provision as to the use of airspace: it provides that, subject to the relevant provisions of the Convention, all States enjoy in the EEZ the freedoms referred to in Article 87 of navigation and overflight.

28.   It is therefore necessary to examine Article 87 which, significantly, is headed "Freedom of the High Seas". The relevant part of the text reads as follows:

> "The high seas are open to all States, whether coastal or land-locked. Freedom of the high seas is exercised under the conditions laid down by this Convention and by other rules of international law. It comprises, *inter alia*, both for coastal and land-locked States:
>
> (a)   freedom of navigation;
> (b)   freedom of overflight;
> (c)   freedom to lay submarine cables and pipe-lines . . . ;
> (d)   freedom to construct artificial islands and other installations . . . ;
> (e)   freedom of fishing . . . ;
> (f)   freedom of scientific research . . ."

29.   It is, therefore, beyond doubt (in your Rapporteur's opinion) that Article 58 of UNCLOS, by applying Article 87 to the right of overflight over the EEZ and using language characteristic of high seas rights, equates the EEZ with the high seas as regards freedom of overflight and is quite incompatible with the suggestion made in the comments of one State[6] that "an effort should be made in the context of the Chicago system to give the EEZ the same conditions as those applicable to land territory and territorial waters with respect to overflight, as provided for in Article 5 of the Chicago Convention (and in IASTA)". Such a suggestion would, in your Rapporteur's view, require an amendment of UNCLOS.

30.   Although Article 39.3 of UNCLOS applies to transit passage through straits and archipelagic waters, it does not extend to overflight of the EEZ. UNCLOS in fact is silent as to the Rules of the Air to be observed by aircraft overflying the EEZ.

31.   The explanation of this silence on the part of UNCLOS about so important a matter may be that, having provided that aircraft overflying the EEZ have the same freedom of overflight as aircraft overflying the high seas, the drafters of UNCLOS thought it unnecessary to provide that aircraft, whether overflying the EEZ or the high seas, must comply with the same Rules of the Air. They may have assumed that this followed as a matter of course from the identity of overflying rights. That, at least, seems to be a reasonable explanation.

32.   The Secretariat's study reaches the same conclusion, though by a somewhat different route: UNCLOS grants the coastal State only rights of economic exploration, exploitation, conservation and management of the resources of the waters and of the sea-bed, together with supporting jurisdiction; it grants no right to regulate air traffic over those waters. Your Rapporteur considers this a convincing argument, and is also impressed by a further argument advanced by the International Federation of Airline Pilots' Associations (IFALPA), which makes a valid point of purposive interpretation:

"The Federation believes that, in the interests of international standardization of safety standards, the rules established under the Chicago Convention should be applicable not only in the airspace above the high seas but also in the airspace above any Exclusive Economic Zone (EEZ) which may have been established by a State either on the basis of UNCLOS or in any other manner".

33.   Your Rapporteur agrees with the Secretariat that it may be appropriate to study this in the Legal Committee with a view to reaching a conclusion. Article 12 of the Chicago Convention provides that "over the high seas the Rules (of the Air) in force shall be those established by this Convention". In its Note to paragraph 2.1.1 of Annex 2 the Council has interpreted this as meaning that "over the high seas these rules apply without exception", i.e. that States cannot file differences. There is, your Rapporteur would suggest, no need for the Legal Committee to become involved in general questions of the status of the EEZ. It is sufficient to take note that, without ambiguity, the same right of freedom of navigation is enjoyed by aircraft over the EEZ as is enjoyed by aircraft over the high seas, which is the plain meaning of Articles 58 and 87 of UNCLOS. It would follow that, as a consequence of Articles 58 and 87 of UNCLOS, the Rules of the Air applying over the EEZ are to be identical with those applying over the high seas.

34.   It is hardly necessary to say that the determination under consideration would be concerned with the rules to be applied, not with the allocation of the duty of administering Flight Information Regions. The normal arrangements for F.I.R.s would not be affected.

35.   The Rules of the Air established by ICAO could, if necessary, make special provision for flight to and from or over artificial islands, installations or structures in the EEZ or in straits or archipelagic waters through which there is a right of transit passage. Whether there is any need to do so would, one would think, be a matter for consideration by the Air Navigation Commission in the first instance.

36.   Your Rapporteur has nothing to add to what the Secretariat's study contains about the Continental Shelf, Land-Locked States and the High Seas. He would, however, draw attention to Article 210 of UNCLOS, which prohibits the pollution of the sea by dumping. Paragraphs 3 and 5 of Article 210 apparently prohibit the dumping of aircraft fuel in the sea without the permission of the competent authorities of States. Paragraph 5, in particular, appears to contemplate the requirement of specific, prior permission. There appears to be no exception

for dumping in an emergency[7], and if so the Article will be likely to interfere with the usual and presumably necessary practice of dumping excess fuel whenever it is possible to do so before attempting an emergency landing. The Committee may wish to consider whether the Council should be recommended to make an interpretative determination to the effect that Article 210 should not be taken to prohibit the dumping of aircraft fuel in an emergency before attempting to land.

Notes

1. Denmark, Finland, Hungary, Sweden and USSR.
2. Federal Republic of Germany.
3. Egypt.
4. Turkey.
5. Argentina, Brazil and Uruguay.
6. Brazil.
7. Contrast Article 39.1(c) of UNCLOS.

- - - - -

IMO Conventions and the London Dumping Convention

Study by the IMO Secretariat	LEG/MISC/1 10/2/86 Extract

Implications of the United Nations Convention on the Law of the Sea, 1982 for the International Maritime Organization (IMO)

I. INTRODUCTION

1.   At its thirteenth regular session the Assembly requested that a careful and detailed examination of the provisions of the United Nations Convention on the Law of the Sea (1982) should be undertaken to assess the implications of the Convention for the conventions and work of IMO and, in particular, to determine the "scope and areas of appropriate IMO assistance to Member States and other agencies in respect of the provisions of the Law of the Sea Convention dealing with matters within the competence of IMO". The examination was also to enable IMO "to develop suitable and necessary collaboration with the Secretary-General of the United Nations on the provision of information, advice and assistance to developing countries on the law of the sea matters within the competence of IMO".

2.   With reference to the future International Sea-Bed Authority, established by the Convention on the Law of the Sea, the Secretary-General of IMO was requested and authorized to provide the advice and assistance which might be required by the Preparatory Commission for the International Sea-Bed Authority on matters falling within the competence of IMO.

3.   By agreement between the Secretary-General of IMO and the Special Representative of the Secretary-General of the United Nations for the Law of the Sea, the Study has been

prepared in full consultation with the relevant officials of the Office of the Special Representative.

IMO and the 1982 Convention on the Law of the Sea

4.   Although it is specifically referred to by name in only one of the Articles of the Convention on the Law of the Sea (Article 2 of Annex VIII), the International Maritime Organization (IMO) is implicitly recognized by the Convention as "the competent international organization" in respect of many important areas. In a number of provisions, the Convention requires States, in exercising powers or rights under the Convention, to conform to or take account of the relevant international regulations and standards adopted "through the competent international organization".

5.   It is generally agreed that the term "competent international organization", when it is used in the singular in provisions of the Convention relating to international regulations and rules applicable to navigation, the prevention, reduction and control of marine pollution from vessels or by dumping, refers to the International Maritime Organization, which is the agency of the United Nations with a global mandate to adopt international standards in matters concerning maritime safety, efficiency of navigation and the prevention and control of marine pollution from ships.

6.   Thus, in affirming and recognizing that the rights and responsibilities of States to regulate navigation and to prevent and control pollution from vessels or by dumping must be exercised and discharged by reference to international standards, the Convention on the Law of the Sea makes the relevant regulations and standards of IMO an integral part of the guidelines by reference to which the Convention's provisions are to be implemented. It is, therefore, right to infer that the Convention on the Law of the Sea recognizes IMO as the appropriate forum for the development of international regulations and rules which are necessary for the effective implementation of the provisions of the Convention relating to navigation and the prevention, control and reduction of marine pollution from vessels or by dumping. Indeed many important provisions of the Convention envisage and expect continuing or new activities by IMO in these fields, and some of the provisions in the Convention will depend on the results of IMO's work for their interpretation and application.

7.   In a number of the provisions dealing with safety of navigation and the prevention, reduction and control of marine pollution, the Convention on the Law of the Sea enjoins or empowers States to "take account of" or "to conform to" or "give effect to" or "implement" certain international standards developed by or through IMO. These are variously referred to as "applicable international rules and standards" or "internationally agreed rules, standards and recommended practices and procedures" or "generally accepted international rules and standards" or "generally accepted international regulations", "applicable international standards", or "applicable international instruments" or "generally accepted international regulations, procedures and practices".

8.   The Convention on the Law of the Sea does not give formal definitions for these expressions, and no clear guidelines are provided as to how the "international regulations and rules, etc." referred to in the Articles may be identified. However, it appears to be generally accepted that the international regulations and standards adopted by IMO constitute a major component of the "generally accepted" international regulations and standards in matters relating to safety of navigation and the prevention and control of marine pollution from vessels

and by dumping. Therefore, these IMO regulations and standards will be of relevance to States and other entities involved in the interpretation or application of provisions of the Convention on the Law of the Sea dealing with such matters.

9.   However, since there are no express provisions in the Convention identifying the regulations and rules which may be considered as "generally accepted" or "applicable" in particular contexts, States and other interested entities will expect some guidance with regard to the status of IMO regulations and standards in relation to the provisions of the Convention on the Law of the Sea. The need for guidance will apply not only in respect of the conventions and treaty instruments of IMO, but also in relation to the large body of important international rules, regulations, standards and recommended practices which have been adopted by IMO and embodied in Recommendations, Codes, Guidelines, General Principles and Manuals, etc.

10.   It is, of course, to be noted that formal and authoritative interpretations of the 1982 Convention's provisions can only be undertaken by the States Parties to that Convention or, in appropriate cases, by judicial or arbitral tribunals provided for that purpose in the Convention itself. Nevertheless the views and suggestions of IMO on these matters may be useful to States, particularly developing countries, in ascertaining the nature and extent of their obligations under the Convention on the Law of the Sea relating to maritime safety and the preservation of the marine environment.

11.   It may also be necessary and useful for IMO to examine the interpretation and application of some of its own rules and standards in the light of the relevant provisions of the Convention on the Law of the Sea. Such an examination may assist Governments in taking measures to implement regulations of IMO while also discharging their responsibilities under the Convention on the Law of the Sea. For example IMO may find, as a result of an examination of the Convention on the Law of the Sea, that further elaboration may be needed regarding the procedures for implementing some of IMO's safety and environmental regulations, or the enforcement of such regulations in a way which is more in harmony with the requirements and objectives of the Convention on the Law of the Sea.

12.   To enable Governments and the appropriate IMO bodies to determine the areas in which such clarifications and harmonization may be necessary or desirable, it would be necessary to identify the provisions of the Convention on the Law of the Sea which deal with matters that are also regulated by the conventions and other international instruments adopted in IMO. Identification of such matters could help the Organization and Governments to determine if there are any actual or potential conflicts between the relevant Articles of the Convention on the Law of the Sea and the corresponding IMO treaty instruments, or whether any gaps may be created by the simultaneous application of the Convention on the Law of the Sea and the relevant IMO instruments. This will enable the appropriate bodies of IMO to determine:

> (i)   whether any IMO treaties or other instruments require to be formally amended, or otherwise revised, in order to bring their provisions into line with the relevant provisions of the Convention on the Law of the Sea;

> (ii)   whether any new tasks, or modifications of current work programmes, may be necessary on the part of IMO as a result of responsibilities assigned directly to IMO by the Convention or of the effects of other provisions of the Convention on the existing activities of IMO;

(iii)   whether it would be necessary or useful for IMO or its organs to establish new or revised procedures in their work, in order to discharge mandates entrusted by the Convention on the Law of the Sea or to perform functions which have to be undertaken as a result of the Convention's provisions of relevance to IMO.

13.   An examination of the impact of the Convention on the Law of the Sea will also enable IMO to determine whether it would be necessary or useful to make suggestions or submit proposals to Governments, the United Nations or specialized agencies, in respect of matters and activities covered by the Convention on the Law of the Sea which are relevant to IMO.

14.   In accordance with the practice in IMO, decisions regarding the need for any revisions in IMO's regulations or instruments, or on proposals to be made by IMO to Governments or other organizations, will be taken by the appropriate inter-governmental bodies, on the basis of proposals from Governments and, where appropriate, international organizations associated with IMO. This Study is, therefore, intended to draw attention to those provisions of the Convention on the Law of the Sea which may have implications for particular areas of IMO's work in order to enable Governments and the inter-governmental bodies of IMO to determine whether, and if so to what extent, further measures by IMO would be necessary or appropriate, and how such measures are to be undertaken.

15.   The Articles of the Convention on the Law of the Sea which relate directly or indirectly to areas within the field of activity of IMO are those which deal with the safety of navigation, the prevention of pollution from ships and by dumping and the regulation by States of the operation of vessels flying their flags or operating within areas subject to their control. The provisions of particular relevance include the Articles of the Convention dealing with the rights and obligations of States and ships in the territorial sea, on the high seas, in the exclusive economic zone, in archipelagic waters, in straits used for international navigation with regard to the promotion of maritime safety and the prevention, reduction and control of marine pollution and the settlement of disputes relating to these rights and obligations.

16.   Other Articles of the Convention which may not be directly relevant to IMO's treaties may, nevertheless have significant implications on certain aspects of the work of the Organization. However, it does not appear useful or feasible to attempt to analyse in detail every Article of the Convention to find out whether it could have some remote relevance to IMO. This Study is, therefore, restricted to the provisions of the Convention on the Law of the Sea whose relevance to IMO is clear and direct. In particular attention is focused on the provisions relating to the following main areas:

(a)   The rights and obligations of flag, port and coastal States in the regulation of shipping activities in

(i)   the territorial sea;
(ii)   the newly-established exclusive economic zone;
(iii) the high seas;
(iv)   straits used for international navigation; and
(v)   archipelagic waters.

(b) The functions and responsibilities of IMO in relation to:

(i) matters already dealt with by the Organization in accordance with its own constitutional mandate;

(ii) matters in respect of which new functions or responsibilities are directly entrusted to IMO, or on which the Organization may consider it useful to undertake work because of certain provisions of the Convention on the Law of the Sea.

17. To supplement the detailed analysis of the main provisions relating to the areas mentioned in paragraph 16 above, a list has been prepared, in tabular form, of the provisions of the 1982 Convention which have direct or indirect implications for IMO and its work. That list appears as an Annex to this Study. Appended to the Annex is a list of the treaty instruments of IMO which deal with matters covered by the respective Articles of the Convention on the Law of the Sea. The Appendix does not include the large number of "non-treaty" international instruments of IMO containing *inter alia*, international regulations, standards, procedures and practices relating to the safety of navigation, the design, construction, equipment and manning of ships, the handling of cargoes on board vessels and in ports, the prevention, control and reduction of marine pollution from ships and by dumping etc. It should nevertheless be noted that the provisions of some of these non-treaty instruments deal with matters of considerable technical importance. In some cases the instruments, such as codes or guidelines, are intended to supplement particular treaty instruments, and to provide necessary guidelines for their effective implementation. It is intended that a detailed and classified list of these non-treaty instruments will be prepared in the near future, in order to give to Governments and other interested parties an indication of the scope and extent of the international regulations and standards contained in these non-treaty instruments which may be of relevance and significance in understanding and applying those Articles of the Convention on the Law of the Sea which relate to the areas of competence of the International Maritime Organization.

II. ANALYSES OF MAJOR PROVISIONS OF THE 1982 UNITED NATIONS CONVENTION ON THE LAW OF THE SEA WHICH HAVE OR MAY HAVE IMPLICATIONS FOR IMO

A. Breadth of the Territorial Sea

18. Article 3 of the Convention on the Law of the Sea states that "every State has the right to establish the breadth of its territorial sea up to a limit not exceeding 12 nautical miles, measured from baselines determined in accordance with this Convention".

19. A number of IMO's conventions and other treaty instruments contain provisions regarding the application of their terms in or in relation to, the territorial seas of States. These instruments were adopted before the adoption of the 1982 Convention and before there was international agreement on the maximum breadth of the territorial sea. The 1982 Convention has now established a specified maximum limit of 12 nautical miles for the breadth of the territorial sea. It may, therefore, be necessary to examine the provisions of IMO's conventions and other instruments concerned, in order to ascertain to what extent their provisions will still be appropriate and adequate for the original purposes, when applied to a territorial sea of twelve nautical miles.

B.   **Rights and obligations of coastal and port States in the regulation of shipping activities in the territorial sea and in ports and terminal installations**

(i)   Regulations for safety of navigation (regulation of innocent passage)

20.   Under Article 21 of the Convention the laws and regulations of the coastal State, regarding the safety of navigation and the regulation of maritime traffic, the protection of navigational aids and facilities must be in conformity with the provisions of the Convention and "other rules of international law", if they are to apply to ships of other States exercising the right of innocent passage through the territorial sea.   Moreover, such laws and regulations shall not apply to "the design, construction, manning or equipment of foreign ships" unless they are "giving effect to generally accepted international rules and standards".   IMO is the only global institution with the mandate in this area, and all existing rules and standards on the design, construction, equipment and manning of vessels have in fact been established in or by IMO.

21.   Article 21, paragraph 4 of the Convention also provides that foreign ships exercising the right of innocent passage through the territorial sea "shall comply with all such laws and regulations (of the coastal State) and all generally accepted international regulations relating to the prevention of collisions at sea".

22.   Article 22 of the Convention requires a coastal State, in designating sea lanes and the prescription of traffic separation schemes for ships exercising the right of innocent passage through its territorial sea, to "take into account the recommendations of the competent international organization" (IMO).

23.   Thus, in respect of the regulation of shipping for the promotion of safety of navigation, the coastal State's rights and obligations under the Convention on the Law of the Sea are significantly affected by:

(a)   IMO's international rules and standards on the design, construction, manning and equipment of ships not flying the flag of the coastal State concerned;

(b)   the provisions of the Convention on the International Regulations for Preventing Collisions at Sea and, through Regulation 10, of that Convention the Traffic Separation Schemes adopted by IMO;

(c)   IMO's principles and procedures regarding the designation or prescription of traffic separation schemes and sea-lanes; and

(d)   other international regulations and standards of IMO which may be deemed to form part of "international law" on the subjects mentioned above.

(ii)   Regulation of shipping for the prevention, reduction and control of marine pollution

(a)   **By the Coastal State:**

24.   Under Article 211, paragraph 4 of the Convention the coastal State is empowered, "in the exercise of (its) sovereignty within (its) territorial sea", to "adopt laws and regulations for the prevention, reduction and control of marine pollution from foreign vessels" but such laws and

regulations must "not hamper innocent passage of foreign vessels" in accordance with Part II, Section 3 of the Convention. Part II, Section 3 includes Article 21, paragraph 2 of which stipulates that the laws and regulations of the coastal State shall not apply to "the design, construction, manning or equipment of foreign ships" unless the laws and regulations of the coastal State are "giving effect to generally accepted international rules and standards".

25. Article 211, paragraph 3 of the Convention provides that a State which establishes particular requirements for the prevention, reduction and control of pollution of the marine environment as a condition for the entry of foreign vessels into its ports or internal waters or for a call at its off-shore terminals must give due publicity to such requirements and also to communicate the requirements to "the competent international organization" (IMO). Furthermore, where such requirements are established in identical form by two or more coastal States in an endeavour to harmonize policy, the communication to IMO should indicate which States are participating in such co-operative arrangements.

(b) By the Port State:

26. Article 218, paragraph 1 gives to the port State the right to undertake investigations and, if the evidence warrants, institute proceedings against a vessel voluntarily in its port or off-shore terminal in respect of discharges in violation *inter alia* of "applicable international rules and standards" established through "the competent international organization" (IMO), even where the discharge concerned took place "outside the internal waters, territorial sea or exclusive economic zone" of the State in question.

27. Paragraph 3 of Article 218 requires a port State to comply, as far as practicable, with a request from any State for investigation of a discharge in violation of "applicable international rules and standards" by a ship in the internal waters, territorial sea or exclusive economic zone of the requesting State, when that ship is voluntarily within a port or at an off-shore terminal of the port State concerned. The port State is also required to comply, as far as practicable, with similar requests from the flag State of the ship concerned, "irrespective of where the violation occurred". Under Article 220, paragraph 1, such a port State has the power to institute proceedings against such a ship in respect of violations within its territorial sea or exclusive economic zone. The port State is also empowered, under Article 220, paragraph 2, to undertake physical inspection of such a ship where there are "clear grounds for believing" that such violation has occurred.

28. Under Article 219 a State which, upon request or on its own initiative, has ascertained that a vessel within its port or off-shore terminal is in violation of "applicable international rules and standards relating to sea-worthiness of vessels", and thereby threatens damage to marine environment is required, as far as practicable, to take administrative measures to prevent the vessel from sailing. The port State may, however, permit the ship to proceed to the nearest appropriate repair yard for the removal of the causes of the violation, after which the ship shall be permitted to continue immediately.

29. IMO is the only global institution with the mandate for establishing international rules and standards relating to "sea-worthiness of ships", and the existing international rules and standards on the subject have in fact been established by IMO.

30. Under Article 223, a port State taking proceedings against a vessel for violations against the laws or regulations of that State, or international regulations or standards, for the

prevention, reduction or control of marine pollution, is obliged to take measures to facilitate *inter alia* the admission of evidence submitted by "the competent international organization" (IMO) and to "facilitate the attendance at such proceedings of official representatives of the competent international organization". Such official representative attending the proceedings shall have such rights and duties as may be provided under national law and regulations or international law.

31.   Under Article 226, a port State investigating a foreign vessel in connection with possible violations of laws and regulations for the prevention, reduction and control of marine pollution is required to follow certain procedures, in particular as regards the examination and acceptability of certificates, records and other documents required by generally accepted international rules and standards, and the grounds and procedures for "physical inspection of the vessel".

   (iii)   Regulation of shipping for the purpose of preventing pollution of the marine
            environment by dumping

32.   The only comprehensive global international treaty for the prevention of marine pollution by dumping is the 1972 Convention for the Prevention of Dumping of Wastes and other Matter at Sea (the London Dumping Convention). The Contracting Parties to the Convention have designated IMO as the "competent organization" responsible for the Secretariat duties in relation to the Convention. In particular, IMO is responsible for organizing and servicing the Consultative Meetings of Contracting Parties which, under the Convention, have the responsibility and authority to keep under continuing review the implementation of the 1972 Convention, including the adoption of amendments to the Convention and its Annexes. The Consultative Meetings are specifically empowered to develop or adopt implementation procedures, including the basic criteria for determining exceptional and emergency situations and procedures for consultative advice and the safe disposal of matter in such circumstances and the designation of appropriate dumping areas. Hence the only global rules, standards and recommended practices and procedures to prevent, reduce and control pollution of the marine environment by dumping are those contained in the London Dumping Convention itself, or in the supplemental rules established by the Contracting Parties in the Consultative Meetings.

33.   Article 210 of the Convention on the Law of the Sea, in requiring States to adopt laws and regulations to prevent, reduce and control marine pollution by dumping in their territorial seas (*inter alia*) also stipulates that the national laws, regulations and measures "shall be no less effective . . . than the global rules and standards (paragraph 6). These global rules and standards are currently those in the London Dumping Convention or developed by the Consultative Meetings of the London Dumping Convention, within the framework of IMO.

34.   Article 216, paragraph 1, of the Convention places an obligation on the coastal State to "enforce" the laws and regulations adopted in accordance with the Convention on the Law of the Sea and "applicable international rules and standards established through competent international organizations or diplomatic conference" for the prevention, reduction and control of marine pollution by dumping. Such enforcement is required of the coastal State with regard to dumping *inter alia* within its territorial sea (paragraph 1(a)).

35.   The provisions in Articles 223 to 233 of the Convention relating to safeguards in connection with proceedings for the enforcement of laws and regulations to prevent, reduce

and control marine pollution, apply also to laws and regulations dealing with pollution by dumping.

C.   Rights and obligations of coastal and port States in the regulation of shipping in the Exclusive Economic Zone (EEZ)

(i)   Regulations for safety of navigation

36.   Under Article 56 of the Convention on the Law of the State, the coastal State has jurisdiction, as provided for in the relevant provisions of the Convention, with regard, *inter alia*, to the "establishment and use of artificial islands, installations and structures". The coastal State has exclusive jurisdiction over such artificial islands, installations and structures with regard *inter alia* to "safety-laws and regulations" (Article 60, paragraph 2). However, the coastal State is obliged under Article 60 of the Convention:

(a)   to give due notice of the construction of such artificial islands, installations or structures and to maintain permanent means for giving warning of their presence (paragraph 3);

(b)   to remove any installations or structures which are abandoned or disused "to ensure *inter alia* safety of navigation, taking into account any generally accepted international standards established in this regard by "the competent international organization" (IMO) (paragraph 3);

(c)   not to extend the breadth of safety zones around such artificial islands, installations or structures beyond 500 metres, except as authorized by generally accepted international standards or as recommended by "the competent international organization" (IMO) (paragraph 5);

(d)   not to establish artificial islands, installations or structures, or safety zones around them, where interference may be caused to the use of recognized sea-lanes essential to international navigation;

(e)   to give due publicity in respect of any artificial islands, installations or structures which are not entirely removed and the extent of any safety zones established round artificial islands, installations or structures.

The above obligations also apply to the establishment of artificial islands, installations and structures on the Continental Shelf (Article 80).

(ii)   Regulation of shipping for the prevention, reduction and control of pollution of the marine environment of the exclusive economic zone

37.   For the purpose of enforcing the applicable regulations for the protection and preservation of the marine environment of its exclusive economic zone, a coastal State is empowered, under Article 211, paragraph 5 of the Law of the Sea Convention, to adopt laws and regulations for the prevention, reduction and control of pollution from vessels conforming to and giving effect to generally accepted international rules and standards established through "the competent international organization" (IMO). The procedures for enforcement in this

regard are set out in Section 6 of part XII of the Convention (Articles 218 to 221) and subject to the relevant provisions in Section 7 of the same part (Safeguards).

38.   The laws and regulations envisaged under Article 211 of the Convention include the laws and regulations to minimize the threat of accidents which might cause pollution of the marine environment (such as those referred to in Article 211, paragraph 1) as well as laws and regulations implementing international rules and standards relating to prompt notification to the coastal State when its coastline or related interests may be affected by incidents, including maritime casualties which involve discharges or probability of discharges (as provided for in Article 211, paragraph 7).

39.   Paragraph 6 of Article 211 empowers the coastal State to adopt "special mandatory measures for the prevention of pollution from vessels" in certain clearly defined areas of its exclusive economic zone, subject to conditions and procedures stipulated in that paragraph. These conditions include:

(a)   appropriate consultations, through "the competent international organization" (IMO), with other States concerned before submitting the proposal with regard to the special measures;

(b)   submission to "the competent international organization" (IMO) by "a communication", of scientific and technical evidence in support of the special measures and submitting also information on necessary reception facilities;

(c)   determination by "the competent international organization" (IMO), within 12 months after receiving such communication, as to whether the conditions in that area correspond to the requirements set out in paragraph 6(a) of Article 211 of the Convention;

(d)   upon determination by "the competent international organization" (IMO) that the necessary conditions are fulfilled, the coastal State may adopt appropriate laws and regulations for the area concerned; however such laws may only implement the international rules and standards or navigational practices as are made applicable, through "the competent international organization" (IMO), for special areas;

(e)   the coastal State may adopt additional laws and regulations (over and above those referred to in sub-paragraph (d) above) provided that:

(i)   the intention to do so has been notified to "the competent international organization" (IMO) at the time when the communication proposing the special measures was sent to that organization;

(ii)   "the competent international organization" (IMO) has agreed to the adoption of the additional laws and regulations within 12 months after the submission of the communication by the coastal State;

(iii)   the additional laws and regulations relate to discharges or navigational practices and do not require foreign vessels to observe design, construction, manning or equipment standards other than generally accepted international rules and standards;

(iv)   the additional laws and regulations shall become applicable to foreign vessels 15 months after the submission of the communication to "the competent international organization"(IMO), and subject to the agreement of the Organization as provided.

(f)   the coastal State is requested to publish the limits of any particular area of its exclusive economic zone in which special mandatory measures have been adopted pursuant to paragraph 6 of Article 211 (paragraph 6(b)).

40.   A State is empowered by Article 220 of the Convention (paragraph 1) to institute proceedings against a vessel voluntarily in its port or at off-shore installations in respect of violations, within the exclusive economic zone of that State, of laws and regulations of the State for the prevention, reduction and control of marine pollution adopted in accordance with the Convention on the Law of the Sea or applicable international rules and standards. Where a State has clear grounds for believing that a vessel navigating in its territorial sea or exclusive economic zone has, in the exclusive economic zone of that State, committed a violation of applicable national or international rules and standards for the prevention, reduction and control of marine pollution, the State may

(a)   require the vessel to give information regarding its identity and port of registry, its last and its next port of call and other relevant information needed to establish whether a violation has occurred (Article 220, paragraph 3);

(b)   undertake physical inspection of the vessel for matters relating to the violation if the vessel has refused to give information or has given information which is manifestly at variance with the evident factual situation and the circumstances of the case justify such an inspection. An inspection is, in any case, permissible only if the violation alleged has resulted in "substantial discharge causing or threatening significant pollution of the marine environment" (Article 220, paragraph 5).

41.   In cases where there is "clear objective evidence" of such violation the State concerned may indeed institute proceedings, including detention of the vessel, in accordance with the laws of the State. But this power may be exercised only if the discharge involved has caused "major damage or threat of major damage to the coastline or related interests of the coastal State, or any resources of its territorial sea or exclusive economic zone" (Article 220, paragraph 6). In this case the State is, nevertheless, obliged to allow the vessel to proceed if the vessel assures compliance with requirements for bonding or other security in accordance with procedures which are established either through "the competent international organization" (IMO) or by agreement between the parties concerned.

42.   The safeguards in respect of proceedings and enforcement measures as provided for in Section 7 of part XII of the Convention (Articles 223 to 233) apply, where appropriate, to proceedings and enforcement measures in respect of violations in the exclusive economic zone.

(iii)   Regulation of shipping for the prevention of pollution of the marine environment by dumping in the exclusive economic zone

43.   The right of the coastal State to permit, regulate or control dumping under Article 210 of the Convention (see paragraph 33 above) applies also to dumping in the exclusive economic zone of that State, and indeed also on the continent shelf of the State. The laws, regulations and measures taken by the State in this respect must be no less effective than the global rules and standards which are established through "the competent international organizations"

(Article 210, paragraph 6), and should be adopted after due consideration of the matter with other States which may be affected (Article 210, paragraph 5).

44.   The coastal State is required to enforce laws and regulations adopted in accordance with the Convention on the Law of the Sea, and applicable international rules and standards established through "competent international organizations" for the prevention of marine pollution by dumping, with regard to dumping within its exclusive economic zone (Article 216, paragraph 1(a)).

C.   **Rights and obligations of States in the regulation of shipping in straits used for international navigation**

   (i)   Regulation of shipping for the safety of navigation

45.   Under Article 41 of the Convention on the Law of the Sea, States bordering a strait used for international navigation (and covered by Article 37 of the Convention) are empowered to designate "sea-lanes" and prescribe "traffic separation schemes" for navigation, where necessary, to promote safe passage of ships. The power extends also to the substitution of sea-lanes or traffic separation schemes. However this power may be exercised subject to certain conditions, namely:

   (a)   The sea-lanes or traffic separation schemes designated or prescribed by the bordering States must conform to generally accepted international regulations (paragraph 3). In this connection it is to be noted that IMO is the only global institution with the mandate to develop international regulations with regard to routeing systems for ships.

   (b)   Before designating sea-lanes or prescribing traffic separation schemes (or substituting existing sea-lanes or traffic separation schemes) the State concerned is required to refer the proposal to "the competent international organization" (IMO), with a view to their adoption. The power of formal "adoption" of the sea-lanes or traffic separation scheme is given by the Convention to IMO; but IMO is empowered to adopt only such sea-lanes or traffic separation schemes as may be agreed with the States bordering the strait concerned. Paragraph 4 of Article 41 states that the State concerned may designate, prescribe or substitute sea-lanes or traffic separation schemes only after such lanes or schemes have been formally adopted by "the competent international organization" (IMO).

   (c)   Where sea-lanes or traffic separation schemes through the waters of two or more States bordering a strait used for international navigation are proposed, the States concerned are required to "co-operate in formulating proposals in consultation with "the competent international organization" (IMO) (paragraph 5).

   (d)   A State designating sea-lanes or prescribing traffic separation schemes in a strait used for international navigation is required to indicate clearly the sea-lanes and traffic separation schemes in question on charts to which "due publicity" must be given. In view of the direct relevance of such publicity for the safety of navigation it appears essential that the publicity be given through IMO, or that IMO be closely involved in the procedure to be adopted, in co-operation with other organizations such as the International Hydrographic Organization (IHO).

(e) Article 42 of the Convention empowers States bordering straits used for international navigation to adopt laws and regulations relating to "transit passage", for the safety of navigation and the regulation of marine traffic as provided in Article 41 - i.e. in conformity with the procedures specified in Article 41 and outlined in sub-paragraphs (a) to (d) above (Article 42, paragraph 1(b)).

(f) Ships in transit passage are required to respect applicable sea-lanes and traffic separation schemes, and laws and regulations established in accordance with Articles 41 and 42. They are also required to comply with generally accepted international regulations, procedures and practices for safety at sea, including the International Regulations for Preventing Collisions at Sea. Accordingly the bordering State is empowered to take necessary measures to ensure compliance of such laws etc. by the ships in transit passage.

(g) States bordering straits used for international navigation are required to give appropriate publicity in respect of laws and regulations adopted by them for the safety of navigation and the regulation of maritime traffic in the strait under Article 41 of the Convention (Article 42, paragraph 1(a)) and any danger to navigation within the strait of which they have knowledge (Article 44).

(h) States bordering straits used for international navigation are not permitted to exercise their powers under Articles 41 and 42 of the Convention in such a way as to have the practical effect of denying, hampering or impairing the right of transit passage (Article 42, paragraph 2).

46. It is worth emphasizing that the provisions of Article 41 and 42 apply in respect of straits used for international navigation in which the régime of transit passage is applicable as provided for under Article 37 of the Convention. In the case of straits which are excluded from the application of the régime of transit passage by virtue of the provision of Article 38, or straits which lie between a part of the high seas or an exclusive economic zone and the territorial sea of a foreign State, the bordering State is under an obligation to apply the régime of innocent passage applicable to its territorial sea (Article 45, paragraph 1).

47. A State bordering a strait used for international navigation may not suspend transit passage or innocent passage as the case may be, through the strait (Articles 44 and 45, paragraph 2).

(ii) Regulation of shipping for the prevention, reduction and control of pollution of the marine environment by vessels

48. Article 42 of the Convention empowers a State bordering a strait used for international navigation to adopt laws and regulations relating to transit passage through the strait in respect of the prevention, reduction and control of pollution, by giving effect to applicable international regulations regarding the discharge of oil, oily wastes and other noxious substances in the strait (paragraph 1(b)). The State is also empowered to enforce such laws, subject to the same safeguards as apply to the enforcement of laws and regulations relating to safety of navigation (see paragraph 45(h) above).

49. Under Article 233 of the Convention, a State bordering a strait used for international navigation has the same powers of enforcement in respect of violations of the laws and

regulations adopted by it under Article 42, where such violation causes or threatens major damage to the marine environment of the strait in question. In such a case the bordering State concerned is empowered to take appropriate enforcement measures, but subject to the safeguards stipulated in Articles 223 to 232 of the Convention (see paragraphs 30 and 31 above).

(iii)   Regulation of shipping for the prevention of pollution by dumping in straits used for international navigation

50.   Under Article 216 of the Convention, States are empowered (and required) to enforce laws and regulations, adopted in accordance with the Convention and applicable international rules and standards established through "competent international organizations" for the prevention, reduction and control of pollution of the marine environment by dumping. Where a strait used for international navigation is otherwise within the jurisdiction of a bordering State for the purpose of pollution prevention, the right and obligation of such a State under Article 216 will also extend to the prevention of pollution by dumping in the strait concerned.

D.   **The rights and obligations of States in regulating shipping in archipelagic waters**

(i)   Regulation of shipping for safety of navigation

51.   The right of an archipelagic State to regulate shipping in its archipelagic waters is subject to the right of "innocent passage" applicable to the territorial sea, as provided for in Article 52 of the Convention.

52.   Article 53 of the Convention gives to an archipelagic State the right to designate sea-lanes suitable for the continuous and expeditious passage of foreign ships through the archipelagic waters and the adjacent territorial sea (paragraph 1), as well as traffic separation schemes for the safe passage of ships through narrow channels in sea-lanes designated by that State (paragraph 6).

53.   The conditions and procedures relating to such sea lanes and traffic separation schemes are prescribed in Article 53. These include:

(a)   Such sea lanes and traffic separation schemes must conform to "generally accepted international regulations" (paragraph 8).

(b)   Proposals for new or revised sea lanes and traffic separation schemes must be referred by the State concerned to "the competent international organization" (IMO), which is empowered to adopt only such sea lanes and traffic separation schemes as may be agreed with the archipelagic State. The archipelagic State may designate, prescribe or substitute the sea lanes or traffic separation schemes only after they have been adopted by "the competent international organization" (IMO) (paragraph 9).

(c)   The archipelagic State is required to indicate clearly the axes of the sea lanes and traffic separation schemes designated or prescribed by it on charts, and due publicity should be given to such charts (paragraph 10).

(d)   Sea-lanes and traffic separation schemes which meet the conditions set in Article 53 must be complied with by ships in "archipelagic sea-lane passage" (Article 53, paragraph 11 and Article 54).   Article 54 provides that the provisions of Article 39 apply to ships in "archipelagic sea-lane passage".   This means that such ships are required to comply with "generally accepted international regulations, procedures and practices" for safety at sea, including the International Regulations for Preventing Collisions at Sea.

(ii)   Regulation of shipping for the prevention of pollution from vessels in archipelagic waters

54.   The right of the State to regulate shipping for the prevention of pollution from vessels in its archipelagic waters is covered by the same restrictions as apply to the coastal State in the regulation of shipping in the territorial sea. (Article 54 and 39(2)(b)).   In particular the laws and regulations adopted by the coastal State in respect of the preservation of the environment and the prevention, reduction and control of pollution must be in conformity with "other rules of international law relating to innocent passage" and such laws shall not apply to the design, construction, manning or equipment of foreign ships unless they are giving effect to generally accepted international rules and standards (Article 52(1), Article 21).

(iii)   Regulation of shipping for the prevention of pollution by dumping

55.   The provisions relating to the prevention of pollution by dumping in the territorial sea and exclusive economic zone (and the continental shelf) apply also to archipelagic waters (see paragraphs 24, 33 to 35 above).

E.   **The right of the coastal State with regard to the avoidance of pollution arising from maritime casualties**

56.   Article 221 of the Convention on the Law of the Sea asserts and safeguards the right of the coastal State to take and enforce measures beyond the territorial sea to protect its coastline or related interests, including fishing from pollution or the threat of pollution resulting from a maritime casualty or acts relating to such casualty which may reasonably be expected to result in major harmful consequences.   The measures taken must be proportionate to the actual or threatened damage.   The Article states that the right of the coastal State may be pursuant to "customary or conventional international law".   In this connection reference may be made to the 1969 International Convention Relating to Intervention on the High Seas in Cases of Oil Pollution Casualties and the 1973 Protocol to it relating to pollution damage by substances other than oil.   These two treaties, adopted under the auspices of IMO, constitute the current "conventional" law on the right of coastal State intervention.   Their application, interpretation and implementation may therefore, be significantly affected by the general rule enunciated in Article 221 of the Convention on the Law of the Sea (see paragraphs 20 and 21 above).

57.   Reference may also be made in this context to Article 211, paragraph 7 of the Convention on the Law of the Sea which envisages the establishment, through "the competent international organization" (IMO) of international rules and standards relating to the prompt notification to coastal States whose coastline or related interests may be affected by incidents, including maritime casualties, which involve discharges or probability of discharges.   The only existing international rules and standards in this respect are those contained in the 1973 International

Convention for the Prevention of Marine Pollution from Ships, as modified by the Protocol of 1978 thereto (MARPOL 73/78) and, in particular, Article 8 and Protocol I to the Convention. Also of relevance are the Guidelines on Reporting and Notification developed by IMO to supplement the provisions of the Convention and its Protocol I. The provisions of the IMO treaties and Guidelines will therefore constitute an important part of the yardstick by which coastal State action in this regard may be assessed. The provisions of the Convention on the Law of the Sea may, in turn, have relevance on the interpretation and application of the scope of the IMO rules.

F.   **Rights and Obligations of Flag States**

   (i) Obligations of the flag State in relation to safety of navigation

58.   Article 94 of the Convention requires a flag State to exercise jurisdiction and control over every ship flying its flag and the master, officers and crew of such a ship in respect, *inter alia*, of administrative and technical matters concerning the ship (paragraph 2(b)), and to take necessary measures in respect of the ship to ensure safety at sea (paragraph 3). The measures specifically referred to in this regard and listed in paragraphs 3 and 4 of Article 94 are those relating to:

   (a)   the construction, equipment and seaworthiness of ships;

   (b)   the manning of ships, labour conditions and the training of crews, taking into account the applicable international instruments;

   (c)   the use of signals, the maintenance of communications and the prevention of collisions;

   (d)   the survey of the ship before registration, and thereafter at appropriate intervals, by a qualified surveyor of ships;

   (e)   the provision on board the ship of such charts, nautical publications and navigational equipment and instruments as are appropriate for the safe navigation of the ships;

   (f)   the need for the ship to be in the charge of a master and officers who possess appropriate qualifications, in particular in seamanship, navigation, communications and marine engineering, with a crew which is appropriate in qualification and numbers for the type, size, machinery and equipment of the ship;

   (g)   the necessity for the master, officers and, to the extent appropriate, the crew to be fully conversant with and required to observe the applicable international regulations concerning the safety of life at sea, the prevention of collisions, the prevention, reduction and control of marine pollution, and the maintenance of communications by radio.

59.   In connection with the maintenance of a register of ships States are relieved of the obligation to register ships which are excluded from "generally international regulations on account of their small size" (Article 94(2)(a)). The regulations which may provide guidance on this point have mostly been developed in IMO. In taking the measures called for in Article 94, the flag State is required to conform to "generally accepted international regulations,

procedures and practices" and take any steps which may be necessary to secure their observance (Article 94, paragraph 5).

60. Under Article 94, paragraph 7, of the Convention the flag State is required to cause an inquiry to be held into every marine casualty or incident of navigation on the high seas involving a ship flying its flag and causing loss of life or serious injury to nationals of another State or serious damage to the ships or installations of another State or serious damage to the marine environment. The flag State is also required to co-operate in the conduct of any inquiry held by the State whose nationals, ships, installations or marine environment have suffered serious damage as a result of the casualty or incident.

61. Under Article 98 the flag State is under an obligation to require the master of a ship flying its flag, in so far as he can do so without danger to the ship, the crew or passengers, to render assistance to any person found at sea and in danger of being lost; to proceed with all possible speed to the rescue of persons in distress, if informed of their need for assistance in so far as such action may reasonably be expected of the master. The flag State must also require the master, in case of a collision involving his ship, to render assistance to the other ship, its crew and passengers (paragraph 1).

62. A number of the provisions of the Convention impose on the flag State, expressly or by implication, the obligation to ensure the compliance by ships flying its flag of requirements imposed for the purpose of promoting maritime safety. These requirements include:

(a) the obligation of foreign ships exercising the right of innocent passage in the territorial sea to comply with appropriate laws and regulations of the coastal State and "all generally accepted international regulations relating to the prevention of collisions at sea" (Article 21, paragraph 4). This obligation also applies to foreign ships in transit passage through straits used for international navigation (Article 39, paragraph 2 and Article 42, paragraph 4); to foreign ships exercising the right of innocent passage in straits used for international navigation which are excluded from the régime of transit passage (Article 45); and to foreign ships exercising the right of archipelagic sea-lane passage in archipelagic waters (Article 39, paragraph 2 and Article 54);

(b) the duty of foreign nuclear powered ships, and ships carrying nuclear or other inherently dangerous or noxious substances, to carry documents and observe special precautionary measures established for such ships by international agreement, when such ships are exercising the right of innocent passage through the territorial sea (Article 23);

(c) the duty of foreign ships exercising the right of transit passage through straits used for international navigation, or archipelagic sea-lane passage in archipelagic waters, to respect applicable sea-lanes or traffic separation schemes (Article 41, paragraph 7 and Article 53, paragraph 11);

(d) the obligation of foreign ships navigating in the exclusive economic zone to comply with "generally accepted international standards" regarding navigation in the vicinity of artificial islands, installations and structures and safety zones properly established around them (Article 60, paragraph 6). The same obligation applies in respect of artificial islands, installations or structures and related safety zones on the continental shelf (Article 80) and presumably also in the Area (see Article 147).

63.   The provisions referred to in sub-paragraphs (a) to (d) of paragraph 62 above do not expressly impose an obligation on the flag State, as such, in respect of the duties specified for the ship. Nevertheless, to the extent that any of the requirements may be considered as part of "the generally accepted international regulations, procedures, and practices" concerning "the safety of life at sea and the prevention of collisions", it may be assumed that the flag State is under an obligation, under Article 94, paragraph 5, "to take any necessary steps which may be necessary to secure their observance".

     (ii)   Obligations of the flag State in relation to the prevention, reduction and control of pollution of the marine environment from vessels

64.   One of the obligations imposed on the flag State by Article 94 of the Convention is that the State shall take such measures for ships flying its flag as are necessary to ensure that "the master, officers and, to the extent appropriate, the crew are fully conversant with and required to observe the applicable international regulations concerning the prevention, reduction and control of marine pollution" (paragraph 4(c)).

65.   Other provisions of the Convention imposing specific obligation on flag States in respect of the prevention and control of marine pollution from vessels flying their flags are the following:

     (a)   Article 211, paragraph 2, requires the flag State to adopt laws and regulations for the prevention, reduction and control of pollution of the marine environment from vessels flying its flag or of its registry. Such laws and regulations shall at least have the same effect as that of "generally accepted international rules and standards" established "through the competent international organization" (IMO).

     (b)   Under Article 217, paragraph 1, a flag State is obliged to ensure compliance by vessels flying its flag, or of its registry, with "applicable international rules and standards, established through the competent international organization" (IMO), as well as the laws and regulations of the flag State, for the prevention, reduction and control of pollution of the marine environment from vessels which have been adopted in accordance with the Convention on the Law of the Sea. The flag State is also required to adopt laws and regulations and take other measures necessary for the implementation of these rules, standards, laws and regulations and to provide for their effective enforcement, irrespective of where a violation occurs.

     (c)   The same Article (217) requires the flag State, in particular, to take appropriate measures to ensure that vessels flying its flag or of its registry are prohibited from sailing, until they can proceed to sea in compliance with the requirements of the international rules and standards established through the "competent international organization" (IMO), including requirements in respect of design, construction, equipment and manning of vessels (paragraph 2). The flag State is also obliged to ensure that vessels flying its flag or of its registry carry on board certificates required by and issued pursuant to international rules and standards and to ensure, further, that the vessels are periodically inspected in order to verify that such certificates are in conformity with the actual condition of the vessels (paragraph 1.3).

(d) The flag State is under a duty to provide for immediate investigation into and, where appropriate, institute proceedings in respect of the alleged violation by its ships of rules and standards established through "the competent international organization" (IMO), irrespective of where the violation occurred or where the pollution caused by such violation has occurred or has been spotted (paragraph 4).

(e) Finally, a flag Stage is required, under Article 217, paragraphs 6 and 7, to investigate any violation alleged to have been committed by vessels flying its flag, if so requested in writing by any State. If satisfied that sufficient evidence is available to enable proceedings to be brought in respect of the alleged violation, the flag State is obliged to institute such proceedings in accordance with its laws. The requesting State and "the competent international organization" (IMO) shall promptly be informed of the action taken and its outcome. Such information shall be available to all States.

(f) The flag State is required to ensure that the penalties provided for by the laws and regulations for vessels flying its flag shall be adequate in severity to discourage violations wherever they occur (Article 217, paragraph 8).

66. Under Article 220, paragraph 4, a flag State is required to adopt laws and regulations and take other measures to ensure that a vessel flying its flag comply with requests for information by a coastal State in whose exclusive economic zone or territorial sea the vessel is navigating, where there are clear grounds for believing that the vessel has committed, in the exclusive economic zone of the coastal State, a violation of applicable international rules and standards or the laws and regulations of the coastal State giving effect to such international rules and standards (paragraphs 3 and 4).

67. Under Article 211 States may, under specified conditions, establish particular requirements for the prevention, reduction and control of pollution as a condition for the entry of foreign vessels into their ports and internal waters, or for calls at their offshore terminals. Two or more States may establish such requirements in identical form in an endeavour to harmonize policy. A flag State is obliged under the Convention to require the master of vessels flying its flag or of its registry to furnish appropriate information (including the State in the region to whose port it is proceeding) to a coastal State participating in such a co-operative arrangement, where the vessel is navigating in the territorial sea of that coastal State and the information has been requested by that State. A coastal State establishing special requirements, whether alone or with other States, is required to communicate such requirements to "the competent international organization " (IMO) and to give due publicity to such requirements (paragraph 3).

68. Article 216 of the Convention imposes on a flag State the obligation to enforce laws and regulations, adopted in accordance with the Convention and "applicable international rules and standards established through competent international organizations" or general diplomatic conference, for the prevention, reduction and control of pollution of the marine environment by dumping with regard to vessels flying its flag or of its registry (paragraph 1(b)).

(iii)   Rights of flag States *vis à vis* other States in respect of ships flying their flag or of their registry

69.   A number of provisions of the Convention on the Law of the Sea stipulate certain rights for the flag State, *vis à vis* other States, with regard to measures taken against the ships of the flag State. In general a flag State has the right, under the Convention, to demand that other States comply with requirements of the Convention when they take or contemplate measures in respect of the ships of the flag State. For example, where the Convention stipulates that a coastal State shall undertake certain obligations, such as the giving of due publicity to their laws or regulations (Article 21(3)), or to dangers of navigation in their territorial seas or exclusive economic zones (Article 24(2) and Article 60), or to special requirements imposed by them as a condition for the entry of foreign ships to their ports or installations (Article 211 (3)), a flag State of a ship affected by the laws or dangers or special requirements in question will be entitled to insist that such publicity is given by the coastal States. Similarly, a flag State has the right to require that a coastal State shall act in accordance with the provisions of the Convention, or the laws of the coastal State in conformity with the Convention or other rules of international law, or in accordance with applicable international rules. Where such coastal State takes any measures against the ships of the flag State; and where the action or measures taken by a coastal State against such ships contravene the provisions of the Convention, the State of the flag or registry of that foreign ship will have the right to invoke on behalf of the ship the procedures in the Convention to defend the rights of the ship.

70.   In addition to this general right of the flag State, certain specific rights of the flag State are expressly stipulated in the provisions of the Convention. These include:

(a)   The flag State has the right to attend proceedings by a coastal State against a vessel of the flag State in respect of alleged violations of applicable rules and standards for the prevention, reduction and control of pollution of the marine environment. The flag State also has the right to present witnesses or evidence at such proceedings (Article 223, paragraph 1).

(b)   The flag State is entitled to be notified, where a vessel of its flag or registry has been detained by a coastal State for violations of applicable laws and regulations or international rules and standards for the protection, reduction and control of pollution of the marine environment, and the vessel has not been released. The flag State may seek the release of the vessel if such release has been refused by the coastal State or if release has been made conditional (Article 226, paragraph 1(c)).

(c)   The flag State has the right to request suspension of proceedings by a coastal State against a ship of the flag State for violations of applicable laws and regulations or international rules and standards relating to the prevention, reduction and control of marine pollution. This request must normally be granted except where certain clearly stipulated conditions, as set out in Article 228, paragraph 1 of the Convention, apply.

(d)   A flag State is entitled to request a port State to institute proceedings against a vessel of that flag State which is in the port or installations of the port State, where the vessel has committed a violation of applicable international rules and standards established through "the competent international organization" (IMO), if the violation occurred outside the internal waters, territorial sea or exclusive economic zone of the port State concerned (Article 218, paragraph 2). The flag State also has the right to request the port State in such cases to investigate the violation, and the port State is obliged to comply, as far as practicable, with such a request from the flag State. The records of the investigation carried out shall be transmitted to the flag State, if so requested (Article 218, paragraphs 3 and 4).

(e) The flag State is exclusively empowered to seek release of a ship flying its flag or of its registry where such ship is detained by another State and release has been refused or made conditional upon the posting of a reasonable bond or other financial security. (Article 220(7), Article 226(1)(c) and Article 292).

G.   **Implications of the Convention on the Law of the Sea for the Functions and Responsibilities of IMO, including the Development, Implementation and Application of the Treaties and other International Instruments adopted through or by IMO**

71. The 1982 Convention on the Law of the Sea was conceived, drafted and adopted as an "umbrella convention" to establish a legal order of the seas and oceans for the achievement of certain general objectives, as set out in the fourth paragraph of the Preamble to the Convention - namely, "the facilitation of international communication and the promotion of the peaceful uses of the seas and oceans, the equitable and efficient utilization of the resources of the seas and oceans, the conservation of their resources and the study, protection and preservation of the marine environment". The Convention does not claim, and it is clearly not intended, to replace or abrogate specific obligations assumed by States under special conventions and agreements concluded previously which relate to particular areas of maritime activity. Indeed the Convention expressly affirms, in its Preamble, that "matters not regulated in this Convention continue to be governed by the rules and principles of general international law". Furthermore Article 311, paragraph 2 of the Convention states that the Convention "shall not alter the rights and obligations of States Parties which arise from other agreements compatible with this Convention and which do not affect the enjoyment by other States Parties of their rights or the performance of their obligations under this Convention. With respect to the protection and preservation of the marine environment, the Convention emphasizes that its provisions are without prejudice to the specific obligations assumed by States under special conventions and agreements . . . . " (Article 237). The provisions of Articles 237 and 311, however, clearly state that the special conventions and agreements which Parties may conclude must be "in furtherance of the general principles set forth in this Convention"; that the special obligations under such agreements "should be carried out in a manner consistent with the general principles and objectives of the Convention"; and that the provisions of such special agreements "should not affect the enjoyment by other States Parties of their rights or the performance of their obligations under this Convention". Thus, the Convention on the Law of the Sea does not preclude the existence or adoption of special rules and regulations by IMO; but in fact presupposes the existence of such IMO rules and regulations and depends on them for the effective implementation of its general principles, in many cases.

72. Accordingly, the Convention on the Law of the Sea does not affect the continued viability and applicability of the international regulations, rules, standards, procedures, practices and principles which have been developed by IMO for the regulation of activities in the marine environment, except to the extent that any of the IMO regulations may be incompatible with the relevant provisions of the Convention. Nor does the Convention call into question the mandate of IMO to develop such international rules and regulations or to review and revise

existing ones, where necessary. In fact the Convention confirms, expressly or by clear implication, that the international regulations and standards developed in IMO in the field of safety of navigation, the prevention, reduction and control of marine pollution from vessels and by dumping are of direct and crucial relevance to the application of the provisions of the Convention on those matters. In a number of Articles of the Convention the international regulations and rules of IMO are declared to constitute, or to be part of, the rules and regulations by reference to which States are required to undertake the measures for implementing the provisions of the Convention. Furthermore, the Convention recognizes IMO as "the competent international organization" through which the international regulations and rules needed for the implementation of many of the Convention's provisions are to be established; and some Articles of the Convention assign or suggest to IMO functions, responsibilities and powers which are deemed to be necessary or desirable for the effective implementation of the particular provisions.

73. However, as has been noted above, the Convention on the Law of the Sea recognizes the validity of the international rules and regulations of IMO only to the extent that such rules and regulations are consistent with the general principles of the Convention and do not affect enjoyment by other States Parties of their rights or the performance of their obligations under the Convention. In the light of the foregoing, it would appear that the implications of the Convention on the Law of the Sea on IMO and its work may be assessed with respect to :

    (a)   the provisions of the Convention which make it necessary or desirable for IMO to consider amendments or other possible modifications to any of the treaty or other instruments adopted within IMO or administered by the Organization;

    (b)   the provisions of the Convention which may make it necessary or useful for IMO to develop new international regulations or rules on particular matters within its competence;

    (c)   such new procedures or revised machinery which IMO may need to establish in order to undertake responsibilities assigned to it by the Convention or otherwise assumed by the Organization as a result of the Convention's provisions.

    (i)   Provisions of the Convention on the Law of the Sea which may result in the need or advisability of revisions or modifications in the treaties of IMO

74. As indicated above, Article 311 of the Convention on the Law of the Sea stipulates that other international agreements entered into by States will not be altered by the Convention provided that the other agreements are compatible with the Law of the Sea Convention. Therefore it appears necessary and useful to examine the treaty instruments of IMO which deal with matters covered by the Convention in order to see if there are any inconsistencies or lack of harmony between any of these instruments and the relevant provisions of the Convention on the Law of the Sea; or if some ambiguities or gaps could result in the application of the IMO treaties and the Convention on the Law of the Sea. If and when any inconsistencies or gaps are identified, consideration will need to be given to the most appropriate procedure for solving the identified problem.

75. The provisions of the Convention on the Law of the Sea in respect of which such examination may be necessary include the following:

(a) **Article 3** - Breadth of the Territorial Sea

Consideration may be given to IMO's treaty instruments which refer specifically to the "territorial sea" of States, in order to determine whether the purpose of these instruments will continue to be effectively served when the maximum breadth of the territorial sea is extended to 12 nautical miles.

(b) **Articles 56 to 60**

The Law of the Sea Convention recognizes for the first time the "exclusive economic zone" (EEZ), with a special legal régime as specified in Article 55. Article 56 sets out the sovereign rights, jurisdiction and duties of the coastal State in the exclusive economic zone, while Article 57 gives the breadth of the zone as not extending "beyond 200 nautical miles from the baselines from which the breadth of the territorial sea is measured".

76. For the purposes of IMO's treaty instruments, the most significant aspects of the jurisdiction of the coastal State in the EEZ relate to:

(a) the protection and preservation of the marine environment; and

(b) the establishment and use of artificial islands, installations and structures.

77. Most of the international regulations, rules and standards of IMO were considered and adopted either before the concept of the EEZ had been accepted or at a time when the nature and extent of the régime had not been sufficiently clarified. Thus, these regulations were generally adopted on the basis of international law as existing before the adoption of the 1982 Convention on the Law of the Sea.

78. Following the general acceptance of the exclusive economic zone with a special status and nature, it would appear necessary and appropriate for IMO to consider whether any of the international instruments of IMO which were intended for application in the "territorial sea" or the "high seas" or "outside the territorial sea" are still adequate in relation to the new exclusive economic zone.

79. In this connection, it may be recalled that the 1973 MARPOL Conference, taking account of the discussions on the Exclusive Economic Zone then taking place in the Committee which was preparing for the Third United Nations Conference on the Law of the Sea, decided to include a provision in the 1973 MARPOL Convention as follows:

The term "jurisdiction" in the present Convention shall be construed in the light of international law in force at the time of application or interpretation of the present Convention". (Article 9, paragraph 3).

80. Article 4, paragraph 2 of MARPOL states that

"Any violation of the requirements of the present Convention within the jurisdiction of any Party to the Convention shall be prohibited and sanctions shall be established therefore under the law of that Party."

The States concerned may deem it necessary to consider within the framework of IMO and, if necessary affirm in a suitable way, the extent to which this provision permits or does not permit States Parties to MARPOL to exercise powers of enforcement in respect of violations of MARPOL in their exclusive economic zones, especially when set against the extensions to, and the limitations which are placed on, the powers of coastal and port States in the enforcement of international regulations and national laws in the exclusive economic zone, as specified in Article 220 of the Convention on the Law of the Sea.

81.   A similar question arises in connection with the 1972 London Dumping Convention, which provides, in its Article VII, paragraph 5,

> "Nothing in this Convention shall affect the right of each Party to adopt other measures, in accordance with the principles of international law, to prevent dumping at sea."

82.   In connection with these two Conventions, it may be noted that Article 56 of the Convention on the Law of the Sea gives to the coastal State jurisdiction, as provided for in the Convention, with regard to the protection and preservation of the marine environment in the exclusive economic zone. Similarly, Article 210, paragraph 3 and Article 216, paragraph 1(b), require and empower the coastal State to control pollution by dumping in its exclusive economic zone and continental shelf, in addition to the territorial sea. It would appear, therefore, that a State Party to MARPOL 73/78 or the 1972 Dumping Convention may apply the provisions of the respective Convention in respect of its exclusive economic zone, to the extent that is has jurisdiction in the exclusive economic zone by virtue of the relevant provisions of the Convention on the Law of the Sea. The powers are however not unlimited. For example the State regulating dumping is required to give due consideration of the matter with other states which may be adversely affected.

83.   This question, however, deserves more detailed consideration by the inter-governmental bodies responsible for the respective treaties.   In the case of the 1972 London Dumping Convention the issue is specifically raised in Article XIII thereof, which envisaged consultation "to define the nature, extent and the right and responsibility of a coastal State to apply the Convention to a zone adjacent to its coast".

84.   Other treaty instruments of IMO which may need to be examined in this regard include the following:

(a)   **Convention on the International Regulations for Preventing Collisions at Sea, 1972 (COLREG 1972)**

Rule 1(a) of the International Regulations provides that "these Rules shall apply to all vessels upon the high seas and in all waters connected therewith navigable by seagoing vessels". It would appear that this formulation is adequate to extend the application of the Convention also to the exclusive economic zone. However, it might be useful for the relevant inter-governmental bodies of IMO to confirm this, if it were deemed necessary to do this to remove any possible doubt on the point.

(b)   **The 1969 Intervention Convention and its 1973 Protocol**

Article I, paragraph 1 of the 1969 Convention provides that

"Parties to the present Convention may take such measures on the high seas as may be necessary to prevent, mitigate or eliminate grave and imminent danger to their coastline or related interests from pollution or threat of pollution of the sea by oil, following upon a maritime casualty or acts related to such a casualty, which may reasonably be expected to result in major harmful consequences."

Article I, paragraph 1 of the 1973 Protocol reproduces the same wording.

85.   In discussions in the Legal Committee of IMO and elsewhere, it has been suggested that the intention of the 1969 Convention was to assert and regulate the right of the coastal State to take measures "in the area beyond its territorial sea". In 1969 the area beyond the territorial sea was generally agreed to constitute the high seas. However, under the 1982 Convention on the Law of the Sea, part of the area beyond the territorial sea of a State, may be designated as the "exclusive economic zone". Upon such designation, that area will not be part of the "high seas", although other States will be entitled to exercise therein certain of the "freedoms" which they have on the high seas, as provided for in the Convention.

86.   In this regard reference may also be made to Article 221 of the Convention on the Law of the Sea dealing with the right of intervention by coastal States to avoid pollution arising from maritime casualties. That article reserves the right of States, pursuant to both customary and conventional international law, to take appropriate and proportionate measures "beyond their territorial sea" to protect their coastline and related interests, including fishing, from pollution or threat of pollution arising from a maritime casualty. It will be noted that specific reference is made in Article 221 to "fishing" as one of the "related interests" which the coastal State may protect by measures of intervention.

87.   It is for consideration, whether the 1969 Convention and its 1973 Protocol need to be revised to provide expressly that the power of the coastal State extends to measures taken in the "exclusive economic zone", and also to clarify, as appropriate, that "fishing interests" are included in the "related interests" covered by the 1969 and 1973 treaties.

88.   It has also been noted that Article 221 of the Convention recognizes the right of intervention to protect "actual or threatened damage" whereas the 1969 Convention referred to measures to prevent "grave and imminent danger".

(c) Instruments on Civil Liability and Compensation

89.   With respect to the status of the exclusive economic zone, reference may be made to the 1984 amendments to the 1969 Civil Liability Convention and the 1971 Fund Convention. The 1969 Convention provided that the Convention "shall apply to exclusively pollution damage caused on the territory including the territorial sea of a Contracting State and to preventive measures taken to prevent or minimize such damage" (Article II).

90.   The corresponding provision (Article 3) of the 1971 Fund Convention stated that the Convention shall apply:

1.   "With regard to compensation according to Article 1, exclusively to pollution damage caused on the territory, including the territorial sea, of a Contracting State, and to preventive measures taken to prevent or minimize such damage;

2.   With regard to indemnification of shipowners and their guarantors according to Article 5, exclusively in respect of pollution damage caused on the territory, including the territorial sea, of a State Party to the Liability Convention by a ship registered in or flying the flag of a Contracting State and in respect of preventive measures taken to prevent or minimize such damage".

91. The 1984 Diplomatic Conference on Liability and Compensation for Damage in connection with the Carriage of Certain Substances by Sea agreed to amend these provisions in order to extend the scope of application of the conventions to cover incidents or damage occurring in the exclusive economic zone or similar zones "established in accordance with international law".

92. The revised provisions adopted for this purpose in the 1984 Protocol to amend the 1969 Civil Liability Convention were the following:

"This Convention shall apply exclusively:

(a)   to pollution damage caused:

   (i)   in the territory, including the territorial sea, of a Contracting State; and
   (ii) in the exclusive economic zone of a Contracting State, established in accordance with international law, or, if a Contracting State has not established such a zone, in an area beyond and adjacent to the territorial sea of that State determined by that State in accordance with international law and extending not more than 200 nautical miles from the baselines from which the breadth of its territorial sea is measured;

(b)   to preventive measures, wherever taken, to prevent or minimize damage" (Article 3 of the 1984 CLC Protocol).

93.   For the Protocol to amend the 1971 Fund Convention the revised provision reads as follows:

"The Convention shall apply exclusively:

(a)   to pollution damage caused:

   (i)   in the territory, including the territorial sea, of a Contracting State; and
   (ii) in the exclusive economic zone of a Contracting State, established in accordance with international law, or, if a Contracting State has not established such a zone, in an area beyond and adjacent to the territorial sea of that State in accordance with international law and extending not more than 200 nautical miles from the baselines from which the breadth of its territorial sea is measured;

(b)   to preventive measures, wherever taken, to prevent or minimize damage" (Article 4 of the 1984 "Fund" Protocol).

94. Although the amended provisions do not make specific references to the 1982 Convention on the Law of the Sea, the discussions at the conference indicated clearly that the

amendments were adopted to extend the scope of application of the conventions to cover damage "in the exclusive economic zone", or "similar zones".

(d) MARPOL 73/78

95. In connection with the powers of enforcement available to States in respect of the prevention, reduction and control of marine pollution from vessels, certain provisions of the Convention on the Law of the Sea will have implications on the interpretation or application of relevant provisions in some treaty instruments of IMO. Of particular significance in this respect are the provisions of Article 4 of IMO's MARPOL 73/78 and its relationship to the corresponding Articles of the 1982 Convention on the Law of the Sea. Under Article 4 of MARPOL 73/78, a State Party is required and empowered to enforce the provisions of the Convention (including the prohibition of violations, the establishment of sanctions under its laws and the taking of proceedings, where there is sufficient evidence) in respect of:

(a) any ship entitled to fly the flag of the Party or operating under the authority of that Party for any violations of the requirements of MARPOL 73/78 by such ship, regardless of where such violations occurred; and

(b) any other ship for violations of the requirements of MARPOL 73/78 by that ship, where the violation occurs within the jurisdiction of that Party.

Article 5, paragraph 6 of MARPOL 73/78 requires Parties to apply the requirements as may be necessary to ensure that the ships of States which are not Parties will be given "no more favourable treatment" than is given to the ships of States Parties.

96. Under Article 220, paragraph 1 of the Convention on the Law of the Sea, the coastal State is entitled and required to enforce the provisions of its laws and regulations, adopted in accordance with applicable international rules and standards, and to institute proceedings in respect of violations of such laws and regulations, where such violations occur in the territorial sea or exclusive economic zone of that coastal State.

97. The coastal State is also authorized, under Article 220, to investigate any such violations by a ship navigating in its territorial sea or exclusive economic zone. The coastal State may request for information and, in specified cases, undertake physical inspection of the ship.

98. Furthermore, Article 218, paragraph 1, gives to a State the power to investigate and to institute proceedings, where warranted, for violations by a ship of applicable international rules and standards established through "the competent international organization" (IMO), even if the violation occurred outside the territorial sea or exclusive economic zone of that State. However, this power can only be exercised in respect of a ship which is voluntarily "within the port of the enforcing State", and the exercise of the power is subject to well-defined right of the flag State, or another coastal State within whose territorial sea or exclusive economic zone the violation may have occurred.

99. Consideration may need to be given to the question whether the rights of the coastal State under the Convention on the Law of the Sea and under MARPOL 73/78 are the same or compatible with each other and, if this is not the case, whether any revisions in MARPOL 73/78 would be necessary or desirable. Reference may be made in this context to the effect, if any, which the provisions of the Convention on the Law of the Sea could have on the

application of the "no more favourable treatment" provision in MARPOL 73/78. The same provision is also to be found in other treaty instruments, such as the 1974 SOLAS Convention as modified by the 1978 Protocol, and the 1978 Convention on Standards of Training, Certification and Watchkeeping of Seafarers (STCW). (See also paragraphs 40 to 41 and paragraphs 79 to 80).

Implications of the Convention on the Law of the Sea with regard to the functions and responsibilities in areas already dealt with by IMO

100.   The Convention on the Law of the Sea may also have significant implications in some areas which are already dealt with by IMO and with some of the decisions of its relevant bodies. It would, therefore, be useful for the appropriate bodies to endeavour to identify any such areas of possible impact in order to determine whether there is the need for IMO to modify its work, or to extend the scope and purpose of its international regulations or procedures to new areas, or to provide clearer or additional guidelines to States or other entities in implementing the provisions of the Convention on the Law of the Sea.

101.   The major areas in which the Convention on the Law of the Sea may result in possible modifications of the work and procedures of IMO include the following:

(a)   **The documentary and special precautionary requirements in respect of nuclear-powered ships and ships carrying nuclear or other inherently dangerous or noxious substances**

Article 23 of the Convention requires foreign-nuclear powered ships and ships carrying nuclear or other inherently dangerous or noxious substances, which are exercising the right of innocent passage through the territorial sea or through straits used for international navigation or in archipelagic waters, to "carry documents and observe special precautionary measures established for such ships by international agreements".

IMO may find it useful to consider to what extent the existing requirements in respect of documentary and other precautionary measures in such cases are appropriate and adequate and, if not, what role IMO should play in the development of the necessary "international agreements".

(b)   **The designation and prescription of the sea-lanes and traffic separation schemes**

The Convention on the Law of the Sea recognizes "sea-lanes" and "traffic separation schemes" as important means for regulating maritime traffic with a view to ensuring safety of navigation and the prevention of pollution of the marine environment. Accordingly, the Convention confers on coastal States the power to designate sea-lanes or prescribe traffic separation schemes in their territorial sea (Article 22) in straits used for international navigation (Article 41) and in archipelagic waters (Article 53). However in all such areas the exercise of the power of the coastal State is subject to certain conditions. These include the holding of consultations with, or the obtaining of the concurrence of, the "competent international organization" (IMO). In the territorial sea the coastal State is required, in designating sea-lanes and prescribing traffic separation schemes, to take into account the recommendations of "the competent international organization" (IMO) (Article 22, paragraph 3(a)). In straits used for international navigation, the sea-lanes designated and the traffic separation schemes prescribed must conform to generally accepted international regulations, and must be designated or prescribed after having been adopted by the "competent international organization" (IMO). However, IMO can only adopt such sea-lanes or traffic separation schemes with the agreement of the coastal State or States concerned (Article 41, paragraphs 3 and 4). Article 41 also requires two or more States bordering straits to co-operate in formulating proposals in consultation with "the competent international organization" (IMO) (paragraph 5). In archipelagic waters, the archipelagic State is empowered to designate sea-lanes and, as necessary, to prescribe traffic separation schemes which shall "conform to generally accepted international regulations". Such sea-lanes and traffic separation schemes are to be designated or prescribed only after they have been adopted by the "competent international organization" (IMO), with the agreement of the archipelagic State concerned (Article 53, paragraphs 1, 6 and 9).

102.   With respect to these provisions, it may be necessary for the relevant bodies of IMO to examine their current procedures in order to determine to what extent the existing regulations and arrangements are adequate for the efficient discharge of the functions expected of IMO under the Convention on the Law of the Sea. In particular consideration may be given to identifying or establishing, as necessary:

   (i)   the recommendations which coastal States have to take into account in prescribing traffic separation schemes or designating "sea-lanes" in their territorial sea;

   (ii)   the international regulations to which traffic separation schemes and "sea-lanes" within straits used for international navigation and in archipelagic waters, must conform;

   (iii) the procedure to be followed by coastal States which wish to refer proposals for traffic separation schemes or sea-lanes in, international straits or archipelagic waters for consideration and adoption by IMO, including procedures and arrangements to facilitate co-operation between two or more States in respect of sea-lanes or traffic separation schemes through the waters of such States.

103.   Consideration may also be given to the extent to which the existing IMO procedures and regulations concerning Ships' Routeing are appropriate and adequate with regard to the designation of "sea-lanes" under the provisions of the Convention on the Law of the Sea. In this connection it may be recalled that some doubts were expressed in IMO and by some delegations and observers at the Third United Nations Conference on the Law of the Sea about the appropriateness of the expression "sea-lanes", as used in the provisions of the Convention on the Law of the Sea dealing with the regulation of maritime traffic.

(c)   **The construction, operation and use of artificial islands, installations and structures in the exclusive economic zone, and the removal of such installations and structures**

104.   Under Article 60 of the Convention on the Law of the Sea, a coastal State has the exclusive right to construct and to authorize and regulate the construction, operation and use of artificial islands, installations and structures in its exclusive economic zone. The coastal State is required to give due notice of such installations and structures and to maintain permanent means for giving warning of their presence, and of safety zones established around them. The coastal State is also required to ensure that installations or structures which are disused shall be removed to ensure safety of navigation. The removal of such installations or

structures shall take into account any generally accepted international standards established in this regard by "the competent international organization" (IMO).

105. In connection with Article 60 the functions expected of IMO may include the consideration, adoption and up-dating as may be necessary of:

    (i)   the "generally accepted" international standards to govern the removal of disused or abandoned installations and structures;

    (ii)   the "generally accepted" international standards or recommendations to be taken into account in determining the breadth of safety zones around installations and structures in cases where the coastal State considers it necessary to exceed the maximum distance for safety zones (500 metres) specified in the Convention;

    (iii)   appropriate guidelines and recommendations in connection with such installations and structures, in particular with regard to:

        (a)   the maintenance of permanent means of warning of their presence;

        (b)   the publicity to be given to such installations and structures, including the depth, position and dimensions of installations or structures which may not be entirely removed;

        (c)   the notice to be given of the existence of safety zones around such installations and structures;

        (d)   the necessary "international standards" regarding navigation in the vicinity of artificial islands, installations, structures and safety zones.

106. The functions and responsibilities of IMO in relation to artificial islands, installations, structures and their removal and safety zones, are the same in respect of similar installations, etc., on the Continental Shelf (Article 80).

(d) **Establishment by coastal States of special requirements for pollution prevention as a condition for the entry of foreign vessels into their ports, internal waters or off-shore installations**

107. In accordance with Article 211, paragraph 3, of the Convention, a coastal State may establish particular requirements for the prevention, reduction and control of pollution of the marine environment as a condition for the entry of foreign vessels into its ports or internal waters or for a call at its off-shore terminals. A coastal State exercising this right is required to give due publicity to such special requirements and to communicate them to the "competent international organization" (IMO).

108. It may be deemed necessary for the relevant IMO bodies to consider whether there is any need for IMO to elaborate specific procedures for receiving such information and for disseminating any such received information to States and other entities to which such information would be useful or necessary.

(e) **Procedures and requirements for bonding or other appropriate financial security in respect of vessels detained by a coastal or port State**

109. Article 220, paragraph 7 obliges a coastal State which has detained a vessel for a violation of international regulations, or national laws, as appropriate, to allow the vessel to proceed if the vessel has complied with the requirements for bonding or other appropriate financial security and the coastal State is bound by the procedures establishing the

requirements in question. The Article also states that the appropriate procedures may be established through "the competent international organization" (IMO). Consideration may, therefore, be given to the possible establishment of "procedures on bonding or financial security" and the suitable mechanism for establishing such procedures.

110.   In this connection it may be noted that Article 292 of the Convention provides for a procedure under which an application may be made by or on behalf of the flag State of a vessel, if it is alleged that the vessel is being detained in contravention of the requirement of the Convention for prompt release, following the posting of a reasonable bond or other financial security. The existence of international procedures in this regard will, accordingly, be of some importance in the implementation of the dispute settlement arrangements in Part XV of the Convention.

(f)   **Establishment by coastal States of special and additional mandatory measures for the prevention of pollution from vessels in respect of clearly defined areas of their exclusive economic zones**

111.   Pursuant to Article 211, paragraph 6, of the Convention a coastal State may, under the conditions stipulated therein, adopt special mandatory laws and regulations for the prevention, reduction and control of marine pollution in a clearly defined area in its exclusive economic zone where such special laws and regulations are required. However, such laws and regulations can only be adopted by the coastal State after a determination by "the competent international organization" (IMO) that the conditions in the area concerned correspond to the requirements set out in Article 211, paragraph 6 of the Convention. Furthermore the State is empowered only to adopt laws and regulations in this regard which implement the international rules and standards or navigational practices which are made applicable, through "the competent international organization" (IMO), for special areas. A similar procedure applies if the State wishes to adopt "additional laws and regulations" on discharges and navigational practices. In particular such laws and regulations should not require foreign vessels to observe design, construction, manning or equipment standards other than generally accepted international rules and standards.

112.   It may be necessary and useful to consider the establishment of special procedures under which coastal States may consult with IMO in this context, and through which IMO may consider and approve the proposals which coastal States may submit. Consideration may also be given to the identification or establishment, as appropriate, of the "international rules and standards or navigational practices" which should be applicable to special areas in the exclusive economic zone of States, in pursuance of Article 211 of the Convention on the Law of the Sea.

(g)   **Role of IMO in proceedings against foreign vessels**

113.   Under Article 223 of the Convention a State which institutes proceedings against a foreign vessel in respect of violations against international or national laws and regulations on marine pollution prevention is required to take measures to facilitate the hearing of witnesses and the admission of evidence submitted by *inter alia* "the competent international organization" (IMO). Such a State is also required to facilitate the attendance of such proceedings by "official representatives" of the "competent international organization" (IMO). Such "official representatives" shall have rights and duties as may be provided for under national law or international law.

114.   The appropriate bodies of IMO may find it necessary to consider the procedures and arrangements required to enable IMO to intervene in such proceedings, including the criteria for determining when such an intervention would be appropriate and the procedure for designating the "official representatives" of the Organization, as envisaged in the Convention on the Law of the Sea.

(h)   **Role of IMO in the implementation and further development of international law relating to liability and compensation for damage**

115.   Article 235 (3) of the Convention provides that "States shall co-operate in the implementation of existing international law and the further development of international law relating to responsibility and liability for the assessment of and compensation for damage" caused by pollution of the marine environment. Where appropriate, States shall co-operate, in the "development of criteria and procedures for payment of adequate compensation, such as compulsory insurance or compensation funds".

116.   In this connection reference may be made to the work already undertaken or contemplated for damage in relation to the carriage of substances by sea. Specifically, the following IMO instruments should be mentioned:

   (a)   International Convention on Civil Liability for Oil Pollution Damage (CLC 1969) and the 1976 Protocol thereto;

   (b)   Protocol of 1984 to amend the International Convention on Civil Liability for Oil Pollution Damage, 1969 (CLC PROT 1984);

   (c)   International Convention on the Establishment of an International Fund for Compensation for Oil Pollution Damage 1971 (FUND 1971).

   (d)   Protocol of 1984 to amend the International Convention on the Establishment of an International Fund for Compensation for Oil Pollution Damage, 1971 (FUND PROT 1984).

117.   Reference may also be made to the work contemplated with regard to the elaboration of a draft convention on liability and compensation in connection with the carriage of noxious and hazardous substances by sea (HNS Convention).

(i)   **Role of IMO in the Special Arbitration Procedure Provided for in Annex VIII of the Convention**

118.   Article 1 of Annex VIII of the Convention (Special Arbitration) provides that disputes concerning the interpretation or application of the articles of the Convention relating to "navigation, including pollution from vessels and by dumping" may be submitted to a special arbitral procedure as provided for in Annex VIII. Under Article 2 of the same Annex special arbitral tribunals to deal with such disputes are to be selected from a "list of experts . . . established and maintained by IMO or by the appropriate subsidiary body concerned to which (IMO) has delegated this function".

119.   IMO may find it necessary to consider how the functions assigned to it under this part of the Convention are to be performed. In particular, consideration will need to be given to

the procedure for establishing and maintaining the list of experts and, if necessary, the designation of an appropriate subsidiary body to perform functions in this regard.

120.   IMO may also consider the need to establish appropriate liaison with:

(a)   States Parties to the Convention on the Law of the Sea which have the right to nominate experts or withdraw experts; and

(b)   the Secretary-General of the United Nations with regard to the constitution of the special arbitration tribunal for particular cases.

(j)   Other possible roles for IMO in connection with the implementation of the Convention on the Law of the Sea

121.   In addition to the new or modified functions and responsibilities directly or indirectly imposed on IMO by the Convention on the Law of the Sea, it may be necessary to consider what, if any, other possible roles may legitimately be played by IMO in connection with the implementation of the provisions of the Convention which deal with matters within the field of competence of IMO, particularly the provisions whose interpretation or application may be assisted by work within IMO. Reference may be made in this connection with the articles of the Convention which relate to safety at sea and the prevention of marine pollution, since many of these articles refer to or presuppose the existence of international regulations and standards adopted by IMO by reference to which States may implement the principles in the Convention on the Law of the Sea.

122.   As indicated above, many articles of the Convention on the Law of the Sea stipulate that the powers and obligations of States are to be exercised or discharged by reference to "generally accepted" or "applicable" international regulations and standards. In some cases, the Convention expressly states that the international rules or regulations involved are those established by "the competent international organization" (IMO) or by "general diplomatic conference". Furthermore, in many other cases the Convention does not even specify the rules and regulations which are to be deemed to be "generally accepted" or "applicable" in the respective contexts. It would therefore be necessary for the appropriate bodies of IMO to consider what guidelines IMO can usefully provide to States in this regard.

123.   The articles and provisions of the Convention on the Law of the Sea which are of particular relevance in this context include those which refer to the following:

(i)   the "generally accepted international rules or standards on the design, construction, manning or equipment" of ships (Article 21, paragraph 2, Article 211, paragraph 4, Article 211, paragraph 6(c));

(ii)   the "generally accepted international regulations relating to the prevention of collisions at sea" (Article 21(4), Article 39(2)).

(iii)   the "recommendations" of "the competent international organization" (IMO) regarding the designation of sea-lanes and the prescription of traffic separation schemes" (Article 22(3)(a), Article 41(3), Article 53(8));.

(iv)   the requirements in respect of documentation and special precautionary measures established by international agreement for foreign nuclear-powered ships and ships carrying nuclear or inherently dangerous or noxious substances (Article 23);

(v) the "generally accepted international standards" with regard to the breadth of safety zones established around artificial islands, installations and other structures in the exclusive economic zone or on the continental shelf, and the "generally accepted international standards regarding navigation in the vicinity of such islands, installations, structures and safety zones" (Article 60, paragraphs 5 and 7, Article 80);

(vi) the "generally accepted international regulations, procedures and practices" relating to the measures to be taken by the flag State to ensure safety at sea and prevention of pollution in respect of ships flying the flag of that State, as specified in paragraphs 3, 4, 5 and 6 of Article 94;

(vii) the "global rules, standards, and recommended practices and procedures" to prevent, reduce and control pollution by dumping (Article 210, paragraphs 4 and 6). Also "applicable rules and standards established through competent international organizations or general diplomatic conference" (Article 216, paragraph 1);

(viii) the "international rules and standards for the prevention, reduction and control of pollution of the marine environment from vessels" (Article 211, paragraphs 1, 2 and 5);

(ix) the "international rules and standards or navigational practices as made applicable through the "competent international organization" (IMO) for special areas" (Article 211, paragraph 6(a));

(x) the "international rules and standards relating to prompt notification to coastal States whose coastline or related interests may be affected by incidents, including maritime casualties, which involve discharges, or probability of discharges" (Article 211(7));

(xi) the "applicable international rules and standards" for the prevention of vessel source pollution established through "the competent international organization" (IMO) which flag States are obliged to enforce with regard to ships flying their flags (Article 217, paragraphs 1 and 2; Article 218, paragraphs 1 and 3; Article 220, paragraphs 1,2,3). Also "certificates (records and other documents)" required by such international rules and standards (Article 217, paragraph 3; Article 226, paragraph 1);

(xii) "applicable international rules and standards relating to sea-worthiness of vessels" (Article 219, Article 226, paragraph 1(c));

124.   In several other areas, the Convention on the Law of the Sea envisages, or suggests the desirability of, international regulations, standards, rules, practices or procedures which would facilitate the implementation of the Convention's provisions. Where such provisions relate to the safety of navigation or the prevention, reduction and control of pollution of the marine environment from vessels or by dumping, IMO may find it necessary to consider whether the regulations and rules previously adopted by it are adequate or whether there is need for the development of new regulations, standards, practices or procedures or the revision of existing ones. The areas in which the need for new or revised international regulations may be considered include the following:

(a)   **Prevention of harmful consequences to vessels and the marine environment as a consequence of the exercise of enforcement powers by States**

125.   Article 225 of the Convention on the Law of the Sea provides that States, when exercising measures of enforcement against foreign vessels, shall not endanger the safety of

navigation or otherwise create any hazard to a vessel, or bring the vessel to an unsafe port or anchorage, or expose the marine environment to an unreasonable risk. Article 226 declares that States shall not delay a foreign vessel longer than is essential for the purposes of the investigations provided for in the Convention. The article lays down the conditions and limits of physical inspections of a vessel, and provides for the release of the vessel, whether absolutely or on conditions as may be appropriate. Paragraph 2 of Article 226 provides that States shall co-operate to develop procedures for "the avoidance of unnecessary physical inspection of vessels at sea."

126. To the extent that it may be considered that any of the procedures envisaged in Article 226, paragraph 2 should be developed on the international plane, IMO would be the appropriate forum for that purpose. In this connection, reference may be made to the provisions in Article 6 of MARPOL 73/78 relating to "Detection of Violations and Enforcement of the Convention". Consideration may be given to whether these provisions provide an appropriate or suitable basis for the elaboration of the necessary international procedures in this regard. Attention may also be given to suitable arrangements or mechanisms for elaborating suitable international procedures in respect of the powers of States regarding various possible violations under the Convention on the Law of the Sea.

(b) **Prevention of interference by marine scientific research installations or equipment with safety of navigation**

127. Article 261 of the Convention on the Law of the Sea states that the deployment and use of any type of scientific research installations or equipment shall not constitute an obstacle to established international shipping routes. Article 262 states that such installations or equipment shall bear identification markings and "shall have adequate internationally agreed warning signals to ensure safety at sea and the safety of air navigation, taking into account rules and standards established by competent international organizations". IMO would appear to be the most appropriate body for developing the international rules and standards to ensure safety at sea. Such elaboration may, of course, need to be undertaken in consultation with other concerned international organizations such as the International Civil Aviation Organization (ICAO), the International Telecommunication Union (ITU), the International Maritime Satellite Organization (INMARSAT), the Inter-governmental Oceanographic Commission (IOC), the International Hydrographic Organization (IHO) and the International Association of Lighthouse Authorities (IALA).

(c) **Possible role of IMO in the facilitation of appropriate publicity with respect to measures for the safety of navigation and the prevention of marine pollution**

128. A number of articles of the Convention on the Law of the Sea impose on States and other entities the obligation to provide publicity with regard to legislative or other measures taken by them, and to publicize information which may become available to them relating to safety of navigation or the prevention of pollution of the marine environment from vessels or by dumping. This publicity is to make States, seafarers and other interested persons aware of the measures or information in question and thus enable them to take appropriate and necessary steps either to prevent infringements of the laws and regulations, or to avoid any dangers which may be presented in particular situations. It is, therefore, essential that the publicity be given in a manner which ensures that the information provided will in fact reach those who are likely to be affected. In some cases the States or other entities required to provide publicity are also enjoined to make the information available to IMO. Even in cases

where reference has been made to another body or bodies, some IMO involvement may be necessary, or at least helpful.

129.   The articles of the Convention relating to "publicity", in respect of matters of possible interest to IMO include the following:

(a)   *Article 21, paragraph 3*: The coastal State is required to give due publicity to its laws and regulations for the regulation of innocent passage in its territorial sea. The same provision applies to the laws and regulations relating to transit passage in straits used for international navigation (Article 42, paragraph 3).

(b)   *Article 22, paragraph 4*: A coastal State is required to indicate clearly the sea-lanes and traffic separation schemes in its territorial sea on charts to which "due publicity" is to be given. The same applies under Article 41, paragraph 6 in relation to transit passage in straits used for international navigation and under Article 53, paragraph 10 in respect of archipelagic sea-lane passage.

(c)   *Article 24, paragraph 2*: The coastal State is required to give publicity to any danger to navigation within its territorial sea of which the State has knowledge. (The same obligation is imposed on States bordering straits used for international navigation under Article 44).

(d)   *Article 41, paragraph 2*: Publicity should be given by States bordering straits used for international navigation in respect of sea-lanes and traffic separation schemes adopted in such straits. The same obligation is imposed by Article 53, paragraph 7 in respect of sea-lanes and traffic separation schemes in archipelagic waters.

(e)   *Article 52, paragraph 2*: An archipelagic State is required to give publicity in respect of suspensions of innocent passage in its archipelagic waters, and suspensions of innocent passage in the territorial sea (Article 25, paragraph 2).

Article 60, paragraph 3: The coastal State is required to give publicity in respect of the depth, position and dimensions of installations or structures in its exclusive economic zone which are not entirely removed. (The same requirements apply in respect of similar installations in the continental shelf, Article 80).

(f)   *Article 60, paragraph 3*: The coastal State is required to give publicity in respect of the extent of safety zones established around artificial islands, installations or structures in its exclusive economic zones. (The same requirement applies to safety zones on the continental shelf, Article 80).

(g)   *Article 211, paragraph 3*: A coastal State which establishes particular require-ments for the prevention, reduction and control of pollution of the marine environment as a condition for the entry of foreign vessels into their ports or internal waters or for a call at their off-shore terminals, must give due publicity of such requirements.

(h)   *Article 211, paragraph 6*: A State which establishes special mandatory measures for marine pollution prevention in a clearly defined area of its exclusive economic zone (paragraph 6, sub-paragraphs (a) and (b); or adopts additional laws and regulations (paragraph 6, sub-paragraph (c)), must give due publicity of such measures.

(i)   *Article 217, paragraph 7*:   A flag State is required to provide IMO with information in respect of action taken by it against a vessel flying its flag for violations of rules and standards adopted through IMO. IMO is required to make such information "available to all States".

130.   In respect of all these provisions, it appears clear that the objective of publicity required will be effectively achieved only if the information in question reaches the States, authorities, entities and persons who are expected to be guided by the information. IMO maintains the most direct and continuing contact with the authorities of States concerned with safety of navigation and the prevention of vessel-source pollution. Accordingly the purpose of the "publicity" is likely to be served by some IMO involvement. To the extent that this involvement is considered necessary and appropriate, it may be useful to consider suitable arrangements by which the Organization may assist or co-operate with the States, or international organizations concerned in ensuring that the publicity given by them will in fact reach the destinations for which it is intended.

131.   IMO's involvement or co-operation in enhancing the effective dissemination of information on maritime safety and pollution prevention measures may extend even to cases in which responsibility for the publicity concerned may have been assigned to specific States or organizations by the Convention. For example, several articles of the Convention, in requiring that States give due publicity to legislation or other measures adopted by them, also stipulate that the information should be deposited with the Secretary-General of the United Nations, who is the depositary of the Convention itself. In line with its normal practice in this regard it must be assumed that the Secretariat of the United Nations will make information deposited with it available to all States concerned. But even in such cases, there may be the need for IMO's involvement in the further dissemination of information, particularly where the information in question may be of significance to ships personnel or other persons operating in the marine environment who are required to take information into account in order to safeguard safety or prevent pollution. IMO may therefore find it useful to consider how it might usefully co-operate with, or assist the United Nations, in making sure that the information will reach ships and other persons who may be more in contact with IMO.

132.   For example Article 147 of the Convention lays down certain conditions for the erection, emplacement and removal of installations used for carrying out activities in the "Area" i.e. "the sea-bed and ocean floor and sub-soil thereof, beyond the limits of national jurisdiction". Among the conditions are that such installations should not interfere with the use of recognized sea-lanes essential to international navigation. It is also provided that permanent means for giving warnings of their presence must be maintained, and safety zones shall be established around the installations, but in a way which does not impede "the lawful access of shipping to particular maritime zones or navigation along international sea-lanes" (Article 147, paragraph 2). The article also stipulates that due notice must be given to the erection, emplacement and removal of such installations.

133.   Also under Article 16, paragraph 2, States are required to give due publicity to the charts showing the baselines for measuring the breadth of their territorial sea, or the lists of geographical co-ordinates of points. Copies of such charts or lists are to be deposited with the

Secretary-General of the United Nations. Similar requirements apply in respect of archipelagic baselines under Article 47, paragraph 9, in respect of the exclusive economic zone under Article 75. There is a similar provision regarding the continental shelf (Article 84, paragraph 2). The primary responsibility for preparing and publicizing these charts will be for the States concerned, but IMO may be in a position to assist in cases where it is deemed that the information may be of relevance to maritime safety or pollution prevention. There is no doubt that some of the information to be publicized under these articles of the Convention can be of considerable relevance to flag States, shipowners and other persons involved in international shipping who will need the information in order fully to discharge their responsibilities to take appropriate measures to ensure safety of navigation and the prevention of accidents which could result in pollution of the marine environment. Accordingly, IMO has a legitimate interest in the most effective dissemination of the information involved. For the purposes of facilitating this effective dissemination of information, IMO may find it necessary or useful to establish mechanisms suitable for channelling information in particular cases to the authorities, institutions or persons directly affected. Any such involvement of IMO will, of course, be in full consultation with the Secretariat of the United Nations or other inter-governmental organizations concerned, or individual States, as appropriate. For it is essential that any role which IMO may play should be such that it does not create unnecessary duplication or proliferation of information and communications on the same subject. Therefore, care should be taken to organize matters in such a way that all concerned recognize clearly that the role of IMO is complementary to the functions of the States, national institutions or international organizations concerned, and not in any way to be regarded as substitutes for those functions.

Other provisions and areas of relevance to IMO

134.   In addition to the provisions to which references have been made in the preceding paragraphs, several other articles and provisions of the Convention on the Law of the Sea may require the initiation of new programmes or procedures by IMO, or the modification of existing work in particular areas. Examples of such provisions are those relating to the following areas:

(a)   **The development and transfer of marine technology and international co-operation (Articles 202 to 203 and 266 to 269)**

135.   The basic objectives of international co-operation, as spelt out in Articles 202 and 268, and especially "the development of human resources through training and education of nationals of developing States and countries ...." are already part of the fundamental aims of IMO and its Technical Co-operation Programme, as provided for in the IMO Convention and in the relevant decisions of its inter-governmental bodies. In implementing these aims, IMO may find it useful to refer, in appropriate cases, to some of the specific arrangements and measures suggested or envisaged in the relevant articles of the Convention on the Law of the Sea, particularly those relating to the transfer of technology and the provision of assistance to developing countries in the maritime field.

(b)   **Promotion of global and regional co-operation for the protection and preservation of the marine environment (Articles 197 to 201)**

136.   IMO, together with other organizations, co-operates in the Regional Seas Programme of the United Nations Environment Programme (UNEP). In particular IMO has played a key

role in the establishment of Regional Arrangements for Combating Marine Pollution. These arrangements are directly pertinent to the provisions of the Convention on the Law of the Sea dealing with global co-operation. Also worth mentioning is the significance of IMO's participation in and contribution to the Group of Experts on Scientific Aspects of Marine Pollution (GESAMP) which brings together several agencies within the United Nations for the expert consideration and the undertaking of appropriate studies on scientific aspects of marine pollution. As the Organization which provides administrative secretariat services to GESAMP, IMO can make significant contribution to the work of the participating organizations in furthering the objectives and purposes outlined in Articles 204 to 206.

(c)   **Development of national and regional marine scientific and technological centers (Articles 275 to 277)**

137.   The provisions relating to the development of national and regional centres as set out in Articles 275 to 277 of the Convention reflect in many respects the programmes which IMO has been promoting for some time in many areas of the world. In this connection, the World Maritime University constitutes a prime example at the global level of the kind of institution envisaged in the Articles, and the experience of the World Maritime University will be of direct relevance in this context.

(d)   **Co-operation among international organizations (Article 278)**

138.   Article 278 enjoins on the competent international organizations to take all appropriate measures to ensure, either directly or in close co-operation among themselves, the effective discharge of their functions and responsibilities. In accordance with its Constitution and pursuant to decisions of its governing organs, IMO has established very co-operative and fruitful arrangements for collaboration with the United Nations and the other agencies and organizations within the United Nations system. However, IMO may need to explore appropriate avenues to promote and facilitate further co-operation with all international organizations whose activities may affect, or be affected by, the measures taken by the Organization with regard to matters dealt with by the Convention. In particular, it may be necessary to review the existing liaison with the Secretary-General of the United Nations and the existing organizations of the United Nations system in respect of matters which pertain to the field of responsibility or interests of the respective organizations. This is particularly so in the light of the views expressed at the IMO Assembly, at its thirteenth regular session, regarding possible "assistance by IMO to Member States and other agencies in respect of the provisions of the Convention on the Law of the Sea dealing with matters within the competence of IMO", and the development of "suitable and necessary collaboration with the Secretary-General of the United Nations on the provision of information, advice and assistance to developing countries on the law of the sea matters within the competence of IMO". Effective and co-ordinated liaison will also be needed with the International Sea-Bed Authority and the International Tribunal for the Law of the Sea when these bodies are established. Any such liaison and co-operation will be subject to the relevant provisions of the Convention on the Law of the Sea, and in accordance with the view of the IMO Assembly that IMO might provide "advice and assistance" to the Preparatory Commission for the International Sea-Bed Authority "on matters falling within the competence of IMO".

    . . .

APPENDIX

TREATY INSTRUMENTS IN RESPECT OF WHICH IMO PERFORMS FUNCTIONS

(1)   International Convention for the Safety of Life at Sea, 1974 (SOLAS 1974)
(2)   Protocol of 1978 relating to the International Convention for the Safety of Life at Sea, 1974 (SOLAS PROT 1978)
(3)   Convention on the International Regulations for Preventing Collisions at Sea, 1972, (COLREG (amended) 1972)
(4)   International Convention for the Prevention of Pollution from Ships, 1973, as modified by the Protocol of 1978 thereto (MARPOL 73/78)
(5)   Convention on Facilitation of International Maritime Traffic, 1965, as amended (FAL 1965)
(6)   International Convention on Load Lines, 1966 (LL 1966)
(7)   International Convention on Tonnage Measurement of Ships, 1969 (TONNAGE 1969)
(8)   International Convention relating to Intervention on the High Seas in Cases of Oil Pollution Casualties, 1969 (INTERVENTION 1969)
(9)   Protocol relating to Intervention on the High Seas in Cases of Pollution by Substances other than Oil, 1973 (INTERVENTION PROT 1973)
(10) International Convention on Civil Liability for Oil Pollution Damage, 1969 (CLC 1969)
(11) Protocol to the International Convention on Civil Liability for Oil Pollution Damage, 1969 (CLC PROT 1976)
(12) Protocol of 1984 to amend the International Convention on Civil Liability for Oil Pollution Damage, 1969 (CLC PROT 1984)
(13) Special Trade Passenger Ships Agreement, 1971 (STP 1971)
(14) Protocol on Space Requirements for Special Trade Passenger Ships, 1973 (SPACE STP 1973)
(15) Convention relating to Civil Liability in the Field of Maritime Carriage of Nuclear Material, 1971 (NUCLEAR 1971)
(16) International Convention on the Establishment of an International Fund for Compensation for Oil Pollution Damage, 1971 (FUND 1971)
(17) Protocol to the International Convention on the Establishment of an International Fund for Compensation for Oil Pollution Damage, 1971 (FUND PROT 1976)
(18) Protocol of 1984 to amend the International Convention on the Establishment of an International Fund for Compensation for Oil pollution Damage, 1971 (FUND PROT 1984)
(19) International Convention for Safe Containers, 1972, as amended (CSC (amended) 1972)
(20) Athens Convention relating to the Carriage of Passengers and their Luggage by Sea, 1974 (PAL 1974)
(21) Protocol to the Athens Convention relating to the Carriage of Passengers and their Luggage by Sea, 1974 (PAL PROT 1976)
(22) Convention on the International Maritime Satellite Organization (INMARSAT) (INMARSAT C)
(23) Operating Agreement on the International Maritime Satellite Organization (INMARSAT) (INMARSAT OA)
(24) Convention on Limitation of Liability for Maritime Claims, 1976 (LLMC 1976)
(25) Torremolinos International Convention for the Safety of Fishing Vessels, 1977 (SFV 1977)

(26) International Convention on Standards of Training, Certification and Watchkeeping for Seafarers, 1978 (STCW 1978)
(27) International Convention on Maritime Search and Rescue, 1979 (SAR 1979)
(28) Convention on the Prevention of Marine Pollution by Dumping of Wastes and Other Matter, 1972 (LDC 1972)

The following four instruments have been superseded by subsequent instruments as indicated below:

(1) International Convention for the Safety of Life at Sea, 1948 (SOLAS 1948)
This Convention was superseded, with effect from 26 May 1965, by the International Convention for the Safety of Life at Sea, 1960, as between the States Parties to the later Convention.
(2) International Convention for the Safety of Life at Sea, 1960 (SOLAS 1960)
This Convention has been superseded, with effect from 25 May 1980, by the International Convention for the Safety of Life at Sea, 1974, as between the States Parties to the later Convention.
(3) International Regulations for Preventing Collisions at Sea, 1960 (COLREG 60)
These Regulations were superseded, with effect from 15 July 1977, by the Regulations annexed to the Convention on the International Regulations for Preventing Collisions at Sea, 1972, as between the States Parties to the later Convention.
(4) International Convention for the Prevention of Pollution of the Sea by Oil, 1954, as amended (OILPOL (amended) 1954)
This Convention has been superseded, with effect from 2 October 1983, by the International Convention for the Prevention of Pollution from Ships, 1973, as modified by the Protocol of 1978 thereto, as between the States Parties to the later instrument.

- - - - -

IMO Assembly   A 15/5(b)/1
15th Session, November 1987   Extract

Consideration of the Reports and Recommendations of the Legal Committee

. . .

13. Committee I noted with satisfaction that the Secretariat of IMO had prepared a Study on the Implications of the United Nations Convention on the Law of the Sea, 1982 for the International Maritime Organization (document LEG/MISC/1), in response to the request of the Assembly at its thirteenth regular session. It was the view of many delegations that the Study would be of benefit both to the Organization and the work of its intergovernmental bodies as well as to individual Member Governments. In this connection it was noted that Member Governments had been invited to submit observations and comments on the Study, and the suggestion was made that any such comments or observations received from Governments might be collated and circulated to all Member States for information and action, as necessary.

. . .

- - - - -

Ninth Consultative Meeting of Contracting Parties   LDC 9/9/2
September 1985   Extract

Report of the Oslo Commission

. . .

IMPLICATIONS OF THE LAW OF THE SEA CONVENTION

4.   Following preliminary discussion at its Ninth Meeting, the Commission considered the possible implications of certain provisions in the Law of the Sea Convention (LOSC) for the Oslo Convention. In general, the Commission considered that for the most part there was agreement between the Oslo Convention and the LOSC and that such minor differences in definitions and provisions as existed did not justify any amendment of the Oslo Convention for its own sake. It was noted, however, that Article 210(5) of LOSC extended the jurisdiction of the coastal State with regard to the protection of the marine environment to that State's Exclusive Economic Zone (EEZ). It was pointed out that the provisions of the LOS Convention are only a legal framework which require specific implementation by national legislation and that therefore the Contracting Parties to the Oslo Convention could lay down in their national legislation that the rules of the Oslo Convention apply to their respective EEZs in order to make them generally effective in these areas.

5.   The Commission concluded that no action should be taken to amend the Oslo Convention expressly for the purpose of implementing the additional provisions of the LOS Convention. It was recognized, however, that action to amend the Convention in this respect might be desirable at an appropriate future date. In particular, an amendment to Article 15(1) could be considered to reflect the extension of the prescriptive jurisdiction of coastal States to the EEZ and Article 2 of the Convention might be amended to expressly mention the EEZ provisions.

. . .

- - - - -

Tenth Consultative Meeting of Contracting Parties   LDC 10/15
October 1986, Report of the Meeting   Extract

. . .

7.   Implications Regarding the Law of the Sea Convention for the London Dumping Convention

7.1   The Secretariat provided a historical outline of considerations by previous Consultative Meetings of the implications regarding the Law of the Sea Convention for the London Dumping Convention, the activities by the United Nations Office for the Law of the Sea, and consideration of the possible implications of the Law of the Sea for the Oslo Convention (LDC 10/7). It also drew attention to Article XIII of the London Dumping Convention which requests the Organization to convene a meeting of Contracting Parties after the Law of the

Sea Conference to consider the right and responsibility of a coastal State to apply the Convention in a zone adjacent to its coast. Attention was also drawn to Article VII(3) of the London Dumping Convention which requested the development of procedures for the effective application of the Convention particularly on the high seas, including procedures for the reporting of vessels and aircraft observed dumping in contravention of the Convention, and to a decision by the Consultative Meeting that this issue be considered in context with Article XIII of the Convention. The Secretariat (LDC 10/7) also indicated that the Oslo Commission considered that for the most part the texts of the Oslo Convention and of the Law of the Sea Convention were compatible and that such minor differences as existed did not justify any amendment to the Oslo Convention although it was recognized that it might be justifiable to amend the Oslo Convention at a future date to reflect the extension of the jurisdiction of coastal States and their exclusive economic zones. The Consultative Meeting was invited to consider the setting up of an intersessional *ad hoc* legal expert group which could report its views on these matters to the Eleventh Consultative Meeting.

7.2   The Secretariat in its paper (LDC 10/7) further drew attention to the question of dismantling, removal and disposal of abandoned or disused off-shore installations and informed the Meeting that whilst aspects related to safety of navigation would be considered by the IMO Sub-Committee on Safety of Navigation at its 23rd session (1216 January 1987) environmental issues related to the disposal of platforms at sea had not yet been discussed at any international forum.

7.3   The representative from the United Nations introduced the Law of the Sea, "Pollution by Dumping, Legislative History of Articles 1, Paragraph 1(5), and Articles 210 and 216" of the United Nations Convention on the Law of the Sea (United Nations publication Sales No.E.85.V.12) (LDC/INF.2). She explained that the Law of the Sea publications programme is designed to produce, on a subject basis, legislative histories, annotations (i.e. information on related conventions, rules, standards, etc.), and collections of national legislation. As an example of the latter, attention was drawn to the collection of "National Legislation on the Exclusive Economic Zone, the Economic Zone and the Exclusive Fishery Zone". The Law of the Sea legislative collection is indexed and computerized. Work on the dumping annotations has been postponed pending decisions of the Contracting Parties to the London Dumping Convention in connection with the present agenda item.

7.4   Work on collecting dumping legislation, and its indexation, would be greatly advanced if Contracting Parties were to furnish copies of their legislation in force. Whatever procedure is adopted for the examination of the implications of the Law of the Sea Convention, the Office of the Special Representative of the Secretary-General for the Law of the Sea would provide every advice and assistance.

7.5   With respect to the legislative history of the Law of the Sea provisions, it was emphasized that it was the clear intention of the Law of the Sea Conference to fully incorporate the London Dumping Convention within its framework. The Office of the Special Representative of the Secretary-General for the Law of the Sea is not therefore unduly concerned about interpretative questions. It is the United Nations primary duty to promote uniform and consistent application of the principles and rules of the Convention. These are generally accepted (as are all parts of the Convention, excepting its part XI, by Signatories and non-Signatories), and since the Law of the Sea Convention depends essentially on the London Dumping Convention for the implementation of the relevant provisions, the United Nations has a special interest in clarifying jurisdictional practices relative to dumping.

7.6   The United Nations Office looks forward to longer-term collaboration with the Consultative Meeting on dumping questions, in view also of the needs of the Preparatory Commission for the future International Sea-Bed Authority concerning environmental regulations for sea-bed mining.

7.7   The Meeting, recognizing the need as expressed in paragraph 7.4 above that Contracting Parties submit their national legislation on dumping for the preparation of a comprehensive study on the implications of the Law of the Sea Convention for the London Dumping Convention, requested its Secretariat to approach the respective national administrations of Contracting Parties with a view to providing the necessary material. In this connection the Meeting recalled that at the Sixth Consultative Meeting Contracting Parties had been requested to submit to the Secretariat copies of legal, governmental or administrative rules on waste disposal at sea or, if possible, summaries of parts of these instruments in one of the working languages of the Consultative Meeting reflecting the national procedures for implementation of the London Dumping Convention. The Secretariat has so far received national legislation on dumping at sea from the following Contracting Parties: Australia, Canada, China, Finland, France, the Federal Republic of Germany, Ireland, Italy, the Netherlands, Papua New Guinea, South Africa, Sweden, Switzerland, the USSR, the United Kingdom and the United States.

7.8   Several delegations expressed the view that further consideration of the implications regarding the Law of the Sea Convention for the London Dumping Convention, as well as other legal aspects including *inter alia* consideration of procedures for the assessment of liability in accordance with the principles of international law regarding State responsibility for damage to the environment of other States or to any other area of the environment resulting from dumping pursuant to resolution LDC.21(9), would benefit from consideration by an intersessional legal experts group.

7.9   The delegation of the United States, noting the fundamental consistency of the London Dumping Convention with the principles of customary international law reflected in the 1982 Law of the Sea Convention, in particular with respect to the rights of a coastal State to regulate dumping, questioned the need for establishing an intersessional working group on the subject of the implications of the Law of the Sea Convention for the London Dumping Convention.

7.10   The delegation of the United Kingdom stated that it could agree in principle with the establishment of a legal experts group subject to the availability of financial resources to be provided by the Organization. It also pointed out that due account should be taken of the progress achieved on items suggested for inclusion in the work programme of such an intersessional group and the need to ensure that the work of such a group is kept in phase with work being undertaken within other fora.

7.11   In a concluding discussion on these matters, the Consultative Meeting agreed that a legal experts meeting should be convened in conjunction with the scheduled inter-governmental panel on the disposal of radioactive wastes at sea (see paragraph 5.32 above). It was further agreed that the legal experts meeting should initially confine its consideration to the implications regarding the Law of the Sea Convention for the London Dumping Convention and the question of the assessment of liability for environmental damage resulting from dumping, as described in paragraph 7.8 above.

7.12   With regard to the dismantling and disposal of off-shore installations, several delegations expressed the view that aside from navigational problems connected with the dismantling and removal of abandoned or disused offshore installations which are being considered by the IMO Sub-Committee on Safety of Navigation, there do exist environmental issues and matters related to the interference with other legitimate uses of the sea (e.g. fishing) which should be addressed by the Consultative Meeting.

7.13   The IUCN observer supported the Secretariat's statements to the effect that no other international bodies were examining directly the environmental considerations pertinent to disposal of offshore platforms. That observer further noted that the deliberate disposal of platforms at sea is dumping under Article III(1)(a)(ii) of the London Dumping Convention and encouraged the Contracting Parties to establish guidelines on this subject at the Eleventh Consultative Meeting.

7.14   The Consultative Meeting agreed that the question of disposal of abandoned or disused offshore structures should be placed on the agenda for its next meeting at which time consideration could be given to this matter in the light of the outcome of consideration by the IMO Sub-Committee on Safety of Navigation. During the intersessional period Contracting Parties were requested to submit to the Secretariat information on State practice regarding the ultimate disposal of offshore installations or platforms to enable it to present a review to the Eleventh Consultative Meeting.

. . .

- - - - -

Ad Hoc Group of Legal Experts on Dumping   LDC/LG 3/4
Report of the Third Meeting, October 1987   Extract

========

. . .

2.   Implications of the United Nations Convention on the Law of the Sea for the London Dumping Convention

2.1   The experts considered the general implications of the United Nations Convention on the Law of the Sea (UNCLOS) for the London Dumping Convention (LDC) and agreed that there were no fundamental inconsistencies between the two conventions suggesting the need to amend the LDC.

2.2   The group agreed that the LDC should be interpreted in the light of developments in international law since its adoption in 1972, including those reflected in Part XII of UNCLOS.

2.3   In this regard, recognizing the right under international law of a coastal State to exercise jurisdiction over dumping in its territorial sea, its exclusive economic zone (EEZ) and onto its continental shelf, the *ad hoc* group concluded that in relation to article XIII of the LDC, a Party could apply, in accordance with international law, the LDC to dumping in its territorial sea and EEZ and onto its continental shelf. There was some divergence of views as to whether the coastal State would have to establish an EEZ before exercising its jurisdiction with regard to dumping in the area within 200 nautical miles from the coast.

2.4   The conclusions of the group referred to in the preceding paragraphs were on the basis of lengthy discussions on various provisions of UNCLOS, e.g. articles 1, 192, 204, 206, 210, 216, 217-221, 237 and 311. The group agreed that they do not present fundamental inconsistencies with the provisions of the LDC.

2.5   The group recognized that a number of provisions of UNCLOS are already accepted as customary international law. However, it was impracticable to analyze each provision to see whether it was part of international law.

2.6   Some experts considered that UNCLOS was a more general and higher convention than the LDC and interpretation of the provisions of the LDC should follow corresponding or relevant provisions of UNCLOS and as referred to in article 237.2 of UNCLOS. However, the group felt that it was not appropriate or necessary to state this (see paragraph 2.2 above), since the Vienna Convention on the Law of Treaties and some provisions of UNCLOS itself, when it enters into force, could make the relationship between UNCLOS and the LDC clear.

    . . .

2.7   In connection with its recommended interpretation of article XIII (see paragraph 2.3 above), the group also considered the meaning of the phrase "in its territory" in articles VI 2(a) and VII 2. With regard to article VI 2(a), the group concluded that the wastes for the purpose of dumping would be loaded in a port "in its territory". Article VII 2 should be construed to mean the obligation of taking measures to prevent and punish conduct in contravention of provisions of the LDC and, therefore, "in its territory" may be seen as an intended limit of the scope of this paragraph and there seems to be no need to amend the article.

- - - - -

ILO Conventions and Recommendations

International Labour Conference   ILO Report I
74th (Maritime) Session 1987   Extract

===

Report of the Director-General

    . . .

INTERNATIONAL INSTRUMENTS

United Nations Convention on the Law of the Sea

In 1982, the Third United Nations Conference on the Law of the Sea adopted the United Nations Convention on the Law of the Sea - a comprehensive treaty on all aspects of this topic. Its 320 articles and nine annexes deal with such questions as territorial and exclusive economic zones, conservation and management of living resources, transfers of marine technology, the deep sea-bed and compulsory dispute settlement. Although the Convention also covers shipping, one of its most significant aspects of concern to the ILO is the provision made for the establishment of an International Sea-Bed Authority to administer the resources of the Area and to organise and control activities therein, and of an Enterprise within the Authority to carry on activities in the Area directly and to transport, process and market minerals recovered from the Area. The ILO's particular interest relates to the conditions of employment and the safety of the personnel employed in ships operated by the Authority or its Enterprise. Specifically, the ILO is interested in ensuring that the labour and social conditions and the safety standards applicable to workers in the Area administered by the Authority are formally fixed at appropriate levels and effectively enforced in the particular context of the Authority and its Enterprise.

Although no provisions on such standards were included in the Convention itself, the need for the same was generally recognized within the Conference, and it was agreed that the matter could be taken up during the preparations for the entry into force of the Convention by the Preparatory Commission. The work of the Preparatory Commission has not yet reached the stage where it is ready to consider this matter . . .

. . .

- - - - -

Antarctic Treaty

UN General Assembly   A/41/722
Forty-first Session   Extract

Question of Antarctica

Report of the Secretary-General

CONTENTS
(Italics denote paragraphs reprinted in this work.)

Paragraphs

. . .

. . .

II. INVOLVEMENT OF THE RELEVANT SPECIALIZED AGENCIES AND
INTERGOVERNMENTAL ORGANIZATIONS IN THE
ANTARCTIC TREATY SYSTEM

A. **Relationship of the Antarctic Treaty system with the specialized agencies of the United Nations and other international organizations**

1. The Antarctic Treaty and Antarctic Treaty Consultative Meetings

(a) **General principles of the relationship of the Antarctic Treaty system with the specialized agencies of the United Nations and other international organizations as established by the Antarctic Treaty and Antarctic Treaty Consultative Meetings**

1. The involvement of the United Nations specialized agencies and other international organizations in the Antarctic Treaty system was first foreseen by the Antarctic Treaty itself. Article III of the Antarctic Treaty, *inter alia*, encourages the establishment of co-operative working relations with those specialized agencies of the United Nations and other international organizations having a scientific or technical interest in Antarctica.

2. In 1961, the First Antarctic Treaty Consultative Meeting recommended to the Governments of the Antarctic Treaty Consultative Parties that they should individually encourage the work of international organizations having a scientific or technical interest in Antarctica, including the specialized agencies of the United Nations, and should promote on a bilateral basis, the establishment and development of co-operative working relations with these organizations (Recommendation I-V).

3. Recommendation XI-1 (1981), made with regard to the future régime on Antarctic mineral resources, the Consultative Meeting suggested that the régime should, *inter alia*, include provisions for co-operative arrangements between the régime and other relevant international organizations. It further suggested that responsibilities that may be exercised in the Antarctic Treaty area by other international organizations should be taken into account in the provisions to be included in the régime so as to ensure that the special responsibilities of the Consultative Parties in respect of the environment in the area are protected.

4. At the Twelfth Consultative Meeting in 1983, a specific responsibility concerning the interaction between the Antarctic Treaty system and the specialized agencies of the United Nations, or other international organizations having a scientific or technical interest in Antarctica, was suggested for the Government of the host country of each Consultative Meeting. According to recommendation XII-6, the Government of such country shall, as and when the representatives of the Consultative Parties consider it appropriate, draw the attention of any of the abovementioned bodies to any part of the report of the Consultative Meeting, or any information document submitted to the Meeting and made available to the public, relevant to the scientific or technical interest which that agency or organization has in Antarctica.

5. The Twelfth Consultative Meeting also came to the conclusion that, as part of the preparation for each regular Consultative Meeting, the Consultative Parties should consider

whether they would be assisted in their discussion of any item of the agenda of the regular Consultative Meeting if a specialized agency of the United Nations or other international organization having a scientific or technical interest in Antarctica were to attend the meeting as an observer when that item was being discussed; and if so, whether the relevant organization should, with the agreement of all Consultative Parties, be invited by the host Government to attend the meeting on that basis.

(b)   **The relationship of the Antarctic Treaty system with the specialized agencies of the United Nations and other international organizations as demonstrated by the Antarctic Treaty Consultative Meetings**

6.   The Antarctic Treaty Consultative Meetings provide the forum where, over the years, a number of legally binding recommendations were adopted by the Consultative Parties in connection with the increasing involvement of the specialized agencies and international organizations in the Antarctic Treaty system.

7.   In this regard, the following measures were recommended to the Governments of the Consultative Parties for approval and subsequent implementation:

(a)   Invitation to an international organization to undertake new Antarctic research, to add new aspects to ongoing research, or to offer advice in specific scientific, technical or environmental fields (recommendations VI-4, VI-5, VII-3, VIII-7, VIII14, IX-3, X-1, X-3, X-4, XII-2, XII-3, XIII-4, XIII-5);

(b)   Encouragement of, and invitation to, an international organization to continue its interest and work in specific fields of Antarctic scientific investigation (recommendations I-IV, III-X, IV-22, VI-4, VI-9, VII-1, VII-2, VIII-10, VIII-11, VIII-14, IX-4, X-7);

(c)   Taking into consideration viewpoints, recommendations, proposals of and measures by the United Nations specialized agencies and international organizations having scientific, technical or environmental interest in Antarctica (recommendations I-XI, II-I, II-II, V-7, VII-1, VII-7, XI-1, XII-1);

(d)   Encouragement of, and invitation to appropriate international organizations to co-operate and consult with each other in specific areas of Antarctic research (recommendations V-3, VIII-11, VIII-13, X-7);

(e)   Invitation to a specialized agency to provide help and advice in the exchange of meteorological data, and to give consideration to and undertake actions in specific aspects of the problem (recommendations VI-3, X-3, XII-1);

(f)   Issuance and adoption as voluntary guidelines of the general rules of conduct with regard to the conservation of Antarctic fauna and flora, as recommended by an international organization (recommendations I-VIII, VII-1);

(g)   Invitation to observers from specialized agencies and appropriate international organizations to attend meetings on Antarctic telecommunications (recommendations I-XI, V-2);

(h) Providing an international organization with specific types of information on Antarctica (recommendations VIII-7, X-3);

(i) Facilitation of the exchange of information regarding plans for scientific programmes carried out through international organizations (recommendation I-I);

(j) Co-ordination of meetings and symposiums organized by the Governments of Consultative Parties on Antarctic logistic problems with similar action undertaken by an international organization (recommendation II-II);

(k) Adoption of specific measures for co-operation in transport in Antarctica, as recommended by an international organization (recommendation IX-4);

(l) Expression of gratitude to an international organization for the devoted service which it has given to the achievement of a better understanding of the Antarctic and to the development of the Antarctic Treaty system (recommendation X-9);

(m) Consideration of requests to meet costs incurred by an international organization when responding to requests for advice by the Antarctic Treaty Consultative Parties (recommendation XII-8);

(n) Invitation to an international organization to appoint its representative as an observer at the Consultative Meetings for the specific purpose of reporting on certain matters within its competence (recommendation XIII-2).

8.   A number of the above-mentioned measures were recommended by the Consultative Meetings with reference to activities, viewpoints, recommendations and decisions of specialized agencies and international organizations concerned with Antarctic research (recommendations III-III, V-2, V-3, VII-2, VII-7, VIII-2, VIII-4, VIII-7, VIII-11, VIII-13, IX-1, IX-3, IX-4, IX-5, X-3, X-6, X-9, XII-1, XII-2, XII-5, XII-8, XIII-4, XIII-5, XIII-7, XIII-8).

9.   According to article IX, paragraph 4, of the Antarctic Treaty, recommended measures "shall become effective when approved by all the Contracting Parties whose representatives were entitled to participate in the meetings held to consider those measures". Among the recommendations referred to in the above paragraphs, the following are not yet in effect:

(a) Recommendations of the thirteenth Consultative Meeting referred to in subparagraphs (a) and (n) of paragraph 7 and paragraph 8 above;

(b) Recommendations of the Twelfth Consultative Meeting referred to in paragraphs 4 and 8, and in subparagraphs (a), (c), (e), and (m) of paragraph 7 above;

(c) Recommendation XI-1 referred to in paragraph 3 and subparagraph (c) of paragraph 7 above;

(d) Recommendations of the Tenth Consultative Meeting referred to in subparagraphs (a), (b), (d), (h) and (l) of paragraph 7 and in paragraph 8 above.

. . .

IV. SIGNIFICANCE OF THE UNITED NATIONS CONVENTION ON THE LAW OF THE SEA IN THE SOUTHERN OCEAN

113.   The General Assembly requested an additional study on, *inter alia*, the "significance" of the United Nations Convention on the Law of the Sea (referred to hereinafter in this section as the Convention) in the Southern Ocean. For the purposes of this study, the Southern Ocean is viewed as being the southern continuation of the Atlantic, Indian and Pacific Oceans. Its northern boundary is considered to be the Antarctic Convergence which generally lies between 45° and 60° south latitude.[4]

114.   The Convention which was opened for signature on 10 December 1982, received a total of 159 signatures by 9 December 1984, the closing date for signature. As at 30 September 1986, 32 instruments of ratification had been deposited with the SecretaryGeneral. The Convention will enter into force 12 months after the date of deposit of the sixtieth instrument of ratification or accession. It is already having a stabilizing effect on the law of the sea at both national and international levels and the recent judgments of the International Court of Justice and arbitral awards have taken into consideration developments in the law of the sea as reflected in the Convention (see A/38/570, A/39/647 and A/40/923).

115.   One of the main objectives of the Convention is to establish a new legal order for the seas and oceans, taking into account recent developments and the needs of the international community. It is a global convention applicable to all ocean space. No area of ocean space is excluded. It follows that the Convention must be of significance to the Southern Ocean in the sense that its provisions also apply to that ocean.

116.   Examination of the significance of the Convention in the Southern Ocean involves the issue of the relationship of the Convention to the other conventions and international agreements applicable to the area. On the general issue of the relationship of the Convention with other conventions and international agreements the Convention states, *inter alia*, that it "shall not alter the rights and obligations of States Parties which arise from other agreements compatible with this Convention and which do not affect the enjoyment by other States Parties of their rights or the performance of their obligations under this Convention".[5]

117.   Of particular importance in this respect is the Antarctic Treaty in force between 32 States (a majority of which have signed the Convention)[6] which sets forth principles and rules to be applied not only to the Antarctic continent, but also to the maritime space of the Antarctic. The Treaty is aimed at furthering the purposes and principles embodied in the Charter of the United Nations by ensuring the use of Antarctica for peaceful purposes only and the continuance of international harmony in Antarctica. It is open for accession by any Member of the United Nations or by any other State that may be invited to accede to it. A network of substantive agreements, including the Antarctic Treaty itself and a body of agreed recommendations, agreed measures and additional instruments have been adopted pursuant to the Antarctic Treaty - all of which constitute the Antarctic Treaty system.[7] For the purposes of the Antarctic Treaty, Antarctica is defined as an area south of 60° south latitude, which embraces a considerable extent of maritime space. Certain conventions of a global character dealing with aspects of the law of the sea also apply to the Southern Ocean.

A. Peaceful uses of the seas

118.   One of the objectives laid down in the preamble of the 1982 Convention is the establishment of a legal order for the seas and oceans which will promote their peaceful uses. This theme is taken up in various parts of the Convention.[8] For instance the Convention states that "the high seas shall be reserved for peaceful purposes" and that the sea-bed and ocean floor and subsoil thereof beyond the limits of national jurisdiction (the Area) "shall be open to use exclusively for peaceful purposes". Installations constructed for carrying out activities in the International Sea-Bed Area (referred to hereafter as the Area) are to be used exclusively for peaceful purposes. The conference, which will be convened to review the operation of the system of exploration and exploitation of the Area, shall ensure, *inter alia*, that the principle of using the Area exclusively for peaceful purposes is maintained. In addition, marine scientific research is to be conducted exclusively for peaceful purposes.

119.   The **leitmotiv** of the Antarctic Treaty is to ensure that Antarctica shall be used exclusively for peaceful purposes and shall not become the scene or object of international discord.[9] Any measures of a military nature, such as "the establishment of military bases and fortifications, the carrying out of military manoeuvres, as well as the testing of any type of weapons" are prohibited.   Thus the Treaty bars all military activities in Antarctica. Furthermore it prohibits any nuclear explosions and the disposal of radioactive waste in Antarctica. To secure these ends the Treaty also provides for a system of observation and inspection.[10] However, the Treaty states that nothing in it shall prejudice or in any way affect the rights, or the exercise of the rights, of any State under international law with regard to the high seas within that area.[11]

B. Marine scientific research

120.   Under the Convention all States have the right to conduct marine scientific research, subject to the rights and duties of other States as provided for in the Convention[12] and States and competent international organizations are enjoined to promote and facilitate the development and conduct of marine scientific research.

121.   The Convention expressly makes freedom of scientific research a freedom of the high seas. States Parties to the Convention have the right to carry out marine scientific research in the Area, exclusively for peaceful purposes and for the benefit of mankind as a whole. The rules of the Convention governing marine scientific research including the powers granted the International Sea-Bed Authority in article 143, apply to the high seas and the international sea-bed area extending south of 60° south latitude.

122.   The Convention has established special régimes for marine scientific research for areas falling under the sovereignty and jurisdiction of coastal States. Coastal States have the exclusive right to regulate, authorize and conduct marine scientific research in their territorial sea. Marine scientific research in the exclusive economic zone and on the continental shelf is subject to the consent régime embodied in the Convention. These special régimes are applicable to the Southern Ocean in so far as such areas exist (see below, para. 139 and ff).

123.   The Antarctic Treaty, embracing a significant part of the Southern Ocean, provides for the freedom of scientific investigation and co-operation towards that end as basic principles, particularly geared to the conditions of Antarctica. It establishes a mechanism for promoting international co-operation in scientific investigation in Antarctica and encourages the

establishment of co-operative relations with those specialized agencies of the United Nations and other international organizations having a scientific or technical interest in Antarctica.[13] To this end, the Consultative Meetings of the Antarctic Treaty have approved a number of recommendations which are binding upon the Treaty Parties if approved by them.

124.   The provisions of the Convention relating to marine scientific research in the high seas apply to those parts of the Southern Ocean which constitute the high seas. However, the position with regard to States not parties to the Antarctic Treaty conducting marine scientific investigation in maritime areas adjacent to claimed territories is not clear.

C. Protection and preservation of the marine environment

125.   The Convention imposes a general obligation on States to protect and preserve the marine environment,[14] with respect to: (a) pollution from land-based sources; (b) pollution from sea-bed activities subject to national jurisdiction; (c) pollution from sea-bed activities beyond national jurisdiction; (d) pollution from activities in the Area; (e) pollution from dumping; (f) pollution from vessels; and (g) pollution from or through the atmosphere.[15]

126.   The measures that States shall take to combat pollution of the marine environment significantly include those necessary to protect and preserve rare or fragile ecosystems as well as the habitat of depleted, threatened or endangered species and other forms of marine life. States are also obliged to take all measures necessary to prevent, reduce and control pollution of the marine environment resulting from the use of technologies under their jurisdiction and control and to avoid introducing alien or new species to a particular part of the marine environment which may cause significant and harmful changes to that environment.

127.   With respect to activities in the Area, appropriate rules, regulations and procedures are required to be adopted, *inter alia*, to prevent, reduce and control pollution, paying particular attention to the need for protection from the harmful effects of such activities as drilling, dredging, excavation, disposal of waste, construction and operation or maintenance of installations, pipelines and other devices related to such activities. Measures should also be adopted to protect and conserve the natural resources of this area and to prevent damage to the flora and fauna of the marine environment.

128.   The Convention deals expressly with the relationship between its part XII (Protection and Preservation of the Marine Environment) and other conventions and agreements relating to the protection and preservation of the marine environment. Specific obligations assumed by States under these conventions and agreements are not prejudiced by the provisions of part XII. However, these obligations should be carried out in a manner consistent with the general principles and objectives of the Convention.[16]

129.   There are measures and regulations concerning protection and preservation of the marine environment applicable to the Southern Ocean that have been approved on the global level under the auspices of the International Maritime Organization, the United Nations Environment Programme, etc. On the regional level such measures have been elaborated within the framework of the Antarctic Treaty (see A/39/583 (Part I), para. 3, sect. III). These rules and regulations are generally compatible with the Convention.

D. Conservation and management of marine living resources

130.   The Convention provides that coastal States have sovereign rights, over all the natural resources to be found in their exclusive economic zones, as well as specific rights and obligations with respect to the conservation and management of living resources.[17]   All States have the right to fish on the high seas - a right which flows from the freedom of the high seas. This right, however, is subject, among other things, to any treaty obligations and to the rights and duties as well as the interests of coastal States provided for, *inter alia*, in article 63, paragraph 2, and articles 64 to 67.   These provisions relate to straddling stocks, highly migratory species, marine mammals, anadromous stocks and catadromous species; they all have effect to a greater or lesser extent on the legal régime of the high seas.

131.   All States have the general duty to co-operate in the conservation and management of the living resources of the high seas.[18] In particular they have a duty, where their "nationals exploit identical living resources or different living resources in the same area", to enter into negotiations with a view to taking the necessary conservation measures and as appropriate establish subregional or regional organizations. In establishing conservation measures it is the duty of States under the Convention to take measures which are designed, on the best scientific evidence available to the States concerned, to maintain or restore populations of harvested species at levels which can produce the maximum sustainable yield, as qualified by relevant environmental and economic factors, including the special requirements of developing States, and taking into account fishing patterns, the interdependence of stocks and any generally recommended international minimum standards, whether subregional, regional or global. The Convention further provides that States shall take into consideration the effects on species associated with or dependent upon harvested species with a view to maintaining or restoring populations of such associated or dependent species above levels at which their reproduction may become seriously threatened. With respect to fishing on the high seas, the Convention expressly declares that States must ensure that the conservation measures and their implementation do not discriminate in form or in fact against the fishermen of any State.

132.   On the initiative of the Antarctic Treaty Consultative Parties two instruments have been adopted for the conservation of Antarctic marine living resources: the Convention for the Conservation of Antarctic Seals (1972) and the Convention on the Conservation of Antarctic Marine Living Resources (CCAMLR, 1980).[19] Neither of these two treaties makes any distinction within the waters of the Antarctic area, but both are specific with regard to the outer limits of the area of application: the Convention for the Conservation of Antarctic Seals applies to areas situated south of 60° south latitude; the area of application of the CCAMLR is the Antarctic Convergence. The application area of the two instruments respectively include all ocean space comprised between each of those limits and the Antarctic coastline.

133.   The CCAMLR states that the term "conservation" includes rational use and it adopts the ecosystem-oriented approach with respect to the conservation of marine living resources. This approach is somewhat different from the notion of "maximum sustainable yield" adopted in the Convention.

134.   The CCAMLR has established a Commission for the Conservation of the Antarctic Marine Living Resources to give effect to its objectives and principles. The Commission shall take into account regulations or measures adopted by existing fisheries commissions responsible for species which may enter the area to which the CCAMLR applies.[20] The Commission must also seek to co-operate with contracting parties exercising jurisdiction in

marine areas adjacent to the area of application of the CCAMLR in respect of the conservation of any stock or stocks of associated species which occur both within those areas and the area of application of the CCAMLR.[21]

135.   Any State interested in research or harvesting activities in relation to Antarctic marine living resources can accede to the CCAMLR. Contracting Parties to CCAMLR not parties to the Antarctic Treaty acknowledge "the special obligations and responsibilities of the Antarctic Treaty Consultative Parties for the protection and preservation of the marine environment of the Antarctic Treaty area".[22] Such States are bound by articles I to VI of this instrument which concerns, *inter alia*, the issues of peaceful purposes and sovereignty.[23] Any acceding State is entitled to membership in the Commission for the Conservation of Antarctic Marine Living Resources as long as it is engaged in research or harvesting activities in relation to the Antarctic marine living resources.[24]

136.   The Convention on the Conservation of Antarctic Seals is designed to promote and achieve the objectives of protection, scientific study and rational use of Antarctic seals, and to maintain a satisfactory balance within the ecological system. It establishes measures which are subject to review in the light of scientific assessment and envisages the establishment of a system of inspection. Since there is no commercial sealing in the area, the Convention plays mostly a preventive role.

137.   The above-mentioned Conventions as well as the International Convention for the Regulation of Whaling (1946), which also applies to the waters of the Southern Ocean, are in accord with the requirements of the Convention.

V. ISSUES OF SOVEREIGNTY AND JURISDICTION

138.   The Convention can be viewed as dividing ocean space into two categories of areas: areas falling under the sovereignty and jurisdiction of coastal States and areas beyond the limits of national jurisdiction. The former includes the internal waters, the territorial sea, the contiguous zone, the exclusive economic zone and the continental shelf. To these may be added the special régimes for islands.[25] The high seas and the international sea-bed area are maritime areas beyond the limits of national jurisdiction.

A. Areas falling within the sovereignty and jurisdiction of States

139.   The question whether the régime embodied in the Convention relating to maritime areas falling under national sovereignty or jurisdiction applies to Antarctica is linked to the legal status of the land masses in Antarctica. Within the Southern Ocean there are islands that are subject to the undisputed sovereignty of various States. The régime of the Convention applies to such islands. Legislative acts concerning the territorial seas and the continental shelves around these islands have to a large extent been enacted by coastal States, and in certain instances declarations on 200 miles exclusive economic or fishery zones have been made.

140.   With respect to Antarctica, seven States parties to the Antarctic Treaty have claimed sovereignty over territories and some of these claims overlap. Two States, while not recognizing any territorial claims in Antarctica, maintain a basis of claims in respect of Antarctic territories. Other States within the system have not made any claims nor do they

recognize claims to sovereignty. A part of the Antarctic continent remains free from claims of national sovereignty.

141.   The Antarctic Treaty has devised a mechanism for dealing with these conflicting positions. This is embodied in article IV which states:

"1.   Nothing contained in the present Treaty shall be interpreted as:

"(a)   a renunciation by any Contracting Party of previously asserted rights of or claims to territorial sovereignty in Antarctica;

"(b)   a renunciation or diminution by any Contracting Party of any basis of claim to territorial sovereignty in Antarctica which it may have whether as a result of its activities or those of its nationals in Antarctica, or otherwise;

"(c)   prejudicing the position of any Contracting Party as regards its recognition or non-recognition of any other State's right of or claim or basis of claim to territorial sovereignty in Antarctica.

"2.   No acts or activities taking place while the present Treaty is in force shall constitute a basis for asserting, supporting or denying a claim to territorial sovereignty in Antarctica or create any rights of sovereignty in Antarctica. No new claim, or enlargement of an existing claim, to territorial sovereignty in Antarctica shall be asserted while the present Treaty is in force."

142.   From the perspective of the Parties to the Antarctic Treaty, the extent to which the various types of maritime jurisdiction can be exercised by claimant States in the Antarctica depends on how article IV of the Antarctic Treaty is interpreted. The Antarctic Treaty Consultative Parties themselves are not in agreement on this question (see also A/39/583 (Part I), sect. II.B, III.F). States which have claimed territorial sovereignty in Antarctica have not renounced their rights. They assert claims to maritime jurisdiction over adjacent waters on the basis that title to territory automatically involves jurisdiction over appurtenant waters and continental shelves. Such rights, in their view, are merely an attribute of their sovereignty. On the other hand non-claimant States do not recognize any claims to territorial sovereignty in the Antarctic area. A number of these States also argue that certain assertions of sovereign rights over resources constitute a new claim or the extension of an existing claim to territorial sovereignty and therefore prohibited by article IV (2) of the Antarctic Treaty.[26] The validity of maritime claims is a broader question than that addressed in the present paragraph. It is not merely dependent on an interpretation of article IV, which is only binding upon the Parties.

143.   The non-recognition of territorial sovereignty in Antarctica by some of the States parties to the Treaty is shared by a number of States not parties to the Antarctic Treaty. Some of these latter States contend that Antarctica should be the common heritage of mankind.[27]

144.   This issue was also dealt with in the CCAMLR. The area of application of this instrument, extended north of 60° south latitude up to a point where the Antarctic Convergence begins covering certain islands over which there was generally undisputed sovereignty. In order to deal with certain problems arising from this extension the mechanism utilized in the Antarctic Treaty was somewhat modified. Article IV of the CCAMLR includes an analogous provision to that of article IV of the Antarctic Treaty with the exception of paragraph 2 (b) which states:

"Nothing in this Convention and no acts or activities taking place while the Convention is in force shall:
   "...

   "(b)   be interpreted as a renunciation or diminution by any Contracting Party of, or as prejudicing, any right or claim or basis of claim to exercise coastal State jurisdiction under international law within the area to which this Convention applies;"

This provision enabled both claimant and non-claimant States to maintain their respective positions with respect to the question of whether attempts to establish fishing or exclusive economic zones were permissible under article IV of the Antarctic Treaty or constituted an enlargement of existing claim. With respect to the right of States to coastal jurisdiction in areas north of 60° south latitude a compromise solution was found through a statement by the Chairman of the Conference regarding the application of the CCAMLR régime to waters adjacent to the islands over which the existence of State sovereignty was recognized by all parties to the Treaty.

145.   In the light of the differences referred to above, the extent to which the provisions of the Convention relating to national sovereignty and jurisdiction apply to the area of application of the Antarctic Treaty, and hence their significance thereto, remains unclear. The application area of the Treaty (the waters south of the 60° south latitude) indicates the limits of the areas within which the parties undertake to regulate their conduct and is not based on any claim of sovereignty or jurisdiction. The manner in which the instruments of the Antarctic Treaty system are applied by the Antarctic Treaty Parties supports this.

146.   With respect to the delineation of baselines, it should be noted that there are unique geophysical conditions prevailing in the Antarctic region which neither the Convention nor any other rule of international law has dealt with. In the case of the Antarctic continent, the low waterline along the coast varies considerably because the ice layer permanently covering the land mass flows outwards and its extension changes depending upon the season.

B.   Areas beyond the national jurisdiction of States

1.   High seas

147.   The provisions of the Convention relating to the high seas apply to all parts of the sea that are not included in the exclusive economic zone, in the territorial sea or in the internal waters of a State or in the archipelagic waters of an archipelagic State. In the high seas all States enjoy, *inter alia*, the freedom of navigation; of overflight; freedom to lay submarine cables and pipelines; to construct artificial islands and other installations; and the freedom of fishing and of scientific research.[28] The general rules relating to the high seas apply to the Southern Ocean.

2.   The International Sea-Bed Area

148.   The international régime under the Convention includes principles and rules governing the exploration and exploitation of the resources of the Area. It establishes an International Sea-Bed Authority - an organization designed to give effect to the principle that "The Area and its resources are the common heritage of mankind".[29] No State may claim or exercise

sovereign rights over any part of the Area or its resources or appropriate any part thereof.[30] Activities in the Area shall be organized, carried out and controlled by the Authority acting on behalf of mankind as a whole and for its benefit.[31]

149.   The ares over which the international régime established in part XI of the Convention will apply is defined as the "sea-bed and ocean floor and subsoil thereof beyond the limits of national jurisdiction".[32]

150.   Since neither the parallel 60° south nor the Antarctic Convergence are limits of national jurisdiction, the Area would extend beyond those lines into the Southern Ocean. This is acknowledged by the Antarctic Treaty parties. At the eleventh Consultative Meeting, the Antarctic Treaty Consultative Parties, a majority of whom are signatories to the Convention, adopted a decision with respect to the régime of Antarctic Mineral Resources which stated that the régime should apply to all mineral resource activities taking place on the Antarctic continent and its adjacent offshore areas "but without encroachment on the deep sea-bed". They further decided that the precise limits of the area of application would be determined by the Antarctic Treaty Consultative Parties in the elaboration of the régime.[33] As the Antarctic mineral resources régime is still under negotiation among the Antarctic Treaty Consultative Parties, it is not possible to analyse at this stage its scope and content nor to consider its relationship with the principles on which the international régime for the Area is based.

151.   On the basis of the definition of the Area the sea-bed and ocean floor and subsoil thereof which lie beyond national jurisdiction are regulated by the international sea-bed régime embodied in the Convention. The precise determination of the limits of the Area in the Southern Ocean presents complex problems. First, there are claimed areas and unclaimed areas in Antarctica. Second, there is the position of claimant and non-claimant States within the Antarctic Treaty system. Third, there is the position of the Antarctic Treaty Consultative Parties referred to in paragraph 150. Fourth, there is the position of a number of States not parties to the Antarctic Treaty which do not recognize claims in Antarctica. And fifth, there is the position of those among the latter which contend that Antarctica should be proclaimed as the common heritage of mankind. As in the case referred to in paragraph 145, therefore, the question of the applicability of the international régime for the sea-bed and ocean floor beyond national jurisdiction to the sea-bed in the Antarctica region, and hence the significance thereto, remains unclear.

Notes

. . .

4.   See report of the Secretary-General (A/39/583 (Part I)). The term Southern Ocean as used in resolution 40/156 is explained by Malaysia (see A/C.1/40/PV.55).
5.   United Nations Convention on the Law of the Sea, art.311, para. 2.
6.   The following parties to the Antarctic Treaty (Consultative and Non-Consultative) have signed the Convention: Argentina, Australia, Belgium, Brazil, Bulgaria, Cuba, Czechoslovakia, Chile, Denmark, Finland, France, German Democratic Republic, Hungary, India, Italy, Japan, Netherlands, New Zealand, Norway, Papua New Guinea, People's Republic of China, Poland, Romania, South Africa, Spain, Sweden, Uruguay and Union of Soviet Socialist Republics. Cuba ratified it. Germany, Federal Republic of, Peru, United Kingdom and the United States of America did not sign it.
7.   See A/C.1/40/PV.48 (Australia).
8.   United Nations Convention on the Law of the Sea, arts. 88; 141; 147, para. 2 (d); 155, para. 2; 143, para. 1; 240 (a); 242, para. 1 and 246, para. 3.
9.   Antarctic Treaty, Preamble and art. I. See A/39/583 (Part I), paras. 66 to 70 and 161 to 170.
10.   Antarctic Treaty, art. VII.
11.   Ibid., art. VI.
12.   United Nations Convention on the Law of the Sea, arts. 238; 239; 87; 143; 245 and 246.
13.   Antarctic Treaty, art. III, para. 2.

14. <u>United Nations Convention on the Law of the Sea</u>, art. 192.
15. <u>Ibid.</u>, part XIII.
16. <u>Ibid.</u>, art. 237.
17. <u>United Nations Convention on the Law of the Sea</u>, arts. 55 to 57 and 61 to 73.
18. <u>Ibid.</u>, arts. 87 and 116 to 119.
19. See also <u>Agreed Measures for the Conservation of Antarctic Fauna and Flora</u> adopted at the
3rd consultative meeting (1964). Further see Report of the SecretaryGeneral A/39/583 (Part 1), sects. II.B, III.F.
20. <u>Ibid.</u>, art. IX, para. 5.
21. <u>Ibid.</u>, art. XI.
22. <u>Ibid.</u>, art. V.
23. <u>Ibid.</u>, articles III and IV.
24. <u>Ibid.</u>, art. VII, para. 2 (b).
25. <u>United Nations Convention on the Law of the Sea</u>, arts. 8; 2; 3; 33; 55 to 58; 76 and 121.
26. See Bush, Antarctica and International Law, A Collection of Inter-State and National Documents, vol. 1, p. 62.
27. See A/C.1/40/PV.48 (Malaysia); A/C.1/40/PV.50 (Bangladesh); <u>Ibid.</u> (Sudan); <u>Ibid.</u> (Libya); <u>Ibid.</u> (Pakistan); <u>Ibid.</u> (Thailand); A/C.1/40/PV.53 (Nepal); <u>Ibid.</u> (Cape Verde); <u>Ibid.</u> (Algeria); <u>Ibid.</u> (Kenya). See the Declaration of the Organization of African Unity (OAU), at its forty-second ordinary session, held in Addis Ababa from 10 to 17 July 1985.
28. <u>United Nations Convention on the Law of the Sea</u>, art. 86 and 87.
29. <u>United Nations Convention on the Law of the Sea</u>, art. 136. See also the Declaration of principles governing the sea-bed and the ocean floor, and the subsoil thereof, beyond the limits of national jurisdiction General Assembly resolution 2749 (XXV) adopted by 108 votes to none, with 14 abstentions.
30. <u>Ibid.</u>, art. 137.
31. <u>Ibid.</u>, art. 140.
32. <u>Ibid.</u>, art. 1, para 1 (i).
33. Eleventh Meeting of the Antarctic Treaty Consultative Parties, Recommendation XI-1, para. 7, IV.

- - - - -

UN General Assembly
Forty-second Session

A/RES/42/46
Extract

<hr>

Resolution 42/46.   Question of Antarctica

. . .

B

The General Assembly,

Having considered the item entitled "Question of Antarctica",

Recalling its resolutions 38/77 of 15 December 1983, 39/152 of 17 December 1984, 40/156 A and B of 16 December 1985 and 41/88 A and B of 4 December 1986,

Recalling the relevant paragraphs of the Political Declaration adopted by the Eighth Conference of Heads of State or Government of Non-Aligned Countries, held at Harare from 1 to 6 September 1986,[1] and the resolution on Antarctica adopted by the Council of Ministers of the Organization of African Unity at its forty-second ordinary session, held at Addis Ababa from 10 to 17 July 1985,[2] as well as the decision of the Council of Ministers of the League of Arab States held at Tunis on 17 and 18 September 1986 and resolution 25/5-P(IS) adopted by the Fifth Islamic Summit Conference of the Organization of the Islamic Conference, held at Kuwait from 26 to 29 January 1987,[3]

Welcoming the increasing awareness of and interest in Antarctica shown by the international community,

Taking into account the debates on this item held at its thirty-eighth, thirty-ninth, fortieth, forty-first and forty-second sessions,

Convinced of the advantages to the whole of mankind of a better knowledge of Antarctica,

Affirming the conviction that, in the interest of all mankind, Antarctica should continue for ever to be used exclusively for peaceful purposes and that it should not become the scene or object of international discord,

Conscious of the significance of Antarctica to the international community in terms, *inter alia*, of international peace and security, environment, economy, scientific research and meteorology,

Reaffirming that the management, exploration, exploitation and use of Antarctica should be conducted in accordance with the purposes and principles of the Charter of the United Nations and in the interest of maintaining international peace and security and of promoting international co-operation for the benefit of mankind as a whole,

Taking note with appreciation of the report of the Secretary-General on the question of Antarctica,[4]

Also taking into account all aspects pertaining to all areas covered by the Antarctic Treaty system,[5]

Reaffirming the principle that the international community is entitled to information covering all aspects of Antarctica and that the United Nations be made the repository for all such information in accordance with General Assembly resolution 41/88 A,

Reaffirming further that any eventual minerals régime on Antarctica should take fully into account the interests of the international community and that a moratorium on the negotiations to establish a minerals régime should be imposed until such time as all members of the international community can participate fully in such negotiations, in accordance with General Assembly resolution 41/88 B,

1.   *Calls upon* the Antarctic Treaty Consultative Parties to invite the SecretaryGeneral or his representative to all meetings of the Treaty parties, including their consultative meetings and the minerals régime negotiations;

2.   *Requests* the Secretary-General to submit a report on his evaluations thereon to the General Assembly at its forty-third session;

3.   *Also calls upon* the Antarctic Treaty Consultative Parties to impose a moratorium on the negotiations to establish a minerals régime until such time as all members of the international community can participate fully in such negotiations;

4.   *Urges* all States Members of the United Nations to co-operate with the Secretary-General and to continue consultations on all aspects relating to Antarctica;

5.   *Decides* to include in the provisional agenda of its forty-third session the item entitled "Question of Antarctica".

Notes

1. A/41/697-S/18392, annex, sect. I, paras. 198-202.
2. A/40/666, annex II, resolution CM/Res.988 (XLII).
3. See A/42/178-S/18753, annex II.
4. A/42/586 and Corr. 1.
5. United Nations, Treaty Series, vol. 402, No. 5778.

85th plenary meeting
30 November 1987

- - - - -

Additional References

Question of Antarctica. UN docs. A/42/586 and A/42/587; UN resolution A/RES/41/88.

Report of the World Commission on Environment and Development. UN doc. A/42/427, Chapter 10.

- - - - -

II

SHIPPING: ECONOMIC AND LEGISLATIVE ASPECTS

1. World Shipping Conditions

2. 1986 United Nations Convention on Conditions for Registration of Ships

3. Effects of "Offshore" Registers

4. Maritime Fraud

5. Consideration of a Draft Convention on Maritime Liens and Mortgages

1

World Shipping Conditions

United Nations Conference on Trade and Development   TD/B/C.4/309
Sales No. E.87.II.D.6
Extract

Review of Maritime Transport 1986
Report by the UNCTAD Secretariat

. . .

Chapter VII

OTHER DEVELOPMENTS

A.   United Nations Convention on a Code of Conduct for Liner Conferences

116.   During 1986 two countries became contracting parties to the Convention, which entered into force on 6 October 1983. Thus, at the end of 1986 the total number of contracting parties stood at 68,[31] accounting for about 50 per cent of relevant world tonnage. The UNCTAD secretariat has continued to give assistance to countries, on request, with respect to the implementation of the Code.

117.   Several documents regarding the implementation of the Code have been prepared by the UNCTAD secretariat.[32] A Review Conference on the Convention on a Code of Conduct for Liner Conference is to be convened in 1988 in accordance with the provisions of article 52 of the Convention.

B.   United Nations Convention on International Multimodal Transport of Goods

118.   The United Nations Convention on International Multimodal Transport of Goods,[33] which was adopted by consensus on 24 May 1980 by the United Nations Conference of Plenipotentiaries, was opened for signature in New York from 1 September 1980 to 31 August 1981 and has remained open for accession thereafter. It will enter into force 12 months after 30 States have become Contracting Parties by definitive signature, ratification or accession. By January 1987 four countries - namely Chile, Malawi, Mexico and Senegal - had ratified or acceded to the Convention, while three countries - namely Morocco, Norway and Venezuela - had signed the Convention subject to ratification.

C.   United Nations Convention on the Carriage of Goods by Sea

119.   This Convention,[34] which was adopted on 30 March 1978 by a conference of plenipotentiaries, was opened for signature in New York from 31 March 1978 to 30 April 1979

and has remained open for accession since then. It will enter into force 12 months after 20 States have become Contracting Parties by definitive signature, ratification or accession. By January 1987 11 countries, namely Barbados, Chile, Egypt, Hungary, Lebanon, Morocco, Romania, Senegal, Tunisia, Uganda and the United Republic of Tanzania, had ratified or acceded to the Convention.

D.   United Nations Conference on Conditions for Registration of Ships

120.   The United Nations Conference on Conditions for Registration of Ships held the fourth part of its session in Geneva from 20 January to 7 February 1986. The Conference was convened pursuant to General Assembly resolution 37/209 of 20 December 1982 to consider the adoption of an international agreement concerning the conditions under which vessels should be accepted on national shipping registers. The Conference completed its work by the adoption on 7 February 1986 of the United Nations Convention on Conditions for Registration of Ships.[35]

121.   The Convention was opened for signature from 1 May 1986 up to and including 30 April 1987 at the Headquarters of the United Nations in New York and will remain open for accession thereafter. The Convention will enter into force 12 months after the date on which not less than 40 States, the combined tonnage of which amounts to at least 25 per cent of world tonnage stipulated in annex III to the Convention, have become Contracting Parties to it.

122.   As at 30 April 1987, the Convention had been signed at United Nations Headquarters in New York by the following 13 States: Algeria, Bolivia, Cameroon, Côte d'Ivoire, Czechoslovakia, Egypt, Indonesia, Libyan Arab Jamahiriya, Mexico, Morocco, Poland, Senegal, and the USSR.

E.   UNCTAD Committee on Shipping

123.   The UNCTAD Committee on Shipping held its twelfth regular session in Geneva from 10 to 21 November 1986. The two-week session was dominated by the problem of excess tonnage in world shipping and surplus world shipbuilding capacity. At the conclusion of the meeting four resolutions were unanimously adopted. In view of the importance of the problem of imbalance in world shipping, it was decided to schedule the next session of the Committee in early 1988 to consider primarily the imbalance between supply and demand in ocean shipping and to recommend practical measures to be taken in order to bring about a balanced situation in the shipping industry.

F.   UNCTAD model clauses on marine hull and cargo insurance

124.   At its twelfth session in November 1986, the Committee on Shipping decided to recommend to the Trade and Development Board that it endorse the UNCTAD non-mandatory model clauses on marine hull and cargo insurance as proposed by the Rapporteur of the Working Group on International Shipping Legislation which adopted the model clauses, and to instruct the UNCTAD secretariat, having assured the correspondence of the text in all languages, to circulate this version to the commercial parties concerned.

125.   The model clauses thus adopted are a truly international legal basis governing the rights and duties of parties to insurance contracts involving international seaborne trade. The model

clauses have maintained a degree of national market flexibility without losing the need for and the benefits gained from international uniformity.

126.   The UNCTAD secretariat has also been requested to prepare explanatory material in order to promote the use of the model clauses.

G.   Maritime liens and mortgages - Joint Intergovernmental Group of Experts on Maritime Liens and Mortgages and Related Subjects

127.   A Joint Intergovernmental Group of Experts on Maritime Liens and Mortgages and Related Subjects has been established by UNCTAD and IMO with a mandate to examine the subject of maritime liens and mortgages, including the possible consideration of:

(a)   The review of the maritime liens and mortgages Conventions and related enforcement procedures, such as arrest;

(b)   The preparation of model laws or guidelines on maritime liens, mortgages and related enforcement procedures, such as arrest;

(c)   The feasibility of an international registry of maritime liens and mortgages.

128.   The first session of the Joint Intergovernmental Group was held in Geneva from 1 to 12 December 1986 and featured a general debate on a number of issues, in particular: the maritime lien to be recognized internationally; identification of the essential characteristics of maritime liens and mortgages, including the need for definitions; relationship between liens and mortgages;   consequences of forced sale; review of enforcement procedures, such as arrest; need for a new international agreement or agreements.

H.   Maritime Fraud

130.   At its twelfth session in November 1986, the Committee on Shipping considered the reports prepared by the UNCTAD secretariat on the various subjects relating to ways and means to combat maritime fraud. The reports cover such subjects as:

Prevention of documentary fraud associated with bills of lading: use of sea waybills;

Measures to improve the exchange of shipping information: establishment of a Maritime Fraud Prevention Exchange;

Measures to increase co-operation in the investigation and prosecution of maritime fraud.

131.   The Committee on Shipping requested the UNCTAD secretariat to monitor the progress made in the establishment of a proposed Maritime Fraud Prevention Exchange, which would be a central collecting point co-ordinating the services of the participating organizations providing information and which would provide shipping interests with immediate access to the existing data banks. The Committee also requested the UNCTAD secretariat to report to it on the progress made in the development of a training programme, in co-operation with the relevant national and international organizations, on measures to combat maritime fraud.   In addition, the UNCTAD secretariat is also undertaking a

comparative study of the different minimum standards for shipping agents and the subsequent preparation of a draft set of standards for shipping agents.

I.   Ad Hoc Intergovernmental Group of Port Experts

132.   This Group was convened in response to decision 54 (XI) of the Committee on Shipping and met in Geneva from 25 February to 5 March 1986. A significant number of Governments sent experts to the meeting and a number of intergovernmental and non-governmental organizations active in the ports field were also present. Of the 46 States members participating, 37 sent officials from transport ministries, port authorities and training institutes. The meeting provided a unique opportunity to analyse, at the intergovernmental level, the problems facing ports in developing countries.

133.   This was the first intergovernmental meeting convened by UNCTAD solely to discuss ports. The secretariat's past programme of work in this field was thoroughly reviewed and recommendations were made for the future programme. The Group was of the opinion that the work carried out by the secretariat had been of great value to the port industry and particularly to ports in developing countries.

134.   The Group identified areas of research and training where further work was required by the secretariat and indicated priorities for this work. The Group recommended that UNCTAD's technical advisory service in the field of ports should be continued and if possible extended. The Group also requested that the dissemination of UNCTAD documents to port managers be improved. The Group prepared a report (TD/B/C.4/298) which was submitted to the twelfth session of the Committee on Shipping. The Committee took note of the report and requested the secretariat to adapt its work programme in the light of the Group's recommendations.

J.   Developments towards the establishment of a common shipping policy and as regards shipbuilding within EEC and OECD

135.   On 22 December 1986, after more than five years of deliberations aimed at the establishment of an EEC common maritime policy, the Council of the European Communities adopted four regulations designed to form the first stage of an EEC shipping policy. (The second stage will consider measures to be taken in order to strengthen the competitive position of the EEC shipping industry.)

136.   The regulations adopted foresee, *inter alia*:

(a)   The application of the principle of freedom to provide services to maritime transport between Member States and between Member States and third countries and the gradual phasing out of existing cargo-sharing arrangements and prohibition of cargo-sharing arrangements in any future agreements between Member States and third countries (subject to certain exemptions in exceptional circumstances);

(b)   Detailed rules for the application of EEC competition policy to maritime transport providing for the anti-trust exemption (exemption from the prohibition of Article 85 (1) of the Treaty of Rome) of liner conferences subject to certain conditions and obligations. The Commission is entrusted with monitoring the exempted agreements with a view to determining whether obligations are being fulfilled and conditions underlying the block exemption are being complied with;

(c)   The application by EEC of measures to protect European shipping from unfair pricing practices by third-country shipowners engaged in international liner shipping;

(d)   The taking of co-ordinated action by EEC countries against a non-Community country, which in accordance with its legislation restricts or threatens to restrict, in the opinion of the EEC Council, the free access of EEC shipping operators to international maritime trade.[36]

137.   The regulations concerning relations between the European Community and third countries and their shipping companies, as well as the application of co-ordinated actions of the EEC countries against them, will enter into force on 1 July 1987.

138.   In February 1987 the OECD Council approved a set of 13 principles concerning a common shipping policy, five of them dealing with a co-ordinated response of OECD countries to protectionist practices of non-member countries. The official recommendation adopted by OECD in this connection calls on member countries to "actively oppose the imposition of régimes which restrict the access to cargo moving internationally by shipping companies adhering to the principle of free competition on a commercial basis".[37]

139.   With respect to subsidies to shipbuilding, it was decided at a top level industry ministers' meeting in December 1986 to fix shipbuilding subsidy limits in the EEC countries at a maximum level of 28 per cent.[38] As regards subsidies to shipbuilding, it was also reported that a target date of end 1989 had been set by OECD for phasing out shipbuilding aid in the member States.[39]

. . .

Notes

. . .

31.   Algeria; Bangladesh; Barbados; Benin; Bulgaria; Cameroon; Cape Verde; Central African Republic; Chile; China; Congo; Costa Rica; Côte d'Ivoire; Cuba; Czechoslovakia;Denmark; Egypt; Ethiopia; Finland; France; Gabon; Gambia; German Democratic Republic; Germany, Federal Republic of; Ghana; Guatemala; Guinea; Guyana; Honduras; India; Indonesia; Iraq; Jamaica; Jordan; Kenya; Kuwait; Lebanon; Madagascar; Malaysia; Mali; Mauritius; Mexico; Morocco; Netherlands; Niger; Nigeria; Norway; Pakistan; Peru; Philippines; Republic of Korea; Romania; Saudi Arabia; Senegal; Sierra Leone; Sri Lanka; Sudan; Sweden; Togo; Trinidad and Tobago; Tunisia; Union of Soviet Socialist Republics; United Kingdom (also on behalf of Gibraltar and Hong Kong); United Republic of Tanzania; Uruguay; Zaire.

32.   Implementation of the United Nations Convention on a Code of Conduct for Liner Conferences (TD/B/C.4/300 and Corr.1); Guidelines towards the application of the Convention on a Code of Conduct for Liner Conferences (UNCTAD/ST/SHIP/1); Implementation of the United Nations Convention on a Code of Conduct for Liner Conferences - Supplemental material (UNCTAD/ST/SHIP/2). These documents are available from the UNCTAD secretariat upon request.

33.   For the text of the Convention, see United Nations Conference on a Convention on International Maritime Transport, vol. I, Final Act and Convention on International Multimodal Transport of Goods (United Nations publication, Sales No. E.81.II.D.7 (vol.I)).

34.   For the text of the Convention, see United Nations Conference on the Carriage of Goods by Sea (United Nations publication, Sales No. E.80.VIII.1).

35.   The text of the Convention is contained in document TD/RS/CONF/23, which is available from the UNCTAD secretariat upon request.

36.   The text of the regulations (Council Regulations (EEC) Nos. 4055, 4056, 4057 and 4058 of 22 December 1986) is contained in Official Journal of the European Communities, L 378, of 31 December 1986.

37.   Lloyd's List (London), 18 February 1987. For the full text of the recommendation and the principles, as well as observations and reservations by member States, see OECD document C(87)11 (Final) of 20 February 1987 (General distribution).

38.   Lloyd's List (London), 23 December 1986.
39.   Fairplay International (London), 17 July 1986.
    . . .

- - - - -

International Labour Conference   ILO Report I
74th (Maritime) Session 1987   Extract

Report of the Director-General

CHAPTER 1. EVOLUTION IN THE SHIPPING INDUSTRY AND TRANSITION IN THE EMPLOYMENT OF SEAFARERS

EVOLUTION IN THE SHIPPING INDUSTRY

. . .

Overtonnage

There have been few sectors of the shipping industry which have not experienced a surplus of ships during the past decade. The causes of this phenomenon are complex. It has already been mentioned that the present oversupply of shipping is largely due to the combined effects of structural changes in industries using large numbers of ships and cyclical downturns which are characteristic of shipping. Furthermore, a lengthy period of inflation and high interest rates, coupled with government guarantees for ship purchases, encouraged many financial institutions to finance the building of ships.

Table 1.	Laid-up tonnage, 1976-86 annual averages	
Year	No. of Ships	Millions dwt
1976	595	35.71
1977	657	43.16
1978	593	30.15
1979	411	11.06
1980	402	9.19
1981	527	27.39
1982	1549	83.76
1983	1663	79.82
1984	1195	64.36
1985	884	48.59
1986	775	35.95

Source: Institute of Shipping Economics and Logistics, Bremen.

Another important cause has been the overcapacity and over expansion of the world's shipbuilding industry, caused in the first place by the demand for large ships in the early seventies and then by the sudden disappearance of this demand after the first petroleum crisis. The sellers' market for ships disappeared in the second half of the 1970s and governments the world over were suddenly faced with the need to support shipbuilding industries which had been forced to cut prices drastically. As employers of large numbers of people, the shipbuilders were successful in attracting government support and favourable credit terms. A number of new shipbuilding industries in certain countries obtained a large share of world ship orders, mainly because of low prices. It was not until very recently that many governments changed their policies of supporting their shipbuilding industries, causing widespread closures of shipyards throughout the world.

Overtonnage can also be traced to the overestimation of demand for dry-bulk carriers, owing to inaccurate forecast of growth in the carriage of coal. Technical changes also led to the oversupply of ships, as replacement tonnage was ordered without scrapping existing ships, far too many of which were sold for further trading.

Also contributing to global overcapacity was the growth in a number of new fleets, as countries not previously associated with ship owning sought to carry a substantial part of their trade in their own ships. The growth in the number of countries offering attractive ship registration conditions, coupled with fiscal incentives to build ships, also encouraged individuals and companies to enter ship operation, adding to the overcapacity. Table 1 indicates the extent of overcapacity.

Changes in size and composition of national fleets

The Report of the Director-General to the 1976 Maritime Session noted that, with few exceptions, the years from 1970 to 1975 had seen virtually all maritime countries increase their fleet tonnages, although the relative growth of the fleets of OECD countries had been very modest. During the following ten years the fleets of the industrialised countries were reduced both in number of ships and tonnage, while the share of the open registry and the developing countries increased. Appendix I shows changes in the size of the merchant fleets of individual countries from 1976 to 1986.

While the flag that a ship flies had in the past generally indicated the nationality of its ownership, the increasing complexity of ship ownership makes the comparison of the sizes of national fleets more difficult. Although the nationality of a major shipping company, public corporation or government shipping line is readily identified, that of a ship owned by an

Table 2.   Merchant fleets of open registry countries (ships of 100 tons gross and upwards)

Country	1976 No. of ships	Millions dwt	1986 No. of ships	Millions dwt
Bahamas	119	0.21	302	10.60
Bermuda	67	2.72	97	1.76
Cyprus	765	4.54	940	18.76
Liberia	2600	142.35	1658	101.59
Panama	2680	25.47	5252	68.35

Source: Lloyd's Register of Shipping: Statistical tables, 1976 & 1986.

international group, financial institution or a small operator is far less so. The flag, whether that of an open registry or even one of the established shipping nations, increasingly gives little indication of a vessel's beneficial ownership.

Nevertheless, even though a high proportion of beneficial ownership of ships has been maintained in the developed industrialised countries, the past five years have seen a great acceleration in the re-registration of ships to less expensive registries, at the expense of the traditional shipping nations. A good part of these flag transfers have been to open registry countries. Table 2 shows the change from 1976 to 1986 in the size of the merchant fleets of the five largest open registry countries, namely Bahamas, Bermuda, Cyprus, Liberia and Panama.

Some of the main reasons for re-registration seem to be the following:

(a)   Taxes on income from the ships' operations are small or non-existent, while dues and fees are nowadays competitive between registers.

(b)   A ship may be registered or deleted from the registry with little formality, and beneficial ownership usually remains confidential.

(c)   The ships can be manned by foreign crews at a lower cost, and nationality requirements for crews are seldom imposed on owners or managers.

(d)   The country of registration has limited powers to enforce national or international regulations concerning the operation of ships.

The combination of lower costs and freedom of operations prove attractive to many owners. Lower crew costs, in particular, generally give the operator substantial advantages.

While there has been an increase in the size of fleets operated by developing maritime countries, this growth has been rather more modest than was generally held some years ago, owing to national economic constraints, a lack of finance for ship procurement and a reluctance of financial institutions to assist unsuccessful shipping projects. There has been a steady growth in joint ventures, although economic conditions have not encouraged such arrangements.

The type of ships operated by the developing maritime countries has also changed. Many high-speed liner ships, which the changing technology of containers and the high price of bunkers had made uneconomical to operate, were sold to developing maritime nations. When difficulties were encountered in running them, more suitable ships were acquired later.

Regulation of national flag shipping in the form of cargo preference measures and other forms of protection and intervention has been a growing feature of shipping during the past ten years; this is not surprising, bearing in mind the poor state of the demand for shipping services during most of this period.

Together with the shift of registration, the decline of the Western European, North American and Japanese fleets and the expansion of shipping in developing countries, there has been a growth in the fleets of Eastern European countries and China. The fleets of the USSR and the German Democratic Republic have been modernized and China's new fleet has made the country practically self-sufficient in shipping.

The advance of technology

The past ten years, though adverse for the shipping industry, have seen a continuing introduction of new technology. However, there has been a considerable change in emphasis from previous years. As the demand for new VLCCs and ULCCs dwindled, a greater emphasis was placed on the improvement of efficiency. The industry has focused the greater part of its efforts on the reduction of operating costs to compensate for the surplus of most types of ships and greatly reduced freight rates. The vessel built in 1987 will probably be not much larger than that of the previous decade, but it will be more efficient, owing to the use of more economical machinery and better hydrodynamics, and it will operate with a smaller crew, thanks to increased automation.

Nevertheless, the construction of large ships, which was particularly characteristic of the tanker sector during the early 1970s, has in many respects been imitated in most other sectors. Certain dry-bulk trades, notably for steam coal, coking coal and iron ore, which depend heavily on long-term contracts, have also favoured very large, specialised ships in recent years. In the liner trades the average size of deep-sea container liners has steadily climbed from the typical first generation 1,200-1,500 20-foot equivalent container unit (TEU) vessel, to that of newer ships capable of carrying upwards of 3,000 containers. Ferries, other specialised ships and even short-sea bulkers have also followed this trend.

But it is in the containment of running costs, prompted by the increase in the cost of fuel, that the most spectacular advances have been made. Most significant has been the move away from the steam turbine as a prime mover for large ships, in favour of the marine diesel; the considerable refinement of the diesel has enabled ships to operate more efficiently on lower quality fuel. This has been achieved largely through significant improvements in the thermal efficiency of machinery and in the reduction of waste heat, and by integrating the main machinery and some of the auxiliaries into a highly efficient unit. Together with other advances such as more efficient propellers and hulls, it has been possible to reduce fuel consumption significantly.

The effect of extensive automation on the size of crews employed on most modern ships has also been considerable. For instance four 50,000 dwt ships of the previous generation would probably employ upwards of 200 seafarers (including leave arrangements). Today's newer 200,000 dwt units can do the same effective work with a fraction of the crew required by the smaller ships. This dramatic reduction has been achieved by a combination of factors. Mechanical and structural maintenance, which required a substantial number of man-hours on less advanced tonnage, has been reduced: the former by more efficient machinery requiring less on-board maintenance, and the latter by such advances as long-life paint coatings and better tools. (Maintenance work has been minimised also by the use of shore-based riding repair teams.) The number of crew members on watchkeeping duties has been reduced by reliance on electronic surveillance and alarm systems, and permitted a greater use of unmanned machinery spaces on virtually every type of modern ship. A single watchkeeper overseeing the entire ship systems from the bridge, generally assisted by a lookout, has become the norm. Peak manpower demands for mooring and unmooring have been reduced by more advanced mooring equipment and the use of multi-skilled ratings from other duties.

The changing nature of modern shipping has also contributed to crew reductions. With container ships and large bulk carriers, much of the onus of cargo supervision, paperwork and planning has been removed from the ships' staff and has become the responsibility of shore people. Although there are specialised ship types which carry considerable amounts of cargo-handling equipment, the tendency is towards greater reliance on terminal equipment and personnel for cargo handling.

Much of the recent emphasis on the development of more efficient port equipment enables a ship to be turned around faster; high-capacity bulk loading and unloading equipment and more efficient container gantry cranes have been developed to service larger bulk carriers and containerships. While the unit size of the container has been constrained by the size of box that can be accommodated on a road trailer or rail wagon, there has been a tendency to look for ways to move beyond the 20 to 40-foot norm.

In the field on navigation much has been made of the development of computer-assisted collision avoidance radars and the increasingly widespread use of navigation equipment using satellites. But even more significant has been the effect of satellite communications and the use of telex and other forms of data transmission, which have all but made the ship an extension of the ship operator's office. This is an area of great interest which will develop significantly in the next few years, and will affect training, education and the working procedures of ship and shore staff alike.

Recent reductions in the price of bunkers may well reduce the emphasis on fuel conservation, but the trend towards still smaller crews is likely to continue. Changes in shipboard organisation and new developments in the reduction of maintenance work are favoured by shipowners seeking competitive advantages.

There is little doubt that technical developments in the shipping industry have had far-reaching effects on the life of the seafarer. For example, while long sea voyages punctuated by short port stays used to be characteristic of tankermen only, today such a situation is typical of seafarers on many types of ships. While ratings capable of working either in the engine room or on deck are common, the difference between the work of navigating and engineering officers continues to diminish in a number of countries. Also, the advent of modern communications has considerably changed the job of the radio officer.

Management changes

The past decade has seen considerable changes in shipping management. Many ship-owning companies which previously supported an extensive in-house structure for the crewing, operation and technical support of their fleets have contracted these activities to ship management firms, crewing agencies, technical maintenance firms and consultants. In addition, shipping companies have hired on ship managers by drawing on surplus shore staff to manage the ships of others, their own fleets having been reduced or sold. The growth of the open registries had tended to encourage this "third party" management, and has given a boost to crewing agencies supplying foreign sea staff to operators running ships under such flags. The supplying of crews has proved attractive to certain countries, as evidenced by the growth of crewing agencies.

Government involvement

Poor trading conditions have traditionally gone hand in hand with an increase in state intervention; the decade under review has been no exception. Governments which have given their support to the establishment of new shipping lines, particularly in developing countries, have felt obliged to intervene to maintain them with subsidy, cargo direction and other protective measures. There has been much emphasis on the protection of shipbuilders, with the provision of favourable credit, soft loans and other fiscal measures to enable threatened yards to obtain orders. There has been an increase in cabotage regulations which have constrained foreign shipping in order to support local coastal fleets.

Government intervention in the field of safety has also increased during the period under review. In particular, this is a consequence of a number of well-publicised catastrophes and growing public awareness of a substandard element in modern shipping operations. Accidents involving pollution of the sea and unqualified personnel on board ships have given rise to important new international standards, including the ILO's Merchant Shipping (Minimum Standards) Convention, 1976 (No. 147), the IMO's International Convention of Standards of Training, Certification and Watchkeeping for Seafarers, 1978, amendments to the International Convention for the Safety of Life at Sea, 1974, and the 1978 Protocol relating to the International Convention for the Prevention of Pollution from Ships, 1973. Similarly, accidents in certain coastal waters have encouraged the extension of traffic routing schemes, and few major ports are now without traffic management schemes for the control of shipping in their waters.

During the past decade international shipping has seen more inter-governmental co-operation and discussion than before, mainly as a result of growing concern over the operation of substandard ships and the difficulty which some flag States have experienced in regulating their ships. The Memorandum of Understanding on Port State Control signed by the maritime authorities of 14 European countries has been an effective deterrent to substandard ships in the ports of the region. During the first three years of this agreement almost 24,000 ships of more than 100 flags were inspected, and more than 1,130 ships were delayed or detained for defects to be made good. Approximately 10 per cent of the deficiencies related to crew conditions; the remainder concerned ship safety in general, including prevention of sea pollution. The effectiveness of such measures has been noted in other parts of the world and it is possible that the systematic inspection of ships by port States could well be established elsewhere.

Other areas of co-operation between European States have concerned vessel information and control, the development of standard practices for traffic management and the tracking of hazardous cargoes.

Regional co-operation is also evolving in other areas of the world, notably in South East Asia where members of the Association of South East Asian Nations (ASEAN) are active in both technical co-operation and the development of common policies. There is increasing intergovernmental co-operation in the Mediterranean on such subjects as marine pollution, and in the Baltic on ice and traffic management. Many other countries are co-operating in such fields as search and rescue.

. . .

- - - - -

Additional References

Major Issues in World Shipping (a) Merchant Fleet Development. UNCTAD report, Committee on Shipping, 12th session. TD/B/C.4/301.

Bibliography, 1983-1987. UNCTAD doc. TD/UNCTAD/CA/2857.

- - - - -

2

1986 United Nations Convention on
Conditions for Registration of Ships

United Nations Conference on Conditions   TD/RS/CONF/23
 for Registration of Ships

===

United Nations Convention on Conditions for Registration of Ships and Resolutions Adopted by the UN Conference on Conditions for Registration of Ships on 7 February 1986

The States Parties to this Convention,

Recognizing the need to promote the orderly expansion of world shipping as a whole,

Recalling General Assembly resolution 35/56 of 5 December 1980, the annex to which contains the International Development Strategy for the Third United Nations Development Decade, which called, *inter alia*, in paragraph 128, for an increase in the participation by developing countries in world transport of international trade,

Recalling also that according to the 1958 Geneva Convention on the High Seas and the 1982 United Nations Convention on the Law of the Sea there must exist a genuine link between a ship and a flag State and conscious of the duties of the flag State to exercise effectively its jurisdiction and control over ships flying its flag in accordance with the principle of the genuine link,

Believing that to this end a flag State should have a competent and adequate national maritime administration,

Believing also that in order to exercise its control function effectively a flag State should ensure that those who are responsible for the management and operation of a ship on its register are readily identifiable and accountable,

Believing further that measures to make persons responsible for ships more readily identifiable and accountable could assist in the task of combating maritime fraud,

Reaffirming, without prejudice to this Convention, that each State shall fix the conditions for the grant of its nationality to ships, for the registration of ships in its territory and for the right to fly its flag,

Prompted by the desire among sovereign States to resolve in a spirit of mutual understanding and co-operation all issues relating to the conditions for the grant of nationality to, and for the registration of, ships,

Considering that nothing in this Convention shall be deemed to prejudice any Provisions in the national laws and regulations of the Contracting Parties to this Convention, which exceed the provisions contained herein,

Recognizing the competences of the specialized agencies and other institutions of the United Nations system as contained in their respective constitutional instruments, taking into account arrangements which may have been concluded between the United Nations and the agencies, and between individual agencies and institutions in specific fields,

Have agreed as follows:

Article 1
Objectives

For the purpose of ensuring or, as the case may be, strengthening the genuine link between a State and ships flying its flag, and in order to exercise effectively its jurisdiction and control over such ships with regard to identification and accountability of shipowners and operators as well as with regard to administrative, technical, economic and social matters, a flag State shall apply the provisions contained in this Convention.

Article 2
Definitions

For the purposes of this Convention:

"Ship" means any self-propelled sea-going vessel used in international seaborne trade for the transport of goods, passengers, or both with the exception of vessels of less than 500 gross registered tons;

"Flag State" means a State whose flag a ship flies and is entitled to fly;

"Owner" or "shipowner" means, unless clearly indicated otherwise, any natural or juridical person recorded in the register of ships of the State of registration as an owner of a ship;

"Operator" means the owner or bareboat charterer, or any other natural or juridical person to whom the responsibilities of the owner or bareboat charterer have been formally assigned;

"State of registration" means the State in whose register of ships a ship has been entered;

"Register of ships" means the official register or registers in which particulars referred to in article 11 of this Convention are recorded;

"National maritime administration" means any State authority or agency which is established by the State of registration in accordance with its legislation and which, pursuant to that legislation, is responsible, *inter alia*, for the implementation of international agreements concerning maritime transport and for the application of rules and standards concerning ships under its jurisdiction and control;

"Bareboat charter" means a contract for the lease of a ship, for a stipulated period of time, by virtue of which the lessee has complete possession and control of the ship, including the right to appoint the master and crew of the ship, for the duration of the lease;

"Labour-supplying country" means a country which provides seafarers for service on a ship flying the flag of another country.

Article 3
Scope of application

This Convention shall apply to all ships as defined in article 2.

Article 4
General provisions

1.   Every State, whether coastal or land-locked, has the right to sail ships flying its flag on the high seas.

2.   Ships have the nationality of the State whose flag they are entitled to fly.

3.   Ships shall sail under the flag of one State only.

4.   No ships shall be entered in the registers of ships of two or more States at a time, subject to the provisions of paragraphs 4 and 5 of article 11 and to article 12.

5.   A ship may not change its flag during a voyage or while in a port of call, save in the case of a real transfer of ownership or change of registry.

Article 5
National Maritime Administration

1.   The flag State shall have a competent and adequate national maritime administration, which shall be subject to its jurisdiction and control.

2.   The flag State shall implement applicable international rules and standards concerning, in particular, the safety of ships and persons on board and the prevention of pollution of the marine environment.

3.   The maritime administration of the flag State shall ensure:

(a) That ships flying the flag of such State comply with its laws and regulations concerning registration of ships and with applicable international rules and standards concerning, in particular, the safety of ships and persons on board and the prevention of pollution of the marine environment;

(b) That ships flying the flag of such State are periodically surveyed by its authorized surveyors in order to ensure compliance with applicable international rules and standards;

(c) That ships flying the flag of such State carry on board documents, in particular those evidencing the right to fly its flag and other valid relevant documents, including those required by international conventions to which the State of registration is a Party;

(d) That the owners of ships flying the flag of such State comply with the principles of registration of ships in accordance with the laws and regulations of such State and the provisions of this Convention.

4. The State of registration shall require all the appropriate information necessary for full identification and accountability concerning ships flying its flag.

Article 6
Identification and accountability

1. The State of registration shall enter in its register of ships, *inter alia*, information concerning the ship and its owner or owners. Information concerning the operator, when the operator is not the owner, should be included in the register of ships or in the official record of operators to be maintained in the office of the Registrar or be readily accessible to him, in accordance with the laws and regulations of the State of registration. The State of registration shall issue documentation as evidence of the registration of the ship.

2. The State of registration shall take such measures as are necessary to ensure that the owner or owners, the operator or operators, or any other person or persons who can be held accountable for the management and operation of ships flying its flag can be easily identified by persons having a legitimate interest in obtaining such information.

3. Registers of ships should be available to those with a legitimate interest in obtaining information contained therein, in accordance with the laws and regulations of the flag State.

4. A State should ensure that ships flying its flag carry documentation including information about the identity of the owner or owners, the operator or operators or the person or persons accountable for the operation of such ships, and make available such information to port State authorities.

5. Log-books should be kept on all ships and retained for a reasonable period after the date of the last entry, notwithstanding any change in a ship's name, and should be available for inspection and copying by persons having a legitimate interest in obtaining such information, in accordance with the laws and regulations of the flag State. In the event of a ship being sold and its registration being changed to another State, log-books relating to the period before such sale should be retained and should be available for inspection and copying by persons having a legitimate interest in obtaining such information, in accordance with the laws and regulations of the former flag State.

6. A State shall take necessary measures to ensure that ships it enters in its register of ships have owners and operators who are adequately identifiable for the purpose of ensuring their full accountability.

7. A State should ensure that direct contact between owners of ships flying its flag and its government authorities is not restricted.

Article 7
Participation by nationals in the ownership and/or manning of ships

With respect to the provisions concerning manning and ownership of ships as contained in paragraphs 1 and 2 of article 8 and paragraphs 1 to 3 of article 9, respectively, and without prejudice to the application of any other provisions of this Convention, a State of registration has to comply either with the provisions of paragraphs 1 and 2 of article 8 or with the provisions of paragraphs 1 to 3 of article 9, but may comply with both.

Article 8
Ownership of ships

1.   Subject to the provisions of article 7, the flag State shall provide in its laws and regulations for the ownership of ships flying its flag.

2.   Subject to the provisions of article 7, in such laws and regulations the flag State shall include appropriate provisions for participation by that State or its nationals as owners of ships flying its flag or in the ownership of such ships and for the level of such participation. These laws and regulations should be sufficient to permit the flag State to exercise effectively its jurisdiction and control over ships flying its flag.

Article 9
Manning of ships

1.   Subject to the provisions of article 7, a State of registration, when implementing this Convention, shall observe the principle that a satisfactory part of the complement consisting of officers and crew of ships flying its flag be nationals or persons domiciled or lawfully in permanent residence in that State.

2.   Subject to the provisions of article 7 and in pursuance of the goal set out in paragraph 1 of this article, and in taking necessary measures to this end, the State of registration shall have regard to the following:

    (a)   the availability of qualified seafarers within the State of registration;

    (b)   multilateral or bilateral agreements or other types of arrangements valid and enforceable pursuant to the legislation of the State of registration;

    (c)   the sound and economically viable operation of its ships.

3.   The State of registration should implement the provision of paragraph 1 of this article on a ship, company or fleet basis.

4.   The State of registration, in accordance with its laws and regulations, may allow persons of other nationalities to serve on board ships flying its flag in accordance with the relevant provisions of this Convention.

5.   In pursuance of the goal set out in paragraph 1 of this article, the State of registration should, in co-operation with shipowners, promote the education and training of its nationals or persons domiciled or lawfully in permanent residence within its territory.

6. The State of registration shall ensure:

(a) that the manning of ships flying its flag is of such a level and competence as to ensure compliance with applicable international rules and standards, in particular those regarding safety at sea;

(b) that the terms and conditions of employment on board ships flying its flag are in conformity with applicable international rules and standards;

(c) that adequate legal procedures exist for the settlement of civil disputes between seafarers employed on ships flying its flag and their employers;

(d) that nationals and foreign seafarers have equal access to appropriate legal processes to secure their contractual rights in their relations with their employers.

Article 10
Role of flag States in respect of the management of
shipowning companies and ships

1. The State of registration, before entering a ship in its register of ships, shall ensure that the shipowning company or a subsidiary shipowning company is established and/or has its principal place of business within its territory in accordance with its laws and regulations.

2. Where the shipowning company or a subsidiary shipowning company or the principal place of business of the shipowning company is not established in the flag State, the latter shall ensure, before entering a ship in its register of ships, that there is a representative or management person who shall be a national of the flag State, or be domiciled therein. Such a representative or management person may be a natural or juridical person who is duly established or incorporated in the flag State, as the case may be, in accordance with its laws and regulations, and duly empowered to act on the shipowner's behalf and account. In particular, this representative or management person should be available for any legal process and to meet the shipowner's responsibilities in accordance with the laws and regulations of the State of registration.

3. The State of registration should ensure that the person or persons accountable for the management and operation of a ship flying its flag are in a position to meet the financial obligations that may arise from the operation of such a ship to cover risks which are normally insured in international maritime transportation in respect of damage to third parties. To this end the State of registration should ensure that ships flying its flag are in a position to provide at all times documents evidencing that an adequate guarantee, such as appropriate insurance or any other equivalent means, has been arranged. Furthermore, the State of registration should ensure that an appropriate mechanism, such as a maritime lien, mutual fund, wage insurance, social security scheme, or any governmental guarantee provided by an appropriate agency of the State of the accountable person, whether that person is an owner or operator, exists to cover wages and related monies owed to seafarers employed on ships flying its flag in the event of default of payment by their employers. The state of registration may also provide for any other appropriate mechanism to that effect in its laws and regulations.

Article 11
Register of ships

1.   A State of registration shall establish a register of ships flying its flag, which register shall be maintained in a manner determined by that State and in conformity with the relevant provisions of this Convention. Ships entitled by the laws and regulations of a State to fly its flag shall be entered in this register in the name of the owner or owners or, where national laws and regulations so provide, the bareboat charterer.

2.   Such register shall, *inter alia*, record the following:

   (a)   the name of the ship and the previous name and registry if any;

   (b)   the place or port of registration or home port and the official number or mark of identification of the ship;

   (c)   the international call sign of the ship, if assigned;

   (d)   the name of the builders, place of build and year of building of the ship;

   (e)   the description of the main technical characteristics of the ship;

   (f)   the name, address and, as appropriate, the nationality of the owner or of each of the owners;

and, unless recorded in another public document readily accessible to the Registrar in the flag State:

   (g)   the date of deletion or suspension of the previous registration of the ship;

   (h)   the name, address and, as appropriate, the nationality of the bareboat charterer, where national laws and regulations provide for the registration of ships bareboat chartered-in;

   (i)   the particulars of any mortgages or other similar charges upon the ship as stipulated by national laws and regulations;

3.   Furthermore, such register should also record:

   (a)   if there is more than one owner, the proportion of the ship owned by each;

   (b)   the name, address and, as appropriate, the nationality of the operator, when the operator is not the owner or the bareboat charterer.

4.   Before entering a ship in its register of ships a State should assure itself that the previous registration, if any, is deleted.

5.   In the case of a ship bareboat chartered-in a State should assure itself that right to fly the flag of the former flag State is suspended. Such registration shall be effected on production of evidence, indicating suspension of previous registration as regards the nationality of the ship under the former flag State and indicating particulars of any registered encumbrances.

Article 12
Bareboat charter

1.   Subject to the provisions of article 11 and in accordance with its laws and regulations a State may grant registration and the right to fly its flag to a ship bareboat chartered-in by a charterer in that State, for the period of that charter.

2.   When shipowners or charterers in States Parties to this Convention enter into such bareboat charter activities, the conditions of registration contained in this Convention should be fully complied with.

3.   To achieve the goal of compliance and for the purpose of applying the requirements of this Convention in the case of a ship so bareboat chartered-in the charterer will be considered to be the owner. This Convention, however, does not have the effect of providing for any ownership rights in the chartered ship other than those stipulated in the particular bareboat charter contract.

4.   A State should ensure that a ship bareboat chartered-in and flying its flag, pursuant to paragraphs 1 to 3 of this article, will be subject to its full jurisdiction and control.

5.   The State where the bareboat chartered-in ship is registered shall ensure that the former flag State is notified of the deletion of the registration of the bareboat chartered ship.

6.   All terms and conditions, other than those specified in this article, relating to the relationship of the parties to a bareboat charter are left to the contractual disposal of those parties.

Article 13
Joint ventures

1.   Contracting Parties to this Convention, in conformity with their national policies, legislation and the conditions for registration of ships contained in this Convention, should promote joint ventures between shipowners of different countries, and should, to this end, adopt appropriate arrangements, *inter alia*, by safeguarding the contractual rights of the parties to joint ventures, to further the establishment of such joint ventures in order to develop the national shipping industry.

2.   Regional and international financial institutions and aid agencies should be invited to contribute, as appropriate, to the establishment and/or strengthening of joint ventures in the shipping industry of developing countries, particularly in the least developed among them.

Article 14
Measures to protect the interests of labour-supplying countries

1.   For the purpose of safeguarding the interests of labour-supplying countries and of minimizing labour displacement and consequent economic dislocation, if any, within these countries, particularly developing countries, as a result of the adoption of this Convention, urgency should be given to the implementation, *inter alia*, of the measures as contained in Resolution 1 annexed to this Convention.

2.   In order to create favourable conditions for any contract or arrangement that may be entered into by shipowners or operators and the trade unions of seamen or other representative seamen bodies, bilateral agreements may be concluded between flag States and labour-supplying countries concerning the employment of seafarers of those labour-supplying countries.

Article 15
Measures to minimize adverse economic effects

For the purpose of minimizing adverse economic effects that might occur within developing countries, in the process of adapting and implementing conditions to meet the requirements established by this Convention, urgency should be given to the implementation, *inter alia*, of the measures as contained in Resolution 2 annexed to this Convention.

Article 16
Depositary

The Secretary-General of the United Nations shall be the depositary of this Convention.

Article 17
Implementation

1.   Contracting Parties shall take any legislative or other measures necessary to implement this Convention.

2.   Each Contracting Party shall, at appropriate times, communicate to the depositary the texts of any legislative or other measures which it has taken in order to implement this Convention.

3.   The depositary shall transmit upon request to Contracting Parties the texts of the legislative or other measures which have been communicated to him pursuant to paragraph 2 of this article.

Article 18
Signature, ratification, acceptance, approval and accession

1.   All States are entitled to become Contracting Parties to this Convention by:

   (a)   signature not subject to ratification, acceptance or approval; or

   (b)   signature subject to and followed by ratification, acceptance or approval; or

   (c)   accession.

2.   This Convention shall be open for signature from 1 May 1986 to and including 30 April 1987, at the Headquarters of the United Nations in New York and shall thereafter remain open for accession.

3.   Instruments of ratification, acceptance, approval or accession shall be deposited with the depositary.

Article 19
Entry into force

1.   This Convention shall enter into force 12 months after the date on which not less than 40 States, the combined tonnage of which amounts to at least 25 per cent of world tonnage, have become Contracting Parties to it in accordance with article 18. For the purpose of this article the tonnage shall be deemed to be that contained in annex III to this Convention.

2.   For each State which becomes a Contracting Party to this Convention after the conditions for entry into force under paragraph 1 of this article have been met, the Convention shall enter into force for that State 12 months after that State has become a Contracting Party.

Article 20
Review and amendments

1.   After the expiry of a period of eight years from the date of entry into force of this Convention, a Contracting Party may, by written communication addressed to the Secretary-General of the United Nations, propose specific amendments to this Convention and request the convening of a review conference to consider such proposed amendments. The Secretary-General shall circulate such communication to all Contracting Parties. If, within 12 months from the date of the circulation of the communication, not less than two-fifths of the Contracting Parties reply favourably to the request, the Secretary-General shall convene the Review Conference.

2.   The Secretary-General of the United Nations shall circulate to all Contracting Parties the texts of any proposals for, or views regarding, amendments, at least six months before the opening date of the Review Conference.

Article 21
Effect of amendments

1.   The decisions of a review conference regarding amendments shall be taken by consensus or, upon request, by a vote of a two-thirds majority of the Contracting Parties present and voting. Amendments adopted by such a conference shall be communicated by the Secretary-General of the United Nations to all the Contracting Parties for ratification, acceptance, or approval and to all the States signatories of the Convention for information.

2.   Ratification, acceptance or approval of amendments adopted by a review conference shall be effected by the deposit of a formal instrument to that effect with the depositary.

3.   Any amendment adopted by a review conference shall enter into force only for those Contracting Parties which have ratified, accepted or approved it, on the first day of the month following one year after its ratification, acceptance or approval by two-thirds of the Contracting Parties. For any State ratifying, accepting or approving an amendment after it has been ratified, accepted or approved by two-thirds of the Contracting Parties, the amendment shall enter into force one year after its ratification, acceptance or approval by that State.

4.   Any State which becomes a Contracting Party to this Convention after the entry into force of an amendment shall, failing an expression of a different intention by that State:

(a) Be considered as a Party to this Convention as amended; and

(b)   Be considered as a Party to the unamended Convention in relation to any Contracting Party not bound by the amendment.

Article 22
Denunciation

1.   Any Contracting Party may denounce this Convention at any time by means of a notification in writing to this effect addressed to the depositary.

2.   Such denunciation shall take effect on the expiration of one year after the notification is received by the depositary, unless a longer period has been specified in the notification.

IN WITNESS WHEREOF the undersigned, being duly authorized thereto, have affixed their signatures hereunder on the dates indicated.

DONE at Geneva on 7 February 1986 in one original in the Arabic, Chinese, English, French, Russian and Spanish languages, all texts being equally authentic.

ANNEX I

Resolution 1
Measures to protect the interests of labour-supplying countries

The United Nations Conference on Conditions for Registration of Ships,

Having adopted the United Nations Convention on Conditions for Registration of ships,

Recommends as follows:-

1.   Labour-supplying countries should regulate the activities of the agencies within their jurisdiction that supply seafarers for ships flying the flag of another country in order to ensure that the contractual terms offered by those agencies will prevent abuses and contribute to the welfare of seafarers. For the protection of their seafarers, labour-supplying countries may require, *inter alia*, suitable security of the type mentioned in article 10 from the owners or operators of ships employing such seafarers or from other appropriate bodies;

2.   Labour-supplying developing countries may consult each other in order to harmonize as much as possible their policies concerning the conditions upon which they will supply labour in accordance with these principles and may, if necessary, harmonize their legislation in this respect;

3.   The United Nations Conference on Trade and Development, the United Nations Development Programme and other appropriate international bodies should upon request provide assistance to labour-supplying developing countries for establishing appropriate legislation for registration of ships and attracting ships to their registers, taking into account this Convention;

4.   The International Labour Organization should upon request provide assistance to labour-supplying countries for the adoption of measures in order to minimize labour displacement

and consequent economic dislocation, if any, within labour-supplying countries which might result from the adoption of this Convention;

5.   Appropriate international organizations within the United Nations system should upon request provide assistance to labour-supplying countries for the education and training of their seafarers, including the provision of training and equipment facilities.

ANNEX II

Resolution 2
Measures to minimize adverse economic effects

The United Nations Conference on Conditions for Registration of Ships,

Having adopted the United Nations Convention on Conditions for Registration of Ships,

Recommends as follows:-

1.   The United Nations Conference on Trade and Development, the United Nations Development Programme and the International Maritime Organization and other appropriate international bodies should provide, upon request, technical and financial assistance to those countries which may be affected by this Convention in order to formulate and implement modern and effective legislation for the development of their fleet in accordance with the provisions of this Convention;

2.   The International Labour Organization and other appropriate international organizations should also provide, upon request, assistance to those countries for the preparation and implementation of educational and training programmes for their seafarers as may be necessary;

3.   The United Nations Development Programme, the World Bank and other appropriate international organizations should provide to those countries, upon request, technical and financial assistance for the implementation of alternative national development plans, programmes and projects to overcome economic dislocation which might result from the adoption of this Convention.

ANNEX III

Merchant fleets of the world
Ships of 500 grt and above
As at 1 July 1985

	Gross registered tons (grt)
Albania	52,698
Algeria	1,332,863
Angola	71,581
Argentina	2,227,252
Australia	1,877,560

Austria	134,225
Bahamas	3,852,385
Bahrain	26,646
Bangladesh	300,151
Barbados	4,034
Belgium	2,247,571
Benin	2,999
Bolivia	14,913
Brazil	5,935,899
Bulgaria	1,191,419
Burma	94,380
Cameroon	67,057
Canada	841,048
Cape Verde	8,765
Chile	371,468
China	10,167,450
Colombia	357,668
Comoros	649
Costa Rica	12,616
Côte d'Ivoire	124,706
Cuba	784,664
Cyprus	8,134,083
Czechoslovakia	184,299
Democratic Kampuchea	998
Democratic Yemen	4,229
Denmark	4,677,360
Djibouti	2,066
Dominica	500
Dominican Republic	35,667
Ecuador	417,372
Egypt	835,995
Equatorial Guinea	6,412
Ethiopia	54,499
Faeroe Islands	39,333
Fiji	20,145
Finland	1,894,485
France	7,864,931
Gabon	92,687
Gambia	1,597
German Democratic Republic	1,235,840
Germany, Federal Republic of	5,717,767
Ghana	99,637
Greece	30,751,092
Guatemala	15,569
Guinea	598
Guyana	3,888
Honduras	301,786
Hungary	77,182
Iceland	69,460
India	6,324,145

Indonesia 1,604,427
Iran (Islamic Republic of) 2,172,401
Iraq 882,715
Ireland 161,304
Israel 541,035
Italy 8,530,108
Jamaica 7,473
Japan 37,189,376
Jordan 47,628
Kenya 1,168
Kiribat 1,480
Korea, Democratic People's Republic of 470,592
Korea, Republic of 6,621,898
Kuwait 2,311,813
Lebanon 461,525
Liberia 57,985,747
Libyan Arab Jamahiriya 832,450
Madagascar 63,115
Malaysia 1,708,599
Maldives 125,958
Malta 1,836,948
Mauritania 1,581
Mauritius 32,968
Mexico 1,282,048
Monaco 3,268
Morocco 377,702
Mozambique 17,013
Nauru 64,829
Netherlands 3,628,871
New Zealand 266,285
Nicaragua 15,869
Nigeria 396,525
Norway 14,567,326
Oman 10,939
Pakistan 429,973
Panama 39,366,187
Papua New Guinea 10,671
Paraguay 38,440
Peru 640,968
Philippines 4,462,291
Poland 2,966,534
Portugal 1,280,065
Qatar 339,725
Rumania 2,769,937
Saint Vincent and the Grenadines 220,490
Samoa 25,644
Saudi Arabia 2,868,689
Senegal 19,426
Singapore 6,385,919
Solomon Islands 1,018

Somalia	22,802
South Africa	501,386
Spain	5,650,470
Sri Lanka	617,628
Sudan	92,700
Suriname	11,181
Sweden	2,951,227
Switzerland	341,972
Syrian Arab Republic	40,506
Tanzania, United Republic of	43,471
Thailand	550,585
Togo	52,677
Tonga	13,381
Trinidad and Tobago	9,370
Tunisia	274,170
Turkey	3,532,350
Uganda	3,394
Union of Soviet Socialist Republics	16,767,526
United Arab Emirates	805,318
United Kingdom of Great Britain and Northern Ireland	13,260,290
Bermuda	969,081
British Virgin Islands	1,939
Cayman Islands	313,755
Gibraltar	568,247
Hong Kong	6,820,100
Montserrat	711
Saint Helena	3,150
Turks and Caicos Islands	513
Total	21,937,786
United States of America	13,922,244
Uruguay	144,907
Vanuatu	132,979
Venezuela	900,305
Viet Nam	277,486
Yugoslavia	2,648,415
Zaire	70,127
Unallocated	4,201,669
World Total	383,533,282

Source: Compiled on the basis of data supplied by Lloyd's Shipping Information Services (London).

Notes

(i)   Types of ship included:
Oil tankers; oil/chemical tankers; chemical tankers; miscellaneous tankers (trading); liquified gas carriers; bulk/oil carriers (including ore/oil); ore and bulk carriers; general cargo ships; containerships (fully cellular and lighter carriers); vehicle carriers; ferries and passenger ships and passenger/cargo ships; livestock carriers.

(ii)   Excluding the reserve fleet of the United States of America and the United States and Canadian Great Lakes Fleets.

- - - - -

Report of the United Nations Conference on   TD/RS/CONF/24
Conditions for Registration of Ships, November 1986   Extract

. . .
Closing Statement at the Fourth Part of the Conference
. . .

205.   The **President** said that the unanimous agreement on the adoption of the United Nations Convention on Conditions for Registration of Ships was an outstanding event.   The Conference had aligned itself with the movement towards a new and more just international maritime order - an essential component of a more balanced new world order - in that throughout its work it had shown itself to be fully conscious of that fundamental requirement expressed in the mandate entrusted to it by United Nations General Assembly resolution 37/209 of 20 December 1982, and that it had always been guided by a respect for the principles of that new order.   The Conference had thus made a major contribution to the emergence of that new international maritime order with the four-fold aim of:

(a)   Increasing or, where appropriate, strengthening safety, discipline, transparency and responsibility in the maritime world and in maritime practices;

(b)   Creating conditions in which shipping would help to bring about the desired expansion of world trade, in an even more orderly and balanced way;

(c)   Imbuing international relations in the vast area of shipping with a renewed spirit of co-operation, characterized by mutual understanding and confidence, and,

(d)   Promoting, through such renewed co-operation, greater and more effective third-world participation in activities directly or indirectly related to world shipping.

Clearly, in these times of surplus maritime tonnage and economic disorder and injustice, international action was imperative if there was to be a more balanced and orderly development of world shipping.

206.   In establishing by international consensus a set of rules and principles on ship registration so as to create a genuine link between the ship and the flag State, the Convention would in fact do a great deal to help set up a system based on justice, respect for legitimate interests, solidarity and, above all, dialogue.   Eighteen months had elapsed since the opening of the United Nations Conference on Conditions for Registration of Ships, during which time the participants had discovered together, session after session, and in contacts between sessions, the enormous difficulty and considerable importance of the mandate entrusted to them by the General Assembly - namely, to agree upon a set of rules and principles on ship registration in order to create a genuine link between the ship and the flag State, a link enabling the flag State to exercise effectively its jurisdiction and control over the ship flying its flag.   An impossible task, some would have said.   It was certainly an overwhelming one.   It had been a genuine gamble to take up so great a challenge in the face of such highly conflicting interests, deep divergences of approach and substantial risks and obstacles in the way of reconciling the views of all concerned.   His confidence had been restored, however, in the unique forum constituted by the United Nations, the result of the efforts of all the members of

the international community to build a more just, interdependent and fraternal world. In accomplishing its task, the Conference had also paid a welcome tribute to the Côte d'Ivoire and its illustrious leader, His Excellency President Houphouët-Boigny. He also praised the role played by the UNCTAD secretariat, its prestige and quality, its readiness to make available to the Conference its own incomparable forum, in which States strove ceaselessly to agree on solutions to the genuine problems of trade and economic development upon which mankind's peace and happiness depended.

207.   He recalled that, after the mission in late 1984 to establish contact with the authorities of many States and interest groups represented at the Conference, the Conference had determined the seven constituent elements of a genuine link between the ship and its flag State, namely:

(a)   The national maritime register;
(b)   The national maritime laws and regulations;
(c)   The national maritime administration;
(d)   The transparency and responsibility of the real owners and operators of ships;
(e)   National participation in the manning of ships;
(f)   National participation in the ownership of ships;
(g)   National participation in the management of shipowning or ship-operating companies.

208.   The Conference had then concluded that, of these seven elements, the last three were essential. The negotiations had centred in these three crucial points and it was around those points that the agreement had been worked out, gradually and arduously no doubt, but fully and in record time.

209.   Referring to the major concessions which, by the second part of the Conference, had broken the stalemate in a situation which had become critical, he said that the concession made by the Group of 77 was the proposal of a package which included a choice between compulsory national participation in the manning of ships and compulsory national participation in the ownership of ships. The concession made by Group B had lain in its willingness from that point onward to negotiate an international agreement, and not, as it had first intended, merely a set of recommendations, which would have greatly reduced the meaning and scope of the work, of the Conference. Group D and China had made concessions on positions of principle, and had shown a positive attitude throughout the negotiations.

210.   What were the major features of the United Nations Convention on Conditions for Registration of Ships which the international community had now arrived at by unanimous agreement of all States Parties? The new Convention resulted from a number of necessary and useful compromises - necessary because they had been called for by General Assembly resolution 37/209 establishing the Conference, useful because they were the prerequisite and *sine qua non* of the success of the Conference. That was the first basic point, compromises had had to be made. Compromises between the interests of the countries of the North and those of the South aspiring to greater prosperity and a greater presence on the seas, between the interests of the suppliers of maritime labour and skills and the international shipping industry; between the interests of the countries with a liberal attitude to registration and the sea-faring developing countries. Thanks to this realistic approach, the Conference had been able to provide the flag States as well as the international community with a new and unique

legal instrument of great historical importance, without which no adequate and viable solutions could be found to any of the current major international shipping problems. That was a second basic point. For almost 30 years the world community had been searching for an internationally acceptable definition of the legal content of the concept of a genuine link. Today, that gap in the law had been filled. He emphasized, however, that the link thus defined was not an end in itself, but a tool available to States and to the international community in the pursuance of their activities and policies, a tool without which none of the current major problems of international shipping could be solved, whether they be questions relating to safety of ships at sea, the protection of the oceans and coasts; the serious problem of surplus world maritime tonnage and the closely related problem of the orderly expansion of international shipping; the movement to and fro of the production factors of international shipping, namely, manpower, capital, know-how and expertise, or all aspects and problems of maritime co-operation among all members of the international community, in particular the question of increased third-world participation in world maritime tonnage.

211.   He was, of course, aware that the new Convention would not radically and immediately change the face of the oceans or the underlying interplay of forces, but it did offer States and the international community an opportunity to bring about the necessary changes, one step at a time, by a gradual but irreversible process. He was convinced that, far from legitimizing current practices, the implementation of the Convention would result in a standardization of national maritime registers - i.e. their gradual transformation into a new type of register in line with the new and orderly international standards resulting from the work of the Conference. Moreover, the genuine link would serve as a tool for the further development of international maritime co-operation, which, through the combinations of interests implied by the constraints of the new Convention, would promote an increasing tendency towards the internationalization of national flags. This new conception of the flag would resemble neither the excessively rigid one of the traditional national flag, nor the excessively lax one of the free flag. The new flag, although everywhere linked to the flag State and able to contribute effectively to national development, would at the same time be more responsive to the evolution of the world shipping industry, and particularly to movements in production factors - factors that had to be evaluated and combined in a clear-sighted and responsible manner in the best interests of all parties concerned, of international development, and ultimately of mankind, as both the means and the end of that development.

. . .

- - - - -

UNCTAD Committee on Shipping   TD/B/1123-TD/B/C.4/307
Report of the 12th Session, November 1986   Extract

. . .

Annex I

RESOLUTIONS ADOPTED BY THE COMMITTEE ON SHIPPING AT ITS TWELFTH SESSION

. . .

(58(XII))   United Nations Convention on Conditions for Registration of Ships

The Committee on Shipping,

Noting the satisfactory outcome of the Conference, which adopted the United Nations Convention on Conditions for Registration of Ships on 7 February 1986 in Geneva,

1.   *Invites* all States which have not yet done so to consider signing the Convention which is open for signature until 30 April 1987 at the United Nations Headquarters in New York;

2.   *Invites* States members of UNCTAD to consider ratifying or acceding to the United Nations Convention on Conditions for Registration of Ships;

3.   *Invites* States members of UNCTAD, when in the process of becoming Contracting Parties and in order to facilitate the implementation of the Convention, to make efforts to refrain from taking steps which are not in conformity with the provisions of the Convention when in force;

4.   *Requests* the UNCTAD secretariat to provide, within existing resources, guidance upon request to Governments concerning the possible implementation of the Convention and to monitor progress made towards the ratification and implementation of the Convention or its provisions and to report periodically thereon to the Committee on Shipping.

- - - - -

IMO Assembly   A 15/30
15th Session, July 1987   Extract

Relations with the United Nations and the Specialized Agencies
Note by the Secretary-General

. . .

(e)   **IMO's participation in the United Nations Conference on Conditions for the Registration of Ships**

10.   As requested by the Council and endorsed by the Assembly at its fourteenth regular session, the Secretary-General made arrangements for IMO to be represented at the last phase of the Conference on Conditions for Registration of ships. The Conference concluded its work with the adoption, on 8 February 1986, of the United Nations Convention on Conditions for the Registration of Ships.   The Conference agreed to incorporate in the preamble of the new Convention a paragraph, as proposed by IMO, which recognized the competence of IMO and other specialized agencies and institutions of the United Nations system, as contained in their constitutional instruments, taking into account arrangements which may have been concluded between the United Nations and the agencies, and between individual agencies and institutions, in specific fields.

11.   The representative of IMO explained IMO's position that the international standards, rules and regulations referred to in the new Convention and dealing with maritime safety, the

competence of ships' personnel and the prevention of marine pollution from ships should be those adopted under the auspices of IMO, which is the organization with the universally recognized competence in these fields. It was also emphasized that the applicability of any such international rules or standards to particular countries should be in accordance with the terms of the relevant instruments in which the standards or rules appeared.

12.   In one of the two resolutions adopted by the Conference, the Conference recommended that IMO, along with UNCTAD and UNDP and other appropriate international bodies, should provide, upon request, technical and financial assistance to those countries which may be affected by the new Convention in order to formulate and implement modern and effective legislation for the development of their fleet in accordance with the provisions of the Convention. The Council noted this request and noted also the view of the Secretary-General that although IMO does not have independent resources to render "financial assistance" to States, the Organization can provide appropriate technical advisory services and assistance in areas within IMO's competence. This was on the assumption that suitable funding would be available from international and national donor agencies, and that requests for such services or assistance would be received from the States concerned in accordance with the applicable procedures.

    . . .

- - - - -

Additional References

Final Act of the Conference. TD/RS/CONF/22.

Composite text as at the close of the third part of the UN Conference on Conditions for Registration of Ships. UNCTAD doc. TD/RS/CONF/19/Add.1.

United Nations Conference on Conditions for Registration of Ships. Report of the Secretary-General of UNCTAD. UN doc. A/41/301.

- - - - -

3

Effects of "Offshore" Registers

IMO Assembly   A 15/5(b)/1
15th Session, November 1987   Extract

Consideration of the Report of the
Administrative, Financial and Legal Committees

. . .

CONSIDERATION OF THE IMPLICATIONS FOR IMO OF "OFFSHORE" REGISTERS

55. Committee I considered a report from the Secretary-General on the question of "offshore" registers and also took account of the comments of the Council. The Secretary-General noted that there was no clear definition of the term "offshore " registers, but for the purpose of consideration of the agenda item it was understood to mean registers established in territories for whose international relations a State was responsible, either with the same or different conditions of registration from those of the State itself.

56. It was noted that there were some implications of "offshore" registers for IMO. As regards the financial implications, note was taken of recent developments which would mean that, with effect from 1 January 1988, merchant shipping tonnage registered in all territories for whose international relations IMO Member States were responsible, would be included in the calculation of contributions to IMO. As regards the technical and related legal implications of the problem, Committee I took note of the Secretary-General's report that a questionnaire had been circulated to Member States and that a report on the responses received would be submitted to the Council for action, as appropriate.

57. In the discussions on this item, a comment was made to the effect that the question also had implications in relation to the implementation of the Declaration of the United Nations General Assembly on the Granting of Independence to Colonial Territories and Peoples. Committee I took note of this comment.

58. Committee I decided to recommend to the Plenary to take note, with satisfaction, that the financial implications of the problem of "offshore" registers had been resolved as far as IMO is concerned. The Plenary might also request the Council to review any technical and related legal implications of the problem, in the light of the report of the Secretary-General.

- - - - -

IMO Council   C/ES.14/10
14th Extraordinary Session, September 1987   Extract

Consideration of the Implications for IMO of "Offshore" Registers
Note by the Secretary-General

1.   At its fifty-eighth session the Council decided to add the agenda item "consideration of the implications for IMO of 'offshore' registers" to the provisional agenda for its fourteenth extraordinary session. The Council also decided to add the item to the provisional agenda of the fifteenth regular session of the Assembly.

2.   The term "offshore register" did not come into regular usage until recently, and there is no clearly agreed definition of its scope. For the purpose of this paper it is understood to mean registers established in territories for whose international relations a State is responsible, either with the same or different conditions of registration from those of the State itself.[1]

3.   One area in which there may be implications for IMO in "offshore registers" or "dual registers" is the question of the extension to ships under these registers of IMO conventions and/or compliance of ships under these registers with IMO conventions. Apart from its records of when a convention has been extended to a territory for whose international relations a State has responsibility, the Organization does not, however, have information on this subject. The Secretary-General has accordingly addressed a circular memorandum to all IMO Member States to enquire as to the current situation. The information gathered from responses received will be circulated in an addendum to this document.

4.   The second area in which there may be implications relates to the calculation of the annual contributions to the IMO regular budget. It will be recalled that under Assembly resolution A.550(13), a total of 90% of the contributions to IMO are based on the merchant tonnage of a Member state as shown in Lloyds Register of Shipping Statistical Tables. The remaining 10% is established by a method predominantly related to the scale of assessments of the United Nations. A copy of the Assembly resolution is attached giving the detailed method of calculation.

5.   The information relating to the tonnage of IMO Member states for purposes of contribution calculations is taken from the relevant line in table 1 of the annual edition of Lloyds Register of Shipping Statistical Tables. It has been the practice since the Statistical Tables were first used for contribution calculations in the earliest days of the Organization to take only the figure shown in the table pertaining to an IMO Member State, and not to include figures shown separately for tonnage registered in territories for whose international relations a Member state is responsible. Recent enquiries with Lloyds have however indicated that their practice does differ in respect of the recording of this information as between States, and the current position is outlined below.

(i)   In the case of all States but three, registrations in territories for whose international relations a State is responsible are included in the total for the registrations of the State and are not identified separately in the statistical Tables. It is understood that Lloyds also intend to adopt this practice in the case of "dual registers".

(ii)   The three remaining States are Denmark, the Netherlands and the United Kingdom.

(iii)   In the case of Denmark, tonnage for the Faroe islands (1986 figure 115.394 Gross Registered Tonnage (GRT)) is shown separately and not included in the figures for Denmark. This has been the case for many years.

(iv)   In the case of the Netherlands, the tonnage for Aruba (128,610 GRT in 1986) is identified separately and not included in the Netherlands. This has been the case, so far, for 1986 only.

(v)   Tonnage for certain territories for whose international relations the United Kingdom is responsible (total tonnage 4.2 million GRT in 1986) is shown under separate headings and not included in the United Kingdom tonnage figure. This has been the case for many years. In addition, Hong Kong is an Associate Member of IMO and therefore does not fall within the scope of this paper.

(vi)   For the States outlined above, it may be noted that not all territories for whose international relations responsibility is exercised are shown separately. In the case of the United Kingdom registrations in the Isle of Man and the Channel Islands are included in the United Kingdom figure. Similarly, registrations in the Netherlands Antilles are included in the Netherlands figure, and registrations in Greenland in the Denmark figure.

6.   The extent of the registrations noted in paragraphs 5(iii) to 5(v) for 1986 has not always been at its present levels. The figure slowly rose from 0.8 million GRT in 1970 to around 2 million in 1980, but fell back again to 0.9 million by 1982. Since then it has risen to the 1986 figure of about 4.5 million.

7.   It can be seen from the method of calculation of contributions at annex that if all registrations in paragraphs 5(iii) to 5(v) were to be included in the calculations of the contribution of the Member State itself, the tonnage contribution of all other Member states would decrease. In 1986, for example, the tonnage contribution of all other Members would have been reduced by just over 1%. The effect on the total contribution of Members would, of course, depend on the relationship between their basic contribution and their tonnage contribution. This would range from no effect at all for those Members with no tonnage assessment to almost the full effect of just over a 1% reduction for those Members with a large tonnage assessment and the minimum basic assessment. There would, of course, be an increase for the three Member States mentioned in paragraph 5.

     . . .

Note

1.   The term "offshore register" has also on occasions been used to describe the practice of a "dual register", which is understood to mean the establishment of an additional register within a State, but with different national conditions of registration from that of the main register.

- - - - -

4

Maritime Fraud

UNCTAD Committee on Shipping   TD/B/1123-TD/B/C.4/307
Report of the 12th Session, November 1986   Extract

. . .

Annex I

RESOLUTIONS ADOPTED BY THE COMMITTEE ON SHIPPING
AT ITS TWELFTH SESSION

(60 (XII))   **Multimodal transport and technological developments, ports, international shipping legislation, technical assistance and training and co-operation among developing countries**

The Committee on Shipping

Recalling Conference resolution 144 (VI) and Committee on Shipping resolutions 51 (XI), 53 (XI), 55 (XI) and decisions 52 (XI), 54 (XI) and 56 (XI),

Recalling also resolution 2(II) of the *Ad Hoc* Intergovernmental Group to Consider Means of Combating All Aspects of Maritime Fraud, including Piracy,

Taking note of the reports of the above meetings contained in documents TD/B/C.4/ISL/53 and TD/B/C.4/296 respectively,

Taking note also of the report of the *Ad Hoc* Intergovernmental Group of Port Experts contained in document TD/B/C.4/298 and annex I,

. . .

III

11.   *Requests* the UNCTAD secretariat;

(a)   To promote the early establishment of the proposed Maritime Fraud Prevention Exchange by the relevant international non-governmental and commercial organizations, and to monitor closely the progress made by participating in the meetings of the preparatory working group of its founder members and operating companies for this purpose, and to report to the Committee on Shipping;

(b)   To monitor the work on the subject of sea waybills, both in liner and tramp shipping, being carried out by the relevant international organizations and to report on the progress made to the Committee on Shipping;

(c)   To report to the Committee on Shipping on the progress made in the development of a training programme, in co-operation with the relevant national and international organizations, on measures to combat maritime fraud;

12.   *Recommends* to the Trade and Development Board to endorse the UNCTAD non-mandatory model clauses on marine hull and cargo insurance as proposed by the Rapporteur to the current session in document UNCTAD/SHIP/608, and to instruct the UNCTAD secretariat, having assured the correspondence of the text in all languages, to circulate this version to the commercial parties concerned; and requests the secretariat subsequently to take the appropriate measures to promote their use by preparing explanatory material;

13.   *Reiterates* that States members of UNCTAD should inform the secretariats of UNCTAD and IMO of the actual commercial and economic consequences they have noted for their merchant ships as a result of port State control at a regional level, and requests the UNCTAD secretariat to inform the Committee on Shipping of any such communication received;

...

- - - - -

Additional References

Resolution 2(II) of the UNCTAD *Ad Hoc* Intergovernmental Group to Consider Means of Combating all Aspects of Maritime Fraud, Including Piracy. In UNCTAD doc. TD/B/C.4/296 - TD/B/C.4/AC.4/10.

"Review and analysis of possible measures to minimize the occurrence of maritime fraud and piracy". UNCTAD doc. TD/B/C.4/AC.4/2.

Report on the feasibility of improving the administrative and legal procedures of prosecuting authorities in cases of maritime fraud. UNCTAD doc. TD/B/C.4/AC.4/8

Work Programme on Shipping and proposals for further work. UNCTAD Committee on Shipping, 12th session. TD/B/C.4/303.

Measures to increase co-operation in the investigation and prosecution of maritime fraud. UNCTAD/ST/SHIP/9.

- - - - -

5

Consideration of a Draft Convention
on Maritime Liens and Mortgages

Joint UNCTAD/IMO Intergovernmental Group of Experts   TD/B/C.4/AC.8/2
on Maritime Liens and Mortgages and Related Subjects
First Session, December 1986   Extract

Consideration of Maritime Liens and Mortgages and
Related Subjects, in Accordance with the Terms of Reference
of the Joint Intergovernmental Group

A new approach to the international régime for maritime securities
Report by the UNCTAD Secretariat

. . .

Chapter I

REVIEW OF CONVENTIONS ON MARITIME LIENS AND MORTGAGES AND
RELATED ENFORCEMENT PROCEDURES SUCH AS ARREST

. . .

18.   The existing international conventions dealing with maritime liens, mortgages and arrest
are briefly reviewed here with a view to determining a need for a new international convention
or conventions.

A.   **International Convention for the Unification of Certain Rules of Law Relating to
          Maritime Liens and Mortgages, signed at Brussels on 10 April 1926**

19.   The UNCTAD secretariat, in its previous report on the subject, provided a thorough
review of this Convention.[11] It pointed out the lack of success achieved by this piece of legislation and tendered numerous explanations for its failure.

20.   The objections made to the 1926 Convention included,[12] *inter alia*, liens securing "claims
resulting from contracts entered into or acts done by the master"; elimination of possessory
liens which include, *inter alia*, a right of retention of the vessel in respect of debts which rank
above mortgages; allowing Contracting States to create or maintain a right of retention in
their domestic law; allowing liens against freight; provisions concerning the system of ranking
"per voyage", set out in Articles 5 and 6, which has led to conflicting interpretation; failure to
deal with the position of long-term charterers; the Protocol to the Convention which
interferes with the international uniformity by allowing contracting States to change to a
certain extent the order of priorities set out in the Convention and to confer certain liens other
than those recognized by the Convention; article 4 dealing with "accessories" which should be
revised; the defective drafting of a number of provisions; the failure to define "maritime
liens"; the failure to define "mortgages".

B.   **International Convention for the Unification of Certain Rules Relating to Maritime Liens and Mortgages, signed at Brussels on 27 May 1967**

21.   The 1967 Convention has been reviewed in the previous reports of both the UNCTAD[13] and the IMO secretariats.[14] It was noted that the Convention was not in force, having been ratified or acceded to by only four States.

22.   Some of the reasons advanced for the failure of the Convention are as follows: failure to define the concepts of "maritime liens" and "mortgages"; although the Convention reduced the number of maritime liens, the list given was stated to be "necessarily arbitrary", criticism directed against article 8 which provided for extinction of maritime liens after a period of one year unless the vessel has been arrested prior to the expiry of such period and the arrest has led to a forced sale; lack of uniformity as regards the type of action which prevents the extinction of maritime liens; lack of uniformity as to the extinction of maritime liens in the case of voluntary sale; the objection raised as regards article 1 which provides that the amount secured by the mortgage should be specified in the register or in the instrument deposited with the registrar, on the ground that in some forms of modern mortgage no figure is mentioned; doubts expressed as to the high ranking given to port, canal, other waterway dues and pilotage dues; the Convention does not deal with other security interests in freight or monies earned by the ship such as charter-hire or insurance monies; failure to deal with long-term ship financing through demise charters; the Convention, in the same way as the 1926 Convention, fails to tie the concepts of maritime liens and mortgages to the concept of arrest (the terminology of the two Liens and Mortgages Conventions has not been aligned with that of the 1952 Arrest Convention); there is no reference to the so-called "sistership" remedy and its relationship with maritime liens, nor to the effect on a maritime lien of lodging bail or other forms of security.[15]

23.   Further, a number of modifications to this Convention, by way of improvement, were suggested.[16] The possible modifications raised included for example the possibility of merging the two Conventions dealing respectively with liens and mortgages, and arrest of ships, into one comprehensive piece of legislation on these three subjects.

24.   It was also stated that an improved 1967 Convention, assuming international support, would achieve some of the objectives which are paramount in the present work (i.e. an increase in international uniformity and promotion of the status of mortgagees).[17] It was suggested that the 1967 Convention could, as a short-term solution, be used as a basis for future work, albeit that some other more radical changes should also be considered.[18]

25.   Further, the UNCTAD secretariat's subsequent report noted[19] that the CMI at its XXIII International Conference in Lisbon made some amendments to the text of the 1967 Convention and agreed upon a Draft Revised Convention.[20] It noted the changes made to the Convention and compared these to the modifications suggested in the earlier report of UNCTAD.[21] It also noted those issues raised in the UNCTAD secretariat's earlier report which have not been tackled and solved by the Draft Revised Convention. These included suggestions for improving the status of mortgagees, complete reformulation of existing terminology and regulating security interests other than mortgages and hypothèques.[22]

26.   The overriding question remains as to whether the modifications made to the demonstrably unsatisfactory and unsuccessful 1967 Convention are sufficiently material to make the Draft Revision more attractive. Even if this question is answered in the affirmative,

a subsidiary but fundamental issue is whether the régime thereby created is the most suitable for all interested parties.

C.   **International Convention Relating to the Arrest of Seagoing Ships, signed at Brussels on 10 May 1952**

27.   This Convention has been reviewed by the UNCTAD secretariat in its previous reports.[23] It was noted that the 1952 Arrest Convention had gained a wide measure of support, having been ratified or acceded to by about 63 countries.

28.   This Convention has also been reviewed by the CMI where a Draft Revised Convention has been agreed upon.[24]   The problems associated with the Convention and modifications made by the CMI were considered in the UNCTAD secretariat report.[25]   It was pointed out that one of the major criticisms directed against the 1952 Arrest Convention was that, in spite of the close linkage between maritime liens, mortgages and arrest of ships, the terminology of this Convention had not been aligned with that of the 1967 Convention on Maritime Liens and Mortgages. However, although this has now been remedied to some extent by the CMI Draft Revised Convention, the outstanding issue of whether the "enforcement" provisions of this Convention should be coupled or combined with the more substantive law of securities in one unified system is considered below.[26]

29.   It should also be mentioned that the consultants considered the Arrest Convention as a compromise between the civil law approach according to which arrest is permissible on any ship of the debtor as security for a claim, subject to certain conditions being fulfilled, and the common law approach, according to which arrest is a measure to acquire admiralty jurisdiction.

D.   **Convention Relating to Registration of Rights in respect of Vessels under Construction, signed at Brussels on 27 May 1967**

30.   The UNCTAD secretariat in its previous reports briefly investigated the aims and effects of this Convention.[27]

31.   The CMI did not revise this Convention, and the only issue of significant importance is whether, perhaps by extending the definition of the ship or vessels to be regulated by a new securities Convention, a ship under construction should be covered under a new Convention.

. . .

Chapter IV

CONCLUDING REMARKS

142.   The previous attempts to achieve international uniformity in the area of maritime liens and mortgages have not been successful. The 1926 Convention has not obtained a great number of ratifications and the 1967 Convention, after 20 years, has not even entered into force. It was pointed out in the previous report of the UNCTAD secretariat[90] that the motivation behind the 1926 Convention was the need for international uniformity in order to enable national systems of shipping to achieve their national objectives more readily. In the case of the 1967 Convention, this need was still recognized but ship-financing by way of mortgages had become a more dominant aspect and, thus, the primary reason for the

Convention had been the need to strengthen the international position of the mortgagees and thus improve the conditions for ship financing at the international level.[91]

143.   The secretariat's previous reports,[92] however, have demonstrated that the current situation concerning maritime liens, mortgages and arrest of ships is far from being unified. It was stated that this situation is a cause of concern for both developed and developing countries in that States may find their national objectives frustrated as the result of differences in the treatment of preferred maritime securities and ensuing uncertainties which surrounds the treatment of such securities. The report went on to say:

> "Developing countries suffer in particular by being unable to obtain sufficient finance for their fleet development and, in the case of States with no settled rules, to develop their national legislation."

> "In the case of developed States with settled rules, the objectives of their national laws may be invalidated by the variations in national legislation on maritime liens and mortgages. This can occur whenever a lien arises in one State and the vessel is arrested in another State - either by the same or another lien-holder - and the second State regards maritime liens as procedural, consequently applying its own laws on the recognition of ranking of such liens. Thus, a lien that arises in one State can be wiped out by the arrest of the vessel in another State if the second State does not recognize the lien."[93]

144.   The investigations carried out by the UNCTAD secretariat of financial institutions and those involved in financing ship purchase and ship-building projects, established that there are many considerations of a commercial, political and legal nature which affect the decision whether or not to advance finance for ship-acquisition. However, registered mortgages continued to be the principal means of ship-financing and there was concern over the lack of uniformity in the area of maritime liens, mortgages and arrest, and over inadequate and non-existent enforcement procedures in some countries. One of the major disincentives in arranging finance for developing countries was the weakness of the enforcement element in their legal systems and the lack of clarity with regard to the priority of claims.[94]

145.   In effect, greater uniformity would enable a lender to make reasonable estimate as to the nature and number of maritime claims which would have priority over his own security.

146.   The review of the activities of UNCTAD, IMO and CMI in the area of maritime liens, mortgages and arrest as presented in this report and in the previous reports of the UNCTAD secretariat,[95] demonstrates that there is a pressing need to improve the current international régime governing this area in order to achieve a greater degree of international uniformity and to give greater protection to the mortgagees.

147.   The previous report of the UNCTAD secretariat[96] puts forward some of the possible options for remedying the current situation. It was suggested that the 1967 Convention could, as a short-term solution, be used as a basis for future reform, but that more radical changes should also be considered.[97] It is, however, doubtful whether modification of the clearly unsuccessful 1967 Convention could provide a satisfactory solution to the present problem.

148.   This report offers a totally new approach to the problem of allowing the ship to be used as a security for claims made against her. It presents a general framework for a single unified

and streamlined legislative instrument designed to regulate the rights of all maritime claimants against a vessel.

149.   This approach has the practical advantage of encouraging greater international uniformity in the whole area of maritime securities and claims enforcement. It offers a régime whereby the registered mortgagee is afforded a high ranking within the list of priorities[98] and a régime which seeks to govern the entire life of a vessel from the moment of being structured or contracted for to the final voyage to the breaker's yard.

150.   The Joint Intergovernmental Group of Experts may wish to give consideration to the new approach presented in this report and request the secretariat to follow up the matter as appropriate.

Notes

. . .

11.   See "Preliminary analysis of possible reforms in the existing international régime of maritime liens and mortgages", (TD/B/C.4/ISL/48), paras. 52-53 and 63-66.

12.   Ibid., paras. 64-65, and International Sub-Committee on Maritime Liens and Mortgages, preliminary report and questionnaire (Hypo-)/1-64), CMI XXVII Conference, New York 1965, pp. 77-82.

13.   See TD/B/C.4/ISL/48, paras. 54, 66-67, 178-181, 185-191.

14.   See "Consideration of work in respect of maritime liens and mortgages and related subjects", IMO document No. LEG/55/4/1 - 18 September 1985, paras. 44-48.

15.   See TD/B/C.4/ISL/48, paras. 66-67.

16.   Ibid., paras. 178-181.

17.   Ibid., paras. 185-191.

18.   Ibid., paras. 190, 185 and TD/B/C.4/ISL/52, para. 33.

19.   See TD/B/C.4/ISL/52, paras. 65-69.

20.   See TD/B/C.4/ISL/L.77 AND TD/B/C.4/ISL/L.79.

21.   TD/B/C.4/ISL/52, para. 73.

22.   Ibid., para. 79.

23.   See TD/B/C.4/ISL/48, paras. 56-61, and TD/B/C.4/ISL/52, paras. 80-94.

24.   See TD/B/C.4/ISL/L.79 and TD/B/C.4.ISL/L.78.

25.   See TD/B/C.4/ISL/52, paras. 86-95.

26.   See paras. 140 et seq.

27.   See TD/B/C.4.ISL/48, para. 55.

. . .

90.   TD/B/C.4/ISL.48, para. 28.

91.   Ibid., paras. 27 and 28.

92.   Ibid., paras. 68-128.

93.   Ibid., paras. 183-184.

94.   See TD/B/C.4/ISL/52, paras. 37-38.

95.   See TD/B/C.4/ISL/52 and TD/B/C.4/ISL/48.

96.   See TD/B/C.4/ISL/48, paras. 129-181.

97.   Ibid., paras. 185 and 190, and TD/B/C.4/ISL/52, para. 33.

98.   See para. 141.

- - - - -

Joint UNCTAD/IMO Intergovernmental Group of Experts   TD/B/C.4/AC.8/3
on Maritime Liens and Mortgages and Related Subjects   Extract
First Session, December 1986

Consideration of Maritime Liens and Mortgages and Related Subjects, in Accordance with the Terms of Reference of the Joint Intergovernmental Group

MARITIME LIENS AND MORTGAGES - ISSUES OF CONSIDERATION PURSUANT
TO THE TERMS OF REFERENCE OF THE JOINT INTERGOVERNMENTAL GROUP
Note by the Secretary-General of IMO

PART I - INTRODUCTION

. . .

9.   At its eleventh session in 1985, the UNCTAD Working Group on International Shipping Legislation discussed the matters and adopted a recommendation to the Trade and Development Board to take the appropriate steps to provide for the convening, jointly with the International Maritime Organization (IMO), of an intergovernmental group of experts.[7] The terms of reference of the group of experts were to "examine the subject of maritime liens and mortgages, including the possible consideration of:

(a)   the review of the maritime liens and mortgages conventions and related enforcement procedures, such as arrest;

(b)   the preparation of model laws of guidelines on maritime liens, mortgages and related enforcement procedures, such as arrest; and

(c)   the feasibility of an international registry of maritime liens and mortgages."

10.   The recommendation of the Working Group was endorsed by the Trade and Development Board at its thirty-second session. The proposal for the convening of a joint intergovernmental group of experts was endorsed by the Legal Committee of IMO at its fifty-sixth session and approved by the Council of IMO at its fifty-sixth session.

11.   The recommendation for the establishment of the joint intergovernmental group was accompanied by a request to the Secretariats of IMO and UNCTAD to prepare the necessary studies and documentation to facilitate the work of the joint intergovernmental group.

. . .

PART II - POINTS WHICH GOVERNMENTS MAY WISH TO CONSIDER IN CONNECTION WITH THE TERMS OF REFERENCE OF THE JOINT INTERGOVERNMENTAL GROUP OF EXPERTS

REVIEW OF CONVENTIONS ON MARITIME LIENS AND MORTGAGES AND RELATED ENFORCEMENT PROCEDURES SUCH AS ARREST WITH SPECIAL REFERENCE TO THE FOLLOWING:

(a) **Need for a new international convention or conventions or other agreement or agreements on maritime liens and mortgages and on arrest of vessels**

In determining the need or desirability for a new international treaty or treaties on the subject, Governments may wish to take account of the purposes which international conventions are intended to serve. The three main principal objectives in this regard are uniformity of law, certainty of law and justice between the parties interested in the issues covered by the treaty in question.

2.   Uniformity of law is desired because it simplifies the law for interested parties in all States, including the legal practitioners and the courts. Uniformity in the law is also useful in eliminating or minimizing the practice of "forum shopping" by which claimants and defendants seek to bring disputes into particular jurisdictions solely because they believe that the laws in such jurisdictions will be more favourable to their cause.

3.   Certainty of law is assisted by an international convention because a convention, by establishing a uniform norm, helps to avoid the conflict of different national laws. This enables interested parties to identify more easily and clearly what their rights and obligations are likely to be, regardless of where the claim may arise or where the issue will be decided.

4.   An international convention can also promote justice by establishing in a clear and fair way rights and obligations for all the parties which have an interest in the subject-matter, including shippers, shipowners, ship operators, charterers, mortgagees and suppliers of services for shipping.

5.   However, for these aims to be achieved by means of an international convention, the convention in question must not cause serious administrative difficulties for Governments or operational problems for the parties which may be affected by them. In particular the implementation of such a convention should not impose on administrations the obligation to take unnecessary measures, nor should it result in inordinate expense for shipowners and operators or uncertainties to claimants and the courts.

   . . .

(b) **The conventions relevant to the subject-matter**
   . . .

(c) **Identification of the essential characteristics of maritime liens**
   . . .

(d) **Identification of the essential characteristics of mortgages**
   . . .

(e) **What should be the role of insurance in determining which liens deserve priority over mortgages**
   . . .

(f) **Is there need for rules on the effects of forced sale on existing securities and charter parties?**
   . . .

(g) **What should be the conditions for and consequences of de-registration of ships?**
...

(h) **Problems associated with conflicts of law**
...

(i) **The desirability and feasibility of dealing with registration of rights with respect to ships under construction in the same international agreement relating to maritime liens and mortgages, or in any other agreement**
...

(j) **The desirability of combined or separate agreements covering maritime liens and mortgages and arrest of vessels**

38. A number of issues require consideration in relation to this question. These include:

(i) In the discussions of this matter a number of advantages and disadvantages of a combined convention on liens and mortgages on the one hand and arrest on the other have been identified.

(a) It was pointed out that one convention only would reduce the number of ratifications since some States might like one part of the convention and not the other parts.

(b) On the other hand it has been suggested that the same objective can be obtained by permitting States to declare to be bound only by the rules on maritime liens and mortgages or by the rules on arrest of ships or by both sets of rules, as the respective States may wish.

(c) It has also been suggested that the objective of a single combined convention could be achieved, at least in part, through a better co-ordination between the two conventions. For example, the two conventions (on maritime liens and mortgages and on arrest of vessels, respectively) could be prepared simultaneously and adopted at the same diplomatic conference, but as separate instruments.

(k) **Review of existing practices with a view to ascertaining the desirability of preparing "guidelines" for national legislation and regulations or "model laws" on maritime liens and mortgages and related enforcement procedures, such as arrest. In particular consideration to be given to the areas and fields in which legislation or other regulations are essential in individual countries to facilitate the procurement of ship-finance for ships registered in those countries**
...

REGISTRATION OF CHARGES AGAINST THE SHIP

(l) **Registration of maritime liens**
...

(m) **The possibility of an international register of maritime liens, mortgages and similar charges**

. . .

OTHER MATTERS

Arrest and Enforcement

45.   The terms of reference of the Joint Group emphasize liens and mortgages. Nevertheless, Governments may wish to consider also the subject of arrest and other forms of enforcement. In this connection, note may be taken of the references to "enforcement procedures, such as arrest" in the terms of reference.

46.   The consideration of the subject of arrest in the context of an examination of maritime liens and mortgages may be justified on the grounds that procedures for the enforcement of claims based on maritime mortgages, hypothèques and maritime liens should be streamlined as much as possible at the international and national levels. It may also be argued that such streamlining, by avoiding uncertainty and removing causes for unnecessary and unreasonable delays, could encourage greater willingness on the part of lending institutions to provide loans for ship-financing.

47.   In considering the need for internationally-acceptable procedures for enforcement, Governments may wish to consider to what extent the 1952 Arrest Convention provides an acceptable compromise between:

(i)   on the one hand, the civil law approach, according to which arrest is permissible, subject to certain conditions, against any ship of the debtor as security for a claim; and

(ii)   on the other hand, the common law approach, according to which arrest is a measure to acquire admiralty jurisdiction

48.   In this connection, it may be noted that the 1952 Arrest Convention has been accepted by over 60 States. It may be assumed that the civil law countries which are Parties have accepted the principle that arrest is permissible only in respect of specified claims of a maritime character and that in certain cases the *forum arresti* is competent for the merits of the case. It may also be assumed that common law countries which are Parties to the 1952 Convention have accepted the principle not only that sister ships may also be arrested, but also that ships which are bare-boat chartered may be arrested in respect of claims against the bare-boat charterer. However, the question whether a vessel may be arrested also in respect of claims against a time-charterer or a voyage-charterer remains in doubt, and may need to be further examined in the context of the mandate of the Joint Intergovernmental Group.

. . .

CONCLUDING REMARKS

. . .

53.   The availability of concrete evidence, based on the practical experience of Governments, shipping operators, financing institutions and international organizations will be of great assistance to Governments in formulating their views and positions on the four major questions which were identified by the Secretariats of IMO and UNCTAD in their consultations. These were:

(a) the principal legitimate objectives by which an international legal régime on maritime liens and mortgages should be evaluated;

(b) the major deficiencies, if any, in the present legal régime as contained in the existing international conventions, and whether any such deficiencies have a significant and adverse impact on the achievement of the objectives agreed upon;

(c) whether any identified deficiencies were likely to be remedied, effectively and in good time, through the adoption of new or revised treaty instruments and, in particular, whether there was a reasonable prospect that any new treaty instrument would receive speedy acceptance by enough States to provide for the needed uniformity of law;

(d) if the adoption of a new or revised treaty were considered to be either unnecessary or inadvisable, what other procedures might be considered to enable a reasonable measure of international uniformity, while permitting individual States to apply rules and procedures in accordance with their respective conditions and requirements.

54. It is noted that these questions are also embodied in principle in the terms of reference of the Joint Intergovernmental Group. It is, therefore, hoped that Governments and organizations concerned will consider it useful and advisable to seek as much information as possible, and make such information available to other participants in the Joint Intergovernmental Group. And it is hoped that the questions and issues outlined in this report will be of assistance to the Government and organizations in collecting and collating such information for the benefit of the Joint Intergovernmental Group.

Note

7. Resolution 6(XI): Report of the Working Group on International Shipping Legislation on its eleventh session, TD/B/C.4/ISL/53, Annex I.

- - - - -

Joint UNCTAD/IMO Intergovernmental Group of Experts   TD/B/C.4/AC.8/9
on Maritime Liens and Mortgages and Related Subjects
Third Session, November 1987   Extract

Consideration of Maritime Liens and Mortgages and Related Subjects, in Accordance with the Terms of Reference of the Joint Intergovernmental Group
Note by the Secretariats of UNCTAD and IMO

DRAFT ARTICLES ON MARITIME LIENS AND MORTGAGES

Article 1[1]
Recognition and enforcement of mortgages, "hypothèques" and charges

Mortgages, "hypothèques" and registerable charges of the same nature, which registerable charges of the same nature will be referred to hereafter as "charges", effected on seagoing vessels by their owners to secure payment of monies shall be enforceable in States Parties provided that:[2]

(a) Such mortgages, "hypothèques" and charges have been effected and registered in accordance with the law of the State in which the vessel is registered;

(b) The register and any instruments required to be deposited with the registrar in accordance with the law of the State where the vessel is registered are open to public inspection, and that extracts of the register and copies of such instruments are obtainable from the registrar; and,

(c) Either the register or any instruments referred to in subparagraph (b) specifies at least the name and address of the person in whose favour the mortgage, "hypothèque" or charge has been effected or that it has been issued to bearer, [the maximum amount secured][3] and the date and other particulars which, according to the law of the State of registration, determine the rank as respects other registered mortgages, "hypothèques" and charges.

Notes

1. See paragraph 5 of the Report on the Work of the Sessional Group, JIGE (II)/3, Annex (hereinafter referred to as "the Report").
2. See paragraph 6 of the Report.
3. See paragraphs 7 to 10 of the Report.

Article 2[1]
Ranking and effects of mortgages, "hypothèques" and charges

The ranking of registered mortgages, "hypothèques" or charges as between themselves and, without prejudice to the provisions of this Convention, their effect in regard to third parties shall be determined by the law of the State of registration; however, without prejudice to the provisions of this Convention, all matters relating to the procedure of enforcement shall be regulated by the law of the State where enforcement takes place.

Note

1. See paragraph 11 of the Report.

Article 3
Change of ownership or registration[1]

1. In the event of a voluntary change of ownership or registration of a vessel, no State Party shall permit the owner to deregister the vessel without the written consent of all holders of registered mortgages, "hypothèques" or charges.[2]

2. A vessel which is or has been registered in a State Party shall not be eligible for registration in another State Party unless either:

(a) A certificate has been issued by the former State to the effect that the vessel has been deregistered, or

(b) A certificate has been issued by the former State to the effect that the vessel will be deregistered when such new registration is effected.

Notes

1. See paragraph 12 of the Report.
2. See paragraphs 13 to 15 of the Report.

Article 4
Maritime liens

1.   Each of the following claims against the owner, demise charterer, manager or operator of the vessel shall be secured by a maritime lien on the vessel:

(i)   Wages and other sums due to the master, officers and other members of the vessel's complement in respect of their employment on the vessel [including social insurance contributions, payable on their behalf];[1]

(ii)   Claims in respect of loss of life or personal injury occurring, whether on land or on water, in direct connection with the operation of the vessel;[2]

(iii) Claims of salvage;[3]

(iv)   Claims based on tort arising out of physical loss or damage caused by the operation of the vessel other than loss of or damage to cargo, containers and passengers, effects carried on the vessel;[4]

(v)   Claims for [wreck removal] [and contribution in general average];[5]

(vi)   [Port, canal, and other waterway dues and pilotage dues].[6 & 7]

2.   No maritime lien shall attach to a vessel to secure the claims as set out in subparagraphs (ii) and (iv) of paragraph 1 of this article which are out of or result from oil pollution[8] or the radioactive properties or a combination of radioactive properties with toxic, explosive or other hazardous properties of nuclear fuel or of radioactive product or waste.

Notes

1. See paragraph 31 of the Report.
2. See paragraph 33 of the Report.
3. See paragraph 32 of the Report.
4. See paragraph 33 of the Report.
5. See paragraph 34 of the Report.
6. See paragraph 35 of the Report.
7. One delegation has proposed the addition of the following subparagraph to this article:
    "(vii) claims in respect of the repair or reconstruction of a vessel".
This text had been proposed on the assumption that paragraph 2 of article 6 is deleted.
8. See paragraph 36 of the Report. Some delegations proposed the insertion of a provision similar to article 3 (b) of the Convention on Limitation of Liability for Maritime Claims, 1976.

Article 5
Priority of maritime liens

1.   The maritime liens set out in article 4 shall take priority over registered mortgages, "hypothèques" and charges and no other claim shall take priority over such maritime liens or over mortgages, "hypothèques" or charges which comply with the requirements of article 1, except as provided in paragraph 2 of article 6.

2.   The maritime liens set out in article 4 shall rank in the order listed, provided however that maritime liens securing claims for salvage, [wreck removal] and [contribution in general average] shall take priority over all other maritime liens which have attached to the vessel prior to the time when the operations giving rise to the said liens were performed.[1]

3.   The maritime liens set out in each of subparagraphs (i), (ii), (iv) [and (vi)] of paragraph 1 of article 4 shall rank *pari passu* as between themselves.

4.   The maritime liens set out in subparagraphs (iii) [and (v)] of paragraph 1 of article 4 shall rank in the inverse order of the time when the claims secured thereby accrued. [Claims for contribution in general average shall be deemed to have accrued on the date on which the general average act was performed]; claims for salvage shall be deemed to have accrued on the date on which the salvage operation was terminated.

Note

1.   Paragraphs 2-4 were not subject to detailed discussion at the second session.

Article 6[1]
Other liens and rights of retention

1.   Each State Party may grant maritime or other liens or rights of retention to secure claims other than those referred to in article 4. Such liens shall rank after the maritime liens set out in article 4 and after registered mortgages, "hypothèques" or charges which comply with the provisions of article 1 and such rights of retention shall not prejudice the enforcement of maritime liens set out in article 4 or registered mortgages, "hypothèques" or charges which comply with the provisions of article 1, nor the delivery of the vessel to the purchaser in connection with such enforcement.

2.   If a lien or right of retention is granted in respect of a vessel in possession of either:

(a)   A shipbuilder, to secure claims for the building of the vessel, or

(b)   A ship repairer, to secure claims for repair, including reconstruction of the vessel effected during such possession,

such lien shall be postponed to, and such right of retention shall not prejudice the enforcement of, all maritime liens set out in article 4, but may take priority over registered mortgages, "hypothèques" or charges on, or be exercisable against, the vessel. Such lien or right of retention shall be extinguished when the vessel ceases to be in the possession of the shipbuilder or ship repairer, otherwise than in consequence of an arrest or seizure.

Note

1.   See paragraphs 43 to 55 of the Report.

One delegation has proposed the following text:

"Each State Party may grant liens or rights to secure claims other than those referred to in article 4. Such liens or rights shall rank after the maritime liens set out in article 4 and after registered mortgages, "hypothèques" or charges which comply with the provisions of Article 1."

This proposal required deletion of article 6 (2).

Article 7^1
Characteristics of maritime liens

[Subject to the provisions of article 11] the maritime liens set out in article 4 follow the vessel notwithstanding any change of ownership or of registration or of flag [except in the case of a forced sale].

Note

1.   See paragraph 56 of the Report.

Article 8^1
Extinction of maritime liens

1.   The maritime liens set out in article 4 shall be extinguished after a period of one year from the time when the claims secured thereby arose unless, prior to the expiry of such period, the vessel has been arrested [or seized], such arrest [or seizure] leading to a forced sale.^{2}

2.   The one-year period referred to in the preceding paragraph shall not be subject to suspension or interruption, provided, however, that time shall not run during the period that the [arrest or seizure of the vessel is not permitted by law] [lien or is legally prevented from arresting the vessel].

Notes

1.   See paragraphs 57 to 66 of the Report.
2.   The following text for paragraph 1 has been proposed by one delegation:
    "1.   A maritime lien set out in article 4 shall be extinguished when any of the following events first occurs:
         (a)   payment of the claim in full; or
         (b)   execution by the lienholder of a discharge of the lien; or
         (c)   arrest or seizure of the vessel, leading to:
            (i)   the giving of bail or other security in respect of the claim; or
           (ii)   a forced sale; or
         (d)   expiration of a period of one year from the time when the claim secured by the lien arose."

Article 9^1
Assignment and subrogation

The assignment of or subrogation to a claim secured by a maritime lien set out in article 4 entails the simultaneous assignment of or subrogation to such maritime lien.

Note

1.   See paragraph 67 of the Report.

Article 10^1
Notice of forced sale

Prior to the forced sale of a vessel in a State Party the competent authority of such State shall give, or cause to be given, at least 30 days written notice of the time and place of such sale to:

(a)   All holders of registered mortgages, "hypothèques", or charges which have not been issued to bearer;

(b)   Such holders of registered mortgages, "hypothèques" and charges issued to bearer and to such holder of maritime liens set out in article 4 whose claims have been notified to the said authority;

(c)   The registrar of the register in which the vessel is registered.

Note

1.   See paragraphs 68 to 70 of the Report.

Article 11[1]
Effects of forced sale

1.   In the event of the forced sale of the vessel in a State Party all mortgages, "hypothèques" or charges except those assumed by the purchaser with the consent of the holders and all liens and other encumbrances of whatsoever nature shall cease to attach to the vessel, provided however that:

(a)   At the time of the sale, the vessel is in the jurisdiction of such State; and

(b)   The sale has been effected in accordance with the law of the said State and the provisions of this Convention.

2.   The costs and expenses arising out of the arrest or seizure and subsequent sale of the vessel and of the distribution of the proceeds shall be paid first out of the proceeds of sale. The balance of the proceeds shall be distributed among the holders of maritime liens, liens and rights of retention mentioned in paragraph 2 of article 6 and registered mortgages, "hypothèques" or charges, in accordance with the provisions of this Convention to the extent necessary to satisfy their claims.[2]

3.   When a vessel registered in a State Party has been the object of a forced sale in a State Party, the competent authority shall, at the request of the purchaser, issue a certificate to the effect that the vessel is sold free of all mortgages, "hypothèques" or charges, except those assumed by the purchaser, and of all liens and other encumbrances provided that the requirements set out in paragraph 1 (a) and (b) have been complied with. Upon production of such certificate the registrar shall be bound to delete all registered mortgages, "hypothèques" or charges except those assumed by the purchaser, and to register the vessel in the name of the purchaser or to issue a certificate of deregistration for the purpose of reregistration, as the case may be.[3]

Notes

1.   See paragraphs 71, 74, 78 and 79 of the Report.
2.   See paragraph 29 of the Report.
3.   See paragraphs 72, 73 and 75 to 77 of the Report.

Article 12[1]
Scope of application

1.   Unless otherwise provided in this Convention, its provisions shall apply to all seagoing vessels registered in a State Party or in a State which is not a State Party.

2.   Nothing in this Convention shall create any rights in, or enable any rights to be enforced against, any vessel owned, operated or chartered by a State and appropriated to public non-commercial services.[2]

Notes

1.   See paragraphs 80 to 82 and 85 of the Report.
2.   One delegation proposed the addition of a further paragraph which would read as follows:
   "3.   Nothing in this Convention shall enable rights on maritime liens to be enforced against a vessel owned by a State and used for commercial purposes if the vessel carries a certificate issued by the appropriate authorities of the State of the vessel's registry stating that the vessel is owned by that State and that the vessel's liability under the claims enumerated in article 4 is covered."
See paragraph 84 of the Report.

Article 13[1]
Communications between States Parties

For the purpose of articles 3, 10, and 11 of this Convention, the competent authorities of the State Parties shall be authorized to correspond directly between themselves.

Note

1.   See paragraph 86 of the Report.

Article 14[1]
Conflict of conventions

Nothing in this Convention shall affect the application of an international convention providing for limitation or of national legislation giving effect there to.

Note

1.   See paragraph 87 of the Report.

- - - - -

Joint UNCTAD/IMO Intergovernmental Group of Experts   TD/B/C.4/AC.8/10
 on Maritime Liens and Mortgages and Related Subjects
Report of the Third Session, December 1987   Extract

=====================

   . . .

Annex I

REPORT OF THE WORK OF THE SESSIONAL GROUP

1.   The Sessional Group had before it the report prepared by the Chairman of the Joint Intergovernmental Group of Experts with the assistance of the secretariats of UNCTAD and IMO, . . . document TD/B/C.4/AC.8/9 . . .

2.   On the basis of this document, the Sessional Group decided to examine the draft articles
. . .

The following is a summary of the discussions and conclusions reached:
. . .

Article 3 - Change of ownership and registration

11.   The Sessional Group noted that, in the light of observations made at the second session, the Chairman had prepared an alternative text for **paragraph 1**. The new text had been worded in such a way as to exclude from its application cases where the change of registration occurred within the same State. One delegation suggested that there might be a need to describe the international scope of application in a general provision. This would serve to clarify whether or not the other provisions of the convention also applied only in international situations.

12.   Most delegations expressed support in principle for the alternative text. Many of these noted, however, that the text needed some improvements of a drafting nature so as to ensure that it also applied to cases where the same owner wished to have his vessel re-registered in another State. There was wide support that this could be achieved by inserting the words "or a voluntary change of registration" after "voluntary change of ownership" in the alternative text.

13.   With regard to the title of the article, it was suggested by some delegations to refer to "voluntary change of ownership or registration". Other delegations, however, were opposed to this proposal. One of these pointed out that paragraph 2 dealt with all cases of registration except those occurring on the basis of a forced sale and applied also to certain transactions that were not voluntary.

14.   In this connection the suggestion was also made to insert the contents of **paragraph 2** in a separate article. One delegation proposed that paragraph 2 be inserted as a new article after article 11 on the effects of forced sale. Other delegations did not favour these suggestions. Several delegations nevertheless noted the close link between this provision and article 11, particularly paragraph 3 thereof. One of these delegations suggested adding the phrase "without prejudice to article 11 (3)" at the beginning of paragraph 2; another delegation felt it might be better to include in article 11.3 a cross-reference to article 3.2.

15.   The Group considered whether it was necessary to retain both subparagraphs of paragraph 2. Several delegations affirmed the need for both provisions, emphasizing at the same time that neither alternative was fully satisfactory. It was noted that under subparagraph (a), on the one hand, there might be a gap between the time of de-registration in the former State and the time of re-registration in the new State. Under subparagraph (b), on the other hand, it could occur that, even for a brief period only, a ship was registered in two different States at the same time. This would be contrary to the provisions of the 1986 Registration Convention. One delegation emphasized that it was important to reach an agreed interpretation of this provision to the effect that the new registration should only become effective at the time the ship was de-registered in the former State of registration. Some delegates felt that progress recently made in the technology in the field of telecommunications would reduce the likelihood and the length of gaps in registration or of an overlap of registrations.

16.   Several delegations proposed to retain only one of the two subparagraphs. Some of these delegations proposed that, in the light of article 11.4 of the 1986 Registration Convention, only

subparagraph (a) should be retained. Some other delegations proposed retention of subparagraph (b) with some amendments.

17. Various suggestions were made to secure simultaneity of deregistration and re-registration. One of these was to amend subparagraph (b) to read as follows:

"A certificate has been issued by the former State to the effect that the vessel is deregistered at such time as the new registration is effected."

18. Another suggestion was to amend subparagraph (b) to read:

"A certificate has been issued by the former State to the effect that the vessel is automatically deregistered with immediate effect at such time as the new registration is effected."

19. A further suggestion was to add at the end of subparagraph (b) the following sentence:

"The date of registration shall be the date of deregistration of the vessel by the former State."

20. The Sessional Group also considered a working paper which had been prepared by the Chairman at the request of a number of delegations (JIGE(III)/WP/3). The working paper, having discussed the question of bareboat charter registration and article 11.5 of the 1986 Registration Convention, put forward a draft article which proposed to extend the protection given to mortgagees by article 3 in case of deregistration of a mortgaged ship also to the case of suspension of registration. The text of this proposed draft article 3 *bis* read as follows:

"1.   In the event of temporary registration of a vessel registered in a State Party in another State Party, the former State shall not permit suspension of registration without the written consent of all holders of registered mortgages, "hypothèques" or charges.

2.   A vessel which is registered in a State Party shall not be eligible for temporary registration in another State Party unless either:

(a)   A certificate has been issued by the former State that the registration of the vessel has been suspended, or

(b)   A certificate has been issued by the former State that the registration of the vessel will be suspended when such temporary registration is effected."

21. Different views emerged from the discussion. Some delegations did not consider that the inclusion of provisions concerning bareboat charter registration was necessary. Other delegations stated that, in view of the increasing practice of bareboat charter registration and for the purposes of clarity, the matter should be dealt with in the draft convention. It was also stressed that the work of the Joint Group should take account of the existing conventions, in particular the 1986 Registration Convention which contained provisions on the subject of bareboat charter registration (articles 11 and 12).

22.   There were, however, differences of opinion as to the interpretation of paragraph 5 of article 11. In the view of some delegations, the paragraph did not provide for total suspension of the original registration, but only dealt with suspension of registration as regards the nationality of the ship. In this context, some delegations stated that, according to the provisions of the 1986 Registration Convention, and in practice, ownership rights, including mortgages/hypothèques, remained in the original register in which the ownership was registered.

23.   One delegation, however, could not envisage how registration could be suspended only as regards the nationality of the ship. In its view, total suspension of registration was intended and not merely suspension of flag, as a State could not have jurisdiction over a ship which was subject to another law. It, therefore, supported the draft article 3 *bis* with deletion of paragraph 2 (b). One delegation stated that the word "suspension" meant "temporary cancellation" and, upon the bareboat charter registration of a ship, all mortgages and hypothèques had to be transferred to the new register.

24.   Some delegations proposed amendments to the proposed article 3 *bis*. One delegation suggested that the provisions dealing with deregistration and suspension of registration be combined in one article, and proposed the following text:

"1.   In the event of a voluntary change of ownership or voluntary change of registration of a vessel, entailing the deregistration of the vessel from the national register of the State party as well as in the event of temporary registration of a vessel, registered in a State party, in another State party in connection with the vessel being bareboat chartered-in, no State party shall permit the owner to deregister the vessel nor permit suspension of registration without the written consent of all holders of registered mortgages, hypothèques or charges.

"2.   A vessel which is or has been registered in a State party shall not be eligible for registration or even temporary registration in another State party unless a certificate has been issued by the former State to the effect that the vessel has been deregistered or that a registration has been suspended."

25.   A large number of delegations suggested that a specific reference to the bareboat charter registration be made, and proposed to replace the words "In the event of temporary registration" in paragraph 1 with the phrase "In the event of bareboat charter-in".

26.   The observer for the International Chamber of Commerce (ICC) stated that the word "suspended" was used in paragraph 5 of article 11 in order to safeguard the mortgages registered in the original register. He further pointed out that the phrase ". . . indicating particulars of any registered encumbrances" was inserted in the paragraph (5) so that a creditor seeking to determine the existence of any mortgage would first refer to the bareboat charter register. This did not mean that mortgages/hypothèques had to be re-registered in the bareboat charter register.

27.   The observer for the International Maritime Committee (CMI) explained that the purpose of article 3 was to protect the security of lenders. He pointed out that the article would need further amendments if the concept of bareboat charter registration were to be introduced into the draft convention in such a way that the new convention would be recognizing the possibility of two registers existing in respect of a ship at the same time. He

stated that at the CMI Lisbon Conference the matter had been discussed and an additional subparagraph was put forward regarding the issue which read as follows: "in case of bareboat charter, the former State and all holders of registered mortgages, 'hypothèques' or charges have consented to such new registration". This proposal had been rejected because it was felt that it would give rise to further problems and that the security of lenders would be seriously damaged if dual registration was recognized.

28.   He recognized that the practice of bareboat charter registration was increasing and could not be ignored and he therefore felt that there was need for an in-depth study of the various existing practices in order to enable the Group to arrive at a satisfactory decision.

29.   The Sessional Group gave further consideration to the question of bareboat charter registration in light of Working Paper JIGE(III)/WP/4 which attempted to examine the question of bareboat charter registration in the context of the work of the Joint Group on maritime liens and mortgages, with particular reference to the provisions of the 1986 Registration Convention. The working paper concluded that the provisions of articles 11 (5) and 12 of the 1986 Registration Convention only provided for what may be termed as a "split jurisdiction" rather than a divided registration, and proposed that all mortgages, hypothèques and charges, in cases of bareboat charter registration of a ship, should be subject to the laws of the State of the original registry of that ship.

30.   Some delegations strongly opposed such an interpretation.   In their view, this interpretation was contradictory to the provisions of the 1986 Registration Convention and the 1982 United Nations Convention on the Law of the Sea. Some of these delegations recognized that article 11 (5) of the 1986 Registration Convention would result in controversial interpretations and had to be interpreted in the light of other provisions of the convention. References were made to articles 4 (4), 11 (4), and 12 (4) which indicated that no ship could be entered in more than one register at a time, that the ship should be deleted from one register before entering it in another register and that the ship was subject to full jurisdiction of the flag State. The delegations pointed out that any exception from the general rule should be interpreted in a strict manner. They further emphasized that there could be no division of jurisdiction and any other view would contradict provisions of the Law of the Sea Convention and the 1986 Registration Convention which spoke of full and exclusive jurisdiction of the flag State.

31.   Some delegations, however, stated that the 1986 Registration Convention only referred to suspension of registration as regards nationality of the ship. It, therefore, envisaged a situation where mortgages, hypothèques and charges remain in the original register and subject to its laws. In their view, the 1986 Registration Convention did not permit deregistration of the mortgages/hypothèques from the original register. They referred to the existing practice in certain countries which permitted bareboat chartering-out; they pointed out that the 1986 Registration Convention intended to accommodate this current practice. They further stated that there were many examples in international law of exceptions to the exclusive jurisdiction of the flag State over its ships. One delegation suggested that on this matter the Group should do no more than warn and protect those prepared to advance monies on the security of a ship.

32.   In the view of some delegations, the new Convention should ensure that the mortgages/hypothèques or charges were not registered in more than one register, whether this be the original register where the ownership is registered or the bareboat charter register. Another delegation suggested that mortgages/hypothèques should be registered in the original

register ("real right register") as opposed to a mere "flag register", and put forward a proposal which was contained in Working Paper JIGE(III)/WP/7. In this context, some delegations stated that the proposal deserved detailed consideration at a later stage.

33.   The Sessional Group decided to consider the subject at its fourth session, on the basis of a study to be prepared by the secretariats of UNCTAD and IMO on the existing practices of States regarding bareboat charter registration. In this connection, delegations were requested to provide the secretariats with the necessary information and national legislations.

Article 4 - Maritime liens

   . . .

48.   As to **subparagraph (iii)**, the Sessional Group agreed to retain salvage claims listed in this subparagraph. Questions, however, were raised as to the ranking of that lien and its relationship with paragraph 2 of article 5. Some delegations suggested that, since salvage preserved the ship for the benefit of all creditors, such claims would rank immediately after claims of wages. Other delegations supported the order of priority given to such claims in draft article 4. In this context the provision of paragraph 2 of article 5 was considered to be appropriate since it dealt with a separate issue, viz. the priority of claims for salvage *vis à vis* other privileged claims.

   . . .

50.   Differing views were expressed regarding **subparagraph (v)**. Some delegations proposed the deletion of claims for wreck removal from the list of maritime liens. In this context some delegations stated that such costs could be covered by the claims referred to in subparagraph (vi). Other delegations suggested that such claims be transferred to article 6 (1) so as to give them lower priority. There was also no consensus as regards contributions in general average. Some delegations favoured deletion of such claims from the list of maritime liens. In this connection, one delegation stated that under its national legislation claims for contribution in general average did not have maritime liens status and, therefore, proposed the deletion of such claims from article 4. Some delegations suggested to transfer these claims to article 6. However, other delegations stated that general average was sometimes analogous to salvage, and should therefore be treated in the same way as salvage claims.

   . . .

52.   With regard to **paragraph 2**, there was wide support for a proposal to narrow the scope of the provision by limiting the exclusion only to claims arising in connection with oil pollution where such damage was within the meaning of the 1969 Convention on Civil Liability for Oil Pollution Damage or the Protocol of 1984 thereto. Accordingly, the Sessional Group agreed to amend paragraph 2 by inserting after the term "oil pollution" the following words:

> ". . . damage within the meaning of the International Convention on Civil Liability for Oil Pollution Damage, dated 29 November 1969 or of any amendment or Protocol thereto which is in force . . . ".

   . . .

Article 5 - Priority of maritime claims

59.   There was wide support for the contents of article 5 as a whole. Differing views were, however, expressed with regard to the references to salvage, wreck removal and contribution in general average contained in **paragraph 2**.

60.   In respect of salvage, several delegations questioned whether there was a need to refer to the existence of a maritime lien in respect of claims for salvage in article 4.1 (iii) in the light of the absolute priority granted to claims for salvage over all other maritime liens which had already attached to the ship. Several delegations emphasized that, in their view, it was important to retain references to salvage in article 4 as well as in article 5. One delegation noted that the special priority given to salvage claims in article 5.2 provided an added incentive for a potential salvor to undertake a salvage operation.

61.   A number of delegations were in favour of deleting the reference to wreck removal from paragraph 2. Some of these noted that since the removal of a wreck occurred mostly under the authority of a public entity, rather than on a voluntary basis, the subject should either not be dealt with in the convention at all or, if necessary, be covered under article 6.1.

62.   A number of other delegations, however, expressed a preference for the retention of a reference to the removal of wrecks in **paragraph 2**. Several of these noted that claims for wreck removal had statutory lien status with a high ranking in their legislation; and, for that reason, they would have to reserve their position if the Sessional Group were to decide to delete the reference to wreck removal from paragraph 2. Some of these delegations also emphasized that such a high priority for claims for wreck removal was justified precisely because wreck removal occurred frequently not only in the interest of removing impediments to international trade and commerce, but also in respect of ensuring maritime safety. Some delegations noted that it was difficult in some situations to draw a dividing line between wreck removal and salvage, and that in some cases wreck removal operations could result in the recovery of a value. Other delegations supported this view and pointed to the fact that often public authorities were not in a position to make a salvage claim because they were responding to a statutorily imposed duty.

63.   Some delegations suggested that claims for salvage and wreck removal should be dealt with together in article 4 as well as in article 5. It was also suggested in this context that the matter might be solved by introducing a definition of the term "wreck", in particular by clarifying the distinction between the salving of a vessel and the removal of a wreck which had no value.

64.   In the light of these diverging views, the Sessional Group agreed to retain, for the time being, the reference to wreck removal in brackets.

65.   In respect of general average many delegations were in favour of deleting the brackets. In the view of some of these delegations, contribution in general average was aimed, like salvage operations, at preserving and maintaining the value of the ship and, in most cases, deserved the same high priority as was accorded to claims for salvage. Some delegations, however, questioned whether this was true in all cases. These delegations therefore wished to maintain the brackets around the term "contribution in general average".

- - - - -

Additional References

Resolution 6(XI) of the UNCTAD Working Group on International Shipping Legislation. 11th session. UNCTAD doc. TD/B/C.4/295 - TD/B/C.4/ISL/53

Draft Revision of the International Convention for the Unification of Certain Rules relating to Maritime Liens and Mortgages. UNCTAD doc. TD/B/C.4/ISL/L.77 (also IMO doc. LEG 55/4).

Draft Revision of the International Convention for the Unification of Certain Rules relating to the Arrest of Sea-going Ships. UNCTAD doc. TD/B/C.4/ISL/L.78.

Report of the IMO Legal Committee, 55th session. IMO doc. LEG 55/11.

Report of the Joint UNCTAD/IMO Intergovernmental Group of Experts on Maritime Liens and Mortgages and Related Subjects, first session. UNCTAD doc. TD/B/C.4/AC.8/4.

Consideration of the subject, in accordance with the terms of reference of the Joint Intergovernmental Group. UNCTAD/IMO Report. UNCTAD doc. TD/B/C.4/AC.8/6.

Report of the Intergovernmental Group on its second session. TD/B/C.4/AC.8/7.

- - - - -

III

MARITIME SAFETY

1. Routeing of Ships

2. Safety of Fishing Vessels

3. Ship Reporting

4. Maritime Communications

5. Ship Identification Numbers

6. Port State Control

7. Maritime Casualties

8. Future Developments

1

Routeing of Ships

IMO Assembly　　　　　　　　　　　　　　　　　　　　　　A 14/Res.572
14th Session, December 1985

Resolution A.572(14)
General Provisions on Ships' Routeing

The Assembly,

Recalling Article 15(j) of the Convention on the International Maritime Organization concerning the functions of the Assembly in relation to regulations and guidelines concerning maritime safety,

Recognizing that the practice of complying with routeing measures adopted by the Organization for international use has contributed to the safety of navigation by reducing the risk of collisions and strandings,

Recognizing further that such practice has consequently reduced the risk of pollution of the marine environment and the risk of damage to marine life resulting from collisions or strandings,

Recalling regulation V/8 of the International Convention for the Safety of Life at Sea, 1974, whereby the Organization is recognized as the only international body for establishing and adopting routeing measures on an international level,

Recalling also rules 1(d) and 10, as amended, of the International Regulations for Preventing Collisions at Sea, 1972, which provide for the adoption of traffic separation schemes by the Organization and the behaviour of vessels in or near such schemes,

Recalling further that the Ninth International Hydrographic Conference charged the International Hydrographic Bureau to deal with matters relating to the presentation on charts and in sailing directions of details of routeing provisions which have been considered, approved and adopted by the Organization for international use,

Recalling additionally resolution A.378(X) on general provisions on ships' routeing and resolution A.428(XI), which authorizes the Maritime Safety Committee to adopt for implementation, subject to confirmation by the Assembly, any amendments to the general provisions on ships' routeing,

Having adopted amendments to resolution A.378(X) by resolutions A.428(XI), A.475(XII) and A.527(13),

Having also adopted resolutions A.376(X) and A.377(X) establishing procedures for the adoption of traffic separation schemes and other routeing systems,

Desiring that all routeing systems including traffic separation schemes thereby adopted conform uniformly to the same general criteria and principles,

Recognizing the need to consolidate and improve the general provisions on ships' routeing, taking account of the International Regulations for Preventing Collisions at Sea 1972, as amended,

Having considered the recommendations made by the Maritime Safety Committee at its forty-ninth and fifty-first sessions,

1.   *Confirms* the amendments to the general provisions on ships' routeing adopted by the Maritime Safety Committee at its forty-ninth and fifty-first sessions;

2.   *Adopts* the consolidated text of the general provisions on ships' routeing set out in the annex to the present resolution;

3.   *Urges* Governments, when planning either to introduce new routeing systems or to amend existing systems, to ensure that such systems comply with the general provisions on ships' routeing set out in the annex to the present resolution;

4.   *Reaffirms* its authorization to the Maritime Safety Committee to adopt for implementation, subject to confirmation by the Assembly, any amendments to the general provisions on ships' routeing and to advise all concerned accordingly,

5.   *Revokes* resolutions A.378(X), A.428(XI), Annex 2 to resolution A.475(XII) and Annex 2 to resolution A.527(13); and

6.   *Requests* the Secretary-General to bring the present resolution to the attention of the International Hydrographic Organization.

ANNEX

GENERAL PROVISIONS ON SHIPS' ROUTEING

1.   OBJECTIVES

1.1   The purpose of ships' routeing is to improve the safety of navigation in converging areas and in areas where the density of traffic is great or where freedom of movement of shipping is inhibited by restricted sea-room, the existence of obstructions to navigation, limited depths or unfavourable meteorological conditions.

1.2   The precise objectives of any routeing system will depend upon the particular hazardous circumstances which it is intended to alleviate, but may include some or all of the following:

.1   the separation of opposing streams of traffic so as to reduce the incidence of head on encounters;

.2   the reduction of dangers of collision between crossing traffic and shipping in established traffic lanes;

.3   the simplification of the patterns of traffic flow in converging areas;

.4   the organization of safe traffic flow in areas of concentrated offshore exploration or exploitation;

.5   the organization of traffic flow in or around areas where navigation by all ships or by certain classes of ship is dangerous or undesirable;

.6   the reduction of risk of grounding to providing special guidance to vessels in areas where water depths are uncertain or critical;

.7   the guidance of traffic clear of fishing grounds or the organization of traffic through fishing grounds.

2.   DEFINITIONS

2.1   The following terms are used in connection with matters related to ships' routeing:

.1   *Routeing system* - Any system of one or more routes or routeing measures aimed at reducing the risk of casualties; it includes traffic separation schemes, two-way routes, recommended tracks, areas to be avoided, inshore traffic zones, roundabouts, precautionary areas and deep-water routes.

.2   *Traffic separation scheme** - A routeing measure aimed at the separation of opposing streams of traffic by appropriate means and by the establishment of traffic lanes.

.3   *Separation zone or line** - A zone or line separating the traffic lanes in which ships are proceeding in opposite or nearly opposite directions; or separating a traffic lane from the adjacent sea area, or separating traffic lanes designated for particular classes of ship proceeding in the same direction.

.4   *Traffic lane** - An area within defined limits in which one-way traffic is established. Natural obstacles, including those forming separation zones, may constitute a boundary.

.5   *Roundabout* - A routeing measure comprising a separation point or circular separation zone and a circular traffic lane within defined limits. Traffic within the roundabout is separated by moving in a counterclockwise direction around the separation point or zone.

.6   *Inshore traffic zone** - A routeing measure comprising a designated area between the landward boundary of a traffic separation scheme and the adjacent coast, to be used in accordance with the Provisions of rule 10(d), as amended, of the International Regulations for Preventing Collisions at Sea (Collision Regulations), 1972.

.7   *Two-way route* - A route within defined limits inside which two way traffic is established, aimed at providing safe passage of ships through waters where navigation is difficult or dangerous.

.8   *Recommended route* - A route of undefined width, for the convenience of ships in transit, which is often marked by centre line buoys.

.9   *Recommended track* - A route which has been specially examined to ensure so far as possible that it is free of dangers and along which ships are advised to navigate.

.10   *Deep-water route* - A route within defined limits which has been accurately surveyed for clearance of sea bottom and submerged obstacles as indicated on the chart.

*   These terms are used in the 1972 Collision Regulations.

.11   *Precautionary area* - A routeing measure comprising an area within defined limits where ships must navigate with particular caution and within which the direction of traffic flow may be recommended.

.12   *Area to be avoided* - A routeing measure comprising an area within defined limits in which either navigation is particularly hazardous or it is exceptionally important to avoid casualties and which should be avoided by all ships, or certain classes of ship.

.13   *Established direction of traffic flow* - A traffic flow pattern indicating the directional movement of traffic as established within a traffic separation scheme.

.14   *Recommended direction of traffic flow* - A traffic flow pattern indicating a recommended directional movement of traffic where it is impractical or unnecessary to adopt an established direction of traffic flow.

3.   PROCEDURES AND RESPONSIBILITIES

Procedures and functions of IMO

3.1   IMO is recognized as the only international body responsible for establishing and recommending measures on an international level concerning ships' routeing.

3.2   In deciding whether or not to adopt or amend a traffic separation scheme, IMO will consider whether:

.1   the aids to navigation proposed will enable mariners to determine their position with sufficient accuracy to navigate in the scheme in accordance with rule 10 of the 1972 Collision Regulations, as amended;

.2   the state of hydrographic surveys in the area is adequate;

.3   the scheme takes account of the accepted planning considerations and complies with the design criteria for traffic separation schemes and with established methods of routeing.

3.3   In deciding whether or not to adopt or amend a routeing system other than a traffic separation scheme, IMO will consider whether the aids to navigation and the state of hydrographic surveys are adequate for the purpose of the system.

3.4   IMO shall not adopt or amend any routeing system without the agreement of the interested coastal States, where that system may affect:

.1   their rights and practices in respect of the exploitation of living and mineral resources;

.2   the environment, traffic pattern or established routeing systems in the waters concerned;

.3   demands for improvements or adjustments in the navigational aids or hydrographic surveys in the waters concerned.

Responsibilities of Governments and recommended practices

3.5   A new or amended routeing system adopted by IMO shall not come into force as an IMO adopted system before an effective date promulgated by the Government that proposed the system, which shall be communicated to IMO by the responsible Government. That date shall not be earlier than six months after the date of adoption of a routeing system by IMO but, when new chart editions necessitate a substantially longer period between adoption and implementation, IMO shall set a later date as required by the circumstances of the case. If the Government that proposed the system is unable at the time of adoption by IMO to declare a definite date of implementation, this information should be communicated to IMO as soon as possible thereafter and the implementation date then declared should not be earlier than four months after the date on which the declaration is made; in the case of a traffic separation scheme the exact time of implementation should also be stated. If there is a protracted delay in making such a declaration, the Government concerned should periodically inform IMO of the situation and forecast when implementation is likely to be possible. Either Notices to Mariners to amend charts, or revised charts to depict the system shall be made available in ample time before the system comes into force.

3.6　The responsible Government implementing a new or amended routeing system should ensure that full and final details of planned changes to aids to navigation, anchorage areas or pilot boarding areas which are closely associated with the system and important to its effective utilization by the mariner are provided to the appropriate hydrographic authority at least six months prior to the date of implementation.

3.7　The selection and development of routeing systems is primarily the responsibility of the Governments concerned.

3.8　A Government proposing a new routeing system or an amendment to an adopted routeing system, any part of which lies beyond its territorial sea, should consult IMO so that such system may be adopted or amended by IMO for international use. Such Government should furnish all relevant information, in particular with regard to the number, edition and where possible the geodetic datum of the reference chart used for the delineation of the routeing system. If appropriate, it should also provide the following additional information:

> .1　the reasons for excluding certain ships or classes of ship from using a routeing system or any part thereof; and
>
> .2　any alternative routeing measures, if necessary, for ships or certain classes of ship which may be excluded from using a routeing system or parts thereof.

Such a system, when adopted, shall not be amended or suspended before consultation with and agreement by IMO, unless local conditions and the urgency of the case require that earlier action be taken. In considering the proposal, IMO shall take account of the objectives, procedures, responsibilities, methods and criteria for routeing systems as set out in these general provisions.

3.9　In an emergency such as might result from the unexpected blocking or obstruction of a traffic lane by a wreck or other hazard, immediate temporary changes in the use of the affected traffic separation scheme may be made by the responsible and sponsoring Government or Governments, with the object of directing traffic flow clear of the new hazard. In such cases, every possible measure shall be taken by the Government or Governments concerned immediately to inform shipping of the hazard and of the temporary changes which have been made.

3.10　Governments are recommended to ensure, as far as practicable, that oil rigs, platforms and other similar structures are not established within routeing systems adopted by IMO or near their terminations. When the temporary positioning of an exploration rig or a similar structure in an adopted traffic separation scheme cannot be avoided, the scheme should, if necessary, be amended temporarily in accordance with the guidelines given in section 7.

3.11 If the above exploration activities lead to the finding of important exploitation prospects, the effect of subsequent exploitation on the safety of marine traffic should be considered carefully. If the establishment of permanent installations within a traffic separation scheme is unavoidable, permanent amendments to the scheme, if deemed necessary, should be submitted to IMO for adoption.

3.12 Governments establishing traffic separation schemes, no parts of which lie beyond their territorial seas, are requested to design them in accordance with IMO criteria for such schemes and submit them to IMO for adoption.

3.13 Where, for whatever reason, a Government decides not to submit a traffic separation scheme to IMO, it should, in promulgating the scheme to mariners, ensure that there are clear indications on charts and in nautical publications as to what rules apply to the scheme.

3.14 Governments establishing routeing systems, other than traffic separation schemes, no parts of which lie beyond their territorial seas, are recommended to follow the same procedure as that set out in paragraphs 3.12 and 3.13 above.

3.15 By rules 10(k) and 10(1) respectively of the 1972 Collision Regulations a vessel restricted in her ability to manoeuvre when engaged in an operation for either the maintenance of safety of navigation or the laying, servicing or picking up of a submarine cable in a traffic separation scheme is exempted from complying with rule 10 to the extent necessary to carry out the operation. The Government or authority responsible for safety of navigation in a traffic separation scheme should ensure that:

.1 the intention of undertaking such an operation is first notified to each Government or appropriate authority concerned;
.2 information about such ships working in a traffic separation scheme is, as far as practicable, promulgated in advance by Notice to Mariners, and subsequently by radionavigation warnings broadcast before and at regular intervals during the operations;
.3 such operations are, as far as possible, avoided in conditions of restricted visibility.

3.16 Nothing in the general provisions on ships' routeing shall prejudice the provisions of the United Nations Convention on the Law of the Sea (1982) nor the present or future claims and legal views of any State concerning the law of the sea and the nature and extent of coastal and flag State jurisdiction.

4. METHODS

In meeting the objectives set out in section 1 the following are among the methods which may be used:

.1 The separation of opposing streams of traffic by separation zones, or lines where zones are not possible . . .
.2 The separation of opposing streams of traffic by natural obstructions and geographically defined objects . . .

.3   The separation of through and local traffic by providing inshore traffic zones. . . Beyond the outside limits of traffic separation schemes, ships may navigate in any direction. Where such areas lie between the traffic separation scheme and the coast they may be designated as inshore traffic zones. . ., with the purpose of keeping local traffic clear of the traffic separation scheme which should be used by through traffic . . .

.4   The sectorial division of adjacent traffic separation schemes at approaches to focal points . . .

.5   The routeing of traffic at focal points and route junctions where traffic separation schemes meet . . .

.6   Other routeing methods . . .

.6.1 deep-water routes . . .

.6.2 areas to be avoided . . .

.6.3 recommended directions of traffic flow . . . , two-way routes . . . and recommended routes and tracks through areas where navigation is difficult or dangerous.

[Note: The above METHODS are illustrated by Figures]

. . .

5.   PLANNING

5.1   Routeing systems should only be established when safety of navigation in the area can thereby be clearly improved.

5.2   The routeing system selected for a particular area should aim at providing safe passage for ships through the area without unduly restricting legitimate rights and practices, and taking account of anticipated or existing navigational hazards.

5.3   When planning, establishing, reviewing or adjusting a routeing system, the following factors shall be among those taken into account by a Government:

.1   their rights and practices in respect of the exploitation of living and mineral resources;

.2   previously established routeing systems in adjacent waters, whether or not under the proposing Government's jurisdiction;

.3   the existing traffic pattern in the area concerned, including coastal traffic, crossing traffic, naval exercise areas and anchorage areas;

.4   foreseeable changes in the traffic pattern resulting from port or offshore terminal developments;

.5   the presence of fishing grounds;

.6   existing activities and foreseeable developments of offshore exploration or exploitation of the sea-bed and subsoil;

.7   the adequacy of existing aids to navigation, hydrographic surveys and nautical charts of the area;

.8   environmental factors including prevailing weather conditions, tidal streams and currents and the possibility of ice concentrations; and

.9   the existence of environmental conservation areas and foreseeable developments in the establishment of such areas.

5.4   Routeing systems should be reviewed, re-surveyed and adjusted as necessary, so as to maintain their effectiveness and compatibility with trade patterns, offshore exploration and resource exploitation, changes in depths of water, and other developments.

5.5   Routeing systems should not be established in areas where the instability of the sea-bed is such that frequent changes in the alignment and positions of the main channels, and thus of the routeing system itself, are likely.

5.6   When establishing areas to be avoided by all ships or by certain classes of ship, the necessity for creating such areas should be well demonstrated and the reasons stated. In general, these areas should be established only in places where inadequate survey or insufficient provision of aids to navigation may lead to danger of stranding, or where local knowledge is considered essential for safe passage, or where there is the possibility that unacceptable damage to the environment could result from a casualty, or where there might be hazard to a vital aid to navigation. These areas shall not be regarded as prohibited areas unless specifically so stated; the classes of ship which should avoid the areas should be considered in each particular case.

5.7   Governments considering establishing a new routeing system or amending an existing one should consult at an early stage with:

   .1   mariners using the area;
   .2   authorities responsible for aids to navigation and for hydrographic surveys and
         nautical publications;
   .3   port authorities; and
   .4   organizations concerned with fishing, offshore exploration or exploitation and
         environmental protection, as appropriate.

This consultation process is implied in paragraphs 3.4, 3.8, 5.3, 5.5 and 6.2.

6.   DESIGN CRITERIA

6.1   The following standards should, so far as the circumstances allow, be applied in the design of ships' routeing measures.

General

6.2   Routes should follow as closely as possible the existing patterns of traffic flow in the areas as determined by traffic surveys.

6.3   The configuration and length of routeing systems which are established to provide for an unobstructed passage through offshore exploration and exploitation areas may differ from the dimensions of normally established systems if the purpose of safeguarding a clear passage warrants such a special feature.

6.4   Course alterations along a route should be as few as possible and should be avoided in the approaches to converge areas and route junctions or where crossing traffic may be expected to be heavy.

6.5   The number of convergence areas and route junctions should be kept to a minimum, and should be as widely separated from each other as possible. Adjacent traffic separation schemes should be placed such that nearly opposing streams of traffic in the adjacent schemes are separated as widely as possible. Route junctions should not be located where concentrated crossing traffic, not following established routes, may be expected, e.g. ferry traffic.

6.6   Routes should be designed to allow optimum use of aids to navigation in the area, and of such shipborne navigational aids as are required or recommended to be fitted by international conventions or by IMO resolutions and recommendations.

6.7   The state of hydrographic surveys within the limits of a routeing system and in the approaches thereto should be such that full information on existing depths of water hazards to surface navigation is available to nautical charting authorities.

6.8   The extent of a traffic separation scheme should be limited to what is essential in the interests of safe navigation.

6.9   Traffic lanes should be designed to make optimum use of available depths of water and the safe navigable areas taking into account the maximum depth of water attainable along the length of the route. The width of lanes should take account of the traffic density, the general usage of the area and sea-room available.

6.10   Where there is sufficient space, separation zones should be used in preference to separation lines to separate opposing streams of traffic and to segregate inshore traffic zones from adjacent traffic lanes. Separation zones or lines may also be used to separate a traffic lane from adjacent sea areas other than inshore traffic zones, in appropriate circumstances, taking into account traffic density and the available means of fixing ships' positions.

6.11   It should be possible for ships to fix their position anywhere within the limits of and in the immediate approaches to a traffic separation scheme by one of the following means, both by day and night:

    .1   visual bearings of readily identifiable objects;
    .2   radar bearings and ranges of readily identifiable objects; and
    .3   D/F bearings.

6.12   When it is concerned essential to provide within a traffic separation scheme an additional lane for ships carrying hazardous liquid substances in bulk, as specified in the International Convention for the Prevention of Pollution from Ships, 1973, in circumstances where it is not possible for ships to fix their position as set out in paragraph 6.11 over the whole area of that lane and an electronic position-fixing system covers that area, the existence of that system may be taken into account when designing the scheme.

6.13   The minimum widths of traffic lanes and of traffic separation zones should be related to the accuracy of the available position-fixing methods, accepting the appropriate performance standards for shipborne equipment as set out in IMO resolutions and recommendations.

6.14   Where space allows the use of traffic separation zones, the width of the zone should, if possible, be not less than three times the transverse component of the standard error (measured across the separation zone) of the most appropriate of the fixing methods listed in paragraph 6.11. Where necessary or desirable, and where practicable, additional separation should be provided to ensure that there will be adequate early indication that traffic proceeding in the opposite direction will pass on the correct side.

6.15   If there is doubt as to the ability of ships to fix their positions positively and without ambiguity in relation to separation lines or zones, serious consideration should be given to providing adequate marking buoys.

Converging and junction areas . . .

. . .

Deep-water routes . . .

7.   TEMPORARY ADJUSTMENTS TO TRAFFIC SEPARATION SCHEMES

7.1   When the temporary positioning of an exploration rig is unavoidable, the design criteria and the provisions for planning should be taken into account before permitting the positioning of the rig or subsequently adjusting a traffic separation scheme.

. . .

7.4   Details of these temporary adjustments should be forwarded to IMO and to appropriate hydrographic offices at least four months before the rig is positioned within an adopted traffic separation scheme so as to allow ample time to inform shipping . . .

7.5   In the event of a temporary adjustment to a traffic separation scheme remaining in force for more than one year, the responsible government should consider whether permanent amendments to the scheme may ultimately become necessary and, if appropriate, initiate timely procedures for IMO to adopt such amendments.

8.   THE USE OF ROUTEING SYSTEMS

8.1   Routeing systems are intended for use by day and by night in all weathers, in ice-free waters or under light ice conditions where no extraordinary manoeuvres or ice breaker assistance are required.

8.2   Routeing systems are recommended for use by all ships unless stated otherwise. Bearing in mind the need for adequate under-keel clearance, a decision to use a routeing system must take into account the charted depth, the possibility of changes in the sea-bed since the time of the last survey, and the effects of meteorological and tidal conditions on water depths.

8.3   A ship navigating in or near a traffic separation scheme adopted by IMO shall in particular comply with rule 10 of the 1972 Collision Regulations to minimize the development of risk of collision with another ship. The other rules of the 1972 Collision Regulations apply in all respects, and particularly the rules of part B, sections II and III, if risk of collision with another ship is deemed to exist.

. . .

9.   REPRESENTATION ON CHARTS

. . .

- - - - -

IMO Assembly　　　　　　　　　　　　　　　　　　　　　　　A 14/Res.578
14th Session, December 1985

Resolution A.578(14)
Guidelines for Vessel Traffic Services

The Assembly,

Recalling Article 15(j) of the Convention on the International Maritime Organization concerning the functions of the Assembly in relation to regulations and guidelines concerning maritime safety and the prevention and control of marine pollution from ships,

Recalling also resolution A.158(ES.IV) entitled "Recommendation on Port Advisory Services" and resolution A.531(13) entitled "General Principles for Ship Reporting Systems",

Bearing in mind that Member Governments are responsible for the safety of navigation and the prevention of pollution in areas under their jurisdiction,

Being informed that vessel traffic services have been provided in a number of areas and have made a valuable contribution to safety of navigation, improved efficiency of traffic flow and reduced risk of pollution,

Being also informed that a number of Governments and international organizations have requested guidance on vessel traffic services,

Recognizing that the level of safety and efficiency in the movement of maritime traffic within a vessel traffic service area is dependent upon close co-operation between those operating the vessel traffic service and participating vessels,

Recognizing also that the use of differing vessel traffic service procedures may cause confusion to masters of vessels moving from one vessel traffic service area to another,

Recognizing further that the safety and efficiency of maritime traffic would be improved if vessel traffic services were established and operated in accordance with internationally approved guidelines,

Having considered the recommendation made by the Maritime Safety Committee at its fifty-first session,

1.　*Adopts* the Guidelines for Vessel Traffic Services set out in the Annex to the present resolution;

2.　*Urges* Member Governments to ensure that vessel traffic services within their territorial seas are operated in accordance with national law and do not prejudice the right of innocent passage through such seas and to ensure that vessels outside territorial seas are able to use, on a voluntary basis, the service provided;

3.   *Recommends* Member Governments to encourage masters of vessels navigating in an area for which a vessel traffic service is provided to make use of such service.

ANNEX

GUIDELINES FOR VESSEL TRAFFIC SERVICES

PREAMBLE

1.   These Guidelines describe operational procedures and planning for vessel traffic services (VTS). The Guidelines do not address liability or responsibility - which should be considered by the authority establishing a VTS - nor do they create new rights to enact legislation which impose requirements on shipping.

2.   VTS authorities are urged to ensure that vessel traffic services within territorial seas are operated in accordance with national law and do not prejudice the right of innocent passage through such waters and to ensure that vessels outside territorial seas are able to use, on a voluntary basis, the service provided.

3.   No provision of these Guidelines shall be construed as prejudicing obligations or rights of vessels established in other international instruments.

4.   VTS authorities or those planning VTS are recommended to follow these Guidelines, as appropriate to their needs, in the interests of international harmonization and improving maritime safety.

5.   These Guidelines describe the possible functions of VTS and provide guidance for designing and operating VTS once it has been decided that such a system, whether simple or highly sophisticated, is necessary. They further aim at international harmonization and address the procedures used by VTS taking into account current practice. They are based on relevant recommendations and resolutions adopted by the Organization, in particular Assembly resolution A.531(13) entitled "General Principles for Ship Reporting Systems".

CHAPTER 1 - OBJECTIVES AND PROCEDURES

1.   **Vessel traffic services**

A VTS is any service implemented by a competent authority, designed to improve safety and efficiency of traffic and the protection of the environment. It may range from the provision of simple information messages to extensive management of traffic within a port or waterway.

1.1   The reasons for establishing a VTS may include:
  - assistance to navigation in appropriate areas;
  - organization of vessel movements to facilitate an efficient traffic flow in the VTS area;
  - handling of data relating to ships involved;
  - participation in action in case of accident;
  - support of allied activities.

1.2   A VTS is particularly appropriate in the approaches to a port, in its access channels and in areas having one or more of the following characteristics:
- high traffic density;
- traffic carrying noxious or dangerous cargoes;
- navigational difficulties;
- narrow channels;
- environmental sensitivity.

2.   VTS authority

2.1   "VTS authority" is the authority operating a VTS. It may include a governmental maritime administration, a single port authority, a pilotage organization or any combination of them.

2.1.1   The authority establishing a VTS should delineate its area of coverage, declare it a VTS area and disseminate to mariners full details concerning the area of operation, including the limits of the areas where participation of vessels is required or recommended, the services provided and the procedures to be followed (see section 5). It should also state the classes of ship which are required or recommended to participate and indicate the VTS centres responsible for the VTS tasks.

2.1.2   The authority should establish appropriate qualifications and training requirements for VTS operators in accordance with section 6.

2.1.3   The VTS authority should ensure that the effects of vessel traffic services, routeing, aids to navigation, pilotage, etc. are fully integrated.

2.1.4   The VTS authority should in general limit the functions of a VTS operating outside port areas and their approach channels to those of providing an information service and navigational assistance service to vessels for the purposes of safety of navigation or the protection of the environment.

2.1.5   Care should be taken that VTS operations do not encroach upon the master's responsibility for the safe navigation of his vessel, or disturb the traditional relationship between master and pilot.

2.1.6   When planning or designing a VTS, the authority should take into account the factors and criteria of chapter 2.

3.   Elements of a VTS

3.1   General

A VTS consists of the following elements:
VTS organization;
vessels using VTS;
communications.

3.2   VTS organization . . .

3.3   **Vessels using a VTS . . .**

3.4   **Communications . . .**

4.   **Functions of a VTS**

. . .

4.3   **Data evaluation**

Data evaluation may include:
- monitoring the manoeuvres of ships for compliance with international, national and local requirements and regulations;
- interpreting the total traffic situation and its developments;
- monitoring the fairway situation (hydrological and meteorological data, aids to navigation);
- co-ordinating the information flow and distributing relevant messages to the participants or organizations concerned;
- collating information for statistical purposes.

4.4   **Information service**

An information service is a service provided by broadcasting information at fixed times, or at any other time if deemed necessary by the VTS centre, or at the request of a vessel and may include:

- broadcasting information about the movement of traffic, visibility conditions or the intentions of other vessels, in order to assist all vessels, including small craft that are participating in the VTS only by keeping a listing watch;
- exchanging information with vessels on all relevant safety matters notices to mariners, status of aids to navigation, meteorological and hydrological information, etc.);
- exchanging information with vessels on relevant traffic conditions and situations (movements and intentions of approaching traffic or traffic being overtaken);
- warning vessels about hindrances to navigation such as hampered vessels, concentrations of fishing vessels, small craft, other vessels engaged in special operations, and giving information on alternative routeing.

4.5   **Navigational assistance service . . .**

4.6   **Traffic organization service . . .**

4.7   **Support of allied activities . . .**

5.   **Procedures**

. . .

6.   **Personnel**

. . .

7.   **VTS Publication for users**

. . .

CHAPTER 2 - PLANNING A VTS

1.   The safety of maritime traffic in a VTS area is necessarily a co-operative activity between those ashore and those at sea. It is therefore important, whenever a VTS is being planned and designed, that, amongst others, the mariner's views on the need for and operation of the service are taken into account. The level of need should also be considered. This will assist in the effective implementation of VTS and facilitate the co-operation of all the future participants and promote confidence in the procedures to be followed.

2.   When considering the introduction of a VTS, the authority should verify that its operation will be in accordance with international and national law.

3.   When planning a VTS, the VTS authority should be guided by criteria such as:

     .1   the general risk of marine accidents and their possible consequences and the density of traffic in the area;

     .2   the need to protect the public and safety of the environment, particularly where dangerous cargoes are involved;

     .3   the operation and economic impact on users of the system and the marine community as a whole;

     .4   the availability of the requisite technology and expertise;

     .5   existing or planned vessel traffic services in adjacent waters and the need for co-operation between neighbouring States;

     .6   existing or proposed traffic patterns or routeing systems in the area, including the presence of fishing grounds and small craft;

     .7   existing or foreseeable changes in the traffic pattern resulting from port or offshore terminal developments or offshore exploration in the area;

     .8   the adequacy of existing communications systems and navigation in the area;

     .9   consultation of interested parties and assessment of prospect procedures;

   .10   meteorological factors such as weather and ice conditions;

   .11   hydrological factors such as tides, tidal ranges and currents; and

   .12   narrow channels, port configuration, bridges and similar areas where the progress of vessels may be restricted.

4.   A VTS area can be divided into sectors but these should be as few as possible. The boundaries should be indicated in appropriate nautical publications.

5.   Area and sector boundaries should not be located where vessels normally alter course or manoeuvre or where they are approaching convergence areas, route junctions or where there is crossing traffic.

6.   VTS centres in an area or sector should use name identifier.

7.   Reporting points should be clearly identified, for example by number, sector, name and a geographical position or description. They should be kept to a minimum and be as widely separated as possible.

- - - - -

IMO Maritime Safety Committee   MSC 53/24
Report of the Fifty-third Session, September 1986   Extract

. . .

Traffic separation scheme "In the Strait of Hormuz"

3.12   Greece (MSC 53/3/3) informed the Committee that it received from time to time reports on infringements by Greek flag vessels of the traffic separation scheme "In the Strait of Hormuz". While Greek legislation provides for penalties for those who contravene the Collision Regulations and every report is investigated, certain cases are judged on the basis of the term "normally" in rule 10(d) of the 1972 Collision Regulations which allows a certain degree of flexibility in the use of a TSS's inshore traffic zone (ITZ). Greece proposed the Sub-Committee on Safety of Navigation study this matter with a view to recommending additional measures which may be necessary to strengthen the safety of navigation in the area and to allow use by through traffic of the ITZ in the scheme.

3.13   Bearing in mind that "the selection and development of routeing schemes is primarily the responsibility of the Governments concerned" (General Provisions on Ships' Routeing - A.572(14)), the Committee deferred consideration of this matter and invited the Government of the Sultanate of Oman to consider MSC 53/3/3 and submit its comments to the Committee's 54th session.

. . .

- - - - -

IMO Maritime Safety Committee   MSC 54/23
Report of the Fifty-fourth Session, May 1987   Extract

. . .

Traffic separation scheme "In the Strait of Hormuz"

. . .

6.2.7   Oman informed the Committee (MSC 54/INF.12) that its Government was satisfied with the operation of the Strait of Hormuz routeing system, including the current traffic separation scheme and inshore traffic zone, and hoped that the system would continue to operate as it does at present. Oman could not support the proposal of Greece and preferred to preserve, without any change, the local character of the inshore traffic zone. Oman considered any change would be antithetical to the current scheme's purpose of promoting maritime safety in the Strait of Hormuz.

. . .

- - - - -

2

Safety of Fishing Vessels

IMO Assembly   A 15/Res.599
15th Session, November 1987

Resolution A.599(15)
Avoidance by Submerged Submarines of
Fishing Vessels and Their Fishing Gear

The Assembly,

Recalling Article 15(j) of the Convention on the International Maritime Organization concerning the functions of the Assembly in relation to regulations and guidelines concerning maritime safety,

Considering the danger to a fishing vessel when its fishing gear is entangled by a submerged submarine,

Taking into account the navigational and safety information available to submarines and fishing vessels and the fact that a fishing vessel would have no information that a submerged submarine is operating in its vicinity and also that a submarine might not have information that a fishing vessel is operating in its vicinity,

Having considered the recommendation made by the Maritime Safety Committee at its fifty-second session,

Recommends that a submerged submarine, if information of the presence of a fishing vessel and its fishing gear is available, should, as far as possible, keep out of the way of that fishing vessel and any fishing gear connected to it unless the submarine is disabled.

- - - - -

3

Ship Reporting

IMO Assembly   A 15/Res.598/Rev.1
15th Session, November 1987

Resolution A.598(15)
General Principles for Ship Reporting
Systems and Ship Reporting Requirements

The Assembly,

Recalling Article 15(j) of the Convention on the International Maritime Organization concerning the functions of the Assembly in relation to regulations and guidelines concerning maritime safety and the prevention and control of marine pollution from ships,

Recalling also resolution 3 of the International Conference on Maritime Search and Rescue, 1979, on the need for an internationally agreed format and procedure for ship reporting systems,

Recalling further article 8 and Protocol I of the International Convention for the Prevention of Pollution from Ships, 1973, as modified by the Protocol of 1978 relating thereto (MARPOL 73/78), as amended, and also the guidelines for reporting incidents involving harmful substances resolution MEPC 22(22),

Considering that current national ship reporting systems may use different procedures and reporting formats,

Considering further that reporting requirements for loss or likely loss of dangerous goods and harmful substances are not identical,

Recognizing that such different procedures and reporting formats could cause confusion to masters of ships moving from one area to another area covered by different ship reporting systems,

Recognizing further that such confusion could be alleviated if ship reporting systems and reporting requirements were to comply as far as practicable with a number of general principles and if reports were made in accordance with a standard format and procedures,

Having considered the recommendation made by the Maritime Safety Committee at its fifty-fourth session and by the Marine Environment Protection Committee at its twenty-fourth session,

1. *Adopts* the General Principles for Ship Reporting Systems and Ship Reporting Requirements set out in the Annex to the present resolution;

2.   *Urges* Member Governments to ensure that ship reporting systems and reporting requirements comply as closely as possible with the general principles specified in the Annex to the present resolution;

3.   *Urges* Member Governments to bring the reporting format and procedures to the notice of shipowners and seafarers as well as the designated authorities concerned;

4.   *Revokes* resolution A.531(13).

ANNEX

GENERAL PRINCIPLES FOR SHIP REPORTING SYSTEMS
AND SHIP REPORTING REQUIREMENTS

Ship reporting systems and reporting requirements are used to provide, gather or exchange information through radio reports. The information is used to provide data for many purposes including search and rescue, vessel traffic services, weather forecasting and prevention of marine pollution. Ship reporting systems and reporting requirements should, as far as practicable, comply with the following principles:

1.   Reports should contain only information essential to achieve the objectives of the system.

2.   Reports should be simple and use the standard international ship reporting format and procedures. Where language difficulties may exist, the languages used should include English, using where possible the Standard Marine Navigational Vocabulary, or alternatively the International Code of Signals. The standard reporting format and procedures to be used are given in the appendix to this Annex.

3.   The number of reports should be kept to a minimum.

4.   No charge should be made for communication of reports.

5.   Safety or pollution related reports should be made without delay; however, the time and place of making non-urgent reports should be sufficiently flexible to avoid interference with essential navigational duties.

6.   Information obtained from the system should be made available to other systems when required for distress, safety and pollution purposes.

7.   Basic information (ship's particulars, on-board facilities and equipment, etc.) should be reported once, be retained in the system and be updated by the ship when changes occur in the basic information reported.

8.   The purpose of the system should be clearly defined.

9.   Governments establishing a ship reporting system should notify mariners of full details of the requirements to be met and procedures to be followed. Details regarding types of ships and areas of applicability, times and geographical positions for submitting reports, shore establishments responsible for operation of the system services provided should be clearly

specified.   Chartlets depicting boundaries of the system and providing other necessary information should be made available to mariners.

10.   The establishment and operation of a ship reporting system should take into account:

.1   international as well as national responsibilities and requirements;

.2   the cost to ship operators and responsible authorities;

.3   navigational hazards;

.4   existing and proposed aids to safety;

.5   the need for early and continuing consultation with interested parties including a sufficient period to allow for trial, familiarization and assessment to ensure satisfactory operation and to allow necessary changes to be made to the system.

11.   Governments should ensure that shore establishments responsible for operation of the system are manned by properly trained persons.

12.   Governments should consider the interrelationship between ship reporting systems and other systems.

13.   Ship reporting systems should preferably use a single operating radio frequency; where additional frequencies are necessary, the number of frequencies should be restricted to the minimum required for the effective operation of the system.

14.   Information provided by the system to ships should be restricted to that necessary for the proper operation of the system and for safety.

15.   Ship reporting systems and requirements should provide for special reports from ships concerning defects or deficiencies with respect to their hull, machinery, equipment or manning, or concerning other limitations which could adversely affect navigation and for special reports concerning incidents of actual or probable marine pollution.

16.   Governments should issue instructions to their shore establishments responsible for the operation of ship reporting systems to ensure that any reports involving pollutions, actual or probable, are relayed without delay to the officer or agency nominated to receive and process such reports, and to ensure that such an officer or agency relays these reports without delay to the flag State of the ship involved and to any other State which may be affected.

17.   States which are affected or likely to be affected by pollution incidents and may require information relevant to the incident should take into account the circumstances in which the master is placed, and should endeavour to limit their requests for additional information.

18.   Danger messages referred to under regulation V/2 of SOLAS 74, as amended, are not included in the appendix to this Annex. The present practice of transmitting such messages should remain unchanged.

19.   The present General Principles for Ship Reporting Systems and Ship Reporting Requirements are intended to supplement, not to replace, the guidelines for reporting incidents involving harmful substances referred to in article V of Protocol I of MARPOL 73/78 (resolution MEPC 22(22) as may be amended).

- - - - -

4

Maritime Communications

IMO Sub-Committee on Safety of Navigation   NAV 33/15
Report of the Thirty-third Session, January 1987   Extract

. . .

5. Matters Concerning Search and Rescue

. . .

Procedures for routeing distress communications

. . .

5.1.23   With respect to the GMDSS implementation and its potential impact on SAR facilities, the Sub-Committee expected the system to offer a unique opportunity to substantially improve the efficiency of SAR resources. It was therefore considered important to implement the GMDSS in an orderly and uniform manner so that a definite target date and universal implementation of the GMDSS are provided. The Sub-Committee invited the Committee to take account of this view when considering the legal procedures for introducing the GMDSS.

. . .

- - - - -

IMO Assembly   A 15/12
15th Session, November 1987   Extract

Consideration of the Reports and Recommendations
of the Maritime Safety Committee
Note by the Secretary-General

. . .

Global maritime distress and safety system (GMDSS)

11.   The Committee made significant progress in the preparatory work for the introduction of the GMDSS. The Committee, at its fifty-fifth session, is expected to finalize the draft text of amendments to the 1974 SOLAS Convention for consideration by the 1988 Conference or expanded Maritime Safety Committee for adoption. The Committee has also approved, or is expected to approve at its fifty-fifth session, the performance standards for the GMDSS equipment and other recommendations and guidelines, supplementary to the revised chapter IV of SOLAS 74.

12.   The Council, at its fifty-seventh session, noted the progress made in the development of the GMDSS and urged early clarification by the Committee of the administrative, financial and operational arrangements necessary for its introduction. The Council, at its fifty-eighth session, reaffirmed this decision.

13.   The Committee has been collecting and reviewing information on financial and administrative implications of the introduction of the GMDSS, including the estimated cost of shipborne installations, the estimated cost for the provision of shore-based facilities, the status of the COSPAS-SARSAT system and its availability for the GMDSS, etc.

14.   The Committee, at its fifty-third session, approved a publication describing the GMDSS which was prepared for the benefit of maritime and telecommunication administrations of countries not regularly participating in IMO meetings. The booklet was circulated to IMO Member Governments and transmitted to the International Telecommunication Union (ITU) for distribution to its Member Governments.

15.   The Committee, at its fifty-second and fifty-third sessions, considered the procedures by which GMDSS provisions should be introduced into the SOLAS Convention. Several delegations favoured the use of the tacit acceptance procedure for the SOLAS amendments adopted by the expanded Maritime Safety Committee while other delegations supported the adoption by a diplomatic conference of amendments by means of a SOLAS protocol.

16.   The Committee, at its fifty-fourth session, continued its consideration of legal procedures to be followed for the introduction of the GMDSS in SOLAS 74, during which various alternative methods for amending chapters I and IV of SOLAS were proposed.

17.   The Committee established an *ad hoc* group to identify practical methods which might be used to amend the SOLAS Convention to introduce the GMDSS, with the following instructions:

.1   the amendment procedure used should ensure that the revised chapter IV would apply to all Contracting Governments to the 1974 SOLAS Convention; and

.2   the date for full implementation of the revised chapter IV by all Governments should be fixed and determined by the Conference.

18.   The Committee noted the report of the group and decided that the subject should be discussed further at its fifty-fifth session so that a decision on legal procedures may be taken at that time.

. . .

- - - - -

IMO Assembly   A 15/Res.606
15th Session, November 1987

Resolution A.606(15)
Review and Evaluation of the Global Maritime
Distress and Safety System (GMDSS)

The Assembly,

Recalling Article 15(j) of the Convention on the International Maritime Organization concerning the functions of the Assembly in relation to regulations and guidelines concerning maritime safety,

Noting the decisions of the WARC-MOB-87, related to the introduction of the GMDSS,

Noting further the provisions of the preliminary draft of a revised chapter IV of the International Convention for the Safety of Life at Sea, 1974, developed for the purpose of establishing the requirements for the introduction of the global maritime distress and safety system (GMDSS),

Recognizing the importance of the GMDSS for the safety of life at sea,

Recognizing also that the GMDSS is provisionally planned to be implemented between 1 August 1991 and 1 February 1997,

Bearing in mind the recommendations contained in resolution A.500(XII), concerning the costs and benefits to the maritime industry of the measures adopted by the Organization,

Bearing also in mind that the investment required for ships to comply with the requirements of the GMDSS may, in many areas, be higher than the investment needed to meet present requirements, in particular for cargo ships of less than 1,600 gross tonnage,

Considering that a review of the requirements for MF DSC, VHF DSC and HF NBDP on cargo ships of less than 1,600 gross tonnage, as set out in this resolution, was a condition for the agreement on GMDSS carriage requirements for these ships and that DSC requirements for ships over 1,600 gross tonnage will be applicable when DSC equipment is available,

Further considering the importance of keeping the operation of the GMDSS and the technical developments related thereto under review,

Requests the Maritime Safety Committee to:

(a) Keep under review the requirements for MF DSC, VHF DSC and HF NBDP on ships of 300 gross tonnage and over but less than 1,600 gross tonnage and for MF DSC and VHF DSC on ships of 1,600 gross tonnage and over, in the light of the cost and demonstrated effectiveness of such facilities compared with alternative systems which may become available prior to the entry into force of the relevant carriage requirements;

(b) Review and evaluate the experience gained with the global maritime distress and safety system (GMDSS) and determine whether, in the future, there is a need to adjust the requirements of the system.

- - - - -

INTERNATIONAL MARITIME SATELLITE ORGANIZATION
ANNUAL REVIEW 1987-1988

ANNUAL REVIEW
1987-1988

1.   Introduction

1.1   The year 1987 was for INMARSAT distinguished by solid progress in a number of key areas. It was also a year in which world-wide interest in mobile-satellite communications continued to grow rapidly a fact which augurs well for all INMARSAT Signatories and Parties in 1988.

1.2   Use of the INMARSAT system grew rapidly. There were 6,488 mobile earth stations commissioned by year end, compared to 4,852 at end 1986. Telephone and telex traffic growth were up 29.6 and 17.8 percent respectively over the previous year's traffic.

1.3   There were many more trails and experiments using INMARSAT by the aviation community. Several new service offerings were announced. The production of avionics and antennas equipment under contract to INMARSAT is proceeding to flight testing in 1988 and early 1989. Pre-operational commercial use of the system is planned to start in 1988, with full commercial aeronautical service coming on stream in 1989.

1.4   The potential for INMARSAT to provide a full range of global mobile-satellite communications services came closer to realization when the Fifth Session of the INMARSAT Assembly encouraged amendment of the Convention and Operating Agreement to give the Organization the institutional competence to provide land mobile-satellite services. Amendments, proposed by the Federal Republic of Germany, are to be considered in 1988. Like the aeronautical amendments to the Convention and Operating Agreement, they confer no monopoly protection. INMARSAT's having the competence to provide land mobile services would be a logical response to the decision of the World Administrative Radio Conference for the Mobile Services in October 1987 to allocate some spectrum for land mobile satellite services.

1.5   The year 1987 also brought five new member countries to INMARSAT, for a total of 53 member countries. Several more are expected to join in the near future. The growing membership provides continuing evidence of the need and benefits of international co-operation.

1.6   Developing countries featured in the recommendations of the Fifth Session of the INMARSAT Assembly held in October 1987. The Assembly recommended development of low cost coast earth stations to extend access to the INMARSAT system and expansion of INMARSAT's technical assignee program for developing countries.

1.7   Although INMARSAT is co-operating with many organizations, the environment in which INMARSAT operates is becoming increasingly competitive. Competition can be welcomed. It should stimulate the development of mobile communications globally and yield many benefits.

1.8   The reality of competition requires INMARSAT to offer the best possible services at the best prices and to appeal to a wide and diversified market in the air, at sea and on land.

1.9   While 1987 brought considerable progress in the development of the INMARSAT system, the challenges of 1988 will be no less formidable - nor any less exciting. Rapid development of the INMARSAT system and services to meet the full force of competition will require major decisions in 1988. As in 1987, solid progress in 1988 will, of course, only be achieved through hard work and co-operation.

    . . .

- - - - -

5

Ship Identification Numbers

IMO Assembly   A 15/12
15th Session, November 1987   Extract

Consideration of the Reports and Recommendations
of the Maritime Safety Committee
Note by the Secretary-General

. . .

Ship identification number scheme

23.   The Committee, for some years, had studied the feasibility of establishing a system of assigning an IMO identification number to each ship which would remain unchanged on change of name or on transfer of flag. The purpose of the scheme is to enhance maritime safety and pollution prevention, and facilitate the prevention of maritime fraud.

24.   The Committee, at its fifty-fourth session, developed a scheme whereby IMO ship identification numbers, using the Lloyd's number, are adopted initially on a voluntary basis and inserted on the ship's certificates. The proposed scheme is forwarded to the Assembly for adoption.

. . .

- - - - -

IMO Assembly   A 15/Res.600
15th Session, November 1987

Resolution A.600(15)
IMO Ship Identification Number Scheme

The Assembly,

Recalling Article 15(j) of the Convention on the International Maritime Organization concerning the functions of the Assembly in relation to regulations and guidelines concerning maritime safety and the prevention and control of marine pollution from ships,

Believing that the enhancement of maritime safety and pollution prevention and the prevention of maritime fraud could be facilitated if a permanent identification number were assigned to a ship which would remain unchanged upon transfer of its flag and would be inserted on ships' certificates,

Having considered the recommendation made by the Maritime Safety Committee at its fifty-fourth session,

1.   *Adopts* the IMO Ship Identification Number Scheme, for implementation on a voluntary basis, as set out in the Annex to the present resolution;

2.   *Invites* Governments concerned to implement the scheme as far as is practicable, and to inform IMO of measures taken in this respect;

3.   *Requests* the Maritime Safety Committee to keep the scheme under review for further improvement as may be necessary.

ANNEX

IMO SHIP IDENTIFICATION NUMBER SCHEME

INTRODUCTION

1.   The purpose of the scheme is to enhance maritime safety and pollution prevention and to facilitate the prevention of maritime fraud. It is not intended to prejudice matters of liability, civil law or other commercial considerations in the operation of a ship. The scheme may be applied by Administrations on a voluntary basis for new and existing ships, under their flag, engaged in international voyages. Administrations may also wish to assign the IMO numbers to ships engaged solely on domestic voyages and to insert the number in the national certificates.

APPLICATION

2.   The scheme applies to seagoing ships of 100 gross tonnage and above, with the exception of the following:

-   vessels solely engaged in fishing;
-   ships without mechanical means of propulsion;
-   pleasure yachts;
-   ships engaged on special service*;
-   hopper barges;
-   hydrofoils, hovercraft;
-   floating docks and structures classified in a similar manner;
-   ships of war and troop ships; and
-   wooden ships in general.

ASSIGNMENT OF IMO NUMBER

3.   The IMO number is a Lloyd's Register (LR) number, allocated at the time of build or when a ship is first included in the register, with the prefix IMO (e.g. IMO 8712345). Administrations which have decided to implement the scheme are invited to assign all appropriate ships flying their flags, or cause them to be assigned, the IMO numbers and to insert them on ships' certificates.

4.   For new ships, the assignment of the IMO number should be made when the ship is registered. For existing ships, the assignment of the IMO number should be made at an early convenient date, such as when the renewal survey is completed or new certificates are issued.

5.   Administrations implementing the scheme are invited to inform the Organization accordingly, for circulation to other Governments.

6.   Official publications and other information from LR and Lloyd's Maritime Information Services (LMIS) are sources for referencing the identification number. If the particulars of a ship do not correspond to those shown in the Register of Ships and its supplement because, for example, the ship had changed its name, or the port State control officer had doubts as to whether the numbers given on the certificates were genuine, further clarification may be sought from Lloyd's Register, the IMO Secretariat or the flag State.

CERTIFICATES ON WHICH THE IMO NUMBER IS TO BE INSERTED

7.   The IMO number should be inserted on a ship's Certificate of Registry which includes the particulars identifying the ship, and on all certificates issued under IMO Conventions when and where appropriate. It is recommended that the IMO number also be inserted in other certificates, such as classification certificates, Suez and Panama tonnage certificates, when and where appropriate. The IMO number should preferably be included in the box headed "Distinctive number or letters" in addition to the call sign.

HOW TO OBTAIN THE IMO NUMBER

8.   The following information indicates how IMO numbers can be obtained for both new and existing ships.

New ships (on order and under construction)

9.   The IMO number can be obtained by one of the following methods:

   .1   Inquiries addressed to the Maritime Information Publishing Group of LR, by telex or facsimile**. In making such inquiry the following particulars, if possible, should be presented:

-    Shipyard and yard number or hull number
-    Ship name (if known)
-    GT/DWT
-    Keel-laid date
-    Owner, operator/manager and flag
-    Basic ship-type***
-    Name and address of inquirer.

Based on the above information, LR will provide the necessary IMO number free of charge. If there are no data in the LR new construction file on the ship concerning which the inquiry is made, a new record on that ship will be created and the LR number will be assigned.

.2   On-line access to the new construction file through SEADATA (IMO has access to this system).

.3   Application through LMIS which will provide a service of regular listings of the order book with selected data items, produced for a client's specification.

Existing ships

10.   The following methods are available for obtaining the IMO number:

.1   The Register of Ships and the 11 cumulative monthly supplements to it published by Lloyd's Register. It is published in 3 volumes and lists details of over 76,000 merchant ships.

.2   The weekly list of alterations to the Register of Ships (non-cumulative) produced by Lloyd's Register.

.3   On-line access to the Lloyd's Register Ship Particulars File through the SEADATA system (IMO has access to this system).

11.   For existing ships, LR is prepared to answer *ad hoc* requests free of charge up to a reasonable point of acceptability.

12.   Any information on charges for services mentioned in paragraphs 9 and 10 may be obtained from Lloyd's Register of Shipping.

Inquiry to the IMO Secretariat

13.   The IMO number may be obtained free of charge from the IMO Secretariat**** which has access to the SEADATA system. In making such an inquiry to the IMO Secretariat, information on particulars of the ship (as in paragraph 9.1) should be provided in writing.

---

*	For example, lightships, floating radio stations, search and rescue vessels.
**	Telex 888379 Telefax (Fax) No. 01-4884796(Group III)
***	Basic ship-types used by LR include:

Passenger	Ferry	General cargo
Specialized cargo	Cellular container	Ro-ro cargo
Bulk	Specialized bulk	Ore carrier
Gas tanker	Gas carrier	Tanker
Specialized tanker	Tug	Factory
Dredger	Sand carrier	ORSV/Supply

(or any combination of these types).

| **** | Telex 23588   Telefax (Fax) No. 5873210 |

- - - - -

6

Port State Control

International Labour Conference   ILO Report I
74th (Maritime) Session, 1987   Extract

Report of the Director-General

. . .

CHAPTER 2. CONDITIONS OF WORK AND LIFE OF SEAFARERS

. . .

Memoranda of Understanding on Port State Control

In pursuance of a resolution adopted by the 1976 Maritime Session of the Conference, the maritime authorities of nine Western European countries decided to introduce a uniform system of port State control of shipping during the interim before entry into force of Convention No. 147. To that end a memorandum on the maintenance of standards of merchant ships (known as the Hague Memorandum) was adopted by a European conference on maritime safety and became effective in 1978. This agreement laid down rules for the enforcement in ports of certain provisions off convention No. 147 and the provisions of a number of IMO Conventions concerning ships' safety and the prevention of marine pollution.

However, owing to continuing maritime accidents in the European region in the succeeding months, a consensus developed that more stringent commitments were necessary which would prevent the operation of substandard ships, while at the same time not creating any distortions of competition between ports. Accordingly, and as referred to previously in this Report, a new Memorandum of Understanding on Port State Control (commonly known as the Paris Memorandum) was signed by representatives of 14 European maritime countries at a Ministerial conference on Maritime Safety, held in Paris in 1982, and came into force during the same year. The scope and area of application of the new Memorandum are broader than those of the earlier one. In addition, a Port State Control Committee was set up to promote effective application of the Memorandum.

At its 24th Session in 1984 the Joint Maritime Commission adopted a resolution which, *inter alia*, requested that information concerning port State inspections and deficiencies be included in the present report. This information is set out below.

During the five years since the Memorandum of Understanding took effect, the number of inspections of visiting foreign flag ships performed by the 14 countries has steadily increased. From July 1985 to June 1986 11,740 inspections were carried out on board 8,721 ships flying the flags of 116 countries and territories. In practical terms this means that a good majority of the ships operating in or visiting the European region are inspected approximately once every six months under the procedures called for by the Memorandum.

Table 3 gives information on ship inspections carried out since July 1983. Although the total number of deficiencies over the three-year period has not tended to decline, the number of ship delays and detentions has significantly decreased. Though this could indicate a decline in serious deficiencies, it is apparent that the objectives of the memorandum to improve compliance with international Conventions will be achieved only gradually.

Table 3.   Inspection of ships by European countries, 1983-86

	Year		
	1983-84	1984-85	1985-86
Number of individual ships inspected	7,686	7,879	8,721
Number of inspections performed	10,227	10,417	11,740
Number of deficiencies	14,011	13,342	15,709
Number of ship delays and detentions	476	356	307
Number of ship delays and detentions as percentage of individual ships inspected	6.19	4.52	3.52

Source: Annual Report on the implementation of the Memorandum of Understanding on Port State Control July 1985-June 1986.

For inspection purposes the nature of deficiencies considered to be clearly hazardous to safety, health or environment are classified into some 20 major categories. These range from ships' safety certificates and navigation equipment to ship manning and crew conditions; they also include the prevention of marine pollution. As a whole, the different categories can be broadly grouped as pertaining to safety of life at sea, working and living conditions on board, and marine pollution. Most subjects in the first two groups closely relate to protection of the health and general welfare of seafarers and their safety. During 1986 the most common deficiencies were found in life-saving appliances (32.22 per cent), fire-fighting apparatus (23.45 per cent), safety in general (musters and drills, gangways and accommodation ladders, means of escape, watertight doors and fittings, etc.) (18.78 per cent), and navigation equipment (16.81 percent). In many instances the deficiencies found involved improper maintenance and poor housekeeping.

Deficiencies within the major categories reported between 1983 and 1986, expressed numerically as percentages of total deficiencies, as a percentage of number of inspections performed and as a percentage of number of individual ships inspected, are set out in table 4.

The ships of some 18 countries or areas were most prominent among all those delayed or detained during the 1985-86 period. The number of such ships expressed as a percentage of the total number of at least 25 ship from those countries which were inspected is indicated in table 5. For comparison purposes, the average rate of delays or detentions of all ships from all 116 countries whose ships were inspected during 1986 was 3.52 per cent.

As regards the types of ships delayed and detained pending the correction of deficiencies, during the 1985-86 period 66.12 per cent were general dry-cargo vessels, 19.87 per cent dry-bulk carriers, 8,79 per cent tankers and combination carriers, 1.63 per cent unitised vessels, 0.98 per cent chemical carriers, and 2.61 per cent other ship types.

. . .

CHAPTER 3. MARITIME ACTIVITIES OF THE ILO, 1976-87

. . .

Memorandum of Understanding on Port State Control

. . .

When the decision was taken in 1980 by the Paris Conference of Ministers to establish a working group to give effect to the common objective of more effective port State control it was also decided to invite the ILO and IMO to take part in the work of the group, since the basis for the enforcement of port State control was Convention No.147 and certain IMO Conventions. Within that group the ILO contributed in particular to the framing of draft procedures and guide-lines for ship inspectors relating to the application of Convention No.147 and of certain Conventions listed in its Appendix. These guide-lines annexed to a Memorandum of Understanding on Port State Control which was signed in 1982. The ILO, together with the IMO, regularly participates with observer status in the work of the Port State Control Committee which was set up in other aspects of the application of the Memorandum. The ILO also takes part in special working groups and in seminars for surveyors and inspectors dealing with technical subjects connected with implementation of the Memorandum.

. . .

- - - - -

7

Maritime Casualties

IMO Legal Committee   LEG 56/9
Report of the 56th Session, April 1986   Extract

. . .

G   Participation in Official Inquiries into Maritime Casualties - Revision of Resolution A.173(ES.IV)

190.   The Committee had before it a revised text of a draft resolution on "co-operation in official inquiries into maritime casualties" submitted by the delegation of Liberia in document LEG 56/7/1. The original text of that draft resolution had been submitted to the Committee at its previous session. The Committee also had before it a draft resolution on "co-operation in maritime casualty investigations" submitted by the United States.

191.   In introducing its proposal, the delegation of Liberia stated that since the two existing IMO resolutions dealing with this subject-matter (resolutions A.173(ES.IV) and A.440(XI)) dated from 1968 and 1979 respectively and antedated the 1982 United Nations Convention on the Law of the Sea, it seemed necessary to restate and clarify the principles contained therein. The main features of the resolution proposed by Liberia were the following:

-       it would also apply in cases where there had not been an incident of pollution;

-       it provided that where an inquiry was held as a matter of course by a flag State, time and place thereof should be communicated to other affected and interested states;

-       it allowed, as in the current resolutions, for hearings to be held in camera where this was required by national law;

-       it omitted from its scope of application preliminary and informal proceedings;

-       it provided for inquiries to be conducted so as to allow representatives of the other States concerned, including, where appropriate, the flag State, to attend;

-       in addition, it allowed States which were seriously affected or substantially interested to participate in the inquiry, at the discretion of the authority holding the inquiry, by entitling them to question witnesses, to view and obtain documents and to obtain a copy of the transcript of evidence;

-       it called for the free exchange of information; and

-       it made provision for notifications to IMO of cases where a State had been denied co-operation and/or facilities.

The delegation explained that the draft resolution differentiated between States "affected" and those "seriously affected" by a casualty and between States being "interested" and those "having a substantial interest" in a casualty. The delegation emphasized that the resolution would of course not be mandatory on States, and noted that the corresponding provision in paragraph 7 of article 94 of the 1982 United Nations Convention on the Law of the Sea (UNCLOS 1982), was considerably broader than what was being proposed by Liberia.

192.   The United States delegation, in introducing its proposal, explained that experience had shown that full international co-operation in maritime casualty investigations was highly beneficial to the improvement of maritime safety. It had, accordingly, prepared a draft resolution which drew upon the existing IMO resolutions but which took into account the solutions adopted by the International Civil Aviation Organization (ICAO) in respect of aircraft incidents as well as the relevant provisions of UNCLOS 1982. The draft resolution suggested that there should be quick consultations at the outset so as to minimize conflicting demands upon evidence of witnesses. It encouraged the holding of a single co-ordinated inquiry. The draft described those situations in which a State "has" a substantial interest and those in which it "may have" a substantial interest. In addition, it also made it possible for a State to establish such substantial interest "based upon the special circumstances of the incident". With respect to the procedures to be applied at the inquiry, the United States proposal followed closely those of Liberia, with the scope of participation depending on the degree of interest of the State in the casualty. In the view of the United States delegation both the Liberian and its own draft resolutions would encourage the exchange of information among and increased participation by States. This would be of benefit to maritime safety. The time was now suitable for updating and improving international co-operation arrangements in this area.

193.   The Committee broadly welcomed the initiative reflected in these drafts and supported the idea of updating and improving the resolutions currently governing co-operation in inquiries into maritime casualties. The Committee invited the two delegations to proceed further with their work on the subject. Most delegations expressed the wish that a single joint draft resolution might be submitted to the Committee for further consideration.

194.   Many delegations emphasized that their support for the proposals was tentative and subject to a more detailed examination of the two draft texts, one of which had only become available during the meeting of the Committee.

195.   One delegation felt that the draft resolutions raised some questions regarding jurisdiction. In the view of that delegation the precedent established by ICAO was not really relevant since it referred to a mode of transport which was much more recent in origin and which involved different criteria. Most maritime nations had developed detailed procedures for the investigation of maritime casualties and the resolutions, though only of a re-commendatory nature, might still create some conflicts with domestic law.

196.   Another delegation, while fully supporting the principle of increased co-operation in this field, emphasized the need to clarify that only those inquiries were meant which had as a purpose to see what changes may be needed in the conventions dealing with maritime safety and the prevention of marine pollution and would not touch upon issues of civil or criminal liability.

197.   One delegation proposed that the principle of reciprocity should be made more explicit in the draft resolutions. The observer of FOEI suggested that in paragraph 4(iii) of the United States' proposal the phrase "including natural resources" be added after "environment". It also suggested that copies of preliminary as well as of final reports on inquiries be transmitted to IMO. Another delegation expressed the view that the definition of "substantially interested States" contained in paragraph 4 of the United States' proposal was too vague. One delegation questioned whether the obtaining of photographs and copies of documents might not create a potential conflict with national procedural laws and suggested that it might be sufficient for all participants to be entitled to view the objects and documents in question.

198.   Responding to questions, the delegate of the United States explained that the phrase "in that State" in paragraph 4(a)(ii) of the draft resolution was intended to cover internal waters and that the reference to "increased safety" in paragraph 4(b)(ii) was meant to take care of situations where a particular State had special expertise, e.g., in a propulsion or hull design, which would aid the inquiry.

199.   The delegations of Liberia and the United States jointly prepared a new draft resolution in the light of the discussions of the Committee. The Committee was not able to give consideration to the new text but agreed to annex it to the present report for consideration at the next session (annex 4). In order to facilitate further work on this, interested Governments and organizations were invited to submit their observations and comments thereon to the United States delegation by 1 June 1986. This would permit the United States, in consultation with Liberia, to discuss the comments with interested States and to prepare an updated draft resolution.

. . .

- - - - -

IMO Legal Committee   LEG 58/12
Report of the 58th Session, October 1987   Extract

. . .

E   Participation in Official Inquiries into Maritime Casualties

100.   The Committee considered a revised draft resolution on co-operation in maritime casualty investigations, submitted jointly by the delegations of Liberia and the United States, together with explanatory notes on the draft, in document LEG 58/5.

101.   In introducing the revised draft resolution, the delegation of the United States emphasized that the draft resolution was intended to relate to the conduct of formal investigations and would not apply to preliminary or informal inquiries. The delegation further noted that the resolution would be non-mandatory and would not prejudice the right of any State to conduct its own investigation. The object of the resolution would encourage a single, co-ordinated investigation where co-ordination was feasible.

102.   The delegation also stated that the draft resolution recognized the diversity of State practice in conducting investigations into maritime casualties, and it had therefore been revised to take into account the comments made by other delegations in that regard.

103. The United Kingdom delegation said its views regarding the draft resolution were contained in document LEG 58/5/1. In general, the United Kingdom's view was that, while co-operation between States interested in a casualty was desirable, the draft resolution did not adequately take into account the political, legal and administrative difficulties which might be faced by Governments in implementing the detailed procedures recommended in the draft resolution.

104. Many delegations supported the revised resolution and felt that it could contribute to improved maritime safety and protection of the marine environment.

105. Several other delegations, while supporting the resolution in principle, expressed doubts as to the urgency and feasibility of the draft document. These delegations noted that implementation of the draft resolution might involve changes in the legislation or procedures in some States. Some of these delegations expressed the view that the draft resolution was not necessary in the light of earlier IMO resolutions on the same subject. Particular reference was made in this connection to resolutions A.173(ES.IV) and A.440(XI).

106. One delegation suggested the nomenclature used to refer to various types of investigations (such as "official", "administrative", "preliminary", etc.) should be examined further to ensure greater clarity.

107. The delegation of Liberia, as a co-sponsor of the draft resolution, stated that the resolution was intended to help the achievement of a goal embodied in the 1982 United Nations Convention on the Law of the Sea. In particular, the delegation referred to article 94, paragraph 7, article 217, paragraphs 5 and 6, and article 218, paragraph 4 of the Convention, which contained provisions relating to co-operation between States in investigating maritime casualties.

108. Following informal consultations among a number of interested delegations, a further revised draft resolution, taking into account the observations and suggestions made in the discussion, was presented to the Committee. The Committee was not able, in the time available, to agree on a draft resolution for submission to the Assembly at its fifteenth regular session. It was agreed to defer discussion of a revised draft to the fifty-ninth session of the Committee, with a view to concluding consideration of the subject either at that session or at the sixtieth session of the Committee. The text of the revised draft resolution is reproduced in annex 3 to this report.

ANNEX 3

REVISED TEXT OF A PROPOSED DRAFT RESOLUTION ON CO-OPERATION IN MARITIME CASUALTY INVESTIGATIONS
(see paragraph 108 of this report)

The Assembly,

Recalling resolution A.173(ES.IV) concerning Participation in Official Inquiries into Maritime Casualties, and further recalling resolution A.440(XI) concerning Exchange of Information for Investigations into Marine Casualties,

Noting the advantages to be gained by improving the procedures and practices contained in the foregoing resolutions to increase the level of co-operation between States in official investigations into maritime casualties, whether or not such casualties result in pollution of coastlines,

Recalling also the provisions of the International Convention for the Prevention of Pollution from Ships, 1973, as modified by the Protocol of 1978 relating thereto (article 12), and the International Convention for the Safety of Life at Sea, 1974 (Annex, chapter I, regulation 21),

Noting also the provisions contained in the United Nations Convention on the Law of the Sea, 1982 (article 94(7); article 223) regarding the conduct of casualty investigations, which reflect an international determination to achieve greater investigative co-operation between States,

Recognizing the importance of maritime casualty investigations in furthering maritime safety and preventing pollution, and the need for full co-operation between States in the conduct of investigations, and for the exchange of information regarding investigations, so that purpose may be fully realized,

With a continuing view to ensuring that all States having a substantial interest in maritime casualties shall have an opportunity of being informed of the facts and represented at formal investigations into such casualties, and

Desiring to encourage consistency in international practice in relation to such official investigations,

Urges States to fulfil their obligations to carry out investigations of maritime casualties,

Bearing in mind resolution A.173(ES.IV) concerning Participation in Official Inquiries into Maritime Casualties and resolution A.440(XI) concerning Exchange of Information for Investigations into Marine Casualties, and

Recommends on the basis of mutual respect for national rules and practices, that States implement the following procedures for the conduct of maritime casualty investigations held for reasons of maritime safety and/or protection of the environment:

1. **Consultation**

(a) States having a substantial interest in a maritime casualty should consult at the earliest opportunity to determine which State or States will conduct an investigation into the casualty and to determine details of co-operation in conducting the investigation(s).

(b) To provide the most efficient use of resources, and minimize conflicts over access to witnesses and evidence, agreement upon a co-ordinated investigation procedure, with attendance and/or participation by other States as provided in paragraph 2, is desirable. However, nothing in this paragraph shall prejudice the right of any State to conduct its own investigation.

(c) If more than one State desires to conduct an investigation of its own, those States should co-ordinate the timing of such investigations to avoid conflicting demands upon witnesses and access to evidence.

2.   **Conduct of the investigation**

(a) An investigation into a maritime casualty, whether held by the flag State or another State, should be so conducted that:

   (i) A State having a substantial interest is allowed to attend and, where practicable, the public is allowed to attend, subject to national rules requiring or permitting hearings or portions of hearings to be held *in camera*;

   (ii) Arrangements are made which allow representatives of States having a substantial interest to participate, subject to national rules and to the reasonable discretion of the authority conducting the investigation, at least to the extent of:

   a.   questioning witnesses or causing questions to be put through the authority conducting the investigation;

   b.   viewing, examining and obtaining photographs of material objects and copies of relevant documents; and

   c.   making submissions in respect of the various elements of the investigation, including suggesting witnesses to be called by the authority conducting the investigation.

   (iii) States with a substantial interest in the casualty participating in the investigation are provided, on a reasonable cost basis, a copy of the transcript of the hearing or its equivalent, where such is prepared for the purposes of the State conducting the investigation, and a copy of the final report. The transcript of proceedings and the report may be withheld if required by national rules for the purpose of criminal proceedings, or its release delayed if, in the determination of the State conducting the investigation, the release will substantially prejudice the rights of a party in subsequent proceedings. The State conducting the investigation should consider the possibility of providing the transcript and final report to other substantially interested, but non-participating States upon an assurance of confidentiality, if necessary, to avoid prejudice to the rights of other parties.

(b) In implementing these procedures, States are encouraged to provide for maximum participation in the investigation by all States with a substantial interest in the casualty.

3.   **Exchange of information**

(a) States should readily exchange, with the State conducting an investigation, any information relevant to the casualty.

(b) If an investigation is being conducted by a substantially interested State, the flag State of a vessel involved in a maritime casualty should, to the extent permitted by its national rules, seek the co-operation of the crew of the vessel with the State conducting the investigation.

4.   **Substantially interested States**

(a) A State has a substantial interest in a maritime casualty if:

    (i)   it is the flag State of a vessel (other than a warship) that is the subject of the investigation; or

   (ii) the casualty occurred within the internal waters of that State or its territorial sea; or

  (iii) the casualty caused or threatened serious harm to the environment of the State or within those areas over which the State may exercise jurisdiction as recognized under international law; or

  (iv) the consequences of the casualty caused, or threatened, serious harm to that State or to artificial islands, installations, or structures over which it may exercise jurisdiction.

(b)   A State may have a substantial interest in a maritime casualty if:

    (i)   the casualty resulted in loss of life or serious injury to the nationals of that State; or

   (ii) that State has at its disposal important information that may be of use to the investigation.

(c)   Nothing in subparagraphs 4(a) and 4(b) precludes a State from establishing a substantial interest in the casualty based upon the special circumstances of the incident.

(d)   Whether a State has a substantial interest in a casualty in circumstances other than those enumerated in subparagraph 4(a) shall be determined by the State conducting the investigation.

5.   Exceptions

(a)   These procedures do not apply to or affect the holding of the following types of proceedings:

    (i)   preliminary or informal investigations into the cause of the casualty (except for the provisions of paragraph 3);

   (ii) criminal proceedings;

  (iii) proceedings conducted exclusively with respect to the revocation or suspension of licenses or certificates; or

  (iv) private litigation to ascertain civil liability for the casualty.

(b)   Notwithstanding subparagraph 5(a)(i), States are encouraged to consult with and permit attendance and/or participation by other States in preliminary or informal investigations where national law or rules allow such participation.

(c)   A State conducting an investigation into a collision involving a vessel flying its flag may conduct such investigation in camera if the other flag State involved does not co-operate in the investigation or the crew of the other vessel is not available to be examined in the investigation.

6.   Compliance

To facilitate compliance with this resolution, States should inform the Organization of the responsible authorities within their Governments that may be contacted regarding co-operation in casualty investigations.

- - - - -

8

Future Developments

IMO Assembly   A 15/Res.631
15th Session, November 1987   Extract

Resolution A.631(15)
Long-Term Plan of the Organization
(Up to 1994)

. . .

MARITIME SAFETY COMMITTEE

I   Objectives

1.   Pursuant to the provisions of Articles 1 and 28 of the Convention on the International Maritime Organization to encourage the general adoption of the highest practicable standards in respect of matters concerning maritime safety and efficiency of navigation including any matter within the scope of the Organization concerned with aids to navigation, construction and equipment of vessels (and other marine vehicles), manning from a safety standpoint, rules for the prevention of collisions, handling of dangerous cargoes, maritime safety procedures and requirements, hydrographic information, log-books and navigational records, marine casualty investigations, salvage and rescue, and any other matter directly affecting maritime safety (e.g. fire safety, training and qualification of seafarers, maritime communications and the safe transport of cargoes generally) and with due regard to the context of resolution A.500(XII).

2.   To provide the necessary machinery for performing any duties assigned to it and to maintain such close relationship with other bodies as may further the purposes of the Organization.

II   Specific subjects

1.   Implementation, technical interpretation and improvement of conventions, codes, recommendations and guidelines.

2.   Procedures for the control of ships including deficiency reports.

3.   Casualty statistics and investigations into serious casualties.

4.   Harmonization of survey and certification requirements and authorization granted to non-governmental organizations to conduct surveys.

5.   Training, watchkeeping and operational procedures for maritime personnel, including seafarers, fishermen, maritime pilots and those responsible for maritime safety in mobile offshore units.

6.   Measures to improve navigational safety, including ships' routeing, requirements and standards for navigational aids and ship reporting systems.

7.   The global maritime distress and safety system and other maritime radiocommunication matters including navigational warning services, shipborne radio equipment and operational procedures.

8.   Survival in case of maritime casualty or distress, and the provision of maritime search and rescue services.

9.   Safe carriage of solid bulk cargoes, timber, grain and other cargoes by sea, including containers and vehicles.

10.   Carriage of dangerous goods in packaged form, portable tanks, unit loads, other transport units, shipborne barges and intermediate bulk containers (IBCs).

11.   Carriage of bulk chemicals in offshore support vessels.

12.   Carriage of irradiated nuclear fuel in purpose built and non-purpose built ships.

13.   Emergency procedures and safety measures for ships carrying dangerous goods, medical first aid in case of accidents involving dangerous goods and the safe use of pesticides in ships.

14.   Safe handling and storage of dangerous goods in port areas.

15.   Intact stability, subdivision, damage stability and load lines of ships.

16.   Tonnage measurement of ships.

17.   Safety considerations for machinery and electrical installations in ships.

18.   Maneuverability of intact and disabled ships.

19.   Control of noise and related vibration levels on board ships.

20.   Matters pertaining to fire safety on board ships.

21.   Safety aspects of the design, construction, equipment and operation of specific types of ships, such as fishing vessels, oil tankers, chemical tankers, gas carriers, dynamically supported craft, mobile offshore drilling units, special purpose ships, offshore supply vessels, nuclear merchant ships, roll-on roll-off ships, barge carriers, barges carrying dangerous chemicals in bulk and diving systems.

22.   Prevention of piracy and unlawful acts against ships.

23.   IMO ship identification number scheme.

24.   Possible revision of the 1977 Torremolinos International Convention.

25.   Co-operation with the United Nations and other international bodies on matters of mutual interest.

26.   A possible single (unified) international instrument (i.e. one comprehensive convention concerning safety of life at sea and marine environment protection) incorporating and superseding relevant conventions and instruments currently applicable, which might include:

> 1974 SOLAS Convention
> 1978 SOLAS Protocol
> 1966 Load Line Convention
> MARPOL 73/78
> International Bulk Chemical Code
> International Gas Carrier Code

LEGAL COMMITTEE

1.   Draft convention on offshore mobile craft.

2.   Arrest of seagoing ships, subject to the results of the work in respect of maritime liens and mortgages and related subjects.

3.   Draft convention on civil jurisdiction, choice of law, recognition and enforcement of judgements in matters of collision at sea.

4.   Consideration of the legal status of novel types of craft, such as air-cushion vehicles, operating in the marine environment.

5.   A possible convention on wreck removal and related issues.

6.   A possible convention on the régime of vessels in foreign ports.

7.   Legal status of ocean data acquisition systems (ODAS).

8.   Possible revision of maritime law conventions in the light of proven need and subject to the directives in resolution A.500(XII), including in particular:

  (a)   revision of the 1974 Athens Convention in order to update the limitation amounts and provide for a procedure for the speedy amendment of those amounts; and

  (b)   revision of the 1976 Convention on Limitation of Liability for Maritime Claims in order particularly to update the limitation figures therein, subject to the conclusions reached in respect of future work on the draft HNS Convention.

- - - - -

Additional References

Reports of the Maritime Safety Committee

Fifty-third session, September 1986. MSC 53/24. Also contains:
New and amended traffic separation schemes;
Revised Code for the Construction and Equipment of Ships Carrying Dangerous Chemicals in Bulk (BCH Code) (adopted by Resolution MSC.9(53));
Amendments to the Procedures for the control of ships;
Ship identification;
Statements on safety of merchant ships in naval exercise areas.
Information on preparations for the 1988 Conference to modify the SOLAS (Safety of Life at Sea) and LL (Load Line) Conventions.

Fifty-fourth session, May 1987. MSC 54/23. Also contains:
Legal procedures for the introduction of GMDSS;
Amended traffic separation schemes and new deep-water routes;
Proposed amendments to Regulations V/16 and III/41.8.18 and Chapter II-2 of the 1974 SOLAS Convention, as amended;
Amendments to the IMOSAR Manual and MERSAR Manual;
Proposed amendment to Rule 1(e) of the 1972 Collision Regulations.
Amendments to the International Code for the Construction and Equipment of Ships Carrying Dangerous Chemicals in Bulk (adopted by Resolution MSC.10(54) (Text of IBC Code also contained in IMO publication Sales No. 100 86.II.E); and
Work programmes of MSC Sub-Committees for 1988-89.

Other Resolutions adopted by the IMO Assembly at its 14th and 15th sessions.

A.596(15)	Safety of passenger ro-ro ferries
A.597(15)	Amendments to the procedures for the control of ships
A.607(15)	Administrative, financial and operational arrangements related to the GMDSS
A.608(15)	Performance standards for ship earth stations capable of two-way communications
A.616(15)	Search and rescue homing capability
A.617(15)	Implementation of the NAVTEX system as a component of the world-wide navigational warning service
A.576(14), A.622(15) & A.623(15)	Watch-keeping standards and requirements with respect to fishing vessels
A.537(14) & A.618(15)	Routeing of ships (add locations)
A.619(15)	Use of pilotage services in the Torres Strait and Great Barrier Reef area
A.620(15)	Navigation through the entrances to the Baltic Sea
A.626(15)	Amendments to the International Regulations for Preventing Collisions at Sea, 1972

Other IMO documents

Status of IMO instruments and Codes. MSC 54/19/3 and 4.

IV

CONDITIONS FOR SEAFARERS

1. 1987 Revision of ILO Conventions
    and Recommendations

2. Workers on Offshore Industrial Installations

1

1987 Revision of ILO Conventions and Recommendations

ILO International Labour Conference   ILO Report I
74th (Maritime) Session 1987   Extract

==========

Report of the Director-General

CHAPTER 1. EVOLUTION IN THE SHIPPING INDUSTRY AND TRANSITION IN THE EMPLOYMENT OF SEAFARERS

. . .

TRANSITION IN THE EMPLOYMENT OF SEAFARERS

Contemporary issues

As mentioned above, the period since 1976 has been marked by recession, a surplus of ships and a poor climate generally for shipping, leading to a variety of cost-cutting measures aimed at preserving the viability of shipping operations. Crew costs have been given priority attention.

In the prevailing economic conditions, with freight rates frequently insufficient to cover ships' operators experiencing financial difficulties. Some of the largest companies in the shipping world, as well as many of the smaller ones, have gone into liquidation. In such circumstances, the situation of crews on board ships arrested or abandoned in foreign ports can be extremely difficult. Sometimes their rights to repatriation and to wage arrears are subordinated to the rights of other creditors.

Another adverse development affecting seafarers has been the spread of piracy and robbery, including violent acts against ships' crews at sea and in certain ports. In some cases local authorities have been unable to take appropriate action. Also, there have been cases of unlawful detention of ships' personnel. Merchant ships trading in war zones constitute an additional hazard for crews who have often become the innocent victims of military action.

General situation of employment

"Almost certainly, employment opportunities for seafarers of many of the industrially developed maritime countries will become increasingly restricted." This prognosis, from the Report of the Director-General to the 62nd Maritime Session, has proved accurate. With very few exceptions, seafarer employment in all developed maritime countries has fallen sharply in the intervening years and there is little evidence that the situation is changing. During the first six years of the current decade, for example, the number of officers serving on British ships fell one-half, while the reduction for ratings was of the order of 40 per cent. During a two-year period ending in 1982, the number of seafarers in France fell by 23 per cent and by 20 per cent in Spain, while that of seafarers employed in the international trades on Japanese ships fell by more than one-third during a five-year period ending in 1985.

In addition to the attrition resulting from economic recession, overtonnage, technical advances and smaller ships' crews, many seafaring jobs in several traditional maritime countries have been lost to seafarers in the Far East and other lower-cost areas: while there were only 36,000 seafarers employed on British ships by 1985 (as compared with 65,000 in 1980), there were no fewer than 36,000 South Korean seafarers serving on board nearly 2,000 ships under 45 flags other than that of their own country; 46,000 Filipino seafarers were similarly employed.

This sharp shift in jobs for seafarers has made manpower planning difficult in several traditional maritime countries. Maritime educational and training establishments in many of these countries have also suffered. The social consequences have in some instances been considerable, as seafarers have been trained for jobs which no longer exist. The shipping industry's poor prospects have reduced promotion opportunities for those fortunate enough to be employed, and discouraged motivated and qualified school-leavers from seeking a career in the industry. The effects upon the industry in the future are likely to be serious, especially as regards efforts to attract new entrants suitable for the more technical jobs.

For seafarers of the developing countries the situation is only marginally less uncertain. The economic situation has been a disincentive to developing countries to invest in shipping, and has hampered the efforts of countries attempting to establish and nurture their own shipping industry, especially since new shipping nations need time to build up a certain adaptability to adverse market conditions. Many developing countries continue to rely on foreign expertise for ship operation. As regards employment, the opportunities for seafarers from the developing countries have been constrained by a surplus of manpower, and further limited by the huge number of ships laid up.

This climate has encouraged a growth in what might be described as an export industry in seagoing labour. Many developing countries with high levels of unemployment have established training facilities to produce seafarers predominantly for export, hoping to benefit from their remittances. The shipping recession, which for example resulted in a drop of about 18,000 Filipino seafarers employed on foreign ships between 1982 and 1986, has led to a more intense competition among labour-supplying countries, some of which are becoming more involved in negotiations with the ultimate employers of their labour. Also, they have intervened to supervise the employment of seafarers on foreign ships a task previously left to private crewing agencies. Measures in this connection include the establishment of seafarers' overseas employment agencies responsible for the registry of seafarers seeking work overseas, the approval of manning agencies, the scrutiny of contract documents and the determination of minimum standards of employment.

Vessels flying the flags of open registries have traditionally been a major source of employment for foreign labour, as few of these nations have had much need for a seagoing labour force. Thus, as the number of open registers continues to increase, it might be expected that the demand for foreign seafarers from labour-supplying countries will also increase. There has been a tendency to believe that, with the considerable differential between the wage rates of seafarers from industrialized countries and those from developing maritime countries, the former would find it increasingly difficult to secure working in this competitive business. However, in the case of an officer from an industrialized country serving on a foreign flag ship, the cost differential is often greatly reduced when the employer does not pay social security contributions and other non-wage costs.

Some countries which previously required that their ships be manned by national seafarers have been forced by the hardships facing ship operators to modify their attitude. Some have permitted a proportion of a ship's crew to be foreign, with the ship remaining under the original flag. Some administrations have permitted foreign crew members "in the absence of suitable nationals". Others have permitted the employment of a certain proportion of foreign seafarers on board ship registered in their dependent territories.

The growth in crewing agencies, both government-sponsored and private, has affected many aspects of seafarers' employment, including training. In general, the cost of seafarers' training is borne either by the government, or by the shipping industry. However, many companies hiring their crews through manning agencies are no longer involved in training. Increasingly, this practice will pose a problem, as the present generation of seafarers, who have been trained in their own countries by traditional methods, age and are replaced. It is a problem that has yet to be properly addressed, especially by the many agencies using personnel trained by others.

Employment opportunities

As mentioned above, job opportunities for seafarers have been affected by the changes that have taken place in national fleets and especially by the lack of opportunity in the traditional maritime fleets and the growth of employment in the fleets of the open registers and of certain developing countries. These developments have affected different categories of seafarers in different ways. While officers from the traditional maritime countries have found it possible to "export" their qualifications and experience, ratings with less formal qualifications have not been so fortunate and many have left the industry. In general, skilled ratings for jobs on certain types of ships - such as chemical or gas carriers - have been more in demand than those for jobs of a more general seafaring nature. Seafarers on passenger ships and ferries have been relatively sheltered from unemployment, although there is a growing tendency to replace catering staff on passenger ships with personnel engaged through concessionaire arrangements, who do not enjoy the same working conditions. Job opportunities for seafarers have also been affected by the large number of tankers that have been laid up for extensive periods. In contrast, few liner-type ships have been laid up although the actual numbers have greatly diminished through the onset of containerisation. The offshore petroleum industry has employed a growing number of seafarers, but recent events have shown that it is not immune to ups and downs, with their inevitable consequences on employment.

While changes in national fleets and the effects of the recession have significantly reduced employment opportunities, a more permanent reduction in the actual number of seagoing jobs has been caused by technical changes. The single, highly productive ship that has replaced a number of ships, multiplied many times over in every trade throughout the world has had a profound effect on the demand for seagoing labour by reducing crew sizes.

The first real reductions in crew numbers took place in the 1960s, with the introduction of remote-controlled machinery and unmanned machinery spaces. The 1970s and the early 1980s have seen the process continue with the introduction of computers at sea and the rationalising of crew functions. Modern ships now feature bridge control centres with rationalised communication systems, collision avoidance radar, optimum displacement and trim selection, main engine remote control and machinery monitoring and diagnostics. Cargo control systems include automatic ballasting and pumping for tankers, loading calculators and remote control of mooring equipment. The number of such modern ships which do not require large crews is significant and growing. In Japan, for example, there are upwards of 150 large ocean-going ships designed to operate with crews of 18, and 15 similar experimental ships with 16-man crews. Several other countries have designed and are testing advanced vessels capable of operating with between 12 and 15 crew members on board.

Similar reductions in crew size have been made in smaller ships and in specialised tonnage; in fact, there is hardly any type of ship which has not seen some changes. No doubt only small further reductions in crew sizes are now possible. However, experiments and studies are now under way in some countries on reducing manning scales in certain ships and on the technology required for a completely unmanned and remote-controlled ship. Many practical, social and even legal problems arise in contemplating such advances.

Technical changes have required seafarers to change many of their traditional skills; they have also changed the régime of life at sea. The small number of people available for tasks on board ship and the increase in the number of specialised ships have caused shipowners to look more closely at working routines on board and to examine the skills that are necessary. Closer supervision from the shore has made many traditional skills of deck officers superfluous, while at the same time placing new demands on them. Similarly, the smaller engine-room complement has made the overhaul of machinery during the voyage impractical and, to some extent, has turned the ships' engineer into a machinery supervisor. The greater reliance on planned maintenance techniques and the use of far more electronic, hydraulic, sensor and control equipment have also changed the working environment and demanded new skills. However, despite all this new technology, ships remain at the mercy of the elements and many traditional skills are still in demand.

Forecasting the need for seagoing manpower is difficult. The swings from oversupply to undersupply frequently happen too suddenly for recruitment and training facilities to anticipate and react. The present recession has added to the difficulty of assessing manpower requirements. In the face of such obstacles, many research programmes have been abandoned, plans for changing the social structure on board ship have been modified, and interest in the long-term trends of seagoing employment has diminished.

Although jobs for seafarers have disappeared in many traditional areas, a number of new job opportunities afloat have appeared in recent years. There has, for example, been considerable growth in trades associated with the international car market, in European ferry operations and in a number of other specialised areas, such as container transshipment.

The offshore petroleum industry, in its manifold forms, continues to require seafaring skills, especially for the various support vessels. Seafarers have adapted to the rather more specialised job requirements of the semi-submersible rig, and of pipelaying and platform maintenance operations. However, the offshore industry seems no less cyclical than the shipping industry.

General trends in employment and working conditions

The conditions of employment of seafarers in the traditional maritime and the developing maritime countries has changed only marginally during the past decade. The recession has not encouraged improvements in this regard. The bargaining position of seafarers, which had been strengthened by a general shortage of ships' crew in the 1970s, has deteriorated owing to the prevailing surplus of seagoing labour. The ability of ship operators to shift their flags from one country to another has jeopardised the job security of seafarers in the traditional maritime countries. Also, the growing number of countries that permit seafarers from any nationality to serve on board their ships has weakened the bargaining position of all seafarers. Even the fleets and crews of countries which do not permit this "flagging out", or the employment of foreigners, have been decimated as a result of the competition with low-cost countries.

In general terms, seafarers from the industrialised world, whether working in their national fleets or seeking work on foreign flag ships, have had to reduce their expectations concerning their working conditions in order to find or keep their job. With few exceptions wage increases and improvements in other conditions have been modest when compared with the improvements achieved in the previous period of full employment. Furthermore, many seafarers have agreed to longer periods of service between leaves, to new pay rates and to full responsibility for their own pension arrangements in order to keep working.

The seafarer's living and working conditions on board ship have, with few exceptions, improved only marginally during the past decade. True, many seafarers enjoy a single cabin and numerous amenities when off duty; but many modern ships, built against strict budgets and specifications designed to save costs, still have certain limitations on living comforts and good working conditions for crews. For example, noise and vibration and cramped machinery spaces continue to plague many modern ships.

Such living and working conditions might be tolerable if periods at sea were interspersed with periods in port, but the far greater productivity of the modern ship has greatly reduced time spent in port. In addition, berths in modern ports are often far from cities or towns, and cargo supervision or maintenance usually preclude much shoregoing. In many respects the pattern of modern shipping has removed many of the former aspects of seagoing life that proved so attractive. Furthermore, with the erosion of pay and leave, the shrinking of crews and the less enjoyable circumstances in work on board ship, many seafarers suffer from loneliness, stress and other psychological problems, made all the worse by the uncertainty surrounding their employment prospects.

. . .

Chapter 2.   CONDITIONS OF WORK AND LIFE OF SEAFARERS

OTHER QUESTIONS

. . .

Seafarers' rights and legal protection

Many maritime countries, considering that seafarers need certain safeguards with regard to their employment, have adopted legislation conferring on them special rights and safeguards in addition to those they may enjoy under labour legislation generally. In particular, precautions are often obligatory in connection with signing of ships' articles of agreement to ensure that the seafarer fully understands his rights and obligations. Articles of agreement cover such matters as the wages the seafarer will be paid, his treatment and care, at the employer's expense, in the event of any sickness or accident occurring during the voyage, his repatriation under certain circumstances and his protection against arbitrary dismissal during a voyage.

In a ship whose crew members are all from the country in which the ship is registered, and where there is a union to defend the crew's interests, the practical significance of these rights is easy to define and they are relatively simple to enforce. However, in the common situation in which a ship is registered in one country and the crew are from other countries (and were possibly engaged in yet other countries), the definition and enforcement of seafarers' rights under the articles binding them can be a complex matter.

In situations of the latter type, a seafarer with a grievance calling for legal redress must determine which national law is applicable. The general rule is that in cases of dispute between a seafarer and his employer, the law of the country of registry of the ship shall apply. However, the ship may be chartered to a national of another country; moreover, the law of the country of registry may grant the rights invoked only to its own nationals and to resident foreigners. Even where the national law in question is applicable and applied, it may not provide an adequate remedy; for instance, it may provide for repatriation to the port of engagement, which may be in a country far distant from the seafarer's home country. Where the seafarer decides to bring an action against his former employer, he must find a lawyer in the employer's home country, or the country of registry of the ship, who is willing to take up his case. By the time the lawyer has instituted proceedings, witnesses may not be available to the courts hearing the case. If the judgement is favourable to the seafarer, he may well find that the lawyer's fees absorb the greater part of the compensation awarded. Finally, the possibility for a seafarer of securing a maritime lien on the ship for the settlement of financial claims is more theoretical than real.

Legislation adopted in the Federal Republic of Germany in 1980 established a procedure under which crew members can lodge complaints against foreign ships; in Norway legislation adopted in 1978 provides a state guarantee for seafarers' wage claims in the event of the operator's insolvency. In Hong Kong, in March 1983, the Seamen's Recruiting Office issued a set of standard clauses and conditions of service to be annexed to the articles of agreement of all Hong Kong seafarers employed in foreign ships; among other things, it establishes a grievance procedure. Panama has set up special maritime tribunals to hear cases brought by seafarers. The international trade union movement has been in a position to intervene successfully on behalf of ships' crews. Certain national unions retain solicitors in foreign ports to take up the cases of their members in the country concerned. But there are still many cases in which a seafarer - and especially a seafarer from a developing country - has the utmost difficulty in obtaining relief.

The previously cited 1986 United Nations Convention on Conditions for Registration of Ships seeks to offer a remedy to the situations described. Its provisions concerning the settlement of civil disputes between seafarers and their employer require flag States to ensure that nationals and foreign seafarers have equal access "to appropriate legal processes to secure their contractual rights in their relations with their employers", and to establish machinery to ensure payment of monies owed to seafarers employed on ships flying their flags if the employer defaults.

Closely related to the questions of the rights and legal protection of seafarers is that of their unlawful detention abroad. Serious cases of such incidents in recent years prompted the 24th Session of the Joint Maritime Commission in 1984 to adopt a resolution requesting the

Office to examine the possibility of asking the appropriate UN body to adopt an instrument which would oblige a State detaining a seafarer or a ship -

(a)   immediately to inform the flag State and the State of nationality of the seafarer and, if interned, allow consular officials immediate access; and

(b)   to deal with the matter expeditiously under the due processes of law and to inform the States specified in (a) above of such developments as they occur.

In the light of an indication from the United Nations that an instrument on the unlawful detention of seafarers could be adopted within the framework of international labour law or international maritime law, and from the IMO that no provisions on the subject are contained in the relevant convention of that organisation, the Office considered it appropriate to include in the proposed Conclusions concerning the contents of a Convention of seafarers' welfare at sea and in port, which was submitted to the Preparatory Technical Maritime Conference, a provision relating to the unlawful detention of seafarers abroad. The Preparatory Conference decided that this provision should be among those contained in a Recommendation of Seafarers' Welfare at Sea and in Port to be considered by the Maritime Session of the International Labour Conference, rather than in a Convention. The draft Recommendation was reviewed by the Legal Committee of the IMO in October 1986; some of its delegations expressed the opinion that the provision concerning detention of seafarers should have appropriate regard to the relevant provisions of the Vienna Convention of Consular Relations - especially those stipulating that the views of the person detained should be taken into account. Other delegations felt that the provision should apply to all cases of detention of seafarers abroad, as it was not always possible to determine in advance whether a detention was lawful or unlawful. Still others were of the view that it would be more appropriate and useful to embody the provisions concerning detention in a Convention instead of in a Recommendation.

- - - - -

ILO Press Release
Geneva   9 October 1987

ILO Maritime Conference adopts
new standards for wellbeing of seafarers

Seafarers throughout the world stand to benefit from higher standards of social protection and welfare and improved working conditions established by the 74th (Maritime) Session of the International Labour Conference which ended here today.

The 16-day session - attended by over 700 government, shipowner and seafarer delegates and advisers from 77 member States of the International Labour Organization - adopted a new Convention and Recommendation on seafarers' welfare at sea and in port, a Convention on social security protection for seafarers - including those serving in ships flying flags other than those of their own country - and a Convention on health protection and medical care. It updated existing standards concerning the repatriation of seafarers by adopting a revised Convention and Recommendation in this field.

All these Conventions are to be applied to commercial maritime fishing to the extent practicable, the decision being taken in each ratifying state after consultation with the representative organizations of fishing vessel owners and fishermen.

Welfare

The Convention and Recommendation adopted by the Conference on seafarers' welfare at sea and in port, which revises previous instruments, seeks to respond to new needs arising from changing conditions of employment and work.

Ratifying States, after consultation with representative organizations of shipowners and seafarers, undertake to ensure that welfare facilities and services - including cultural, recreational and information services - are provided and financed both in appropriate ports and on board ship. These services should be available to all seafarers without discrimination and reviewed frequently to ensure they are adapted to changing needs. Member States and the parties "engaged and interested" should co-operate in this field.

The Recommendation states that in the implementation of these measures account should be taken of the special needs of seafarers in respect of their safety, health and spare-time activities, especially when in foreign countries and when entering war zones. It recommends the establishment of welfare boards to ensure co-ordination between services and to see that facilities correspond to needs.

Governments should ensure adequate and regular financial support is provided, the instrument states.

Seafarers should be kept informed of all facilities available in the port of call, and special attention should be given to the protection of foreign seafarers, particularly in cases of detention.

In a resolution, the Conference asked that social and welfare services for seafarers' families be examined by the next session of the ILO's Joint Maritime Commission.

Social security

The Convention adopted in this field - revising existing instruments on social security and sickness insurance for seafarers - requires ratifying States to provide seafarers with social security protection not less favourable than that enjoyed by shore workers for which it has legislation in force.

Member States would be bound to apply either minimum standards (as specified in the Social Security [Minimum Standards] Convention, No. 102) or superior standards (as laid down in other ILO instruments) relating to contingencies to be covered and benefits to be provided, in at least three of nine branches of social security: medical care and sickness, unemployment, old age, employment injury, family, maternity, invalidity and survivors' benefit.

Shipowners' liabilities cover medical care, board and lodging and repatriation of seafarers where required. The instrument also makes provision for the payment of wages of seafarers who by reason of their condition are left behind on a voyage or who are repatriated or landed in the territory of the competent member State.

The Convention extends protection to foreign or migrant seafarers, setting out rules designed to avoid conflicts of laws and to ensure equality of treatment and the maintenance of rights, subject to inter-State agreement. It guarantees the provision of certain benefits, pensions and death grants, to beneficiaries who are nationals of another member State or refugees or stateless persons, irrespective of their place of residence.

Health protection and medical care

A new Convention in this field aims at providing seafarers with health protection and medical care comparable to that which is generally available to workers ashore. It guarantees seafarers the right to visit a doctor in ports of call and stresses the development of health promotion and health education programmes.

Every ship shall carry a medicine chest and a medical guide and have access to a round-the-clock medical advice system by radio or satellite communication, available free of charge.

All ships carrying 100 or more seafarers and ordinarily engaged on international voyages of more than three days' duration shall carry a medical doctor, the Convention states. In other ships, one or more specially trained crew members shall be put in charge of medical care and the administering of medicines as part of their regular duties.

Separate hospital accommodation shall be provided on ships of 500 or more gross tonnage, carrying 15 or more seafarers and engaged in a voyage of more than three days' duration.

States ratifying the Convention shall co-operate with one another in promoting protection of the health of seafarers and medical care for them on board ship.

Repatriation

The Conference adopted a Convention and Recommendation which guarantee seafarers repatriation rights in a variety of circumstances. It takes into account developments in the shipping industry and revises instruments on this subject adopted over 60 years ago.

The Convention lists the circumstances in which repatriation rights shall apply, including cessation of employment, illness, shipwreck and bankruptcy of the shipowner. It sets out the means for prescribing, at the national level, the maximum duration of service periods on board following which a seafarer is entitled to repatriation; such periods shall be less than 12 months and the national authorities shall seek wherever possible to reduce them.

The destinations to which seafarers may be repatriated - prescribed by national laws - shall include the place at which the seafarer agreed to enter into the engagement, the place stipulated by collective agreement, the seafarer's country of residence or such other place as may be mutually agreed at the time of engagement.

The shipowner shall be responsible for arranging repatriation by appropriate and expeditious means, and for bearing the cost. If he fails to meet these obligations, the responsibility for repatriation shall fall on the competent authority of the State in whose territory the ship is registered; if it fails to do so, the State from which the seafarer is to be repatriated or the State of which he or she is a national may arrange repatriation, the Convention says. The Recommendation underlines this last clause.

The Conference also adopted a resolution urging governments to take steps to expedite legal procedures in cases of abandonment of seafarers - and particularly the sale of arrested vessels - so as to enable the swift repatriation of stranded seafarers and to guarantee the payment of their wages.

Resolutions

Governments of maritime countries were urged in a Conference resolution to make known to seafarers the danger of infection from AIDS and its measures of prevention. The ILO was asked to study this question and to convene a meeting of the Joint ILO/WHO Committee on the Health of Seafarers to deal with priority questions regarding seafarers' health, the AIDS problem in particular.

Another resolution asked the ILO to give high priority to seafarers' welfare questions, and to seek ways of associating the International Committee on Seafarers' Welfare in its work in this field.

Concerned that in some parts of the world recruitment practices were in operation which were unfavourable to both seafarers and responsible shipowners, the Conference asked that the question of updating ILO standards on the placing of seamen be considered by the next session of the Joint Maritime Commission, and asked member States to ensure the regulation and proper licensing of fee-charging employment agencies.

A fourth resolution requested the ILO to study changes in the shipboard environment and in the characteristics of seafarer' employment, with a view to identifying measures to improve living and working conditions on board ship.

In a further resolution the Conference expressed serious concern that armed conflict endangered merchant shipping and had already led to the death and injury of seafarers in some regions. It appealed to ILO member States to use their influence to persuade warring States to refrain from attacking merchant shipping in international waters and to put an end to armed conflicts.

A sixth resolution underlined the importance of the "landmark" Convention (No. 147) on Merchant Shipping (Minimum Standards) adopted at the 1976 maritime session of the Conference, and asked governments to report on measures taken to implement that Convention. It also urged States which had not yet done so to take expeditious action to apply the provisions of that instrument.

- - - - -

ILO International Labour Conference   Provisional Record No.15
74th (Maritime) Session, October 1987   Extract

. . .

Resolution concerning the expediting of legal proceedings in cases of abandonment of seafarers and in the sale of arrested vessels

The General Conference of the International Labour Organisation,

Conscious that in many cases of abandonment of seafarers the recourse of the seafarers with regard to costs of their repatriation and recovery of their unpaid wages is limited to arrests of the ship and the final consequence of *in rem* legal proceedings, and

Being further conscious that in a significant number of cases where repatriation is immediately available the seafarers, very concerned about losing their accrued wages and leave pay, none the less insist upon remaining with the vessel until she is sold and they are paid off from the proceeds, and

Noting that lengthy delays in such *in rem* legal proceedings are common, that such delays inevitably result in increased costs of litigation (including the costs taxed by the court for the keeping of the ship in custody) and also the result in deterioration of the ship with consequent loss of value, both of which effects act to diminish radically the chances of full satisfaction of the seafarers' claims,

Urgently recommends the governments of member States to take the initiative in framing laws not only for the speedy disposal of suits through summary proceedings at nominal legal fees, but also for the speedy disposal of vessels and the payment of wages on a priority basis from sale proceeds; and to take such measures within their territories as are necessary to expedite legal procedures in cases of abandonment of seafarers, and particularly to expedite the sale of arrested vessels, and to distribute or make interim provision from the proceeds of such sales so as to enable the swift repatriation of stranded seafarers and to secure their claims for unpaid wages;

Requests the Director-General to communicate this resolution to the IMO/UNCTAD Joint Intergovernmental Group of Experts on Maritime Liens and Mortgages and Related Subjects, so that the problem may be taken into account when drafting the relevant new international instruments.

- - - - -

ILO International Labour Conference
74th (Maritime) Session, Geneva, October 1987

Provisional Record No. 15
Extract

...

Recommendation concerning the Repatriation of Seafarers

The General Conference of the International Labour Organization,

Having been convened in Geneva by the Governing Body of the International Labour Office and having met at its Seventy-fourth Session on 24 September 1987, and

Having decided upon the adoption of certain proposals with regard to the revision of the Repatriation of Seamen Convention, 1926 (No. 23), and of the Repatriation (Ship Masters and Apprentices) Recommendation, 1926 (No. 27), which is the fifth item on the agenda of the session, and

Having determined that these proposals shall take the form of an international Recommendation supplementing the Repatriation of Seafarers Convention (Revised), 1987:

Adopt this ____ day of October of the year one thousand nine hundred and eighty-seven the following Recommendation which may be cited as the Repatriation of Seafarers Recommendation, 1987;

Whenever a seafarer is entitled to be repatriated pursuant to the provisions of the Repatriation of Seafarers Convention (Revised), 1987, but both the shipowner and the Member in whose territory the ship is registered fail to meet their obligations under the Convention to arrange for and meet the cost of repatriation, the State from which the seafarer is to be repatriated or the State of which he or she is a national should arrange for his or her repatriation, and recover the cost from the Member in whose territory the ship is registered in accordance with Article 5, paragraph 1(a), of the Convention.

- - - - -

ILO International Labour Conference
74th (Maritime) Session, Geneva, October 1987

Provisional Record No. 16
Extract

...

Resolution concerning the application of international Conventions and Recommendations and the more widespread ratification of the Merchant Shipping (Minimum Standards) Convention, 1976 (No. 147)

The General Conference of the International Labour Organization,

Recalling the resolution adopted at the 24th Session of the Joint Maritime Commission concerning the need for more widespread ratification of the Merchant Shipping (Minimum Standards) Convention, 1976 (No. 147),

Considering that the adoption of this Convention, and the supplementary Merchant Shipping (Improvement of Standards) Recommendation, 1976 (No. 155), resulted from the international resolve to eliminate substandard merchant ships,

Considering that the number and tonnage of vessels registered in countries which have not ratified Convention No. 147 and the number of seafarers from such countries have continued to increase,

Considering that the International Labour Organization has a responsibility to encourage the acceptance and practical application of the international labour standards which it adopts,

Informed that a great many ILO Conventions and Recommendations, particularly Convention No. 147, as well as the fundamental principles of the United Nations, are not applied under a great many flags;

Requests the Governing Body of the International Labour Office:

(a) to remind each member State of the ILO that Conventions create an imperative obligation for member States which have ratified them to give effect to their provisions, and that Recommendations provide guidance on matters of general policy, legislation and practice;

(b) to ask the governments of member States, within the provisions of Article 19 of the Constitution of the International Labour Organization, to report on the measures that have been taken in their respective countries to implement the Merchant Shipping (Minimum Standards) Convention, 1976 (No. 147), and the Merchant Shipping (Improvement of Standards) Recommendation, 1976 (No. 155), and to arrange for an analysis of the governments' replies to be submitted by the International Labour Office to the next session of the Joint Maritime Commission, which should consider what further action, including measures designed to implement the social standards, might be necessary in the light of this information;

(c) to urge member States which have not done so to take expeditious and effective action to implement the provisions of the Merchant Shipping (Minimum Standards) Convention, 1976 (No. 147), and to give effect to the provisions of the Merchant Shipping (Improvement of Standards) Recommendation, 1976 (No. 155);

(d) to request the Director-General to continue and intensify the efforts of the Office to promote more widespread ratification of Convention No. 147.

- - - - -

. . .

Resolution concerning conditions of employment for seafarers

The General Conference of the International Labour Organization

Recalling the resolution concerning the environment on board ships, adopted by the 62nd (Maritime) Session of the International Labour Conference,

Recalling the Prevention of Accidents (Seafarers) Convention, 1970 (No.134),

Recalling further the provisions of the Wages, Hours of Work and Manning (Sea) Convention (Revised), 1958 (No.109) and the Wages, Hours of Work and Manning (Sea) Recommendation, 1958 (No.109),

Bearing in mind that Convention No.109 has not received the required number of ratifications for entry into force,

Considering that during the past decade a rapid evolution has taken place in the shipping industry which is continuing unabatedly and has given rise to technological, economic, structural and geographical changes in ships' operation,

Considering that the aforementioned evolution has had and continues to have consequences in respect of industrial relations, seafarers' employment conditions, manning scales, the organisation of the shipboard workload, has effected considerable reductions in manning scales in many maritime countries, and affects profoundly the shipboard environment,

Considering that IMO has presently under discussion the question of fatigue of watchkeeping personnel,

Considering further that working conditions and prevention of shipboard accidents come under the scope of ILO;

Requests the Governing Body of the International Labour Office:

(a) to arrange for a comprehensive study to be undertaken of the changes in the shipboard environment and in the characteristics of seafarers' employment with a view to identifying areas of possible ILO activities including any possible measures which may need to be taken to improve minimum standards in regard to living and working conditions of seafarers on board ship and to submit the results of this study to the first meeting of the Joint Maritime Commission after the present General Conference;

(b)　to instruct the Director-General in co-operation with the Secretary-General of IMO to arrange for an early session of the IMO/ILO Joint Committee on Training to consider the question of fatigue in the manning and safety of ships.

- - - - -

Additional References

Reports of the 74th Maritime Session of the International Labour Organization, 1987:

Report II, Seafarers' welfare at sea and in port;
Report III (1) and (2), Social security protection for seafarers, including those serving in ships flying flags other than those of their own country;
Report IV, Health protection and medical care for seafarers;
Report IV, The Merchant Shipping (Minimum Standards Convention, 1976) (No. 147));
Mechanism for incorporating new convention in the appendix;
Report V, Revision of the Repatriation of Seamen Convention, 1926 (No.23) and of the Repatriation (Ship Masters and Apprentices) Recommendation, 1926 (No.27).

- - - - -

2

Workers on Offshore Industrial Installations

ILO International Labour Conference   Report III
72nd Session, 1986   (Part 4A)

===

Report of the Committee of Experts on the
Application of Conventions and Recommendations

. . .

General questions concerning the application of Conventions
Application of Conventions to offshore industrial installations

38.   Since 1981, the Committee has been considering the applicability of international labour Conventions to offshore industrial installations used in the exploration and extraction of mineral and petroleum resources at sea.   Within the framework of reports submitted under article 22 of the Constitution, in 1985 the Committee again invited governments to submit information on the extent to which and the manner in which the Conventions they had ratified were applied, where relevant, to work in such installations.   It also expressed the hope that employers' and workers' organizations would communicate their comments on these matters.

39.   In 1985, 12 governments provided replies, three of which were initial responses.   This brought the total number of governments replying since 1981 to 56.   The Committee also received comments from one workers' organization.   In addition, in reports submitted under article 22 of the Constitution for ratified Conventions, two Governments (Norway and the United Kingdom) and one workers' organization (the United Kingdom Trades Union Congress), provided information on the application of the Merchant Shipping (Minimum Standards) Convention, 1976 (No. 147) to offshore industrial installations.

40.   In its initial reply, the Government of Gabon indicated that the national legislation applies to offshore industrial installations.   The Government of Bulgaria, for its part, stated that there are no offshore industrial installations in that country.

41.   The Government of Turkey, also giving its initial reply, noted that there are no offshore industrial installations of a permanent nature on the seas surrounding Turkey, although the Turkish Petroleum Corporation from time to time concludes agreements with foreign drilling contractors to explore petroleum and mineral resources for a specific period of time.   The Government also states that there is no special legislation governing labour conditions in such installations and that the national labour legislation is fully applicable.   It is possible, however, to include special terms and conditions of employment in the agreements made with the contracting firms.   Labour inspection services are undertaken by the State.   Provided that there is no provision to the contrary in contracting agreements, it is not possible to employ workers of Turkish nationality.   Foreign nationals employed in drilling installations are not generally insured under the Turkish social security legislation, but they are covered for invalidity, old-age and survivor's insurance, if they submit an application to the Social

Insurance Institution (SSK). Foreign nationals who are the citizens of those countries that have signed bilateral social security agreements with Turkey are automatically covered for invalidity, old-age and survivor's pensions, even without such an application. Moreover, the workers employed by the operators and the contracting firms are insured by some large foreign insurance companies against all risks. According to the Government, under section 29, paragraph 3, of the Collective Labour Agreements, Strikes and Lock-Outs Act (No. 2822), it is unlawful to call a strike or order a lock-out in the exploration, production, refining or purification of gas, coal, natural gas and petroleum. In case of a labour dispute, the parties may apply to the Supreme Arbitration Board or may go to a private arbitrator (see also the Committee's observation under Convention No. 98). Finally, the seafarers engaged in the sea-going vessels running between the shore and the mobile or fixed platforms at sea are subject to the legislation and regulations concerning maritime employment.

42. The Government of New Zealand stated that in general, the national legislation does not apply directly to offshore industrial installations. In most instances, however, the provisions of that legislation apply in so far as there exists a registered award or agreement having coverage of the installations and associated industries. The Government provided several sample agreements which cover a broad range of topics; wages, hours of work, overtime, holidays, annual leave, sick pay, termination of employment, transportation, the resolution of disputes and grievances, and so forth. The samples which were forwarded expressly excluded the rates of remuneration provided for in the agreements from the coverage of the Cost of Living Allowance Regulations 1984. As the Government noted, awards and collective agreements covering this industry contain detailed health and safety requirements, which are usually based upon existing legislative provisions. In addition, the Accident Compensation Act 1982 applies in respect of any installation or drilling rig on or above the continental shelf. Also applicable is the Petroleum Act 1937, which is administered by the Ministry of Energy. Inspectors may visit offshore installations at any time, but most visits are in response to a serious accident or a written complaint. Inspectors have the power to stop mining or drilling operations if there is immediate danger to the workers.

43. The Government of the United Kingdom provided detailed information in regard to the points which the Trades Union Congress (TUC) had raised last year (see 1985 report, paragraph 34). The Government forwarded a list of United Kingdom legislation relating to offshore installations in the fields of health and social security, employment, energy and health and safety. It also stated that the Continental Shelf, over which the Government exercises sovereign rights only for limited purposes, cannot be regarded as part of the United Kingdom's land territory, or of its territorial sea. In the Government's view, for an international labour Convention to apply to the Continental Shelf, it must contain express provision to that effect. The Government summarises its position as follows: to the extent that employment and social security legislation puts into effect international labour Conventions which the United Kingdom has ratified, then to that extent the substance of a particular Convention is implemented in practice in United Kingdom offshore installations. Similarly, amendments to social security acts and various social security regulations have extended the social security system to offshore installations. The Government notes that from 1976 to 1984 several orders have applied the provisions of almost all employment legislation to United Kingdom offshore installations. The Department of Energy has the responsibility for all health and safety matters offshore; it is advised by the Health and Safety Commission. In addition to enforcing the Health and Safety at Work etc. Act (HSWA), as agents for the Health and Safety Commission, the Department of Energy administers and enforces its own safety regulations. The HSWA already applies to offshore installations in designated areas of the Continental

Shelf and in territorial waters. In the view of the Health and Safety Commission, in general, proposed legislation "packages" (regulations, accompanied and supported by approved codes of practice and guidance notes) which apply to all kinds of work and workers should be applied offshore unless there are good reasons against doing so. The question of offshore application is considered at an early stage in the development of new regulations. Finally, the Government points out that the Oil Industry Advisory Committee was set up by the Health and Safety Commission to advise on health and safety matters in both the on- and off-shore side of the industry. Its membership is drawn from the CBI and the TUC, and the Government departments concerned. The TUC has sent further comments concerning offshore installations which were communicated by the Office to the Government in February 1986. The Committee will return to the matter at its next session when any comments that the Government may wish to make have been received.

44. Several governments referred to or essentially repeated information which they had furnished in previous years (Austria, Bahrain, Burma, Guyana, Sri Lanka and the United States). In a follow-up reply, the Government of the Congo stated that social protection of seafarers, who are governed by the merchant shipping code, and non-seafaring personnel employed on offshore petroleum installations, who have their conditions of work fixed by the Labour Code, is assured by the National Social Insurance Fund.

45. The Committee once again invites governments to continue sending information on these matters which would be of help in clarifying certain difficult problems, in particular as to the legal status of off-shore industrial installations, the legislation applicable to the workers concerned, the manner in which jurisdiction is exercised and the effect of these factors on the scope of application of the ILO Conventions concerned. ...

    . . .

- - - - -

ILO International Labour Conference   ILO Report I
74th (Maritime) Session, 1987   Extract

Report of the Director-General

    . . .

Chapter 2. Conditions of Work and Life for Seafarers

    . . .

Seafarers in the offshore oil and gas industry

The development of offshore activities - and in particular those relating to exploration and production of petroleum - has provided employment on board mobile offshore rigs, drilling ships and supply ships for considerable numbers of seafarers who have found it difficult to obtain seagoing jobs or who wish to leave the sea. These seafarers face special problems in their new employment.

Although conditions of work and life on a mobile offshore drilling unit are in some ways similar to those on board ship, they demand a considerable effort of adaption on the part of most seafarers. Hours of work are radically different; a typical pattern is 12 hours on, 12 hours off, two weeks on the rig, two weeks on shore leave. The occupational hazards inherent in the work are much greater, and there is less security of employment than in seafaring. Above all, the mix of marine and industrial skills required are extremely complex, as are the chains of command.

A number of accidents in which mobile drilling units have capsized and sunk have given rise to demands for the establishment of standards on manning levels and the qualifications required for persons in positions of responsibility on board. In this connection some countries are establishing certification requirements: in the United States, for instance, the establishment of certificates of competency for the positions of offshore installation manager, barge supervisor and ballast control operator have been proposed. In addition, several countries have requested the IMO to establish uniform standards on certification.

Problems also arise concerning the applicability of social legislation to persons working on board mobile drilling units. In particular, there is the question of whether the social legislation of the country of registry or that of the country in the territory (or exclusive economic zone) in which the unit is operating should apply. In addition, all the problems of ensuring the legal protection and social security coverage for multinational crews on board ship affect mobile drilling units as well, with the additional complication that many of the employees on board are not seafarers in the strict sense of the term. Norway has dealt with the problem by extending the provisions of the Seamen's Act to employees on drilling vessels and other mobile units in the sea associated with oil; however, workers engaged by any person other than the master, the platform manager or the shipowner may be exempted if their contracts are subject to the national legislation of another country.

- - - - -

Additional Reference

International Labour Conference, 71st Session. ILO Report III, Part 4A.

- - - - -

V

OFFSHORE STRUCTURES AND INSTALLATIONS

1

Removal of Disused Offshore Platforms

Ninth Consultative Meeting of Contracting
  Parties to the London Dumping Convention
September 1985

LDC 9/9/2
16 August 1985
Extract

Report of the Oslo Commission

. . .

PLATFORMS AND PIPELINES

6.   In the context of Article 60 of UNLOSC, which requires abandoned or disused offshore oil and gas platforms to be removed in such a way as to ensure safety of navigation, the Commission considered the scope of the Oslo Convention and the role of the Oslo Commission in this respect.   It was suggested that although the Oslo Convention did not explicitly include the dumping of platforms in its definition of dumping (Article 19(1)), the provisions of Annex II concerning the dumping of bulky wastes together with past practice regarding the issue of permits for the disposal of bulky wastes all pointed towards the conclusion that the dumping of platforms into the sea was within the competence of the Oslo Commission.

7.   The Commission agreed that all Contracting Parties should consider with their national legal experts whether the current provisions of the Oslo Convention could be construed as controlling the dumping of platforms or whether a specific amendment to the Oslo Convention text is desirable.   Concerning the questions raised, there was no consensus as to whether the present text of the Oslo Convention can be construed as controlling the dumping of platforms. Many Contracting Parties were of the opinion that the scope of the Convention either definitely or probably could be construed as covering such dumping; one delegation was of the opinion that such dumping is not covered.   In the view of this delegation it would be premature to consider such an amendment of the Convention text.

8.   Regarding the national requirements governing the dismantling and removal of platforms, which were submitted by Contracting Parties, it appeared that common features were an obligation on the operator to "clear the site" after operations have ceased so that no obstruction or danger to navigation remains.   In most cases, the national authorities require installations to be physically removed after operations have ceased and allow no dumping of the platform in situ.   Similar provisions apply to the removal of pipelines although in many cases the physical removal of an entire pipeline after use is not automatically required.

9.   In the light of this information, the Commission considered whether the dismantling and removal of platforms should be discussed further in the Oslo Commission or whether the primary discussions would better take place in other fora.   It was pointed out that under the provisions of the Continental Shelf Convention there is an obligation to remove platforms after use; however, the provisions of the Law of the Sea Convention (UNLOSC) do not seem

to exclude the option of leaving the platform *in situ* under certain conditions. The "competent international organization" referred to in Article 60(3) of UNLOSC is IMO on the basis of its competence in matters related to maritime safety. After discussion, the Commission agreed that its concern about the future disposal of platforms, particularly if there was any intention to dump the platforms or parts of them in Oslo Convention waters, should be addressed by the appropriate IMO body. The Commission agreed to request IMO to keep the Commission informed of developments within the Maritime Safety Committee or other appropriate organs of the Organization.

10.   The Commission also considered whether the dismantling and removal of platforms, on the one hand, or the laying and removal of pipelines, on the other hand, should be the subject of an Oslo Commission Recommendation or Decision. It was agreed that the possibility of agreeing to an explicit Recommendation should be considered at the Commission's Twelfth Meeting in 1986. If such a Recommendation can be agreed, outlining the Commission's policy on these matters, it could be of value to other organizations, such as IMO, who also have an interest in this problem.

   . . .

- - - - -

IMO Maritime Safety Committee
52nd Session

MSC 52/26/5
22 November 1985
Extract

Removal of redundant offshore oil and gas platforms
Submitted by the Oslo Commission

Introduction

1.   The 1970s saw a huge development in the North Sea for the exploitation of its oil and gas resources. This development is continuing but many of the older platforms will reach the end of their working life towards the end of this decade. The operators - and the national authorities under whose jurisdiction they operate - will then be faced with the problem of how to dispose of these redundant platforms in a safe and environmentally satisfactory manner.

Environmental aspects

2.   If the disposal of redundant platforms is to be solved by the "dumping" at sea of the platforms (either as a whole or in part), such disposal would fall under the provisions of two international conventions, as well as any national measures which might apply. The two international conventions concerned are the Convention on the Prevention of Marine Pollution by Dumping of Wastes and Other Matter (the London Dumping Convention, 1972) and the Convention for the Prevention of Marine Pollution by Dumping from Ships and Aircraft (the Oslo Convention, 1972). The London Dumping Convention (LDC) provides the global framework controlling dumping at sea, the Secretariat services for which are provided by the International Maritime Organization. The Oslo Convention is a regional convention

whose area of application is confined to the North-East Atlantic Ocean and whose membership includes all the maritime States of western Europe.

3.   Article III, paragraph 1(a)(ii) of the London Dumping Convention includes within its definition of dumping "any deliberate disposal at sea of vessels, aircraft, platforms or other man-made structures at sea". Approval to dump a platform would require a special permit under the "bulky wastes" provisions of Annex II, paragraph C of the Convention.

4.   Similar provisions apply in the framework of the Oslo Convention, although the definition of dumping in Article 19(1) is more ambiguous than in the London Dumping Convention; the emphasis is clearly on dumping **by** or **from** ships or aircraft (which by definition in the Convention includes platforms) and no specific reference is made to the dumping **of** platforms *per se*. However, the fact that the definition of dumping includes "any deliberate disposal into the sea" could be cited in support of the argument that the spirit and intention of the Oslo Convention embraces the dumping of platforms. This viewpoint is shared by most, but not all, of the Contracting Parties to the Oslo Convention.

5.   If the scope of the Oslo Convention is taken to apply to the dumping of platforms, the "bulky waste" provisions of the Convention entail more stringent requirements than those of the London Dumping Convention. Such wastes should always be deposited in deep water, at depths not less than 2,000 metres, and not less than 150 nautical miles from the nearest land.

International provisions concerning the removal of platforms

6.   Under the provisions of the Continental Shelf Convention there is an obligation to remove platforms after use. However, the provisions of the 1982 Law of the Sea Convention (UNCLOS) do not seem to exclude the option of leaving the platform *in situ* under certain conditions. Article 60(3) states:

> "...Any installations or structures which are abandoned or disused shall be removed to ensure safety of navigation, taking into account any generally accepted international standards established in this regard by the competent international organization. Such removal shall also have due regard to fishing, the protection of the marine environment and the rights and duties of other States. Appropriate publicity shall be given to the depth, position and dimensions of any installations or structures not entirely removed."

The "competent international organization" referred to in Article 60(3) is IMO on the basis of its competence in matters related to maritime safety.

Request of the Oslo Commission

7.   At the Eleventh Meeting of the Oslo Commission (Mariehamn, 11-13 June 1985), the Commission considered whether problems related to the dismantling and removal of platforms should be discussed further within the Oslo Commission or whether the primary discussions would better take place in other fora. Recognizing that IMO is the competent organization referred to in Article 60(3) of UNCLOS, the Commission agreed that the question should be addressed by the appropriate IMO body.

8.   The Oslo Commission has agreed that its concern about the future disposal of platforms, particularly if there is any intention to dump the platforms or parts of them in Oslo

Convention waters, should be taken into account by IMO. The Commission has also asked to be kept informed of developments within the Maritime Safety Committee or other appropriate organs of the Organization.

9.   At its next meeting, in June 1986, the Oslo Commission will consider whether to adopt a legally binding Decision, or a Recommendation to Contracting Parties, incorporating its policy on the dismantling and removal of platforms within the Oslo Convention area.

. . .

- - - - -

IMO Sub-Committee on Safety of Navigation   NAV 33/15
Report of the Thirty-third Session, January 1987   Extract

. . .

7.   Removal of Disused Offshore Platforms

7.1   The Sub-Committee recalled that at its thirty-second session (NAV 32/13, paragraph 12.3.2) it had invited Members to consider the comments of the Oslo Commission (MSC 52/26/5) with respect to removal of abandoned or disused offshore oil and gas platforms and to submit their comments and proposals to its thirty-third session when initial consideration could be given to this matter.

7.2   In this respect, the Sub-Committee considered proposals submitted by the E and P Forum (NAV 33/7) aiming at establishing "International standards on removal of abandoned or disused offshore installations for safety of navigation" as the basis of a relevant recommendation to the Committee, as well as draft general requirements for the protection of all interests, for consideration by coastal States when regulating the removal of offshore installations. The E and P Forum proposed that, to ensure safe navigation where removal of disused offshore platforms is necessary from locations transversed by shipping, there should be an unobstructed water depth of at least 40 metres measured at the lowest astronomical tide.

7.3   In this regard, the Federal Republic of Germany (NAV 33/7/2), noting that abandoned offshore structures in general constitute a navigational hazard and that the number of such structures is likely to increase in the future, considered that the proposed international standards, referred to in paragraph 7.2 above, did not take due account of the interests of fishermen, sub-surface navigation, marine research or the marine environment since they do not include provisions for complete removal of such structures. The Federal Republic of Germany also informed the Sub-Committee that, under its Federal Mining Act of 13 August 1980, each and every operational installation, including those in the sub-soil of the sea-bed, erected in the territorial waters or in the waters superjacent to its continental shelf, shall be completely removed following termination of offshore activities.

7.4   The United States (NAV 33/7/1) submitted a proposed draft Assembly resolution - Recommendation for the removal of offshore installations and structures in the exclusive economic zone and on the continental shelf, which would establish an international requirement for the removal of abandoned or disused installations and structures to ensure safety of navigation and other legitimate uses of the high seas, with exemption being limited to

2% or an agreed specification that would limit the amount of such installations not completely removed.

7.5 In this regard, Norway (NAV 33/7/3) proposed that the Sub-Committee should, at this session, limit its consideration to purely navigational safety issues and invite the Committee to decide on other aspects related to the removal of disused offshore installations.

7.6 ACOPS, representing also the views of the fishing industry, urged Members contemplating unilateral legislation, which would allow partial removal of disused platforms, to refrain from passing any rules prior to the development of international standards. They emphasized that, if any exceptions to the complete removal of such platforms were to be contemplated, it should be ensured that short-term financial interests were not allowed to harm the fishing industry, which will continue to generate revenue long after hydrocarbon resources are exhausted.

7.7 Some Members supported the views of the E and P Forum, whilst others supported, in general, the views of the United States.

7.8 The delegation of Japan was of the opinion that it is premature to decide upon total removal of offshore installations and structures because further study of the necessary technology for total removal is needed and because partially removed installations or structures could be no hazard to surface navigation as long as a sufficient unobstructed water column is provided.

7.9 The delegation of Mexico supported the proposal made by the E and P Forum adding that, in its view, bearing in mind the cost implications of the removal of disused platforms, whether partial or total, platforms in waters under Mexican jurisdiction should, in the first place and in accordance with international maritime regulations, be properly marked with buoys and charted and also timely warning given to mariners. A radar transponder might be installed on each of them as a safety measure for navigation without prejudice to subsequent compliance with future IMO provisions.

7.10 The delegation of the United Kingdom considered that the criteria upon which the standards for the removal of disused offshore platforms should be based, ought to be functional rather than numerical or arbitrary, i.e. not based on a number or percentage of platforms, and that coastal States concerned should be allowed to exercise their discretion in deciding which platforms should be, entirely or partially, removed on a case-by-case basis. They could not accept all the arguments put forward by ACOPS on behalf of the fishing industry, particularly the implication that loss of access should be equated to loss of catch. They also expressed the view that a policy calling for the entire removal of all disused platforms would clearly be contrary to article 60.3 of the United Nations Convention on the Law of the Sea from which IMO's mandate for establishing standards flowed. They regretted that some delegations were apparently not yet ready to carry forward IMO's remit on this matter and, reminding the Sub-Committee that both the Oslo Commission and the Parties to the London Dumping Convention were awaiting IMO's recommendations before initiating their own consideration of the matter, urged Members to proceed with substantive consideration of these important issues.

7.11   The delegation of the USSR was of the opinion that exemption from total removal should not be extended to installations and structures in shallow seas where the water depth is less than 300 metres.

7.12   The Sub-Committee, taking account of the documents submitted and statements made during the session, prepared, basically from a safety of navigation point of view, preliminary draft guidelines and standards for the removal of offshore installations and structures in the exclusive economic zone and on the continental shelf and, in order to keep the Committee informed of its progress on this subject, decided to attach these draft guidelines and standards to the present report as Annex 6.

7.13   In considering these preliminary draft guidelines, the Sub-Committee accepted that any decision taken on the removal of disused offshore platforms would have implications for the safety of surface navigation (including safety of navigation of fishing vessels) and sub-surface navigation. It was therefore agreed that the effect such a decision may have on the safety of navigation of all types of ships should be taken into account.

7.14   In addition, the Sub-Committee expressed the view that a recommendation on removal of disused offshore platforms should cover a broader area than that falling purely within the purview of the safety of navigation (encompassing aspects such as legal, environmental and technical other than navigational). In drafting Annex 6, it therefore placed all aspects of the subject going beyond its competence in square brackets for consideration by the Committee. Paragraph 3.6 of the draft guidelines and standards was also placed in square brackets because a consensus could not be reached within the Sub-Committee.

7.15   The Sub-Committee agreed to further consider annex 6 at its thirty-fourth session and invited Members to submit comments and proposals thereon to that session.

. . .

- - - - -

IMO Maritime Safety Committee   MSC 54/23
Report of the Fifty-fourth Session, May 1987   Extract

. . .

6.5   Removal of disused offshore platforms

6.5.1   The Committee considered the preliminary draft guidelines and standards for the removal of offshore installations and structures in the exclusive economic zone and on the continental shelf (NAV 33/15, annex 6) which had been prepared by the Sub-Committee basically from the point of view of safety of navigation of surface and submersible vessels including those engaged in fishing.

6.5.2   The Committee noted the view of the Sub-Committee (NAV 33/15, paragraph 7.14) that a recommendation on removal of disused offshore platforms should take into account aspects other than safety of navigation, such as legal, environmental and other technical considerations. The Committee noted that those aspects, considered as being beyond the Sub-

Committee's competence, had been placed in square brackets together with paragraph 3.6 of annex 6 of NAV 33/15 on which consensus had not been reached.

6.5.3   FOEI (MSC 54/6/3) and ACOPS (MSC 54/6/5) were of the opinion that, whereas the Sub-Committee should consider matters related to safety of navigation, environmental considerations should be evaluated by the MEPC as well as UNEP and Contracting Parties to the London Dumping Convention (LDC), which already had this subject on its agenda (LDC 10, agenda item 7), and the Legal Committee should consider the legal aspects. ACOPS also considered it essential that FAO should be represented at relevant meetings to consider the effect of the guidelines on fishing interests.

6.5.4   With regard to the legal background of decommissioning platforms, ACOPS (MSC 54/6/5/Add.1) drew the Committee's attention to legal decisions which ACOPS considered clarified the status of the 1958 Geneva Convention on the Continental Shelf and its relationship with the 1982 United Nations Law of the Sea Convention.

6.5.5   The Committee agreed that the MEPC should be invited to consider the preliminary draft guidelines and standards (NAV 33/15, annex 6) and the comments of FOEI and ACOPS in so far as they relate to its particular competence. Several delegations were of the opinion that, in order to expedite the work, the relevant documents should be referred to the MEPC for consideration at its next session.

6.5.6   Several delegations were also of the opinion that some provisions of the preliminary draft guidelines and standards have certain legal aspects beyond the competence of the Sub-Committee and the Committee, and proposed that the draft guidelines and standards must also be considered by the Legal Committee.

6.5.7   Other delegations considered that the Sub-Committee should first complete its work on the substance of the guidelines so that the Committee could consider their complete content before involving other IMO Committees, or consulting with any other international organization or deciding the form in which the guidelines should be issued by the Organization.

6.5.8   After discussion, the Committee decided to refer the draft guidelines and standards, together with the FOEI and ACOPS comments to the next session of the MEPC for consideration of the matters under its purview. The MEPC was invited to submit any comments and advice directly to the thirty-fourth session of the NAV Sub-Committee.

6.5.9   The Sub-Committee was instructed to take account of the comments and proposals received in its revision of the draft guidelines and standards.

6.5.10   The Committee agreed that when the Sub-Committee had completed its work on the draft text, the Committee would decide which bodies and organizations the draft text need be referred to before being approved by the Committee.

     . . .

- - - - -

IMO Marine Environment Protection Committee   MEPC 25/19
25th Session, December 1987   1 July 1987
                                                                        Extract

---

Removal of disused offshore platforms
Note by the Secretariat

1.   The Maritime Safety Committee (MSC) at its fifty-fourth session (27 April to 1 May 1987) considered preliminary draft guidelines and standards for the removal of offshore installations and structures in the exclusive economic zone and on the continental shelf which had been prepared by the Sub-Committee on Safety of Navigation (NAV 33/15, annex 6). In this connection, the Committee was informed that the Sub-Committee had prepared its recommendations basically from the view of safety of navigation, and that other aspects, such as those related to legal, environmental and technical aspects would need to be considered by other bodies.

2.   After discussion, the Maritime Safety Committee decided to refer the draft guidelines and standards, together with comments made thereon by Friends of the Earth International (FOEI) (MSC 54/6/3) and the Advisory Committee on Pollution of the Sea (ACOPS) (MSC 54/6/5, MSC 54/6/5/Add.1) to the twenty-fifth session of the Marine Environment Protection Committee for consideration of matters under its purview. The MEPC was invited to forward any comments and advice directly to the thirty-fourth session of the NAV Sub-Committee (MSC 54/23, paragraph 6.5.8).

3.   The Oslo Commission, at its thirteenth session (June 1987), was informed of the progress made in the development of guidelines and standards. The Commission noted that environmental aspects related to the removal of platforms and structures were of particular importance for its future work and it therefore welcomed the information that the MEPC has been invited to consider such aspects at its twenty-fifth session. The Oslo Commission also adopted a questionnaire asking its members to provide information on number, types, and positions of platforms, in the Oslo Convention area, as well as national removal and disposal strategies.

4.   In addition to the activities of the Oslo Commission described above, attention is also drawn to the decision of the Tenth Consultative Meeting of Contracting Parties to the London Dumping Convention to consider the disposal at sea of offshore platforms at the Eleventh Consultative Meeting (September/October 1988) (LDC 10/15, paragraph 12.2).

5.   At the fifty-fourth session of the Maritime Safety Committee, several delegations expressed the view that certain legal aspects were beyond the competence of the technical committees and sub-committees and that therefore the Legal Committee should be asked for advice. It has also been pointed out that, in developing international standards, the potential effects on the interests of fisheries would have to be taken into account and that therefore the United Nations Food and Agriculture Organization (FAO) should be consulted. With regard to environmental aspects it has been proposed that besides the MEPC, the United Nations Environment Programme (UNEP) should also be asked for advice. However, the Committee agreed that it would decide, after completion of the work on the draft guidelines and standards

by the Sub-Committee on Navigation, which bodies and organizations should be asked for advice before final approval of the guidelines and standards by MSC.

6.   The MEPC is invited to consider, from the environmental point of view, the draft guidelines and standards for the removal of offshore installations and structures in the exclusive economic zone and on the continental shelf as prepared by the Sub-Committee on Safety of Navigation (NAV 33/15, annex 6), taking into account the comments submitted to the fifty-fourth session of MSC by FOEI (MSC 64/6/3) and ACOPS (MSC 54/6/5, MSC 54/6/5/Add.1). The comments and advice of the MEPC would be forwarded directly to the thirty-fourth session of the NAV Sub-Committee (8-12 February 1988).

IMO Marine Environment Protection Committee   MEPC 25/19/3
25th session, December 1987   12 October 1987
                                                  Extract

Removal of disused offshore platforms

Note by the Oil Industry International Exploration and Production Forum
(E & P Forum)

. . .

The E & P Forum notes that the Maritime Safety Committee decided during its 54th session to invite MEPC 'to consider the preliminary draft guidelines and standards (developed at the 33rd session of the Navigation (NAV) Sub Committee) and the comments of FOEI and ACOPS in so far as they relate to its particular competence...' and to submit any comments and advice directly to the 34th session of the NAV Sub Committee.

The E & P Forum has devoted considerable efforts to the subject through the organization of industry wide surveys and seminars. Individual members of the Forum have already been involved in the removal of small installations and in studies on the feasibility and engineering of full or partial removal of larger structures. In view of the Forum's extensive involvement in all aspects of the issues we consider it appropriate to provide MEPC with our perception of the background of the Preliminary Draft Guidelines and some technical information on specific measures that would be taken to protect the marine environment.

Background

There is general agreement that the abandonment of offshore platforms should be undertaken with proper regard for:

i)   safety of navigation,

ii)   protection of other interests during the removal operation and from any residues remaining at the platform location, and

iii)   protection of all interests from the marine disposal (dumping) of offshore platforms (or parts thereof) at other locations.

Development of 'Preliminary Draft Guidelines'

This subject was brought to the attention of IMO at the 52nd session of the Maritime Safety Committee by the Oslo Commission - an intergovernmental body with responsibilities in the N.E. Atlantic area for the marine disposal aspect. ((iii) above.)

The Oslo Commission in their submission to MSC stated that:-

> "The competent international organisation" referred to in Article 60(3) is IMO on the basis of its competence in matters related to maritime safety (MSC 52/26/5 para 6).

The Navigation Sub Committee, on instructions from MSC 52, duly considered a number of submissions on this topic at its 33rd session and prepared the Preliminary Draft Guidelines and Standards for the Removal of Offshore Installations and Structures in the Exclusive Economic Zone and on the Continental Shelf (hereafter referred to as the Preliminary Draft Guidelines) which have been submitted to this Committee as the Annex to MEPC 25/19.

These Preliminary Draft Guidelines are mainly concerned with aspect (i) (safety of navigation) but also touch in general terms on aspect (ii) (protection of the marine environment) and at one point on aspect (iii) (in para 3.11 - marine disposal to create artificial reefs for fisheries enhancement).

The Oslo Commission and the corresponding governing body for the global London Dumping Convention have each decided to delay consideration of aspect (iii), until the work in IMO is complete.

Protection of other interests during the removal operation etc. - aspect (ii)

One of the papers considered in the preparation of the Preliminary Draft Guidelines was that from the E & P Forum (NAV 33/7). In this paper the E & P Forum although recommending that the standards developed by IMO be solely concerned with safety of navigation (with coastal states having the separate additional responsibility to control individual removal operations for the protection of the marine environment and fishing on their respective continental shelves) also attempted to identify the concerns of other interests. These are summarised in Table 1.

It is clear from an examination of this table that many of the measures necessary to ensure safety of navigation (subsequently incorporated in the Preliminary Draft Guidelines) will substantially limit any potential adverse effects on other interests viz:-

-    since most of the world's platforms are in relatively shallow waters, they will in most cases need to be completely removed to ensure safety of navigation. Such structures would not generally qualify as candidates for possible non or partial removal under para 3.4 of the Preliminary Draft Guidelines. The E & P Forum estimates that over 90% of the world's platforms are in that category,

- partial removal would only be allowable where "any remaining materials will remain on location on the sea bed and not move. . . "(para 3.9 of the Preliminary Draft Guidelines),

- the location and dimensions of any remaining residues not entirely removed would be indicated in nautical charts (para 3.8).

Thus application of the Preliminary Draft Guidelines to the existing 6000 offshore platforms should lead to the creation of only a limited number of precisely charted, finite contained masses of non polluting material. This can be compared with 20,000 recorded shipwrecks in the United Kingdom Hydrographer's data bank for just the seas around the UK - the precise location and depths of some 8000 has yet to be determined.

Additional Specific Measures to Protect the Marine Environment

The potential for pollution from oil production installations offshore or onshore arises from:

i)   the oil wells themselves,
ii) the inventory of hydrocarbons in pipework and tankage,
iii) stocks of chemicals used in connection with oil and gas production e.g. drilling mud constituents, corrosion inhibitors, de-emulsifiers.

A plan for the full or partial removal of a disused offshore platform would need to ensure that prevention of pollution from these sources is fully addressed.

Sealing the Wells

Exploration and production wells are plugged and capped prior to abandonment in accordance with long established industry practices. An extract from the widely used American Petroleum Institute's recommended practice on plugging and abandonment of wells is attached at Annex 1.

Flushing of Tanks and Pipework

Tanks and pipework would have to be flushed to remove residual hydrocarbons. Procedures have been developed for such cleaning which are regularly exercised in the preparation of pipework for cutting or other such work in potentially flammable atmospheres. An Outline is shown at Annex 2.

The object of the cleaning in these instances is primarily to eliminate the explosion and fire risk associated with hydrocarbon residues. Prior to the cutting up of structures for full or partial removal it would be necessary to follow a procedure similar to that outlined in Annex 2 and thereby eliminate this potential source of pollution.

Removal of Residual Chemicals

The principal use of chemicals on offshore installations is as additives in drilling muds while drilling the wells in the early phases of an oil or gas field development. It would be unlikely for there to be any such chemicals left on a platform at the time of removal.

Table 1: Concerns of key interests involved and possible answers to same

| CONCERNS OF FOLLOWING INTERESTS | | | | | |
Surface Navigation	Submarine Navigation	Fishing	Protection of Marine Environment	Other Users of Sea	Possible Measure to Meet Concerns
Possible collision					Installations to continue to be illuminated in accordance with international standards until decommissioning complete
Collision with residues following decommissioning (deepest vessel 28.6., semi-submersibles 25m)					Complete removal of virtually all shallow water installations (greater than 40 m). Adequate water depth over deepest remaining residues, even under lowest tide conditions (e.g., 40m l.a.t.).
	Collision with residues at installation locations	Trawl snags on residues at installation locations		Laying and operation of sub-marine pipelines and cables	Location and height of any remaining residues to be promptly marked on mariners' charts
	Collision with residues at uncharted locations	Debris at surrounding locations			Checks made on bottom currents to ensure any deposited residues do not move under normal or severe storm conditions. All light material to be removed during decommissioning. Surrounding area to be surveyed on completion of decommissioning.
		Harm to fish populations	Damage to marine environment		Seal wells to prevent leaks. Removal of all toxic potentially harmful chemicals. Efficient flush out of oil and oily residues from tanks, pipes and pipelines.
	Collision during silent navigation in narrow straits	Fishing grounds of special importance			Site specific requirements over and above norm.

However, in the event of small quantities of chemicals remaining on the platform, e.g. corrosion inhibitors, such materials would be shipped back, preferably in their original containers, for disposal at appropriate reception facilities onshore.

Survey of Sea-bed in Vicinity of Platforms

Oil and gas production over a prolonged period could result in there being debris in the immediate vicinity of the installation (well within the 500m radius safety zone). Should such materials be likely to cause problems for future fishing activities it would be appropriate, following the full or partial removal operation, for the vicinity to be surveyed by an approved technique (e.g. side scan sonar, trawling) and for any remaining residues which could damage nets to be removed. Numerous studies of the sediments around the bases of deep water offshore platforms have revealed that in most cases bottom currents are not sufficiently strong to move 'pea' size rock particles let alone larger obstacles that could snag nets.

Such a requirement would greatly reduce but not completely eliminate the 'no go' areas for bottom trawling. The base area of the largest offshore structure is around 0.01 km^2. However even if one allowed a 500 m radius (0.78 km^2) around remaining residues it can be calculated that in the North Sea, for example, the remains of at least 80 platforms would have to be left behind to occupy as much as 0.01% of the sea-bed area. In many parts of the world such residues would be regarded not as possible hazards to fishing activities, but as potential benefits to such through the creation of artificial reefs.

Conclusion

The Committee is invited to note that: -

- the adoption of the Preliminary Draft Guidelines in their present form would substantially mitigate any potential adverse inputs to the marine environment,

- there are established industry techniques which would eliminate the sources of potential pollution from sub sea wells and remaining residues - most of these would have to be adopted in any event for safety reasons,

- the area lost to commercial trawling would be kept to a very low level - there is at present no scientific evidence to equate loss of access with loss of catch.

. . .

- - - - -

IMO Marine Environment Protection Committee   MEPC 25/20
Report of the Twenty-fifth Session, December 1987   Extract

. . .

Removal of disused offshore platforms

. . .

19.13 Paragraphs 19.14 to 19.19 below record a number of points emerging from discussion of this matter by the Committee.

19.14 The Mexican delegation pointed out that line three of paragraph 3.2 of the Standards should refer to the IALA "recommendations", not "regulations", and expressed the hope that the E & P Forum would provide information on the experience gained by its members on the removal of small installations and the costs involved. Similarly, the delegation considered that the specific measures to protect the marine environment, mentioned by the E & P Forum in its document (MEPC 25/19/3, pages 4, 5 and 6), were adequate.

19.15 The observer of FOEI, *inter alia*, expressed the view that the environmental impact of the use of explosives in dismantling operations should be addressed.

19.16 The Canadian delegation stated that in planning the construction of platforms for operations in deep water off the east coast of Canada, consideration was being given to incorporation of design features which would facilitate eventual removal.

19.17 In putting forward the views of its member from the European Association of Fishermen, the observer of ACOPS provided some quantitative estimates of the impact of offshore operations on the fishing industry, including the effects of debris and abandoned pipelines. The view was expressed that partially dismantled platforms should be inspected annually and the outcome made generally known.

19.18 The delegations of Trinidad and Tobago and Mexico expressed the view that "the competent international organization" mentioned in article 60(3) of UNCLOS could be interpreted as referring to other organizations, such as FAO and UNEP, working conjointly with IMO. It, therefore, hoped that the Guidelines and Standards would be referred by the MSC to FAO and UNEP for their consideration.

19.19 In the view of the Swedish delegation, the Guidelines and Standards should be referred by the MSC to FAO, UNEP and the London Dumping Convention before passing to the IMO Assembly for adoption as a resolution.

19.20 In declining to enter into discussion on the papers on this subject, the Danish delegation stated that no agreement had been reached in its country concerning the acceptability of allowing abandoned or disused offshore installations to remain in the position where they had been used. Denmark's immediate reaction was to stress that there seemed to be no benefit to the marine environment in allowing offshore installations to remain in the sea after they had been abandoned. Denmark also stressed that no decision had been made to solve the question of whether allowing offshore installations to remain in the sea can be interpreted as dumping, falling under the provisions of the London Dumping and Oslo Conventions. The Danish policy on dumping was that this is an unacceptable disposal method which must be substituted by alternate land-based solutions. Therefore, Denmark will not allow offshore platforms to remain in the sea if this idea can be interpreted as falling under the definition of "dumping" in the said Conventions. The Danish delegation requested that its statement be recorded in the report of the Committee.

19.21 After an extensive discussion, during which several delegations expressed support for the United States proposal for amendments contained in documents MEPC 25/19/6 and MEPC 25/19/6/Corr.1 and other delegations support for the Swedish proposal contained in document MEPC 25/19/5, the Committee approved as a compromise the preliminary draft Guidelines and Standards developed by the Sub-Committee on Safety of Navigation with the amendments proposed by the United States, as shown in annex 17. The Committee agreed to transmit the preliminary draft Guidelines and Standards to the Sub-Committee on Navigation.

19.22 In noting that certain of the amendments proposed by Sweden, in MEPC 15/19/5, dealt with safety and matters not related to the protection of the marine environment, the Committee referred them to the Sub-Committee on Safety of Navigation for further consideration.

19.23 The Committee recommended to the Maritime Safety Committee that the draft Guidelines and Standards, after completion of the work of the MSC and before finalization by the Assembly, be referred to FAO, UNEP and the Contracting Parties to the London Dumping Convention for comments.

. . .

ANNEX 17

PRELIMINARY DRAFT GUIDELINES AND STANDARDS FOR THE REMOVAL OF OFFSHORE INSTALLATIONS AND STRUCTURES IN THE EXCLUSIVE ECONOMIC ZONE AND ON THE CONTINENTAL SHELF
(revised by MEPC 25)

1. General removal requirement

1.1 Abandoned or disused offshore installations or structures are required to be removed, except where non-removal or partial removal is consistent with the following guidelines and standards.

1.2 Information giving details of such non-removal or partial removal should be forwarded to the Organization.

2. Guidelines for decisions governing removal

2.1 The decision to allow an offshore installation, structure, or parts thereof to remain on the sea-bed should include a case-by-case evaluation, by the coastal State with jurisdiction over the installation or structure, of the following matters:

    .1   any potential effect on the safety of surface or subsurface navigation;
    .2   the rate of deterioration of the material and its present and possible future effect on the marine environment;

.3   the potential effect on the marine environment, including living resources;

.4   the risk that the material will shift from its position at some future time;

[.5   the costs, technical feasibility, and risks of personal injury associated with removal of the installation or structure;

.6   the potential assignment of liability for damages resulting from any installation or structure or part thereof left on the sea-bed;]

.7   the determination of a genuine new use or other reasonable justification for allowing the installation or structure, or parts thereof, to remain on the sea-bed; and

.8   identification of the party responsible for maintaining the aids to navigation, if deemed necessary, to mark the position of any obstruction to navigation and for monitoring the condition of remaining material.

2.2   The determination of any potential effect on safety of surface and subsurface navigation should be based on the number, type and draft of vessels expected to transit the area in the foreseeable future; the cargoes being carried in the area; the tide, current, general hydrographic conditions and potentially extreme climate conditions; the proximity of designated or customary sea lanes and port access routes; the aids to navigation in the vicinity; [the location of commercial fishing areas;] the width of the available navigable fairway; and whether the area is an approach to an international strait or a route used for international navigation through archipelagic waters.

2.3   The determination of any potential effect on the marine environment should be based upon scientific evidence taking into account the effect on water quality; geologic and hydrographic characteristics; the presence of endangered or threatened species; existing habitat types; local fishery resources; the potential for pollution or contamination of the site by residual products from or deterioration of the offshore installation or structure.

2.4   The process for allowing an offshore installation or structure, or parts thereof, to remain on the sea-bed should also include the following actions by the coastal State with jurisdiction over the installation or structure: specific official authorization identifying the conditions under which an installation or structure, or parts thereof, will be allowed to remain on the sea-bed; a specific plan, adopted by the coastal State, to monitor the accumulation and deterioration of material left on the sea-bed to ensure there is no subsequent adverse impact on navigation or the marine environment; advance notice to mariners as to the specific depth, position and dimensions and markings of any installations or structures not entirely removed from the sea-bed; and advance notice to appropriate hydrographic services to allow for timely revision of nautical charts.

3.   Standards

The following standards should be taken into account when a decision is made regarding the removal of an offshore installation or structure.

3.1   The coastal State having jurisdiction over the installation or structure should ensure that it is removed in whole or in part in conformity with these standards once it is no longer serving the primary purpose for which it was originally designed and installed, or a subsequent genuine new use. Such removal should be performed as soon as reasonably practicable after abandonment or disuse of such installation or structure.

3.2 Removal should be performed in such a way as to cause no significant adverse effects upon navigation or the marine environment. Installations should continue to be lit in accordance with IALA regulations following the end of production activity and prior to the completion of any partial or complete removal that may be required. Details of the position and dimensions of any installations remaining after the removal operations should be promptly passed to the relevant national authority and to one of the World Charting Hydrographic Authorities. The means of removal or partial removal should not cause a significant adverse effect on living resources of the marine environment, especially threatened and endangered species.

3.3 In situations where an existing installation or structure, or part thereof, will serve a genuine new purpose if permitted to remain wholly or partially in place on the sea-bed (such as enhancement of a living resource), or can be left there without causing unjustifiable interference with other uses of the sea, the coastal State may determine that the installation or structure need not be entirely removed.

3.4 In situations where entire removal is technically unfeasible or would involve extreme cost, or an unacceptable risk to personnel or marine environment even though no genuine new purpose can be identified for a disused installation or structure, or parts thereof, the coastal State may determine that it need not be entirely removed.

3.5 In cases referred to in paragraphs 3.3 and 3.4, an unobstructed water column sufficient to ensure safety of navigation should be provided above any partially removed installation or structure which does not project above the surface of the sea.

3.6 [Partial removal of installations and structures should be limited by using a functional or objective standard.]*

3.7 Installations or structures which no longer serve the legitimate primary purpose for which they were originally designed or installed and are located in approaches to or in international straits or routes used for international navigation through archipelagic waters, in customary deep draught sea lanes, in or immediately adjacent to routeing systems which have been adopted by the Organization, should be entirely removed and should not be subject to any exceptions.

3.8 The coastal States should ensure that the position, depth and dimensions of material from any installation or structure which has not been entirely removed from the sea-bed are indicated on nautical charts and, where necessary, properly marked with aids to navigation. The coastal State should also ensure that advance notice of at least 120 days is issued to advise mariners and appropriate hydrographic services of the change in the status of the installation or structure.

3.9 Prior to giving consent to the partial removal of any installation or structure, the coastal State should satisfy itself that any remaining materials will remain on location on the sea-bed and not move under the influence of waves, tides, currents, storms or other foreseeable natural causes so as to cause a hazard to navigation.

---

*   This standard or principle requires further consideration by the Sub-Committee.

3.10   The coastal State should ensure that legal title to installations and structures which have not been totally removed from the sea-bed is unambiguous, and that responsibility for maintenance and the financial ability to assume liability for future damages are clearly established.

3.11   Where living resources can be enhanced by the placement on the sea-bed of material from removed installations or structures (e.g. to create an artificial reef), such material should be located well away from customary traffic lanes, taking into account these guidelines and standards and other relevant standards for the maintenance of maritime safety. The coastal State should ensure that the responsible party conducts periodic monitoring to ensure continued compliance with these guidelines and standards.

3.12   Unless otherwise stated, these standards should be applied to existing as well as future installations or structures.

3.13   All future installations or structures in the exclusive economic zone, or on the continental shelf should, as an essential component of their design, provide for their effective and expeditious removal, as long as the features intended to expedite removal do not unreasonably compromise the operational safety and survivability of the structures or installations in the environment in which they are to be located.

3.14   Nothing in these guidelines and standards is intended to preclude a coastal State from imposing more stringent removal requirements for existing or future installations or structures in its exclusive economic zone or on its continental shelf.

- - - - -

Additional References

Report of the Oslo Commission to the Tenth Meeting of Consultative Parties to the London Dumping Convention. IMO doc. LDC 10/11/1.

Notes submitted by Governments and Observers to the Sub-Committee on Navigation, 33rd session: NAV 33/7(E & P Forum), NAV 33/7/1(United States), NAV 33/7/2(Federal Republic of Germany), NAV 33/7/3 (Norway).

Notes submitted by Observers to the Maritime Safety Committee, 54th session: Friends of the Earth International (MSC 54/6/3) and the Advisory Committee on Pollution of the Sea (ACOPS)(MSC 54/6/5/Add.1).

Notes submitted by Governments to the Marine Environment Protection Committee, 25th session: MEPC 25/19/5(Sweden), MEPC 25/19/6 and Corr.1(United States).

- - - - -

2

Infringement of Safety Zones

IMO Marine Safety Committee	MSC 54/23
Report of the 54th Session, May 1987	Extract

. . .

6.6   Prevention of infringement of safety zones around offshore structures

6.6.1   In considering the draft Assembly resolution on measures to prevent infringement of safety zones around offshore structures (NAV 33/15, annex 7), the Committee noted that reservations had been expressed by some delegations in the Sub-Committee with regard to operative paragraphs (d) and (e).

6.6.2   In this regard, France (MSC 54/6/6) proposed amendments to reflect that the coastal State:

.1 is competent to take action against and penalize violations of the rules concerning safety zones around offshore structures coming under its jurisdiction;
.2 may transmit a report on the infringement to the ship's flag State in accordance with the procedure set forth in the draft resolution; and
.3 should be informed of the flag State's intended follow-up to a report communicated under .2 above.

6.6.3   Norway (MSC 54/6/4) was of the opinion that the recommendation should not imply that vessels may enter the safety zone around offshore structures at their own discretion and proposed removal of "stress of weather" from operative paragraph (e).

6.6.4   The Committee concurred, in principle, with the proposals of France and Norway but recognized that some drafting improvement would be needed. In addition, the USSR delegation proposed certain amendments to the draft Assembly resolution.

. . .

- - - - -

IMO Assembly   A 15/Res.621
15th Session, November 1987

. . .

Resolution A.621(15)
Measures to Prevent Infringement of Safety Zones Around Offshore Installations or Structures

The Assembly,

Recalling Article 15(j) of the Convention on the International Maritime Organization concerning the functions of the Assembly in relation to regulations and guidelines concerning maritime safety and the prevention and control of marine pollution from ships,

Having considered articles 60 and 80 of the United Nations Convention on the Law of the Sea, 1982,

Noting article 5 of the Geneva Convention on the Continental Shelf, 1958,

Recalling requirements for ships to maintain a continuous listening watch on VHF Channel 16 prescribed by regulation IV/8 of the International Convention for the Safety of Life at Sea, 1974 (the 1974 SOLAS Convention), as amended in 1981,

Recalling also requirements for ships to carry adequate and up-to-date charts, notices to mariners and other nautical publications prescribed by regulation V/20 of the 1974 SOLAS Convention,

Recalling further:

(a)   resolution A.341(IX) containing recommendations on dissemination of information, charting and manning of drilling rigs, production platforms and other similar structures,

(b)   resolution A.379(X) containing a recommendation for the establishment of safety zones in offshore exploration areas,

(c)   resolution A.572(14) on General Provisions on Ships' Routeing, and

(d)   resolution A.578(14) on Guidelines for Vessel Traffic Services,

Being informed of infringements by vessels of safety zones around offshore installations or structures,

Being concerned about the safety of personnel and the risk of serious damage to offshore installations or structures, vessels and the environment in the event of a collision,

Being further informed that:

(a) some flag States do not consistently take action, in accordance with resolution A.379(X), when complaints of infringements of safety zones around offshore installations or structures by their vessels are received,

(b) on occasion, vessels do not respond to radiotelephone calls initiated by offshore installations or structures and that near misses and collisions could have been avoided if vessels maintained a continuous listening watch on VHF Channel 16,

(c) vessels identified as having infringed safety zones around offshore installations or structures have, on occasion, been found not to be carrying adequate and up-to-date charts of the area, in violation of regulation V/20 of the 1974 SOLAS Convention,

Being also informed that not all offshore installations or structures are adequately equipped with devices that would help prevent vessels infringing on the safety zones established around them, including lights and sound signals, racons and means for permanent visual look-out and radar watch, and that not all of them listen for and warn vessels on appropriate VHF channels,

Being also aware that safety zone regulations are applied by coastal States to protect MODUs* on station, production platforms, artificial islands, accommodation platforms, units and ancillary equipment referred to herein as installations or structures,

Desiring to bring an end to the infringement of safety zones established around offshore installations or structures,

Having considered the recommendation made by the Maritime Safety Committee at its fifty-fourth session,

1. *Recommends*:

(a) vessels which are passing close to offshore installations or structures to:

(i) navigate with care when passing near offshore installations or structures giving due consideration to safe speed and safe passing distances taking into account the prevailing weather conditions and the presence of other vessels or dangers;

(ii) where appropriate, take early and substantial avoiding action when approaching such installation or structure to facilitate the installation's or structure's awareness of the vessel's closest point of approach and provide information on any possible safety concerns, particularly where the offshore installation or structure may be used as a navigational aid;

(iii) use any designated routeing systems established in the area; and

(iv) maintain a continuous listening watch on the navigating bridge on VHF Channel

---

*   For the purpose of this resolution mobile offshore drilling units (MODUs) used for exploratory drilling operations offshore are considered to be vessels when they are in transit and not engaged in a drilling operation, but are considered to be installations or structures when engaged in a drilling operation.

16 when navigating near offshore installations or structures to allow radio contact to be established between such installations or structures, vessel traffic services and vessels so that any uncertainty as to a vessel maintaining an adequate passing distance from the installations or structures can be alleviated;

(b)   every coastal State which authorizes and regulates the operation and use of offshore installations and structures under its jurisdiction to:

    (i)   issue early notices to mariners by appropriate means to advise vessels of the location or intended location of offshore installations or structures, the breadth of any safety zones and the rules which apply therein, and any fairways available;

    (ii)   require operators of MODUs to provide advance notice of change of their location to the appropriate authority of the coastal State so as to allow timely issue of notices to mariners;

    (iii)   require operators of offshore installations or structures to take adequate measures to prevent infringement of safety zones around such offshore installations or structures; such measures may include effective lights and sound signals, racons, permanent visual look-out and radar watch, listening for and warning vessels on appropriate VHF channels, and the establishment of vessel traffic services;

    (iv)   request operators of offshore installations or structures to report actions by vessels which jeopardize safety including infringement of safety zones;

(c)   every coastal State which is aware of an infringement of the regulations relating to safety zones around offshore installations or structures within its jurisdiction to take action in accordance with international law and, where it considers necessary, to notify the flag State of the infringement allegedly committed by the vessel concerned and provide available factual evidence to substantiate the allegation as follows:

    (i)   name, flag and call sign of the vessel;

    (ii)   course and speed of the vessel;

    (iii)   identification of the installation or structure and its operators;

    (iv)   description of the operational status of the offshore installation or structure (i.e. position latitude/longitude, purpose of being on station, length of time on station, breadth of the safety zone, text and date of notice to mariners giving warning of the offshore activity and rules applicable to the safety zone);

    (v)   weather conditions at time of the alleged infringement,.

    (vi)   details of attempts by installation or structure personnel or personnel on service vessels to contact the approaching vessel including radio frequencies used and the interval between attempts;

    (vii)   description of any communications with the vessel;

    (viii)   statement as to the exhibiting on the installation or structure of the proper signal lights and the sounding of appropriate fog signals;

    (ix)   inclusion of photographic evidence or a complete and detailed radar plot, or both, and indication of whether a radar beacon or other warning device was in operation;

    (x)   any possible contravention of any other regulation or convention by the intruding vessel such as the International Regulations for Preventing Collisions at Sea, 1972, or the 1974 SOLAS Convention; and

    (xi)   name of the Government official to contact regarding the complaint;

(d) every flag State which receives a complaint of an infringement of a safety zone by any of its vessels to make inquiries and take action, where appropriate, in accordance with its national legislation, in the light of relevant information, giving due consideration to the rules of the safety zones infringed, the opportunities available to the vessel of being informed of the safety zone, the facts provided in the complaint and the results of any inquiry;

(e) every flag State which has received a report of an infringement to inform, as appropriate, the coastal State concerned of the follow-up action it has taken;

(f) every flag State to take appropriate measures, if necessary, to ensure that suitable procedures exist to take action against the owner, master or any person at the time being responsible for the conduct of any of its vessels which commit an infringement against any duly established safety zone, and to inform the coastal State concerned of the follow-up action taken;

(g) that the prohibition on vessels, other than those involved in rendering services related to the operation of the offshore installation or structure, should not apply to vessels entering or remaining in the safety zone:

    (i) when in distress;
   (ii) for the purpose of saving or attempting to save life or property; or
  (iii) in cases of *force-majeure*;

(h) That the attention of seafarers should be drawn to the need, in such cases, to make early radio contact with the offshore installation or structure, vessel traffic services and vessels;

2. *Requests* the Maritime Safety Committee, in consultation with the Legal Committee, to keep the present resolution under review and to report to the Assembly as necessary.

VI

SALVAGE AND RELATED ISSUES

1.   Preparation of a Draft Convention

1

Preparation of a Draft Convention

IMO Assembly   A 15/13
15th Session, November 1987   Extract

Consideration of the Reports and
Recommendations of the Legal Committee
Note by the Secretary-General

. . .

Consideration of the question of salvage and related issues

5.   At the request of the Assembly and the Council, the Legal Committee continued to assign the highest priority to its work on the preparation of a new convention on salvage and related issues. The Committee concluded a third reading of the draft articles for the new convention at its fifty-sixth session; and undertook a fourth and final reading of the draft articles at the fifty-seventh session. At the end of the fifty-seventh session the Legal Committee agreed that it had concluded the substantive work on the draft for the convention. The Committee accordingly, decided to recommend to the Council to make appropriate provision for a diplomatic conference to be convened during the 1988-1989 biennium to consider and adopt the new convention.

. . .

7.   The Legal Committee also considered certain "public law" aspects of salvage, in particular problems associated with notification requirements in respect of incidents which posed threats of pollution of the marine environment. In this connection the Legal Committee took note of the work of the Marine Environment Protection Committee (MEPC) on requirements for notification of casualties to interested coastal States. The Legal Committee considered whether the requirements being elaborated by the MEPC also met the particular requirements of coastal States in the context of salvage operations or whether additional or separate provisions would be necessary in this respect. The Legal Committee was of the opinion that duplication of rules and guidelines should be avoided and that it would not be desirable to establish a separate reporting system dealing exclusively with salvage. The Committee hoped that the amended provisions of Protocol I of MARPOL 73/78 and the revised Guidelines for Reporting Incidents Involving Harmful Substances, would also meet the requirements of coastal States in respect of the reporting and notification of incidents involving salvage.

8.   The Legal Committee noted, at its fifty-seventh session, that the MEPC had included in the revised Guidelines for Reporting Incidents Involving Harmful Substances certain "notification requirements on a master engaged or requested to engage in a salvage operation relating to the ship involved in an incident creating a threat of pollution." Some delegations expressed regret that the requirements on salvage had not been included in the amended text of Protocol I of 1973/78 MARPOL itself; but some delegations expressed understanding for the reasons why it had not been possible to do so. The Legal Committee expressed the hope

that individual States would take the necessary steps to ensure that the Guidelines would be effectively implemented.

...

- - - - -

IMO Legal Committee   LEG 58/12, Annex 2
Report of the Fifty-eighth Session, October 1987   Extract

===

...

Draft Articles for a Convention on Salvage

Chapter I - General Provisions

Article 1
Definitions

For the purpose of this Convention:

(a) "Salvage operations" means any act or activity undertaken to assist a vessel or any other property in danger in navigable waters or in any other waters whatsoever.

(b) "Vessel" means any ship, craft or structure capable of navigation.

(c) "Property" means any property not permanently and intentionally attached to the shoreline and includes freight for the carriage of the cargo, whether such freight be at risk of the owner of the goods, the shipowner or the charterer.

(d) "Damage to the environment" means substantial physical damage to human health or to marine life or resources in coastal or inland waters or areas adjacent thereto, caused by pollution, contamination, fire, explosion or similar major incidents.

(e) "Payment" means any reward, remuneration, compensation or reimbursement due under this Convention.

Article 2
Scope of application

This Convention shall apply whenever judicial or arbitral proceedings relating to matters dealt with in this Convention are brought in a Contracting State.

Article 3
Salvage operations controlled by Public authorities

1.   This Convention shall not affect any provisions of national law or an international convention relating to salvage operations by or under the control of public authorities.

2.   Nevertheless, salvors carrying out such salvage operations shall be entitled to avail themselves of the rights and remedies provided for in this Convention in respect of salvage operations.

3.   The extent to which a public authority under a duty to perform salvage operations may avail itself of the rights and remedies provided for in this Convention shall be determined by the law of the State where such authority is situated.

Article 4
Salvage contracts

1.   This Convention shall apply to any salvage operations save to the extent that the contract otherwise provides expressly or by implication.

2.   The master shall have the authority to conclude contracts for salvage operations on behalf of the owner of the vessel. The master or the owner of the vessel shall have the authority to conclude such contracts on behalf of the owner of the property on board the vessel.

3.   Nothing in this article shall affect the application of article 5 nor duties to prevent or minimize damage to the environment.

Article 5
Annulment and modification of contracts

. . .

Article 6
Duty of the owner and master and duties of the salvor

1.   The salvor shall owe a duty to the owner of the vessel or other property in danger:

   (a) to exercise due care to salve the vessel or other property in danger;
   (b) to carry out the salvage operations with due care;
   (c) in performing the duties specified in subparagraphs (a) and (b) to exercise due care to prevent or minimize damage to the environment;
   (d) whenever circumstances reasonably require, to seek assistance from other salvors; and
   (e) to accept the intervention of other salvors when reasonably requested to do so by the owner or master of the vessel or other property in danger; provided however that the amount of his reward shall not be prejudiced should it be found that such a request was unreasonable.

2.   The owner and master of the vessel or other property in danger shall owe a duty to the salvor:

   (a) to co-operate fully with him during the course of the salvage operations;
   (b) in so doing to exercise due care to prevent or minimize damage to the environment;
   (c) when the vessel or other property has been brought to a place of safety, to accept redelivery when reasonably requested by the salvor to do so.

Article 7*
Duty to render assistance

1. Every master is bound, so far as he can do so without serious danger to his vessel and persons thereon, to render assistance to any person in danger of being lost at sea.

2. The Contracting States shall adopt the measures necessary to enforce the duty set out in paragraph 1.

3. The owner of the vessel shall incur no liability for a breach of the duty of the master under paragraph 1.

Article 8
Co-operation of Contracting States

A Contracting State shall, whenever regulating or deciding upon matters relating to salvage operations such as admittance to ports of vessels in distress or the provision of facilities to salvors, take into account the need for co-operation between salvors, other interested parties and public authorities in order to ensure the efficient and successful performance of salvage operations for the purpose of saving life or property in danger as well as preventing damage to the environment in general.

Chapter III - Rights of salvors

Article 9
Conditions for reward

. . .

Article 10
Criteria for assessing the reward

. . .

Article 11
Special compensation

1. If the salvor has carried out salvage operations in respect of a vessel which by itself or its cargo threatened damage to the environment and failed to earn a reward under article 11 at least equivalent to the compensation assessable in accordance with this article, he shall be entitled to compensation from the owner of that vessel equivalent to his expenses as herein defined.

2. If, in the circumstances set out in paragraph 1, the salvor by his salvage operations has prevented or minimized damage to the environment, the compensation payable by the owner to the salvor under paragraph 1 may be increased, if and to the extent that the tribunal considers it fair and just to do so, bearing in mind the relevant criteria set out in article 11.1, but in no event shall it be [more than . . .].**

3. "Salvor's expenses" for the purpose of paragraphs 1 and 2 means the out-of-pocket expenses reasonably incurred by the salvor in the salvage operation and a fair rate for equipment and personnel actually and reasonably used in the salvage operations, taking into consideration the criteria set out in article 11.1(g), (h) and (i).

4.   Provided always that the total compensation under this article shall be paid only if and to the extent that such compensation is greater than any reward recoverable by the salvor under article 11.

5.   If the salvor has been negligent and has thereby failed to prevent or minimize damage to the environment, he may be deprived of the whole or part of any payment due under this article.

6.   Nothing in this article shall affect any rights of recourse on the part of the owner of the vessel.

Article 12
Apportionment between salvors

     . . .

Article 13
Salvage of persons

     . . .

Article 14
Services rendered under existing contracts

     . . .

Article 15
The effect of salvor's misconduct

     . . .

Article 16
Prohibition by the owner or master of the vessel

     . . .

Chapter IV - Claims and actions

Article 17
Maritime lien

1.   Nothing in this Convention shall affect the salvor's maritime lien under any international convention or national law.

2.   The salvor may not enforce his maritime lien when satisfactory security for his claim, including interest and costs, has been duly tendered or provided.

Article 18
Duty to provide security

     . . .

Article 19
Interim payment

     . . .

Article 20
Limitation of actions

     . . .

Article 21
Jurisdiction

     . . .

Article 22
Interest

. . .

Article 23
Publication of arbitral awards

. . .

Article 24
(article X in the report of the Legal Committee's 58th session - LEG 58/12)
Reservations

1.   Any State may, at the time of signature, ratification, acceptance, approval or accession, reserve the right not to apply the provisions of this Convention:

   (a)   when all vessels involved are vessels of inland navigation;
   (b)   when all interested parties are nationals of that State;
   (c)   whenever the property is permanently attached to the sea-bed for hydrocarbon production, storage and transportation.

2.   Reservations made at the time of signature are subject to confirmation upon ratification, acceptance or approval.

3.   Any State which has made a reservation to this Convention may withdraw it at any time by means of a notification addressed to the Secretary-General. Such withdrawal shall take effect on the date the notification is received. If the notification states that the withdrawal of a reservation is to take effect on a date specified therein, and such a date is later than the date the notification is received by the Secretary-General, the withdrawal shall take effect on such later date.

Article 25
(article Y in the report of the Legal Committee's 58th session - LEG 58/12)
State-owned vessels

1.   This Convention shall not apply to warships or to other vessels owned or operated by a State Party and being used at the time of the salvage operations exclusively on governmental non-commercial services, unless the State Party decides otherwise.

2.   Where a State Party decides to apply the Convention to its warships or other vessels owned or operated by that State an being used at the time of the salvage operations exclusively on governmental non-commercial services, it shall notify the Secretary-General thereof specifying the terms and conditions of such application.

APPENDIX

Proposed text for an additional provision:***

"Cargoes owned by a State or carried on board either a vessel described in article Y.1 or on a commercial vessel for a governmental and non-commercial purpose shall not be seized, arrested or detained under any legal process whatsoever nor under any legal process *in rem* nor under any provision of this Convention. Consistent with these principles, such cargoes and the State owners thereof shall not be subject to, or be affected by articles [3, 4.2, 17, 18, 19, 20, 21, 22].

---

*   This article was numbered as article 8 in the annex to document LEG 58/4, following the decision of the Legal Committee, at its fifty-seventh session, to combine the principle of the previous article 7 into the present article 6 (LEG 57/12, paragraph 135).

**   In the draft convention prepared by the CMI, the phrase at the end of this paragraph was "but in no event shall it be more than doubled".

***   At its fifty-eighth session the Legal Committee was not able to agree on the inclusion of this proposed text in the draft Convention. The Committee, however agreed that the above text should be submitted to the diplomatic conference in an annex to the basic conference document (LEG 58/12, paragraphs 48 to 53).

- - - - -

Additional References

Text of first draft in IMO doc. LEG 55/3, Annex I.

Consideration of the question and revision of draft Convention. Reports of the IMO Legal Committee at its 56th and 57th sessions, LEG 56/9 and LEG 57/12.

Proposals submitted by delegations to the Legal Committee, 58th session. LEG 58/4/1 (China), LEG 58/4/2 (Mauritius), LEG 58/WP.1, 2 and 4 (United States of America), LEG 58/WP.5 and 6 (Federal Republic of Germany), LEG 58/WP.7 (German Democratic Republic).

Report of the Chairman of the Working Group on article 2.2(e). LEG/58/WP.3.

"The draft of a new salvage convention and the salvage of wrecks" by F. Berlingieri. LEG 58/INF.2, Annex.

- - - - -

VII

SPECIAL ISSUES

1. Illicit Drug Trafficking

2. Unlawful Acts Against the Safety
   of Navigation and Offshore Platforms

3. Attacks Against Merchant Shipping

4. Asylum-Seekers in Distress at Sea

1

Illicit Drug Trafficking

Preparation of a Draft Convention

UN Commission on Narcotic Drugs   E/CN.7/1986/2
Ninth Special Session, February 1986   9 September 1985
                                                                          Extract

Comments and Proposals Received from Governments Concerning A Draft Convention on Illicit Traffic in Narcotic Drugs and Psychotropic Substances
Note by the Secretary-General

. . .

Chapter III. IDENTIFICATION OF ELEMENTS

. . .

Illicit drug traffic on the high seas

118.   It is observed[145] that, while the concept of interception on the high seas of vessels involved in drug trafficking may be considered worthy of inclusion in the draft convention, its implementation may prove difficult. Importance is attached by one Government[146] to maintaining the principle of free right of passage for ships on the high seas. Consequently, if the new convention were to include a provision allowing the stopping and boarding of vessels on the high seas, it would have to make such intervention conditional upon the consent of the flag State.[147]

119.   Reference is made to resolution 1983/4 of the Economic and Social Council entitled "Measures to improve international co-operation in the maritime interdiction of illicit drug traffic" which calls for improved systems of registration of vessels and requests Governments to respond promptly to inquiries made for law enforcement purposes by other states regarding the registry of vessels. It is suggested[148] that a provision along the lines of that resolution could be included in the draft convention.

120.   It is also suggested[149] that consideration be given to a provision inviting Governments to make it a punishable offence for any person to organize, participate in, or be in any way concerned in the carriage of controlled drugs on the high seas other than in the course of bona fide trade.

121.   Attention is drawn to article 108 of the United Nations Convention on the Law of the Sea (1982), which provides that "all States shall co-operate in the suppression of illicit traffic in narcotic drugs and psychotropic substances engaged in by ships on the high seas contrary to international conventions" and that "any state which has reasonable grounds of believing that a ship flying its flag is engaged in illicit traffic in narcotic drugs or psychotropic substances may

request the co-operation of other States to suppress such traffic". It is suggested[150] that these provisions could be elaborated upon in the new convention.

122.   In this connection, it is further suggested[151] that illicit traffic on the high seas might be assimilated to piracy and treated as such under applicable international law.

123.   Accordingly, the convention should provide that a State may request another State authority to board a vessel flying the latter's flag and seize, arrest and prosecute as appropriate when there are reasonable grounds to believe that such vessel is engaged in drug trafficking. Upon receipt of such a request, the flag State would be required to take action to insure that the vessel is not engaged, or permitted to engage further, in trafficking.[152]

124.   In addition to possible provisions relating to illicit traffic on the high seas, it is suggested by one Government[153] that the proposed convention could also cover cases of illicit traffic in the territorial sea and in the contiguous zone. Reference is made in this respect to article 27 of the Convention on the Law of the Sea which authorizes the coastal State to exercise criminal jurisdiction on board a foreign ship passing through the territorial sea "if such measures are necessary for the suppression of illicit traffic in narcotic drugs and psychotropic substances". Article 33 of the same Convention, which enables the coastal State to exercise in a contiguous zone to its territorial sea the control necessary to prevent infringement of its sanitary laws and regulations, could be made applicable to infringement of national drug legislation as it forms part of sanitary laws.

---

145. Australia. 146. United Kingdom. 147. Turkey, United Kingdom, United States. 148. Turkey, United Kingdom. 149. United Kingdom. 150. Egypt, Spain. 151. Egypt, United States. 152. United States. 153. Egypt.

. . .

- - - - -

UN Commission on Narcotic Drugs   E/CN.7/1986/2/Add.1
Ninth Special Session, February 1986   24 December 1985
                                                                       Extract

---

Comments and Proposals Received from Governments Concerning A Draft Convention on Illicit Traffic in Narcotic Drugs and Psychotropic Substances
Note by the Secretary-General

. . .

Chapter III. IDENTIFICATION OF ELEMENTS

. . .

Illicit traffic on the high seas

47.   One Government[61] considered it important to adopt provisions for the suppression of illicit trafficking on the high seas, particularly by arresting vessels suspected of being involved in illicit drug trafficking. In this connection attention is drawn to paragraph 20 of the Report of

the International Narcotics Control Board for 1985 (E/INCB/1985/1) in which the Board recommended that consideration be given to incorporating in the new instrument provisions aimed at facilitating the exercise of criminal jurisdiction on board vessels passing through the territorial seas or on the high seas. It also suggested inclusion of provisions enabling any state which has reasonable grounds to believe that a ship flying its flag is engaged in drug trafficking to request the co-operation of other States in suppressing this activity. Provisions to this effect are already included in article 27, paragraph 1(d), and article 108, paragraph 2, of the Convention on the Law of the Sea.

48. One Government[62] suggested that, in the law enforcement procedures against trafficking by ships on the high seas, court action should be directed against the responsible crew members rather than against the carrier itself. It indicated that it was not in favour of provisions for strict liability against shipping lines. It also emphasized that any provision addressing the subject in the new convention should be consistent with the provisions of the Convention on the Law of the Sea.

49. One replying Government[63] suggested that a provision along the lines of resolution 1983/4 of the Economic and Social Council entitled "Measures to improve international co-operation in the maritime interdiction of illicit drug traffic" could be included in the draft convention. The resolution called for improved international co-operation, particularly with regard to the registration of vessels.

50. One Government proposed that efforts should be made to promote the adoption by the international community of an instrument dealing specifically with illicit drug trafficking on the high seas.[64]

---

61. Italy. 62. Canada. 63. Venezuela. 64. Italy.

- - - - -

UN Commission on Narcotic Drugs   E/CN.7/1986/11/Add.3
Ninth Special Session, February 1986   24 December 1985
                                                Extract

Report of the Expert Group on Countermeasures to Drug Smuggling by Air and Sea

. . .

IV. CONSIDERATION OF "COMMENTS AND PROPOSALS RECEIVED FROM GOVERNMENTS CONCERNING A DRAFT CONVENTION ON ILLICIT TRAFFIC IN NARCOTIC DRUGS AND PSYCHOTROPIC SUBSTANCES" (E/CN.7/1986/2)

. . .

24. In respect of countering **illicit traffic via commercial carriers**, the group again fully supported the high priority that had been given to this element as meriting support for inclusion in the draft Convention.

25. In this context, the group noted the initiatives taken by ICAO. They welcomed the proposals approved by the Council of ICAO, in pursuit of General Assembly resolution 39/143, to work more closely with the Division and to become involved not only in the preparation of the new draft convention, but also in assessing the need for any appropriate guidance materials. The group also examined and commended to the attention of the Commission the Memorandum of Understanding entered into between the CCC and ICS, which is attached as Annex III. The group also noted that a similar Memorandum of Understanding between the CCC and IATA was being developed.

26. Participants debated in depth the need to achieve a proper balance between safety rules and practices and the full searching of aircraft and vessels which was necessary to ensure the most effective action against drug smuggling by sea and air. The group agreed that, despite all the disadvantages to society of drug trafficking, it was nevertheless essential to ensure that the safety of passengers travelling by plane or vessel was paramount. In accordance with this principle, the group suggested that the Commission commend to the attention of Governments the desirability of ensuring that complete agreement be reached between Customs or other concerned authorities and carriers relating to procedures for carrying out thorough searches. The kind of agreement which had proved valuable in the connection, in the opinion of a number of participants, was one which ensured that carriers made certified airframe mechanics or other experts with similar qualifications and experience available to co-operate with Customs and other authorities. By these means safety was guaranteed while thorough searches were nevertheless possible.

27. The group agreed that in this, as in other areas where it was necessary to achieve a balance between legitimate commercial interests and drug law enforcement, there was a great and continuing need for those agencies which were concerned with drug law enforcement to hold regular contact meetings with representatives of commercial carriers. This might usefully be done by expanding or adjusting the arrangements made at the national level for co-ordinating preventive action against the illicit traffic under the provisions of article 35 of the Single Convention on Narcotic Drugs, 1961, and under the provisions of article 21(a) of the Convention on Psychotropic Substances. Through contacts of this kind it might, for instance, be possible to persuade commercial carriers to avoid "peaking" the arrival and departure of planes at the same busy period at international airports. If such arrivals and departures could be staggered as a result of negotiation, the load on customs, immigration, and other authorities concerned with drug law enforcement would be spread over a reasonable period. This would provide more time for examination of passengers and goods and permit greater concentration on exploiting any intelligence which had been received regarding any passengers or goods. The problem of "peaking" aircraft arrivals and departures was often particularly acute in some of the smaller transit States where the national economy depended heavily on tourism. The group noted that under these circumstances traffickers and their associates were increasingly using the territory of the States concerned as points from which the traffic could be organized, even though the drugs themselves did not necessarily pass through the territories of the States concerned.

. . .

30. In respect of further elements: **co-operation across frontiers** and **investigative and judicial assistance** which had been identified by many Governments as meriting support for inclusion in the draft Convention, the observer from the CCC drew attention to the provisions of the International Convention on mutual administrative assistance for the prevention, investigation and repression of Customs offences (Nairobi Convention) and, in particular, to

Annex X thereof. He suggested that the Commission be asked to suggest to Governments that they consider adhering to this Convention and, in particular, to Annex X. The group accepted this suggestion, believing that the provisions of Annex X could be of value in supporting more co-ordinated action against smuggling by sea, by air and by land routes.

...

41.   Also in the context of elements which, in the view of the group merited inclusion in the new convention, was the illicit drug traffic on the high seas. The group noted the provisions of articles 27.1(d) and 108 of the United Nations Convention on the Law of the Sea and believed that consideration might usefully be given to the inclusion of equivalent provisions in the new convention. The group recognized and debated possible practical difficulties in applying such provisions. Account was taken of the successes that had been achieved in countering drug smuggling in the Caribbean as a result of prior consultation through diplomatic channels between the Governments of States concerned. Such prior consultation, which had resulted in either formal or informal agreements, had enabled numerous ships to be intercepted either on the high seas or when they entered the territorial waters of States in the Caribbean in an attempt to evade pursuit.

...

ANNEX III

Memorandum of Understanding between the Customs Co-operation Council and the International Chamber of Shipping

Recognizing that offences against Customs laws, particularly drug smuggling, are prejudicial to the economic, social, fiscal and security interests of states and to the interests of all parties involved in legitimate international trade, and that such offences may involve the use of any transportation facility including merchant vessels and their cargoes,

Noting that the escalation in drug trafficking necessitates Customs authorities to increase their surveillance and controls,

Aware that such increased controls could result in additional expense and costly delays to operators of merchant vessels engaged in legitimate trade,

Believing that increased co-operation between shipowners and Customs authorities could significantly assist those authorities in gathering of information and other aspects of combating Customs fraud, in particular drug smuggling,

Believing also that such co-operation would be of benefit to all parties in legitimate trade including shipping companies and their agents,

The Customs Co-operation Council and the International Chamber of Shipping have agreed as follows:

(i)   To strengthen further the co-operation between the two organisations,

(ii)   To examine and develop together ways in which co-operation and consultation between shipowners and Customs authorities could be improved with a view to combating Customs fraud, in particular drug smuggling,

(iii)   To seek to ensure a better understanding by shipowners of Customs authorities' tasks and problems and vice-versa, thereby facilitating a productive exchange of information between the two parties,

(iv)   To consider practical ways in which the personnel of shipping companies and their agents might assist Customs authorities in the detection of Custom offences, in particular those relating to drug smuggling.

- - - - -

UN Commission on Narcotic Drugs   E/1986/23, also
Report on the Ninth Special Session   E/CN.7/1986/13
February 1986   Extract

...

Chapter II

Preparation of A Draft Convention Against Illicit Traffic in Narcotic Drugs

...

24.   Several representatives and observers proposed that the following elements grouped in category B should also be considered for inclusion in the draft convention:

- Special problems of transit States
- Illicit drug traffic on the high seas
- Smuggling of drugs through the mails

The special problems of the transit States should be given high priority, they said.   One observer suggested that such a provision should recognize the collective responsibility of States affected by illicit production and demand, as well as the transit States, in combatting the illicit transit traffic.

25.   Several representatives and observers supported the inclusion of provisions allowing for appropriate intervention on the high seas in cases of illicit drug traffic. Improved co-operation and bilateral and regional agreements in this field should also be encouraged.   Some representatives pointed out that provisions in the new instrument should be in conformity with those of the United Nations Convention on the Law of the Sea (1982).

...

Chapter X

Resolutions and Decisions Adopted
by the Commission at its Ninth Special Session

A. Resolutions

**1 (S-IX). Guidance on the drafting of an international
convention to combat drug trafficking**

The Commission on Narcotic Drugs,

Recalling General Assembly resolution 39/141 of 14 December 1984 in which the commission was requested to initiate the preparation of a draft convention against illicit drug traffic, as a matter of high priority,

Recalling further resolution 1 (XXXI) of the Commission on Narcotic Drugs in which the Secretary-General was requested to compile and consolidate comments and proposals submitted by Governments on elements they would like to have incorporated in the draft convention,

Noting the Commission's request, in its resolution 1 (XXXI), that the Economic and Social Council include this item on the provisional agenda of the ninth special session, so that the Commission might consider, at that session, the report of the Secretary-General and reach decisions on those elements which could be included in the draft convention, as well as on the modalities for preparing the text of the draft convention,

Emphasizing the fundamental relationship between the consumption of narcotic drugs and psychotropic substances and the trafficking of those substances, and the necessity to adopt effective measures to reduce the demand for these substances in order to make more effective the measures to combat drug trafficking,

Bearing in mind General Assembly resolution 40/120 of 13 December 1985, in which the Economic and Social Council is requested to instruct the Commission to decide on the elements that could be included in the convention and to request the Secretary-General to prepare a draft on the basis of those elements,

Taking note of resolution 2 entitled "Struggle against illicit drug trafficking" adopted by the Seventh United Nations Congress on the Prevention of Crime and the Treatment of Offenders, and of the relevant parts of the report of that Congress,

Recognizing that a new convention should serve to supplement the existing international instruments - such as the Single Convention on Narcotic Drugs, 1961, that Convention as amended by the 1972 Protocol amending the Single Convention on Narcotic Drugs, 1961, and the 1971 Convention on Psychotropic Substances - which provide the existing international legal framework for combatting illicit drugs and drug abuse, and which the Commission urges all States which have not yet done so to adhere to,

Convinced that the new convention should take into consideration the priority interests of all countries concerned so that it can be effective, widely acceptable and enter into force at the earliest possible time,

Convinced further that the report of the Secretary-General on "Comments and proposals received from Governments concerning a draft convention on illicit traffic in narcotic drugs and psychotropic substances" (E/CN.7/1986/2 and Corr. 1 and 2 and Add. 1-3) illustrate the high priority accorded this endeavour by States, and their interest in the early conclusion of a draft convention,

1.   *Expresses its appreciation* to those States which responded to the request of the Secretary-General for comments and proposals on elements for inclusion in a draft convention;

2.   *Commends* the Secretary-General for his comprehensive report on those responses;

3.   *Recommends* that the following elements be included in an initial draft convention:

(a)   Definition, as required for the purpose of the convention,

(b)   Identification, tracing, freezing and forfeiture of proceeds of drug trafficking,

(c)   Strengthening of the obligations concerning extradition for offences relating to drug trafficking;

(d)   Measures to monitor or control specific chemicals, solvents and precursors used in the illegal processing or manufacture of controlled drugs,

(e)   Measures to ensure that commercial carriers are not used to transport illicit narcotic drugs and psychotropic substances, including the development of a system of sanctions,

(f)   Means of co-operation among countries, particularly among law enforcement agencies, for the exchange of information as well as the establishment of joint communications links, training assistance and the exchange of expertise, including the posting of drugs liaison officers as needed, taking into consideration the special problems of transit States,

(g)   Strengthening co-operation among countries to provide mutual legal and judicial assistance in cases relating to drug trafficking, and promotion of mutual assistance in investigative and prosecutorial matters,

(h)   Controlled delivery,

(i)   Adequacy of sanctions for offences relating to drug trafficking,

(j)   Strengthening mutual co-operation among States in the suppression of illicit drug trafficking on the high seas,

(k)   Measures to curtail the illicit and uncontrolled cultivation of narcotic plants, including prevention, crop substitution and eradication,

(l)   Extension of controls in free trade zones and free ports,

(m)   Prevention of receipt, possession and transfer of equipment for the purpose of illegal manufacturing, compounding or processing of narcotic drugs and psychotropic substances,

(n)   Prevention of the use of the mails for the illegal transport of narcotic drugs and psychotropic substances;

4.   *Requests* the Secretary-General to prepare a preliminary draft of a convention containing the elements specified in paragraph 3, and to circulate that draft to Members of the Commission and other interested Governments by 15 August 1986;

5.   *Invites* Members of the Commission and other interested Governments to submit their comments on and/or proposed textual changes in the draft to the Secretary-General by 30 October 1986;

6.   *Requests* the Secretary-General to compile these comments and/or proposed textual changes and to circulate them for consideration at the thirty-second session of the Commission, so that the Commission may give direction on the further development of the draft convention.

- - - - -

UN, Open-Ended Intergovernmental Expert Group	DND/DCIT/WP.12
Meeting on the Preparation of a Draft Convention Against	22 July 1987
Illicit Traffic in Narcotic Drugs and Psychotropic Substances	Extract

Interim Report of the Meeting, July 1987

Chapter II.   Review of The Draft Convention

. . .

Article 12

107.   Several representatives expressed support for the general tenor of the draft article. However, it was noted by some representatives that a number of its provisions might give rise to problems from the point of view of criminal law or the international law of the sea. One representative emphasized that any action against ships by States other than the flag State in cases where the evidence of illicit traffic was not clear and manifest could lead to abuses and might undermine legal principles which were important. A treaty provision waiving the flag State's consent could lead to traffickers merely having their vessels registered under a flag of convenience and consequently such treaties would probably not serve the purposes intended.

108.   The Group approved, without amendment, the text of paragraph 1 which sets out the general obligation for States to co-operate to the fullest extent possible to suppress the illicit traffic.

109.   In connection with paragraph 2, it was suggested that it would be desirable to extend its provisions to cover unregistered ships which are required to be registered, as well as registered ships. It was also suggested that rather than speaking of "registered under its laws" it would be preferable to use in that paragraph, and throughout the article, the expression "flying its flag" which was the common term of the art.

110.   The Group approved for paragraph 2 a revised formulation, taking into account the above suggestions.

111.   The reference in the draft to the United Nations Convention on the Law of the Sea was not considered appropriate by some delegations as that convention, after its entry into force, might not be binding on all Parties to the present instrument. Divergent views were expressed

regarding the use of the expression "high seas" in paragraph 3. Some representatives were in favour of retaining that term while others objected to it and deemed it preferable to rely on the concept of territorial sea or waters. In lieu of the term "high seas" the Group agreed to refer instead to the area "beyond the external limits of the territorial sea" without prejudice to any rights enjoyed by the coastal State seaward of those limits. Some representatives recalled the existence of a contiguous zone in which States had exclusive rights in respect of matters relating to customs, taxation, health and immigration. The Group agreed that the reservation concerning the rights of the coastal State in the new text included that zone. Some representatives expressed reservations with regard to this formulation, in view of the fact that, as signatories of the United Nations Convention on the Law of the Sea, they would construe and implement the provisions of this article in a way compatible with their obligations under that instrument.

112. The Group approved the proposal made by several representatives that with regard to vessels flying the flag of another Party, the prior consent of the flag State must be given before a vessel may be boarded, searched and seized. In the case of seizure, it was emphasized that this action should be contemplated only if evidence of the vessel being engaged in illicit traffic was discovered. Paragraph 3 was amended to reflect these requirements. In view of the inclusion of the requirement for prior permission, the reference to vessels flying the flag of the boarding State was considered superfluous, as a flag State had jurisdiction over its vessels in the situation envisaged in that paragraph. Similarly, reference to vessels not displaying a flag or markings of registry was unnecessary as the question of prior permission did not arise in such cases. Subparagraphs (a) and (c) were consequently deleted.

113. It was pointed out that the authority to be designated by each Party, in accordance with paragraph 4, would not necessarily be competent to act upon requests from another Party, but only to respond to them in an expeditious manner. The wording was amended accordingly. The Group also approved a proposal to amend the second and third sentences of paragraph 4 so as to indicate more precisely at what time the flag State should designate an authority to receive and respond to requests from other Parties for the purposes of paragraph 3, as well as the time limit for the notification of the designation to all other Parties.

114. The Group agreed to amend paragraph 5 so as to cover existing as well as future treaties, whether they be multilateral or bilateral. In conformity with the corresponding deletion made in paragraph 3, the Group agreed to delete subparagraph (a) referring to judicial requirements where the vessel in custody was flying the flag of the boarding State.

115. The Group approved a proposal to delete paragraph 6 as the Provision which conferred to one Party alone the right to call in question an agreement or arrangement was not in keeping with international practice.

116. In order to emphasize and safeguard the overall interest of the flag state in any action undertaken pursuant to the provisions of the article, the Group agreed to add a new paragraph 6 to the effect that the flag State concerned should be informed of the results of such action.

117. Several representatives supported a proposal to include an indemnity clause similar to that in article 110, paragraph 3, of the United Nations Convention on the Law of the Sea, relating to piracy, to cover the loss or damage which may be sustained by vessels subjected to searches which prove unwarranted. Many representatives objected to the proposed inclusion, pointing out that the situation in article 12, where prior permission from the flag State was

required, was different from that in article 110 and that such a provision would inhibit action by States in the fight against the illicit traffic. The proposal was not agreed upon. One delegation expressed the opinion that the convention should contain a liability clause which would, among other provisions, clearly stipulate the obligations of the requesting and requested Parties.

Article 13

118.   During its consideration of article 13, which the Commission on Narcotic Drugs at its thirty-second session had agreed to retain as formulated in the preliminary text, one representative referred to the proposal of his Government for a more comprehensive draft as reproduced in paragraph 867 of document DND/DCIT/WP.1. There was general agreement that those proposed provisions were too detailed and would be difficult to implement because of their complexity. It was decided that the initial version of article 13 should remain the basic text for discussion in the Expert Group.

119.   It was agreed that in order to ensure the effectiveness of the measures envisaged to suppress the illicit traffic in free trade zones and free ports, which were particularly vulnerable to the illicit traffic, paragraph 1 should be amended to indicate that such measures should be "no less stringent" than those applied in other parts of the national territory.

120.   The Group agreed that the wording in subparagraph 2(a) should be amended to take into account the fact that it was within the normal competence of States to empower their appropriate authorities to perform search operations. It was also agreed not to limit the provisions to "incoming and outgoing vessels" but to cover "cargoes" as well.

121.   The Group agreed to extend the provisions of the article to include the "search of crew members and passengers and their baggage" in free trade zones and free ports. It was pointed out that systematic or indiscriminate search operations would raise practical difficulties and might have legal implications as regards respect for the rights of individuals. It was therefore agreed that the provision of subparagraph 2(b) should refer to the search of crew members and passengers only "when appropriate".

        . . .

ANNEX I

REFORMULATION OF ARTICLES CONSIDERED BY THE EXPERT GROUP
        . . .

Article 12
Illicit Traffic by Sea

1.   The Parties shall co-operate to the fullest extent possible to suppress the illicit traffic by sea.

2.   If a Party, which has reasonable grounds to suspect that a vessel flying its flag or not displaying a flag or markings of registry is being used for the illicit traffic, requests the assistance of other Parties in suppressing its use for that purpose, the Parties so requested shall render such assistance, within the means available to them.

3.   Without prejudice to any rights provided for under general international law, a Party, which has reasonable grounds for believing that a vessel that is beyond the external limits of the territorial sea of any State and is flying the flag of another Party is engaged in illicit traffic, may, if that Party has received prior permission from the flag State, board, search and, if evidence of illicit traffic is discovered, seize such a vessel.

4.   For the purposes of paragraph 3 of this article, a Party shall respond in an expeditious manner to requests from another Party to determine whether a vessel is registered under its laws and to requests for permission made pursuant to the provisions in that paragraph. At the time of adhering to the Convention, each Party shall designate an authority to receive and respond to such requests. The authority designated by each Party for this purpose shall be notified through the Secretary-General to all other Parties within one month of the designation.

5.   Where evidence of illicit traffic is found, the Party having custody of the vessel shall take appropriate action with respect to the vessel and persons on board, in accordance with treaties, where applicable, or any prior agreement or arrangement otherwise reached with the flag State.

6.   A Party which has taken any action contemplated in this article shall promptly inform the flag State concerned of the results of that action.

7.   The Parties shall consider entering into bilateral and regional agreements or arrangements to carry out, or to enhance the effectiveness of the Provisions of this article.

. . .

- - - - -

UN Commission on Narcotic Drugs   E/1987/17, also
Report on the Thirty-second Session   E/CN.7/1987/18
February 1987   Extract

. . .

Chapter II

Preparation of A Draft Convention Against the Illicit Traffic in Narcotic Drugs and Psychotropic Substances

. . .

42.   One representative said that article 12 should be strengthened to make the high seas "off limits" to drug traffickers. An observer suggested that the article should not only give the right to seize ships on the high seas, but also aircraft in countries' air space. Another observer proposed that the provisions concerning search and seizure of vessels should be deleted, because of the serious implications which their implementation could have in certain areas of international trade and also in view of their possible abuse by certain States.

. . .

- - - - -

UN General Assembly   A/42/489
Forty-second Session   25 August 1987
                                                                  Extract

Draft convention against illicit traffic in narcotic drugs and psychotropic substances
Report of the Secretary-General

. . .

II. ACTION BY THE ECONOMIC AND SOCIAL COUNCIL AND THE COMMISSION ON NARCOTIC DRUGS

. . .

7.   At its first regular session of 1987, the Economic and Social Council adopted on 26 May 1987 Commission on Narcotic Drugs draft resolution I as Council resolution 1987/27. In paragraph 3 of that resolution, the Council requested the Secretary-General to prepare a working document that would consolidate the draft prepared by the Secretary-General, the comments made by Governments, the comments made by States participating in the thirty-second session of the Commission, as reflected in its report, and information on the results of the session, and to circulate it to States by 1 May 1987. The document was also to include "a draft preambular part, a section on the implementation mechanism and draft final provisions".

8.   In paragraph 4 of resolution 1987/27, the Economic and Social Council decided to establish "an open-ended intergovernmental expert group to meet in 1987, twice if necessary (perhaps in July and October), each session lasting one to two weeks, within available resources, to review the working document, to reach agreement on the articles of the convention, wherever possible, and to prepare a revised working document".

9.   In paragraph 6 of resolution 1987/27, the Council reiterated the request contained in paragraph 4 of General Assembly resolution 41/126, addressed to the Secretary-General to report to the International Conference on Drug Abuse and Illicit Trafficking on the progress made in preparing the draft convention. In paragraph 7, the Secretary-General was requested to distribute, by 1 November 1987, the expert group's revised draft to States for review. In paragraph 8, the Secretary-General was further requested to report to the Commission on Narcotic Drugs at its next session on the results of the expert group's meetings and to provide any comments from Governments on the expert group's revised draft. In paragraph 9, the Council requested the Commission on Narcotic Drugs to consider at its next session "the report of the Secretary-General on the progress achieved by the expert group and the comments from Governments on the work of the group, and to make recommendations on the steps to be followed in the further elaboration of the draft convention, including the possibility of convening a plenipotentiary conference in 1988 to adopt it".

. . .

- - - - -

UN General Assembly   A/RES/42/111
Forty-second Session   19 January 1988

Resolution 42/111. Preparation of a draft convention against illicit traffic in narcotic drugs and psychotropic substances

The General Assembly,

Recalling its resolutions 33/168 of 20 December 1978, 35/195 of 15 December 1980, 36/132 of 14 December 1981, 36/168 of 16 December 1981, 37/168 of 17 December 1982, 37/198 of 18 December 1982, 38/93 and 38/122 of 16 December 1983, 39/141 and 39/143 of 14 December 1984, 40/120, 40/121 and 40/122 of 13 December 1985, 41/125, 41/126 and 41/127 of 4 December 1986 and other relevant provisions,

Recalling also the provisions of its resolution 41/126, in which it is recognized that the preliminary draft convention prepared by the Secretary-General in compliance with Commission on Narcotic Drugs resolution 1 (S-IX) of 14 February 1986[1] constitutes a positive step in the preparation of the convention and that the elements included in the draft correspond to many of the interests of the international community in its efforts to confront the problem of illicit drug trafficking,

Emphasizing the importance of the contribution that will be made by the convention in supplementing the existing international instruments on the subject, namely the Single Convention on Narcotic Drugs of 1961, as amended by the 1972 Protocol Amending the Single Convention on Narcotic Drugs of 1961,[2] and the Convention on Psychotropic Substances of 1971,[3]

Recalling that in paragraph 3 of its resolution 41/126 it requested the Commission on Narcotic Drugs to continue the preparation of the draft convention so that it might be effective, and widely acceptable, and enter into force at an early date,

1.   *Expresses its appreciation to and commends* the Secretary-General for the report[4] submitted to the International Conference on Drug Abuse and Illicit Trafficking on progress achieved in the preparation of a new convention against illicit traffic in drugs;

2.   *Underlines* the importance of the appeal made by the Conference in paragraph 3 of its Declaration,[5] in which it called for the urgent but careful preparation and finalization, taking into account the various aspects of illicit trafficking, of the draft convention against illicit traffic in narcotic drugs and psychotropic substances to ensure its entry into force at the earliest possible date as a complement to existing international instruments;

3.   *Welcomes* the report of the meeting of the Intergovernmental Expert Group on the preparation of the draft convention,[6] in accordance with Commission on Narcotic Drugs resolution 1 (XXXII) of 10 February 1987,[7] and urges Member States to submit in due course their observations on the draft revised by the Expert Group;

4.   *Requests* the Secretary-General, using existing resources, to consider the possibility of convening the Intergovernmental Expert Group for a period of two weeks immediately

prior to the tenth special session of the Commission on Narcotic Drugs in order to continue revision of the working paper on the draft convention against illicit traffic in narcotic drugs and psychotropic substances and, if possible, to reach agreement on the convention;

5.   *Requests* the Commission on Narcotic Drugs, through the Economic and Social Council, to consider and, if possible, approve at its tenth special session the draft convention against illicit traffic in narcotic drugs and psychotropic substances, and to prepare recommendations on the next measures to be taken with a view to concluding the preparation of the convention, including the possibility of convening a plenipotentiary conference in 1988 for its adoption;

6.   *Requests* the Secretary-General to make the necessary administrative arrangements for the convening of any agreed plenipotentiary conference in 1988 for the signing of the convention against illicit traffic in narcotic drugs and psychotropic substances;

7.   *Once again* urges all States that have not yet done so to ratify or to accede to the Single Convention on Narcotic Drugs of 1961, as amended by the 1972 Protocol Amending the Single Convention on Narcotic Drugs of 1961, and the Convention on Psychotropic Substances of 1971;

8.   *Requests* the Secretary-General to report to the General Assembly at its forty-third session on the implementation of the present resolution.

93rd plenary meeting
7 December 1987

Notes

1. See Official Records of the Economic and Social Council, 1986, Supplement No. 3 (E/1986/23), chap. X, sect. A.
2. United Nations, Treaty Series, vol. 976, No. 14152.
3. Ibid., vol. 1019, No. 14956.
4. A/CONF.133/5.
5. A/CONF.133/12, chap. I, sect. B.
6. E/CN.7/1988/2 (part II).
7. See Official Records of the Economic and Social Council, 1987, Supplement No. 4 (E/1987/17), chap. VIII, sect. A.

- - - - -

Control Measures

UN Commission on Narcotic Drugs:	A/CONF.133/PC/10
Preparatory Body for the International Conference on Drug Abuse and Illicit Trafficking Report of the Second Session, February 1987	Extract

. . .

Chapter III   Draft Comprehensive Multidisciplinary Outline of Future
Activities in Drug Abuse Control

. . .

E.   **Consideration of chapter III: Suppression of illicit trafficking**

. . .

. . .

111.   Some delegations suggested that separate treatment in the CMO be given to questions relating to aircraft and ships so as to reflect or take into account the technical and legal differences between aviation and shipping.

112.   One representative was concerned that the recommendations regarding control over ships and aircraft might be abused by States for purposes other than the interdiction of drug traffickers. He suggested that the recommendations should be deleted or, otherwise, that they should be adequately reworded so as to reflect their purposes more clearly and to cover the responsibility of the State whose ship carried out the boarding operation for the damage caused to the other ship during the operation. He also expressed the view that in any event the shipowner's prior and express authorization would be needed before the other ship could be boarded.

. . .

- - - - -

Report of the International Conference	A/CONF.133/12
on Drug Abuse and Illicit Trafficking, June 1987	Extract

A.   Comprehensive Multidisciplinary Outline of Future Activities
in Drug Abuse Control

INTRODUCTION

1.   The Comprehensive Multidisciplinary Outline of Future Activities in Drug Abuse Control is a repertory of recommendations addressed to Governments and to organizations setting forth practical measures which can contribute to the fight against drug abuse and to the suppression of illicit trafficking. At the national level, it is for each Government to determine

which of the recommendations could be useful in its country in the light of economic and social conditions and to the extent consistent with national law. The Comprehensive Multidisciplinary Outline is not and was not designed to be a formal legal instrument; it does not create either rights or obligations of an international character. Its purpose will be achieved when the text is used as a handbook by national authorities and by interested organizations as a source of ideas to be selected and translated into action appropriate to local circumstances in the manner considered fit by these authorities and organizations. The text is accordingly drafted in non-mandatory style as a working guide, rather than as a package to be accepted in its entirety.

2.   The recommendations have been drafted in terms fully consistent with the principal international instruments concerned with drug abuse control, that is, the Single Convention on Narcotic Drugs, 1961, as amended by the 1972 Protocol amending the Single Convention on Narcotic Drugs[1], and the 1971 Convention on Psychotropic Substances of 1961[2].

3.   In addition, with a view to safeguarding the principle of the sovereignty of the State and the primacy of the fundamental principles of the law and constitution of the State, many recommendations include a proviso concerning respect for these principles.

    . . .

Chapter III. SUPPRESSION OF ILLICIT TRAFFICKING

    . . .

Target 26. Surveillance of land, water and air approaches to the frontier

The problem

308.   Frontiers are particularly difficult to keep under effective surveillance and offer smugglers many opportunities for evasion. Similarly, in some countries possibilities for building private air strips and for effecting parachute deliveries in remote areas have been widely exploited by traffickers. To supplement the controls applied by the police and customs authorities at official points of entry, more complete coverage of frontiers, airspace and remote areas is needed to protect societies from the nefarious activities of the illicit traffickers in drugs.

Suggested courses of action

At the national level

309.   The forces which are responsible for or have jurisdiction over the controls at point of entry and other related agencies with responsibility in this area could develop, implement and, as appropriate, co-ordinate plans for the surveillance of air and water approaches by appropriate means and equipment in order that suspect movements may be reported promptly to customs and other law enforcement agencies. The coast guard or similar agencies could be authorized, on reasonable grounds of suspicion of illicit carriage of drugs, to stop and search vessels and aircraft within and over their territorial waters, without prejudice to the safety of such vessels and aircraft.

310.   The appropriate authorities should strictly enforce the existing domestic and international regulations regarding the registration of all aircraft - commercial or private - and

enforce the obligation of all aircraft operators to operate strictly in accordance with approved flight plans and in conformity with the instructions of the air traffic control agencies.

311.   The appropriate ministry or authority could consider making regulations (where they do not already exist) requiring all privately owned boats, including pleasure craft, arriving from abroad outside any official port of entry, to report immediately to the nearest designated authority, giving full details of port of origin, cargo, passengers, owners and master of the ship or skipper, in order to request permission to refuel and obtain supplies. An aircraft entering or leaving the territory of the State should be strictly required to land at, or take off from, a designated customs airport (article 10 of the Convention on International Civil Aviation)[5]; the appropriate authorities of each State have an internationally recognized right, without unreasonable delay, to search any aircraft on landing or departure, and to inspect the certificates and other documents prescribed by national law and/or by international conventions.   The non-observance of such regulations would be punishable.   Persons or companies providing fuel or supplies to such craft without verifying that they have permission would be liable to fines or other penalties.

312.   The appropriate ministry or authority should ensure that law enforcement agencies responsible for combating illicit trafficking are provided with efficient communication networks and means of transport and that their staff is trained to deal with drug trafficking between official points of entry.   In countries that lack the financial resources to develop the necessary installations, networks, equipment and facilities for training, the Government might propose projects qualifying for multilateral or bilateral assistance or for assistance from UNFDAC for the purpose of obtaining them.

313.   Non-governmental associations of amateur pilots, yachtsmen and owners of pleasure craft and owners of private aircraft, boats and ferries, as well as associations of commercial and private fishermen and hunters and their individual members, are urged to co-operate with law enforcement authorities by reporting to these authorities suspected drug trafficking activities.

314.   Law enforcement agencies could consider the possibility of establishing telephone "hot lines" that are free of charge and connected to a permanently manned office, so that any person may report suspect drug-related occurrences without fear of reprisal.

315.   The appropriate ministry or authority could establish and maintain a system of licensing for private boats and marinas. The appropriate authorities should strictly enforce the existing domestic and international regulations concerning the registration of aircraft, the issuance of operator's permits and the use of properly designated airports or airstrips. Private operators and their organizations should be encouraged to report to law enforcement agencies suspected drug trafficking activity.

316.   The appropriate authorities could consider arranging for civic recognition or awards to individuals and non-governmental associations that have made outstanding contributions to the protection of the national frontiers against illicit drug trafficking.

At the regional and international levels

317.   The air traffic control agencies and other authorities concerned should strengthen flight control regulations in co-operation with their counterparts in the region and on a world-wide basis.

318.   The ministry or authority concerned, together with law enforcement agencies at the national and local levels, may wish to ensure that clear and effective channels of communication with corresponding agencies in other countries are established and maintained.

319.   Regional seminars should be organized to facilitate the exchange of ideas and techniques designed to strengthen frontier controls.

320.   The ministries or authorities concerned should take full advantage of regional and interregional co-operative mechanisms, of the sessions of the Commission on Narcotic Drugs and its Sub-Commission on Illicit Drug Traffic and Related Matters in the Near and Middle East, regional meetings of Heads of National Drug Law Enforcement Agencies, and of ICAO, IMO, CCC and ICPO/Interpol and IATA, in order to ensure maximum co-operation and consistency of implementation and training methods in safeguarding and strengthening the security of frontiers.

. . .

Target 28. Controls over ships on the high seas and aircraft in international airspace

The problem

326.   Vessels and aircraft are utilized for the illicit transport of drugs between countries, outside national boundaries, on the high seas and in international airspace. As numerous countries may be affected by the international shipment of drugs, appropriate co-operative procedures for interception need to be devised which do not interfere with legitimate passage and commerce, subject to compliance with existing relevant international conventions.

Suggested courses of action

At the national level

327.   Should the ministry or authority concerned have reasonable grounds for suspecting that a vessel or aircraft registered under the laws of the State is illicitly carrying drugs, it may request another State to assist in carrying out a search: for example, that other State may be asked to direct its authorities to board and inspect the vessel and, if drugs are found, to seize them and arrest persons involved in the trafficking. In such circumstances, the State's own authorities may board or seize a vessel or aircraft registered under its laws.

328.   Subject to the provisions of international law, the law enforcement authorities should, to the fullest extent permitted by national law, undertake to board and seize a vessel unlawfully carrying drugs, provided that the authorization of the State of registry and, when applicable, of a coastal State has been obtained. A State should endeavour to respond promptly when asked for permission to stop, board and search a vessel under its registry for reasons of illicit drug trafficking control. Subject to the same considerations, an aircraft may be subject to search upon landing at a designated airport.

329.   The appropriate ministry or authority should, after the seizure of such a vessel or aircraft, deal promptly with illicit drugs and traffickers found thereon under the country's own laws if the conveyance is registered under that country's laws or, if registered under the laws of

another State, pursuant to such agreement as is reached with the State of registry without unnecessary delay.

330.   States could authorize the appropriate agency or responsible authority to take appropriate action in these matters. This action might include the prompt communication of information indicating whether a particular vessel or aircraft is registered under the laws of the requested State and also authority to empower a requesting State to seize the suspect vessel or aircraft.

At the regional and international levels

331.   International bodies and States could consider whether international standards can be established for the identification, seizure and disposition of vessels and aircraft on the surface suspected of carrying drugs illicitly, and of the drugs and traffickers found thereon. States should also make every effort to conclude bilateral, multilateral and regional agreements to strengthen such co-operation between States.

332.   Existing intergovernmental forums, including the transport and shipping programmes of the regional commissions, should consider the question of illicit drug movement, the need to co-ordinate efforts to halt it, and the importance of support for the new convention.

. . .

B.   DECLARATION OF THE INTERNATIONAL CONFERENCE ON DRUG ABUSE AND ILLICIT TRAFFICKING

. . .

8.   Recognizing the magnitude and extent of the world-wide drug problem, we agree to intensify efforts against drug abuse and illicit trafficking. As an extension of our commitment, we also agree to promote inter-regional and international co-operation in:

(a)   Prevention and reduction of demand;
(b)   Control of supply;
(c)   Suppression of illicit trafficking; and
(d)   Treatment and rehabilitation.

For this purpose, we consider that the following, *inter alia*, should guide the development of our actions:

. . .

(c)   Suppression of illicit trafficking:

(i)   Develop bilateral and other instruments or arrangements for mutual legal assistance which might include among other things, if appropriate, extradition and tracing, freezing and forfeiture of assets, and for enhancing international legal or law enforcement co-operation in this field;

(ii)   Improve dissemination of information to national and international law enforcement bodies, especially concerning profiles and methods of operation of drug trafficking organizations, and further develop international, financial, technical and operational co-operation in investigation and training for officers and prosecutors.

. . .

Notes

1. United Nations Treaty Series, vol. 976, No. 14152, p.106.
2. Ibid., vol. 1019, No. 14956, p.176.
   . . .
5. United Nations Treaty Series, vol. 15, p.295.

- - - - -

Additional References

International Conference on Drug Abuse and Illicit Trafficking. UN resolutions A/RES/40/122, A/RES/41/125 and A/RES/42/112.

Commission on Narcotic Drugs: Preparatory Body for the International Conference on Drug Abuse and Illicit Trafficking. Report of the first session. UN doc. A/CONF.133/PC/6.

International Conference on Drug Abuse and Illicit Trafficking. Provisional Comprehensive Multidisciplinary Outline of Future Activities. UN doc. A/CONF.133/4.

International campaign against traffic in drugs. UN resolutions A/RES/41/127, and A/RES/42/113 and doc. A/42/490.

"The Council of Europe Co-operation Group to Combat Drug Abuse and Illicit Trafficking in Drugs (the Pompidou Group)". UN Bulletin on Narcotics, Vol. XXXIX, No.1, 1987.

Guidelines on co-operation between customs authorities and shipping companies on the prevention of drug smuggling on vessels engaged in international trade. IMO doc. FAL.5/Circ.1.

- - - - -

2

Unlawful Acts Against the Safety of Navigation and Offshore Platforms

Preventive Measures

IMO Maritime Safety Committee
53rd Session, September 1986

MSC/Circ. 443, incl. MSC 53/24
Extract

Measures to Prevent Unlawful Acts Against Passengers and Crews on Board Ships

At its fifty-third session (MSC 53/24, paragraph 17.3), the Maritime Safety Committee approved the measures to prevent unlawful acts against passengers and crews on board ships (MSC 53/24, annex 14), the text of which is attached hereto.

These measures are intended to assist Member Governments when reviewing and strengthening, as necessary, port and onboard security in accordance with resolution A.584(14). Member Governments are requested to bring the measures to the attention of concerned organizations and interested parties.

MSC 53/24, ANNEX 14

1. INTRODUCTION

1.1 Assembly resolution A.584(14) directed that internationally agreed measures should be developed, on a priority basis, by the Maritime Safety Committee to ensure the security of passengers and crews on board ships and authorized the Maritime Safety Committee to request the Secretary-General to issue a circular containing information on the agreed measures to governments, organizations concerned and interested parties for their consideration and adoption.

1.2 The text of Assembly resolution A.584(14) is attached at appendix 1.

2. Definitions

For the purpose of these measures:

.1 DESIGNATED AUTHORITY means the organization or organizations or the administration or administrations identified by or within the Government as responsible for ensuring the development, implementation and maintenance of port facility security plans or flag State ship security plans, or both.

.2   PORT FACILITY means a location within a port at which commercial maritime activities occur affecting ships covered by these measures.

.3   PASSENGER TERMINAL means any area within the port facility which is used for the assembling, processing, embarking and disembarking of passengers and baggage.

.4   PORT FACILITY SECURITY PLAN means a comprehensive written plan for a port facility which identifies, *inter alia*, regulations, programmes, measures and procedures necessary to prevent unlawful acts which threaten the passengers and crews on board ships.

.5   PORT FACILITY SECURITY OFFICER means the person in a port responsible for the development, implementation and maintenance of the port facility security plan and for liaison with the ships' security officers.

.6   OPERATOR means the company or representative of the company which maintains operational control over the ship while at sea or dockside.

.7   SHIP SECURITY PLAN means a written plan developed under the authority of the operator to ensure the application of measures on board ship which are designed to prevent unlawful acts which threaten passengers and crews on board ships.

.8   OPERATOR SECURITY OFFICER* means the person designated by the operator to develop and maintain the ship security plan and liaise with the port facility security officer.

.9   SHIP SECURITY OFFICER* means the master or the person on board the ship responsible to the master and operator for on-board security, including implementation and maintenance of the ship security plan and for liaison with the port facility security officer.

3.   General provisions

3.1   Governments, port authorities, administrations, shipowners, operators, shipmasters and crews should take all appropriate measures against unlawful acts threatening passengers and crews on board ships. The measures implemented should take into account the current assessment of the likely threat together with local conditions and circumstances.

3.2   It is desirable that there be appropriate legislation or regulations which, *inter alia*, could provide penalties for persons gaining or attempting to gain unauthorized access to the port facility and persons committing unlawful acts against passengers or crews on board ships. Governments should review their national legislation, regulations and guidance to determine their adequacy to maintain security on board ships.

3.3   The measures contained in this document are intended for application to passenger ships engaged on international voyages** of 24 hours or more and the port facilities which serve them. Certain of these measures may, however, also be appropriate for application to other ships or port facilities if the circumstances so warrant.

3.4 Governments should identify a designated authority responsible to ensure the development, implementation and maintenance of ship and port facility security plans. The designated authority should co-ordinate with other relevant domestic agencies to ensure that specific roles and functions of other agencies and departments are agreed and implemented.

3.5 Governments should notify the Secretary-General of progress made in the implementation of security measures. Any useful information, which might assist other governments in their implementation of measures, on any difficulties and problems which arose and were overcome during implementation of the security measures, should be forwarded with the notification. The designated authority should co-operate with similar authorities of other governments in the exchange of appropriate information.

3.6 Governments concerned with an act of unlawful interference should provide the Organization with all pertinent information concerning the security aspects of the act of unlawful interference as soon as practicable after the act is resolved. Further information and a reporting format is given in appendix 2.

3.7 In the process of implementing these measures, all efforts should be made to avoid undue interference with passenger services and take into account applicable international conventions.

3.8 Governments and port authorities should ensure the application of these measures to ships in a fair manner.

4.   Port facility security plan

4.1 Each port facility should develop and maintain an appropriate port facility security plan adequate for local circumstances and conditions and adequate for the anticipated maritime traffic and the number of passengers likely to be involved.

4.2 The port facility security plan should provide for measures and equipment as necessary to prevent weapons or any other dangerous devices, the carriage of which is not authorized, from being introduced by any means whatsoever on board ships.

4.3 The port facility security plan should establish measures for the prevention of un-authorized access to the ship and to restricted areas of the passenger terminal.

4.4 The port facility security plan should provide for the evaluation, before they are employed, of all persons responsible for any aspect of security.

4.5 A port facility security officer should be appointed for each port facility. The port facility security plan should identify the security officer for that port facility.

4.6 The responsibilities of the port facility security officer should include, but not be limited to:

    .1   conducting an initial comprehensive security survey in order to prepare a port facility security plan, and thereafter regular subsequent security inspections of the port facility to ensure continuation of appropriate security measures;

.2   implementing the port facility security plan;

.3   recommending modifications to the port facility security plan to correct deficiencies and satisfy the security requirements of the individual port facility;

.4   encouraging security awareness and vigilance;

.5   ensuring adequate training for personnel responsible for security;

.6   maintaining records of occurrences of unlawful acts which affect the operations of the port facility;

.7   co-ordinating implementation of the port facility security plan with the competent operator security officers; and

.8   co-ordinating with other national and international security services, as appropriate.

4.7 Security measures and procedures should be applied at passenger terminals in such a manner as to cause a minimum of interference with, or delay to, passenger services, taking into account the ship security plan.

5.   Ship security plan

5.1 A ship security plan should be developed for each ship. The plan should be sufficiently flexible to take into account the level of security reflected in the port facility security plan for each port at which the ship intends to call.

5.2 The ship security plan should include measures and equipment as necessary to prevent weapons or any other dangerous devices, the carriage of which is not authorized, from being introduced by any means whatsoever on board a ship.

5.3 The ship security plan should establish measures for the prevention of unauthorized access to the ship and to restricted areas on board.

5.4 A ship security officer should be appointed on each ship. The ship security plan should identify the ship security officer.

5.5 The operator security officer should be responsible for, but not be limited to:

.1   conducting an initial comprehensive security survey and thereafter regular subsequent inspections of the ship;

.2   developing and maintaining the ship security plan;

.3   modifying the ship security plan to correct deficiencies and satisfy the security requirements of the individual ship.,

.4   encouraging security awareness and vigilance;

.5   ensuring adequate training for personnel responsible for security; and

.6   co-ordinating implementation of the ship security plan with the competent port facility security officer.

5.6   The ship security officer should be responsible for, but not limited to:

.1   regular inspections of the ship;

.2   implementing and maintaining the ship security plan;

.3   proposing modifications to the ship security plan to correct deficiencies and satisfy the security requirements of the ship;

.4   encouraging security awareness and vigilance on board;

.5   ensuring that adequate training has been provided for personnel responsible for security;

.6   reporting all occurrences or suspected occurrences of unlawful acts to the port facility security officer and ensuring that the report is forwarded, through the master, to the operator for submission to the ship's flag State's designated authority; and

.7   co-ordinating implementation of the ship security plan with the competent port facility security officer.

6.   Annexes

The annexes attached hereto contain information which may be useful when developing or improving security measures.

---

*   The operator security officer functions may be assigned to the ship security officer on board the ship.
**   Voyages include all segmented voyages.

. . .

APPENDIX 1

RESOLUTION A.584(14)
(adopted on 20 November 1985)

MEASURES TO PREVENT UNLAWFUL ACTS WHICH THREATEN THE SAFETY OF SHIPS AND THE SECURITY OF THEIR PASSENGERS AND CREWS

The Assembly,

Recalling Article 1 and Article 15(j) of the Convention on the International Maritime Organization concerning the purposes of the Organization and the functions of the Assembly in relation to regulations and guidelines concerning maritime safety,

Noting with great concern the danger to passengers and crews resulting from the increasing number of incidents involving piracy, armed robbery and other unlawful acts against or on board ships, including small craft, both at anchor and under way,

Recalling resolution A.545(13) which urged action to initiate a series of measures to combat acts of piracy and armed robbery against ships and small craft at sea,

Recognizing the need for the Organization to assist in the formulation of internationally agreed technical measures to improve security and reduce the risk to the lives of passengers and crews on board ships,

1. *Calls upon* all Governments, port authorities and administrations, shipowners, ship operators, shipmasters and crews to take, as soon as possible, steps to review and, as necessary, strengthen port and on-board security;

2. *Directs* the Maritime Safety Committee, in co-operation with other committees, as required, to develop, on a priority basis, detailed and practical technical measures, including both shoreside and shipboard measures, which may be employed by Governments, port authorities and administrations, shipowners, ship operators, shipmasters and crews to ensure the security of passengers and crews on board ships;

3. *Invites* the Maritime Safety Committee to take note of the work of the International Civil Aviation Organization in the development of standards and recommended practices for airport and aircraft security;

4. *Authorizes* the Maritime Safety Committee to request the Secretary-General to issue a circular containing information on the measures developed by the Committee to Governments, organizations concerned and interested parties for their consideration and adoption.

   . . .

- - - - -

UN General Assembly   A/RES/42/159
Forty-second Session   Extract

Resolution 42/159. Measures to prevent international terrorism which endangers or takes innocent human lives or jeopardized fundamental freedoms and study of the underlying causes of those forms of terrorism and acts of violence which lie in misery, frustration, grievance and despair and which cause some people to sacrifice human lives, including their own, in an attempt to effect radical changes:

(a) Report of the Secretary-General;

(b) Convening under the auspices of the United Nations, of an international conference to define terrorism and to differentiate it from the struggle of peoples for national liberation.

The General Assembly,

. . .

5. *Urges* all States to fulfil their obligations under international law and to take effective and resolute measures for the speedy and final elimination of international terrorism and, to that end:

(a) To prevent the preparation and organization in their respective territories, for commission within or outside their territories, of terrorist acts and subversive acts directed against other States and their citizens;

(b) To ensure the apprehension and prosecution or extradition of perpetrators of terrorist acts;

(c) To endeavour to conclude special agreements to that effect on a bilateral, regional and multilateral basis;

(d) To co-operate with one another in exchanging relevant information concerning the prevention and combating of terrorism;

(e) To harmonize their domestic legislation with the existing international conventions on this subject to which they are parties;

. . .

10. *Also welcomes* the work undertaken by the International Maritime Organization on the problem of terrorism on board or against ships, and the initiative under way to draft instruments on the suppression of unlawful acts against the safety of maritime navigation and of fixed platforms on the continental shelf;

. . .

94th plenary meeting
7 December 1987

- - - - -

Preparation of a Draft Convention

IMO Legal Committee 1st Extraordinary Session, October 1987	LEG/ES.1/3 Extract

. . .

ANNEX 1

DRAFT CONVENTION FOR THE SUPPRESSION OF UNLAWFUL ACTS AGAINST THE SAFETY OF MARITIME NAVIGATION

The States Parties to this Convention,

Having in mind the purposes and principles of the Charter of the United Nations concerning the maintenance of international peace and security and the promotion of friendly relations and co-operation among States,

Recognizing in particular that everyone has the right to life, liberty and security of person, as set out in the International Declaration of Human Rights and the International Covenant on Civil and Political Rights,

Deeply concerned about the world-wide escalation of acts of terrorism in all its forms, which endanger or take innocent human lifes, jeopardize fundamental freedoms and seriously impair the dignity of human beings,

Considering that unlawful acts against the safety of maritime navigation jeopardize the safety of persons and property, seriously affect the operation of maritime services, and undermine the confidence of the peoples of the world in the safety of maritime navigation,

Considering that the occurrence of such acts is a matter of grave concern to the international community as a whole,

Being convinced of the urgent need to develop international co-operation between States in devising and adopting effective and practical measures for the prevention of all unlawful acts against the safety of maritime navigation, and the prosecution and punishment of their perpetrators.

Recalling resolution 40/61 of 9 December 1985, of the General Assembly of the United Nations in which, *inter alia*, the International Maritime Organization was invited "to study the problem of terrorism aboard or against ships with a view to making recommendations on appropriate measures",

Recalling further resolution A.584(14) of 20 November 1985, of the Assembly of the International Maritime Organization, which called for development of Measures to Prevent Unlawful Acts which Threaten the Safety of Ships and the Security of their Passengers and Crews,

Affirming the desirability of monitoring rules and standards relating to the prevention and control of unlawful acts against ships and persons on board ships, with a view to updating them as necessary, and, to this effect, taking note with satisfaction, of the Measures to Prevent Unlawful Acts Against Passengers and Crews on Board Ships, recommended by the Maritime Safety Committee of the International Maritime Organization,

Affirming further that matters not regulated by this Convention continue to be governed by the rules and principles of general international law,

Having agreed as follows:

Article 1

For the purposes of this Convention, "ship" means a vessel of any type whatsoever not permanently attached to the sea-bed, including dynamically supported craft, submersibles, or any other floating craft.

Article 2

1.   This Convention shall not apply to:

(a) a warship or a ship owned or operated by a State when being used
     as a naval auxiliary or for customs or police purposes; or

(b) a ship which has been withdrawn from navigation or laid up.

2.   Nothing in this Convention shall affect the immunities of warships and other Government
ships operated for non-commercial purposes.

Article 3

1.   Any person commits an offence if that person unlawfully and intentionally:

(a) by force or threat thereof or any other form of intimidation seizes or exercises
     control over a ship; or

(b) performs an act of violence against a person on board a ship if that act is likely to
     endanger the safe navigation of the ship; or

(c) destroys a ship or cause damage to a ship or to its cargo which is likely to endanger
     the safe navigation of the ship; or

(d) places or causes to be placed on a ship, by any means whatsoever, a device or
     substance which is likely to destroy that ship, or cause damage to that ship or its
     cargo which endangers or is likely to endanger the safe navigation of the ship; or

(e) destroys or seriously damages maritime navigational facilities or seriously interferes
     with their operation, if any such act is likely to endanger the safe navigation of ships;
     or[1]

(f) communicates information which he knows is false, thereby endangering the safe
     navigation of ships; or[1]

(g) injures or kills any person, in connection with the commission or the attempted
     commission of any of the offences set force in subparagraphs (a) to (f).

2.   Any person also commits an offence if that person:

(a) attempts to commit any of the offences set force in paragraph 1 if that attempt is
     likely to endanger the safe navigation of the ship; or

(b) abets the commission of any such offence perpetrated by any person or is otherwise
     an accomplice of a person who commits such an offence; or

(c) threatens to commit any of the offences set forth in paragraph 1, subparagraphs (b)
     and (c), if that threat is likely to endanger the safe navigation of the ship.

Article 4

1.   This Convention shall apply if the ship is navigating in waters beyond the outer or lateral
limits of the territorial seas of the flag State or its schedule includes navigation in those waters.

2.   In cases where the Convention does not apply pursuant to paragraph 1, it shall nevertheless apply, with the exception of articles 13, 14, and 15, if the offender or the alleged offender is found in a State Party other than the flag State.

Article 5

1.   A State may at the time of signature or ratification, acceptance or approval of this Convention or accession thereto declare that it shall not apply the Convention where the ship is navigating in internal waters and its schedule does not include navigation beyond the outer or lateral limits of the territorial sea.

2.   A State may at the time of signature or ratification, acceptance or approval of the Convention or accession thereto declare that it shall apply the Convention where the ship is navigating in straits used for international navigation in cases not covered by article 4, paragraph 1.

3.   Any State which has made a declaration in accordance with paragraph 1 or 2 may at any time withdraw that declaration by notification to the Secretary-General of the International Maritime Organization (hereinafter referred to as the Secretary-General).

Article 6

Each State Party shall make the offences set force in article 3 punishable by appropriate penalties which take into account the grave nature of those offences.

Article 7

1.   Each State Party shall take such measures as may be necessary to establish its jurisdiction over the offences set forth in article 3 when the offence is committed:

    (a)   against or on board a ship flying the flag of the State at the time the offence is committed; or

    (b)   in the territory of that State, or inside the outer or lateral limits of its territorial sea; or

    (c)   by a national of that State.

2.   A State Party may also establish its jurisdiction over any offence when:

    (a)   it is committed by a stateless person whose habitual residence is in that State;

    (b)   during its commission a national of that State is seized, threatened, injured or killed;

    (c)   it is committed in an attempt to compel that State to do or abstain from doing any act; or

    [(d)   the demise-charterer in possession of the ship concerned in the offence [is a national of that State and] has its principal place of business in that State.]

3.   Each State party shall take such measures as may be necessary to establish its jurisdiction over the offences set forth in article 3 in cases where the alleged offender is present in its territory and it does not extradite him to any of the States Parties which have established their jurisdiction in accordance with paragraphs 1 and 2 of this article.

4.   This Convention does not exclude any criminal jurisdiction exercised in accordance with national law.

Article 8

1.   Upon being satisfied that the circumstances so warrant, any State Party in the territory of which the offender or the alleged offender is present, shall take him into custody or take other measures to ensure his presence for such time as is necessary to enable any criminal or extradition proceeding to be instituted.

2.   Such State shall immediately make a preliminary enquiry into the facts, in accordance with its own legislation.

3.   Any person regarding whom the measures referred to in paragraph 1 are being taken shall be entitled to:

    (a)   communicate without delay with the nearest appropriate representative of the State of which he is a national or which is otherwise entitled to establish such communication or, if he is a stateless person, the State in the territory of which he has his habitual residence;

    (b)   be visited by a representative of that State.

4.   The rights referred to in paragraph 3 shall be exercised in conformity with the laws and regulations of the State in the territory of which the offender or the alleged offender is present, subject to the proviso that the said laws and regulations must enable full effect to be given to the purposes for which the rights accorded under paragraph 3 are intended.

5.   When a State Party, pursuant to this article, has taken a person into custody, it shall immediately notify the States which have established jurisdiction in accordance with article 7, paragraph 1 and, if it considers it advisable, any other interested States of the fact that such person is in custody and of the circumstances which warrant his detention. The state which makes the preliminary enquiry contemplated in paragraph 2 of this article shall promptly report its findings to the said States and shall indicate whether it intends to exercise jurisdiction.

Article 9

Nothing in this Convention shall be construed as affecting in any way the existing rules of international law pertaining to the competence of States to exercise investigative or enforcement jurisdiction on board ships not flying their flag.

Article 10

1.   The State Party in the territory of which the offender or the alleged offender is found shall, in cases to which article 7 applies, if it does not extradite him, be obliged, without

exception whatsoever and whether or not the offence was committed in its territory, to submit the case without delay to its competent authorities for the purpose of prosecution, through proceedings in accordance with the laws of that State. Those authorities shall take their decision in the same manner as in the case of any ordinary offence of a grave nature under the law of that State.

2. Any person regarding whom proceedings are being carried out in connection with any of the offences set forth in article 3 shall be guaranteed fair treatment at all stages of the proceedings, including enjoyment of all the rights and guarantees provided for such proceedings by the law of the State in the territory of which he is present.

Article 11

1. The offences set forth in article 3 shall be deemed to be included as extraditable offences in any extradition treaty existing between any of the States Parties. States Parties undertake to include such offences as extraditable offences in every extradition treaty to be concluded between them.

2. If a State Party which makes extradition conditional on the existence of a treaty receives a request for extradition from another State Party with which it has no extradition treaty, the requested State shall consider this Convention as a legal basis for extradition in respect of the offences set forth in article 3. Extradition shall be subject to the other conditions provided by the law of the requested State.

3. States Parties which do not make extradition conditional on the existence of a treaty shall recognize the offences set forth in article 3 as extraditable offences subject to the conditions provided by the law of the requested State.

4. If circumstances require, the offences set forth in article 3 shall be treated, for the purposes of extradition between States Parties, as if they had been committed not only in the place in which they occurred but also in a place within the jurisdiction of the State Party requesting extradition.

5. A State Party which receives more than one request for extradition from States which have established jurisdiction in accordance with article 7 and which decides not to prosecute shall, in selecting the State to which the offender or the alleged offender is to be extradited, pay due regard to the interests and responsibilities of the State Party whose flag the ship was flying at the time of the commission of the offence.

Article 12

1. States Parties shall afford one another the greatest measure of assistance in connection with criminal proceedings brought in respect of the offences set forth in article 3, including the supply of the evidence at their disposal necessary for the proceedings.

2. States Parties shall carry out their obligations under paragraph 1 in conformity with any treaties on mutual judicial assistance that may exist between them.

Article 13

1.   States Parties shall co-operate in the prevention of the offences set forth in article 3, particularly by:

   (a)   taking all practicable measures to prevent preparation in their respective territories for the commission of those offences within or outside their territories;

   (b)   exchanging information in accordance with their national law, and co-ordinating administrative and other measures taken as appropriate to prevent the commission of offences set forth in article 3.

2.   When, due to the commission of an offence set forth in article 3, the passage of a ship has been delayed or interrupted, any State Party in whose territory the ship or passengers or crew are present shall be bound to exercise all possible efforts to avoid a ship, its passengers, crew or cargo being unduly detained or delayed.

Article 14

   Any State Party having reason to believe that an offence set forth in article 3 will be committed shall, in accordance with its national law, furnish any relevant information in its possession to those States which it believes would be the States establishing jurisdiction in accordance with article 7.

Article 15

1.   Each State Party shall, in accordance with its national law, provide to the Secretary-General as promptly as possible, any relevant information in its possession concerning:

   (a)   the circumstances of the offence;

   (b)   the action taken pursuant to article 13, paragraph 2;

   (c)   the measures taken in relation to the offender or the alleged offender, and, in particular, the results of any extradition proceedings or other legal proceedings.

2.   The State Party where the alleged offender is prosecuted shall, in accordance with its national law, communicate the final outcome of the proceedings to the Secretary-General.

3.   The information transmitted in accordance with paragraphs 1 and 2 shall be communicated by the Secretary-General to all States Parties, to members of the International Maritime Organization (hereinafter referred to as the Organization), to the other States concerned, and to the appropriate international intergovernmental organizations.

Article 16

1.   Any dispute between two or more States Parties concerning the interpretation or application of this Convention which cannot be settled through negotiation within a reasonable time shall, at the request of one of them, be submitted to arbitration. If within six months from the date of the request for arbitration, the parties are unable to agree on the organization

of the arbitration any one of those parties may refer the dispute to the International Court of Justice by request in conformity with the Statute of the Court.

2.   Each State may at the time of signature or ratification, acceptance or approval of this Convention or accession thereto declare that it does not consider itself bound by paragraph 1. The other States Parties shall not be bound by paragraph 1 with respect to any State Party which has made such a reservation.

3.   Any State which has made a reservation in accordance with paragraph 2 may at any time withdraw that reservation by notification to the Secretary-General.

Article 17

1.   This Convention shall be open for signature by all States at the Headquarters of the Organization from . . . to . . .[2] and shall thereafter remain open for accession. States may become Parties to this Convention by:

(a) signature without reservation as to ratification, acceptance or approval; or

(b) signature subject to ratification, acceptance or approval, followed by ratification, acceptance or approval; or

(c) accession.

2.   Ratification, acceptance, approval or accession shall be effected by the deposit of an instrument to that effect with the Secretary-General.

Article 18[3]

1.   This Convention shall enter into force ninety days following the date on which fifteen States have either signed it without reservation as to ratification, acceptance or approval, or have deposited an instrument of ratification, acceptance, approval or accession in respect thereof.

2.   For a State which deposits an instrument of ratification, acceptance, approval or accession in respect of this Convention after the conditions for entry into force thereof have been met, the ratification, acceptance, approval or accession shall take effect ninety days after the date of such deposit.

Article 19

1.   This Convention may be denounced by any State Party at any time after the expiry of one year from the date on which this Convention enters into force for that State.

2.   Denunciation shall be effected by the deposit of an instrument of denunciation with the Secretary-General.

3.   A denunciation shall take effect one year, or such longer period as may be specified in the instrument of denunciation, after the receipt of the instrument of denunciation by the Secretary-General.

Article 20

1.   A conference for the purpose of revising or amending this Convention may be convened by the Organization.

2.   The Secretary-General shall convene a conference of the States Parties to this Convention for revising or amending the Convention, at the request of one third of the States Parties, or ten States Parties, whichever is the higher figure.

3.   Any instrument of ratification, acceptance, approval or accession, deposited after the date of the entry into force of an amendment to this Convention, shall be deemed to apply to the Convention as amended, unless a contrary intention is expressed in the instrument.[4]

Article 21

1.   This Convention shall be deposited with the Secretary-General.

2.   The Secretary-General shall:

  (a) inform all States which have signed this Convention or acceded thereto, and all Members of the Organization, of:

     (i)   each new signature or deposit of an instrument of ratification, acceptance, approval or accession, together with the date thereof;
     (ii) the date of the entry into force of this Convention;
     (iii) the deposit of any instrument of denunciation of this Convention together with the date on which it is received and the date on which the denunciation takes effect;
     (iv) the receipt of any declaration or notification made under articles 5 and 16;

  (b) transmit certified true copies of this Convention to all States which have signed this Convention or acceded thereto.

3.   As soon as this Convention enters into force, a certified true copy thereof shall be transmitted by the Depositary to the Secretary-General of the United Nations for registration and publication in accordance with Article 102 of the Charter of the United Nations.

Notes

1. Subparagraphs (e) and (f), are to be reviewed in light of the text finally agreed for article 4.
2. The Committee suggests that the Convention remain open for signature for one year.
3. This article was approved by the Committee subject to further discussion as to the number of States required to bring the Convention into force.
4. The view was expressed in the Committee that the words "unless a contrary intention is expressed in the instrument" should be given further consideration.

ANNEX 2

DRAFT PROTOCOL FOR THE SUPPRESSION OF UNLAWFUL ACTS AGAINST THE SAFETY OF FIXED PLATFORMS LOCATED ON THE CONTINENTAL SHELF

The States Parties to this Protocol,

Being Parties to the Convention for the Suppression of Unlawful Acts Against the Safety of Maritime Navigation,

Recognizing that the reasons for which the Convention was elaborated also apply to fixed platforms located on the continental shelf,

Taking account of the provisions of that Convention,

Have agreed as follows:

Article 1

1.   The provisions of article 6 and of articles 8 to 16 of the Convention for the Suppression of Unlawful Acts Against the Safety of Maritime Navigation (hereinafter referred to as the Convention) shall apply also to the offences set forth in article 2 of this Protocol where such offences are committed on board or against fixed platforms located on the continental shelf.

2.   For the purposes of this Protocol, "fixed platform" means an artificial island, installation or structure permanently attached to the sea-bed for the purpose of exploration or exploitation of resources or for other economic purposes.

Article 2

1.   Any person commits an offence if that person unlawfully and intentionally:

   (a) by force or threat thereof or any other form of intimidation seizes or exercises control over a fixed platform; or

   (b) performs an act of violence against a person on board a fixed platform if that act is likely to endanger its safety; or

   (c) destroys a fixed platform or causes damage to it which is likely to endanger its safety; or

   (d) places or causes to be placed on a fixed platform, by any means whatsoever, a device or substance which is likely to destroy that fixed platform or likely to endanger its safety; or

   (e) injures or kills any person in connection with the commission or the attempted commission of any of the offences set forth in subparagraphs (a) to (d).

2.   Any person also commits an offence if that person:

(a)   attempts to commit any of the offences set forth in paragraph 1 if that attempt is likely to endanger the safety of the fixed platform; or

(b)   abets the commission of any such offence perpetrated by any person or is otherwise an accomplice of a person who commits such an offence; or

(c)   threatens to commit any of the offences set forth in paragraph 1(b) and (c) if that threat is likely to endanger the safety of the fixed platform.

Article 3

1.   Each State Party shall take such measures as may be necessary to establish its jurisdiction over the offences set forth in article 2 when the offence is committed:

(a)   against or on board a fixed platform while it is located on the continental shelf of that State; or

(b)   by a national of that State.

2.   A State Party may also establish its jurisdiction over any such offence when:

(a)   it is committed by a stateless person whose habitual residence is in that State;

(b)   during its commission a national of that State is seized, threatened, injured or killed; or

(c)   it is committed in an attempt to compel that State to do or abstain from doing any act.

3.   Each State Party shall take such measures as may be necessary to establish its jurisdiction over the offences set forth in article 2 in cases where the alleged offender is present in its territory and it does not extradite him to any of the States Parties which have established their jurisdiction in accordance with paragraphs 1 and 2 of this article.

4.   This Protocol does not exclude any criminal jurisdiction exercised in accordance with national law.

Article 4

Nothing in this Protocol shall be construed as affecting in any way the existing rules of international law pertaining to the competence of States to exercise investigative or enforcement jurisdiction on fixed platforms located on their continental shelf.

Article 5

1.   This Protocol shall be open for signature at the Headquarters of the International Maritime Organization (hereinafter referred to as the Organization) from . . . to . . . and shall thereafter remain open for accession. States may become Parties to this Protocol by:

(a)   signature without reservation as to ratification, acceptance or approval; or

(b)   signature subject to ratification, acceptance or approval, followed by ratification, acceptance or approval; or

(c)   accession.

2.   Ratification, acceptance, approval or accession shall be effected by the deposit of an instrument to that effect with the Secretary-General of the Organization (hereinafter referred to as the Secretary-General).

3.   Only States which have signed the Convention without reservation as to ratification, acceptance or approval, or have ratified, accepted, approved or acceded to the Convention may become a Party to this Protocol.

Article 6

1.   This Protocol shall enter into force ninety days following the date on which two States have either signed it without reservation as to ratification, acceptance or approval, or have deposited an instrument of ratification, acceptance, approval or accession in respect thereof, or on the date on which the Convention enters into force, whichever is the later date.

2.   For any State which deposits an instrument of ratification, acceptance, approval or accession in respect of this Protocol after the conditions for entry into force thereof have been met, the ratification, acceptance, approval or accession shall take effect ninety days after the date of such deposit.

Article 7

1.   This Protocol may be denounced by any State Party at any time after the expiry of one year from the date on which this Protocol enters into force for that State.

2.   Denunciation shall be effected by the deposit of an instrument of denunciation with the Secretary-General.

3.   A denunciation shall take effect one year, or such longer period as may be specified in the instrument of denunciation, after the receipt of the instrument of denunciation by the Secretary-General.

4.   A denunciation of the Convention by a State Party shall be deemed to be a denunciation of this Protocol by that Party.

Article 8

1.   A conference for the purpose of revising or amending this Protocol may be convened by the Organization.

2.   The Secretary-General shall convene a conference of the States Parties to this Protocol for revising or amending the Protocol, at the request of [one third of the States Parties] [or . . . States Parties, whichever is the higher figure].[1]

3.   Any instrument of ratification, acceptance, approval or accession, deposited after the date of the entry into force of an amendment to this Protocol, shall be deemed to apply to the Protocol as amended, unless a contrary intention is expressed in the instrument.[2]

Article 9

1.   This Protocol shall be deposited with the Secretary-General.

2.   The Secretary-General shall:

> (a)   inform all States which have signed this protocol or acceded thereto, and all Members of the Organization, of:

>> (i)   each new signature or deposit of an instrument of ratification, acceptance, approval or accession, together with the date thereof;
>> (ii)   the date of the entry into force of this Protocol;
>> (iii)   the deposit of any instrument of denunciation of this Protocol together with the date on which it is received and the date on which the denunciation takes effect;
>> (iv)   the receipt of any declaration or notification made under article 16 of the Convention, concerning this Protocol;

> (b)   transmit certified true copies of this Protocol to all States which have signed this Protocol or acceded thereto.

3.   As soon as this Protocol enters into force, a certified true copy thereof shall be transmitted by the Depositary to the Secretary-General of the United Nations for registration and publication in accordance with Article 102 of the Charter of the United Nations.

Notes

1. This matter was not discussed by the Committee.
2. The view was expressed in the Committee that the words "unless a contrary intention is expressed in the instrument" should be given further consideration.

- - - - -

IMO Legal Committee   LEG/ES.1/5
Report of the 1st Extraordinary Session, October 1987   Extract

===

. . .

C. Consideration of The Draft Convention for the Suppression of Unlawful Acts Against the Safety of Maritime Navigation

8.   The Committee had before it a document LEG/ES.1/3 prepared by the Secretariat, containing, in annexes 1 and 2 respectively, the texts of the draft **Convention for the Suppression of Unlawful Acts Against the Safety of Maritime Navigation** and of the draft

Protocol for the Suppression of Unlawful Acts Against the Safety of Fixed Platforms Located on the Continental Shelf, as prepared by the *Ad Hoc* Committee on the Suppression of Unlawful Acts Against the Safety of Maritime Navigation (document LEG/ES.1/3).

9.   The Committee noted that the Council had invited the Committee to consider the draft convention and the draft protocol, and to make such comments as it deemed fit. In particular, the Council had also drawn the Committee's attention to the following four matters:

     (a)   the reference to "demise or bareboat" charterer in article 7 of the draft convention;

     (b)   the issue concerning the obligation of States Parties to accept alleged offenders detained by the master of a ship, as raised in article 10 of the draft convention;

     (c)   the question regarding the handling of crew discipline and its relationship with the scope of application of the draft convention; and

     (d)   the question of harmonization of the terminology of the draft instruments with that of the United Nations Convention on the Law of the Sea.

10.   The Committee agreed to consider the above four issues and to consider any other matters which might be raised by delegations in the remaining time available to it.
    . . .

(d) **Harmonization of the terminology of the draft instrument with that of the United Nations Convention on the Law of the Sea**

49.   The Committee examined articles of the draft convention with a view to identifying any terms which appeared to conflict with the relevant terminology in the provisions of the United Nations Convention on the Law of the Sea. In particular, the Committee's attention was drawn to article 4, paragraph 1; article 5, paragraphs 1 and 2; article 7, paragraph 1(b); article 8, paragraph 1; article 10, paragraph 1; and article 13, paragraph 2.

50.   The Committee took note of the statement by the representative of the Office of Ocean Affairs and Law of the Sea, to the effect that the Office had discovered no major disharmonies between the terminology of the draft convention and the Law of the Sea Convention. The representative observed, however, that the Office had noted that the draft convention used the phrase "lateral limits" of a State's territorial sea, that the words "lateral limit" were not used in the United Nations Convention on the Law of the Sea.

51.   One delegation proposed that, in article 4, paragraph 1, article 5, paragraph 1, and article 7, paragraph 1(b), the words "the outer or lateral limits of" should be deleted. Several delegations supported this proposal.

52.   One delegation proposed that the draft convention should be consistent in its use of the word "territory" and that this applied to both land territory and territorial sea in accordance with the Convention on the Law of the Sea. The delegation cited in particular articles 7.1(b), 10.1 and 13.2 of the draft convention where different terminology had been used for the same substance. He noted that article 7.1(b) referred to the "territory of that State, or inside . . . its territorial sea", while article 10.1 referred only to "the territory", and article 13.2 referred to a "State Party in whose territory the ship or passengers or crew are present".

53.   The representative from the Office of Ocean Affairs and the Law of the Sea said the Office noted the issue of harmonization in this case would involve article 2 ("land territory") and article 33 ("within its territory or territorial sea") of the Law of the Sea Convention. The term "territory", according to the representative, included internal waters.

54.   Several delegations did not agree with the suggestion that the term "territory" should be used in place of "territory or territorial sea".

55.   One delegation explained the use of different terminology in different articles was appropriate.   The delegation pointed out that article 7.1 concerned the establishment of jurisdiction, and it was, therefore, appropriate to refer to both territory and territorial sea, whereas article 10 concerned the exercise of jurisdiction and consequently was appropriately confined to "territory" only.   This delegation cited article 27 of the Law of the Sea Convention to support this difference in terminology, by noting that article 27 imposed limits on the exercise of criminal jurisdiction by the coastal State over foreign flag vessels in the territorial sea, whereas there were no such limits to the jurisdiction in the territory of the State.

56.   This analysis was supported by several delegations.

57.   One delegation observed that this analysis was not accurate; the fact that the coastal State cannot exercise jurisdiction over foreign flag vessels in its territorial sea does not mean that article 10 should not be applied if a person is actually found within the territorial sea, for example on board a small sailing boat or another vessel which for some reason is not entitled to innocent passage.   In the view of that delegation, "territory" (whenever this word occurs) in article 10.1 should include the territorial sea.

58.   One delegation also explained that the use of the terms "territory" and "territorial waters" was appropriate.   That delegation pointed out that the reference to territory and to the territorial sea in article 7.1 corresponded to the distinction made by the Law of the Sea Convention which introduced a specific régime for territorial waters.   Thus, article 27 of that Convention provided for limited penal jurisdiction of the coastal State within territorial waters. On the other hand, in article 10 of the draft convention it was sufficient to refer merely to territory since in that case it was a matter of criminal proceedings undertaken by a State.

59.   One delegation observed that the terminology "territory or territorial sea" and "territory including the territorial sea" had been used in other conventions, *inter alia*, the Convention on the Prevention of Marine Pollution by Dumping of Wastes and Other Matter, 1972, and the International Convention on Civil Liability for Oil Pollution Damage, 1969.

60.   Several delegations observed that in article 10.1, the term "territory" is used twice in the same sentence with a slightly different meaning.   One delegation pointed out that it might be useful to include appropriate definitions at the beginning of the convention.

61.   The Legal Committee agreed that the drafting committee of the diplomatic conference should be required to examine the matter and to determine the appropriate terminology to be used.

62.   Several delegations expressed their concern over the contents of article 5.2.   Some of these delegations expressed doubts about the need for such a provision.   Several delegations felt that the provision was superfluous since they understood that, as drafted, it stated the right

of the coastal State to apply the Convention to ships flying its flag when navigating in its own territorial sea in a strait used for international navigation.

63.   The delegation of Spain expressed opposition to the inclusion of article 5.2 on substantive grounds and pointed out that that paragraph was contrary to the provisions of article 34 of the 1982 United Nations Convention on the Law of the Sea in that it made distinctions within the territorial sea of one and the same State.

64.   Other delegations, however, did not agree with that opinion.

65.   The Committee concluded that the difference of opinion regarding article 5.2 was essentially of a political nature and did not involve a conflict of terminology. It was noted that the *Ad Hoc* Preparatory Committee had agreed to leave the issue for solution by the diplomatic conference.

   . . .

(e)   **Other matters**
   . . .

   (iii)   **Clarification of the term "Fixed Platform"**

77.   The delegation of Australia referred to the draft **Protocol for the Suppression of Unlawful Acts against the Safety of Fixed Platforms located on the Continental Shelf** and expressed the view that the term "Fixed Platform" had to be defined more clearly. According to this delegation, there was the possibility of confusion between the concept of a "ship" as used in the draft convention and the concept of "permanently attached" platforms as used in the draft protocol. Particular reference was made to the case of a ship engaged in exploration for minerals, a platform being towed to a place to be attached, and a floating hotel. The delegation suggested that these concepts needed to be considered to ensure that no gap existed between the draft convention and the draft protocol. These structures were extremely vulnerable to the kind of offences covered by the convention, and care should be taken that they were not left out of protection.

78.   This concern was shared by another delegation.
   . . .

- - - - -

Additional References

Consideration of a draft Convention for the suppression of unlawful acts against the safety of maritime navigation. IMO Council, fifty-seventh session. IMO document C 57/25.

Measures to prevent international terrorism which endangers or takes innocent human lives or jeopardizes fundamental freedoms and study of the underlying causes of those forms of terrorism and acts of violence which lie in misery, frustration, grievance and despair and which cause some people to sacrifice human lives, including their own, in an attempt to effect radical changes. UN docs. A/RES/40/61, A/42/519 and Add.1, A/42/201 and A/42/336.

- - - - -

3

Attacks Against Merchant Shipping

UN Security Council   S/RES/582 (1986)
2666th Meeting, February 1986

Resolution 582 (1986)
(Adopted by the Security Council at its 2666th meeting on 24 February 1986)

The Security Council,

Having considered the question entitled "The situation between Iran and Iraq",

Recalling that the Security Council has been seized with the question of the situation between Iran and Iraq for almost six years and that decisions have been taken thereon,

Deeply concerned about the prolongation of the conflict between the two countries resulting in heavy losses of human lives and considerable material damage and endangering peace and security,

Recalling the provisions of the Charter and in particular the obligation of all Members to settle their international disputes by peaceful means in such a manner that international peace and security and justice are not endangered,

Noting that both Iran and Iraq are parties to the Protocol for the prohibition of the use in war of asphyxiating, poisonous or other gases, and of bacteriological methods of warfare done at Geneva on 17 June 1925,

Emphasizing the principle of the inadmissibility of the acquisition of territory by force,

Taking note of the efforts of mediation pursued by the Secretary-General,

1.   *Deplores* the initial acts which gave rise to the conflict between Iran and Iraq and deplores the continuation of the conflict;

2.   *Also deplores* the escalation of the conflict, especially territorial incursions, the bombing of purely civilian population centres, attacks on neutral shipping or civilian aircraft, the violation of international humanitarian law and other laws of armed conflict and, in particular, the use of chemical weapons contrary to obligations under the 1925 Geneva Protocol;

3.   *Calls upon* Iran and Iraq to observe an immediate cease-fire, a cessation of all hostilities on land, at sea and in the air and withdrawal of all forces to the internationally recognized boundaries without delay;

4.   *Urges* that a comprehensive exchange of prisoners-of-war be completed within a short period after the cessation of hostilities in co-operation with the International Committee of the Red Cross;

5.   *Calls upon* both parties to submit immediately all aspects of the conflict to mediation or to any other means of peaceful settlement of disputes;

6.   *Requests* the Secretary-General to continue his ongoing efforts, to assist the two parties to give effect to this resolution and to keep the Council informed;

7.   *Calls upon* all other States to exercise the utmost restraint and to refrain from any act which may lead to a further escalation and widening of the conflict and, thus, to facilitate the implementation of the present resolution;

8.   *Decides* to remain seized of the matter.

- - - - -

Report of the Secretary-General   A/42/1
on the Work of the Organization   9 September 1987
                                                    Extract

. . .

. . . Various conflicts in recent years have extended to the sea, raising the possible need for a United Nations role in ensuring the safety of civilian ships and in maintaining peace at sea as an element in bringing a war to an end. Any peace maintenance operation in the ocean area would differ in key respects from peace-keeping on land, although the same broad principles would apply. At present it would be difficult to mount such operations as quickly on an *ad hoc* basis as has been the case with land-based operations. There is, therefore, need to plan and be prepared for such eventualities, a process for which the advice of experts in the international academic and defense communities could usefully be sought.

. . .

- - - - -

ILO International Labour Conference   Provisional Record No.16
74th (Maritime) Session, October 1987   Extract

. . .

Resolution concerning attacks on merchant shipping

The General Conference of the International Labour Organization

Recalling that the 24th Session of the Joint Maritime Commission (Geneva, 1984) called on all governments to make every effort to find peaceful solutions to conflicts that are threatening the lives of seafarers,

Believing that the right of safe navigation by merchant shipping in international waters, free from the risks of armed attacks by States, constitutes a seafarers' inalienable right,

Expressing its serious concern that armed conflict endangers merchant shipping and has already led to the death and injury of seafarers in some regions;

Appeals to all member States of the International Labour Organization to use their influence in their diplomatic and commercial dealings with warring States to persuade the latter to refrain from attacking merchant shipping in international waters and put an end to armed conflicts.

- - - - -

4

Asylum-Seekers in Distress at Sea

IMO Council   C 54/D
54th Session, June 1985   Extract

===

Summary of Decisions

. . .

17. Relations with the United Nations and the Specialized Agencies

. . .

(d) Proposal submitted by the United Nations High Commissioner for Refugees

17(d).1   The Council considered the report on the work undertaken by the Maritime Safety Committee at the request of the Council as presented in document C 54/17(d).

17(d).2   The Council noted the long-established maritime tradition of rescue at sea, and in particular,

- regulation 10, chapter V of the Annex to the International Convention for the Safety of Life at Sea, 1974;
- article 12 of the Geneva Convention on the High Seas, 1958;
- paragraph 2.1.10, chapter 2 of the Annex to the International Convention on Maritime Search and Rescue, 1979; and
- the principles contained in article 98 of the United Nations Convention on the Law of the Sea, 1982.

17(d).3   The Council recalled the principles of Assembly resolution A.433(XI) on "Decisions of the shipmaster with regard to maritime safety and marine environment protection" and, in particular, the invitation to Governments to ensure that the shipmaster is not constrained by the shipowner, charterer or any other person from taking in this respect any decisions which, in the professional judgement of the shipmaster, is necessary.

17(d).4   The Council also recalled Assembly resolution A.545(13) on "Measures to prevent acts of piracy and armed robbery against ships".

17(d).5   The Council was aware of the appeals made to Governments and organizations concerned by the Secretary-General and the United Nations High Commissioner for Refugees in 1977, 1978 and 1983 regarding the rescue of persons in distress at sea.

17(d).6   The Council noted with concern the continuing plight of persons at sea, particularly those in small craft which are not suitably constructed, equipped or manned and who may be in need of protection from the perils of the sea or possible acts of piracy and armed robbery.

17(d).7   The Council decided:

    (a)   to urge Governments, organizations and shipowners concerned to intensify their efforts in ensuring that necessary assistance is provided to any person in distress at sea;

    (b)   to recommend that Governments and shipowners take all suitable measures, in the context of the applicable international conventions and resolutions, to facilitate actions by a shipmaster which, in his professional judgement, are necessary for the rescue of persons in distress at sea; and

    (c)   to request shipmasters to maintain due vigilance and take all possible steps to assist and, as necessary, rescue any person found to be in distress at sea.

17(d).8   The Council requested the Secretary-General to continue his consultations with all appropriate bodies of the United Nations, including the United Nations High Commissioner for Refugees, in order to further the objectives of these decisions.

17(d).9   The Council requested the Secretary-General to communicate these decisions of the Council to all Governments, bodies and organizations concerned.

Reference documents: C 54/17(d) (substantive document); C 54/SR.6.

   . . .

- - - - -

UN High Commissioner for Refugees   A/40/12/Add.1
Report of the Executive Committee, 36th Session, October 1985   Extract

---

1985 UNHCR Executive Committee Conclusion No.38 (XXXVI) "Rescue of Asylum-Seekers in Distress at Sea"

115.   **Conclusions of the Committee**

   . . .

(3)   Rescue of asylum-seekers in distress at sea

The Executive Committee:

    (a)   Reaffirmed the fundamental obligation under international law for shipmasters to rescue all persons, including asylum-seekers, in distress at sea;

    (b)   Recalled the conclusions adopted by the Executive Committee at previous sessions recognizing the need to promote measures to facilitate the rescue of asylum-seekers in distress at sea;

(c) Expressed satisfaction that the rescue of asylum-seekers in distress at sea had increased significantly in 1985, but at the same time expressed concern that many ships continued to ignore asylum-seekers in distress at sea;

(d) Welcomed the fact that the provision of an appropriate number of resettlement places had made it possible for the Rescue at Sea Resettlement Offers (RASRO) scheme to commence on a trial basis as from May 1985;

(e) Welcomed the wide-ranging initiatives undertaken by UNHCR to promote the rescue of asylum-seekers in distress at sea and the support given to these initiatives by States;

(f) Strongly recommended that States maintain their support of UNHCR action in this area and, in particular, that they:

     (i) Join or renew contributions to the DISERO (Disembarking Resettlement Offers) and to the RASRO schemes, or to either of them, as soon as possible;
    (ii) Request shipowners to inform all shipmasters in the South China Sea of their responsibility to rescue all asylum-seekers in distress at sea.

. . .

- - - - -

VIII

PEACEFUL USES OF THE SEA

1. Naval Armaments and Disarmament

2. Nuclear-Free-Zones & Zones of Peace

1

Naval Armaments and Disarmament

UN General Assembly   A/40/535
Fortieth Session   17 September 1985
UN Publication Sales   No. E.80.IX.3, Extract

General and Complete Disarmament

Study on the naval arms race
Report of the Secretary-General

CONTENTS

(Italics denote paragraphs reprinted in this work.)

CHAPTER I

GENERAL BACKGROUND AND SETTING

1. By resolution 38/188 G of 20 December 1983 the General Assembly requested the Secretary-General, with the assistance of qualified governmental experts, to carry out a comprehensive study on the naval arms race, on naval forces and naval arms systems, including maritime nuclear-weapons systems, as well as on the development, deployment and mode of operation of such naval forces and systems. The same operative paragraph made clear that

the study should be carried out with a view to analysing the possible implications of these factors for international security, for the freedom of the high seas, for international shipping routes and for the exploitation of marine resources, thereby facilitating the identification of possible areas for disarmament and confidence-building measures.

2.   The present report has been prepared pursuant to that resolution and contains eight chapters. . . .

A. Purposes and objectives of the study

3.   Some 71 per cent of the earth's surface is sea, and over two thirds of the world's human inhabitants live within 300 kilometres (km) of a sea coast, yet for the very large majority, the significance of the sea, its resources, its present and potential benefits and the impact of developments at sea apparently deserve only passing consideration.

4.   To date, little attention has been paid in multilateral disarmament negotiations to the continuing development of naval forces and naval arms systems and the added dimension and implications this has given to the problems of international security. However, the modernization and expansion of navies and the increased sophistication of naval-based arms systems in general have created new and enlarged operational capabilities, especially among nuclear-weapon States and other militarily significant States, and have given rise to concern among many nations. They are concerned about the possible effects on the prospects for global disarmament and on the freedom of the high seas, the principle of non-interference with international sea communications for trade and shipping and with the economic exploitation of marine resources.

5.   One reason for the lack of attention to the naval arms race in multilateral disarmament negotiations has been the difficulty in discussing such matters as long as negotiations on the law of the sea had not been concluded and the legal situation was unclear. The Convention on the Law of the Sea, which was signed at Montego Bay, Jamaica, on 10 December 1982, embodied existing and new principles in the legal régime governing the use of ocean space.[1] It is now in the process of ratification by States. Once the Convention is in force, discussions pertaining to the issues of the naval arms race, measures for naval disarmament and related questions might thus be carried out on a firmer basis. This matter is addressed in more detail in chapter V.

6.   In resolution 38/188 G, the General Assembly has underlined the paramount importance, for the security and well-being of all nations, for international trade and shipping and for the economic exploitation of marine resources, of preserving the freedom of the high seas and of keeping open international sea communications for trade and shipping in a manner consistent with the Charter of the United Nations and with the principles of international law. These considerations, together with recent developments in the law of the sea, are reflected in the purposes of the study, which are as follows:

   (a) To draw attention to an aspect of the competitive accumulation of arms which carries major implications for international security;

   (b) To describe the various factors and interactive effects of certain major developments in the maritime environment;

(c) To analyse the implications for international security, for the freedom of the high seas, for international shipping routes and for the exploitation of marine resources.

7.   The objectives of the study are twofold:

(a) To promote a wider international understanding of the issues involved;

(b) To facilitate the identification of possible areas for negotiation of confidence-building and disarmament measures on the world's seas as a constituent part of the disarmament process as a whole.

B.   Relevant principles of the Final Document and the United Nations Convention on the Law of the Sea

8.   The Final Document adopted by consensus by the General Assembly at its tenth special session, the first special session devoted to disarmament, in 1978 was of major significance in that it set out an international disarmament strategy.[2]

9.   In declaring that the ultimate objective of the efforts of States in the disarmament process is general and complete disarmament under effective international control, the Final Document states that progress requires the conclusion and implementation of agreements on the cessation of the arms race and on genuine measures of disarmament, taking into account the need of States to protect their security. Among such measures, effective measures of nuclear disarmament and the prevention of nuclear war have the highest priority.

10.   The Final Document further states that, together with negotiations on nuclear disarmament measures, negotiations should be carried out on the balanced reduction of armed forces and conventional armaments, based on the principle of undiminished security of the parties with a view to promoting or enhancing stability at a lower military level, taking into account the need of all States to protect their security. These negotiations should be conducted with particular emphasis on armed forces and conventional weapons of nuclear-weapon States and other militarily significant countries.

11.   In order to promote the peaceful use of, and to avoid an arms race on, the sea-bed and the ocean floor and the subsoil thereof, the Final Document requested the Committee on Disarmament - now the Conference on Disarmament - to proceed promptly with the consideration of further measures in the field of disarmament for the prevention of an arms race in that environment. In this regard, the Conference on Disarmament was requested to take action in consultation with the States parties to the Treaty on the Prohibition of the Emplacement of Nuclear Weapons and Other Weapons of Mass Destruction on the Sea-Bed and the Ocean Floor and in the Subsoil Thereof .

12.   Among the other principles set out in the Final Document, many of which can be seen to have a bearing on limiting and reversing the naval arms race, the General Assembly called for the resolute pursuit of agreements or other measures on a bilateral, regional and multilateral basis with the aim of strengthening peace and security at a lower level of forces. The Final Document suggested that such measures might include bilateral, regional and multilateral consultations and conferences, as appropriate, and consultations among major arms suppliers and recipient countries on the limitation of all types of international transfer of conventional weapons, based in particular on the principle of undiminished security of the parties with a

view to promoting or enhancing stability at a lower military level, taking into account the need of all States to protect their security as well as the inalienable right to self-determination and independence of peoples under colonial or foreign domination and the obligations of States to respect that right.

13.   As noted above, the Final Document is a disarmament strategy covering all aspects of the arms race.   As the naval arms race in itself embraces many of the features of the world's competitive accumulation of arms, the principles cited in the paragraphs above are not the only facets of the Final Document applicable to the naval scene.   In fact, it may be said that much of the Final Document can be seen as having direct application to measures to halt and reverse the naval arms race.

14.   The Convention on the Law of the Sea does not provide for disarmament measures.   It does explicitly uphold the peaceful utilization of the various areas of the sea as a fundamental norm.   Under the Convention, peaceful uses of the seas is a recurrent theme: as a general rule (art. 301), on the high seas (art. 88), in the exclusive economic zone (art. 58), on the international sea-bed area (art. 141) and in the conduct of marine scientific research (art. 240).

15.   There is also a widespread, but not unanimous, belief that consideration will have to be given to the substantive broadening of naval disarmament agreements which are indirectly but clearly related to the Convention on the Law of the Sea if the principle in the Convention of the peaceful uses of the seas is to be implemented effectively.   A case in point is the broadening in scope of the aforementioned Treaty on the Prohibition of the Emplacement of Nuclear Weapons and Other Weapons of Mass Destruction on the Sea-Bed and the Ocean Floor and in the Subsoil Thereof.

16.   The Convention on the Law of the Sea applies the principle of the peaceful uses of the seas to the high seas and the exclusive economic zone.   The waters of both these areas are to be reserved for peaceful purposes.   The international sea-bed area shall also be open to use exclusively for peaceful purposes.   Its development means in effect the peaceful use of the sea-bed beyond national jurisdiction.   This is the reason for the importance of the Convention régime governing the sea-bed and ocean floor and subsoil thereof beyond national jurisdiction (known as the "Area") and its resources as the "common heritage of mankind" (art. 136).   This régime provides that activities in the Area shall be carried out for the benefit of mankind as a whole, taking into particular consideration the interests and needs of developing States and of peoples who have not attained full independence or other self-governing status.   In this respect, the régime makes an integral contribution to fulfilling the requirements of a new international economic order.

17.   The Convention on the Law of the Sea is discussed in greater detail in chapter V, but there can be little doubt that its entry into force, 12 months after ratification or accession by 60 States, will have a major impact on the conduct of international relations related to the uses and exploitation of ocean space.

. . .

D.   The sea and its resources and their value to mankind

. . .

1. Fisheries

36.   The advent of 200-mile exclusive economic zones, introduced by the Convention on the Law of the Sea, will provide a new dimension to national rights and duties and present a number of States with opportunities to exploit new resources but also with problems of how to develop maritime capabilities to protect their interests and enforce the obligations of other States fishing in their respective zones. In turn, the development will also present a number of other States with the problem of how to maintain access to traditional fishing grounds with historic rights which will now fall under different jurisdiction.   One example of new arrangements has been the establishment in January 1983 of a common fisheries policy for the European Communities, providing, *inter alia*, for yearly decisions on the allowable catch of each type of fish for each member State.

37.   Globally, a major event was the FAO Conference on World Fisheries Management and Development held in Rome from 27 June to 6 July 1984. The Conference adopted a resolution entitled "The Strategy for Fisheries Management and Development" comprising guidelines and principles which are to be taken into account by Governments and organizations when planning and implementing fisheries management and development. The Conference also approved an integrated package of five Programmes of Action to assist developing countries to increase fish production and improve their individual and collective self-reliance in fisheries.

38.   In sum, it may be seen that ocean fisheries represent a major resource. With an increasing human population there will be rising demands for protein from the sea which will best be met by a judicious use of modern technology and methods and a combination of international and national management of available and potential fish resources. Furthermore, the increased rights and duties of States in their respective exclusive economic zones arising from the Convention on the Law of the Sea will stimulate significant national interest in and requirements for the development of improved methods and tools for management in the respective areas of the fishing industry.

2.   Mineral resources of the sea-bed

. . .

40.   The exploitation of the resources of the deep sea-bed was the subject of much discussion and negotiation during the preparation of the Convention on the Law of the Sea. Using the term the "Area", meaning the sea-bed and ocean floor and subsoil thereof beyond the limits of national jurisdiction, the Convention declares in Part XI that the Area and its resources are the common heritage of mankind, and it sets out provisions governing activities in the Area. International support for the Convention, although very considerable, was not completely unanimous. The principles were accepted, but some of the objections from a number of industrialized countries concerned the effects of the provisions of Part XI.

3.   Energy from the sea and the sea-bed

. . .

4.   Sea-borne trade and shipping

. . .

5. Pollution

50. Mounting concern has been expressed in recent years at the rise in pollution in the world's oceans and associated seas. The Convention on the Law of the Sea (art. 1, pars. 1 (4)) defines pollution of the marine environment as:

> ". . . the introduction by man, directly or indirectly, of substances or energy into the marine environment, including estuaries, which results or is likely to result in such deleterious effects as harm to living resources and marine life, hazards to human health, hindrance to marine activities, including fishing and other legitimate uses of the sea, impairment of quality for use of sea water and reduction of amenities".

51. Although much of the open oceans remain as yet not seriously threatened, this is not the case closer to shore. The major sources of marine pollution, accounting for some 80 per cent, are land-based activities. Chemicals enter the sea from coastal industries and via rivers, e.g. insecticides and fertilizers from agricultural run-off; or by atmospheric deposit; or by dumping at sea of chemical wastes. Heavy metals are carried down rivers from mining operations and industrial processes. Sewage is discharged into the seas either directly from sewage systems or dumped from barges. Oil and other petroleum products find their way to the seas as a result of accidental spillage, industrial waste, urban run-off or deliberate tank-cleaning operations by ships. Radioactive pollution occurs from industrial outfalls, dumping of packaged industrial radioactive waste, discharge of low-level nuclear waste from coastal nuclear installations or from earlier nuclear tests.

52. Measures to limit and control marine pollution have been the subject of several multilateral efforts, both within and outside the United Nations and it is clear that these will have to be continued if the value of the seas to mankind is to be protected. Maritime forces, both afloat and air-borne, can and do provide considerable assistance in pollution control, particularly in areas be prime responsibility ascribed to States in the Convention on the Law of the Sea. The International Convention for the Prevention of Pollution from Ships, 1973 (MARPOL), which was modified by the Protocol of 1978 relating thereto (generally referred to as MARPOL 73/78), provides the basis for such action.

CHAPTER II

DEVELOPMENT OF NAVAL CAPABILITIES

A. Motivations for States to develop naval capabilities

. . .

54. . . . Many States have major interests in sea-borne trade, in the continued viability of shipping routes and in the protection of those routes and the ships that ply them in times of peace and war. The preservation of sea lines of communication during war can become vital to a nation's survival, as can the denial of the use of the sea to adversaries. Traditionally, this has been the principal motivation for acquiring naval capabilities. States that have identified the need for a maritime strategy, and have been able to afford one, have taken steps to develop naval forces accordingly. Another motivation for States to acquire navel capabilities has been to protect themselves from aggression from the sea or from the effects of piracy.

. . .

56.   The changes in the uses of ocean space and the exploitation of the sea's resources, identified in the 1960s by the international community\and now embodied in the Convention on the Law of the Sea, will bring new rights and responsibilities to many States and the need to police and protect them. There are therefore additional motivations for States, including those that may not previously have had any naval capabilities, to develop such forces.

57.   Separately, the existence of a much greater number of sovereign States and their inherent rights of self-defence are likely to lead to perceptions on the part of some that naval capability is required in order to be able to exercise those rights and to resist interference and intervention, particularly in the absence of an effective system of international security.

58.   Above all, the most significant technological change has been the advent of nuclear weapons.   The sea has now become the operational environment of ballistic missile submarines, each of which has been estimated to be carrying the equivalent of more explosive power than was used by all the combatants in the Second World War.   The combination of missile and warhead design, nuclear propulsion power, highly accurate navigation and guidance systems and sophisticated hull design and construction techniques has provided the opportunity for the development of an entirely new naval capability of awesome specific purpose.

59.   The spur to deploy such capabilities, and to continue to improve them, has been the political confrontation between certain major Powers and their respective allies, which has been in evidence since 1945. In order to maintain the effectiveness of those strategic nuclear forces and the levels of general-purpose naval capability that each side has considered to be necessary, naval forces of significant strength - and cost - have been developed.

60.   The motivations for developing naval capabilities are thus several. They vary from local self-defence to the potential for strategic nuclear use; from preparation of the capacity for overseas intervention to establishment of seaboard protection and security; from traditional protection of commerce and national interests to newly established areas of exclusive economic jurisdiction. In addition to these major reasons there are other aspects, such as national prestige, the protection of territorial integrity, affirmation of an overseas presence, support for friendly or allied States, defence against subversion by sea, coercion and intimidation of adversaries or efforts to counterbalance adversaries' ability to take action in a certain area. Naval forces also continue to be used in the context of the global rivalry between the two leading nuclear-weapon States and their allies. Together, and according to differing national economic strengths and assessments of priorities, these factors lead some States to expend considerable resources on the development of naval forces and weapons.

61.   The possession and continued development of maritime forces in all their forms constitute a part of the global arms race, the overall cost of which was estimated to amount to over $800 billion in 1984.[12] Though national security and the needs of self-defence are recognized to be of prime importance to States, such a sum represents a massive diversion of valuable resources away from helping to meet the economic and social needs of a troubled world. Furthermore, by using for military purposes large amounts of human effort, material and financial resources which could be used more productively elsewhere, expenditures on arms and armed forces often represent a significant burden on the economic health of a country.

B. Sea power in the general political, economic and security context

62.   It is generally agreed by writers on maritime strategy that sea power encompasses many interlocking elements. Mahan identified six factors as being necessary for a State to develop a naval capability: geographical position (astride sea lanes); physical properties (natural harbours etc.); extent of territory (large enough to support a navy but not so large as to encourage a continental strategy); number of population; national character; and character of Government (willing to support a maritime policy). With such factors, a State would have the constituents for the development of merchant shipping and a beneficial overseas trade, the acquisition of bases and for the construction of a navy to protect the sea lines of communication. A more modern commentator, S. G. Gorshkov, Admiral of the Fleet of the Soviet Union and Commander-in-Chief of the Soviet Navy, has described a State's sea power as possibilities for the State to explore the ocean and harness its wealth, the status of the merchant and fishing fleets and their ability to meet the needs of the State and also the presence of a navy matching the interests of that State.[13] In this sense, naval forces *per se* are part of a wider, more comprehensive sea power which can have significant political, economic and security implications.   Primarily, however, it remains true that a naval force is a declaration by a nation that it has specific maritime interests and has the political will to protect them.

63.   In common with other instruments of military force, navies have to be designed, built, equipped and trained for war yet spend most of their time in a peacetime environment. Their purposes and tasks in peace often differ from those in war. While a State will endeavour to give primacy to its navy's preparedness and effectiveness in war, in practice various compromises often have to be made to accommodate the conflicting requirements of peacetime responsibilities.   The general contexts of navel forces need therefore to be considered in these two different sets of conditions although there are inevitably functions which are applicable to both.

64.   A fundamental distinction exists between war on land and war at sea. Historically, at issue on land is the actual possession and occupation of territory, whereas at sea the issue is the unhampered use of the sea. The oceans do not, in general, lend themselves to the notion of occupation but are infinitely available as a medium of communication. Thus, the objective of first obtaining and then maintaining maritime superiority - preferably by decisive battle - becomes a matter of achieving the unhampered ability to use the sea for one's own purposes and/or of denying that use to one's enemy. Having achieved that condition in ocean areas that are considered vital, naval force can then be used to promote and protect such interests and priorities as the State considers necessary to the success of its wider politico-military aims on land, such as successful invasion of foreign territory, effective blockade of an enemy's sea-borne supplies or movements, or assuring a State's own logistic supply routes of food and war materials. In political terms, therefore, supremacy at sea is not an end in itself. Ultimately it may be a means of ensuring national survival or a means towards the end of achieving victory on land. From this general position, it follows that States which consider their security in war to depend on unhampered use of sea lines of communication will take steps to develop a naval capability to safeguard those lines. In so doing, they may develop naval forces which are perceived as capable of threatening the security or interests of that States, thus leading to the construction of a naval force, to counter the perceived threat. The result can be a naval arms race, a phenomenon which history has witnessed before and which is at present being repeated.

65. In peace, naval forces have several roles. In the first instance, a strong naval force capable of operating far from its home bases offers a significant capacity for becoming involved in regional disputes or conflicts. Its presence and strength therefore provide options for action, either by vigorous involvement or coercion or as a restraint on action by others which would not be available if such a force did not exist. This role, and its attendant ability to support land or air operations against shore targets if necessary, is known as "power projection".

66. The unique characteristic of naval power is that influence can be exercised by simple presence in an area without necessarily having to land any forces on the territory of another State. Naval influence in peacetime environment is often exercised not by actively denying use of the oceans to others but by ensuring their availability to one's own maritime traffic and to that of other nations. This activity is the role of "naval presence", whereby the knowledge that a force of warships is consistently in the area becomes a factor in the politics of the region. Thus, such elements as protection of interests, naval presence abroad (often exercised by courtesy visits to foreign ports known as "showing the flag") and maritime policing are seen by maritime States as important naval functions. The demonstration of the ability to deploy sea power in all its forms - naval force, merchant shipping, oceanographic vessels, fishing fleets etc. - can make a deep political impression, particularly now that the development of maritime resources is becoming the subject of increased national and international attention.

67. The possession in peacetime by maritime powers of naval forces sufficiently strong to carry out their wartime tasks constitutes a factor that has its own momentum. The average hull-life of a warship is at least 20 years and some will serve over 30. A new class of warship can take 10 years from its design to operational service. The provision of a naval force available to perform its allotted war tasks can therefore involve large economic resources in peacetime. Research and development, production, fitting-out, upkeep, maintenance, modernization and replacement particularly in these days of high-technology weapon systems and equipment, have become a very expensive and persistent commitment. These expenditures are quite separate from the very considerable costs of manpower, at sea and ashore, and the day-to-day operating costs of naval forces.

68. Above all other considerations, the advent of nuclear weapons and the decision to use the oceans as the medium for the deployment of a large number of strategic and tactical nuclear-armed forces have introduced an entirely new and particularly dangerous element into naval operations. Although these weapons are in the hands of five nations, they nevertheless can carry grave implications for the security of all. The nature of the strategic nuclear deployments by the navies of nuclear-weapon States will be discussed later in the report.

C. Levels of navies

69. The world's navies are of differing sizes, strengths and compositions, reflecting the different strategies, responsibilities and economic strengths of States. For the purposes of this study, it is convenient to consider navies to be at three levels:

(a) **World-wide navies**, those that can be, and often are, deployed in most oceans of the globe on a continuous basis. Such operations necessitate reliable access to overseas bases and friendly port facilities, a strong logistic support system and sufficient numbers of warships to be able to maintain a presence far from home notwithstanding the need for regular periods off-task for maintenance, repair, refit and modernization. At present only two States possess such navies: the United States and the Soviet Union.

(b) **"Blue-water" navies**, those that are normally deployed in waters surrounding the State concerned, although often out to a significant distance from shore, and which also possess the capacity to conduct occasional deployments and limited operations in force distant from bases at home. There are perhaps some 15 navies that may be considered to be at this level.

(c) **Coastal navies**, those that are almost exclusively deployed in waters immediately adjacent to a nation's land territory executing traditional naval tasks such as maritime self-defence, protection of sovereign interests in territorial waters, protection of national economic interests in offshore waters, maritime policing and counter-smuggling duties, local search and rescue etc. Such navies may undertake only occasional deployments further afield and then usually in small numbers for courtesy visits. Most navies are at this level, although there exists a wide range of capabilities.

70. A numerical comparison between the navies of the Soviet Union and the United States has only limited use as each State has its own historical background and geopolitical situation which have given rise to different maritime strategies. The United States is bordered by two oceans and has extensive coastlines which, for the most part, are ice-free and permit access to the open sea at all times of the years. The Soviet Union, on the other hand, has a very large land area with restricted access to the oceans, and much of its coastline is subject to severe ice conditions each year. Historically, the United States has been a significant naval power for many years whereas the Soviet Union has developed long-range naval capabilities comparatively recently, although the Soviet Navy has been numerically large for much longer. Both countries, like many others, have significant interest in maintaining the principle of the freedom of the high seas and the right of innocent passage through territorial waters.

71. The development of massive sea-borne strategic nuclear forces by each State, and the activities which that development has involved in the sense of each countering the perceived threats of the other, have had a considerable influence on the composition and mode of operation of their forces. Again, however, there are significant asymmetries which render numerical comparisons of doubtful value. In addition to their strategic nuclear missions, both navies are deployed on a world-wide basis and have a potent capacity for general operations far from their home waters. It is their ability to conduct a strategic nuclear exchange, the possibility of conflict at sea including the use of tactical nuclear weapons and their capacity for intervention abroad that cause concern on the part of many other States.

72. The "blue-water" navies vary considerably in size, as do the States themselves, and in military capability. Some of the States concerned still have territorial responsibilities in distant parts of the world or arrangements with friendly States which involve naval manoeuvres and exercises from time to time. In a number of cases the States depend heavily on sea-borne trade and open sea lines of communication which they would seek to defend in time of war in order to survive. Three States (China, France and the United Kingdom) possess maritime strategic nuclear forces and, presumably, also a tactical nuclear weapon capacity. These capabilities, although small in comparison with those of the Soviet Union and the United States, nevertheless form part of the world's stock of nuclear weapons.

73. Finally, over 125 nations are capable of carrying out almost solely coastal operations although many to only a very small degree. Again, the navies vary considerably in size and fire-power, and numerical comparison would be of little value. Although some warships and weapons are not modern and the total naval capability of a State may be minor, it may well be quite sufficient for the limited tasks set by national policy. In other cases, however, modern ship design, together with up-to-date sensors and weapons, provide very effective capabilities over a restricted distance. For example, highly accurate missiles can be put to sea on small and inexpensive ships and thereby can constitute a significant naval force in a limited engagement. Despite increasing facilities for indigenous production in various parts of the world, most of these navies, particularly those of developing countries, are often dependent on arms suppliers abroad for ships and such naval equipment as well as for training assistance.

D. Transfers of naval arms

74. There are many reasons for States to consider it necessary to have some form of naval force. The composition of the force, its size, the numbers of vessels and other components and the capabilities of its weapon systems vary according to the tasks it may be called upon to perform. However, for other than comparatively simple warships, the large majority of nations often have to seek shipbuilding and weapon expertise elsewhere. There is therefore a thriving international market in the transfer of naval arms.

. . .

Chapter III

NAVAL FORCES AND NAVAL ARMS SYSTEMS

. . .

4. Conventional naval forces

. . .
. . .

5. Support services

(a) Seagoing logistic support

130. Extended operations at sea demand efficient and reliable logistic support. Navies which are sufficiently large and well organized to be able to contemplate such operations require supplies of fuel of various kinds, ammunition, food and general supplies, and the ships carrying them, in turn, have to be defended. The result is that the navies of the United States and the Soviet Union, and some of the blue-water navies mentioned earlier, have developed considerable numbers of seagoing replenishment ships, tankers, specialized repair and maintenance vessels, missile support ships and miscellaneous craft. The larger the navy and the more its long-range commitments, the greater - and more costly - its support organization must be. Indeed, any navy which seeks to become a blue-water navy has to develop such logistic support capabilities.

131. Merchant ships in commercial use are not part of naval strength, but some States have an integrated command structure controlling all merchant ship activities, with close association, at the time of ship design and construction, between fleet requirements and the ability of the class of ship concerned to meet some of those or other demands if and when so required. Thus, the provision of cargo-hatch sizes of certain dimensions, a specific crane capacity, repair facilities or helicopter landing facilities may have more to do with potential

Table 2. Selected conventional naval strengths (active service) **a**/

	Aircraft-carriers **b**/	Battleships	Cruisers	Destroyers and frigates	Corvettes/FAC **c**/ (missile)	FAC (torpedo)/ FAC (gun)	Submarines (excl. Ballistic Missile Subs.)
Argentina	1	—	—	11	7/-	2/2	3
Brazil	1	—	—	18	16/-	-/3	7
China	—	—	—	41	14/222	250/345	103
France	2	—	2	43	-/5	-/-	19
India	1	—	1	28	3/16	-/-	8
Indonesia	—	—	—	10	-/4	2/-	2
Italy	2	—	2	19	8/-	4/-	10
Japan	—	—	—	52	-/-	5/-	14
Spain	1	—	—	26	5/-	-/-	9
Sweden	—	—	—	2	-/30	6/-	12
Turkey	—	—	—	17	-/14	5/1	17
Union of Soviet Socialist Republics	4	—	41	263	59/105	10/-	279
United Kingdom	2	—	4	56	-/-	-/-	27
United States of America	14	2	28	168	-/-	-/-	99

Source: Jane's Fighting Ships 1984-85, pp. 150-151.

a/ Excluding ships in reserve or under construction or modernization.

b/ The term "aircraft-carrier" is used in a broad sense; some of the vessels so classified carry mostly helicopters. The Soviet classification is "tactical aircraft-carrying cruiser".

c/ Fast Attack Craft (see para. 129 below.)

military use than with normal commercial operation. It is also possible to design containers of weapons systems or maintenance equipment that can be placed on board merchant ships at very short notice. The ability quickly to divert merchant ships to naval-support activities in time of war is a naval asset of very great value and one that is really available only to States possessing a flag merchant fleet of substantial size.

132.   Large or medium-sized navies also have the services of certain specialist ships. The importance of anti-submarine warfare (ASW), particularly strategic ASW (i.e. the detection and tracking of SSBNs) has led to a considerable need for better knowledge of the contours of the sea-bed, the direction and speed of ocean currents, the salinity and temperature of the sea at various depths, the movements of sea-ice and other oceanographic details. Separately, there are requirements for powerful ice-breakers, missile-range instrumentation ships, salvage vessels, deep-sea rescue vessels, ocean-going tugs, intelligence-gathering vessels, cable-repair ships, submarine tenders and a large number of auxiliaries and harbour craft. All these are part of the seagoing "tail" that lies behind the effectiveness of the "teeth" of the warships themselves. . . .

. . .

CHAPTER IV

APPLICATIONS AND USES OF NAVAL CAPABILITIES

. . .

D. Sea control and sea denial

. . .

146.   For all navies, the tasks of coastal protection in time of war are of great importance and include such duties as protection against attacks on coastal shipping, guarding against covert or open incursions against shore targets and anti-mining and minesweeping operations. States with overseas territorial responsibilities have also to take into account the need to offer those territories the same level of protection as the homeland in the event of a threat to their security. This aspect raises various political perceptions which are discussed in more detail in chapter VI.

. . .

F. Affirmation of sovereignty, naval presence and surveillance

153.   In peacetime, naval presence and surveillance are very important missions. A navy is an attribute and symbol of sovereignty and many coastal States tend therefore to have navies; this is likely to increase with the added responsibilities of the exclusive economic zone. Other specific factors also play a role: reaction to the naval acquisitions of a neighbour and perhaps a desire to be able, using a State's own forces, to prevent an influx of subversive elements arriving by sea, as has happened in a number of African and Asian countries. These factors vary in importance but all tend to lead to the strengthening of the means of surveillance.

154.   To assist in this task of surveillance, many Governments have established separate Coast Guard forces. A Coast Guard is often responsible for civilian maritime affairs in the coastal area, whereas a navy generally deals with purely military missions at sea. Often the Coast Guard is not part of the ministry or department of defence but is assigned to a civilian ministry (transport, fisheries or interior). At the same time, most Coast Guards have a military structure and return to the control of the navy in the event of armed conflict. This is

widely practiced, particularly in Latin America, but it can lead to duplication of functions with the navy and this, in turn, can result in conflicts of responsibilities.

155.   Besides the task of surveillance in coastal areas there is also that of presence on the high seas. To some extent this involves what is now sometimes referred to as public service, which is described later in this chapter. There is also, however, the purely political aspect of what is often called naval diplomacy. Gunboat diplomacy in its traditional form has fortunately become a rarity but the political use of naval forces continues to be common. The motivations may be very different and may include co-operation, such as protocol visits, friendly visits and joint manoeuvres; different forms of coercion, such as naval presence in protection of nations or threatened interests; or affirmation of sovereignty over disputed territory or even intervention. There are many types of examples and the large number of such occurrences each year involving navies demonstrates that navies continue to be of great political importance. By maintaining strong fleets in various parts of the world, capable of taking offensive or intervention action, the naval forces of certain States are able to play a deterrent role in many circumstances, thereby bringing the threat or use of military force to bear on the course of situations far from their own shores. Examples of this activity may be seen currently in the Mediterranean, the Indian Ocean, the China Sea, the South Atlantic and in Central American waters.

G. Public service

156.   In addition to their war-fighting and other military duties, naval ships perform other very valuable tasks. The different aspects of public service described in this section are not only a matter of national policy; they also reflect that States increasingly strive for co-operation in this field in order to discharge themselves of the responsibilities allocated to them by international agreements and to meet their legitimate concern about activities outside areas under their national jurisdiction. It should be borne in mind that military assistance rendered in the public service is mostly carried out under the responsibility of the ministries concerned, for instance, the ministry of justice in the case of counter-terrorism. The prerequisites for such activities are formulated by civil authorities. Navies are, in this context, therefore instruments of civilian policy.

1. Law enforcement actions

Protection of economic resources
(counter-smuggling, fishery protection, counter-terrorism, counter-piracy)

157.   The protection of economic resources covers a wide area of responsibilities, and each country tends to adopt different and individual approaches according to circumstance.

158.   Although not protection of marine resources, efforts to counter smuggling provide a long-standing demonstration of naval activities designed to protect a nation's economic trade. Smuggling, which takes place off many coasts, can in certain commodities have major harmful effects on national economic and other interests.

159.   Naval involvement in fishery protection is more than simple protection. It is enforcement of the rules on size and type of fish caught and minimum net mesh used; guarding against unlawful fishing in prohibited areas or by those not permitted to fish in protected areas; and a police function concerned with avoiding the catching of fish that are

temporarily or permanently protected. These protection duties and police functions are supported by many national and international treaties and agreements.

160. Another essential and difficult area of protection of resources is defence against possible terrorist attacks on offshore installations. Nations with offshore assets normally have plans to counter this type of threat. Naval presence is considered to be of great value in deterring potential attacks of this nature. Planning between government, naval forces and industry, from time to time supported by an exercise, is now regularly carried out by a number of countries.

161. In some parts of the world piracy continues to be a significant problem; it has been reported to be on the increase in certain areas.[24] In general, merchant shipping companies and seamen's unions have resisted suggestions that merchant ships should be armed. The task of controlling and eradicating piracy therefore falls on naval forces, and in most cases on those that have comparatively little capacity to maintain the continuous patrols and availability of high-speed reaction that success in counter-piracy operations demands.

2. Miscellaneous activities (hydrography and oceanography, pollution control, disaster relief, search and rescue)

162. Many navies in the world add to the safety of international shipping by making a consistent, high-quality contribution to the international hydrographic effort and to the subsequent publication of charts, books and other material.

163. In the past two decades, the task of survey has become increasingly specialized with the development of deep-diving submarines, deep-draught tankers and the special needs of the offshore industry. Routing through confined waters is a normal procedure today to increase the safety of navigation and it, too, often requires special planning and charting by the hydrographic offices of co-operating countries.

164. In addition to the hydrographic activities of States and international organizations, a considerable effort is concentrated on oceanographic survey. States, with the Soviet Union and the United States providing the major efforts, carry out surveys of the oceans, covering the total range of scientific research the sea and the sea-bed. It is clear that these surveys have considerable economic, military and environmental significance and so for many countries the national interest in them is understandably high. In many countries the tasks are given to special branches of navies which plan and co-ordinate activities nationally and internationally and often operate the survey vessels involved.

165. The seriousness of the world-wide ocean pollution problem dates from the time when rapid development of industry, agriculture and shipping came into conflict with the intensifying use of the riches of the oceans, as described in chapter I. Over the past 30 years a number of international conventions have been adopted in efforts to control pollution, and the United Nations has been active in these multilateral efforts. The Convention on the Law of the Sea provides a comprehensive framework of rules covering all sources of marine pollution (see part XII of the Convention).

166. Many national systems of pollution control involve the resources of navies. Whether by carrying out surveillance patrols, reporting culprits, or escorting them to anchorages for further investigation when pollution accidents occur, naval forces can assist in many different

ways.   A typical example was when minesweepers with high-definition sonar equipment searched for and found drums of a very dangerous toxic substance on the bottom of the sea. Earlier the drums had been lost overboard from a merchant ship in heavy weather. Similarly, special teams trained to retrieve explosive ordnance from the sea bottom have proved to be necessary, especially in areas shallow enough for fishing, exploration and exploitation.

167.   Another aspect of pollution control sometimes appropriate for naval vessels and aircraft is the peaceful surveillance of maritime commercial traffic in busy areas.   By encouraging compliance with rules of navigation and safe use of traffic separation lanes, the risks of collisions which might then lead to pollution can be reduced.

168.   With the introduction of offshore production platforms for oil and gas, States have had to consider the consequences of accidents on these platforms. The two main elements, the importance of which has been recognized in the Convention on the Law of the Sea, are safety and the rescue of human lives and control of the pollution resulting from this type of accident. Navies with fixed-wing aircraft and helicopters, proper command and control arrangements and communication facilities are obvious choices for these kinds of operations as well as other kinds of assistance and police operations. With their well-tried liaison capacity with national and international authorities, and their capabilities for quick and effective action, naval resources are often the best fitted to take effective emergency action which can then be supplemented, at a later stage, by outside assistance from appropriate experts.

169.   The combination of organizational expertise, fire-fighting capabilities, technical and medical skills and general capabilities enables naval forces to render valuable assistance at times of disaster at sea or ashore in coastal areas. In such incidents and events as mercantile collisions or breakdowns, rescue operations, earthquakes or hurricanes, naval ships have been ready sources of emergency assistance and civil support. They can also bring supplies of essential commodities to stricken areas. Such operations often involve ships of several nations and close co-ordination with governmental authorities and international organizations.

170.   In sum, it can be stated that naval forces are eminently suited for many different peacetime tasks in the public service when the situation demands, the majority of which tasks are often above the level of national interest and are to the benefit of the international community at large.

CHAPTER V

MARITIME LEGAL CONTEXT

171.   So far, the study has presented an overview of the maritime environment, its uses and resources, and the general nature and disposition of naval forces and naval arms systems, including maritime nuclear weapons. Before addressing the security and other implications of these factors, it is necessary to consider in broad terms the maritime legal context. In particular, the importance and scope of the Convention on the Law of the Sea should be noted. Although it has not yet entered into force, it is significant that since the opening of the Convention for signature an important additional number of States have become signatories (see para. 182 below). In addition, several States have incorporated, or are in the process of incorporating, into their national legislation rules similar to those of the Convention, especially with regard to such aspects as territorial seas and the exclusive economic zone. Some States are also engaged in modifying their legislation to reflect relevant provisions contained in the

Convention. In consequence, the Convention on the Law of the Sea provides in the present circumstances a solid basis for further development of the existing rules of customary law.

172.   The following paragraphs present only a brief discussion of complex legal subjects. The observations contained therein are not intended to prejudice any existing laws and agreed principles, nor to trespass on matters that may be currently under negotiation in any international forum.

A. General rules of international law restricting the use of force, right of self-defence and collective self-defence at sea

173.   The use of force in general international law is governed by the provisions of the Charter of the United Nations, in particular by Article 2, paragraph 4, and Article 51, which read as follows:

Article 2, paragraph 4,

"All Members shall refrain in their international relations from the threat or use of force against the territorial integrity or political independence of any State, or in any other manner inconsistent with the Purposes of the United Nations."

Article 51

"Nothing in the present Charter shall impair the inherent right of individual or collective self-defence if an armed attack occurs against a Member of the United Nations, until the Security Council has taken measures necessary to maintain international peace and security. Measures taken by Members in the exercise of the right of self-defence shall be immediately reported to the Security Council and shall not in any way affect the authority and responsibility of the Security Council under the present Charter to take at any time such action as it deems necessary in order to maintain or restore international peace and security."

174.   A distinction should be made in maritime matters between the use of force in self-defence and the lawful use of force to enforce jurisdiction. The latter has assumed particular importance in the new law of the sea.

175.   One of the significant features of the new law of the sea is that coastal States have been extending their sovereignty and jurisdiction over adjacent maritime areas. The 1958 Geneva Conventions had already given coastal States sovereign rights over the natural resources of their continental shelves and had codified the right of hot pursuit and the right of warships to board ships on the high seas in certain circumstances. The 1982 Convention on the Law of the Sea continued this process, for instance by granting coastal States sovereign rights over all the resources in their exclusive economic zones and giving archipelagic States sovereignty over their archipelagic waters. The question of the degree to which force may be used to enforce these recognized rights of sovereignty and jurisdiction is therefore of some importance.

176.   The Charter in Article 51 recognizes that States have the inherent right of individual or collective self-defence. It also recognizes that Members of the United Nations may exercise collectively what is their individual right. To this end States have entered into collective security arrangements in various parts of the world, among them the following:

In the Americas

Inter-American Treaty of Reciprocal Assistance (Rio Treaty), 1947

In Europe and the North Atlantic

Treaty between Belgium, France, Luxembourg, the Netherlands and the United Kingdom (Brussels Treaty, 1948

North Atlantic Treaty (NATO), 1949

Warsaw Treaty of Friendship, Co-operation and Mutual Assistance (Warsaw Treaty), 1955

In the Middle East

Collective Security Pact between States of the Arab League, 1950

In the Pacific area

Security Treaty between Australia, New Zealand and the United States (ANZUS Treaty), 1951

These treaties envisage taking measures of collective self-defence at sea since their zones of application cover maritime areas.

177.　The legal validity of these arrangements are all expressly based on the Charter of the United Nations, in some cases in particular on Article 51 of the Charter. Specific reference to Article 51 is found in the Rio Treaty, the Brussels Treaty, the NATO Treaty and the Warsaw Treaty. No such reference is made in the ANZUS Treaty. However, it is expressly declared in that Treaty that the rights and obligations of any of the Parties under the Charter are not affected and the responsibility of the United Nations for the maintenance of international peace and security is not prejudiced.

178.　In the exercise of the right of collective self-defence it is clear that parties to these security arrangements may use force upon the high seas, within the limits prescribed by international law, to protect their armed forces, public vessels or aircraft. As always in the case of legitimate self-defence, the use of force shall not exceed a proportional response to the armed attack, taking into account its nature and magnitude.

179.　The principle of non-intervention in international law is embodied in the Charter of the United Nations. Armed intervention is prohibited by the general prohibition of force in Article 2, paragraph 4, and various forms of indirect intervention are prohibited by the provisions of Article 1, paragraph 2 (calling for respect for the principle of equal rights and self-determination of peoples) and by Article 2, paragraph 1 (setting forth the principle of the sovereign equality of States). In the Declaration on Principles of International Law concerning Friendly Relations and Co-operation among States in accordance with the Charter of the United Nations (see General Assembly resolution 2625 (XXV), annex), an authoritative interpretation of the Charter was established, according to which the principle of non-intervention should be given a wide scope of application. The Declaration covers all forms of interference or threats against "the personality" of States. Modern naval capabilities permit the political use of naval forces new and subtle forms which do not have to be explicit in order to be perceived as coercion.

180.   One example of prohibited activity - prohibited in the interests of maintaining international peace and security - is the blockade. In its definition of aggression, adopted without a vote in 1974 in resolution 3314 (XXIX) of 14 December 1974, the General Assembly, *inter alia*, specifies that, "the blockade of the ports or coasts of a State by the armed forces of another State" qualifies as an act of aggression (annex, art. 3 (c)). Such a blockade is, in the absence of a Security Council decision to that effect, not even permitted as a form of reprisal against a State which has committed a crime against international law.

B.   The Convention on the Law of the Sea

181.   The Convention on the Law of the Sea confirms to a large extent the régime established by the four Geneva Conventions of 1958. It clarifies the law in many respects, setting a clear limit for the territorial sea and introducing definitive limits to the continental shelf. It also introduces new concepts into maritime law: the exclusive economic zone and archipelagic waters. Above all, it gives practical expression to the principle of the common heritage of mankind set out in General Assembly resolution 2749 (XXV) of 17 December 1970, which contains *inter alia*, three guidelines:

(a)   That the area declared to be the common heritage of mankind shall not subject to appropriation by national means or to any claim of sovereignty or sovereign rights over any part thereof;

(b)   That the exploitation of the sea-bed and ocean floor, and the subsoil thereof, shall be carried out for the benefit of mankind as a whole, taking into consideration the interests and needs of the developing countries;

(c)   That the area shall be reserved exclusively for peaceful purposes. Resolution 2749 (XXV) implies, therefore, the recognition of the need for disarmament and the right to development.

182.   The Convention, adopted on 30 April 1982, was opened for signature on 10 December 1982. As of 9 December 1984, the closing for signature, it had been signed by 159 States and entities. As of 19 July 1985, 21 States and entities had ratified the Convention. The Convention will enter into force 12 months after receipt of 60 ratifications or accessions.

1.   Freedom of navigation

183.   One of the main tasks facing the Third United Nations Conference on the Sea was to establish a legal maritime order which accommodated the needs of developing countries and the maritime interests of the developed countries. It was clear that only by such an accommodation could the important aspects of the peaceful uses of the seas and the freedom of navigation be promoted.

184.   There were three important interests, among others, which had to be reconciled by the Conference: on the one hand, the security interests of coastal States and the need to protect the mainly resource-oriented interests of the developing coastal States and on the other hand,

the necessity of preserving the freedom of navigation of ships and aircraft. In this the Conference was successful as the Convention on the Law of the Sea has managed to balance these interests.

185.   One of the dominant reasons for restricting the sovereignty and jurisdiction of coastal States to a fairly narrow band of water known as the territorial sea was to ensure that the freedom of navigation, whether commercial or military, was not affected by any extensions. Thus the new Convention has reaffirmed the freedom of navigation. There are two developments in the new law of the sea with respect to areas falling under the sovereignty of coastal States which could particularly affect the freedom of navigation: first, the adoption of a 12-mile territorial sea and second, the acceptance of the notion of archipelagic waters. Both these developments are embodied in the Convention on the Law of the Sea, but in both cases, the Convention has sought to mitigate the consequences of these developments on the freedom of navigation.

2.   Peaceful uses of the seas

186.   The peaceful uses of the seas has been a recurring theme before successive United Nations forums on the law of the sea for almost four decades. At the Conference on the Law of the Sea held at Geneva in 1958, the testing of nuclear weapons on the high seas was a very live issue. It was argued that such tests violated the principle of the freedom of the high seas, and proposals were submitted to the Conference with the intent of obliging States to refrain from testing nuclear weapons on the high seas. The Conference finally accepted a resolution which, while recognizing the serious and genuine apprehension on the part of many States that nuclear explosions constituted an infringement of the freedom of the seas, decided to refer the matter to the General Assembly, in particular to the Disarmament Commission. It may be noted that the Treaty Banning Nuclear Weapon Tests in the Atmosphere, in Outer Space and under Water was opened for signature in 1963 and entered into force later the same year.

187.   One of the objectives laid down in the preamble of the 1982 Convention on the Law of the Sea is the establishment of a legal order for the seas and oceans which will promote their peaceful uses. This theme is taken up in various parts of the Convention, in marked contrast to the 1958 Geneva Conventions on the Law of the Sea where no such reference can be found. For instance, it is quite clearly stated that "the high seas shall be reserved for peaceful purposes" (art. 88) and that the sea-bed and subsoil beyond the limits of national jurisdiction (the Area) "shall be open to use exclusively for peaceful purposes" (art. 141). Installations constructed for carrying out activities in the Area are to be used exclusively for peaceful purposes (art. 147, para. 2 (d)). The conference which will be convened to review the operation of the system of exploration and exploitation of the Area "shall ensure", *inter alia*, "that the principle of using the Area exclusively for peaceful purposes is maintained" (art. 155, para. 2). In addition, under the new Convention marine scientific research is to be conducted exclusively for peaceful purposes. This point is stated in several provisions of the Convention: in article 143, paragraph 1; 240 (a); 242, paragraph 1; and 246, paragraph 3. The Convention also reiterates a general principle of international law already embodied in the Charter of the United Nations: that States shall settle their disputes, in this case those concerning the interpretation or application of the Convention, by peaceful means. The Convention itself has provided a mechanism for the settlement of such disputes.

188.   The Convention declares that "the high seas shall be reserved for peaceful purposes", but it does not contain a definition of "peaceful purposes". The Convention may however have

provided the answer when, under the heading of peaceful uses of the seas (art. 301), it declares that

> "in exercising their rights and performing their duties under this Convention, States Parties shall refrain from any threat or use of force against the territorial integrity or political independence of any State, or in any manner inconsistent with the principles of international law embodied in Charter of the United Nations."

Thus, military activities which are consistent with the principles of international law embodied in the Charter of the United Nations, in particular with Article 2, paragraph 4, and Article 51, are not prohibited by the Convention on the Law of Sea.

3. Internal waters

189.   Before considering the territorial sea it is necessary to deal briefly with the régime of internal waters. Internal waters are situated on the landward side of the baseline from which the breadth of the territorial sea is measured. Internal waters include waters within ports, watercourses and certain gulfs and bays. The principal feature which distinguishes internal waters from territorial sea is that under customary international law the sovereignty of the coastal state in these waters is not limited by a right of innocent passage in favour of shipping. The only exception is the special case in which straight baselines have been drawn across deeply indented or island-fringed coastlines enclosing waters which had not previously been considered internal waters. The right of innocent passage exists in such waters.

4. Territorial sea

190.   By virtue of the Convention on the Law of the Sea, coastal States may extend their territorial sea up to a breadth of 12 miles. This has settled a long-standing controversy concerning the breadth of the territorial sea with claims varying from 3 to 200 miles. Coastal States are thus empowered to exercise sovereignty over the territorial sea up to a distance of 12 miles, its sea-bed, subsoil and superjacent airspace.

191.   All ships enjoy the right of innocent passage through the territorial sea. Under the régime of innocent passage there is however no freedom of overflight for foreign aircraft, and submarines were required to navigate on the surface and show their flags. The Convention in article 19 clarifies the meaning of innocent passage by enumerating activities which can be considered not innocent, many of which fall within the category of military or quasi-military activities. They include, for instance:

> "(a)   any threat or use of force against the sovereignty, territorial integrity or political independence of the coastal State, or in any other manner in violation of the principles of international law embodied in the Charter of the United Nations;

> "(b)   any exercise or practice with weapons of any kind;

> "(c)   any act aimed at collecting information to the prejudice of the defence or security of the coastal State;
> "...
> "(e)   the launching, landing or taking on board of any aircraft;

"(f)   the launching, landing or taking on board of any military device;

"...

"(l)   any other activity not having a direct bearing on passage."

192.   A coastal State may require foreign ships exercising the right of innocent passage to use sea lanes and traffic separation schemes as it may designate or prescribe for the regulation of the passage of ships (art. 22).   This requirement applies particularly to tankers, nuclear-powered ships and ships carrying nuclear or other inherently dangerous or noxious substances or materials.   Moreover, such ships, when exercising the right of innocent passage, must carry documents and observe special precautionary measures established for them by international agreements.

193.   A coastal State may adopt laws and regulations relating to innocent passage with respect to, for instance, (a) the safety of navigation and the regulation of maritime traffic; (b) the protection of navigational aids and installations; (c) the protection of cables and pipelines; and (d) marine scientific research and hydrographic surveys.   In exercising the right of innocent passage, foreign ships must comply with such laws and regulations.

194.   A coastal State must not hamper the innocent passage of foreign ships.   It may suspend such passage temporarily for reasons of security.   It must not discriminate on the basis of the nationality of such ships or the destination or origin of their cargo.   The coastal State is under an obligation to give publicity to any danger to navigation of which it has knowledge within its territorial sea.

5.   Straits used for international navigation

195.   The general adoption of the new limit of 12 miles for the territorial sea will change (and has already changed) the legal status of several straits used for international navigation.   Such straits will fall completely within the territorial seas and hence within the sovereignty of the States bordering the straits.   Thus, in areas where freedom of navigation previously existed, the régime of innocent passage will obtain.   This will particularly affect the passage of military vessels and aircraft since first, there is no innocent passage for aircraft in the territorial sea and second, submarines are required to navigate on the surface and show their flag. ...

196.   Where straits used for international navigation fall within the territorial sea of the States bordering straits the Convention provides for the right of transit passage for all ships and aircraft.   All ships and aircraft exercising the right of transit passage enjoy the freedom of navigation and overflight solely for the purpose of continuous and expeditious transit and subject to the observance of certain duties during their passage.   Such duties include, *inter alia*, the obligations to proceed without delay through or over the strait; to refrain from any threat or use of force against the sovereignty, territorial integrity or political independence of States bordering the strait, or in any other manner in violation of the principles of international law embodied in the Charter of the United Nations; and to refrain from any activities other than those incident to their normal modes of continuous and expeditious transit unless rendered necessary by *force majeure* or distress.   In particular, ships in transit passage must observe the generally accepted international rules with respect to safety at sea and the prevention, reduction and control of pollution from ships.

197.   States bordering straits have the right to designate sea lanes and traffic separation schemes for navigation in straits used for international navigation and they may require foreign

ships exercising the right of transit passage to use such sea lanes and traffic separation schemes.

198.   States bordering straits have the right to enact laws and regulations concerning transit passage. Such laws may relate, for example, to the safety of navigation, the protection and preservation of the marine environment and the prevention of fishing. Such laws must not be discriminatory nor may they in effect deny or impede the right of transit passage. There shall be no suspension of transit passage. Where straits used for international navigation are not covered by the Provisions of the Convention - for example, in a strait used for international navigation between a part of the high seas or an exclusive zone and the territorial sea of a foreign State - the right of innocent passage obtains. Innocent passage through straits may not be suspended.

199.   Transit passage is a new concept in the law of the sea resulting from the extension of the breadth of the territorial sea up to 12 miles. The provisions of the Convention concerning straits used for international navigation do not affect the legal régime of straits which are regulated by "long-standing international conventions in force specifically relating to such straits" (art. 35 (c)). In this connection, the general rule embodied in article 311, paragraph 3, should be borne in mind. This provision states, *inter alia*, that States parties may conclude bilateral or multilateral agreements modifying or suspending provisions of the Convention on the Law of the Sea provided that such agreements are compatible with the Convention and that they do not affect the rights and obligations of other States parties under the Convention. Long-standing international conventions remain outside the régime established in the Convention for straits used for international navigation. Examples are the Convention concerning the régime of straits, signed at Montreux in 1936, which regulated transit and navigation in the Straits of the Dardanelles, the Sea of Marmara and the Bosphorus; and the 1881 Treaty between Argentina and Chile, defining the boundaries between the two countries and, *inter alia*, regulating the legal régime of the Magellan Straits; Copenhagen Convention on the Sound and the Belts, 1857, defining a régime for the strait between Sweden and Denmark; and the 1921 Convention relating to the non-fortification and neutralization of the Aaland Islands and, *inter alia*, regulating the régime of part of the strait between Finland and Sweden.

6. Archipelagic waters

200.   The Convention recognizes the concept of an archipelagic State - that is, a State constituted wholly by one or more archipelagos. Such a State may under certain conditions draw straight baselines joining the outermost islands and drying reefs of the archipelago. These lines, known as "archipelagic baselines", are used to measure the breadth of the State's territorial sea, contiguous zone, exclusive economic zone and continental shelf. The waters enclosed within archipelagic baselines are known as "archipelagic waters" and the archipelagic State exercises sovereignty over such waters, their sea-bed, subsoil and superjacent airspace.

201.   Through these waters ships of all States enjoy the right of innocent passage similar to that enjoyed in the territorial sea. An archipelagic State may designate sea lanes and air routes through or over its archipelagic waters for the passage of foreign ships and aircraft. All ships and aircraft enjoy the right of "archipelagic sea lanes passage" in such sea lanes and air routes.

202.   Archipelagic sea lanes passage means the exercise "of the rights of navigation and overflight in the normal mode solely for the purpose of continuous, expeditious and

unobstructed transit between one part of the high seas or an exclusive economic zone and another part of the high seas or an exclusive economic zone" (art. 53, para. 3). The archipelagic State may define sea lanes and air routes by axis lines from the entry points to the exit points of such routes. Ships and aircraft may not deviate more than 25 miles to either side of the axis lines. The rules relating to transit passage through straits used for international navigation with respect to the duties of ships and aircraft apply, *mutatis mutandis,* in archipelagic sea lanes passage. Where an archipelagic State does not designate sea lanes or air routes, the right of archipelagic sea lanes passage may be exercised through the route normally used for international navigation.

203.   An archipelagic State must respect existing agreements and recognize traditional fishing rights and other legitimate interests of "the immediately adjacent neighbouring State" in their archipelagic waters. Upon receiving due notice, it shall permit other States to maintain and replace existing submarine cables which do not touch the land and which have been laid by them in waters which may now be considered archipelagic waters.

7. The exclusive economic zone

204.   The concept of the exclusive economic zone represents for many coastal States the most important development in the new law of the sea. It was established to meet a demand by coastal States, particularly developing States, most of which are without the means to take advantage of the freedoms governing the high seas and, what is more, have long-distance fishing vessels of other nations harvesting marine resources close to their coasts.

205.   In the exclusive economic zone - a zone which may extend up to 200 miles from the baseline from which the territorial sea is measured - a coastal State has sovereign rights with respect to the natural resources, whether living or non-living, of the waters superjacent to the sea-bed and of the sea-bed and its subsoil, and with regard to other economic activities for the exploration and exploitation of the zone.

206.   A coastal State has certain competences under the Convention which go beyond its sovereign rights over resources. In particular it has jurisdiction in accordance with the relevant provisions of the Convention with regard to (a) the establishment and use of artificial islands, installations and structures; (b) marine scientific research; and (c) the protection and preservation of the marine environment.

207.   It is useful to examine more closely the nature of a coastal State's competence over artificial islands, installations and structures in the exclusive economic zone. A coastal State has the exclusive right to construct and to authorize and regulate the construction, operation and use of artificial islands, installations and structures constructed for economic purposes; and installations and structures which may interfere with the exercise of the rights of the coastal State in the zone. Installations and structures which do not interfere with these rights are outside the exclusive jurisdiction of the coastal State.

208.   All other States enjoy in the exclusive economic zone freedom of navigation and over-flight and freedom to lay submarine cables and pipelines, and other internationally lawful uses of the sea related to these freedoms, such as those associated with the operation of ships, aircraft and submarine cables and pipelines.

209.   The question arises whether those uses of the seas which are not mentioned in the Convention (the residual rights) remain with the international community or belong to the coastal State. The Convention itself offers a solution in article 59, which states that where the Convention "does not attribute rights or jurisdiction to the coastal State or to other States within the exclusive economic zone, and a conflict arises between the interests of the coastal State and any other State or States, the conflict should be resolved on the basis of equity and in the light of all the relevant circumstances, taking into account the respective importance of the interests involved to the parties as well as to the community as a whole" (art. 59). Thus the Convention acknowledges that there are uses of the sea over which it has given competence neither to the coastal State nor to other States in the exclusive economic zone and it has provided important substantive guidelines for resolving conflicts of competence over uses which are not mentioned in the Convention.

210.   Under the Convention the exclusive economic zone is subject to a specific legal régime. The legal régime of the exclusive economic zone is different from that of the territorial sea or the high seas. It is a zone which partakes of the characteristics of both régimes and belongs to neither. In short it is *sui generis*.

211.   It is expressly stated that "articles 88 to 115 and other pertinent rules of international law apply to the exclusive economic zone in so far as they are not incompatible with this Part" (art. 58, para. 2). This provision has in fact transported almost all the provisions of the high seas régime, except those dealing with the conservation and management of the living resources of the high seas, into the exclusive economic zone.

212.   Certain observations can be made on these provisions. First, some of these provisions are of general application since they deal with issues concerning ships: nationality of ships, status of ships, ships flying the flag of the United Nations, its specialized agencies or the International Atomic Energy Agency, duties of the flag State; and so on. Second, other provisions deal with the prohibition of the transport of slaves, drugs, piracy and unauthorized broadcasting. These issues are of international concern and must, it seems, necessarily apply to the exclusive economic zone. Finally, two provisions apply to the régime of the exclusive economic zone: article 88 which states that "the high seas shall be reserved for peaceful purposes" and article 89 which prohibits States from subjecting "any part of the high seas" to their sovereignty.

213.   A coastal State is under an obligation to have due regard to the rights and duties of other States and to act in a manner compatible with the provisions of the Convention when exercising its rights and performing its duties under the Convention. Other States, i.e. non-coastal States, were under a similar obligation.

214.   In exercising their rights and performing their duties under the Convention in the exclusive economic zone, States shall have due regard to the rights and duties of the coastal State and shall comply with the laws and regulations adopted by the coastal State in accordance with the provisions of the Convention and other rules of international law in so far as they are not incompatible with the régime of the exclusive economic zone (art. 58, para. 3). The Convention also provides for compulsory procedures entailing binding decisions "when it is alleged that a coastal State has acted in contravention of the provisions of the Convention in regard to the freedoms and rights of navigation, overflight or the laying of submarine cables and pipelines, or in regard to other internationally lawful uses of the sea specified in Article 58" (art. 297, para. 1 (a)). There will also be a resort to compulsory procedures entailing

binding decisions when a State in exercising the freedoms, rights or uses granted to non-coastal States contravenes the Convention or contravenes laws or regulations adopted by the coastal State in conformity with the Convention and other rules of international law not incompatible with the Convention.

8. The continental shelf

215.   Under the Convention on the Law of the Sea, the continental shelf of a coastal State comprises the sea-bed and subsoil of the submarine areas that extend beyond the limit of the territorial sea throughout the natural prolongation of its land territory, or to a distance of 200 miles from the baselines from which the territorial sea is measured.

216.   Where the continental shelf extends beyond 200 miles, a coastal State may choose to determine the outer edge of its continental margin either by (a) reference to the outermost fixed points at each of which the thickness of sedimentary rocks is at least 1 per cent of the shortest distance from such point to the foot or the continental slope or (b) a line connecting fixed points not more than 60 miles from the foot of the continental slope. In such cases the outer limits of the continental self may not extend beyond 350 miles from the baselines or 100 miles from the 2,500-m isobath. Coastal States shall establish the definitive limits of the continental shelf on the basis of recommendations by a Commission on the Limits of the Continental Shelf.

217.   The coastal State has sovereign rights for the purpose of exploring and exploiting the natural resources of the continental shelf. These rights do not effect the legal status of the waters or that of the airspace above the shelf. Thus the freedoms of navigation and overflight have not been affected by the régime of the continental shelf.

9. High seas

218.   The high seas are all parts of the sea that are not included in the economic zone, the territorial sea or the internal waters of a State or in the archipelagic waters of an archipelagic State. On the high seas all States enjoy the freedoms of navigation and overflight; the freedom to lay submarine cables and pipelines and to construct artificial islands and other installations; and the freedom of fishing and of scientific research. The new régime for the sea-bed and subsoil beyond national jurisdiction - identified in the Convention as the Area - does not affect the legal status of the high seas.

10. Enforcement measures

219.   A coastal State is entitled to take certain measures to enforce its laws and regulations applicable to the various maritime zones falling under its jurisdiction. For instance, a warship may be required to leave the **territorial sea** immediately if it fails to comply with the laws and regulations of the coastal State concerning passage through the territorial sea.

220.   In the **contiguous zone** - a zone which may not extend beyond 24 miles from baselines from which the breadth of the territorial sea is measured - a coastal State may exercise the control necessary to prevent infringement of its customs, fiscal, immigration or sanitary laws and regulations within its territory or territorial sea, and also to punish infringements of such laws and regulations committed within its territory or territorial sea.

221.   In the exercise of its sovereign rights over the living resources in the **exclusive economic zone**, the coastal State is empowered under article 73 of the Convention to take a wide range of enforcement measures. They include inspection, arrest and judicial proceeding. In this respect the coastal State has certain obligations. Arrested vessels and their crews must be released upon the posting of reasonable bond and security. Moreover, the penalties for violating fisheries laws and regulations may not include, in the absence of agreement, imprisonment or other form of corporal punishment. The coastal State is also under a duty to notify the flag State of any action taken or penalty imposed in the matter.

222.   A coastal State may adopt laws and regulations in the **exclusive economic zone** in order to combat pollution from vessels. Such laws and regulations must conform and give effect to generally accepted international rules and standards. The coastal State is entitled to take certain measures to enforce these laws. In particular, a vessel may be required to give information regarding its identity and port of registry, its last and next port of call and so on where there are clear grounds for believing that the vessel has violated the pollution laws and regulations of the coastal State. In cases in which the violation results in major damage, the coastal State may detain the vessel and institute proceedings against it.

223.   A foreign ship may be pursued **on the high seas** if the coastal State has good reason for believing that the ship has violated the laws and regulations enacted by the State with respect to the various maritime zones under its sovereignty and jurisdiction - the territorial sea, contiguous zone, exclusive economic zone and continental self. This right of hot pursuit ceases when the ship pursued enters the territorial sea of its own State or that of a third State. Only warships, military aircraft or other government ships may exercise this power of enforcement.

224.   States are empowered to take police action **on the high seas** in order to protect certain international community interests such as the suppression of piracy and unauthorized broadcasting and the prohibition of slavery. In particular, a warship is justified in boarding a foreign ship if the ship is engaged in piracy, in the slave trade, in unauthorized broadcasting, the ship is without nationality or though flying a foreign flag or refusing to show its flag, the ship is in reality of the same nationality as the warship.

11. Warships and other government ships operated for non-commercial purposes

225.   In article 29 of the Convention, a warship has been defined as:

". . . a ship belonging to the armed forces of a State bearing the external marks distinguishing such ships of its nationality, under the command of an officer duly commissioned by the government of the State and whose name appears in the appropriate service list or its equivalent, and manned by a crew which is under regular armed forces discipline."

Some navies are often assisted or accompanied by government-owned ships whose tasks are specifically those of naval support or other non-commercial functions. Such ships, unless they meet the definition of article 29, are not warships for the purposes of the Convention.

226.   Warships and other government ships operated for non-commercial purposes on the high seas enjoy complete immunity from the jurisdiction of any State other than the flag State. In particular, the provisions of the Convention regarding the protection and preservation of

the marine environment do not apply to any warship, naval auxiliary, other vessels or aircraft owned or operated by a State and used, for the time being, only on government non-commercial service (art. 236). By the operation of article 58, paragraph 2, this immunity extends to the exclusive economic zone. In the territorial sea, such ships also enjoy immunity with such exceptions applicable to all ships as are incorporated in the régime of innocent passage.

227.   There are two other notable exceptions. First, there is the sanction of expulsion from the territorial sea if any warship does not comply with the laws and regulations of a coastal State concerning passage through the territorial sea, as has already been noted. Second, a flag State is liable for any loss or damage to the coastal State resulting from a warship's not complying with the laws and regulations of the coastal State or with the provisions of the Convention or other rules of international law. The flag State is also liable when such loss or damage occurs during transit passage.

12.   Other relevant multilateral regional and bilateral agreements

228.   There are certain relevant multilateral treaties or bilateral arrangements which have significant effects on the legal régime of the oceans. On the relationship of the Convention on the Law of the Sea with other conventions and international agreements, article 311 states, *inter alia*, that:

> "1.   This Convention shall prevail, as between States Parties, over the Geneva Conventions on the Law of the Sea of 29 April 1958.

> "2.   This Convention shall not alter the rights and obligations of Parties which arise from other agreements compatible with this Convention and which do not affect the enjoyment of other States Parties of their rights or the performance of their obligations under this Convention."

The Convention on the Law of the Sea thus prevails as between States parties over the 1958 Geneva Conventions on the Law of the Sea but as between States Parties does not affect other agreements which are compatible with it.

C. Multilateral treaties since 1945

1.   The Antarctic Treaty (1959)[25]

229.   The Antarctic Treaty raises two issues of relevance to the law of the sea. First, there is a clear prohibition against the carrying out of any military activities in Antarctica. For the purposes of this Treaty, Antarctica is defined as the area south of 60° south latitude, which embraces a large extent of high seas. According to article I, Antarctica is to be used for peaceful purposes only. Any measures of a military nature, such as "the establishment of military bases and fortifications, the carrying out of military manoeuvres, as well as the testing of any type of weapons" are prohibited. Article V prohibits in Antarctica any nuclear explosions or the disposal of radioactive waste.

230.   It should be noted that "nothing in the Treaty shall prejudice or affect the rights, or the exercise of the rights, of any State under international law with regard to the high seas within that area" (art. VI).

231.   The Treaty contains provisions on the promotion of international scientific co-operation in Antarctica. It also facilitates scientific research and provides for the rights of inspection in Antarctica (arts. VII and IX).

2. Treaty Banning Nuclear weapon Tests in the Atmosphere, in Outer Space and under Water (Partial Test Ban Treaty) (1963)[25]

232.   By the Partial Test Ban Treaty the parties are obliged to prohibit, to prevent, and not to carry out any nuclear explosion at any place under their jurisdiction or control whether it takes place in the atmosphere; beyond its limits, including outer space; or under water, including territorial waters or high seas; or in any other environment if such explosion causes radioactive debris to be present outside the territorial limits of the State under whose jurisdiction or control such explosion is conducted (art. I).

3. Treaty on the Prohibition of the Emplacement of Nuclear Weapons and Other Weapons of Mass Destruction on the Sea-Bed and the Ocean Floor and in the Subsoil Thereof (Sea-Bed Treaty) (1971)[25]

233.   The Sea-Bed Treaty was concluded during the deliberations of the Committee on the Peaceful Uses of the Sea-Bed and the Ocean Floor beyond the Limits of National Jurisdiction - the precursor, as it were, of the Third United Nations Conference on the Law of the Sea. At a certain stage the debates on the issue of the peaceful uses of the oceans in the Sea-Bed Committee ran parallel with those conducted in the Conference of the Committee on Disarmament. It can be said that the adoption of the Sea-Bed Treaty to a certain extent stilled the debate on this issue in the context of the Conference transactions, although there was a brief debate in that Conference on this issue in 1976.

234.   The Sea-Bed Treaty forbids the emplanting or the emplacement on the sea-bed and the ocean floor and in the subsoil thereof beyond a 12-mile sea-bed zone of "any nuclear weapons or any other type of weapons of mass destruction as well as structures, launching installations or any other facilities specifically designed for storing, testing or using such weapons" (art. I, para. 1).

235.   Article II defines the meaning of the expression "beyond the outer limit of a sea-bed zone". It states "for the purpose of this Treaty, the outer limit of the sea-bed zone shall be coterminous with the 12-mile outer limit of the zone referred in part II of the Convention on the Territorial Sea and the Contiguous Zone, signed at Geneva on 29 April 1958, and shall be measured in accordance with the provisions of part I, section II, of that Convention and in accordance with international law".

236.   States parties have the right to verify through observation the activities of other States parties on the sea-bed and the ocean floor and in the subsoil thereof beyond the 12-mile limit zone provided that observation does not interfere with such activities (art. III, para. 1). Verification activities pursuant to the Treaty must not interfere with activities of other States parties and "shall be conducted with the regard for rights recognized under international law, including the freedoms of the high seas and the rights of coastal States with respect to the exploration and exploitation of their continental shelves" (art. III, para. 6).

237.   By article V of the Treaty, the States parties undertook "to continue negotiations in good faith concerning further measures in the field of disarmament for the prevention of an

arms race on the sea-bed, the ocean floor and the subsoil thereof". At both subsequent Review Conferences of the Treaty, held in 1977 and 1983, article V has been reaffirmed. Noting that negotiations on such measures had not yet taken place, the Review Conference requested the Conference on Disarmament to proceed promptly with consideration of further disarmament measures in consultation with the States parties to the Treaty, and taking into account existing proposals and any relevant technological developments. A third Review Conference is expected to take place between 1988 and 1990.

4. Treaty for the Prohibition of Nuclear Weapons in Latin America (Treaty of Tlatelolco) (1967)[25]

238.   The objective of the Treaty of Tlatelolco is the military denuclearization of Latin America, this being understood to mean the creation of a nuclear-weapon-free zone so that the region will be, in the words of the preamble, "forever free from nuclear weapons". In article 1, paragraph 1, the Treaty states:

"1.   The Contracting Parties hereby undertake to use exclusively for peaceful purposes the nuclear material and facilities which are under their jurisdiction, and to prohibit and prevent in their respective territories:

"(a)   The testing, use, manufacture, production or acquisition by any means whatsoever of any nuclear weapons, by the Parties themselves, directly or indirectly, on behalf of anyone else or in any other way, and

"(b)   The receipt, storage, installation, deployment and any form of possession of any nuclear weapons, directly or indirectly, by the Parties themselves, by anyone on their behalf or in any other way."

239.   For the purposes of the Treaty, the term "territory" includes the sea, airspace and any other space over which the State exercises sovereignty in accordance with its own legislation (art. 3). The zone of application is in article 4, and under certain conditions, that is when certain requirements are fulfilled, the terms of the Treaty could apply to extensive areas of the high seas.

240.   The Treaty of Tlatelolco has a number of very important characteristics, including the following:

(a)   In the fourth preambular paragraph, it is recognized that militarily denuclearized zones are not an end in themselves but rather a means for general and complete disarmament at a later stage. That the establishment of nuclear-weapon-free zones on the basis of arrangements freely arrived at among States of the region concerned constitutes an important disarmament measure was recognized by the General Assembly in paragraph 60 of the Final Document of the Tenth Special Session in 1978;

(b)   The zone of application is regionally contiguous (the Antarctic quadrant adjacent to South America) with the zone of peace established for Antarctica by the Antarctic Treaty of 1959 (specifically prohibiting nuclear weapons);

(c)   The Treaty is compatible, from the regional point of view, with the Inter-American Treaty of Reciprocal Assistance (TIAR), even though that instrument does not constitute a military alliance but rather a collective defence pact;

(d)   The Treaty provides regional support and complementarity for the Convention on the Law of the Sea, with regard to the peaceful uses covered by the Treaty;

(e)   Once the provisions of the Treaty have been fully implemented, the zone of application provided for in that instrument will be much greater than the sum of the maritime areas of the States parties for which the Treaty has entered or may enter into force.

5.   Final Act of the Conference on Security and Co-operation in Europe (1975)[26]

241.   The Final Act of the Conference, generally known as the Helsinki Declaration, prescribes pre-notification of "major military manoeuvres exceeding a total of 25,000 troops, independently or combined with any possible air or naval components (in this context the word 'troops' includes amphibious and air-borne troops)".   Notification will be given of such manoeuvres taking place on the territory in Europe of States participating in the agreement as well as, if applicable, in the adjoining sea area and air space.

D.   Bilateral agreements[27]

1.   Agreement between the Government of the United States
of America and the Government of the Union of Soviet
Socialist Republics on the Prevention of Incidents
on and over the High Seas (1972)

242.   By this Agreement the two States concerned sought to "assure the safety of navigation of the ships of their respective armed forces on the high seas and flight of their military aircraft over the high seas" (preamble).   The parties agreed to observe strictly the letter and spirit of the International Regulations for Preventing Collisions at Sea (the Rules of the Road).   In a Protocol to this Agreement signed in 1973 the parties agreed not to simulate attacks against non-military ships.

243.   It is noteworthy that in article II of this instrument the parties recognized "that their freedom to conduct operations on the high seas is based on the principles established under recognized international law and codified in the 1958 Geneva Convention on the High Seas".

2.   Treaty on the Limitation of Anti-Ballistic Missile Systems
(ABM Treaty) and SALT I and SALT II Agreements

244.   In one Treaty and two bilateral agreements the United States and the Union of Soviet Socialist Republics have undertaken certain limitations which have maritime effects.   In the ABM Treaty, which entered into force in 1972, the parties pledged, *inter alia*, not to develop, test, or deploy ABM systems or components which are sea-based (art. V, para. 1).   In the Interim Agreement on Certain Measures with Respect to the Limitation of Strategic Offensive Arms (known as the SALT I Agreement) which came into force in 1972, the parties agreed to limit submarine-launched ballistic missile (SLBM) launchers and modern ballistic missile submarines.   The understanding as expressed in the Protocol to the Interim Agreement was that the United States should not have more than 44 modern ballistic missile submarines and

710 SLBMs while the Soviet Union should not have more than 62 modern ballistic missile submarines and 950 SLBMs.

245.   Further limitations on and reductions in strategic offensive arms were envisaged in the Treaty between the United States and the Union of Soviet Socialist Republics on the Limitation of Strategic Offensive Arms (SALT II, 1979).   However, this Treaty has not formally entered into force although both parties state that they have been abiding by the provisions of the agreement.   The Treaty was to have remained in force until 31 December 1985.

E.   Declarations

1.   Declaration of Ayacucho

246.   The Declaration of Ayacucho, which was signed by Argentina, Bolivia, Chile, Colombia, Ecuador, Panama, Peru and Venezuela in 1974 and ratified by the parties in 1978, and the Conference on Conventional Weapons held at Mexico City in 1978 are noteworthy regional contributions with regard, *inter alia*, to arms control, including naval arms, and the peaceful settlement of international disputes and the prohibition of the threat of use of force and of armed aggression or of economic or financial aggression in relations between States.   There has been no further progress in either case except for the two years' work on elaboration of projects of arms control accomplished by experts of the Andean Group within the framework of the Declaration of Ayacucho.

2.   Declaration on the Denuclearization of Africa

247.   At its first regular session, held at Cairo from 17 to 21 July 1964, the Assembly of Heads of State and Government of the Organization of African Unity (OAU) adopted a declaration on the denuclearization of Africa in which the Heads of State and Government announced their readiness to undertake, in an international treaty to be concluded under the auspices of the United Nations, not to manufacture or acquire control of nuclear weapons. Since that date, the General Assembly has repeatedly called upon all States to consider and respect the continent of Africa, including the continental African States, Madagascar and other islands surrounding Africa, as a nuclear-weapon-free zone.[28]

248.   On that occasion the African States have stated that, recognizing that the denuclearization of the African continent constitutes a practical measure for impeding the proliferation of nuclear weapons in the world and for permitting the attainment of general and complete disarmament and the achievement of the objectives of the Charter of the United Nations, they reaffirm their appeal to all States, particularly those of the nuclear club, to respect the continent of Africa as a nuclear-weapon-free zone.   The African States have also reaffirmed their long-standing attachment to nuclear disarmament and to the prevention of a nuclear war as well as to the non-proliferation of nuclear weapons, in particular to the prevention of the introduction of nuclear weapons in the Continent.   The African States have considered that any non-proliferation régime depends essentially on the attitude of the States members of the nuclear club.   If those States wish to move forward in this field, the African States have declared, they should not advocate non-proliferation while, at the same time, reinforcing their own nuclear stocks, or directly or indirectly helping their allies, in particular South Africa, whose military and nuclear capabilities threaten international peace and security.

3. Declaration of the Indian Ocean as a Zone of Peace

249. The Declaration of the Third Conference of Heads of State or Government of Non-Aligned Countries, held at Lusaka from 8 to 10 September 1970, called upon all States to consider and respect the Indian Ocean as a zone of peace from which great Power rivalries and competition as well as bases conceived in the context of such rivalries and competition should be excluded, and declared that the area should also be free of nuclear weapons. Subsequently, the General Assembly adopted resolution 2832 (XXVI) of 16 December 1971, by which the Indian Ocean, within limits to be determined, together with the airspace above and the ocean floor subjacent thereto, was designated for all time as a zone of peace. The Assembly also called upon the great Powers to enter into consultations with the littoral States of the Indian Ocean with a view to halting the further escalation of their military presence there and to eliminating from the area all bases, military installations and logistical supply facilities, nuclear weapons and other weapons of mass destruction. Furthermore, it called upon the littoral and hinterland States, the permanent members of the Security Council and other major maritime users of the Indian Ocean to enter into consultations aimed at the implementation of the Declaration whereby (a) warships and military aircraft would not use the Indian Ocean for any threat or use of force against any littoral or hinterland State; (b) the right to free and unimpeded use of the zone by the vessels of all nations would be ensured; and (c) international agreement would be reached for the maintenance of the Indian Ocean as a zone of peace.

250. In 1972, by resolution 2992 (XXVII) of 15 December 1972, the General Assembly established the *Ad Hoc* Committee on the Indian Ocean and, since 1973, the Assembly has generally considered the question of the Indian Ocean, and the matter of holding a conference on the issues, in connection with the annual reports of the *Ad Hoc* Committee. The number of *Ad Hoc* Committee members has been increased, at various dates, from 15 to 48, and the General Assembly has adopted many resolutions on the subject.[29] On 11 December 1979 it was decided, by General Assembly resolution 34/80 B, to convene a Conference on the Indian Ocean at Colombo as a necessary step for the implementation of the Declaration of the Indian Ocean as a Zone of Peace. The preparatory work relating to the Conference is at present being discussed by the *Ad Hoc* Committee on the Indian Ocean.

4. South-East Asia as a Zone of Peace and Nuclear-Weapon-Free Zone

251. In November 1971, the member States of the Association of South East Asian Nations (ASEAN), comprising at that time Indonesia, Malaysia, the Philippines, Singapore and Thailand, issued a Declaration pronouncing their intent to secure international recognition of, and respect for, South-East Asia as a zone of peace, freedom and neutrality. Since then, the ASEAN States have been actively engaged in the further elaboration of the principles, objectives and elements of such a zone, which would embrace the entire region of South-East Asia and within which a nuclear-weapon-free zone would form an essential part. Subsequently, the Seventh Conference of Heads of State or Government of Non-Aligned Countries, held at New Delhi in March 1983, in its Political Declaration "noted with approval the efforts being made for the early establishment of a zone of peace, freedom and neutrality in the region and called upon all States to give those efforts their fullest support". Considering the vast sea areas and strategic international waterways that would be encompassed by such a zone, ASEAN countries believe that its eventual establishment in conformity with the provisions of the Convention on the Law of the Sea would constitute another significant

regional contribution to the lessening of the naval arms race and the enhancement of economic co-operation and development in a vital region of the world.

5. Security and co-operation in the Mediterranean

252.   Questions relating to security and co-operation in the Mediterranean were considered, *inter alia,* by the Conference on Security and Co-operation in Europe (CSCE) between July 1973 and August 1975. The outcome of that consideration was reflected in the Mediterranean Chapter of the Final Act of the Conference in which the participating States declared a number of intentions in recognition of the fact that security in Europe was closely linked with security in the Mediterranean area as a whole. Further consideration was given to the issues at the CSCE follow-up meetings held at Madrid between November 1980 and September 1983.

253.   Within the United Nations, the General Assembly in recent years has adopted several resolutions on the subject of strengthening security and co-operation in the Mediterranean region.[30] Separately, action has been taken by some of the Mediterranean States themselves, and the first ministerial meeting of the Ministers for Foreign Affairs of the Mediterranean members of the Non-Aligned Movement was held at Valletta on 10 and 11 September 1984. In the Final Declaration of that meeting (see A/39/526-S/16758) it was stated, *inter alia*, that:

> "The Ministers also considered that the freedom of the high seas in a closed sea like the Mediterranean should be exercised scrupulously and exclusively for the purposes of peace, and that naval deployment, particularly by States outside the region, that directly or indirectly threatened the interests of non-aligned Mediterranean members should be excluded." (see para. 13)

6. South Pacific Forum

254.   Meeting at Tuvalu in August 1984, the countries of the South Pacific Forum, comprising Australia, Cook Islands, Federated States of Micronesia (as an observer), Fiji, Kiribati, Nauru, New Zealand, Niue, Papua New Guinea, Solomon Islands, Tonga, Tuvalu, Vanuatu and Western Samoa, agreed on the desirability of establishing a nuclear-free zone in the region at the earliest possible opportunity in accordance with certain principles. Bearing in mind the geographical features of the region, it is clear that such a zone, if established, will embrace large areas of the seas.

CHAPTER VI

IMPLICATIONS FOR SECURITY AND THE PEACEFUL USES OF THE SEAS

A. Implications for international security

255.   The foregoing chapters of this study have described, in general terms, the nature of the competitive accumulation and qualitative development of arms taking place in the oceans and seas of the world that constitute the naval arms race. This phenomenon is a part of the global arms race; in turn, the global arms race is a reflection of the political perceptions of States and the continued absence of a condition of international security. However, while being an integral part of the global arms race, the naval arms race has its own characteristics and, in part, its own intrinsic motivations: one of the unique features of the naval arms race is that a great part of naval operations takes place on the high seas. These waters are open for use by

all who have interests in the peaceful uses of the sea and the peaceful development and exploitation of its resources. To many of the States seeking to use the oceans for such peaceful purposes, particularly if such States do not have strong naval forces of their own, naval operations conducted on the high seas can in certain situations create anxiety and insecurity rather than reassurance.

256. The unremitting quest for security has been at the forefront of the activities of the United Nations since its inception in 1945, as recognized by the fact that the very first purpose of the United Nations expressed in Article I of the Charter of the organization is: "to maintain international peace and security" (Art. 1). That the quest has been one of long standing was indicated by the General Assembly in the opening words of the Final Document of the Tenth Special Session, adopted by consensus in 1978: "The attainment of the objective of security, which is an inseparable element of peace, has always been one of the most profound aspirations of humanity." (Para. 1). Additionally, it could be noted that the Convention on the Law of the sea is also seen as contributing to the strengthening of security, as reflected in the preamble: The States parties to this Convention believing that "the codification and progressive development of the law of the sea achieved in this Convention will contribute to the strengthening of peace, security, co-operation and friendly relations among all nations".

257.   Yet the goal of security has persistently eluded humanity's grasp. In its continued absence, States have instead accumulated weapons in an apparent effort to guarantee by arms what international negotiation and co-operation have so far failed to provide. The advent of nuclear weapons and the constant technological progress in their means of delivery, their accuracy and their lethality have brought greatly increased dangers to the survival of the entire human race. The threats to basic survival, and the harmful effects of the unproductive and spiralling arms race on economic and social progress in both developing and developed countries, have been fully described in the Final Document, in previous United Nations disarmament studies and in many other governmental and non-governmental statements and publications.

258. The implications for security of the burgeoning quantitative and qualitative developments taking place in the world's navies are many. First and foremost, there is the threat to world security represented by the strategic nuclear weapons st sea. By one estimate amounting to more than 7,200 SLBM warheads,[31] some 40 per cent of the estimated world total of strategic nuclear warheads are designed for naval deployment. Owing to the operating cycles of SSBNs, this total cannot be operationally available at sea all at once, but even so there is no doubt that significant numbers are continuously at sea. According to the same source, at any one time from 17 to 20 United States, 10 Soviet, 2 French and 1 to 2 British SSBNs may be on station, carrying some 3,100 nuclear warheads. On submerged patrol in the oceans, including under the Arctic ice-cap, every endeavour is made by SSBNs to remain entirely undetected at all times, despite the considerable efforts that are made to locate and trail them from the moment they leave harbour to their return at the end of their patrols. These activities, which up to now have taken place continuously in the world's northern oceans and seas, arouse concerns on the part of States which do not participate in them.

259.   In that world security is held hostage to the strategic nuclear policies of the nuclear-weapon States, in particular those of the Soviet Union and the United States, the unceasing deployment of such strategic nuclear forces at sea constitutes the most potent naval capability endangering international peace and security. The arguments on the part of some that such deployments represent successful mutual deterrence are to others insubstantial and

inadequate protection against the prospect of misunderstanding, technical fault or human error unleashing a nuclear exchange which would affect the whole world. In brief, in the view of the overwhelming majority of States, the possible consequence are too disastrous to warrant the smallest risk and therefore measures of nuclear disarmament are urgently needed.

260.   At a different level, the numbers and extent of the deployment of tactical nuclear weapons also give rise to vary great concern. As indicated in chapter III, many of the warships, submarines and aircraft of the nuclear-weapon States can be considered nuclear-capable and, as far as can be ascertained, there would appear to be a wide availability in service of tactical nuclear weapons, including short-range missiles. In the wide-open spaces of the ocean it is possible to use tactical nuclear weapons in a military encounter without direct damage to civilian life or property. Notwithstanding the existence of rigorous control procedures, it is possible to envisage circumstances in which such use might be initiated. Such possibilities might easily lead to a highly dangerous reaction or response which could have grave implications for international security as a whole. In addition, there are important questions concerning custody on board, safety in cases of collision and the absolute reliability of control systems in peacetime, even though the nuclear-weapon States maintain that in fact their safety record to date has been sound. Overall, very serious doubts remain on the part of non-nuclear-weapon States concerning the assurances given by the present five nuclear-weapon States on these issues.

261.   There is also the very real difficulty of externally identifying which ships, submarines or aircraft are actually carrying tactical nuclear warheads. In addition, with submerged submarines there is the further difficulty of identifying even their nationality and of establishing communications with them. In this regard the development of sea-launched cruise missiles, or torpedoes, capable of carrying either a nuclear or a conventional warhead creates extremely complex verification problems. While accepting that because a ship is nuclear-weapon-capable it does not necessarily mean that such weapons are on board, the wide availability of tactical nuclear weapons that now appears to exist, and the custom of certain nuclear-weapon States neither to confirm nor to deny the presence on board of nuclear weapons, will raise very deep misgivings on the part of non-nuclear-weapon States when requested to allow such vessels to pay port visits or enter their territorial waters. Therefore, for several reasons, early consideration should be given by the nuclear-weapon States to agree on effective measures of curtailing the numbers and deployment of tactical nuclear weapons.

262.   The world-wide capabilities of the general-purpose naval forces of the United States and the Soviet Union also have significant international security implications. To a lesser extent, there can be similar effects from the activities of some of the blue-water navies.

263.   In the first instance, as part of their respective alliance arrangements the navies of the member States of NATO and WTO regularly conduct exercises, including amphibious exercises, and take part in training. While such activities are considered by their respective participants as part of their collective defence arrangements, States outside those alliances often consider them to be demonstrations of military force which are more provocative to the other side than reassuring. As such, in the opinion of non-aligned and neutral States, naval exercises and training of this nature are more likely to unsettle international security than to consolidate it: this may be particularly so in the case of large-scale exercises, especially if world-wide, which are clearly designed to create exercise conditions and incidents close to those anticipated in the event of actual conflict. There have been instances of unduly prolonged naval manoeuvres which, even though carried out with the approval of an adjacent

coastal State, have in effect constituted a risk to the region or sub-region involved, including the potential aggravation of conflicts.

264.   The principle of freedom of navigation on the world's oceans makes a coastal State the neighbour across the sea of every other coastal State, including all significant naval Powers. While naval forces have the recognized legal right to cruise and operate off the coasts of foreign States, coastal States, particularly those which are small or medium in size, have on the other hand a legitimate claim for a reasonable "seaboard security" and should not be subjected to power projection possibly originating from such activities. It should be noted in this regard that the Convention on the Law of the Sea includes balanced provisions which would meet security needs of both flag States and coastal States provided they are strictly implemented. It should also be noted that the security of both categories of States could be further enhanced by means of agreed confidence- and security-building measures in harmony with the Convention and customary international law.

265.   It is true that naval exercises are not limited to the naval forces of the two main alliances: exercises and co-operative manoeuvres take place between the navies of many countries, but for the most part such activities are seen as more regional or subregional in nature and they do not have the potential for global confrontation.

266.   When employed on normal deployments as part of national peacetime tasks, activities by world-wide and blue-water navies outside their own territorial and regional areas can become a significant political factor in regional and local situations. As stated previously, the knowledge that there is a strong naval presence in the area, particularly if it is known to have the capability of projecting military force on shore, can become an important political factor in regional and local situations. Many regional States may become concerned at the implications of such deployments for regional security and strongly dislike the implied threat, real or perceived, of external intervention in the regional or internal affairs of other States.

267.   Extra-regional States may consider that they have specific national interests in the area concerned that necessitate naval presence. In this context it is relevant to consider the nature of such naval presence in areas that are often far from the national territory of the State or States concerned.

268.   In the first category, there are such activities as routine co-operation in times of peace between the navies of maritime Powers and those of coastal States. These can take the form of joint manoeuvres and other traditional activities arising from bilateral or multilateral agreements of co-operation, support or assistance between States.

269.   The second category arises from the development of serious local conflicts not directly linked to any confrontation between major Powers. In such cases there may be legitimate interests by extra-regional States in the maintenance of the freedom of navigation and the continuation of maritime trade in order to facilitate the transportation of vital commodities, to the extent that such naval activities remain in conformity with the Charter of the United Nations and the provisions of the Convention on the Law of the Sea.

270.   A third category is that in which confrontation between the two principal military States is projected to other regions through naval presence. There would appear to be certain cases in which such confrontation has been spread to distant geographical areas which were previously free of external involvement. It is widely believed that the dispatch of warships as a

"show of force", or as a form of coercion or other pressure, particularly to areas of international tension, can often have harmful rather than helpful effects on regional security.

271.   Finally, there is the category in which open conflict takes place and in which one of the parties is a significant naval Power acting in a theatre of operations distant from the scope of application of its own military alliance although perhaps with the support, in different ways and to different extents, of other members of that alliance and with the most sophisticated military means, including the hypothetical, but not *a priori* discounted, utilization of nuclear weapons in that conflict.

272.   In connection with the above-mentioned forms of naval presence, the continued establishment and/or reinforcement of military bases abroad, particularly foreign naval bases, constitute a problem deserving particular attention. In most cases foreign naval bases are established as a result of bilateral arrangements between sovereign States; recent years have witnessed a decline in the number of such bases owing to a variety of factors. However, to a large majority of States, foreign naval bases are perceived as generating greater points of friction and tension in the regions concerned rather than contributing to greater stability and security. These States therefore regard the continuing presence of foreign naval bases as an unwelcome factor of destabilization to regional security and hence as a potential threat to international peace and security. Bases and other military installations in Non-Self-Governing Territories give rise to additional problems to which the Special Committee on the Situation with regard to the Implementation of the Declaration on the Granting of Independence to Colonial Countries and Peoples and the Fourth Committee of the General Assembly have devoted continuing attention for a number of years and which have been the subject of numerous resolutions receiving wide support in the General Assembly.

273.   At the local level, the existence of naval forces has often tended to prompt the use of force in the settlement of disputes, in direct contravention of the Charter of the United Nations. Incidents of open conflict have occurred in several parts of the world in the past few years, and the conjunction of a greater number of sovereign States, each with the inherent right of self-defence, and larger sea areas which fall under national jurisdiction gives cause for the belief that there may be more rather than fewer such incidents in the future. Moreover, in addition to incidents on the high seas, there may be increased risk of incidents in coastal waters or violations of coastal security along the shoreline itself; this may be particularly the case in the light of the proliferation of light, missile-armed warships. There is even greater need, therefore, for the exercise of moderation and restraint on the part of all, and recourse to the machinery provided in the Charter of the United Nations, if further threats to security are to be contained.

B. Implications for the freedom of navigation and international shipping routes

274.   In one particular sense, the activities of naval forces represent something of a paradox with regard to the freedom of navigation and international shipping routes. To some States, naval forces represent a menace to such liberties, in their use of the oceans to demonstrate their mobility and power and in their capacity for the application of force in various ways; whereas, to other States particularly those that have traditionally depended on overseas trade and free access to maritime resources - naval forces are seen as an essential means of safeguarding their interests in such freedoms. It is believed that this apparent paradox might

be resolved by full and positive application of the elements reflected in the following paragraphs.

275.   As stated previously, the extension of territorial waters, the introduction of exclusive economic zones and the designation of rules for rights of passage through territorial waters, archipelagic waters and straits used for international navigation, as set out in the Convention on the Law of the Sea, are expected to have interactive effects on the deployment and activities of naval forces.

276.   In a growingly interdependent world the freedom of the high seas is as important as it has ever been; indeed, in some respects it may well be even more important, than hitherto. Article 87 of the Convention on the Law of the Sea stipulates:

> "the high seas are open to all States, whether coastal or land-locked. Freedom of the high seas is exercised under the conditions laid down in the Convention and by other rules of international law" (para. 1).

The Article lists specific freedoms, such as that of navigation and overflight, then continues:

> "These freedoms shall be exercised by all States with due regard for the interests of other States in their exercise of the freedom of the high seas . . ." (para. 2).

Article 88 states simply:

> "The high seas shall be reserved for peaceful purposes."

The provisions of articles 87 and 88 apply also to the exclusive economic zone.

277.   In the light of such provisions in the Convention on the Law of the Sea to promote freedom of navigation and protection of international shipping routes, the harmful impact of naval activities that curtail the free and open use of sea lanes cannot be over-emphasized. In this context, the applicability of the 1907 Hague Conventions in time of war should be noted. Although the following activities may sometimes be justified on the grounds that they safeguard the ships of States not involved in disputes, such activities as mining, covert submarine operations in coastal waters, blockades, the imposition of restrictions on the use of certain areas of the high seas, the establishment of maritime exclusion zones as a result of conflict and similar practices may constitute interference with the peaceful uses of the sea. The nature of such interference may include interruption of hazard to commercial shipping, activities directed against a State's coastal security or denial of access to traditional fishing grounds. The part that naval force may play in the exercise of the inherent right to individual or collective self-defence or in actions against terrorism, piracy or smuggling is recognized, but States cannot expect to enjoy the freedom of the high seas and the uncritical support of the international community if at times they deny those freedoms to other States using the seas for peaceful purposes. For States not participating in an ongoing conflict, securing the right to use the seas in times of crisis is an important objective.

C. Implications for the exploitation of marine resources

278.   With greater interest in the exploitation of marine resources and the introduction of the exclusive economic zone, the number of offshore and other commercial activities will continue

to increase. Although ordinary commercial accidents such as tanker collisions can have major pollution effects, accidents at sea involving a nuclear-armed or nuclear-powered vessel could have very major harmful effects on marine resources, particularly if resulting radiation led to extensive contamination of the sea area concerned; the risk of this possibility is of major importance given the significance of the sea as one of the principal sources of life on the planet. Separately, grave damage to the living resources of the sea could be caused by naval confrontation or attacks on offshore oilrigs. Instances of extensive pollution and damage to marine resources, or interruption of such activities as fishing, have already resulted in recent years from naval activities of a warlike nature.

279.   On the other hand, the growing complexity of offshore activities will call for much-improved national and international management arrangements if marine resources are to be exploited in a rational and orderly manner to the benefit of mankind. It has been noted that some maritime States have found their existing bureaucracies unequal to the task: the United States has some 40 overlapping agencies concerned with the offshore estate, the United Kingdom over 20.[32] New resources, new developments, new activities, new responsibilities - all will demand more co-ordinated maritime policies, administrative machinery and policing capabilities. There are likely to be more, not fewer, disputes over fishing rights and laws and the activities of trawlers. There will probably be increased competition between various parties endeavouring to exploit the same area for different resources. More sea traffic and greater industrialization will create a greater need for more effective pollution controls and improved protection of the marine environment. Other effects of greater sea traffic may include an increased incidence of collisions at sea, more salvage and wreck clearance, an extended need for traffic separation systems and a greater need for search and rescue services in the protection of human life. In many of these aspects much has already been achieved in recent years through the valuable work of IMO.

280.   Within this growing range of activities, there is much that appropriately equipped naval vessels could do. There are also many ways in which the greater experience and capacities of the maritime Powers that at present have world-wide and blue-water navies could assist coastal States, if so requested and without interfering in their affairs, in dealing with this entirely new range of problems. In doing so, they would be diverting some of their political and military energies away from a highly expensive naval arms race and towards greater international co-operation to the social and economic benefit of the international community at large.

281.   A particular instance that has received much attention in the General Assembly has been the question of Namibia. It is important to recall that since resolution 1803 (XVII), of 14 December 1962, the General Assembly has reaffirmed many times in other resolutions the permanent sovereignty of States, territories and peoples subject to foreign occupation, colonial domination or the régime of **apartheid**, over their natural wealth and resources, notably the obligation to compensate them for the exploitation, the loss or the exhaustion of their natural resources. The situation becomes more complex in Non-Self-Governing Territories and colonial Territories such as Namibia, where military bases and installations have been established and colonial domination is being exercised over that Territory while its renewable and non-renewable natural resources are being exploited. Moreover, the Charter of the United Nations contains a "Declaration regarding Non-Self-Governing Territories" (Art. 73). In connection with this Article, the Conference on the Law of the Sea declared, in resolution III annexed to its Final Act:

   "...

"(a) In the case of a territory whose people have not attained full independence or other self-governing status recognized by the United Nations, or a territory under colonial domination, provisions concerning rights and interests under the Convention shall be implemented for the benefit of the people of the territory with a view to promoting their well-being and development.

"..."

CHAPTER VII

POSSIBLE MEASURES OF DISARMAMENT AND CONFIDENCE-BUILDING

282.   In resolution 38/188 G, the General Assembly requested the preparation of a comprehensive study on the naval arms race and an analysis of its possible implications in order to facilitate the identification of possible areas for disarmament and confidence-building measures. Several of the comments of Member States, addressed to the Secretary-General in response to resolution 38/188 G, included remarks to the effect that the value of the study would be undermined if it led only to the gathering of information on naval armaments, the description of their technical details and methods of comparing naval forces. From the comments submitted by Member States, there was a widespread view that the Group of Experts should endeavour to identify areas of difficulty and possible measures for discussion and negotiation in the appropriate forums.

283.   The major significance of the Final Document of the Tenth Special Session of the General Assembly, the first special session devoted to disarmament, held in 1978, has been described in paragraphs 8 and 13 of the present report. The objectives of measures of disarmament and confidence-building in the naval context are as follows:

(a) To strengthen international peace and security in accordance with the purposes and principles of the Charter of the United Nations;

(b) To contribute to the international disarmament strategy set out in the Final Document;

(c) To promote the peaceful uses of the seas and oceans, the equitable and efficient utilization of their resources, the conservation of their living resources and the study, protection and preservation of the marine environment.

284.   In accordance with the Final Document, agreements or other measures should be resolutely pursued on a bilateral, regional and multilateral basis with the aim of strengthening peace and security at a lower level of forces and taking into account the need of States to protect their security. Among the other guiding Principles of the Final Document that are relevant, it should be noted that the nuclear-weapon States have a primary responsibility for nuclear disarmament and, together with other militarily significant States, for halting and reversing the arms race.

285.   Whenever arms control and disarmament in the maritime domain are under discussion, some factors should be considered axiomatic. First, disarmament measures should be balanced and should not diminish the security of any State. But as naval forces are not independent of other military forces, they should be considered in their general military context. There is no such thing as an independent naval balance or parity. Disarmament

measures in the maritime field should thus be balanced in that general sense. Second, this fact combined with the vary differing geographical situations of States could require multilateral measures of restriction for naval forces and weapons to be numerically asymmetrical in order to maintain an overall military situation in balance. Third, because of the universal nature of the Convention on the Law of the Sea, such measures should not take the legal form of amendments to the Convention. They should be embodied in separate legal instruments in harmony with the Convention. Fourth, as in all arms control and disarmament, appropriate verification and compliance procedures are essential for the proper implementation of agreed measures.

286.   Just as this study of the naval arms race has been a wide-ranging consideration of very complex issues, similarly there exists a wide range of possible measures of disarmament and confidence-building. Some may be of general application, while others may be applicable in narrow circumstances such as specific weapon systems or in specific geographical areas. Separately, possible measures that may find favour in one quarter may not be attractive in another, or perhaps may be more acceptable at some point in the future but are not regarded as susceptible to negotiation at present. The following survey of possible measures is presented as an illustrative, though not exhaustive, list of matters that might be considered for negotiation. For convenience, they are grouped as follows:

Quantitative restraints;
Qualitative or technological restraints;
Geographic and/or mission restraints;
-   Confidence-building measures;
-   Modernization of the laws of sea warfare.

Some of the possible measures relate to more than one group.

A. Quantitative restraints

287.   Since the Washington Naval Treaty of 1922, there has been long-standing interest in quantitative restraints that place numerical limits on certain types of naval vessels and weapons. More recent examples of quantitative restraints were the numerical limits on ballistic missile launchers on submarines and on modern ballistic missile submarines agreed in the 1972 SALT I Interim Agreement, and the aggregate limits on strategic offensive arms set by the 1977 SALT II Treaty. Difficulties with quantitative restraints could arise from the subsequent tendency on the part of States to pursue vigorously construction programmes in categories of ships or weapons not covered by the agreed restrictions. Even so, quantitative restraints should not be lightly discarded as they are the most direct means of limiting and reducing the competitive accumulation of arms. It has been suggested that quantitative restraints might include:

(a)   A freeze on the manufacture of naval nuclear weapons;

(b)   Limitations on numbers of SLBM launchers and nuclear warheads;

(c)   Limitations on the introduction of new SLBM systems;

(d)   Specific reductions in ballistic missile submarines and in SLBMs;

(e)   Prohibition of or limitations on sea-launched cruise missiles with nuclear warheads;

(f)   Specific reductions in on-board tactical nuclear weapons, either by numbers or types or by types of ship;

(g)   Limitations on numbers of naval ships of main types;

(h)   Limitation on amphibious capabilities.

It should be clearly understood that the Group of Experts has not listed these suggestions with a view to legitimizing the continuance of nuclear weapons but on the contrary offers them as means of starting a process of progressive and balanced reductions leading ultimately to the complete eradication of nuclear weapons from naval operations within the overall objective of general and complete disarmament under strict and effective international control.

B. Qualitative or technological restraints

288.   The rapid pace of technological advance has been highly evident in recent years. The constant pressure to gain qualitative advantage has resulted in massive diversion of resources to research and development by those States able to afford such activities. In producing significant technological progress, the efforts create a cycle of competition that is very difficult to stop; they are also undertaken at a great cost and can have destabilizing results. The concept of numerical restraints may also present other difficulties owing to some of the asymmetries described earlier in this report. Measures to restrain technological improvements are generally very difficult to verify unless a particular technological development is altogether banned, but on the other hand, technology itself may make possible ways of controlling elements of the naval arms race or the effects of certain weapons. Suggested measures of restraint have included:

(a)   Limitations on dual-capable missiles (i.e. those able to carry either nuclear or conventional warheads);

(b)   Systems for ensuring that naval armaments have a method for deactivation which will disable them if they do not explode;

(c)   Methods for neutralizing, minimizing or banning the emplacement of monitoring systems in or on the sea-bed or ocean floor;

(d)   Prohibition on the development and production of new SLBM systems.

289.   In the matter of naval arms transfers the diversion of scarce resources to the acquisition or development of arms by countries often has harmful economic effects. For this reason, there may also be merit in considering the applicability of agreed-controls on arms transfers and the transfer of technology for naval application, *inter alia*, as a complement to the prohibition of certain arms developments. Such restraints should not impede a State's ability to acquire arms in order to discharge its right to self-defence, nor should such means be used to deny access on the part of developing States to technological or industrial progress. Qualitative and/or quantitative limitations on arms transfers could be of significant value, but the difficulties and sensitivities, some of which were described in the recent United Nations

Study on Conventional Disarmament,[33] should be given consideration if satisfactory progress in this area is to be achieved.

C. Geographic and/or mission restraints

290. Limitations of this type have had some success in the past, the best known perhaps being the Rush-Bagot Agreement of 1817 and the Montreux Convention of 1936. A key ingredient of any limitation measure, and of its subsequent success and longevity, rests in the fact that it must contain something of great value to each and every signatory. Without this ingredient, a State may consider that the gain to be had from the proposed agreement is not worth the concessions that have to be made. Furthermore, progress in such negotiations cannot proceed in a political vacuum but is subject to the general pressures and climate of international relations between States.

291. Another important factor to be borne in mind in the consideration of possible geographic and/or mission restraints is the unique mobility and flexibility of naval forces. States may wish to exercise the principle of the freedom of the high seas yet recognize that certain limitations to deployments - for instance, temporary deployments may be permitted but not permanent stationing of naval forces - may provide specific benefits. In other circumstances, it may be possible to negotiate limitations on certain kinds of naval deployment, or naval missions, that would lessen the chances of confrontation in areas of possible regional conflict.

292. There would appear to be considerable interest on the part of many States in the limitation of the deployment of nuclear weapons. Given that the present policies of nuclear-weapon States are neither to confirm nor deny the presence on board of nuclear weapons, one of the major difficulties to be overcome is the matter of identifying which ships, submarines or naval aircraft are carrying nuclear weapon at any particular time. The efforts to introduce nuclear-weapon-free zones, such as in Latin America by the Treaty of Tlatelolco and in Antarctica by the Antarctic Treaty, could provide stepping-stones towards the consideration of new areas in which nuclear weapons would be prohibited. In this respect, it may be possible to give consideration to agreements for extending existing areas that are free of nuclear weapons, e.g. increasing the nuclear-weapon-free régime to cover all sea areas presently demarcated by the Antarctic Treaty at the latitude of 60° south (see article VI of the Treaty, which has the effect of excluding the high seas within the area). There have also been proposals to introduce a contiguous nuclear-weapon-free area at sea between 60° south and some other latitude as may be agreed.

293. Other types of geographical restraint could be the confinement of missile submarines to agreed-areas, disengagement arrangements achieved by limitations on naval deployments in certain oceans or seas or reductions in the level of military presence in appropriate regions distant from home territory; limitations on the length or size of naval manoeuvres in certain areas; and reduction of existing, and prohibition of new, foreign naval bases.

294. Where it is agreed that restrictions and confidence-building measures are to apply to a specific region, there are two general ways in which the area of application might be defined. One is a definition in geographical terms as was done in the case of the Treaty of Tlatelolco. The other is a definition in functional terms as envisaged in the agreed-mandate for the Conference on Confidence- and Security-building Measures and Disarmament in Europe.

295.   In recent years, various ideas have been put forward for discussion. These include:

(a)   A ban on the transit and transport of nuclear weapons in international waters, globally, by area or by categories of ships;

(b)   The withdrawal of vessels carrying nuclear weapons from certain ocean and sea areas, e.g. the Indian Ocean and the Mediterranean Sea;

(c)   The establishment of peace zones, or nuclear-weapon-free zones, with ocean or sea areas as their primary constituents, e.g. the Indian Ocean, the Mediterranean Sea, the Baltic Sea, South-East Asia, the South Pacific;

(d)   The prohibition of the transit and transport of nuclear weapons through peace zones or through nuclear-weapon-free zones;

(e)   The removal of missile submarines from extensive areas of combat patrol and the confinement of their patrol areas within agreed limits;

(f)   The restriction of naval activities by the creation of maritime zones within which the rights of non-coastal States of individual zones would be restricted;

(g)   The restricting and lowering of the level of military presence and military activity in appropriate regions. In this context, it has been suggested that such restraints may be applicable in many areas such as the Atlantic, the Indian or the Pacific Oceans, in the Mediterranean Sea or in the Gulf, and in sea areas adjacent to northern Europe;

(h)   The prohibition on the establishment of new, and the gradual elimination of existing, foreign naval bases;

(i)   Various geographical limitations on naval exercises and manoeuvres.

D. Confidence-building measures

296.   It has long been argued that one of the best ways of encouraging States to negotiate measures of disarmament is to take steps to increase mutual trust and confidence. In the United Nations **Comprehensive Study on Confidence-building Measures**, the Group of Experts concluded that "the overall objective of confidence-building measures is to contribute towards reducing or, in some instances, even eliminate the causes for mistrust, fear, tensions, and hostilities as significant factors behind the international arms build-up".[34]

297.   It has also long been recognized that confidence-building measures cannot be substitutes for specific disarmament measures. They assist and support disarmament initiatives and they can create an atmosphere conducive to progress, but they are not a replacement for real disarmament action.

298.   Confidence-building measures can be agreed in many forms. In the naval context they can be political and/or military. They can be global, regional or subregional, and they can be negotiated multilaterally or bilaterally or even adopted as unilateral initiatives. Among the types of measures that have been suggested in recent years as appropriate to the naval arms

race are the following, some of which may be closely related to measures listed in other groups:

(a)   Extension of existing confidence-building measures to seas and oceans, especially to areas with the busiest sea lanes;

(b)   Agreements not to expand naval activities in areas of tension or armed conflict;

(c)   As a corollary of (b), withdrawal of foreign naval forces to specified distances from regions of tension or armed conflict;

(d)   Agreements between two or more extra-regional States to forgo on a reciprocal basis some or all forms of naval deployment, activity and/or transit in a particular area;

(e)   Restraints on the use of foreign naval bases;

(f)   Restraints on the use of certain weapon systems;

(g)   The promotion of mutual trust and confidence by more openness between States concerning their naval strengths, activities and intentions, e.g. prior notification of and exchanges of information on naval exercises or manoeuvres or on major movements of naval, including amphibious, forces; the presence of observers during exercises or manoeuvres; notification of the passage of submarines, especially in regions of high international tension;

(h)   International agreements to prevent incidents between naval forces on or over the high seas, similar to the existing US/USSR Agreement on the prevention of incidents on and over the high seas of 1972;

(i)   Measures related to the non-proliferation of certain technologies of maritime warfare.

E. Verification

299.   As stated in the Final Document of the Tenth Special Session of the general Assembly, "Disarmament and arms limitation agreements should provide for adequate measures of verification satisfactory to all parties concerned in order to create the necessary confidence and ensure that they are being observed by all parties" (para. 31). Verification has important political and technical aspects - political because States are often very reluctant to allow verification to be carried out on their own national territory because the nature of the activities may be unacceptably intrusive, technical because there are ways in which certain forms of verification can be carried out reliably by national technical means, and because such means can work adequately without necessitating on-site inspection.

300.   Verification of naval disarmament and associated measures has certain features which can be different from verification of such measures on land. In the first place, verification carried out at sea does not raise the aspect of intrusion or violation of land territory or territorial airspace if it is carried out on the high seas, and no on-site inspection is involved. Second, naval vessels and aircraft are finite units; their presence and movements can under certain circumstances be readily and precisely identified. Third, the international nature of the oceans - indeed, the freedom of the seas - renders observation more practicable, provided that

the necessary technical and physical means are available. In this respect, however, significant problems will have to be addressed concerning such aspects as submarines and as the identification of which ships are, or may be, carrying nuclear weapons. On the other hand, some confidence-building measures providing for openness and the transfer of information could contribute to more effective verification.

301.　There are wide possibilities for the choice of how verification might be carried out and by whom, depending on the matter to be verified. Technical means might include detection devices on satellites, aircraft or other vessels or deployed underwater. Verification teams could be drawn from the States participating in the measures, or they could be representatives of international or regional organizations or representatives of neutral or other States from within, or outside, the area concerned. There is almost no limit to the types of verification methods that might be used without being intrusive, provided that States demonstrate the necessary political readiness to consider the measures needed to ensure the mutual confidence of States in fulfilling their obligations.

F.　Modernization of the laws of sea warfare

302.　Most of the treaty law which regulates naval warfare is very old, for example the Paris Declaration of 1856 relating to merchant shipping in wartime and the Hague Conventions of 1907[35] which today are partly obsolete. The only comparatively modern document on war at sea is the second Geneva Convention of 1949[36] on the protection of wounded, sick and shipwrecked members of armed forces at sea. However, the long tradition and existence of old treaties in force suggest that this issue should be considered in some detail.

303.　The recent revision of, and additions to, the rules of international humanitarian law applicable in armed conflict (the 1977 Protocols Additional to the Geneva Conventions of 1949)[37] did not fully address the laws of war at sea. The second Geneva Convention does not regulate warfare as such but only the protection of victims of naval war. In the light of the many changes and developments that have taken place in the naval sphere, there seems to be a need for modernization in this field of international law. A complete revision and updating of the relevant Hague Conventions and other older instruments would probably not be a realistic undertaking. However, it should be possible to single out certain issues of particular interest and of pressing urgency and consider the adoption of separate brief protocols on them. The conclusion and adoption of such protocols could mean, first, a progressive development of international law in this field and, second, a degree of protection for civilians and civilian values which, if adhered to by the major military Powers, could have considerable confidence-building effects. For instance, the problems of identification and communication at sea could probably be studied in the framework of the International Telecommunication Union, the International Maritime Organization and the International Civil Aviation Organization.

304.　The following is a list of suggested topics that might be dealt with in international instruments:

(a)　**Zonal restrictions.** In order to reflect current circumstances, there is a need for further development of international law concerning such concepts as "interception areas", "war zones", "blockade zones" or "total exclusion zones". Maritime powers have long been resorting to various zonal concepts in crisis and in times of war. For States that are not parties to the conflict, such acts can involve enforced curtailment of the principle of the freedom of the high seas. The need for freedom of navigation and for keeping international sea communications open, in times of crisis and war as well as in peace, should be given due regard. The possibility and practicability of geographical and functional restrictions could be investigated. Merchant and fishing vessels (on condition that they are not engaged in unneutral services) should always be legally protected from armed attack, even if they must enter the zone at the risk of unintentional or collateral damage.

(b) **Long-range weapons**. Modern long-range missiles and torpedoes pose certain problems for the implementation of the general prohibition against indiscriminatory methods and means of warfare that has long been an established principle in international humanitarian law applicable in armed conflicts. When weapons are fired from such great distances it can be very difficult to select and identify targets. There is a danger of accidental strikes on units which are protected under international law, such as hospital ships and neutral merchant ships. In order to prevent disastrous mistakes in warfare and protect peaceful shipping, new practical measures in the context of the laws of sea warfare should be developed.

(c) **Sea mines**. The 1907 Hague Convention Relative to the Laying of Automatic Submarine Contact Mines (Convention VIII) is of limited value today. Its definition of mines does not accommodate later developments, i.e. modern mines which rely on magnetic, acoustic or pressure effect or a combination thereof. Convention VIII provides for neutralizing mechanisms (art. 1) and information regarding danger zones (art. 3). A new treaty could usefully build on the same concepts, adding requirements on recording the position and type of minefields in order to protect the peaceful uses of the marine environment.

(d) **Protection of the marine environment**. Part XII of the United Nations Convention on the Law of the Sea is entitled "Protection and preservation of the marine environment". Given the nature of the Convention, there are no explicit provisions therein offering protection of the marine environment against the consequences of armed attacks. As recent events in the Gulf have shown, oil pollution emanating from military operations can have unpredictable and very harmful consequences for the marine environment. According to the 1977 Protocol Additional to the Geneva Conventions of 12 August 1949, and relating to the Protection of Victims of International Armed Conflicts (Protocol I) it is prohibited to employ methods or means of warfare which are intended, or may be expected, to cause widespread, long-term and severe damage to the natural environment (art. 35). Although Protocol I specifically applies to warfare on land or in the air, it is for consideration that this general rule could usefully be extended to cover naval warfare through a specific protocol.

G. Relation to the Law of the Sea

305. Some States have noted that the Convention on the Law of the Sea and the Sea-Bed Treaty are not entirely in accord. As the Third Review Conference of the latter will take place not earlier than 1988 and not later than 1990, it might be appropriate for that Review Conference to give consideration to the matter, with a view to deciding what action, if any, should be taken. It is also for consideration that any future relevant arms limitation and/or disarmament agreements should be in harmony with the United Nations Convention on the Law of the Sea.

. . .

CHAPTER VIII

SUMMARY AND CONCLUSIONS

308.   In carrying out a comprehensive study, as requested by the General Assembly in resolution 38/188 G, the Group of Experts has had to cover a broad compass. In essence, this report is an overview of a very wide and complex subject from which several significant conclusions of a general nature may be drawn.

309.   It is useful to recall that some 71 per cent of the earth's surface is sea and over two thirds of the world's human population live within 300 kilometres of a sea coast.   The importance of the sea, its uses and resources, to the human race cannot be over-emphasized. A major proportion of the world's international trade goes by sea; fisheries provide a vital source of protein to many hundreds of millions of people; an increasing amount of the world's energy supplies are derived from sea areas; and as technology develops and expands so, too, will the means of further developing the mineral resources of the sea-bed and the sea itself. The world's oceans have already played an important role in human exploration and development, and it can be expected that the role they will play in the future will be of even greater significance to mankind.

310.   The specific value of the sea to an individual State varies widely from country to country according to geographical situation, extent of development, maritime outlook, economic dependence or independence and many other factors. Some States accord great importance to their sea lines of communication and marine industries and consequently will go to great lengths to protect them, both politically and if necessary militarily. To others, the seas often represent a challenging opportunity for the fulfillment of some of their basic aspirations for economic advancement. To many, the seas can also represent a potential source of threat to their national security and territorial integrity.

311.   Into this picture, the advent of the Convention on the Law of the Sea has introduced a series of major and interconnected new elements. Large areas of what have been parts of the high seas will now become subject to the specific legal régime of the exclusive economic zone in which coastal States will enjoy full economic rights while recognizing important freedoms of the high seas. The provision by which coastal States may extend their territorial sea up to a breadth of 12 miles; the new concept of "transit passage"; the introduction of "archipelagic waters"; the definition of "the continental shelf"; the provisions of the Convention concerning the development of the sea-bed and ocean floor and subsoil thereof, beyond the limits of national jurisdiction - all these are new factors. Although some of these aspects have not yet received acceptance by all States, without doubt the implementation of the Convention on the Law of the Sea will have far-reaching effects on the international conduct of maritime affairs.

312.   In addition to these factors and of particular relevance to the present study, there is the use of the seas by the navies of the world. The majority of the world's States possess naval forces, albeit of widely differing capabilities. The existence of such forces in the exercise of sovereign rights is legitimate and recognized by the Group; however, there are sometimes conflicts of interest between naval activities and non-military uses of the sea, just as there are conflicts between latent security threats and the freedom of navigation. Naval activities should take account, *inter alia*, of the legitimate interests of coastal States, and it is important that such activities should be compatible with the provisions of the Convention on the Law of the Sea.

313. Naval presence and activities are not new, but recent years have witnessed several fundamental technological developments which have had major effects on the international maritime situation. The most important of these changes, in a technical sense, has been the development of nuclear energy. In its uses for ship propulsion, particularly in submarines, and for nuclear warheads, it has multiplied the capabilities of naval vessels and the weapons they carry. In specific form, these are represented by the nuclear-armed ICBMs deployed on board the nuclear-powered submarines of five States. As stated earlier in this report, some 40 per cent of the combined United States and Soviet potential totals of strategic missiles are sea-borne. Together with the strategic nuclear warheads distributed among the navies of the other three nuclear-weapon States, a significant proportion of the world's strategic nuclear capability is at sea, by far the largest part of it on board United States and Soviet SSBNs.

314. The threat to international security represented by these weapons, and the continuing development of improved SLBMs with enhanced guidance and greater accuracy, make even more urgent the need for successful bilateral and multilateral negotiations leading to effective measures of nuclear disarmament.

315. In addition to strategic nuclear forces, there are large numbers of tactical nuclear weapons at sea. This fact, coupled with ever-diminishing warning time within which a prospective target must react, imparts a particularly dangerous dimension to the arms race at sea. Whereas strategic missiles are carried by submarines of specific design and purpose, tactical nuclear weapons may be on board a wide variety of ships, submarines, aircraft or helicopters of the navies of the five nuclear-weapon States. Furthermore, in the near future the situation will be made more complex by the arrival in operational service of versatile, comparatively inexpensive, highly accurate, sea-launched cruise missiles. These missiles, able to carry either conventional or nuclear warheads for use against naval or shore targets, will greatly complicate the difficulties of verification and therefore also the difficulties of negotiating effective measures of disarmament.

316. The proliferation of nuclear weapons at sea, particularly the aspect of geographical dispersion of such weapons, will give rise to mounting concern, particularly among many non-nuclear-weapon States which in being States parties to the Treaty on the Non-Proliferation of Nuclear Weapons or otherwise have declared their intentions not to acquire or develop nuclear weapons themselves yet find that such policies have not stemmed the widening circles of nuclear-weapon deployments.

317. Rapid technological innovation and development, particularly in missiles and electronics, have greatly enhanced the war-fighting capabilities of navies, as described in some detail in chapter III. The navies of the United States and the Soviet Union in this respect are much more powerful than the navies of other States and have the capacity, not possessed by other navies, for prolonged operations in all the oceans of the world. At the same time, however, there are many asymmetries between the two navies, and between the naval forces of their allies, which do not render meaningful any efforts to make direct comparisons. These asymmetries include differing concepts of sea power, different geographical factors, different peacetime and wartime tasks, differing naval compositions in the nature of the vessels and aircraft that make up the respective fleets, and different policies towards national security within which the individual navies discharge their responsibilities. To an extent these asymmetries are also present in some of the world's coastal navies which, by means of technological advance, are in the process of acquiring a small but potent ability to carry out naval actions close to their own shores.

318.   In discharging its mandate to assist the Secretary-General in carrying out a comprehensive study, the Group of Experts has endeavoured to present a survey of naval strengths and activities as they exist against a backcloth of the maritime situation as a whole. Navies have their legitimate parts to play in the exercise by States of the inherent right of individual or collective self-defence. However, the development of naval capabilities to carry out such duties has, in the geopolitical circumstances since 1945, become a competitive accumulation and qualitative refinement of arms with a momentum of its own. It is this aspect, as described earlier in this report, which constitutes the naval arms race. In turn, this is itself part of the general arms race described by the General Assembly in the Final Document of the Tenth Special Session in 1978 and which consumes unproductively so much of the world's human, financial and material resources.

319.   Naval strength, which by some is seen as an essential guarantor of the protection of vital economic, political or security interests, is sometimes seen by others as a source of threat to international security or a means of potential intervention or interference in the internal affairs of States. The latter perceptions are particularly true for States that do not have strong naval forces of their own. In this context, as has been described in chapter VI, certain naval practices are considered to be inimical to the maintenance of international security and to be incompatible with the rights of those who have interests in the peaceful uses of the sea and the peaceful development and exploitation of its resources.

320.   In the context of naval activities, the security régime at sea is based on three pillars of international law: the general restrictions on the use of force, customary law of the sea, and arms control and disarmament treaties agreed between States. The entry into force of the Convention on the Law of the Sea will give strong additional support to this structure. To give further support, the rules on the non-use of force should be strengthened; existing arms restrictions should be carefully maintained and new measures negotiated; and the early entry into force and full implementation of the Convention on the Law of the Sea should be encouraged.

321.   As this century approaches its close, the need for improved and more effective internationally accepted ocean management policies will become ever more apparent. In no way must the widened national responsibilities that will be introduced by the entry into force of the Convention on the Law of the Sea be misused as justification for the expansion and utilization of naval force. Yet within a framework of improved international security, there is much that might be done by naval ships and aircraft to assist in the peaceful uses of the sea for the benefit of humanity. There is also much that could be done by the experienced maritime States to assist in promoting such endeavours.

322.   There are thus two basic objectives for action. The first is the achievement by negotiation of (a) effective measures of nuclear disarmament at sea in order to halt and reverse the nuclear arms race until the total elimination of nuclear weapons and their delivery systems has been achieved and (b) measures to achieve security and stability at significantly lower levels of conventional naval arms and armed forces. This objective is within the ultimate objective of the efforts of States in the disarmament process of achieving general and complete disarmament under strict and effective international control. It follows, therefore, that measures of naval arms limitation and reduction - both nuclear and conventional must be considered in the overall context of halting and reversing the arms race in general, but this should not be an excuse for failing to address the resolution of specific problems of naval disarmament, or the agreement of measures of confidence-building in the naval environment,

or negotiation of mutually acceptable measures to limit the transfers of certain naval arms or specific technologies. In these contexts, for instance, consideration should be given to making multilateral the existing bilateral agreement between the Soviet Union and the United States on the Prevention of Incidents on and over the High Seas, to continuing negotiations in good faith on further measures for the prevention of an arms race on the sea-bed in accordance with article V of the Sea-Bed Treaty; to giving full effect to the nuclear-weapon-free régime of the Antarctic Treaty by applying it to the seas within its area of application (south of 60° south), and to modernizing the laws of sea warfare.

323.   Chapter VII of the present report reflects a large number of measures that have been suggested in various recent publications, papers and governmental statements. The Group recommends that the measures should be given close attention with a view to discussion and negotiation as appropriate. As, however, their acceptability and priority will probably vary according to political judgements, the Group expresses no opinion other than to urge that the proposals involving measures of nuclear-weapon limitation and disarmament should be given priority.

324.   The second objective should be the investigation of possible ways in which naval organization, capabilities and experience might make positive contributions to the establishment of improved and more effective ocean management policies for the peaceful uses of the world's seas in the years ahead, so that future generations may use to best advantage the resources of the sea for the benefit of all mankind. In the sense that security is not a narrow concept confined solely to the military situation but has a broader meaning embracing economic and social development, there is much that might be achieved in the improvement of policies of ocean management which, in turn, could contribute to the promotion of social progress and to better standards of life in larger freedom.

325.   It has been said that without development there will be no peace, and without peace there will be no development. Security in the maritime environment is therefore not just military in nature but includes such other facets as food security, resource security, job security and ocean management security. It has significant legal, political, military, organizational and practical implications. As described in earlier paragraphs, international discussion and co-operation are already in hand it several important technical fields in the form of such endeavours as the work of IMO and the establishment of the Strategy for Fisheries Management and Development through FAO. There are also some notable regional initiatives such as the recent Conference on Economic, Scientific and Technical Co-operation in the Indian Ocean held at Colombo from 15 to 20 July 1985 and the OAU Conference for Security and Co-operation in Africa in conformity with the Plan of Action of Lagos, held at Addis Ababa from 18 to 20 July 1985. The view has been expressed in the Group of Experts, however, that there may be considerable merit in holding, at an appropriate time, a global conference on the theme of "Security in the Maritime Environment" as a means of bringing together the disparate threads of these complex issues and determining what further steps might be taken by the international community.

326.   With these two objectives in mind, the Group has in this study addressed a wide range of sensitive, complicated and often interrelated topics. Many issues deserve greater attention in the appropriate forums within and outside the United Nations, globally and - where appropriate - regionally. It is the Group's hope that the considerations expressed in this report will be of assistance in such discussions.

Notes

1.   The Law of the Sea: United Nations Convention on the Law of the Sea with Index and Final Act of the Third United Nations Conference on the Law of the Sea (United Nations publication, Sales No. E.83.V.5).
2.   The Final Document is contained in resolution S-10/2. For the full text of the resolution, see The United Nations Disarmament Yearbook, vol.3:1978, appendix I (United Nations publication, Sales No. E.79.IX.3). The text has also been published in leaflet form (DPI/679).

. . .

12.   The calculation of world military expenditure is of necessity imprecise owing to such variables as differences in exchange rates, secrecy of information, problems of deciding how to allow for differences in the system and costing of military production and difficulties in how to allow for price changes in the civilian and military sectors of the economy. A useful reference point may be SIPRI Yearbook, 1985, p. 223, which gave a figure of $800 to $820 billion for the year 1984, measured in 1984 dollars.
13.   S. G. Gorshkov, Morskaya mosch gosudarstaya (Moscow, Voennoe Izdatel'stvo Ministerstva Oborony SSR, 1976). Published in English as The Sea Power of the State (Oxford, Pergamon Press, 1979).

. . .

24.   Christopher Mayer, "Piracy today", Lloyd's Nautical Year Book 1985 (Lloyd's of London Press, 1984).
25.   For the texts of the multilateral treaties referred to in paragraphs 229-240, see Status of Multilateral Arms Regulation and Disarmament Agreements, 2nd ed. (United Nations publication, Sales No. E.83.IX.5).
26.   Sea Cmnd. 6198 (London, H.M. Stationery Office, 1975).
27.   For the texts of the bilateral agreements referred to in paragraphs 242-245, see Goldblat, op. cit.
28.   The earliest General Assembly resolution on the subject of Africa as a denuclearized zone was 1652 (XVI) of 24 November 1961. Thereafter, other resolutions have been 2033 (XX) of 3 December 1965, 32/81 of 12 December 1977, 33/63 of 14 December 1978, 34/76 A of 11 December 1979, 35/146 B of 12 December 1980, 36/86 B of 9 December 1981, 37/74 A of 9 December 1982, 38/181 A of 20 December 1983 and 39/61 of 12 December 1984.
29.   In addition to resolution 2832 (XXVI) of 16 December 1971, and resolution 2992 (XXVII) of 15 December 1972, other resolutions adopted have been 3080 (XXVIII) of 6 December 1973, 3259 A (XXIX) of 9 December 1974, 3468 (XXX) of 11 December 1975, 31/88 of 14 December 1976, 32/86 of 12 December 1977, S-10/2 of 30 June 1978, 33/68 of 14 December 1978, 34/80 A and B of 11 December 1979, 35/150 of 12 December 1980, 36/90 of 9 December 1981, 37/96 of 13 December 1982, 38/185 of 20 December 1983 and 39/149 of 17 December 1984.
30.   See, for example, resolutions 36/102 of 9 December 1981, 37/118 of 16 December 1982, 38/189 of 20 December 1983 and 39/153 of 17 December 1984.
31.   Arkin and others, op. cit.
32.   Geoffrey Till and others, Maritime Strategy in the Nuclear Age. 2nd ed. (New York, St. Martin's Press, 1984), p. 203.
33.   See note 14.
34.   Comprehensive Study on Confidence-building Measures (United Nations publication, Sales No. E.82.IX.3), para. 160.
35.   Goldblat, op. cit., pp. 122-131.
36.   United Nations, Treaty Series, vol. 75, No. 971.
37.   Goldblat, op. cit., pp. 239-252.

- - - - -

UN Disarmament Yearbook,
Volume 10: 1985

UN Publication
Sales No. E.86.IX.7
Extract

. . .

Chapter II   The question of general and complete disarmament

. . .

Consideration by the General Assembly, 1985

. . .

Of the 15 resolutions adopted, 6 are discussed in this chapter and 9 in subsequent chapters . . .

(a)   In this chapter . . .
    (i)   40/94 I (Curbing the naval arms race; limitation and reduction of naval arma-
          ments and extension of confidence building measures to seas and oceans),
          below;
    (ii) 40/94 J (Further measures in the field of disarmament for the prevention of an
          arms race on the sea-bed, the ocean floor and in the subsoil thereof) . . .
    (iii) 40/94 K (Objective information on military matters) . . .
    (iv) 40/94 L (Compliance with arms limitation and disarmament agreements) . . .
    (v)   40/94 N (Disarmament and the maintenance of international peace and
          security) . . .
    (vi) 40/94 O (Review of the role of the United Nations in the field of disarma-
          ment) . . .

(b)   In subsequent chapters
    (i)   40/94 A (Conventional disarmament on a regional scale) . . .
    (ii)   40/94 B (Study of the question of nuclear-weapon-free zones in all its aspects)
           . . .
    (iii) 40/94 C (Study on conventional disarmament) . . .
    (iv)   40/94 D (Prohibition of the development, production, stockpiling and use of
           radiological weapons) . . .
    (v)   40/94 E (Comprehensive study of concepts of security) . . .
    (vi)   40/94 F (Study on the naval arms race) . . .
    (vii) 40/94 G (Prohibition of the production of fissionable material for weapons
           purposes) . . .
    (viii) 40/94 H (Nuclear-weapon freeze) . . .
    (ix)   40/94 M (Third Review Conference of the Parties to the Treaty on the Non-
           Proliferation of Nuclear Weapons) . . .

    . . .

On 7 November, Bulgaria, Democratic Yemen, the German Democratic Republic, the Lao People's Democratic Republic, Poland, the Syrian Arab Republic and Viet Nam submitted a draft resolution entitled "Curbing the naval arms race: limitation and reduction of naval armaments and extension of confidence-building measures to seas and oceans", which was later also sponsored by the Libyan Arab Jamahiriya.

In introducing the draft resolution on 11 November, Bulgaria emphasized the urgent need to take international concerted measures to limit naval armaments both quantitatively and qualitatively while it was still possible, and drew attention to several places where the wording of the draft differed from the previous year's version. The eighth preambular paragraph was new and reflected the view that such measures should be worked out and implemented with due regard to the principle of not harming the legitimate security interests of any State. The thirteenth and fourteenth preambular paragraphs took note of the United Nations study on naval armaments just completed with the assistance of a group of qualified governmental experts, and considered that the discussion at the 1985 session of the Disarmament Commission constituted a valuable initial step for the endeavour envisaged in the draft. Regarding the operative part of the draft, Bulgaria stressed the new element in operative paragraph 5, which called for the continued consideration of the question by the Disarmament Commission in an appropriate subsidiary body, taking due account of the views expressed by Member States on the subject in various United Nations documents as well as of future initiatives, with a view to submitting recommendations to the Assembly at its forty-first session.

On 12 November, the sponsors submitted a revised draft resolution, in which the words "as a matter of priority" had been added to operative paragraph 5 (see below).

On 18 November, the First Committee adopted the draft resolution by a recorded vote of 56 to 19, with 56 abstentions. Eight States explained their positions on the draft.

The United Kingdom, which cast a negative vote, expressed surprise at the sponsors' persistence in pursuing the initiative, which it considered flawed and irrelevant, cutting across the United Nations study on the same subject. It pointed out that despite initial indications of interest, the Soviet Union and Bulgaria had declined to participate in the group preparing that study, but that the former had unilaterally put forward proposals on the subject which the United Kingdom regarded as discriminatory, designed to limit naval deployments only in areas which were extensively used by Western navies, but not mentioning areas used by the Soviet navy. While naval activities were undoubtedly of legitimate international concern, the United Kingdom did not share the view that the world was in the midst of some dangerous escalation of a "naval arms race" which posed a volatile threat. The Western alliance did have substantial naval forces, as its component elements were separated by two oceans and depended on sea-borne trade, while the Soviet Union and its allies constituted a large contiguous land mass. The United Kingdom considered that what it perceived as an extensive Soviet naval buildup, particularly the expansion of the Soviet submarine fleet, posed a potential and growing threat to Western lines of communication and trade and was, therefore, inherently destabilizing. The Netherlands, which also voted against the draft, believed it was superfluous in view of the submission of a draft resolution on the naval arms study (see chapter XXIV). Moreover, the Netherlands pointed out that the text did not take into account existing geographical disparities between major naval Powers. It also believed that some notions in the preambular paragraphs provided an insufficient basis for fruitful consideration of the issues in a multilateral disarmament body.

The Soviet Union, supporting the draft, stressed that together with other socialist countries it had consistently advocated that the issue of curbing the arms race on the seas and oceans be brought down to a practical level and had repeatedly taken initiatives in that regard. It stressed that the draft resolution in question was also aimed at bringing about negotiations on the subject and that it appealed to all member States, in particular nuclear-weapon States and other major naval Powers without discrimination, to refrain from increasing their naval presence and activities in areas of conflict or tension, or far from their own shores. The Soviet Union shared the alarm, expressed in the draft, at what it considered the increasingly frequent use of fleets or other naval formations for the demonstration or use of force and as a means of exerting pressure.

Among the non-aligned States voting in favour, Argentina, Benin and Democratic Yemen explained their positions. Argentina drew attention to the same appeal that the Soviet Union had, stating that Argentina fully supported it in respect of naval activities in the South Atlantic. Benin rejected an assertion by the United Kingdom that pressures had been brought to bear upon members of the Group of African States to have them vote in favour. Democratic Yemen likewise criticized some aspects in the United Kingdom's view of the draft. Among the non-aligned countries abstaining, India stated that it was unable to understand the rationale of detaching the issue of the naval arms race from the wider issues of the nuclear arms race and of general and complete disarmament. Colombia supported the curbing of the naval arms race, but could not accept many of the formulations in the text.

On 12 December, the General Assembly adopted the draft resolution by a recorded vote of 71 to 19 (mainly Western States), with 59 abstentions, as resolution 40/94 I. It reads as follows:

The General Assembly,

Recalling its resolutions 38/188 F of 20 December 1983 and 39/151 I of 17 December 1984,

Convinced that all channels of the arms race, in particular the nuclear-arms race, should be effectively covered by the efforts to halt and reverse it,

Disturbed by the growing threat to peace, international security and global stability posed by the continuing escalation of the naval arms race,

Alarmed by the even more frequent use of naval fleets or other naval formations for demonstrations or use of force and as an instrument to exert pressure against sovereign States, especially developing States, to interfere in their internal affairs, to commit acts of armed aggression and intervention and to preserve the remnants of the colonial system,

Aware that the growing presence of naval fleets and the intensification of the naval activities of some States in conflict areas or far from their own shores increase tensions in these areas and could adversely affect the security of the international sea lanes in these areas, the freedom of navigation and the exploitation of maritime resources,

Firmly convinced that the undertaking of urgent steps to curb military confrontation at sea would be a significant contribution to preventing war, especially nuclear war, and to strengthening peace and international security,

Aware of the numerous initiatives and concrete proposals to undertake effective measures aimed at limiting naval activities, limiting and reducing naval armaments and extending confidence-building measures to seas and oceans,

Convinced that such measures should be worked out and implemented with due regard to the principle of not harming the legitimate security interests of any State concerned,

Stressing once again the importance of relevant measures of a regional character, such as the implementation of the Declaration of the Indian Ocean as a Zone of Peace and the transformation of the Mediterranean into a zone of peace, security and co-operation,

Reaffirming once again that seas and oceans, being of vital importance to mankind, should be used exclusively for peaceful purposes in accordance with the régime established by the 1982 United Nations Convention on the Law of the Sea,

Taking note of the report of the Secretary-General and other documents, submitted in pursuance of resolutions 38/188 F and 39/151 I, which contain the replies of Member States, including a major naval Power, in the modalities for negotiations, as well as various specific ideas and new proposals for joint measures on curbing the naval arms race and naval activities,

Noting with satisfaction that the prevailing view expressed in these replies strongly favours an early commencement of negotiations aimed at curbing the naval arms race and naval activities, strengthening confidence and security at sea and reducing naval armaments,

Taking note of the United Nations study on the naval arms race carried out with the assistance of a group of qualified governmental experts,

Considering that the discussion on the subject that has taken place at the 1985 substantive session of the Disarmament Commission constitutes a valuable initial step in the common search for ways and means which could ensure proper conditions for more detailed and thorough consideration of the issue of curbing the naval arms race, with a view to holding appropriate negotiations,

1.   *Appeals once again* to all Member States, in particular to nuclear-weapon States and other major naval Powers, to refrain from enlarging their naval presence and activities in areas of conflict or tension, or far from their own shores;

2.   *Reaffirms once again* its recognition of the urgent need to start negotiations with the participation of the major naval Powers, in particular the nuclear-weapon States, and other interested States on the limitation of naval activities, the limitation and reduction of naval armaments and the extension of confidence-building measures to seas and oceans, especially to areas with the busiest international sea lanes or to regions where the probability of conflict situations is high;

3.   *Invites* Member States, particularly the major naval Powers, including the nuclear-weapon States, to consider the possibility of holding direct consultations, bilateral and/or multilateral, with a view to preparing the opening at an early date of such negotiations;

4.   *Also invites* Member States, especially those that have not yet done so, to communicate to the Secretary-General not later than April 1986 their views concerning the modalities for holding the multilateral negotiations referred to above, including the possibilities for holding them at the Conference on Disarmament at Geneva;

5.   *Requests* the Disarmament Commission to continue the consideration of this question as a matter of priority in an appropriate subsidiary body, taking due account of the proposals made and the views expressed on the subject-matter contained in the replies of Member States to the Secretary-General, in the verbatim records of the Disarmament Commission, in the working papers and the United Nations study on this question, as well as of future initiatives, with a view to submitting its recommendations to the General Assembly at its forty-first session;

6.   *Decides* to include in the provisional agenda of its forty-first session the item entitled "Curbing the naval arms race: limitation and reduction of naval armaments and extension of confidence-building measures to seas and oceans".

On 7 November, Poland, Romania and the Ukrainian SSR submitted a draft resolution entitled "further measures in the field of disarmament for the prevention of an arms race on the sea-bed, the ocean floor and the subsoil thereof". On 12 November, the sponsors, joined by Cameroon, submitted a revised draft resolution. Among other things, it noted, in a new third preambular paragraph, that the Third United Nations Conference on the Law of the Sea had concluded and the Convention on the Law of the Sea had been opened for signature on 10 December 1982. It emphasized, in a new fourth preambular paragraph, the interest of all States, including specifically developing ones, in the progress of the exploration and use of the sea-bed and the ocean floor and its resources for peaceful purposes.

On 18 November, the above-mentioned countries and Canada, as a new sponsor, submitted a second revision, in which a request to the Conference on Disarmament to report on its continued consideration of the subject to the General Assembly at its forty-third session was deleted from operative paragraph 1. Likewise, the whole of operative paragraph 2, by which the Assembly would have decided to include an item on the subject in the provisional agenda of the forty-third session, was deleted.

Also on 18 November, the Ukrainian SSR introduced the draft and its various revisions. It stated that the text derived from the 1978 Final Document, specifically its paragraph 79, and the Final Declaration of the Second Review Conference of the Parties to the Treaty on the Prohibition of the Emplacement of Nuclear Weapons and Other Weapons of Mass Destruction on the Sea-Bed and the Ocean Floor and in the Subsoil Thereof[23]. It was designed to continue the work of the thirty-eighth session, at which the Assembly, by resolution 38/188

B, had requested the Conference on Disarmament to consider further measures for the prevention of an arms race in the marine environment and to report on the matter to the Assembly at its fortieth session, which it did[24]. The Ukrainian SSR explained that in the course of consultations with the sponsors of resolution 38/188 B, particularly Norway, it had been learned that, at a future session of the Assembly, they would submit a draft resolution fully covering the question of the preparation and convening of a third review conference of the parties to the sea-bed Treaty. Last-minute consultations had thus led to the changes embodied in the second revision, as outlined above.

At the same meeting, the First Committee approved the twice revised draft resolution without a vote. On 12 December, the General Assembly adopted the draft resolution, also without a vote, as resolution 40/94 J. It reads as follows:

The General Assembly,

Recalling its resolution 38/188 B of 20 December 1983, in which it reiterated its expressed hope for the widest possible adherence to the Treaty on the Prohibition of the Emplacement of Nuclear Weapons and Other Weapons of Mass Destruction on the Sea-Bed and the Ocean Floor and in the Subsoil Thereof, called again upon all States to refrain from any action which might lead to the extension of the arms race to the sea-bed and ocean floor, and also requested the Conference on Disarmament to proceed promptly with consideration of further measures in the field of disarmament for the prevention of an arms race on the sea-bed, the ocean floor and in the subsoil thereof,

Taking note of the report of the Conference on Disarmament on its consideration of further measures in the field of disarmament for the prevention off an arms race on the sea-bed, the ocean floor and in the subsoil thereof,

Noting that the Third United Nations Conference on the Law of the Sea had concluded and that the United Nations Convention on the Law of the Sea was opened for signature on 10 December 1982,

Emphasizing the interest of all States, including specifically the interest of developing States, in the progress of the exploration and use of the sea-bed and the ocean floor and its resources for peaceful purposes,

Requests the Conference on Disarmament, in consultation with the States parties to the Treaty on the Prohibition of the Emplacement of Nuclear Weapons and Other Weapons of Mass Destruction on the Sea-Bed and the Ocean Floor and in the Subsoil Thereof, taking into account existing proposals and any relevant technological developments, to continue its consideration of further measures in the field of disarmament for the prevention of an arms race on the sea-bed, the ocean floor and in the subsoil thereof.

. . .

Notes

. . .

23.   SBT/CONF.II/20, part II.
24.   Official Records of the General Assembly, Fortieth Session, Supplement No.27 (A/40/27 and Corr.1), paras. 112 and 113.

. . .

CHAPTER XXIV   United Nations disarmament studies programme

Study on the naval arms race

By resolution 38/188 G of December 1983, the General Assembly had requested the Secretary-General, with the assistance of qualified governmental experts, to carry out a comprehensive study on the naval arms race, on naval forces and naval arms systems, including maritime nuclear-weapons systems, as well as on the development, deployment and mode of operation of such naval forces and systems, all with a view to analysing their possible implications for international security, for the freedom of the high seas, for international shipping routes and for the exploitation of marine resources, thereby facilitating the identification of possible areas for disarmament and confidence-building measures. The Assembly further requested the Secretary-General to submit the final report to the Assembly at its fortieth session, in 1985.

Pursuant to that resolution, the Secretary-General, in early 1984, appointed the Group of Governmental Experts to Carry Out a Comprehensive Study on the Naval Arms Race, Naval Forces and Naval Arms Systems, composed of experts from China, France, Gabon, Indonesia, the Netherlands, Peru and Sweden. The Group of Experts held two sessions in 1984 and two in 1985, namely, from 4 to 15 March and from 17 to 26 July.

By a letter dated 26 July, the Chairman of the Group, Mr. Ali Alatas of Indonesia, transmitted the study,[15] which had been adopted by consensus by the experts, to the Secretary-General. It was submitted to the General Assembly, annexed to the report of the Secretary-General, on 17 September.

The study states that, to date, little attention has been paid in multilateral negotiations to the continuing development of naval forces and naval arms systems and the added dimension and implications this has given to the problems of international security. However, the modernization and expansion of navies and the increased sophistication of naval-based arms systems in general have created new and enlarged operational capabilities, especially among nuclear-weapon States and other militarily significant States, and have given rise to concern among many nations.

Noting that some 71 per cent of the Earth's surface is sea, and over two thirds of the world's human inhabitants live within 300 kilometres of the sea coast, the study outlines some of the significant benefits offered by the sea to mankind. A major portion of the world's international trade goes by sea; fisheries provide many hundreds of millions of people with a source of protein; an increasing amount of the world's energy supplies are derived from sea areas; and as technology develops and expands so, too, will the means of further developing the mineral resources of the sea-bed and the sea itself. The world's oceans have already played an important role in human exploration and development, and it can be expected that the role they will play in the future will be of even greater significance.

The Group of Experts observes that there are several motivations for States to develop naval capabilities, varying from local self-defence to the potential for strategic nuclear use; from an ability to carry out overseas intervention to establishment of seaboard protection and security; from protection of commerce and national interests to policing newly established areas of exclusive economic jurisdiction. Primarily, however, according to the study, a naval force is a declaration by a nation that it has specific maritime interests and the political will to protect them. In so doing, States may develop naval forces which are perceived as capable of threatening the security or interests of other States, thus leading to the construction of a naval force to counter the perceived threat. The result can be a naval arms race, which is the current situation.

Addressing the naval forces and naval arms systems at present in service, the Group notes the major developments of the past 50 years, principally the nuclear revolution, the electronic revolution and advances in weapons systems.

The study contains a description of existing naval forces compiled from published sources. The Group cautions that the information is for illustrative purposes only, in order to present a broad picture of naval forces and their capabilities without attempting any form of numerical comparison.

The experts observe that the deployment of naval vessels and the duties such vessels are called upon to perform are many and varied. Although only a few States posses extensive naval capabilities, most navies can carry out some functions, even if only to a limited extent. As described in the study, such functions include strategic nuclear deterrence, power projection (naval force operating in areas distant from home bases and able to support forces on shore), sea control and sea denial, and specialized operation in sea areas covered by ice. More traditional modes of operation in peace-time are activities in affirmation of sovereignty, naval presence and surveillance. In addition, naval forces are eminently suited for many different peace-time tasks in the public service when the situation demands.

The report describes, in broad terms, the maritime legal context and notes in particular the importance and scope of the Convention on the Law of the Sea[16]. Although it has not yet entered into force, many States have become signatories and several are engaged in amending their national legislation to reflect provisions of the Convention. In their report, the experts discuss briefly many of the Convention's main provisions affecting the use of the seas by navies, including such aspects as the freedom of navigation, peaceful uses of the sea, international waters territorial seas, straits used for international navigation, archipelagic waters, exclusive economic zones, the continental shelf and the high seas. The Group also outlines other multilateral treaties since 1945, bilateral agreements, and declarations affecting the maritime situation.

Having described the nature of the competitive accumulation and qualitative development of arms taking place in the oceans and seas of the world that constitute the naval arms race, the study declares that phenomenon to be a part of the global arms race. One of the unique features of the naval arms race is that a great part of naval operations takes place on the high seas. The implications for security, according to the report, of the burgeoning quantitative and qualitative developments taking place in the world's navies are many. First and foremost, there is the threat to world security represented by the strategic nuclear weapons at sea. At a different level, the numbers and extent of the deployment of tactical nuclear weapons also give rise to very great concern in view of the many warships, submarines and aircraft of the nuclear-weapon States which can be considered nuclear-capable. In addition, the problems of verification which are already difficult will be further complicated by the development of sea-launched cruise missiles and/or torpedoes, capable of carrying either a nuclear or a conventional warhead.

The world-wide capabilities of the general-purpose naval forces of the United States and the Soviet Union also have significant international security implications. the Group also considers differing categories of naval presence in areas that are often far from the national territory of the State or States concerned.

The Group of Experts states that whenever arms control and disarmament in the maritime domain are under discussion, some factors should be considered axiomatic. First, disarmament measures should be balanced and should not diminish the security of any State, but, at the same time, there is no such thing as a naval balance or parity independent of other military forces. Secondly, that fact together with geographical factors could require measures of restriction for naval forces and weapons to be numerically asymmetrical in order to maintain an overall military situation in balance. Thirdly, such measures should be embodied in legal instruments in harmony with the Convention on the Law of the Sea. Fourthly, as in all arms control and disarmament, appropriate verification and complaints procedures are essential for the proper implementation of agreed measures.

The study presents a survey of possible measures of disarmament and confidence-building grouped under the following headings: quantitative restraints; qualitative or technological restraints; geographic and/or mission restraints; confidence-building measures; verification; and modernization of the laws of sea warfare.

After summarizing their findings, the experts identify two basic objectives for action. The first is the achievement by negotiation of: (a) effective measures of nuclear disarmament at sea in order to halt and reverse the nuclear arms race until the total elimination of nuclear weapons and their delivery systems has been achieved; and (b) measures to achieve security and stability at significantly lower levels of conventional naval arms and armed forces. Measures of naval arms limitation and reduction - both nuclear and conventional- must be considered in the overall context of halting and reversing the arms race in general.

The second objective, according to the study, is the investigation of possible ways in which naval organization, capabilities and experience might make positive contributions to the establishment of improved and more effective ocean management policies for the peaceful uses of the world's seas in the years ahead, so that future generations might use to best advantage the resources of the sea for the benefit of all mankind.

With those two objectives in mind, the Group observes that many of the issues addressed in the study deserve greater attention in the appropriate forums within and outside the United Nations, globally and - where appropriate - regionally and subregionally. The Group expresses its hope that the considerations set out in the study will be of assistance in such discussions.

During the course of the debate in the First Committee,[17] the study on the naval arms race was mentioned by a number of States, including Bulgaria, Democratic Kampuchea, Gabon, the Netherlands, Peru, Sri Lanka, the Soviet Union, Sweden and Viet Nam. The representative of Indonesia, who had served as Chairman of the Group of Experts, introduced the study. He stated that the Group hoped that it would be seen as a serious effort to bring together many disparate aspects of the naval scene and to present a reasoned and nonpolemical account of the current naval situation. Having summarized the main findings of the study, he stated that the Group of Experts had drawn several significant conclusions of a general nature. Thus, while recognizing the traditional freedoms of the high seas, it observed that the proliferation of nuclear weapons at sea, in particular the aspect of geographical dispersion of such weapons, would give rise to mounting concern. The Group recognized that navies had legitimate parts to play in the exercise by States of the inherent right of individual or collective self-defence, but the development of naval capabilities had become a competitive accumulation and qualitative refinement with a momentum of its own. In conclusion, he recalled the two basic objectives for action identified in the report; nuclear disarmament at sea and a lowering of the level of conventional naval arms, as well as improved national and international policies of ocean management.

In a separate statement, Indonesia declared that as a maritime nation and a non-nuclear State, it had viewed with concern the disquieting trends of increasing naval buildup and deployment of new naval systems. In its opinion, such ominous developments had added a potentially destabilizing dimension to the overall arms race. It viewed the establishment of the Group of Experts to carry out a study on the naval arms race and to analyse its ramifications as most opportune and expressed its hope that the experts' findings and recommendations would generate concerted and concrete action by Member States, primarily through the negotiation of measures of nuclear disarmament and confidence-building at sea.

The Netherlands, speaking on behalf of the ten member States of the European Community as well as Portugal and Spain, pointed out that most of these States were coastal, and that historically seas and oceans had played an important role in their development. It welcomed the study as a useful and valuable contribution to the debate on many problems connected with the question of naval armament. In the view of the States that the Netherlands represented, the content of the study, with regard to both factual information on military and other naval activities and its conclusions, provided a source of material to draw upon in considering possible further action by the international community in the field. Sri Lanka, as an island nation, was particularly interested in the study, which revealed that a significant proportion of the world's strategic nuclear capabilities was sea-borne, largely on United States and Soviet vessels. The proliferation of nuclear weapons at sea was particularly alarming and that, together with other findings in the study, seemed to Sri Lanka added reason to implement urgently the Declaration of the Indian Ocean as a Zone of Peace.

On 7 November in the First Committee, Australia, Austria, China, Finland, France, Gabon, Iceland, Indonesia, Mexico, the Netherlands, Peru, Sri Lanka, Sweden and Yugoslavia submitted a draft resolution entitled "Study on the naval arms race". In introducing it on 13 November, Sweden stated that it shared the belief of the Chairman of the Group of Experts that the study contained enough information to give a useful picture not only of naval forces and naval arms systems, but also of the resources of the sea and the vital importance they represented to the human race. By the draft, Member States would be invited to communicate their views on the study to the Secretary-General. He would then submit a compilation of their responses to the Disarmament Commission, which would be requested to consider the issues of the study in their entirety. The mainly procedural draft also contained a provision by which an item entitled "Naval armaments and disarmament" would be included in the provisional agenda of the General Assembly at its forty-first session.

On 18 November, the First Committee approved the draft by a recorded vote of 131 to 1 (United States), with 3 abstentions (Egypt, India and Israel).

In connection with the vote, four States that voted in favour explained their positions. Argentina considered that the study was a useful contribution to the analysis of an important subject which, in its view, had not thus far been duly considered by the United Nations. Argentina would transmit its views on the study to the Secretary-General, and it hoped that the deliberations of the Disarmament Commission would contribute to gathering the back ground information necessary to draw the attention of the Conference on Disarmament to the matter. Bulgaria recalled its general approach to the question of curbing the naval arms race, which basically consisted in taking practical steps to limit and reduce armaments and activities and to extend confidence-building measures to the seas and oceans, especially to areas with the busiest international sea lanes or to regions where the probability of conflict situations was high. In spite of some reservations regarding certain conclusions of the study, it had decided to support the draft resolution. While noting with satisfaction that many of its proposals regarding concrete measures for curbing naval activities and naval armaments had been reflected in the study, the Soviet Union could not agree with a number of points made in the document. It held that many of its arguments were unbalanced and that it contained unjustified attempts to blame the Soviet Union for the naval arms race. The Soviet Union further criticized the study for what it considered the tendentiousness and inaccuracy of its statistics, giving a distorted picture of the actual situation. In spite of such reservations, it supported the draft resolution because it felt that the consideration of the question of naval armaments in the Disarmament Commission could help to open up serious negotiations on the matter with the participation of all the major naval Powers and other interested States. The United Kingdom stated that it did not necessarily share all the views expressed on the subject. However, it believed that the resolution, which was supported by a broadly based group of countries, offered a generally acceptable and reasonable basis for work on the subject of naval issues by the Disarmament Commission.

India explained its abstention. It failed to understand the rationale for detaching a limited issue from the wider, central issues of the nuclear arms race and general and complete disarmament, on which no progress had been made. In its view, the draft tended to distort established priorities in the field of disarmament.

The United States explained its negative vote, stating that it was not engaged in a naval arms race. It felt that any study that focused on naval forces in isolation, ignoring the threats which made maritime forces necessary, would be skewed against those nations and groups of States with vital maritime interests that must be defended. It had opposed the resolution calling for the study and had not participated in it. It therefore did not support the draft, which would divert the Disarmament Commission's attention from more appropriate pursuits.

On 12 December,[18] the General Assembly adopted the draft resolution by a recorded vote of 146 to 1 (United States), with 3 abstentions (Grenada, India, St. Christopher and Nevis), as resolution 40/94 F. It reads as follows:

The General Assembly,

Recalling its resolution 38/188 G of 20 December 1983, by which it requested the Secretary-General, with the assistance of qualified governmental experts, to carry out a comprehensive study on the naval arms race,

Reaffirming its concern about the naval arms systems,

Having examined the report of the Secretary-General transmitting the study carried out by the Group of Governmental Experts to Carry Out a Comprehensive Study on the Naval Arms Race, Naval Forces and Naval Arms Systems,

    1.   *Takes note with satisfaction* of the study on the naval arms race;

    2.   *Expresses its appreciation* to the Secretary-General and to the Group of Governmental Experts to Carry Out a Comprehensive Study on the Naval Arms Race, Naval Forces and Naval Arms Systems which assisted him in preparation of the study;

    3.   *Commends* the study and its conclusions to the attention of all Member States;

    4.   *Invites* all Member States to inform the Secretary-General, no later than 5 April 1986, of their views concerning the study;

5.   *Requests* the Secretary-General to make the necessary arrangements for the reproduction of the study as a United Nations publication and to give it the widest possible distribution;

6.   *Requests* the Secretary-General to prepare for the Disarmament Commission at its substantive session in May 1986 a compilation of the views received from Member States regarding this issue;

7.   *Requests* the Disarmament Commission to consider, at its forthcoming session in 1986, the issues contained in the study on the naval arms race, both its substantive content and its conclusions, taking into account all other relevant present and future proposals, with a view to facilitating the identification of possible measures in the field of naval arms reductions and disarmament, pursued within the framework of progress towards general and complete disarmament, as well as confidence-building measures in this field, and to report on its deliberations and recommendations to the General Assembly at its forty-first session;

8.   *Decides* to include in the provisional agenda of its forty-first session an item entitled "Naval armaments and disarmament".

. . .

Notes

. . .

15.   A/40/535, annex. Subsequently, the study was issued as a United Nations publication, Sales No. E.86.IX.3.

16.   Official Records of the Third United Nations Conference on The Law of the Sea, vol. XVII, document A/CONF.62/122. For the text of the Convention, see The Law of the Sea: United Nations Convention on the Law of the Sea with Index and Final Act of the Third United Nations Conference on the Law of the Sea (United Nations publication, Sales No. E.83 V.5).

17.   Official Records of the General Assembly, Fortieth Session, First Committee, 3rd to 36th and 40th meetings, and ibid., Sessional Fascicle, corrigendum.

18.   Ibid., Plenary Meetings, 113th meeting.

. . .

- - - - -

UN Disarmament Commission   A/CN.10/102
Substantive Session, May 1987   Extract

Naval Armaments and Disarmament: Chairman's Paper on Agenda Item 8

1.   At its forty-first session, the General Assembly by resolution 41/59 K of 3 December 1986, entitled "Naval armaments and disarmaments", *inter alia*, requested the Disarmament Commission to continue, at its forthcoming session in 1987, the substantive consideration of the question and to report on its deliberations and recommendations to the General Assembly at its forty-second session.

2.   In its consideration of the item, the Commission had before it the following documents:

    (a)   Report of the Secretary-General containing the study on the naval arms race (A/40/535);

    (b)   Chairman's paper on agenda item 8 (A/CN.10/83);

    (c)   Working paper submitted by Finland (A/CN.10/90);

    (d)   Working paper submitted by Bulgaria, the German Democratic Republic and the Union of Soviet Socialist Republics (A/CN.10/92).

(e)   Working paper submitted by Sweden (A/CN.10/101).

3.   On 4 May 1987, the Disarmament Commission decided to follow last year's course of action and hold substantive and open-ended consultations on the subject. Pursuant to that decision, the Chairman delegated the actual conduct of the substantive and open-ended consultations to a "friend of the Chairman", *in casu*, the representative of Indonesia. The Consultation Group held seven meetings on the item.

4.   In the course of the consultations participants continued their consideration of various aspects of the question including the possibility of measures of naval arms limitation and disarmament, as well as the desirability of applying confidence-building measures at sea.

5.   Participants reaffirmed that the significant elements and principles that were identified in the paper arising from the consultations held in 1986 (A/CN.10/83) remained valid and provided a good basis for further consideration of the subject. It was acknowledged that, as stated in the Final Document of the Tenth Special Session, in the task of achieving the goals of nuclear disarmament, all nuclear-weapon States, in particular those among them which possess the most important nuclear arsenals, bore a special responsibility, and that States with the largest military arsenals also had a special responsibility in pursuing the process of conventional arms reductions: these principles were equally applicable to the naval dimension of the global arms race and related issues.

6.   It was recognized that, as stated in the Study on the Naval Arms Race, naval forces are not independent of other military forces and that they should be considered in their general military context. There is no such thing as an independent naval balance or parity. By the same token, the reduction of naval nuclear forces and naval non-nuclear forces falls within the framework of nuclear and conventional disarmament respectively, and therefore should follow the general approaches of nuclear and conventional disarmament efforts.

7.   There was widespread concurrence of view that, at this stage, confidence-building measures of various kinds, both in the global and the regional context, would be more amenable to further consideration and possible negotiation in the appropriate forums. It was recognized that a fundamental feature of the global maritime environment, both military and non-military, was freedom of navigation and that naval confidence-building measures should be in harmony with current law of the sea.

8.   In this regard, suggestions of initiatives that might be of relevance included: extension of existing confidence-building measures to seas and oceans especially to areas with the busiest sea-lanes; prior notification of naval activities; the invitation of observers to naval exercises or manoeuvres; limitations on the number or scale of naval exercises in specific regions; exchange of information on naval matters; greater openness on naval matters in general; and strict observance of existing maritime measures designed to build confidence.

9.   It was felt that the possibility should be pursued of negotiating a multilateral agreement concerning the prevention of incidents at sea beyond the territorial sea in addition to existing agreements. A multilateral agreement of this nature should be formulated in such a way as to respond to the needs of all interested nations for enhancing safety at sea without diminishing the traditional freedom of navigation.

10.   A number of participants highlighted the benefits to be derived from the maritime aspects of existing proposals for zones of peace in certain regions, together with recent developments such as the declaration by the General Assembly of a zone of peace and co-operation in the South Atlantic. The positions of participants on this issue were noted.

11.   Further discussion took place on the issue of the practicability of updating some of the existing laws of sea warfare. In this connection specific mention was made of the possibility of updating the Hague Convention VIII of 1907 on Laying of Automatic Submarine Contact Mines, and the possibility of further work on the development of international law concerning exclusion zones with particular reference to the safety of non-belligerent vessels engaged in peaceful maritime activities. It was noted that these issues need extensive consideration in the appropriate forums.

12.   In the consideration of possible measures, it was suggested that a useful way of categorizing such measures was by identifying the objectives or purposes that they would serve. In this regard such objectives as peacetime security, security for non-military activities at sea and seaboard security could well be achieved through effective and relevant confidence-building measures.

13.   It was recognized that the harmful effects that conflict at sea could have on the freedom of navigation and other uses of the sea, in accordance with current international law, for States neutral to or otherwise not involved in an ongoing conflict, have been amply demonstrated in recent years. The maintenance of freedom of navigation and other uses of the sea is an important objective for all States neutral to or otherwise not involved in such conflicts.

14.   The proliferation of nuclear weapons at sea, particularly the aspect of geographical dispersion of such weapons, has given rise to mounting concern on the part of many States. It was recognized that most strategic nuclear weapons are already the subject of certain bilateral negotiations. The view was expressed that early consideration should by given by States to effective measures of curtailing the numbers and deployment of tactical weapons at sea but some participants noted that such weapons could not be seen in isolation from the overall military balance.

15.   Participants felt that the subject of naval armaments and disarmament should continue to be the subject of further discussion by the Disarmament Commission at its next substantive session.

- - - - -

UN General Assembly   A/RES/42/38
Forty-second Session, 30 November 1987   Extract

Resolution 42/38.   General and complete disarmament

. . .

K

Naval armaments and disarmament

The General Assembly,

Recalling its resolution 38/188 G of 20 December 1983, by which it requested the Secretary-General, with the assistance of qualified governmental experts, to carry out a comprehensive study on the naval arms race,

Recalling its resolution 40/94 F of 12 December 1985, by which it requested the Disarmament Commission to consider the issues contained in the study on the arms race,[16] both its substantive content and its conclusion, taking into account all other relevant present and future proposals, with a view to facilitating the identification of possible measures in the field of naval arms reductions and disarmament, pursued within the framework of progress towards general and complete disarmament, as well as confidence-building measures in this field,

Recalling also its resolution 41/59 K of December 1986, by which it requested the Disarmament Commission to continue, at its forthcoming session in 1987, the substantive consideration of the question and to report on its deliberations and recommendations to the General Assembly at its forty-second session,

Having examined the report of the Chairman of the Disarmament Commission on the substantive consideration of the question of the naval arms race and disarmament during the 1987 session of the Commission,[17] which met with the approval of all delegations participating in the substantive consultations and which, in their view, could form the basis of further deliberations on the subject,

1.   *Notes with satisfaction* the report on the substantive consideration of the question of the naval arms race and disarmament by the Chairman of the Disarmament Commission;

2.   *Requests* the Disarmament Commission to continue, at its forthcoming session in 1988, the substantive consideration of the question and to report on its deliberations and recommendations to the General Assembly not later than at its forty-third session;

3.   *Also requests* the Disarmament Commission to inscribe on the agenda for its 1988 session the item entitled "Naval armaments and disarmament";

4.   *Decides* to include in the provisional agenda of its forty-third session the item entitled "Naval armaments and disarmament".

Notes

16.　A/40/535, annex. The study was subsequently issued with the title The Naval Arms Race (United Nations publication, Sales No. E.86.IX.3).
17.　A/CN.10/102.

- - - - -

Additional References

Study on the naval arms race. Replies from Governments. UN docs. A/CN.10/77 and Adds. 1, 2 and 3; A/CN.10/82.

Study on the naval arms race. Working Papers submitted by Governments: A/CN.10/78 (China); A/CN.10/80 (Bulgaria, German Democratic Republic and Union of Soviet Socialist Republics).

Substantive consideration of the question of naval arms race and disarmament. Chairman's Paper. UN doc. A/CN.10/83.

Naval armaments and disarmament. In UN resolution A/RES/41/59.

Naval armaments and disarmament. Working Papers submitted by Governments: A/CN.10/90 (Finland), A/CN.10/92 (Bulgaria, German Democratic Republic and Union of Soviet Socialist Republics), A/CN.10/101 (Sweden).

Status of multilateral disarmament agreements. Report of the Secretary-General. UN doc. A/41/644.

Consideration of Other Areas Dealing with the Cessation of the Arms Race and Disarmament and Other Relevant Measures. Report of the Conference on Disarmament, 1985 session, parag. 113. GAOR, 40th session, Suppl. No. 27 (A/40/27).

2

Nuclear-Free Zones & Zones of Peace

South Pacific Nuclear Free Zone Treaty and Related Protocols[1]

Preamble

The Parties to this Treaty,

United in their commitment to a world at peace;

Gravely concerned that the continuing nuclear arms race presents the risk of nuclear war which would have devastating consequences for all people;

Convinced that all countries have an obligation to make every effort to achieve the goal of eliminating nuclear weapons, the terror which they hold for humankind and the threat which they pose to life on earth;

Believing that regional arms control measures can contribute to global efforts to reverse the nuclear arms race and promote the national security of each country in the region and the common security of all;

Determined to ensure, so far as lies within their power, that the bounty and beauty of the land and sea in their region shall remain the heritage of their peoples and their descendants in perpetuity to be enjoyed by all in peace;

Reaffirming the importance of the Treaty on the Non-Proliferation of Nuclear Weapons (NPT) in preventing the proliferation of nuclear weapons and in contributing to world security;

Noting, in particular, that Article VII of the NPT recognizes the right of any group of States to conclude regional treaties in order to assure the total absence of nuclear weapons in their respective territories;

Noting that the prohibitions of emplantation and emplacement of nuclear weapons on the seabed and the ocean floor and in the subsoil thereof contained in the Treaty on the Prohibition of the Emplacement of Nuclear Weapons and Other Weapons of Mass Destruction on the Seabed and the Ocean Floor and in the Subsoil Thereof apply in the South Pacific;

Noting also that the prohibition of testing of nuclear weapons in the atmosphere or under water, including territorial waters or high seas, contained in the Treaty Banning Nuclear Weapon Tests in the Atmosphere, in Outer Space and Under Water applies in the South Pacific;

Determined to keep the region free of environmental pollution by radioactive wastes and other radioactive matter;

Guided by the decision of the Fifteenth South Pacific Forum at Tuvalu that a nuclear free zone should be established in the region at the earliest possible opportunity in accordance with the principles set out in the communiqué of that meeting;

Have agreed as follows:

Article 1
Usage of Terms

For the purpose of this Treaty and its Protocols:

(a) "South Pacific Nuclear Free Zone" means the areas described in Annex 1 as illustrated by the map attached to that Annex;

(b) "territory" means internal waters, territorial sea and archipelagic waters, the seabed and subsoil beneath, the land territory and the airspace above them;

(c) "nuclear explosive device" means any nuclear weapon or other explosive device capable of releasing nuclear energy, irrespective of the purpose for which it could be used. The term includes such a weapon or device in unassembled and partly assembled forms, but does not include the means of transport or delivery of such a weapon or device if separable from and not an indivisible part of it;

(d) "stationing" means emplantation, emplacement, transportation on land or inland waters, stockpiling, storage, installation and deployment.

Article 2
Application of the Treaty

1. Except where otherwise specified, this Treaty and its Protocols shall apply to territory within the South Pacific Nuclear Free Zone.

2. Nothing in this Treaty shall prejudice or in any way affect the rights, or the exercise of the rights, of any State under international law with regard to freedom of the seas.

Article 3
Renunciation of Nuclear Explosive Devices

Each Party undertakes:

(a) not to manufacture or otherwise acquire, possess or have control over any nuclear explosive device by any means anywhere inside or outside the South Pacific Nuclear Free Zone;

(b) not to seek or receive any assistance in the manufacture or acquisition of any nuclear explosive device by any State.

(c) not to take any action to assist or encourage the manufacture or acquisition of any nuclear explosive device by any State.

Article 4
Peaceful Nuclear Activities

Each Party undertakes:

(a)   not to provide source or special fissionable material, or equipment or material especially designed or prepared for the processing, use or production of special fissionable material for peaceful purposes to:

(i)   any non-nuclear-weapon State unless subject to the safeguards required by Article III.1 of the NPT, or

(ii)   any nuclear-weapon State unless subject to applicable safeguards agreement with the International Atomic Energy Agency (IAEA).

Any such provisions shall be in accordance with strict non-proliferation measures to provide assurance of exclusively peaceful non-explosive use;

(b)   to support the continued effectiveness of the international non-proliferation system based on the NPT and the IAEA safeguards systems.

Article 5
Prevention of Stationing of Nuclear Explosive Devices

1.   Each Party undertakes to prevent in its territory the stationing of any nuclear explosive device.

2.   Each Party in the exercise of its sovereign rights remains free to decided for itself whether to allow visits by foreign ships and aircraft to its ports and airfields, transit of its airspace by foreign aircraft, and navigation by foreign ships in its territorial sea or archipelagic waters in a manner not covered by the rights of innocent passage, archipelagic sea lane passage or transit passage of straits.

Article 6
Prevention of Testing of Nuclear Explosives Devices

Each Party undertakes:

(a)   to prevent in its territory the testing of any nuclear explosive device;

(b)   not to take any action to assist or encourage the testing of any nuclear explosive device by any State.

Article 7
Prevention of Dumping

1.   Each Party undertakes:

(a)   not to dump radioactive wastes and other radioactive matter at sea anywhere within the South Pacific Nuclear Free Zone;

(b)   to prevent the dumping of radioactive wastes and other radioactive matter by anyone in its territorial sea;

(c)   not to take any action to assist or encourage the dumping by anyone of radioactive wastes and other radioactive matter at sea anywhere within the South Pacific Nuclear Free Zone;

(d)   to support the conclusion as soon as possible of the proposed Convention relating to the protection of the natural resources and environment of the South Pacific region and its Protocol for the prevention of pollution of the South Pacific region by dumping, with the aim of precluding dumping at sea of radioactive wastes and other radioactive matter by anyone anywhere in the region.

2.   Paragraphs 1 (a) and 1 (b) of this Article shall not apply to areas of the South Pacific Nuclear Free Zone in respect of which such a Convention and Protocol have entered into force.

Article 8
Control System

1.   The Parties hereby establish a control system for the purpose of verifying compliance with their obligations under this Treaty.

2.   The control system shall comprise:

(a)   reports and exchange of information as provided for in Article 9;

(b)   consultations as provided for in Article 10 and Annex 4 (1);

(c)   the application to peaceful nuclear activities of safeguards by the IAEA as provided for in Annex 2;

(d)   a complaints procedure as provided for in Annex 4.

Article 9
Reports and Exchanges of Information

1.   Each Party shall report to the Director of the South Pacific Bureau for Economic Co-operation (the Director) as soon as possible any significant event within its jurisdiction affecting the implementation of this Treaty. The Director shall circulate such reports promptly to all Parties.

2.   The Parties shall endeavour to keep each other informed on matters arising under or in relation to the Treaty. They may exchange information by communicating it to the Director, who shall circulate it to all Parties.

3.   The Director shall report annually to the South Pacific Forum on the status of this Treaty and matters arising under or in relation to it, incorporating reports and communications made under paragraphs 1 and 2 of this Article and matters arising under Articles 8 (2) (d) and 10 and Annex 2 (4).

Article 10
Consultations and Review

Without prejudice to the conduct of consultations among Parties by other means, the Director, at the request of any Party, shall convene a meeting of the Consultative Committee established by Annex 3 for consultation and co-operation on any matter arising in relation to this Treaty or for reviewing its operation.

Article 11
Amendment

The Consultative Committee shall consider proposals for amendment of the provisions of this Treaty proposed by any Party and circulated by the Director to all Parties not less than three months prior to the convening of the Consultative Committee for this purpose. Any proposal agreed upon by consensus by the Consultative Committee shall be communicated to the Director who shall circulate it for acceptance to all Parties. An amendment shall enter into force thirty days after receipt by the depositary of acceptances from all Parties.

Article 12
Signature and Ratification

1.   This Treaty shall be open for signature by any Member of the South Pacific Forum.

2.   This Treaty shall be subject to ratification. Instruments of ratification shall be deposited with the Director who is hereby designated depositary of this Treaty and its Protocols.

3.   If a Member of the South Pacific Forum whose territory is outside the South Pacific Nuclear Free Zone becomes a Party to this Treaty, Annex 1 shall be deemed to be amended so far as is required to enclose at least the territory of that Party within the boundaries of the South Pacific Nuclear Free Zone. The delineation of any area added pursuant to this paragraph shall be approved by the South Pacific Forum.

Article 13
Withdrawal

1.   This Treaty is of a permanent nature and shall remain in force indefinitely, provided that in the event of a violation by any Party of a provision of this Treaty essential to the achievement of the objectives of the Treaty or of the spirit of the Treaty, every other Party shall have the right to withdraw from the Treaty.

2.   Withdrawal shall be effected by giving notice twelve months in advance to the Director who shall circulate such notice to all other Parties.

Article 14
Reservations

This Treaty shall not be subject to reservations.

Article 15
Entry into Force

1.   This Treaty shall enter into force on the date of deposit of the eighth instrument of ratification.

2.   For a signatory which ratifies this Treaty after the date of deposit of the eighth instrument of ratification, the Treaty shall enter into force on the date of deposit of its instrument of ratification.

Article 16
Depositary Functions

The depositary shall register this Treaty and its Protocols pursuant to Article 102 of the Charter of the United Nations and shall transmit certified copies of the Treaty and its Protocols to all Members of the South Pacific Forum and all States eligible to become Party to the Protocols to the Treaty and shall notify them of signatures and ratifications of the Treaty and its Protocols.

In witness whereof the undersigned, being duly authorized by their Governments, have signed this Treaty.

Done at Rarotonga, this sixth day of August, One thousand nine hundred and eighty-five, in a single original in the English language.

ANNEX 1

South Pacific Nuclear Free Zone

A.   The area bounded by a line:

(1)   commencing at the point of intersection of the Equator by the maritime boundary between Indonesia and Papua New Guinea;

(2)   running thence northerly along that maritime boundary to its intersection by the outer limit of the exclusive economic zone of Papua New Guinea;

(3)   thence generally north-easterly, easterly and south-easterly along that outer limit to its intersection by the Equator;

(4)   thence east along the Equator to its intersection by the meridian of Longitude 163 degrees East;

(5)   thence north along that meridian to its intersection by the parallel of Latitude 3 degrees North;

(6)   thence east along that parallel to its intersection by the meridian of Longitude 171 degrees East;

(7)   thence north along that meridian to its intersection by the parallel of Latitude 4 degrees North;

(8)   thence east along that parallel to its intersection by the meridian of Longitude 180 degrees East;

(9)   thence south along that meridian to its intersection by the Equator;

(10)   thence east along the Equator to its intersection by the meridian of Longitude 165 degrees West;

(11)   thence north along that meridian to its intersection by the meridian of Latitude 5 degrees 30 minutes North;

(12)   thence east along that parallel to its intersection by the meridian of Longitude 154 degrees West;

(13)   thence south along that meridian to its intersection by the Equator;

(14)   thence east along the Equator to its intersection by the meridian of Longitude 115 degrees West;

(15)   thence south along that meridian to its intersection by the parallel of Latitude 60 degrees South;

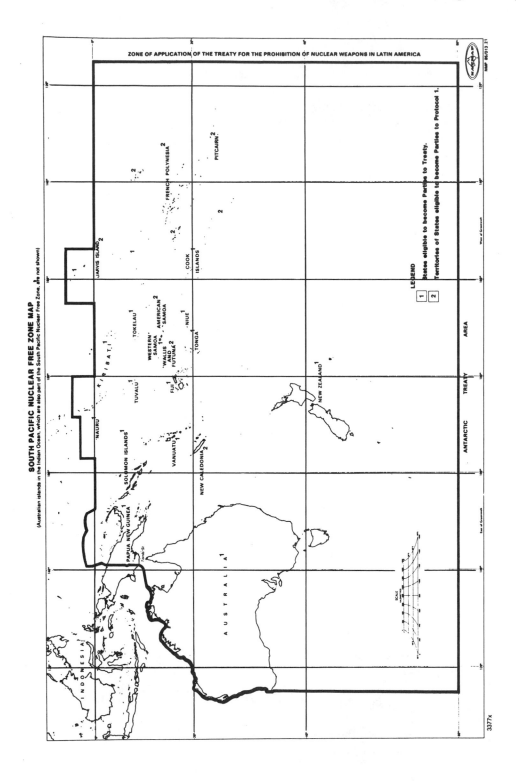

SOUTH PACIFIC NUCLEAR FREE ZONE MAP
(Australian islands in the Indian Ocean, which are also part of the South Pacific Nuclear Free Zone, are not shown)

ZONE OF APPLICATION OF THE TREATY FOR THE PROHIBITION OF NUCLEAR WEAPONS IN LATIN AMERICA

LEGEND

1 States eligible to become Parties to Treaty.

2 Territories of States eligible to become Parties to Protocol 1.

ANTARCTIC   TREATY   AREA

3377x

(16)   thence west along that parallel to its intersection by the meridian of Longitude 115 degrees West;

(17)   thence north along that meridian to its southernmost intersection by the outer limit of the territorial sea of Australia;

(18)   thence generally northerly and easterly along the outer limit of the territorial sea of Australia to its intersection by the meridian of Longitude 136 degrees 45 minutes East;

(19)   thence north-easterly along the geodesic to the point of Latitude 10 degrees 50 minutes South, Longitude 139 degrees 12 minutes East;

(20)   thence north-easterly along the maritime boundary between Indonesia and Papua New Guinea to where it joins the land border between those two countries;

(21)   thence generally northerly along that land border to where it joins the maritime boundary between Indonesia and Papua New Guinea, on the northern coastline of Papua New Guinea; and

(22)   thence generally northerly along that boundary to the point of commencement.

B.   The areas within the outer limits of the territorial seas of all Australian islands lying westward of the area described in paragraph A and north of Latitude 60 degrees South, provided that any such areas shall cease to be part of the South Pacific Nuclear Free Zone upon receipt by the depositary of written notice from the Government of Australia stating that the areas have become subject to another treaty having an object and purpose substantially the same as that of this Treaty.

ANNEX 2

IAEA Safeguards

1.   The safeguards referred to in Article 8 shall in respect of each Party be applied by the IAEA as set forth in an agreement negotiated and concluded with the IAEA on all source or special fissionable material in all peaceful nuclear activities within the territory of the Party, under its jurisdiction or carried out under its control anywhere.

2.   The agreement referred to in paragraph 1 shall be, or shall be equivalent in its scope and effect to, an agreement required in connection with the NPT on the basis of the material reproduced in document INFCIRC/153 (Corrected) of the IAEA. Each Party shall take all appropriate steps to ensure that such an agreement is in force for it not later than 18 months after the date of entry into force for that Party of this Treaty.

3.   For the purposes of this Treaty, the safeguards referred to in paragraph 1 shall have as their purpose the verification of the non-diversion of nuclear material from peaceful nuclear activities to nuclear explosive devices.

4.   Each Party agrees upon the request of any other Party to transmit to that Party and to the Director for the information of all Parties a copy of the overall conclusions of the most

recent report by the IAEA on its inspection activities in the territory of the Party concerned, and to advise the Director promptly of any subsequent findings of the Board of Governors of the IAEA in relation to those conclusions for the information of all Parties.

ANNEX 3

Consultative Committee

1.   There is hereby established a Consultative Committee which shall be convened by the Director from time to time pursuant to Articles 10 and 11 and Annex 4 (2). The Consultative Committee shall be constituted of representatives of the Parties, each Party being entitled to appoint one representative who may be accompanied by advisers. Unless otherwise agreed, the Consultative Committee shall be chaired at any given meeting by the representative of the Party which last hosted the meeting of Heads of Government of Members of the South Pacific Forum. A quorum shall be constituted by representatives of half the Parties.   Subject to the provisions of Article 11, decisions of the Consultative Committee shall be taken by consensus or, failing consensus, by a two-thirds majority of those present and voting. The Consultative Committee shall adopt such other rules of procedure as its sees fit.

2.   The costs of the Consultative Committee, including the costs of special inspections pursuant to Annex 4, shall be borne by the South Pacific Bureau for Economic Co-operation. It may seek special funding should this be required.

ANNEX 4

Complaints procedure

1.   A Party which considers that there are grounds for a complaint that another Party is in breach of its obligations under this Treaty shall, before bringing such a complaint to the Director, bring the subject matter of the complaint to the attention of the Party complained of and shall allow the latter reasonable opportunity to provide it with an explanation and to resolve the matter.

2.   If the matter is not resolved, the complaint Party may bring the complaint to the Director with a request that the Consultative Committee be convened to consider it. Complaints shall be supported by an account of evidence of breach of obligations known to the complainant Party. Upon receipt of a complaint the Director shall convene the Consultative Committee as quickly as possible to consider it.

3.   The Consultative Committee, taking account of efforts made under paragraph 1, shall afford the Party complained of a reasonable opportunity to provide it with an explanation of the matter.

4.   If, after considering any explanation given to it by the representatives of the Party complained of, the Consultative Committee decides that there is sufficient substance in the complaint to warrant a special inspection in the territory of that Party or elsewhere, the Consultative Committee shall direct that such special inspection be made as quickly as possible by a special inspection team of three suitably qualified special inspectors appointed by the

Consultative Committee in consultation with the complained of and complainant Parties, provided that no national of either Party shall serve on the special inspection team. If so requested by the Party complained of, the special inspection team shall be accompanied by representatives of that Party. Neither the right of consultation on the appointment of special inspectors, nor the right to accompany special inspectors, shall delay the work of the special inspection team.

5.   In making a special inspection, special inspectors shall be subject to the direction only of the Consultative Committee and shall comply with such directives concerning tasks, objectives, confidentiality and procedures as may be decided upon by it. Directives shall take account of the legitimate interests of the Party complained of in complying with its other international obligations and commitments and shall not duplicate safeguards procedures to be undertaken by the IAEA pursuant to agreements referred to in Annex 2 (1). The special inspectors shall discharge their duties with due respect for the laws of the Party complained of.

6.   Each Party shall give to special inspectors full and free access to all information and places within its territory which may be relevant to enable the special inspectors to implement the directives given to them by the Consultative Committee.

7.   The Party complained of shall take all appropriate steps to facilitate the special inspection, and shall grant to special inspectors privileges and immunities necessary for the performance of their functions, including inviolability for all papers and documents and immunity from arrest, detention and legal process for acts done and words spoken and written, for the purpose of the special inspection.

8.   The special inspectors shall report in writing as quickly as possible to the Consultative Committee, outlining their activities, setting out relevant facts and information as ascertained by them, with supporting evidence and documentation as appropriate, and stating their conclusions. The Consultative Committee shall report fully to all Members of the South Pacific Forum, giving its decisions as to whether the Party complained of is in breach of its obligations under this Treaty.

9.   If the Consultative Committee has decided that the Party complained of is in breach of its obligations under this Treaty, or that the above provisions have not been complied with, or at any time at the request of either the complainant or complained of Party, the Parties shall meet promptly at a meeting of the South Pacific Forum.

- - - - -

PROTOCOL 1

The Parties to this Protocol,
Noting the South Pacific Nuclear Free Zone Treaty (the Treaty),
Have Agreed as follows:

Article 1

Each Party undertakes to apply, in respect of the territories for which it is internationally responsible situated within the South Pacific Nuclear Free Zone, the prohibitions contained in Articles 3, 5 and 6, insofar as they relate to the manufacture, stationing and testing of any nuclear explosive device within those territories, and the safeguards specified in Article 8(2)(c) and Annex 2 of the Treaty.

Article 2

Each Party may, by written notification to the depositary, indicate its acceptance from the date of such notification of any alteration to its obligation under this Protocol brought about by the entry into force of an amendment to the Treaty pursuant to Article 11 of the Treaty.

Article 3

This Protocol shall be open for signature by the French Republic, the United Kingdom of Great Britain and Northern Ireland and the United States of America.

Article 4

This Protocol shall be subject to ratification.

Article 5

This Protocol is of a permanent nature and shall remain in force indefinitely, provided that each Party shall, in exercising its national sovereignty, have the right to withdraw from this Protocol if it decides that extraordinary events, related to the subject matter of this Protocol, have jeopardised its supreme interests.   It shall give notice of such withdrawal to the depositary three months in advance. Such notice shall include a statement of the extraordinary events it regards as having jeopardised its supreme interests.

Article 6

This Protocol shall enter into force for each State on the date of its deposit with the depositary of its instrument of ratification.

In Witness Whereof the undersigned, being duly authorised by their Governments, have signed this Protocol.

Done at *Suva*, this Eighth day of August, One thousand nine hundred and eighty-six, in a single original in the English language.

- - - - -

PROTOCOL 2

The Parties to this Protocol,
Noting the South Pacific Nuclear Free Zone Treaty (the Treaty),
Have Agreed as follows:

Article 1

Each Party undertakes not to use or threaten to use any nuclear explosive device against:

(a)   Parties to the Treaty; or

(b)   any territory within the South Pacific Nuclear Free Zone for which a State that has become a Party to Protocol 1 is internationally responsible.

Article 2

Each Party undertakes not to contribute to any act of a Party to the Treaty which constitutes a violation of the Treaty, or to any act of another Party to a Protocol which constitutes a violation of a Protocol.

Article 3

Each Party may, by written notification to the depositary, indicate its acceptance from the date of such notification of any alteration to its obligation under this Protocol brought about by the entry into force of an amendment to the Treaty pursuant to Article 11 of the Treaty or by extension of the South Pacific Nuclear Free Zone pursuant to Article 12(3) of the Treaty.

Article 4

This Protocol shall be open for signature by the French Republic, the People's Republic of China, the Union of Soviet Socialist Republics, the United Kingdom of Great Britain and Northern Ireland and the United States of America.

Article 5

This Protocol shall be subject to ratification.

Article 6

This Protocol is of a permanent nature and shall remain in force indefinitely, provided that each Party shall, in exercising its national sovereignty, have the right to withdraw from this Protocol if it decides that extraordinary events, related to the subject matter of this Protocol, have jeopardised its supreme interests.   It shall give notice of such withdrawal to the depositary three months in advance. Such notice shall include a statement of the extraordinary events it regards as having jeopardised its supreme interests.

Article 7

This Protocol shall enter into force for each State on the date of its deposit with the depositary of its instrument of ratification.

In Witness Whereof the undersigned, being duly authorised by their Governments, have signed this Protocol.

Done at *Suva*, this Eighth day of August, One thousand nine hundred and eighty-six, in a single original in the English language.

- - - - -

PROTOCOL 3

The Parties to this Protocol,
Noting the South Pacific Nuclear Free Zone Treaty (the Treaty),
Have Agreed as follows:

Article 1

Each Party undertakes not to test any nuclear explosive device anywhere within the South Pacific Nuclear Free Zone.

Article 2

Each Party may, by written notification to the depositary, indicate its acceptance from the date of such notification of any alteration to its obligation under this Protocol brought about by the entry into force of an amendment to the Treaty pursuant to Article 11 of the Treaty or by extension of the South Pacific Nuclear Free Zone pursuant to Article 12(3) of the Treaty.

Article 3

This Protocol shall be open for signature by the French Republic, the People's Republic of China, the Union of Soviet Socialist Republics, the United Kingdom of Great Britain and Northern Ireland and the United States of America.

Article 4

This Protocol shall be subject to ratification.

Article 5

This Protocol is of a permanent nature and shall remain in force indefinitely, provided that each Party shall, in exercising its national sovereignty, have the right to withdraw from this Protocol if it decides that extraordinary events, related to the subject matter of this Protocol, have jeopardised its supreme interests.   It shall give notice of such withdrawal to the depositary three months in advance. Such notice shall include a statement of the extraordinary events it regards as having jeopardised its supreme interests.

Article 6

This Protocol shall enter into force for each State on the date of its deposit with the depositary of its instrument of ratification.

In Witness Whereof the undersigned, being duly authorised by their Governments, have signed this Protocol.

Done at *Suva*, this Eighth day of August, One thousand nine hundred and eighty-six, in a single original in the English language.

Notes

1. Text submitted to the Conference on Disarmament and reproduced in its report, Official Records of the General Assembly, Fortieth Session, Supplement No. 27 (A/40/27 and Corr.1), appendix II (CD/642), vol IV, document CD/633 and Corr.1.

- - - - -

Sixteenth South Pacific Forum   A/40/672-S/17488
Rarotonga, Cook Islands, August 1985   Extract

Forum Communiqué

. . .

2.   The main issues discussed were as follows:

. . .

REGIONAL NUCLEAR MATTERS

South Pacific Nuclear-Free Zone Treaty

15.   The Forum considered the report of the Chairman of the Working Group of officials on a South Pacific Nuclear-Free Zone and the agreed text of a draft South Pacific Nuclear-Free Zone Treaty annexed to the report. It was noted that the draft Treaty incorporated all the principles on a South Pacific Nuclear-Free Zone adopted by the Fifteenth Forum in Tuvalu. The Forum endorsed the text of the Treaty produced by the Working Group and opened it for signature at the Forum by those countries in a position to do so, it being understood by the Forum that some countries would not be in a position to sign the Treaty, at least until they had subjected it to their normal constitutional processes. Heads of Government of Australia, Cook Islands, Fiji, Kiribati, New Zealand, Niue, Tuvalu and Western Samoa signed the Treaty.

16.   The Forum also considered the three draft Protocols to the SPNFZ Treaty. Since the Protocols involve countries outside the region it was agreed that consultations should be held with all the countries eligible to sign the Protocols before they were finalized. The Forum commissioned the Working Group on a South Pacific Nuclear-Free Zone to organize these consultations and to make recommendations to Forum leaders concerning the adoption of the Protocols at the next meeting of the Forum in 1986 or earlier if practicable.

17.   The Forum observed that endorsement of the South Pacific Nuclear-Free Zone Treaty, which would establish only the second nuclear-weapon-free zone in a permanently inhabited area, reflected the deep concern of all Forum members at the continuing nuclear-arms race and the risk of nuclear war. In this context, the Forum welcomed the resumption of arms control talks between the super-Powers and expressed its hope that these talks would achieve their declared objective of a reduction in nuclear weapons and to their eventual elimination as well as to the prevention of an arms race in space. The Forum also noted that the Third Review Conference of the Nuclear Non-Proliferation Treaty would be held at Geneva from 27 August to 24 September 1985 and that the South Pacific Nuclear-Free Zone Treaty is in accordance with article VII of the Non-Proliferation Treaty concerning regional arrangements to ensure the absence of nuclear weapons. The Forum agreed that the Review Conference be informed of the progress made on the establishment of the zone.

18.   The Forum expressed support for Australia's initiative at the Review Conference to require that application of full scope International Atomic Energy Agency safeguards to all nuclear exports to non-nuclear-weapon States and noted that the initiative was fully consistent with article 4 of the Zone Treaty. The Forum affirmed its support for the NPT as the most important means of preventing the spread of nuclear weapons to additional countries.

19.   Forum leaders noted that the southern boundary to which the South Pacific Nuclear-Free Zone will apply is the area governed by the Antarctic Treaty which provides for the Antarctic to remain demilitarized, free of nuclear weapons, for there to be a ban on nuclear testing and the disposal of nuclear wastes.   Interest was expressed in the continued viability of the Antarctic Treaty system which complemented in an adjacent area their own efforts to establish a South Pacific Nuclear-Free Zone.

. . .

Dumping of radioactive waste

21.   The Forum reaffirmed its strong opposition to the dumping of radioactive waste in the oceans of the region.   Forum members were committed to the early conclusion of the Convention and Protocols being negotiated under the auspices of the South Pacific Regional Environment Program (SPREP) which would, among other things, preclude the dumping at sea of radioactive waste in the region.   The Forum noted that this commitment was also enshrined in the South Pacific Nuclear-Free Zone Treaty.

22.   The Forum welcomed the statement by the Prime Minister of Japan that Japan had no intention of dumping radioactive waste in the Pacific Ocean in disregard of the concern expressed by the communities of the region.

23.   The Forum considered further the proposal, made by Nauru at the Fifteenth Forum at Tuvalu, to strengthen the London Dumping Convention including the report of the Chairman of the South Pacific Nuclear-Free Zone Working Group recording the Working Group's consideration of the Nauru proposal.

24.   The Forum noted that the next meeting of parties would take place from 23 to 27 September 1985.   In the light of their shared opposition to radioactive waste dumping at sea, it was agreed that those Forum members participating in the London Dumping Convention Meeting would consult closely about approaches to this issue at that meeting.   It was recognized that it would be desirable to achieve a common approach. The advantages were noted of having additional Forum members adhere to the London Dumping Convention, so as to increase the number of parties to that Convention which shared South Pacific regional concerns.

- - - - -

Seventeenth South Pacific Forum
Suva, Fiji, 8-11 August 1986   Extract

Forum Communiqué

. . .

South Pacific Nuclear Free Zone

14.   The Forum recalled that it had endorsed the text of the Treaty and opened it for signature on 6 August 1985 in Rarotonga.   It was noted that ten Forum Members had now

signed the Treaty and four had already ratified it. The Forum was pleased with the favourable international reaction to the conclusion of the Treaty and looked forward to the Treaty coming into force in the near future when eight instruments of ratification had been lodged. The Forum reiterated its view that the Treaty was a significant addition to the existing arms control and disarmament régime and would make an important contribution to protecting the region's favourable security environment.

15.   The Forum finalized the Protocols to the Treaty and agreed that they should be opened for signature when the Treaty came into force or on 1 December 1986, whichever came first. It further agreed that if at any future time the Forum decided to amend the Treaty in ways that might affect the obligations of States that had signed the Protocols the Forum would, at the appropriate time, consult with the States concerned. The Forum also agreed to the inclusion of a specific withdrawal clause to enable signatories to the Protocols to withdraw in the event of any unforeseen circumstances arising which would jeopardize their national interests.

16.   The Forum agreed that the deeply-felt concerns and aspirations of all its Members in regard to the acquisition, stationing and testing of nuclear weapons and the dumping at sea of nuclear waste were addressed in the Treaty of Rarotonga. It expressed the strong hope that the States eligible to sign the Protocols would acknowledge these concerns and aspirations and adhere to the Protocols when they were opened for signature. The Forum noted with pleasure that some States eligible to sign the Protocols had already indicated that signature would receive prompt and favourable consideration.

. . .

- - - - -

UN General Assembly   A/RES/41/11
Forty-first Session

Resolution 41/11.   Declaration of a zone of peace and co-operation of the South Atlantic

The General Assembly,

Conscious of the determination of the peoples of the States of the South Atlantic region to preserve their independence, sovereignty and territorial integrity and to preserve their relations under conditions of peace and liberty,

Convinced of the importance of promoting peace and co-operation in the South Atlantic for the benefit of all mankind and, in particular, of the peoples of the region,

Convinced further of the need to preserve the region from measures of militarization, the arms race, the presence of foreign military bases and, above all, nuclear weapons,

Recognizing the special interest and responsibility of the States of the region to promote regional co-operation for economic development and peace,

Fully conscious that the independence of Namibia and the elimination of the fascist régime of **apartheid** are conditions essential to guaranteeing the peace and security of the South Atlantic,

Recalling the principles and norms of international law applicable to ocean space, in particular the principle of the peaceful uses of the oceans,

Convinced that the establishment of a zone of peace and co-operation in the South Atlantic would contribute significantly to the strengthening of international peace and security and to promoting the principles and purposes of the United Nations,

1.   *Solemnly declares* the Atlantic Ocean, in the region situated between Africa and South America, a "Zone of peace and co-operation of the South Atlantic";

2.   *Calls upon* all States of the zone of the South Atlantic to promote further regional co-operation, *inter alia*, for social and economic development, the protection of the environment, the conservation of living resources and the peace and security of the whole region;

3.   *Calls upon* all States of all other regions, in particular the militarily significant States, scrupulously to respect the region of the South Atlantic as a zone of peace and co-operation, especially through the reduction and eventual elimination of their military presence there, the non-introduction of nuclear weapons or other weapons of mass destruction and the non-extension into the region of rivalries and conflicts that are foreign to it;

4.   *Calls upon* all States of the region and of all other regions to co-operate in the elimination of all sources of tension in the zone, to respect the national unity, sovereignty, political independence and territorial integrity of every State therein, to refrain from the threat or use of force, and to observe strictly the principle that the territory of a State shall not be the object of military occupation resulting from the use of force in violation of the Charter of the United Nations, as well as the principle that the acquisition of territories by force is inadmissible;

5.   *Reaffirms* that the elimination of **apartheid** and the attainment of self-determination and independence by the people of Namibia, as well as the cessation of all acts of aggression and subversion against States in the zone, are essential for peace and security in the South Atlantic region, and urges the implementation of all United Nations resolutions pertaining to colonialism, racism and **apartheid**;

6.   *Requests* the Secretary-General to submit to the General Assembly at its forty-second session a report on the situation in the South Atlantic and the implementation of the present declaration, taking into account the views expressed by Member States;

7.   *Decides* to include in the provisional agenda of its forty-second session the item entitled "Zone of peace and co-operation of the South Atlantic".

50th plenary meeting
27 October 1986

- - - - -

Additional References

Zone of peace and co-operation of the South Atlantic.   General Assembly resolution A/RES/42/16.

Implementation of the declaration of the Indian Ocean as a zone of peace. UN resolutions A/RES/41/87 and A/RES/42/43.

Strengthening of security and co-operation in the Mediterranean region. UN doc. A/41/486 and resolutions A/RES/41/89 and A/RES/42/90.

- - - - -

IX

LAND - LOCKED STATES

Land-Locked States

Third ACP-EEC Convention
Lomé, 8 December 1984

Extract

. . .

TITLE V

*General provisions for the least-developed, landlocked
and island ACP States
Article 255*

Special attention shall be paid to the least-developed, land-locked and island ACP States and the specific needs and problems of each of these three groups of countries in order to enable them to take full advantage of the opportunities offered by this Convention.

In this spirit, the following Articles contain specific provisions and adjustments to the general provisions applicable to all ACP States, with details of derogations from such provisions in different fields.

CHAPTER 1

*Least-developed ACP States
Article 256*

The least-developed ACP States shall be accorded special treatment in order to enable them to overcome the serious economic and social difficulties hindering their development.

Article 257

1.   The following shall be considered least-developed ACP States for the purposes of this Convention:

Antigua and Barbuda, Belize, Benin, Botswana, Burkina Faso, Burundi, Cape Verde, Central African Republic, Chad, Comoros, Djibouti, Dominica, Equatorial Guinea, Ethiopia, Gambia, Grenada, Guinea, Guinea-Bissau, Kiribati, Lesotho, Malawi, Mali, Mauritania, Mozambique, Niger, Rwanda, Saint Christopher and Nevis, Saint Lucia, Saint Vincent and the Grenadines, Sao Tomé and Principe, Seychelles, Sierra Leone, Solomon Islands, Somalia, Sudan, Swaziland, Tanzania, Togo, Tonga, Tuvalu, Uganda, Vanuatu, Western Samoa.

2.   The list of least-developed ACP States may be amended by decision of the Council of Ministers where:

-     a third State in a comparable situation accedes to this Convention;

- the economic situation of an ACP State undergoes a significant and lasting change, either so as to necessitate its inclusion in the category of least-developed ACP States or so that its inclusion in that category is no longer warranted.

Article 258

The provisions laid down pursuant to Article 256 in respect of the least-developed ACP States are contained in the following Articles:

- Agricultural co-operation and food security: Article 36 first indent, Article 37(3)
- Industrial development: Article 74 second and third paragraph
- Transport and communications: Article 93
- Development of trade and services: Article 96(3)
- Regional co-operation: Article 111
- General trade arrangements: Article 142
- Stabilization of export earnings from agricultural commodities: Article 155(2) and 3(c), Article 161(2), Article 162(2), Article 172
- Mining products: special financing facility (Sysmin): Article 180, Article 184
- Financial and technical co-operation: Article 185 under (i), Article 188(2)(c), Article 190(2) second indent, Article 196(2)(c), Article 197(11), Article 201(4), Article 219(6)
- Investment: Article 246
- Rules of origin: Protocol 1: Articles 29 and 30(4) and (8)(a).

CHAPTER 2

Landlocked ACP States
Article 259

Specific provisions and measures shall be established to support landlocked ACP States in their efforts to overcome the geographical difficulties and obstacles hampering their development.

Article 260

1. The landlocked ACP States are:

Botswana, Burkina Faso, Burundi, Central African Republic, Chad, Lesotho, Malawi, Mali, Niger, Rwanda, Swaziland, Uganda, Zambia, Zimbabwe.

2. The list of landlocked ACP States may be amended by decision of the Council of Ministers where a third State in a comparable situation accedes to this Convention.

Article 261

The provisions laid down pursuant to Article 259 in respect of the landlocked ACP States are contained in the following Articles:

- Agricultural co-operation and food security: Article 36 second indent
- Industrial development: Article 74 second paragraph
- Transport and communications: Article 93

- Development of trade and services: Article 96(3)
- Regional co-operation: Article 111
- General trade arrangements: Article 142
- Stabilization of export earnings from agricultural commodities: Article 155(2) and (3)(c), Article 161(2), Article 162(2)
- Mining products: special financing facility (Sysmin): Article 180
- Financial and technical co-operation: Article 185 under (i), Article 190(2) second indent, Article 197(11)
- Investment: Article 246

CHAPTER 3

Island ACP States
Article 262

Specific provisions and measures shall be established to support island ACP States in their efforts to overcome the specific natural and geographical difficulties and obstacles, such as their fragmentation and the consequences of natural disasters, hampering their development.

Article 263

1. The island ACP States are:

Antigua and Barbuda, Bahamas, Barbados, Cape Verde, Comoros, Dominica, Fiji, Grenada, Jamaica, Kiribati, Madagascar, Mauritius, Papua New Guinea, Saint Christopher and Nevis, Saint Lucia, Saint Vincent and the Grenadines, Sao Tomé and Principe, Seychelles, Solomon Islands, Tonga, Trinidad and Tobago, Tuvalu, Vanuatu, Western Samoa.

2. The list of island ACP States may be amended by decision of the Council of Ministers where a third State in a comparable situation accedes to this Convention.

Article 264

The provisions laid down pursuant to Article 262 in respect of the island ACP States are contained in the following Articles:

- Agricultural co-operation and food security: Article 36, third indent
- Industrial development: Article 74 second paragraph
- Transport and communications: Article 93
- Development of trade and services: Article 96(3)
- Regional co-operation: Article 111
- General trade arrangements: Article 142
- Stabilization of export earnings from agricultural commodities: Article 155(2), Article 161(2), Article 162(2)
- Mining products: special financing facility (Sysmin): Article 180
- Financial and technical co-operation: Article 185 under (i), Article 190(2) second indent, Article 197(11)
- Investment: Article 246

. . .

- - - - -

UNCTAD Trade and Development Board   TD/B/1107
33rd Session, September 1986   Extract

Progress in the Implementation of Specific Action Related to the Particular Needs and Problems of Land-Locked Countries
Report by the UNCTAD Secretariat

. . .

Chapter I. OVERALL ASSESSMENT OF THE SPECIFIC ACTIONS TAKEN IN FAVOUR OF LAND-LOCKED DEVELOPING COUNTRIES

. . .

8.   Donor countries and institutions should make more deliberate efforts to address themselves to the transit-transport problem in their overall assistance programmes. This can be most effectively accomplished by giving greater direct support in critical areas related to the transit-transport sector. These include the development and maintenance of transit-transport infrastructure and services, the improvement of management practices in transit-transport operations, training, the simplification of customs and trade procedures and strengthening of institutions in the transit-transport sector.

9.   Land-locked countries and their transit neighbours will need to be fully committed in their efforts to establish bilateral and subregional, legal institutional and administrative mechanisms to regulate the smooth flow of transit cargo. These commitments are indeed reflected in the programme of activities related to transport and communications in the SADCC group of countries and in the Northern Corridor Agreement recently signed by Burundi, Kenya, Rwanda and Uganda. To help implement such efforts effectively much more financial and technical assistance would be needed.

. . .

- - - - -

Meeting of the Co-ordinating Bureau of the   A/41/341 - S/18065
Movement of Non-Aligned Countries, April 1986   Extract

. . .

Annex II Economic Declaration

. . .

XXIV. LAND-LOCKED DEVELOPING COUNTRIES

141.   The Ministers recalled earlier appropriate decisions of the Non-Aligned Movement in respect of land-locked developing countries and affirmed that these should be implemented urgently in order to ensure their right of free access to and from the sea and freedom of transit, as provided for in article 125 of the United Nations Convention on the Law of the Sea, and in order to provide for necessary international assistance to meet their special needs. They further recognized that the right of access to and from the sea and freedom of transit

should be realized in compliance with sub-articles 2 and 3 of article 125 of the United Nations Convention on the Law of the Sea so that any programme or action in respect of such transit facilities should be undertaken in consultation with, and with the approval of, the transit country concerned.

. . .

- - - - -

UNCTAD

TD/B/1120
UN Sales No.E.86.II.D.7
Extract

The Least Developed Countries 1986
Report by the UNCTAD Secretariat

. . .

Special problems of land-locked least developed countries

Sixteen out of 37 LDCs are land-locked and face additional transport bottlenecks in their international trade. The distances from the principal towns in LDCs to the main ports vary from 670 km to 2,690 km (see table 15). The international trade of these countries is dependent on the transit-transport infrastructures and services along the transit routes. The land-locked countries have little control, however, over the development and operations of such facilities within their transit neighbours. Furthermore, the latters' ability to improve, from their own resources, the transit-transport infrastructures and services in the ports and along the transit corridors is very limited because many of them are themselves developing countries. This underscores the need for international support in the development of the transit-transport systems in developing countries.

UNCTAD studies have indicated that transport costs (which include storage costs along the transit routes, insurance costs, costs due to extra documentation, etc.) in the international trade of land-locked countries are in many cases very significant because of the inadequacy of the facilities available. In 1982, freight costs as a percentage of the value of imports for land-locked countries constituted about 15.7 per cent as compared to 10.7 per cent of all developing countries. These high transportation costs reduce export earnings and increase import costs. In order to lessen these additional transport costs, land-locked countries will have to further promote co-operative arrangements with their transit neighbours with the aim of establishing a more efficient transit-transport system by, among other means, improving management practices in the movement of transit cargo along the transit corridors and in the ports, and harmonizing procedures and technical standards for the smooth inter-state movement of commercial road transport vehicles and trains.

. . .

- - - - -

UN General Assembly   A/42/537
Forty-second Session   30 September 1987
                                                                     Extract

Development and International Economic Co-operation: Trade and Development

Progress in the implementation of specific action related to the
particular needs and problems of the land-locked developing countries
Note by the Secretary-General

. . .

I. SALIENT FEATURES OF THE CURRENT TRANSIT-TRANSPORT SITUATION

A. The transit corridor systems[a]

1.   The fact that overseas trade plays an important role in the trade pattern of developing countries in general and that land-locked developing countries have no access to the sea and are remotely situated from world markets implies that such countries are faced with an additional challenge in their development efforts.   Indeed, this challenge constitutes a particularly heavy burden because of the limited resource base of these countries, most of which are also least developed. Although the transit countries share the burden of developing and maintaining viable transit corridors, their resource capabilities are limited since most of them are also developing countries.   Hence, it is important that the donor countries and institutions pay special attention to the particular needs and problems of land-locked developing countries within their assistance programmes.

2.   The problems facing land-locked developing countries have been accentuated during recent years by the external shocks associated with the deterioration of the world economic situation.   Furthermore, most of the land-locked developing countries are situated in the African region, where natural disasters have crippled economies that are already highly vulnerable. Land-locked developing countries and their transit neighbours have therefore not only had a limited capacity to expand the network of transit corridor systems but have also failed to maintain existing facilities.

3.   The impact of these developments on the various corridors serving land-locked developing countries varies by region and subregion. This is a reflection of a number of factors.

(a)   The degree of remoteness of the land-locked developing countries from the ocean ports

Although all land-locked developing countries lack proprietary or sovereign access to the ocean, an overview of the transit corridors currently in use reveals wide variations in their distances from world markets. For example, the port nearest to the capital city or major commercial centre of Bolivia, the Lao People's Democratic Republic, Malawi, Swaziland and Zimbabwe is less than 750 kilometres away, whereas in the case of Afghanistan, Burundi, the

Central African Republic, Chad, Paraguay, Uganda and Zambia, the corridor distance is at least 1,130 kilometres (see appendix, table 1).

(b) Physical structure of the transit-transport network

The degree of segmentation varies in the routes linking the ocean ports and the internal destinations in the land-locked developing countries. Some of the rail corridors are linked to the interior destinations only by road or water. This necessitates trans-shipments *en route*, which results in long delays and damage to cargo. The main transit corridors of Bhutan, Burundi, the Central African Republic, Chad, the Lao People's Democratic Republic, Niger and Rwanda are rail/road, rail/water or road/water/rail routes (see appendix, table 1,).

(c) Relative importance of the transit traffic in the total cargo being handled in the transit ports

In the past, the transit corridors linking Malawi, Zambia and Zimbabwe with the Mozambican ports of Beira and Maputo, for example, had a relatively good record of efficiency since the service industry related to the movement of transit cargo from these land-locked States generated considerable revenue for the Mozambican economy. By contrast, the transit cargo of such countries as Bhutan and Nepal makes up a very minor portion of the cargo moving through the Indian port of Calcutta. This has an influence on the decisions to undertake special measures to meet the requirements for moving and handling transit traffic.

(d) Historical ties between land-locked developing countries and their transit neighbours

The development of the transit corridors linking the Sahelian land-locked countries in the west and central African subregion with the coastal States previously administered by France benefited from the fact that these corridors served common commercial and political interests during the colonial era. Similarly, the transit corridor linking Uganda and Kenya had, during the colonial period and briefly after independence, jointly owned and administered transit-transport infrastructure systems and services. Recent acute shortfalls in resources, combined with the overall economic mismanagement during the 1970s in Uganda, have decreased the efficiency of transit-transport operations in these subregions.

(e) Availability of alternative routes

Although many land-locked developing countries have several potential routes to ocean ports, in practice most of them are heavily dependent on one main route because of limited resources to develop and maintain alternative outlets.[b] This situation has rendered many of the land-locked developing countries highly vulnerable to disruptions of transit routes resulting from technical breakdowns, natural disasters, labour disputes, political upheavals or international conflicts. The emergence of monopolies - with their high transit cost implications - is an additional risk of heavy dependence on one outlet. For example, the main corridor linking Rwanda to the port of Mombasa in Kenya was interrupted on several occasions following political unrest in Uganda during the late 1970s and early 1980s. Rwanda was compelled for some considerable time to airlift part of its cargo to and from Mombasa. More recently, Rwanda began using a new corridor via Lake Victoria to Mombasa. Although it is a high-cost road/water/rail route, whose physical infrastructure is underdeveloped, it is a vital "insurance route". Another route linking Rwanda with the Tanzanian rail system, which provides access to the port of Dar-es-Salaam, is being developed. Malawi has also had to divert some of its transit cargo from the traditional corridor, the Mozambican ports of Beira and Nacala, to the port of Dar-es-Salaam following political disturbances in Mozambique. At present, countries in the southern African subregion are examining the feasibility of diverting all transit cargo from the routes through South Africa to the east African ports of Dar-es-Salaam and Mombasa should South Africa close its borders in retaliation for sanctions by the international community.

B. Summary of current key bottle-necks along the transit corridors

4.   Over the past few years, the United Nations Conference on Trade and Development (UNCTAD) has been carrying out three subregional transit-transport technical assistance projects in Africa and one regional project in Asia with the aim of alleviating operational problems along the transit corridors and helping to speed up the movement of transit cargo at a minimum cost (see paras. 44 and 45 below). In spite of these efforts, there are areas where increased assistance is still urgently required.

(a)   Shortages of experienced and skilled manpower

This problem affects the operational efficiency of the whole transit-transport system. Although the problem is most serious in the ports, railway and road transport operations are also affected, particularly in the African region. One solution is to establish regional training institutions, or where they already exist, to provide them with adequate staffing, teaching aids and equipment so that systematic training programmes can be implemented. A major prerequisite is to identify training needs by function and category in all areas of transit-transport. The training programmes should involve specialized workshops and seminars for trainers, operational staff and transit-transport managers and policy-makers, and they should be supplemented by on-the-job training arrangements. Where feasible and desirable, opportunities for formal training in more advanced institutions should be made available. In this connection, UNCTAD has been supporting training programmes within the framework of its technical assistance projects.

(b)   Poor and deteriorating physical condition of transport infrastructure

This problem is principally due to poor maintenance, which in turn stems from a lack of adequate spare parts and experienced and skilled personnel. A number of programmes supported by international organizations are under way in the different regions to upgrade and develop transit-transport infrastructures. Many programmes in the African region are associated with the United Nations Transport and Communications Decade in Africa. In the southern African subregion, the Southern African Transport and Communications Commission is also playing a major role in carrying out transit-transport projects. Among the major donor efforts is the work to rehabilitate the Beira corridor, linking the land-locked countries in the southern African subregion with the Mozambican port of Beira, and the Tazara corridor, linking Zambia with the Tanzanian port of Dar-es-Salaam. In the east and central African subregion, international assistance is being provided to develop the crucial alternative road/rail route to Dar-es-Salaam for Rwanda and to rehabilitate the Kigoma-Dar-es-Salaam rail route and the Uganda road routes to the Kenyan border. Efforts under way in the west and central African subregion include the rehabilitation of the railway through the Burkina Faso-Abidjan corridor, the road route between Burkina Faso and Benin, the road along the Bangui-Cameroon corridor, the Bangui-Congo river/rail corridor, the Bamako-Dakar-Abidjan road corridor and the Niger-Cotonou rail/road link. In the Asian region, there is a multilateral project to develop containerization along the Nepal-Indian corridor. Plans are also being made to develop and improve the alternative route through Bangladesh.

(c)   Poor communications facilities between the transit and land-locked developing countries

This is one of the major constraints in the transit-transport operations. The remoteness of the land-locked developing countries from sea ports and overseas markets, coupled with inadequate communication links with various commercial centres in these countries and between ports and overseas markets, continues to hamper the movement of transit cargo. Unreliable information about the arrival and departure times of cargo has led to long delays in moving cargo in and out of the ports in recent years. The costs caused by such delays can be considerable. This problem is particularly serious in the Mozambican and west African ports. In the southern and east African subregions, efforts are being made to establish cargo-tracking centres in the transit and land-locked developing countries and eventually to link them through a computer system so as to provide a regular interchange of information on the movement of transit traffic. This will considerably reduce delays and additional costs and improve transit-transport operations.

(d)   Inadequate bilateral and subregional agreements to facilitate transit-transport

There are a number of regional and subregional agreements concerning transit, but most are too broad and poorly implemented. For example, implementation of the recently ratified Northern Transit Corridor Agreement between Burundi, Kenya, Rwanda, Uganda and Zaire, which is designed to streamline transit-transport operations along the corridor linking the land-locked countries in the subregion with the Kenyan port of Mombasa, still requires considerable substantive and administrative assistance. Furthermore, there are now some 20 international conventions regarding transit, but many land-locked developing countries and transit countries have not yet ratified or acceded to them.[c] Doing so would help them to remove some of the bottle-necks currently restraining transit-transport traffic.

(e)   Inadequate port facilities

This problem is especially critical in the Mozambican ports of Maputo and Beira. Operations in the Tanzanian port of Dar-es-Salaam have also been hindered by poor facilities in recent years. In the late 1970s, the majority of Zambian cargo had to be diverted to southern African transit routes because of acute congestion. Some corrective measures are now being taken to meet the growing demand for port services at Dar-es-Salaam by the land-locked countries of the southern African and east and central African subregions. The very poor facilities in the port of Asunción (Paraguay) also remain a major bottle-neck. Cargo handling facilities in these ports, as well as in many other transit ports in the west African subregion, are generally not adapted to modern technology. Damage, deterioration and loss of cargo are still quite common in many transit ports, and delays in cargo loading/unloading sometimes result in large surcharges. Berth capacity in these ports is often inadequate, and in some cases the demand for berth/handling facilities for specialized cargo cannot be met. These inefficiencies have led to increased demand for storage facilities in many transit ports, which in many cases are also inadequate.

(f)   Cumbersome documentation and customs procedures

The movement of transit cargo out of the ports is often delayed by complex documentation requirements, which increases the costs for many land-locked developing countries, particularly in the African and Asian regions.   One important initiative recently taken within the framework of UNCTAD technical assistance projects in the African region is the introduction of a road transit customs declaration document, which is designed to replace multiple transit documents. If it is effectively and widely used, this document will contribute to the speedier and cheaper movement of transit cargo across national frontiers. It is now in use in the east and central African subregion. In order to overcome the complex documentation problems related to transit payments such as road tolls, commercial vehicle guarantee and third party insurance, which are now settled through the central banking systems, a simple transit expenses coupon system has been introduced in the southern African subregion.

Notes

a.   A more detailed analysis of the corridor systems in the African region was made by the Economic Commission for Africa in a recent report prepared for the Economic and Social Council, which was based on work carried out by the UNCTAD secretariat as a contribution to the United Nations Transport and Communications Decade in Africa. See E/ECA/CM.13/49.
b.   Afghanistan, Chad, Mongolia, Niger, Paraguay and Zambia have at least three main routes. Bolivia and Zimbabwe have six or seven outlets. Almost all other land-locked developing countries have at least two routes.
c.   For a more detailed analysis, see TD/B/1007.

APPENDIX — **Statistical tables**

Table 1 — Main access to the sea for land-locked developing countries

Originating point	Transit		Distance (kilometres)	Means
	Port	Country or territory		
Africa				
Botswana	Gaborone	Johannesburg/Durban	South Africa	880	Rail
Burkina Faso	Ouagadougou	Abidjan	Côte d'Ivoire	1 150	Rail
Burundi	Bujumbura	Dar-es-Salaam	United Republic of Tanzania	1 500	Rail and water
	Bujumbura-Kigali	Kampala	Uganda	1 800	Rail and water
Central African Republic	Bangui	Pointe-Noire	Congo	820	Rail and water
	Bangui	Douala	Cameroon	1 300	Road and rail
Chad	Fort Lamy	Lagos	Nigeria	2 050	Road and rail
	Fort Lamy	Pointe-Noire	Congo	3 000	Road and water-rail
	Abéché	Port Sudan	Sudan	2 660	Road and rail
Lesotho	Maseru	Durban	South Africa	740	Road
Malawi	Blantyre	Beira	Mozambique	560	Rail
	Salima	Beira	Mozambique	810	Rail
Mali	Bamako	Dakar	Senegal	1 240	Rail
	Bamako	Abidjan	Côte d'Ivoire	1 250	Road and rail
Niger	Niamey	Cotonou	Dahomey	1 060	Road and rail
	Niamey	Abidjan	Côte d'Ivoire	1 650	Road and rail
	Zinder	Lagos	Nigeria	1 400	Road and rail
Rwanda	Kigali	Dar-es-Salaam	United Republic of Tanzania	1 840	Road, water and rail
	Kigali-Kampala	Mombasa	Kenya	1 800	Road and rail
Swaziland	Mbabane	Maputo	Mozambique	200	Rail
Uganda	Kampala	Mombasa	Kenya	1 300	Rail
Zambia	Lusaka	Beira	Mozambique	2 026	Rail
	Lusaka	Maputo	Mozambique	2 035	Rail
	Lusaka	Dar-es-Salaam	United Republic of Tanzania	2 045	Rail
Zimbabwe	Harare	Beira	Mozambique	602	Rail
	Harare	Maputo	Mozambique	1 481	Rail
	Harare	Nacala	Mozambique	1 400	Road and rail
	Harare	Durban	South Africa	2 070	Rail
	Harare	Elizabeth	South Africa	2 380	Rail
	Harare	Dar-es-Salaam	United Republic of Tanzania	2 500	Road and rail

Table 1 (continued)

| Originating point | Transit | | | |
	Port	Country or territory	Distance (kilometres)	Means
Asia				
Afghanistan .... Kabul	Karachi	Pakistan	2 000	Road and rail
Kabul	Bandar Abbas	Islamic Republic of Iran	2 000	Road
Kabul	Leningrad	USSR (via Hairaton)	5 575	Road and rail
Kabul	Riga	USSR (via Hairaton)	5 753	Road and rail
Bhutan .... Punakha	Calcutta	India	600	Road and rail
Kandahar	Karachi	Pakistan	950	Road and rail
Lao People's Democratic Republic.......... Vientiane	Bangkok	Thailand	670	Road, water and rail
Mongolia .... Ulan Bator	Leningrad	USSR	5 000	Rail
Mongolia .... Ulan Bator	Nakhodka	USSR	4 040	Rail
Mongolia .... Ulan Bator	Tiamjin	China	1 580	Rail
Nepal .... Kathmandu	Calcutta	India	890	Road and rail
Latin America				
Bolivia .... La Paz	Arica	Chile	450	Rail
La Paz	Antofagasta	Chile	1 130	Rail
La Paz	Matarani	Peru	800	Rail and water
Sicasica	Arica	Chile	350	Pipeline
Camiri	Yacuiba	Argentina	250	Pipeline
Santa Cruz — Corumba	Santos	Brazil	2 550	Rail
Santa Cruz — Yacuiba	Buenos Aires	Argentina	2 470	Rail
Paraguay .... Asunción	Buenos Aires	Argentina	1 600	River
Asunción	Paranagua	Brazil	1 130	Road
Asunción	Montevideo	Uruguay	1 700	River

Source: Updated information from UNCTAD questionnaire.

UN General Assembly   A/RES/42/174
Forty-second Session   11 December 1987

Resolution 42/174.   Specific action related to the particular needs
and problems of land-locked developing countries

The General Assembly,

Reiterating the specific actions related to the particular needs of the land-locked developing countries set out in United Nations Conference on Trade and Development resolutions 63 (III) of 19 May 1972,[1] 98 (IV) of 31 May 1976,[2] 123 (V) of 3 June 1979[3] and 137 (VI) of 2 July 1983[4] and Trade and Development Board resolution 319 (XXXI) of 27 September 1985,[5]

Recalling the provisions of its resolutions 31/157 of 21 December 1976, 32/191 of 19 December 1977, 33/150 of 20 December 1978, 34/198 of 19 December 1979, 35/58 of 5 December 1980, 36/175 of 17 December 1981, 39/209 of 18 December 1984 and 40/183 of 17 December 1985 and other resolutions of the United Nations relating to the particular needs and problems of land-locked developing countries,

Bearing in mind that the land-locked developing countries, most of which are also least developed countries, have been severely affected by the current socio-economic crisis,

Recalling the relevant provisions of the Final Act adopted by the United Nations Conference on Trade and Development at its seventh session,[6]

Recalling also the United Nations Convention on the Law of the Sea,[7] adopted on 10 December 1982,

Noting that the report of the *Ad Hoc* Group of Experts to Study Ways and Means of Improving Transit-transport Infrastructures and Services for Land-locked Developing Countries[8] and the recommendations therein, and the various views and comments of Governments on the report, could be a basis for an approach towards resolving the problems that the land-locked developing countries face,

Recognizing that the lack of territorial access to the sea, aggravated by remoteness and isolation from world markets, and prohibitive transit, transport and trans-shipment costs and risks impose serious constraints on export earnings, private capital inflow and domestic resource mobilization of the land-locked developing countries and therefore adversely affect their growth and socio-economic development,

Recognizing also that most transit countries are themselves developing countries facing serious economic problems, including the lack of adequate infrastructure in the transport sector,

Noting with concern that the measures taken thus far have not adequately addressed the problems of land-locked developing countries,

1.   *Reaffirms* the right of access of land-locked countries to and from the sea and freedom of transit through the territory of transit States by all means of transport, in accordance with article 125 of the United Nations Convention on the Law of the Sea;

2.   *Appeals* to all States, international organizations and financial institutions to implement, as a matter of urgency and priority, the specific actions related to the particular needs and problems of land-locked developing countries envisaged in United Nations Conference on Trade and Development resolutions 63 (III), 98 (IV), 123 (V) and 137 (VI) and the Final Act adopted by the Conference at its seventh session, in the International Development Strategy for the Third United Nations Development Decade,[9] in the Substantial New Programme of Action for the 1980s for the Lesser Developed Countries[10] and in other relevant resolutions of the United Nations;

3.   *Urges* the international community, in particular donor countries and multilateral financial and development organizations, to provide land-locked and transit developing countries with appropriate financial and technical assistance in the form of grants or concessional loans for the construction, maintenance and improvement of their transport and transit infrastructures and facilities, including alternative routes;

4.   *Invites* transit countries and the land-locked developing countries to co-operate effectively in harmonizing transport planning and in promoting joint ventures, where appropriate, in the fields of transport and communications at the regional, subregional and bilateral levels;

5.   *Urges* the international development bodies, in particular the United Nations Development Programme, the United Nations Conference on Trade and Development and the regional commissions, to further expand their support, including technical assistance programmes in the transport and communications sectors of the land-locked developing countries;

6.   *Appeals* to the international community to make available to all transit and land-locked developing countries, as required and on appropriate terms, including concessional arrangements, new scientific and technological know-how relating to specific transit-transport and communication problems;

7.   *Appeals* to the international community and, in particular, donor countries, multilateral financial and development institutions, the United Nations Conference on Trade and Development and the regional commissions, to extend all possible support to land-locked developing countries in their efforts to implement economic measures and policies designed to promote a pattern of growth that renders their economies less vulnerable to adverse consequences of their land-locked situation;

8.   *Welcomes* the report of the Secretary-General of the United Nations Conference on Trade and Development on progress in the implementation of specific action related to the particular needs and problems of land-locked developing countries,[11] submitted pursuant to resolution 40/183, and requests him to prepare another report, taking into account the provisions of the present resolution, for submission to the General Assembly at its forty-fourth session.

96th plenary meeting
11 December 1987

Notes

1. See Proceedings of the United Nations Conference on Trade and Development, Third Session, vol. I, Report and Annexes (United Nations publication, Sales No. E.73.II.D.4), annex I.A.
2. Ibid., Fourth Session, vol. I, Report and Annexes (United Nations publication, Sales No. E.76.II.D.10 and corrigendum), part one, sect. A.
3. Ibid., Fifth Session, vol. I, Report and Annexes (United Nations publication, Sales No. E.79.II.D.14), part one, sect. A.
4. Ibid., Sixth Session, vol. I, Report and Annexes (United Nations publication, Sales No. E.83.II.D.6), part one, sect. A.
5. See Official Records of the General Assembly, Fortieth Session, Supplement No. 15 (A/40/15), vol. II, sect. I.
6. See TD/351, part one, sect. I.
7. Official Records of the Third United Nations Conference on the Law of the Sea, vol. XVII (United Nations publication, Sales No. E.84.V.3), document A/CONF.62/122.
8. Official Records of the Trade and Development Board, Twenty-ninth Session, Annexes, agenda item 6, document TD/B/1002.
9. Resolution 35/56, annex.
10. Report of the United Nations Conference on the Least Developed Countries, Paris, 1-14 September 1981 (United Nations publication, Sales No. E.82.I.8), part one, sect. A.
11. A/42/537, annex.

- - - - -

Additional References

Land-locked developing countries: their characteristics and special development problems. UNCTAD doc. UNCTAD/ST/LDC/5.

Land-locked developing countries. Progress report by the UNCTAD secretariat. UNCTAD doc. TD/B/1007.

Progress in the implementation of specific action related to the particular needs and problems of land-locked developing countries. UNCTAD doc. TD/B/1107

- - - - -

X

PROTECTION AND PRESERVATION OF THE MARINE ENVIRONMENT

1

General Issues

Future Perspectives

UN General Assembly   A/RES/42/184
Forty-second Session   Extract

Resolution 42/184.   International co-operation in the field of the environment

The General Assembly,

Having considered the report of the Governing Council of the United Nations Environment Programme on the work of its fourteenth session,[1]

Having also considered the report of the Executive Director of the United Nations Environment Programme on international conventions and protocols in the field of the environment,[2]

Taking note of the Environmental Perspective to the Year 2000 and Beyond[3] and the report of the World Commission on Environment and Development,[4]

. . .

5.   *Welcomes* the annual reports on the state of the world environment, in particular the report for 1987,[8] fifteen years after the United Nations Conference on the Human Environment, and requests that these reports be given wide dissemination and be drawn upon fully in the preparation of reports within the United Nations system on the world economic and social situation;

6.   *Agrees* with the Governing Council that the United Nations Environment Programme should attach importance to the problem of global climate change and that the Executive Director should ensure that the Programme co-operates closely with the World Meteorological Organization and the International Council of Scientific Unions and maintains an active, influential role in the World Climate Programme;

. . .

10.   *Welcomes* Governing Council decision 14/30 of 17 June 1987,[7] in which it approved the Cairo Guidelines and Principles for the Environmentally Sound Management of Hazardous Wastes,[9] and the steps taken by the United Nations Environment Programme to develop a global convention on environmentally sound transboundary movement of hazardous wastes, supports the Goals and Principles of Environmental Impact Assessment[10] adopted by the Governing Council in its decision 14/25 of 17 June 1987 and its recommendations regarding their application, welcomes the adoption by the Governing Council in its decision 14/27 of 17

June 1987 on the London Guidelines for the Exchange of Information on Chemicals in International Trade[11] and encourages further steps in this regard;

. . .

19. *Agrees* with the Governing Council on the importance it attached, in the annex to its decision 14/12 of 18 June 1987,[7] to the preparation of the system-wide medium-term environment programme for the period 1990-1995, guided by the Environmental Perspective to the Year 2000 and Beyond, and urges the Administrative Committee on Co-ordination to develop an effective way of monitoring the implementation of the system-wide programme and of evaluating critical programmes therein that involve a number of organizations;

. . .

Notes

1. Official Records of the General Assembly, Forty-second Session, Supplement No.25 (A/42/25 and Corr.1).
2. UNEP/GC.14/18 and Corr.1 and Add.1.
3. Official Records of the General Assembly, Forty-second Session, Supplement No.25 (A/42/25 and Corr.1), annex II.
4. A/42/427, annex.

. . .

7. Official Records of the General Assembly, Forty-second Session, Supplement No.25 (A/42/25 and Corr.1), annex I.
8. UNEP/GC.14/6 and Add.1-3. Also UN publication Sales No. E.87.III.D.1.
9. UNEP/GC.14/17, annex II.
10. Ibid., annex III.
11. Ibid., annex IV.

- - - - -

Additional Reference

UNEP Register of international treaties and other agreements in the field of the environment. UNEP/GC/INFORMATION/11/Rev.1/Supplement 1.

- - - - -

UN General Assembly   A/RES/42/186
Forty-second Session   Extract

Resolution 42/186. Environmental Perspective to the Year 2000 and Beyond

. . .

The General Assembly,

. . .

Welcoming the Environmental Perspective to the Year 2000 and Beyond, prepared by the Intergovernmental Inter-sessional Preparatory Committee on the Environmental Perspective to the Year 2000 and Beyond of the United Nations Environment Programme, referred to in General Assembly resolution 38/161, considered further by the Governing Council of the United Nations Environment Programme at its fourteenth session and adopted in its decision

14/13 of 19 June 1987, as a basis for the further elaboration of its programme and operations, while acknowledging that different views exist on some aspects,

Appreciating that concepts, ideas and recommendations contained in the report of the World Commission on Environment and Development have been incorporated into the Environmental Perspective,

. . .

2.   *Adopts* the Environmental Perspective to the Year 2000 and Beyond, contained in the annex to the present resolution, as a broad framework to guide national action and international co-operation on policies and programmes aimed at achieving environmentally sound development, and specifically as a guide to the preparation of further system-wide medium-term environment programmes and the medium-term programmes of the organizations and bodies of the United Nations system, in the light of Governing Council decision 14/13;

3.   *Notes* that the perceptions generally shared by Governments of the nature of environmental problems, and their interrelationships with other international problems, and of the efforts to deal with them include the following:

(a)   An international atmosphere of peace, security and co-operation, free from the presence and the threat of wars of all types, especially nuclear war, in which intellectual and natural resources are not wasted on armaments by any nation, would greatly enhance environmentally sound development;

(b)   The imbalance of present world economic conditions makes it extremely difficult to bring about sustained improvement in the world's environmental situation; accelerated and balanced world development and lasting improvements in the global environment require improved world economic conditions, especially for the developing countries;

(c)   Since mass poverty is often at the root of environmental degradation, its elimination and ensuring equitable access of people to environmental resources are essential for sustained environmental improvements;

(d)   The environment puts constraints on as well as provides opportunities for economic growth and social well-being; environmental degradation, in its various forms, has assumed such proportions as can cause irreversible changes in ecosystems, which threaten to undermine human well-being; environmental constraints, however, are generally relative to the state of technology and socio-economic conditions, which can and should be improved and managed to achieve sustained world economic growth;

(e)   Environmental issues are closely intertwined with development policies and practices, consequently, environmental goals and actions need to be defined in relation to development objectives and policies;

(f)   Although it is important to tackle immediate environmental problems, anticipatory and preventive policies are the most effective and economical in achieving environmentally sound development;

(g) The environmental impacts of actions in one sector are often felt in other sectors; thus internalization of environmental considerations in sectoral policies and programmes and their co-ordination are essential for the achievement of sustainable development;

(h) Since conflicts of interest among population groups, or among countries, are often inherent in the nature of environmental problems, the participation of the concerned parties is essential in determining effective environmental management practices;

(i) Environmental degradation can be controlled and reversed only by ensuring that the parties causing the damage will be accountable for their actions, and that they will participate, on the basis of full access to available knowledge, in improving environmental conditions;

(j) Renewable resources, as part of complex and interlinked ecosystems, can have sustainable yields only if used while taking into account system-wide effects of exploitation;

(k) The safeguarding of species is a moral obligation of humankind and should improve and sustain human well-being;

(l) Building awareness at various levels of environmental conditions and management, through the provision of information, education and training, is essential for environmental protection and improvement;

(m) Strategies to deal with environmental challenges have to be flexible and should allow for adjustments to emerging problems and evolving environmental management technology;

(n) International environmental disputes which are growing in number and variety, need to be resolved by peaceful means;

. . .

7. *Calls* special attention to section IV of the Environmental Perspective, which spells out instruments of environmental action, to be used as support in addressing, as appropriate, problems dealt with in previous sections of the Environmental Perspective;

. . .

12. *Requests* the governing bodies of relevant United Nations organizations to report regularly to the General Assembly on the progress made in achieving the objectives of environmentally sound and sustainable development in line with paragraph 114 of the Environmental Perspective;

. . .

96th plenary meeting
11 December 1987

ANNEX

Environmental Perspective to the Year 2000 and Beyond

. . .

III. OTHER ISSUES OF GLOBAL CONCERN

69. This section discusses briefly the major environmental issues of global concern that have not been adequately dealt with in previous sections.

A. Oceans and seas

70. Oceans and seas are being polluted extensively. The rising pollution levels and degradation of coastal ecosystems threaten the life-support capacities of oceans and seas and undermine their role in the food chain. Efforts to monitor the state of oceans and seas, including those of the United Nations Environment Programme and other international organizations, confirm that there is cause for concern. This problem is particularly serious for coastal waters and semi-enclosed seas that border highly populated and industrialized zones. The situation will get much worse unless concerted action is undertaken now. The ongoing monitoring effort is far from comprehensive and, where it has advanced, it has not yet led to adequate change in the practices causing environmental damage.

71. The challenge is to control and decrease marine pollution, and establish or strengthen régimes of environmental management of oceans and seas through international co-operation and national action.

72. A comprehensive data base should be established over time on which action programmes to restore and preserve the environmental balance in the world's oceans and seas can be based. Among others, the Global Environmental Monitoring System, Global Resource Information Data Base and the oceans and coastal programmes of the United Nations Environment Programme should intensify efforts towards this end.

73. Conventions and agreements to monitor and manage human activities with view a to ensuring environmental protection of the seas and oceans should be ratified and implemented by all concerned countries. Where such legal instruments do not exist, they should be negotiated. Governments should strengthen or introduce policies and measures aimed at preventing practices harmful to marine ecosystems and ensuring environmentally sound development of inland areas. Such policies and measures should include control of the discharge of industrial effluents and sewage, dumping of wastes, including hazardous and radioactive materials, disposal of hazardous residues and operational wastes from ships, incineration at sea, and oil spills from tankers and off-shore platforms. Environmentally sound land-based technology for the disposal of hazardous wastes should be developed and promoted. The United Nations Environment Programme should continue to collaborate in this work with the Intergovernmental Oceanographic Commission, the International Maritime Organization, and other appropriate international organizations.

. . .

IV. INSTRUMENTS OF ENVIRONMENTAL ACTION

. . .

C. Legislation and environmental law

100. Increasingly, environmental legislation has been providing practical frameworks at the national level for implementing environmental standards and regulating the activities of enterprises and people in the light of environmental objectives. At the international level, conventions, protocols and agreements have been providing a basis for co-operation among countries at bilateral, regional and global levels for the management of environmental risks, control of pollution and conservation of natural resources.

101.   There is a need to expand the number of accessions to and ratifications of these conventions and to institute mechanisms at the national level to ensure their application. The present momentum should be maintained of concluding conventions in fields such as hazards relating to chemicals, treatment and international transport of hazardous wastes, industrial accidents, climate change, protection of the ozone layer, protection of the marine environment from pollution from land-based sources and protection of biological diversity, in which the United Nations Environment Programme has been playing an active part.

102.   Groundwork has been prepared over the last 15 years under the aegis of the United Nations Environment Programme to establish legal frameworks to manage regional seas. Governments should intensify their efforts to implement legislative measures and other policies at national levels so that the policy sources of the environmental problems of the regional seas are effectively tackled. ...

103.   The Montevideo Programme for the Development and Periodic Review of Environmental Law,[9] prepared under the auspices of the United Nations Environment Programme, should be implemented fully.   Development of international environmental law should continue, with a view to providing a strong basis for fostering co-operation among countries. The progressive emergence of general environmental norms and principles and the codification of existing agreements could lead to a global convention on protection and enhancement of the environment.

104.   Governments should settle their environmental disputes by peaceful means, making use of existing and emerging agreements and conventions. The International Court of Justice, the International Court of Arbitration and regional mechanisms should facilitate peaceful settlement of environmental disputes.
    ...

Note

...
9.   UNEP/GC.10/5/Add.2 and Corr. 1 and 2, annex, chap. II.

- - - - -

UN General Assembly   A/42/427
Forty-second Session   Extract

Report of the World Commission on Environment and Development
Note by the Secretary-General

1.   The General Assembly, in its resolution 38/161 of 19 December 1983, *inter alia*, welcomed the establishment of a special commission that should make available a report on environment and the global *problématique* to the year 2000 and beyond, including proposed strategies for sustainable development.   The commission later adopted the name World Commission on Environment and Development.   In the same resolution, the Assembly decided that, on matters within the mandate and purview of the United Nations Environment Programme, the report of the special commission should in the first instance be considered by

the Governing Council of the Programme, for transmission to the Assembly together with its comments, and for use as basic material in the preparation, for adoption by the Assembly, of the Environmental Perspective to the Year 2000 and Beyond.

2.   At its fourteenth session, held at Nairobi from 8 to 19 June 1987, the Governing Council of the United Nations Environment Programme adopted decision 14/14 of 6 June 1987, entitled "Report of the World Commission on Environment and Development" and, *inter alia*, decided to transmit the Commission's report to the General Assembly together with a draft resolution annexed to the decision for consideration and adoption by the Assembly.

3.   The report of the World Commission on Environment and Development, entitled "Our Common Future"*, is hereby transmitted to the General Assembly. Decision 14/14 of the Governing Council, the proposed draft resolution and the comments of the Governing Council on the report of the Commission can be found in the report of the Governing Council on the work of its fourteenth session.[1]

. . .

Note

*   The 1987 WCED report, "Our Common Future", has been published by and is available through Oxford University Press.

1.   Official Records of the General Assembly, Forty-second Session,Supplement No.25 (A/42/25)

- - - - -

Additional Reference

Legal principles for environmental protection and sustainable development adopted by the World Committee on Environment and Development (WCED) Expert Group on Environmental Law. WCED/86/23/Add.1.

- - - - -

UN Economic and Social Council   E/1988/42
Report of the Administrative Committee   23 March 1988
on Co-ordination for 1987   Extract

International Co-operation and Co-ordination
Within the United Nations System

. . .

E.   **International co-operation in the field of the environment**

26.   The ACC considered the relevant aspects of the report of the World Commission on Environment and Development (A/42/427) and, in welcoming the emphasis placed in the report on sustainable development, stressed that greater efforts to integrate this dimension in the activities of the system were essential. The report required a major re-orientation of

policies which the United Nations system could support and facilitate, but which depended, first, on the will and determination of Governments and peoples, in whose hands primarily such re-orientation lay. The availability of significant additional resources would facilitate the re-orientation. ACC believed that the mechanism of the Designated Officials for Environmental Matters could be instrumental in keeping under review the progress made by the United Nations system towards sustainable development and in co-ordinating its appropriate efforts.

. . .

28.   The importance of the integration of environmental considerations into development planning and policies continued to be stressed by the ACC, which agreed that the United Nations system should, in a few countries at this stage, initiate a process by which they would, upon request, assist the countries in the fulfillment of this task. It was thought important to learn from experience how theoretical approaches would work in practice and develop guidelines which could be replicated and used more broadly.

. . .

- - - - -

UN General Assembly   A/RES/42/187
Forty-second Session   Extract

Resolution 42/187.   Report of the World Commission on Environment and Development

. . .

Recalling that, in its resolution 38/161 of 19 December 1983 on the process of preparation of the Environmental Perspective to the Year 2000 and Beyond to be prepared by the Governing Council of the United Nations Environment Programme, it welcomed the establishment of a special commission, which later assumed the name World Commission on Environment and Development, to make available a report on environment and the **global problématique** to the year 2000 and beyond, including proposed strategies for sustainable development,

. . .

Taking note of Governing Council decision 14/14 of 19 June 1987 transmitting the report of the Commission to the General Assembly,

Noting that the Environmental Perspective to the Year 2000 and Beyond has taken account of the main recommendations in the Commission's report,

. . .

3.   *Agrees* with the Commission that while seeking to remedy existing environmental problems, it is imperative to influence the sources of those problems in human activity, and economic activity in particular, and thus to provide for sustainable development;

. . .

6.   *Decides* to transmit the report of the Commission to all Governments and to the governing bodies of the organs, organizations and programmes of the United Nations system,

and invites them to take account of the analysis and recommendations contained in the report of the Commission in determining their policies and programmes;

. . .

10. *Requests* the Secretary-General, through the appropriate existing mechanisms, including the Administrative Committee on Co-ordination, to review and co-ordinate on a regular basis the efforts of all the organs, organizations and bodies of the United Nations system to pursue sustainable development, and to report thereon to the General Assembly through the Governing Council of the United Nations Environment Programme and the Economic and Social Council,

. . .

18. *Invites* the governing bodies of the organs, organizations and programmes of the United Nations system to report, as appropriate, through the Economic and Social Council, to the General Assembly, not later than its forty-fourth session, on progress made in their organizations towards sustainable development, and to make such reports available to the Governing Council of the United Nations Environment Programme at its next regular session;

. . .

- - - - -

UN Economic Commission for Europe	ENV/R.195
Senior Advisers to ECE Governments	March 1987
on Environmental Problems	Extract

Draft Regional Strategy for Environmental Protection and Rational Use of Natural Resources in ECE Member Countries Covering the Period Up to the Year 2000 and Beyond

. . .

II. ENVIRONMENTAL PROBLEMS AND TRENDS

. . .

B.(2)   The seas around Europe

43. ECE Governments have registered concern for the status of, and the trends in, pollution of the seas and near-shore marine environments of Europe including pollution from land-based sources as well as that arising from marine navigation including the dumping of wastes. The view is broadly shared that there is a fundamental need to ensure the productivity of marine ecosystems and to increase the living resources of the seas and the continental shelf as well as to explore and make use of the resources of the sea-bed in an environmentally sound manner.

44. In certain parts of the seas in the ECE region, eutrophication has become a serious problem. Heavy metals, chlorinated hydrocarbons and chlorinated organic compounds are also of great concern. Eutrophication is to a great extent caused by the increased use of fertilizers and leakage of nitrogen. The precipitation of airborne pollutants is also of

considerable proportion, with deposits being made both directly into the seas and via watercourses.

. . .

III. GOALS

. . .

A. Medium-term goals

. . .

79. (c) Pollution abatement in the seas and near-shore marine environments of Europe:

   (i)   substantial reduction in the input of pollution from land and ships to the seas and near-shore marine environments of Europe via rivers and coastal waters;

   (ii) further development of monitoring programmes and data bases in the field of marine protection;

   (iii) reduction of transboundary marine pollution;

   (iv) reduction of air-borne pollutants, particularly nitrogen and chlorinated compounds;

   (v)   further development of the control of international trans-shipment of hazardous substances and compounds;

   (vi) promotion of the elaboration of a European Coastal Charter;

   (vii) total ban on waste disposal and incineration at sea.

. . .

   (g) Efficient management of wastes and toxic and hazardous chemicals and improvement of technologies:

. . .

   (h) Improvement of environmental management:

. . .

   (iv) further development of environmental impact assessment as a planning instrument and as a procedure for use in the decision-making process;

   (v)   further development of risk assessment as an instrument for use in the decision-making process;

. . .

B. Long-term goals

80. . . .

   (i)   Prevention of pollution of seas and near-shore marine environments.

. . .

   (o) Creation of a region-wide, comprehensive system of international legal obligations for effective protection of major ecosystems and for prevention or significant reduction of major adverse impacts on the natural environment. At the regional level, if possible, the harmonization of existing international legal rules, where appropriate and necessary, by the adoption of new rules in order to protect the environment.

- - - - -

Management and Control of Hazardous Wastes

UNEP Governing Council   A/42/25, Annex I
Report of the 14th Session, June 1987   Extract

Decisions adopted by the Governing Council at its fourteenth session

14/30. **Environmentally sound management of hazardous wastes**

The Governing Council,

Recalling the recommendations of the *Ad Hoc* Meeting of Senior Government Officials Expert in Environmental Law, held at Montevideo from 28 October to 6 November 1981, which considered the transport, handling and disposal of toxic and hazardous wastes as a priority matter and foresaw, at the world level, the preparation of guidelines, principles or conventions as appropriate,

Further recalling its decision 10/24 of 31 May 1982, pursuant to which an *Ad Hoc* Working Group of Experts on the Environmentally Sound Management of Hazardous Wastes was established to consider guidelines or principles regarding the environmentally sound transport, handling (including storage) and disposal of toxic and dangerous wastes,

. . .

3.   *Approves* the Cairo Guidelines and Principles for the Environmentally Sound Management of Hazardous Wastes, as well as the recommendations adopted at the third session of the *Ad Hoc* Working Group, . . . contained in the report of the Working Group ...;[60]

4.   *Calls upon* Governments and international organizations concerned to use the Cairo Guidelines and Principles in the process of developing appropriate bilateral, regional and multilateral agreements and national legislation for the environmentally sound management of hazardous wastes;

5.   *Notes with satisfaction* the active co-operation between the *Ad Hoc* Working Group and other United Nations organizations and bodies, the Organization for Economic Co-operation and Development and other international organizations outside the United Nations system, as well as non-governmental organizations;

6.   *Welcomes* the important work undertaken by the above-mentioned organizations in relation to the environmentally sound management of hazardous wastes, including the appropriate control of trans-frontier movements of such wastes;

7.   *Stresses* the need to extend international measures to guarantee the environmentally sound management of hazardous wastes and, in particular, the control of trans-frontier movements of such wastes;

. . .

9.   *Also authorizes* the Executive Director to convene in consultation with Governments, within available resources, a working group of legal and technical experts with a mandate to prepare a global convention on the control of transboundary movements of hazardous wastes, drawing on the conclusions of the *Ad Hoc* Working Group and the relevant work of national, regional and international bodies;

. . .

12.   *Requests* the Executive Director to convene in early 1989 a diplomatic conference for the purpose of adopting and signing a global convention on the control of transboundary movements of hazardous wastes;

. . .

Note

. . .

60.   UNEP/WG.122/3

- - - - -

UNEP Publication   Environmental Law Guidelines and Principles No. 8

Cairo Guidelines and Principles for the Environmentally Sound Management of Hazardous Wastes
(Decision 14/30 of the Governing Council of UNEP of 17 June 1987)

Introduction

This set of guidelines and principles is addressed to Governments with a view to assisting them in the process of developing policies for the environmentally sound management of hazardous wastes. They have been prepared on the basis of common elements and principles derived from relevant existing bilateral, regional and global agreements and national regulations, drawing upon experience already gained through their preparation and implementation. Special importance is attached to respect for the balance achieved in principle 21 of the Stockholm Declaration on the Human Environment between the rights and duties of States concerning their natural resources and the environment.

These general guidelines cover the management of hazardous wastes from their generation to their final disposal and, in particular, the problem of transfrontier movements of such wastes, which calls for international co-operation between exporting and importing countries in the light of their joint responsibility for the protection of the global environment.

These guidelines are without prejudice to the provisions of particular systems arising from international agreements in the field of hazardous waste management. They have been developed with a view to assisting States in the process of developing appropriate bilateral, regional and multilateral agreements and national legislation for the environmentally sound management of hazardous wastes. The guidelines deal mainly with the administrative aspects of the environmentally sound management of hazardous wastes, and do not claim to give specific guidance on the more technical aspects of dealing with hazardous wastes.

At the present time, waste management differs substantially in different regions of the world, particularly according to their state of economic development. This imbalance necessitates co-operation to improve the management of hazardous wastes in the interest of the environment, especially as regards actual and potential transfrontier movements of such wastes.

Although the guidelines have not been prepared specifically to address the situation of developing countries, they nevertheless provide a framework for effective and environmentally sound hazardous waste management policies in those countries. Implementation of the guidelines should thus help them to avoid serious and costly environmental problems due to mismanagement of hazardous wastes. By implementing the guidelines, countries could incorporate a sound waste management policy into their national economic development policies.

PART I - GENERAL PROVISIONS

1. Definitions

For the purposes of the present guidelines and principles:

(a) "Wastes" means any materials considered as wastes or legally defined as wastes in the State where they are situated or through or to which they are conveyed;

(b) "Hazardous wastes" means wastes other than radioactive wastes which, by reason of their chemical reactivity or toxic, explosive, corrosive or other characteristics causing danger or likely to cause danger to health or the environment, whether alone or when coming into contact with other wastes, are legally defined as hazardous in the State in which they are generated or in which they are disposed of or through which they are transported;

(c) "Management" means the collection, transport (including transfrontier movements), storage (including storage at transfer stations), treatment and disposal of hazardous wastes;

(d) "Transport" means the movement of hazardous wastes from the place at which they are generated until they arrive at an approved site or facility for disposal;

(e) "Disposal" means final disposal;

(f) "Approved site or facility" means a site or facility for the storage, treatment or disposal of hazardous wastes which has been the subject of a prior written authorization or operating permit for this purpose from a competent authority in the State where the site or facility is located.

(g) "Competent authority" means a governmental authority with appropriate qualifications designated or established by a State to be responsible, within such geographical area and with such jurisdiction as the State may think fit, for the planning, organization, authorization and supervision of the management of hazardous wastes;

(h) "Pollution" means the introduction by man, directly or indirectly, of any hazardous wastes into the environment as a result of which there arises any hazard to human health, plant or animal life, harm to living resources or to ecosystems, damage to amenities or interference with other legitimate uses of the environment;

(i) "Contingency" means any accident or other event occurring during the management of hazardous wastes which gives rise to or presents a threat of pollution;

(j) "Territory" means areas over which a State has jurisdiction for the protection of the environment;

(k) "Export" means the movement of hazardous wastes beyond the territory of the State in which they were generated;

(l) "State of export" means a State in which hazardous wastes which are the subject of an export are generated;

(m) "State of import" means a State in which hazardous wastes are received for disposal;

(n) "Transit State" means a State, not being the State of export or of import, through the territory of which a movement of hazardous wastes takes place.

2. General principles

(a) States should take such steps as are necessary, whether by legislation or otherwise, to ensure the protection of health and the environment from damage arising from the generation and arrangement of hazardous wastes. To this end, States should, *inter alia*, ensure that transfrontier movements of hazardous wastes are kept to the minimum compatible with the efficient and environmentally sound management of such wastes.

(b) States should take all practicable steps to ensure that the management of hazardous wastes is conducted in accordance with international law applicable in matters of environmental protection.

3. Non-discriminatory control of hazardous wastes

Each State should ensure that, within its jurisdiction, hazardous wastes to be exported are controlled no less stringently than those remaining within its territory.

4. International co-operation

Without prejudice to the other provisions of these guidelines and principles, States should, in a manner appropriate to their needs and capabilities, initiate and co-operate in:

(a) The achievement and improvement of the environmentally sound management of hazardous wastes;

(b) The development and implementation of new environmentally sound low-waste technologies and the improvement of existing technologies with a view to reducing the generation of hazardous wastes and achieving more effective and efficient methods of ensuring their management in an environmentally sound manner, including the study of the economic, social and environmental effects of the adoption of such new or improved technologies;

(c)   Monitoring the effects of the management of hazardous wastes on health and the environment;

(d)   Exchanges of information, whether on a bilateral or multilateral basis, with a view to promoting the environmentally sound management of hazardous wastes.

5.   Transfer of technology

States should, in a manner appropriate to their needs and capabilities, whether directly or through the appropriate international organizations, promote actively and in accordance with their legitimate interests the transfer on fair and reasonable conditions of technology related to the environmentally sound management of hazardous wastes. They should also promote the technical capacity of States, especially of developing States, which may need and request technical assistance in this field.

6.   Transfer or transformation of pollution

States and persons involved in the management of hazardous wastes should recognize that protection of health and the environment is not achieved by the mere transformation of one form of pollution into another, nor by the mere transfer of the effects of pollution from one location to another, but only by the use of the waste treatment option (which may include transformation or transfer) which minimizes the environmental impact.

PART II - GENERATION AND MANAGEMENT OF HAZARDOUS WASTES

7.   Preventive measures

(a)   States should take such steps as are appropriate to ensure that the generation of hazardous wastes within their territories is reduced to a minimum.

(b)   States should ensure that persons involved in the management of hazardous wastes take such steps as are necessary to prevent pollution arising from such management and, if pollution should occur, to minimize the consequences thereof for health and the environment.

(c)   In particular, States should take such steps as are necessary to promote the development and employment of low-waste technologies applicable to activities generating hazardous wastes and the recycling and reuse of hazardous wastes unavoidably produced by such activities.

8.   Establishment of competent authorities

Each State should designate or establish one or more competent authorities as defined in guideline 1.

PART III - CONTROL OVER DISPOSAL OF HAZARDOUS WASTES

9.   Disposal plans for hazardous wastes

(a)   States should ensure that each competent authority prepares, in its area of responsibility, in consultation with the other public authorities concerned and with the participation of the public as appropriate, a plan for the management of hazardous wastes describing the arrangements for implementing that plan.

(b) Such plans should be reviewed by the competent authorities to ensure their continuing adequacy in the light of experience in the operation of the plans and of changes in circumstances, including changes in the state of scientific knowledge.

10.   Separation of hazardous wastes

The competent authorities should ensure that persons concerned in the management of hazardous wastes keep them separate from other wastes where it is necessary to do so for their environmentally sound management.

11.   Collection of hazardous wastes

States should promote the establishment of a system of collection of hazardous wastes, including those that are generated in small quantities.

12.   Duty to ensure safe disposal

States should ensure that persons engaged in activities in the course of which hazardous wastes are generated are required to make appropriate arrangements for the disposal of those wastes in an environmentally sound manner. In particular, they should satisfy themselves as to the capability and reliability of persons and facilities involved in the management of such wastes.

13.   Use of best practicable means

States should ensure that persons involved in the management of hazardous wastes employ the best practicable means in all aspects of such management.

14.   Approved sites and facilities

(a)   States should take such steps as are necessary to require that the storage, treatment and disposal of hazardous wastes take place only at approved sites or facilities.

(b)   An authorization or operating permit for approved sites or facilities should be granted only if:

(i)   An assessment undertaken by or at the request of the competent authority has established that no significant adverse effects on health or the environment are to be expected as a result of such storage, treatment or disposal;

(ii)   The competent authority is satisfied as to the suitability of the operator of the facility at which such storage, treatment or disposal is to be carried out, including the technical knowledge and financial means of that operator to carry out the operations in respect of which the authorization or operating permit is sought to be granted and to take the appropriate safety measures in respect thereof.

15. International listing of approved sites and facilities

For the guidance of their competent authorities and to ensure the optimal use of their disposal facilities in conformity with guideline 2, States should consider the establishment, on a bilateral or multilateral basis, of lists of approved sites and facilities in their respective territories.

16. Transfrontier effects of approved sites and facilities - Pre-authorization information

(a) States should ensure that, where it is proposed to grant an authorization or operating permit under guideline 14 in respect of activities which may have significant effects on health or the environment in another State (hereinafter referred to as "the State concerned"), the State concerned is provided in a timely manner by the State entitled to grant the authorization or operating permit (hereinafter referred to as "the authorizing State") with sufficient information, in conformity with the laws and regulations of the latter State, to enable it to evaluate accurately the likely effects of those activities.

(b) The State concerned should respect the confidentiality of the information transmitted to it under paragraph (a) above.

17. Transfrontier effects - consultation

In the circumstances described in guideline 16, the authorizing State and the State concerned should, prior to the adoption of any decision in the authorizing State as to the granting of the authorization or operating permit, enter into consultations which shall be conducted in good faith. These consultations should take place promptly and should be concluded within a reasonable time.

18. Transfrontier effects - equal access and treatment

In the circumstances described in guideline 16, the authorizing State should accord to the public authorities and nationals of the State concerned the same rights of participation in the administrative and judicial proceedings related to the granting of authorizations or operating permits and in any appeal or review thereof as those which are accorded to its own public authorities and nationals.

PART IV - MONITORING, REMEDIAL ACTION AND RECORD-KEEPING

19. Monitoring

(a) States should ensure that the operators of sites or facilities at which hazardous wastes are managed are required, as appropriate, to monitor the effects of those activities on health and the environment and to supply the competent authorities with the results of such monitoring, either periodically or on demand. States should ensure that the protection of abandoned sites or closed facilities against the subsequent unauthorized disposal of hazardous wastes, and the monitoring of such sites or facilities for effects on health and the environment, continue after their abandonment or closure.

(b) States should ensure that the competent authorities have the power to enter upon the sites or facilities mentioned in paragraph (a) above and upon such other premises as may be necessary for the purposes of monitoring the effects upon health and the environment of the activities carried out at those sites or facilities. States should also ensure that the competent authorities have the power to order the cessation, limitation or modification of those activities if it is determined that adverse effects on health and the environment are taking place, or are likely to take place.

(c)   States should ensure that appropriate remedial action is taken in cases where monitoring gives indications that management of hazardous wastes has resulted in adverse effects on health or the environment.

(d)   States should ensure that persons involved in the management of hazardous wastes keep accurate and precise records, as appropriate, of the relevant information concerning wastes, including the type, quantity, physical and chemical characteristics, origin and location within the site or facility of such wastes.

20.   Public access to information

States should ensure that competent authorities keep a record of the authorizations or operating permits issued by them under guideline 14, and that the public have access to information concerning the number and types of those authorizations or permits and the conditions attached thereto.

PART V - SAFETY AND CONTINGENCY PLANNING

21.   Instruction of workers

States should ensure that persons employed at sites or facilities at which hazardous wastes are managed receive, on a continuing basis, information on the conditions attached to authorizations or permits and full and appropriate instruction as to the safety precautions necessary to ensure the protection of health and the environment, including the actions to be taken by them in any contingency.

22.   Contingency plans

States within whose territories hazardous wastes are managed should recognize the need for studies on the risks of sites or facilities, and contingency plans prepared by operators of sites or facilities, or by the competent authorities, as appropriate, and the application of such plans as and when necessary. These plans should take into account any potential adverse effects on health and the environment in other States.

23.   Contingency plans - transfrontier effects

(a)   If a State has reason to believe that a contingency which has arisen within its territory is likely to have significant adverse effects on health and the environment in another State, that State should as soon as practicable supply the other State with the information necessary to enable it to adopt effective countermeasures.

(b)   States should provide such assistance as they can reasonably make available to other States in which a contingency has occurred.

PART VI - TRANSPORT OF HAZARDOUS WASTES

24. Transport rules

States should ensure that the transport of hazardous wastes is conducted in a manner compatible with international conventions and other international instruments governing the transport of hazardous materials or wastes.

25. Transport documentation

To ensure that hazardous wastes are safely transported for disposal, and to maintain records of the transport and disposal of such wastes, States should establish a system by which all transport of such wastes should be accompanied by a hazardous wastes movement document from the point of generation to the point of disposal. This document should be available to the competent authorities and to all Parties involved in the management of such wastes.

26. Notification and consent procedure in respect of transfrontier movements of hazardous wastes

(a) States should establish a system which ensures that all States involved in a transfrontier movement of hazardous wastes receive full information sufficiently in advance to enable them to assess the proposed movement properly.

(b) A State of export should take such steps as are necessary to ensure that a request from a State of import or transit State for relevant information concerning the transfrontier movement in question elicits a constructive and timely response.

(c) In the absence of bilateral, regional or multilateral arrangements, States should provide that it shall not be lawful for any person to initiate a transfrontier movement of hazardous wastes until the State of import and any transit State have given their consent to that movement.

(d) The consent of the State of import referred to in paragraph (c) above should take the form of an explicit consent, provided always that States may by bilateral or multilateral arrangements adopt a tacit consent procedure.

(e) Any transit State should be notified in a timely manner of a proposed movement, and may object to it within a reasonable time in accordance with its national laws and regulations. The consent of a transit State referred to in paragraph (c) above may also take the form of a tacit consent.

(f) The State of export should not permit a transfrontier movement of hazardous wastes to be initiated unless if it is not satisfied that the wastes in question can be managed in an environmentally sound manner, at an approved site or facility and with the consent of the State of import.

(g) In order to facilitate implementation of this guideline, each State should designate an agency which shall be the focal point to which the notifications and inquiries mentioned in the foregoing paragraphs may be addressed.

(h)   Nothing in this guideline shall be so construed as to affect the sovereign right of a State to refuse to accept within its territory hazardous wastes originating elsewhere.

27.   State of export to readmit exports

Where a State of import or transit State, in conformity with its laws and regulations, opposes a transfrontier movement of hazardous wastes into its territory, and where the hazardous wastes which are the subject of the transfrontier movement have already left the State of export, the latter should not object to reimport of the wastes.

28.   States to co-operate in the management of hazardous wastes

States should, in pursuance of guideline 2, enter into bilateral, regional or multilateral agreements for the management of their hazardous wastes in order to ensure the optimal use of their treatment and disposal facilities.

PART VII - LIABILITY AND COMPENSATION

29.   Liability, insurance and compensation for damage caused by hazardous wastes

States should ensure that provision is made in their national laws and regulations for (a) liability, (b) insurance and (c) compensation and/or other remedies for damage arising from the management of hazardous wastes, and they should take such steps as are necessary to ensure the compatibility and, where appropriate, the harmonization of such laws and regulations.

- - - - -

UN General Assembly
Forty-second Session

A/RES/42/183
Extract

Resolution 42/183.   Traffic in toxic and dangerous products and wastes

The General Assembly,

Taking note of decisions 14/19 on the International Register of Potentially Toxic Chemicals, 14/27 on environmentally sound management of chemicals, in particular those that are banned and severely restricted in international trade, and 14/30 on environmentally sound management of hazardous wastes, ...

Taking note also of Economic and Social Council resolution 1987/54 of 28 May 1987 on the work of the Committee of Experts on the Transport of Dangerous Goods,

...

Convinced that the London Guidelines for the Exchange of Information on Chemicals in International Trade[2] and the Cairo Guidelines and Principles for the Environmentally Sound Management of Hazardous Wastes represent a significant step forward,

Concerned that part of the international movement of toxic and dangerous products and wastes is being carried out in contravention of existing national legislation and relevant international legal instruments, to the detriment of the environment and public health of all countries, particularly of developing countries,

. . .

Welcoming the convening of a diplomatic conference in Switzerland in 1989 for the purpose of adopting a global convention on control of transboundary movement of hazardous wastes . . .

1. *Requests* the Secretary-General to prepare a comprehensive report on the question of illegal traffic in toxic and dangerous products and wastes - that is, traffic in contravention of national legislation and relevant international legal instruments - as well as traffic not carried out in compliance with internationally accepted guidelines and principles in this field, and its impact on all countries, in particular developing countries, for submission to the General Assembly at its forty-fourth session, . . . ;

. . .

Note

. . .

2. UNEP/GC.14/17, annex IV.

- - - - -

Environmental Impact Assessment

UNEP Governing Council
Report of the 14th session, June 1987

A/42/2, Annex I
Extract

. . .

Decisions adopted by the Governing Council at its fourteenth session

14/25. Environmental impact assessment

The Governing Council,
. . .

Mindful that the environmental impacts of development activities, which may on occasion reach beyond national boundaries, can significantly affect the sustainability of such activities,

Convinced that the integration of environmental and natural resources issues into planning and programme implementation is indispensable in a process of sustainable development,

Considering that environmental impact assessment is a valuable means of promoting the integration of environmental and natural resources issues into planning and programme implementation and thereby helps to avoid potential adverse impacts,

1.   *Adopts* the Goals and Principles of Environmental Impact Assessment, as developed by the Working Group of Experts on Environmental Law;

. . .

3.   *Requests* the Executive Director to bring the Goals and Principles, together with the report of the Working Group, to the attention of all States and relevant international organizations, including multilateral development banks, and that, in doing so, he should inform them of the recommendation of the Governing Council that the Goals and Principles should be considered for use as a basis for preparing appropriate national measures, including legislation, and for international co-operation in the field of environmental impact assessment, including further international agreements, where appropriate;

4.   *Further requests* the Executive Director to this end:

(a)   To assist States, as appropriate, in implementing the Goals and Principles;

(b)   To conduct a survey of States and relevant international organizations on their experience in applying the Goals and Principles;

(c)   To investigate measures which could be undertaken to further international co-operation and agreement in the field, including the application of environmental impact assessment to development projects with possible transboundary environmental effects;

(d)   To report to the Governing Council at its next regular session on these matters.

. . .

- - - - -

UNEP Publication   Environmental Law Guidelines and Principles No. 9

Goals and Principles of Environmental Impact Assessment
(Decision 14/25 of the Governing Council of UNEP, of 17 June 1987)
Environmental Impact Assessment (EIA)[1]

EIA means an examination, analysis and assessment of planned activities with a view to ensuring environmentally sound and sustainable development.

The EIA goals and principles set out below are necessarily general in nature and may be further refined when fulfilling EIA tasks at the national, regional and international levels.

GOALS

1.   To establish that before decisions are taken by the competent authority or authorities to undertake or to authorize activities that are likely to significantly affect the environment, the environmental effects of those activities should be taken fully into account.

2.   To promote the implementation of appropriate procedures in all countries consistent with national laws and decision-making processes, through which the foregoing goal may be realized.

3.   To encourage the development of reciprocal procedures for information exchange, notification and consultation between States when proposed activities are likely to have significant transboundary effects on the environment of those States.

PRINCIPLES

Principle 1

States (including their competent authorities) should not undertake or authorize activities without prior consideration, at an early stage, of their environmental effects. Where the extent, nature or location of a proposed activity is such that it is likely to significantly affect the environment, a comprehensive environmental impact assessment should be undertaken in accordance with the following principles.

Principle 2

The criteria and procedures for determining whether an activity is likely to significantly affect the environment and is therefore subject to an EIA, should be defined clearly by legislation, regulation, or other means, so that subject activities can be quickly and surely identified, and EIA can be applied as the activity is being planned.[2]

Principle 3

In the EIA process the relevant significant environmental issues should be identified and studied. Where appropriate, all efforts should be made to identify these issues at an early stage in the process.

Principle 4

An EIA should include, at a minimum:

(a)   A description of the proposed activity;

(b)   A description of the potentially affected environment, including specific information necessary for identifying and assessing the environmental effects of the proposed activity;

(c)   A description of practical alternatives, as appropriate;

(d)   An assessment of the likely or potential environmental impacts of the proposed activity and alternatives, including the direct, indirect, cumulative, short-term and long-term effects;

(e)   An identification and description of measures available to mitigate adverse environmental impacts of the proposed activity and alternatives, and an assessment of those measures;

(f)   An indication of gaps in knowledge and uncertainties which may be encountered in compiling the required information;

(g)   An indication of whether the environment of any other State or areas beyond national jurisdiction is likely to the affected by the proposed activity or alternatives;

(h)   A brief, non-technical summary of the information provided under the above headings.

Principle 5

The environmental effects in an EIA should be assessed with a degree of detail commensurate with their likely environmental significance.

Principle 6

The information provided as part of EIA should be examined impartially prior to the decision.

Principle 7

Before a decision is made on an activity, government agencies, members of the public, experts in relevant disciplines and interested groups should be allowed appropriate opportunity to comment on the EIA.

Principle 8

A decision as to whether a proposed activity should be authorized or undertaken should not be taken until an appropriate period has elapsed to consider comments pursuant to principles 7 and 12.

Principle 9

The decision on any proposed activity subject to an EIA should be in writing, state the reasons therefor, and include the provisions, if any, to prevent, reduce or mitigate damage to the environment.

This decision should be made available to interested persons or groups.

Principle 10

Where it is justified, following a decision on an activity which has been subject to an EIA, the activity and its effects on the environment or the provisions (pursuant to Principle 9) of the decision on this activity should be subject to appropriate supervision.

Principle 11

States should endeavour to conclude bilateral, regional or multilateral arrangements, as appropriate, so as to provide, on the basis of reciprocity, notification, exchange of information, and agreed-upon consultation on the potential environmental effects of activities under their control or jurisdiction which are likely to significantly affect other States or areas beyond national jurisdiction.

Principle 12

When information provided as part of an EIA indicates that the environment within another State is likely to be significantly affected by a proposed activity, the State in which the activity is being planned should, to the extent possible:

(a)   notify the potentially affected State of the proposed activity;

(b)   transmit to the potentially affected State any relevant information from the EIA, the transmission of which is not prohibited by national laws or regulations; and

(c)   when it is agreed between the States concerned, enter into timely consultations.

Principle 13

Appropriate measures should be established to ensure implementation of EIA procedures.

Notes

1.   In this document an assessment of the impact of a planned activity on the environment is referred to as an environmental impact assessment (EIA).

2.   For instance, this principle may be implemented through a variety of mechanisms, including:

    (a)   Lists of categories of activities that by their nature are, or are not, likely to have significant effects;

    (b)   Lists of areas that are of special importance or sensitivity (such as national parks or wetland areas), so that any activity affecting such areas is likely to have significant effects;

    (c)   Lists of categories of resources (such as water, tropical rain forests, etc.), or environmental problems (such as increased soil erosion, desertification, deforestation) which are of special concern, so that any diminution of such resources of exacerbation of such problems is likely to be "significant";

    (d)   An "initial environmental evaluation", a quick and informal assessment of the proposed activity to determine whether its effects are likely to be significant;

    (e)   Criteria to guide determinations whether the effects of a proposed activity are likely to be significant.

If a listing system is used, it is recommended that States reserve the discretion to require the preparation of an EIA on an ad hoc basis, to ensure that they have the flexibility needed to respond to unanticipated cases.

- - - - -

Additional References

UNEP Governing Council decision l3/18/III. UNEP doc. UNEP/GC.13/16 (also A/40/25).

UNEP Working Group of Experts on Environmental Law. Reports of the first and second sessions. UNEP/WG.107/3 and UNEP/WG.152/4.

Proposed principles and guidelines (by the Working Group). UNEP/WG.152/2.

Environmental Series 1 of the UN Regional Economic Commission for Europe(ECE). UN doc. ECE/ENV/50 (also Sales No. E.87.II.E.14.).

General References

UNEP 1986 Annual Report of the Executive Director, Part One. UNEP/GC.14/3 (Also Sales No. E.87.III.D.2).

Proposed scope and approach of the cross-organizational programme analysis of the activities of the United Nations system in the area of the environment. Report of the Secretary-General. Committee for Programme and Co-ordination, 27th session, May 1987. UN doc. E/AC.51/1987/5.

Proceedings of the Governing Council at its fourteenth session.   UNEP doc. UNEP/GC.14/26.

Other decisions adopted by the Governing Council at its 14th session and related documents:

14/1.   Programme policy and implementation
A.   Policy matters and future orientation of the work of UNEP
B.   New initiatives
C.   International conferences on the environment
(See UNEP/GC.14/4/Add.4)
14/2.   Reports of the Administrative Committee on Co-ordination
(See UNEP/GC.14/8 and UNEP/GC.14/12)
14/7.   Environment and financial institutions: co-operation between UNEP and the Committee of International Development Institutions on the Environment
(See UNEP/GC.14/2, chap.IV; UNEP/GC.14/3, chap.IV; UNEP/GC.14/4/Add.5)
14/9.   State-of-the-environment reports
A.   Health and the environment
B.   The state of the world environment 1987
C.   Emerging environmental issues
D.   Environmental events
E.   State of the environment in developing countries
(See UNEP/GC.14/5 and UNEP/GC.14/6)
14/12.   In-depth study of the UN intergovernmental structure and functions in the economic and social fields
14/16.   Promotion of the transfer of environmental protection technology
14/18.   The International Environmental Information System (INFOTERRA)
14/19.   International Register of Potentially Toxic Chemicals
14/20.   Global climate change
(See Resolution 3.20 (Cg-X) of the WMO Tenth Congress)
14/24.   Improvement and harmonization of environmental measurement
14/27.   Environmentally safe management of chemicals, in particular those that are banned and severely restricted in international trade
(See UNEP/GC.14/17, annex IV)
14/28.   Protection of the ozone layer
14/29.   International conventions and protocols in the field of the environment
(See UNEP/GC.14/18 and Add.1)
14/32.   List of selected environmentally harmful chemical substances, processes and phenomena of global significance
(See UNEP/GC.14/19)

- - - - -

Nuclear Safety

First Special Session of the IAEA   GC(SPL.1)RESOLUTIONS/(1986)
General Conference, September 1986

Final Document of the Special Session of the General Conference

The General Conference, at its special session on nuclear safety and radiological protection:

Role of Nuclear Energy

- Recognizes that nuclear power will continue to be an important source of energy for social and economic development.

- Emphasizes that the highest level of nuclear safety will continue to be essential to the use of this energy source.

Responsibility of States

- Reaffirms that each country engaged in nuclear energy activities is itself responsible for ensuring the nuclear and radiation safety, physical security and environmental compatibility of its nuclear facilities and activities.

International Co-operation

- Appeals for a strengthening of international co-operation, at both the bilateral and the multilateral level, with regard to nuclear safety, radiological protection, physical security and environmental compatibility.

Role of the IAEA

- Reaffirms the central role of the Agency, under its Statute, in encouraging and facilitating international co-operation in the peaceful uses of nuclear energy, including nuclear safety and radiological protection.

- Reaffirms the usefulness of the Agency's continuing programmes for enhanced nuclear safety and radiological protection, and urges all Members to co-operate fully in the implementation of these programmes.

- Underlines the importance of and need for future increased efforts within the Agency, and in co-operation with other concerned international organizations, to promote the safe application of nuclear power.

Post-Accident Review

- Expresses its satisfaction with the post-accident review meeting conducted from 25 to 29 August 1986 under the auspices of the Agency.

- Expresses its appreciation to the participating experts from the Soviet Union for providing, in the context of this meeting, valuable information for understanding the accident.

- Takes note of the report on the post-accident review meeting and requests the Board of Governors to consider carefully any proposals for enhanced nuclear safety and radiological protection activities in its future review of the regular Agency programme, taking into consideration - *inter alia* - the valuable information and recommendations resulting from that meeting.

Conventions on Notification and Assistance

- Adopts the texts of the Convention of Early Notification of a Nuclear Accident and the Convention on Assistance in the Case of a Nuclear Accident or Radiological Emergency, which are attached, and decides to open the Conventions for signature on 26 September 1986

- Takes note of the statements made by several States as to the need for early notification of all nuclear accidents with radiological safety significance and of the declarations made by several States on their readiness to notify also nuclear accidents other than those specified in Article 1 of the Convention on Early Notification.

- Recognizes the role entrusted to the Agency in the implementation of the Convention.

- Appeals to all States to sign and become Party to the Conventions as promptly as possible.

- Appeals to all Signatory States for which the Conventions will not enter into force immediately to declare, whenever possible, that they will provisionally apply either or both of the Conventions pending their entry into force for such States.

RESOLUTION ON MEASURES TO STRENGTHEN INTERNATIONAL CO-OPERATION IN NUCLEAR SAFETY AND RADIOLOGICAL PROTECTION

The General Conference,

(a) *Having adopted* the texts of the Convention on Early Notification of a Nuclear Accident, the Convention on Assistance in the Case of a Nuclear Accident or Radiological Emergency, and the final document of this special session,

(b) *Taking note* of the statements and proposals made during this special session, and

(c) *Convinced that* the subject-matter of international co-operation in the field of nuclear safety has not yet been exhausted and that further consideration should be given to the above-mentioned statements and proposals,

1. *Decides* that all statements and proposals made during the general debate and in the Committee of the Whole which relate to the subject-matter* shall be referred to the Board of Governors;

2.   *Requests* the Board of Governors to pursue the discussion of the above-mentioned statements and proposals, including the proposals submitted by Mexico on behalf of the Group of 77, by all interested Member States; and

3.   *Requests* the Board of Governors to submit to the General Conference at its 31st regular session a report on the implementation of the two above-mentioned Conventions and of this resolution.

---

*   These include the proposals reflected in the relevant summary records (GC(SPL.1)/OR.1-8 and GC(SPL.1)/COM.5/OR.1-3) and in the following Conference documents submitted by Governments: GC(SPL.1)/5; 6 and 7(Mexico on behalf of the Group of 77), 8, 9, 10, 12, 13, 14, and 16.3.

- - - - -

Convention on Early Notification of A Nuclear Accident
(entered into force 27 October 1986)
IAEA GC(SPL.I)/Resolutions(1986)

The States Parties to This Convention,

Aware that nuclear activities are being carried out in a number of States,

Noting that comprehensive measures have been and are being taken to ensure a high level of safety in nuclear activities, aimed at preventing nuclear accidents and minimizing the consequences of any such accident, should it occur,

Desiring to strengthen further international co-operation in the safe development and use of nuclear energy,

Convinced of the need for States to provide relevant information about nuclear accidents as early as possible in order that transboundary radiological consequences can be minimized,

Noting the usefulness of bilateral and multilateral arrangements on information exchange in this area,

Have Agreed as follows:

Article 1
Scope of application

1.   This Convention shall apply in the event of any accident involving facilities or activities of a State Party or of persons or legal entities under its jurisdiction or control, referred to in paragraph 2 below, from which a release of radioactive material occurs or is likely to occur

and which has resulted or may result in an international transboundary release that could be of radiological safety significance for another State.

2.   The facilities and activities referred to in paragraph 1 are the following:

(a)   any nuclear reactor wherever located;

(b)   any nuclear fuel cycle facility;

(c)   any radioactive waste management facility;

(d)   the transport and storage of nuclear fuels or radioactive wastes;

(e)   the manufacture, use, storage, disposal and transport of radioisotopes for agricultural, industrial, medical and related scientific and research purposes; and

(f)   the use of radioisotopes for power generation in space objects.

Article 2
Notification and information

In the event of an accident specified in article 1 (hereinafter referred to as a "nuclear accident"), the State Party referred to in that article shall:

(a)   forthwith notify, directly or through the International Atomic Energy Agency (hereinafter referred to as the "Agency"), those States which are or may be physically affected as specified in article 1 and the Agency of the nuclear accident, its nature, the time of its occurrence and its exact location where appropriate; and

(b)   promptly provide the States referred to in sub-paragraph (a), directly or through the Agency, and the Agency with such available information relevant to minimizing the radiological consequences in those States, as specified in article 5.

Article 3
Other Nuclear Accidents

With a view to minimizing the radiological consequences, States Parties may notify in the event of nuclear accidents other than those specified in article 1.

Article 4
Functions of the Agency

The Agency shall:

(a)   forthwith inform States Parties, Member States, other States which are or may be physically affected a specified in article 1 and relevant international intergovernmental organizations (hereinafter referred to as "international organizations") of a notification received pursuant to sub-paragraph (a) of article 2; and

(b)   promptly provide any State Party, Member State or relevant international organization, upon request, with the information received pursuant to sub-paragraph (b) of article 2.

Article 5
Information to be provided

1.   The information to be provided pursuant to sub-paragraph (b) of article 2 shall comprise the following data as then available to the notifying State Party:

(a)   the time, exact location where appropriate, and the nature of the nuclear accident;

(b)   the facility or activity involved;

(c)   the assumed or established cause and the foreseeable development of the nuclear accident relevant to the transboundary release of the radioactive materials;

(d)   the general characteristics of the radioactive release, including, as far as is practicable and appropriate, the nature, probable physical and chemical form and the quantity, composition and effective height of the radioactive release;

(e)   information on current and forecast meteorological and hydrological conditions, necessary for forecasting the transboundary release of the radioactive materials;

(f)   the results of environmental monitoring relevant to the transboundary release of the radioactive materials;

(g)   the off-site protective measures taken or planned;

(h)   the predicted behaviour over time of the radioactive release.

2.   Such information shall be supplemented at appropriate intervals by further relevant information on the development of the emergency situation, including its foreseeable or actual termination.

3.   Information received pursuant to sub-paragraph (b) of article 2 may be used without restriction, except when such information is provided in confidence by the notifying State Party.

Article 6
Consultations

A State Party providing information pursuant to sub-paragraph (b) of article 2 shall, as far as is reasonably practicable, respond promptly to a request for further information or consultations sought by an affected State Party with a view to minimizing the radiological consequences in that State.

Article 7
Competent authorities and points of contact

1.   Each State Party shall make known to the Agency and to other States Parties, directly or through the Agency, its competent authorities and point of contact responsible for issuing and

receiving the notification and information referred to in article 2. Such points of contact and a focal point within the Agency shall be available continuously.

2.   Each State Party shall promptly inform the Agency of any changes that may occur in the information referred to in paragraph 1.

3.   The Agency shall maintain an up-to-date list of such national authorities and points of contact as well as points of contact of relevant international organizations and shall provide it to States parties and Member States and to relevant international organizations.

Article 8
Assistance to States Parties

The Agency shall, in accordance with its Statute and upon a request of a State Party which does not have nuclear activities itself and borders on a State having an active nuclear programme but not a Party, conduct investigations into the feasibility and establishment of an appropriate radiation monitoring system in order to facilitate the achievement of the objectives of this Convention.

Article 9
Bilateral and multilateral arrangements

In furtherance of their mutual interests, States Parties may consider, where deemed appropriate, the conclusion of bilateral or multilateral arrangements relating to the subject matter of this Convention.

Article 10
Relationship to other international agreements

This Convention shall not affect the reciprocal rights and obligations of States Parties under existing international agreements which relate to the matters covered by this Convention, or under future international agreements concluded in accordance with the object and purpose of this Convention.

Article 11
Settlement of disputes

1.   In the event of a dispute between States Parties, or between a State Party and the Agency, concerning the interpretation or application of this Convention, the parties to the dispute shall consult with a view to the settlement of the dispute by negotiation or by any other peaceful means of settling disputes acceptable to them.

2.   If a dispute of this character between States Parties cannot be settled within one year from the request for consultation pursuant to paragraph 1, it shall, at the request of any party to such dispute, be submitted to arbitration or referred to the International Court of Justice for decision. Where a dispute is submitted to arbitration, if, within six months from the date of the request, the parties to the dispute are unable to agree on the organization of the arbitration, a party may request the President of the International Court of Justice or the Secretary-General of the United Nations to appoint one or more arbitrators. In cases of conflicting requests by the parties to the dispute, the request to the Secretary-General of the United Nations shall have priority.

3.   When signing, ratifying, accepting, approving or acceding to this Convention, a State may declare that it does not consider itself bound by either or both of the dispute settlement procedures provided for in paragraph 2. The other States Parties shall not be bound by a dispute settlement procedure provided for in paragraph 2 with respect to a State Party for which such a declaration is in force.

4.   A State Party which has made a declaration in accordance with paragraph 3 may at any time withdraw it by notification to the depositary.

Article 12
Entry into force

1.   This Convention shall be open for signature by all States and Namibia, represented by the United Nations Council for Namibia, at the Headquarters of the International Atomic Energy Agency in Vienna and at the Headquarters of the United Nations in New York, from 26 September 1986 and 6 October 1986 respectively, until its entry into force or for twelve months, whichever period is longer.

2.   A State and Namibia, represented by the United Nations Council for Namibia, may express its consent to be bound by this Convention either by signature, or by deposit of an instrument of ratification, acceptance or approval following signature made subject to ratification, acceptance or approval, or by deposit of an instrument of accession. The instruments of ratification, acceptance, approval or accession shall be deposited with the depositary.

3.   This Convention shall enter into force thirty days after consent to be bound has been expressed by three States.

4.   For each State expressing consent to be bound by this convention after its entry into force, this Convention shall enter into force for that State thirty days after the date of expression of consent.

5.   (a) This Convention shall be open for accession as, provided for in this article, by international organizations and regional integration organizations constituted by sovereign States, which have competence in respect of the negotiation, conclusion and application of international agreements in matters covered by this Convention.

(b) In matters within their competence such organizations shall, on their own behalf, exercise the rights and fulfil the obligations which this Convention attributes to States Parties.

(c) When depositing its instrument of accession, such an organization shall communicate to the depositary a declaration indicating the extent of its competence in respect of matters covered by this Convention.

(d) Such an organization shall not hold any vote additional to those of its Member States.

Article 13
Provisional application

A State may, upon signature or at any later date before this Convention enters into force for it, declare that it will apply this Convention provisionally.

Article 14
Amendments

1.   A State Party may propose amendments to this Convention. The proposed amendment shall be submitted to the depositary who shall circulate it immediately to all other States Parties.

2.   If a majority of the States parties request the depositary to convene a conference to consider the proposed amendments, the depositary shall invite all States Parties to attend such a conference to begin not sooner than thirty days after the invitations are issued. Any amendment adopted at the conference by a two-thirds majority of all States Parties shall be laid down in a protocol which is open to signature in Vienna and New York by all States Parties.

3.   The protocol shall enter into force thirty days after consent to be bound has been expressed by three States. For each State expressing consent to be bound by the protocol after its entry into force, the protocol shall enter into force for that State thirty days after the date of expression of consent.

Article 15
Denunciation

1.   A State Party may denounce this Convention by written notification to the depositary.

2.   Denunciation shall take effect one year following the date on which the notification is received by the depositary.

Article 16
Depositary

1.   The Director General of the Agency shall be the depositary of this Convention.

2.   The Director General of the Agency shall promptly notify States Parties and all other States of:

(a)   each signature of this Convention or any protocol of amendment;

(b)   each deposit of an instrument of ratification, acceptance, approval or accession concerning this Convention or any protocol of amendment;

(c)   any declaration or withdrawal thereof in accordance with article 11;

(d)   any declaration of provisional application of this Convention in accordance with article 13;

(e)   the entry into force of this Convention and of any amendment thereto; and

(f)   any denunciation made under article 15.

Article 17
Authentic texts and certified copies

The original of this Convention, of which the Arabic, Chinese, English, French, Russian and Spanish texts are equally authentic, shall be deposited with the Director General of the International Atomic Energy Agency who shall send certified copies to States Parties and all other States.

In Witness Whereof the undersigned, being duly authorized, have signed this Convention, open for signature as provided for in paragraph 1 of article 12.

Adopted by the General Conference of the International Atomic Energy Agency meeting in special session at Vienna on the Twenty-sixth day of September one thousand nine hundred and eighty-six.

- - - - -

Convention on Assistance in the Case of a Nuclear Accident or Radiological Emergency
(entered into force 26 February 1987)
IAEA GC(SPL.I)/Resolutions(1986)

The States Parties to This Convention,

Aware that nuclear activities are being carried out in a number of States,

Noting that comprehensive measures have been and are being taken to ensure a high level of safety in nuclear activities, aimed at preventing nuclear accidents and minimizing the consequences of any such accident, should it occur,

Desiring to strengthen further international co-operation in the safe development and use of nuclear energy,

Convinced of the need for an international framework which will facilitate the prompt provision of assistance in the event of a nuclear accident or radiological emergency to mitigate its consequences,

Noting the usefulness of bilateral and multilateral arrangements on mutual assistance in this area,

Noting the activities of the International Atomic Energy Agency in developing guidelines for mutual emergency assistance arrangements in connection with a nuclear accident of radiological emergency,

Have Agreed as follows:

Article 1
General provisions

1.   The States Parties shall cooperate between themselves and with the International Atomic Energy Agency (hereinafter referred to as the "Agency") in accordance with the provisions of this Convention to facilitate prompt assistance in the event of a nuclear accident or radiological emergency to minimize its consequences and to protect life, property and the environment from the effects of radioactive releases.

2.   To facilitate such cooperation States Parties may agree on bilateral or multilateral arrangements or, where appropriate, a combination of these for preventing or minimizing injury and damage which may result in the event of a nuclear accident or radiological emergency.

3.   The States Parties request the Agency, acting within the framework of its Statute, to use its best endeavours in accordance with the provisions of this Convention to promote, facilitate and support the cooperation between States parties provided for in this Convention.

Article 2
Provisions of assistance

1.   If a State Party needs assistance in the event of a nuclear accident or radiological emergency, whether or not such accident or emergency originates within its territory, jurisdiction or control, it may call for such assistance from any other State Party, directly or through the Agency, and from the Agency, or, where appropriate, from other international intergovernmental organizations (hereinafter referred to as "international organizations").

2.   A State Party requesting assistance shall specify the scope and type of assistance required and, where practicable, provide the assisting party with such information as may be necessary for that party to determine the extent to which it is able to meet the request. In the event that it is not practicable for the requesting State Party to specify the scope and type of assistance required, the requesting State Party and the assisting party shall, in consultation, decide upon the scope and type of assistance.

3.   Each State Party to which a request for such assistance is directed shall promptly decide and notify the requesting State Party, directly or through the Agency, whether it is in a position to render the assistance requested, and the scope and terms of the assistance that might be rendered.

4.   States Parties shall, within the limits of their capabilities, identify and notify the Agency of experts, equipment and materials which could be made available for the provision of assistance to other States Parties in the event of a nuclear accident or radiological emergency as well as the terms, especially financial, under which such assistance could be provided.

5.   Any State Party may request assistance relating to medical treatment or temporary relocation into the territory of another State Party of people involved in a nuclear accident or radiological emergency.

6.   The Agency shall respond, in accordance with its Statute and as provided for in this Convention, to a requesting State Party's or a Member State's request for assistance in the event of a nuclear accident or radiological emergency by:

(a)   making available appropriate resources allocated for this purpose;

(b)   transmitting promptly the request to other States and international organizations which, according to the Agency's information, may possess the necessary resources; and

(c)   if so requested by the requesting State, co-ordinating the assistance at the international level which may thus become available.

Article 3
Direction and control of assistance

Unless otherwise agreed:

(a)   the overall direction, control, co-ordination and supervision of the assistance shall be the responsibility within its territory of the requesting State. The assisting party should, where the assistance involves personnel, designate in consultation with the requesting State, the person who should be in charge of and retain immediate operational supervision over the personnel and the equipment provided by it. The designated person should exercise such supervision in cooperation with the appropriate authorities of the requesting State;

(b)   the requesting State shall provide, to the extent of its capabilities, local facilities and services for the proper and effective administration of the assistance. It shall also ensure the protection of personnel, equipment and materials brought into its territory by or on behalf of the assisting party for such purpose;

(c)   ownership of equipment and materials provided by either party during the periods of assistance shall be unaffected, and their return shall be ensured;

(d)   a State Party providing assistance in response to a request under paragraph 5 of article 2 shall co-ordinate that assistance within its territory.

Article 4
Competent authorities and points of contact

1.   Each State Party shall make known to the Agency and to other States Parties, directly or through the Agency, its competent authorities and point of contact authorized to make and receive requests for and to accept offers of assistance. Such points of contact and a focal point within the Agency shall be available continuously.

2.   Each State Party shall promptly inform the Agency of any changes that may occur in the information referred to in paragraph 1.

3.   The Agency shall regularly and expeditiously provide to States Parties, Member States and relevant international organizations the information referred to in paragraphs 1 and 2.

Article 5
Functions of the Agency

The States Parties request the Agency, in accordance with paragraph 3 of article 1 and without prejudice to other provisions of this Convention, to:

(a) collect and disseminate to States Parties and Member States information concerning:

    (i) experts, equipment and materials which could be made available in the event of nuclear accidents or radiological emergencies;

    (ii) methodologies, techniques and available results of research relating to response to nuclear accidents or radiological emergencies;

(b) assist a State Party or a Member State when requested in any of the following or other appropriate matters:

    (i) preparing both emergency plans in the case of nuclear accidents and radiological emergencies and the appropriate legislation;

    (ii) developing appropriate training programmes for personnel to deal with nuclear accidents and radiological emergencies;

    (iii) transmitting requests for assistance and relevant information in the event of a nuclear accident or radiological emergency;

    (iv) developing appropriate radiation monitoring programmes, procedures and standards;

    (v) conducting investigations into the feasibility of establishing appropriate radiation monitoring systems;

(c) make available to a State Party or a Member State requesting assistance in the event of a nuclear accident or radiological emergency appropriate resources allocated for the purpose of conducting an initial assessment of the accident or emergency;

(d) offer its good offices to the States Parties and Member States in the event of a nuclear accident or radiological emergency;

(e) establish and maintain liaison with relevant international organizations for the purposes of obtaining and exchanging relevant information and data, and make a list of such organizations available to States Parties, Member States and the aforementioned organizations.

Article 6
Confidentiality and public statements

1.   The requesting State and the assisting party shall protect the confidentiality of any confidential information that becomes available to either of them in connection with the assistance in the event of a nuclear accident or radiological emergency. Such information shall be used exclusively for the purpose of the assistance agreed upon.

2.   The assisting party shall make every effort to coordinate with the requesting State before releasing information to the public on the assistance provided in connection with a nuclear accident or radiological emergency.

Article 7
Reimbursement of costs

1.   An assisting party may offer assistance without costs to the requesting State. When considering whether to offer assistance on such a basis, the assisting party shall take into account:

    (a)   the nature of the nuclear accident or radiological emergency;

    (b)   the place of origin of the nuclear accident or radiological emergency;

    (c)   the needs of developing countries;

    (d)   the particular needs of countries without nuclear facilities; and

    (e)   any other relevant factors.

2.   When assistance is provided wholly or partly on a reimbursement basis, the requesting State shall reimburse the assisting party for the costs incurred for the services rendered by persons or organizations acting on its behalf, and for all expenses in connection with the assistance to the extent that such expenses are not directly defrayed by the requesting State. Unless otherwise agreed, reimbursement shall be provided promptly after the assisting party has presented its request for reimbursement to the requesting State, and in respect of costs other than local costs, shall be freely transferrable.

3.   Notwithstanding paragraph 2, the assisting party may at any time waive, or agree to the postponement of, the reimbursement in whole or in part. In considering such waiver or postponement, assisting parties shall give due consideration to the needs of developing countries.

Article 8
Privileges, immunities and facilities

1.   The requesting State shall afford to personnel of the assisting party and personnel acting on its behalf the necessary privileges, immunities and facilities for the performance of their assistance functions.

2.   The requesting State shall afford the following privileges and immunities to personnel of the assisting party or personnel acting on its behalf who have been duly notified to and accepted by the requesting State:

    (a)   immunity from arrest, detention and legal process, including criminal, civil and administrative jurisdiction, of the requesting State, in respect of acts or omissions in the performance of their duties; and

(b)   exemption from taxation, duties or other charges, except those which are normally incorporated in the price of goods or paid for services rendered, in respect of the performance of their assistance functions.

3.   The requesting State shall:

(a)   afford the assisting party exemption from taxation, duties or other charges on the equipment and property brought into the territory of the requesting State by the Assisting party for the purpose of the assistance; and

(b)   provide immunity from seizure, attachment or requisition of such equipment and property.

4.   The requesting State shall ensure the return of such equipment and property. If requested by the assisting party, the requesting State shall arrange, to the extent it is able to do so, for the necessary decontamination of recoverable equipment involved in the assistance before its return.

5.   The requesting State shall facilitate the entry into, stay in and departure from its national territory of personnel notified pursuant to paragraph 2 and of equipment and property involved in the assistance.

6.   Nothing in this article shall require the requesting State to provide its nationals or permanent residents with the privileges and immunities provided for in the forgoing paragraphs.

7.   Without prejudice to the privileges and immunities, all beneficiaries enjoying such privileges and immunities under this article have a duty to respect the laws and regulations of the requesting State. They shall also have a duty not to interfere in the domestic affairs of the requesting State.

8.   Nothing in this article shall prejudice rights and obligations with respect to privileges and immunities afforded pursuant to other international agreements or the rules of customary international law.

9.   When signing, ratifying, accepting, approving or acceding to this Convention, a State may declare that it does not consider itself bound in whole or in part by paragraphs 2 and 3.

10.   A State Party which has made a declaration in accordance with paragraph 9 may at any time withdraw it by notification to the depositary.

Article 9
Transit of personnel, equipment and property

Each State Party shall, at the request of the requesting State or the assisting party, seek to facilitate the transit through its territory of duly notified personnel, equipment and property involved in the assistance to and from the requesting State.

Article 10
Claims and compensation

1. The States Parties shall closely cooperate in order to facilitate the settlement of legal proceedings and claims under this article.

2. Unless otherwise agreed, a requesting State shall in respect of death or of injury to persons, damage to or loss of property, or damage to the environment caused within its territory or other area under its jurisdiction or control in the course of providing the assistance requested:

    (a) not bring any legal proceedings against the assisting party or persons or other legal entities acting on its behalf;

    (b) assume responsibility for dealing with legal proceedings and claims brought by third parties against the assisting party or against persons or other legal entities acting on its behalf;

    (c) hold the assisting party or persons or other legal entities acting on its behalf harmless in respect of legal proceedings and claims referred to in sub-paragraph (b); and

    (d) compensate the assisting party or persons or other legal entities acting on its behalf for:

        (i) death of or injury to personnel of the assisting party or persons acting on its behalf;
        (ii) loss of or damage to non-consumable equipment or materials related to the assistance;

except in cases of willful misconduct by the individuals who caused the death, injury, loss or damage.

3. This article shall not prevent compensation or indemnity available under any applicable international agreement or national law of any State.

4. Nothing in this article shall require the requesting State to apply paragraph 2 in whole or in part to its nationals or permanent residents.

5. When signing, ratifying, accepting, approving or acceding to this Convention, a State may declare:

    (a) that it does not consider itself bound in whole or in part by paragraph 2;

    (b) that it will not apply paragraph 2 in whole or in part in cases of gross negligence by the individuals who caused the death, injury, loss or damage.

6. A State Party which has made a declaration in accordance with paragraph 5 may at any time withdraw it by notification to the depositary.

Article 11
Termination of assistance

The requesting State or the assistant party may at any time, after appropriate consultations and by notification in writing, request the termination of assistance received or provided under this Convention. Once such a request has been made, the parties involved shall consult with each other to make arrangements for the proper conclusion of the assistance.

Article 12
Relationship to other international agreements

This Convention shall not affect the reciprocal rights and obligations of States Parties under existing international agreements which relate to the matters covered by this Convention, or under future international agreements concluded in accordance with the object and purpose of this Convention.

Article 13
Settlement of disputes

1. In the event of a dispute between States Parties, or between a State Party and the Agency, concerning the interpretation or application of this Convention, the parties to the dispute shall consult with a view to the settlement of the dispute by negotiation or by any other peaceful means of settling disputes acceptable to them.

2. If a dispute of this character between States Parties cannot be settled within one year from the request for consultation pursuant to paragraph 1, it shall, at the request of any party to such dispute, be submitted to arbitration or referred to the International Court of Justice for decision. Where a dispute is submitted to arbitration, if, within six months from the date of the request, the parties to the dispute are unable to agree on the organization of the arbitration, a party may request the President of the International Court of Justice or the Secretary-General of the United Nations to appoint one or more arbitrators. In cases of conflicting requests by the parties to the dispute, the request to the Secretary-General of the United Nations shall have priority.

3. When signing, ratifying, accepting, approving or acceding to this Convention, a State may declare that it does not consider itself bound by either or both of the dispute settlement procedure provided for in paragraph 2 with respect to a State Party for which such a declaration is in force.

4. A State Party which has made a declaration in accordance with paragraph 3 may at any time withdraw it by notification to the depositary.

Article 14
Entry into force

1. This Convention shall be open for signature by all States and Namibia, represented by the United National Council for Namibia, at the Headquarters of the International Atomic energy Agency in Vienna and at the Headquarters of the United Nations in New York, from 26 September 1986 and 6 October 1986 respectively, until its entry into force or for twelve months, whichever period is longer.

2.   A State and Namibia, represented by the United Nations Council for Namibia, may express its consent to be bound by this Convention either by signature, or by deposit of an instrument of ratification, acceptance or approval following signature made subject to ratification, acceptance or approval, or by deposit of an instrument of accession. The instruments of ratification, acceptance, approval or accession shall be deposited with the depositary.

3.   This Convention shall enter into force thirty days after consent to be bound has been expressed by three States.

4.   For each State expressing consent to be bound by this Convention after its entry into force, this Convention shall enter into force for that State thirty days after the date of expression of consent.

5.   (a)   This Convention shall be open for accession, as provided for in this article, by international organizations and regional integration organizations constituted by sovereign States, which have competence in respect of the negotiation, conclusion and application of international agreements in matters covered by this Convention.

      (b)   In matters within their competence such organizations shall, on their own behalf, exercise the rights and fulfil the obligations which this Convention attributes to States Parties.

      (c)   When depositing its instrument of accession, such an organization shall communicate to the depositary a declaration indicating the extent of its competence in respect of matters covered by this Convention.

      (d)   Such an organization shall not hold any vote additional to those of its Member States.

Article 15
Provisional application

A State may, upon signature or at any later date before this Convention enters into force for it, declare that it will apply this Convention provisionally.

Article 16
Amendments

1.   A State Party may propose amendments to this Convention. The proposed amendment shall be submitted to the depositary who shall circulate it immediately to all other State Parties.

2.   If a majority of the States Parties request the depositary to convene a conference to consider the proposed amendments, the depositary shall invite all States Parties to attend such a conference to begin not sooner than thirty days after the invitations are issued. Any amendment adopted at the conference by a two-thirds majority of all States Parties shall be laid down in a protocol which is open to signature in Vienna and New York by all States Parties.

3.   The protocol shall enter into force thirty days after consent to be bound has been expressed by three States. For each State expressing consent to be bound by the protocol after its entry into force, the protocol shall enter into force for that State thirty days after the date of expression of consent.

Article 17
Denunciation

1.   A State Party may denounce this Convention by written notification to the depositary.

2.   Denunciation shall take effect one year following the date on which the notification is received by the depositary.

Article 18
Depositary

1.   The Director General of the Agency shall be the depositary of this Convention.

2.   The Director General of the Agency shall promptly notify States Parties and all other States of:

(a)   each signature of this Convention or any protocol of amendment;

(b)   each deposit of an instrument of ratification, acceptance, approval or accession concerning this Convention or any protocol of amendment;

(c)   any declaration or withdrawal thereof in accordance with articles 8, 10 and 13;

(d)   any declaration of provisional application of this Convention in accordance with article 15;

(e)   the entry into force of this Convention and of any amendment thereto; and

(f)   any denunciation made under article 17.

Article 19
Authentic texts and certified copies

The original of this Convention, of which the Arabic, Chinese, English, French, Russian and Spanish texts are equally authentic, shall be deposited with the Director General of the International Atomic Energy Agency who shall send certified copies to States Parties and all other States.

In Witness Whereof the undersigned, being duly authorized, have signed this Convention, open for signature as provided for in paragraph 1 of article 14.

Adopted by the General Conference of the International Atomic Energy Agency meeting in special session at Vienna on the twenty-sixth day of September one thousand nine hundred and eighty-six.

- - - - -

Report of the United Nations Conference   A/CONF.108/7
for the Promotion of International Co-operation   Extract
in the Peaceful Uses of Nuclear Energy, April 1987

. . .

IV. Summary of the General Debate

. . .

70. All speakers emphasized the importance of nuclear safety. Several noted that the problem of ensuring nuclear safety could not be a matter pertaining to only one country, but had to be dealt with by the whole international community. Some speakers advocated the creation of an international system for the safe development of nuclear power. A number of speakers recalled that the safety of nuclear installations was the exclusive responsibility of the State concerned, a responsibility which could not be delegated without jeopardizing the safety itself. Stressing the need for international co-operation in this matter, they noted that such co-operation should have as a primary goal assistance to States in undertaking their national responsibilities. Other speakers stated that the transboundary effects of possible nuclear accidents required international co-operative measures.

71. In that regard, several speakers suggested that international nuclear safety co-operation needed to be strengthened. They expressed satisfaction with the two Conventions concluded in 1986 under the aegis of the IAEA - namely, the Convention on the Early Notification of a Nuclear Accident and the Convention on Assistance in the Case of a Nuclear Accident or Radiological Emergency. It was noted that the recent adoption of those two Conventions was further evidence of the competence and efficacy of the IAEA. Several speakers said that there was a need to supplement the two Conventions with bilateral and regional agreements, *inter alia*, by establishing civil liability with respect to those countries which were not engaged in nuclear energy production.

72. None the less, a number of speakers emphasized that those Conventions were not by themselves enough. While the Conventions were aimed at mitigating the consequences of an accident, reducing the risk of an accident was even more important, it was stated. It had become evident that there was need for closer co-operation of a long-term and comprehensive nature, relating to the safe development of nuclear power in its totality and embracing all stages from planning to designing, siting and operation, to waste disposal and health and environmental concerns. A suggestion made was that binding rules should be established to guide safety at nuclear installations on a global basis.

73. Many countries, both developing and developed, shared the view that regional co-operation could also assist their nuclear energy programmes. In particular, the benefits could be seen in terms of reduced costs of construction and maintenance and other factors. It was suggested that regional environmental monitoring systems be established in Africa and Asia, under the IAEA, in order to provide radiological monitoring. It was also proposed that the management of disposal of radioactive wastes should be undertaken on a regional basis.

74. There was also support given by participants to regional arrangements covering, *inter alia*, the CMEA countries, the OECD countries, EURATOM, the Nordic countries, the IAEA Regional Co-operative Agreement for Asia and the Pacific, and ARCAL for Latin American

countries. The goals of economic and technical co-operation among developing countries, particularly within regions, were also seen to be relevant.

75.   Another aspect of regional co-operation was the support given by some speakers to the creation of nuclear weapon-free zones. In addition to the existing Tlatelolco Treaty, which is intended to cover Latin America and the Caribbean, it was recalled that the Treaty of Rarotonga had come into force in December 1986, creating a nuclear-free zone in the South Pacific region. Some speakers expressed support for the establishment of such zones in the Balkans, Central Europe, South Asia, Southeast Asia, the Middle East and Africa. Reference was also made to the importance of the proposal to create a nuclear-free peace zone on the Korean Peninsula and efforts for its realization. According to another view, this proposal lacked practicability.

   . . .

80.   Several speakers proposed that the Agency's future attention should include the questions of international safety standards, liability for transboundary effects of a nuclear accident, and an internationally accepted mechanism covering all treatment and disposal of spent fuel.

   . . .

- - - - -

Additional Reference

United Nations Conference for the Promotion of International Co-operation in the Peaceful Uses of Nuclear Energy. UN General Assembly resolution A/RES/42/24.

- - - - -

2

Pollution from Ships

MARPOL 73/78 Convention and Related Codes

IMO Assembly   A 15/14
15th Session, November 1987   Extract

===

Consideration of the Reports and Recommendations of the
Marine Environment Protection Committee
Note by the Secretary-General

. . .

Adoption of amendments to Annex II of MARPOL 73/78 and date of implementation of this Annex

9.   Following intense preparatory work over several sessions and approval of the draft texts of amendments to Annex II of MARPOL 73/78 on 5 December 1985, the Committee, during its twenty-second session adopted, under cover of resolution MEPC 16(22), amendments to MARPOL 73/78, Annex II (MEPC 22/21, annex 2). In accordance with article 16(2)(f)(iii) of the 1973 Convention, the amendments were deemed to have been accepted on 5 October 1986 and no objections have been communicated. Therefore, in accordance with article 16(2)(g)(ii) of the 1973 Convention, the amendments entered into force. By virtue of Resolution MEPC 17(22) of 5 December 1985, the Committee decided in accordance with Article II of the 1978 Protocol that Parties shall be bound by the provisions of Annex II of MARPOL 73/78 as amended from 6 April 1987.

. . .

Adoption of revised text of the P & A Standards and amendments to the IBC and BCH Codes

10.   On 5 December 1985 the Committee, at its twenty-second session, adopted under cover of resolution MEPC 18(22) the new Standards for Procedures and Arrangements for the Discharge of Noxious Liquid Substances.

11.   The IBC (International Code for the Construction and Equipment of Ships Carrying Dangerous Chemicals in Bulk) and BCH (Code for the Construction and Equipment of Ships Carrying Dangerous Chemicals in Bulk) Codes were extended to cover marine pollution aspects and adopted by MEPC at its twenty-second session, by resolutions MEPC 19(22) and MEPC 20(22) of 5 December 1985, respectively.

12. Both the Marine Environment Protection Committee and the Maritime Safety Committee agreed that the IBC Code should be mandatory under MARPOL 73/78 and the 1974 SOLAS Convention, and remain identical.

13. The IBC and BCH Codes, including amendments, have been published in the 1986 Editions (IMO Publication, Sales Numbers: 100 86.11.E and 772 86.12.E, respectively).

14. The text of Annex II of MARPOL 73/78 incorporating the amendments adopted by MEPC on 5 December 1985, together with Unified Interpretation of the Provisions of Annex II and the Standards for Procedures and Arrangements for the Discharge of Noxious Liquid Substances, has been published in "Regulations for the Control of Pollution by Noxious Liquid Substances in Bulk" (IMO Publication, Sales Number: 512 86.13.E.).

. . .

- - - - -

IMO Marine Environment Protection Committee MEPC 24/19
Report of the Twenty-fourth Session, March 1987 Extract

. . .

6. Updating of the List of Chemicals

6.1 The Committee considered a report of the informal meeting of experts which was convened at IMO Headquarters from 13 to 17 October 1986 to assign pollution categories and minimum carriage requirements to as many substances as possible based on the outcome of the twentieth session of the GESAMP Working Group on the Evaluation of the Hazards of Harmful Substances (MEPC 24/6).

6.2 The Committee reviewed the lists prepared by the meeting of experts and found that for a number of substances the pollution category and carriage requirements had been revised as a result of change in their GESAMP Hazard Profile. Recalling its decision on the treatment of substances the pollution categories of which have been upgraded or downgraded (MEPC 22/21, paragraph 3.7), the Committee agreed to remove those substances which were upgraded from the approved list, together with those considered controversial by a Member, and referred all of those substances to the BCH Sub-Committee for review.

6.3 The Committee approved the lists of substances set out in annex 6 in the form of entries for chapters VI and VII of the BCH Code, for substances categorized on the basis of GESAMP hazard profiles and those provisionally assessed by the meeting of experts. The Secretariat was requested to produce equivalent IBC entries on the basis of approved entries for the BCH Code and to invite the MSC to approve the lists. The Secretariat was further requested to combine these entries with those approved at the Committee's twenty-third session and to circulate these lists as a new circular. Equivalent amendments to appendices II and III of Annex II would also be prepared in time for formal adoption of amendments to the Code.

6.4 The Committee reconsidered its previous decision (MEPC 22/21, paragraph 3.7) with respect to the treatment of substances for which the category has changed, based on a revision of the GESAMP hazard profile. The delegations of Japan, Sweden and the United States felt that it would be a violation of the Convention to implement a downgraded requirement without awaiting the formal entry into force of the amendment. The Swedish delegation, supported by the delegations of Japan and the United States, expressed the view that it is not appropriate for the Organization to recommend implementation of downgraded requirements pending the formal entry into force of the amendment. The Committee agreed to maintain its decision with respect to the treatment of upgraded or downgraded substances for the time being, but agreed to reconsider this issue at its next session. In this connection, Japan reserved its position and expressed the view that with respect to substances listed in appendix II to Annex II of MARPOL 73/78 Japan would not implement the downgraded requirement until the formal entry into force of the amendment.

6.5 The Committee agreed that upgraded requirements for substances which will be included in a future amendment should be circulated for information purposes so that new requirements can be taken into consideration by the chemical transportation industry.

6.6 The Committee noted the observation of the experts that the GESAMP Working Group's profiles are based on the intrinsic toxicity to marine life, and that properties such as solubility and volatility which could play an important role in reducing the length of time marine organisms are exposed to threat of harm are not taken into account. In this connection, the Group recalled that the toxic effects on living organisms depend not only on the nature of the compound or the intrinsic toxicity of the compound, but also on the exposure concentration and, in particular, on the duration of the exposure. The Committee agreed that the BCH SubCommittee should be instructed to consider development of guidelines to adjust the present system for determining pollution categories and ship-types in order to obtain a more realistic assessment of pollution hazard.

. . .

- - - - -

IMO Marine Environment Protection Committee,   MEPC 25/20, Annex 7
Report of the Twenty-fifth Session, December 1987   Extract

Annex 7

GUIDELINES FOR THE FUTURE AMENDMENTS TO THE IBC AND BCH CODES

General

1. Amendments to the IBC and BCH Codes should normally be considered for adoption at intervals of two years[1] except where, in special circumstances, the adoption of amendments is urgently needed.

2. To commence formal action for amendments, the BCH Sub-Committee should prepare a set of proposed amendments to the IBC and BCH Codes which the Secretary-General, on behalf of Parties to SOLAS 74 and MARPOL 73/78, should circulate to the Governments concerned under the six-months' rule, in accordance with article VIII(b)(i) of SOLAS 74 and article 16(2)(a) of MARPOL 73/78, as applicable.

3. As a general rule, proposed amendments which could not be agreed upon by the BCH Sub-Committee by consensus, should not be included in the above-mentioned set for

circulation but should be forwarded to the MSC and the MEPC for consideration and action, as appropriate.

4.   Proposed amendments to be circulated under the six-months' rule should include provisions for the application of the amendments to new and existing ships.

Amendments to the IBC Code

5.   The MEPC[2] (if the meeting is held after the end of the six-months' period) should formally adopt the proposed amendments in accordance with article 16(2)(d) of MARPOL 73/78, and determine the period of tacit acceptance based on the date of adoption by the MSC, e.g. amendments would be deemed to have been accepted 12 months after the date of adoption by the MSC. If, however, the MEPC agreed to introduce substantial changes to the proposed amendments, the MEPC should normally postpone the formal adoption of the amendments until its next session and refer the changes in question to the MSC for concurrence. Alternatively, the proposed amendments in question should be referred back to the BCH Sub-Committee for reconsideration.

6.   The amendments should be formally adopted by the expanded MSC in accordance with article VIII(b)(iv) of SOLAS 74, with the same acceptance date determined as for the MARPOL purpose.

7.   The amendments should enter into force at a specific date for both SOLAS and MARPOL purposes, subject to compliance with the conditions for tacit acceptance, in accordance with the relevant articles of the Conventions.

8.   Normally, the minimum acceptance period, i.e., twelve months after the adoption by the MSC or ten months after the adoption by the MEPC, may be specified. If, however, the BCH Sub-Committee considers that a longer period for the entry into force of amendments should be required, because of the nature of the amendments, appropriate recommendations to the MSC and the MEPC should be made by that Sub-Committee.

9.   If amendments adopted by the MEPC were rejected by the MSC, such amendments should not enter into force for either SOLAS or MARPOL purposes. This may be effected by the inclusion of an appropriate proviso when the MEPC determines the date of tacit acceptance, as mentioned in paragraph 5, for instance:

"In accordance with article 16(2)(f)(iii) of MARPOL 73/78, the MEPC determines that the amendments shall be deemed to have been accepted on [date[3]], or the date determined by the MSC on which corresponding amendments for the purpose of SOLAS 74 are deemed to have been accepted in accordance with article VIII(b)(vi)(2) thereof, whichever occurs later, unless prior to that date not less than one third of the Parties to MARPOL 73/78, or the Parties the combined merchant fleets of which constitute not less than fifty per cent of the gross tonnage of the world's merchant fleet, have communicated to the Organization their objections to the amendments."

10. For amendments to the BCH Code, similar procedures should be followed, except that formal adoption is needed under MARPOL only and the date of entry into force of the amendments is based on the date of adoption of amendments by the MEPC.

11. The amendments to the BCH Code will, in many cases, be considered and adopted together with the corresponding amendments to the IBC Code. In such cases, the acceptance date should be set to coincide with that of the IBC amendments.

Miscellaneous

. . .

13. The present guidelines may be modified, as necessary, in individual cases to meet particular circumstances.

Notes

1.   At sessions of the BCH Sub-Committee, when no amendments are being prepared for circulation in accordance with paragraph 2, any proposed amendments should be submitted to the MSC and the MEPC for approval, in principle, and subsequently circulated to the Governments concerned for information.
2.   For the sake of simplicity, it is assumed that the MEPC will meet first. If the meeting of the MSC takes place first, the reference to the MSC and the MEPC and to SOLAS and MARPOL in subparagraphs 5, 6 and 9 should be interchanged.
3.   Calendar date not earlier than twelve months after the last day of the session of the MSC at which the same amendments are considered for adoption.

- - - - -

IMO Marine Environment Protection Committee
Report of the 23rd Session, July 1986

MEPC 23/22, Annex 3
Extract

. . .

Resolution MEPC. 26(23)

PROCEDURES FOR THE CONTROL OF SHIPS AND DISCHARGES UNDER ANNEX II OF THE INTERNATIONAL CONVENTION FOR THE PREVENTION OF POLLUTION FROM SHIPS, 1973, AS MODIFIED BY THE PROTOCOL OF 1978 RELATING THERETO (MARPOL 73/78)

THE MARINE ENVIRONMENT PROTECTION COMMITTEE,

Recalling Article 38 of the Convention of the International Maritime Organization concerning the functions of the Committee,

Noting that Annex II of the International Convention for the Prevention of Pollution from Ships, 1973, as modified by the Protocol of 1978 relating thereto (MARPOL 73/78), as amended, is expected to take effect on 6 April 1987,

Recalling also that the Parties to MARPOL 73/78 have undertaken to give effect to its provisions in order to prevent pollution of the marine environment by the discharge of, *inter alia*, noxious liquid substances in contravention of that Convention,

Recalling also that the Parties to MARPOL 73/78 have undertaken to give effect to its provisions in order to prevent pollution of the marine environment by the discharge of, *inter alia*, noxious liquid substances in contravention of that Convention,

Noting the Procedures for the Control of Ships and Discharges under Annex I of MARPOL 73/78 introduced by the Assembly resolution A.542(13),

Reaffirming its desire to ensure that ships comply at all times with the marine pollution standards prescribed by MARPOL 73/78,

Having considered the proposals of the Member Governments:

1.   *Adopts* the Procedures for the Control of Ships and Discharges under Annex II of MARPOL 73/78 as set out in the Annex to this resolution;

2.   *Invites* Member States and Parties to MARPOL 73/78 to implement the procedures when Annex II of MARPOL 73/78 takes effect and thereby to contribute towards the attainment of the objectives of that Convention;

3.   *Requests* Governments concerned to provide information on action taken in respect of ships found to be deficient in relation to Annex II of MARPOL 73/78 in their role as either port or flag State administration;

4.   *Further requests* the Secretariat to collect and update when necessary the information referred to above for circulation to the Governments concerned.

ANNEX

PREAMBLE

1.   The Parties to the International Convention for the Prevention of Pollution from Ships, 1973, as modified by the Protocol of 1978 relating thereto, (MARPOL 73/78) have undertaken to give effect to its provisions in order to prevent the pollution of the marine environment by the discharge of, *inter alia*, noxious liquid substances or mixtures containing such substances in contravention of that Convention.

2.   The provisions cover the design and equipment of ships, the execution of surveys and inspections in order to ensure that the design and equipment comply with the relevant international standards and cover the operations of ships in so far as this concerns the protection of the marine environment.

3.   The primary responsibility for securing that objective in relation to any particular ship rests with the Administration of the flag State. No attempt is made in this document to lay down guidelines for Administrations in this respect.

4.   In some cases, and this applies especially to the operational provisions, it may be difficult for the Administration to exercise full and continuous control over some ships entitled to fly the flag of its State. Such ships for instance may not call regularly at ports or offshore terminals under the jurisdiction of the flag State.

5.   The problem can be and has been overcome partly by appointing surveyors at foreign ports or authorizing classification societies to act on behalf of the flag State. In addition MARPOL 73/78 includes a number of provisions, supplemented by guidelines on specific control procedures, for States other than the flag State to exercise control over foreign ships visiting port or off-shore terminals under their jurisdiction. In this document the provisions and guidelines for port and coastal State control are drawn together.

6.   Parties should make effective use of the opportunities that port State control provides for identifying deficiencies and substandard operations, if any, in visiting foreign ships which may render them pollution risks and for ensuring that remedial measures are taken. The purpose of these guidelines is to assist Parties to exercise effective port and coastal State control and thereby to contribute towards the attainment of the objectives of MARPOL 73/78.

7.   Nothing in these guidelines should be construed as derogating from the powers of any Party to take measures within its jurisdiction in respect of any matter to which MARPOL 73/78 relates or as extending the jurisdiction of any Party.

8.   For the inspections carried out under these control procedures article 7 of MARPOL 73/78 applies in that:

    .1   all possible efforts shall be made to avoid a ship being unduly detained or delayed; and

    .2   when a ship is unduly detained or delayed under the control procedures it shall be entitled to compensation for any loss or damage suffered.

CHAPTER 1 - INTRODUCTION

1.1   This document sets out procedures for the control of ships under MARPOL 73/78 and contains guidelines for port States and, where appropriate, for coastal States to ensure that a ship continues to comply with the relevant provisions of Annex II to MARPOL 73/78 (hereinafter referred to as Annex II).

1.2   A number of factors may cause the condition of a ship to be considered as posing a threat of harm to the marine environment rendering the ship involved a pollution risk. These factors fall into categories which include:

    .1   non-compliance with the construction or equipment requirements of the Convention;

    .2   inoperative or malfunctioning equipment; and

    .3   non-compliance with the operational requirements of the Convention.

The control procedures aim to identify such a pollution risk and to provide the basis for remedial action.

1.3   Of necessity these control procedures have been divided into different categories each of which is dealt with in a separate chapter. It must, however, be kept in mind that one category may involve another so that for a certain ship more than one chapter of this document may be applicable.

1.4 Chapter 2 contains guidance aimed at ascertaining whether a ship holds a valid Certificate of Fitness (COF) or International Pollution Prevention Certificate for the Carriage of Noxious Liquid Substances in Bulk (NLS) as called for by Annex II and is built, equipped and operating in compliance with the relevant provisions of Annex II.

1.5 Chapter 3 contains guidance on the gathering of evidence of violations of the discharge provisions in Annex II.

1.6 Chapter 4 contains control procedures on in-port inspections of unloading, stripping and prewashing operations as required by regulation 8 of Annex II. This regulation requires that Parties to Annex II shall, in giving effect to the provisions of the regulation, apply the procedures developed by the Organization.

1.7 Chapter 5 contains guidance on control measures for ships of non-Parties.

1.8 Chapter 6 contains guidance on the dissemination of information obtained as a result of exercising these control procedures.

1.9 In five appendices to this document, detailed guidelines are given for officials charged with carrying out the control procedures referred to above.

. . .

- - - - -

IMO Assembly
15th Session, November 1987

A 15/14
Extract

Consideration of the Reports and Recommendations of the Marine Environment Protection Committee
Note by the Secretary-General

. . .

Annex III of MARPOL 73/78

15. In preparation for the entry into force and implementation of Annex III of MARPOL 73/78, the Committee, recalling its agreement at its twenty-first session that the only logical way of implementing Annex III would be by means of the IMDG Code, agreed in principle on a revised text of Annex III (MEPC 22/21, annex 9) which, *inter alia*, clarifies the relationship between Annex III and the IMDG Code.

16. The Committee, in view of the entry into force of Protocol I which requires reporting of discharge or probable discharge of harmful substances in packaged form and defines "harmful substances" in packaged form as those identified as marine pollutants in the IMDG Code, approved a new section 23, Marine Pollutants, of the General Introduction to the Code. In the appendix to section 23 of the IMDG Code is a list of 174 substances identified as marine pollutants. This section 23 was adopted by the MSC at its fifty-third session as an interim amendment to the IMDG Code. It was the intention of both Committees that further

amendment to section 23 and individual schedules should be developed to cover the marine pollution aspects and adopted in time for the entry into force of Annex III of MARPOL 73/78.

. . .

- - - - -

IMO Marine Environment Protection Committee	MEPC 25/20
Report of the Twenty-fifth Session, December 1987	Extract

. . .

8.   Implementation of Annex III of MARPOL 73/78 and Amendments to the IMDG Code to Cover Pollution Aspects
. . .

Amendments to Annex III

8.11   The Committee, after having considered the report of the drafting group set up in accordance with paragraph 8.6 above (MEPC 25/WP.7), agreed on the amendment hereunder, necessary to reflect that an appendix to contain the guidelines will be added to Annex III:

> "(1.2)   Guidelines for the identification of harmful substances in packaged form are given in the appendix to this Annex."

Existing paragraph (1.2) to be renumbered accordingly.

8.12   The Committee considered and approved the guidelines for the identification of harmful substances in packaged form given in annex 15 to this report in the format of an "appendix" which would be appended to Annex III, as agreed by the Committee at its twenty-third session (MEPC 23/22, paragraph 8.9.3.10).

. . .

- - - - -

IMO Marine Environment Protection Committee	MEPC 25/9/4
Twenty-fifth Session, 19 November 1987	

Implementation of Annexes V and IV of MARPOL 73/78
Note by the Secretariat

1.   At its twenty-fourth session, the MEPC gave consideration to a note by the Secretariat regarding the implementation of Annexes V and IV of MARPOL 73/78, annexed to which was a report of a working group, regarding Annex IV, which had met during the twenty-third session of the MEPC. The Committee noted the explanations contained therein regarding the admissibility of reservations to the Optional Annexes of MARPOL 73/78 and welcomed the

offer of the Secretariat to examine the matter further. As promised, the Secretariat is pleased to provide the following information for consideration by the MEPC.

2. Article 19 of the Vienna Convention on the Law of Treaties sets out the provides as follows:

"A State may, when signing, ratifying, accepting, approving or acceding to a treaty, formulate a reservation unless:

(a) the reservation is prohibited by the treaty;
(b) the treaty provides that only specified reservations, which do not include the reservation in question, may be made; or
(c) in cases not falling under subparagraphs (a) and (b), the reservation is incompatible with the object and purpose of the treaty".

3. MARPOL 73/78 does not explicitly prohibit the making of a reservation, nor does it specify any particular reservations which would be permissible to the exclusion of any other reservations. Accordingly, the question whether reservations may be made to the treaty is to be answered by reference to subparagraph (c) of article 19 of the Vienna Convention which provides that a reservation may be made unless it is "incompatible with the object and purpose" of the Convention. The question whether a particular reservation is incompatible or not with the object and purpose of MARPOL 73/78 is to be determined by the Parties to MARPOL 73/78, in accordance with the procedures set out in articles 20 and 21 of the Vienna Convention. The relevant provisions of those articles read as follows:

Article 20

"4. In cases not falling under the preceding paragraphs and unless the treaty otherwise provides:

(a) acceptance by another Contracting State of a reservation constitutes the reserving State a Party to the treaty in relation to that other State if or when the treaty is in force for those States;
(b) an objection by another Contracting State to a reservation does not preclude the entry into force of the treaty as between the objecting and reserving States unless a contrary intention is definitely expressed by the objecting State;
(c) an act expressing a State's consent to be bound by the treaty and containing a reservation is effective as soon as at least one other Contracting State has accepted the reservation.

5. For the purpose of paragraphs 2 and 4 and unless the treaty otherwise provides, a reservation is considered to have been accepted by a State if it shall have raised no objection to the reservation by the end of a period of twelve months after it was notified of the reservation or by the date on which it expressed its consent to be bound by the treaty, whichever is later."

Article 21

"3. When a State objecting to a reservation has not opposed the entry into force of the treaty between itself and the reserving State, the provisions to which the reservation relates do not apply as between the two States to the extent of the reservation."

4.   Reference has been made in this context to paragraph 1 of article 14 of MARPOL 73/78 which reads as follows:

> "(1)   A State may at the time of signing, ratifying, accepting, approving or acceding to the present Convention declare that it does not accept any one or all of Annexes III, IV and V (hereinafter referred to as "Optional Annexes") of the present Convention. Subject to the above, Parties to the Convention shall be bound by any Annex in its entirety."

The suggestion has been made that this prohibition means that reservations may not be made in respect of any Optional Annex. If this view were accepted, the only course available to a State which accepts MARPOL 73/78 would be either to declare its non-acceptance of any Optional Annex in relation to which the State had some difficulties or, alternatively, to be bound by that Optional Annex without the possibility of any reservations. This would be the case even if a proposed reservation related to a matter which had no significant implications for the other States which have agreed to be bound by the Optional Annex in question.

5.   However, it may be noted that the Vienna Convention differentiates between, on the one hand, partial acceptance by States of a treaty, i.e. agreement to be bound by only a part or parts of a treaty and, on the other hand, acceptance of a treaty in its entirety, but subject to a reservation. The law regarding partial acceptance of a treaty is contained in article 17, paragraph 1 of the Vienna Convention which provides that "the consent of a State to be bound by part of a treaty is effective only if the treaty so determines or the other Contracting States so agree". This provision states that it is "without prejudice" to the provisions of the same Convention on reservations. Accordingly, it would appear that, while a State which agrees to be bound by an Optional Annex will be bound by that Annex in its entirety, such a State may, nevertheless, make a reservation to that Optional Annex. However, such a reservation should satisfy the condition stipulated in subparagraph (c) of article 19 of the Vienna Convention, i.e. the reservation should not be "incompatible with the object and purpose" of the Optional Annex or of MARPOL 73/78 as a whole.

6.   In this connection, it may be recalled that the 1973 MARPOL Conference considered proposals for the inclusion of a provision on reservations in the 1973 MARPOL Convention. The Conference decided against the inclusion of any of the provisions proposed. It is, therefore, reasonable to assume that the Conference did not intend to prohibit the making of reservations in respect of any part of the 1973 Convention. This approach was not affected by the 1978 MARPOL Protocol.

7.   On this assumption, the better view would appear to be that reservations may be made by States to MARPOL 73/78, including any of the Annexes thereto, subject only to the general treaty law on reservations specified in the Vienna Convention.

8.   In accordance with the Vienna Convention, it will be for determination whether any particular reservations to an Optional Annex would be incompatible with the object and purpose of that Annex, or of MARPOL 73/78 as a whole. A decision on this point must be based on the precise nature of the specific reservation and its likely implications on the implementation of the Annex in question, or the MARPOL treaty in general.   Such a determination will be made by the Parties to MARPOL 73/78 which are also bound by the Optional Annex concerned, either collectively in the MEPC or individually, as appropriate.

9.   If the MEPC were to accept the view that the provision in paragraph 1 of article 14 of MARPOL 73/78 does not completely preclude the making of reservations to the Optional Annexes, then the Committee might conclude that a State which does not declare its non-acceptance of an Optional Annex at the time of ratification, etc., or which subsequently withdraws such a declaration, may nevertheless make a reservation in respect of that Optional Annex.   However, such a reservation will be subject to the general law regarding the acceptability and application of reservations, as codified in the 1969 Vienna Convention on the Law of Treaties.

- - - - -

IMO Marine Environment Protection Committee
Report of the Twenty-fifth Session, 1987

MEPC 25/20
Extract

. . .

9.   Implementation of Annexes V and IV of MARPOL 73/78

. . .

9.11   In considering the report of the Working Group (MEPC 25/WP10), the Committee:

1.   agreed to the scope and content of the Guidelines with the understanding that some editorial improvement may be required, and therefore requested the Secretariat to issue the draft Guidelines as a document, . . . inviting comments thereon . . . ;

2.   instructed the Secretariat to solicit, through an appropriate mechanism, the views of Member Governments on the need for early development of an "Annex VI", its possible scope and content, and other means of solving the problems associated with cargo residue disposal.

. . .

- - - - -

Additional References

Documents submitted by delegations: MEPC 25/9 (Canada), MEPC 25/9/1 (Spain), MEPC 25/9/3, containing draft guidelines for the implementation of Annex V (United States).

- - - - -

Hazardous Waste Reception Facilities

IMO Assembly   A 14/Res.585
14th Session, 1985   Extract

===

Resolution A.585(14)
Provision of Facilities in Ports for the Reception of Oily Wastes from Ships

The Assembly,

Recalling Article 15(j) of the Convention on the International Maritime Organization concerning the functions of the Assembly in relation to regulations concerning the prevention and control of marine pollution from ships,

Recalling also that regulations 10(7) and 12 of Annex I of the International Convention for the Prevention of Pollution from Ships, 1973, as modified by the Protocol of 1978 relating thereto (MARPOL 73/78), establish the latest dates by which States Parties to MARPOL 73/78 undertake to ensure that reception facilities for oily residues and mixtures are provided in loading terminals, repair ports and other ports of Parties,

Conscious that the provision of facilities in ports for the reception of oily wastes from ships is vital to the effective implementation of MARPOL 73/78,

Noting further the outcome of recent initiatives at the regional* level,

Noting also that oil tankers and tank barges are being utilized for the reception of oily wastes and mixtures as an immediate measure as a complement to shore reception facilities, or as an alternative means of providing such facilities, on the grounds of technical and economic viability,

1.   *Urges* Member Governments and States Parties to the International Convention for the Prevention of Pollution from Ships, 1973, as modified by the Protocol of 1978 relating thereto (MARPOL 73/78), to review the adequacy of existing reception facilities and, where appropriate, to give the concept of floating reception facilities their serious consideration and evaluation;

2.   *Invites* Member Governments to submit information to the Marine Environment Protection Committee on the operation and use of floating reception facilities in order that their effectiveness may be reviewed and so that others may benefit from the experience gained;

3.   *Further invites* the Marine Environment Protection Committee and the Maritime Safety Committee to consider whether the present safety and pollution prevention standards

---

* The recommendation of the Fourth Ordinary Meeting of the Contracting Parties to the Convention for the Protection of the Mediterranean Sea against Pollution and its related Protocols which took place in Genoa in September 1985 on the creation of floating reception facilities in the Mediterranean area (Reproduced in this Volume at pages 720 - 724).

applicable to ships and oil tankers, when converted to floating reception facilities, are adequate.

. . .

- - - - -

IMO Assembly   A 15/14/Add.1
15th Session, 5 September 1987   Extract

Consideration of the Reports and Recommendations of the Marine Environment Protection Committee
Note by the Secretary-General

. . .

Maritime Safety Committee

3.   The Maritime Safety Committee at its fifty-second session noted the invitation by the Assembly in resolution A.585(14) to consider whether the present safety and pollution prevention standards applicable to ships and oil tankers, when converted to floating reception facilities, are adequate and instructed the Sub-Committee on Ship Design and Equipment and the Sub-Committee on Fire Protection to consider the above problem taking also into account the possibility that the tanker undergoing such conversion might have been laid up for a considerable time and, therefore, does not necessarily comply with all international requirements currently in force for a tanker of the size in question. The Maritime Safety Committee underlined that, in the absence of guidelines dealing with the subject, adequate safety and pollution prevention measures remain the responsibility of the flag State and, if necessary, the port State.

4.   . . .   The Sub-Committees . . . concluded that:

   .1   when the vessel is permanently moored, the requirements of the port State should be adhered to;

   .2   when the vessel undertakes short voyages, or voyages in exceptional circumstances, as prescribed in regulation I/4(a) of SOLAS, the requirements of the SOLAS Convention and those of the flag and port State involved should be complied with, as appropriate;

   .3   where the regular operations of the vessel as a reception facility include international voyages under its own power, the vessel should comply fully with the requirements of the SOLAS Convention.

5.   The Maritime Safety Committee agreed fully with the foregoing conclusions.

Marine Environment Protection Committee

. . .

7. . . . The Committee at its twenty-third session noted that there were three types of discharges arising from floating reception facilities upon which a standard should be imposed, *viz*:

- discharges from machinery spaces
- ballast water resulting from variations in oil cargo
- oily waste received from other ships and water effluent derived from the treatment of such wastes.

8. The Committee agreed that the first two of these were regulated by MARPOL 73/78, with the discharge criteria applicable in any situation corresponding to unconverted ships and tankers operating under similar circumstances. The Committee considered that the third type of discharge was subject to the provisions of the London Dumping Convention, 1972, such discharges falling within the definition of dumping contained in article III(1)(a)(i) of that Convention (MEPC 23/22, paragraph 6.5).

9. The Secretariat was requested to convey the Committee's opinion to Contracting Parties to LDC and at the same time to point out that if discharges of such water effluent were regulated by MARPOL 73/78 the oil content would not exceed 15 ppm.

10. The Tenth Consultative Meeting of Contracting Parties to LDC noted that "oily water and water effluents derived from the treatment of such wastes" fell under the provisions of Annex I, paragraph 5 of that Convention. In taking into account paragraph 9 of Annex I ("trace contaminants" exemption), it was agreed that the standard "not exceeding 15 ppm" could fulfil the conditions of the trace contaminants exemption clause when issuing dumping permits to operators of floating reception facilities.

11. In this connection Contracting Parties to LDC were requested to take full account of the Guidelines for the Implementation of Paragraphs 8 and 9 of Annex I to the London Dumping Convention (LDC 10/15, paragraph 13.19). The meeting also agreed that the application of the trace contaminants provision of Annex I, paragraph 9 to discharge from floating reception facilities be considered by the Scientific Group on Dumping.

12. . . . The Scientific Group on Dumping expressed the view that oily effluents with oil contents of less than 15 ppm could be regarded as falling under the trace contaminants clause if the effluent is discharged through an oil discharge monitoring meter approved by the responsible national administration in accordance with the specifications recommended by IMO (resolution A.393(X)).

- - - - -

r

IMO Marine Environment Protection Committee   MEPC 25/20
Report of the Twenty-fifth Session, December 1987   Extract

. . .

Reception facilities for noxious liquid substances

. . .

6.10   In consideration of the observations and suggestions made by INTERTANKO (MEPC
25/6/1), based upon experience in implementing Annex II of MARPOL 73/78, the
Committee made the following observations and decisions in consideration of the points
raised:

> **Dissemination of information:**   The Committee concurred with the view that ports
> should disseminate information on reception facilities to the shipping industry and local
> shipping agencies, this matter having been specifically addressed by the Committee in
> paragraph 6.5 above.   The Committee further concurred that port regulations and by-
> laws respecting the use of reception facilities should be made known . . .

> **Pre-wash Techniques:**   The Committee requested the BCH Sub-Committee to consider
> the development of a unified interpretation on the acceptance of recycling techniques,
> taking into account all safety aspects involved, in order to reduce the amount of pre-
> wash slops to be delivered ashore;

> **Authorized surveyors for the purpose of regulation 8 of Annex II:**   The Committee
> agreed that to ensure no undue delay is caused by inspections and mandatory
> endorsements of cargo record books, the names, addresses and telephone numbers of
> authorized surveyors should be made known to local shipping agencies and shipping
> industries.   The question of whether this information should also be communicated by
> Governments to IMO for dissemination to its Members is addressed in paragraph 6.8
> above;

> **Facilities at unloading terminals for the reception of cargo strippings at low back
> pressure:**   The Committee generally concurred with INTERTANKO's view on this
> subject and agreed that this should be brought to the attention of the BCH Sub-
> Committee;

> **Reports on alleged inadequacies in respect of port reception facilities:**   The
> Committee recalled that MEPC/Circ.184 contained a form for reporting difficulties
> encountered in the disposing of NLS residue/water mixtures from ships.   The
> Committee could not agree that the identity of reporting ships should not be disclosed,
> since such information was essential if follow-up inquiries were to be made.

. . .

- - - - -

Reporting and Combating of Incidents

IMO Assembly　　　　　　　　　　　　　　　　　　　　　　　　　A 15/14
15th Session, November 1987　　　　　　　　　　　　　　　　　　　Extract

Consideration of the Reports and Recommendations of the Marine Environment Protection Committee
Note by the Secretary-General

. . .

Reporting of incidents involving harmful substances under MARPOL 73/78

22.　After due consideration of the various proposals, MEPC at its twenty-second session, agreed upon a revised text of Protocol I to MARPOL 73/78 and formally adopted amendments giving effect to this new text under cover of resolution MEPC 21(22) dated 5 December 1985.　No objections were reported by 5 October 1986.　Therefore, in accordance with article 16(2)(g)(ii) of MARPOL 73/78, Protocol I, as amended, entered into force on 6 April 1987.

23.　As requested by the Assembly at its fourteenth session, MEPC also finalized at its twenty-second session, new Guidelines for Reporting Incidents Involving Harmful Substances, which supersede the Interim Guidelines contained in resolution A.447(XI).　These new Guidelines were adopted by MEPC on 5 December 1985 by resolution MEPC 22(22).　The Committee recommended Parties to MARPOL 73/78 to implement these new Guidelines.

24.　Protocol I, as amended, and new Guidelines were published in IMO Publication "Provisions Concerning the Reporting of Incidents Involving Harmful Substances under MARPOL 73/78" (Sales Number: 516 86.14.E).

. . .

- - - - -

IMO Marine Environment Protection Committee　　　　　　MEPC 25/20, Annex 18
Report of the 25th Session, December 1987　　　　　　　　　　　　Extract

. . .

Resolution MEPC. 30(25)
Guidelines for Reporting Incidents Involving Harmful Substances

THE MARINE ENVIRONMENT PROTECTION COMMITTEE,

Recalling Article 38 of the Convention on the International Maritime Organization concerning the functions of the Committee,

Recalling also article 8 and Protocol I of the International Convention for the Prevention of Pollution from Ships, 1973, as modified by the Protocol of 1978 relating thereto (MARPOL 73/78), concerning reports on incidents involving harmful substances,

Recalling further resolution MEPC 21(22) by which it adopted amendments to Protocol I of MARPOL 73/78,

Recognizing that States Parties to the International Convention relating to Intervention on the High Seas in Cases of Oil Pollution Casualties (1969) and the Protocol Relating to Intervention on the High Seas in Cases of Marine Pollution by Substances other than Oil (1973) may take such measures on the high seas as may be necessary to prevent, mitigate or eliminate grave and imminent danger to their coastline or related interests from pollution or threat of pollution of the sea by oil and substances other than oil following upon a maritime casualty or acts related to such a casualty, which may reasonably be expected to result in major harmful consequences,

Recognizing also the need for coastal States to be informed by the master of an assisting ship undertaking salvage of particulars of action taken and the incident,

Recognizing further that an incident involving damage, failure or break down of the ship, its machinery or equipment could give rise to a significant threat of pollution to coastlines or related interests,

Noting resolution MEPC.22(22) by which the Committee established the Guidelines for Reporting Incidents Involving Harmful Substances,

Noting also resolution A.598(15) by which the Assembly adopted General Principles for Ship Reporting Systems and Ship Reporting Requirements,

Having considered proposals for a revision of the Guidelines,

1. *Adopts* the Guidelines for Reporting Incidents Involving Harmful Substances, the text of which is set out in the Annex to the present resolution to supersede the Guidelines contained in resolution MEPC.22(22);

2. *Recommends* Member Governments and States Parties to the Protocol of 1978 relating to the International Convention for the Prevention of Pollution from Ships, 1973 to implement the Guidelines, in accordance with paragraph (2) of article V of Protocol I.

ANNEX

GUIDELINES FOR REPORTING INCIDENTS INVOLVING HARMFUL SUBSTANCES

1. INTRODUCTION

The intent of these guidelines is to enable coastal States and other interested parties to be informed without delay of any incident giving rise to pollution, or threat of pollution, of the marine environment, as well as of assistance and salvage measures, so that appropriate action may be taken.

2.   HOW TO MAKE REPORTS

The report should be transmitted in accordance with the Annex of resolution A.598(15).

3.   CONTENTS OF REPORTS

The report should contain the specific information listed in section 3.2 or 3.3 as appropriate of the appendix to the Annex of resolution A.598(15).

4.   SUPPLEMENTARY REPORT

4.1   Immediately following or as soon as possible after the transmission of the information referred to in section 3 above, as much as possible of the information essential for the protection of the marine environment as appropriate to the incident should be reported. The information should include items P, Q, R, S and X as listed in section 3.2 or 3.3 as appropriate of resolution A.598(15).

5.   PROBABILITY OF DISCHARGE

5.1   The probability of a discharge resulting from damage to the ship or its equipment is a reason for making a report. In judging whether there is such a probability and whether the report should be made, the following factors, among others, should be taken into account:

.1   the nature of the damage, failure or breakdown of the ship, machinery or equipment; and

.2   sea and wind state and also traffic density in the area at the time and place of the incident.

5.2   It is recognized that it would be impracticable to lay down precise definitions of all types of incidents involving probable discharge which would warrant an obligation to report. Nevertheless, as a general guideline, the master of the ship should make reports in cases of:

.1   damage, failure or breakdown which affects the safety of ships. Examples of such incidents are collision, grounding, fire, explosion, structural failure, flooding, cargo shifting; and

.2   failure or breakdown of machinery or equipment which results in the impairment of the safety of navigation. Examples of such incidents are failure or breakdown of steering gear, propulsion plant, electrical generating system, essential shipborne navigational aids.

6.   REPORTS ON ASSISTANCE OR SALVAGE

6.1   Whenever a ship is engaged in or requested to engage in an operation to render assistance to or undertake salvage of a ship involved in an accident referred to in subparagraph 1(a) or 1(b) of article II of Protocol I of MARPOL 73/78, as amended, the Master of the former ship should report without delay the particulars of the action undertaken or planned. In addition, he should report, as far as practicable, on the items referred to in sections 3 and 4. Reports should be made in accordance with section 2 and the coastal State should be kept informed regarding developments.

7.   ACTION BY GOVERNMENTS

7.1   Governments should be guided by paragraphs 16 and 17 of the Annex of resolution A.598(15).

. . .

- - - - -

IMO Marine Environment Protection Committee   MEPC 25/20
Report of the Twenty-fifth Session, December 1987   Extract

. . .

12.   Enforcement of Pollution Conventions: . . .

. . .

12.2   The Committee was informed by the Secretary that the mandatory annual reports received . . . show that 1,005 illegal discharges are reported in the statistical report and 441 cases were referred to the flag State.   The statistical report also records 447 violations concerning the oil record book and 29 concerning the IOPP Certificate, and 82 others. According to the annual assessment report of the effectiveness of port State control, 21,595 ships were boarded in 1986, which constitute some 29% of the world fleet and compliance rates were approximately 97%.

. . .

- - - - -

IMO Assembly   A 14/Res.587
14th Session, 1985

Resolution A.587(14)
Arrangements for Combating Major Incidents
or Threats of Marine Pollution

The Assembly,

Recalling Article 15(j) of the Convention on the International Maritime Organization concerning the functions of the Assembly in relation to regulations concerning the prevention and control of marine pollution from ships,

Recalling also resolution A.349(IX) affirming the desirability of continuing to enhance the activity of IMO, within the limits of its resources and budget, for providing technical assistance in the field of marine pollution and requesting *inter alia* the Marine Environment Protection Committee to take all possible steps to further this objective,

Recognizing the roles of the United Nations Environment Programme (UNEP) and the United Nations Development Programme (UNDP) in the protection of the marine environment and their long-standing co-operation with the Organization in this area,

Recognizing also that bilateral and multilateral arrangements are a valuable and economical way of supplementing national arrangements in the effective combating of major spillages of oil or noxious substances,

Recalling further resolution A.448(XI) urging Governments to develop or improve national contingency arrangements to the extent feasible and to develop, as appropriate, joint contingency arrangements at a regional, subregional or sectoral level or on a bilateral basis, if they have not already done so, and requesting the Council, the Marine Environment Protection Committee and the Secretary-General to take all possible steps to develop and pursue programmes which would assist in promoting regional antipollution arrangements,

Noting with appreciation that IMO has, in co-operation with UNEP and relevant regional organizations, developed and supported the adoption and implementation of regional agreements and arrangements on co-operation in combating pollution of the sea in cases of emergency,

1.   *Invites* the Secretary-General, in co-operation with UNEP, UNDP and other organizations concerned, as appropriate, to undertake on a priority basis an evaluation of the problems of countries faced with the threat of major marine pollution from spillages of oil and other hazardous substances, taking into consideration the roles of the respective organizations in dealing with these problems;

2.   *Requests* the Marine Environment Protection Committee on the basis of this evaluation to take steps and to make recommendations, as appropriate and as soon as possible;

3.   *Requests further* the Council and the Secretary-General to take all possible steps to implement these recommendations and to report to the Assembly at its fifteenth session.

- - - - -

IMO Assembly   A 15/14/Add.1
15th Session, 1987   Extract

===

Consideration of the Reports and Recommendations of the Marine Environment Protection Committee
Note by the Secretary-General

. . .

Arrangements for combating major incidents or threats of marine pollution (Resolution A.587(14)

13.   The Committee at its twenty-second session noted that by resolution A.587(14) the Assembly had invited the Secretary-General, in co-operation with UNEP, UNDP and other organizations concerned as appropriate, to undertake on a priority basis an evaluation of the

problems of countries faced with the threat of major marine pollution from spillages of oil and other hazardous substances. It was also noted that the Assembly had requested the Committee, on the basis of this evaluation, to take steps and to make recommendations as appropriate and as soon as possible.

. . .

15. . . . the Secretary-General convened a small Advisory Group . . .

16. The recommendations of the Advisory Group referred to in its report (MEPC 23/Inf.6) were endorsed by the Committee at its twenty-third session and are shown in annex 12 to its report (MEPC 23/22). In particular the Committee, recalling that at its twenty-second session it had endorsed a procedure whereby the IMO Secretariat would collect and circulate information on international co-operation in combating marine pollution, agreed with the Advisory Group's suggestion that such information should take the form of a guide to international assistance in marine pollution emergencies which would facilitate the provision of such assistance and advice. The Secretariat has circulated a "Questionnaire on International Assistance in Marine Pollution Emergencies" (MEPC/Circ. 173, 29 August 1986) to collect information which will form the basis for the guide . . .

17. Noting the success of IMO, UNEP and UNDP in establishing a subregional response capability covering the Celebes Sea, the Advisory Group also suggested that IMO, in co-operation with UNEP and with the financial support of UNDP and other potential sources, explore the possibility of establishing similar arrangements in other sub-regions of the world, such as the Gulf of Aden.

. . .

19. At the request of the Committee, the attention of all Member Governments was drawn to the problem of timely clearance of material and equipment needed to respond to major marine pollution incidents and Governments were recommended to make every effort to make appropriate arrangements to facilitate transfrontier movement of marine pollution response resources during emergency situations (MEPC /Circ, l62, 27 February 1986).

20. Pursuant to decisions taken at the twenty-fourth session of the Committee, the Secretary General has exchanged correspondence with the Secretary-General of the International Civil Aviation Organization (ICAO) concerning the facilitation of air transport for marine pollution control material and equipment and as a result the Facilitation Committee (September 1987) will consider at its seventeenth session whether to suggest a draft amendment to the Annex of the ICAO (Chicago) Convention relating to this subject.

21. The Facilitation Committee will also consider at its seventeenth session a proposed amendment to the Annex of the Facilitation Convention submitted by Sweden (FAL/7/6) relating to the facilitation of the arrival and departure of ships engaged, *inter alia*, in combating or prevention of marine pollution and the facilitation of the entry and clearance of persons, cargo, including material and equipment required to deal, *inter alia*, with combating and prevention of marine pollution.

22. The Marine Environment Protection Committee at its twenty-fourth session agreed upon the draft text of a resolution on arrangements for the entry and clearance of marine pollution response resources, which appears at annex to document A 15/14. This draft text is being brought to the attention of the Facilitation Committee at its seventeenth session. If there are

any amendments proposed by the Facilitation Committee they will be incorporated in a revised draft text and submitted to the Assembly.

. . .

- - - - -

IMO Assembly   A 15/14/2
15th Session, November 1987   Extract

Consideration of the Reports and Recommendations of the Marine Environment Protection Committee
Note by the Secretary-General

1.   Reference is made to paragraphs 21 and 22 of document A 15/14/Add.1 . . .
. . .

3.   The Facilitation Committee, at its seventeenth session (14-18 September 1987), considered the text and expressed concern over the difference between the wording of the amended Standards 5.11 and 5.12 in the Annex to the Facilitation Convention, adopted at that session, which would apply only to Contracting Governments, and that of the draft resolution which was addressed to all Governments. The Committee therefore agreed to a revised text for the draft Assembly resolution which is annexed to its report (FAL 17/18) for transmission through the Council, for consideration at the fifteenth session of the Assembly.   In recommending the text of the resolution, the Committee agreed that the reference to "salvage related and pollution combating material and equipment", in the second operative paragraph, should be understood to mean equipment needed to deal with a pollution incident or threat thereof.

. . .

- - - - -

IMO Assembly   A 15/Res.625
15th Session, November 1987

Resolution A.625(15)
Arrangements for the Entry and Clearance of Marine Pollution Response Resources During Emergency Situations

The Assembly,
. . .

Recalling also resolution A.448(XI) and resolution A.587(14) concerning the development, as appropriate, of joint marine pollution contingency arrangements at a regional or subregional level, or on a bilateral basis, and concerning the need to address the problems of countries faced with the threat of major marine pollution from spillages of oil and other hazardous substances, respectively,

Being aware of the problem of timely clearance of material and equipment needed to respond to a marine pollution incident; of the consequent need for Governments to make every effort to make appropriate arrangements to facilitate transfrontier movement of marine pollution response resources during emergency situations; and of MEPC/Circ.162 relating thereto,

Noting that the Facilitation Committee at its seventeenth session adopted amendments to Standards 5.11 and 5.12 of the Annex to the Convention on Facilitation of International Maritime Traffic, 1965, as amended,

Noting also the recommendations made by the Marine Environment Protection Committee at its twenty-second, twenty-third and twenty-fourth sessions,

1.   *Invites* Contracting Parties to the above-mentioned Facilitation Convention to implement the amendments adopted at the seventeenth session of the Facilitation Committee annexed to the present resolution pending their entry into force,

2.   *Urges* Member Governments to make every effort to establish prior arrangements to expedite the customs clearance and, where applicable, the temporary importation of all salvage related and pollution combating material and equipment and the rapid entry of technical personnel required to deal with a major marine pollution incident or threat thereof.

ANNEX

AMENDMENTS TO THE ANNEX TO THE CONVENTION ON FACILITATION OF INTERNATIONAL MARITIME TRAFFIC, 1965, AS AMENDED, RELATED TO ARRANGEMENTS FOR THE ENTRY AND CLEARANCE OF MARINE POLLUTION RESPONSE RESOURCES DURING EMERGENCY SITUATIONS, ADOPTED BY THE FACILITATION COMMITTEE ON 17 SEPTEMBER 1987

Amend Section 5F to read:

"F.   EMERGENCY ASSISTANCE

5.11   Standard. Public authorities shall facilitate the arrival and departure of ships engaged in disaster relief work, the combating or prevention of marine pollution, or other emergency operations necessary to ensure maritime safety, the safety of the population or the protection of the marine environment.

5.12   Standard. Public authorities shall, to the greatest extent possible, facilitate the entry and clearance of persons, cargo, material and equipment required to deal with situations described in Standard 5.11."

- - - - -

Special Areas and Particularly Sensitive Sea Areas

IMO Marine Environment Protection Committee   MEPC 25/20
Report of the Twenty-fifth Session, December 1987   Extract

. . .

5. Uniform Interpretation and Amendments of MARPOL 73/78, Including Special Area Status for the Gulf of Aden

Designation of the Gulf of Aden as a Special Area under Annex I of MARPOL 73/78

5.1 As agreed at its last session, the Committee considered the proposed amendments to regulation 10 of Annex I of MARPOL 73/78, the text of which was formulated by the Committee at its last session to provide for the designation of the Gulf of Aden as a special area (MEPC 25/5). The Committee also received a paper prepared by the Secretariat upon the request of the Committee at its last session, summarizing the information submitted by the coastal States indicating the rationale for the designation of the Gulf of Aden as a special area and the information on the availability and adequacy of the reception facilities (MEPC 25/5/10) as well as the additional information submitted by Somalia (MEPC 25/5/10/Add.1).

5.2 The Committee also noted that the fifteenth Assembly expressed its hope that the Committee will be able to finalize these amendments during this session.

5.3 The proposed amendments were unanimously adopted by the Parties to MARPOL 73/78 present in the Committee by resolution MEPC.29(25) which is shown in annex 9. The Committee expressed the hope that the three coastal States would accede to MARPOL 73/78 as soon as possible. The three States should inform the Organization of the availability of adequate reception facilities so that the special area provisions could become applicable to the Gulf of Aden as soon as possible. The delegations of Democratic Yemen, Djibouti and Somalia expressed their appreciation to the Committee and said that they now had the incentive necessary to become Party to MARPOL 73/78 as soon as possible and to provide adequate reception facilities in accordance with regulation 10 of Annex I.

. . .

ANNEX 9

RESOLUTION MEPC.29(25)

ADOPTION OF THE AMENDMENTS TO THE ANNEX OF THE PROTOCOL OF
1978 RELATING TO THE INTERNATIONAL CONVENTION FOR THE
PREVENTION OF POLLUTION FROM SHIPS, 1973
(Designation of the Gulf of Aden as a Special Area)

THE MARINE ENVIRONMENT PROTECTION COMMITTEE,

Noting the functions which article 16 of the International Convention for the Prevention of Pollution from Ships, 1973 (hereinafter referred to as the "1973 Convention") and resolution

A.297(VIII) confer on the Marine Environment Protection Committee for the consideration and adoption of amendments to the 1973 Convention,

Noting further article VI of the Protocol of 1978 relating to the International Convention for the Prevention of Pollution from Ships, 1973 (hereinafter referred to as the "1978 Protocol"),

Having considered at its twenty-fifth session amendments to the 1978 Protocol proposed and circulated in accordance with article 16(2)(a) of the 1973 Convention,

1.   *Adopts* in accordance with article 16(2)(d) of the 1973 Convention amendments to the Annex of the 1978 Protocol, the text of which is set out in the Annex to the present resolution;

2.   *Determines* in accordance with article 16(2)(f)(iii) of the 1973 Convention that the amendments shall be deemed to have been accepted on 1 October 1988 unless prior to this date one third or more of the Parties or the Parties, the combined merchant fleets of which constitute fifty per cent or more of the gross tonnage of the world's merchant fleet, have communicated to the Organization their objections to the amendments;

3.   *Invites* the Parties to note that in accordance with article 16(2)(g)(ii) of the 1973 Convention the amendments shall enter into force on 1 April 1989 upon their acceptance in accordance with paragraph 2 above;

4.   *Requests* the Secretary-General in conformity with article 16(2)(e) of the 1973 Convention to transmit to all Parties to the 1978 Protocol certified copies of the present resolution and the text of the amendments contained in the Annex;

5.   *Further requests* the Secretary-General to transmit to the Members of the Organization which are not Parties to the 1978 Protocol copies of the resolution and its Annex.

ANNEX

AMENDMENTS TO THE ANNEX OF THE PROTOCOL OF 1978 RELATING TO THE INTERNATIONAL CONVENTION FOR THE PREVENTION OF POLLUTION FROM SHIPS, 1973

ANNEX I

Regulations for the Prevention of Pollution by Oil

Regulation 10

Methods for the Prevention of Oil Pollution from Ships while operating in Special Areas

The existing text of paragraph (1) is replaced by the following:

"(1)   For the purposes of this Annex the special areas are the Mediterranean Sea area, the Baltic Sea area, the Black Sea area, the Red Sea area, the "Gulfs area" and the Gulf of Aden area, which are defined as follows:

(a)   The Mediterranean Sea area means the Mediterranean Sea proper including the gulfs and seas therein with the boundary between the Mediterranean and the Black Sea constituted by the 41°N parallel and bounded to the west by the Straits of Gibraltar at the meridian 5°36'W.

(b)   The Baltic Sea area means the Baltic Sea proper with the Gulf of Bothnia, the Gulf of Finland and the entrance to the Baltic Sea bounded by the parallel of the Skaw in the Skagerrak at 57°44.8'N.

(c)   The Black Sea area means the Black Sea proper with the boundary between the Mediterranean and the Black Sea constituted by the parallel 41°N.

(d)   The Red Sea area means the Red Sea proper including the Gulfs of Suez and Aqaba bounded at the south by the rhumb line between Ras si Ane (12°28.5'N, 43°19.6'E) and Husn Murad (12°40.4'N, 43°30.2'E).

(e)   The Gulfs area means the sea area located north west of the rhumb line between Ras al Hadd (22°30'N, 59°48'E) and Ras Al Fasteh (25°04'N, 61°25'E).

(f)   The Gulf of Aden area means that part of the Gulf of Aden between the Red Sea and the Arabian Sea bounded to the west by the rhumb line between Ras si Ane (12°28.5'N, 43°19.6'E) and Husn Murad (12°40.4'N, 43°30.2'E) and to the east by the rhumb line between Ras Asir (11°50'N, 51°16.9'E) and Ras Fartak (15°35'N, 52°13.8'E)."

The existing text of paragraph 7(b) is replaced by the following:

"(b)   Red Sea area, Gulfs area and Gulf of Aden area:".

- - - - -

Tenth Consultative Meeting of Contracting Parties   LDC 10/13/2
to the Convention on the Prevention of Marine Pollution   22 August 1986
by Dumping of Wastes and Other Matter   October 1986

Identification of particularly sensitive sea areas
Note by the Secretariat

1.   The Marine Environment Protection Committee at its twenty-third session (7-11 June 1986) considered ways and means for identifying particularly sensitive sea areas, taking into account resolution 9 of the International Conference on Tanker Safety and Pollution Prevention (TSPP) (London, February 1978) which invited the Organization to initiate studies with a view to making an inventory of particularly sensitive sea areas around the world and assessing the extent and type of protective measures that might be required with regard to the prevention and control of marine pollution from ships and dumping of wastes. For easy reference, the resolution is shown in annex hereto.

2.   The Consultative Meeting will recall that a lengthy debate took place at the Third Consultative Meeting on this issue (LDC III/12, chapter 10). The outcome of that debate has been reported to the twenty-third session of MEPC as follows:

"   During discussion of TSPP resolution 9 by the Third Consultative Meeting of Contracting Parties to the London Dumping Convention, views were expressed that "sensitive" zones could be identified by criteria related to the control of undesirable effects of dumping in areas outside specific dumping sites. Further, referring to article IV of the LDC concerning the issuance of permits for waste disposal at sea, the opinion was expressed that the considerations set out in Annex III to the Convention (provisions to be considered when establishing criteria for the issue of permits) implied that dumping is prohibited in particularly sensitive areas. Concern was also expressed that by designating areas sensitive to dumping activities the impression might be given that dumping elsewhere would not lead to damage to the marine environment.

One delegation pointed out that most dumping took place in coastal waters and that a sensitive area might be very restricted and therefore it would be illogical to define whole sea areas as sensitive. It was recommended that GESAMP should be requested to update GESAMP Reports and Studies No.3 entitled "Scientific Criteria for the Selection of Sites for the Dumping of Wastes into the Sea" in order to facilitate the selection of sites which will minimize the effect on the marine environment of the particular waste or other matter which is to be dumped and to compile a bibliography.

The Meeting concluded that as regards the London Dumping Convention these views should be conveyed to GESAMP, which should be requested to develop further the scientific criteria for the selection of sites which will minimize the effect on the marine environment of the particular waste or other matter which is to be dumped. It also suggested that GESAMP should be requested to compile a bibliography of available material." (MEPC 23/16/2).

3.   In light of the above, the Working Group established by the twenty-third session of MEPC to consider this subject concluded that no further action would be undertaken on this matter by the Consultative Meeting in that within the London Dumping Convention "environmental sensitivity" is covered by the criteria adopted for selecting dumping sites (MEPC 23/WP.5, paragraph 2.3).

4.   With regard to pollution from ships (and related maritime activities), MEPC adopted a draft Circular containing a questionnaire for distribution to IMO member States and appropriate international organizations inviting them to provide information on the criteria used in identifying protected sea areas. The Secretariat would prepare a summary report on the basis of information received for consideration by the Committee at its twenty-fifth session.

5.   The Consultative Meeting is invited to take note of the above information and to review the position of the Third Consultative meeting as summarized in Paragraph 2 above. In this connection, the Consultative Meeting may wish to consider the role of regional conventions which in their areas restrict dumping and incineration activities (e.g. Helsinki Convention, Barcelona Convention) or which include specific provisions concerning the establishment of protected areas (e.g. Protocol Concerning Mediterranean Specially Protected Areas, Protocol Concerning Protected Areas and Wild Fauna and Flora in the Eastern African Region).

ANNEX

RESOLUTION 9

PROTECTION OF PARTICULARLY SENSITIVE SEA AREAS

The Conference,

Noting with appreciation the work being carried out by the Inter-Governmental Maritime Consultative Organization concerning the protection of the marine environment against pollution from ships and from dumping of wastes,

Noting further the action taken by the International Conference on Marine Pollution, 1973, to include in the International Convention for the Prevention of Pollution from Ships, 1973, (MARPOL Convention) special mandatory provisions to prevent pollution of the sea in certain defined special areas, including the Mediterranean Sea area, the Baltic Sea area, the Black Sea area, the Red Sea area and the "Gulfs" area, because of their particular oceanographic characteristics and ecological significance,

Noting also that, under Article VIII of the Convention on the Prevention of Marine Pollution by Dumping of Wastes and Other Matter, 1972 (the London Dumping convention), Contracting Parties with common interests to protect in the marine environment in a given geographical area shall endeavour, taking into account characteristic regional features, to enter into regional agreements consistent with that convention for the prevention of pollution, especially by dumping,

Being aware of continuing activities in special regions including the Mediterranean Sea, the Red Sea, the "Gulfs" area, the Gulf of Guinea, the Caribbean and South East Asian Waters, within the United Nations system under the co-ordination of the United Nations Environment Programme and with the participation of IMCO,

Being aware also of the need for measures aiming at the protection of particularly sensitive sea areas against pollution from ships and dumping of wastes,

Realizing that this need cannot be met without special studies undertaken as a matter of priority,

Recognizing the competence of the Organization in the field of the prevention and control of marine pollution from ships and dumping of wastes, and the competence of other international organizations in the field of the marine environment,

Invites the Organization:

(a) to pursue its efforts in respect of the protection of the protection of the marine environment against pollution from ships and dumping of wastes:

(b) to initiate, as a matter of priority and in addition to the work under way, studies, in collaboration with other relevant international organizations and expert bodies, with a view to:

(i)   making an inventory of sea areas around the world which are in special need of protection against marine pollution from ships and dumping, on account of the areas' particular sensitivity in respect of their renewable natural resources or in respect of their importance for scientific purposes;

(ii) assessing, inasmuch as possible, the extent of the need of protection, as well as the measures which might be considered appropriate, in order to achieve a reasonable degree of protection, taking into account also other legitimate uses of the seas;

(c)   to consider, on the basis of the studies carried out accordingly and the results of other work undertaken, what action will be needed in order to enhance the protection of the marine environment from pollution from ships and dumping of wastes;

(d)   to take action, when appropriate, in accordance with the established procedure, with a view to incorporating any necessary provisions, within the framework of relevant conventions, as may be identified as a result of the above studies;

(e)   to formulate a recommendation to the Consultative Meeting of Contracting Parties that appropriate steps be taken within the framework of the London Dumping Convention, to protect such particularly sensitive sea areas from pollution caused by dumping.

- - - - -

IMO Marine Environment Protection Committee,   MEPC 25/20
Report of the Twenty-fifth Session, December 1987   Extract

. . .

15.   Identification of Particularly Sensitive Areas, Including Development of Guidelines for Designating Special Areas under Annexes I, II and V

Particularly sensitive areas

15.1   The Committee was informed of the material received by the Secretariat in response to MEPC/Circ.171 and MEPC/Circ.171/Corr.1 by which information had been requested regarding the criteria which are being used for the designation of protected marine areas, the measures taken for the protection of such areas, as well as the geographical location of protected areas which extend beyond the territorial seas.

15.2   The Federal Republic of Germany pointed out that it has initiated a wide range of measures to protect the German Bight from pollution caused by maritime transport as well as from other sources of marine pollution (MEPC 25/15). The delegations from Norway (MEPC 25/15/1), Sweden (MEPC/ 25/15/20), the United Kingdom (MEPC 25/15/3), the United States (MEPC 25/15/4) and Canada (MEPC 25/15/7) also informed the Committee of criteria used in their countries for establishing protected marine areas, the measures taken for the protection of such areas and the location of particularly sensitive areas. The Committee noted that, in most countries, different categories of protected marine areas have been established, e.g. marine sanctuaries, critical habitats, marine reserves, etc., which are subject to different protection measures.

15.3 The delegation of Ecuador informed the Committee of the establishment of an ecological protection zone in the region of the Galapagos Archipelago which is to be avoided by merchant ships (MEPC 25/15/6). Ecuador will submit further details of its measures to this Committee, and also to the Sub-Committee on Safety of Navigation for consideration, with a view to their adoption.

15.4 The Committee was also informed of the material prepared by the Secretariat during the intersessional period (MEPC 25/INF.2, MEPC 25/INF.7) which included information provided by the Food and Agriculture Organization (FAO), the World Health Organization (WHO), the Intergovernmental Oceanographic Commission (IOC) of Unesco, the United Nations Environment Programme (UNEP), the Helsinki Commission, the International Whaling Commission, the Permanent Commission for the South Pacific (CPPS), the Regional Organization for the Protection of the Marine Environment (ROPME), the South Pacific Commission (SPC) and the International Commission of Scientific Unions (ICSU). The Permanent Commission for the South Pacific (CPPS), in a separate submission (MEPC 25/INF.7/Add.1), introduced its regional atlas of the South-east Pacific containing information on areas which need particular protection, as well as criteria for the identification of such areas.

15.5 The Committee expressed its appreciation to the international organizations which had provided the material. The observer from Friends of the Earth International (FOEI) informed the Committee that the Fourth World Wilderness Congress, in September 1987, adopted several recommendations regarding the establishment of marine protected areas. Among the international organizations requested to take action in this field, particular mention had been made of IMO.

15.6 Several delegations, stressing the importance of developing criteria for the identification of particularly sensitive areas, expressed the view that this be carried out with high priority. Other delegations, although recognizing the importance of establishing particularly sensitive areas, warned against the proliferation of sensitive areas which might lead to the disorientation and bewilderment of seafarers. They rather preferred to make the current provisions of MARPOL 73/78 more stringent, thus following the original desire of Parties to the Convention, namely the "complete elimination of international pollution of the marine environment" (preamble to MARPOL 73/78).

15.7 The Committee reconvened its Working Group on Particularly Sensitive Areas to consider the material submitted in response to MEPC/Circ.171 and to advise the Committee on the steps to be taken for identifying sea areas which are in special need of protection against marine pollution. The consideration of the proposals made by the Working Group is reflected in paragraphs 15.9 and 15.11 below.

. . .

Consideration of proposals made by the Working Group on Particularly Sensitive Sea Areas

15.9   The Committee noted that its Working Group on Particularly Sensitive Sea Areas, in its report (MEPC 25/WP.14), had defined "particularly sensitive sea areas" as areas which need special protection because of their "significance for ecological, socio-economic or scientific reasons, and which are vulnerable to damage by maritime activities". The Committee also took note of the draft criteria for the identification of particularly sensitive sea areas (MEPC 25/WP.14, annex 2). Members of the Committee were invited to submit their comments on the draft criteria to the twenty-sixth session of the Committee. The IOC Group of Experts on Effects of Pollutants (GEEP), which is co-sponsored by IMO, was also invited to comment on the proposed criteria.

15.10   With regard to the designation of special areas under MARPOL 73/78, the Committee noted the set of draft criteria prepared by its Working Group on Particularly Sensitive Sea Areas (MEPC 25/WP.14, annex 1). Members of the Committee were invited to submit their comments on the draft criteria for consideration at its twenty-sixth session and to utilize the draft criterion in the interim period as a basis for the formulation of proposals for designating special areas.

15.11   With regard to the envisaged measures for control of the protection of special areas, it was noted that, in addition to measures under MARPOL, it would be possible for IMO to adopt special routeing measures according to resolution A.377(X) "Procedures for adoption and amendment of routeing systems other than traffic separation schemes". With some further minor amendments, the Working Group's report was adopted.

- - - - -

IMO Marine Environment Protection Committee   MEPC 25/WP.14
Twenty-fifth Session, 3 December 1987   Extract

Identification of Particularly Sensitive Areas, Including Development of Guidelines for Designating Special Areas Under Annexes I, II AND V
Report of the Working Group

. . .

2.   **Terms of Reference**

. . .

Special Areas

1.   Establish criteria for the designation of Special Area status.

Particularly sensitive sea areas

1.   Formulate a definition for "particularly sensitive areas";

2.   Develop a set of general criteria which could be applied to determine which marine areas are particularly sensitive;

3.   Develop a set of specific criteria which would be more technical in nature in that they would need to be supported by marine scientific research;

4.   Identify appropriate regulatory measures in the maritime field for the protection of sensitive areas; and

5.   Identify particularly sensitive areas beyond the territorial seas using the criteria developed with a view to establishing an inventory of such areas.

3.   Special Areas

The Working Group considered criteria for special area designation using MEPC 25/15/5 as a basis. The Working Group agreed that special area designation for a given area should be evaluated separately for Annexes I, II and V of the Convention. The proposed criteria for special area designation are set out in Annex 1 to this report. The Working Group recommends that the Committee note the proposed criteria with a view to finalizing the criteria at its next session.

4.   Particularly sensitive sea areas

4.1   Definition and criteria for particularly sensitive sea areas

4.1.1   The Working Group considered the definition for a particularly sensitive area in the context of resolution 9 of the TSPP Conference and agreed that a particularly sensitive area is an area which needs special protection because of its significance mainly for ecological, socio-economic or scientific reasons and which may be vulnerable to damage by maritime activities.

    . . .

4.1.3   The criteria developed by the Working Group are set out in Annex 2 to this report. The Working Group recommends that the Committee note the Working Group's progress in developing criteria for particularly sensitive sea areas with a view to further development at its next session. The Working Group also recommends that the IOC Group of Experts on Effects of Pollutants (GEEP) be invited to comment on the proposed criteria. It is also suggested that GEEP endeavour to test the criteria listed in Annex 2 against well studied sensitive areas in different climatic zones (e.g. Morrocoy Park, Wadden Sea, and a higher latitude ecosystem).

4.2   Development of more specific criteria

Due to time constraints the Working Group could not give detailed consideration to this item. However, the Working Group noted that GEEP is considering methods for assessment of, and criteria for defining the vulnerability of particularly sensitive areas and recommends that, if appropriate, more specific technical, site-specific criteria based on experiences from case studies be proposed. The Working Group recommends that the Group formulate its criteria in a manner consistent with the general criteria developed by the Committee.

5.   Measures of control

5.1   The Working Group considered what measures of control could be taken by the Organization to provide protection for particularly sensitive sea areas. In this connection the Working Group noted examples of measures identified at the twenty-third session of the Committee, which included:

1. to designate the area as a special area in Annexes I, II and V under MARPOL 73/78; and

2. to adopt, under COLREG, special routeing measures near or in the area or designate the area as an "area to be avoided".

5.2 The Working Group agreed that in some cases protection could be afforded to a particularly sensitive sea area by establishing a buffer zone around the area and by restricting marine activities in the particularly sensitive sea area and its buffer zone. The Working Group, recalling the suggestion made in plenary regarding the tightening of discharge criteria (for example, changing the Annex I, Regulation 9, 100 ppm discharge criteria to 15 ppm) as an option to consider in lieu of providing additional protection for particularly sensitive sea areas, agreed that such a measure could obviate the need for some protective measures. Owing to time constraints the Working Group was unable to give this item further detailed consideration.

. . .

ANNEX 1

CRITERIA FOR THE DESIGNATION OF SPECIAL AREA STATUS

Introduction

MARPOL 73/78, in Annexes I, II and V, defines certain sea areas as "Special Areas", relative to the type of pollution controlled by each Annex. "Special Area" is defined as "a sea area where for recognized technical reasons in relation to its oceanographical and ecological condition and to the particular character of its traffic the adoption of special mandatory methods for the prevention of sea pollution by oil (noxious liquid substances, garbage, as applicable) is required". Under the Convention these Special Areas are provided a higher level of protection than other areas of the sea. A Special Area should generally be considered a sea area of such an extent that a discharge of a harmful substance could otherwise be made from a ship in accordance with the discharge criteria established for open sea areas under Annexes I, II and V of the Convention. Certain criteria must be satisfied in order for an area to be given Special Area status. These criteria are grouped into the following categories:

1. oceanographic conditions;
2. ecological conditions;
3. vessel traffic characteristics.

Special Area designation for a given area should be evaluated separately for Annexes I, II and V of the Convention. Generally, in order to be designated a Special Area, one of the criteria in each category should be satisfied. However, it may be necessary to take additional conditions into account.

Criteria for designation of Special Area status

1. Oceanographic conditions

Conditions which would cause the concentration or retention of pollutants of harmful substances in the waters or sediments of the area, including:

.1 particular circulation patterns, such as convergence zones and gyres;

    .2   long residence time caused by low flushing rates;

    .3   ice state; and

    .4   adverse wind conditions.

2.   Ecological conditions

Conditions indicating that protection of the area from harmful substances is needed to protect:

    .1   depleted, threatened or endangered marine species;

    .2   commercially or recreationally important fisheries;

    .3   areas of high productivity such as spawning, breeding and nursery areas; and

    .4   rare or fragile ecosystems, such as coral reefs, mangroves and wetlands.

3.   Vessel traffic characteristics

The sea area is used by ships to an extent that the discharge of harmful substances by ships when operating in accordance with non-Special Area requirements of the Convention would be unacceptable in light of oceanographic and ecological conditions that exist in the area.

4.   Other considerations

4.1 The threat to amenities posed by the discharge of harmful substances from ships operating in accordance with the Convention requirements for non-Special Areas may strengthen the argument for designating an area as a Special Area.

4.2 Proposals for the designation of Special Areas would be strengthened by information that measures are being or will be taken to prevent, reduce and control pollution of the marine environment by sources other than shipping.

ANNEX 2

CRITERIA FOR PARTICULARLY SENSITIVE SEA AREAS

Introduction

1.   Resolution 9 of the TSPP Conference invites the Organization, *inter alia*, to make an inventory of sea areas in need of special protection from ships and dumping due to their sensitivity in respect of their renewable natural resources or their importance for scientific research. Accordingly, MEPC, at its twenty-third session, decided to develop criteria for identification of particularly sensitive sea areas in need of special protection from ships.

2.   The following draft criteria with regard to designation of a particularly sensitive sea area which could receive additional protection from harmful substances originating from ships were consequently developed. It should be noted that criteria for identification of areas to be protected from dumping activities would not necessarily be the same as those listed below.

3.   The criteria below relate to particularly sensitive sea areas within and beyond the limits of the territorial sea. They can be used by the Organization to identify particularly sensitive sea areas beyond the territorial seas with a view to bringing about the development of international protective measures regarding pollution from ships. These criteria can also be

used by national Administrations to identify particularly sensitive sea areas within their territorial waters for the same purpose.

4. A particularly sensitive sea area is defined as an area which needs special protection because of its significance for ecological, socio-economic or scientific reasons and which may be vulnerable to damage by maritime activities.

Characteristics which contribute to giving an area special significance

5. **Ecological criteria**

5.1 The area has rare or fragile ecosystems and provides habitats for depleted, threatened or endangered species (uniqueness and endangered species).

5.2 The ecological processes of an area provide essential support for species or an ecosystem. Certain species may have seasonal dependence on the area (dependency).

5.3 The area is virtually undisturbed by human activities (naturalness).

5.4 The area is highly representative of ecological processes, or community or habitat types or other natural characteristics (representativeness).

5.5 The area has a high variety of species, and a rich ecosystem (diversity).

5.6 The area is highly biologically productive (productivity).

6. **Social and economic criteria**

6.1 The area is of particular importance to utilization of living marine resources (economic benefit).

6.2 The area has special significance for recreation and tourism (recreation).

6.3 The area has importance for aquaculture (economic benefit).

7. **Scientific and educational criteria**

7.1 The area has high scientific interest (research).

7.2 The area provides suitable baseline conditions with regard to biota or environmental characteristics (baseline and monitoring studies).

7.3 The area offers opportunity to demonstrate particular natural phenomena (education).

Factors contributing to the vulnerability of an area

8. The presence of oceanographic and meteorological factors could cause an area to be vulnerable or increase its vulnerability, i.e. by causing the concentration or retention of harmful substances in the waters or in the sediment of the area, or by otherwise exposing the area to harmful substances. These conditions include circulation patterns such as convergence zones, oceanic fronts and gyres, long residence times caused by low flushing rates, as well as adverse ice states and wind conditions.

9.   An area already subject to environmental stress owing to human activities or natural phenomena (e.g. oil seepage) may be in need of special protection from further stress, including from maritime activities.

Other considerations

10. In designating an area as a particularly sensitive area and considering what special protective measures should be taken, consideration may be given to the degree to which actions already underway may indicate the need for further special protective measures and consideration should also be given to the beneficial effects that such measures will have.

- - - - -

Additional References

Report of the Tenth Consultative Meeting of Contracting Parties to the London Dumping Convention. LDC 10/15, Section 13.

Identification of particularly sensitive areas, including development of guidelines for designating special areas under MARPOL Annexes I, II and V. MEPC 25/INF.2 and 7.

Papers submitted to MEPC by Governments: MEPC 25/15/4 and 5 (USA), MEPC 25/15/3 (UK), MEPC 25/15/2 (Sweden), MEPC 25/15/1 (Norway), MEPC 25/15/6 (Ecuador), MEPC 25/15 (FRG) and MEPC 25/15/7 (Canada).

- - - - -

Future Developments

IMO Assembly   A 15/Res.631
15th Session, November 1987   Extract

Resolution A.631(15)
Long-Term Work Plan of the Organization
(Up to 1994)

. . .

ANNEX

. . .

MARINE ENVIRONMENT PROTECTION COMMITTEE

I.   Principal objectives

1.   Solution of problems involved in the implementation of . . . MARPOL 73/78 including examination of the problems of implementation of MARPOL 73/78 in relation to the protection of the marine environment in special areas.

2.   Development of suitable procedures for the enforcement of conventions relating to marine pollution.

3. Promotion of technical co-operation, including the development of regional arrangements on co-operation to combat pollution in cases of emergency.

4. Entry into force of the optional Annexes to MARPOL 73/78.

II. Specific Subjects

1. Uniform interpretation and application of the provisions of MARPOL 73/78 and possible amendments thereto.

2. Reception facilities for residues.

3. Oily-water separators and oil discharge monitoring and control systems including those for light refined oils and oil-like substances.

4. Procedures for the control of ships and certificates and the control of discharge from ships.

5. Surveys and certification of ships under MARPOL 73/78.

6. Penalties for infringement of convention provisions.

7. Casualty investigations in relation to marine pollution.

8. Arrangements for combating major incidents or threats of marine pollution.

9. Promotion of regional arrangements for combating marine pollution.

10. Development and updating of anti-pollution manuals.

11. Identification of particularly sensitive sea areas.

12. Categorization of noxious liquid substances and harmful substances.

13. Prevention of pollution by noxious solid substances in bulk.

14. Measures on board ships to minimize the escape of pollutants in the case of accidents.
    . . .

- - - - -

General Reference

Status of IMO Conventions relating to marine pollution (as of 25/10/1987). IMO doc. MEPC 25/2.

- - - - -

3

Pollution from Dumping

Annexes to the London Dumping Convention

Report of the Ninth Consultative Meeting of Contracting   LDC 9/12
Parties to the London Dumping Convention, 1985   Annex 2

===

Resolution LDC. 19(9)
Criteria for the Allocation of Substances to the Annexes

THE NINTH CONSULTATIVE MEETING,

. . .

1.   *Adopts* a new set of Guidelines containing criteria for assigning substances to Annexes I and II to the Convention as shown in the Annex to this resolution;

2.   *Requests* its Scientific Group on Dumping to consider any proposals from Contracting Parties for additions or amendments to the Annexes in light of the new guidelines.

ANNEX

GUIDELINES FOR ALLOCATION OF SUBSTANCES TO THE ANNEXES TO THE
LONDON DUMPING CONVENTION

These guidelines are intended to allow the Scientific Group on Dumping to take into account the best available scientific and technical information, recognizing that an element of further interpretation and judgement will enter the final deliberations and decisions of the Consultative Meeting. These guidelines are not intended for use as rigid rules but should nevertheless be used as the basis for the considerations of the Scientific Group and be experimented with and adapted as necessary.

1.   **Criteria of relevance to risk evaluation**

1.1   In the evaluation of the risks arising from the disposal of any substance, the criteria listed in paragraph 2.2 below are relevant in considering the allocation of substances to the Annexes. It should also be noted that matters related to **radioactivity** do not fall within the terms of reference of the Scientific Group and were referred by agreement to other fora, bodies or organizations (e.g. the IAEA). They are not considered further in these Guidelines.

2.   **Classification of substances**

2.1   The Annexes classify defined substances or groups of substances rather than wastes. In evaluating the risks from sea dumping of substances for the purpose of classification to or between the Annexes the following steps are required:

.1 evaluation of hazard potential;

.2 evaluation of environmental exposure; and

.3 conclusions on potential scale of effects and decision on classification.

2.2 In evaluating hazard potential the following factors must be taken into account:

.1 **Persistence/degradability**:

persistence is a property of a substance which reflects the degree to which it will remain in a particular state or form. In this regard elements are of course persistent but will occur in the environment in many different forms and in compounds of differing persistence and biological properties. For elements, therefore, information is needed only on the formation and transformation of bio-available and toxic forms. The term "degradable" applies only to organic compounds and refers to the breakdown of a substance by physical, chemical or biological means. While it is possible in a laboratory to assess the intrinsic degradability of a substance by means of standardized tests, it is necessary for the purposes of the Convention to carry out additional tests which more adequately reflect the physical and chemical conditions likely to pertain in the sea. In particular, the concentration of test substances, and conditions related to organic materials and bacterial inoculum require special attention. Tests should be carried out with respect to all relevant environmental compartments;

.2 **Bioaccumulation potential**:

bioaccumulation potential is generally determined by a comparison between uptake and elimination of a substance by an organism under controlled test conditions or through field observations. Bioaccumulation potential can provide a useful estimate of whether or not body burdens might reach levels that may present a hazard, either to the organism itself or to its predators. Bioaccumulation per se is however not necessarily harmful to the organism and is, for example, necessary in the uptake of essential elements by organisms;

.3 **Toxicity to marine life**:

toxicity testing is the measurement of deleterious biological effects of a substance under acute or under chronic exposure conditions (the latter resulting from either a continuous input of a non-persistent substance or a single input of a persistent substance). As a minimum, to assess the potential hazard of a substance to marine life, data on lethal toxicity under chronic (or at least long term) exposure conditions are needed. Preferably data on sub-lethal effects (including effects on reproduction) should also be considered, especially if chronic exposure may occur. A second minimum requirement is that these data should refer to representative organisms from at least three trophic levels (e.g. algae, crustacea and fish). Harmful effects to marine life may result from chemical and physical factors other than toxicity, and should also be considered, e.g. effects on photosynthesis, exchange of nutrients, gas, etc.;

.4 **Toxicity to man, domestic animals, marine mammals and birds preying on marine organisms:**

where persistent and bioaccumulative substances are concerned, information on toxicity to man, domestic animals or marine mammals is of relevance where a significant pathway through the marine environment exists. "Significance" in this respect may be related to a contribution to the acceptable daily intake (ADI) as recommended by WHO/FAO and other international organizations and agencies;

.5   **Carcinogenicity and mutagenicity:**

the state-of-the-art does not yet permit testing of carcinogenicity or mutagenicity to marine organisms; there is no hard evidence that these factors play a significant role in the marine environment. These factors are therefore for the moment considered to be relevant primarily in terms of possible marine pathways for the transfer to man of substances demonstrating mammalian carcinogenicity or mutagenicity;

.6   **Ability to interfere with other legitimate uses of the sea:**

substances may exert such effects not only through physical interference with legitimate uses of the sea but also may have aesthetic effects. This interference includes the tainting of fish and shellfish.

2.3   The factors described under points .2 to .4 above . . . apply to the original compound as well as to the persistent metabolites or other products of organic substances and to the different forms in which elements are present. Where tests are used to evaluate bioaccumulation, bio-availability and toxicity to marine life . . . , these tests must have been undertaken using realistic concentrations, and test conditions must have adequately reflected the physical and chemical condition pertaining in the sea, especially in so far as these affect bio-availability. The chemical state and physical form of substances have an important effect on their bio-availability, toxicity, persistence and bioaccumulation potential.

2.4   Whether or not a substance is of **non-natural origin** is not in itself a criterion for designation to the Annexes. However, in combination with a very low degree of (bio) degradability, extra caution may be required. This extra caution is warranted in light of the fact that substances which do not naturally occur by definition cannot be dispersed or diluted to natural back-ground levels in the environment. Such alien substances might impose unexpected stress on marine biota and should therefore be subjected to adequate testing.

2.5   By "evaluation of environmental exposure" as referred to in paragraph 2.1.2 above, is meant the measurement or estimation of actual or potential distribution and concentration (including trends in these factors) of a substance in all relevant ecological and geographical compartments and the estimation of actual or potential contribution of dumping to local, regional or global flux. There has been a degree of confusion in earlier discussions on the relative significance of **concentration, quantity** or **flux** (that is the rate of throughput of a substance, defined as mass per unit area per unit time). For the purposes of these Guidelines the **contribution by dumping to local, regional or global flux** is a relevant criterion. Measurement of **concentration** is required for estimating exposure, which together with a knowledge of the relationship between effects and concentration, enable a hazard assessment to be made.

2.6   On the basis of these considerations, the potential scale of effects of dumping of a substance can be determined and decisions can be taken as to whether such substances should be included in the Annexes and to which Annex they should be designated. The criteria for making these distinctions are addressed in the following paragraphs. In taking these decisions, several elements should be borne in mind in determining the appropriate safety margin to be applied. Firstly, there is a time lag between the introduction of controls and the effects of these controls becoming evident in the environment. Secondly, there are limitations to the current ability to fully predict the consequences of any disposal to the sea. Thirdly, as noted in paragraph 2.4 above, the synthetic origin of a substance may indicate the need for a more cautious approach.

3.   **Allocation to Annexes I and II**

3.1   Substances should be allocated to the Annexes if:

   .1   they are, or are proposed to be, dumped; and if
   .2   significant environmental exposure may result; and if
   .3   they possess any combination of the properties listed in paragraph 2.2 above in significant degree.

3.2   Annex I substances will be those for which dumping will or may result in, or contribute significantly to environmental exposure on a wide scale, extending far beyond the original location and time of disposal. Such substances will have in common a high degree of persistence coupled with:

   .1   the ability to accumulate to levels significant in terms of toxicity to marine organisms and their predators, to domestic animals or to man; or

   .2   the ability to accumulate through marine pathways to levels significant in terms of carcinogenicity or mutagenicity to domestic animals or to man; or

   .3   the ability to cause a high degree of interference with fisheries, amenities or other legitimate uses of the sea.

3.3   Annex II substances will be all those considered suitable for inclusion in the Annexes except for those allocated to Annex I.

- - - - -

Report of the Tenth Consultative Meeting of Contracting
   Parties to the London Dumping Convention, 1986

LDC 10/15
Extract

. . .

Application of the Annexes to Dredged Material

3.3   . . . Draft Guidelines for the Application of the Annexes to the Disposal of Dredged Material . . . were presented . . . together with a draft resolution for their adoption by the Consultative Meeting (LDC/SG.9/13).

3.4 . . . It was recognized that there may be exceptional circumstances in which a detailed consideration of Annex III, Section C4 indicates that sea disposal is the option of least detriment to the environment. While the draft Guidelines suggested that it would be acceptable under such circumstances to issue a permit for sea disposal, the Convention does not presently allow such an interpretation. Although there was considerable support for the principle that the disposal option of least detriment should be the preferred option, the Meeting agreed to delete the respective paragraphs for the time being, and further agreed that the Scientific Group should be requested to study mechanisms by which this principle could be accommodated within the framework of the Convention.

. . .

3.6 . . . The Consultative Meeting adopted resolution LDC.23(10) and the Guidelines on the Application of the Annexes to the Disposal of Dredged Material annexed thereto. This is shown at annex 2 to this report.

3.7 The Consultative Meeting noted the advice of the Scientific Group that, consequent on the adoption of special guidelines on dredged material, it was necessary to amend the Interim Guidelines for the Implementation of Paragraphs 8 and 9 of Annex I to the London Dumping Convention (LDC IV/12, annex 5) by deleting any references to the disposal at sea of dredged material. The revised Interim Guidelines and an accompanying resolution proposed by the Secretariat (LDC 10/3/2) were adopted by the Consultative Meeting and are given at annex 3 to this report.

. . .

Review of the Annexes to the London Dumping Convention

. . .

3.18 The Consultative Meeting recalled that at its Ninth Meeting it had noted a recommendation by the Scientific Group to include a paragraph in Annex III, Section A of the Convention (characteristics and composition of the matter) similar to that in paragraph B9 of Annex III. . . . The Meeting adopted resolution LDC.26(10), as shown at annex 5, which in keeping with established procedures, designated the Twelfth Consultative Meeting as the date for formal adoption of this amendment.

. . .

3.20 In connection with the difficulties expressed by the Scientific Group in developing a sound scientific rationale to support the current structure of the Annexes, and the various key terms contained therein, the Consultative Meeting noted that the Chairman of the Scientific Group in his submission (LDC 10/3/6) explained the background to these difficulties in the work of the Convention. The Chairman of the Scientific Group informed the Meeting that, in the opinion of many scientists, future progress with the interpretation and implementation of the Convention would be constrained by certain ambiguities in the structure and content of the Annexes, and by restricting the consideration of the Scientific Group to the assessment of sea disposal. With regard to the latter point, it was an important consideration under Annex III of the Convention that comparative assessments of all disposal options should be carried out and, as a consequence, it was equally important that decisions concerning the regulation of waste disposal at sea should be supported by scientific advice which took into account the effects of land-based alternatives. In such a way it would be possible to identify the option of least detriment to the environment . . .

. . .

3.22 ... The Consultative Meeting invited the Chairman of the Scientific Group to prepare a draft resolution on the future work programme of the Group. ... Resolution LDC.27(10) is shown at annex 6.

...

ANNEX 2

RESOLUTION LDC.23(10)

GUIDELINES FOR THE APPLICATION OF THE ANNEXES TO THE DISPOSAL OF DREDGED MATERIAL

THE TENTH CONSULTATIVE MEETING,

...

Recognizing that the major part of the sediments dredged from the waterways of the world are either not polluted or may possess mitigative properties that diminish the development of adverse environmental impacts after disposal at sea,

Recognizing further that the major cause of the contamination of sediments requiring to be dredged is the emission of hazardous substances into internal and coastal waters and that problems will continue until such emissions are controlled at source,

Recognizing also the need for maintaining open shipping lanes and harbours for maritime transport and that undue burden should be avoided with regard to the interpretation and application of the provisions of the ... London Dumping Convention,

...

Recognizing that for the disposal of dredged material at sea not all of the factors listed in Annex III and their corresponding interpretations are applicable,

...

Having considered the draft Guidelines for the Application of the Annexes to the Disposal of Dredged Material at Sea prepared by the Scientific Group on Dumping,

1.   *Adopts* the Guidelines for the Application of the Annexes to the Disposal of Dredged Material at Sea as set out at Annex hereto;

2.   *Resolves* that Contracting Parties to the Convention when assessing the suitability of dredged material for disposal at sea shall take full account of the Guidelines ... ;

3.   *Agrees* to review the Guidelines ... within five years time in light of experience gained by Contracting Parties with these guidelines, in particular with regard to the application of the terms "trace contaminants", "rapidly rendered harmless" and "special care" as defined for disposal of dredged material at sea;

4.   *Requests* Contracting Parties to submit to the Organization for distribution to all Contracting Parties information on their experience gained with the above guidelines, including case studies;

5. *Calls upon* Contracting Parties to take all practicable steps to reduce pollution of marine sediments, including control of emissions of hazardous substances into internal and coastal waters.

ANNEX

GUIDELINES FOR THE APPLICATION OF THE ANNEXES TO THE DISPOSAL OF DREDGED MATERIAL

1. INTRODUCTION

1.1 In accordance with article IV(1)(a) of the Convention, Contracting Parties shall prohibit the dumping of dredged material containing substances listed in Annex I unless the dredged material can be exempted under paragraph 8 (rapidly rendered harmless) or paragraph 9 (trace contaminants) of Annex I.

1.2 Furthermore, in accordance with article IV(1)(b) of the Convention, Contracting Parties shall issue special permits for the dumping of dredged material containing substances described in Annex II and, in accordance with Annex II, shall ensure that special care is taken in the disposal at sea of such dredged material.

1.3 In the case of dredged material not subject to the provisions of articles IV(1)(a) and IV(1)(b), Contracting Parties are required under article IV(1)(c) to issue a general permit prior to dumping.

1.4 Permits for the dumping of dredged material shall be issued in accordance with article IV(2) which requires careful consideration of all the factors set forth in Annex III. In this regard, the Eighth Consultative Meeting in adopting Guidelines for the Implementation and Uniform Interpretation of Annex III (resolution LDC.17(8)) resolved that Contracting Parties shall take full account of these Guidelines in considering the factors set forth in that Annex prior to the issue of any permit for the dumping of waste and other matter at sea.

1.5 With regard to the implementation of paragraphs 8 and 9 of Annex I to the Convention, the Fourth Consultative Meeting adopted Interim Guidelines (LDC IV/12, annex 5) which provide advice concerning the conditions under which permits may be issued for dumping wastes containing Annex I substances, and concerning the evaluation of the terms "trace contaminants" and "rapidly rendered harmless".

1.6 Notwithstanding the general guidance referred to in paragraphs 1.4 and 1.5 above, subsequent deliberations by Contracting Parties have determined that the special characteristics of dredged material warrant separate guidelines to be used when assessing the suitability of dredged material for disposal at sea. Such guidelines would be used by regulatory authorities in the interpretation of paragraphs 8 and 9 of Annex I, and in the application of the considerations under Annex III. These Guidelines for the Application of the Annexes to the Disposal of Dredged Material have been prepared for this purpose and, more specifically, are intended to serve the following functions:

    .1   to replace the Interim Guidelines for the Implementation of paragraphs 8 and 9 of Annex I as they apply to dredged material; and

.2   to replace **section A** of the Guidelines for the Implementation and Uniform Interpretation of Annex III (resolution LDC.17(8)).

2.   CONDITIONS UNDER WHICH PERMITS FOR DUMPING OF DREDGED MATERIAL MAY BE ISSUED

. . .

3.   ASSESSMENT OF THE CHARACTERISTICS AND COMPOSITION OF DREDGED MATERIAL

. . .

4.   DISPOSAL MANAGEMENT TECHNIQUES

4.1   Ultimately, the problems of contaminated dredged material disposal can be controlled effectively only by control of point source discharges to waters from which dredged material is taken. Until this objective is met, the problems of contaminated dredged material may be addressed by using disposal management techniques.

4.2   The term "disposal management techniques" refers to actions and processes through which the impact of Annex I or Annex II substances contained in dredged material may be reduced to, or controlled at, a level which does not constitute a hazard to human health, harm to living resources, damage to amenities or interference with legitimate uses of the sea. In this context they may, in certain circumstances, constitute additional methods by which dredged material containing Annex I substances may be "rapidly rendered harmless" and which may constitute "special care" in the disposal of dredged material containing Annex II substances.

4.3   Relevant techniques include the utilization of natural physical, chemical and biological processes as they affect dredged material in the sea; for organic material these may include physical, chemical or biochemical degradation and/or transformation that result in the material becoming non-persistent, non-toxic and/or non-biologically available. Beyond the considerations of Annex III sections B and C, disposal management techniques may include burial on or in the sea floor followed by clean sediment capping, utilization of geochemical interactions and transformations of substances in dredged material when combined with sea water or bottom sediment, selection of special sites such as in abiotic zones, or methods of containing dredged material in a stable manner (including on artificial islands).

4.4   Utilization of such techniques must be carried out in full conformity with other Annex III considerations such as comparative assessment of alternative disposal options and these guidelines should always be associated with post-disposal monitoring to assess the effectiveness of the technique and the need for any follow-up management action.

ANNEX 5

RESOLUTION LDC.26(10)

AMENDMENTS TO ANNEX III TO THE LONDON DUMPING CONVENTION

THE TENTH CONSULTATIVE MEETING,

. . .

Noting that a number of wastes which have been proposed for dumping at sea were ill-defined and that problems have been encountered when assessing the impact of such wastes to marine life and human health,

Emphasizing the need for careful consideration of all the factors set forth in Annex III, including characteristics and composition of the matter to be dumped:

1. *Agrees* to approve in principle the inclusion in Annex III, section A of the following text:

   "In issuing a permit for dumping, Contracting Parties should consider whether an adequate scientific basis exists concerning characteristics and composition of the matter to be dumped to assess the impact of the matter to marine life and to human health",

2. *Invites* Contracting Parties to implement the amendment on a voluntary basis,

3. *Invites* further Contracting Parties to indicate in writing to the Secretary-General of the International Maritime Organization if they do not expect to be in a position to adopt formally the amendment at the Consultative Meeting designated for formal adoption, and

4. *Designates* the Twelfth Consultative Meeting to be held in 1989 for formal adoption of the above amendment.

ANNEX 6

RESOLUTION LDC.27(10)

FUTURE WORK PROGRAMME OF THE SCIENTIFIC GROUP ON DUMPING

THE TENTH CONSULTATIVE MEETING,

. . .

Concerned to maintain the value afforded . . . by the present systems for the classification of wastes for disposal at sea in terms of the Annexes to the Convention,

Wishing to avail itself of advances in technical knowledge and practical understanding which might enable the protection of the marine environment to be further enhanced,

Conscious that significant inputs of pollutants into the marine environment may directly or indirectly arise from sources other than the dumping of waste at sea,

Mindful that, in making decisions on the protection of the marine environment from the adverse effects of dumping, due regard should be taken of the impact of alternative disposal options and the various pathways by which waste materials may be transported from the land into the sea,

. . .

Agrees to invite the Scientific Group on Dumping to review the operational procedures of the Convention, with particular regard to the structure of the Annexes, and any potential ambiguities arising from the application thereof,

Requests the Scientific Group to submit to the Twelfth Consultative Meeting, any recommendations for alternative procedures for the classification and assessment of wastes to be dumped at sea which would afford better protection of the total environment against the adverse impacts of waste,

. . .

- - - - -

LDC Scientific Group on Dumping   LDC/SG.10/11
Report of the Tenth Meeting, May 1987   Extract

. . .

2.   Review of the Annexes to the London Dumping Convention

2.1 Alternatives to the current black list/grey list approach with regard to the regulation of substances considered for disposal at sea

2.3.1 . . . The Chairman . . . emphasized the importance of the task given to the Scientific Group by the Tenth Consultative Meeting as detailed in resolution LDC.27(10) (LDC/SG.10/2). For a number of years the Group had been expressing difficulties in developing scientific advice for the Consultative Meeting due to certain inconsistencies and ambiguities related to the structure of the Annexes to the Convention. The opportunity had now been given to explore alternative structures which might overcome these difficulties, and which would afford better protection of the whole environment against the adverse impacts of wastes. The outcome of this work might not only affect the implementation of the London Dumping Convention, but also those regional conventions on marine pollution which had adopted similar systems for the classification and assessment of wastes to be dumped at sea. . .

2.3.2 In response to the request of the ninth meeting of the Scientific Group for information on the control strategies used by IMO and other organizations in the protection of the marine environment, the Secretariat described some of the principles underlying other conventions, such as MARPOL 73/78 and the approaches taken by GESAMP and UNEP (LDC/SG.10/2/5) . . . The Secretary informed the Group that concepts of environmental capacity frequently formed the basis of pollution control strategies, for example the Montreal Guidelines (1985) developed by UNEP to assist Governments in the process of developing international agreements and national legislation on pollution from land-based sources. The ICES Advisory Committee on Marine Pollution (ACMP) had recently published an account of the principles of ACMP assessments and the assimilative capacity concept (LDC/SG.10/2/4). The Group recognized the importance of this document and noted that the principles of radiological protection developed by ICRP (1977), namely "justification" of a practice and "optimization" of measures to reduce exposure, had been discussed in the context of assimilative capacity.

2.3.6 . . . The different views expressed during the discussion are summarized as follows:

    .1   Some delegations considered that application of the assimilative capacity approach to the regulation of dumping would lead to a more permissive attitude towards this practice. These delegations also stated that the approach lacked clear definition, was more idealistic than practical and might be costly to implement. They further expressed the view that assimilative capacity was not completely a scientific concept - its application includes considerations of the political and economic fields. Whereas it might be effectively applied to localized inputs of degradable wastes in semi-enclosed bays and coastal areas, there was no evidence to show that it could be used to predict the consequences of large-scale contamination by persistent substances in larger areas of the sea e.g. adjacent seas. For these reasons, the above delegations felt that assimilative capacity was a potentially dangerous concept and should not be the basis of any proposals for re-structuring of the Annexes.

.2   Other delegations stressed the need for a concept which would provide a working basis for the assessment and control of environmental impacts due to wastes. These delegations felt that the assimilative capacity concept could be used in conjunction with regulatory tools, such as water quality objectives and emission standards, to manage waste inputs so that harmful effects were avoided. Acceptability of environmental changes would always be a balance between scientific and political judgement. The principles of justification and optimization, when used in conjunction with the assimilative capacity approach would provide a basis for an effective waste management policy. Uncertainly existed in every decision-making process and it was not reasonable to reject a management approach on the grounds of uncertainty alone.

. . .

2.3.8 The Group then considered a number of possibilities for restructuring the present black list/grey list system for classification of potentially harmful substances including the deletion of the grey list and a more central role for the present Annex III. While there was general agreement that the need for a "prohibited" category or black list would always exist, there was some support for the incorporation of the "special care" or grey list substances into a remodelled Annex III . . .

2.3.9 . . . The present debate had shown that there was an element of agreement on a number of important issues, in particular with regard to the basic importance of waste management principles, comparative assessments, complex wastes and the changing magnitude of waste disposal problems.

2.3.10 . . . The Group agreed . . . to convene a small intersessional group of experts . . .

2.3.11 . . . The intersessional group of experts should:

1.   seek to integrate current approaches to environmental and waste management into the operational procedures of the Convention, taking into account concepts and principles underlying the Convention as outlined in resolution LDC.27(10);

2.   give due recognition to the importance of:

     - comparative assessments of alternative waste management and disposal options;

     - management of complex wastes as well as substances; and

- temporal and spatial aspects of controls over dumping, e.g. related to the changing magnitude of waste disposal problems, and the balance between present options and the future development of improved technologies; and

3. make recommendations to the Scientific Group concerning alternatives to the current structures of the Annexes.

- - - - -

Report of the Second Meeting of the Joint   LDC/OSCOM/IAS 2/9
LDC/OSCOM Group of Experts on Incineration at Sea, May 1987   Extract

---

. . .

4.   Alternative Technologies for the Treatment and Disposal of Hazardous Wastes, Including Their Risks and Costs

. . .

4.5   Comparative assessment of land and sea alternatives in relation to waste management principles

4.5.1   . . . The Working Group had recognized that regulatory agencies responsible for evaluating proposals to incinerate wastes at sea, would need to consider a range of environmental, health, safety, economic and technological factors before reaching a decision to use this form of waste disposal. The requirements in this regard were embodied in Regulation 2(2) of the Regulations for the Control of Incineration of Wastes and Other Matter at Sea, and were further elaborated within Annex III, section C4 and the Guidelines thereto (resolution LDC.17(8)).   Nevertheless, the Working Group considered that, to assist regulatory authorities in carrying out comparative assessments of land- and sea-based alternatives, some further guidance might be included in section C4 of the Annex III Guidelines, directed specifically at wastes proposed for incineration at sea.

. . .

4.5.4   . . . The Working Group agreed that it would be both appropriate and helpful to incorporate the hierarchy of waste management into a new section C4 of the Annex III Guidelines which would be used by regulatory authorities, in accordance with Article IV(2), specifically when evaluating applications for permits for the incineration of wastes at sea. The proposed text of this new section C4 is shown at annex 9 . . .

. . .

4.5.6   Based upon the scientific and technical information submitted to the meeting, the Working Group concluded that alternative techniques are available for a number of wastes incinerated at sea. Those technologies that are higher on the hierarchy of waste management techniques are expected to be environmentally preferable and should be evaluated in each case. Additional highly promising technologies can be expected on a commercial scale within a few years. Taking into account the above, it is recommended that all Contracting Parties incinerating wastes at sea promote the application of the above-mentioned technologies through their waste management strategies.

. . .

ANNEX 9

PROPOSED NEW SECTION C4 OF THE GUIDELINES FOR THE IMPLEMENTATION AND UNIFORM INTERPRETATION OF ANNEX III TO THE LONDON DUMPING CONVENTION FOR USE SPECIFICALLY IN RELATION TO WASTES PROPOSED FOR INCINERATION AT SEA

4.   The practical availability of alternative land-based methods of treatment, disposal or elimination, or of treatment to render the matter less harmful for dumping at sea.

Interpretation

Recognizing the provisions of Regulation 2(2) of the Regulations for the Control of Incineration of Wastes and Other Matter at Sea, the appropriate authorities should ensure that, before considering the incineration of wastes at sea, every effort has been made to determine the practical availability of alternative land-based methods of treatment, disposal or elimination for the wastes concerned. In this regard, the authorities should take appropriate steps to ensure that the generators of those wastes that are proposed for incineration at sea have applied the generally accepted hierarchy of waste management in determining the practical availability of alternative land-based methods.

The hierarchy is described as follows:

Existing and developing methods for managing hazardous wastes are commonly organized into a hierarchy that accords preferred status to methods that reduce risk by reducing the quantity and degree of hazard of a waste.

The highest tier in the hierarchy includes those methods - collectively referred to as reduction - that actually avoid the generation of waste. Techniques that reuse or recover wastes after they are generated occupy the next tier. Techniques that treat or destroy wastes are preferred over those that merely contain or actually disperse wastes into the environment.

Specific technological approaches which have been shown to achieve significant reductions in the amounts of hazardous waste generated include process and equipment changes, chemical substitution, product reformulation, as well as a variety of maintenance, operational and housekeeping changes as well as waste reuse.

In applying the hierarchy of waste management, alternatives to incineration of wastes at sea should be considered in the light of a comparative assessment of:

-     Human health risks;
-     Environmental costs;
-     Hazards (including accidents) associated with treatment, packaging, transport and disposal;
-     Economics (including energy costs);
-     Exclusion of future uses of disposal areas

for both incineration at sea and the alternatives.

If the foregoing analysis shows the ocean alternative to be less preferable, a licence for incineration at sea should not be given.

- - - - -

Additional References

Amendment to the list of substances contained in Annex II to the London Dumping Convention. Resolution LDC.25(10). In LDC 10/15, annex 4.

Alternatives to the current black list/grey list approach with regard to the regulation of substances considered for disposal at sea. LDC/SG.10/2.

- - - - -

Dumping and Incineration Operations

Tenth Consultative Meeting of Contracting Parties to the London Dumping Convention, 1986	LDC 10/11/1 Extract

Report of the Oslo Commission

. . .

50.   . . . The Commission agreed:

.1   that the authorities which have issued a Form of Approval for an incineration vessel shall carry out checks on a regular basis in order to control the conditions laid down in the Form of Approval;

.2   that the control of the composition and quantity of the waste shall in principle be carried out by the country of origin of the waste. If transfrontier movement of waste takes place, Contracting Parties shall inform each other as far as possible in order to promote an adequate control of the composition and quantity of the waste;

.3   that recurrent checks on heavy metals and on compounds included in the list of substances shall be carried out as appropriate by the appropriate authorities;

.4   that checks on the adequate working of control devices shall be carried out by the appropriate authorities of the country in whose port the wastes are loaded for incineration and the authorities which issued the Form of Approval, acting in close cooperation.   The division of responsibilities, the development of appropriate protocols for inspection of incineration vessels and the arrangements for exchanging information on the outcome of these exercises should be settled by bilateral negotiation between these authorities.

- - - - -

IMO Marine Environment Protection Committee   MEPC 25/20
Report of the Twenty-Fifth Session, 1987   Annex 5

Interpretation of Annex II of MARPOL 73/78 in Respect of Ships Engaged in Dumping Operations and Explanatory Notes Thereto

For the purpose of the application of Annex II in respect of ships engaged in the dumping operation of liquid wastes under the London Dumping Convention, the regulations of Annex II should be interpreted as follows.

Interpretation:

Regulation 1(2)

Clean ballast means ballast water carried in a tank which, since it was last used to carry liquid wastes for the purpose of dumping at sea under the London Dumping Convention, has been cleaned and the residues therefrom have been discharged and the tank emptied in accordance with the appropriate provisions as identified under the interpretation of regulation 8(1).

Regulation 2(1)

Annex II applies to ships designed, equipped and operated to dump at sea liquid wastes which are deemed under regulation 3 to be noxious liquid substances.

Regulation 3(4)

For the purpose of the application of Annex II, liquid wastes carried by ships for the purpose of dumping at sea under the London Dumping Convention, shall be treated as category A noxious liquid substances, irrespective of the actual evaluated category.

Regulation 5(1)

Dumping ships may discharge cargo tank washings and cargo pump-room bilges either into the sea at the dumpsite under the permit issued under the London Dumping Convention, or to a shore reception facility.

No discharge into the sea from the cargo area or cargo pump-room bilges are permitted whilst the ship is in route to or from the dumpsite.

The P and A Manual for dumping ships should reflect their specialized operations and contain only the applicable information in appendix D to the Standards for Procedures and Arrangements.

Regulation 5(7)

This regulation does not apply to ships engaged in dumping at sea since no discharge to the sea within special areas is allowed.

Regulation 5A

This regulation does not apply to vessels engaged in dumping operations under the London Dumping Convention since wastes are treated as category A noxious liquid substances.

Regulation 7

The Party that loads liquid chemical wastes aboard a dumping ship for dumping at sea should ensure that the loading port has adequate reception facilities to receive cargo tank washings and cargo pump-room bilges, or should ensure that adequate facilities are available at another port. Since dumping ship cargoes are generally compatible, allowing reloading and other waste cargo, reception facilities will normally only be required for purposes in connection with the inspection of cargo tanks or repair of dumping ships.

Regulation 8(1)

The Party who issues a permit for dumping under the London Dumping Convention should undertake to ensure that tank cleaning operations are performed in accordance with the ship's P and A Manual and that the cargo tank washings and cargo pump-room bilges are either dumped at the dumpsite or discharged to a reception facility.

Regulation 8(2)

At the request of a ship's master, the Government of the port State in which the liquid wastes are loaded aboard a dumping ship may exempt, prior to the ship's departure from the loading port, the ship from the requirements in regulation 8(2)(a) if it is satisfied that the conditions in regulation 8(2)(b)(i) or (ii) are met. For consecutive voyages from the same loading port, a single exemption would suffice.

Regulation 9

Ships engaged in dumping operations under the London Dumping Convention should be provided with a Cargo Record Book. Information that is recorded in another official ship's document need not be recorded in the Cargo Record Book.

Regulation 10

Ships engaged in the dumping of liquid wastes containing noxious liquid substances should be surveyed, taking into account the present interpretations of Annex II for dumping vessels.

Regulation 13

Ships engaged in dumping operations should, as a minimum, comply at least with the Guidelines for the Construction and Equipment of Ships Carrying Hazardous Liquid Wastes in Bulk for the Purpose of Dumping at Sea (Assembly resolution A.582(14) as adopted on 20 November 1985).

Explanatory notes:

1.   Although the actual dumping of harmful substances into the sea within the meaning of LDC is not subject to the discharge provisions of MARPOL 73/78 by virtue of its article 2(3)(b)(i), ocean dumping ships as such are subject to the requirements of MARPOL 73/78 by virtue of article 3(1)(a).

2.   Since cargoes carried by ships engaged in dumping operations may contain noxious liquid substances of various categories or mixtures containing these substances, Annex II by virtue of its regulation 2(1) also applies to these ships. This implies that the carriage requirements of Annex II, and the operational requirements in respect of discharges other than dumping, are applicable to ocean dumping ships.

3.   Since it is impracticable to evaluate each cargo of liquid wastes carried for dumping for the purpose of Annex II categorization, and as these wastes may only be dumped into the sea at the dumpsite under the conditions of the dumping permit issued under LDC, it is recommended that all liquid waste cargoes carried for dumping at sea are treated as if they were category A substances under Annex II. In doing so, anomalies between the two Conventions will be avoided as no discharges into the sea would be allowed other than dumping at the dumpsite. Although LDC does not regulate the discharge of tank washings and pump-room bilges, this also implies that wash water and bilge water contaminated with wastes have to be discharged either at sea, together with the cargo of wastes, at the dumpsite, or to a shore reception facility.

4.   Since it is also known that many liquid wastes carried for dumping at sea, if fully evaluated, would pose less harm to the marine environment than category A noxious liquid substances, certain flexibility, as provided for under the interpretations for regulations 1(2) and 8(1), is justified.

5.   In view of the unique operations of ocean dumping ships, it is recommended that, in respect of the carriage requirements, compliance with . . . Assembly resolution A.582(14) should be regarded for these ships as compliance with regulation 13 of Annex II.

- - - - -

Additional References

Interpretation of Annex II of MARPOL 73/78 in respect of Incinerator Ships.
Report of the 23rd session of the IMO Marine Environment Protection Committee, 1986.
Doc. MEPC 23/22, Annex 7.

Interim provisions for the surveillance of cleaning operations carried out at sea on board incineration vessels. Resolution LDC 20(9). In LDC 9/12, Annex 3.

Proposed resolution on new guidelines for the surveillance of cleaning operations carried out at sea on board incineration vessels. IMO doc. LDC 10/15, Section 4 and Annex 9.

Risks of transport of hazardous wastes. In LDC/OSCOM/IAS 2/9, para. 4.

Discharges from floating oil reception facilities. In LDC 10/15, Section 13 and LDC/SG.10/11, Section 7.

- - - - -

Monitoring and Control of Dumping Activities

Report of the Tenth Consultative Meeting of Contracting Parties to the London Dumping Convention, 1986	LDC 10/15 Extract

. . .

3.27   The Consultative Meeting expressed its concern that some Contracting Parties had not submitted reports on dumping activities as required by Article VI(4) and that, as a result, the Secretariat had not been able to prepare fully comprehensive summaries of dumping statistics. The Scientific Group had reviewed the draft report on permits issued in 1983 and had made a number of proposals . . . In particular, the Group recommended that no further efforts should be made to compile reports on the actual amounts of waste dumped because the returns were not complete and it was not possible to obtain accurate statistics on the amounts of contaminants in bulky wastes such as dredged material and sewage sludge. . . .

3.28   A number of delegations indicated that they regarded the compilation of data on actual amounts of waste dumped to be an important activity within the Convention. . . . The Consultative Meeting agreed to discontinue the preparation of reports on actual amounts of waste dumped but urged Contracting Parties to continue to provide information in the existing format so that alternative approaches to summarization might be considered at a future meeting of the Scientific Group. . . . The Consultative Meeting once again stressed the importance of "nil" returns from Contracting Parties not engaged in dumping activities.

. . .

- - - - -

Tenth Consultative Meeting of Contracting Parties to the London Dumping Convention	LDC.2/Circ.174 10 February 1987

The purpose of monitoring within the framework of the London Dumping Convention and the reporting of monitoring activities to the Secretariat
(LDC Articles VI(1)(d) and VI(4))

. . .

The (Tenth) Consultative Meeting urged Contracting Parties to submit information on monitoring carried out in accordance with Article VI(4) of the Convention, taking into account annotations for interpreting Article VI(4) of the London Dumping Convention prepared by the Scientific Group on Dumping as follows:

1. Monitoring ". . . the conditions of the seas for the purposes of this Convention" (as required in article VI(1)(d)) refers to those measurements performed by Contracting Parties, alone or in collaboration, to demonstrate the acceptability and compliance of their permitted at-sea dumping practices with the overall intent of the Convention and the requirements of the Annexes.

2. Monitoring the general condition of regional seas over large areas that may be affected cumulatively by human activities other than at-sea dumping is not a requirement of the Convention, unless it is necessary to demonstrate the acceptability and compliance of permitted dumping practices.

3. Monitoring, for the purposes of the Convention, should be designed primarily to document that the magnitude, scale, and duration of environmental effects related to a permitted dumping activity do not exceed those expected and accepted as a result of the pre-permit assessments performed in accordance with the Annex III Guidelines.

4. The specific design of monitoring programmes developed by Contracting Parties in compliance with the Convention is highly dependent upon the characteristics of the waste and the disposal location, on the method of disposal, and on the other legitimate uses of the sea in the vicinity of the disposal activity. These factors are the primary considerations of the Annex III Guidelines (resolution LDC.17(8)). These Guidelines establish a framework for evaluating the potential effects of a proposed disposal activity. If a permit is issued, monitoring should be performed to confirm the reliability of the Annex III assessment.

5. General guidelines for measurements to be included in a dump site monitoring programme for the purposes of the Convention can be developed effectively only in the specific context of the Annex III Guidelines. The existing Annex III Guidelines should therefore be reviewed and revised where appropriate to incorporate additional mention and instruction relating to implications for monitoring requirements.

6. In accord with article VI(4) of the Convention, Contracting Parties are to report to the Secretariat on the status of at-sea dumping activities within their jurisdiction. The purpose of these reports is to demonstrate compliance with the Convention. Because of the highly variable nature of at-sea dumping circumstances and their potential effects, detailed reporting requirements cannot be specified for many categories of relevant information.

7. While not specifically required under the Convention, monitoring long-term trends of environmental quality and marine resource quality on large regional scales can provide a useful context for interpreting the effects of specific dumping activities, especially in regions of intensive use. Such programmes are encouraged.

Contracting Parties are invited to submit to the Secretary-General of this Organization information and results of their monitoring activities in using either the original format (Part 1 of the annex) or those provisions referred to on monitoring in the new format (Part 2, section 3 of the annex).

...

- - - - -

Reporting of Incidents and Force Majeure

| Tenth Consultative Meeting of Contracting Parties to the London Dumping Convention, 1986 | LDC 10/11/1 Extract |

Report of the Oslo Commission

...

DEVELOPMENT OF COOPERATION AND REPORT PROCEDURES

...

11.   Regarding the undertaking by Contracting Parties to assist one another in dealing with pollution incidents involving dumping at sea (Article 15(4)) and the undertaking to develop cooperative procedures for the application of the Convention, particularly on the high seas (Article 15(5)), it was suggested that it was difficult to envisage a pollution incident involving dumping in the usual sense since such materials would presumably have been licensed for disposal at sea, although an incident involving an incineration vessel could be imagined. In the case of a pollution incident in the North Sea, the Bonn Agreement procedures would enter into play. The following options appeared to be open:-

1.   those Contracting Parties which are not members of the Bonn Agreement could take the initiative to request membership;

2.   the Contracting Parties could simply reaffirm their pledge already given under Article 15(4);

3.   the Oslo Commission could itself develop pollution combating procedures;

4.   the Commission could agree that no specific further action is called for under Article 15(5).

12.   After discussion, the Commission decided that the only immediate action that could be taken was for Contracting Parties to reaffirm their pledge, already given by ratifying the Convention, to assist one another as appropriate in dealing with pollution incidents involving dumping at sea, and to exchange information on methods of dealing with such incidents. The Commission agreed that the most practical way in which it could give effect to strengthening the commitment in Article 15(4) was by agreeing to maintain and keep up to date the list of national contact points which can be contacted in case of emergency. The Commission also confirmed that no further action is called for regarding the development of co-operative procedures under Article 15(5) of the Convention ...

...

- - - - -

Tenth Consultative Meeting of Contracting Parties   LDC 10/9
to the London Dumping Convention

Interpretation of the *Force Majeure* Provisions
(Article V(1)) With Regard to the Deliberate Disposal at Sea of Ships' Cargoes in Cases of Incidents
Note by the Secretariat

Introduction

1.   The Secretariat in a note to the Ninth Consultative Meeting drew attention to the need for authoritative advice and clarification concerning the interpretation of Article V(1) of the Convention referring to cases of *force majeure* where dumping at sea is necessary to secure human life or the safety of vessels (LDC 9/11/2). In this connection attention was also drawn to cases where cargo has been spoiled by seawater intake, breakdown of technical devices or by long unforeseeable delays during a journey or in ports. The key question was as to whether such incidents and cases should be considered as "incidental to, or derived from the normal operations of vessels", and therefore be excluded from the provisions of the London Dumping Convention.

Discharges to secure human life and safety of vessels - outcome of consideration by MEPC

2.   The Ninth Consultative Meeting agreed that before considering in detail the question as to whether the jettisoning overboard of cargo from non-dumping vessels in cases where this was necessary to secure human life or the safety of vessels would fall under the *force majeure* provisions of Article V(1) of the Convention or not, advice should be sought from the IMO Marine Environment Protection Committee, taking into account the *force majeure* provisions set out in MARPOL 73/78. . . .

3.   . . . The MEPC noted that the definition of "dumping" as contained in the London Dumping Convention (Article III(1)) excluded the disposal at sea of materials incidental to, or derived from, the normal operations of vessels. Accordingly, the Committee concluded that the *force majeure* requirements of Article V(1) of the London Dumping Convention would apply only to vessels loaded for the purpose of dumping (or incineration) of waste or other matter at sea and would not extend to situations in which cargo (i.e. loaded solely for the purpose of transport) was jettisoned overboard in cases where the safety of the vessel or of life at sea were at risk. In this connection attention was also drawn to the fact that requirements concerning the discharge from ships into the sea of oil and other hazardous substances in cases where it is necessary to secure the safety of a ship or to save life at sea are contained in every Annex of MARPOL 73/78, thus covering incidents related to normal operations of vessels (MEPC 22/21, paragraphs 20.22 and 20.23).

4.   The Committee did not respond to questions related to the discharge or jettisoning overboard directly from ships or spoilt cargo which might be caused either by delays during transport or unloading, by seawater intake, by failure of cooling or heating devices, or by fire fighting media.

Outcome of Consideration by the Oslo Commission

5.   The above interpretation provided by MEPC was the subject of detailed discussion at the twelfth meeting of the Oslo Commission (June 1986). It may be noted in this regard that the Oslo Convention in its Article 8(1) contains the same *force majeure* provisions as set out in Article V(1) of the London Dumping Convention. After discussion, the Oslo Commission agreed:

.1   that, with the exception of the Federal Republic of Germany and the United Kingdom, all other Contracting Parties accepted that the *force majeure* provisions of Art.8(1) should be interpreted widely and should apply to all ships and aircraft;

.2   that it was necessary for all *force majeure* incidents to be reported to the Oslo Commission, partly because of the requirement in the Convention text and also because of the need to know about the input of contaminants to Convention waters;

.3   that all Contracting Parties should take the necessary action at the national level to ensure that the appropriate dumping authorities are informed by the national shipping authorities whenever *force majeure* discharges and dumpings are reported to the nearest coastal State;

.4   that a report form at Annex 5* should be used by the national dumping authorities to report *force majeure* incidents immediately to the Commission as required by Art.8(1);

.5   that the observer from IMO should bring the Commission's discussion on this matter to the attention of the next meeting of MEPC. In this respect, the Commission recalled that the reporting requirements of MARPOL did not supersede the obligation of Contracting Parties to report *force majeure* incidents to the Oslo Commission.

Matters for consideration by the Consultative Meeting

6.   The Tenth Consultative Meeting when considering this item may wish to take into account the following:

.1   Article V(1), if applicable to any cargoes, including those loaded onboard merely for transport would oblige the master of a vessel flying the flag of a Contracting Party to report immediately, either directly or through the responsible maritime authority, to his national authority responsible for dumping, the jettisoning overboard of any matter in cases where this would appear to be the only way of averting a threat to the ship and human life;

.2   a requirement to report the jettisoning of any cargo at sea in cases of incidents would be much stricter than that foreseen by the provisions of MARPOL 73/78,

---

*   Name of vessel; Date of Dumping; Geographical co-ordinates; Details of cargo jettisoned (substances and amounts); Description of circumstances leading to force majeure dumping; Description of any follow-up action.

which covers the reporting of "harmful substances" only. Further, the London Dumping Convention requests that such reports be submitted immediately to the Organization which shall convey to Contracting Parties such notifications (Article XIV(3)(d));

.3   in case the Consultative Meeting would follow the advice provided by MEPC, i.e. that Article V(1) would be applicable to dumping vessels and incineration ships only (in situations where discharges and dumping operations are to be carried out under conditions which differ from those prescribed in a permit), a situation would arise in which the same requirements in two legal instruments (the London Dumping Convention and the Oslo Convention) with similar aims and objectives would be interpreted in different ways.

. . .

- - - - -

Report of the Tenth Consultative Meeting of Contracting   LDC 10/15
Parties to the London Dumping Convention, 1986   Extract

. . .

9. Interpretation of the *Force Majeure* Provisions (Article V(1)) With Regard to the Deliberate Disposal at Sea of Ships' Cargoes in Cases of Incidents
. . .

9.9   ... During the discussions the following points were expressed:

.1   that the question of *force majeure* reporting under Article V(1) of the London Dumping Convention and the disposal of spoiled or damaged cargo are separate issues;

.2   that there are differences of legal interpretations among Contracting Parties with some expressing the view that the *force majeure* reporting requirements under the London Dumping Convention apply only to ships operating under a dumping permit to dispose of waste or other matter at sea, and other Contracting Parties expressing the view that the London Dumping Convention *force majeure* provisions apply to all ships, whether or not the material was originally loaded on board for the purpose of disposal at sea;

.3   that under the former of the interpretations contained in .2 above only the jettisoning of non-harmful substances that did not constitute a direct danger to navigation would not require reporting under MARPOL 73/78, the London Dumping Convention or SOLAS 74/78. In addition, there would not be any reporting requirements for the disposal of non-harmful material in non-*force majeure* situations, except with respect to reporting dangers to navigation.

9.10   . . . The most appropriate course of action would be to request the Contracting Parties to provide information on the following:

    .1   national laws and procedures for reporting the disposal at sea of material in *force majeure* situations and in non-*force majeure* situations involving damaged or spoiled cargo;

    .2   the number of reports received regarding *force majeure* disposal operations and cases where spoiled or damaged cargo had been dumped at sea, including the types and quantities of material disposed.

    . . .

9.12   The Consultative Meeting . . . agreed that Contracting Parties should provide the information requested in paragraph 9.10 above, and any other relevant information they may have on this issue . . .

- - - - -

Import/Export of Wastes for Disposal at Sea

Tenth Consultative Meeting of Contracting Parties to the London Dumping Convention, 1986	LDC 10/6 and Add.1

Problems Relating to the Import/Export
of Wastes for Their Disposal at Sea
Submitted by the OECD Secretariat

**OECD Council Decision-Recommendation on Exports
of Hazardous Wastes from the OECD Area**
(Adopted by the Council at its 644th Meeting on 5th June 1986)

THE COUNCIL

    . . .

Having regard to the Decision and Recommendation of the Council of 1st February 1984 on Transfrontier Movements of Hazardous Waste (C(83)180(Final)) and without prejudice to that Decision and Recommendation;

Having regard to the Resolution of the Council of 20th June 1985 on International Cooperation Concerning Transfrontier Movements of Hazardous Wastes (C(85)100), by which it has been decided to develop an international system for effective control of transfrontier movements of hazardous wastes, including an international agreement of a legally binding character;

Considering the European Communities Council Directive of 6th December 1984 on the Supervision and Control within the European Community of the Transfrontier Shipment of

Hazardous Waste (84/631/EEC), supplemented by the Decision of the Council of the European Communities of 6th March 1986;

Considering the work carried out within the United Nations Environment Programme on the environmentally sound management of hazardous wastes;

Considering the particular nature of wastes and the distinction between wastes and products which are traded internationally;

Convinced that the exports of hazardous wastes may, if not properly monitored and controlled, result in serious risks to human health and the environment;

On the proposal of the Environment Committee:

I.   *Decides* that Member countries shall:

(i)   Monitor and control exports of hazardous wastes to a final destination which is outside the OECD area; and for this purpose shall ensure that their competent authorities are empowered to prohibit such exports in appropriate instances;

(ii)   Apply no less strict controls on transfrontier movements of hazardous wastes involving non-Member countries than they would on movements involving only Member countries;

(iii)   Prohibit movements of hazardous wastes to a final destination in a non-Member country without the consent of that country and the prior notification to any transit countries of the proposed movements;

(iv)   Prohibit movements of hazardous wastes to a non-Member country unless the wastes are directed to an adequate disposal facility in that country.

II.   *Recommends* that, to implement this Decision, Member countries should:

(i)   Seek to conclude bilateral or multilateral agreements with non-Member countries to which frequent exports of hazardous wastes are taking place or are foreseen to take place;

(ii)   Apply the measures set out below concerning the control of exports of hazardous wastes to a final destination outside the OECD area.

III.   *Instructs* the Environment Committee to take account of the elements of this Decision-Recommendation in developing the draft international agreement referred to in the Resolution of the Council on International Cooperation Concerning Transfrontier Movements of Hazardous Wastes (C(85)100)).

MEASURES CONCERNING THE CONTROL OF
EXPORTS OF HAZARDOUS WASTES

1.   The following measures are designed to facilitate the harmonisation of policies concerning transfrontier movements of hazardous wastes to a final destination outside the OECD area. They do not prejudice the implementation of stricter measures which have been or might be adopted at national, regional or world level to reduce the dangers associated with the transport and disposal of hazardous wastes.

2.   These measures should apply in the absence of a bilateral or multilateral agreement concerning transfrontier movements of hazardous wastes between the exporting Member country and the importing non-Member country concerned, and should be taken into account in the negotiation of such an agreement.

3.   Member countries should require, with respect to any export of hazardous wastes to a final destination outside the OECD area, that the measures set out below be taken by the exporter or by the competent authorities of the exporting country.

4.   **The exporter should:**

(a)   provide the competent authorities of the importing country (and of any transit countries) with at least the same information that he would provide them if they were Member countries;

(b)   inform the competent authorities of the importing country of any specific disposal methods legally required or forbidden for such wastes in the exporting country;

(c)   provide to the competent authorities of the exporting country:

   (i)   the information used by the exporter to assure himself that the proposed disposal operation can be performed in an environmentally sound manner;
   (ii)   certification that the proposed disposal facility may, under the laws and regulations of the importing country, dispose of the kinds of wastes whose export is proposed;
   (iii) a copy of an undertaking by the operator of the proposed disposal facility that he will dispose of the wastes as foreseen in the disposal contract, and in the facility specified therein;
   (iv)   a copy of the information transmitted to the competent authorities of the importing country to obtain their written consent to the import and disposal of the wastes;
   (v)   a copy of the written consent of the competent authorities of the importing country, and confirmation that the competent authorities of any transit countries have received delivery of notification;

(d)   demand and receive from the disposer documents confirming that the wastes have been handed over to the disposer and disposed of as foreseen, and put these documents at the disposition of the competent authorities of the exporting country.

5.   Member countries may choose to charge their competent authorities instead of the exporter with some of the tasks listed above.

6.   **The competent authorities of the exporting country should:**

(a)   before any final decision is taken, inform the competent authorities of the importing country when they have specific environmental concerns regarding the proposed disposal operation;

(b) prohibit the export of the hazardous wastes whenever:

    (i)   they are not satisfied with the information provided under 4.(c) above;

    (ii) an objection is made by any country of transit and no appropriate alternative route can be found by the exporter;

    (iii) the proposed disposal operation is not in conformity with applicable international law;

(c) prohibit additional exports of hazardous waste to a given destination when the documents specified in 4.(d) above were not provided to the exporter by the disposer after a previous export to the same destination;

(d) notify the exporter promptly whether or not they object to the proposed transfrontier movement;

(e) notify the competent authorities of the importing country if they have prohibited the export of the wastes.

Definitions

For the purpose of the Decision-Recommendation:

(a) "Waste" means any material considered as waste or legally defined as waste in the country where it is situated or through or to which it is conveyed;

(b) "Hazardous waste" means any waste other than radioactive waste considered as hazardous or legally defined as hazardous in the country where it is situated or through or to which it is conveyed, because of the potential risk to man or the environment likely to result from an accident or from improper transport or disposal;

(c) "Transfrontier movement of hazardous wastes" means any shipment of wastes from one country to another, where the wastes are considered as being hazardous wastes in at least one of the countries concerned. Hazardous wastes arising from the normal operation of ships, including slops and residues, shall not be considered a transfrontier movement covered by this Decision-Recommendation;

(d) "Exporting country" means any country from which a transfrontier movement of hazardous wastes is initiated or is envisaged;

(e) "Importing country" means any country to which a transfrontier movement of hazardous wastes takes place or is envisaged for purpose of disposal (treatment, landfill, storage, dumping or incineration at sea);

(f) "Transit country" means any country other than the exporting or importing country across which a transfrontier movement of hazardous wastes takes place or is envisaged;

(g) "Exporter" means the generator of the wastes or the person in the exporting country who arranges for exporting the wastes at the request and on behalf of the generator;

(h)   "OECD area" means all land or marine areas under the national jurisdiction of any OECD Member country.

- - - - -

Disposal of hazardous waste in marine areas outside any national jurisdiction
Note submitted by the OECD Secretariat

1.   INTRODUCTION

The OECD Council Decision-Recommendation on Exports of Hazardous Wastes from the OECD Area . . . deals with the exports of hazardous wastes to a final destination outside the OECD area, i.e. to a final destination in a non-Member country **or** to a final destination outside any national jurisdiction. In practice, the latter case concerns mainly marine areas outside any national jurisdiction, e.g. dumping or incineration in areas beyond the exclusive economic zones. For the purpose of this note, we shall describe this as "disposal on the high seas"[1].

The purpose of this note is to describe how this new Decision-Recommendation could be applied in case of disposal on the high seas and what effect it could have on the protection of the marine environment which States have the obligation to protect according to Article 192 of the Convention on the Law of the Sea (not yet in force).

2.   DECISION

The "Decision" part of Decision-Recommendation (C(86)64(Final)) is binding on OECD Member countries, while the "Recommendation" part is only submitted to Member countries for consideration in order that they may, if they consider it opportune, provide for their implementation[2].

In matters of "disposal on the high seas", this Decision requires that Member countries ensure that their competent authorities are **empowered to prohibit exports of hazardous waste for disposal on the high seas in appropriate instances**. In practice this is not yet the case because most national laws concerning dumping and/or incineration at sea deal with wastes loaded in a harbour of the same country (or loaded on a ship under the flag of the same country when the country of loading is not a party to the appropriate dumping convention). Thus, competent authorities in many Member countries may find it difficult to prohibit an export of hazardous wastes by road when such wastes are to be loaded on a ship in another country for disposal on the high seas.

A second obligation under this Decision might be that the country of loading (transit country when loading is not taking place in the exporting country) be notified of the proposed movement. While this conclusion would be reasonable[3], it would be preferable to derive the obligation to notify the transit country from Decision and Recommendation of the OECD Council on Transfrontier Movements of Hazardous Waste (C(83)180(Final)) ("provision of adequate and timely information concerning transfrontier movements of hazardous waste").

3.   RECOMMENDATION

The new OECD Act also contains a series of recommended measures for implementing the Decision.

3.1   Control of the proposed disposal operation

According to the Recommendation, "the exporter should provide to the competent authorities of the exporting country the information used by the exporter to assure himself that the proposed operation can be performed in an **environmentally sound manner**" and "the competent authorities of the exporting country should prohibit the export of the hazardous wastes whenever:

(a)   they are not satisfied with the information provided (by the exporter) . . .

(b)   the proposed disposal operation is not in conformity with applicable international law."

This text leaves open the question of how to ascertain whether a proposed disposal operation on the high seas is "environmentally sound".

The primary consideration in making such a determination is probably that the competent authorities should prohibit the export if they are not satisfied with the information provided by the exporter. For example, it is very doubtful that a proposed disposal operation on the high seas which would not be authorized or which would be prohibited for environmental reasons when loading takes place in the exporting country[4], would be seen as being environmentally sound by the exporting country when loading takes place in a harbour in another country. In such a case, the exporter is not likely to satisfy his authorities that he made a good assessment and such authorities could prohibit the export.

Furthermore, it would seem that the exporter should examine and report to his authorities whether the proposed disposal operation on the high seas meets all existing environmental requirements which result from international agreements which are in force and cover the site of the proposed disposal operation, **whether or not the exporting country is a party to these agreements.**

If the competent authorities of the exporting country have specific concerns regarding the proposed disposal operation on the high seas and wish to prohibit it, they could also seek a legal basis for their decision on the ground that the proposed disposal operation is not in conformity with applicable international law, i.e. conventions and agreements in force in the exporting country concerning dumping and/or incineration at sea[5] **as well as customary international law related to the protection of the marine environment.** In this connection Article 210 of the Convention on the Law of the Sea could be pertinent for determining the content of customary international law as well as the London Dumping Convention which can be viewed as having set "global rules" to prevent pollution of the sea from dumping.

3.2 Follow up

According to the new Decision-Recommendation, the exporter should also provide to his competent authorities a copy of the undertaking by the operator of the proposed disposal facility (i.e. master of the ship) that he will dispose of the wastes as foreseen in the disposal contract (e.g. at the agreed site for dumping or incineration and with the agreed incineration efficiency), and in the facility specified therein (e.g. with the incinerator ship as specified). Furthermore the exporter should receive documents confirming that the wastes have been disposed of as foreseen. If the exporter does not receive these documents after a previous export, it is recommended that further exports to such a disposer would be prohibited. This "penalty" for lack of documents would probably also apply if disposal did not take place as foreseen, but the Decision-Recommendation does not mention this case.

3.3 Links with the London Dumping Convention[6]

As stated in the Recommendation, the OECD system does not prejudice "the implementation of stricter measures . . ." in the marine environment. It suggests measures which are additional to existing measures under the dumping conventions, such as control by the exporting State and follow-up measures.

If the wastes are loaded in the exporting country and if that country is a party to the conventions dealing with dumping in the area where the disposal operation is foreseen, the new Decision introduces only additional follow-up measures.

If the wastes are loaded in an exporting country which is not a party to the pertinent dumping conventions, the new Decision would not require the exporting country to prohibit the disposal operation because it is contrary to a convention to which it is not a party. However, the exporting country could prohibit loading of the wastes if the proposed disposal operation is contrary to customary international law applicable in that country (or to Article 8 of the London Dumping Convention if the exporting country is party to this Convention but not to the pertinent regional dumping convention).

If the wastes are loaded in a transit country (i.e. not in the exporting country), the new Decision includes additional control whether or not the loading country is a party to the London Dumping Convention. In this instance both the exporting country and the loading country may make an objection to the proposed disposal operation[7]. If the loading country (which must be notified) makes an objection, the exporting country should prohibit export and take all practicable steps to ensure that the projected export is **not initiated** (on the basis of Decision and Recommendation C(83)180, para. 8). Implementation of these Decisions would mean that no export for disposal on the high seas could be initiated without providing both the exporting and the loading countries with necessary information and obtaining the necessary permits.

In practice this means that a country which does not allow certain hazardous wastes to be dumped at sea when loading takes place in that country, should prohibit the export of such wastes to another country where loading would take place prior to dumping at sea[8].

Notes

1. Disposal in the exclusive economic zone or onto the continental shelf would be considered in this Decision as disposal in the coastal country concerned (see Art. 210(5) and 216(1)(a) of the Convention on the Law of the Sea) as this country has jurisdiction with regard to the protection and preservation of the marine environment in the exclusive economic zone (Art. 56) and sovereign rights for the purpose of exploiting the natural resources of the continental shelf (Art. 77).
2. Extract from OECD Rules of Procedure (Rule 18).

3. Some sections of the Decision-Recommendation are only applicable to transfrontier movements of hazardous wastes, i.e. movements between an exporting Member country and an importing non Member country in which the disposal operation would take place. Although dumping or incineration operations performed outside the limits of national jurisdiction are under the control of the flag State (personal jurisdiction of the flag State over the ship, see Art. 94(4)(c) and 216(1)(b) of the Law of the Sea Convention), it does not seem reasonable to assume that these operations are performed "in" an importing country.
4. Either on the basis of a national law applicable to ships flying its flag or as a result of conventions for the protection of the marine environment in force in the exporting country.
5. e.g., London Dumping Convention and regional dumping conventions (Oslo, Barcelona, Helsinki, etc.)
6. In force in all OECD countries except Austria, Luxembourg and Turkey. Turkey, however, is a Party to the Barcelona Convention and its Protocol on Dumping in the Mediterranean Sea while Luxembourg is Party to the Paris Convention on Land-based Pollution and implements many relevant Community Directives.
7. Art. 216(2) of the Convention on the Law of the Sea does not preclude actions by the exporting State.
8. This conclusion is in line with the non-discrimination principle adopted in Decision and Recommendation C(83)180(Final), para. 4.

- - - - -

Report of the Tenth Consultative Meeting of Contracting
Parties to the London Dumping Convention, 1986

LDC 10/15
Extract

. . .

6.   Problems Relating to the Import/Export of Wastes for Disposal at Sea
. . .

6.2   The Secretary introduced the so-called Cairo Guidelines and Principles for the Environmentally Sound Management of Hazardous Wastes developed by a UNEP *ad hoc* Working Group (LDC 10/6/1)* and drew particular attention of the Contracting Parties to paragraphs 26 and 28 of the Guidelines (Notification and consent procedure in respect of transfrontier movement of hazardous wastes; Co-operation in the management of hazardous wastes).

6.3   The United States delegation reported on the outcome of intersessional work . . . (LDC 10/6/2 and Adds.1 and 2). The study covered the relationship between actions necessary for the effective implementation of the London Dumping Convention and the work of other international organizations, division of responsibilities between exporting, transit and importing countries, relationship between private entities and national authorities and the need for additional measures to be taken under the London Dumping Convention.

6.4   The Meeting noted the activities of other organizations such as UNEP, EEC, OECD and the Oslo Commission in developing binding rules and recommendatory guidelines on the transboundary movement of hazardous wastes. It was also noted that the work undertaken in some of these organizations may ultimately lead to an international convention on all aspects of the transboundary movement of hazardous wastes. The Meeting nevertheless agreed that action by the Consultative Meeting was necessary to ensure that sea disposal of wastes was carried out in compliance with the requirements of the London Dumping Convention.
. . .

6.7   . . . The resolution . . . was adopted as resolution LDC.29(10) on Export of Wastes for Disposal at Sea. The text of which is set out at annex 13 to this report.

6.8 . . . Several Parties indicated that they would only permit export of wastes to States **Party** to the London Dumping Convention.

. . .

_____

* The text of the Cairo Guidelines is on pages 526 - 534 of this Volume.

ANNEX 13

RESOLUTION LDC. 29(10)
Export of Wastes for Disposal At Sea

THE TENTH CONSULTATIVE MEETING,

Recognizing the obligation of Contracting Parties to promote, individually and collectively, the effective control of all sources of pollution of the marine environment,

Recognizing further the increasing movement of wastes across national boundaries for a variety of purposes such as storage, recycling, treatment, or final disposal,

Recalling the recommendation of the London Dumping Convention Task Team 2000 Report (LDC 8/4) that Contracting Parties address the problem of the transboundary movement of wastes for disposal at sea,

Recalling further resolution LDC Res.11(V) concerning the export of wastes for incineration at sea,

Acknowledging that protection of the marine environment in connection with the transboundary movement of wastes for disposal at sea is a shared responsibility between exporting and receiving countries,

Noting the activities of such organizations as UNEP, EEC, OECD, and the Oslo Commission in developing rules and guidelines on the transboundary movement of hazardous wastes, and their value in advancing the objectives of the London Dumping Convention,

Bearing in mind that the work undertaken in some of these organizations may ultimately lead to an international convention on all aspects of the transboundary movement of hazardous wastes,

Believing that pending the creation of such an international convention it is useful to make recommendations to Contracting Parties on transboundary movements of hazardous wastes destined for disposal at sea,

Recognizing the right of individual States to apply rules governing the export of wastes for sea disposal that are more stringent than international rules and guidelines,

Desiring that any disposal at sea be conducted in accordance with the requirements of the London Dumping Convention, and appropriate regional conventions,

Agrees to work toward the widespread acceptance and effective application of the Convention,

Agrees further to recommend that Contracting Parties not export wastes for sea disposal, particularly those containing substances listed in Annex I and II of the London Dumping Convention, to States not Party to the Convention or to an appropriate regional convention unless there are both compelling reasons for such export and clear evidence that the wastes would be disposed of in compliance with the requirements of the London Dumping Convention and such regional conventions,

Calls on Contracting Parties exporting wastes for sea disposal to:

1. provide advance notification of any intended movement of such wastes to the receiving country and any other country which may exercise authority over their transport or disposal in sufficient time for an informed assessment;

2. obtain the prior consent of the appropriate national authorities in any country receiving wastes and issuing the required permit for sea disposal,

Urges Contracting Parties to endeavour to ensure that wastes exported for a purpose other than sea disposal are not ultimately disposed of at sea unless done in compliance with the requirements of the Convention,

Requests that Contracting Parties provide the Organization with the names of the national authorities in their country responsible for receiving advance notification of the transboundary movement of wastes for sea disposal, and requests the Organization to circulate this information among the Contracting Parties,

Urges Contracting Parties to take account of this resolution when negotiating any future international convention on the transboundary movement of hazardous wastes.

- - - - -

Radioactive Waste Disposal

Report of the Ninth Consultative Meeting of Contracting   LDC 9/12, Annex 4
Parties to the London Dumping Convention, 1985

Resolution LDC. 21(9)
Dumping of Radioactive Wastes at Sea

THE NINTH CONSULTATIVE MEETING,

Recognizing that the marine environment and the living resources of the sea are of vital importance to all nations and that the objective of the London Dumping Convention is to prevent the pollution of the seas by dumping,

Considering that the Convention should continue to provide an effective global forum for the Contracting Parties in which to pool the advances of science and technology in their effort to combat marine pollution,

Taking note of the increasing concern of a growing body of public opinion, and in particular among the populations living near present or potential dumping sites, with regard to the dumping of radioactive wastes at sea,

Recognizing that dumping of radioactive wastes at sea may adversely affect the environment of other nations and of regions located beyond the limits of national jurisdiction in contravention with Principle 21 of the UN Declaration on the Human Environment adopted in Stockholm in June 1972,

Recognizing that, under Article I of the Convention, Contracting Parties have pledged themselves specially to take all practicable steps to prevent the pollution of the seas by the dumping of wastes and other matter that is liable to create hazards to human health, to harm living resources and marine life, to damage amenities or to interfere with other legitimate uses of the sea,

Recalling that the Seventh Consultative Meeting in February 1983 adopted resolution LDC.14(7) which called for the suspension of all dumping at sea of radioactive materials pending the presentation to the Contracting Parties of the final report of an expert meeting on radioactive matters related to the London Dumping Convention,

Recognizing that the practice of dumping radioactive wastes at sea has been limited to a few States which have halted such dumping since the adoption of resolution LDC.14(7) . . . ,
. . .

Noting that the Expert Panel on the Disposal at Sea of Radioactive Wastes recognizes deficiencies in scientific information that need to be resolved for a rigorous and precise assessment of the consequences of sea dumping of radioactive wastes,

Accepting that, as noted by the Expert Panel, in the comparison between options, social, economic, scientific and technological factors are difficult to quantify on a common basis, especially where the social factors have international dimensions; and that . . . in the final analysis social and related factors may outweigh those of a purely scientific and technical nature,

Noting also the absence of comparison between land-based and sea dumping options,

1. *Agrees* to a suspension of all dumping at sea of radioactive wastes and other radioactive matter to permit time for the further consideration of issues which would provide a broader basis for an informed judgement on proposals for the amendment of the Annexes of the Convention. This suspension will continue pending the completion of the studies and assessments referred to in paragraphs 2 to 5 hereunder;

2. *Requests* that additional studies and assessments of the wider political, legal, economic and social aspects of radioactive waste dumping at sea be undertaken by a panel of experts to complement the existing Expanded Panel Report;

3. *Requests* that further assessments examine the issue of comparative land-based options and the costs and risks associated with these options;

4.　*Requests* that studies and assessments examine the question of whether it can be proven that any dumping of radioactive wastes and other radio-active matter at sea will not harm human life and/or cause significant damage to the marine environment;

5.　*Requests* the IAEA to advise Contracting Parties with respect to certain outstanding scientific and technical issues relating to the sea dumping of radioactive wastes, specifically:

(a)　To determine whether additional risks to those considered in the revised IAEA Definition and Recommendations justify re-examination of the definition of radioactive wastes and other radioactive matter unsuitable for dumping at sea for certain individual radionuclides;

(b)　To establish source (dose) upper bounds appropriate to the practice of radioactive waste dumping under the Convention;

(c)　To define quantitatively the exempt levels of radionuclides for the purposes of the Convention;

6.　*Requests* the Organization to approach appropriate international agencies to establish and maintain an inventory of radioactive wastes from all sources entering the marine environment;

7.　*Calls upon* Contracting Parties to develop, as envisaged in Article X, procedures for the assessment of liability in accordance with the principles of international law regarding State responsibility for damage to the environment of other States or to any other area of the environment resulting from dumping.

- - - - -

Report of the Tenth Consultative Meeting of Contracting　　　　LDC 10/15
Parties to the London Dumping Convention, 1986　　　　　　　　　　Extract

===

. . .

5.　The Disposal of Radioactive Wastes at Sea

Disposal into the sea-bed of high-level radioactive wastes

. . .

5.2　The Meeting emphasized that consensus had already been reached on the most crucial points, namely that:

.1　The Consultative Meeting of the Contracting Parties to the London Dumping Convention is the appropriate international forum to address the question of the disposal of high-level radioactive wastes and matter into the sea-bed, including the question of the compatibility of this type of disposal with the provisions of the London Dumping Convention; and that

.2　no such disposal should take place unless and until it is proved to be technically feasible and environmentally acceptable, including a determination that such wastes and matter can be effectively isolated from the marine environment, and a regulatory mechanism is elaborated under the London Dumping Convention to govern the disposal into the sea-bed of such radioactive wastes and matter.

5.3   The Meeting also recognized that the key question still to be resolved was as to whether the current text of the Convention would permit the emplacement of high-level radioactive materials into the sea-bed for the purpose of experiments designed to explore the future potential of sea-bed emplacement as an environmentally sound waste disposal option, taking into account Article III(1)(b)(ii) of the London Dumping Convention.

. . .

5.7   The Meeting considered that the actions taken to date by previous Consultative Meetings were sufficient to cover any situation that may arise and that in the light of the lack of current activity on the subject, no additional action was needed at this stage. Consultative Parties were requested, however, to inform any future Consultative Meeting of plans to conduct experiments that would involve the emplacement of high-level radioactive wastes into the sea-bed.

. . .

IAEA Revised Definition and Recommendations

5.13   In introducing the new Revised Definition and Recommendations, published as IAEA Safety Series No. 78, a safety standard which had been distributed at the Meeting under LDC 10/INF.9, the representative of the IAEA briefly explained the changes made in the present revision. She pointed out major changes in structure and the impact of the use of new models, assumptions and data on the release rate limits. She also emphasized the relationship between Safety Series No. 78 and its supporting documents such as Safety Series Nos. 61, 65 and 66, as well as future subsidiary documents such as those on exemption rules and source upper bounds. She pointed out that the newly calculated release rate limits, although based on different models, data and dose limits, do not change the annual release rate limits for alpha-emitters, reduced the limits slightly for beta/gamma-emitters of half-lives greater than a year and reduced by approximately a factor of 100 the limits for short-lived beta/gamma emitters and tritium . . .

5.14   The IAEA representative further pointed out that the limits set in the Definition are those above which dumping may not take place. This does not imply that dumping below those limits is automatically permitted. The Recommendations, including environmental assessments, site selection and operational requirements are to be implemented and the actual radiation doses predicted from proposed dumping must be a small fraction of the limit used to define what is unacceptable for dumping.

5.15   In order to effectively solve the problem of *de minimis* or exempt levels of radioactivity, i.e. materials which could be considered as non-radioactive for the purposes of the London Dumping Convention and therefore be dumped under a general rather than a special permit, the Agency is undertaking two parallel activities. The first is the support of a group of experts in coastal modelling under GESAMP (IMO/FAO/UNESCO/WMO/WHO/IAEA/UN/UNEP Joint Group of Experts on the Scientific Aspects of Marine Pollution). It is expected that it would take about two years for the expert group to complete its task, at which time the Agency is expected to have completed work on the second part of the parallel activity, guidance on principles of exemptions from regulatory requirements. The Agency will then be in a position to apply these principles to the models and to develop additional guidance for the Convention in this regard.

5.16   The Meeting considered ways and means on how recognition should be given to the Revised Definition and Recommendations prepared by the IAEA. In this connection the Chairman explained the procedure used at a previous Consultative Meeting when dealing with a revision of the IAEA Definition and Recommendations and suggested the adoption of a similar text. The Meeting, after minor amendments to the text proposed by the Chairman, agreed to the following:

.1   to take note of the IAEA Revised Definition and Recommendations, published as Safety Series No. 78, an IAEA Safety Standard;

.2   to request the Organization to circulate the document to Contracting Parties for the purposes of implementation of the London Dumping Convention, as a replacement of the 1978 IAEA Definition and Recommendations (INFCIRC 205/Add.1/Rev.1) and, in so doing, inform them that the Definition and Recommendations should not be construed as encouraging in any way the dumping at sea of radioactive wastes and other radioactive matter; and that IAEA Safety Series No. 78 shall not prejudice the review of relevant issues by the Intergovernmental Panel constituted in accordance with resolution LDC.21(9);

.3   to request the Organization to circulate at the same time to the Contracting Parties an invitation to comment on the above document;

. . .

.5   to consider at a subsequent meeting any revisions in the Definition and Recommendations in light of the comments received . . .

. . .

- - - - -

IAEA Board of Governors   LDC 10/INF.9
(Submitted to the Tenth LDC Meeting), 5 August 1985   IAEA Safety Series No.78

Revision of the Definition required by Annex I (paragraph 6) to the Convention and of the Recommendations required by Annex II (section D)

. . .

APPENDIX 1

. . .

SECTION I

INTRODUCTION

Background

1.   This document was prepared by the International Atomic Energy Agency (IAEA) as required by the Convention on the Prevention of Marine Pollution by Dumping of Wastes and Other Matter (. . . LDC):

- to define high-level radioactive waste or other high-level radioactive matter unsuitable for dumping at sea listed in Annex I to the Convention; and

- to recommend a basis for issuing special permits for dumping radio-active materials listed in Annex II to the Convention.

The "Definition" presented in this document of radioactive matter unsuitable for dumping at sea is formulated, in part, in qualitative terms, and, in part, in numerical terms, based on the principles of radiation protection and on scientific modeling.

Interpretation of the term radioactive waste

2.   Virtually all materials contain some radionuclides, but it is clearly not the intention of the Convention that all materials be treated as radioactive when considering their suitability for sea dumping.   For example: sewage sludge, dredge spoils, fly ash, agriculture wastes, construction materials, vessels which are not nuclear powered, artificial reef building materials and other such materials that have not been contaminated with radionuclides of anthropogenic origin (except global fall out from nuclear weapons testing) are not considered to be radioactive for the purposes of sea disposal. If there is a question as to whether the material to be dumped should be considered non-radioactive for the purposes of the Convention, the Parties shall take into account the relevant recommendations, standards and guidelines being developed by the IAEA. The IAEA is at present working towards the formulation of advice on this subject.   Until advice is provided, national authorities should exercise discretion in deciding whether materials are radioactive waste, bearing in mind the principles and purposes of the Convention.

Principles of radiation protection

3.   The principles of radiation protection used as the basis for the "Definition and Recommendations" in this document are derived from the recommendations of the International Commission on Radiological Protection[1] and the IAEA/WHO/ILO/NEA (OECD) Basic Safety Standards for Radiation Protection[2].

Comparison of options

4.   It is presumed that before issuing special permits, competent authorities have identified, assessed and compared to the extent practicable options for the disposal of the waste and that it has been established that disposal at sea is the preferred option on a balance of radiological and other environmental factors; and social and economic grounds.

Cumulative effects - international involvement

5.   The cumulative effects of dumping by one or more than one State at any given site or in a single ocean basin must be addressed. This can be done only if the relevant information is shared amongst interested parties in a timely manner.   Prior notification, observation and surveillance of dumping operations; review of assessments; coordination of monitoring activities and record keeping are best accomplished through multilateral or international mechanisms.

Limitation of dumping site

6.   In order not to prejudice future uses of the ocean floor, it is desirable that both the area of any given dumping site and the number of sites should be small.

Derivation of the quantitative Definition

7.   The quantitative Definition of radioactive waste unsuitable for dumping at sea (see Section II) has been derived using models recommended by GESAMP[3], and a data base assembled by the IAEA[4,5]. It is based on the assumptions *inter alia*, that dumping takes place in a single ocean basin of volume $10^{17} m^3$, at a site where the average water depth is 4000 metres, at a rate of 10^8 kg per year, and continues for a 1,000 years. It is also assumed that radionuclides are released instantaneously as soon as the waste reaches the ocean floor. In addition, the quantitative Definition is based on an annual dose limit for individuals of 1 mSv; this limit is applied to the critical group of the population. Full details of the procedures and data used to derive the quantitative Definition are given in reference[6].

Applicability of the Definition

8.   The "Definition" applies to packaged waste, or waste in solid form, waste dumped in the deep ocean to a minimum depth of 4000 metres and is subject to review and revision by the Agency, as and when appropriate in the light of technological developments and increased scientific knowledge. The assumptions regarding the nature of ocean dumping practices for radioactive waste disposal that have been made in the derivation of the "Definition" and the formulation of the "Recommendations" in this document are given in paragraph 7. Other methods of radioactive waste dumping in the ocean, that are inconsistent with these and other assumptions made in this document, shall not be authorized until appropriate recommendations and advice, pertinent to these other methods of disposal, have been formulated by the IAEA, transmitted to the IMO, and presented to the Contracting Parties to the Convention.

Adoption of more stringent requirements

9.   The Recommendations set forth in the document should not be interpreted as precluding the adoption of more restrictive requirements by any Party to the Convention or appropriate national authorities, pursuant to Article IV.3 and VI.3 of the Convention. Nothing in this document shall be construed as encouraging the dumping at sea of radioactive waste and other radioactive matter. When dumping radioactive materials covered by Annex II to the Convention, it is emphasized that the Definition merely sets limits above which material may not be dumped.

SECTION II

DEFINITION OF HIGH-LEVEL RADIOACTIVE WASTE OR OTHER HIGH-LEVEL
RADIOACTIVE MATTER UNSUITABLE FOR DUMPING AT SEA

. . .

SECTION III

RECOMMENDATIONS REQUIRED BY ANNEX II OF THE CONVENTION PERTAINING TO THE DUMPING OF RADIOACTIVE WASTES

Introduction

12. The Definition specifies only what radioactive matter shall not be dumped at sea. Guidance as to the nature and quantities of material that may be dumped at any given dump site, under the provisions of the LDC is contained in these recommendations, together with guidance on dumping procedures.

Dose upper bound

13. It should be noted that although a dose of 1 mSv a^{-1} to individuals was used for the purpose of arriving at the quantitative definition, this does not imply that 1 mSv a^{-1} from actual dumping operations is acceptable. Members of the public will be receiving doses from other sources and it is therefore necessary to restrict doses from ocean dumping *per se*. This can be achieved by setting an upper bound to the dose received from that practice. A value for this upper bound has not been internationally established; however, it should be substantially lower than 1 mSv a^{-1}.

14. It is essential that the optimisation principle is also implemented[7]. The implementation of these procedures should ensure that the doses actually received by individuals from sea dumping will be only a small fraction of 1 mSv a^{-1}. Site specific models and realistic parameter values and assumptions should be used in calculating doses to be compared with the upper bound, and in optimization exercises. The doses to be compared with the upper bound are the peak individual doses from past and foreseeable future dumping.

15. As noted above no dose upper bound for sea dumping has yet been established. Until this has been achieved, it would be prudent for national authorities to use as an upper bound a value which is substantially lower than 1 mSv a^{-1}. It is recommended that upper bounds for dumping in specific ocean basins be established through consultations within multilateral mechanisms. It is further recommended that a global upper bound for all dumping be established through appropriate mechanisms.

Environmental assessment

16. The appropriate national authorities shall not grant a special permit for dumping of radioactive waste unless a detailed environmental assessment gives reasonable assurance that such dumping can be accomplished in accordance with the objectives and provisions of the Convention and these Recommendations. In addition to the relevant factors specified in Annex III of the Convention due consideration should be given in the environmental assessment to the guidance provided in IAEA Safety Series 65.[7]

17. The environmental assessment shall be based to the extent possible on site-specific parameters and models and contain information to assist national authorities to decide whether or not dumping at sea is the preferred option. The assessment therefore should include a comparison with other waste management options on radiological protection and other grounds, and also address the following:

(1) descriptive matter, such as waste quantities, waste form and activity concentrations for significant nuclides;

(2) the optimization of the radiological impact of both the operational and post-disposal phases of sea dumping;

(3) the consequence of major accidents;

(4) effects on ecosystems;

(5) compliance of the operation with national and international provisions on sea dumping of radioactive waste; and

(6) compliance of the operation with national regulations with respect to radiological protection.

18. Before granting a special permit, the appropriate national authorities shall ensure that the proposed dumping operation complies with the radiation protection requirements set forth in the IAEA/WHO/ILO/NEA(OECA) Basic Safety Standards for Radiation Protection[2].

Environmental evaluation of total dumping

19. In addition to the environmental assessment prepared in support of a specific application for a special permit for dumping, the appropriate national authorities shall take the following factors into account in determining whether each proposed dumping operation is acceptable:

(1) Periodic reviews of the total dumping which has been carried out under permits issued by them;

(2) Dumping which is known to have been carried out by other States; and

(3) Prospective dumping which may reasonably be expected.

20. This evaluation will be facilitated through the establishment of regional agreements and other appropriate forms of international co-operation.

21. In addition to the factors specified in Annex III to the Convention, the following requirements shall be met by the appropriate national authorities in the selection of a site for the dumping of packaged waste; further guidance on selection of sites has been provided in Safety Series No.61.[8]

(1) Dumping shall be restricted to those areas of the oceans between latitudes 50°N and 50°S. The area shall have an average depth greater than 4000 metres. Recognizing that variations in sea-bed topography do exist, this restriction should not be interpreted to exclude those sites within which there are localized areas with water depths of 3600 metres;

(2) Sites should be located clear of continental margins and open sea islands, and not in marginal or inland seas. Nor should they be situated in areas of volcanic activity,

ocean trenches, mid-ocean ridges and associated fracture zones and plate bound-aries, or areas associated with other natural phenomena that would make the site unsuitable for dumping;

(3) The area must be chosen so as not to interfere with other legitimate uses of the seas; in particular it shall avoid areas crossed by submarine cables in current use, and areas that have potential sea-bed resources that may be exploited either directly by mining or by the harvest of marine products, or indirectly (e.g. spawning) as feeding grounds for marine organisms, important to man;

(4) The area must be suitable for the safe conduct of the dumping operation and shall be chosen to avoid undue navigational hazard and to minimize the risk of collision with other traffic during maneuvering.

22. The dumping site shall be defined by geographical coordinates. It should also be as small as practicable, consistent with operational flexibility and no larger than 10^4 square kilometres.

23. The number of dump sites shall be kept to a minimum. Any dumping site satisfying the exclusionary criteria specified above should not be deemed acceptable in the absence of the detailed environmental assessment required under paragraph 16. The selection, use and surveillance of dump sites should be carried out under multilateral or international arrangements.

The control of sea dumping operations

24. The dumping of unpackaged liquid radioactive waste into the deep sea shall be prohibited since such waste would not be sufficiently dense or immiscible with sea-water to descend to and remain on the sea bed. The dumping of packaged liquid radioactive waste into the deep sea is excluded except as described in Paragraph 28 [6]. Solid radioactive wastes where the radioactivity is intrinsically contained in a relatively insoluble matrix and which can be shown not to disperse before reaching the sea-bed, do not require packaging and may be dumped in the deep sea under the same requirements as for packaged solid waste.

25. The direct discharge of radioactive gases and vapour to the oceanic atmosphere from incineration at sea shall not be authorized until appropriate recommendations for such practices have been formulated.*

26. The dumping operation shall be subject to strict control. A number of factors must be taken into consideration. They concern, in particular, the conditioning and packaging of the waste in order to ensure safe transport and handling, and minimization of the risk of accidental recovery of packages after disposal. This is covered by operational measures dealing with the choice of a suitable dumping site, the design and construction of waste packages, the choice of an appropriate ship able to dispose of the waste at the given dumping site, provisions for radiation protection of the crew, and an adequate supervision of the dumping operations by competent escorting officers. All these operational requirements shall, therefore, be specified in the special permits issued by the appropriate national authorities in accordance with the Convention.

A. HANDLING AND TRANSPORT

27. The relevant provisions of the IAEA Transport Regulations[9] shall be complied with, together with any applicable national and international transport regulations for dangerous goods. In particular, the packages shall be designed to ensure adequate containment of the waste during handling and transport.

B. PACKAGING AND WASTE FORM

28. The packages shall conform to the standards in IAEA TECDOC-240 [10] and shall be designed to ensure that the contents are retained within them during descent to the sea-bed.
. . .

29. Continued isolation and containment of radioactive waste after descent to the sea-bed should be pursued through the use of suitable packaging to minimize to the extent reasonably achievable the radioactivity which might ultimately be released, thereby preventing unnecessary contamination of the marine environment. ⋅

30. The number and weight of packages and the nature and quantities of radioactive content of the material to be dumped shall be recorded and kept by the competent national authority.

C. MONITORING

31. Monitoring, including environmental research, of environmental media for effects of dumped radioactive wastes in the vicinity of the dumping site should be conducted, to the extent feasible and meaningful, taking into full account the relevant guidance provided in IAEA Safety Series No. 61[8] and ICRP Publication 43 [11], to evaluate environmental pathway models, assess effects on marine organisms, and provide information to ensure compliance with procedures and requirements for dumping operations.

D. APPROVAL OF THE SHIP AND ITS EQUIPMENT

32. Certain special requirements are necessary for ships engaged in the dumping of packaged radioactive wastes. These include the following requirements:

(1) The ships shall be capable of safely carrying the approved** consignment to the designated dumping site;

(2) The ships shall be provided with operable satellite navigational equipment and communication equipment suitable for use in the particular dumping area;

(3) An adequate supply of dunnage and equipment shall be provided to ensure that the packages can be suitably stowed;

(4) The ships shall be provided with suitable handling gear, including gear to recover any debris which does not sink, which shall be functional during dumping operations;

(5) Provisions for decontaminating the holds and bilges shall be available; and

(6)   The ship shall be available for inspection and approved by the appropriate national authorities before an approved dumping operation is carried out and thereafter as necessary.

E.   ESCORTING OFFICERS

General

33.   The dumping operation shall be supervised by approved escorting officers representing the national authorities granting the dumping permits.

   . . .

Record keeping/Reporting

37.   Approved records of the nature and quantities of all materials dumped, and the location, time and method of dumping shall be kept and reported to the International Maritime Organization (IMO) and to other parties as appropriate.

38.   Notification of the intention to dump should be provided to IMO or an appropriate regional organization 6 months prior to the anticipated date of dumping.   This notification should include the environmental assessment prepared in support of the issue of a special permit for the proposed dumping (Paragraph 16), or all relevant information available at the time of such notification to be followed as soon as possible by the full environmental assessment, which is to be submitted prior to the dumping operation.

39.   The periodic reviews of dumping required under Paragraph 19 should be submitted to IMO.

International co-operation and observation

40.   Dumping should preferably be carried out within the framework of regional co-operation agreements as provided for by Article VIII of the Convention.

41.   International co-operation in the selection and use of dumping sites is encouraged.

42.   In order to further the objectives and provisions of the Convention, the IAEA is of the opinion that the Parties to the Convention, IMO, and the appropriate national authorities should provide for international or multilateral observation of loading and disposal at sea of radioactive waste or other radioactive matter to satisfy themselves that these operations are carried out in accordance with the Convention and with the "Recommendations" set out in this Document.

---

*   The discharge of gases and vapours to the oceanic atmosphere by incineration is subject to the provisions of the Incineration at Sea Regulations under the London Dumping Convention.   Annex II, paragraph E of LCD III/12 (Report of the Third Consultative Meeting 14 October 1978).
**   Throughout this section the term "approved" means approved by the appropriate national authorities within the meaning of the Convention.

ANNEX

(Contains background information and assumptions for the derivation of the quantitative Definition)

APPENDIX 2

(Contains a listing of the meetings held and the documentation produced for the second revision)

Notes

1. INTERNATIONAL COMMISSION ON RADIOLOGICAL PROTECTION, Recommendations of the International Commission on Radiological Protection (ICRP), ICRP Publication 26, Pergamon Press, Oxford (1977).
2. INTERNATIONAL ATOMIC ENERGY AGENCY, Basic Safety Standards for Radiation Protection, 1982 Edition, Safety Series No.9, IAEA, Vienna (1982).
3. GESAMP - IMO/FAO/UNESCO/WMO/WHO/IAEA/UN/UNEP Joint Group of Experts on the Scientific Aspects of Marine Pollution, An Oceanographic Model for the Dispersion of Wastes Disposed of in the Deep Sea, Reports and Studies No.19, IAEA, Vienna (1983).
4. Sediment K_dS and Concentration Factors for Radionuclides in the Marine Environment, Technical Reports Series No.247, IAEA, Vienna (1985).
5. The Oceanographic and Radiological Basis for the Definition of High Level Wastes Unsuitable for Dumping at Sea, Safety Series No.66, IAEA, Vienna (1984).
6. Procedures and Data for the Evaluation of Ocean Disposal of Radioactive Waste. To be published as IAEA Technical Reports Series (Working Draft).
7. INTERNATIONAL ATOMIC ENERGY AGENCY, Environmental Assessment Methodologies for Sea Dumping of Radioactive Wastes, Safety Series No.65, Vienna (1984).
8. INTERNATIONAL ATOMIC ENERGY AGENCY, Control of Radioactive Waste Disposal into the Marine Environment, Safety Series No.61, IAEA, Vienna (1983).
9. INTERNATIONAL ATOMIC ENERGY AGENCY, Regulations for the Safe Transport of Radioactive Materials - 1985 Edition, Safety Series No.6, IAEA, Vienna (1985), and INTERNATIONAL ATOMIC ENERGY AGENCY, Advisory Material for the Application of the IAEA Transport Regulations, Safety Series No.37 (1973)(under revision).
10. INTERNATIONAL ATOMIC ENERGY AGENCY, Packaging of Radioactive Wastes for Sea Disposal, TECDOC-240, IAEA, Vienna (1981).
11. INTERNATIONAL COMMISSION ON RADIOLOGICAL PROTECTION, Principles of Monitoring for the Radiation Protection of the Population, ICRP Publication 43, Ann. ICRP 15 (1) Pergamon Press, Oxford (1985).

- - - - -

Report of the Tenth Consultative Meeting of
Contracting Parties to the London Dumping Convention, 1986

LDC 10/15
Extract

. . .

Council of Europe

11.7 The Meeting noted that the Parliamentary Assembly of the Council of Europe had adopted a resolution (847(1985))(LDC 10/INF.4) calling on the Governments of Member States currently or prospectively engaged in nuclear energy programmes to --

.1 continue to refrain from the sea-dumping of low-level and medium-level radioactive waste, in the light of the conclusion drawn by the Contracting Parties to the London Dumping Convention, and

.2 develop alternative methods to sea-dumping for the safe disposal of low-level and medium-level radioactive wastes.

. . .

- - - - -

Report of the Tenth Consultative Meeting of   LDC 10/15
Contracting Parties to the London Dumping Convention, 1986   Extract

. . .

Establishment of an inter-governmental panel of experts

. . .

5.32   Despite the efforts of Contracting Parties during the course of the debate to achieve
consensus, several delegations had reservations and reserved their positions on the resolution.
Nevertheless there was a consensus that a vote should be avoided and the resolution be
adopted without division. The Meeting accordingly adopted resolution LDC.28(10) setting up
an inter-governmental panel and its programme of work, together with the questionnaire to be
directed to Contracting Parties. That resolution is shown in annex 11 to this report.

5.33   Countries not fully in agreement with the resolution wished to express their
reservations in this report. The statements received in this regard are shown in annex 12.

    . . .

ANNEX 11

RESOLUTION LDC.28(10)

STUDIES AND ASSESSMENTS PURSUANT TO RESOLUTION LDC.21(9)

THE TENTH CONSULTATIVE MEETING,

Recalling the findings of the Expanded Panel of Experts on the Disposal at Sea of
Radioactive Wastes . . . (LDC 9/4),

Recalling further that pursuant to resolution LDC.21(9) it had been agreed that dumping
at sea of radioactive wastes and other radioactive matter should be suspended pending the
completion of further studies and assessments,

Decides that:

1.   An inter-governmental panel of experts on radioactive waste disposal at sea be established in accordance with resolution LDC.21(9).

2.   The panel be requested to examine or undertake further studies and assessments, taking
account of the work of other competent international and national bodies, on the
following:

    .1   the wider political, legal, economic and social aspects of radioactive waste dumping
at sea;

    .2   the issue of comparative land-based options and the costs and risks associated with
these options;

.3   the question of whether it can be proven that any dumping of radioactive wastes and other radioactive matter at sea will not harm human life and or cause significant damage to the marine environment;

3.   The panel should take account of information provided, and of work carried out, by international organizations and agencies as requested in the operative paragraphs 5 and 6 of resolution LDC.21(9);

4.   The preliminary questionnaire attached to this resolution be circulated immediately to all Contracting Parties inviting their comments on the studies and assessments which the panel will examine or undertake as provided above;

     . . .

6.   The panel be requested to submit a preliminary report to the Eleventh Consultative Meeting . . .

     . . .

- - - - -

Report of the First Meeting of the LDC   LDC/IGPRAD 1/6
Inter-Governmental Panel of Experts on   Extract
Radioactive Waste Disposal at Sea, October 1987

. . .

3.   Additional Material Needed for Examining or Undertaking Studies and Assessments on the General Areas of Study Requested in Paragraph 2 of Resolution LDC.28(10)

3.1   The wider political, legal, economic and social aspects of radioactive waste dumping at sea

3.1.1   The Panel agreed that the following issues concerning the wider political, legal, economic and social aspects of radioactive waste dumping at sea should be further discussed, examined or undertaken:

3.1.1.1   Legal issues

.1   Study of the possible procedures for establishing liability and indemnification for establishing loss or damage caused by dumping.

.2   Examine the provisions of other existing conventions and international law regarding the uses of the sea relating to pollution across or outside national frontiers that might assist Contracting Parties in deciding on actions related to dumping of wastes at sea . . .

.3   Examine international consultative and multilateral mechanisms, in particular with regard to internationally recognized duties to consult on the dumping at sea of radioactive wastes . . .

.4   Evaluate as to whether international law requires that any State that dumps radioactive wastes at sea has the duty to monitor the effects of such dumping on the marine environment and also has to take all feasible steps to mitigate any damage to the biosphere caused by such dumping . . .

.5 Consider as to whether the results of the studies carried out by the LDC PRAD* meetings with respect to health impacts have affected the applicability of principles of customary and conventional international law to dumping of radioactive wastes at sea . . .

3.1.1.2 Political issues

.1 Collect information concerning countries which have developed policies on sea dumping and storage of radioactive wastes. What were and are the main factors in influencing such policies?

.2 Collect opinions expressed in international white papers on disposal of radioactive wastes at sea, e.g. in the 1987 Report of the World Commission on Environment and Development: Our Common Future.

.3 Examine by what means information on dumping of radioactive wastes at sea is available to the public. How is public opinion formed? What are the channels for the formation, public participation in, and expression of this opinion?

.4 Collect views expressed by public opinion concerning the dumping of radioactive wastes at sea.

.5 Does the public perception of the risks associated with the acceptability of radioactive wastes intended for dumping at sea change with the origin of such wastes, i.e. whether these wastes derive from military or civilian uses?

.6 Evaluate which political factors are important in balancing dumping of radioactive wastes at sea versus land-based disposal options.

.7 Determine what improvements could be made, if any, to international consultative mechanisms concerning the dumping of radioactive wastes at sea.

3.1.1.3 Social and economic aspects

.1 Assess the social and economic costs and benefits of dumping of radioactive wastes at sea and discuss the implications of separating costs and benefits of sea dumping with special attention being given to the costs or benefits for non-dumping countries.

.2 Decide what social and economic factors can be assessed, quantified (wherever feasible), and compared. Public concerns and perceptions should be taken into account.

.3 Study the economic and social impacts of sea dumping of radioactive wastes, such as difficulties in exploiting sea resources, on other legitimate uses of the sea.

---

* Viz. meetings culminating in the Meeting of the Expanded Panel on the Review of Scientific and Technical Considerations relevant to the proposal for the Amendment of the Annexes to the London Dumping Convention related to the Dumping of Radioactive Wastes, IMO Headquarters, 3-7 June 1985.

.4　　Evaluate the general social and economic problems related to the possible or perceived harm or detriment to health of humans from dumping of radioactive wastes at sea.

.5　　Consider assessment approaches taken for various toxic substances in order to decide as to whether a common and specially comparable policy can be developed covering all hazardous substances being dumped at sea.

.6　　Consider how the burden of proof regarding safety can be effectively shifted to prospective dumping nations.

3.2　**The issues of comparative land-based options and the costs and risks associated with these options**

. . .

3.2.6　. . . The Panel agreed on terms of reference for further work as follows:

.1　　to evaluate the comparative assessments of the disposal on land and dumping at sea options for the management of low-level radioactive wastes submitted by Contracting Parties. Such an evaluation should, inter alia, examine the extent to which they follow relevant international guidance on this topic (particularly IAEA Safety Series No.65 and taking due account of the explicit requirement to consider the distribution of potential risks in space and time) and identify similarities and differences which exist between the approaches adopted, the nature and results of the component assessments and the criteria for drawing conclusions; and

.2　　to examine the parallels between the regulatory approaches to, and environmental assessments of, the dumping at sea of both radioactive and non-radioactive wastes to identify opportunities for developing a common, comprehensive and holistic framework for the regulation of dumping at sea of all wastes.

. . .

3.3　**The question of whether it can be proven that any dumping of radioactive wastes and other radioactive matter at sea will not harm human life and/or cause significant damage to the marine environment**

. . .

3.3.　. . . The Panel agreed on terms of reference for further studies as follows:

.1　　to develop operational definitions of such terms as "harm", "safety", "proof", "significance" and other terms which may be required to address operative paragraph 2.3 of resolution LDC.28(10);

.2　　to review and summarize available scientific information on estimates of risks, both voluntary and involuntary, to human well-being that result from various human activities in order to provide a basis for comparison with those risks estimated in the Report of the Expanded Panel (LDC 9/4) to result from the dumping at sea of radioactive wastes carried out under the provisions of the London Dumping Convention and pursuant to the Recommendations of the IAEA. Where possible, risk estimates from other human uses, applications, disposals and dissemination of potentially hazardous substances should be included. All measures of risk should be carefully defined so that uniform bases of comparison can be developed;

.3   to develop, as appropriate, in terms understandable to the layman:

   .3.1   an explanation of the basis of the assumption of a linear dose/effect relationship which underlies an assessment of radiological risks;

   .3.2   an opinion as to whether it is possible to define radiation doses below which no
   deleterious effects can be demonstrated in man and other organisms.

. . .

ANNEX 2

(Contains a Summary of the Responses to the Questionnaire on Radioactive Wastes)(Resolution LDC.28(10))

- - - - -

Additional References

Statements made in connection with the vote on resolution LDC.21(9). IMO doc. LDC 9/12,
Annex V.

Statements made by Contracting Parties in the discussion and Statements expressing
reservations on Resolution LDC.28(10). In LDC 10/15, Annexes 10 and 12.

Summary of the responses to the questionnaire pursuant to Res. LDC.28(10). IMO doc.
LDC/IGPRAD 1/6, Annex 2.

Evaluation of responses to the questionnaire. Papers submitted by Portugal (LDC/IGPRAD
1/3) and Nauru (LDC/IGPRAD 1/3/19).

- - - - -

Hazards Caused by Synthetic Materials

Report of the Ninth Consultative Meeting of Contracting   LDC 9/12, Annex 6
Parties to the London Dumping Convention, 1985

Resolution LDC. 22(9)
Environmental Hazards Caused by the Disposal at Sea of Persistent
Plastics and Other Persistent Synthetic Materials (Including Fishing Nets)

THE NINTH CONSULTATIVE MEETING,

Recognizing that the Convention . . . prohibits the dumping at sea of persistent plastics
and other persistent synthetic materials (including fishing nets and ropes) which may float or
may remain in suspension in the sea in such a manner as to interfere materially with fishing,
navigation or other legitimate uses of the sea;

Recognizing further that Annex V of . . . MARPOL 73/78, when in force, would prohibit
the disposal into the sea of all plastics, including but not limited to synthetic ropes, synthetic
fishing nets and plastic garbage bags, derived from the normal operation of vessels;

Recalling Article I of the Convention . . . which calls upon Contracting Parties to individually and collectively promote the effective control of all sources of pollution of the marine environment, and which pledges the Contracting Parties to take all practicable steps to prevent the pollution of the sea by dumping of waste and other matter that is liable to create hazards to human health, to harm living resources and marine life, to damage amenities or to interfere with other legitimate uses of the sea;

Recalling Article XII of the Convention which, *inter alia*, pledges Contracting Parties to promote, within the competent specialized agencies and other international bodies, measures to protect the marine environment against pollution caused by wastes generated in the course of operation of vessels, aircraft, platforms and other man-made structures at sea;

Recognizing the harm from entanglement and ingestion to living resources and marine life caused by disposal at sea of persistent plastics and other persistent synthetic materials (including fishing nets);

Believing that the hazard to living resources and marine life from entanglement and ingestion resulting from the interaction with persistent plastics and other persistent synthetic materials (including fishing nets) requires further attention by competent international bodies;

1.   *Requests* the Secretariat to bring to the attention of the Marine Environment Protection Committee, to the Food and Agriculture Organization and to other competent international bodies this resolution and other information available from Contracting Parties . . . and to report any actions taken by those bodies . . . ;

2.   *Offers* to respond to any request for technical assistance from the Marine Environment Protection Committee, the Food and Agriculture Organization and other competent international bodies . . . ;

3.   *Pledges* to co-ordinate activities with the . . . other . . . bodies; and

4.   *Urges* Contracting Parties to consider measures for collecting and disseminating information on the hazards to living resources and marine life caused by the disposal of persistent plastics and other persistent synthetic materials (including fishing nets) and to identify practicable means to reduce these hazards.

- - - - -

FAO Committee on Fisheries, 17th Session   COFI/87/8
(Submitted also to the Tenth LDC Consultative   MEPC 25/INF.3
Meeting and the Twenty-fifth session of the Marine   LDC.2/Circ.192
Environment Protection Committee)   Extract

Protection of Living Resources From
Entanglement in Fishing Nets and Debris
Study by the FAO Secretariat

. . .

DESCRIPTION OF THE PROBLEM

2.   The interaction of marine living resources with active fishing nets or derelict fishing gear and other debris can be through collision or ingestion. Collision may result in the animal being entrapped (e.g. in traps), gilled (e.g. fish in gillnets), girdled (e.g. in ring-shaped material such as binding straps) or eventually being able to escape from the net or plastic debris. Such interactions through collision will be referred to hereafter as "entanglement".

. . .

4.   This paper only considers the non-targeted animals that are initially captured unintentionally through entanglement in derelict debris or during fishing operations and the ingestion of debris by these animals. As so defined, entanglement in active fishing gear should also include all unintentional capture of non-targeted fish; however, this is outside the purpose of the present study, which will mainly focus on marine mammals.

Active fishing . . .

Derelict fishing gear and debris . . .

ASSESSMENT OF THE ENTANGLEMENT OF LIVING RESOURCES

12.   A summary of the information collected by FAO through its questionnaire and other inquiries is presented in Appendix I.

13.   While approaching the issue of entanglement of marine mammals in active fishing, a question arises regarding the true nature and extent of the inter-actions between various species of marine mammals and fisheries. The juxtaposition between a perceived threat to highly prized wildlife such as marine mammal populations and the food resource and dependent livelihoods creates a conflict of interests that presents a variety of controversies. Assessing how commercial fisheries should be conducted and setting quotas for maximum incidental captures to avoid depletion of marine mammal populations relies on the concept of "optimum sustainable yield"; at the same time there is a tremendous lack of knowledge of the biology, distribution and population size of marine mammals. So far, sustainable yields for marine mammals have generally been poorly estimated, and the stocks are ineffectively monitored. Another factor to consider in assessing the number of animals entangled in gear is the health of the marine mammal. Since all animals swim much faster than the moving gear (e.g. when observing seals entangled in trawls) the question of the physical conditions of the

animal arises (disease etc.). A rational approach to determine the magnitude of the entanglement problem cannot be made without considering the population trends of potentially susceptible species and this limitation should be kept in mind.

14. The joint FAO/UNEP Global Plan of Action for the Conservation, Management and Utilization of Marine Mammals (endorsed in 1984) is concerned with the biological aspect of marine mammal management and includes the question of incidental capture in its recommendations (including the legislative and policy-making issues); these recommendations offer means of addressing the entanglement problem, including the biological investigations which are indispensable for the evaluation of the impact of entanglement on marine mammal populations and their management.

15. Although evidence exists regarding the growing amount of plastic debris and its impact on marine living resources, it is extremely difficult to assess the magnitude of the problem. Debris is often reported as a number of pieces of plastic (or fishing gear fragments) regardless of the initial volume of plastic involved or its disintegration. Furthermore, even in the case of the northern fur seal, which is the best studied as to mortality caused by debris, there are still uncertainties about the mortality caused by entanglement and other factors (e.g. by diseases).

16. The data available suggest that there is a large quantity of plastic litter . . . in the sea but only a minor part lost or discarded fishing gear. . . .

EXISTING METHODS AND MODIFICATIONS TO REDUCE ENTANGLEMENT
   . . .

PROPOSED FISHING GEAR MODIFICATIONS TO REDUCE ENTANGLEMENT
   . . .

PERTINENT LEGAL MEASURES

34. . . . When examining activities leading to entanglement situations and *a fortiori* measures dealing with such activities and situations, a distinction must be made . . . between deliberate disposal of fishing gear and accidental loss of fishing gear. . . .

(a) **Controls over incidental catches of non-targeted fish and other living marine resources by fishing gear**

International Agreements

35. There are no international agreements that deal specifically with the incidental entanglement of marine mammals in fishing gear during the course of fishing operations. However, the stated objectives and functions of a number of international bodies are sufficiently broad to accommodate discussions and actions with respect to this problem and, in fact, the matter has been discussed in numerous fora.
   . . .

37. Marine mammals are dealt with generally in the 1982 United Nations Convention on the Law of the Sea, though without specific reference to the problem of incidental catches. Relevant provisions are Articles 56-62 establishing the sovereign rights of coastal States over the living resources in the exclusive economic zones and criteria for conservation and

utilization, Article 63 providing for cooperation in the conservation and development of stocks commonly exploited, and Article 64 providing for cooperation in the conservation and utilization of highly migratory species. Articles 65 and 120 safeguard the rights of coastal States and the competence of international organizations as appropriate to prohibit, limit or regulate the exploitation of marine mammals in the exclusive economic zone and on the high seas more strictly than as provided for elsewhere in the Convention with respect to commercial fish stocks.

National Legislation

38. A few countries have legislation dealing specifically with incidental catches of marine mammals. Examples are the US Marine Mammal Protection Act which provides for permits for the incidental taking of marine mammals in the course of commercial fishing operations. . . . Mexico bans the capture of marine mammals and has issued detailed instructions for releasing those that have been accidentally captured during tuna fishing operations. In a number of countries, e.g. New Zealand and Malaysia, the taking of marine mammals in general is prohibited. . . . Australia has recently acted to restrict the maximum length of pelagic gillnets by both Australian and foreign fishermen . . .

(b) **Controls over the deliberate disposal of fishing gear and other materials**

International agreements concerning controls over dumping

39. General provisions requiring States to take measures to control pollution of the marine environment are included in Part XII of the United Nations Law of the Sea Convention. Directly relevant are Articles 210 and 211 requiring States to take measures to abate and control pollution of the marine environment resulting from dumping and the operation of ships. The substance of the measures to be taken is spelt out in more detail in a series of conventions dealing with dumping and pollution from ship operations.

40. The London Dumping Convention . . . prohibits the dumping at sea of persistent plastics and other persistent synthetic materials, including netting and ropes, which may float or remain in suspension in the sea in such a manner as to interfere materially with fishing, navigation or other legitimate uses of the sea (Article IV and Annex I, paragraph 4). Contracting Parties are required to take effective measures, individually and collectively, to implement this prohibition.

41. The London Dumping Convention is a global agreement covering dumping operations in all parts of the world. It is supplemented by a series of regional conventions dealing with the control of dumping in the North Sea, Baltic Sea and Mediterranean Sea. . . . A number of other conventions on marine pollution have been adopted for other regions of the world's seas under the UNEP Regional Seas Programme. All of these regional conventions contain general provisions requiring the Contracting Parties to take appropriate measures to prevent, reduce and control pollution caused by dumping in the area covered by the convention. The measures are not, however, spelt out in detail as in the Oslo Convention, the Barcelona Protocol on Dumping and the Helsinki Convention.

International agreements concerning controls over operational pollution from shipping

42. . . . Annex V of the MARPOL Convention (one of the so-called optional annexes) deals with the disposal of garbage from ships and bans the disposal into the sea of all plastics, including synthetic ropes and synthetic fishing nets. The ban does not apply to accidental loss of synthetic fishing nets or synthetic material incidental to the repair of such nets, provided that all reasonable precautions have been taken to prevent such loss. . . .

43. The prohibition on the disposal of garbage from shipping is reiterated at the regional level in Annex IV of the Helsinki Convention. . . . General provisions requiring contracting States to take measures to prevent, abate and combat pollution caused by discharges from shipping are included in the various regional conventions concluded under the UNEP Regional Seas Programme.

44. While no legally binding measures have been adopted, discussions have also been held at the North Pacific Fur Seal Commission on entanglement of fur seals in lost or discarded fishing nets.

. . .

FURTHER LEGAL MEASURES REQUIRED

47. Any discussion of further legal measures required to combat the problem of entanglement must deal separately with each of the problem areas dealt with above.

48. The problem of incidental catches of non-targeted fish and other marine resources, in particular marine mammals in fishing, is already being dealt with in a number of international fora. Given the different impacts of fishing operations on different fish and marine mammal resources and the different management objectives and approaches followed with respect to the affected resources in different parts of the world, the issue would seem more appropriately approached at the regional level through the competent regional organizations than at the global level. Similarly, the approach taken toward controlling the incidental catch of marine mammals in gillnetting and tuna purse-seining operations in national legislation will also depend upon the management and conservation objectives and criteria adopted by the coastal States, taking into account their obligations of cooperation under the United Nations Convention on the Law of the Sea.

49. Problems of discarded nets and net fragments are already covered by the global and regional conventions on dumping and garbage pollution from shipping. They should, it is suggested, continue to be treated as part of the more general problem of marine pollution. In this context, however, emphasis should be placed on increased participation in the London Dumping Convention and on bringing into force as soon as possible Annex V of MARPOL 73/78. In addition, efforts might be made to promote the adoption of further regional conventions or protocols dealing with the control of pollution. Emphasis should also be placed on the development of effective national legislation for the implementation of these agreements.

50. The one problem area where little has been done in the form of legal controls at either the international or the national level is that of reducing the dangers of entanglement from accidentally lost nets and net fragments. For the most part, the adoption of legal controls at either national or international levels will depend upon the outcome of technical measures.

. . .

- - - - -

Committee on Fisheries   CL 91/7
Report of the Seventeenth Session, May 1987   Extract

. . .

Protection of Living Resources From
Entanglement in Fishing Nets and Debris

84.   In discussing the questions raised in document COFI/87/8 the Committee pointed to the difference between entanglement in marine debris and the incidental capture of living resources other than those targeted by the fishery. It was felt that these two issues could be usefully separated.

85.   As regards entanglement in marine debris, the Committee felt that this could best be pursued on a global basis, with one or more international bodies collecting data on the extent and the nature of the phenomenon. The application of the provisions of anti-dumping legislation, e.g. the London Dumping Convention, the Barcelona Convention and the International Convention for the Prevention of Pollution from Ships (MARPOL) were of paramount importance in this context and the Committee felt that IMO could take a leading role in monitoring of entanglement in marine debris.

86.   As regards incidental capture, the Committee noted that regional fishery commissions and other bodies with related responsibilities could be the appropriate fora to recommend follow-up actions, such as monitoring incidental catches of marine mammals, turtles, birds and other organisms . . .

. . .

- - - - -

Additional References

Protection of living resources from entanglement in fishing nets and debris. FAO doc. COFI.85/7.

Report of the Tenth LDC Meeting. LDC 10/15, Section 8.

- - - - -

General Reference

The provisions of the Convention on the Prevention of Marine Pollution by Dumping of Wastes and Other Matter, 1972 and decisions made by the Consultative Meetings of Contracting Parties. IMO doc. LDC 9/INF/2.

- - - - -

4

Marine Pollution from Other Sources

UNEP Publication: Environmental Law Guidelines and Principles No. 7

Montreal Guidelines for the Protection of the
Marine Environment Against Pollution from Land-Based Sources

Introduction

This set of guidelines is addressed to Governments with a view to assisting them in the process of developing appropriate bilateral, regional and multilateral agreements and national legislation for the protection of the marine environment against pollution from land-based sources.   They have been prepared on the basis of common elements and principles drawn from relevant existing agreements, drawing upon experience already gained through their preparation and implementation.   Principal among these agreements are the United Nations Convention of the Law of the Sea (Part XII), the Paris Convention for the Prevention of the Marine Pollution from Land-Based Sources, the Helsinki Convention on the Protection of the Marine Environment of the Baltic Sea Area, and the Athens Protocol for the Protection of the Mediterranean Sea against Pollution from Land-Based Sources.

These guidelines are suggested as a broad framework for the development of similar agreements in those regions where such agreements are called for; for the guidance of Governments in areas which are not at present covered by any regional agreements; and for the preparation in the long term, should the need arise, of global convention on pollution from land-based sources designed to strengthen international institutional arrangements to ensure the harmonization and application of global and regional rules, criteria, standards and recommended practices and procedures and to review the effectiveness of measures taken.

The guidelines are of a recommendatory nature.   They are presented as a check-list of basic provisions rather than a model agreement, which Governments may select from, adapt or elaborate upon, as appropriate, to meet the needs of specific regions.   They are without prejudice to the elaboration of cross-sectoral guidelines/principles within the framework of the Montevideo Programme for the Development and Periodic Review of Environmental Law, as recommended by the UNEP *Ad Hoc* Meeting of Senior Government Officials Expert in Environmental Law.

The guidelines were drafted, in response to UNEP Governing Council decision 10/24 of 31 May 1982, by an *Ad Hoc* Working Group of Experts on the Protection of the Marine Environment against Pollution from Land-based Sources which met between 1983 and 1985 and adopted them in Montreal, Canada, on 19 April 1985.   In the light of the Working Group's report (UNEP/WG.120/3), the Governing Council by decision 13/18 (II) of 24 May 1985 encouraged "States and international organizations to take the Montreal Guidelines for the Protection of the Marine Environment against Pollution from Land-based Sources into account in the process of developing bilateral, regional and, as appropriate, global agreements in this field".

1. **Definitions**

For the purposes of these guidelines:

(a) "Pollution" means the introduction by man, directly or indirectly, of substances or energy into the marine environment which results or is likely to result in such deleterious effects as harm to living resources and marine ecosystems, hazards to human health, hindrance to marine activities, including fishing and other legitimate uses of the sea, impairment of quality for use of sea water and reduction of amenities;

(b) "Land-based sources" means:

　(i) Municipal, industrial or agricultural sources, both fixed and mobile, on land, discharges from which reach the marine environment, in particular:
　　a.　From the coast, including from outfalls discharging directly into the marine environment and through run-off;
　　b.　Through rivers, canals of other watercourses, including underground watercourses; and
　　c.　Via the atmosphere:
　(ii) Sources of marine pollution from activities conducted on offshore fixed or mobile facilities within the limits of national jurisdiction, save to the extent that these sources are governed by appropriate international agreements.

(c) "Marine environment" means the maritime area extending, in the case of watercourses, up to the freshwater limit and including inter-tidal zones and salt-water marshes;

(d) "Freshwater limit" means the place in watercourses where, at low tide and in a period of low freshwater flow, there is an appreciable increase in salinity due to the presence of sea water.

2. **Basic obligation**

States have the obligation to protect and preserve the marine environment. In exercising their sovereign right to exploit their natural resources, all States have the duty to prevent, reduce and control pollution of the marine environment.

3. **Discharges affecting other States or areas beyond the limits of national jurisdiction**

States have the duty to ensure that discharges from land-based sources within their territories do not cause pollution to the marine environment of other States or of areas beyond the limits of national jurisdiction.

4. **Adoption of measures against pollution from land-based sources**

(a) States should adopt, individually or jointly, and in accordance with their capabilities, all measures necessary to prevent, reduce and control pollution from land-based sources, including those designed to minimize to the fullest possible extent the release of toxic, harmful or noxious substances; especially those which are persistent, into the marine environment. States should ensure that such measures take into account internationally agreed rules, criteria, standards and recommended practices and procedures.

(b) In taking measures to prevent, reduce and control pollution from land-based sources, States should refrain, in accordance with international law, from unjustifiable interference with activities carried out by other States in the exercise of their sovereign rights and in pursuance of their duties in conformity with internationally agreed rules, criteria, standards and recommended practices and procedures.

5. **Co-operation on a global, regional or bilateral basis**

(a) States should undertake, as appropriate, to establish internationally agreed rules, criteria, standards and recommended practices and procedures to prevent, reduce and control pollution from land-based sources, with a view to co-ordinating their policies in this connection, particularly at the local and regional level. Such rules, criteria, standards and recommended practices and procedures should take into account local ecological, geographical and physical characteristics, the economic capacity of States and their need for sustainable development and environmental protection, and the assimilative capacity of the marine environment, and should be reviewed from time to time as necessary;

(b) States not bordering on the marine environment should co-operate in preventing, reducing and controlling pollution of the marine environment originating or partially originating from releases within their territory into or reaching water basins or watercourses flowing into the marine environment or via the atmosphere. To this end, States concerned should as far as possible, and, as appropriate, in co-operation with competent international organizations, take necessary measures to prevent, reduce and control pollution of the marine environment from land-based sources;

(c) If discharges from a watercourse which flows through the territories of two or more States or forms a boundary between them are likely to cause pollution of the marine environment, the States concerned should co-operate in taking necessary measures to prevent, reduce and control such pollution.

6. **Duty not to transfer or transform pollution from land-based sources**

In taking measures to prevent, reduce and control pollution from land-based sources, States have the duty to act so as not to transfer directly or indirectly, damage or hazards from one area to another or transform such pollution into another type of pollution.[1]

7.   **Specially protected areas**

(a)   States should, in a manner consistent with international law, take all appropriate measures, such as the establishment of marine sanctuaries and reserves, to protect certain areas to the fullest possible extent from pollution, including that from land-based sources, taking into account the relevant provisions of annex I;

(b)   States should, as practicable, undertake to develop, jointly or individually, environmental quality objectives for specially protected areas, conforming with the intended uses, and strive to maintain or ameliorate existing conditions by comprehensive environmental management practices.

8.   **Scientific and technical co-operation**

States should co-operate, directly and/or through competent international organizations, in the field of science and technology related to pollution from land-based sources, and exchange data and other scientific information for the purpose of preventing, reducing and controlling such pollution, taking into account national regulations regarding the protection of confidential information. They should, in particular, undertake to develop and co-ordinate to the fullest possible extent their national research programmes and to co-operate in the establishment and implementation of regional and other international research programmes.

9.   **Assistance to developing countries**

(a)   States should, directly and/or through competent international organizations, promote programmes of assistance to developing countries in the fields of education, environmental and pollution awareness, training, scientific research and transfer of technology and know-how, for the purpose of improving the capacity of the developing countries to prevent, reduce and control of pollution from land-based sources and to assess its effects on the marine environment;

(b)   Such assistance should include:

(i)   Training of scientific and technical personnel;
(ii)   Facilitation of the participation of developing countries in relevant international programmes;
(iii) Acquisition, utilization, maintenance and production by those countries of appropriate equipment; and
(iv)   Advice on, and development of, facilities for education, training, research, monitoring and other programmes;

(c)   States should, directly and/or through competent international organizations, promote programmes of assistance to developing countries for the establishment, as necessary, of infrastructure for the effective implementation of applicable internationally agreed rules, criteria, standards and recommended practices and procedures related to the protection of the marine environment against pollution from land-based sources, including the provision of expert advice on the development of the necessary legal and administrative measures.

10. **Development of a comprehensive environmental management approach**

States should undertake to develop, as far as practicable, a comprehensive environmental management approach to the prevention, reduction and control of pollution from land-based sources, taking into account relevant existing programmes at the bilateral, regional or global level and the provisions of annex I. Such a comprehensive approach should include the identification of desired and attainable water use objectives for the specific marine environments.

11. **Monitoring and data management**

States should endeavour to establish directly or, whenever necessary, through competent international organizations, complementary or joint programmes for monitoring, storage and exchange of data, based, when possible, on compatible procedures and methods, taking into account relevant existing programmes at the bilateral, regional or global level and the provisions of annex III, in order to:

(a) Collect data on natural conditions in the region concerned as regards its physical, biological and chemical characteristics;

(b) Collect data on inputs of substances or energy that cause or potentially cause pollution emanating from land-based sources, including information of the distribution of sources and the quantities introduced to the region concerned:

(c) Assess systematically the levels of pollution along their coasts emanating from land-based sources and the fates and effects of pollution in the region concerned; and

(d) Evaluate the effectiveness of measures in meeting the environmental objectives for specific marine environments.

12. **Environmental assessment**

States should assess the potential effects/impacts, including possible transboundary effects/impacts, of proposed major projects under their jurisdiction or control, particularly in coastal areas, which may cause pollution from land-based sources, so that appropriate measures may be taken to prevent or mitigate such pollution.

13. **Development of control strategies**

(a) States should develop, adopt and implement programmes and measures for the prevention, reduction and control of pollution from land-based sources. They should employ an appropriate control strategy or combination of control strategies, taking into account relevant international or national experience, as described in annex I,

(b) States should, as appropriate, progressively formulate and adopt, in co-operation with competent international organizations, standards based on marine quality or on emissions, as well as recommended practices and procedures, taking into account the provisions of annex I;

(c)   Where appropriate, States should undertake to establish priorities for action, based on lists of substances pollution by which should be eliminated and of substances pollution by which should be strictly limited on the basis of their toxicity, persistence, bioaccumulation and other criteria as elaborated in annex II, or in relevant international agreements.

14.   Pollution emergencies arising from land-based sources

States and, as appropriate, competent international organizations should take all necessary measures for preventing and dealing with marine pollution emergencies from land-based sources, however caused, and for reducing or eliminating damage or the threat of damage therefrom. To this end States should, as appropriate, individually or jointly, develop and promote national and international contingency plans for responding to incidents of pollution from land-based sources and should co-operate with one another and, whenever necessary, through competent international organizations.

15.   Notification, information exchange and consultation

Whenever releases originating or likely to originate from land-based sources within the territory of a State are likely to cause pollution to the marine environment of one or more other States or of areas beyond the limits of national jurisdiction, that State should immediately notify such other State or States, as well as competent international organizations, and provide them with timely information that will enable them, where necessary, to take appropriate action to prevent, reduce and control such pollution. Furthermore, consultations deemed appropriate by States concerned should be undertaken with a view to preventing, reducing and controlling such pollution.

16.   National laws and procedures

(a)   Each State should adopt and implement national laws and regulations for the protection and preservation of the marine environment against pollution from land-based sources, taking into account internationally agreed rules, criteria, standards and recommended practices and procedures, and take appropriate measures to ensure compliance with such laws and regulations;

(b)   Paragraph (a) above is without prejudice to the right of States to take more stringent measures nationally or in co-operation with each other to prevent, reduce and control pollution from land-based sources under their jurisdiction or control;

(c)   Each State should, on a reciprocal basis, grant equal access to and non-discriminatory treatment in its courts, tribunals and administrative proceedings to persons in other States who are or may be affected by pollution from land-based sources under its jurisdiction or control.

17.   Liability and compensation for pollution damage emanating from land-based sources

(a)   States should ensure that recourse is available in accordance with their legal systems for prompt and adequate compensation or other relief in respect of damage caused by pollution of the marine environment by natural or juridical persons under their jurisdiction;

(b)   To this end, States should formulate and adopt appropriate procedures for the determination of liability for damage resulting from pollution from land-based sources. Such procedures should include measures for addressing damage caused by releases of a significant scale or by the substances referred to in guideline 13 (c).

18. **Implementation reports**

States should report, as appropriate, to other States concerned, directly or through competent international organizations, on measures taken, on results achieved and, if the case arises, on difficulties encountered in the implementation of applicable internationally agreed rules, criteria, standards and recommended practices and procedures. To this end, States should designate national authorities as focal points for the reporting of such measures, results and difficulties.

19. **Institutional arrangements**

(a)   States should ensure that adequate institutional arrangements are made at the appropriate regional or global level, for the purpose of achieving the objectives of these guidelines, and in particular for promoting the formulation, adoption and application of international rules, criteria, standards, and recommended practices and procedures, and for monitoring the condition of the marine environment;

(b)   The functions of such institutional arrangements should include:

(i)   Periodic assessment of the state of the specific marine environment concerned;

(ii)   Formulation and adoption, as appropriate, of a comprehensive environmental management approach consistent with the provisions of guidelines 7 and 10;

(iii)   Adoption, review and revision, as necessary, of the lists referred to in guideline 13;

(iv)   Development and adoption, as appropriate, of programmes and measures consistent with the provisions of guidelines 10 and 13;

(v)   Consideration, where necessary, of the reports and information submitted in accordance with guidelines 15 and 18;

(vi)   Recommendation of appropriate measures to be taken for the prevention, reduction and control of pollution from land-based sources, such as assistance to developing countries, the strengthening of regional co-operation mechanisms, consideration of aspects of transboundary pollution, and the difficulties encountered in the implementation of agreed rules; and

(vii)   Review of the implementation of relevant internationally agreed rules, criteria, standards and recommended practices and procedures, and of the efficacy of the measures adopted and the advisability of any other measures.

Annex I

STRATEGIES FOR PROTECTING, PRESERVING AND ENHANCING THE QUALITY OF THE MARINE ENVIRONMENT

INTRODUCTION

In controlling marine pollution from land-based sources, an overall approach to the uses and the natural values of the marine environment should be taken, while still considering the needs of populations and industries for waste disposal. It is important to note that for many types of waste, the use of the marine environment is only one option among several. However, in some instances, marine disposal may be a feasible alternative. The present annex describes a number of strategies which can be employed to protect the marine environment against pollution from land-based sources and, where necessary, restore areas that have been affected. The goal is to protect the marine ecosystem by maintaining its quality within acceptable levels as determined on the basis of scientific, institutional, social and economic factors. It should be recognized that there are many activities competing to derive benefits from the marine environment. None of these activities, save the perpetuation of a marine ecosystem as a vital component of global life support, should be regarded as having guaranteed rights. Compromise and consideration of all alternatives must always be considered. Consequently, in the course of the decision-making process determining the use of a particular sector of the marine environment, social, economic and political factors, as well as natural environmental factors must be taken into account.

Once decision-makers have determined the desired present, interim and long-term uses and associated objectives for a water body, a number of control strategies may be employed to achieve those objectives. Flexibility will be an important consideration in the strategies or regulatory instruments implemented for various water bodies, reflecting their different environmental capacities and other properties and differences in regional socio-economic conditions. The principal strategies in use are based on marine quality standards, on emission standards and on environmental planning. Experience shows that a combination of strategies is often needed. Practical constraints may prevent full implementation of a strategy based on quality standards. Where such an approach cannot be fully implemented, other strategies should be employed.

1.0   CONTROL STRATEGIES

Pollution control strategies in use have been categorized as follows:

(a)   Those based on marine environmental quality standards;

(b)   Those based on emission standards;

(c)   Those based on environmental planning.

Priorities for control are often established by the classification of substances into a "black" and a "grey" list. Substances are assessed according to the criteria described an annex II. States undertake to eliminate pollution by those substances in the black list and strictly to limit pollution by those in the grey list.

1.1   Strategies based on marine quality standards

Such strategies relate directly to the quality of water, biota or sediments that must maintained for a desired level of quality and intended use. Several applications of such quality-based strategies exist.

1.1.1   Direct derivation from quality objectives

Technical assessments are conducted to determine the maximum allowable inputs that will ensure that the desired levels of environmental quality are met. The assessments consider the fates and effects of various contaminants, amounts of input, and the existing natural characteristics of the relevant marine ecosystem. Numerical standards are then established, to which concentrations measured in the receiving environment may be compared. They are usually more restrictive than numbers derived from the technical assessment to allow for monitoring and enforcement capabilities and safety requirements. They may apply to water, sediment, fish or the tissues, health or community composition of organisms in the marine ecosystem.

Monitoring is required to detect changes and compliance with the standards. Changes in the items monitored, after adjustment for natural fluctuation, may signal a need to reduce inputs further and vary existing standards and controls.

1.1.2. No change above ambient

Standards are set based on existing levels which must not be exceeded. This strategy is employed in situations where the aim is to prevent any increase in prevailing specific contaminant levels. It is an interim strategy to allow time to develop a solid scientific base on which more precise quality criteria may be employed for a specific use. It does not imply that an existing state of the environment is satisfactory, nor does it eliminate the need for its improvement.

1.1.3 Dilution

Some contaminants discharged at the source are assumed to attenuate as they spread from that source. Dynamic characteristics of the receiving environment are employed to determine the rate and level of dilution. Standards are derived from measured parameters taken at given distances from the discharging source. This strategy may accept short-term or local excess of a potential pollutant at the source of discharge. Application is generally used with effluent that is considered biodegradable, and avoided where scientific evidence suggests that the effluent may accumulate in a given receiving environment.

1.1.4 Loading allocations

These impose priority of control on the larger sources in consideration of the most cost-effective solutions. Allowable discharge are measured in terms of the total allowable for an entire receiving environment, regardless of specific site quality. Application is suited to relatively self contained receiving environments, such as lagoons and semi-enclosed bodies of water. It allows flexibility of contaminant output, in that certain sources may emit more than adjacent ones as long as loading limits are not exceeded. All these strategies may employ criteria for water, air or sediment quality, as well as criteria related to specific marine life. Receiving environment quality standards are most prevalent for uses - e.g. swimming, direct harvesting of fish for human consumption - where sound scientific criteria exist to determine levels of harm. Emissions of potential pollutants are usually controlled to ensure that the desired quality is achieved. If the quality needs to be upgraded, additional controls are placed on allowable emissions.

1.2 Strategies based on emission standards

These strategies may be based on:

(a)   A general principle of pollution control;
(b)   Achievable technology;

(c)   Distribution of control costs;

(d)   Enforceability.

They differ from strategies based on marine quality in that the standards set are not primarily determined by the level of contaminant in the environment.

1.2.1. Technology-based standards

These standards are usually applied on a sectoral basis, thus providing a means of imposing similar costs across a particular sector. Alternatively, they may be determined on a case-by-case basis. The standards will need to be reviewed periodically in the light of developing technology.

Standards may be based on:

1.2.1.1. Best practicable technology

This reflects the application of demonstrable and sound treatment technology or a spectrum of technologies which is affordable by the sector concerned.

1.2.1.2. Best available technology

This reflects state-of-the-art technology in use in contaminant control. In general, the standards set would reflect a more stringent level of control as compared to best practicable technology. Application is generally for the control of emissions of the most noxious substances or to protect a sensitive environmental use.

1.2.1.3 As low as reasonably achievable

This is mainly applied to radio-nuclides, and is based on the principles of "optimization". This, as defined by the International Commission on Radiological Protection, requires radiation doses to be kept to levels that are "reasonably achievable", by technological improvements and by a suitable choice among alternative options. "Reasonably achievable" takes into account both the ease with which the technology can be applied and the balance between the benefits, in terms of dose deduction, and the social and economic costs of its application.

1.2.1.4 Zero discharge

In a situation where stringent protection of a sensitive marine environment is deemed appropriate, consideration may be given to the denial of any release of a contaminant to the environment.

1.2.2. Uniform regional emission standards

Such standards are usually applied in situations where there are existing pollution problems of a similar nature and there is an urgent need to reduce pollution. They do not give primary consideration to the nature of sources, their economic base, or the receiving environment.

1.3 Planning strategies

This set of strategies draws in part on those mentioned in section 1.1 and 1.2 above and will often be used to supplement then (the reverse is also true). Planning strategies allow an approach to the management and protection of particular environments which may involve restrictions on, or modification of, activities and sites as well as discharges.

1.3.1 Activity management

Certain activities are deemed inappropriate or inconsistent with the value or uses of an environment. Consideration should be given to whether the activity is essential, and if so, whether it can be accommodated elsewhere or in a different manner.

1.3.1.1. Use designation

Use of the receiving environment is the determining factor for pollution control standards as well as the basis for regulations or guidelines affecting other activities. For example, if the desire is to maintain or develop a shellfish harvest (a socio-economic decision), then quality standards and uses are developed with this in mind.

This application may result from a perceived threat to an established economic base or cultural value, or a conscious effort to change the existing use of a receiving environment.

1.3.1.2 Environmental assessment of activities

Siting of any activity significantly affecting the marine environment is subject to a comprehensive analysis and assessment of:

(a)   The ecological characteristics of the receiving environment;

(b)   The direct and indirect potential effect/impacts of the activity on the environment; and, as appropriate,

(c)   The direct and indirect potential effects/impacts on the environment of any reasonable alternative to the activity.

1.3.2 Regional planning

Plans are drawn up for particular regions, taking into account socio-economic and ecological factors, which are then used as a basis for development.

1.3.2.1. Coastal zone management

The strategy employs planning capabilities to make the best use of the coastal zone.

It is not use-specific or source-specific but area-specific. Potential activities are assessed as components of a coastal zone. Planning is based on regional socio-economic and ecological considerations. Zoning and other land use restrictions or modifications are major regulatory tools. Many States make use of regional planning authorities or councils which are given the task of managing overall resource planning within a particular coastal area.

1.3.2.2 Watershed or drainage basis planning

This strategy acknowledges that a large proportion of pollution enters the marine environment via watercourses. It does not necessarily account for inputs via the atmosphere, though air management areas have also been employed for control purposes.

Through consideration of socio-economic and environmental factors, taking the area of a drainage system as the planning unit, the desired uses and level of quality that can be attained for any given marine water body are determined.

Pollution via watercourses is controlled through regulation of point and diffuse sources of such pollution within the given watershed.

1.3.2.3 Specially protected areas

This strategy involves the identification of unique or pristine areas, rare or fragile ecosystems, critical habitats and the habitat of depleted, threatened or endangered species and other forms of marine life.

Those areas to be protected or preserved from pollution, including that from land-based sources, are selected on the basis of a comprehensive evaluation of factors, including conservational, ecological, recreational, aesthetic and scientific values.

States should notify an appropriate international organization of the establishment of an any modification to such areas, with a view to the inclusion of such information in an inventory of specially protected areas.

2.0 CONTROL INSTRUMENTS

This section outlines the various types of mechanism which can be invoked to implement control strategies:

2.1 Regulations

Regulations are developed pursuant to enabling legislation and can exist in forms such as:

2.1.1. Emission standards (air/water)

Standards based on best practicable technology, best available technology, geographical area, etc.

2.1.2. Environmental quality standards

Standards for the receiving environment which vary according to its intended use.

2.2 Guidelines/codes of practice

These are descriptions of practices and abatement technologies that may be developed to meet the pollution control needs of various point and non-point sources. They provide a listing of basic requirements that may be implemented or adopted by industry or local authorities.

2.3 Permits

Legislation may require a discharger to have a permit to satisfy the requirements for the release of pollutants. These requirements can be based on standards in the form of emission control regulations, guidelines, codes of practice or specific requirements derived from environmental quality standards prescribed to protect the receiving environment.

2.4 Equipment standards certification

Environmental considerations may be incorporated directly in association with particular equipment. To this end, the equipment or configuration of equipment may be designed, manufactured, tested and certified to comply with the requirements for source releases of pollutants.

2.5 Product controls

If a particular substance or assemblage of substances in the form of a commercial product is deemed to be of environmental significance, a restriction may be placed on the production, use and export/import of the product.

2.6 Planning restrictions

Under planning law or practice, restrictions may be placed on the use of certain land.

2.7 Economic measures

These may take a variety of forms, e.g. tax incentives, subsidies and effluent charges. To be effective, the incentive offered must be strong enough or the charge levied high enough to persuade the discharger or user that it is in his own financial interest to limit his discharge or use of the substance concerned.

3.0 FACTORS INFLUENCING CHOICE OF STRATEGIES AND CONTROL INSTRUMENTS

There is a wide range of strategies and control instruments which can be utilized either individually or in combination to address pollution of the marine environment from land-based sources. A number of factors may influence such a choice. In general terms, they may be categorized as economic, scientific/technical or social/cultural/political, as follows:

3.1 Economic

General economic conditions and trends (deficit, balance of trade, inflation,etc.);
Availability of public financing;
Availability of external funding;
Unemployment;
Economic viability of various sectors;
The "polluter pays" principle;
Availability of institutions and infrastructure.

Environmental Protection

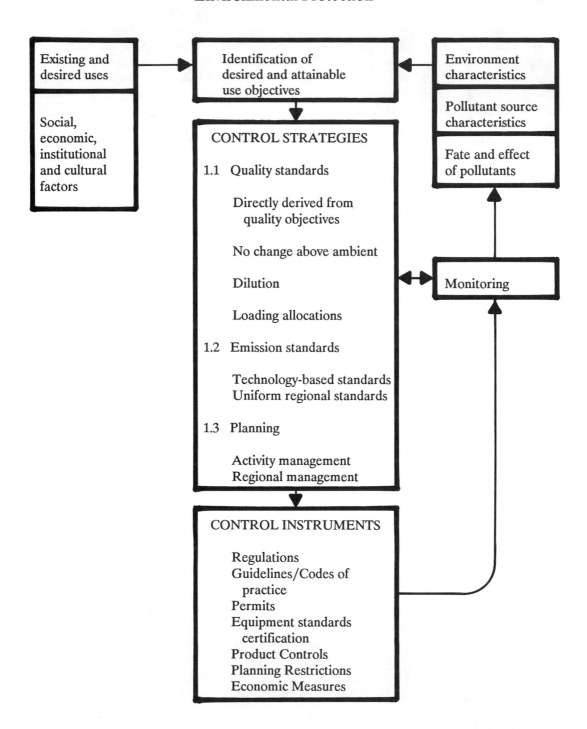

3.2 Scientific/technical

3.2.1. Availability/accessibility of scientific data, including:

Physical characteristics affecting flushing and mixing;
Natural nutrient cycles and geochemical cycles;
Biological processes and nature of communities.

3.2.2. Availability/accessibility of technology, including:

Basic information on industry types and on total effluent releases, and specific date on waste stream constituents;
Availability of expertise;
Capability for monitoring;
Existing engineering infrastructure;
Experience with implementation of strategies or instruments elsewhere;
Sensitivity of ecosystems to be affected;
Climatic considerations;
Current level of pollution of the receiving environment and identified trends in municipal, agricultural and industrial waste releases.

3.3 Social/cultural/political

Infrastructure;
Existing and proposed uses of the marine environment;
Political realities;
Social/cultural awareness of the population;
Perception of environmental, social and cultural values.

Annex II

CLASSIFICATION OF SUBSTANCES

INTRODUCTION

Substances may be classified into a black list of those substances pollution by which should be eliminated and a grey list of those substances pollution by which should be strictly limited and reduced.

The basic criteria to be taken into account in allocating substances to one of these lists are:

(a) Persistence;
(b) Toxicity or other noxious properties;
(c) Tendency to bioaccumulations.

These criteria are not necessarily of equal importance for a particular substance or group of substances. Other factors such as location and quantities of discharge may need to be considered.

1.0 BLACK LIST

Substances may be included in this list:

(a) Because they are not readily degradable or rendered harmless by natural processes; and
(b) Because they may either:
   (i) Give rise to dangerous accumulation of harmful material in the food chain; or
   (ii) Endanger the welfare of living organisms causing undesirable changes in the marine ecosystems; or
   (iii) Interfere seriously with harvesting of sea foods or with other legitimate uses of the sea; and
(c) Because it is considered that pollution by these substances necessitates urgent action.

The substances that fulfil these criteria may include:

1.1 Certain organic biocides (e.g. organohalogen compounds and substances which may form such compounds in the marine environment);

1.2 Persistent hydrocarbons of petroleum origin;

1.3 Certain metals and their compounds (e.g. mercury);

1.4 Persistent synthetic materials which may seriously interfere with legitimate use of the sea;

1.5 Radioactive materials;

1.6 Substances which have been proved to possess carcinogenic properties in or via the aquatic environment;

1.7 Materials in whatever form (e.g. solid, liquid, semi-liquid, gaseous or in a living state) produced for biological and chemical warfare.

2.0 GREY LIST

Substances may be included in this list because, although exhibiting similar characteristics to the substances in the black list and requiring strict control, they seem less noxious or are more readily rendered harmless by natural processes. The substances to which this may apply include:

2.1 Organic biocides not included in the black list;

2.2 Hydrocarbons of petroleum origin and their derivatives not included in the black list;

2.3 Certain elements and their compounds (e.g. fluorides and cyanides);

2.4   Inorganic and synthetic organic materials, other than those included in the black list, which are likely to produce harmful effects on marine organisms or to make edible marine organisms unpalatable, as well as chemicals which may lead to the formation of such substances in the marine environment;

2.5   Acid and alkaline compounds of such composition and in such quantity that they may seriously impair the quality of the marine environment;

2.6   Substances which, though not producing toxic effects, may become harmful because of the concentrations or quantities in which they are discharged, or which are liable to reduce amenities seriously or to endanger human life or marine organisms or to impair other legitimate uses of the sea;

2.7   Pathogenic micro-organisms which are or may become harmful because of the concentrations and quantities in which they are discharged or which are liable to endanger human life or marine organisms, or to impair other legitimate uses of the marine environment and coastal waters in particular.

Annex III

MONITORING AND DATA MANAGEMENT

1.0   MONITORING

In the protection of the marine environment against pollution from land-based sources, monitoring can be defined as the measurement of a pollutant or its effects on either man or marine resources for the purposes of assessing and controlling exposure to that pollutant. Thus monitoring is used to assess, first, the need for pollution prevention measures, and subsequently the effectiveness of any protection measures introduced. If monitoring is to meet these objectives and be cost-effective it must be carefully designed and implemented.

1.1   Resources to be protected

One of the first things to ascertain is what resources need protecting in the area concerned and the various pollutant sources and ways in which each could possibly be threatened. For example, the well-being of a nature reserve, fish hatchery or fish resource might be threatened by a variety of substances. Similarly, the suitability of fish or shellfish for human consumption might be affected by other substances such as mercury or arsenic which may adversely affect man whilst not affecting fisheries.

1.2   Information on inputs

It is also important at an early stage to establish for each area the activities already practised and the pollutants likely to reach the sea via point, non-point and riverine sources.

A knowledge of the resources to be protected and the pollutants which are most likely to affect them will allow attention to be focused on those substances which appear most likely to be of concern, thereby reducing the amount of effort devoted to establishing a data base on inputs. Information on inputs can also be used to focus environmental monitoring efforts on those pollutants most likely to be encountered in each area. If possible the scale of input should also be established, at least in order of magnitude terms. This will normally be fairly easy but more accurate qualification will require improvements in the quality of data on both concentration and flow.

Information on inputs from direct discharges may be determined from descriptions of unit processes in use. If permit programmes have been established, information on controlled pollutants should be available from the permit issuing authority. Inputs from non-point sources are generally estimated by employing accepted formulae describing land use in the watershed and the associated run-off. In estimating inputs from point and non-point sources, the pollutants of concern may include a broad range of substances, for example, toxicants and nutrients.

1.3　Establishing baseline concentrations

Having decided what needs to be monitored, on the basis of what resources must be protected and which pollutants are likely to be of interest, the concentrations actually present in the environment can be established. This information can then be used to assess those protection measures necessary and their effectiveness. The need for control measures may be judged by comparing the concentrations found either with some form of water quality criteria, for example maximum permissible concentration, or with similar data from other areas known not to be contaminated.

When baseline concentrations are being ascertained, the most appropriate substrate should be selected. Three options exist: water, biota and sediments. Only rarely should it be necessary to analyse samples of all three. The choice will depend on the pollutant concerned, the water quality criteria selected and the nature of the pathways exposed. For example, water would be most suitable for nutrients, biochemical oxygen demand 9B(BOD), pH and certain metals, but biota would be more appropriate for polychlorinated biphenyls (PCBs) or mercury, and undisturbed sediments can be particularly useful in timer spatial trend assessments.

1.4　Ongoing monitoring

Monitoring will be required to establish the effectiveness of pollution protection measures. Even if no reductions in inputs are deemed necessary, it may be desired to check that the situation does not deteriorate. Whatever their purpose, monitoring programmes should be designed to consider the receiving capacity of the environment as well as inputs. This means considering present water quality in relation to the desired quality, and the scale of environmental protection measures taken in relation to the existing concentrations, the nature of the pollutants present, the scale of their input and their removal processes. On this basis it will be possible to define what should be monitored and with what frequency.

1.5　Sampling and analysis

The number and nature of the samples collected should be representative of the substrate being monitored. Water quality, biological tissues and sediments can all be very variable even over short distances, and the sampling strategy should, when necessary, be tested statistically to ensure it is sound. The programme design should take account of the hydrographic characteristics of the area so as to avoid sampling the same body of water at different places as it moves under the influence of a current. Finally, the sample collected must be adjusted to the form in which the pollutant occurs in the environment or in the discharge streams.

Once a suitable sampling programme has been designed, it may be possible to bulk samples for analysis in order to reduce the analytical workload and costs. This will inevitably lead to the loss of some information, and should be considered only if the complexity of the analytical technique demands it, the loss of information can be tolerated or the monitoring is to be used only to pick up abnormalities, as in compliance monitoring.

1.6 Resource monitoring

In addition to monitoring the pollutants of interest in the selected substrate, it is essential that the state of the resource(s) be monitored. However, if adverse changes do occur it should not be assumed the protection measures taken were inadequate. For example, fish stocks decline due to fishing effort as well as pollution and undesirable plankton blooms occur for reason other than nutrients enrichment. Monitoring of biological effects is desirable but very few techniques can be applied routinely on a wide scale and most give unspecific responses. Once suitable effect monitoring techniques are available, they may be more attractive alternatives than purely chemical monitoring in environmental matrices.

2.0 DATA AND DATA MANAGEMENT

Before the data from any monitoring programme are used, it is important that confidence limits be established and reported in order to ensure that the confidence with which recorded numbers and handled and interpreted is not misplaced. It is also necessary to decide how the data should be handled for future reference and use.

2.1 Limitations in the data and the extent to which they can be tolerated

The results obtained from any monitoring programme will be subject to errors of accuracy and precision, the size of which must be quantified. If precision is high and accuracy poor then all results for a set of analyses of the same sample will be very close together, for example, differing by no more than 1 per cent, though they may differ from the true result by much more, possibly by as much as an order of magnitude. Some errors will derive from the nature of the samples. These can be minimized by proper statistical design of the sampling procedures and attention to the collection of uncontaminated samples.

All analytical procedures have inherent errors in precision and accuracy. To a greater or lesser extent either or both types of error can be compounded by operator or laboratory errors, which are often not recognized. However, by using good analytical equipment and methods and following rigorous analytical quality assurance scheme, it should be possible to achieve high accuracy and precision for all analytical data, and allow quantification of the scale errors.

2.2 Intercomparability requirements

In most cases where monitoring programmes are operated on a multilateral basis it is essential that the results obtained by all contributors are truly comparable. Establishing comparable monitoring programmes may prove difficult. However, it is desirable that targets be set for comparability of the data.

Analytical comparability is only one aspect of monitoring data. The actual programmes run by different countries must also be comparable. It obviously will not be possible to compare results from three countries if one analyses water, another a fish species and another sediments. Even when agreement is reached on whether to sample water, biota or sediments it will be necessary to agree, for example, which species of fish should be used, whether the water should be filtered before analysis or whether whole sediment should be analysed or only a particular size fraction.

2.3 Requirements for analytical quality control

It may be impossible to arrange that all contributors use identical analytical procedures. Even if they do, for the reasons given previously, intercomparability is not guaranteed. To establish whether differences do exist and to minimize them a programme of intercalibration is essential. Each laboratory should assure the quality of its data by participating in intercalibration exercises and analysing at intervals reference materials containing certified concentrations of the pollutants of interest in appropriate matrices and concentrations.

2.4 Data storage, retrieval and exchange

Depending on the scale of the monitoring programme various methods of data storage and transfer may be appropriate. It is essential that the design of the storage/retrieval system be carefully worked out to reflect the end use of the data in both raw and interpreted form. The most efficient method in many respects is to use a computer. It is essential that the limitations of any set of data be instantly recognizable when it is retrieved. To this end, information such as performance in a recognized intercalibration exercise, analysis of reference materials, etc., should be retrievable with the data. Ideally the data should be freely accessible by all contributors and the scientific community in general. However, if a country or group of countries wish certain types of data to be available only to a limited audience that wish must be safeguarded.

Regions may exhibit different natural background or baseline concentrations, have different resources to be protected and be exposed to different pollutants. As a consequence their monitoring programmes may differ - for example, different fish species may be used as indicators, permissible limits differ according to exposure patterns and different targets may be set for sampling and analytical accuracy. Therefore it will probably be more practical and effective, at least initially, to organize monitoring programmes and data storage on a regional rather than a global basis.

Once a satisfactory level of regional comparability has been achieved, interregional comparability should follow as a logical progression.

Note

1. Guideline 6 does not prevent the transfer or transformation of pollution in order to prevent, reduce and control pollution of the environment as a whole.

- - - - -

UNEP Governing Council,   A/42/25, Annex 1
Report of the 14th Session, 1987

Decisions adopted by the Governing Council at its fourteenth session

14/31. Shared natural resources and legal aspects of offshore mining and drilling.

The Governing Council,

1.   *Takes note* of the report of the Executive Director on shared natural resources and legal aspects of offshore mining and drilling[61] and authorizes the Executive Director to transmit it on behalf of the Council, together with any comments made by delegations thereon, to the General Assembly at its forty-second session in accordance with General Assembly resolution 40/200 of 17 December 1985;

2.   *Calls upon* Governments and international organizations to take further action to implement the principles of conduct in the field of the environment for the guidance of States in the conservation and harmonious utilization of natural resources shared by two or more States, and the conclusions of the study of the legal aspects concerning the environment related to the offshore mining and drilling;

3.   *Invites* the Executive Director to keep the matter under review and to report to the Governing Council at its next regular session.

Note

...

61.   UNEP/GC.14/25 and Corr. 1 and 2.

- - - - -

Additional References

Offshore Mining and Drilling.   UNEP publication Environmental Law Guidelines and Principles No. 4.

Final Report of the *Ad Hoc* Working Group of Experts on the Protection of the Marine Environment Against Pollution from Land-Based Sources.   UNEP doc. UNEP/WG.120/3.

- - - - -

5

Liability for Pollution Damage

Carriage of Hazardous and Noxious Substances

IMO Legal Committee   LEG 55/5
55th Session, 1985   Extract

Consideration of a Report on the Draft Convention on Liability and Compensation in Connection with the Carriage of Noxious and Hazardous Substances by Sea (Draft HNS Convention)
Note by the Secretary-General

. . .

D.   DISCUSSIONS AT THE DIPLOMATIC CONFERENCE

44.   . . . The main issues on which consensus was not considered feasible at the Conference were:

1.   GEOGRAPHICAL SCOPE OF APPLICATION: whether the convention should be extended to apply to damage caused beyond "the territory, including the territorial sea" of Contracting States. The consensus reached on this issue in respect of the 1984 CLC and FUND Protocols may provide a solution in the HNS Convention (annex 2, section A).

. . .

ANNEX 2

SUMMARIES OF ARGUMENTS, OBSERVATIONS AND SUGGESTIONS MADE DURING THE DISCUSSIONS AT THE DIPLOMATIC CONFERENCE IN RESPECT OF THE RESPECTIVE ISSUES LISTED IN PARAGRAPH 44 OF THIS DOCUMENT

. . .

Section A - Geographical scope of application

(i)   The arguments made in favour of extending the Convention to cover damage beyond the territorial sea included the following:

1.   The Convention should have a broad geographical scope and should be extended to cover damage caused in all maritime areas in which the coastal State has sovereign rights. It would be illogical to envisage drawing an imaginary line across an area in which a State exercised sovereign rights, implying that the Convention provided compensation for damage on one side of that line, and not on the other.

2.   There is no reason why damage outside the limit of the territorial sea of a Contracting State should not be compensated under the revised CLC and the revised Fund Convention as well as the HNS Convention.

3.   Since the movements of ships could not be restricted, it is inconsistent to seek to restrict the geographical coverage of the Convention.

4.   The extension of the scope of application is in complete accordance with the Law of the Sea Convention. As the EEZ is now part of international law, the scope of application of the HNS Convention should be extended to cover that zone.

5.   It is quite normal to cover damage in the EEZ, and there is no question of increasing any State's rights in that zone. After the Law of the Sea Conference the EEZ cannot be ignored now.

6.   Seeking to limit the scope of the Convention is as definite a step backwards as to retain the liability limits provided for under the 1969 Civil Liability Convention.

(ii) The arguments advanced to support restricting the Convention to damage in the "territory including the territorial sea" included the following:

1.   The main purpose of the Convention is to offer protection against personal injury, which is usually caused in the territory and territorial sea of a State. From the environmental point of view it is sufficient to restrict the scope of application to the territorial sea. In most cases damage to property, personal injury and death only occur close to the coast, and pollution would have a greater impact nearer the coast. The limitation of the scope to the territorial sea would link the text of the Convention more closely to those areas for which the régime covering the carriage of noxious and hazardous substances by sea is considered necessary.

2.   In the Law of the Sea Convention there are no sovereign rights over the natural resources of the EEZ, but only for the purpose of the exploration, development and conservation of natural resources, and not in connection with the natural resources themselves. The EEZ has been created on the clear understanding that it is part of the high seas. The Conference must not give increased rights to coastal States by making the EEZ part of their territorial waters. An extension of the scope of application to the EEZ is not possible for pollution risks, since such claims could only be made in an area where States have rights which are protected. The rights of a coastal State in the EEZ are not the same as those rights in its territory. The Law of the Sea Convention gives coastal States certain rights within the EEZ, but other States also have rights in that zone and many States still consider the EEZ part of the high seas. The power to take preventive measures is all that is required to protect the interests of a coastal State. Inclusion of the EEZ would enable States to recover for damage to a considerable area off their coastline, over which they have exclusive rights of exploitation. The legal rights and obligations of States with regard to the EEZ are not yet entirely clear in international law.

3.   To extend the scope to a wider and possibly indeterminate area would weaken the effectiveness of the régime and possibly have a disastrous effect on market capacity; on the contrary, a narrower scope of application would provide for greater clarity, simplicity and foreseeability. The extension of the scope of application to the EEZ will have the effect that insurance premiums will increase and capacity could become more restricted.

4. The text of the article in the draft HNS Convention would create legal uncertainty, if the bracketed words were to be retained. The reference to "international law" does not preclude the possibility of differences of interpretation appearing in regard to the extent of territorial waters or zones in which rights to natural resources are exercised. A clear definition of territorial application is essential so that all parties concerned with the carriage of HNS as well as States will know precisely the extent of the special rules imposed by the proposed Convention.

5. The limitation of the scope of application to the territorial sea and coastal areas is preferable in order to ensure the ratification of the HNS Convention.

* * *

Reference may be made to the solution adopted by the Conference, in respect of the same issue, in the Protocol of 1984 to amend the International Convention of Civil Liability for Oil Pollution Damage, 1969 and the Protocol of 1984 to amend the International Convention on the Establishment of an International Fund for Compensation for Oil Pollution Damage, 1971. Under the compromise adopted by the Conference, the 1984 Protocols extend the scope of application of the 1969/71 régime to cover pollution damage caused "in the exclusive economic zone of a Contracting State, established in accordance with international law, or, if a Contracting State has not established such a zone, in an area beyond and adjacent to the territorial sea of that State determined by that State in accordance with international law and extending not more than 200 nautical miles from the baselines from which the breadth of its territorial sea is measured". This solution may therefore be considered for application in the context of the HNS Convention.

- - - - -

IMO Legal Committee LEG 58/6
58th Session, 1987 Extract

Consideration of the Question of Liability for Damage Caused
by the Maritime Carriage of Hazardous and Noxious Substances
Note by the Secretariat

1. The 1984 International Conference on Liability and Compensation for Damage in Connection with the Carriage of Certain Substances by Sea did not find it feasible, in the time available, to resolve the many complex issues in the draft Convention on Liability and Compensation in Connection with the Carriage of Noxious and Hazardous Substances by Sea (HNS Convention) which was one of the draft instruments submitted to the Conference. However, there was general recognition of the need for an international agreement on the subject. Accordingly, the Conference decided, in a resolution, to send the draft HNS Convention back to IMO for such further action as might be deemed appropriate, taking account of the views and proposals presented during the discussions at the Conference. Specifically, the Conference recommended that IMO, after requesting such opinions as it

might consider necessary, arrange to "prepare a new and more widely acceptable draft for submission to a diplomatic conference which may be convened in the future". The Conference further recommended that IMO assign priority to the preparation of such a new draft. The text of the resolution of the Conference on the matter is reproduced in the annex.

2.　　The recommendations of the 1984 diplomatic conference on the HNS Convention were considered by the Council at its fifty-second and fifty-third sessions. At the fifty-third session, the Council "noted that the discussions of the Conference revealed a number of fundamental issues on which wide differences of opinion remained". The Council invited the Secretary-General to prepare an analysis of these fundamental issues and submit them to the Legal Committee for consideration. The Legal Committee was, in turn, invited to present appropriate recommendations and proposals to the Council on this subject.

3.　　As requested by the Council, the Secretary-General arranged for a study to be prepared on the fundamental issues on which differences of opinion remained. This study was presented in document LEG 55/5 . . .

4.　　After considering the study, the Legal Committee expressed the hope that "Governments and interested organizations might, through informal consultations where appropriate, consider possible new approaches and solutions to the fundamental issues identified in the Secretariat report and submit concrete proposals for consideration by the Legal Committee" (LEG 55/11, paragraph 164). The Committee agreed to consider the subject when such "concrete proposals had been received for resolving the outstanding problems which emerged at the diplomatic conference in 1984". This conclusion was endorsed by the Council, at its fifty-sixth session in June 1986.

5.　　At its fifty-seventh session, the Legal Committee agreed that it might be necessary to give consideration to some aspects of the draft HNS Convention during the 1988-1989 biennium. The Committee, accordingly, recommended the inclusion of the draft HNS Convention on the work programme for that biennium. The Committee noted that work on the draft HNS Convention might involve consideration of certain other subjects, in particular revision of the 1976 Convention on Limitation of Liability for Maritime Claims and the question of compensation for damage from fire and explosion on board nuclear tankers. It was again emphasized in the Committee that "substantive work would be undertaken only on the basis of concrete proposals for resolving the outstanding problems from the 1984 Diplomatic Conference".

. . .

ANNEX

INTERNATIONAL CONFERENCE ON LIABILITY
AND COMPENSATION FOR DAMAGE IN CONNECTION WITH THE
CARRIAGE OF CERTAIN SUBSTANCES BY SEA

RESOLUTION ON THE DRAFT CONVENTION ON LIABILITY AND
COMPENSATION IN CONNECTION WITH THE CARRIAGE OF NOXIOUS AND
HAZARDOUS SUBSTANCES BY SEA

THE CONFERENCE,

Having considered the draft submitted by the International Maritime Organization (IMO)(LEG/CONF.6/3) and noting that there are differing points of view about many complex issues raised by this draft, and their implications,

Conscious of the risks posed by the carriage of hazardous and noxious substances by sea and the need to adopt uniform international rules to deal with issues of liability and compensation in respect of damage caused by such substances,

Noting with appreciation the strenuous efforts made by the Organization in preparing the draft HNS Convention and the useful work undertaken by Committee of the Whole I and its Chairman during the Conference,

1.   *Decides* that the draft be sent to IMO so that the Organization, taking into consideration all that has been stated in Committee of the Whole I, and after requesting such opinions as it may consider necessary, may arrange to prepare a new and more widely acceptable draft for submission to a diplomatic conference which may be convened in the future;

2.   *Recommends* that the Organization assign priority to the preparation of such a new draft, and arrange for a diplomatic conference to examine the new draft at the earliest possible time.

- - - - -

IMO Legal Committee
Report of the 58th Session, October 1987

LEG 58/12
Extract

. . .

F. Consideration of the Question of Liability for Damage Caused by the Maritime Carriage of Hazardous and Noxious Substances

. . .

110.   The Committee used, as the basis of its discussions, document LEG 58/6/1 which had been submitted by the delegations of Canada, Denmark, Finland, France, the German Democratic Republic, the Federal Republic of Germany, the Netherlands, Poland, Sweden and Switzerland.

. . .

112.   Most delegations expressed support for the "basic requirements for any new system of liability" as set out in paragraph 6 of document LEG 58/6/1 which were that:

  (i)   packages should be covered by the new instrument;
  (ii)   liability should rest with an easily identifiable party;
  (iii)   as far as practicable, liability should be strict; and
  (iv)   any limit of liability should be sufficiently high to provide adequate compensation for HNS damage.

113.   Some delegations were of the view that packaged goods should not be included in the convention. One of these delegations doubted whether it was practicable to arrange insurance

for all packaged dangerous goods carried by sea or to require the shipowner to ensure that all HNS packages carried on his ship would be covered by appropriate insurance.

114.   The suggestion was made that the inclusion of packaged substances in the scope of application of a new HNS convention could have far-reaching implications which deserved serious study.

    . . .

116.   Many delegations expressed a preliminary preference for placing the liability on the shipowner alone, without involving the shipper or cargo interests. Some delegations favoured the system of shared shipper and shipowner liability which, in their view, took account both of risks posed by transportation as well as risks posed by hazards inherent in certain substances. For these reasons some of these latter delegations considered that it would be unfair to impose liability either solely on the shipowner or entirely on the cargo interests.

117.   The observer from the European Council of Chemical Manufacturers Federation (CEFIC) as well as the French delegation referred to a similar draft which had been prepared by the International Institute for the Unification of Private Law (UNIDROIT) regarding the carriage of HNS substances by land and inland navigation, and stated that the legal responsibility and liability for HNS damage should lie in the right place, i.e. on the carrier.

118.   Some delegations expressed keen interest in the approach under which damage caused by HNS substances would be covered by a revision of the Convention on Limitation of Liability for Maritime Claims, 1976, with a view either to raising the existing global limitation ceiling to cover HNS damage, or to establishing a special layer of liability for HNS damage on top of the global limitation. In this connection, many delegations expressed the view that any such increased limitation amount, should be sufficient to compensate victims adequately for HNS damage, as well as meeting claims for other damage.

119.   One delegation, however, warned against any increase in the global limitation of the 1976 Convention to such a high extent that it had the effect of imposing unlimited liability for most incidents. This delegation suggested that, to avoid this, it might be useful to consider applying higher limits for any damage which occurred "during the carriage" of HNS by sea, unless the shipowner was able to prove that the carriage of HNS was irrelevant to the incident causing the damage and to any damage resulting therefrom.

120.   One delegation expressed the view that the options presented in document LEG 58/6/1 did not represent new approaches for resolving the fundamental issues which had emerged at the diplomatic conference in 1984.

121.   Some delegations stated that certain issues, other than those enumerated in LEG 58/6/1, would need to be addressed in any future work on the HNS Convention. The additional issues suggested for consideration included a definition for hazardous or noxious substances, the possible coverage of damage by fire and explosion, and the geographical scope of application of any new convention.

    . . .

125.   Many delegations were in favour of further work toward an international system of liability. In their view, it was preferable for IMO to develop such a system without waiting for a major catastrophe involving HNS substances. Furthermore, the establishment of such a

system internationally would discourage and prevent the proliferation of unilateral and unco-ordinated national systems.

. . .

128.   The vast majority of the Legal Committee accepted that work on the HNS Convention should be kept on the work programme for the 1988-1989 biennium, and that the subject should retain its priority.

. . .

- - - - -

Additional References

Protocol of 1984 to Amend the 1969 International Convention on Civil Liability for Oil Pollution Damage; Protocol of 1984 to Amend the 1971 International Convention on the Establishment of an International Fund for Compensation for Oil Pollution Damage; Resolution on the Draft Convention on Liability and Compensation in Connection with the Carriage of Noxious and Hazardous Substances by Sea. IMO publication Sales No. 456.85. 15.E.

1984 Protocols to the Civil Liability Convention and Fund Convention. Treaty Law Aspects of the Revision of the CLC and IOPC Fund Convention. LEG 55/10.

Proposals submitted by the International Association of Classification Societies (IACS). LEG 58/6/2.

Consideration of the question of liability for damage caused by the maritime carriage of hazardous and noxious substances. "Liability for damage caused by the escape of dangerous cargoes from ships" by Z.Brodecki. LEG 58/6/3.

- - - - -

Dumping and Incineration at Sea

Ad Hoc Group of Legal Experts on Dumping   LDC/LG 3/4
Report of the Third Meeting   22 October 1987
                                                             Extract

===

. . .

3.   Procedures for the Assessment of Liability for Environmental Damage Resulting From Dumping and Incineration of Wastes and Other Matter at Sea (LDC Article X)

3.1   The group had before it papers submitted by Spain (LDC/IGPRAD 1/3/18), Australia (LDC/LG 3/INF.2) and Nauru (LDC/IGPRAD 1/3/19). . . .

. . .

3.3   Some experts felt that the wording "procedures for the assessment of liability" in article X of the LDC was obscure; the Chairman, however, explained that article X had been included because of difficulties in solving problems of liability at the time of the 1972 Conference and that the phrase should be taken to mean a régime of liability as such for the purpose of the Convention.

3.4   The group agreed that the liability régime envisaged under article X of the LDC is concerned with the damage caused by dumping conducted under the LDC. The group recognized that if such a régime were to be developed, it would involve very difficult and complex issues. One expert thought that the issues were not insurmountable and a régime could be developed expeditiously, if there is a will.

3.5   Some experts considered that the all embracing provision of article II of the LDC concerning the effectiveness of the measures taken under the Convention would apply to whatever liability régime, if any, is established. They also doubted whether any régime which might be established at this stage would be effective and felt that preventive measures are more effective and useful and priority should therefore be given to preventive and/or regulatory activities.

3.6   Other experts thought that in the absence of collectively effective measures established under Article II of the LDC, the problem of developing a régime for liability and compensation should be studied in order to eventually establish such a system.

3.7   It was pointed out that in the 11 years of the existence of the LDC, there had been no established record of international claims being made concerning damages caused by authorized dumping. This could be due to the fact that any dumping conducted under the requirements of the LDC had been authorized and permitted after careful consideration by national authorities.

3.8   Some other experts argued that the reasons for no claims having been presented might have been due to the absence of rules of liability and that there were cases of dumping of wastes causing harm to the marine environment. A number of cases of nuclear accidents or incidents (although not from dumping activities) were cited. They felt that there is a proven need for a régime of liability under the LDC and stressed that the work of elaboration of such a régime should be undertaken without awaiting a future disaster.

3.9   The expert from Spain stated that the development of procedures for the assessment of liability, in accordance with the principles of international law regarding State responsibility for damage to the environment resulting from dumping, constitutes for the Contracting Parties to the LDC, a legal commitment which is expressed in a variety of legal texts, in particular, point 7 of resolution LDC 21(9). In his view resolution LDC 21(9) constitutes the beginning of a new phase in the history of the LDC, in which phase new attention is to be paid to States' responsibility and liability for damages resulting from dumping.

3.10   With regard to the question of what other international treaties were available or being formulated in the field of liability régimes considered by the group, the group was informed of the experience of Baltic States which, under article 17 of the Helsinki Convention, are considering the issue of developing rules concerning responsibility for damage in the marine environment of the Baltic Sea area. Their experience showed that if a régime were to be developed under the LDC, it would require long and concentrated efforts and that the elaboration of a régime in the LDC forum may be helpful to the regional organizations. Furthermore, the group was informed that an "Inventory concerning existing international agreements and international work currently in progress pertaining to liability for damage caused by marine pollution" had been prepared within the Helsinki Commission in 1983 and that the inventory is expected to be updated by the Helsinki Commission Secretariat.

3.11   The group then decided to discuss further the present state of international law, in order to ascertain the need for development of a new liability régime.   The group was informed of the work done within other fora which may cover certain aspects of the work envisaged by article X of the LDC, such as in the International Law Commission (international liability for injurious consequences arising out of acts not prohibited by international law as well as State responsibility) and the matter of State liability for nuclear damage was also being considered by IAEA.

3.12   The group was informed by the IMO Legal Officer of the present status of developments of the proposed international convention on the liability for damage caused by the maritime carriage of hazardous and noxious substances (HNS). . . .

3.13   The representative of OECD/NEA provided information regarding the application of nuclear civil liability conventions to the dumping of radioactive waste.   The régime of civil liability for nuclear damage is based mostly on the 1960 Paris Convention (entered into force in 1968), grouping 15 countries in Western Europe, and the world-wide 1963 Vienna Convention (entered into force in 1977) which has at present 10 Contracting Parties. Both Conventions, which have very similar provisions, establish a system of strict and inclusive liability of the nuclear operator.   As it appears from the work of competent international organizations, these Conventions cover damage likely to result from radioactive waste disposed at sea, since radioactive wastes are nuclear materials in the meaning of the Conventions.   Both Conventions apply also to the high seas.   It was recently confirmed by the Parties to the Paris Convention that the latter applied to the final disposal of radioactive waste and, as a consequence, to the sea dumping of such waste.

3.14   The OECD/NEA representative indicated, however, that implementation of the Paris and Vienna Civil Liability Conventions in the context of dumping might raise certain difficulties such as:

-   Identification of the operator liable when there are wastes of different origins;
-   Determination of damage effectively suffered, in particular in the case of extra-patrimonial damage to the marine environment;
-   Limitation in time of the operator's liability and the related question of obtaining insurance cover on the market.

3.15   The OECD/NEA representative also indicated that for dumping operations of low-level radioactive waste which took place in the North Atlantic in the years 1967/1982, a financial guarantee had been obtained to cover liability for nuclear damage.   In fact, with the exception of one country, all countries taking part in such operations were Parties to the above Paris Convention.   He also added that his statement was not in any way intended to imply a judgement concerning the merits and desirability of an international State liability system.

3.16   The expert from Spain was of the opinion that according to articles VI and VII of the LDC, dumping activities are always "State conduct", that is to say activities attributable to the authorizing and controlling State in the light of the rules of international law. He referred to the work of the UN International Law Commission, concerning international responsibility of States (see also the Spanish submission). The OECD/IAEA liability Conventions, however, refer only to questions of civil liability of private parties under national laws and not to matters of international responsibility and liability of States under public international law, a point which is formally excluded both by the Paris Convention (Annex II) and the Vienna Convention (article XVIII).

3.17   The expert from Spain, therefore, felt that the Paris and Vienna Conventions do not provide an appropriate legal framework for dealing with matters concerning a State's responsibility and liability resulting from dumping at sea. In his view the legal focus of these conventions is not clearly on dumping, therefore they could only be taken into consideration in a very dubious and distorted way (by analogy) and they consider only matters of civil damage but not the damage to the marine environment or ecological damage which constitutes the specific concern of the LDC. The expert from Nauru supported the views and opinions expressed by the Spanish expert . . .

3.18   Some experts considered that the Paris and Vienna Conventions and other international principles were relevant. Furthermore, note was made of the recourse under national law. In this respect, mention was made of article 235.2 of UNCLOS which says that States shall ensure that recourse is available in accordance with their legal systems for prompt and adequate compensation or other relief in respect of damage caused by pollution of the marine environment by natural or juridical persons under their jurisdiction. Also, some experts stated that if a liability régime were to be established under the LDC, the concept of State liability concerning dumping operations conducted by private persons or companies would be unacceptable.

3.19   A clear division of views persisted throughout the discussion of this agenda item, in that some experts considered that by resolution LDC.21(9), paragraph 7, the group was given a clear instruction to develop a régime of liability in accordance with article X of the LDC, while most of the experts considered either that elaboration of a liability régime was not needed, or that it remained an open question and that it would be premature to embark upon the exercise of establishing such a régime.

3.20   Because of the above-mentioned majority view there was no substantive discussion of the papers submitted. The group, nevertheless, agreed that the valuable work done by Australia, Nauru and Spain should be retained for any further consideration of the liability régime under the LDC.

. . .

- - - - -

6

Developments in Regional Seas Agreements

East Africa Region

Register of International Treaties and
   Other Agreements in the Field of the Environment

UNEP/GC/INFORMATION/
11/Rev.1/Supplement 1
1 April 1987

Convention for the Protection, Management and Development of the Marine and Coastal Environment of the Eastern African Region

Objectives

To protect and manage the marine environment and coastal areas of the Eastern African region.

Provisions

The parties agree to:

(a) Take all appropriate measures to prevent, reduce and combat pollution of the Convention area (art. 4), particularly pollution from ships (art. 5), pollution caused by dumping (art. 6), pollution from land-based sources (art. 7), pollution from sea-bed activities (art. 8), and airborne pollution (art. 9);

(b) Protect and preserve rare or fragile ecosystems as well as the habitat of depleted, threatened or endangered species and other marine life in specially protected areas (art. 10);

(c) Co-operate in dealing with pollution emergencies in the Convention area (art. 11)

(d) Take all appropriate measures to prevent, reduce and combat environmental damage in the Convention area resulting from dredging, land reclamation, and other engineering activities (art. 12);

(e) Develop guidelines for the planning of major development projects in the Convention area, assess the environmental effects of development projects likely to cause significant adverse changes in the Convention area, and develop procedures for dissemination of information and consultation among the parties in such assessments (art. 13);

(f) Co-operate in scientific research and monitoring in the Convention area, and in the exchange of data collected (art. 14);

(g) Co-operate in the development of rules and procedures to govern liability and compensation for damage caused by pollution in the Convention area (art. 15);

(h)   Designate UNEP to discharge secretariat functions under the Convention (art. 16);

The Convention includes an annex, establishing arbitration procedures for resolution of disputes between the contracting parties.

Membership

Open to any State invited as a participant to the Conference of Plenipotentiaries on the Protection, Management and Development of the Marine and Coastal Environment of the Eastern African Region, held at Nairobi from 17 to 21 June 1985, and to any regional intergovernmental integration organization invited to the Conference which exercises competence in the fields covered by the Convention and having at least one member which belongs to the Eastern African region.

- - - - -

PROTOCOL CONCERNING PROTECTED AREAS AND WILD FAUNA AND FLORA IN THE EASTERN AFRICAN REGION

Objective

To provide for the protection of threatened and endangered species of flora and fauna, and important natural habitats, in the Eastern African region.

Provisions

The parties agree to:

(a)   Take all appropriate measures to protect the endangered species of flora and fauna listed in annexes I and II to the Protocol against capture, killing, destruction of habitat, possession, and sale (arts. 3 and 4);

(b)   Regulate the harvest and sale of threatened or depleted fauna species, listed in Annex III, and protect critical habitats of breeding stocks of such species (art. 5);

(c)   Co-ordinate efforts to protect the migratory species listed in annex IV (art. 6);

(d)   Take measures to prevent the introduction of potentially harmful alien or new species (art. 7);

(e)   As necessary, establish protected areas to safeguard important ecosystems, including particularly those ecosystems that provide habitat for species of fauna and flora that are endangered, endemic, migratory, or economically important (art. 8), taking into account traditional activities of local populations (art. 12);

(f)   Co-operate in development of guidelines for selection and management of protected areas (arts. 9 and 10), and co-ordinate the establishment of such areas to ensure adequate protection for frontier areas and the creation of a representative network of protected areas in the region (arts. 13 and 16);

(g) Take measures to ensure that the public is informed about protected areas, and has the opportunity to participate in protection efforts (arts. 14 and 15), and to encourage scientific research (art. 17);

(h) Provide the Convention secretariat with information about their activities under the Protocol and the results of relevant scientific research, and co-operate in providing technical and management assistance to each other (arts. 18 and 19).

The Protocol has four annexes, listing the protected species of wild flora (annex I), the species of wild fauna requiring special protection (annex II), the harvestable species of wild fauna requiring protection (annex III), and the protected migratory species (annex IV).

Membership

Open to contracting parties to the Convention for the Protection, Management and Development of the Marine and Coastal Environment of the Eastern African Region.

- - - - -

PROTOCOL CONCERNING CO-OPERATION IN COMBATING MARINE POLLUTION IN CASES OF EMERGENCY IN THE EASTERN AFRICAN REGION

Objective

To provide a framework for co-ordinated response in the event of major spillages of oil and other harmful substances in the Convention area.

Provisions

The parties agree to:

(a) Co-operate in undertaking all necessary measures to prevent and remedy marine pollution incidents, including the development of legislation and contingency plans, and the exchange of relevant information (arts. 3 and 4);

(b) Establish procedures for the rapid reporting of marine pollution incidents (art. 5);

(c) Provide assistance to each other in the event of a marine pollution incident (art. 6);

(d) Provide for prompt response to marine pollution incidents, through such measures as assessment, notification, consultation, and remedy of the incident (art. 7), to be undertaken through subregional agreements, as appropriate (art. 8);

(e) The Convention secretariat (UNEP) shall co-ordinate and otherwise assist activities under the Protocol (art. 9);

The Protocol has one annex, specifying guidelines for reporting marine pollution incidents pursuant to article 5.

Membership

Open to contracting parties to the Convention for the Protection, Management and Development of the Marine and Coastal Environment of the Eastern African Region.

- - - - -

South Pacific Region

Communiqué of the Seventeenth South Pacific Forum
Suva, Fiji, 8-11 August 1986   **Extract**

. . .

South Pacific Regional Environment Programme (SPREP)

17. The Forum reaffirmed its strong opposition to the dumping of all radio-active waste at sea and to nuclear testing. The Forum examined progress on the negotiation of a SPREP Convention and reaffirmed its commitment to an early conclusion.

18. The Forum directed officials, in addition to working for a total prohibition of dumping of radio-active waste, to deal with the question of testing in the SPREP Convention as follows:

(a) They should ensure that the Conference made clear that the opposition of Forum countries to testing continues unchanged.

(b) They should endeavour to negotiate general agreement, including the agreement from France, that the SPREP Convention will prohibit environmental pollution from nuclear testing.

(c) If (b) is not acceptable to all, officials should revert to pressing for a complete ban on testing as such.

19. The Forum noted that once that Convention was adopted and entered into force it would complement Article 7 of the South Pacific Nuclear Free Zone Treaty which would prohibit sea dumping in areas not covered by the SPREP Convention.

. . .

- - - - -

Convention for the Protection of the Natural Resources and Environment of the South Pacific Region

The Parties,

Fully aware of the economic and social value of the natural resources of the environment of the South Pacific Region;

Taking into account the traditions and cultures of the Pacific people as expressed in accepted customs and practices;

Conscious of their responsibility to preserve their natural heritage for the benefit and enjoyment of present and future generations;

Recognizing the special hydrological, geological and ecological characteristics of the region which require special care and responsible management;

Recognizing further the threat to the marine and coastal environment, its ecological equilibrium, resources and legitimate uses posed by pollution and by the insufficient integration of an environmental dimension into the development process;

Seeking to ensure that resource development shall be in harmony with the maintenance of the unique environmental quality of the region and the evolving principles of sustained resource management;

Realizing fully the need for co-operation amongst themselves and with competent international, regional and subregional organizations in order to ensure a co-ordinated and comprehensive development of the natural resources of the region;

Recognizing the desirability for the wider acceptance and national implementation of international agreements already in existence concerning the marine and coastal environment;

Noting, however, that existing international agreements concerning the marine and coastal environment do not cover, in spite of the progress achieved, all aspects and sources of marine pollution and environmental degradation and do not entirely meet the special requirements of the South Pacific Region;

Desirous to adopt the regional convention to strengthen the implementation of the general objectives of the Action Plan for Managing the Natural Resources and Environment of the South Pacific Region adopted at Rarotonga, Cook Islands, on 11 March 1982;

Have agreed as follows:

Article 1
GEOGRAPHICAL COVERAGE

1.   This Convention shall apply to the South Pacific Region, hereinafter referred to as "the Convention Area" as defined in paragraph (a) of article 2.

2.   Except as may be otherwise provided in any Protocol to this Convention, the Convention Area shall not include internal waters or archipelagic waters of the Parties as defined in accordance with international law.

Article 2
DEFINITIONS

For the purposes of this Convention and its Protocols unless otherwise defined in any such Protocol:

(a)   The "Convention Area" shall comprise:

   (i)   the 200-nautical-mile zones established in accordance with international law off:

   American Samoa; Australia (East Coast and Islands to eastward including Macquarie Island); Cook Islands; Federated States of Micronesia; Fiji; French Polynesia; Guam; Kiribati; Marshall Islands; Nauru; New Caledonia and Dependencies; New Zealand; Niue; Northern Mariana Islands; Palau; Papua New Guinea; Pitcairn Islands; Solomon Islands; Tokelau; Tonga; Tuvalu; Vanuatu; Wallis and Futuna; and Western Samoa;

   (ii)   those areas of high seas which are enclosed from all sides by the 200-nautical-mile zones referred to in subparagraph (i);

   (iii)   areas of the Pacific Ocean which have been included in the Convention Area pursuant to article 3;

(b)   "dumping" means:

   -   any deliberate disposal at sea of wastes or other matter from vessels, aircraft, platforms or other man-made structures at sea;

   -   any deliberate disposal at sea of vessels, aircraft, platforms or other man-made structures at sea;

"dumping" does not include:

   -   the disposal of wastes or other matter incidental to, or derived from the normal operations of vessels, aircraft, platforms or other man-made structures at sea and their equipment, other than wastes or other matter transported by or to vessels, aircraft, platforms or other man-made structures at sea, operating for the purpose of disposal of such matter or derived from the treatment of such wastes or other matter on such vessels, aircraft, platforms or structures;

   -   placement of matter for a purpose other than the mere disposal thereof, provided that such placement is not contrary to the aims of this Convention;

(c)   "wastes or other matter" means material and substances of any kind, form or description;

(d)   The following wastes or other matter shall be considered to be non-radioactive: sewage sludge, dredge spoil, fly ash, agricultural wastes, construction materials, vessels, artificial reef building materials and other such materials, provided that they have not been contaminated with radio nuclides of anthropogenic origin (except dispersed global fall-out from nuclear weapons testing), nor are potential sources of naturally occurring radio nuclides for commercial purposes, nor have been enriched in natural or artificial radio nuclides;

If there is a question as to whether the material to be dumped should be considered non-radioactive, for the purposes of this Convention, such material shall not be dumped unless the appropriate national authority of the proposed dumper confirms that such dumping would not exceed the individual and collective dose limits of the International Atomic Energy Agency general principles for the exemption of radiation sources and practices from regulatory control. The national authority shall also take into account the relevant recommendations, standards and guidelines developed by the International Atomic Energy Agency;

(e) "vessels" and "aircraft" means waterborne or airborne craft of any type whatsoever. This expression includes air-cushioned craft and floating craft, whether self-propelled or not;

(f) "pollution" means the introduction by man, directly or indirectly, of substances or energy into the marine environment (including estuaries) which results or is likely to result in such deleterious effects as harm to living resources and marine life, hazards to human health, hindrance to marine activities, including fishing and other legitimate uses of the sea, impairment of quality for use of sea water and reduction of amenities;

In applying this definition to the Convention obligations, the Parties shall use their best endeavours to comply with the appropriate standards and recommendations established by competent international organizations, including the International Atomic Energy Agency;

(g) "Organization" means the South Pacific Commission;

(h) "Director" means the Director of the South Pacific Bureau for Economic Co-operation.

Article 3
ADDITION TO THE CONVENTION AREA

Any Party may add areas under its jurisdiction within the Pacific Ocean between the Tropic of Cancer and 60 degrees south latitude and between 130 degrees east longitude and 120 degrees west longitude to the Convention Area. Such addition shall be notified to the Depositary who shall promptly notify the other Parties and the Organization. Such areas shall be incorporated within the Convention Area ninety days after notification to the Parties by the Depositary, provided there has been no objection to the proposal to add new areas by any Party affected by that proposal. If there is any such objection the Parties concerned will consult with a view to resolving the matter.

Article 4
GENERAL PROVISIONS

1. The Parties shall endeavour to conclude bilateral or multilateral agreements, including regional or subregional agreements, for the protection, development and management of the marine and coastal environment of the Convention Area. Such agreements shall be consistent with this Convention and in accordance with international law. Copies of such agreements shall be communicated to the Organization and through it to all Parties to this Convention.

2. Nothing in this Convention or its Protocols shall be deemed to affect obligations assumed by a Party under agreements previously concluded.

3.   Nothing in this Convention and its Protocols shall be construed to prejudice or affect the interpretation and application of any provision or term in the Convention on the Prevention of Marine Pollution by Dumping of Wastes and Other Matter, 1972.

4.   This Convention and its Protocols shall be construed in accordance with international law relating to their subject-matter.

5.   Nothing in this Convention and its Protocols shall prejudice the present or future claims and legal views of any Party concerning the nature and extent of maritime jurisdiction.

6.   Nothing in this Convention shall affect the sovereign right of States to exploit, develop and manage their own natural resources pursuant to their own policies, taking into account their duty to protect and preserve the environment. Each Party shall ensure that activities within its jurisdiction or control do not cause damage to the environment of other States or of areas beyond the limits of its national jurisdiction.

Article 5
GENERAL OBLIGATIONS

1.   The Parties shall endeavour, either individually or jointly, to take all appropriate measures in conformity with international law and in accordance with this Convention and those Protocols in force to which they are party to prevent, reduce and control pollution of the Convention Area, from any source, and to ensure sound environmental management and development of natural resources, using for this purpose the best practicable means at their disposal, and in accordance with their capabilities. In doing so the Parties shall endeavour to harmonize their policies at the regional level.

2.   The Parties shall use their best endeavours to ensure that the implementation of this Convention shall not result in an increase in pollution in the marine environment outside the Convention Area.

3.   In addition to the Protocol for the Prevention of Pollution of the South Pacific Region by Dumping and the Protocol Concerning Co-operation in Combating Pollution Emergencies in the South Pacific Region, the Parties shall co-operate in the formulation and adoption of other Protocols prescribing agreed measures, procedures and standards to prevent, reduce and control pollution from all sources or in promoting environmental management in conformity with the objectives of this Convention.

4.   The Parties shall, taking into account existing internationally recognized rules, standards, practices and procedures, co-operate with competent global, regional and subregional organizations to establish and adopt recommended practices, procedures and measures to prevent, reduce and control pollution from all sources and to promote sustained resource management and to ensure the sound development of natural resources in conformity with the objectives of this Convention and its Protocols, and to assist each other in fulfilling their obligations under this Convention and its Protocols.

5.   The Parties shall endeavour to establish laws and regulations for the effective discharge of the obligations prescribed in this Convention. Such laws and regulations shall be no less effective than international rules, standards and recommended practices and procedures.

Article 6
POLLUTION FROM VESSELS

The Parties shall take all appropriate measures to prevent, reduce and control pollution in the Convention Area caused by discharges from vessels, and to ensure the effective application in the Convention Area of the generally accepted international rules and standards established through the competent international organization or general diplomatic conference relating to the control of pollution from vessels.

Article 7
POLLUTION FROM LAND-BASED SOURCES

The Parties shall take all appropriate measures to prevent, reduce and control pollution in the Convention Area caused by coastal disposal or by discharges emanating from rivers, estuaries, coastal establishments, outfall structures, or any other sources in their territory.

Article 8
POLLUTION FROM SEA-BED ACTIVITIES

The Parties shall take all appropriate measures to prevent, reduce and control pollution in the Convention Area resulting directly or indirectly from exploration and exploitation of the sea-bed and its subsoil.

Article 9
AIRBORNE POLLUTION

The Parties shall take all appropriate measures to prevent, reduce and control pollution in the Convention Area resulting from discharges into the atmosphere from activities under their jurisdiction.

Article 10
DISPOSAL OF WASTES

1.   The Parties shall take all appropriate measures to prevent, reduce and control pollution in the Convention Area caused by dumping from vessels, aircraft, or man-made structures at sea, including the effective application of the relevant internationally recognized rules and procedures relating to the control of dumping of wastes and other matter. The Parties agree to prohibit the dumping of radioactive wastes or other radioactive matter in the Convention Area. Without prejudice to whether or not disposal into the sea-bed and subsoil of wastes or other matter is "dumping", the Parties agree to prohibit the disposal into the sea-bed and subsoil of the Convention Area of radioactive wastes or other radioactive matter.

2.   This article shall also apply to the continental shelf of a Party where it extends, in accordance with international law, outward beyond the Convention Area.

Article 11
STORAGE OF TOXIC AND HAZARDOUS WASTES

The Parties shall take all appropriate measures to prevent, reduce and control pollution in the Convention Area resulting from the storage of toxic and hazardous wastes. In particular, the Parties shall prohibit the storage of radioactive wastes or other radioactive matter in the Convention Area.

Article 12
TESTING OF NUCLEAR DEVICES

The Parties shall take all appropriate measures to prevent, reduce and control pollution in the Convention Area which might result from the testing of nuclear devices.

Article 13
MINING AND COASTAL EROSION

The Parties shall take all appropriate measures to prevent, reduce and control environmental damage in the Convention Area, in particular coastal erosion caused by coastal engineering, mining activities, sand removal, land reclamation and dredging.

Article 14
SPECIALLY PROTECTED AREAS AND PROTECTION OF WILD FLORA AND FAUNA

The Parties shall, individually or jointly, take all appropriate measures to protect and preserve rare or fragile ecosystems and depleted, threatened or endangered flora and fauna as well as their habitat in the Convention Area. To this end, the Parties shall, as appropriate, establish protected areas, such as parks and reserves, and prohibit or regulate any activity likely to have adverse effects on the species, ecosystems or biological processes that such areas are designed to protect. The establishment of such areas shall not affect the rights of other Parties or third States under international law. In addition, the Parties shall exchange information concerning the administration and management of such areas.

Article 15
CO-OPERATION IN COMBATING POLLUTION IN CASES OF EMERGENCY

1.   The Parties shall co-operate in taking all necessary measures to deal with pollution emergencies in the Convention Area, whatever the cause of such emergencies, and to prevent, reduce and control pollution or the threat of pollution resulting therefrom. To this end, the Parties shall develop and promote individual contingency plans and joint contingency plans for responding to incidents involving pollution or the threat thereof in the Convention Area.

2.   When a Party becomes aware of a case in which the Convention Area is in imminent danger of being polluted or has been polluted, it shall immediately notify other countries and territories it deems likely to be affected by such pollution, as well as the Organization. Furthermore it shall inform, as soon as feasible, such other countries and territories and the Organization of any measures it has itself taken to reduce or control pollution or the threat thereof.

Article 16
ENVIRONMENTAL IMPACT ASSESSMENT

1.   The Parties agree to develop and maintain, with the assistance of competent global, regional and subregional organizations as requested, technical guidelines and legislation giving adequate emphasis to environmental and social factors to facilitate balanced development of

their natural resources and planning of their major projects which might affect the marine environment in such a way as to prevent or minimize harmful impacts on the Convention Area.

2.   Each Party shall, within its capabilities, assess the potential effects of such projects on the marine environment, so that appropriate measures can be taken to prevent any substantial pollution of, or significant and harmful changes within, the Convention Area.

3.   With respect to the assessment referred to in paragraph 2, each Party shall, where appropriate, invite:

(a)   Public comment according to its national procedures;
(b)   Other Parties that may be affected to consult with it and submit comments.

The results of these assessments shall be communicated to the Organization, which shall make them available to interested Parties.

Article 17
SCIENTIFIC AND TECHNICAL CO-OPERATION

1.   The Parties shall co-operate, either directly or with the assistance of competent global, regional and subregional organizations, in scientific research, environmental monitoring, and the exchange of data and other scientific and technical information related to the purposes of the Convention.

2.   In addition, the Parties shall, for the purposes of this Convention, develop and co-ordinate research and monitoring programmes relating to the Convention Area and co-operate, as far as practicable, in the establishment and implementation of regional, subregional and international research programmes.

Article 18
TECHNICAL AND OTHER ASSISTANCE

The Parties undertake to co-operate, directly and when appropriate through the competent global, regional and subregional organizations, in the provision to other Parties of technical and other assistance in fields relating to pollution and sound environmental management of the Convention Area, taking into account the special needs of the island developing countries and territories.

Article 19
TRANSMISSION OF INFORMATION

The Parties shall transmit to the Organization information on the measures adopted by them in the implementation of this Convention and of Protocols to which they are Parties, in such form and at such intervals as the Parties may determine.

Article 20
LIABILITY AND COMPENSATION

The Parties shall co-operate in the formulation and adoption of appropriate rules and procedures in conformity with international law in respect of liability and compensation for damage resulting from pollution of the Convention Area.

Article 21
INSTITUTIONAL ARRANGEMENTS

1.   The Organization shall be responsible for carrying out the following secretariat functions:

(a)   To prepare and convene the meetings of Parties;

(b)   To transmit to the Parties notifications, reports and other information received in accordance with this Convention and its Protocols;

(c)   To perform the functions assigned to it by the Protocols to this Convention;

(d)   To consider enquiries by, and information from, the Parties and to consult with them on questions relating to this Convention and the Protocols;

(e)   To co-ordinate the implementation of co-operative activities agreed upon by the Parties;

(f)   To ensure the necessary co-ordination with other competent global, regional and subregional bodies;

(g)   To enter into such administrative arrangements as may be required for the effective discharge of the secretariat functions;

(h)   To perform such other functions as may be assigned to it by the Parties; and

(i)   To transmit to the South Pacific Conference and the South Pacific Forum the reports of ordinary and extraordinary meetings of the Parties.

2.   Each Party shall designate an appropriate national authority to serve as the channel of communication with the Organization for the purposes of this Convention.

Article 22
MEETINGS OF THE PARTIES

1.   The Parties shall hold ordinary meetings once every two years. Ordinary meetings shall review the implementation of this Convention and its Protocols and, in particular, shall:

(a)   Assess periodically the state of the environment in the Convention Area;

(b)   Consider the information submitted by the Parties under article 19;

(c) Adopt, review and amend as required annexes to this Convention and to its Protocols, in accordance with the provisions of article 25;

(d) Make recommendations regarding the adoption of any Protocols or any amendments to this Convention or its Protocols in accordance with the provisions of articles 23 and 24;

(e) Establish working groups as required to consider any matters concerning this Convention and its Protocols;

(f) Consider co-operative activities to be undertaken within the framework of this Convention and its Protocols, including their financial and institutional implications and to adopt decisions relating thereto;

(g) Consider and undertake any additional action that may be required for the achievement of the purposes of this Convention and its Protocols; and

(h) Adopt by consensus financial rules and budget, prepared in consultation with the Organization, to determine, *inter alia*, the financial participation of the Parties under this Convention and those Protocols to which they are party.

2.   The organization shall convene the first ordinary meeting of the Parties not later than one year after the date on which the Convention enters into force in accordance with article 31.

3.   Extraordinary meetings shall be convened at the request of any Party or upon the request of the Organization, provided that such requests are supported by at least two thirds of the Parties. It shall be the function of an extraordinary meeting of the Parties to consider those items proposed in the request for the holding of the extraordinary meeting and any other items agreed to by all the Parties attending the meeting.

4.   The Parties shall adopt by consensus at their first ordinary meeting, rules of procedure for their meetings.

Article 23
ADOPTION OF PROTOCOLS

1.   The Parties may, at a conference of plenipotentiaries, adopt Protocols to this Convention pursuant to paragraph 3 of article 5.

2.   If so requested by a majority of the Parties, the Organization shall convene a conference of plenipotentiaries for the purpose of adopting Protocols to this Convention.

Article 24
AMENDMENT OF THE CONVENTION AND ITS PROTOCOLS

1.   Any Party may propose amendments to this Convention. Amendments shall be adopted by a conference of plenipotentiaries which shall be convened by the Organization at the request of two thirds of the Parties.

2. Any Party to this Convention may propose amendments to any Protocol. Such amendments shall be adopted by a conference of plenipotentiaries which shall be convened by the Organization at the request of two thirds of the Parties to the Protocol concerned.

3. A proposed amendment to the Convention or any Protocol shall be communicated to the Organization, which shall promptly transmit such proposal for consideration to all the other Parties.

4. A conference of plenipotentiaries to consider a proposed amendment to the Convention or any Protocol shall be convened not less than ninety days after the requirements for the convening of the Conference have been met pursuant to paragraphs 1 or 2, as the case may be.

5. Any amendment to this Convention shall be adopted by a three-fourths majority vote of the Parties to the Convention which are represented at the conference of plenipotentiaries and shall be submitted by the Depositary for acceptance by all Parties to the Convention. Amendments to any Protocol shall be adopted by a three-fourths majority vote of the Parties to the Protocol which are represented at the conference of plenipotentiaries and shall be submitted by the Depositary for acceptance by all Parties to the Protocol.

6. Instruments of ratification, acceptance or approval of amendments shall be deposited with the Depositary. Amendments shall enter into force between Parties having accepted such amendments on the thirtieth day following the date of receipt by the Depositary of the instruments of at least three fourths of the Parties to this Convention or to the Protocol concerned, as the case may be. Thereafter the amendments shall enter into force for any other Party on the thirtieth day after the date on which that Party deposits its instruments.

7. After the entry into force of an amendment to this Convention or to a Protocol, any new Party to the Convention or such protocol shall become a Party to the Convention or Protocol as amended.

Article 25
ANNEXES AND AMENDMENT OF ANNEXES

1. Annexes to this Convention or to any Protocol shall form an integral part of the Convention or such Protocol respectively.

2. Except as may be otherwise provided in any Protocol with respect to its annexes, the following procedures shall apply to the adoption and entry into force of any amendments to annexes to this Convention or to annexes to any Protocol:

(a) Any Party may propose amendments to the annexes to this Convention or annexes to any Protocol;

(b) Any proposed amendment shall be notified by the Organization to the Parties not less than sixty days before the convening of a meeting of the Parties unless this requirement is waived by the meeting;

(c) Such amendments shall be adopted at a meeting of the Parties by a three-fourths majority vote of the Parties to the instrument in question;

(d)   The Depositary shall without delay communicate the amendments so adopted to all Parties;

(e)   Any Party that is unable to approve an amendment to the annexes to this Convention or to annexes to any Protocol shall so notify in writing to the Depositary within one hundred days from the date of the communication of the amendment by the Depositary. A Party may at any time substitute an acceptance for a previous declaration of objection, and the amendment shall thereupon enter into force for that Party;

(f)   The Depositary shall without delay notify all Parties of any notification received pursuant to the preceding subparagraph; and

(g)   On expiry of the period referred to in subparagraph (e) above, the amendment to the annex shall become effective for all Parties to this Convention or to the Protocol concerned which have not submitted a notification in accordance with the provisions of that subparagraph.

3.   The adoption and entry into force of a new annex shall be subject to the same procedure as that for the adoption and entry into force of an amendment to an annex as set out in the provisions of paragraph 2, provided that, if any amendment to the Convention or the Protocol concerned is involved, the new annex shall not enter into force until such time as that amendment enters into force.

4.   Amendments to the Annex on Arbitration shall be considered to be amendments to this Convention or its Protocols and shall be proposed and adopted in accordance with the procedures set out in article 24.

Article 26
SETTLEMENT OF DISPUTES

1.   In case of a dispute between Parties as to the interpretation or application of this Convention or its Protocols, they shall seek a settlement of the dispute through negotiation or any other peaceful means of their own choice. If the Parties concerned cannot reach agreement, they should seek the good offices of, or jointly request mediation by, a third Party.

2.   If the Parties concerned cannot settle their dispute through the means mentioned in paragraph 1, the dispute shall, upon common agreement, except as may be otherwise provided in any Protocol to this Convention, be submitted to arbitration under conditions laid down in the Annex on Arbitration to this Convention. However, failure to reach common agreement on submission of the dispute to arbitration shall not absolve the Parties from the responsibility of continuing to seek to resolve it by means referred to in paragraph 1.

3.   A Party may at any time declare that it recognizes as compulsory *ipso facto* and without special agreement, in relation to any other Party accepting the same obligation, the application of the arbitration procedure set out in the Annex on Arbitration. Such declaration shall be notified in writing to the Depositary who shall promptly communicate it to the other Parties.

Article 27
RELATIONSHIP BETWEEN THIS CONVENTION AND ITS PROTOCOLS

1.   No State may become a Party to this Convention unless it becomes at the same time a Party to one or more Protocols. No State may become a Party to a Protocol unless it is, or becomes at the same time, a Party to this Convention.

2.   Decisions concerning any Protocol pursuant to articles 22, 24 and 25 of this Convention shall be taken only by the Parties to the Protocol concerned.

Article 28
SIGNATURE

This Convention, the Protocol Concerning Co-operation in Combating Pollution Emergencies in the South Pacific Region, and the Protocol for the Prevention of Pollution of the South Pacific Region by Dumping shall be open for signature at the South Pacific Commission Headquarters in Noumea, New Caledonia on 25 November 1986 and at the South Pacific Bureau for Economic Co-operation Headquarters, Suva, Fiji from 26 November 1986 to 25 November 1987 by States which were invited to participate in the Plenipotentiary Meeting of the High-Level Conference on the Protection of the Natural Resources and Environment of the South Pacific Region held at Noumea, New Caledonia from 24 November 1986 to 25 November 1986.

Article 29
RATIFICATION, ACCEPTANCE OR APPROVAL

This Convention and any Protocol thereto shall be subject to ratification, acceptance or approval by States referred to in article 28. Instruments of ratification, acceptance or approval shall be deposited with the Director who shall be the Depositary.

Article 30
ACCESSION

1.   This Convention and any Protocol thereto shall be open to accession by the States referred to in article 28 as from the day following the date on which the Convention or Protocol concerned was closed for signature.

2.   Any State not referred to in paragraph 1 may accede to the Convention and to any Protocol subject to prior approval by three fourths of the Parties to the Convention or the Protocol concerned.

3.   Instruments of accession shall be deposited with the Depositary.

Article 31
ENTRY INTO FORCE

1.   This Convention shall enter into force on the thirtieth day following the date of deposit of at least ten instruments of ratification, acceptance, approval or accession.

2.   Any Protocol to this Convention, except as otherwise provided in such Protocol, shall enter into force on the thirtieth day following the date of deposit of at least five instruments of ratification, acceptance or approval of such Protocol, or of accession thereto, provided that no Protocol shall enter into force before the Convention. Should the requirements for entry into force of a Protocol be met prior to those for entry into force of the Convention pursuant to paragraph 1, such Protocol shall enter into force on the same date as the Convention.

3.   Thereafter, this Convention and any Protocol shall enter into force with respect to any State referred to in articles 28 or 30 on the thirtieth day following the date of deposit of its instrument of ratification, acceptance, approval or accession.

Article 32
DENUNCIATION

1.   At any time after two years from the date of entry into force of this Convention with respect to a Party, that Party may denounce the Convention by giving written notification to the Depositary.

2.   Except as may be otherwise provided in any Protocol to this Convention, any Party may, at any time after two years from the date of entry into force of such Protocol with respect to that Party, denounce the Protocol by giving written notification to the Depositary.

3.   Denunciation shall take effect ninety days after the date on which notification of denunciation is received by the Depositary.

4.   Any Party which denounces this Convention shall be considered as also having denounced any Protocol to which it was a Party.

5.   Any Party which, upon its denunciation of a Protocol, is no longer a Party to any Protocol to this Convention, shall be considered as also having denounced this Convention.

Article 33
RESPONSIBILITIES OF THE DEPOSITARY

1.   The Depositary shall inform the Parties, as well as the Organization:

    (a) Of the signature of this Convention and of any Protocol thereto and of the deposit of instruments of ratification, acceptance, approval or accession in accordance with articles 29 and 30;

    (b) Of the date on which the Convention and any Protocol will come into force in accordance with the provisions of article 31;

    (c) Of notification of denunciation made in accordance with article 32;

    (d) Of notification of any addition to the Convention Area in accordance with article 3;

    (e) Of the amendments adopted with respect to the Convention and to any Protocol, their acceptance by the Parties and the date of their entry into force in accordance with the provisions of article 24; and

(f)   Of the adoption of new annexes and of the amendments of any annex in accordance with article 25.

2.   The original of this Convention and of any Protocol thereto shall be deposited with the Depositary who shall send certified copies thereof to the Signatories, the Parties, to the Organization and to the Secretary-General of the United Nations for registration and publication in accordance with Article 102 of the United Nations Charter.

In Witness Whereof the undersigned, being duly authorized by their respective Governments, have signed this Convention.

Done at Noumea, New Caledonia on the twenty-fourth day of November in the year one thousand nine hundred and eighty-six in a single copy in the English and French languages, the two texts being equally authentic.

ANNEX ON ARBITRATION

Article 1

Unless the agreement referred to in article 26 of the Convention provides otherwise, the arbitration procedure shall be in accordance with the rules set out in this Annex.

Article 2

The claimant Party shall notify the Organization that the Parties have agreed to submit the dispute to arbitration pursuant to paragraph 2, or that paragraph 3 of article 26 of the Convention is applicable. The notification shall state the subject-matter of the arbitration and include the provisions of the Convention or any Protocol thereto, the interpretation or application of which is the subject of disagreement. The Organization shall transmit this information to all Parties to the Convention or Protocol concerned.

Article 3

1.   The Tribunal shall consist of a single arbitrator if so agreed between the Parties to the dispute within thirty days from the date of receipt of the notification for arbitration.

2.   In the case of the death, disability or default of the arbitrator, the Parties to a dispute may agree upon a replacement within thirty days of such death, disability or default.

Article 4

1.   Where the Parties to a dispute do not agree upon a Tribunal in accordance with article 3 of this Annex, the Tribunal shall consist of three members:

(a)   One arbitrator nominated by each Party to the dispute, and

(b)   A third arbitrator who shall be nominated by agreement between the two first named and who shall act as its Chairman.

2.   If the Chairman of a Tribunal is not nominated within thirty days of nomination of the second arbitrator, the Parties to a dispute shall, upon the request of one Party, submit to the Secretary-General of the Organization within a further period of thirty days, an agreed list of qualified persons. The Secretary-General shall select the Chairman from such list as soon as possible. He shall not select a Chairman who is, or has been, a national of one Party to the dispute except with the consent of the other Party to the dispute.

3.   If one Party to a dispute fails to nominate an arbitrator as provided in subparagraph 1 (a) within sixty days from the date of receipt of the notification for arbitration, the other Party may request the submission to the Secretary-General of the Organization within a period of thirty days of an agreed list of qualified persons. The Secretary-General shall select the Chairman of the Tribunal from such list as soon as possible. The Chairman shall then request the Party which has not nominated an arbitrator to do so. If this Party does not nominate an arbitrator within fifteen days of such request, the Secretary-General shall, upon request of the Chairman, nominate the arbitrator from the agreed list of qualified persons.

4.   In the case of the death, disability or default of an arbitrator, the Party to the dispute who nominated him shall nominate a replacement within thirty days of such death, disability or default. If the Party does not nominate a replacement, the arbitration shall proceed with the remaining arbitrators. In the case of the death, disability or default of the Chairman, a replacement shall be nominated in accordance with paragraphs 1 (b) and 2 within ninety days of such death, disability or default.

5.   A list of arbitrators shall be maintained by the Secretary-General of the Organization and composed of qualified persons nominated by the Parties. Each Party may designate for inclusion in the list four persons who shall not necessarily be its nationals. If the Parties to the dispute have failed within the specified time-limits to submit to the Secretary-General an agreed list of qualified persons as provided for in paragraphs 2, 3 and 4, the Secretary-General shall select from the list maintained by him the arbitrator or arbitrators not yet nominated.

Article 5

The Tribunal may hear and determine counter-claims arising directly out of the subject-matter of the dispute.

Article 6

The Tribunal may, at the request of one of the Parties to the dispute, recommend interim measures of protection.

Article 7

Each Party to the dispute shall be responsible for the costs entailed by the preparation of its own case. The remuneration of the members of the Tribunal and of all general expenses incurred by the arbitration shall be borne equally by the Parties to the dispute. The Tribunal shall keep a record of all its expenses and shall furnish a final statement thereof to the Parties.

Article 8

Any Party which has an interest of a legal nature which may be affected by the decision in the case may, after giving written notice to the Parties to the dispute which have originally initiated the procedure, intervene in the arbitration procedure with the consent of the Tribunal which should be freely given. Any intervenor shall participate at its own expense. Any such intervenor shall have the right to present evidence, briefs and oral arguments on the matter giving rise to its intervention, in accordance with procedures established pursuant to article 9 of this Annex, but shall have no rights with respect to the composition of the Tribunal.

Article 9

A Tribunal established under the provisions of this Annex shall decide its own rules of procedure.

Article 10

1. Unless a Tribunal consists of a single arbitrator, decisions of the Tribunal as to its procedure, its place of meeting, and any question related to the dispute laid before it shall be taken by majority vote of its members. However, the absence or abstention of any member of the Tribunal who was nominated by a Party to the dispute shall not constitute an impediment to the Tribunal reaching a decision. In case of equal voting, the vote of the Chairman shall be decisive.

2. The Parties to the dispute shall facilitate the work of the Tribunal and in particular shall, in accordance with their legislation and using all means at their disposal:

(a) Provide the Tribunal with all necessary documents and information, and

(b) Enable the Tribunal to enter their territory, to hear witnesses or experts, and to visit the scene of the subject-matter of the arbitration.

3. The failure of a Party to the dispute to comply with the provisions of paragraph 2 or to defend its case shall not preclude the Tribunal from reaching a decision and rendering an award.

Article 11

The Tribunal shall render its award within five months from the time it is established unless it finds it necessary to extend that time-limit for a period not to exceed five months. The award of the Tribunal shall be accompanied by a statement of reasons for the decision. It shall be final and without appeal and shall be communicated to the Secretary-General of the Organization, who shall inform the Parties. The Parties to the dispute shall immediately comply with the award.

- - - - -

PROTOCOL FOR THE PREVENTION OF POLLUTION OF THE SOUTH PACIFIC REGION BY DUMPING

THE PARTIES TO THE PROTOCOL,

Being parties to the Convention for the Protection of the Natural Resources and Environment of the South Pacific Region . . . ;

Recognizing the danger posed to the marine environment by pollution caused by the dumping of waste or other matter;

Considering that they have a common interest to protect the South Pacific Region from this danger, taking into account the unique environmental quality of the region;

Desiring to enter into a regional agreement consistent with the Convention on the Prevention of Marine Pollution by Dumping of Wastes and Other Matter, 1972, as provided in article VIII thereof, according to which the Contracting Parties to that Convention have undertaken to endeavour to act consistently with the objectives and provisions of such regional agreement;

Have agreed as follows:
. . .

Article 2
GEOGRAPHICAL COVERAGE

The area to which this Protocol applies, hereinafter referred to as the "Protocol Area", shall be the Convention Area as defined in article 2 of the Convention together with the continental shelf of a Party where it extends, in accordance with international law, outward beyond the Convention Area.

Article 3
GENERAL OBLIGATIONS

1.   The Parties shall take all appropriate measures to prevent, reduce and control pollution in the Protocol Area by dumping.

2.   Dumping within the territorial sea and the exclusive economic zone or onto the continental shelf of a Party as defined in international law shall not be carried out without the express prior approval of that Party, which has the right to permit, regulate and control such dumping taking fully into account the provisions of this Protocol, and after due consideration of the matter with other Parties which by reason of their geographical situation may be adversely affected thereby.

3.   National laws, regulations and measures adopted by the Parties shall be no less effective in preventing, reducing and controlling pollution by dumping than the relevant internationally recognized rules and procedures relating to the control of dumping established within the framework of the Convention on the Prevention of Marine Pollution by Dumping of Wastes and Other Matter, 1972.

Article 4
PROHIBITED SUBSTANCES

1.   The dumping in the Protocol Area of wastes or other matter listed in Annex I to this Protocol is prohibited except as provided in this Protocol.

2.   No provision of this Protocol is to be interpreted as preventing a Party from prohibiting, insofar as that Party is concerned, the dumping of wastes or other matter not mentioned in Annex I. That Party shall notify such measures to the Organization.

Article 5
SPECIAL PERMITS

The dumping in the Protocol Area of wastes or other matter listed in Annex II to this Protocol requires, in each case, a prior special permit.

Article 6
GENERAL PERMITS

The dumping in the Protocol Area of all wastes or other matter not listed in Annexes I and II to this Protocol requires a prior general permit.

Article 7
FACTORS GOVERNING THE ISSUE OF PERMITS

The permits referred to in articles 5 and 6 shall be issued only after careful consideration of all the factors set forth in Annex III to this Protocol. The Organization shall receive records of such permits.

Article 8
ALLOCATION OF SUBSTANCES TO ANNEXES

Substances are allocated to Annexes I and II of this Protocol in accordance with Annex IV.

Article 9
FORCE MAJEURE

The provisions of articles 4, 5 and 6 shall not apply when it is necessary to secure the safety of human life or of vessels, aircraft, platforms or other man-made structures at sea in cases of *force majeure* caused by stress of weather, or in any case which constitutes a danger to human life or a real threat to vessels, aircraft, platforms, or other man-made structures at sea, if dumping appears to be the only way of averting the threat and if there is every probability that the damage consequent upon such dumping will be less than would otherwise occur. Such dumping shall be so conducted as to minimize the likelihood of damage to human or marine life. Such dumping shall immediately be reported to the Organization and, either through the Organization or directly, to any Party or Parties likely to be affected, together with full details of the circumstances and of the nature and quantities of the wastes or other matter dumped.

Article 10
EMERGENCIES

1.   A Party may issue a special permit as an exception to article 4, in emergencies arising in the Protocol Area, posing unacceptable risk relating to human health and admitting no other feasible solution. Before doing so the Party shall consult any other country or countries that are likely to be affected and the Organization which, after consultating other Parties, and international organizations as appropriate, shall in accordance with article 15 promptly recommend to the Party the most appropriate procedures to adopt. The Party shall follow these recommendations to the maximum extent feasible consistent with the time within which action must be taken and with the general obligation to avoid damage to the marine environment and shall inform the Organization of the action it takes. The Parties pledge themselves to assist one another in such situations.

2.   This article does not apply with respect to materials in whatever form produced for biological and chemical warfare referred to in paragraph 6 of Section A of Annex I.

3.   Any Party may waive its rights under paragraph 1 at the time of, or subsequent to ratification, acceptance or approval of, or accession to this Protocol.

Article 11
ISSUANCE OF PERMITS

1.   Each Party shall designate an appropriate authority or authorities to:

(a) Issue the special permits provided for in article 5 and in the emergency circumstances provided for in article 10;

(b)   Issue the general permits provided for in article 6;

(c)   Keep records of the nature and quantities of the wastes or other matter permitted to be dumped and of the location, date and method of dumping; and

(d) Monitor individually, or in collaboration with other Parties, and competent international organizations, the condition of the Protocol Area for the purposes of this Protocol.

2.   The appropriate authority or authorities of each Party shall issue the permits provided for in articles 5 and 6 and in the emergency circumstances provided for in article 10 in respect of the wastes or other matter intended for dumping:

(a)   Loaded in its territory or at its offshore terminals; or

(b)   Loaded by vessels flying its flag or vessels or aircraft of its registry when the loading occurs in the territory or at the offshore terminals of a State not party to this Protocol.

3.   In issuing permits under paragraphs 1 (a) and (b) the appropriate authority or authorities shall comply with Annex III together with such additional criteria, measures and requirements as they may consider relevant.

Article 12
IMPLEMENTATION AND ENFORCEMENT

1.　Each Party shall apply the measures required to implement this Protocol to all:

　(a)　Vessels flying its flag and vessels and aircraft of its registry;

　(b)　Vessels and aircraft loading in its territory or at its offshore terminals wastes or other matter which are to be dumped; and

　(c)　Vessels, aircraft and fixed or floating platforms believed to be engaged in dumping in areas under its jurisdiction.

2.　Each Party shall take in its territory appropriate measures to prevent and punish conduct in contravention of the provisions of this Protocol.

3.　The Parties agree to co-operate in the development of procedures for the effective application of this Protocol particularly on the high seas, including procedures for the reporting of vessels and aircraft observed dumping in contravention of the Protocol.

4.　This Protocol shall not apply to those vessels and aircraft entitled to sovereign immunity under international law.　However, each Party shall ensure by the adoption of appropriate measures that such vessels and aircraft owned or operated by it act in a manner consistent with the object and purpose of this Protocol and shall inform the Organization accordingly.

Article 13
ADOPTION OF OTHER MEASURES

Nothing in this Protocol shall affect the right of each Party to adopt other measures, in accordance with the principles of international law, to prevent dumping.

Article 14
REPORTING OF DUMPING INCIDENTS

Each Party undertakes to issue instructions to its maritime inspection vessels and aircraft and to other appropriate services to report to its authorities any incidents or conditions in the Protocol area which give rise to suspicions that dumping in contravention of the provisions of this Protocol has occurred or is about to occur.　That Party shall, if it considers it appropriate, report accordingly to the Organization and to any other Party concerned.

Article 15
INSTITUTIONAL ARRANGEMENTS

The Parties designate the Organization to carry out the following functions:

　(a)　To assist the Parties, upon request, in the communication of reports in accordance with articles 9 and 14;

　(b)　To convey to the Parties concerned all notifications received by the Organization in accordance with articles 4 (2) and 10;

(c) To transmit to the International Maritime Organization as the Organization responsible for the secretariat functions under the Convention on the Prevention of Marine Pollution by Dumping of Wastes and Other Matter, 1972, records and any other information received in accordance with article 7;

(d) To keep itself informed on evolving international standards and the results of research and investigation, and to advise meetings of Parties to the Protocol of such developments and any modification of the Annexes which may become desirable; and

(e) To carry out other duties assigned to it by the Parties.

Article 16
MEETINGS OF THE PARTIES

1.   Ordinary meetings of the Parties to this Protocol shall be held in conjunction with ordinary meetings of the Parties to the Convention held pursuant to article 22 of the Convention. The Parties to this Protocol may also hold extraordinary meetings in conformity with article 22 of the Convention.

2.   It shall be the function of the meetings of the Parties to this Protocol to:

(a) Keep under review the implementation of this Protocol, and to consider the efficacy of the measures adopted and the need for any other measures, in particular in the form of annexes;

(b) Study and consider the records of the permits issued in accordance with articles 5, 6, 7 and the emergency situation in article 10, and of the dumping which has taken place;

(c) Review and amend as required any annex to this Protocol taking into account Annex IV;

(d) Adopt as necessary guidelines for the preparation of records and procedures to be followed in submitting such records for the purposes of article 7;

(e) Develop, adopt and implement in consultation with the Organization and other competent international organizations procedures pursuant to article 10 including basic criteria for determining emergency circumstances and procedures for consultative advice and the safe disposal, storage or destruction of matter in such circumstances;

(f) Invite, as necessary, the appropriate scientific body or bodies to collaborate with and to advise the Parties and the Organization on any scientific or technical aspects relevant to this Protocol, including particularly the content and applicability of the Annexes; and

(g) Perform such other functions as may be appropriate for the implementation of this Protocol.

3.   The adoption of amendments to the Annexes to this Protocol pursuant to article 25 of the Convention shall require a three-fourths majority vote of the Parties to this Protocol.

Article 17
RELATIONSHIP BETWEEN THIS PROTOCOL AND THE CONVENTION

1.   The provisions of the Convention relating to any protocol shall apply with respect to the present Protocol.

. . .

ANNEX I

- A -

The following substances and materials are listed for the purposes of article 4 of this Protocol.

1.   Organohalogen compounds.

2.   Mercury and cadmium compounds.

3.   Cadmium and cadmium compounds.

4.   Persistent plastics and other persistent synthetic materials, for example, netting and ropes, which may remain in suspension in the sea in such a manner as to interfere materially with fishing, navigation or other legitimate uses of the sea.

5.   Crude oil and its wastes, refined petroleum products, petroleum distillate residues and any mixtures containing any of these taken on board for the purpose of dumping.

6.   Materials in whatever form (e.g. solids, liquids, semi-liquids, gases, or in a living state) produced for biological and chemical warfare.

7.   Organophosphorous compounds.

- B -

Section A does not apply to substances, other than substances produced for biological or chemical warfare, which are rapidly rendered harmless by physical, chemical or biological processes in the sea provided they do not:

-    make edible marine organisms unpalatable; or

-    endanger human health or that of marine biota.

The consultative procedure provided for under article 10 shall be followed by a Party if there is doubt about the harmlessness of the substance.

- C -

This Annex does not apply to wastes or other materials, such as sewage sludges and dredged spoils, containing the matters referred to in paragraphs 1 - 5 of Section A as trace contaminants. The dumping of such wastes shall be subject to the provisions of Annexes II and III as appropriate.

ANNEX II

The following substances and materials requiring special care are listed for the purposes of article 5 of this Protocol.

- A -

Wastes containing a significant amount of the matters listed below:

arsenic)
lead   )
copper)   and their compounds
zinc   )

organosilicon compounds
cyanides
fluorides
pesticides and their by-products not covered in Annex I.

- B -

In the issue of permits for the dumping of acids and alkalis, consideration shall be given to the possible presence in such wastes of the substances listed in section A to the following additional substances:

beryllium)
chromium)
nickel   )   and their compounds
vanadium)

- C -

Containers, scrap metal and other bulky wastes liable to sink to the sea bottom which may present a serious obstacle to fishing or navigation. Substances which, though of a non-toxic nature, may become harmful due to the quantities in which they are dumped, or which are liable to seriously reduce amenities.

ANNEX III

Provisions to be considered in establishing criteria governing the issue of permits for the dumping of matter at sea, taking into account article 7 of this Protocol, include:

- A -

Characteristics and Composition of the Matter

1.   Total amount and average composition of matter dumped (e.g. per year).

2.   Form, (e.g. solid, sludge, liquid, or gaseous).

3.   Properties: physical (e.g. solubility and density), chemical and biochemical (e.g. oxygen demand, nutrients) and biological (e.g. presence of viruses, bacteria, yeasts, parasites).

4.   Toxicity.

5.   Persistence: physical, chemical and biological.

6.   Accumulation and biotransformation in biological materials or sediments.

7.   Susceptibility to physical, chemical and biochemical changes and interaction in the aquatic environment with other dissolved organic and inorganic materials.

8.   Probability of production of taints or other changes reducing marketability of resources (e.g. fish, shellfish, etc.).

9.   In issuing a permit for dumping, Parties should consider whether an adequate scientific basis and sufficient knowledge of the composition and characteristics of the waste or other matter proposed for dumping exist for assessing the impact of such material on the marine environment and human health.

- B -

Characteristics of Dumping Site and Method of Deposit

1.   Location (e.g. co-ordinates of the dumping area, depth and distance from the coast), location in relation to other areas (e.g. amenity areas, spawning, nursery and fishing areas and exploitable resources).

2.   Rate of disposal per specific period (e.g. quantity per day, per week, per month).

3.   Methods of packaging and containment, if any.

4.   Initial dilution achieved by proposed method of release.

5.   Dispersal characteristics (e.g. effects of currents, tides and wind on horizontal transport and vertical mixing).

6.   Water characteristics (e.g. temperature, pH, salinity, stratification, oxygen indices of pollution - dissolved oxygen [DO], chemical oxygen demand [COD], biochemical oxygen demand [BOD] - nitrogen present in organic and mineral form including ammonia, suspended matter, other nutrients and productivity).

7.   Bottom characteristics (e.g. topography, geochemical and geological characteristics and biological productivity).

8.   Existence and effects of other dumpings which have been made in the dumping area (e.g. heavy metal background reading and organic carbon content).

9.   In issuing a permit for dumping, Parties should consider whether an adequate scientific basis exists for assessing the consequences of such dumping, as outlined in this Annex, taking into account seasonal variations.

- C -

General Considerations and Conditions

1.   Possible effects on amenities (e.g. presence of floating or stranded materials, turbidity, objectionable odor, discolouration and foaming).

2.   Possible effects on marine life, fish and shellfish culture, fish stocks and fisheries, seaweed harvesting and culture.

3.   Possible effects on other uses of the sea (e.g. impairment of water quality for industrial use, underwater corrosion of structure, interference with ship operations from floating materials, interference with fishing or navigation through deposit of waste or solid objects on the sea floor and protection of areas of special importance for scientific or conservation purposes).

4.   The practical availability of alternative land-based methods of treatment, disposal or elimination, or of treatment to render the matter less harmful for dumping at sea.

- D -

References

Reference should also be made to "Guidelines for the Implementation and Uniform Interpretation of Annex III" as adopted by the Consultative Meeting of Contracting Parties to the Convention on the Prevention of Marine Pollution by Dumping of Wastes and Other Matter, 1972.

ANNEX IV

ALLOCATION OF SUBSTANCES TO ANNEXES

1.   Substances are allocated to Annexes I and II on the grounds of any combination of the following criteria:

Persistence and degradability,
Bioaccumulation potential,
Toxicity to marine life,
Toxicity to man, domestic animals, marine mammals and birds preying on marine organisms,
Carcinogenicity and mutagenicity,
Ability to interfere with other legitimate uses of the sea.

2.   Annex I substances are those which have a high degree of persistence coupled with:

(a)   The ability to accumulate to harmful levels in terms of toxicity to marine organisms and their predators, to domestic animals or to man; or

(b)   The ability to accumulate through marine pathways to levels harmful in terms of carcinogenicity or mutagenicity to domestic animals or to man; or

(c)   The ability to cause interference with fisheries, amenities or other legitimate uses of the sea.

3.   Annex II substances are all those considered suitable for inclusion in the Annexes except for those allocated to Annex I.

- - - - -

PROTOCOL CONCERNING CO-OPERATION IN COMBATING POLLUTION EMERGENCIES IN THE SOUTH PACIFIC REGION

THE PARTIES TO THIS PROTOCOL,

Being parties to the Convention for the Protection of the Natural Resources and Environment of the South Pacific Region . . . ;

Conscious that the exploration, development and use of offshore and near-shore minerals and the use of hazardous substances, as well as related vessel traffic, pose the threat of significant pollution emergencies in the South Pacific Region;

Aware that the islands of the region are particularly vulnerable to damage resulting from significant pollution due to the sensitivity of their ecosystems and their economic reliance on the continuous utilization of their coastal areas;

Recognizing that in the event of a pollution emergency or threat thereof, prompt and effective action should be taken initially at the national level to organize and co-ordinate prevention, mitigation and clean-up activities;

Recognizing further the importance of rational preparation and mutual co-operation and assistance in responding effectively to pollution emergencies or the threat thereof;

Determined to avert ecological damage to the marine environment and coastal areas of the South Pacific Region through the adoption of national contingency plans to be co-ordinated with appropriate bilateral and subregional contingency plans;

Have agreed as follows:

Article 1
DEFINITIONS

For the purposes of this Protocol:

(a) "Convention" means the Convention for the Protection of the Natural Resources and Environment of the South Pacific Region . . . ;

(b) "South Pacific Region" means the Convention Area as defined in article 2 of the Convention and adjacent coastal areas;

(c) "related interests" of a Party refer, *inter alia*, to:

  (i)   maritime, coastal, port, or estuarine activities;
  (ii) fishing activities and the management and conservation of living and non-living resources, including coastal ecosystems;
  (iii) the cultural value of the area concerned and the exercise of traditional customary rights therein;
  (iv) the health of the coastal population;
  (v)   tourist and recreational activities;

(d) "pollution incident" means a discharge or significant threat of a discharge of oil or other hazardous substance, however caused, resulting in pollution or an imminent threat of pollution to the marine and coastal environment or which adversely affects the related interests of one or more of the Parties and of a magnitude that requires emergency action or other immediate response for the purpose of minimizing its effects or eliminating its threat.

Article 2
APPLICATION

This Protocol applies to pollution incidents in the South Pacific Region.

Article 3
GENERAL PROVISIONS

1.   The Parties to this Protocol shall, within their respective capabilities, co-operate in taking all necessary measures for the protection of the South Pacific Region from the threat and effects of pollution incidents.

2.   The parties shall, within their respective capabilities, establish and maintain, or ensure the establishment and maintenance of, the means of preventing and combating pollution incidents, and reducing the risk thereof. Such means shall include the enactment, as necessary, of relevant legislation, the preparation of contingency plans, the development or strengthening of the capability to respond to a pollution incident and the designation of a national authority responsible for the implementation of this Protocol.

Article 4
EXCHANGE OF INFORMATION

Each Party shall periodically exchange with other Parties, either directly or through the Organization, current information relating to the implementation of this Protocol, including the identification of the officials charged with carrying out the activities covered by it, and information on its laws, regulations, institutions and operational procedures relating to the prevention and the means of reducing and combating the harmful effects of pollution incidents.

Article 5
COMMUNICATION OF INFORMATION CONCERNING, AND REPORTING OF, POLLUTION INCIDENTS

1. Each Party shall establish appropriate procedures to ensure that information regarding pollution incidents is reported as rapidly as possible and shall, *inter alia*:

(a) Require appropriate officials of its government to report to it the occurrence of any pollution incident which comes to their attention;

(b) Require masters of vessels flying its flag and persons in charge of offshore facilities operating under its jurisdiction to report to it the existence of any pollution incident involving their vessel or facilities;

(c) Establish procedures to encourage masters of vessels flying its flag or of its registry to report, to the extent practicable, the existence of any pollution incident involving their vessel to any coastal State in the South Pacific Region which they deem likely to be seriously affected;

(d) Request masters of all vessels and pilots of all aircraft operating in the vicinity of its coasts to report to it any pollution incident of which they are aware.

2. In the event of receiving a report regarding a pollution incident, each Party shall promptly inform all other Parties whose interests are likely to be affected by such incident as well as the flag State of any vessel involved in it. Each Party shall also inform the Organization and, directly or through the Organization, the competent international organizations. Furthermore, it shall inform, as soon as feasible, such other Parties and organizations of any measures it has itself taken to minimize or reduce pollution or the threat thereof.

Article 6
MUTUAL ASSISTANCE

1. Each Party requiring assistance to deal with a pollution incident may request, either directly or through the Organization, the assistance of the other Parties. The Party requesting assistance shall specify the type of assistance it requires. The Parties whose assistance is requested under this article shall, within their capabilities, provide this assistance based on an agreement with the requesting Party or Parties and taking into account, in particular in the case of pollution by hazardous substances other than oil, the technological means available to them. If the Parties responding jointly within the framework of this article so request, the Organization may co-ordinate the activities undertaken as a result.

2. Each Party shall facilitate the movement of technical personnel, equipment and material necessary for responding to a pollution incident, into, out of and through its territory.

Article 7
OPERATIONAL MEASURES

Each Party shall, within its capabilities, take steps including those outlined below in responding to a pollution incident:

(a) Make a preliminary assessment of the incident, including the type and extent of existing or likely pollution effects;

(b) Promptly communicate information concerning the situation to other Parties and the Organization pursuant to article 5;

(c) Promptly determine its ability to take effective measures to respond to the pollution incident and the assistance that might be required and to communicate any request for such assistance to the Party or Parties concerned or the Organization in accordance with article 6;

(d) Consult, as appropriate, with other affected or concerned Parties or the Organization in determining the necessary response to a pollution incident;

(e) Carry out the necessary measures to prevent, eliminate or control the effects of the pollution incident, including surveillance and monitoring of the situation.

Article 8
SUBREGIONAL ARRANGEMENTS

1.   The Parties should develop and maintain appropriate subregional arrangements, bilateral or multilateral, in particular to facilitate the steps provided for in articles 6 and 7 and taking into account the general provisions of this Protocol.

2.   The Parties to any arrangements shall notify the other Parties to this Protocol as well as the Organization of the conclusion of such subregional arrangements and the provisions thereof.

Article 9
INSTITUTIONAL ARRANGEMENTS

The Parties designate the Organization to carry out the following functions:

(a) Assisting Parties, upon request, in the communication of reports of pollution incidents in accordance with article 5;

(b) Assisting Parties, upon request, in the organization of a response action to a pollution incident, in accordance with article 6;

(c) Assisting Parties, upon request, in the following areas:

  (i) the preparation, periodic review, and updating of the contingency plans, referred to in paragraph 2 of article 3, with a view, *inter alia*, to promoting the compatibility of the plans of the Parties; and
  (ii) the identification of training courses and programmes;

(d) Assisting the Parties upon request, on a regional or subregional basis, in the following areas;

  (i) the co-ordination of emergency response activities; and
  (ii) the provision of a forum for discussions concerning emergency response and other related topics;

(e)   Establishing and maintaining liaison with:

   (i)   appropriate regional and international organizations; and
   (ii) appropriate private organizations, including producers and transporters of substances which could give rise to a pollution incident in the South Pacific Region and clean-up contractors and co-operatives;

(f)   Maintaining an appropriate current inventory of available emergency response equipment;

(g)   Disseminating information related to the prevention and control of pollution incidents and the removal of pollutants resulting therefrom;

(h)   Identifying or maintaining emergency response communications systems;

(i)   Encouraging research by the Parties, as well as by appropriate international and private organizations, on the environmental effects of pollution incidents, the environmental effects of pollution incident control materials and other matters related to pollution incidents;

(j)   Assisting Parties in the exchange of information pursuant to article 4; and

(k)   Preparing reports and carrying out other duties assigned to it by the Parties.

Article 10
MEETINGS OF THE PARTIES

1.   Ordinary meetings of the Parties to this Protocol shall be held in conjunction with ordinary meetings of the Parties to the Convention, held pursuant to article 22 of the Convention. The Parties to this Protocol may also hold extraordinary meetings as provided for in article 22 of the Convention.

2.   It shall be the function of the meetings of the Parties:

(a)   To review the operation of this Protocol and to consider special technical arrangements and other measures to improve its effectiveness;

(b)   To consider any measures to improve co-operation under this Protocol including, in accordance with article 24 of the Convention, amendments to this Protocol.

Article 11
RELATIONSHIP BETWEEN THIS PROTOCOL AND THE CONVENTION

1.   The provisions of the Convention relating to any Protocol shall apply with respect to the present Protocol.

   . . .

- - - - -

Additional Reference

Report of the Fourth Meeting of Experts on a Draft Convention on the Protection and Development of the Natural Resources and Environment of the South Pacific Region. UNEP/South Pacific Commission doc. SPREP/Expert Meeting 4/Report.

- - - - -

Mediterranean Sea

Report of the Fourth Ordinary Meeting
of the Contracting Parties to the Convention
for the Protection of the Mediterranean Sea
Against Pollution and its Related Protocols

UNEP/IG.56/5
30 September 1985

Extract

. . .

II. Genoa Declaration on the Second Mediterranean Decade

The Contracting Parties to the Convention for the Protection of the Mediterranean Sea against Pollution and its Related Protocols, meeting in Genoa on 9-13 September 1985;

-       having reviewed their co-operation in the framework of the Mediterranean Action Plan over the past ten years and the role of the United Nations Environment Programme (UNEP) therein;

. . .

6.   *Reaffirm* their determination to co-operate for the protection of the Mediterranean environment and the rational use of its resources, especially through the harmonization of legislation and developing common standards; strengthening research and monitoring centres; the establishment of training programmes; the transfer of know-how; and broadening the scope of technical co-operation with developing countries of the region to enable them to meet their obligations in the protection of the Mediterranean;

. . .

8.   *Commit themselves* to increase investment to combat pollution and to increase their vigilance on the application and adherence to the legislation on the protection of the environment;

. . .

17.   *Adopt* the following ten targets to be achieved as a matter of priority during the second decade of the Mediterranean Action Plan:

(a)   Establishment of reception facilities for dirty ballast waters and other oily residues received from tankers and ships in ports of the Mediterranean;

(b) Establishment as a matter of priority of sewage treatment plants in all cities around the Mediterranean with more than 100,000 inhabitants and appropriate outfalls and/or appropriate treatment plants for all towns with more than 10,000 inhabitants;

(c) Applying environmental impact assessment as an important tool to ensure proper development activities;

(d) Co-operation to improve the safety of maritime navigation and to reduce substantially the risk of transport of dangerous toxic substances likely to affect the coastal areas or induce marine pollution;

(e) Protection of the endangered marine species (e.g. Monk Seal and Mediterranean sea turtle);

(f) Concrete measures to achieve substantial reduction in industrial pollution and disposal of solid waste;

(g) Identification and protection of at least 100 coastal historic sites of common interest;

(h) Identification and protection of at least 50 new marine and coastal sites or reserves of Mediterranean interest;

. . .

(j) Substantial reduction in air pollution which adversely affects coastal areas and the marine environment with the potential danger of acid rains.

III. RECOMMENDATIONS APPROVED BY THE CONTRACTING PARTIES

A. FRAMEWORK CONVENTION AND RELATED PROTOCOLS

The Contracting Parties:

. . .

2. *Invite* Contracting Parties to ratify the Protocol on Land-based sources.

3. *Invite* Contracting Parties to ratify the Protocol on Specially Protected Areas.

4. *Invite* the Contracting Parties to ratify . . . MARPOL 73/78.

5. *Invite* the Contracting Parties to ratify all international conventions relevant to the protection of the environment.

6. *Request* the Secretariat to initiate preparation for a Protocol on the protection of the Mediterranean Sea against pollution from off-shore exploration and exploitation.

7. *Invite* the EEC to provide the Secretariat with documents and information on liability and compensation for damages resulting from pollution other than hydrocarbons.

8. *Recommend* that adequate port reception facilities be provided in the Mediterranean as required by the MARPOL 73/78 Convention.

. . .

B.   CO-OPERATION IN CASES OF EMERGENCIES

The Contracting Parties:

1.   *Recommend* that all Coastal States develop and adopt national contingency plans, which are an essential prerequisite to building multilateral and sub-regional arrangements for mutual assistance in cases of emergency.

2.   *Recommend* that the Regional Oil Combating Centre develops proposals for sub-regional co-operation arrangements in case of emergencies involving oil pollution.
. . .

C.   INSTITUTIONAL ARRANGEMENTS
. . .

D.   FINANCIAL ARRANGEMENTS
. . .

E.   INTEGRATED PLANNING AND MANAGEMENT OF THE RESOURCES OF THE MEDITERRANEAN BASIN
. . .

1.   BLUE PLAN
. . .

(g) *Request* an in-depth review by the Contracting Parties of the results of the Blue Plan, and examination of its relevance for national development strategies (by 1988/1989).

3.   SPECIALLY PROTECTED AREAS

The Contracting Parties:

(a) *Invite* the Regional Activity Centre for Specially Protected Areas to formulate, in co-operation with the Secretariat and other relevant international organizations, common guidelines for the selection, establishment and management of Specially Protected Areas;
. . .

F.   LONG-TERM PROGRAMME FOR POLLUTION MONITORING AND RESEARCH
. . .

4.   TECHNICAL IMPLEMENTATION OF THE DUMPING PROTOCOL
. . .

(1)   Administrative matters.

(a)   The Contracting Parties which have not yet done so should designate without delay "competent authorities", in accordance with article 10 of the Protocol.

(b) On the basis of information provided by the Contracting Parties, the Secretariat should prepare and circulate a roster of experts and institutions capable of providing technical assistance on matters of dumping of wastes at sea and on alternative methods for waste disposal.

(2) Reporting and notification.

(a) Reports transmitted by the Contracting Parties to the Secretariat in accordance with Article 20 of the Convention should include copies, or alternatively summaries, of legal or administrative rules referring to implementation of the Protocol. The Secretariat should prepare and circulate annual reports summarizing submissions made by the Contracting Parties.

(b) The Contracting Parties concerned should transmit to the Secretariat "NIL reports" when no dumping permits were issued and no dumping has taken place during the period for which reports on permits issued and on actual dumping have to be submitted.

(c) The Contracting Parties should amend the Provisional Prior Consultation Procedure adopted by the Second Meeting of the Contracting Parties so that its opening sentence would read: "The following procedure **which does not apply to sewage sludge and dredge spoils** is recommended . . ." (appendix 1).

(3) Definition of terms mentioned in annex I and criteria for application of article 5 of the Protocol.

(a) The Contracting Parties should adopt, on a provisional basis, the definitions set forth in paragraphs 1(a) and 1(b) of appendix 2 for the terms "non toxic", "rapidly converted in the sea into substances which are biologically harmless", "rapidly rendered harmless by physical, chemical or biological processes in the sea", and "trace contaminants" mentioned in annex I of the Protocol. The implication of these definitions should be taken into account when the Provisional Prior Consultation Procedure is applied.

(b) The Contracting Parties should adopt, on a provisional basis, the definition set forth in paragraph 1(c) of appendix 2 for the expression "acid and alkaline compounds of such composition and in such quantity that they may seriously impair the quality of sea-water" mentioned in paragraph 8 of annex I of the Protocol. The Secretariat should develop and circulate practical guidelines for dumping of acid and alkaline compounds covered by annex II of the Protocol.

(c) The Contracting Parties should urge the International Atomic Energy Agency to complete its work on the definition of the *de-minimis* level of radioactivity for wastes and other matter of low-level radioactivity and to make it available for the Contracting Parties.

(4) Monitoring and research

. . .

Appendix 1. Provisional prior consultation procedure

. . .

Appendix 2. Provisional definitions of terms mentioned
in Annex I and provisional criteria for
application of article 5 of the Protocol

. . .

5.   INTERIM ENVIRONMENTAL QUALITY CRITERIA FOR MERCURY

. . .

6.   INTERIM ENVIRONMENTAL QUALITY CRITERIA FOR BATHING WATERS

. . .

G.   CREATION OF FLOATING RECEPTION FACILITIES IN THE
MEDITERRANEAN SEA

The Contracting Parties:

. . .

Whereas the Mediterranean is designated as a "special area" under MARPOL 73/78 for which special mandatory methods for the prevention of sea pollution by oil are required;

Whereas Article 6 of the Barcelona Convention concerning pollution from ships calls upon Contracting Parties to take all measures in conformity with international law to prevent, abate and combat pollution of the Mediterranean Sea Area caused by discharges from ships and to ensure the effective implementation in the Area of the "rules that are generally recognized at the international level" in this regard;

Conscious of the lack of reception facilities in many areas; and that their construction on shore takes a long time;

. . .

Invite Governments to participate actively in the implementation of one or several floating reception facilities in the vicinity of ports or sheltered areas in which important maritime traffic of tankers may need such facilities in order to comply with stringent discharge requirements;

Apply the necessary control procedures, in accordance with international regulations formulated by the International Maritime Organization (IMO), to ensure that vessels use the reception facilities for discharging their dirty ballast water and oil residues in a reception facility and to report periodically to the Mediterranean Action Plan (MAP).

H.   PARTICIPATION TO ACTION COST 301 CONCERNING THE REDUCTION OF
THE RISK OF MARITIME CASUALTIES AND THE PREVENTION OF
POLLUTION IN THE MEDITERRANEAN SEA THROUGH A REGIONAL
NETWORK OF VESSEL TRAFFIC SERVICES CENTRES (RVTS)

. . .

Urge all the Contracting Parties to participate actively in the Action COST 301 in order to ensure that all the Mediterranean Sea can be adequately covered by an effective Regional Network of Vessel Traffic Services Centres (RVTS).

. . .

- - - - -

Caribbean Region

Report of the Fifth Meeting of the Monitoring Committee on the Action Plan for the Caribbean Environment Programme, May 1987	UNEP/IG.67/5, Annex I Extract

Decisions of the Fifth Meeting of the Monitoring Committee

The Fifth Meeting of the Monitoring Committee on the Action Plan for the Caribbean Environment Programme,

Taking note of the entry into force of the Convention on the Protection and Development of the Marine Environment of the Wider Caribbean Region and its associated Protocol concerning Co-operation in Combating Oil Spills in the Wider Caribbean Region,

. . .

Decides:

. . .

Legal Agreements

15.   To urge those Governments which have not yet ratified or acceded to the Cartagena Convention and Protocol to do so as soon as possible and to deposit their instruments of ratification with the depositary Government, the Government of Colombia.

16.   To convey to the First Meeting of Contracting Parties its concern that consideration be given to a formula that will integrate the financial and institutional mechanisms for the implementation of the legal agreements and those in existence for the implementation of the Caribbean Action Plan, in order to avoid the creation of another Trust Fund and the unnecessary duplication of institutional arrangements.

17.   To recommend to UNEP and the Caribbean Action Plan Governments which are parties to the Cartagena Convention that they take the necessary steps prior to the First Meeting of Contracting Parties in order to move forward in preparing protocols on land-based sources of pollution and specifically protected areas and wildlife, in case the meeting of Parties decides to develop them as additional instruments.

. . .

- - - - -

European Region

Contracting Parties to the Convention
for the Prevention of Marine Pollution from
Land-based Sources (Paris Convention)

Official Journal of the
European Communities
No.L 24. 1/27/87

Protocol Amending the Convention for the Prevention
of Marine Pollution from Land-Based Sources

The Contracting Parties to the Convention for the prevention of marine pollution from land-based sources, done at Paris on 4 June 1974 (hereinafter referred to as "the Convention");

Recalling Article 1 of the Convention, in which the Contracting Parties pledge themselves to take all possible steps to prevent pollution of the sea;

Recognizing that the Convention does not contain provisions referring to the prevention of pollution of the maritime area through the atmosphere;

Desiring to extend the scope of the Convention to such pollution;

Have agreed as follows:

Article I

The following is inserted in Article 3 of the Convention after iii of subparagraph c:

"iv) by emissions into the atmosphere from land or from man-made structures as defined in subparagraph iii above".

Article II

The first sentence of Article 4, paragraph 3, is amended by inserting "and emissions into the atmosphere", after "discharges into watercourses".

Article III

The following is inserted at the beginning of Article 16 d of the Convention:

"to examine the feasibility of and, as appropriate".

Article IV

1.   This Protocol shall be open for signature at Paris from 26 March 1986 until 30 June 1986 by the States which are parties to the Convention on the date of the opening for signature of this Protocol, and by the European Economic Community.

2.   This Protocol shall be subject to ratification, acceptance or approval.

Article V

After 30 June 1986 this Protocol shall be open for accession by any State referred to in Article 24 of the Convention and by the European Economic Community.

Article VI

1.   This Protocol shall enter into force on the first day of the second month following the date on which the last of the contracting parties referred to in Article IV of this Protocol has deposited its instrument of ratification, acceptance, approval or accession.

2.   For any other State becoming party to this Protocol after its entry into force, this Protocol shall enter into force on the first day of the second month following the date on which that State has deposited its instrument of accession.

3.   Any State which becomes a contracting party to this Protocol without being a contracting party to the Convention shall be considered as a contracting party to the Convention as amended by this Protocol as of the date of entry into force of this Protocol for that State.

4.   Any State which becomes a contracting party to the Convention after the entry into force of this Protocol shall be considered as a contracting party to the Convention as amended by this Protocol.

5.   The instruments of ratification, acceptance, approval or accession shall be deposited with the Government of the French Republic.

Article VII

The Depository Government shall inform the Contracting Parties and those States referred to in Article 22 of the Convention of signature of this Protocol, of the deposit of instruments of ratification, acceptance, approval or accession, made pursuant to Articles IV, V and VI, and of the date of entry into force of this Protocol.

Article VIII

The original of this Protocol, of which the English and French texts shall be equally authentic, shall be deposited with the Government of the French Republic.

In Witness Whereof, the undersigned, duly authorized by their respective Governments, have signed this Protocol.

Done in Paris, this 26 March 1986.

- - - - -

UN Economic Commission for Europe   E/ECE/(42)/L.19
Report of the 42nd Session, April 1987   Extract

Decision F (42)   Co-operation in the Field of Protection and
                   Improvement of the Environment

The Economic Commission for Europe,

   . . .

Confirming that protection of the environment is one of the ECE priorities,

   1.   *Notes* with satisfaction the publication by the Senior Advisers to ECE Governments on Environmental Problems of the Report on Environmental Trends and Policies in the ECE Region as a first part of the long term regional strategy for environmental protection and rational use of natural resources, and *invites* the Senior Advisers to finalize the Regional Strategy prior to their sixteenth session;

   . . .

   3.   *Expresses* its satisfaction with the progress made in the implementation of the Convention on the Long-range Transboundary Air Pollution and *appeals* to Parties to the Convention to make every effort for prompt ratification of the protocols adopted under the Convention, or to those that are not in a position to ratify the Protocol on Sulphur Dioxide to take effective action to reduce further their sulphur emissions, taking into account the commitments entered into at Helsinki in July 1985;

   4.   *Welcomes* the decision taken by the fourth session of the Executive Body of the Convention on Long-range Transboundary Air Pollution concerning the mandate of the Working Group on Nitrogen Oxides and *calls upon* the Working Group to elaborate a draft protocol to the Convention concerning control of emissions of nitrogen oxides or their transboundary fluxes as soon as possible, . . .

   5.   *Calls upon* the Senior Advisers to take all necessary efforts for the implementation of the provisions contained in the Declaration on Low- and Non-waste Technology and Re-utilization and Recycling of Waste;

   6.   *Invites* the Senior Advisers to continue their activities in the field of treatment and final storage of hazardous wastes, taking into account the work done in this area by other fora;

   7.   *Invites* the Senior Advisers to continue their activities in the field of environmental impact assessment, . . .

   8.   *Invites* the Senior Advisers . . . to finalize as soon as possible the elaboration of the Declaration on the Protection of Flora, Fauna and their Habitats, bearing in mind the need to adhere to existing agreements as well as the need to avoid overlapping with the activities of other competent international organizations in this area;

   . . .

10. *Invites* member States to consider improving the use of effective control technologies taking into account the necessity to co-operate effectively in the prevention and combating of pollution and to preserve and improve the environment in the ECE region;

11. *Requests* member States to promote the commercial exchange of available technology as well as direct industrial contacts in the field of environmental protection.

. . .

- - - - -

Additional References

Annual Report of the Economic Commission for Europe. UN doc. E/1986/31.

Principles regarding co-operation in the field of transboundary waters. Decision I(42) of the Economic Commission for Europe. In E/ECE(42)/L.19.

Application of Environmental Impact Assessment. ECE Environmental Series 1. UN doc. ECE/ENV/50 (also Sales No. E.87.II.E.14).

- - - - -

IMO Marine Environment Protection Committee   MEPC 25/20
Report of the 25th Session, December 1987   Extract

. . .

Second International Conference on the Protection of the North Sea

19.1   The United Kingdom delegation, on behalf of the delegations of the North Sea countries of Belgium, Denmark, the Federal Republic of Germany, France, the Netherlands, Norway, Sweden, the United Kingdom, and of the Commission of the European Communities, informed the Committee on the outcome of the second Ministerial Conference on the Protection of the North Sea, held in London during 24 and 25 November 1987. . . .

19.2   The Conference resulted in a Ministerial Declaration based on a Quality Status Report of the North Sea as prepared for the Conference. . . .

19.3   The Ministerial Declaration includes specific measures aimed at the reduction of pollution of the North Sea. These measures are in relation to:

- inputs via rivers and estuaries of substances that are persistent, toxic and liable to bioaccumulate;
- inputs of nutrients;
- inputs of pollutants via the atmosphere;
- dumping and incineration at sea;
- pollution from ships;
- pollution from offshore installations;
- co-operation on airborne surveillance.

19.4   In respect of the measures in relation to pollution from ships, the Ministers agreed, *inter alia*, to the following:

.1   to implement Annex V of MARPOL 73/78 on a regional basis as from 31 December 1988 if the conditions for its entry into force are not met before 31 December 1987;

.2   to continue their efforts within IMO to bring Annexes III and V of MARPOL 73/78 into force;

.3   to initiate the necessary action within IMO for designating the North Sea a special area for the purpose of Annex V of MARPOL 73/78;

.4   to continue to co-operate under the Memorandum of Understanding on port State control so that after the detection of operational violations all reports on alleged pollution incidents are dealt with speedily and effectively, so as to ensure that ships reported in respect of an alleged pollution incident will be subject to stringent and wide-ranging inspection procedures in ports, that the prosecution of a violation under MARPOL 73/78 will be facilitated, and that the documentation for prosecution of a violation under MARPOL 73/78 will be improved;

.5   to continue to ensure the availability of adequate reception facilities in ports bordering the North Sea for oily and chemical wastes from ships and for garbage prior to the implementation of Annex V of MARPOL 73/78;

.6   to initiate actions within international bodies such as IMO and the International Standards Organization (ISO) in order to improve quality standards of marine heavy fuel oil so as to achieve a reduction of marine and atmospheric pollution.

19.5   The Ministers further agreed to hold a third Conference on the Protection of the North Sea in the Netherlands, in early 1990 . . .

   . . .

19.7   . . . The observer of ICS referred to the Quality Status Report of the North Sea . . . This Report acknowledged that the input of pollutants, in particular oil, resulting from shipping operations in the area did not have a significant adverse effect on the overall quality of the North Sea. By comparison with other sources of pollution, in particular riverborne effluents, the Status Report showed that the amount of oil pollution in the North Sea, attributable to shipping operations as a whole, was very small.

19.8   The observer of ICS, supported by several other delegations, therefore, expressed the hope that the Governments of the North Sea would also turn their attention to dealing with the other identified sources of pollution in the area with the same diligence that had been, and continued to be, applied by IMO in the marine field.

- - - - -

XI

FISHERIES MANAGEMENT AND DEVELOPMENT

1

GLOBAL ASPECTS

World Fisheries Situation

FAO Committee on Fisheries   COFI/87/2
Seventeenth Session, May 1987   Extract

===

World Fisheries Situation and Outlook

INTRODUCTION

1.   At earlier sessions of the Committee, the opportunity was given to review, from time to time, trends and outlook for world fisheries. This subject has not appeared as a major item on the agenda since the Committee's Eleventh Session in 1977 . . .

. . .

Exclusive Economic Zones and Trade

17.   Prior to the extension of jurisdictions, the total value of the distant-water fishing harvest approximated $US 7 300 million (1978 prices). Excluding oceanic pelagics, however, two-thirds of this harvest was taken off the coasts of developed countries and most of the remaining third off Northwest Africa, leaving little more than five percent for developing countries elsewhere. Besides gaining twice the amount of fishery resources, the developed countries possessed an industrial organization and infrastructure that enabled them readily to expand their harvest, and trade in the products, of those resources.

18.   For the distant-water fishing countries, the effects of EEZ establishment included (a) a reduction in fleet size and a rationalization of craft mix and deployment, (b) a search for alternative resources and fishing grounds on the high seas and within EEZs and (c) negotiation of fishing agreements with coastal States. The result for some of these countries is a reduction in harvest and/or a switch to the harvesting of lower-valued species.

19.   The impact of coastal State extensions of jurisdiction (EEZs) in the later seventies, which was expected to bring about a major realignment of the international fish trade, has been masked by the 30 percent increase in overall production during the subsequent period. It had been expected that countries previously with large foreign fleets operating off their coasts would benefit most from the establishment of EEZs, the areas identified being the Northeast Pacific and Northwest Atlantic (for developed countries) and the Southwest, East Central and Southeast Atlantic (for developing countries). Some of the countries involved have increased their exports. Several countries which have lost access to fishing grounds have also increased their exports.

. . .

SOME IMPLICATIONS OF PRESENT TRENDS

Fishery management

38. The above outlook for the world's fisheries raises issues of policy that concern politicians, administrators, entrepreneurs and other decision-makers concerned with the fisheries sector. The fifties and sixties, in most parts of the world, were a period of rapid growth, brought about by fleet expansion and the use of innovative technologies. As resource stocks became fully exploited and then overfished, however, there emerged an interest in problems of fishery management, although not yet a generalized conviction that action in this field was widely necessary.

39. By the seventies, there were few resource stocks left to which fishing effort could be transferred and, in the middle years of the decade, increased fuel costs rendered many fishery resources unprofitable, temporarily or permanently. More recently, rising prices for fish in real terms has compensated, at least partially, for cost increases. If this process were to continue, however, as seems probable, the task of fishery-management authorities might be made more difficult to accomplish, as price increases attract more fishing effort despite declining yields.

40. With establishment of EEZs, some problems of fishery management have been simplified - others e.g., those relating to trans-boundary matters, may have been exacerbated. Moreover, coastal State control does not of itself ensure effective management of fisheries, even of those based on stocks occurring exclusively within national zones. Administrators, as well as political leaders (with whom the ultimate decisions rest) and donors often prefer an expansionist policy; the benefits of such a policy being perceived as immediate and tangible whereas those of good management often are long-term and hypothetical. As in the past, pressures of this kind may continue to frustrate a rational approach to fishery management.

41. Management must be concerned with the overall economic performance of the fisheries. To this end, government intervention in fisheries must include measures that reduce fishing costs, improve revenues and satisfy social objectives. For example, the use of fossil fuels in fishing can represent 90 percent of the cost of production and measures can be taken to lower these costs. . . . In the same way, considerable savings can be achieved by reducing the search time required for finding productive shoals of fish. . . . Other areas for consideration by governments are the targeting of fisheries on animals where prices are significantly higher. . . .

42. Social considerations often require conscious allocation of limited fish resources to particular groups of fishermen which is most commonly achieved by legislating protective areas for the use by specified fishing gears or fishermen. . . . It is particularly important to protect and enhance small-scale or artisanal fisheries, which produce over 20 million tons of fish a year, almost all of which is used for direct human consumption. . . .

43. In addition, environmental degradation will become increasingly a serious problem in maintaining important fishery resources in coastal waters. More effort will be required to adopt measures to enhance productivity, such as stricter monitoring and prevention of environmental degradation, pollution, protection of nursery grounds and juvenile fish, stocking of appropriate species in suitable areas and strategic placement of artificial reefs.

. . .

CONCLUSIONS

56.   The projected increase in demand for direct human consumption of an additional 30 million tons by the year 2000 might therefore be answered by better fisheries management (10 million tons), possible increases from aquaculture (about 5 to 10 million tons), and improved utilization of resources (15 to 20 million tons).   Delays in improving management and therefore alleviating supply constraints can be expected to increase prices which in turn will improve the viability of aquacultural production.

57.   For capture fisheries, with the natural resources under mounting pressure, the need for management is becoming acute if production is to be enhanced, let alone maintained, to the year 2000.   Without management, fisheries development becomes increasingly difficult to sustain.   Indeed, once fishery resources become fully exploited, catches fall and the potential wealth of an over-exploited fishery is dissipated in higher than necessary costs.   In resolving this issue both technical assistance and capital investment under concessionary terms have important roles.

58.   Within the context of technical assistance in support of fisheries management, a need of many developing countries is for a greater support of research on tropical fisheries; included under this heading is the provision of statistical services.   In general, the quality of such services has been deteriorating over a long period.

59.   Governments and donors may wish also to give further consideration to the ways in which capital aid may be directed towards alleviation of the problems of conflict, over-capacity and dissipation of economic rents which will facilitate the progression of the fishing sectors to a more orderly and sustainable industry.   Governments without access to funds for compensating fishermen for losses incurred from management measures will continue to be unable to achieve significant changes in the conduct of fishing.   In the inshore areas of most tropical fisheries, the consequences of a fisheries closure has extreme economic implications on the livelihood of artisanal fishermen.   More attention is required to the need for matching fishing effort to the sustainable yield from the resources, whereby direct control over fishing effort can relieve fishing pressure, improve incomes to fishermen as well as providing them with important collateral for credit acquisition.

60.   Just as the extension of fisheries jurisdictions to 200 miles nationalized fisheries that were previously under free and open access, national fisheries will also require division into areas for exclusive use by specified fishing gears or fishermen if conflicts are to be avoided and the national consequences of "open" access overcome.   The enforcement of these areas will require a greater "at sea" physical presence than has been the case so far and, indeed, the concept of fisheries protection vessels should be viewed from the same perspective as that of fences for agricultural lands.

61.   While the production levels from capture fisheries can be improved through management within the time period under study, so the costs of production can be reduced by immediate attention given to energy-saving methods directed at engine-efficiency horsepower limits, and reductions in search time for productive shoals of fish.   Particular attention is required for improving the living standards of small-scale fishermen in recognition of their important contribution to sustained supplies of fish for direct human consumption.

62. Without sufficient government infrastructures to undertake fisheries management, the fisheries sector will fail to reach its potential. In the past, it has not been a priority of many governments to improve the capability of their fishery institutions significantly faster than those of other sectors. Governments, however, may wish to consider the dangers to their fisheries in not undertaking as quickly as possible the strengthening of their fishery institutions to enable them to undertake the complex tasks of fisheries management.

   . . .

64. A significant contribution to increased supplies could also result from making better use of what is already caught. Ensuring that the present discards from trawl fisheries are landed for human consumption, investing in facilities to reduce post-harvest losses and fully utilizing the small pelagic species as food could all have an impact. However, the contribution from all the above sources to the increased food fish demand in the year 2000 will only be possible if governments address the needs now.

   . . .

- - - - -

FAO Committee on Fisheries
Report of the Seventeenth Session, May 1987

CL 91/7
Extract

   . . .

World Fisheries Situation

The Committee welcomed the opportunity to review the present world fisheries situation and outlook for the future and suggested that such a review should be placed regularly on the agenda of the Committee, preferable at four-year intervals. It agreed that the likely gap between demand and supply by the year 2000 dictated the need for major efforts by FAO as well as by Member Governments, particularly in: (1) the improvement of fisheries management; (2) the effective development of aquaculture; and (3) the improved utilization of fish, including the reduction of post-harvest losses.

   . . .

15. The Committee noted the continued growth in the world catch of fish but expressed concern that much of the recent growth had been in the catches of small pelagic species which were generally of lower value and subject to wide natural fluctuations and utilized generally for fish meal. The Committee thought that the future outlook presented in the paper (COFI/87/2) was realistic and that the likely gap between demand and supply dictated the need for major efforts by FAO as well as Member Governments.

   . . .

17. In achieving the task of improved management, one of the most critical needs was improved information. FAO's role in providing such information was recognized as being of crucial importance.   The role of FAO's regional and sub-regional fishery bodies was particularly valued in helping governments to improve their information base. Concern was expressed that some governments were not providing statistical data of an acceptable quality with regard to some of their fisheries and it was hoped that this could be overcome.

. . .

19. It was generally agreed that there was a strong need for training in the acquisition of information and in the development of management expertise. Some delegations noted that there was considerable disparity among countries in their approaches to fisheries management and FAO was encouraged to examine the conditions that would be conducive to the adoption of better management practices.

. . .

21. Many delegations stressed the importance of ensuring rational exploitation of the resources in their exclusive economic zones for the benefit of their countries. A number of countries expressed concern about the difficulties of monitoring fishing operations and of ensuring that foreign fishing vessels were not violating their zones. Several delegations noted that the costs of controlling fishing in their exclusive economic zones were high and requested assistance in the development of appropriate cost-effective monitoring, control and surveillance systems.

. . .

- - - - -

Follow-up to the 1984 FAO World Conference on Fisheries Management and Development

---

FAO Conference   C 85/REP
Twenty-third Session, November 1985   Extract

Resolution 6/85
Follow-up to the World Conference on Fisheries Management and Development

THE CONFERENCE,

Recalling its Resolution 4/79 supporting the proposal to hold an FAO Conference on Fisheries Management and Development,

Having considered the Report of the World Conference on Fisheries Management and Development, held in Rome from 27 June to 6 July 1984,

Aware that fish is an important part of daily diets in many countries and provides nearly one-quarter of the world's supply of animal protein and that in many countries fisheries are important sources of employment, income and foreign exchange,

Convinced that by optimum use of the resources at present being exploited, through improved production, management and conservation and reduced wastage, and by greater production from under-used or unexploited marine species and aquaculture, fisheries can increase their contribution to national economic, social and nutritional goals, and to world food security,

Recognizing that the new régime of the oceans has created opportunities to promote the sustained development and rational management of the world's marine fish resources and that the role of inland water fisheries and aquaculture can also be further enhanced, both as sources of food and within the overall context of rural development,

Noting with appreciation Resolution 39/225 of the General Assembly of the United Nations endorsing the Strategy for Fisheries Management and Development and the associated Programmes of Action adopted by the World Fisheries Conference, and inviting FAO in collaboration with the organs, organizations and bodies concerned within the United Nations system, to continue to play its important role in assisting states in their efforts toward the improved management and development of fishery resources,

1.   *Commends* the Director-General for having taken the initiative of convening the FAO World Conference on Fisheries Management and Development;

2.   *Welcomes* the adoption by the World Fisheries Conference of a Strategy for Fisheries Management and Development and five associated Programmes of Action;

3.   *Stresses* that primary responsibility for implementing the Strategy at the national level rests with Member Governments but that international assistance, in particular by FAO, will continue to be needed by a number of developing countries;

4.   *Expresses its appreciation* for the extra-budgetary and other forms of support already provided for the implementation of the Programmes of Action and *calls upon* all bilateral and multilateral donor agencies and financing institutions to provide the further support required to ensure their effective implementation;

5.   *Notes with satisfaction* the measures taken or planned by the Director-General in follow-up to the World Fisheries Conference and *invites* him to submit a report to the Twenty-fourth Session of the FAO Conference on the progress achieved in implementing the Strategy and Programmes of Action;

6.   *Urges* States, international and regional organizations to cooperate with the Director-General in the preparation of such reports.

(Adopted 27 November 1985)

- - - - -

FAO Committee on Fisheries,   COFI/87/3
Seventeenth Session, May 1987   Extract

Progress in the Implementation of the Strategy for Fisheries Management and Development

INTRODUCTION

1.   The 1984 FAO World Fisheries Conference endorsed a Strategy for Fisheries Management and Development and invited States and international organizations to take into

account the principles and guidelines contained in the Strategy when planning the management and development of fisheries. In Resolution No.3 adopted by the Conference, the Director-General of FAO was requested to provide the FAO Committee on Fisheries and the Organization's governing bodies with periodic reports on the progress achieved in implementing the Strategy; the Resolution further encouraged States, international and regional organizations to collaborate with the Director-General in the preparation of such reports.

. . .

OVERALL COMMENTARY AND CONCLUSIONS

12. The detailed analysis set out in Appendix A demonstrates, above all, the difficulties of presently attempting to evaluate, certainly in any quantitative manner, the "progress" achieved in "implementing" the Strategy adopted by the World Fisheries Conference in 1984. In the first instance, the Conference took great care when endorsing the Strategy to emphasize its flexible and non-mandatory nature, the extent to which any government or organization may or may not wish to take the Strategy's guidelines and principles into account is thus entirely a matter within its own prerogative.

. . .

16. . . . A number of fisheries administrations, in both large and small countries, have found the text of the Strategy to be a most valuable advocate when seeking the allocation of higher priorities to the fishery sector. . . . The Strategy, embodying international consensus on the best courses for fisheries management and development, has frequently been used, in whole or in part, as a valuable authority and point of reference by Directors of Fisheries in the work of their own departments and in relations with other government bodies.

17. . . . It is encouraging to observe that, following the Conference, certain governments took direct action to strengthen their fisheries administrations and/or to review and, in some cases, re-formulate their plans for the fisheries sector in the light of the Strategy's recommendations. In this connection, an important feature has been the steps taken, before or after the Conference, to involve industry representatives and others engaged in various aspects of the fisheries, in the formulation and execution of development plans and management schemes . . .

. . .

19. The review further illustrated the serious attempts being made to design and implement schemes for the better management and utilization of the fish resources. Attention was drawn to the need for - and frequent lack of - sufficient data, both biological and socio-economic, when elaborating and introducing management measures. Many governments also referred to the problems encountered in establishing effective systems for the control and surveillance of the fishing operations and to the need for further assistance in ensuring compliance with management schemes.

. . .

23. Finally, great importance continues to be attached by both developing and developed countries to technical and economic cooperation in fisheries and to mechanisms for collaboration in research, development and management. The many bilateral agreements, joint ventures and other cooperative arrangements described by respondents illustrates the thrust being given to world fisheries development through international collaboration.

The Supplementary Data Sheets

. . .

25.   Significant trends emerging from the data provided have been noted in the relevant text of Appendix A. What is clearly indicated is the effort which remains to be made to improve national capabilities to collect and analyse even the basic data required for fisheries planning, development and management, especially with regard to the socio-economic aspects of the sector.

. . .

Appendix A

REVIEW OF REPLIES RECEIVED FROM GOVERNMENTS

. . .

Strategy element III: Principles and practices for the rational management
and optimum use of fish resources

19.   From the replies received from governments on this subject, it is clear that the need for rational management is a matter of major concern and priority in many countries. Some respondents described in detail the management measures which had been introduced or were under consideration. Canada referred to the criteria of economic efficiency and reviewed the system, operating in the Atlantic offshore demersal fishery since 1982, of quasi-property rights, i.e., enterprise allocations. An analagous system was described by New Zealand where, after a period of open access which had led to over-capitalization, the mechanism of Individual Transferable Quotas was introduced in 1986, creating tradeable property rights in respect of seven key inshore finfish species. The USA noted major changes in policies and plans so as to develop management régimes that are market-oriented as well as biologically-based.

20.   Other countries, for example, the Philippines, noted that the introduction of management measures was constrained by the lack of insufficient data and of clearly defined fishing rights. Seychelles similarly observed that the first task of its newly created Fisheries Authority was to establish the data base required for the planning and management of its fisheries. The need for appropriate data as a pre-requisite for management was also emphasized by other respondents, for example, Togo and Sri Lanka. The benefits to be gained from efficient management were illustrated by Cyprus which reported a 60 percent increase in production after the introduction, with the assistance of FAO, of new measures to control its trawl fishery.

21.   A number of countries made special reference to the problems of attempting to apply conventional management techniques to multispecies fisheries. Japan, for example, advised that because of these difficulties it does not attempt to regulate through the use of Total Allowable Catches but uses instead a variety of techniques, particularly licensing and the fishing rights system. The use of improved management practices is clearly a widespread matter of concern and interest. Mexico, for example, noted that it had reviewed both existing domestic management systems and experience elsewhere, especially multilateral attempts to control overfishing, and has recognized the need to seek a proper balance between exploitation and conservation.

22. Many responses emphasized the widespread concern regarding the difficulties encountered in establishing systems for the monitoring, control and surveillance of fishing operations, i.e. of ensuring compliance with management measures once introduced. Nigeria

noted that measures had been adopted to promote the rational management of its resources but that the growth in fishery activities had not been matched by the government's capacity to introduce adequate control systems. Ghana also advised that it had created a new control and surveillance unit in response to the high priority it now attached to enforcement of hitherto often ignored management measures. Many developing countries clearly need and expect continued assistance, notably from FAO, in introducing cost-effective monitoring, control and surveillance systems, as well as management schemes.

23. There was widespread appreciation of the benefits which accrue from involving all groups concerned in the process of formulating and implementing management measures. Australia, Japan, New Zealand, Panama, the Philippines, Sri Lanka, the UK and the USA were among those governments who made particular reference to the establishment of formal consultative mechanisms providing for the participation of representatives from the fishery industry in the design and execution of management schemes and in the settlement of disputes. Samoa drew attention to its education programme through various media to create awareness among fishermen and the public of the dangers of uncontrolled, illegal fishing methods and the need to conserve and protect the resources.

24. Steps to control pollution and avoid environmental degradation were described by many respondents. Canada noted its new federal policy for fish habitat management, including pollution control. Nigeria referred to the problems arising from the use of water resources for purposes other than fishing whilst Toga drew attention to its collaboration with Benin in the battle against coastal erosion and marine pollution and Bahrain to its programmes designed to restore mangrove areas.

. . .

- - - - -

FAO Committee on Fisheries CL 91/7
Report of the Seventeenth Session, May 1987 Extract

===

. . .

Progress in the implementation of the Strategy for fisheries management and development

The Committee considered the preliminary progress report prepared in response to the request of the World Fisheries Conference as instructive, with valuable information, reflecting many of the trends in fisheries. It noted steps taken by several countries in improving the legal, administrative and institutional frameworks for fisheries management and development and actions taken to review or revise their policies and programmes for the fisheries sector in the light of the recommendations of the Strategy. It agreed that the World Fisheries Conference's Strategy provided a useful tool to both governments and international organizations in their endeavours to improve the contributions of fisheries to national, economic, social and nutritional goals. It recommended that further progress reports be prepared, using the same format, for submission to the Committee on Fisheries at four-yearly intervals. FAO was requested to assist developing countries which might request the Organization's help and advice in preparing their national reports.

. . .

31. The Committee noted that the review by FAO (COFI/87/3) re-affirmed the critical importance of training, transfer of technology and financial resources so as to improve the self-reliance of developing countries in planning and executing fisheries development and management programmes. It also welcomed the emphasis placed in the report upon the vital need for better and more comprehensive data, both biological and socio-economic. . . .

. . .

34. The Committee recommended that further progress reports should be prepared at four-yearly intervals. . . . It was considered that such future evaluations of the usefulness and relevance of the Strategy might be made jointly with overviews of the overall state and prospects of the world's fisheries, similar to that presented in document COFI/87/2 . . .

- - - - -

Additional References

Report of the FAO World Conference on Fisheries Management and Development, Rome, 27 June-6 July 1984. FAO publication.

Resolution of the European Parliament on the follow-up to the FAO World Conference on Fisheries, 19 April 1985.

Report of the FAO Committee on Fisheries, 16th session. FAO doc. CL 87/7 and COFI/87/Inf.8.

Documents of the 17th session of the FAO Committee on Fisheries, May 1987:
    COFI/87/4   Progress in the implementation of the Programmes of Action.
    COFI/87/5   Progress in the implementation of the Resolutions concerning specific aspects of fisheries management and development.
    COFI/87/6   Sub-Committee on Fish Trade: Report on First Session, October 1986.
    COFI/87/10   The work of FAO in fisheries during 1988-1989.
    COFI/87/Inf.4   Review of the state of world fishery resources. Regional reviews.
    COFI/87/Inf.5   Fishery commodity situation and outlook 1985-1986.

- - - - -

Fisheries Policy and Legislation

THIRD ACP-EEC CONVENTION
Lomé, 8 December 1984   Extract

. . .

Part Two
The areas of ACP-EEC co-operation

. . .

CHAPTER 3
Co-operation on agricultural commodities

. . .

TITLE II
Development of fisheries

Article 50

The ACP States and the Community recognize the urgent need to promote the development of fishery resources of ACP States both as a contribution towards the development of fisheries as a whole and as a sphere of mutual interest for their respective economic sectors.

Co-operation in this field shall promote the optimum utilization of the fishery resources of ACP States, while recognizing the rights of landlocked States to participate in the exploitation of sea fisheries and the right of coastal States to exercise jurisdiction over the living marine resources of their exclusive economic zones in conformity with current international law and notably the conclusions of the third United Nations Conference on the Law of the Sea.

Article 51

To encourage the development of the exploitation of the fishery resources of the ACP States, all the mechanisms for assistance and co-operation provided for in this Convention, notably financial and technical assistance in accordance with the terms set out in Title III, Part Three, of this Convention shall be applied to fisheries.

The priority objectives of such co-operation shall be to:

-       encourage the rational exploitation of the fishery resources of the ACP States and the resources of high seas in which the ACP States and the Community share interests;

-       increase the contribution of fisheries to rural development, by giving importance to the role they play in strengthening food security, improving nutrition and rural living standards;

-    increase the contribution of fisheries to industrial development by increasing catches, output and exports.

Article 52

Assistance from the Community for fisheries development shall include support in the following areas:

(a)   fisheries production, including the acquisition of boats, equipment and gear, the development of infrastructure for rural fishing communities and the fishing industry and support for aquaculture projects, notably by providing specific lines of credit to appropriate ACP institutions for onlending to the operators concerned;

(b)   fisheries management and protection, including the assessment of fish stocks and of aquaculture potential, the improvement of environmental monitoring and control and the development of ACP coastal States' capacities for the management of the fishery resources in their exclusive economic zone;

(c)   processing and marketing of fishery products, including the development of processing, collection, distribution and marketing facilities and operations; the reduction of post-harvest losses and the promotion of programmes to improve fish utilization and nutrition from fishery products.

Article 53

Particular attention shall be paid in fishery resource development co-operation to the training of ACP nationals in all areas of fisheries, to the development and strengthening of ACP research capabilities and to the promotion of intra-ACP and regional co-operation in fisheries management and development.

Article 54

The ACP States and the Community recognize the need for direct or regional co-operation or, as appropriate, co-operation through international organizations, with a view to promoting conservation and the optimum use of the living resources of the sea.

Article 55

The Community and the ACP States recognize that coastal States exercise sovereign rights for the purpose of exploring, exploiting, conserving and managing the fishery resources of their respective exclusive economic zones in conformity with current international law. The ACP States recognize that there is a role for Community Member States' fishing fleets, operating lawfully in waters under ACP jurisdiction, in the development of ACP fishery potential and in economic development in general in the coastal ACP States. Accordingly, the ACP States declare their willingness to negotiate with the Community fishery agreements aimed at guaranteeing mutually satisfactory conditions for fishing activities of vessels flying the flag of one of the Member States of the Community.

In the conclusion or implementation of such agreements, the ACP States shall not discriminate against the Community or among the Member States, without prejudice to special arrangements between developing States within the same geographical area, including reciprocal fishing arrangements, nor shall the Community discriminate against ACP States.

Article 56

Where ACP States situated in the same subregion as territories to which the Treaty establishing the European Economic Community (hereinafter referred to as the Treaty) applies wish to engage in fishing activities in the corresponding fishing zone, the Community and the ACP States shall open negotiations with a view to concluding a fishery agreement in the spirit of Article 55, taking account of their specific situation in the region and of the objective of strengthening regional co-operation between those territories and the neighbouring ACP States.

Article 57

The Community and the ACP States recognize the value of a regional approach to fisheries access and shall support moves by ACP coastal States towards harmonized arrangements for access for fishing vessels.

Article 58

The Community and the ACP States agree to take all appropriate steps to ensure that the efforts undertaken in fisheries co-operation under this Convention shall be effective, taking into account notably the Joint Declaration on the origin of fishery products.

As regards exports of fishery products to the markets of the Community, due account shall be taken of Article 284.

Article 59

The mutually satisfactory conditions referred to in Article 55 shall bear in particular on the nature and the scale of the compensation to be received by the ACP States concerned under bilateral agreements.

Compensation shall be additional to any allocation relating to projects in the fisheries sector pursuant to Title III, Part Three, of this Convention.

Compensation shall be provided for partly by the Community as such and partly by the shipowners and shall take the form of financial compensation which may include licensing fees and, where appropriate, any other elements agreed upon by the parties to the fishery agreement, such as obligatory landing of part of the catch, employment of ACP nationals, the taking on board of observers, transfer of technology, research and training grants.

Compensation shall relate to the scale and value of the fishing opportunities provided in the exclusive economic zones of the ACP States.

In addition, with regard to the fishing of highly migratory species, the particular character of such fisheries shall be taken into account in the respective obligations under the agreements, including the financial compensation.

The Community shall take all necessary measures to ensure that its vessels comply with the provisions of the agreements negotiated and with the laws and regulations of the ACP State concerned.

- - - - -

FAO Fisheries Law Advisory Programme   Circular No. 2, Rev.1
                                                        October 1986

Forms of Foreign Participation in Fisheries: Coastal-State Policy
by Lawrence C. Christy

Coastal-state policy toward foreign participation in fisheries is partly a function of general economic policies and partly of factors peculiar to fisheries. These policies and factors will differ greatly from one country and fishery to another, but there are certain principles that can be used generally to analyse the problem.

All countries regulate foreign participation in their economies, although not all in the same way. Even those that advertise an "open door" to foreign investment do not usually allow it in all sectors, nor do they allow free immigration and unrestricted imports of equipment and supplies. In most countries, there is no pretense that the door is wide open, although capital inflows are usually encouraged. Investments must be approved in order for profits and interest to be repatriated, and the sectors in which an investment will be approved are usually limited. Some, such as retail sales or real estate, may be closed even to resident foreigners. The conditions under which an investment will be approved often include local ownership of a certain share (in effect a joint venture), employment of nationals, local processing, restrictions on local sales and many others. Frequently special conditions, including both exemptions from and additions to the normal rules, are provided where the size of an investment or the characteristics of a particular sector justify them (e.g., petroleum).

Similar considerations apply to fisheries, but the role of the state is magnified by its responsibilities as the manager of the resource. A sovereign state is free to choose any policy it wishes from a centrally managed economy to unbridled *laissez faire*. In the case of fisheries, however, the state is obligated to take responsibility for management, no matter what its general economic policies are. As resource manager it must decide on the uses and limits of foreign participation in the fishery.

It is assumed that a basic goal of coastal states is to maximize the net benefits they derive from their fisheries. "Net benefits" is intentionally a rather elastic term, in recognition both that what is perceived as a benefit in one country may not be so welcome elsewhere and that all the costs of producing benefits must be deducted before the final balance can be drawn up. Before these factors were understood, many countries' fisheries policy was simply to maximize the total catch that could be sustained over time (maximum sustainable yield). It has since been realized that while this may maximize employment and food supplies, it also has high costs, including the diversion of financial resources from areas where they could be more productively employed.   Thus countries are increasingly looking to more sophisticated measures of the benefits they obtain from their fisheries.

Foreign fishing, like other fishery activities, may have both costs and benefits. The costs have been a particularly unpleasant discovery for many countries that have recently extended their fisheries jurisdiction, only to find that traditional methods of fisheries patrol would cost far more than any conceivable fees from fishing. Competition with national fishermen has been another cost of foreign fishing. Potential benefits include not only fees and, in some countries, increased food supply, but also the spin-off effects of shore activities. Even as simple an operation as trans-shipping can be a significant source of employment and revenues.

Some countries have even built up successful fishing bases, trans-shipping depots, processing and repair facilities which are used largely or exclusively to support fishing operations outside their jurisdiction. Although some interference with local fisheries is possible and should be analysed and treated accordingly, for the port state a fishing base is more like any non-fisheries foreign investment, with the added advantage that the products and services are mainly exported. For the states in whose waters fishing takes place, on the other hand, foreign basing and support represents a loss of one of the potential benefits of foreign fishing. Although not analysed below among the forms of foreign participation, the possibility of independent shore activities should always be considered by both port and fishery states.

There are three broad approaches that a state with fishery resources may take toward foreign participation in its fisheries. These are to prohibit or discourage any foreign participation, to grant access to wholly-foreign operations (licensing), and to permit foreign access only in association with national partners (joint ventures) or national operations (over-the side sales).

These must be seen as broad categories, not as uniquely defined choices. None of them is truly exclusive; even a policy to exclude foreign participation will have exceptions dictated by the need for foreign inputs and markets, the presence of immigrant foreigners, the difficulty of defining and controlling the activities prohibited to foreigners. Nonetheless, each of the three might properly be described as the dominant policy of a coastal state toward foreign participation in fisheries.

1.   Excluding foreign participation

Several countries have, officially at least, no foreign participation in fisheries under their jurisdiction and others seem bent on eliminating foreign participation to the extent possible. The ostensible reason for such a policy is to improve catches and opportunities for national fishermen.

Excluding foreign fishing can have a beneficial effect in several ways, but whether the benefits will be realized and whether they will exceed the costs are complex questions which will have very different answers in different fisheries. In a crowded, homogeneous fishery, the exclusion of some (foreign) fishermen is likely to improve catches for those (local) fishermen that remain. The effect may be nullified if new fishermen then enter the fishery, but even so there may be benefits through increased employment, local procurement and marketing. Where the fishery is lightly exploited, reducing foreign fishing may have no discernible immediate effect on local catches, although in the long run less foreign fishing would normally increase opportunities for local effort to expand.

Where there are fisheries on different stocks or different segments of the same stock, the effects of excluding foreign fishing are not so direct or predictable. For example, an offshore fishery for adults of a species might have no immediate effect on the inshore fishery for juveniles, although the eventual effect on recruitment might be large. To the extent the foreign fishery exploits totally different species, there should be no immediate effect on local fisheries, but here again there may be considerable overlap, with the target species of the local fishery forming a significant by-catch in the foreign fishery.

To the extent that factors determining the effect of foreign on local fishing are known, access arrangements can frequently be structured to minimize adverse effects. A foreign fishery may be confined to a certain zone or distance from shore where overlap with local fisheries is less significant. Or special gear restrictions (e.g. larger mesh size) can be imposed on the foreign fleet in order to lessen competition with local fisheries. These measures naturally have to be evaluated in terms of their effects on the profitability of foreign operations as well.

Whether or not reduced foreign fishing improves national fisheries, it may be very useful in avoiding conflict between different gear and different groups of fishermen. In the typical gear conflict, it is the local fishermen who are most likely to suffer losses, so the government's interest in reducing conflict is quite clear. Even where there are no competitive or conflicting effects of foreign fishing, it may be strongly disliked by national fishermen. A government may thus have good political reasons for reducing foreign fishing or at least making it less visible.

Foreign fishing is normally seen as a source of revenue and other benefits, against which any adverse effects on local fishing must be weighed. In some cases, however, the costs of administering and policing foreign fishing may make it unattractive regardless of effects on local fishing. Vigorous exclusion would itself impose costs of policing; a state might well decide to pursue no active policy, neither allowing foreigners to fish nor expending any effort to prevent them. This is not a rare policy in other areas of law enforcement.

As there are benefits in excluding foreign fishing, there are also costs. The greatest is the danger that a coastal state will be led into industrial fishing developments for which it may possess few of the necessary elements beyond the resource itself. It may then confront the need simultaneously to create economic organizations, import equipment, learn techniques, train personnel and find markets. Any one of these is a heavy burden, and attempting them all at once can easily lead to commercial disaster.

Even where a country is not lured into unprofitable ventures, total exclusion of foreigners may cost it opportunities. Flexible arrangements with foreigners can be a buffer that allows fisheries management to respond relatively quickly to changing circumstances, to utilize unconventional resources, to take advantage of fluctuations in abundance, to complement local skills.

In the end, rigid prohibition of foreign fishing may be desirable in one set of circumstances, but it may as easily work against the interests of the coastal state where circumstances change. Weighing the costs and benefits over the long run, therefore, most states choose a fairly flexible policy toward foreign fishing, emphasizing one or another form according to the situation.

2.   Access arrangements for foreign fishing: Commercial licensing

Access arrangements for foreign fishing may be governed by bilateral agreements, licences, contracts or some combination of the three. They may be reciprocal or one-way. They may provide for foreign fishing as such or for some form of association. (Considerations peculiar to joint ventures and other associated arrangements are discussed below; in this section it is assumed that the fishing operation is entirely foreign.)

Commercial licensing may or may not be based on a bilateral agreement, and in fact it may or may not even involve an actual licence, but we shall retain the term "licensing" for non-reciprocal access by wholly foreign fishing operations.

The first issue of commercial licensing is not the form, but whether to have it or not. The great advantages of commercial licensing arrangements are that they can be set up quickly, the terms can be renegotiated relatively easily and frequently, and they can be discontinued when necessary. This provides an opportunity to adjust the amount and nature of fishing effort without social and economic dislocations in the local fishing community. If management is sufficiently effective, temporary licences are a valuable tool for increasing fishing effort to take advantage of fluctuations in abundance. Licenses can also be used to phase out foreign fishing when increases in local capacity are foreseen.

The typical benefit of commercial licensing is fees, which may be paid in cash or product. A major benefit which is harder to measure is the spin-off effects on the coastal-state economy if the foreign fishing is locally based.

Financially, commercial licensing represents less risk than either national fishing or joint ventures. The fees can be structured to provide a known and steady income which comes off the top of the operation (i.e. is not susceptible to financial manipulation through hidden profit taking) and is not subject to commercial risks. It is a rent paid directly to the coastal-state government and can be used for development or other purposes at that government's discretion. Where foreign fishermen have a comparative economic advantage, this could be determinative. A related advantage of commercial licensing is that the coastal state's financial commitment is minimal whereas development of national capacity normally requires capital.

The major disadvantage of commercial licence is the ease with which the licensed fleet can simply sail away. If the foreign fishing has generated significant shore-based activity, this can seriously disrupt the local economy. Since this is a function of the flexibility of commercial licensing, which has just been described as an advantage, it encourages the coastal state either to limit the scale of commercial licensing or to find ways to induce greater stability.

The basic problem of commercial licensing is how to extract fees or other benefits from the foreign fishing activities without incurring costs of enforcement that exceed the benefits. Every state that wants to gain economically from its fisheries will have to solve this problem.

Many of the solutions first considered concentrated on physical enforcement through ships, airplanes and in-port inspections. It is becoming apparent, however, that for many states the costs of physical enforcement would exceed obtainable benefits from foreign fishing. Where the costs are placed on the foreign fisherman (in-port inspections, carrying observers) they substantially reduce the fees he is willing (or able) to pay. Even where enforcement costs do not actually exceed revenues, it is still advantageous to reduce them.

There is a growing consensus that reduced enforcement costs depend on enhanced self-regulation, on the engagement of flag-state responsibility for compliance with coastal-state conditions and on better information about the fishery. It also happens that these conditions encourage a longer-term commitment from foreign fishermen, thus tending to stabilize the foreign fishing activity. Realizing these conditions is not simple, however, since they may conflict with each other, for example, persuading the flag state to accept an enforcement role may have the effect of reducing the reliability of flag-state statistics; it surely will have this effect as soon as fishermen realize their returns will be used against them.

Notwithstanding the uncertainties and complexities, there are four important directions the coastal state can pursue to encourage self-regulation, flag-state responsibility and information-production. These are:

> (a) reasonable licence conditions;
> (b) longer-term licences;
> (c) bilateral agreements; and
> (d) regional co-operation.

(a) Reasonable conditions

The chances of catching an unlicensed fishing vessel are very slim in most EEZs. This greatly reduces the deterrent effect of harsh penalties. The coastal state must therefore make it relatively attractive for foreign fishermen to take out licences and to comply with their conditions. The major way to accomplish this is to make the conditions as little burdensome as possible. Especially to be avoided are conditions that burden fishermen without benefiting the coastal state. These would include administrative complexities and delays in general, as well as such requirements as reporting more information than the coastal state was prepared to handle or carrying observers despite a lack of suitable candidates.

Many other conditions may be difficult or even impossible for particular fisheries. An example is the requirement that a tuna long liner report its entry into an EEZ 24 hours in advance. Since the long-liner is following the fish and can travel 250 miles in 24 hours, it simply cannot make an accurate prediction of entry time and location. A coastal trawler, on the other hand, would probably experience no difficulty.

(b) Licence term

As coastal states gain experience with fisheries management and development in extended zones, it is likely that many of them will see a longer-term role for commercial licensing. The use of short-term licences as a management tool may continue, but it really depends on the availability of surplus vessels that can economically be moved into a fishery on short notice. For the fisheries where a continuing foreign presence is desirable, it will sooner or later be necessary to attract new investment. This is complemented by the necessity of obtaining as much voluntary compliance with the fisheries régime as possible. Only if the fisherman has some assurance of continued access can he be expected to make investments in either equipment or good resource management.

Unless coastal states can accept very high management costs and very low effective investment, they will have to grant longer-term licences or concessions. A typical use would be for those fisheries that are not exploited by the coastal state and which coastal-state fishermen are not likely to be able to exploit at competitive costs. An example in developing countries is fisheries that can economically be exploited only by industrial methods. Given the costs - almost all in foreign exchange - and risks of industrial fishing, many countries will experience direct losses in either national or joint venture exploitation. If they can find a way to realize appropriate benefits from a long-term licensing arrangement, this can be the best - even the only - way to exploit the fishery.

Longer-term licences can also provide certain benefits, such as training and the establishment of related industries, that are not so likely to be gained through short term arrangements. Indeed, a properly structured commercial licensing arrangement could provide for very similar developmental activities to what joint ventures are usually expected to bring. Licence conditions can include training, employment, local landing and processing, always assuming that these are feasible in the first place. Long-term licences will pose difficulties in setting fees for an unpredictable future, but these should not be insurmountable.

(c)   Bilateral agreements

The use of a bilateral agreement in conjunction with commercial licensing has considerable potential for gaining flag-state co-operation in compliance control, which may be enhanced by a regional network of harmonized agreements. Bilateral agreements are also a useful way to provide for transfer of non-cash benefits (such as training) from the flag state, and they may even increase the cash benefits available. The EEC, for example, appears to use Community cash payments for access rights as a method of subsidizing Community vessels. Agreements also facilitate the allocation of surplus under the Convention on the Law of the Sea, which is essentially conceived in terms of inter-state obligations. It should be noted that agreements between coastal states and non-governmental fishing associations are also commonly used, both instead of and in addition to state-to-state agreements. The licence itself is normally issued by the coastal state under its national legislation, but this is not always the case.

Special considerations apply to reciprocal fishing agreements. Many fisheries are effectively internationalized by the coastwise movements of fishermen, who sometimes acquire a semi-local status. In other cases, seasonal or other factors make it economic to use the same fleet in the waters of two countries. Where such conditions obtain and political factors are favourable, the utility of reciprocal fishing agreements is clear. Actually reaching and implementing an agreement is not so easy, however. The two sides may not gain equally in the exchange; there may be difficulty defining the vessels eligible to benefit from the agreement; there may simply be too much friction and too little trust to allow the agreement to work.

Reciprocal access agreements can also represent a trap for the coastal state if it is not in a position to fish in the other party's waters. This may be the case in an agreement with a distant-water fishing nation, but is also found in regional agreements where only one party has off-shore capability or surplus resources. As long as nothing is conceded in the name of an unrealizable reciprocity, no harm is done by the form of words. But several countries have legislation which automatically grants national status to vessels operating under reciprocal agreements; they must be careful about the agreements they make.

(d) Regional co-operation

There are at least three ways in which regional co-operation can increase coastal states' net benefits from foreign fishing. The first (and probably the first stage of co-operation) is to improve information on the fishery through exchange. This is obviously facilitated through harmonized reporting requirements and forms. In a more advanced stage, information on fishing operations can be centralized through a regional register and self-reporting can be supplemented by regional surveillance. A second way coastal states can gain from co-operation is to reduce the difficulties of compliance by standardizing forms, vessel markings and gear regulations for common resources. The third, more difficult use of regional co-operation is to improve bargaining power by presenting a united front on certain fees and conditions. As we are constantly seeing, it is difficult for states with different interests to join together this way, but the benefits can be substantial.

3.   **Association with nationals**

There are a variety of arrangements under several legal forms that associate foreign fishing interests with coastal-state citizens and entities. These include equity joint ventures, joint operations with or without profit-sharing, charters, over-the-side sales and others yet to be identified. All of these can be used in combination with each other and disguised as each other. National policies, however, frequently distinguish between joint ventures - which may qualify as local - and other arrangements which may or may not have any special status.

(a) Joint ventures

For a long time joint ventures have been favoured by developing countries as a means of developing their own fishing industries. They have also, perhaps more commonly, resulted from foreign fishermen seeking access in the face of measures to limit foreign fishing. If a local company or a certain percentage of local ownership is required, a company can be established or a partner found. Other joint ventures have been formed in fisheries - as in other sectors - for financial, commercial or technical reasons that had little to do with government policy.

The peculiar attraction of joint ventures to coastal countries is as a means of development. The joint venture allows the coastal country to participate in an industrial enterprise according to its capacities without first having to master the technical and managerial skills needed to run it. The capacities of local managers and technicians may be increased as a result, allowing gradually greater participation.

The developmental objective is not inconsistent with another advantage of joint ventures complementarity. The different skills, costs, markets of two countries or companies may be combined to maximum advantage. This is easily seen where a country can offer resources, shore facilities and low-cost labour, and a foreign company possesses capital, management and market access.

The drawbacks of joint ventures may be as great as the hopes placed in them. The greatest is risk, both commercial risk, which is generally high in fishing, and the risk of financial manipulation by the dominant partner. Both risks are especially significant to developing countries which can least afford losses and generally have less sophistication in preventing them, although experience with development incentives in the industrialized countries shows that they, too, can be the victims of misplaced confidence. Another drawback of joint ventures is their potential for evading restrictions on foreign fishing.

The situations in which a joint venture offers good prospects are relatively few because of the number of conditions that must be fulfilled. The first is an adequate, marketable resource. Unfortunately most of the known, easily marketed resources are already heavily fished and the under-exploited resources are not easily marketed nor well explored. Even if a marketable resource is identified, it may require careful choice of foreign partner to assure access to the most favourable markets for that resource.

The technical feasibility of a joint venture is much more complex than that of a foreign distant-water operation. The technology used is typically that possessed by the foreign partner, which is frequently poorly suited to the aptitudes and technical preparation of the local labour force. The foreign technology will also usually require elaborate infrastructure (assuming a locally-based operation), which few developing countries possess. Attempts to create the infrastructure as part of the joint venture have frequently turned out to be more than the enterprise could afford. Attempts to do without the infrastructure have run into very high operating costs and/or loss of production due to excessive repair time.

A final major requisite for a successful joint venture is capable management. What constitutes good management is endlessly debatable, but the effects of bad management are not: loss of sea time, inability to keep good skippers, lower catches, poor product quality, lower prices and large losses. Many coastal states are under the impression that the foreign partner will supply the management. If the partner is well chosen, this is true to a certain extent, but the local partner must contribute to good management as well. If he does not, he is unlikely either to assure himself proportionate benefits from the enterprise (he will be cheated) or to assimilate the techniques introduced by it. An inexperienced partner can also interfere with the competent management provided by the other partner, thus nullifying its effects.

Countries which have neither a well developed private sector nor an efficient public sector are not likely to provide suitable partners for a joint venture. They would therefore be wiser to avoid them, even where the resource, market and techniques are favourable.

In adopting its general position toward joint ventures, a coastal state has to concentrate on the substance of an arrangement and not on the words that describe it. It has to recognize that no matter what percentage of local ownership it insists on, there is still a real foreign interest - often a dominant foreign interest - in the venture.

Accordingly the coastal state should analyse joint ventures in much the way it analyses commercial licensing: how will it affect local fishing, what will the fees and other measurable benefits be, what are the long-term benefits, how can the benefits be extracted without excessive cost?

These questions have to be answered by each state, and re-asked as circumstances change. Only two general statements are offered here: coastal states should insist on a fishing fee and they should realize that compliance control is harder, not easier, with joint ventures. The importance of the fee is that many fishing operations are not profitable (processing and marketing may make up for losses on the catching side). Joint ventures are also subject to more and less subtle financial manipulations, which further reduce the chances of profit. It is for the most part illusory, therefore, to count on profits instead of a fee.

The compliance control problem is slightly different: it should actually be easier to know what the fleet is doing, but when coastal-state investment is at risk, the number and complexity of transactions it wants to know about are much greater. Joint ventures may thus improve conventional compliance control, but they are a high-risk way to do it.

(b)   Other forms of association

This is an open category, covering at least three kinds of arrangement. One, typified by joint fisheries operations, involves foreign vessels fishing under foreign control. A middle category comprises foreign contractual services, including chartering of vessels, to a national company. Finally, there are arrangements typified by over-the-side sales whereby foreign interests conduct ancillary operations but do not participate in the actual catching of fish.

To the extent that these hybrid arrangements allow complementary skills and resources to be combined to mutual advantage, they must be seen as beneficial to both the coastal state and foreigners. This is easily seen in but not limited to - over-the-side sale of products without an attractive local market. These offer an especially interesting possibility for development of artisanal fisheries in response to favourable world markets.

These miscellaneous forms of association have two principal disadvantages. One is that the foreigner will be attracted by the most profitable aspects of an operation, assuming the marketing role, for example, and leaving catching to the locals. Even where the balance between the parties is fair, the coastal state may suffer from the loss of national value added. For example, even if chartering foreign boats is cheaper for the fisherman, it reduces the sales of local shipyards.

The second disadvantage of these arrangements, in common with joint ventures, is their use to evade measures designed to limit foreign - and favour local - fishing. Local ownership requirements are easily evaded through the use of straw men and creative charter, sales and financing agreements. This in turn allows foreigners to benefit from favourable conditions that might be intended for nationals.

(c)   Legal regulation of association with nationals

Despite possible disadvantages, the general approach of a coastal state toward foreign association with nationals must be to regulate rather than prohibit it. It is very difficult in the modern world to exclude all foreign participation in fishing, and as soon as some foreign equipment, financing, technicians or markets become involved, it is very difficult to define "fishing" in such a way that foreigners cannot evade restrictions on their activities. They can buy company shares, enter long-term contracts, acquire processing plants, and do other perfectly legitimate things that have the effect of placing them in the fishery. There is an advantage, therefore, in a policy that recognizes this and aims at setting the most beneficial conditions.

There are several different approaches a coastal state can take to regulating such a heterogeneous category. One is to deal with it as a whole by defining "fishing" or "foreign investment" very broadly and then regulating all of their manifestations. Within such an approach different positions can be taken toward different kinds of arrangements or individual judgements can be made in each case. The disadvantage of this approach is that it creates a considerable administrative burden. It may, however, be the most appropriate in a relatively small country where even modest investments would affect important national interests.

A more common method is to regulate not in terms of the category, but of particular elements of fishing. Typically these would be the definition of "fishing" or "fishing boat" and the definition of nationality. Thus if "fishing" only includes catching, foreign mother-ship operations would be possible, but not if fishing includes catching, transporting and processing. If the nationality of a fishing boat is defined by the nationality of its operator, it may be possible to charter a foreign-owned boat and fish on local terms. If nationality is defined in terms of the owner, skipper and place of construction, chartered and even purchased foreign vessels would fall into the foreign category.

The disadvantage of depending on prior definitions is that they are too static. As soon as a regulated element is defined, arrangements are invented to circumvent it. And if the definition is tight enough, it may then prevent arrangements that would be in the general interest. But this is probably unavoidable in regulating a major industry.

4. **Choosing the policy**

It is evident from the foregoing discussion that any coastal state's policy toward foreign participation in its fisheries will depend on a combination of factors that is likely to be unique, both to the state and to the time. Each state therefore faces the necessity of developing its own policy and of constantly up-dating it. Nonetheless, there are some principles that seem to have more general application.

One is that the calculation of costs and benefits is complex. This is largely based on the proposition that there is likely to be a significant interaction between foreign and local fisheries, even when they seem to be concentrated on different stocks. The problem is compounded by the fact that different fishermen and governments are all likely to have different combinations of fishery objectives, which are not easily weighed on the same scale.

Another general principle is the need for a flexible policy to meet changing circumstances. Resource situations may be poorly known or variable or both; the fishery will change in response to general economic developments as well as to the resource situation; both local and foreign fishermen will alter the situation further by reacting to the fishery policy itself. To the extent these factors dominate any fishery, policy would tend to favour those forms of foreign participation that are easiest to control and to eliminate where necessary. Where there is enough stability to favour long-term development, more stable forms of foreign participation might be enlisted in aid of it. The necessity of longer-term guarantees for longer term investments does not, however, eliminate the need for continually up-dating the policy.

In all but very simple situations, coastal states will probably find that there is a use for all of the forms of foreign participation as well as for its exclusion from some fisheries. Where resources are unexplored or very lightly exploited, commercial licensing might be the best way to use them while learning about them. Where local fishermen are unable to dispose of catches for lack of processing or marketing facilities, arrangements with foreign companies for either shore or ship based processing may be the answer. Where a qualified local partner and other conditions exist for a major commitment to a particular venture with a suitable foreign partner, a joint venture can be the right form.

- - - - -

FAO Fisheries Law Advisory Programme   Circular No. 5, 1986

Principles of Fisheries Legislation Under the New Law of the Sea
by Gerald Moore

1.   Introduction

The new legal régime that has emerged from the Third United Nations Conference on the Law of the Sea has had a revolutionary impact on the management of fisheries. With the extension of national jurisdiction over fisheries to 200 miles, almost all conventional fish resources, with the exception of some tuna and marine mammals, now fall within the exclusive management powers of the coastal states. Many of these resources were originally taken by foreign fishing fleets. The new régime gives substantial new opportunities to coastal states to derive increased benefits from fisheries in their exclusive economic zones, both by developing their own fishing operations and by eliciting fees or other forms of payment from foreign fishing operations. It also places on coastal states a degree of responsibility for the management of fisheries that for many developing countries must be almost overwhelming.

These changes and the need to respond to the new opportunities and responsibilities have led most coastal states to review relevant policies and laws. The first product of this review has been a spate of legislation establishing extended jurisdiction; to date 96 independent coastal states have declared 200-mile zones and a further 7 have extended their jurisdiction up to agreed boundaries or median lines. The second phase, now in full flow, has been the revision of basic fisheries laws. The main thrust of this review has been to deal in more depth with the two new issues thrown up by the changes in the law of the sea, namely to strengthen controls over foreign fishing operations in the extended zone and to provide a more rational basis for fisheries management. Together with this new impetus has come a new and broader view of the role of law in fisheries management and indeed in the management of all renewable natural resources. Turning their backs on colonial type legislation, whose primary concern was to detail activities of individuals that should be prohibited and to give broad and unfettered discretionary powers to the fisheries administration, many countries are now seeking to incorporate more positive guidelines and criteria for decision-making by the fisheries administration itself in their new legislation. The objective, it appears, is to provide a legislative framework for a fisheries management system, and to ensure, so far as possible, that both the private sector and the public administration perform their roles within that framework. The aim of the present paper is to consider some of the issues involved in the treatment of the two main issues of management and controls over foreign fishing in new fisheries legislation and then to discuss briefly some of the other provisions that may need to be included in such legislation. But first a word about approaches to the regulation of fisheries in the new exclusive economic zone and the respective roles of fisheries and EEZ legislation.

2.   **Fisheries Law and Exclusive Economic Zone Legislation**

No sector of human activity or of nature can be considered in isolation. Taking too narrow a view of any sector can result in inconsistencies of policy with respect to the management of natural resources and the environment, and conflicts with other sectors. It is partly this line of thought that has led a number of countries to try to deal with the problems of management of all the resources of the exclusive economic zone in a single piece of legislation. The idea is seductive. Authority is lent to it by the fact that the concept of the exclusive economic zone has arisen out of the Law of the Sea Convention and that legislation providing for the implementation of the Convention has for the most part been drawn up by the same Ministries of Foreign Affairs that were responsible for its negotiation. In practice, however, the concept has some limitations. Firstly, dealing with all the matters in the exclusive economic zone covered by the Law of the Sea Convention, while gaining coherence in the treatment of these subjects, means creating artificial divisions with related matters outside the confines of the exclusive economic zone or the Convention. To give a practical example, the marine spaces legislation of Fiji deals with the establishment of the territorial sea and the exclusive economic zone, and, following the Convention, provides for the licensing and control of foreign fishing operations in the zone. It also empowers the Minister responsible for fisheries matters to make regulations for the conservation of resources in the zone. The Act specifically does not deal with foreign fishing in the territorial sea. Nor does it apply to local fishing activities in the zone or beyond. Hence any conservation measures required for marine fisheries off the coast of Fiji will have to be promulgated both under the Marine Spaces Act, for application to foreign fishing operations in the exclusive economic zone, and under the basic Fisheries Act, for application to local and foreign fishing operations in the territorial sea and to local fishing vessels in the exclusive economic zone and beyond. The situation is aggravated in some other states, where responsibility for the promulgation of regulations under the exclusive economic zone legislation is vested with the Minister for Foreign Affairs or Prime Minister, rather than the Fisheries Minister.

As mentioned above, arguments for a comprehensive treatment of all resources in the exclusive economic zone are based in part on the concept of the close interrelationship of all marine resources. In a sense this is true. Both navigation and sea-bed mining, for example, can have a negative impact on fisheries. However, the interactions among the sectoral uses of the ocean are not universal. On closer analysis, it appears that conflicts among the various uses of ocean resources are more within each distinct sector, as opposed to among the sectors. The conflicts are more of overcrowding of navigation and the need for shipping lanes, overfishing and the need for conservation measures, and problems of allocating limited sites for sea-bed mining activities, than they are of conflicts among mineral exploitation, shipping and fishing. The plane on which all the sectoral uses do conflict tends to be limited to that of marine pollution. An exception is in clearly defined ecologically vulnerable areas subject to intensive use, such as the so-called coastal zone.

The above analysis, then, suggests the appropriateness of comprehensive fisheries and other sectoral legislation, coupled with marine pollution control and coastal conservation laws. The analysis appears to have been accepted and followed in a number of countries that originally adopted comprehensive exclusive economic zone legislation and are now finding the need to integrate that legislation more with their general system of fisheries management.

3.   **Management Issues**

The question of fisheries management is becoming increasingly important as most of the world's conventional fisheries resources become fully or over-exploited. The great increases of the world fisheries catch in the 1960's and the early 1970's came from the exploitation of hitherto untapped resources. It has been predicted that any substantial increases in the future can only come through improved management of currently exploited fisheries. This, coupled with the reallocation of jurisdiction and management authority under the new Law of the Sea Convention, places the onus for improved management squarely on the coastal state. This will in turn call for much more vigorous provisions dealing with management in the basic fisheries legislation.

a)   Management planning

Typically, a Fisheries Act will set out the main lines of the fisheries administration, the general responsibilities of the Minister and the executive head of the administration, the structure and role of any advisory machinery, licensing powers, enforcement powers of authorized officers, and regulation-making powers of the Minister. Traditional legislation tends to limit itself to this type of provision. More modern legislation, however, will tend to include more positive criteria and guidelines for the fisheries administration in approaching the task of fisheries management. In a few cases broad management objectives have been set out in the law, either in the substantive provisions or through the definition of leading terms and concepts. For the most part, however, it will be difficult for the basic legislation to include anything more than very general management objectives, given that detailed management objectives may vary from sector to sector, from fishery to fishery, and from time to time. Nevertheless, it is important that these objectives be formulated if any consistent scheme of management is to be applied. The proper role of fisheries legislation, it is suggested, should be to ensure that the process of formulating management objectives is carried out and carried out in a rational way. One way increasingly being used is to require the preparation of fisheries management and development plans.

The nature and use of these plans will inevitably vary considerably from country to country, depending on the sophistication of the fisheries administration, the need for active management of particular fisheries and the degree of public participation called for. The US, for example, requires the preparation of complex and lengthy plans for all exploitable fisheries. The new Vanuatu legislation calls for the formulation of fisheries management and development plans for all exploitable fisheries, but these are far more brief and simple, particularly in areas where no active management measures are as yet contemplated. The new New Zealand legislation, on the other hand, requires the formulation of plans only for those fisheries where substantial management action is anticipated.

The process of formulating simple fisheries management and development plans, it is suggested, can be a distinctly useful one. First and foremost, it provides an opportunity and an occasion for the fisheries administration to think in terms of their management responsibilities, to examine the management basis for proposed development programmes and to be able to present the results of that thinking in a coherent way, even if it may not always be palatable to interests dedicated to "development at all costs". It also provides a framework for consultation with the fishing community and other interested sectors of the public on the needs for management and serves to elicit the understanding and support for any measures finally adopted, without which they would have little chance of success. The plans provide a framework and a reason for conservation measures eventually adopted and a dynamic means of shifting into active schemes of management such as limitations entry for particular fisheries. For developing countries, they may also form a focal point for attracting technical aid in the formulation and review of management policies and schemes.

While the content of fisheries management and development plans will vary, the following are some suggestions based on recent legislative practice in a number of developing countries. For all significant fisheries, the plans should record the state of knowledge concerning the fishery, including in that term the fishermen and dependent activities as well as the resources themselves, the management objectives and the general management intentions with respect to that fishery, i.e. whether there should be expansion of the fishery and/or active management measures taken with respect to the fishery, and the need for and type of further information required concerning the fishery. Where active management measures may be required for any fishery, these would be spelled out in the relevant plan, including the details of any catch or effort limitation schemes, criteria for the issuance of licences, and other relevant matters, such as the transferability or non-transferability of licences in limited entry schemes. Management plans would be drawn up in consultation with the fishermen and local authorities in the areas concerned, thus allowing them the necessary say in the formulation of the management schemes that they will be required to observe. The management plans themselves may be accorded direct regulatory force. This is done, for example, in the recent New Zealand legislation. For most developing countries, however, it is not suggested that regulatory force be accorded directly to fisheries management and development plans in view of the consequent need to specify in detail and rigidly, the procedures for the adoption of the plans, and the likelihood of uncertainty or ambiguity in the wording of the plans. It is suggested rather that legal force should stem only from regulations drawn up in the normal way on the basis of the management and development plans as necessary.

b)   Catch limitations

The traditional method of fisheries management in western developed countries has been through the enforcement of total allowable catches. It is not proposed to enter into a polemical discussion of the merits and demerits of this type of control, beyond noting some of the difficulties associated with its administration and legal enforcement. Apart from the scientific and political difficulties in arriving at suitable and timely figures for the total allowable catch, the main problems seem to lie in the economic effects of management systems based solely on the enforcement of unallocated total allowable catches, and the tendency to encourage over-capitalization as each participant in the fishery seeks to increase his capacity to take a larger share of the TAC. More importantly for the fisheries lawyer are the severe problems encountered in the administration and enforcement of such management systems. These practical difficulties are exacerbated in developing countries, where there may be a dearth of trained scientific staff to carry out the necessary stock assessment and to make the necessary recommendations and analyses, a lack of clear management policy objectives that would enable proper decisions to be made on the size of the TAC, and the lack of adequate administrative machinery to ensure an accurate and timely flow of statistical information on catches, including by-catches and to administer any cut-off of fishing once a TAC has been reached. A number of solutions have been put forward to deal with the economic effects of catch limitation schemes. The favourite, at least in the eyes of free market economists, is currently the allocation of individual quotas to fishing enterprises, quotas that may be traded on the open market. This approach is being tried in a number of developed countries, (e.g. Canada and Australia). However, as pointed out by Troadec (1983), the implementation of such a system is likely to be even more demanding of credible administrative control and is thus unlikely to be a workable approach for many developing countries for some time to come. The problems of administration from the point of view of monitoring of catches can, it has been suggested, (Beddington, 1983) be eased by applying controls at the point of first sale. This will certainly be so in some cases particularly where a large number of small scale producers are involved with the product being funnelled through a limited number of collection or trading points. A typical example would be trochus fisheries where controls are usually most appropriately applied at the point of collection, processing or export. For other fisheries where the domestic markets are widespread and not all products pass through established markets, the problems are likely to persist.

The above discussion of the problems associated with the administration and enforcement of catch limits does not in any way deny the necessity of setting total allowable catches for managed fisheries; the scientific and policy aspects of the process will need to be gone through in any case. The concept, for fisheries in the exclusive economic zone, is also embodied in Article 61 of the Law of the Sea Convention. But what the discussion does suggest, is that for some developing countries the administrative controls used to contain fishing mortality within the limits of the TAC, and hence the legal provisions used to define and apply those controls, will need to be expressed in terms of other measures that are easier to administer, whether these be controls over fishing effort applied through restrictive licensing schemes or through the recognition of exclusive proprietary use rights, etc.

c) Closed Seasons

Closed seasons can be used in a number of different ways. They can be used as a measure to protect certain species during periods of their life cycle when they are particularly vulnerable, they can be used as a means of generally reducing the period of time to which they are subjected to fishing, and they can be used as a means of enforcing catch limitation schemes. The different objectives will have consequences from the point of view of the legal way in which such measures are promulgated. Closed seasons of the first two types will normally be applied through regulations made under the basic fisheries act. The flexibility afforded by the medium of regulations will be required, as the dates and existence of closed seasons may need to be varied from time to time with new knowledge and to meet the changing exigencies of fisheries management. There will normally, however, be no need for rapid action in the closure of a fishing season for these objectives, although there are examples of closure of fishing seasons being used in a more flexible way to protect stocks once evidence of spawning becomes apparent. For the closure of seasons required to administer total allowable catch restrictions or in the examples given above, very rapid "over-night" action may be required, calling for even greater flexibility than that afforded by the medium of fisheries regulations. This can be achieved through the delegation to the Minister or chief fisheries administrator of the power to close the fishing season for a particular fishery or for all fisheries by means of a notice, or a notification relating to the conditions of a fishing licence.

d) Closed Areas

Closed areas again can serve a number of purposes. They can be used to protect certain vulnerable areas such as nursery grounds for particular species of fish. They, and their obverse mechanism, the permitted fishing areas or windows or boxes as they are known as, can also be used as a mechanism for reducing overall fishing effort (though not always with great success) or for controlling fishing operations, and in particular foreign fishing operations) by herding them into accessible areas which can be more easily monitored. Closed areas would normally be set in regulations made under the fisheries act, and would not normally require the mechanism for rapid action that the closure of seasons would call for. Both closed areas and permitted fishing areas can also be set in licence conditions, a device which can be useful if individual areas are to be set aside, for example, for fishing vessels of different nationalities.

e)   Mesh sizes and species sizes

These again will normally be set in fisheries regulations, bearing in mind the need for review of the standards set. While flexibility is thus required, too rapid changes in the regulations will result in undue hardship to fishermen. Any lead-in time for the introduction of new specifications will therefore need to take into account the use-life of nets in which the fishermen have already invested. As the results of introducing mesh regulations are not always easily demonstrated (Beddington, 1983), the introduction of new mesh specifications will need to be preceded by extensive practical trials by the fisheries authorities and extensive public consultation with the fishermen - yet a further argument for the adoption of the concept of fisheries management and development plans in which the factor of public participation is built in. Mesh specifications will need to be accompanied with clear provisions dealing with the method of measurement, and supported by provisions regarding the stowage of nets that are carried on board a fishing vessel but not intended for use in the regulated fishery. Species sizes will also need to be supported by clear provisions dealing with methods of measurement, and, in the case of net fisheries, the amount of proportion of undersized fish that will constitute an infraction.

f)   Licensing

Central to any management measures, and indeed to any fisheries law, will be the system of licensing. Licensing usually performs a dual function. The first is to provide a means of obtaining government revenue. But licensing also has the important function of providing a linkage between the administration and the fishing operations. Through that linkage the administration has a means of controlling the conduct of those operations by means of licence conditions, of obtaining information on fishing activities, and, by the decision of whether or not to grant a licence, to control the amount of effort in fisheries or in a particular fishery. Traditionally, the emphasis has been mostly on the first function. Recently, given the increasing number of fully or over exploited fisheries, more emphasis is being placed on the management functions of licensing.

The consideration of licensing raises a number of issues. The first is the distinction between registration and licensing, particularly where fishing vessels are concerned. At times the two terms seem to be used interchangeably, with the objectives of the two not clearly defined. There is indeed no magic in a name, and the true function of any system of prior authorization of the use of a vessel for fishing operations is not necessarily determined by the title given to the system. Nevertheless the following distinction between registration and licensing is usually observed. Registration is concerned mainly with questions of ownership, nationality and safety standards, i.e. the fishing vessel as a vessel. Licensing, on the other hand, will be more concerned with questions related to the use of the fishing vessel for fishing operations. In many systems, the function of registration will be undertaken by the authorities responsible for merchant shipping, although normally only for vessels over a certain size. Registration of vessels under that size may need to be carried out by the fisheries administration, particularly where required in order to support a system of financial assistance to the fishing industry based on subsidies or credits for the purchase, construction or improvement of fishing vessels.

A second issue concerns the unit to be licensed, which may be the fishermen, the fishing vessels and/or the fishing gear to be used. No generally applicable answers can be given, as the design of any licensing system will depend on the situation of the particular country, and indeed the particular fishery, concerned. But it can be said that, of all these units, the fishing vessel with its gear will normally be treated as the most basic unit of fishing effort and thus the focus for any licensing system. Whether or not licensing should be extended to fishing gear as such, independently of fishing vessels, will depend on the nature of the fishery, and in particular whether strict controls over the use of certain gear, such as gill nets or traps, are required that cannot be achieved through licensing controls over the fishing vessel itself. Whether licensing controls should be extended to individual fishermen, will again depend on the nature of the fisheries to be managed, in particular those fisheries not necessarily involving the use of fishing vessels, the assessment of the usefulness of fishermen's licences in achieving more effective compliance control, and their usefulness as a means of delimiting the category of persons eligible for financial or other assistance schemes.

The usefulness of a licensing system for management purposes will depend to a large extent on the criteria for the issuance of the licence on the one hand and the conditions attached to the licence on the other hand. Of these issues, the former raises the most difficulties. For the most part, traditional fisheries legislation has been reticent on criteria for the issuance of licences apart from those criteria linked to the criminal record of the applicant or the seaworthiness of the vessel. Management considerations have tended to be overlooked. In a sense this is understandable, since the denial of a licence to fish to any national, though not to foreign vessels, is a serious matter: the delimitation of the group that is to receive preferential access to publicly controlled natural resources is a task from which most politicians have tended to resile. It is for this reason that most management systems in the past have tended to be based on non-discriminating measures such as the establishment of minimum mesh or species sizes, closed seasons and areas and the setting of global, i.e. unallocated, catch limits.

As noted above, however, management systems based on such measures alone do suffer from grave limitations, particularly from the point of view of the economic effects on the fishing industry and the tendency towards overcapitalization.

g)   Other measures

The fisheries law will also need to provide generally for prohibition or control of certain ecologically dangerous methods of fishing, such as the use of poisons and explosives. These are normally provisions that will not change from time to time, and thus there is no particular reason why they should not be included in the basic fisheries law itself. Indeed in most cases they are so included.

h)   The handling of management measures in fisheries legislation

What then does all this analysis mean from the point of view of the drafting of fisheries legislation?

It means first of all that for most developing countries, the legislation will need to be drafted in such a way as to be flexible, not to preclude a likely approach but allowing for the growth of management systems along the above paths. In most cases, unless the legislation is being drawn up specifically with a proposed management system for particular fisheries in mind like the new New Zealand Fisheries Act, it will be impossible and undesirably restrictive, for the basic legislation to try to determine in advance, detailed criteria for all management systems for all fisheries. More specifically, it will mean providing for a basic system of licensing, initially centred on the licensing of fishing vessels, but extensible to fishing gear and fishermen, together with some dynamic mechanism for formulating detailed management schemes and the criteria required to implement those schemes. One such dynamic mechanism increasingly being recommended for, and adopted by, developing countries, is the fisheries management and development plan referred to earlier in this paper.

4.   **Control Over Foreign Fishing**

    . . .

5.   **Other Provisions of Fisheries Legislation**

    a)   Fisheries related research operations

Marine scientific research operations are dealt with in some detail in Part XIII of the new Law of the Sea Convention. The right of states and competent international organizations to conduct marine scientific research is safeguarded under the Convention subject to certain provisos and conditions. These include the sovereign right of the coastal state to authorize research operations in its territorial sea. Marine scientific research operations in the exclusive economic zone and on the continental shelf are to be conducted only with the consent of the coastal state. Such consent is not to be unreasonably withheld by the coastal state, in normal circumstances and for general scientific research. However the coastal state does have discretion to withhold its consent where the project is of direct significance for the exploration and exploitation of the natural resources of the zone. This, by definition, would include all fisheries related research operations. The Convention provides for the kinds of information to be supplied to the coastal state on proposed research projects and sets down certain conditions relating to the conduct of those projects. These include the right of the coastal state on request to participate in the project, and to be provided with preliminary reports and the final results and conclusions of the project. Other provisions deal with circumstances in which the consent of the coastal state to marine scientific research operations in its exclusive economic zone may be implied.

The procedures for authorizing marine scientific research may often be set out in special legislation dealing with the whole topic. Some reference, however, will need to be made to fisheries related marine research operations in the fisheries legislation, if only to exempt authorized research operations from the general licensing requirements applicable to commercial operations. Where no separate legislation on marine scientific research exists, then it will be necessary to spell out the procedures for authorization of fisheries related research and survey operations in the fisheries legislation itself. Typical elements of such a system would be a prohibition on unauthorized research operations, a provision enabling the Minister or executive head of the fisheries authority to authorize such operations, the kind of information and research and survey plans to be submitted together with an application for authority to conduct fisheries related research, and the general conditions, on which such operations once authorized can be carried out. These latter conditions will normally include the supply of information and results to the coastal state and its participation in the conduct of the operations.   Provision may also be made for exemption from certain conservation measures where necessary for the research operations, such as the use of smaller mesh sizes.

b)   Marine Reserves

A number of countries are now introducing the concept of marine reserves into their legislation and administration.   These can be particularly important for countries with potentially vulnerable coastal areas, attractive coastal sites, such as coral reefs or wrecks, and a significant tourist sector. They should not however be confused with the concept of protected or closed fishing areas, which will have a narrower and specifically fisheries management objective. Marine reserves can be handled as part of the general legislation dealing with national parks, and it is so dealt with in many countries. Others, including Trinidad and Tobago and Barbados have preferred to have separate legislation dealing with marine parks and reserves specifically. In other cases, where no other suitable legislation exists, provision is often made for the establishment of marine reserves in the basic fisheries legislation. In some ways this may be more appropriate, in view of the fact that the expertise on marine biology and ecology required to manage a marine reserve will normally be located with the national fisheries authorities rather than the national park and terrestrial reserves administration. Wherever the provisions are located, they will need to include certain basic elements. These will be procedures for the designation of marine areas and the surrounding land areas, including consultation with local authorities and inhabitants in the areas concerned, prohibitions on certain acts within the areas, such as fishing, dredging for sand and gravel, and procedures for the management of the reserves.

c)   Marine pollution

Marine pollution can constitute a significant threat to living resources as well as to the tourist and health interests of coastal states. For this reason, general provisions on the control of marine pollution are not infrequently included in the basic legislation dealing with marine fisheries. While not in any way denying the need for controls over marine pollution, the fisheries legislation is in most cases not the most suitable place to locate those controls. The reasons for this are numerous. In the first place, the type of controls that will be introduced are complex and need to cover not only ship-source pollution, such as oil pollution from tankers and other shipping, contingency planning for pollution incidents, and the implementation of global and regional marine environment protection conventions, but also land-based sources of pollution, such as local sewerage outlets, industrial plant pollution and river borne pollution including agricultural run-off. To cover all these sources of pollution properly in a fisheries law, would change substantially the primary thrust of that law. On the other hand, merely to introduce general provisions into the fisheries act will normally result in ineffective controls, while giving the misleading impression that the problem has been tackled and solved. Secondly, the inclusion of pollution controls into fisheries legislation will normally mean that the fisheries authorities will have to bear the brunt of administering those controls. Fisheries, however, are only one of the interests affected by pollution; health and tourism interests will also be affected, often more strongly. Administration of pollution controls will also often place the fisheries authorities, not always the most powerful of voices, in opposition to the industrial development interests of the country. Their voices will also be heard, in most cases, only after investment has been made, for example, in the construction of a brewery or industrial plant. For these reasons, then, it is suggested that pollution controls should rather be located in separate marine pollution or environmental quality legislation and administered by an authority that brings together the interests affected by pollution and allows their views to be taken into account in the planning stage of any industrial or urban development.

d)   Aquaculture

For a number of countries aquaculture offers the prospect of a sustained source of marine products to feed the hungry and contribute positively to the balance of payments. In countries with high land prices and low standards of living, however, aquaculture aimed at the local markets may have limited prospects compared to capture fisheries.   Where the development of aquaculture operations is contemplated, a number of legal issues may arise which may need to be covered in the fisheries legislation, or in legislation aimed specifically at aquaculture. These provisions can be divided broadly speaking into those aimed at facilitating, those aimed at protecting and those aimed at controlling aquaculture operations. Facilitating provisions are aimed generally at the problem of making available land on sufficiently long leases to enable entrepreneurs to make the necessary capital investments.   In many cases adequate procedures may already exist in the crown lands legislation to deal with these problems.   Protecting provisions will normally be aimed at protecting the rights of aquaculturists in the products they raise; without such provisions, for example, any person would be free to take oysters from an oyster bed on the foreshore. The same problem, of course, does not arise with aquacultural operations undertaken on private land. Controlling provisions are mainly concerned with health and disease control and general environmental effects. Closely related are the controls over the importation of live fish which will normally be found in a basic fisheries act. The objective of such controls will be to guard against the spread of communicable fish diseases and, perhaps more importantly, to guard against the introduction of exotic species, whose release into the wild might have undesirable or even disastrous effects on the ecology of the area.

e)   Controls over Fish Processing Establishments

The question of controls over fish processing establishments inevitably raises a number of issues, including in particular the division of responsibility between the national authorities responsible for fisheries management and those responsible for health matters and to a lesser extent, those responsible for the formulation and implementation of export standards. The main interests of the fisheries management authorities are twofold; the need to preserve quality control in order to protect the good name of the country's products in export markets and secondly the need to control the amount of processing capacity in order to avoid excessive pressure on the resources. This second function can be particularly important where fish products collected from a large number of small scale producers are involved, as for example in processing of trochus shells. Controls over the amount of fish products passing through the establishments may, in practice, prove the only cost-effective means of management open to the fisheries authorities. The health authorities' main interests, on the other hand, tend to be limited to protecting the health of local consumers. The national standards institutes' interests will reflect the fisheries authorities' interests in protecting the good name of the country's products in export markets. Any division of responsibilities in the control of fish processing establishments in any country will need to take into account these divergent interests. Above all, however, the maxim "if it works, don't change it", should it is suggested, always prevail. In countries where the health authorities are already exercising effective control over food processing establishments generally, and they can be persuaded to make allowance for the protection of export markets, then it is probably better to leave the operation of the system of control to those authorities. Where the controls are not properly implemented, then there may be reason for introducing a system of controls into the fisheries legislation. Crucial elements of such a system would include the licensing of fish processing establishments, the enforcement of construction and operating standards for those establishments, procedures for certifying the quality of exported products, and provisions for the furnishing of statistics on the operation of the establishments.

f)   Enforcement

Proper enforcement provisions are of course fundamental to any fisheries law. Where legislated provisions cannot be or are not in practice enforced, then the law itself loses its credibility. In such a situation, it is not always the provisions on enforcement narrowly defined that may be at fault, but more generally the way in which the substantive provisions are drawn up.

Perhaps the first issue in dealing with enforcement provisions, is to decide on the category of persons who will be given enforcement powers. In this connection, it is a common adage of government fisheries officers that their main functions should be to assist the fishermen and not to enforce fisheries legislation. That being so, there are few, if any, fisheries services who when faced with the final choice exclude fisheries officers from the category of authorized enforcement officers under the basic fisheries legislation. Other groups normally included in the category of enforcement officers would be police officers, officers of the government defence force and coastguard, and customs officers. In all cases it may be desirable to specify some limitation of rank. As to the powers to be accorded to enforcement officers, the main principle, as with any piece of legislation, is to achieve a satisfactory balance between the need for effective enforcement and the protection of the rights of individuals. This is a prime consideration when dealing with powers of arrest and entry on to private land. Most countries will debate long and hard, for example, over powers of enforcement officers to enter hotels and restaurants and to check the contents of freezers to ascertain whether closed season restrictions are being observed. Where the line is finally drawn will depend upon the importance attached to effective enforcement of this type of provision and the legal traditions of the country concerned. Whatever those traditions are, the powers accorded to enforcement officers must include certain powers of entry without a warrant onto private land, where an offence is reasonably suspected, though not into private houses. They must also include powers to stop, board and inspect fishing vessels in jurisdictional waters, powers to inspect catch, gear and documents relating to the navigation and fishing operations of the vessel, and powers to take samples of fish on board and copies of relevant documents. They will also need to include powers to seize vessels, catches and gear, and to take the vessels and their crew to the nearest or most convenient port, though not necessarily to arrest the master or crew of an "offending" vessel. Somewhere in the legislation of the country should be provisions relating to the exercise of hot pursuit by enforcement aircraft and vessels, though this may often be found in legislative texts restricted to the enforcing agencies, rather than in the basic fisheries law itself. It is also not usual, though it is certainly not unknown, for the fisheries legislation to contain detailed procedures for the stopping of fishing vessels and prescriptions dealing with the use of force in such circumstances. These matters are, for the most part, dealt with in administrative instructions circulated to the police and armed forces alone. Where regional surveillance and enforcement schemes are contemplated, special provisions may be required in the enforcement provisions, enabling enforcement officers from the regional scheme or from another state to be accorded powers under the fisheries act and for their evidence to be admissible in national courts.

Regarding sanctioning procedures, many countries are now turning to the use of civil penalties and administrative procedures in addition to the traditional criminal sanctioning processes, particularly in cases involving foreign fishing violations. In countries where administrative penalties are still viewed with suspicion, a similar effect has been produced by the use of the rather archaic procedure of the compounding of offences, or, in French based law, by the procedure of "transactions". On a number of issues, the sanctioning procedures may need to be supported by the judicious use of presumptions, in order, for example, to change the burden of proof on such issues as whether or not a licence was held, whether or not fish found on board a fishing vessel found committing an offence had been caught in the course of the offence, and concerning the introduction of evidence relating to the cause of death of dynamited fish.

g)   Enabling powers

As noted earlier in this paper, the success of fisheries legislation will depend, at least in part, on its flexibility in dealing with changing management situations. For this reason it is essential that the enabling clause in the legislation should be broad enough to allow the Minister to make regulations to meet those changing circumstances. It should, on the other hand, not be so broad as to give him unfettered power to impinge unduly on the rights of private citizens. In short the main lines of the management system and licensing requirements should be set out in the basic fisheries act, leaving it to the regulations to fill in the details of the system and adapt the detailed measures to the dynamic needs of fisheries management.

h)   Definitions

The definitions in a fisheries law will of course depend on the content of the substantive provisions of the law. Nevertheless the content of certain definitions can have a substantive effect. In a number of recent laws, for example, the objectives of fisheries management are set out in the definitions of concepts such as conservation and management, optimum yield or total allowable catch. Similarly the definition of such concepts as local as opposed to foreign fishing vessels, or artisanal as opposed to industrial fishing operations, will determine the groups that are given preferential access to resources or other benefits. Definitions may also bear on the geographical scope of the legislation, and on the characterization of offences. In the latter context, the new trend seems to be to extend the definition of fishing to include preparatory acts, such as searching for fish, and sequential acts such as processing and collection of fish. The extension of the definition will have a significant substantive effect, *inter alia*, on the design of the coastal state's system for the licensing and control of foreign fishing.

6.   **Some Final Points on the Structure of Fisheries Legislation**

The design of fisheries legislation, like that of any other kind of legislation, will of necessity differ from country to country, in line with each country's policy objectives and legislative traditions. Some points, however, are universal. The first is the need for clarity and simplicity. The law, if it is to be followed, will need to be understood by the people at which it is directed, in particular by the fishing community. Secondly and relatedly, the law will need to be easy to implement. Some provisions may look attractive on paper, but may turn out to be completely unenforceable or unworkable in practice. A law is only as good as the results that it produces, and if it does not produce the intended result, in the most costeffective way, then the law is not successful. The third point is the need for flexibility in the law. The main lines of the administrative system proposed must be set down in the basic law. The details of the system, however, will need to have a certain flexibility if they are to respond to the changing needs of fisheries management. This will mean relegating the specification of rules and detailed rules that are liable to require frequent modification, to some form of subsidiary legislation. In practice the determination of the appropriate level at which individual measures should be expressed will be dependent on the degree of flexibility and universality required. General powers of enforcement officers, for example, will need to be set out clearly in the basic legislation. The specification of fee levels for licences, on the other hand, will need to be expressed in regulations. So also will detailed conservation measures, such as minimum mesh or species sizes or closed areas or seasons. Even more flexibility may be required in instances where closure of a fishing season is used for implementing total allowable catch or quota restrictions; in such cases it may be necessary to provide for the closure of seasons by means of ministerial notices. Other requirements relating to local or foreign fishing operations may be more properly expressed in terms of licence conditions, or in the case of foreign fishing operations, as provisions in an access agreement, whether or not supported by licence conditions.[1]

Note

1.   On this point see Moore, G. The respective roles of laws, regulations, access agreements and licence conditions, WP/8.

References

Beddington, J.R. and R.B. Rettig, Approaches to the regulation of 1984 fishing effort. FAO Fish. Tech. Pap., (243): 39 p.

Troadec, J-P, Practices and prospects for fisheries development 1983 and management: The case of Northwest African Fisheries, in Global Fisheries: Perspectives for the 1980's, ed. B.J. Rothschild, Springer-Verlag, New York 1983.

- - - - -

FAO Fisheries Law Advisory Programme   Circular No. 6, 1986
                                                                      Extract

Flag State Measures to Ensure Compliance
with Coastal State Fisheries Regulations
The United States, Japanese and Spanish Experience
by Eugene R. Fidell, Morio Okatsu, & José Luis Meseguer

PREFACE

. . . Where . . . access is granted, whether under access agreements with the flag state or direct licensing arrangements with foreign fishing companies, the coastal state will face the problem of establishing effective control over those foreign fishing operations. For many developing coastal states, with only limited financial and man-power resources, these problems will often be substantial. Many such states are looking for new ways of achieving practical control over foreign operations that do not entail costly expenditures on sea-borne enforcement capabilities. The cost of operation of a normal patrol craft, for example, quite apart from capital costs, can often exceed the total revenue that the coastal state may expect to receive from foreign fishing operations. Many of these new compliance control mechanisms are based on regional cooperation, such as the regional register of foreign fishing vessels recently established in the South Pacific under the aegis of the Forum Fisheries Agency. Other techniques are being tried out both at the bilateral and regional level. One such approach is the concept of flag state responsibility for compliance control. The essence of the concept is that a flag state, if it has entered into an agreement with a coastal state for access by its vessels to the fish resources in that coastal state's waters, should accept a degree of responsibility for ensuring that its vessels comply with the terms of the agreement and with the relevant fishery laws of the coastal state concerned. The concept received approval at the recent FAO World Conference on Fisheries Management and Development (Rome 1984) as one of the **Principles and Practices for the Rational Management and Optimum Use of Fish Resources**:

> (xvii)   Where access is granted to foreign fishing vessels, the flag States themselves should take measures to ensure compliance with the terms of access agreements and with coastal State fisheries laws and regulations. Coastal States should consider including provisions to this effect in bilateral access agreements.

In current practice, many states do include general provisions regarding flag state responsibility for compliance control in bilateral access agreements. However few of these agreements provide for detailed mechanisms for implementing the concept in practice. Indeed, the degree to which it can be implemented effectively will depend very much on the laws and administrative controls in force in and available to the flag state. The present series of studies examines the experiences of three major fishing countries with controls over the operations of their fishing vessels abroad, and evaluates the potential for practical implementation of the concept of flag state responsibility for compliance control in those countries.

Gerald Moore

THE UNITED STATES EXPERIENCE
by Eugene R. Fidell

Introduction

. . .

The purpose of this study is to summarize the law and practice of the United States with respect to ensuring compliance by U.S.-flag vessels with other nations' fisheries regulatory programs. The United States has appropriate legislation and subsidiary legislation in place, but the implementation of the program has been the target of political and other pressures that could threaten its effectiveness. In addition, it is not clear that flag states with different legal traditions would particularly benefit from using the American machinery as a model. Finally, the program currently in place omits the potentially useful option of imposing sanctions against the vessel's documentation or the mariner's licences of offending personnel. Without such provisions, the effectiveness of the American program may be open to question.

. . .

The Lacey Act

. . . In 1981, Congress passed the Lacey Act Amendments of 1981[9]. Under that legislation, a tighter and more comprehensive system was created, including civil penalties, forfeitures, criminal sanctions and permit sanctions - all for the purpose of ensuring that U.S.-flag vessels and their operators would meet their obligations under, among other things, foreign fishing laws and international conventions. While fishing as such is not covered, the list of prohibitions is so sweeping ("to import, export, transport, sell, receive, acquire, or purchase in interstate or foreign commerce. . . any fish. . . taken, possessed, transported, or sold in violation of. . . any foreign law")[10] that as a practical matter fishing is within its sweep, and the statute has been so interpreted.

. . .

Conclusion

The United States experience is not particularly encouraging as a demonstration of what a flag state can do to ensure that its vessels comply with coastal state fisheries regulatory measures. For one thing, with the exception of a single fishery (the Gulf of Mexico shrimp fishery), there is virtually no administrative experience in implementation of the Lacey Act. The experience that fishery, in turn, has been one of political wrangling and domestic efforts to minimize United States steps in support of foreign fishing laws. Communications between the two neighbours have been sporadic, so far as can be determined, and there is little reason to believe that the amount of resources applied to the problem by United States authorities reflects a reasoned process of evaluating the needs of the resource.

The availability of reimbursement of foreign fines out of the Fishermen's Guaranty Fund poses a potential threat to American efforts to ensure compliance with foreign fisheries regulatory programs. If United States vessel owners and operators know that they have a chance, at least, of being reimbursed for such fines or other penalties if they are able to persuade the Department of State that the coastal state's regulations are unreasonable, even those who might not otherwise risk seizure or other foreign sanctions might nonetheless be willing to take the chance.

In particular the recent creation of a potential loophole which might permit reimbursement of even proper fines under the San José Agreement (if only it appears that the offense is not so serious as to thwart the purposes of the Agreement) shows that domestic political considerations may erode the Government's commitment even to agreed-upon international cooperative efforts, much less to the principle of assuring compliance with individual coastal states' regulatory measures.

Based on the information available, the most important steps that could be taken by the United States (if it were disposed to do so, which is a valid question) would be (a) to ensure that its Lacey Act machinery is known to coastal states, (b) to emphasize its willingness to invoke that statute vigorously against any vessel found to be in violation, (c) to press meritorious cases appropriately and inform coastal state authorities promptly of the results, and (d) to make arrangements with coastal states (especially those with common maritime borders with the United States) with regard to the sensible allocation of United States surveillance and enforcement assets, so that detection of offenders does not remain the sole responsibility of the coastal state. The United States might also want to consider putting in

---

9.   Pub. L. No. 97-79, 16 U.S.C. sec. 3371 et seq. (1982 & Supp. III 1985).
10. 16 U.S.C. sec. 3372(a)(2)(B)(1982).

. . .

place an arrangement for the derating of licensed merchant mariners involved in violations of the Lacey Act, thereby adding a special disincentive to potential offenders against foreign regulatory measures.

It remains to be seen, of course, whether the impediments to flag state efforts to secure compliance with coastal state requirements can ever be truly successful. Surveillance assets will perforce always be allocated, in the final analysis, by the flag state according to its priorities, informed - at best - by the views of the coastal state. Domestic political considerations will almost inevitably have an impact on both the legal framework and the amount of effort expended towards securing such compliance, and the cost and feasibility of judicial or administrative trials at a place distant from the *situs* of the offence (and perhaps before a tribunal that on balance is sympathetic with the offender) will remain a source of concern.

All this is not necessarily intended to suggest an entirely gloomy prognosis. Given the realities of international relations and the competition for increasingly scarce marine resources, however, it would be unreasonable to expect that flag states will exhaust themselves, particularly in times of governmental budget squeezes such as that currently affecting the United States, in an effort to help some other country's problem. Nonetheless, a useful purpose is served by establishing a credible framework for flag state enforcement - not, it should be emphasized, for the purpose of lulling the coastal state into a false sense of security or to distract it from its ultimately nondelegable responsibility for management of its own resources - but rather at least to reduce the potential drain on coastal state financial resources that would be required to shoulder the entire burden of ensuring compliance by foreign fishing vessels.

JAPANESE CONTROLS OVER THEIR DISTANT WATER FISHING OPERATIONS
by Morio Okatsu

Introduction

The effective control of foreign fishing under extended national jurisdiction places a considerable administrative burden on developing coastal states. In one respect the adoption of effective controls can be viewed as a question of the protection of national sovereign rights over the resources of its 200-mile exclusive economic zone, which should not be dependent on the outcome of any cost benefit analysis. In practice many developing coastal states are viewing critically the outlay of financial resources and manpower required and are unwilling to spend more on surveillance and enforcement than they are likely to gain in benefits from effective controls.

Faced with the need to reach some form of balance or indeed surplus in their favour, a number of coastal states are looking to new ways of reducing costs and increasing the effectiveness of coastal state compliance control measures. One of these ways is through regional cooperation. The institution of the regional register of foreign fishing vessels in the South Pacific is one example of such a cooperative mechanism. A further approach, now finding increasing acceptance throughout the world, is the concept of placing some of the responsibility on the flag state for ensuring that its vessels comply with the terms of any agreement between it and the coastal state relating to fisheries in the coastal states zone - the so-called principle of flag state responsibility.

A number of flag states already take some action to ensure that their vessels do comply with coastal state fishing laws. Japan is one of these countries.

It is the aim of this paper to examine the manner in which Japan, under its fisheries laws and administrative practices, does exercise controls over its distant-water fishing vessels and the extent to which these controls can mesh with coastal state compliance control systems.
    . . .

IV. Access Agreements and Compliance Control
    . . .

. . . The consequences of the enforcement of these Notices [The texts of these Notices are Japanese laws instituted by the Minister under Article 90(2)-1 of the Ministerial Order.] by the Japanese Government are far different from those resulting from the enforcement of coastal states' laws by the coastal states. What Japan is enforcing is Japanese legislation concerning the jurisdiction of coastal states on the basis of the fishery agreements between Japan and those coastal states. On the other hand, if coastal states want more enforcement, such as the return of the violators (or violating vessels) into the jurisdiction of the coastal state for the enforcement of its own laws, they will find that no such provisions exist in Japanese legislation.

. . . Japan prohibits illegal entry into coastal states' waters only where fishery agreements exist with the coastal states concerned. Japan's enforcement of laws against illegal entry assumes that legal entry exists and is authorized by the fishing agreement. This sort of give-and-take policy seems quite apparent in the style of these Notices.

Another noteworthy point is that it is only intergovernmental agreements that have the effect of triggering the enforcement provisions in the Japanese legislation. Many countries have concluded fishery agreements with Japanese fishery associations. Like the intergovernmental agreements,[2] those non-governmental agreements also include provisions placing responsibility on the associations to ensure the compliance of their members with the terms of the agreements and with the coastal states' laws.[3]

However, these non-governmental agreements have no triggering effect on Japanese legislation. In other words, if coastal states wish to enlist Japan's own law enforcement to control illegal fishing, or at least illegal entry by Japanese fishing vessels into their coastal waters, they can only do it through the medium of a fishing agreement to which the Japanese Government is a party.

---

2. For example, Agreement on Fisheries between the Government of New Zealand and the Government of Japan signed on 1 September 1978, Article IV states: The Government of Japan shall take measures, in accordance with the relevant laws and regulations of Japan, to ensure:
    (a) that nationals and fishing vessels of Japan refrain from fishing for living resources within the New Zealand Zone, unless licenced . . . ;
    (b) that all fishing vessels of Japan licensed to fish within the New Zealand Zone comply with the relevant laws and regulations of New Zealand in respect of fisheries . . .
3. Agreement between the Palau Maritime Authority and the Fisheries Association of Japan concerning Fishing in the Waters of Palau, signed 5 November 1983, Article IV 2 and 3, states:
    2) The Association shall ensure that their members will not fish in the Fishery Zones of Palau without first obtaining fishing permits from the Authority.
    3) The Association shall ensure that their members will comply with applicable fisheries laws and regulations
    . . .

Conclusions and Recommendations

A) Background matters

As has been seen, Japanese distant-water fisheries are subject to both Government and voluntary self-regulatory controls. Most of Japan's own effort to control its fishery may not seem to be relevant to the coastal states' interests. However, such controls cannot be totally dismissed in view of the impact they may have, even if indirectly, on the Japanese vessels fishing in other states' waters.

Japan has a strong motivation to control its own fisheries, that is the protection of existing Japanese fishery interests given the shrinking opportunities for distant-water fishing operations. In many cases, the first and most clear result of such control seems to be the reduction of the number of vessels. This is particularly true for the typical examples of distant-water fisheries, both distant-water and near seas tuna fishery and southern trawlers (part of distant-water trawlers).

A second result of the controls is that competition among Japanese fishermen, in the same categories as well as between the different categories of fisheries, will likely increase. For each Japanese vessel, the right to gain access to fishing grounds will be limited and thus the value of that right to access will increase. Illegal fishing operations, whether in areas restricted by Japanese voluntary controls or by the extension of coastal state jurisdiction, are likely to be resented by Japanese fishermen who have taken the necessary action to acquire legal fishing rights in those areas.

B) The basis for compliance control is always the Japanese legislation itself

From the basis of the above analysis it is obvious that too great expectations in the sense of enforcement of coastal state regulations should not be placed on the Japanese system of controls over its distant-water fishing vessels. However, the fact that such a system does exist, that unauthorized entry into state fishery waters covered by a fishing agreement is an offence under Japanese laws, that Japan does maintain controls over the location of its fishing vessels and does maintain an investigatory and enforcement capability, and above all the fact that there is a strong tradition of voluntary intra-industry self-regulation, do offer certain opportunities for the development and implementation of the concept of flag state responsibility. The direction which this development could most easily take would seem to be linked to the following concepts:

(a) the conclusion of agreements, including perhaps regional or subregional arrangements, that could trigger the mechanisms of Japanese law prohibiting unauthorized entry into coastal state fishery waters. The mechanism of regional or subregional arrangements might allow for even coastal states that did not wish to permit fishing activities to claim the protection of these mechanisms.

(b) an accent on surveillance activities by the coastal states linked to a procedure for investigation of and reporting on violations by the Japanese authorities or associations.

LEGAL AND ADMINISTRATIVE CONTROL OF DISTANT WATER FLEETS IN
SPANISH LAW
by José Luis Meseguer

I.   BACKGROUND CONSIDERATIONS

. . .

. . . Recent legislation, . . . , has . . . introduced an important innovation affecting the
exercise of state jurisdiction in fishery matters. This is that the personal jurisdiction of the
Spanish state may be exercised over its own nationals for offences committed against Spanish
legislation in waters coming under the sovereignty or jurisdiction of other States.

The only limitation here is to be found in the legal maxim *non bis in idem*. Offences
committed in the waters of another state may be punished by the Spanish authorities only
where such offences have not been punished by the authorities of the state in whose waters
they were so committed. Moreover, under the Penalties Act[2] jurisdiction of the kind can only
be exercised on two specific premises, namely that the offences militate against or might place
at risk the normal performance of a bilateral or multilateral fisheries convention entered into
by Spain, and that the fishing is engaged in without the requisite temporary fishing licence or
where such a licence is misused, i.e., where the fishing is done in areas other than those
authorized by the licence.

II.   GENERAL PRINCIPLES UNDERLYING THE RULES GOVERNING
DISTANT-WATER FLEETS

There are two criteria laid down in Spanish legislation regulating fishing activities of
offshore and distant-water vessels, namely the quota system as regard fishing areas and
temporary fishing licensing.

. . .

IV.   APPLICABILITY OF SPANISH LAW IN WATERS OF OTHER STATES
AND ON THE HIGH SEAS

. . . guideline (No. xvii of the principle and guidelines adopted by the FAO World
Conference on Fisheries Management and Development, Rome 27 June - 6 July 1984) is more
in the nature of an aspiration for the future than the reflection of hallowed State practice. At
the same time, certain States with long-distance fishing fleets have recently introduced a
practice which, given time, may indeed favour the consolidation of this guideline as a
customary principle of international law.

Where Spain is concerned, and as noted in Part I of this paper, legislation introduced an
important innovation as regards the exercise of state jurisdiction. In addition to territorial
jurisdiction over vessels fishing in Spanish waters and to the personal jurisdiction over Spanish
vessels operating on the high seas, the Spanish State has looked with favour on the possibility
of exercising that jurisdiction over Spanish vessels in the case of offences committed under its

---

2.   Act No. 53/1.982 relative to offences in maritime fisheries matters committed by foreign vessels in waters under
Spanish jurisdiction irrespective of the provisions thereby contravened or of the penalties applicable thereto. -
Boletín Oficial del Estado (BOE) No. 181, 3 July 1982.

. . .

own legislation or under fisheries agreements in waters coming within the sovereignty or jurisdiction of another State.

The extension of jurisdiction, however, demands that it be accepted by the coastal State. Once this extension was formalized, in 1980, it proved to be both the result and the cause of treaty practice with potential repercussions at the international level. In bilateral treaty practice Spain has followed two approaches in seeking to secure compliance with the laws of the coastal State by foreign fleets. The juridical consequences, however, differ in the respective cases.

Thus, certain agreements (with Angola, Cape Verde, Norway, Portugal and South Africa) lay down the requirement that Spanish vessels authorized to engage in fishing must comply with the fisheries legislation of the coastal State. Here the territorial jurisdiction of the coastal State is exclusive over vessels authorized to engage in fishing, and offences may be punished by the authorities of that coastal State. The Spanish authorities will be able to punish, under Spanish law, only vessels that are not authorized to fish in those waters on the grounds of unlawful use of the temporary fishing licence.

The other agreements referred to introduce the novel element of requiring the Spanish Government to undertake to guarantee compliance with the agreement only (Canada), with the agreement and the laws of the coastal State (Mauritania, Senegal and Seychelles) or only with national legislation (Guinea-Bissau and United States of America). None of these bilateral fisheries agreements, however, has entailed the next logical step, from this requirement, of establishing a procedure for reporting or applying penalties whereby the Spanish authorities are enabled to cooperate by invoking their personal jurisdiction in order to lend support to the territorial jurisdiction of the coastal State. When all is said and done, these prove to be imperfect obligations and are destined to come to nothing because they are not accompanied by any machinery to guarantee their performance.

In order to make good this shortcoming, Act No. 53/1.982, of 13 July 1982, introduced an international element in the definition of administrative offence in marine fisheries. Thus, under section 1 (1),

"An administrative offence in the sea fisheries and shellfish fisheries shall be an act or omission so qualified in this Act and in any provision of Spanish laws or regulations in force in these matters or in any bilateral or multilateral fisheries agreements in force between Spain and any other State that have been published in the **Boletín Oficial del Estado**."

However, this rule, too, contains a further rule of the kind described as being "juridically left blank" in the sense that the fisheries agreement can be enforced directly only where express provision has been or will be made for the type of sanction (according to whether the offence is minor, serious or very serious). Otherwise, only those offences will lead to prosecution proceedings being taken where they are offences of illegal fishing (unlawful use of fishing licence) in the waters of the coastal State with which Spain has a fisheries agreement or offences constituting "the contravention of obligations established in a bilateral or multilateral fisheries agreement entered into by Spain whenever failure to comply with such an obligation by the owner of a vessel or any group of such owners militates against or places at risk the performance of the agreement".

- - - - -

FAO Fisheries Law Advisory Programme   Circular No. 8
                                                             March 1987

Maritime Hot Pursuit
by Eugene R. Fidell

Introduction

. . . The topic is one of concern to all coastal states struggling to achieve effective control over the living (and non-living) resources of adjacent seas. While effective use of the right of hot pursuit is by no means a cure-all for the suppression of illegal foreign fishing, it is an important tool that should be available not only for actual use in appropriate cases, but also to lend credibility to coastal state positions in negotiations and promulgation of fisheries regulatory measures.

. . .

Hot Pursuit: The General Concept

The basic idea behind hot pursuit is the notion that a governmental authority whose jurisdiction is limited to a particular territory must have some way of apprehending wrongdoers who seek to flee that territory. A state's laws in general have no extraterritorial application, at least as to persons or vessels of other nations. Hence, some mechanism is necessary to ensure that the purposes of a state's legislation are not thwarted by the simple expedient of flight by the criminal.

The concept has widespread application to the exercise of governmental authority. For example, the doctrine has been invoked as a justification for crossing national land boundaries in pursuit of criminals who maraud without regard to those boundaries, and who might not otherwise be brought to justice. The doctrine can also have application even within a single country, as, for example, in the case of nations organized along federal lines.

Maritime Hot Pursuit

Hot pursuit as a doctrine has long been recognized by customary international law. In addition, detailed provisions were set down in Article 23 of the 1958 Convention on the High Seas. Today the corresponding provisions appear in Article 111 of the United Nations Convention on the Law of the Sea (UNCLOS). As will appear from the following discussion, a number of potentially thorny questions exist for which UNCLOS does not furnish clear answers. For these, one must still have resort to customary law of the sea and state practice.

Because this paper is intended to have as practical an application as possible, the discussion below identifies and responds to what are believed to be the issues most likely to be addressed by fisheries law administrators.

1.   **What is the purpose of hot pursuit?**   The purpose of hot pursuit is only to preserve the coastal state's ability to enforce its laws with respect to foreign vessels. It creates an exception

to the territorial concept of jurisdiction so that foreign vessels may not escape punishment simply by fleeing.

2.   **To what vessels does hot pursuit apply?** The doctrine of hot pursuit has no application to vessels of the coastal state. Such a vessel may be pursued and boarded, subject to whatever constraints the flag state may impose on itself through domestic legislation, anywhere other than in the territorial sea of a third state. Thus, there is, with respect to a vessel flying the flag of the coastal state no need to maintain continuous pursuit after the vessel's offense has been observed. Moreover, a vessel may not assert, with respect to enforcement measures undertaken by its own flag state authorities, that it is in innocent passage.

3.   **How often is hot pursuit employed?** Hot pursuit is no longer a rarity. Modern navigational aids such as radar permit foreign vessels to be alert to at least some of the operational enforcement efforts of coastal states, making it that much likelier that they will take steps to flee to beyond the limits of coastal state authority when they sense that they may be apprehended.

4.   **Which officials can exercise the right of hot pursuit?** The right of hot pursuit, as governed by international as opposed to domestic law,[1] looks not to the identity of the official, but the character of the platform from which the right is to be exercised[2]. Hot pursuit, that is, is exercised "by" a ship or aircraft, rather than "by" its commander. As indicated below, however, in certain situations, the official status of the person in charge of the enforcement craft, or even the crew, could invalidate the pursuit.

5.   **Which vessels can be used to initiate or continue hot pursuit?** UNCLOS Article 111(5) provides that hot pursuit "may be exercised only by warships or military aircraft, or other ships or aircraft clearly marked and identifiable as being on government service and authorized to that effect." The "warships or military aircraft" clause is readily understood. Article 29 defines "warship" as "a ship (1) belonging to the armed forces of a State (2) bearing the external marks distinguishing such ships of its nationality, (3) under the command of an officer (4) duly commissioned by the government of the State and (5) whose name appears in the appropriate service list or its equivalent, and (6) manned by a crew which is under regular armed forces discipline" (numbering inserted). This imposes considerable limitations. Subclause (4) seems to require that the vessel be under the command of a "commissioned" officer, rather than a military person serving under a "warrant" or a noncommissioned or "petty" officer. Subclause (5) calls upon the coastal state to maintain an orderly list of its officers. Subclause (6) would exclude vessels manned by "civil servants", even if commanded by a naval officer.[3]

These limitations are quite easily avoided under the other clause of Article 111(5), dealing with "other ships or aircraft (1) clearly marked and (2) identifiable as being on government service and (3) authorized to that effect" (numbering added). If the vessel is not clearly identifiable as being on government service, charges that the offender failed to heave to may be rejected in court.[4] Some states have deemed it prudent to pass specific legislation indicating which of its vessels are authorized to initiate hot pursuit. The designation should be gazetted or otherwise made a matter of public record, and should, one would think, be generic as to classes of vessels (e.g., all customs vessels, police vessels, fisheries department vessels) rather than naming particular craft.

Related to the foregoing is the question whether neighboring coastal states - for example, states whose enforcement resources were limited - might join together and arrange to cooperate in exercising the right of hot pursuit. Article 111 proceeds on the assumption that the pursuit will be effected by warships or specially authorized vessels belonging to the coastal state whose law is thought to have been violated. As to warships, this conclusion seems inescapable. However, it is conceivable that an international agreement could be negotiated under which vessels of a state other than the coastal state would be deemed "other ships . . . clearly marked and identifiable as being on government service and authorized to that effect" for the purposes of Article 111(5). Such an arrangement, which assumes that a vessel could qualify under Article 111(5) even if it did not meet the "genuine link" requirement set in Article 91(1) for vessel nationality, would somewhat reduce the chances of escape by offenders by permitting the states in the region, in effect, to pool their resources.

In order to minimize the chances that such an arrangement would be found to violate international law, special measures would probably have to be taken to give the matter due publicity, lest fleeing offenders be able to contend that they reasonably believed their pursuers were unauthorized. If the basic premise is correct that the purpose of Article 111(5) is simply to ensure due notice to the affected private interests, it would seem that a neighboring state's warships could qualify as "other vessels" for purposes of the coastal state's hot pursuit authority under Article 111.

6.   **Can hot pursuit be initiated by an aircraft?**   Yes. Hot pursuit may be initiated, maintained or consummated (i.e., a seizure effected) from an aircraft. There is at least one known case in which a helicopter arrested a vessel.[5] There has also been a case in which a submarine (Libyan) arrested a foreign (Italian) fishing vessel.

7.   **What is required to initiate hot pursuit?**   In order to initiate hot pursuit, the pursuing vessel or aircraft must first satisfy itself "by such practicable means as may be available that the ship pursued or one of its boats or other craft working as a team and using the ship pursued as a mother ship is within the limits of the territorial sea, or, as the case may be, within the contiguous zone or the exclusive economic zone or above the continental shelf".[6] Once that conclusion has been drawn, the pursuing unit must give "a visual or auditory signal to stop at a distance which enables it to be seen or heard by the foreign ship". The signal, which must be given while the offending vessel is still within the maritime zone on which jurisdiction is predicated,[7] may be by loudspeaker, voice, flag hoist, blank warning shots, ship's whistle, siren or other means. The International Code of Signals, which is widely used,[8] includes appropriate signals in this regard[9]. Specific signal may also be set forth in coastal state legislation, access agreements or permit terms. Radio transmissions do not satisfy the requirements of international law for initiation of hot pursuit.[10]

Implied in Article 111(4) of UNCLOS is the notion that after the visual or auditory signal, the pursuer or some unit working with it **must actually pursue**; i.e., it cannot simply give the signal and consider the pursuit to be in effect. This point is expressly made with respect to aircraft-effected pursuits in UNCLOS Art. 111(6)(b), but it is to be assumed that the same principle applies to cases in which the signal is given by a vessel. See UNCLOS Art. 111(4).

The duty to give a visual or auditory signal applies to hot pursuit initiated by an aircraft. Common methods of giving the signal to stop from an aircraft include dropping message blocks, radio transmission, and flashing lights. It is unclear whether dipping wings or other airborne maneuvers will suffice if the meaning of those maneuvers is not established in advance in publicly available regulations. It is, however, understood that in practice a number of countries use the procedures set out in Regulation 16 of Chapter V of the Annex to the International Convention for the Safety of Life at Sea, 1974.

The enforcement vessel or aircraft need not itself be in or over the territorial sea, EEZ or continental shelf in order to initiate or continue hot pursuit. (UNCLOS Art. 111(1); *see generally* N. Poulantzas, *supra*, at 198-99).

8.   **What is required to continue hot pursuit?**   The pursuit must be uninterrupted. [UNCLOS Art. 111(1)].   In narrow circumstances, such as a storm, brief interruptions will apparently not terminate the pursuit provided there is no reasonable doubt as to whether the target is the same as the vessel identified prior to the hiatus. *(See generally* N. Poulantzas, *supra*, at 210-15).   It has been held that a delay to pick up small boats working with the pursued vessel is not an interruption, and a pause to board and attempt (without success) to review the vessel's papers has also been deemed not an interruption. (*Id*. at 213).   The foremost expert in this area considers that the case would be altered if the ship's papers had been made available for inspection during the boarding, "since the purpose of pursuit has been practically attained by making all enquiries". (*Id*. at 214).

9.   **What happens if the hot pursuit is interrupted?** Hot pursuit that has been interrupted is deemed abandoned. This is particularly the case if the interruption is such that there can no longer be reasonable certainty that a pursued vessel is the same one that was being pursued prior to the interruption. Arrest of a vessel following such an interruption would violate international law and give rise to liability for damages.

If the pursued vessel enters the haven of its own flag state's territorial sea or the territorial sea of a third state, the pursuit has ended; it is not simply suspended until such time as the vessel leaves those waters, even if the pursuing unit(s) remain on the scene. [UNCLOS Art. 111(3)]. One would think that the purpose of this provision is not so much to create safe havens for offenders but to respect the juridical rights of flag states and third states. Those states could therefore presumably relinquish the benefits of this provision by treaty, but there appears to be no direct authority on the point thus far, although there is at least one instance in which neighboring states have, by treaty, agreed that coastal state enforcement measures may continue in the territorial seas of an adjacent and opposing coastal state.[11] Neighboring coastal states wishing to collaborate in matters of fisheries enforcement might wish to pursue the matter in regional negotiations.[12]

10. **What happens if the pursued vessel is apprehended?**   Once the vessel has been apprehended, the coastal state has authority to see to it that it is brought to an appropriate port for adjudication. Actual navigation may be left to the usual crew if they will cooperate. If they refuse to cooperate, the vessel may be towed to port. Crewmembers may be removed from the vessel if necessary or appropriate. The coastal state has an obligation to exercise due care for the vessel while it is in custody, and has a duty to release the vessel promptly, under UNCLOS Article 73(2), "upon the posting of reasonable bond or other security". The precise details of which agency of the coastal state shall have responsibility for custody during the pendency of any litigation is a matter for coastal state determination, and this may well differ depending on the organization of functions relating to national defense, port security, police and so on.

If the seized vessel is escorted across the EEZ or high seas for the purpose of coastal state legal proceedings, and that route was necessary in the circumstances, that fact does not entitle the vessel to be released. UNCLOS Art. 111(7).

11. **What is the status of a seized vessel?** The status of the seized vessel turns in part on international legal considerations and in part on domestic coastal state legal considerations. The vessel remains a vessel of the flag state, although it is subject to the control of the coastal state for the time being. The vessel is not, however, a "prize", since that concept applies only to vessels seized by a belligerent in wartime. Thus, the law enforcement personnel responsible for the seized vessel should be referred to as a "boarding party" rather than a "prize crew".

12. **What happens if the pursued vessel escapes?** If the pursued vessel escapes, the coastal state may nonetheless protest to the flag state, and invoke any sanctions that may be available as regards flag state fishing quotas or permit revocation. If so provided in the access agreement or in the flag state's domestic legislation, the flag state may have the duty and power to impose sanctions itself on the offender. Extradition is not currently a practical option for fisheries offenses[13], but there is no reason why countries could not negotiate agreements for the extradition of fisheries offenders who are fortunate or crafty enough to elude coastal state capture. If the offending vessel subsequently returns to the jurisdiction of the coastal state other than in the course of innocent passage, UNCLOS Art. 28(2), or perhaps as a vessel in distress, the coastal state could arrest it for the prior offense, subject to application of the coastal state's statute of limitations. It cannot, however, simply be pursued anew, absent a further violation of coastal state law.[14]

13. **Can the pursuing vessel use force?** Yes, but the force must be reasonable in the circumstances. First, the use of force must be distinguished from the use of firearms for the purpose of signalling. If signals are ineffective in securing compliance with the order to stop, any force used must be extremely carefully controlled, since human life may easily be endangered.

> "Only when [visual and sound signals] are clearly ineffective may gunfire be used, and then it must be in the form of blank shots, or shots deflected across the bow; and only when these measures are also clearly ineffective may a ship be fired into. But in that case a solid shot with a minimal effect and of the lowest feasible calibre must be used. Unless arrest is resisted by return fire, explosive shot should not be used." (D. O'Connell, *supra*, at 1072).

Specific guidelines should therefore be in place and observed not only as to the type of weapons and projectile to be employed, but also how any fire is to be directed. In addition, fire should be so directed that the ship's ability to navigate is affected. This means fire should be aimed at the rudder first.

It should be stressed that excessive force is not only to be avoided out of respect for human life and because international law currently condemns the mainstay of the penal process - imprisonment - as a sanction for fisheries offenses, *see* UNCLOS Art. 73(3), but also because excess can give rise to international frictions and substantial pecuniary liability.

Article 31 provides that the flag state "shall bear international responsibility for any loss or damage to the coastal State resulting from the non-compliance by a warship or other government ship operated for non-commercial purposes with . . . the provisions of this

Convention or other rules of international law." Conversely, the coastal state would bear international responsibility for loss or damage arising from misapplication of its authority under Article 111. In this vein, Article 111 (8) states that "where a ship has been stopped or arrested outside the territorial sea in circumstances which do not justify the exercise of the right of hot pursuit, it shall be compensated for any loss or damage that may have been thereby sustained"[15].

14. Can more than one vessel or aircraft join in the pursuit? Yes. The pursuit may be "passed" in relays from one vessel or aircraft to another vessel or aircraft; it can also be "passed" from an aircraft to a vessel and back. The passage, however, must be such that the pursuit remains continuous, even though the particular pursuer may change.

15. Is the consent of the flag state of the vessel required in order to conduct hot pursuit? No. On the other hand, the flag state should be promptly notified when one of its vessels has been apprehended as a result of hot pursuit. Such notification is required by UNCLOS Article 73(4) for any seizure of a foreign vessel[16].

Flag states may well assert their vessels' interests by claiming that the pursuit was invalid for one reason or another.

In addition, when a foreign vessel successfully evades apprehension involving hot pursuit, the coastal state may well want to lodge a diplomatic protest over the matter. If an access agreement or permit are in force, the coastal state would be justified in taking into account the flight in determining whether to revoke the permit, assess a civil penalty (if authorized), reduce quotas, or take other retaliatory action, particularly if the flag state fails or refuses to take punitive action itself against the offender.

16. What happens if the pursued vessel enters the EEZ or contiguous zone of the flag state or a third state? The UNCLOS does not expressly answer this question, but a strong *expressio unius* argument can be made that the safe haven provision of Article 111(3), under which the right of hot pursuit ceases when the pursued vessel enters the territorial sea of its flag state or a third state, necessarily implies that mere entry into a contiguous zone, EEZ or waters superjacent to the flag state or third state's continental shelf would have no effect on the coastal state's right to pursue. As far as state practice is concerned, it is understood that in at least one case UK enforcement craft have continued hot pursuit into the 200-mile Irish exclusive fishery limits, although this is not a general practice[17].

17. Can hot pursuit be initiated from a (a) fisheries zone, (b) EEZ, or (c) continental shelf? Yes. Item (a) is the subject of a reported decision of a court in the United States, involving a Japanese fishing vessel seized off Maine[18]. Items (b) and (c) are covered expressly in UNCLOS Article 111(2). It should be added, however, that for cases in which the continental shelf exceeds 200 miles from the baseline from which the territorial sea is measured, hot pursuit may be exercised only in respect of violations involving creatures of the continental shelf; that is, it may be that the vessel and its continental shelf fishery resources catch will be subject to forfeiture, but not any finfish that were on board.

Article 111(1) expressly authorizes hot pursuit from archipelagic waters (as well as internal waters, territorial sea and contiguous zone).

18. **Can the coastal state make a refusal to heave to an offense?** Yes[19]. If the foreign fishing vessel is caught as a result of the hot pursuit, or if there is in place some other mechanism that permits enforcement measures to be taken even if a vessel is not in the custody of the coastal state, the coastal state may treat the fishing vessel's attempt to flee as a refusal to allow a boarding authorized by coastal state law. Thus, for example, United States foreign fishing regulations make it a violation for a vessel to fail to stop when directed to do so. 50 C.F.R. sec. 611.6(c)(2) (1985). The same regulations prohibit refusals "to allow an authorized officer to board [a foreign fishing vessel] for purposes of conducting any search or inspection in connection with enforcement of" the fisheries law, the applicable access agreement, the regulations or a fishing permit. *Id*. sec. 611.7(a)(2). The regulations also make it an offense to "interfere with, obstruct, delay, oppose, impede, intimidate, or prevent by any means any boarding, investigation or search, wherever conducted, in the process of enforcement" the statute, an access agreement, the regulations or a fishing permit. *Id*. sec. 611.7(a)(6). Similar provisions are to be found in the legislation of some of the coastal states in the subregion, e.g. Guinea, Guinea-Bissau[20].

19. **What steps should a coastal state take to maximize its ability to exercise the right of hot pursuit?** The steps that can and should be taken to maximize the coastal state's ability to exercise the right of hot pursuit include:

(a) Having the ships, aircraft, communications and navigational equipment, and arms needed to maintain a credible patrol and apprehension operation;

(b) Having in place appropriate detailed instructions concerning when and how the right of hot pursuit may be exercised;

(c) Ensuring that maritime law enforcement personnel are appropriately trained to exercise the right of hot pursuit, including in particular training and guidance concerning the use of force;

(d) Ensuring that maritime law enforcement personnel have access to timely, expert legal advice as needed on an emergency basis in connection with exercise of the right of hot pursuit;

(e) Ensuring that arrangements are in place for policy and operational coordination among the coastal state officials responsible for national defense, foreign affairs and fisheries regulation;

(f) Ensuring that agreement has been reached with adjacent coastal states with respect to lateral seaward boundaries, so that the geographical limits applicable to the exercise of the right of hot pursuit may be known to all concerned before any incidents arise;

(g) Determining whether nearby coastal states can waive the provision of UNCLOS Article 111(3) terminating hot pursuit when the offending vessel enters another state's territorial sea, and if so, whether and under what circumstances those nearby states would be disposed to waive that provision; and

(h) Negotiating regional arrangements for hot pursuit, so that pursuit of an offender could be "passed" from vessels or aircraft of one nation to vessels or aircraft of another (i) in exigent circumstances or (ii) as a means of minimizing one coastal state's exercise of enforcement powers in another coastal state's EEZ.

Conclusion

As should be apparent from the foregoing, the right of hot pursuit can be critical to the implementation of a credible coastal state fisheries regulatory program. To be effective, the right requires a substantial commitment of resources so that ships and aircraft can be on scene when needed, and legal proceedings can be brought to a successful conclusion in keeping with both domestic and international standards. While bilateral or multilateral fisheries agreements can go far to ensure that foreign fishing vessels comply with the requirements of coastal state laws, for example, by providing for real sanctions to be administered by the offender's flag state authorities, such arrangements will never fully protect against those who are truly determined to enrich themselves regardless of the interests of coastal states. This is, of course, particularly true with respect to the "pure" poacher, i.e., the fishing vessel that flies the flag of a country with which the coastal state has no access agreement.

Because of the expense involved in mounting a credible at-sea surveillance and enforcement program, coastal states in the CECAF subregion may want to explore arrangements under which these costs can be shared, as well as arrangements to make certain that none of the waters over which they have jurisdiction are turned into a safe haven for those who would defy the fisheries laws of neighboring states. Putting appropriate cooperative measures into effect for these purposes will represent an unusual challenge to coastal states in the subregion, and may require the exploration of unresolved issues of international law. But the benefits of addressing the matter would seem to be beyond debate.

Finally, in order to avoid embarrassment as well as the danger of responsibility for damages, it is important that enforcement agencies be fully trained in the limitations international law places on the exercise of the right of hot pursuit. Any maritime law enforcement operation is potentially hazardous, and fleeing poachers are unlikely to make the enforcement officials' task any easier. In order to be effective, the hot pursuit function should be the subject of regular drills, and detailed instructions, reviewed by national legal authorities, should be in place before the power is exercised. These should make clear to those responsible for enforcement the sequence of events that is necessary to invoke the power, but also should include practical guidance that will instill confidence in the pursuing/boarding units and maximize the prospects for a successful prosecution.

Notes

1. Domestic legal rules of the coastal state may impose additional constraints. N. Poulantzas, The Right of Hot Pursuit in International Law (1969). For an examination of such potential constraints under domestic United States law see Fidell, Fisheries Legislation: Naval Enforcement, 7 J. Mar. L. & Com. 351, 361-65 (1976).
2. Fidell, Enforcement of the Fisheries Conservation and Management Act of 1976: The Policeman's Lot, 52 Wash. L. Rev. 513, 568 & No. 304 (1977).
3. Similar factors would be applied, mutatis mutandis, to military aircraft. Cf. UNCLOS Arts. 110(4), 111(6) (a).
4. Eg., Regina v. Cauley, 14 Can. Crim. Cas. 2d 573 (N.S. Magis. 1973).
5. Fishing News Int'l, Mar. 1975, at 17-18 (arrest of Danish fishing vessel Oryx by UK helicopter), noted in Fidell, Fisheries Legislation: Naval Enforcement, supra, at 356 No. 19. The case was later dropped as a borderline violation.
6. A vessel outside the geographical reach of the coastal state but working with smaller vessels within that state's reach is deemed to be constructively present and therefore subject to pursuit. N. Poulantzas, supra, at 243-51.
7. United States v. Postal, 589 F.2d 862, 872 (5th Circ. 1979).
8. N. Poulantzas, supra, at 206.

9. Some coastal states specify the signals to be given. See 2 D. O'Connell, The International Law of the Sea 1072 No. 68 (1984).

10. N. Poulantzas, supra, at 204-05, 212 No. 19.

11. See N. Poulantzas, supra, at 191, and D. O'Connell, supra at 1090 & No. 164 (both citing Convention for the Repression of Contraband in Alcoholic Liquors between Denmark and Sweden, Oct. 28, 1935, 166 L.N.T.S. 299). Senegalese fisheries law also contemplates pursuit across marine boundaries if permitted by treaty. Law No. 76-89, July 2, 1976, Art. 32, noted and reproduced in Tavares de Pinho, Compendium des Législations des Etats Membres de la Commission Sous-Régionale des Pêches, FAO Fisheries Law Advisory Programme Doct. No. FL/COPACE/87/19/1987. It is believed that the right has not yet been exercised.

12. Note that the Conference of Plenipotentiaries on Cooperation in the Protection and Development of the Marine and Coastal Environment of the West and Central African Region in Abidjan, 1981, called on states parties to the Convention to cooperate in "granting the right of hot pursuit in all waters within the geographical scope of the Convention in respect of vessels caught in the act of polluting in waters falling under their jurisdiction". The geographical scope of the Convention includes the territorial seas of the states parties to the Convention.

13. Poulantzas refers briefly (at 231) to the possibility of extradition, but state practice in the extradition area does not typically extend to fisheries offenses. Moreover, some nations decline to extradite their own nationals.

14. See N. Poulantzas, supra, at 231-32.

15. The language is not believed to preclude additional claims on behalf of the vessel's flag state as well.

16. Earlier law was not mandatory. In 1969 Poulantzas commented (at 237 No. 94) that "the importance of the incident requiring notification or not should be left to the discretion of the competent department of the coastal State if not otherwise provided for in Consular Conventions or generally in Treaties between the States concerned."

17. See U.K. 5th report of the House of Commons Expenditure Committee, Session 1977-78, The Fishing Industry. House of Commons Publication No. 356, 1978, p. 75.

18. United States v. Taiyo Maru No. 28, 395 F. Supp. 413 (D. Me. 1975), 70 Am. J. Int'l L. 138-39 (1976), discussed in Fidell, Hot Pursuit from a Fisheries Zone, 70 Am. J. Int'l L. 95 (1976); see also Ciobanu, Comment, 70 Am. J. Int'l L. 549 (1976), and Fidell, Letter, id. at 554.

19. See, eg., Regina v. Cauley, supra; see also N. Poulantzas, supra, at 205-06 & No. 325 (collecting statutes authorizing pursuit if vessel fails to comply with order to stop).

20. See Compendium des Legislations des Etats Membres de la Commission sous-régionale des Pêches, pp. 84-129.

- - - - -

Additional References

Coastal State Requirements for Foreign Fishing. FAO Legislative Study No. 21, Rev.2, 1985.

Fisheries Development. Review of support by the United Nations Development Programme, UNDP Publication 1986.

- - - - -

Marking and Identification of Fishing Vessels

FAO Committee on Fisheries   COFI/87/7
Seventeenth Session, May 1987   Extract

Marking and Identification of Fishing Vessels

1. . . . The 1984 FAO World Conference on Fisheries Management and Development recommended in its report that "States should adopt standard specifications with respect to the identification and the marking of fishing vessels in cooperation with competent international organizations".

. . .

4.   . . . The Director-General convened an Expert Consultation on the Technical Specifications for the Marking of Fishing Vessels in Rome, 16-20 June 1986. The Consultation
established the following criteria as the basis for the Technical Specifications:

  (i)   the use of an established international system from which the identity and national-
        ity of vessels can be readily determined, irrespective of size and tonnage, and for
        which a register is maintained on a worldwide basis;
  (ii) they should be without prejudice to international conventions, national and bilateral
        practices;
  (iii) their implementation and maintenance will be at minimum cost to governments and
        fishing vessel owners; and
  (iv) they facilitate marine search and rescue operations.

5.   The specifications prepared by the Experts at the Rome Consultation are contained in
Part II of document COFI/87/Inf.12. Paragraph 37 of Part I of document COFI/87/Inf.12
states: "given the provisions set out in paragraphs 34 and 35, the Specifications developed at
the Consultation and given in Part II meet the criteria established in paragraph 6 (above) and
can be adopted as a standardized marking system for the identification of fishing vessels
operating, or likely to operate in waters other than those of the flag State".

    . . .

8.   The Committee is further invited to consider the recommendation of the Consultation
contained in paragraph 27 of document COFI/87/Inf.12 which states: "In the same way, it was
decided that, where it was necessary to identify certain types of fishing gear deployed at sea
and unattended for a period of time, the gear markers should also display the same mark as
the fishing vessel to which the gear belongs, in order that the owner of the gear can be
identified". In addition, the recommendation contained in paragraph 38(b) of document
COFI/87/Inf.12 states: "in order to identify the authority vested in monitoring, control and
surveillance vessels and aircraft, coastal States should clearly mark such vessels and aircraft in
at least as prominent a way as that required of fishing vessels" . . . .

- - - - -

FAO Committee on Fisheries   CL 91/7
Report of the Seventeenth Session, May 1987   Extract

    . . .

Marking and identification of fishing vessels

    The Committee supported the concept of a uniform system for the marking of fishing
vessels and considered the draft specifications, prepared at an Expert Consultation convened
by the Director-General in June 1986, a good basis for implementing such a system. Whilst
noting that several delegations stated that their governments would require time to review the
proposed marking system, the Committee suggested that the matter be further considered by
both the Committee on Fisheries and the FAO Council.

    . . .

79.   Some delegations expressed reservations as to applying the marking system to a large number of small artisanal fishing vessels. It was explained that the system was primarily intended for vessels operating, or likely to operate, in waters other than those of the flag States and the cost of the system proposed would be minimal to governments and fishing vessel owners and mainly consist of maintaining a register.

80.   The Committee was advised that the draft had been elaborated in close consultation with other international organizations, such as IMO, ITU and ICAO. The recent meeting of the IMO Maritime Safety Committee (54th session, April 1987) had confirmed that the FAO proposals did not overlap with or contradict the IMO proposal on ship identification numbers which had been developed to serve a different purpose and explicitly excluded fishing vessels.

81.   As regards a standardized system for the marking of fishing gear, the Committee felt that the complexities of this issue were large and that it would be difficult to discuss the matter at this stage without further studies.

   . . .

83.   It was noted that the system would be without prejudice to international conventions and to national or bilateral practices or requirements.

- - - - -

Additional References

Report of the Expert Consultation on the Technical Specifications for the Marking of Fishing Vessels. FAO Fisheries Report No. 367.

Report of the Expert Consultation on the Technical Specifications for the Marking of Fishing Vessels. June 1986. Seventeenth session of the FAO Committee on Fisheries. FAO document COFI/87/Inf.12.

- - - - -

2

Regional Developments

FAO Committee on Fisheries   COFI/87/9
Seventeenth Session, May 1987   Extract

Review of the FAO Regional Fishery Bodies

A. INTRODUCTION

1.   Nine regional fishery bodies have been established by FAO with responsibilities for conservation and management of fish resources and for fishery development. They cover about 50 percent of the total area of the world's oceans and the inland waters of Africa, Latin America, Asia and Europe. One hundred and thirty-four Member Nations of FAO are members of at least one of these bodies.

2.   The first bodies of this type were created nearly 40 years ago: the Indo-Pacific Fisheries Commission (IPFC) in 1948 and the General Fisheries Council for the Mediterranean (GFCM) in 1949. Others were gradually established: the European Inland Fisheries Advisory Commission (EIFAC) in 1957; the Regional Fisheries Advisory Commission for the Southwest Atlantic (CARPAS) (which has been inactive for a number of years) in 1961; the Fishery Committee for the Eastern Central Atlantic (CECAF) and the Indian Ocean Fisheries Commission (IOFC) in 1967; the Committee for Inland Fisheries of Africa (CIFA) in 1971; the Western Central Atlantic Fishery Commission (WECAFC) in 1973 and the Commission for Inland Fisheries of Latin America (COPESCAL) in 1976.

3.   The role of regional fishery bodies is recognized in the 1982 United Nations Convention on the Law of the Sea. The Convention accords sovereign rights to coastal States to explore, exploit, conserve and manage natural resources within their exclusive economic zones. The Convention also contains a number of provisions regarding cooperation among coastal States and competent international organizations whether sub-regional, regional or global, with respect to conservation of living resources within the exclusive economic zone (Arts. 61-70) and in the high seas (Arts. 116 to 120), though the nature of the respective role to be played in these areas differs.

4.   The FAO Conference has often echoed the interest shown by the Organization's Member Nations in the activities of these bodies. At its Sixteenth Session in 1971, for example, it was agreed that regional arrangements represented the most viable solution for the rational utilization of fishery resources, and their strengthening should be of high priority[1]. More recently, at its Twenty-third Session in 1985, the Conference reaffirmed that the Organization should give high priority to providing technical support to these bodies in order to ensure that they would continue to play a leading role in the conservation and management of fisheries[2].

5.   Since its creation more than 20 years ago, the Committee on Fisheries has, at varying intervals, discussed in detail questions affecting all FAO fishery bodies, for example at its Third, Fifth and Twelfth Sessions held respectively in 1968, 1970 and 1978. Taking into

account the development of world fisheries since 1978, it now appears advisable that the Committee should again review the activities of these bodies in order to ensure that they are suited to the present situation. This document provides up-to-date information on these bodies, and notes the principal problems they have had to deal with in recent years.

---

1. Report of the Sixteenth Session of the Conference of FAO, para. 62
2. Report of the Twenty-third Session of the Conference of FAO, para. 161

B. LEGAL BACKGROUND

6.   Bearing in mind the implications for the composition, functions, competence and resources of the various regional bodies of FAO, it may be useful first to review briefly their legal status. In this respect, they may be divided into four distinct categories:

(a) Commission open to all Member Nations created under Article VI.1 of the Constitution

7.   Two fishery bodies were established on this basis: the Indian Ocean Fisheries Commission (IOFC) and the Western Central Atlantic Fishery Commission (WECAFC). Such Commissions, which may be established by the Conference or Council, are open to all Member Nations of the Organization and are responsible for providing advice on the formulation and implementation of policies, and coordinating their implementation. They do not constitute entities distinct from FAO. They are subsidiary bodies whose Secretariat is provided by the Organization and whose expenses are covered by the FAO Regular Programme. Their reports and recommendations are transmitted to the Director-General, who takes them into account when preparing the Organization's Programme of Work and Budget, and also draws the attention of the Conference to recommendations which could have an effect on the Organization's policy or finances. The Director-General also communicates the reports and relevant recommendations to all Member Nations of the Commission. This is particularly important when these recommendations are directly addressed to these nations.

(b) Regional commissions established under Article VI.1 of the Constitution

8.   Three fishery bodies were created under these provisions: The Regional Fisheries Advisory Commission for the Southwest Atlantic (CARPAS), the European Inland Fisheries Advisory Commission (EIFAC), and the Commission for Inland Fisheries of Latin America (COPESCAL). The main feature of these Commissions is that they are only open to those FAO Member Nations whose territories are wholly or partly situated within a given region[1]. Apart from this, they have the same characteristics as the other Commissions under Article VI.1 mentioned above as regards their legal nature, their functions, their Secretariat, their source of finance and the transmission of their reports and recommendations.

---

1. For COPESCAL it was laid down that the Commission was open to Member Nations served by the Regional Office for Latin America and the Caribbean.

(c) **Committees composed of selected Member Nations established under Article VI.1 of the Constitution**

9.   Two Committees concerned with fisheries have so far been established on the basis of Article VI.2: the Fishery Committee for the Eastern Central Atlantic (CECAF) and the Committee for Inland Fisheries of Africa (CIFA). This Article provides the possibility of creating committees composed of selected Member Nations to study and report on matters pertaining to the purpose of the Organization. Their statutes usually include criteria for selection of their members[2]. This solution was adopted when these committees were created in order to overcome certain historical difficulties. With the exception of their composition, these committees have the same characteristics as the commissions created under Article VI.1.

---

2.   The members of CECAF are chosen from FAO Member Nations in Africa whose territory borders the Atlantic Ocean from Cape Spartel to the mouth of the Congo River and such other Member Nations fishing or carrying out research in the sea area concerned or having some other interest in the fisheries thereof and whose contribution to the work of the Committee is deemed by the Director-General to be essential or desirable. CIFA is composed of African Member Nations of the Organization selected by the Director-General on the basis of their active interest in inland fishery development and of their potential contribution to the effective discharge of the functions of the Committee.

(d) **Commissions or committees established by agreements concluded under Article XIV of the Constitution**

10.   Commissions and committees can be established by international agreements prepared by Member Nations of specific geographical areas, approved by the FAO Conference and submitted for consideration by these nations in accordance with the provisions of Article XIV of the Constitution. There are at present two bodies of this type concerned with fisheries: the Indo-Pacific Fishery Commission (IPFC) and the General Fisheries Council for the Mediterranean (GFCM). As bodies created by international agreements, IPFC and GFCM constitute entities distinct from FAO. However, since they were established by and function within the framework of the Organization, they are not completely independent of it. Any FAO Member Nation that so wishes may become a party to the agreements creating these bodies by depositing an instrument of accession with the Director-General. Nations that are not members of FAO but are members of the UN or a specialized agency may be admitted, subject to the approval of the body created by the agreement. These nations must, however, pay a proportionate share of Secretariat expenses, which is fixed by the Organization. At its Ninth Session, the Conference of FAO laid down that the creation of a body under Article XIV is only justified if the agreement envisages acceptance by Member Nations of precise obligations going beyond mere participation in the work of the body established, and includes financial or other obligations going beyond those already assumed under the Constitution of the Organization.

11.   As regards sources of finance, bodies established by the agreements concluded under Article XIV of the Constitution may belong to one of the following three categories: (a) bodies entirely financed by FAO; (b) bodies financed by FAO and which may also undertake cooperative projects financed by their members; (c) bodies financed by FAO and which also have an autonomous budget. FAO provides them with the necessary administrative support, as in the case of commissions and committees created under Article VI of the Constitution. Similarly, the Secretaries of these bodies are appointed by the Director-General and are administratively responsible to him.

12.   Lastly, it may be noted that some independent commissions have been established under conventions concluded on the initiative of FAO. These are, for example, the International Commission for the Conservation of Atlantic Tunas (ICCAT) and the International Commission for the Southeast Atlantic Fisheries (ICSEAF). As regards these two bodies, the direct role of FAO was limited to preparing and convening conferences of plenipotentiaries responsible for adopting the conventions that created them. The Director-General of FAO is the depositary of these conventions.

C.   GEOGRAPHICAL COVERAGE

13.   All the bodies reviewed in the present document have specific regional competences. It is, however, important to point out that, unlike the situation with most other regional bodies established by FAO under the above-mentioned provisions of the Constitution, the areas covered by the "regional" marine fishery bodies do not always correspond to the "regions" defined by the Organization for its field activities. These areas have in fact been defined in terms of oceans rather than continents. Thus, for example, African nations are concerned with three distinct FAO bodies concerned respectively with fisheries in the Mediterranean, the Eastern Central Atlantic and the Indian Ocean. On the other hand, it will be noted that the IOFC area of competence is bordered by countries served by three FAO Regional Offices (Africa, Near East, Asia and the Pacific). This approach is justified by the technical requirements of rational management of fish stocks. The socio-economic and other affinities of coastal communities have not, however, been overlooked and, to take them into account, subsidiary sub-regional Committees have been created within several bodies, i.e., in the Lesser Antilles, in the South China Sea, in the Bay of Bengal, etc. (see Section G below).

14.   Some bodies exclusively concerned with marine fisheries have an area of competence defined in their statutes by geographic coordinates or precise indications. This is the case with GFCM, IOFC, WECAFC and CECAF, whose areas of competence also coincide, apart from a few details, with statistical areas that have long been recognized internationally. It should, however, be borne in mind that CECAF recommended an extension southwards[1], or alternatively the elimination[2], of the southern boundary of its area of competence in order to facilitate participation by Angola and Namibia. On the advice of the Council[3] and the Committee on Fisheries[4], it was decided to postpone any decision in this respect until these two Member Nations had made their intentions known.

15.   For IPFC the situation is a little less clear. Under the terms of the agreement of 1948 which created it, this Commission performs its functions in both marine and inland fisheries of the Indo-Pacific Region. The marine area has, however, never been precisely defined. As long as IPFC was the only international fishery body in the region, this uncertainty raised no major problems. Nations who acceded to the agreement were within the Pakistan-New Zealand-Japan triangle. No African nation on the Indian Ocean acceded to IPFC; at that time the South Pacific Islands were all administered by member nations of IPFC. With the creation of IOFC, and then the South Pacific Forum Fishery Agency (FFA), the risks of overlapping have become more real.

16.   When the Committee on Fisheries recommended that the Council create IOFC, it concluded that it would be undesirable to divide responsibility for the consideration of the fisheries problems of the Indian Ocean between more than one body[5]. For its part, the Council noted that the creation of IOFC might lead to a withdrawal of interest in the Indian Ocean by IPFC[6]. At present five Member States bordering the Indian Ocean but without

coastlines on the Pacific continue to be members of IPFC. However, in recent years, they have reduced their participation in the IPFC activities relating to marine resources although keeping a strong interest in the work of IPFC concerned with inland fisheries, aquaculture, post-harvest technology and marketing. At their joint session in 1982, IOFC and IPFC envisaged the possibility of defining more clearly their respective areas of competence, to minimize cases of dual membership. No decision was taken then. Several delegations did, however, express the wish that the possibility of merging IOFC and IPFC in a single body might be again considered at future sessions[7].

17. On the Pacific Ocean side, none of the island nations that became independent during the last 15 years succeeded to the IPFC agreement. These nations decided to join with Australia and New Zealand to form FFA. The eastern boundary of the IPFC area is therefore rather difficult to determine with precision. In an area where there are substantial stocks of highly migratory species, such uncertainty could lead to difficulties.

---

1. Report of the Fifth Session of CECAF, para. 62
2. Report of the Seventh Session of CECAF, para. 99
3. Report of the Seventy-fourth Session of the Council, para. 34
4. Report of the Fourteenth Session of the Committee on Fisheries, para. 75
5. Report of the Second Session of the Committee on Fisheries, para. 33
6. Report of the Forty-eighth Session of the Council, para. 41
7. Report of the Joint Session of IOFC (Seventh Session) and IPFC (Twentieth Session), para. 114

D. MEMBERSHIP

18. As mentioned above (paras. 6 to 12), membership depends on the legal status of the bodies concerned. Their present composition is shown in the Annex to document COFI/87/Inf.7.

19. The new Law of the Sea has affected the composition of several regional fishery bodies. This is because coastal States now have sovereign rights as regards exploration, conservation and management of resources within a 200-mile limit off their coasts. Accession by non-coastal States to several international fishery bodies constituted outside the aegis of FAO has therefore often been restricted. The FAO bodies (particularly CECAF, WECAFC, IPFC and IOFC) have adopted a slightly different solution: without modifying the statutory provisions in force with regard to membership, these bodies have decided to create subsidiary bodies composed only of the coastal States and specifically responsible for studying questions of resource management in a sub-region.

20. Broadly speaking, the degree of membership in FAO fishery bodies is satisfactory, since most of the nations concerned have decided to become members. For example, the African States bordering the Eastern Central Atlantic, are, without exception, members of CECAF. In the Western Central Atlantic, WECAFC includes 26 of the 29 nations with coastlines on its area of competence. The same situation pertains in the Mediterranean, where only one FAO coastal Member Nation is not a member of GFCM. Due to the importance of their work and their reputation for impartiality, these bodies are in a unique position to encourage cooperation among all nations in the same region as regards resource management and fishery development. The only two cases of incomplete membership are IPFC (of which China is not at present a member) and COPESCAL (from which Brazil is absent). In these two cases,

however, experts from these countries participate in some of the technical working parties organized by these commissions.

21.   Mention must be made of a problem affecting some marine fishery bodies (particularly IOFC and, to a lesser extent, CECAF); this is the problem of inactive members. Some Member Nations, which decided a long time ago to join certain bodies, have since ceased to attend meetings, either because they have transferred their competence in the matter (the case of some Member Nations of the EEC), or because they no longer have fishing interests in the region concerned. Legally, however, they continue to be members of these bodies, which creates difficulties in obtaining the quorum needed for decisions. It is suggested that these nations might be invited to re-examine their situation and perhaps either participate more actively in the work of the bodies of which they are members, or else formally withdraw. ·

22.   Lastly, it should be recalled that full participation in FAO fishery bodies is reserved for nations. However, in the last 10 years Member States of EEC have transferred certain important aspects of their competence as regards fisheries to the Community. It is the latter that is now competent to take measures to conserve the living resources of the sea in areas subject to the jurisdiction of Member States covered by the EEC Treaty. Under Community law, the Community reserves to itself the competence to take measures to conserve the living resources of the sea, through contractual commitments with third countries and in the framework of international organizations. These regulatory powers also cover distant-water fishing by vessels flying the flag of EEC Member States. EEC Members Countries and EEC observers at meetings of FAO fishery bodies have several times drawn attention to this problem, for which no easy solution can be envisaged.

E.   FUNCTIONS

23.   The FAO bodies and their various subsidiaries also form one of the major interfaces between the fisheries administrations of the member countries and the Regular Programme of FAO. Their discussions provide an opportunity for the collection of the opinions of national fisheries workers on topics and priorities for technical work which are essential to framing the Programme of Work of the Fisheries Department.

24.   Compared with most other international fishery bodies, almost all the FAO bodies have the peculiarity of operating in tropical or sub-tropical areas and, apart from EIFAC, the majority of their members are developing countries. Unlike the independent bodies established for the North Atlantic or the North Pacific, FAO bodies must, therefore, be concerned not only with resource management but also with development and training. As recognized by the FAO Conference at its last Session in 1985, they are in a position to play a particularly active role in the promotion of economic cooperation among developing countries (ECDC) and technical cooperation among developing countries (TCDC)[1].

25.   The mandates given to these bodies have been conceived to meet the specific needs of each region served. They are thus necessarily different from one body to another. One may, however, discern a number of common points. This comparison is important in that it can assist in identifying gaps or inadequacies.

26.   A number of fields are covered by practically all the mandates; these are (i) the collection, diffusion and analysis of statistical, scientific or other information; (ii) encouragement of education, training and extension work; and (iii) promotion and

coordination of national and international research and development efforts. Other aspects are specifically mentioned in only some of the mandates: liaison and cooperation with the competent institutions in the region (CARPAS, CECAF and EIFAC), the examination of economic and social aspects (GFCM, IPFC and COPESCAL), the promotion of fish and fishery product processing and marketing activities (IPFC, CIFA and COPESCAL). Several mandates, however, contain relatively broad provisions with regard to the functions of the bodies they govern. As a result, the absence of a specific reference to one type of activity does not necessarily imply that the body in question cannot be concerned with this activity.

---

1.   Report of the Twenty-third Session of the Conference of FAO, para. 161.

27. All the statutory texts provide for resource management functions. The table below summarizes the main relevant provisions.

RESOURCE MANAGEMENT FUNCTIONS

CARPAS	To advise on the evolution of an organized approach in respect of the rational exploitation of fisheries.
EIFAC	To advise on the evolution of an organized approach toward the development of inland fisheries.
GFCM	To formulate and recommend appropriate measures (i) for the conservation and rational management of resources and (ii) for the implementation of these recommendations.
IPFC	To formulate and recommend appropriate measures to conserve and manage resources.
CECAF	To assist Member Governments in establishing the scientific basis for regulatory measures for the conservation and improvement of resources.
WECAFC	To promote the development, conservation, rational management and best utilization of resources that are of interest to two or more countries.
COPESCAL	To formulate regulatory measures for the conservation and improvement of resources and to make appropriate recommendations for the adoption and implementation of these measures.
CIFA	To formulate regulatory measures for resource conservation and improvement and to make appropriate recommendations for the adoption and implementations of these measures.
IOFC	To examine management problems, with particular reference to offshore resources.

28. It can be seen that there are considerable differences among these different mandates regarding management. Those of GFCM and IPFC are clear and precise: these bodies are responsible for formulating and recommending management measures. The functions of IOFC and CECAF are, however, relatively more limited since the former must in principle restrict itself to "examining management problems" and the latter can only "assist governments in establishing the scientific basis for regulatory measures". However, the differences in the texts are not necessarily reflected in practice, for example, IOFC[1] and CECAF[2] have now formulated and recommended specific management measures, whereas IPFC, whose mandate is more explicit, has so far not done so. The time may come to bring the various texts and practices more closely into line. This could prove all the more necessary since the status of exploitation of certain stocks in the Indian Ocean and the Eastern Central Atlantic may in the near future require the adoption of other economic zones (EEZs) of several coastal States, or in both an EEZ and an area adjacent to it. The present record of success in management could be improved substantially by focusing the work of management subsidiary bodies of sub-regional level, by developing national capacity in management through training, institution promoting, and development of research on resources and fisheries economics at national level.

---

1. At its Second Session in 1979, the IOFC Committee for the Development and Management of the Fishery Resources of the Gulfs recommended the establishment of a five-month closed season for shrimp fishing and an immediate reduction in the amount of fishing effort for shrimp. These measures were brought forward again at the following sessions and effectively implemented by the coastal States concerned, with the flexibility required by local conditions.

2. At its Sixth Session in 1979, CECAF recommended the adoption of a 60mm mesh size for the exploitation of all demersal species. This measure was introduced into the legislation of most CECAF countries although it is not yet enforced generally. At its last session (Tenerife, Spain, 24-28 November 1986) CECAF recommended also reductions of fishing effort on several overfished stocks.

F.   POWERS

29. All international fishery bodies have consultative powers in the sense that they can only formulate recommendations, which are not binding on the States. This principle - which is valid both for independent bodies and for those established within FAO - has been implemented in various ways.

30. The most interesting procedure is that of potentially binding recommendations, subject to objection. Briefly, this formula is applied in the following way: after having received notification of the measure recommended, Member States are allowed a certain time (from 3 to 6 months as the case may be) to lodge objections. If no objection has been lodged within this time, the recommendation becomes binding on all Member States. If one Member State makes an objection, the entry into force of the recommendation is delayed and a new period is granted to enable other Member States to reconsider their position in the light of the new situation. Once the additional period has expired, the recommendation becomes binding on all Member States who have not made objections. However, if the number of objections is too high, the recommendation does not come into force, subject to agreement between certain States to give effect to it. Outside of FAO this procedure is applied *inter alia* by the Commission for the Conservation of Antarctic Marine Living Resources, the International Whaling Commission, the International Commission for the Conservation of Atlantic Tunas, and the Northwest Atlantic Fisheries Organization.

31. In FAO this procedure was adopted in 1976 by GFCM. IPFC has also envisaged using it and at its Twenty-first Session in 1984 agreed that the question could be taken up at a later session as soon as reliable data were available as a basis for the preparation of management measures[1]. All other FAO fishery bodies can make simple recommendations which are transmitted to Member Nations by the Director-General. For legal reasons, only those bodies established under Article XIV of the Constitution (GFCM and IPFC) can use the objection procedure described above. Should the seven other bodies wish to adopt it they would have first to be reconstituted on the appropriate legal basis.

---

1. Report of the Twenty-first Session of IPFC, para. 94.

G.   INTERNAL STRUCTURE

32. In view of the diversity of the problems dealt with, and/or the extent of the areas covered, all FAO fishery bodies have had to create subsidiary bodies. Since the parent bodies only meet on average every two years and for a limited time, the bulk of the technical work is done in the inter-sessional period by more specialized groups.

33. There are various types of subsidiary bodies: four bodies (IPFC, GFCM, EIFAC and COPESCAL) have, under their statutes, an Executive Committee composed of the Chairman and Vice-chairman, which keeps track of all ongoing work in between the sessions. Most of the bodies have also created committees (or sub-committees) composed of Member Nations and responsible either for management and development matters in a specific sub-region, or for specific problems. Subsidiary sub-regional bodies have been established by:

IPFC: -   Committee for the Development and Management of Fisheries in the South China Sea;

WECAFC: -   Committee for the Development and Management of Fisheries in the Lesser Antilles;

CIFA: -   Sub-Committee for the Protection and Development of the Fisheries in the Sahelian Zone;
          -     Sub-Committee for the Development and Management of the Fisheries of Lake Victoria;
          -     Sub-Committee for Lake Tanganyika;

IOFC: -   Committee for the Development and Management of the Fishery Resources of the Gulfs;
          -     Committee for the Development and Management of Fisheries in the Southwest Indian Ocean;
          -     Committee for the Development and Management of Fisheries in the Bay of Bengal.

Subsidiary bodies responsible for specific problems have also been established by:

EIFAC: -   Sub-Commission on Fishery Biology and Management;
          -     Sub-Commission on Fish Culture and Diseases;
          -     Sub-Commission on Fish and Polluted Waters;

GFCM: -   Committee on Resources Management;

IPFC: -   Special Committee on Management of Indo-Pacific Tuna;
       -   Standing Committee on Resources Research and Development;

CECAF: -   Sub-Committee on Management of Resources within the Limits of National Jurisdiction;
       -   Sub-Committee on Fishery Development;

IOFC: -   Committee for the Management of Indian Ocean Tuna.

In addition to this set of intergovernmental subsidiary bodies, there are some thirty working parties and technical consultations composed of experts (appointed either by their country or by the Director-General) responsible, in principle for limited periods, for studying specific technical questions. The total number of subsidiary bodies is thus around 45.

34. As regards Executive Committees, practices have varied considerably from one body to another. The EIFAC Executive Committee has not been convened for several years. The normal work of this Commission is monitored by the Chairman, in close cooperation with the Secretary. The Executive Committee of IPFC, on the other hand, has met very frequently. It held its Sixty-third Session in September 1986. This is mainly due to the fact that all the subsidiary bodies of IPFC (with the exception of the Special Committee on Management of Indo-Pacific Tuna) report to the Commission through the Executive Committee. In order to promote closer contact between technical and decision-making levels, this procedure could be modified. While at the Twentieth Session of the Commission in 1982 it was in fact proposed that the Executive Committee be abolished, it was subsequently considered that a decision on this subject could only be taken later. GFCM and COPESCAL have adopted a pragmatic approach and only convened their Executive Committees when circumstances so required. This flexibility appears to have given satisfaction to Member Nations, and might serve as an example to other bodies.

35. Subsidiary bodies with sub-regional competence are generally relatively recent creations. Most of them were established after the FAO Conference recognized at its Twentieth Session in 1979 the need for an adjustment of structures at sub-regional level to take account of the needs of groups of nations sharing stocks or fisheries, or who had common problems or opportunities or other natural affinities[1]. They are all composed exclusively of nations with a coastline on the relevant area, and have, in their areas of competence, functions similar to those of their parent bodies. In this connection, two issues deserve attention:

-   In the Indian Ocean, neither the Red Sea nor the Arabian Sea are covered by an IOFC sub-regional committee. Taking into account the financial implications, it would at present be difficult to create a new committee exclusively for these areas. However, the area of competence of the present Committee for the Development and Management of the Fishery Resources of the Gulfs might perhaps be extended to strengthen sub-regional cooperation among the States of the Northwest Indian Ocean.

-   In the Eastern Central Atlantic, the CECAF Sub-Committees on Management of Resources within the Limits of National Jurisdiction and on Fishery Development each cover a vast area more than 10,000 km long stretching from Morocco to Zaire.

Since fisheries in the Gulf of Guinea are very different from those of West Africa, these two subsidiary bodies could perhaps be abolished and be substituted by two sub-committees covering for each sub-region not only resources management but also, like in many other FAO fishery bodies, fishery development.

---

1.   Report of the Twentieth Session of the Conference, para. 129, and Resolution 4/79 of the Conference.

36.   As regards the subsidiary bodies responsible for specific problems throughout the area of competence of their parent organization, it may be noted that the IOFC and IPFC Committees responsible respectively for management of tuna stocks in the Indian Ocean and in the Indo-Pacific, for many years met jointly. In 1984/85 the two Commissions decided to end this arrangement. Since then, the IOFC Committee has been very active.

     . . .

J.   COOPERATION WITH OTHER INTERNATIONAL ORGANIZATIONS

58.   Over the last decade, the number of international organizations concerned with fisheries has increased. Not only have new organizations concerned exclusively with fisheries been created (the South Pacific Forum Fisheries Agency in 1979, the Commission for the Conservation of Antarctic Marine Living Resources in 1980, the North Atlantic Salmon Conservation Organization and the Latin American Organization for Fisheries Development in 1982, the Regional Fishery Committee for the Gulf of Guinea in 1984, the Sub-Regional Commission for Fisheries (West Africa) in 1985) but also many regional economic development organizations have intensified their activities in the field of fisheries. This has been the case particularly with the European Economic Community, the Association of South-East Asian Nations, the Caribbean Community, etc. Bilateral aid agencies from Western Europe, the Nordic countries, North America and Japan are executing a number of projects throughout the world. Within a region or sub-region, international cooperation in fisheries can be conducted through (i) FAO marine fishery and inland fishery bodies, (ii) regional economic cooperation bodies, (iii) non FAO fishery bodies, (iv) regional field projects executed by FAO, (v) projects executed directly by bilateral donors.

59.   Although most FAO bodies have the mandate to promote and coordinate international aid, it is not always possible for them to play this role fully, particularly *vis à vis* bilateral aid. Since in any event resources are limited, it is important to avoid their dissipation and to ensure better coordination of international efforts. The FAO fishery bodies, which usually include all the States in one region or sub-region, can provide an ideal forum for exchanging information and, if necessary, harmonizing different actions undertaken or envisaged. Encouragement should therefore be given to all organizations and programmes acting in a given region to participate more frequently and more actively in meetings of FAO fishery bodies.

60.   The membership of regional economic groupings is in general based on linguistic, economic or political affinities and does not always coincide with natural management areas. These bodies do not therefore provide from a strictly technical point of view an adequate geographical framework for cooperation in the proper management of fish stocks. However, given the strong links among their members, they can play a very important role in the development process. FAO fishery bodies should thus be encouraged to increase further their cooperation with them, particularly in development matters.

SUGGESTED ACTION BY THE COMMITTEE

61.   The Committee is invited to examine the various issues raised in this document, and make recommendations to the Secretariat or to the relevant FAO fishery bodies, particularly as regards:

(i)   the geographical areas covered (paras. 14 to 17);
(ii)   the participation of Member Nations (paras. 20 and 21) and the status of regional economic cooperation bodies to which Member Nations have transferred some of their competences (para. 22);
(iii)   the management functions (para. 28);
(iv)   the scope of recommendations made (para. 31);
(v)   the operation of subsidiary bodies (paras. 34 to 37);
(vi)   organization of meetings (paras. 41 to 43);
(vii)   administrative and technical assistance (paras. 49-57); and
(viii) the cooperation with other international organizations concerned with fisheries (paras. 58 to 60).

- - - - -

FAO Committee on Fisheries   COFI/87/Inf.7
Seventeenth Session, May 1987   FAO Fisheries Circular No. 807

Activities of International Organizations Concerned with Fisheries

. . .

1. MARINE FISHERY BODIES

Atlantic Ocean and Adjacent Seas

International Council for the Exploration of the Sea (ICES)

. . .

4.   . . . the Council considered the scientific papers and reports on a wide range of co-operative research activities in the fields of fisheries, mariculture, marine pollution and oceanography being undertaken by scientists in its member countries under the Council's aegis.   Prominent amongst these activities was the appraisal and assessment of exploited fishery resources in the North-East Atlantic and Baltic Sea and the associated provision, through the Council's Advisory Committee on Fishery Management (ACFM), of scientific advice on their conservation and management to member governments and international bodies. Attention was drawn to the serious problems created in the assessment work by the deterioration in the coverage of reported catch and other statistics for some of the main fisheries in the area. This and other elements of the advisory system were also discussed at the Fifth Dialogue Meeting held in association with the North-East Atlantic Fisheries Commission (NEAFC) and the International Baltic Sea Fishery Commission (IBSFC) in October 1985. . . .

. . .

North-East Atlantic Fisheries Commission (NEAFC)

   . . .

9.   At the Fourth Annual Meeting, the Commission discussed the latest report of the *Ad Hoc* Committee on Technical Conservation Measures and accepted the Committee's recommendation to publish a Manual of the technical conservation measures in force in the waters under the fisheries jurisdiction of the Contracting Parties.

10.   . . . On blue whiting, the Commission . . . agreed on a recommendation for a minimum mesh size of 35 mm applicable when using pelagic trawls in the NEAFC regulatory area. Concerning the blue whiting stock, consideration was also given to the possibility of formally establishing a total allowable catch (TAC).

   . . .

International Baltic Sea Fishery Commission (IBSFC)

   . . .

17.   During the . . . [Twelfth] Session, the Commission adopted changes in its Fishery Rules with regard to mesh-sizes and minimum landing sizes in the Baltic fisheries. . . .

   . . .

North Atlantic Salmon Conservation Organization (NASCO)

   . . .

21.   At its Third Annual Meeting, the Report of the AFCM [ICES Advisory Committee on Fisheries Management] was presented to the Council. The West Greenland Commission adopted a proposal for a total allowable catch (TAC) at West Greenland of 850 tonnes in both 1986 and 1987 and the North American Commission adopted a regulatory measure closing the Newfoundland and Labrador fishery on 15 October 1986. The Council considered progress made on developing a format for the analysis of catch statistics for salmon stocks, as well as progress on provision to the Secretary by each Contracting Party of laws, regulations and programmes in force relating to the conservation, restoration, enhancement and rational management of salmon stocks. The Council agreed that its Secretary, in consultation with ICES, should review the status of the existing Atlantic salmon management, tagging programmes and investigate the desirability of establishing a central repository for all tagging information.

Northwest Atlantic Fisheries Organization (NAFO)

   . . .

25.   . . . the Scientific Council informed the Fisheries Commission on the status [of the harp and hooded seal populations in the Northwest Atlantic], and provided scientific advice for the management of certain stocks outside and overlapping the Canadian 200-mile fishery zone.

26.   In 1985, the NAFO Fisheries Commission adopted TACs and allocated quotas for 1986 for fish stocks in the Regulatory Area and for fish stocks overlapping national fishing limits. The Commission also considered proposals for revision and improvement of some of the rules for the management and conservation of stocks in the Regulatory Area. In 1986, a working group to revise the NAFO Enforcement Measures was formed.

27. At both Annual Meetings, the Council continued the study of its Rules of Procedure and of the problems resulting from the presence in the Regulatory Area of vessels belonging to non-member States.

. . .

Joint Fishery Commission (JFC)

29. During the period under review, the Joint Fishery Commission (JFC) continued the activities of the joint international expeditions on board Polish, Bulgarian and Soviet vessels with the participation of experts from Cuba and the German Democratic Republic. The purpose of these expeditions was to develop further the studies of the main resources of the Northeast Atlantic outside the 200-mile limit. . . .

30. Further investigations and experiments were carried out by the Commission regarding new fishing techniques and processing equipment for traditional and new species. Progress had been made in the exchange of scientific and technical information using computer techniques. . . .

General Fisheries Council for the Mediterranean (GFCM)

. . .

34. The Council took initial steps to make extensive surveys of stocks exploited in common by several countries in the Western Mediterranean. It discussed in detail the management of the coastal areas and their protection against indiscriminate trawling, the creation of artificial reefs and open sea mariculture structures. The Council also noted that better utilization of small pelagic species could constitute an alternative to the over-exploited demersal resources and offer prospects for increased fish production in the area.

. . .

Mixed Commission for Black Sea Fisheries

. . .

38. . . . Decisions taken at [the Seventeenth] Session included the extension of the ban on dolphin catching and new measures to be taken to preserve the existing turbot stock. The Commission advised its members to consider amendments to the Convention with respect to the extension of jurisdiction to 200 miles in the Black Sea.

. . .

Fishery Committee for the Eastern Central Atlantic (CECAF)

. . .

42. On fishery statistics, the Committee observed that a number of maritime boundaries were now being agreed upon between countries in the region and that it might be possible to introduce a statistical grid on this basis. It noted that an improved grid based on resources and ecological considerations would be of more use to scientists engaged in stock assessment and lead to better management on a stock-by-stock basis. The Committee approved a resolution urging Member coastal States who entered into bilateral agreements to request their partners (in particular USSR) to improve statistical data submitted to them and to intensify scientific cooperation.

43.   On the management of resources, the Committee noted the significant progress made by several countries with regard to information on resources and recommended that consideration be given to striking a balance between the presence of foreign fleets and the development of national fisheries capacity, as well as the protection of the artisanal fisheries sector from unfavourable competition with industrial fisheries.

. . .

Sub-Regional Fishery Commission for West Africa

. . .

49.   [At] the Sixth Session of the Conference of Ministers . . . 1986. A programme of work for 1986/87 was adopted which includes the following activities:

   (a)   development of sub-regional cooperation in the field of control and surveillance of vessels fishing in the waters under the jurisdiction of Member States;
   (b)   preparation of a detailed project document for the setting up of a sub-regional system for collecting and processing fisheries statistics data;
   (c)   harmonization of national requirements on mesh sizes of fishes at first capture; and
   (d)   elaboration of a joint fisheries research programme.

The Commission requested FAO to provide assistance regarding the implementation of some of its programmes.

Western Central Atlantic Fishery Commission (WECAFC)

. . .

52.   . . . The . . . main recommendations [of the WECAFC Committee for the Development and Management of Fisheries in the Lesser Antilles] included standardization of methodology for data collection and training courses for fishermen and boat builders.

53.   The Fifth Session of the Working Party on Assessment of Marine Resources . . . identified areas which needed more cooperative research such as mapping and protection of the critical habitats, measures to reduce adverse impacts of fish trapping practices and mechanisms for collection and exchange of data on shared resources.

54.   The Fourth Session of the Working Party on Fishery Statistics . . . made recommendations for the improvement of biological and socio-economic data and the reduction of systematic errors in catch and effort statistics. It also considered the desirability of establishing national and regional data centres.

. . .

Regional Fishery Advisory Commission for the Southwest Atlantic (CARPAS)

56.   No session of this Commission was held during the period under review.

Joint Technical Commission for the Argentina/Uruguay Maritime Front (CTMFM)

. . .

60.   The Commission prepared an agreement on cooperation between the two countries on pollution. It also considered the question of mesh sizes used by fishing vessels and a survey on selectivity is planned for 1987.

International Commission for the Conservation of Atlantic Tunas (ICCAT)

. . .

62.   The Commission reviewed the conservation measures currently in force and . . . decided to maintain its regulatory measures on bluefin, yellowfin and bigeye tunas. . . .

63.   Because of the increase in the stock abundance in yellowfin tuna brought about by a decrease in purse seine effort, a special research endeavour, the "Yellowfin Year Program", had been put into effect by the Commission. The Program Plan was drawn up in late 1985/early 1986 and the results of the first year's activities were reported to the Commission at the 1986 meeting. This Program will be continued in 1987.

64.   The Commission also approved a "Program of Enhanced Research for Billfish" to correct deficiencies in basic data on growth, mortality and stock structure of billfish species. Special research will be carried out in 1987 on swordfish to assess the current status of this stock.

. . .

International Commission for the Southeast Atlantic Fisheries (ICSEAF)

. . .

68.   The Commission continued its scientific studies on the state of the fish resources off the southwest coast of Africa. It adopted certain measures for the protection of the resources, including limitations on the total allowable catches of hake, Cape horse mackerel, chub mackerel and snook. In addition, the Commission decided to continue the following regulatory measures: the reporting system to monitor catches of Cape horse mackerel, chub mackerel and horse mackerel; the closed area within 25 km of the coast, and the minimum mesh sizes of 110 mm for hake fisheries and 60 mm for all other trawl fisheries. The Commission noted that only five countries had notified the Secretariat of inspectors and inspection vessels operating in the Convention areas. It recognized that a larger number of countries should perform this important function and hoped that other countries in the area would participate in inspection tasks in the future.

69.   At the Seventh Special Meeting of the Commission, it was agreed to reduce the total catch of hake and mackerel by 14 percent and 10 percent respectively for 1987. With reference to the enforcement of catch quotas of protected species, an *ad hoc* working group was set up to establish the relationship between fishing effort and national quotas . . .

. . .

Indian Ocean and Indo-Pacific Area

Indian Ocean Fishery Commission (IOFC)

　. . .

72.　The Commission discussed the state of marine fisheries in the Indian Ocean. . . Fishing craft and gear were developing slowly and further improvements could be achieved through technical cooperation with developing countries. The Commission discussed various ways in which FAO could assist member countries, particularly as regards the establishment or improvement of data collection systems and the formulation of management plans.

73.　On fish utilization and marketing, the Commission noted that the problems of fish quality control and inspection was causing severe economic losses and considered that it was necessary to improve handling and processing and to strengthen national quality control and inspection systems.

　. . .

Indo-Pacific Fishery Commission (IPFC)

　. . .

81.　The Committee noted that FAO technical assistance in respect of the resources of the region was being provided through the Organization's Regular Programme work on the assessment of multispecies resources in the Indo-Pacific region. In addition, FAO was planning to organize a regional workshop/consultation on the assessment of multispecies resources and multi-gear fisheries in the Indo-Pacific region in the second half of 1987. The Committee also reviewed country statements outlining the state of national fisheries, policy objectives, major strategies adopted for management and development by Hong Kong, Indonesia, Malaysia, the Philippines and Thailand.

　. . .

Pacific Ocean

International North Pacific Fisheries Commission (INPFC)

　. . .

84.　. . . the Commission reviewed the results of conservation programmes and scientific research on North Pacific fishery resources. It agreed that continued emphasis should be placed on coordinated research to determine the continent of origin of salmon found south of latitude 46°N and in other parts of the Convention area. The Commission reviewed the work of the *Ad Hoc* Committee on Marine Mammals which is responsible for studies with respect to marine mammals incidentally caught in the Convention area when fishing for anadromous species.

　. . .

International Pacific Halibut Commission (IPHC)

　. . .

91.　. . . The Commission, on the basis of the status of stocks of Pacific halibut after the 1985 season, recommended a total catch limit of 66.4 million pounds for 1986. The Commission once more expressed its concern over the incidental catch of Pacific halibut and submitted recommendations to control the problem.

　. . .

Pacific Salmon Commission (PSC)

. . .

96.   Negotiation of the harvest allocation for fisheries of one country, subject to intercepting stocks originating in the other country's waters, is a major activity of the Commission. Allocation agreements for most fisheries were written into the Treaty for its two years (1985 and 1986) making the 1987 season the first major negotiations undertaken by the new Commission. These were expected to be completed by March 1987 when the Commission would submit its recommendations to each country for ratification.

North Pacific Fur Seal Commission (NPFSC)

. . .

99.   The Commission reviewed the fur seal research carried out by the scientists of member countries and recommended that pelagic, land and general research on fur seals should continue in 1985. . . .

100.   The Fourth Workshop on Population Trends of Northern Fur Seals . . . concluded that the population of northern fur seals on the Pribilof Islands was declining, while the populations on San Miguel Island and Bogoslof Island remained relatively stable. The workshop recommended that problems related to the population decline should be approached from a broad prospective.

Inter-American Tropical Tuna Commission (I-ATTC)

. . .

103.   . . . The Commission . . . received a brief account of the programme in which the I-ATTC staff is encouraging the vessels to use high-power lights to illuminate the backdown channel of their nets at nights, which appears to reduce the mortality of dolphins caught in the nets.

104.   The Commission's Secretariat recommended a minimum quota of 175 000 short tons for 1986 with provisions for two increments of 15 000 tons each, one or both of which could be added to the minimum quota at the discretion of the Director.

. . .

South Pacific Permanent Commission (SPPC)

. . .

108.   The Permanent Commission reviewed the implementation of the Regional Study of El Niño Phenomenon (ERFEN) which is supervised by a special scientific committee. It stressed the importance of greater involvement of experts from the region in the evaluation of the various effects of the phenomenon and recommended that a study on the socio-economic consequences be undertaken. The Commission also approved basic principles for the harmonization of national legislation on marine research by foreign vessels.

. . .

South Pacific Forum Fisheries Agency (FFA)

. . .

116.   FAO continues to work closely with the FFA on a regional approach to assisting the South Pacific Island States in the management and further development of their fisheries, in particular, harmonization of access agreements for foreign fishing.

117.   The UNDP/FAO South Pacific Regional Development Programme is an important conduit of FAO's collaboration with the FFA. The Programme offers an important input to FFA's training programme through jointly executed workshops and courses. . . .

Other Areas

Latin American Organization for the Development of Fisheries (OLDEPESCA)

. . .

121.   In 1985, an agreement was signed between FAO and OLDEPESCA. The agreement provides for: (a) exchange of information and documents on subjects of common interest; (b) consultation on planning and implementation of programmes of interest to both organizations; (c) undertaking of joint studies; and (d) implementation of scientific and technical cooperation in the field of research on resources, catch, processing and marketing of fishery products.

. . .

Commission for the Conservation of Antarctic Marine Living Resources (CCAMLR)

. . .

127.   At the 1985 meeting, stock assessments of commercial fish species were reviewed and updated. The Commission adopted several conservation measures, in particular, for Antarctic marbled cod (*Notothenia rossii*).

128.   . . . The Commission, at its 1986 meeting, adopted further measures aimed at the protection of marbled cod in all areas where it had been commercially fished. It adopted a conservation measure which would permit the Commission, at its 1987 meeting, to fix limitations of catch on any species for the 1987/88 season as a binding measure, and permit a similar procedure to be used after 1987/88.

129.   No attempt was made to assess the krill resources. The krill catch increased in the 1985/86 season to the second largest on record. Several projects aiming at making krill assessment possible are being executed or are planned. . . .

. . .

International Whaling Commission (IWC)

. . .

134.   Following the Commission's decision in 1982 that the catch limits for commercial whaling would be set at zero from the 1986 coastal season and the 1985/86 pelagic season. The Commission did not discuss catch limits for commercial whaling at its Thirty-seventh and Thirty-eighth Annual Meetings. This decision is to be kept under review and it was agreed that, by 1990 at the latest, the Commission would undertake a comprehensive assessment of

the effects of the decision on whale stocks and consider modification of this provision and the establishment of other catch limits.

135.   At its Thirty-seventh Annual Meeting, the report of a working group on the future activities of the Commission during the pause in commercial whaling was discussed by the Commission. It included plans for the comprehensive assessment of the whale stocks and the effects (including socio-economic) of the zero catch limits. Plans were also developed for a review of the Indian Ocean Sanctuary in 1987; the integration of a Second International Decade of Cetacean Research as the Whale component of the FAO/UNEP Global Plan of Action for Marine Mammals; a review procedure for scientific research catches under special permit; and humane killing studies in aboriginal subsistence fisheries.

136.   At both Annual Meetings, the Commission set catch limits for aboriginal subsistence whaling which are not subject to the pause in commercial whaling. The Commission discussed proposals regarding the revision of the 1946 Convention. . . .

   . . .

- - - - -

Additional Reference

Activities of Regional Fishery Bodies and other international organizations concerned with fisheries. FAO Committee on Fisheries, fifteenth session. FAO document COFI/85/Inf.6, February 1985.

- - - - -

FAO Committee on Fisheries   CL 91/7
Report of the Seventeenth Session, May 1987   Extract

   . . .

Review of the Activities of FAO Regional Fishery Bodies

90.   The Committee expressed its satisfaction that this topic had been placed on the agenda, particularly as it had not been discussed at recent sessions . . . It requested that this item be placed again on the Agenda of its Eighteenth Session, and that the next report should also include a detailed and functional analysis of the scope, objectives and achievements of the various bodies. . . .

91.   The Committee unanimously recognized the key role of the FAO regional fishery bodies as fora to exchange information and experience and to recommend measures for the development and management of fisheries and to facilitate the harmonization of policies. . . .
   . . .

92.   To ensure the efficient functioning of the regional fishery bodies it was recognized that it was desirable for all member countries to participate in their sessions.

93. The European Economic Community (EEC) expressed its interest in the work of the FAO regional fishery bodies and the wish to collaborate more directly in the activities of some of them. Attention was drawn to the special circumstances involved in such participation by EEC and reference was made to the effective implementation of stock management measures and to bilateral fisheries agreements between EEC and the developing countries in order to provide a sustained financial contribution. It was recognized that this problem was beyond the competence of the Committee. It was felt, however, that solutions to this problem should, for the time being, be sought on a case-by-case basis.

94. With the expansion of world fisheries and the consequent need for improved management, some bodies were being required to exercise an increasing role in this regard.
. . .

97. The Committee was informed of the close collaboration that existed with non-FAO regional bodies such as the Latin American Organization for Fisheries Development (OLDEPESCA), the Commission for the Conservation of Antarctic Marine Living Resources (CCAMLR), the International Commission for the South-east Atlantic Fisheries (ICSEAF), the Permanent Commission for the South Pacific (CPPS) and the South Pacific Forum Fisheries Agency (FFA). It was noted that the scope and activities of FAO regional fishery bodies did not overlap with these and other international and bilateral organizations involved with fisheries but were complementary. For this reason the Committee requested that efforts be made to increase the involvement of such organizations in the work of FAO regional fishery bodies. Furthermore, some delegations pointed out that the number of international organizations dealing with fisheries had increased considerably over the last decade while budgetary resources were insufficient thus detracting from chances of reaching fisheries management agreements.

- - - - -

FAO Fisheries Law Advisory Programme

TCP/RLA/6652(T)
FL/WECAFC/86/12
Extract

Report of the FAO/WECAFC/CARICOM Workshop on Fisheries Legislation in CARICOM Member States
May 1986
. . .

THE CONVENTION ON THE LAW OF THE SEA AND ITS IMPLICATIONS FOR FISHERIES LEGISLATION
. . .

2. Under UNCLOS, coastal states may assume sovereignty over the management and exploitation of the living and non-living resources of an area of sea up to 200 miles from its baselines. The state must, in its management of that area, avoid over-exploitation and must conserve those resources. Meeting this obligation will imply substantial costs in the areas of management, surveillance and enforcement.

3.   On the question of management, not merely biological, but also social, economic and political factors may be taken into account. This is particularly relevant in connection with decisions on total allowable catch and the existence and extent of a surplus over national harvesting capacity. In such situations, the influence of local fishermen will be a political factor which has to be taken into account.

4.   A major issue is whether the provisions of UNCLOS, particularly Articles 61 and 62, should be reflected in domestic law and, if so, the extent to which they should be reflected. These articles deal with the conservation of living resources, the need to use best available scientific evidence, the maintenance of stock to produce the maximum sustainable yield as qualified by environmental and economic factors and the optimum utilization of such living resources including access to surplus stock by other countries.

5.   There are two schools of thought on this subject. One is the approach whereby the provisions of Articles 61 and 62 would be incorporated verbatim into domestic legislation. The other approach would provide for implementation of the concept but not its inclusion in a detailed manner as part of domestic legislation. While inclusion would have the advantage of providing management guidelines, the disadvantages of inflexibility and justiciability in a domestic context may outweigh any advantages, bearing in mind that non-inclusion in legislation does not entail a rejection or negation of the concept.

6.   A problem also to be considered is that of "translating" an international obligation couched in language often deliberately loose into domestic legislation which by its nature needs careful definitive drafting. Often what is an acceptable form of expression in an international agreement is an unacceptable form of expression in domestic legislation, leading to many unanswerable questions in an application for judicial review. This may be all the more so bearing in mind that a state could not mandatorily be brought to book for non-implementation of this international obligation since Article 297(3)(a) of UNCLOS expressly excepted those provisions from those for which a coastal state must accept submission of a dispute for settlement.

7.   It was considered that, on balance, it is preferable to use the provisions of Articles 61 and 62 as the basis for domestic legislation rather than to incorporate the provisions verbatim into the domestic legislation.

8.   The question of penalties attracted discussion. Particular attention was paid to Article 73 of UNCLOS under which arrested boats must be released on payment of a bond as security while penalties preclude imprisonment or other forms of corporal punishment in the absence of an agreement to the contrary. On the first point it was noted that it may be possible to distinguish between an "arrested vessel" and a "convicted vessel" so as to allow forfeiture for the latter. Another approach would be to require a bond of such sum as would compensate for the departure of the boat. It may be necessary to make it mandatory for the courts to release vessels on the posting of a satisfactory bond or other form of security. On the second point, it was noted that while the approach among states towards imprisonment as a penalty was about equal, the recent trend had been toward not imposing sentences of imprisonment.

9.   The question was also raised of the extent of Exclusive Economic Zones particularly of countries whose coasts lie close to each other and which would require delimitation agree-ments. While some statutes provided for an interim approach of median line delimitation subject to agreement, this approach might weaken a state's negotiating position.

10.   It was noted that the United Nations Convention on the Law of the Sea (UNCLOS) had been opened for signature in 1982 though it was not yet in force. This fact is important for its implications on future fisheries legislation.

11.   While some aspects of UNCLOS were representative of state practice and thus could be regarded as part of customary international law there was some doubt as to the status of other aspects of UNCLOS such as the concept of the Exclusive Economic Zone. Such aspects could be regarded more as a creation of UNCLOS than as an example of customary international law. This would have important implications, bearing in mind that UNCLOS was not yet in force.

. . .

FISHERIES LEGISLATION AND ITS CO-ORDINATION
AND HARMONIZATION IN THE REGION

. . .

11.   The workshop noted that the Law of the Sea Convention made it necessary for most countries to revise their fisheries legislation. However, the legal input was only a part of the process as adequate information was required on the resource itself. If this information is not available, legislation will have to be revised or redrafted when the information is known.

12.   The need for harmonization of fisheries legislation was discussed. It was noted that CARICOM member states did not form a natural fisheries management area, but were somewhat disparate, both in terms of geography and resources. There was thus little need for harmonization of fisheries legislation at the CARICOM level, at least so far as management systems and conservation measures were concerned.

13.   The need for harmonization of legislation and management systems did arise, however, at a subregional level where stocks were shared or interrelated. For the most part these sub-regions were not confined to CARICOM member states but would involve co-operation and harmonization among neighbouring CARICOM and non-CARICOM member states. The delegation of Guyana indicated that the question of harmonization of fisheries legislation in the context of subregional management of shared stocks was presently receiving intense consideration by their country. The main harvested resource of shrimp seemed to be diminishing and Guyana was considering the adoption of management measures to deal with this situation. Elements of the proposed management plan would include limited trawling for shrimp in specified areas and a possible closed season. The management plan should be developed in concert with the other countries sharing the same shrimp resource, namely Suriname, French Guiana, Guyana, Venezuela and Trinidad and Tobago. The Guyana delegation suggested the convening of an inter-Guiana meeting to deal effectively with this issue.

14.   The FAO representative emphasized the need for contact, discussions and negotiation between countries that shared stocks.

. . .

19.   The workshop noted that in addition to harmonization as it related to subregional management of shared stocks there might be other areas where the countries of the region could benefit from greater co-operation and harmonization at the CARICOM level. These included the trade of fishery products and the protection of endangered species.

20. Harmonization of quality standards was not considered to be a major factor in the problems of promoting intra-regional trade in fish and fish products. Other factors were far more important. However, harmonization of import and export controls could be of great use in providing support for conservation measures in neighbouring countries and in dealing with the problem of illegal export of fish. The experience of the European Economic Community with respect to harmonization, trade measures and minimum species size regulations was noted. The workshop appointed a working group to formulate specific recommendations on this issue. The report of the working group . . . recommends that the CARICOM Standing Committee of Ministers responsible for Agriculture call on member countries to introduce legislation requiring imports of the more important and valuable species of fish, such as shrimp and lobsters, to be accompanied by certificates of origin attesting that the fish had been legally caught and exported.

21. The problem was raised of states licensing foreign vessels to fish in their waters and these vessels, in turn, straying into the waters of other states. Some delegations felt that some harmonization of legislation was needed to control this. In discussions on this point it was noted that it might be difficult and unrealistic to incorporate into a country's law that licensed foreign vessels will not violate the laws of neighbouring countries. The experience of other regions with Regional Registers of fishing vessels as a compliance control mechanism was noted.

22. Discussions followed on the advantages and disadvantages of having a comprehensive Exclusive Economic Zone Act in which provisions dealing with foreign fishing in the EEZ were also included or incorporating these provisions in a comprehensive Fisheries Act. It was noted that there were two divergent approaches. From a historical point of view early legislation on the Exclusive Economic Zone or Exclusive Fisheries Zone was introduced, usually by the Ministry of Foreign Affairs and tended to include fisheries provisions based on Articles 61 and 62 of the Convention. This legislation was in addition to the Fisheries Act. The implementation of the provisions of both acts can present difficulties and there is now a tendency in many countries towards the adoption of a comprehensive Fisheries Act that incorporates the fisheries aspects of the Law of the Sea Convention. When looked at in practice the differences in powers vested in a country over the control of its fisheries resources in its Territorial Sea and within its Exclusive Economic Zone are probably not sufficiently diverse as to necessitate two separate pieces of fisheries legislation or indeed completely separate treatment in a single piece of legislation. These differences relate to the obligation of the coastal state to manage properly the fishery resources of its EEZ, the obligation to give access to surplus resources in the EEZ and not to impose the penalty of imprisonment for fishery offences in the EEZ. It was noted that the integration of all fisheries provisions and mechanisms into a comprehensive Fisheries Act would alone provide the coastal state with a proper legal framework for fisheries management that would allow it to meet its management obligations under the Convention. Mechanisms for allowing for access to surplus could also be provided for under a comprehensive piece of fisheries legislation. With respect to imprisonment, the new tendency is for most coastal states to remove it as a penalty for fisheries offences for nationals as well as foreigners.

23. Under the Law of the Sea Convention there are additional matters relating to mineral resources, navigation, free passage, etc. which may be best dealt with under separate Legislation to that dealing with fisheries.

LEGISLATIVE PROVISIONS RELATING TO THE MANAGEMENT
AND DEVELOPMENT OF FISHERIES

. . .

5.   In debating the desirability of providing for management and development plans in legislative proposals, the workshop agreed that, wherever possible, the concept of management and development plans should be institutionalized by entrenchment in legislation. Any tendency to over-exploit the fishery resource could be resisted by the fishery administrator, who would have a proper legal basis and right to make known the facts relating to the state of the fishery resources. The institution of fishery management plans as a central concept of the fisheries legislation would place proper emphasis on fisheries management and provide an appropriate legal framework for fisheries management and development. It would also create a dynamic mechanism within the fisheries legislation that would enable the legislation to respond to new needs such as the introduction of limited entry schemes in fully or over-exploited fisheries, without having to amend the basic legislation. The details of any such scheme would be worked out in the appropriate management plan, with public participation, and legal consequences in such areas as the transferability of fishing licences would flow from the adoption of such schemes. It was noted that the introduction of limited entry schemes would require decisions on a large number of issues and that such issues could not all be addressed in advance and in detail in the basic legislation. It was important however that limited entry schemes could be introduced without the need to adopt new legislation, to avoid a rush of new entrants into an already overcrowded fishery.

6.   The subject of the establishment of a National Fisheries Advisory Board or Committee comprised of representatives from all fisheries sectors, advisory to the government on fisheries management and development issues was discussed by the group. The view was expressed that management and development plans were so crucial to the survival of the fishing industry in any country that there should be legislative provisions to facilitate a public input in the formulation of such plans and that a National Fisheries Advisory Board was a vehicle through which, by consultation with interested parties, the views of the industry could be conveyed to the responsible Minister.

. . .

9.   The issue of legislative provisions dealing with the involvement of local fisheries communities in the establishment of conservation measures and means for the avoidance and settlement of conflicts among different groups of fishermen was discussed by the group. Members reviewed the provisions relating to the establishment of local fisheries management areas and authorities in the OECS harmonized legislation and related their individual experiences in attempts made to settle disputes between fishermen and fishing communities. Although damage to the fishing gear of artisanal fishermen by industrial fishing vessels sometimes gave rise to disputes, the majority of disputes arose because of poaching or exploitation of fishing stocks from areas which some fishermen regarded as their special preserve. In such conflicts reconciliation through fishermen's co-operatives was frequently successful. It was agreed that legislative measures could lend force and effectiveness to the methods employed by fishermen co-operatives or other local fishermen's communities to resolve disputes.

LICENSING OF FISHING OPERATIONS AND OTHER
CONSERVATION METHODS

. . .

Nationality Criteria

1.   The workshop examined the criteria for distinguishing between foreign fishing vessels and national fishing vessels. Some countries in the region have very strict nationality criteria, in the sense that local vessels were required to be owned 100% by resident nationals, or companies wholly owned by resident nationals. Other countries required ownership by local citizens or companies whose shareholding was at least 51% owned by nationals. Yet other countries did not go behind the veil of incorporation of locally established companies to require any local shareholding. In some cases the nationality of the vessel for fishing purposes was left to be determined by the normal flag registration criteria applied by the Marine Board or shipping authorities for all merchant ships.

2.   It was noted that the decision on nationality criteria for the purpose of fishing was different from that of according flag nationality to a vessel. In the case of fishing vessels, the decision was essentially one regarding preferential access to the coastal states fish resources.

3.   The workshop concluded that the criteria for establishing nationality will depend upon the policy of the coastal state concerned. In countries where the policy may be to encourage foreign fishing operations landing to local processing operations, criteria for classification as a national vessel may sometimes be set more flexibly than in a situation where the coastal state wishes to control strictly, or discourage foreign fishing. The example of Fiji was noted which classified all locally based foreign vessels landing to local canneries as local fishing vessels, because Fiji wishes to encourage such landings.

4.   The workshop recommended that governments look closely into the question of nationality criteria for fishing vessels when revising their national fisheries legislation, to ensure that criteria appropriately reflect their national fisheries policies.

Licensing of foreign fishing operations

5.   The licensing of foreign fleets may be necessary in some instances to exploit the resources that the coastal state cannot yet exploit; to provide employment, to generate revenue to a coastal state by the payment of fees, or to supply raw material to processing plants. Licensing of foreign fleets may create difficulties where the resource can be efficiently exploited by nationals. Each country will normally wish to give priority to the development of its own national fishing fleets.

6.   The workshop noted the obligation placed on coastal states under Article 62 of UNCLOS to permit foreign fishing vessels access to their EEZs to exploit the surplus of the allowable catch that is not exploited by the coastal state. The workshop noted, however, the flexibility in the discretion left to the coastal state in determining the level of the allowable catch, its own harvesting capacity and hence the level of the surplus.

7.   The workshop noted that no country in CARICOM has sufficient information on the resources in its EEZ to determine the optimum yield and consequently to determine whether

or not they have surpluses. However, some countries have been permitting foreign fishing while others have recognized the need to start preparing to deal with this issue.

8. The group then examined some aspects of foreign fishing operations. The differences were recognized between distant-water foreign fishing operations, where vessels enter the EEZ of coastal states, conduct fishing activities and return to their base which is not in the coastal state and, on the other hand, locally based foreign fishing operations where the foreign fleet conducts fishing activities from a base within the coastal state. It was recommended that this distinction could be usefully reflected in national legislation with separate rules and possibly fee structures, for distant-water and locally-based foreign fishing operations.

9. With respect to distant-water foreign fishing operations, the importance of requiring umbrella intergovernmental access agreements was recognized. This type of arrangement, supported by individual vessel licensing, can have several advantages, including those of providing a framework for the payment of additional financial aid by the flag state, and of placing a certain amount of responsibility on the flag state for ensuring that its vessels comply with the terms and conditions of the negotiated access arrangement - the so-called concept of flag state responsibility for compliance control.

10. Locally based foreign fishing operations usually call for a more flexible approach to regulation on an individual company/vessel licensing arrangement. In such cases the requiring of a bilateral access agreement might well be irrelevant and unnecessarily inflexible. Provision should also be made in national legislation for test fishing operations, which may require similar flexibility in regulation.

11. On the question of controlling the activities of foreign fishing fleets the group referred to the need for surveillance. Marking of vessels was considered and it was agreed to circulate the report on the "Report of the Expert Consultation and Fishing Vessel Markings", Halifax, Canada, 1985. It was reported that a further technical consultation would be held in June this year to consider the detailed formulation of a recommended marking standard.

12. The particular problems of methods of authorizing foreign fishing was considered. It was noted, in particular, that quotas are difficult and costly to monitor and that coastal states may wish to consider other systems such as permitting a fixed number of vessels or fishing days. An identified problem was that foreign fishing fleets based in one coastal state may violate the laws of the neighbouring coastal state by entering and conducting fishing activities in the EEZ of the neighbouring coastal state.

13. A working group to consider draft legislation on this issue was set up. The draft legislative provisions are set out as Appendix G to this Report.

Licence fees for foreign fishing

14. Basically, four methods of fixing fees were discussed. Coastal states may charge lump-sums. This system, which has been commonly used in the South Pacific, places most of the risk on the foreign fleet, as their catch may not reach the level for which the fees were assessed. On the other hand it places the least administrative burden on the coastal state, which can easily administer this system and immediately know the level of revenue expected from the operations of the foreign fleet.

15.   Secondly, there is a fee based on the level of the fishing effort, i.e. the size or capacity of vessels, number of vessels, number of fishing days, etc. Sometimes this system may be tied into the market value of the catch. This system places less risk on the foreign fleet and is more difficult to administer.

16.   The third method is to compute fees based on actual catch. This method requires maximum administration and places the maximum risks on the coastal state. It could result in false statistics being supplied to the coastal states.

17.   The fourth method is a relatively new concept whereby the foreign fleet is paid an effort fee and the catch remains the property of the coastal state. This type of fee structure is probably more appropriate for countries with a state fishing or marketing company that could take the property in the fish.

18.   It was observed that the fee could be cash, a percentage of the catch or even aid to the coastal state.

19.   The workshop felt that the most appropriate system would have to be decided on by the coastal state, taking into account the above factors.

Licensing of local fishing operations

20.   The workshop agreed that it is necessary to license local operations since, primarily, it provides vital information on the local fishing industry.

21.   The units of type of activity being licensed may well vary among the countries. The main unit of fishing effort to be licensed will normally be the fishing vessel. In some cases it may also be necessary or desirable to license fishing gear and fishermen. In many cases it may be desirable to include also licensing controls over processing plants and exports, in order to control the level of pressure on resources.

22.   The distinction between the functions of vessel registration (i.e. controls over the fishing vessel as a unit of navigation) and fishing vessel licensing (i.e. controls over the fishing vessel as a unit of fishing effort) was noted. In most cases, the fishing vessels must be registered before being granted a license and a number to be displayed.

23.   Registration of fishing vessels was handled by the Fisheries Department in some countries, the Harbour Master in others and by a Marine Board in another. However, all fishing licences, where in force, were and should be granted by the Fisheries Department. Registration tended to relate to ownership, certification of seaworthiness, inspection, equipment on board, etc. Licensing usually related to the control of fishing operations and conditions of fishing, markings, etc.

24.   The workshop considered the best way of structuring licensing systems for the eventual development of schemes for limitation of local fishing effort.

25.   Limited entry was not in force in any of the countries but the need existed. The experiences of the participants revealed the difficulties of mustering political will to introduce limited entry. Unemployment and the fact that people who lose their jobs tend to gravitate into fishing may influence the political situation.

26.   The workshop thought that the fisheries legislation should provide for the possibility of adopting schemes for the limitation of fishing effort. Some public participation in the form-ulation of such schemes would be essential. The fisheries management plans recommended for inclusion in the legislation might provide a vehicle and legal framework for this.

27.   Most countries had not examined schemes for limited entry. Examples of other methods of controlling fishing mortality were given, such as increasing licence fees, reducing or eliminating subsidies, having transferable quotas, etc. The difficulties of administering transferable quotas in developing countries were recognized. One country was encouraging the exploitation of unexploited stocks to diversify fishing activities and spread the fishing effort.

. . .

34.   The workshop reaffirmed the crucial importance of obtaining true and accurate statistics and supported the requirement of having some authority to demand statistics.

35.   In general the Minister should have the right of making regulations regarding the keeping of statistics. However, some aspects could be legislated while others could be set as conditions of licences.

36.   The requirements for the completion and submission of daily fishing log books by skippers could be legislated for or made a condition of fishing licences. The supply of information on sports fishing from clubs or tournaments could be legislated for, as could reports from processing plants and exporters. Data collectors may require legislative support to visit landing sites and obtain information, e.g. the power to require fishermen to present their catches for weighing and answer questions relating to catch and effort.

37.   A view was expressed that voluntary encouragement or incentives should be used to obtain data rather than legal coercion since operators may present false and/or inaccurate information.

38.   It was agreed that information should be collected from as many sources as possible to facilitate crosschecking and verification to establish the quality of the statistics. The fishermen are the first line of information while plants, vendors, etc. represent the second line of information. Generally for the second line of information, licences conditions may be appropriate for obtaining information.

. . .

40.   Regulations regarding mesh size regulations, closed season, quotas, etc. require to be changed periodically. Since they are subject to changes, a great degree of flexibility is required and they should be put into subsidiary legislation rather than in the Act. For closed seasons used to implement total allowable catches in certain fisheries, even greater flexibility may be required so as to be able to close season "over-night". This flexibility can be achieved by giving the fisheries administration the power to close and open seasons by means of notices or announcements in the local press.

MARINE SCIENTIFIC RESEARCH RELATED TO FISHERIES

. . .

2.   The view was expressed that, in view of the number and complexity of the provisions in the Convention on marine scientific research, it would be necessary to give further

consideration to the treatment of scientific research in the draft fisheries legislation and the need for interministerial consultations was stressed. It was however pointed out that the provisions dealing with marine scientific research operations in the draft Barbados Law dealt only with scientific research and survey operations related to fisheries. As such, under Article 246(5), the powers of the coastal state with respect to the controls over scientific research in the exclusive economic zone were much greater than with respect to other scientific research operations not "of direct significance for the exploration and exploitation of natural resources". The only provisions of the Convention which were not intended to be reflected in the draft law were those relating to the concept of implied consent under Article 252, which it was felt, should be handled as a matter of the coastal states international obligations rather than dealt with in the context of national legislation.

3.   On the issue of local research institutions it was suggested that individual approvals of research projects were not necessary but that Government should approve a list of projects and impose conditions with respect to reports.

4.   It was suggested that the provisions being complicated, a working group should be formed to redraft the provisions of Sections 25 and 26 of the Barbados draft Bill to produce a model that may be applicable to all the states. The provisions are set out in Appendix J to this report.

   . . .

OFFENCES AND LEGAL PROCEEDINGS

   . . .

1.   In accordance with the workshop prospectus the discussion on agenda item 10, Offences and Legal Proceedings, centered on the range of offences and the level of penalties, the court system which would enforce the penalties and deal with offences occurring beyond the limits of the territorial sea and the rebuttable presumptions which would assist in proving that an offence has been committed.

2.   A differentiation was made between the type of penalty to be imposed for an offence committed by a local as opposed to a foreign fishing vessel. Where it was a foreign fishing vessel not based in the coastal state or licensed to fish in the EEZ, it was felt that, as a penalty for the offence of fishing illegally, the vessel should be seized and the catch forfeited.

3.   Article 73 of the United Nations Convention on the Law of the Sea precludes imprisonment for violations of fisheries laws and regulations in the EEZ and requires prompt release of the vessel and its crew upon posting of a reasonable bond or other security. The penalty still existed in most countries albeit in a round-about way, in that imprisonment may be imposed for non-payment of fines.

4.   Where a fine is imposed it has to be meaningful in order to have an impact. Territories sharing common or related stocks should have not gross disparities in the level of penalties imposed as this might tend to divert fishing effort from one area to another in the same way as differences in fee levels.

5.   It was recognized that prompt handling of fisheries offences was necessary. The system of handling penalties administratively instead of through the courts was examined. This system obtains in Suriname. Compounding of offences was suggested as an alternative because the former tended to be seen in many common-law countries as the executive

encroaching on the judiciary and as contrary to the doctrine of the separation of powers. The concept of compounding is usually to be found in the Customs Law, the Inland Revenue and Forestry laws of some territories so the idea is not repugnant, as it is agreed that offences must be dealt with quickly. The concept of release of foreign vessels on the posting of a satisfactory bond was considered. The amount of the bond would have to be proportionate to the worth of the vessel so that if the vessel is not returned, the bond would cover the loss.

6. In the United Kingdom there is no power to confiscate the vessel. The courts have the power to forfeit gear and catch. The gear and catch is normally sold back to the owner.

7. Forfeiture of a vessel would normally be applicable only to foreign fishing vessels. If the courts are given powers to forfeit, these should not be mandatory, as this might well place the Government in an embarrassing situation. The legislation should also provide for forfeiture of catch. It was suggested that forfeiture of catch could be made mandatory for foreign vessels fishing illegally.

Court Systems

8. Consideration was given to the following points:

(a) That extended jurisdiction would have to be given to magistrates in order for them to deal with offences committed outside the territorial sea.

(b) One area of difficulty was establishing that a vessel was within the fisheries zone or EEZ and therefore fishing illegally. It was recommended that countries include a provision in their laws that the place of the offence as revealed in the log book of the enforcement vessel be *prima facie* evidence of the place of the offence.

(c) There was a need for education of persons dealing with fisheries offences, especially magistrates, to make them aware of the seriousness of certain offences so as to make the penalty commensurate with the crime. Also as this was a relatively new area, provision should be made for assessors to advise the court on the level at which a bond should reasonably be set.

(d) Traditionally the Crown does not appeal against criminal convictions. Appealing could be an effective method of combatting the system where slight penalties were imposed for serious offences. It was felt, however, that it would be difficult to break tradition in this respect, although some countries in the region do already have such an appeal system in place.

(e) Fines for fisheries offences should be set at an appropriately high level. It was suggested that to allow a magistrate to impose fines which would be over their limit would require an extension of their jurisdiction. This might be viewed as an encroachment on the jurisdiction of the High Court. Some offences may therefore have to be tried by the High Court.

Presumptions

9. It was noted that in the OECS Legislation, where a fishing vessel is caught fishing illegally, it is presumed that all the fish on board was caught in the course of the commission of the offence. Some countries went even further in presuming that the fish on board a vessel passing through the exclusive economic zone had been taken in the zone, even where no offence was known to have been committed. It was felt, however, that this presumption of an

offence would be too onerous and might be viewed as an improper limitation on the right of free navigation through the exclusive economic zone.

ENFORCEMENT

. . .

2.   The primary role of the police, coast-guard and various defense organizations in enforcement was recognized. The need was felt to educate them on the relevant legislation and the importance of proper enforcement of conservation and other fisheries regulations.

3.   Much debate surrounded the question dealing with powers of inspection of premises in search of illegally caught fish. It was felt that a balance should be drawn between the need for enforcement mechanisms to be effective, and the need to respect the basic rights of citizens. The workshop was of the view that the power of entry of fisheries officers into premises should depend upon the officer having "reasonable grounds" to suspect that an offence has been or is in the process of being committed.

4.   Certain measures can and do facilitate enforcement such as standardized markings, radio equipped boats, reports of entry into and exit out of a state's waters, and the use of log books reflecting catch, area of catch and type. Use can be made of observers when and where necessary. Local fishermen could also be a useful source of fisheries information to surveillance and enforcement services.

5.   Attention was paid to section 21 of the Barbados draft (WP/13). That section deals with powers of inspection of local fishing vessels and gives an authorized officer the right of inspection to satisfy himself of the seaworthiness, sanitary condition and safety equipment of such vessels.

6.   The Workshop recognized that the work of the Harbour Master or merchant shipping authorities frequently tended to overlap with that of the Fisheries Division. The need for co-operation between them was widely recognized and accepted.

7.   As far as possible fisheries authorities should confine their responsibilities to dealing with fishing vessels as fishing units, leaving the control of vessels as navigational units to the merchant shipping authorities. However in practice controls over the seaworthiness and safety equipment of the smaller fishing vessels tended to fall to the Fisheries Administration.

8.   Particular attention was paid to the provisions of the Law of the Sea Convention as it affects national legislation in respect of seizure and forfeiture of boats and catch.

9.   Provision for the release of arrested vessels on the posting of a satisfactory bond was a useful device as the bond could be forfeited instead of the ship in the event of a conviction and order of forfeiture by the court. Indeed such a procedure of release on bond is required by the Convention. It was suggested that assessors could be used to advise the court on the value of the vessel and catch and thus of the bond to be set.

10. Finally the need for relatively high levels of penalties for illegal fishing was recognized, in view of the high value of catches, particularly where species such as shrimp or lobster were concerned. It was felt that magistrates should be sensitized as to the economic aspects of fishery offences.

GENERAL

. . .

2.   Some of the OECS concerns at the time of drawing up the Regulations were regulating the functions of the fishery advisory committee; the registration and licensing of fishing boats, both local and foreign; fisheries management and conservation measures; fishing gear, explosives, etc.

Harmonization

3.   It was recognized that it was difficult to deal with fishery regulations in detail since each country has different and varying needs depending on environmental conditions among other things. However, it was felt that harmonization of regulations might be important with respect to the condition of fishing vessels, sharing fleets with other countries and conservation measures when sharing stocks.

4.   The regulations recommended for the OECS in respect of foreign fishing regulations might serve as a checklist for other countries when drawing up similar regulations.

Flexibility

5.   The view was expressed that there was a need for flexibility so that matters might be dealt with expeditiously. The best way to achieve this is by regulations rather than by an enabling Act which, because of parliamentary procedures, would take more time. Certain matters, such as control of fishing vessels, might even be dealt with in licence conditions giving even greater flexibility.

. . .

ENVIRONMENTAL CONSIDERATIONS

. . .

1.   The environment of the Region is, in general, healthy, and tends to be taken for granted. Accordingly, environmental considerations are not given their due weight. However, this attitude should be guarded against. As in other parts of the world, the marine environment is increasingly affected by human activities such as:

(a)   The use of fertilizers and pesticides in agriculture on an increasing scale, resulting in higher concentrations of these chemicals in run-offs;
(b)   The disposal of industrial waste;
(c)   Sewage disposal;
(d)   Off-shore oil-drilling; the shipment and refining of oil;
(e)   Land-development projects along coast-lines or rivers, resulting in the disappearance of mangrove stands and erosion;
(f)   Discharge of bilge by sea-going vessels.

2.   Legislation should give due regard to the adverse effects of these activities on fish-stocks. The workshop considered whether provisions, specifically aimed at the preservation of fish-stocks, should be inserted in fishery legislation or whether comprehensive legislation, covering all aspects of environmental protection, including that of the preservation of fish-stocks, should

be enacted. It was noted that the choice between these alternatives seems to be influenced greatly by the political clout of the fisheries interests.

3.   It was felt that in most countries of the region, the fisheries interest is clearly subservient to others (e.g. tourism, industrial and agricultural development, etc.). In these circumstances, provisions concerning the preservation of marine ecology within general fisheries legislation do not seem to be effective and enforcement might be a virtual impossibility. On the other hand, it was observed that the same circumstances might prevent the enactment of comprehensive legislation, which gives due regard to the fishery aspect of environmental protection. When comprehensive legislation is not possible the insertion of a clause concerning the preservation of fish stocks might be accepted in so far as it does not seem to stand in the way of higher priority interests.

4.   In some countries of the region, however, comprehensive environmental legislation is preferred.

5.   Observations were made to the effect that legislation should provide for the consideration of environmental aspects of projects at the planning stage so as to avoid the adverse effects of the implementation of ill-conceived projects.

6.   It was further observed that legislation should provide for multidisciplinary advisory agencies in which all the concerned interests would be represented. Such a provision should not be inserted in fishery legislation since it would result in confining the scope of activities of the advisory body to the representation of the fishing interest. In case of conflict between this interest and another the fisheries interest might well suffer because of lack of political support.

7.   The importance of harmonization of legislation concerning the protection of the environment was drawn to the attention of the workshop. A recommendation that a workshop should be held to deal with this subject was proposed and agreed upon.

    . . .

APPENDIX F

MODEL PROVISIONS ON FISHERIES MANAGEMENT AND DEVELOPMENT

ADMINISTRATION OF FISHERIES

3.   There shall be appointed a Chief Fisheries Officer and such Fisheries Officers, Assistant Fisheries Officers and other officers as may be necessary to give effect to this Act.

FISHERIES MANAGEMENT AND DEVELOPMENT SCHEMES

4.   (1) The Chief Fisheries Officer shall progressively develop and keep under review schemes for the management and development of significant fisheries in the waters of Barbados.

(2)   Each fisheries schemes shall include:

(a)   an identification of the fishery concerned and the assessment of the present state of its exploitation;

(b)   a statement of the objectives to be achieved in the management and development of the fishery;

(c)   the specification of any management and development measures to be taken;

(d)   an indication of the main requirements for statistical information on the fishery and the means to be used to obtain such information; and

(e)   the specification, where appropriate, of any licensing programmes to be followed for the fishery, any limitations to be applied to local fishing operations and the amount of fishing, if any, to be allocated to foreign fishing vessels.

(3)   In preparing and reviewing a fisheries schemes the Chief Fisheries Officer shall consult with the local fishermen, local authorities, any other persons affected by the fishery scheme and with any Fisheries Advisory Committee appointed under Section #.

(4)   Each fisheries scheme and each review thereof shall be submitted to the Minister for approval.

FISHERIES ADVISORY COMMITTEE

5.   (1)   The Minister may appoint a Fisheries Advisory Committee to advise on the management and development of fisheries with the objective of ensuring the optimum utilization of the fisheries resources in the waters of Barbados for the benefit of the people of Barbados.

(2)   Any Fisheries Advisory Committee appointed under this Section shall include the Chief Fisheries Officer and such other persons as the Minister may consider capable of advising on the management and development of fisheries.

APPENDIX G

MODEL PROVISIONS ON FOREIGN FISHING

FISHERIES ACCESS AGREEMENTS

7.   (1)   The Government of Barbados may enter into access agreements with other states and with associations representing foreign fishing vessels owners or charterers, providing for the allocation of fishing rights to vessels from those states or associations.

(2)   The fishing rights allocated under agreements entered into under subsection (1) shall not exceed the total resources or amount of fishing allowed to the appropriate category of foreign fishing vessels under the appropriate fisheries scheme.

(3)   Any agreement entered into under subsection (1) shall include a provision establishing the responsibility of the foreign state or association to take necessary

measures to ensure compliance by its vessels with the terms and conditions of the agreement and with the laws relating to fishing in the waters of Barbados.

(4)   For the purposes of this Section and Section # the term "state" shall include any regional organization to which the power to negotiate access agreements has been delegated by the member countries of that organization.

FOREIGN FISHING VESSEL LICENCES

8.   (1)   No foreign vessel shall be used for fishing or related activities in the waters of Barbados without a valid foreign fishing vessel licence issued under this Section.

(2)   Subsection (1) shall not apply to any foreign fishing vessel used purely for the purpose of sport fishing or fisheries related research operations.

(3)   An application for a foreign fishing vessel licence shall be made, in the prescribed form, to the Minister.

(4)   Subject to the provisions of the Act and any regulations made under this Act, the Minister may issue a foreign fishing vessel licence in the prescribed form authorizing a foreign fishing vessel to be used in the waters of Barbados for such fishing or related activities as may be specified in the licence.

(5)   Subject to Sub-Section (6), no foreign fishing vessel licence shall be issued to any foreign fishing vessel unless there is in force with the Government of the flag state of the vessel or with an association of which the owner or charterer is a member, an access agreement to which the Government of Barbados is a party.

(6)   A licence may be issued in respect of:

(a)   test fishing operations; or
(b)   a locally based foreign fishing vessel, notwithstanding the absence of an access agreement otherwise required under subsection (5).

(7)   Where a fishing vessel is used in contravention of Sub-Section (1) or of any condition of the foreign fishing vessel licence the master, owner and charterer of that vessel is each guilty of an offence and shall be liable on summary conviction to a fine not exceeding _____ dollars.

STOWAGE OF FISHING GEAR

9.   (1)   The fishing gear of any foreign fishing vessel which is prohibited from fishing in the waters of Barbados under section 8 shall be stowed in the prescribed manner while the vessel is within the waters of Barbados.

(2)   Where a foreign fishing vessel is licensed to fish by means of a particular type of fishing gear in any specific area of the waters of Barbados, any other fishing gear on board the vessel shall be stowed in the prescribed manner while the vessel is within that area or within any other area of the waters of Barbados where it is not licensed to fish.

(3)   Where a foreign fishing vessel contravenes Sub-Section (1) the master, owner and charterer of that vessel is each guilty of an offence.

. . .

APPENDIX J

MODEL PROVISIONS ON FISHERIES RELATED RESEARCH AND SURVEY OPERATIONS

FISHERIES RESEARCH

25.   (1)   Subject to sub-section (#), no person shall undertake fisheries related research or survey operations in the waters of Barbados except with the prior permission of the Minister.

(2)   Sub-section (1) shall not apply to fisheries related research or survey operations undertaken -

(a)   in the waters of Barbados by an approved local research institution within the meaning of section #.

(b)   in the exclusive economic zone of Barbados by an international organization or agency of which Barbados is a member under and in accordance with a detailed international project to which the Government of Barbados has given its formal approval.

(3)   An application to undertake fisheries related research or survey operations in the waters of Barbados shall be made to the Minister in the prescribed form and shall be supported by a detailed plan of the research or survey operations to be undertaken.

(4)   The Minister [, with the approval of the Cabinet,] may grant permission for any vessel or person to undertake fisheries related research and survey operations in the waters of Barbados and in doing so may exempt such vessel or person from any of the provisions of this Act.

(5)   It shall be a condition of any permission given by the Minister under subsection # that -

(a)   such scientific observers or other personnel as the Minister may designate shall be allowed on board the research or survey vessel and shall be allowed to participate fully in the research or survey project both on board the vessel and on shore;

(b)   copies of any raw data generated by the research or survey operations shall be submitted to the Chief Fisheries Officer at the end of the operations or during the course of such operations;

(c)   the results and conclusions of the research or survey operations shall be submitted to the Chief Fisheries Officer as soon as practicable following the completion of the operations and in any case no later than the time specified for the submissions of the results and conclusions in the written permission given by the Minister;

(d) no results of the research and survey operations shall be published or otherwise made internationally available without the prior agreement of the Minister.

(6) The Minister may attach such other conditions as he deems fit to any permission granted under Sub-Section (1).

(7) Where any of the conditions set out in paragraph (5) has been breached, no further permissions for fisheries related research or survey operations shall be granted to the person concerned until such time as the corrective action has been taken to the satisfaction of the Minister.

(8) Any person who undertakes or assists in any fisheries research in the waters of Barbados:

(a) without permission under Sub-Section (1); or
(b) in contravention of any condition or conditions attached to the permission under subsection (5) or (6),

is guilty of an offence.

(9) Any permission or exemption granted under this Section shall be in writing.

APPROVED LOCAL RESEARCH INSTITUTIONS

26. (1) The Minister may designate any local scientific or academic institution as an approved local research institution for the purposes of section # (2).

(2) Any designation under subsection (1) shall be in writing.

(3) It shall be a condition of the designation of an institution under sub-section (1), that the institution shall -

(a) submit to the Chief Fisheries Officer, at least once a year, a list of research projects undertaken during the previous year together with a summary of the results of any such projects completed during that period;
(b) give the Chief Fisheries Officer or any fisheries officer designated by the Chief Fisheries Officer, access to the results of any completed research project and any data generated by or during the course of the project;
(c) submit to the Chief Fisheries Officer such other information regarding research projects as he may require; and
(d) comply with such other conditions as the Chief Fisheries Officer may require in relation to the proper management of fisheries, the protection of the environment and the observance of the international obligations of Barbados.

. . .

SUMMARY OF RECOMMENDATIONS

The FAO/WECAFC/CARICOM workshop on Fisheries meeting in Bridgetown, Barbados, on 6-12 May 1986, adopted the following recommendations:

1.   That CARICOM member states and other states observing the workshop should take prompt measures to review their fisheries legislation to bring it into line with the Law of the Sea Convention and to provide a proper legal basis for the management and development of fisheries embodied where possible in a single comprehensive Fisheries Act;

2.   That such legislation should enable both coastal and flag states to implement their obligations and take advantage of their rights under the Convention, though all the provisions of the Convention establishing such international rights and obligations should not necessarily be repeated verbatim in national legislation;

3.   That states sharing common or related stocks with neighbouring states, whether members of CARICOM or not, should seek to harmonize their fisheries legislation with the neighbouring states and that this need should be brought to the attention of the various working groups on shared stocks including those scheduled to meet under the auspices of WECAFC;

4.   That states may wish to take into account the common principles and guidelines set out in the report of the workshop in drawing up new fisheries legislation;

5.   That CARICOM member states should consider including in their legislation a requirement that imports from CARICOM and non-CARICOM member states of fish and fish products of designated species, including shrimp and lobsters, should be accompanied by a valid certificate of origin from the country of export, attesting that the fish have been inspected and found to be in conformity with the conservation and export requirements of the exporting country;

6.   That CARICOM member states should seek to establish schemes requiring fishermen to carry suitable identification documents where these are not yet in force;

7.   That CARICOM member states should follow the work on standardization of marking requirements for fishing vessels being carried out under the auspices of the Canadian Government and FAO, to facilitate both surveillance and enforcement by coastal states, and air/sea rescue operations to protecting the lives of fishermen at sea;

8.   That CARICOM member states should press for the convening of a workshop on the drafting of legislation for the protection of the marine environment within the framework of the Action Plan for the wider Caribbean region adopted under the Cartagena Agreement.

- - - - -

Report and Proceedings of the Expert   FAO Fisheries Report No. 383
Consultation on Shared Fishery Resources
of the Lesser Antilles Region, September 1986   Extract

Part 1.   Report of the Expert Consultation

. . .

Objectives

The need for some kind of co-ordinated approach to assessment and management of shared stocks in the eastern Caribbean has become of increasing concern for several reasons:

(a) Large pelagics, whose mobility and distribution make them the most obviously shared resources, have been identified as showing the greatest potential to support fishery expansion in the region.

(b) Significant advances in fishery research and research capability in the region.

(c) Extended jurisdiction, which has been claimed by most countries in the region, has brought increased awareness of the responsibilities of coastal states for both local and regional management of resources occurring wholly or partially within their EEZs.

Consequently, the need to review the available information on shared stocks in the region, and to propose appropriate strategies for their assessment and management, was considered a priority issue by the WECAF Committee for the Development and Management of Fisheries in the Lesser Antilles, in 1985 at its second session (FAO Fish. Rep. No. 349). On the basis of a recommendation by that committee, FAO organized the present "Expert Consultation on Shared Fishery Resources of the Lesser Antilles Region".

The above concerns with shared stock problems are not limited to the Lesser Antilles sub-region, nor are many of the stocks which will be considered at this meeting restricted to this area. However, for practical purposes the scope of the meeting has been confined to this area.

The Lesser Antilles sub-region, which extends from the U.S. Virgin Islands south to Grenada, comprises one of the most compact aggregations of nations in the world. In addition to seven independent island nations (St. Kitts and Nevis, Antigua and Barbuda, Dominica, St. Lucia, Barbados, St. Vincent and the Grenadines, and Grenada); there are the dependencies of the United Kingdom, (British Virgin Islands, Anguilla, Montserrat); and the Netherlands (St. Maarten and St. Eustatius); Departments of France (Guadeloupe, St. Martin, St. Barthelemy and Martinique) and territories of the United States of America (US Virgin Islands). Fishing in the region is not solely by the above states. Commercial, distant-water fleets of Japan, Taiwan, Korea, Cuba, Venezuela and the U.S.A. have been active in the region for several decades, fishing mainly for tuna and other large pelagic species.

In view of the number of nations participating in the fisheries of the region, attempts at shared stock management will be faced with a plethora of problems in both major arenas for co-operation; research/assessment, and allocation/enforcement. In the first arena, early problems will relate to information. Standardisation of techniques and subsequently, agreement on appropriate analysis and interpretation will come into the picture. In the second arena, delimitation of EEZs, historical fishing rights, management objectives will be at issue.

At this first meeting on shared stocks in the region, the general objectives were:

(a) to obtain an overview of the extent to which the major resources may be shared by the islands of the region;

(b) to determine the information required to more accurately assess the degree to which stocks are shared;

(c) to review the organisational requirements for acquiring and analysing this information;

(d) to plan for the implementation of the required activities, i.e. proposals.

In order to properly address the above questions it is necessary to first review the types of shared stock situation which may be encountered, and to consider appropriate approaches to managing these stocks.   Only with these in mind is it possible to discuss appropriate assessment techniques and information requirements.

The consultation briefly reviewed the provisions of the text for the Law of the Sea as they relate to sharing of stocks (United Nations, 1983), noting in particular interpretations by Burke (1982), and Garcia *et al* (1986).   Participants also noted that the list of highly migratory species did not include some migratory species of importance in the Lesser Antilles region; notably, rainbow runner, *Elagatis bipinnulatus*, and fourwing flyingfish, *Hirundichthys affinis*.

Finally, whereas the above objectives are the immediate or proximate ones for this meeting, the ultimate aim should be kept in mind.   That is, to develop a well reasoned, well documented, convincing scenario which will stimulate action on the part of senior fishery managers and administrators.

. . .

General considerations on the management of shared stocks

The overall picture of activities involved in shared stock management was considered under four headings: stock identification, assessment and data requirements, allocation, and surveillance and enforcement (Mahon, 1987).

Two considerations relating to the above activities were emphasized:

(a) The need for discussion and consensus among participating countries.

(b) That interim conservation measures may frequently be required while agreed upon measures or research programmes are being implemented.

The difficulties in defining fish stocks precisely, and the need for participants in the fishery to agree on management units, were recognized.

Two main approaches to managing shared stocks were noted.   The first was the allocation of a total allowable catch (TAC) or total allowable effort (TAE) and the second was co-ordinated conservation-oriented regulations such as size limits, seasonal closures etc.

It is presumed that management of shared resources that occur in several EEZs would need to be discussed and decided upon in an international forum set up within the sub-region to address matters relating to shared resources; other than perhaps, those of a bilateral nature.

As a management strategy, the advantage of a TAE over a TAC is that it is more easily measured.   However, allocation of TAE requires that there be agreement on conversion factors between various types of vessels and gear.   These will need to be updated frequently.

The ways of arriving at TACs or TAEs were reviewed. These ranged from the most complex, data intensive approach involving yield per recruit analysis and estimation of recruitment, through surplus production modelling, to TACs based on past catch and effort.

The latter approach was discussed extensively as being the most likely candidate for application in the manpower and data limited situation of the Lesser Antilles. Implementation could involve allocating catches or effort to participants on the basis of their most recent catches or fleet size; recognizing however that in the long-term, the final national shares would come to reflect more closely the proportion and availability of the stock in each national zone; using for example some of the criteria spelled out by Caddy (1982). Any changes to the *status quo* could be negotiated. Proposals to increase catch and effort ideally require supporting information as to the anticipated impact of the increase on the stock.

Therefore, although the past catch and effort approach was seen as a possibility for early implementation of shared stock management, it was clear that several factors are missing for immediate implementation. These include the capability for monitoring and evaluation of stock status. A forum would also be required for on-going negotiations.

The meeting recognized that in most fisheries the minimum data requirements would be catch and effort. The most effective way of acquiring the latter is through licensing schemes which can also provide ancillary economic data. . . .
    . . .

Foreign fishing activities

Foreign fishing activities in the Lesser Antilles region were reviewed (Joseph, 1987). Although it was clear that numerous distant-water fishing countries had been active in the region there is currently little or no documentation of present levels of foreign fishing activity.

Estimation of foreign catch and effort is an important aspect of evaluating the resource potential of the region. In shared stock negotiations, precise, documented knowledge of foreign fishing activities play a significant role.

Documentation of foreign fishing activities could be achieved by requesting coastguard units, fishermen and local airlines to record and report any foreign fishing vessels. . . .

The options for dealing with foreign fishing activities were presented, and the pros and cons discussed.
    . . .

Option 1: The Status Quo

In most cases, foreign vessels are fishing without permission. Notable exceptions are some of the U.S. swordfish longliners fishing in the waters of the British Virgin Islands. Consequently, coastal states are losing the opportunity to acquire significant revenues from their resources. In the British Virgin Islands, licences are U.S. $7,000.00 per vessel/season. The total amount of revenue from 13 vessels would constitute a significant proportion of the budget of most island fishery divisions.

Option 2: Licensing

Licensing arrangements are the most common in dealing with foreign fishing activities. The conditions of the license may vary considerably according to the requirements of the coastal state; for example, training can be specified, or by-catch may be claimed by the licensing country. It is also possible to require some explanatory fishing in specified areas.

For licensing to be successful there must be the capability to monitor the licensee's compliance with the conditions of the licence. In the Lesser Antilles region, capabilities for surveillance and enforcement at sea are limited. Even where there are coastguard vessels, fisheries enforcement is seldom their top priority.

The alternative of requiring foreign vessels to carry observers is a viable one. The comfort and safety of observers must be provided for in the licensing agreement, as must adequate recompense for long periods at sea.

Surveillance and enforcement are one area where regional co-operation is likely to be most fruitful. Information-sharing on vessel locations and activities could alert countries as a vessel enters their EEZ from that of another country. Further co-operation could involve sharing the cost of regional surveillance vessels or aircraft.

A regional licensing system could greatly simplify surveillance, even by individual islands, and would simplify the process of acquisition of licences by foreign vessels. However, it may be necessary to design a system in which the final decision for allowing fishing in each EEZ is left with the government of that country.

Option 3: Joint Venture

Such operations often include the establishment of processing facilities in the country. However, in the case of high-priced species for the fresh fish market, transshipment may be all that is required.

Joint ventures may result in the establishment of a fishery infrastructure which is not subsequently supportable by the resource base. However, it does provide the coastal state with more easy control of catches, access to on-board training, and possibilities for establishing a data base on the resources of their EEZ. Landings from joint ventures contribute to the national catch record.

. . .

CONCLUDING SESSION: RECOMMENDATIONS AND PROPOSALS FOR DEFINITION AND MANAGEMENT OF SHARED STOCKS

While it is recognized that countries within whose zones a shared resource may occur have shared ownership and management responsibility for that resource, it is suggested under LOS (Article 63, 64) that they consider co-operative management with other part owners of the resource through an appropriate regional or sub-regional body. The extent to which management of the major fishery resources of the Lesser Antilles region may require such co-operation is shown in Table 7 (see page 832).

Co-operative Mechanisms for Research and Management on Shared Resources?

The consultation noted that Article 63 of the LOS Convention directs that two or more coastal States shall seek, either directly or through appropriate sub-regional or regional organisations, to consult on conservation and development of shared resources both adjacent coastal States and those fishing the same resource beyond EEZ. Article 64 addresses the situation of highly migratory species in a similar fashion, but in addition directs coastal States and other harvesting nations to set up an appropriate international organisation where one does not exist.

Interpretation of these two articles differ significantly between countries, and in practise several different approaches to management exist.

The consultations observed that the easiest case (Category II) is that for transboundary stocks, where two adjacent states can solve the problem by direct negotiation, although the use of the sub-regional forum for discussing the scientific basis for such measures may be useful in alerting other countries to the needs for management and the approaches that prove successful.

Several organisations which bring together groups of states, and which already have concerns for fisheries, already exist in the region. These are: OECS, CARICOM, ICCAT, WECAFC, and the Lesser Antilles Committee of WECAFC.

The membership of these groupings is shown in Figure 7 (p. 833), which makes clear that no single organisation represents all states involved in fisheries in the west Atlantic, although WECAFC comes closest to doing so, and the Lesser Antilles Committee represents all coastal states in the sub-region.

ICCAT

Discussion centered on the desirability of OESC being a member of ICCAT: this could be effected immediately in observer status, and the consultation recommended that this be done if possible. The desirability of full membership, as and when ICCAT completes ratification of a new convention allowing supernational organisations to do so, is felt to be less clearly a priority at this time, and the effectiveness with which OECS States could achieve their management objectives solely within ICCAT was not considered to be very high. At the same time, the ICCAT meeting allows the OECS States to encounter most participants in the Atlantic distant-water fishery, and it was believed this could lead to useful informal contacts outside the Commission sessions: in particular, to notify these states of access conditions, licensing or joint venture arrangements etc. The possibility of accrediting a tuna scientist of international stature to represent sub-regional interests in the very technical discussions in the scientific committee at this forum, also seems worth considering. Only Category IV stocks would need to be considered by ICCAT: recognizing that for the tunas at least most catches come from outside Lesser Antilles EEZs. This makes scientific assessment of stock status and management of stock exploitation by the Lesser Antilles countries alone essentially impossible.

WECAFC

This forum obviously provides a possible venue for discussions among all of the coastal states in the region, and at least some of the distant-water fishing interests, although it has not so far been used for concrete issues of this kind. Category III stocks falling outside the Lesser Antilles chain could be discussed here; and possibly also some Category IV resources.

The consultation felt however that as presently constituted, WECAFC has serious drawbacks as a forum for negotiation on shared resources. These are: the biennial nature of WECAFC meetings, and more seriously, the lack of a secretariat in the region. The presence of an outposted officer goes some way towards providing an effective presence though this position is only found on a temporary basis.

The Lesser Antilles Committee also appears to provide a valuable forum where the four main states or groups of states, the United States, Barbados, France and the OECS (with affiliation of Dutch and U.K. territories) are all represented. The same critical comments are valid, as they have been expressed for WECAFC. This grouping however, would be well situated to discuss management measures for category III, and if requested, categories I and II stocks also.

Considering WECAFC and its subsidiary bodies, the consultation recognized that, with modification in the way described above, it could perform the functions described below, as a series of steps.

Step 1:   Two or more countries refer a question relating to shared resources management to a regional secretariat.

Step 2:   The resident scientist, with assistance from the fisheries departments of concerned states, gathers the necessary data and carries out the research required.

Step 3:   The WECAFC Working Party on Marine Resources discusses the data and any assessment made.

Step 4:   This assessment is referred to either the Lesser Antilles Committee (Category II and III stocks) or to WECAFC (Category IV stocks).

Step 5:   These two bodies make recommendations to member countries for implementation.

OECS States

The desirability of a degree of co-ordination of national work on Category II and III stocks, especially through the proposed OESC desk, was recognized; although 2-way data exchange (shown by arrows in Figure 7) would be desirable.

CARICOM

Barbados and Trinidad and Tobago are not members of OECS, but are members of a wider organization, CARICOM. (Trinidad and Tobago is not a member of the Lesser Antilles Committee, but with OECS and CARICOM, is invited to attend its next meeting in observer status). CARICOM can evidently play an important role in co-ordination over the full range of its Member States.

Table 7.   Summary of relationships of major demersal and pelagic species to EEZs within the Lesser Antilles region . . .

Species	Category				
	I	II		III	IV
	Within one EEZ	Transboundary (a) adults	(b) larvae	Migratory, within EEZs of region	Migratory, partly within EEZs
Demersals					
conch	0	0*	o		
lobster	0	0*	o		
snapper/grouper	0	0*	o		
Pelagics					
dolphin				0	o
swordfish				o	0
white marlin					0
blue marlin					0
sailfish					0
yellowfin tuna					0
skipjack tuna					0
bigeye tuna					0
little tuna				o	o
blackfin tuna				0	o
bonito				0	o
wahoo				o	0
king mackerel		o		0	
flyingfish				o	o
jacks - coastal	0	0*	o		
- pelagic		o		o	

0 = probable Category, o = possible Category
* only in the case of shared island shelves

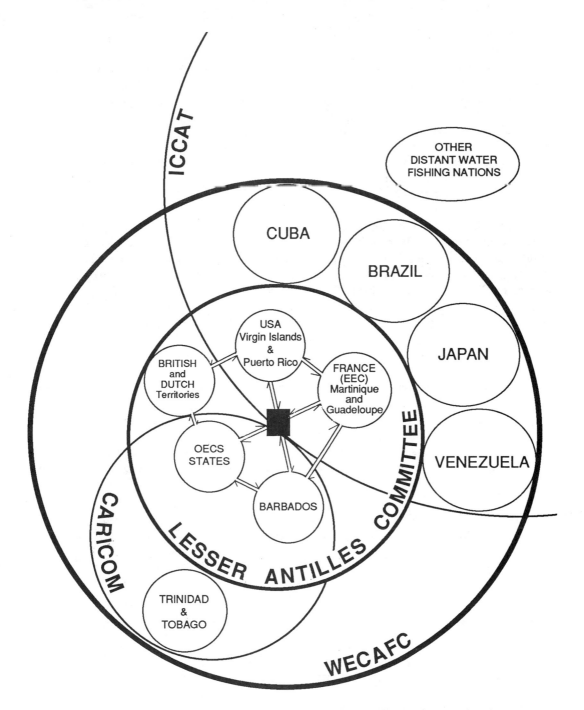

Figure 7. The interrelationships among the countries and organizations relevant to fisheries in the eastern Caribbean

A new organisation?

The possibility of setting up a quite new organisation was discussed, but the consultation felt that this would not be necessary at this time, at least until the other options above have been fully exploited.

A possible mechanism for co-ordination among bodies

The exchange of data on shared stocks could to some extent be co-ordinated through the WECAFC Secretariat if it were located within the region (represented by the square in the centre of Figure 7, page 833).

Clearly the mechanisms discussed here are purely hypothetical and to be effective, would need co-ordinated action by member states, as well as significantly increased funding. Funding might come from various donors initially, but a degree of self funding, such as that provided for example, by a fraction of licence revenues, or by national contributions would have to supplement limited funds available to FAO for current activities within the region.

In the immediate future, focus should be placed on three main objectives:

(1) Collecting more reliable catch and effort data nationally.

(2) Better training in species identification, including on the spot training and development of a field manual for Lesser Antilles species, based on the FAO Identification Sheets.

(3) Improved capabilities in both data exchange and analysis, and increased awareness at all governmental levels of the nature and extent of sharing of resources, and their practical implications in the LOS context.

- - - - -

South Pacific Forum Fisheries Agency - CIDA/FFA
Second Regional Legal Consultation,
Goroka, Papua New Guinea, 24-26 June 1986   Extract

. . .

Domestic Implications of Ratification of the
United Nations Convention on the Law of the Sea (UNCLOS)

3.   . . . The following major issues were identified.

(a) The extent to which UNCLOS reflects customary international law. The meeting recognized that while many of the principles embodied in UNCLOS represent customary international law, much of the detail does not. An example of this is Part V of UNCLOS, which deals with the Exclusive Economic Zone.

(b) The consultation considered that there is uncertainty as to the extent to which those parts of UNCLOS which do form part of customary international law are already incorporated into the domestic laws of FFA member States.

(c) The meeting recognized that the only certain means of incorporating UNCLOS into domestic law is by legislation. To that end, the following legislation options were identified:

    (i) legislation incorporating UNCLOS language or interpreting that language.

    If legislation incorporates UNCLOS language, the meeting considered interpretation of such language at the domestic level may require reference to interpretation at the international level and to other parts of UNCLOS which may not appear in domestic legislation.

    (ii) comprehensive or sectoral legislation.

    A comprehensive approach to give effect to EEZ rights would involve a single piece of legislation, whereas a sectoral approach would deal with different EEZ rights in separate pieces of legislation, for example fisheries acts. The meeting preferred a sectoral approach.

(d) The consultation also considered whether it would be necessary to have the implementing legislation referred to in paragraph 3 in place before ratifying UNCLOS, or whether it would be possible, by relying on Article 310, to ratify UNCLOS before enacting such legislation. It would appear that the situation would depend on each country's interpretation of Article 310 and its treaty implementation practice.

(e) The consultation noted that before ratification, a review of domestic legislation with a view to determining the need for amending or new legislation, in addition to implementing legislation, would be desirable.

(f) The consultation considered the role of domestic courts in giving effect to customary international law of treaty law, particularly the extent to which courts might review administrative decisions of a discretionary nature. The consultation considered that there were potential difficulties in judicial review displacing a government's legitimate and necessary role in determining its international obligations.

(g) It was reported that the financial implications of ratification have not yet been determined, but it is likely that an approach is being taken through the UN to ensure that costs will be set conservatively.

. . .

Review of Multilateral Fisheries Agreement with the United States

4. . . . The following major issues were identified.

(a) The consultation noted that the provisions in the draft agreement relating to reporting and observers amount to recognition by the United States of Pacific Island parties' jurisdiction over tuna, and no further express declaration of jurisdiction would be necessary or desirable.

(b) The process of ratification of the agreement by the United States and the effect of US budget cutbacks on the agreement was discussed.

(c) The consultation considered that the US Fishermens' Protective Act, if applied to US fishing vessels arrested and fined pursuant to the agreement, could result in the reimbursement of any fines imposed, and therefore reduce the effectiveness of the agreement. Further consideration should be given to including a provision in the draft agreement preventing US fishermen from receiving benefits under that Act if thcy havc violated the agreement, especially in view of the US implementing legislation for the Eastern Pacific Ocean agreement, which permits the Act to apply in certain circumstances.

(d) The consultation considered the application of forfeiture provisions of Pacific Island parties to US vessels which have violated the agreement, and concluded that the draft agreement is satisfactory in this respect.

(e) The consultation recommends that provisions relating to unlicensed fishing be reviewed with a view to clarification.

(f) The consultation noted the relationship between the draft agreement and the United Nations Convention on the Law of the Sea, in particular articles 64 and 116.

(g) Domestic implementation of the agreement was addressed, and the meeting considered the different approaches which could be taken. There are three basic approaches:

    (i) A comprehensive approach.

    This approach would seek to incorporate in detail the obligations and benefits of the agreement into domestic law.

    (ii) An approach of minimal amendment.
    (iii) Incorporation of the terms of agreement itself into domestic law.

    There was agreement that whichever approach is adopted, it would have to include legislation:

    (i) disapplying the requirement for a license issued by the coastal States;
    (ii) giving effect to a regional license and enforcement of that license; and
    (iii) taking into account a regional observer programme.

. . .

Regional Cooperation in Controls over Foreign Fishing Operations

5.   . . . The consultation considered a number of existing and possible regional mechanisms of control over foreign fishing vessels, including the Regional Register, flag State compliance

control, administrative sanctions, harmonization of marking and penalties and cooperative enforcement.

(a) Regional Register

The consultation noted that the Regional Register had attracted favourable attention in other regions. Possible improvements and different uses to which the Regional Register might ultimately be put were canvassed.

The consultation considered revised language for the criteria for withdrawal of good standing, and recommended that the language in Attachment F be recommended by the Secretariat to FFC members for approval, noting that it covers civil and criminal offences and, although the standard of proof would therefore be lowered, there are safeguards in the procedures which would ensure that the criteria would be used prudently. Some delegations expressed reservations about the continued use of the word 'serious' in 5.1(a), and one delegation expressed reservation about the appropriateness of the language, given the reference to civil penalties.

(b) Flag State Compliance Control

The consultation recognized that the dissemination of up to date coastal State laws is an essential element of a system of flag State compliance control, when such control is required by agreement, as in the multilateral fisheries agreement with the United States. To that end, the consultation agreed that FFA member States should ensure that up to date fisheries legislation is forwarded promptly to the FFA for inclusion in the FAO Regional Compendium of Legislation.

(c) Legal Aspects of Joint Surveillance and Enforcement Operations

The consultation recommended that legal aspects of the following matters be considered in the development of a surveillance and enforcement programme:

(i)   cross-authorization and protection of enforcement officers;
(ii) identification and marking of enforcement vessels and aircraft; and
(iii) standardization and use of evidence.

. . .

- - - - -

Treaty on Fisheries Between the Governments of Certain Pacific Island States and the Government of the United States of America

The Governments of the Pacific Island States party to this Treaty and the Government of the United States of America:

Acknowledging that in accordance with international law, coastal States have sovereign rights for the purposes of exploring and exploiting, conserving and managing the fisheries resources of their exclusive economic zones or fisheries zones;

Recognizing the strong dependence of the Pacific Island parties on fisheries resources and the importance of the continued abundance of those resources;

Bearing in mind that some species of fish are found within and beyond the jurisdiction of any of the parties and range throughout a broad region; and

Desiring to maximize benefits flowing from the development of the fisheries resources within the exclusive economic zones or fisheries zones of the Pacific Island parties;

Have agreed as follows:

Article 1
DEFINITIONS AND INTERPRETATION

1.1. In this Treaty:

(a) "Administrator" means that person or organization designated by the Pacific Island parties to act as such on their behalf pursuant to this Treaty and notified to the Government of the United States;

(b) "final judgement" means a judgement from which no appeal proceedings have been initiated within sixty days;

(c) "fishing" means:

  (i)   searching for, catching, taking or harvesting fish;
  (ii) attempting to search for, catch, take or harvest fish;
  (iii) engaging in any other activity which can reasonably be expected to result in the locating, catching, taking or harvesting of fish;
  (iv) placing, searching for or recovering fish aggregating devices or associated electronic equipment such as radio beacons;
  (v)   any operations at sea directly in support of, or in preparation for any activity described in this paragraph; or
  (vi) aircraft use, relating to the activities described in this paragraph except for flights in emergencies involving the health or safety of crew members or the safety of a vessel;

(d)   "fishing vessel of the United States" or "vessel" means any boat, ship or other craft which is used for, equipped to be used for, or of a type normally used for commercial fishing, which is documented under the laws of the United States;

(e)   "Licensing Area" means all waters in the Treaty Area except for:

    (i)   waters subject to the jurisdiction of the United States in accordance with international law; and

    (ii)   waters closed to fishing by fishing vessels of the United States in accordance with Annex I;

(f)   "operator" means any person who is in charge of, directs or controls a vessel, including the owner, charterer and master;

(g)   "Pacific Island party" means a Pacific Island State party to this Treaty and "Pacific Island parties" means all such States from time to time;

(h)   "Pacific Island State" means a party to the South Pacific Forum Fisheries Agency Convention, 1979;

(i)   "party" means a State party to this Treaty, and "parties" means all such States, from time to time;

(j)   "this Treaty" means this Treaty, its Annexes and Schedules; and

(k)   "Treaty Area" means all waters north of 60 degrees south latitude and east of 90 degrees east longitude, subject to the fisheries jurisdiction of Pacific Island parties, and all other waters within rhumb lines connecting the following geographic co-ordinates, designated for the purposes of this Treaty, except for waters subject to the jurisdiction in accordance with international law of a State which is not a party to this Treaty:

2° 35' 39" S	141° 00' 00" E
1° 01' 35" N	140° 48' 35" E
1° 01' 35" N	129° 30' 00" E
10° 00' 00" N	129° 30' 00" E
14° 00' 00" N	140° 00' 00" E
14° 00' 00" N	142° 00' 00" E
12° 30' 00" N	142° 00' 00" E
12° 30' 00" N	158° 00' 00" E
15° 00' 00" N	158° 00' 00" E
15° 00' 00" N	165° 00' 00" E
18° 00' 00" N	165° 00' 00" E
18° 00' 00" N	174° 00' 00" E
12° 00' 00" N	174° 00' 00" E
12° 00' 00" N	176° 00' 00" E
5° 00' 00" N	176° 00' 00" E
1° 00' 00" N	180° 00' 00"
1° 00' 00" N	164° 00' 00" W
8° 00' 00" N	164° 00' 00" W
8° 00' 00" N	158° 00' 00" W

0° 00' 00"	150° 00' 00" W
6° 00' 00" S	150° 00' 00" W
6° 00' 00" S	146° 00' 00" W
12° 00' 00" S	146° 00' 00" W
26° 00' 00" S	157° 00' 00" W
26° 00' 00" S	174° 00' 00" W
40° 00' 00" S	174° 00' 00" W
40° 00' 00" S	171° 00' 00" W
46° 00' 00" S	171° 00' 00" W
55° 00' 00" S	180° 00' 00"
59° 00' 00" S	160° 00' 00" E
59° 00' 00" S	152° 00' 00" E

and north along the 152 degrees of east longitude until intersecting the Australian 200 nautical mile limit.

1.2   Nothing in this Treaty shall be deemed to affect the applicability of any provision of a Pacific Island party's law which is not identified or otherwise described in this Treaty.

Article 2
BROADER CO-OPERATION

2.1   The Government of the United States shall, as appropriate, co-operate with the Pacific Island parties through the provision of technical and economic support to assist the Pacific Island parties to achieve the objective of maximizing benefits from the development of their fisheries resources.

2.2   The Government of the United States shall, as appropriate, promote the maximization of benefits generated for the Pacific Island parties from the operations of fishing vessels of the United States licensed pursuant to this Treaty, including:

(a)   The use of canning, trans-shipment, slipping and repair facilities located in the Pacific Island parties;

(b)   The purchase of equipment and supplies, including fuel supplies, from suppliers located in the Pacific Island parties; and

(c)   The employment of nationals of the Pacific Island parties on board licensed fishing vessels of the United States.

Article 3
ACCESS TO THE TREATY AREA

3.1   Fishing vessels of the United States shall be permitted to engage in fishing in the Licensing Area in accordance with the terms and conditions referred to in Annex I and licences issued in accordance with the procedures set out in Annex II.

3.2   It shall be a condition of any licence issued pursuant to this Treaty that the vessel in respect of which the licence is issued is operated in accordance with the requirements of Annex I. No fishing vessel of the United States shall be used for fishing in the Licensing Area without a licence issued in accordance with Annex II or in waters closed to fishing pursuant to Annex I, except in accordance with paragraph 3 of this article, or unless the vessel is used for fishing albacore tuna by the trolling method in high seas areas of the Treaty Area.

3.3   A Pacific Island party may permit fishing vessels of the United States to engage in fishing in waters under the jurisdiction of that party which are:

(a)   Within the Treaty Area but outside the Licensing Area; or

(b)   Except for purse seine vessels, within the Licensing Area but otherwise than in accordance with the terms and conditions referred to in Annex I,

in accordance with such terms and conditions as may be agreed from time to time with the owners of the said vessels or their representatives. In such a case, if the Pacific Island party gives notice to the Government of the United States of such arrangements, and if the Government of the United States concurs, the procedures of articles 4 and 5.6 shall be applicable to such arrangements.

Article 4
FLAG STATE RESPONSIBILITY

4.1   The Government of the United States shall enforce the provisions of this Treaty and licences issued thereunder. The Government of the United States shall take the necessary steps to ensure that nationals and fishing vessels of the United States refrain from fishing in the Licensing Area and in waters closed to fishing pursuant to Annex I, except as authorized in accordance with article 3.

4.2   The Government of the United States shall, at the request of the Government of a Pacific Island party, take all reasonable measures to assist that party in the investigation of an alleged breach of this Treaty by a fishing vessel of the United States and promptly communicate all the requested information to that party.

4.3   The Government of the United States shall ensure that:

(a)   Each fishing vessel of the United States licensed pursuant to this Treaty is fully insured against all risks and liabilities;

(b)   All measures are taken to facilitate:

    (i)   Any claim arising out of the activities of a fishing vessel of the United States, including a claim for the total market value of any fish taken from the Licensing Area without authorization pursuant to this Treaty, and the prompt settlement of that claim;

    (ii)   The service of legal process by or on behalf of a national or the Government of a Pacific Island party in any action arising out of the activities of a fishing vessel of the United States;

    (iii) The prompt and full adjudication in the United States of any claim made pursuant to this Treaty;

    (iv)   The prompt and full satisfaction of any final judgement or other final determination made pursuant to this Treaty; and

(v)   The provision of a reasonable level of financial assurances, if, after consultation with the Government of the United States, all Pacific Island parties agree that the collection of any civil or criminal judgement or judgements or determination or determinations made pursuant to this Treaty has become a serious enforcement problem;

(c)   An amount equivalent to the total value of any forfeiture, fine, penalty or other amount collected by the Government of the United States incurred as a result of any actions, judicial or otherwise, taken pursuant to this article is paid to the Administrator as soon as possible following the date that the amount is collected.

4.4   The Government of the United States shall, at the request of the Government of a Pacific Island party, fully investigate any alleged infringement of this Treaty involving a vessel of the United States, and report as soon as practicable and in any case within two months to that Government on that investigation and on any action taken or proposed to be taken by the Government of the United States in relation to the alleged infringement.

4.5   In the event that a report provided pursuant to paragraph 4 of this article shows that a fishing vessel of the United States:

(a)   While fishing in the Licensing Area did not have a licence to fish in the Licensing Area, except in accordance with paragraph 2 of article 3; or

(b)   Was involved in any incident in which an authorized officer or observer was allegedly assaulted with resultant bodily harm, physically threatened, forcefully resisted, refused boarding or subjected to physical intimidation or physical interference in the performance of his or her duties as authorized pursuant to this Treaty; or

that there was probable cause to believe that a fishing vessel of the United States:

(c)   Was used for fishing in waters closed to fishing pursuant to Annex I, except as authorized in accordance with paragraph 3 of article 3;

(d)   Was used for fishing in any Limited Area described in Annex I, except as authorized in accordance with that Annex I;

(e)   Was used for fishing by any method other than the purse seine method, except in accordance with paragraph 2 of article 3;

(f)   Was used for directed fishing for southern bluefin tuna or for fishing for any kinds of fish other than tunas, except that other kinds of fish may be caught as an incidental by-catch;

(g)   Used an aircraft for fishing which was not identified on a form provided pursuant to Schedule 1 of Annex II in relation to that vessel; or

(h)   Was involved in an incident in which evidence which otherwise could have been used in proceedings concerning the vessel has been intentionally destroyed;

and that such vessel has not submitted to the jurisdiction of the Pacific Island party concerned, the Government of the United States shall, at the request of that party, take all necessary measures to ensure that the vessel concerned leaves the Licensing Area and waters closed to fishing pursuant to Annex I immediately and does not return except for the purpose of submitting to the jurisdiction of the party, or after action has been taken by the Government of the United States to the satisfaction of that party.

4.6   In the event that a report provided pursuant to paragraph 4 of this article shows that a fishing vessel of the United States has been involved in a probable infringement of this Treaty, including an infringement of an applicable national law as identified in Schedule 1 of Annex I, other than an infringement of the kind described in paragraph 5 of this article, and that the vessel has not submitted to the jurisdiction of the Pacific Island party concerned, the Government of the United States shall, at the request of that party, take all necessary measures to ensure that the vessel concerned:

(a)   Submits to the jurisdiction of that party; or

(b)   Is penalized by the Government of the United States at such level as may be provided for like violations in United States law relating to foreign fishing vessels licensed to fish in the exclusive economic zone of the United States but not to exceed the sum of $US 250,000.

4.7   Financial assurances provided pursuant to this Treaty may be drawn against by any Pacific Island party to satisfy any civil or criminal judgement or other determination in favour of a national or the Government of a Pacific Island party.

4.8   Prior to instituting any legal proceedings pursuant to this article concerning an alleged infringement of this Treaty in waters within the jurisdiction, for any purpose, as recognized by international law, of a Pacific Island party, the Government of the United States shall notify the Government of that Pacific Island party that such proceedings shall be instituted. Such notice shall include a statement of the facts believed to show an infringement of this Treaty and the nature of the proposed proceedings, including the proposed charges and the proposed penalties to be sought. The Government of the United States shall not institute such proceedings if the Government of that Pacific Island party objects within 30 days of the effective date of such notice.

4.9   The Government of the United States shall ensure that an agent is appointed and maintained in accordance with the requirements of subparagraphs (a) and (b) of this paragraph, with authority to receive and respond to any legal process issued by a Pacific Island party in respect of an operator of any fishing vessel of the United States (identified in the form set out in Schedule 1 of Annex II) and shall notify the Administrator of the name and address of such agent, who:

(a)   Shall be located in Port Moresby for the purpose of receiving and responding to any legal process issued in accordance with this article; and

(b)   Shall, within 21 days of notification that legal process has been issued in accordance with this article, travel to any Pacific Island party, at no expense to that party, for the purpose of receiving and responding to that process.

Article 5
COMPLIANCE POWERS

5.1   It is recognized that the respective Pacific Island parties may enforce the provisions of this Treaty and licences issued thereunder, including arrangements made pursuant to article 3.3 and licences issued thereunder, in waters under their respective jurisdictions.

5.2   The Governments of the Pacific Island parties shall promptly notify the Government of the United States of any arrest of a fishing vessel of the United States or any of its crew and of any charges filed or proceedings instituted following the arrest, in accordance with this article.

5.3   Fishing vessels of the United States and their crews arrested for breach of this Treaty shall be promptly released upon the posting of a reasonable bond or other security. Penalties applied in accordance with this Treaty for fishing violations shall not be unreasonable in relation to the offence and shall not include imprisonment or corporal punishment.

5.4   The Government of the United States shall not apply sanctions of any kind including deductions, however effected, from any amounts which might otherwise have been paid to any Pacific Island party, and restrictions on trade with any Pacific Island party, as a result of any enforcement measure taken by a Pacific Island party in accordance with this article.

5.5   The Governments of the parties shall adopt and inform the other parties of such provisions in their national laws as may be necessary to give effect to this Treaty.

5.6   Where legal proceedings have been instituted by the Government of the United States pursuant to article 4, no Pacific Island party shall proceed with any legal action in respect of the same alleged infringement as long as such proceedings are maintained. Where penalties are levied or proceedings are otherwise concluded by the Government of the United States pursuant to article 4, the Pacific Island party which has received notice of such final determination shall withdraw any legal charges or proceedings in respect of the same alleged infringement.

5.7   During any period in which a party is investigating any infringement of this Treaty involving a fishing vessel of the United States, being an infringement which is alleged to have taken place in waters within the jurisdiction, for any purpose, as recognized by international law, of a Pacific Island party, and if that Pacific Island party so notifies the other parties, any licence issued in respect of that vessel shall, for the purposes of article 3, be deemed not to authorize fishing in the waters of that Pacific Island party.

5.8   If full payment of any amount due as a result of a final judgement or other final determination deriving from an occurrence in waters within the jurisdiction, for any purpose, of a Pacific Island party is not made to that party within sixty (60) days, the licence for the vessel involved shall be suspended at the request of that party and that vessel shall not be authorized to fish in the Licensing Area until that amount is paid to that party.

Article 6
CONSULTATIONS AND DISPUTE SETTLEMENT

6.1   At the request of any party, consultations shall be held with any other party within sixty (60) days of the date of receipt of the request. All other parties shall be notified of the request for consultations and any party shall be permitted to participate in such consultations.

6.2   Any dispute between the Government of the United States and the Government of one or more Pacific Island parties in relation to or arising out of this Treaty may be submitted by any such party to an arbitral tribunal for settlement by arbitration no earlier than one hundred and twenty (120) days following a request for consultations under article 6.1. Unless the parties to the dispute agree otherwise, the Arbitration Rules of the United Nations Commission on International Trade Law, as at present in force, shall be used.

6.3   The Government or Governments of the Pacific Island party or parties to the dispute shall appoint one arbitrator and the Government of the United States shall appoint one arbitrator. The third arbitrator, who shall act as presiding arbitrator of the tribunal, shall be appointed by agreement of the parties to the dispute. In the event of a failure to appoint any arbitrator within the time period provided in the Rules, the arbitrator shall be appointed by the Secretary-General of the Permanent Court of Arbitration at The Hague.

6.4   Unless the parties to the dispute agree otherwise, the place of arbitration shall be Port Moresby. The tribunal may hold meetings at such other place or places within the territory of a Pacific Island party or elsewhere within the Pacific Islands region as it may determine. An award or other decision shall be final and binding on the parties to the arbitration, and, unless the parties agree otherwise, shall be made public. The parties shall promptly carry out any award or other decision of the tribunal.

6.5   The fees and expenses of the tribunal shall be paid half by the Government or Governments of the Pacific Island party or parties to the arbitration and half by the Government of the United States, unless the parties to the arbitration agree otherwise.

Article 7
REVIEW OF THE TREATY

7.   The parties shall meet once each year for the purpose of reviewing the operation of this Treaty.

Article 8
AMENDMENT OF THE TREATY

8.   The following procedures shall apply to the adoption and entry into force of any amendment to this Treaty:

(a)   Any party may propose amendments to this Treaty;

(b)   A proposed amendment shall be notified to the depositary not less than forty five (45) days before the meeting at which the proposed amendment will be considered;

(c)   The depositary shall promptly notify all parties of such proposal;

(d) The parties shall consider proposed amendments to this Treaty at the annual meeting described in article 7, or at any other time that may be agreed by all parties;

(e) Any amendment to this Treaty shall be adopted by the approval of all the parties, and shall enter into force upon receipt by the depositary of instruments of ratification, acceptance or approval by the parties;

(f) The depositary shall promptly notify all parties of the entry into force of the amendment.

Article 9
AMENDMENT OF ANNEXES

9. The following procedures may apply to the adoption and entry into force of any amendment to an Annex of this Treaty, at the request of the party proposing the amendment, in lieu of the procedure set out in article 8, unless otherwise provided in the Annex:

(a) Any party may propose an amendment to an Annex of this Treaty at any time by notifying such proposal to the depositary, which shall promptly notify all parties of the proposed amendment;

(b) A party approving a proposed amendment to an Annex shall notify its acceptance to the depositary, which shall promptly notify all the parties of each acceptance. Upon receipt by the depositary of notices of acceptance from all parties, such amendment shall be incorporated in the appropriate Annex and shall have effect from that date, or from such other date as may be specified in such amendment. The depositary shall promptly notify all parties of the adoption of the amendment and its effective date.

Article 10
NOTIFICATION

10.1 The Administrator and each party shall notify the depositary of their current addresses for the receipt of notices given pursuant to this Treaty, and the depositary shall notify the Administrator and each of the parties of such addresses or any changes thereof. Unless otherwise specified in this Treaty, any notice given in accordance with this Treaty shall be in writing and may be served by hand or sent by telex or, where either method cannot readily be effected, by registered airmail to the address of the party or the Administrator as currently listed with the depositary.

10.2 Delivery by hand shall be effective when made. Delivery by telex shall be deemed to be effective on the business day following the day when the "answer back" appears on the sender's telex machine. Delivery by registered airmail shall be deemed to be effective twenty-one (21) days after posting.

Article 11
DEPOSITARY

11. The depositary for this Treaty shall be the Government of Papua New Guinea.

Article 12
FINAL CLAUSES

12.1   This Treaty shall be open for signature by the Governments of all the Pacific Island States and the Government of the United States of America.

12.2   This Treaty is subject to ratification by the States referred to in paragraph 1 of this article. The instruments of ratification shall be deposited with the depositary.

12.3   This Treaty shall remain open for accession by States referred to in paragraph 1 of this article. The instruments of accession shall be deposited with the depositary.

12.4   This Treaty shall enter into force upon receipt by the depositary of instruments of ratification by the Government of the United States and by the Governments of ten Pacific Island States which shall include the Federated States of Micronesia, the Republic of Kiribati and Papua New Guinea.

12.5   This Treaty shall enter into force for any State ratifying or acceding after the entry into force of this Treaty on the thirtieth day after the date on which its instrument of ratification or accession is received by the depositary.

12.6   This Treaty shall cease to have effect at the expiry of one year following the receipt by the depositary of an instrument signifying withdrawal or denunciation by the United States, any of the Pacific Island States named in article 12.4, or such number of Pacific Island States as would leave fewer than ten such States as parties.

12.7   This Treaty shall cease to have effect for a party at the expiry of the sixth month following the receipt by the depositary of an instrument signifying withdrawal or denunciation by that party, except that where this Treaty would cease to have effect under the last preceding paragraph as the result of the receipt of the said instrument, it shall cease to have effect for that party in the manner provided in the last preceding paragraph.

12.8   Any licence in force pursuant to this Treaty shall not cease to have effect as a result of this Treaty ceasing to have effect either generally or for any party, and articles 1, 3, 4 and 5 shall be regarded as continuing in force between the United States and the Pacific Island State party in respect of such licence until such licence expires in accordance with its terms.

12.9   No reservations may be made to this Treaty.

12.10   Paragraph 9 of this article does not preclude a State, when signing, ratifying or acceding to this Treaty, from making declarations or statements, provided that such declarations or statements do not purport to exclude or modify the legal effect of the provisions of this Treaty in their application to that State.

Done at Port Moresby on the second day of April, 1987.

ANNEX I

PART 1

INTRODUCTORY

1.   In this Annex:

(a)   "applicable national law" means any provision of a law, however described, of a Pacific Island party which governs the fishing activities of foreign fishing vessels, being a law identified in Schedule 1, and which is not inconsistent with the requirements of this Treaty and shall be taken to exclude any provision which imposes a requirement which is also imposed by this Treaty;

(b)   "Closed Area" means an area of a Pacific Island party as described in Schedule 2;
(c)   "Limited Area" means an area described in Schedule 3; and

(d)   "the vessel" means the vessel in respect of which a licence is issued.

2.   Schedule 1 may be amended from time to time by the inclusion by any Pacific Island party of any applicable national law and, for the purposes of this Treaty, except as provided in this paragraph, the amendment shall take effect from the date that the amended Schedule has been notified to the Government of the United States. For the purposes of any obligation on the United States pursuant to paragraphs 4 and 5 of article 4, the amendment shall take effect sixty (60) days from the date that the amended Schedule has been notified to the Government of the United States. The Government of the Pacific Island party shall use its best endeavours to provide advance notice to the Government of the United States of the amendment.

3.   Nothing in this Annex and its Schedules, nor acts or activities taking place thereunder, shall constitute recognition of the claims or the positions of any of the parties concerning the legal status and extent of waters and zones claimed by any party. In the claimed waters and zones, the freedoms of navigation and overflight and other uses of the sea related to such freedoms are to be exercised in accordance with international law.

. . .

- - - - -

Indian Ocean Fishery Commission   IOFC:TM/86/Inf.8
Committee for the Management of Indian Ocean Tuna   Extract
Ninth Session, December 1986

Bilateral Arrangements Between Coastal
Countries and Distant-Water Fishing Nations

INTRODUCTION

1.   Tuna fishing by artisanal fleets of pole-and-line boats, gillnet boats or trollers is a traditional activity in many areas of the Indian Ocean such as the Maldives, Sri Lanka or

Sumatra (Indonesia). Foreign fleets from eastern Asia using longlines and pole and lines began to operate in the region in the mid-fifties. More recently, French and Spanish fleets started large-scale purse seine fishing in the Southwest Indian Ocean. As a result of the activities of these newcomers to the fishery, the catch of tuna and tuna-like species increased from 234 000 t in 1979 to 455 000 t in 1985. This was due, in particular, to the dramatic increase in the catches of yellowfin and skipjack which are caught mainly by non-locally-based vessels. Indeed, from 1980 to 1985 the catches of these two species increased from 21 700 t to 132 000 t.

2.   Until the mid-seventies Japanese and Korean longline and pole-and-line vessels operated mainly outside the areas under national jurisdiction which were generally not wider than 12 miles. Thus very few access agreements were concluded during this period. The general adoption of the 200-mile limit coincided with the arrival in the region of large purse seiners which resulted in the conclusion of a number of bilateral agreements. So far, five coastal States have entered into such agreements with foreign governments[1]: Australia (with Japan and the Republic of Korea), France (with Japan and the Republic of Korea for the French islands around Madagascar for which competence has not been transferred to EEC), Madagascar (with EEC), Mozambique (with Spain), and the Seychelles (with EEC, France and Spain). Some East African coastal countries are currently negotiating further agreements with EEC. Less formal access arrangements have been entered into by India, Indonesia, Malaysia, and Seychelles and Somalia with foreign partners.

3.   This paper analyses the main provisions of the intergovernmental agreements concluded so far. Some of them are no longer in force but they are referred to given their interest from a practical and legal point of view.

GENERAL CHARACTERISTICS

(a)   Bilateral Agreements and the Law of the Sea

4.   The United Nations Convention on the Law of the Sea includes a number of provisions which have to be taken into account when negotiating access agreements[2]. Although the Convention was open for signature in December 1982, most of its provisions concerning fisheries had been agreed upon in 1975. It is interesting to compare the bilateral agreements concluded in the Indian Ocean since the mid-seventies with the key provisions on fisheries of the Convention.

5.   Several agreements mention, in general terms, in their preamble, that the Parties took into account the work of the Third United Nations Conference on the Law of the Sea. Coming to detailed provisions, it is first to be noted that the concept of exclusive economic zones is not frequently referred to as such. To designate the 200-mile off the coastal countries, the Parties have so far preferred to use alternative wordings such as "the zone under the fishery jurisdiction of" (e.g., agreements France/Korea and France/Japan) or "the juris- dictional waters of" (e.g., agreement Mozambique/Spain) or "the fishing zone of" (e.g., agreement Seychelles/Spain). It is clear, however, that even if the words "Exclusive Economic Zone" are not used the sovereign rights of the coastal States over the fishery resources of their 200-mile zones are *de facto* recognized.

6.   Another important concept of the Convention which can hardly be found in the access agreements concluded so far in the region is that of surplus. Under the provisions of the

Convention, coastal States are required to promote the objective of optimum utilization of the living resources in exclusive economic zones. To this end, they have to fulfil a number of obligations, the most important of which can be summarized as follows:

- coastal States have to determine the allowable catch of the living resources in their exclusive economic zone;

- they must then determine their own capacity to harvest these resources;

- where coastal States do not have the capacity to harvest the entire allowable catch, they have to give other States access to the surplus. They have, however, considerable freedom in determining the conditions governing such access.

7.   These provisions of the Convention on the Law of the Sea are of obvious interest to a region such as the Indian Ocean where most of the coastal States do not yet have the necessary means to exploit fully the abundant tuna resources of the waters under their jurisdiction. It is true that the Convention has not yet entered into force, but one can already see that, as in other regions bordered by developing countries[3], the agreements providing for access by foreign fleets to the living resources of the Indian Ocean's EEZs do not generally make reference to the concept of surplus. It is interesting to note that the only agreement including such a reference has been concluded between two developed countries (Australia and Japan).

(b) Types of Agreements

8.   As mentioned above (see paragraphs 2 and 3), this document concentrates on bilateral agreements concluded between governments. In some cases, however, it will refer to provisions of agreements entered into by coastal countries with private interests (e.g., the agreement between the Government of the Seychelles and the French Syndicate national des armateurs de thoniers congélateurs). Moreover, in a few cases foreign tuna boats were given licences outside the framework of any formal agreements.

9.   Several agreements cover only tuna fishing (e.g., EEC/Seychelles; France/Republic of Korea) while others deal with other types of fishing as well. In these cases, the provisions concerning tuna are either included in a protocol which is appended to the main agreement and has the same duration (e.g., EEC/Madagascar) or are the subject of the subsidiary agreement renegotiated each year (e.g., Australia/Japan).

10.   The duration of the agreements varies from one to five years. It should however be noted that several one-year agreements have been regularly extended over several years (e.g., France/Japan and France/Republic of Korea) and that five-year agreements (such as the one between Mozambique and Spain) are implemented by protocols which are concluded for one year only. An intermediate solution has been agreed upon in the two agreements concluded by the EEC which are valid for three years (including their annexes and implementing protocols).

(c) Institutional Framework

11.   All the agreements concluded for more than one year provided for periodic consultation between the Parties regarding the implementation of the agreement. These consultations are frequently organized within the framework of a commission set up by the agreement. These

bodies are generally entrusted with ensuring the correct application of the agreement. They meet in principle at regular intervals and alternatively in either one of the countries. In most cases the functions assigned to them are described in general terms: they are entrusted with responsibility for ensuring the correct application of the agreement. The agreement concluded by Spain with Mozambique goes further and provides that the commission must formulate the annual programme for cooperation which is embodied in the annual implementing protocols.

(d) Settlement of Disputes

12.   With regard to disputes concerning the interpretation or application of the agreements, all the agreements analysed for the purpose of this paper include only provisions of a general nature.   They stipulate that in the case of any difference of opinion arising from the interpretation or application of the agreement, the Parties "will enter into consultation" (EEC/Seychelles) or "will examine it in the most objective and conciliatory spirit with a view to overcoming the difficulty" (EEC/Madagascar). A similar requirement is found in a slightly elaborated form in the 1979 agreement between Australia and Japan in which the Parties agreed to settle any dispute by means of "negotiations which are to be initiated 60 days after one Party receives a request" for the opening of negotiations from the other.

13.   With respect to the settlement of disputes arising from incidents occurring during fishing operations, the same agreement provides that the Government of Japan shall take all necessary measures to facilitate prompt and adequate settlement of a claim for loss or damage for which Japanese fishing vessels are responsible while within the Australian fishing zones for the purpose of fishing operations.

REGULATION AND CONTROL OF FISHING OPERATIONS

14.   Article 62 paragraph 4 of the Convention on the Law of the Sea provides that nationals of other States fishing in the exclusive economic zone of the coastal State shall comply with the conservation measures and with the other terms and conditions established in its laws and regulations.   It then indicates that national legislation must be consistent with the Convention and, without being exhaustive, lists a series of points which may be included in the laws and regulations governing access.   In practice, these points are either covered directly in the provisions of bilateral agreements or the latter limit themselves to making cross-references to the relevant national legislation. They will be reviewed below.

(a) Specific Requirements

15.   The first main requirement is always the obtaining of the licence before starting tuna fishing operations.   Usually the procedure for the submission of applications for and the issuance of licences is not included in bilateral agreements since it is dealt with in national legislation. However, the procedure is outlined in an annex to the agreement between EEC and Madagascar. In the agreement between Spain and Seychelles a standard application form listing all the required information on the applicant and his vessel is given in an annex. The licence is usually delivered for a period of one year, but there are several other possibilities. Thus, Korean longlines operating in the Seychelles exclusive economic zone are licensed on a monthly basis.   The tuna fishing licences issued by Madagascar to EEC purse-seiners correspond to the period of validity of the agreement, i.e. three years. In all cases, licences are issued in respect of fishing vessels. However, the subsidiary agreement on tuna long line

fishing between Australia and Japan also provides for the licensing of persons intended to engage in fishing on board each of the vessels licensed under the subsidiary agreement.

16.   In all cases the agreements considered herein or the annexes or protocols thereto prescribe the number and type of the tuna vessels authorized to operate. In some cases, such as the 1973 agreement between France and Madagascar, the vessels are listed by name. More commonly the agreements merely indicate the maximum number of authorized vessels. For instance in both of the EEC agreements mentioned above, the limit has been set at 27 ocean-going freezer tuna boats. This maximum number does not however reflect the actual fishing effort being applied on the stocks since the agreements stipulate that the number of such vessels fishing simultaneously may not exceed 18. Taken in association with other regulatory measures (such as closed areas) the reduction of the fishing effort through a limitation of the number of authorized vessels is an efficient management measure which can be implemented by coastal States. Thus when the number of Japanese longliners authorized to operate in the Australian fishing zone was reduced in 1983 the Australian authorities explained that this reduction reflecting *inter alia* their concern about the status of the stocks of southern bluefin tuna. Finally it should also be noted that many of the agreements expressly exclude the possibility of transferring a licence from the initially authorized vessel to another. This prohibition aims at avoiding that such a transfer be made in favour of a vessel of a much greater capacity thereby increasing the fishing effort which was originally planned. However, in a few cases (e.g., EEC/Madagascar) and particularly in the event of *force majeure* a vessel's fishing licence may be replaced by a licence for another vessel the capacity of which does not exceed that of the vessel to be replaced.

17.   It is customary for bilateral agreements to ensure that the fishing operations of foreign vessels will not adversely affect the interest of the fishermen of the coastal State. The exclusion of foreign vessels from areas close to the shore is particularly important in the case of trawling but it is sometimes also necessary for tuna fishing. In the latter case such measures are aimed at avoiding gear conflicts with local trawlers or at protecting breeding areas. Thus the annex to the agreement between Spain and Seychelles provides that, in order to avoid adverse effect on small-scale fisheries in Seychelles, fishing by seiners shall not be authorized in the continental shelf area as defined by the 200 metric isobath or within three mile limits around the rafts placed by Seychelles fishermen. Similarly around Madagascar, EEC tuna vessels are excluded from the first two nautical miles of the waters under Malagasy jurisdiction.

18.   The agreement containing the most sophisticated provisions on closed areas is the subsidiary agreement between Australia and Japan concerning Japanese longline fishing. At each yearly renegotiation of this agreement the Contracting Parties agreed that very substantial areas of the Australian fishing zone would be permanently or seasonally closed to Japanese longliners. Depending on the areas, these measures were justified by the need (i) to reduce competition with Australian tuna vessels, (ii) to protect game fishermen, (iii) to avoid conflicts with Australian trap and trawl fishermen to allow for the development of specific fisheries, and (iv) to reduce the fishing effort on some stocks in danger of being overexploited. The rules concerning the closure of the areas are not absolutely rigid and the agreement stipulates that, as long as it cannot be reasonably avoided, the drifting of a part of a longline into a closed area is not to be considered as a violation of the agreement.

19.   The allocation of catch quotas is a practice requiring adequate scientific, administrative and enforcement capabilities as well as logistical facilities. So far this type of management

measure has not been frequently adopted by developing countries. In the Indian Ocean the agreements concluded by developing coastal States do not include any provision of that kind. On the other hand, the agreements concluded by Australia and France with Japan do provide for such measures. Off the French Islands of the Indian Ocean the annual quotas granted to Japanese longliners have always been rather low (a few hundred tons). On the eastern side of the ocean, Japan has accepted since 1985 to restrict its catches of bluefin tuna in Australian waters to 23 150 tons. Both countries agreed on a range of strict operational controls and reporting requirements.

(b) Provisions to ensure compliance with regulations

20. Many bilateral agreements include general provisions in which the flag State undertakes to take all appropriate steps to ensure that its vessels observe the provisions of the agreement and the rules governing fishing in the exclusive economic zone of the coastal State. Most of the Indian Ocean coastal States do not have the required naval and aerial enforcement equipments. To overcome this difficulty they have imposed detailed obligations on the tuna vessels operating under agreement in the areas under their jurisdiction. The purpose of these measures is to facilitate the task of the coastal State in monitoring the geographical position of the foreign vessels and in controlling the amount of fish caught.

21. Thus foreign vessels are required to notify the coastal State's authorities each time they enter into or leave from the exclusive economic zone. In the case of the agreement between Australia and Japan the notification of the intention to enter the zone is to be made 12 hours in advance. In order to avoid problems in case of controls the foreign vessels are also frequently requested to report the quantity of fish held on board when entering the zone (e.g., Seychelles/Spain; France/Republic of Korea). During their stay in the coastal State's zone the foreign vessels are normally obliged to report at given intervals on their position and on the results of their fishing activities. Details on the frequency and nature of such reports are often specified in the annexes to the agreements. It should however be borne in mind that, in addition, the vessels are bound by the relevant provisions of the national legislation of the coastal State. Under the two agreements concluded by the EEC in the region, reports on position and catches must be sent to the coastal State concerned every three days. The frequency of such reports is six days in the Australia/Japan agreement and seven days in the two agreements concluded by France with Japan and the Republic of Korea. Australian radio reporting requirements are particularly detailed. They are appended to the present document for information.

22. These radio reports must often be complemented by consolidated statistical information covering longer periods to be forwarded by the competent authorities of the flag State. Thus, in the agreement between Seychelles and Spain, Spanish tuna vessels are required to provide every three months complete statistics on their catches, using the ICCAT statistical form. Under the agreement between the Republic of Korea and France, the Korean Government agreed to forward annually to the French Government statistical information, for each month, on the activities of Korean vessels in the French zone including (i) the catch of each vessel per area (by quantities and by species), (ii) the average number of vessels per area, (iii) the number of hooks, and (iv) the areas of capture (by 5 degree). Under the Australia/Japan agreement the following data must be provided to the Australian authorities not later than 90 days after the vessels return to their own port: (a) a copy of the original data sheets of the report of tuna longline fishing which, in accordance with Japanese regulations, each Japanese tuna vessel is required to make and relating to its fishing operation in the Australian zone, and

(b) details of the main "target-species" of each vessel and a description of the dimension of its longline gear. Moreover the vessels are obliged to maintain a catch record on logbooks which are collected from time to time by Australian inspectors or forwarded by post by the vessel at the first port of call following operations in the zone.

23.   Many agreements include provisions on the systematic monitoring conducted by observers taken on board for greater or lesser periods of time. The observers are frequently scientists of the coastal States (e.g., agreement Seychelles/Spain). In some cases the coastal States ask a local fisherman member of the crew to carry out the role of observer over and above his seaman's duties (e.g., EEC/Seychelles). The observers are normally paid by the coastal State but, in the agreement between EEC and Madagascar, it is specified that the shipowner of the foreign vessel must pay 10 ECUs to the Malagasy Government for each day spent by an observer on board a tuna boat. The same agreement provides that, when a tuna boat with a Malagasy observer on board leaves the Madagascar fishing zone, every step must be taken to ensure that the observer returns to Madagascar as soon as possible, at the shipowners' expense.

FORM OF COMPENSATION

24.   The most common form of compensation in the Indian Ocean is the payment of a fee by the shipowner. This element is often complemented by contributions which are granted by the flag State authorities. Thus, comparing the level of fishing fees agreed upon in various agreements it is not always meaningful since the actual overall benefit gained by the coastal State must be evaluated taking into account other forms of compensation.

(a)   **Obligations of the shipowners**

25.   Several methods have been used in the region to calculate the fees to be paid by the tuna shipowners. They may be broadly divided into two categories: those linking directly the amount of the fee to the actual result of the fishing operations and those providing for lump sums agreed upon before the commencement of the fishing campaign.

26.   The two agreements so far concluded by the EEC and the agreement between the Seychelles and Spain belong to the first category. The fee to be paid by the EEC shipowners has been fixed at 20 ECUs per ton caught in the coastal State's exclusive economic zone. Under the agreement with Spain, the Government of the Seychelles receives a given percentage of the value of the catches. In both cases the crucial problem arises from the need to determine the percentage of the total catches taken by foreign vessel within the EEZ of the coastal State. Because of the highly migratory pattern of tuna stocks large purse seiners are frequently obliged to pursue the fish in several national exclusive economic zone's as well as on the high seas. In the EEC agreements the parties agreed that the basis for the percentage taken in the exclusive economic zone of the coastal State would be the catch statements drawn up by the shipowners. A final statement is drawn up each year by the EEC Commission, taking into account available scientific opinion, particularly by experts from FAO and other experts based in the region. In the Seychelles/Spain agreement, the parties agreed to assume that 50 percent of the Spanish purse seiner's catches would be deemed to come from the Seychelles exclusive economic zone. It is understood that, at the time of drafting the present document, these agreements were being re-negotiated.

27. In the Australia/Japan and the France/Japan agreements the fees are agreed upon before the beginning of the fishing campaign. In the case of the former, a review of the outcome of the annual negotiations shows that a number of factors are taken into account by the Parties when reaching agreement on the lump sum to be paid by the Japanese industry. In short, the amount to be paid depends on (i) the number of licensed vessels, (ii) the opening or closure of certain fishing grounds of particular interest to Japanese fishermen, (iii) the price of tuna products on the Japanese market, and (iv) the acceptance by Japan of various conservation measures such as catch quotas. In the France/Japan agreement, the amount is obtained by applying a fee to a quota established for each fishing season. Thus, for example for the 1982/83 fishing season the quota or the EEZ of the French islands of the Indian Ocean was 200 t and the fishing fee was 0,36 French Francs per kilo of tuna. The lump sum was therefore 72.000 French Francs.

28. An important difference between the system of payment described in paragraph 26 and the one described in paragraph 25 is that the Japanese industry is committed to pay the entire fee independently of the actual results of the fishing operations. In the case of the EEC agreements, the final payment can only be made when the exact quantity of fish caught by the flag State vessel is known. It should, however, be noted that in both cases, upon the agreement coming into force, the shipowners are obliged to pay a sum as an advance on the fees and that, if the amount of the fees due for the actual fishing operations does not equal the advance payment, the corresponding sum shall not be reimbursed.

29. In addition to the payment of fees, the shipowners are sometimes committed to give preference to a port nominated by the coastal State for the landing or the transshipment of catches (e.g., Seychelles/Spain). Developing coastal States also frequently impose on the shipowners the placement of trainees on board tuna fishing vessels. For example, each EEC purse seiner operating in Malagasy waters must employ two Malagasy seamen for the duration of the fishing year. The relevant agreement also provides that, should the Malagasy side not have any applicant to propose, this commitment must be replaced by a flat-rate sum equivalent to 50 percent of the wages of these seamen in proportion to the duration of the season; this sum is to be used for the training of Malagasy fishermen.

30. Finally, in addition to the requirements identified above, some of the agreements require that the shipowners be represented by agents residing in the coastal States' territories. These agents are to bear full or partial responsibility with regard to the fishing activities conducted by the foreign fishing vessels. More generally, they are to represent the shipowners in their relationships with the coastal States.

(b) Commitments of the Flag State

31. Besides committing themselves to take all appropriate measures in order to facilitate the enforcement of the coastal States' laws and regulations by their nationals, the flag States frequently agree to provide the coastal States with economic, financial and/or technical assistance.

32. Thus in its agreement with Madagascar and the Seychelles, the EEC agreed to contribute to the execution of projects connected with the development of the local fishing industries. In both agreements the amount of this contribution has been fixed at a rate of at least 900 000 ECUs. This amount corresponds to an estimated catch weight of 6 000 tons of tuna in the

EEZ of the coastal State. Should the amount of tuna caught exceed the agreed quantity, the level of the contribution must be increased accordingly without exceeding 3 million ECUs.

33. The EEC also agreed to contribute toward financing of scientific programmes to increase knowledge of the tuna stocks in the regions of the Indian Ocean surrounding the Seychelles and Madagascar. At the request of the coastal country, this contribution (350 000 ECUs in each case) may go toward the cost of international meetings to improve both the aforesaid knowledge and the management of fishery resources.

34. Trade matters are more and more frequently included in bilateral agreements. They are an important element of the negotiations between Australia and Japan. The subsidiary agreements concerning Japanese tuna longlining fishing include assurances from the Japanese side that access to the Japanese market would continue to be available for commercially competitive Australian fish and fish products. This is of particular importance to the developing Australian sashimi tuna industry.

Notes

1. For the purpose of this paper, when a reference is made to a government, it shall be deemed to include equally EEC to which EEC member countries transferred their competence for negotiating fishery agreements.
2. See J.E Carroz: "Les problèmes de la peche dans la Convention sur le droit de la mer et de la pratique des Etats" In "Le nouveau droit international de la mer", ouvrage collectif publié sous la direction de D. Bardonnet et M. Virally; Ed. Pedone, Paris, 1983, pp. 177-230.
3. For the West African region see J.E. Carroz and M.J. Savini: "Les accords de pêche conclus par les Etats africains riverains de l'Atlantique", annuaire Français de Droit International, Vol. XXIX, 1983, Paris, CNRS 1984, pp. 674-709.

- - - - -

FAO Legislative Study No. 42, 1987   Extract

Regional Compendium of Fisheries Legislation
(Indian Ocean Region) Vol. I

INTRODUCTION

. . .

The present compendium deals with the major aspects of fisheries legislation in the Indian Ocean, including fisheries management and conservation, and coastal fisheries. In view of the particular characteristics of the fisheries of the region, however, special attention is given in the present analysis to the problems of controls over foreign fishing operations.

The Extent of National Jurisdiction

In 1969 an FAO survey showed that almost all of the countries bordering the Indian Ocean claimed fisheries jurisdiction limits of 12 miles or less. Now, following adoption of the UN Convention on the Law of the Sea, almost all the countries that have a potential 200-mile fishery zone have claimed it. Only Tanzania (50 miles) and British Indian Ocean Territory (3 miles) have failed to exercise a 200-mile claim, and in the latter case, Mauritius has claimed an

EEZ around the same islands, the Chagos Archipelago. Of the 14 countries in more constricted geographical situations, 6 have extended fisheries jurisdiction to an agreed or median line or, in the case of Egypt, an unspecified distance. Most of these claims are in terms based on the Convention. Thus 27 States of the region have established 12-mile territorial seas. Of the remainder, 7 claim territorial seas of 6 miles or less, one of 50 miles and one of 200 miles. Twenty-one states have established fishing zones, ranging from a median line to 200 miles in the case of Australia.

So far as the implications of extended national jurisdiction over fisheries are concerned, most of the countries in the IOFC region base their fishing industries mainly on their own resources, but a growing number also operate in neighbouring and high-seas waters. Notable in this regard are Thailand, which possesses a sizeable middle-water fishing fleet, Mauritius, which has the nucleus of an oceanic tuna fleet, and Seychelles and Madagascar, which serve as bases for oceanic purse-seiners. In addition to the purse-seiners (mainly French and Spanish) foreign fishing is represented by Japanese, Korean and Taiwanese long-liners fishing in Seychelles and on the high seas, Soviet trawlers in Mozambique and Yemen P.D.R., and a variety of fishing activities by East Asian vessels in Australia and Indonesia.

Legislation for extended fisheries jurisdiction

The status of legislation to implement extended fisheries jurisdiction varies considerably, from relatively elaborate maritime zones acts to simple proclamations of jurisdiction without any implementing legislation whatever. Since there has been a tendency for extended zones to be proclaimed by the executive first and only made subject of legislation later, it can be expected that the number of countries which have extended their jurisdiction without legislation will diminish as implementing laws are adopted.

There is one cluster of EEZ laws which stands out both for its completeness and for the striking similarity of the laws to each other. The group comprises India, Mauritius, Pakistan, Seychelles and Sri Lanka. Each of these countries' law establishes a 12-mile territorial sea limit and provides for innocent passage of foreign ships. Each of the laws except for Mauritius and Seychelles also provides for the establishment of a contiguous zone for security purposes. They all provide for the delimitation of the continental shelf. Finally, all the laws provide for the establishment of exclusive economic zones of 200 miles, in which the rights of the coastal states are described in almost identical language, based generally on the Convention on the Law of the Sea. Each of the states requires exploration and exploitation activities within the economic zone to be licensed, although all but Pakistan and Sri Lanka specifically provide that these controls are not to apply to fishing by local nationals. In addition, India, Pakistan and Seychelles provide for the establishment of designated areas within the economic zone in which further controls may be exercised. Provisions are included on offences and sanctions in the laws of all but Sri Lanka. This group of laws also creates the power to extend any act to the EEZ and continental shelf, a power which could go beyond the rights of coastal states in the EEZ under UNCLOS.

Similarly complete maritime zones legislation also exists in Bangladesh, Burma, Comoros, Djibouti and Yemen P.D.R., although the details vary.

Both Indonesia and Malaysia have rather extensive laws, although limited to the EEZ and (Malaysia) continental shelf. The Malaysian law has particularly extensive provisions on the marine environment and on scientific research.

France, Mozambique and Oman, on the other hand, only define the zones, leaving other legislation to regulate activities.

Madagascar's new EEZ law has slightly more substance in adding to the definition of maritime zones the general prohibition against foreigners' exploiting the EEZ without permission.

Even the most elaborate maritime zones laws require regulations to make them effective, and they usually contemplate further legislation or the extension of existing laws as well. These laws and regulations have taken a variety of forms, depending both on the nature of the texts establishing extended jurisdiction and on the nature of the activities to be regulated. Several countries in the region have adopted specific legislation on foreign fishing (Comoros, India, Seychelles, Sri Lanka); others have revised their general fisheries legislation to meet new circumstances (Indonesia, Malaysia, Oman, Qatar, Yemen P.D.R.); while a third group has relied on existing legislation extended to the new areas, or measures taken under the authority of extended jurisdiction laws and proclamations. The tendency is to revise general fisheries legislation to apply to extended zones. In one case, Seychelles, all approaches have been used, culminating in 1986 in a new fisheries law of general application.

The remainder of the introduction will concentrate on the substance of fisheries legislation in the Indian Ocean, in whatever form it is embodied.

RESOURCE MANAGEMENT

(a) Management planning

The extension of national jurisdiction over fisheries places increasing importance on sound management planning by the coastal state. Indeed, the Convention charges the coastal state with legal responsibility for managing the resources in its 200-mile economic zone and for promoting the objective of the optimum utilization of resources. While it is not strictly essential that machinery, procedures and criteria be set up by legislation (as opposed to administrative action), it is essential that the problem of how such management planning should be carried out, be properly confronted. As an example of how this problem is being approached in one country outside the region, the legislation implementing the U.S. 200-mile fishery conservation zone provides for the drawing up of management plans for each fishery by regional fishery management councils, working on the basis of national standards and criteria.

Within the Indian Ocean, management planning provisions and criteria are increasingly found in the fisheries legislation. Australia provides for management planning including for joint state federal management authorities to undertake fisheries management planning and exercise management powers. Malaysia, Oman, Qatar and Seychelles all provide explicitly for fisheries management planning. In Australia and Malaysia, plans are to seek the "optimum utilization" of fishery resources, which is not defined; in the other countries, planning goals are less clearly stated. Kuwait, Sri Lanka and Yemen Arab Republic all have provisions for co-ordination which may be adapted to planning as well, and Bangladesh legislation mentions fisheries management and development plans as a criterion for granting licences although it does not provide explicitly for anybody to compile the plans. Legislation now under consideration in Kenya and Mauritius also provides for management planning.

A new development in planning provisions is a provision for consultation or co-ordination of plans with neighbouring countries. This first appeared in the IOFC region in the legislation of Oman in 1981, soon followed by very similar provisions in Qatar in 1983. The recently adopted legislation in Seychelles and that under consideration in Mauritius also provide for regional consultation on fisheries plans.

Resource information

The greatest source of fisheries resource information is in the statistical returns of fishermen. Most of the countries in the IOFC area make some provision in their laws for the collection of statistics. The statistics may also have a compliance-control purpose, but that is more apparent in requirements for real-time reporting, usually by radio or telex, which are discussed below. A typical resource information requirement is to maintain a fishing log. This is either required or authorized to be required by the laws and regulations of Australia, Bangladesh, Comoros, French dependent territories, India, Indonesia, Madagascar, Malaysia, Mozambique, Oman, Seychelles and Sri Lanka. More general reporting requirements in Bahrain, Egypt, Kuwait, Maldives, Pakistan, Qatar, Saudi Arabia and Somalia may be applied so as to require maintenance of a log.

Requirements of written returns do not usually apply to artisanal fishermen, but even they are usually subject to requirements to give information as requested, to present their catch for weighing or to land it at designated points where statistics are kept. This is the case in Kenya and Mauritius, for example.

A second source of resource information is research and survey work. Several countries allow for exemptions from normal licensing and management measures for research or scientific fishing. There has been some dissatisfaction with the genuineness of scientific purpose of some experimental fishing and with the timeliness and completeness of data supplied, which has prompted at least one country (Seychelles) to require an approved research plan and transmission of raw data as a condition of scientific fishing.

Fisheries management may be pursued for several sometimes incompatible objectives and uses a variety of means. Traditionally management has sought first to protect the resource against damage or destruction, and within that task to distribute the opportunities to fish. More recently countries have begun to adopt management schemes for the express purpose of maximizing economic benefits (to the state or to a defined group of fishermen) from the fishery. Pursuit of this goal frequently requires limitation of fishing effort. Since it is very difficult to limit fishing effort by nationals, there are relatively few examples of national fisheries management for economic goals. But the growth of foreign fishing has given a major role to management measures designed to maximize economic benefits. These have ranged from high fees to quantitative limitations on catch and effort.

Traditional management measures include prohibitions of ecologically harmful methods such as explosives, minimum sizes of fish, gear restrictions, closed seasons and closed fishing areas. Any of these measures may be applied as a condition of individual fishing licences discussed below, and to that extent they potentially exist under most fisheries law. As distinct legislative or regulatory provisions, however, they are not so nearly universal. In the IOFC area, the most common measure is a prohibition of ecologically dangerous methods, found in Bahrain, Bangladesh, Egypt, India, Indonesia, Iran, Iraq, Israel, Jordan, Kuwait, Maldives,

Mauritius, Oman, Pakistan, Qatar, Seychelles, Sri Lanka, Sudan, Tanzania, Thailand, Yemen Arab Republic and Yemen Democratic Republic.

Mesh size regulations are authorized in the laws of many countries, but apparently only applied in Australia, Bangladesh, Egypt, Indonesia, Iran, Israel, Kuwait, Madagascar, Malaysia, Mauritius, Mozambique, Qatar, Saudi Arabia and Sudan. They are also probably applied by state legislation in India. Minimum fish sizes, restrictions on taking berried female lobsters and other catch characteristics are found in Australia, Iran, Israel, Kenya (oysters), Kuwait, Madagascar, Mauritius, Oman ("small fish"), Pakistan, Qatar, Seychelles, Sri Lanka (spiny lobster) and Sudan.

Closed seasons are applied in Mauritius for different gear and in several countries for shrimp. The most interesting of these provisions was jointly adopted by the members of the IOFC Gulfs Fisheries Committee to prohibit shrimping during the critical period of the year (roughly February to June, although the dates of national regulations vary). Pakistan also has a closed season for shrimp, June and July. A number of laws authorize closed areas for conservation and other purposes, but most of those have been applied for the purpose of restricting certain gear in coastal or local-fishing areas. Thus Malaysia restricts trawlers to distances of from 3 to 12 miles, depending on their size, and also prohibits night fishing by the small trawlers. Egypt, Kuwait, Madagascar also restrict trawling in terms of distance or geographical areas. Bangladesh, Oman, Qatar and Saudi Arabia all prohibit the use of certain gear in shallow water. Iran includes a combination of distance and depth criteria for the operation of trawls and certain other gear.

Programmes to limit catch and effort are relatively rare, except for the perhaps unintended effect of the special conditions applied to foreign fishing. A notable exception is Australia, which has considerable experience with controlled-entry fisheries. Malaysia is making efforts in this direction and a number of countries in the IOFC area have instituted some basic provisions which would facilitate limitation schemes.

The essential provision, and the heart of any effective management system, is licensing. An appropriately designed licensing allows the fisheries administration to limit entry into a fishery both quantitatively and in terms of the kind of fishing that will be allowed and the way it can be conducted. Licensing provides the basis for the collection of statistics, for collecting fees, for imposing other conditions and for controlling compliance with the fisheries régime.

Not surprisingly, most of the countries in the IOFC region have some sort of licensing system, although it may be limited to certain kinds of fishing or sizes of vessels. In some cases the requirement is in terms of "registration" rather than licensing (Kenya, Sri Lanka) but the provisions are similar in substance. It is suspected even where the legislation is not available that all countries in the Indian Ocean in fact require authorization for foreign fishing. Quite a few known to have licensing requirements, on the other hand, do not require a licence for certain categories of local vessels (Bahrain, Djibouti, Indonesia, Israel, Jordan, Kenya). And very few countries require a licence for fishing without a vessel, except for certain kinds of net and special products such as cockles, bêche-de-mer and turtles.

Simply requiring licences is not in itself a means of controlling catch and effort, which depends on the criteria for granting licences. Traditionally, there have been three main strains of licensing criterias in fisheries legislation. One has been to leave licensing to the broad discretion of a licensing officer, frequently exercised according to administrative instructions or standard practices (e.g. Iraq). A second, almost opposite strain has been the automatic licence, in which the licensing officer apparently has no power to refuse a correctly submitted application (e.g. Tanzania). In practice, where there is no policy of limiting licences, the two approaches may produce the same result. Such licences are not well suited for a limitation scheme because there is no reasoned legal basis for distinguishing among potential licensees.

A third approach, which has usually been applied to fixed gear and inland fisheries, limits the number and kind of licences. Bahrain explicitly cites interference with other fish barriers as a ground for refusing a licence for a new barrier. But the power to limit licences has obvious uses in a general limitation of fishing effort, and much of the legislation in the region now provides explicitly or allows for such use of licensing. Bahrain itself allows licences to be refused if use of the proposed vessel or barrier would be harmful to fisheries resources.

Refusal or cancellation of licences for the proper management of fisheries (expressed in different ways) is increasingly found in legislation in the IOFC area (e.g. Australia, Comoros, Sri Lanka). Legislation in Bangladesh and Malaysia and the newly adopted fisheries law of Seychelles go somewhat further and require licensing decisions to conform to the fisheries plan. In addition both Oman and Qatar have provisions for planning and limiting the number of licences, although the two are not linked in the legislation.

Actually fixing limits of catch and effort requires some determination of the desirable or permissible level. At least nine countries' laws require that the level be set for some - usually foreign - or all fisheries (e.g. Bangladesh, Egypt, France, Indonesia, Kuwait, Maldives, Oman, Qatar, Seychelles), and eight others allow limits on either catch or effort to be established (Australia, Comoros, Iraq, Israel, Madagascar, Malaysia, Sri Lanka, Tanzania).

At least six countries have published laws or regulations actually setting allowable catches or levels effort for given fisheries. Indonesia has stated a total allowable catch for several species in accordance with its fisheries law; it is now required to establish the number and equipment of vessels allowed to take the TAC. Madagascar has established a commission which advises on the issue of large-vessel licences and established quotas for small-vessel licences. Iran, Mauritius, Mozambique and Saudi Arabia have all established effort limitations by law or regulation without a separate enabling provision. In addition, Kuwait has adopted a temporary policy of not issuing new fishing licences while it considers more permanent limitations.

FOREIGN FISHING

The extension of national jurisdiction over fisheries implies increasing problems of allocating and controlling access by foreign vessels and enforcing conservation measures. While the attitude of countries in the region towards foreign fishing in waters under national jurisdiction varies over a wide range, it is the intention here to look not so much at the general governmental policy as the mechanics of implementation and enforcement of that policy.

(a) Nationality criteria

One basic point in controls over foreign fishing is the definition of what constitutes a national or foreign vessel. This determines whether an operation can qualify for national treatment and avoid the more onerous conditions of foreign fishing altogether. Differences in definition have, on occasion, been the cause of substantial mis-understandings between countries interested in negotiating reciprocal fishing agreements.

In most countries in the region the basic nationality criterion is the ownership of the boat. The differences arise mainly where ownership is shared among nationals and foreigners, or where the vessel is owned by a company in which shares are held by non-nationals. The traditional rule in countries having a common-law tradition has been not to go behind the "veil of incorporation" to ascertain the ownership of company shares, but to treat any company incorporated under the local law as a local company, wherever **actual** control lies. Thus, the **Australian** Fisheries Act, for example defines an Australian boat as one wholly owned by a person resident of, or company incorporated in Australia, provided that the operations of the boat are based in Australia and that the boat was built in Australia or lawfully imported or forfeited there. Similarly in **Ethiopia** any vessel owned by a local company is at present treated as a national vessel.

It has become increasingly clear, however, that the criterion of vessel ownership is not sufficient to define nationality for the purpose of preferred access to national resources, including fisheries. A number of countries have therefore added requirements concerning the ownership of companies that own vessels. In **Malaysia**, a local fishing vessel is defined as one wholly owned by the Government of Malaysia or the Government of a State in Malaysia; or by Malaysian citizens; or a statutory corporation established under any of the laws of Malaysia; or a body corporate or unincorporate whether established in Malaysia or not, provided that it is wholly owned by any of the former persons or bodies. In **India**, 60% of the share capital of the company is to be held by Indian citizens. In a number of other countries, local management is also a criterion. Thus, in **Thailand**, a majority of the directors must be nationals, if a limited company is to claim local status for its fishing vessels. In **Madagascar** a majority of the share capital must be owned by nationals, the principal office must be in Madagascar and the general manager or managers, the chairman, and a majority of the board of directors must all be nationals. Other countries with nationality requirements for company shareholders and directors include Bangladesh, Comoros, France, Iran, Seychelles, Sri Lanka and Yemen Arab Republic. Several countries in the IOFC area define nationality in such a way that foreign-owned vessels operated by - or under contract to - local nationals are treated as local vessels. In the case of France, this is only permitted where nationals have full control of the vessel and it can relinquish the flag of ownership. Mauritius, Oman and Qatar require specific approval of charter arrangements; Saudi Arabia does not.

(b) Coastal State requirements for foreign fishing

Within the region, only Thailand seems to exclude the possibility of fishing by foreign vessels within waters under their jurisdiction. Although the law allows for fishing by foreign vessels under intergovernmental agreements, it also requires all vessels fishing within those limits to hold a fishing licence, and forbids the issue of such licence to non-nationals or foreign-controlled companies.

Where an element of foreign fishing is allowed, this is sometimes subject to the same general requirements and system of licensing as national fishing. In **Pakistan**, for example, the Territorial Waters and Maritime Zones Act, 1976, provides that fishing operations in the 200-mile exclusive economic zone are to be regulated by the provisions of the Exclusive Fishing Zone (Regulation of Fishing) Act, 1975, which applies alike to national and foreign craft. Bahrain and Yemen People's Republic also treat nationals and foreigners the same in their fishing legislation, although Yemen applies very different conditions to foreign vessels through bilateral agreements.

In other countries in the region a separate set of requirements applies to foreign fishing. These may be imposed by separate legislations as in India, Sri Lanka and until recently in Seychelles, or merely under special provisions of general fisheries law.

The issue of a foreign licence is frequently subject to special procedures, including issue by a different authority from local licences. This is frequently the Minister or director of fisheries instead of a fisheries officer (in Burma, India and Sri Lanka, for example).

One of the decisions of principle to be made by coastal state governments is whether foreign fishing operations are to be authorized only under the framework of an inter-governmental fishing agreement or whether individual applications should be entertained, and, conversely, whether individual licences or permits should be required even where bilateral "umbrella" agreements are in force. As evidenced by trends in other regions of the world, the requirement of both "umbrella agreements" and individual licensing seems to be viewed as the most effective basis for compliance control. Some of the States of the region have opted for that procedure. Seychelles recently adopted legislation will require both as a general rule, as does Australia, French departments and dependent territories, Kuwait, Malaysia and Thailand.

North and South Yemen require either a licence or an agreement, and Iran requires only an agreement. In addition, agreements will in practice be the rule for fishing by EEC vessels, which already fish in Madagascar and Seychelles and have expressed interest in having agreements with Comoros, Kenya, Mozambique, Somalia and Tanzania.

The contents of agreements are not usually specified, but recent legislation in both Malaysia and Seychelles provides that agreements shall include an undertaking by the Government of the flag state to ensure compliance by its vessels with the fisheries laws of the coastal state. It is worth noting the recent fishing agreements both in the Indian Ocean and elsewhere generally do contain such an undertaking.

Conditions relating to benefits from foreign fishing

The benefits available from foreign fishing may be realized in a number of ways, but the most common and the easiest to compare is fishing fees. Foreign fishing in the IOFC area is subject to the payment of fees that vary enormously, which is not surprising given the great variety of conditions in the region. One of the greatest beneficiaries of fishing fees, Seychelles, does not include the amounts in its regulations, but they are available from agreements. Under the agreement with Spain for purse-seining the fee amounts to a total of 5 per cent of the value of catches from anywhere in the Indian Ocean. The agreement with the EEC, on the other hand is expressed in tonnages and provides for total payments of ECU 70 per tonne caught in Seychelles waters, in addition to certain other payments.

Somalia, which has had extensive experience with foreign and joint-venture fishing, has promulgated a special scale of fees for joint ventures, which range up to $10,000 a year for a 50/50 joint venture in addition to a vessel fee of up to $1600 per month for a tuna vessel. Foreign vessel fees are $80 per year per horsepower unit plus a royalty on catch ranging from $49 a tonne for finfish to $420 a tonne for deep-sea lobster.

Other countries calculate fees in a variety of ways. Bangladesh and Indonesia charge according to the carrying capacity of the vessel. The amount ranges from $25 to $334 per vessel in Bangladesh. In Indonesia it is from $44 to $85 per cubic meter of hold capacity, depending on the type of vessel. Indonesia also has a schedule of fees for joint venture vessels, up to $1000 per vessel plus royalties of up to 2% of catch value. India charges foreign fishing fees based on the tonnage of catch allowed, ranging up to $158 per tonne for trawl fish.

A number of other countries appear to have very low foreign fishing fees, but they tend either not to have significant foreign fishing or to impose other conditions, including fees paid under agreements. Thus Oman has fees applicable to local and foreign operators alike that do not exceed $700 per vessel, yet it has long collected one of the highest payments in kind (30 per cent) anywhere.

Other forms of benefit are mentioned in some of the legislation in the IOFC region, including training, employment, landing of catches. While these are not all applied, several countries in fact receive these kinds of benefit from foreign fishing. Thus both Seychelles and Somalia have succeeded in obtaining employment of local nationals aboard foreign vessels. Several countries have joint venture arrangements which are in fact linked to parallel foreign fishing operations, although the joint venture is not a legislative requirement for foreign vessels. South Yemen has arrangements for the landing and local processing of catch from the licensed foreign fleet.

There are also certain conditions designed more to prevent a loss than to gain a benefit. Foremost are provisions to exclude foreign fishing vessels from areas exploited by local fishermen. Indonesian legislation provides for zoning of certain areas according to type of fishing in order to protect traditional fisheries. Several countries, including Seychelles and Comoros, forbid foreign fishing within their territorial waters (12 miles). Malaysia prohibits foreign trawlers within 30 miles of the coast and Maldives goes somewhat further and only authorizes foreign fishing beyond 75 miles from its shores.

Conditions relating to enforcement

The problem of enforcing legislation in a maritime zone 200 miles wide has not been simple for coastal states, especially for developing countries that do not have and cannot afford expensive means of air and sea patrol. This has caused them to seek more cost-effective means. There have been consequent innovations in criminal law, including the increased use of presumptions, of civil or compounded penalties and of course of high fines and forfeitures. One of the most interesting developments on the enforcement front, however, has been the increasing attention paid in some parts of the world to the use of licence conditions to improve compliance with fisheries régimes.

The use of bilateral agreements is in some respects a compliance control measure, giving the coastal state leverage it would not otherwise have over both licensed vessels and also other vessels of the flag state. Even without reaching the point of prosecution, the threat of losing all fishing opportunities for its vessels can cause a flag state to apply considerable pressure on its vessels to comply with coastal state legislation.

Conditions of fishing licences which aid compliance control are potentially infinite, but countries have recently tended to emphasize reporting. It is felt that self-reporting by a well identified group of vessels, such as those under licence, should be a relatively cheap source of information on their activities. Reports of position and catch should be easily verified by occasional surveillance and by port inspections, either occasionally or at the beginning and end of a trip. To be effective, though, the reports must be transmitted by radio or telex. More complicated regulations, such as by-catch and type of gear are less amenable to enforcement on the basis of vessel reports and would require other means of enforcement.

Legislation in the Pacific, where control of unauthorized fishing has higher priority than enforcement of management regulations, not surprisingly emphasizes reporting of vessel activities. West African legislation devotes much less attention to this aspect. In the Indian Ocean, radio reports are required or at least authorized by Australia (also a Pacific country), Bangladesh, France, Indonesia, Malaysia, Seychelles and Sri Lanka. This requirement is likely to become more common with the development of purse-seining in the Indian Ocean.

Other compliance-control conditions include requirements to land or trans-ship in a coastal-state port, to come into port for inspection, to carry observers, to fly the home-state flag and to display required markings. All of these are found in a number of IOFC countries' legislation.

ENFORCEMENT

While licence conditions are useful in fisheries compliance control, they do not obviate the need for traditional law enforcement. This has been greatly complicated by the extension of jurisdiction and some new approaches have been developed to aid law enforcement in extended zones. Given the different legal traditions and judicial procedures in the various countries of the Indian Ocean area, no attempt will be made to deal here with all aspects of this problem. General comments will be made only on aspects of enforcement relating to foreign fishing.

In most of the enactments establishing 200-mile economic zones in the region, provisions dealing with enforcement are usually drafted in general terms if not inexistent. However, an increasing number of laws provide for specific penalties for violation of the law by foreign fishing vessels. In **Malaysia**, if found guilty, the owner or master of a foreign fishing vessel is liable to a fine not exceeding one million ringgit and each and every member of the crew is liable to a fine of one hundred thousand ringgit. Whereas in all other cases, there is a liability to a fine not exceeding fifty thousand ringgit or a term of imprisonment not exceeding two years or both. In **India**, the nature of the penalty depends on whether the contravention takes place on the territorial waters or in the exclusive economic zone. In the first case, the owner or the master of the vessel is punishable with imprisonment for a term not exceeding three years or with a fine not exceeding rupees 1,5 million or with both. In the second, the penalty is less severe since such persons are only punishable with fines not exceeding 300,000 rupees. In **Bangladesh** the skipper owner and charter of a foreign fishing vessel found in the fisheries waters illegally are liable to rigorous imprisonment for a term not exceeding three years and to a fine not exceeding 100,000 taka. In addition, the vessel in question is deemed to be forfeited to the Government. In **Sri Lanka**, contravention of the relevant provision of the law carries a fine not exceeding one million five hundred rupees. In addition to fines and imprisonment, many countries empower the courts to order the forfeiture of vessel, gear and catch (e.g. Egypt, India, Indonesia, Kenya, Kuwait, Madagascar, Qatar, Seychelles, Sri Lanka, Tanzania).
. . .

The potential conflict between the navigation rights of shipping and the enforcement needs of coastal states is dealt with in several ways. The most common requirements expressly sanctioned by UNCLOS, is the stowage of gear by unlicensed vessels.

In addition, some countries, such as **Australia, Indonesia** and **Tanzania**, in effect prohibit unauthorized entry of foreign fishing vessels into jurisdictional waters, except for a limited right of passage ("innocent passage" as opposed to "free navigation") or some such other purpose such as distress. In **Burma, Australia** and **Madagascar**, it is required that passage be direct and by the shortest practicable route, while in the case of **Indonesia**, specific routes are stipulated for innocent passage by fishing vessels. Mozambique prohibits "preparing to fish", which is defined in such a way as to require expeditious passage through Mozambican waters. Both the **Madagascar** and the **Tanzanian** legislation require vessels to carry clear identification. In **Malaysia**, the master of the vessel is required to notify by radio the name, the flag state, location, route and destination of the vessel, along with the type and amount of fish it is carrying while exercising the right of innocent passage. In addition to making unauthorized fishing or entry into jurisdictional zones, offences, the **Australian** legislation prohibits unauthorized carrying or processing of fish within jurisdictional waters (i.e., mother-ship operations), while the **Tanzanian** legislation, with the same aim in view, prohibits the unauthorized transhipment of fish within the limits.

So far as enforcement is concerned, most countries provide broadly similar powers of stopping, boarding, inspection or seizure and arrest in the event of suspected contraventions. However, very few indications are given of the specific procedures for arrest and seizure of foreign vessels. Of more interest is the introduction in several laws in the area of provisions relating to hot pursuit, following article 111 of the United Nations Conventions on the Law of the Sea which, subject to certain conditions, recognizes the right of coastal States to undertake the hot pursuit of foreign vessels which are believed to have violated their laws and regulations including those relating to their exclusive economic zones. **Burma** was one of the first States of the region to introduce in their legislation provisions for hot pursuit from the territorial sea and other zones, including the exclusive economic zone (1977). In **Seychelles**, there is specific provision for the hot pursuit of foreign fishing vessels following the committing of an offence against the applicable law relating to fishing in the exclusive economic zone. In **Malaysia**, where it is believed that a vessel has contravened the applicable law, such vessel may be pursued beyond the limit of the exclusive economic zone "to the extent allowed by international law". The right of hot pursuit ends as soon as the vessel enters the territorial sea or exclusive economic zone of its own State or any third State except when it is provided otherwise by an agreement to which Malaysia is a party. Where cooperative enforcement procedures are contemplated in regional fishing agreements between neighbouring countries in the region, an issue of particular importance may be rights of pursuit into the territorial sea or economic zone of the neighbouring country, where traditional "hot pursuit" normally ends.

Enforcement of controls over fishing in extended zones of national jurisdiction presents a number of evidentiary problems. In this connection, it is interesting to note the increasing use of presumptions in national legislation. One form of "factual" presumption consists in equating failure to stow gear properly with fishing, either as sufficient proof of fishing or as a separate offence with the same (high) penalty. Another frequent presumption concerns fish aboard a vessel. In the new legislation in Seychelles, fish found aboard a vessel which has committed an offence are rebuttably presumed to have been caught in the commission of the offence and are thus subject to forfeiture. In the previous Seychelles legislation, as well as in that of India and Malaysia, fish found on board a vessel is presumed, without direct evidence of an offence, to have been caught in jurisdictional waters. In Australia, mere possession of fish can be an offence, to which proof that it was caught outside the fishing zone is a defence. This considerably eases the burden of proving illegal fishing, but it could also be applied to restrict rights of navigation.

    . . .

- - - - -

UN General Assembly, 41st Session   A/41/863
Security Council, 41st year   S/18468
                                          Extract

Falkland Islands (Malvinas)

. . .

APPENDIX
Excerpt from the statement made on 21 November 1985 by the
Assistant Director-General of the FAO Fisheries Department
at the twelfth meeting of Committee I at the twenty-third
session of the FAO Conference

With the support of some delegations who spoke in plenary last week, the Director-General has agreed that FAO will carry out, within the limits of its competence and mandate as a specialized technical agency, an assessment of the state of fish stocks in the South West Atlantic, including migratory stocks on the Patagonia shelf.

Its report will also cover as far as possible the impact of fishing on the ecosystem of the area. Indeed, we have been following developments closely since 1983, and the document on the state of world fishery resources submitted to our Committee on Fisheries in April of this year draws attention to the seriousness of the situation. There are indications that the level of fishing efforts in the area might increase significantly in the forthcoming fishing season.

- - - - -

UN Special Committee on the Situation with Regard
   to the Implementation of the Declaration   A/AC.109/878
   on the Granting of Independence to Colonial   6 August 1986
   Countries and Peoples   Extract

Falkland Islands (Malvinas)
Secretariat Working Paper

. . .

C. Fisheries

71. According to the Food and Agriculture Organization of the United Nations (FAO), the waters around the Falkland Islands (Malvinas) are one of the richest fishing grounds in the

world. The waters particularly abound in hake, squid, blue whiting and krill, although no precise scientific information exists so far about the size and composition of the present catch or about the sustainable yield of fish stocks. The Falkland Islands (Malvinas) are one of the few remaining areas in the world where a 200-mile fishery zone has not been proclaimed, enabling fishing trawlers to fish at will, particularly within the 150-mile "Protection Zone" and usually up to the limit of the 200-mile fishery zone off the Argentine mainland, without being subject to any regulation or licence. As a result there has been an enormous growth in the number of vessels fishing in those waters in the four years since the end of the South Atlantic conflict, leading to fears about the consequences for the conservation of stocks resulting from such an increase. Although no exact figures are available, the number of vessels arriving and clearing in Stanley and Berkely Sound in the Falkland Islands (Malvinas) provides some indication about the level of fishing activity. In 1975 the total number of vessels was 49; that number peaked to a total of 312 in 1980, was down to 227 in 1982 - the year of the conflict - and had reached the figure of 903 in 1985.

. . .

74.   In November 1985, FAO decided to undertake a preliminary technical study on the state of fish stocks which is expected to be concluded by the end of the summer of 1986. The Government of the United Kingdom has supported the FAO initiative and in the meantime has sought to enter into arrangements with some of the main fishing countries in order to obtain voluntary limits on the size of the catches made by their fishing fleets.

75.   The Government of Argentina has also expressed increasing concern at the problem which, Foreign Minister Dante Caputo stated, posed "a risk of squandering a major natural resource and creating serious disruptions in world markets" (see A/40/PV.92). It has also agreed to the FAO study referred to above, though it has not committed itself to entering into the kind of multilateral régime favoured by the Government of the United Kingdom.

. . .

- - - - -

FAO Committee on Fisheries   CL 91/7
Report of the Seventeenth Session, May 1987   Extract

===

. . .

World Fisheries Situation

. . .

18.   The Committee noted that a study of the Patagonian fishery resources and the off-shore fisheries in the South-West Atlantic, an important part of the FAO statistical Area 41, had recently been published by FAO. Recognizing the importance of the fisheries in statistical Area 41 and that under the present circumstances FAO is uniquely capable of collating and analysing fisheries data, the Committee requested the Secretariat to continue to monitor the area, within its mandate as a specialized technical agency, and in particular to update the study as appropriate. To this end, the countries fishing in the area were invited to co-operate with the Secretariat, particularly through the provision of all catch and effort data and biological information on the fishery resources.

. . .

- - - - -

UN Special Committee on the Situation with Regard   A/AC.109/920
to the Implementation of the Declaration   3 August 1987
on the Granting of Independence to Colonial   Extract
Countries and Peoples

Falkland Islands (Malvinas)
Secretariat Working Paper

. . .

V. POSITIONS OF THE GOVERNMENTS OF THE UNITED KINGDOM AND ARGENTINA

A. United Kingdom

. . .

22.   Announcing before the House of Commons on 29 October 1986 the United Kingdom Government's decision to establish the Falkland Islands Interim Conservation and Management Zone (FICZ) (see paras. 57-60), the Secretary of State for Foreign and Commonwealth Affairs stated that such a measure was justified by the concern for the conservation of fish stocks, which were being depleted by the rapid increase in fishing in the south-west Atlantic; by the failure of some fishing nations to co-operate fully with the study undertaken and the United Kingdom's initiative by the FAO which had retarded its completion and by a series of Argentine actions which undermined the multilateral approach favoured by the United Kingdom Government. Sir Geoffrey singled out in particular the "aggressive patrolling" by Argentina more than 200 miles from Patagonia and within 200 miles of the Falkland Islands (Malvinas), its conclusion of bilateral fisheries agreements with Bulgaria and the Soviet Union through which Argentina purported to exercise jurisdiction that, as a matter of international law, was the entitlement of the Territory. He further stated that the United Kingdom remained ready and willing to achieve a multilateral régime without prejudice to the respective positions on sovereignty, as soon as it could be achieved. He added that the Falkland Island's entitlement to a 200-mile fishery zone, subject to delimitation on the south-western side with Argentina, within which the Falkland Islands Interim Conservation and Management Zone was being established, did not depend on the United Nations Convention on the Law of the Sea (which the United Kingdom had not signed) but on customary international law as the International Court of Justice had accepted.[18]

. . .

B. Argentina

. . .

28.   In a press communiqué issued on 29 October 1986, the Argentine Government rejected the United Kingdom's declaration on south-west Atlantic fisheries as a claim that was "juridically and politically inadmissible because it encroaches on waters over which the Argentine Republic exercises rights of sovereignty and jurisdiction" and stated that the conservation of fishing resources invoked by the United Kingdom Government was actually "a pretext . . . to appropriate not only the waters and its resources but the marine soil and subsoil".[21] At the same time, in a note transmitted on 31 October 1986 to the United Kingdom

through the Brazilian Embassy at Buenos Aires, the Argentine Government formally rejected the United Kingdom declaration and reaffirmed "its sovereignty over the Malvinas Islands, the South Georgia and South Sandwich Islands and its rights of sovereignty and jurisdiction over the surrounding maritime waters, sea-bed and marine subsoil".[22]

. . .

IX. ECONOMIC CONDITIONS

. . .

C. Fisheries

57. On 29 October 1986, the United Kingdom Government issued a "declaration on south-west Atlantic fisheries" thereby declaring that "in order to create the necessary conditions for ensuring conservation of the fish stocks around the Falkland Islands":

(a) Effective immediately, the Falkland Islands (Malvinas) were entitled "under international law to fishery limits of a maximum of 200 nautical miles from the baselines from which the breadth of the Falkland Islands is measured", subject to the need for a boundary with Argentina in areas where arcs of 200 nautical miles from Argentina and the Islands overlapped. In the absence of any agreement, the boundary was that prescribed by the rules of international law concerning delimitation of maritime jurisdiction;

(b) The continental shelf around the Falkland Islands (Malvinas) extended to a distance of 200 nautical miles from the baselines from which the breadth of the territorial sea of the Falkland Islands was measured or to such other limits as "prescribed by the rules of international law, including those concerning the delimitation of maritime jurisdiction between neighbours";

(c) Legislative measures would be taken "to ensure the conservation and management of living resources in accordance with international law . . . on an interim basis pending internationally agreed arrangements for the south-west Atlantic fishery as a whole". Such measures would apply to the Falkland Islands Interim Conservation and Management Zone (FICZ) the limits of which would be defined by legislation (see para. 22).

58. In his statement before the House of Commons, the United Kingdom Secretary of State for Foreign and Commonwealth Affairs announced that limits of FICZ would generally be of 150 miles radius from the Falkland Islands (Malvinas), an area approximately co-extensive with the Falkland Islands Protection Zone. FICZ would be administered by the Falkland Islands Government which was to introduce the necessary legislation with effect from 1 February 1987, when the next fishing season began. Licensing reflecting conservation needs would be the responsibility of the Falkland Islands Government, which would use its own civilian fisheries protection vessels and surveillance aircraft . . .

. . .

60. According to United Kingdom Government reports, the total number of fishing vessels that have been licensed to fish within FICZ has been limited to 220, compared with 600 in 1986. The majority of vessels belonged to companies registered (in descending order of numbers) in Japan, the Republic of Korea, the authorities in Taiwan, Spain and Poland.[42]

. . .

62.   The technical study on the state of fish stocks in the south-west Atlantic by FAO, the preparation of which was reported in the 1986 working paper (A/AC.109/878), was finalized and published early in 1987.[45]

. . .

Notes

18.   Parliamentary Debates, House of Commons, 29 October 1986, cols. 323-326.
21.   A/41/784 - S/18438.
22.   A/41/788 - S/18441, annex.
42.   Parliamentary Debates, House of Commons, 5 February 1987, col. 740
45.   Ccinko, J., The Patagonian fishery resources and the off-shore fisheries in the South-West Atlantic. FAO Fisheries Technical Paper (286).

- - - - -

Additional References

Indian Ocean

Reports of the Eighth and Ninth Sessions of the Committee for the Management of Indian Ocean Tuna. FAO Fisheries Reports Nos. 351 and 382.

South Pacific

South Pacific Forum Fisheries Agency. Communiqué of the Sixteenth South Pacific Forum. UN doc. A/40/673.

South-West Atlantic

The Patagonian fishery resources and the offshore fisheries in the South-West Atlantic. FAO Technical Paper 286, 1987.

Question of the Falkland Islands (Malvinas) with reference to fisheries:

Declaration on South-West Atlantic Fisheries by the United Kingdom, 29 October 1986. UN doc. A/41/777, Annex. See also Letter of 21 November 1986, A/41/868.

Resolution adopted by the Permanent Council of the Organization of American States, 11 November 1986. UN doc. A/41/828, Annex.

Declaration by the Argentine Government, 17 November 1986. UN doc. A/41/845, Annex. See also Letter of 3 November 1986, A/41/788.

General Assembly resolution, UN doc. A/RES/42/19.

Antarctica

See Reports of the Secretary-General, UN docs. A/41/722 and A/42/586.

Mediterranean

Report of the General Fisheries Council for the Mediterranean, 1986. GFCM Report 18, FAO.

- - - - -

3

Marine Mammals

Conference of the Parties to the Convention on the   CMS Proceedings
Conservation of Migratory Species of Wild Animals   Vol. I
Proceedings of the First Meeting, October 1985   Extract

. . .

Resolution 1.4
Composition and Functions of the Scientific Council

**The Conference of the Parties to the Convention on the
Conservation of Migratory Species of Wild Animals,**

Taking into account that article VIII of the Convention calls for the establishment of a Scientific Council at the first meeting of the Conference of the Parties,

. . .

6.   *Directs* the Scientific Council to address the following questions and tasks, in order of priority:

(a)   To assist in the development of indicative and exemplary agreements between Range States according to the Convention;

(b)   To formulate guidelines for the application of such terms of the Convention as "endangered" and "migratory species";

(c)   To review, in the light of these guidelines, the existing list of species on the appendices of the Convention;

(d)   To recommend, in accordance with article VIII, paragraph 5(c), of the Convention, species to be included in the appendices I or II, such additions to be made according to a clear, defined set of principles;

(e)   To develop a comprehensive and consistent candidate list of species which could benefit by future inclusion in appendices I and II, as they are put forward;

(f)   To provide information, channelled through the secretariat, to all Range States of particular species, with a view to encouraging all non-party Range States to become Parties to the Convention and to participate in its implementation.

. . .

Resolution 1.6
AGREEMENTS

**The Conference of the Parties to the Convention on the
Conservation of Migratory Species of Wild Animals,**

Recognizing the importance of demonstrating the effectiveness of the Convention,

Aware of the particular need to conclude Agreements for appendix II species,

1.   *Instructs* the secretariat to take appropriate measures to develop Agreements for the following species and groups of migratory animals:

   a.   European species of Chiroptera;
   b.   *Ciconia c. ciconia*;
   c.   Western palearctic Anatidae;
   d.   North and Baltic Sea populations of *Phocoena phocoena* and *Tursiops truncatus*;

2.   *Recommends* that progress on these Agreements should be reviewed at meetings of the Standing Committee and Scientific Council, and reported on at the second meeting of the Conference of the Parties;

3.   *Further recommends* that full account be taken of the record of discussions on the development of exemplary Agreements during the first meeting of the Conference of the Parties.

Resolution 1.7
SMALL CETACEANS

**The Conference of the Parties to the Convention on the
Conservation of Migratory Species of Wild Animals,**

Noting the advice of the Scientific Committee that the small cetaceans be considered for inclusion in appendix II of the Convention at the forthcoming second meeting of the Conference of the Parties,

Recognizing that a working group on marine migratory animals during the present first meeting of the Conference of the Parties has drafted a paper on biological elements for an agreement on certain small cetaceans,

Directs the secretariat to set up, in consultation with the Scientific Council and appropriate national and international organizations, a working group on small cetaceans.

- - - - -

UNEP Regional Seas Reports and Studies No.55   1985
                                                                Extract

. . .

A. Global Plan of Action for the Conservation,
Management and Utilization of Marine Mammals
Summary

1.   For the purpose of the Plan, marine mammals are taken to include those mammals which spend all or a large proportion of their time in the sea and obtain their food predominantly from it. They also include a few species whose ancestors were marine but which have moved into fresh waters.

2.   These marine mammals belong to four groups: cetaceans, pinnipeds, sirenians and some others. The populations of many of these animals have been severely depleted by human activities, mainly by hunting, but also by incidental catches in fishing nets, destruction of their habitats and disturbance of breeding colonies; pollution has also had serious effects on some species in some areas.

3.   The most seriously depleted large whales are the right and bowhead whales and, to a lesser extent, the blue and humpback whales. The fin and sei whales, although less depleted, are well below their most productive levels in most areas. The minke whale has in most areas been relatively little affected by exploitation. The status of sperm whales is particularly difficult to assess, but the population seems to be still very large.

4.   There is some uncertainty about the status of a number of the small cetaceans, but probably those in the most critical condition are some of the freshwater forms whose habitats have been gravely impoverished by the construction of dams, siltation and water pollution.

5.   Many of the pinnipeds which were seriously reduced by hunting in the past have made good recoveries, and the forms in greatest danger at present are the several species of monk seals, whose habitat requirements make them particularly susceptible to coastal modification and disturbance, and some fur seals and sea lions.

6.   The sirenians, which live in coastal and fresh waters in tropical areas, have been severely reduced throughout much of their range as a result of hunting (mainly subsistence but locally some commercial), habitat modification and disturbance.

. . .

11.   The steps needed to achieve effective conservation, management and utilization of marine mammals are numerous and complex, and cannot be fully identified at present. Therefore, although the total plan is seen as a long-term project of indefinite duration, the activities listed in the financial plan cover the medium-term period devoted to taking specific steps to deal with some urgent situations which can currently be identified, to improving in a number of areas the existing conservation mechanisms relating to marine mammals, and to obtaining information which will be needed as the implementation of the plan proceeds. A

Review Meeting is proposed to be held at the end of the first biennium to examine the results obtained and develop further plans for implementation.

12.   For the purpose of the Plan, "conservation" is taken to include rational exploitation, as well as the management of human activities which affect the marine mammals directly or indirectly, including exploitation.   It includes also actions related to trade in products from marine mammals, to the various threats to their well-being and to the realization of human values from them on a sustainable basis.   The term "management" is used to mean the positive actions which may be undertaken to achieve the conservation of a species, population or ecosystem.   It embraces, for example, creation of sanctuaries, prohibition of public access to breeding areas, catch limits and other restrictions on exploitation.   Thus, while conservation is a concept, management is a means by which that concept is put into effect.

13.   The Plan puts forward a series of Recommendations which are summarized and classified in table 1, with an indication of the bodies which it is proposed should implement each Recommendation.   In addition to those relating to establishing the machinery described in paragraph 10 above, the Recommendations deal with the following general areas of activity:

(a)   Identification of conservation and management objectives;

(b)   Actions to meet present critical situations;

(c)   Actions to increase present knowledge so as to provide a basis for further stages of the Plan;

(d)   Actions to improve the overall machinery of conservation, including:

(i)   Improvement in the availability of information;
(ii)   Increase in the number of scientists working on marine mammals;
(iii)   Increase in scientific activities;
(iv)   Development of concepts and mechanisms for the establishment of protected areas of marine mammals;
(v)   Improvement of public understanding of marine mammals and their conservation.

14.   In the area of objectives, an interim definition of "optimum population level" is proposed for use as a guideline in the first biennium of the Plan.   It is recommended that the Review Meeting should consider means by which a review of information, concepts and alternatives for global objectives for the conservation of marine mammals could be undertaken as the implementation of the Plan progresses.

. . .

16.   A series of studies, by consultants or in other ways, are proposed as means of obtaining the information needed to develop further activities for implementation.   These studies relate to:

(a)   Exploitation of marine mammals not under international control;

(b)   International killing of marine mammals for reasons other than direct exploitation, and the associated effects of marine mammals on the fisheries concerned;

(c)   Incidental killing of marine mammals in other fisheries;

(d)   Occurrence of contaminants in marine mammals and their environments;

(e)   Man-induced changes in breeding areas;

(f)   Effects on marine mammals of fisheries for their food species or for species competing with them for food;

(g)   Management of resources shared between two or more nations.

17.   Improvement in the availability of information refers both to increased speed and coverage in the publication of information on catches of marine mammals and trade in products derived from them and to improvement of the systems for the storage and availability of scientific information relating to marine mammals and their environments.

    . . .

20.   The problems relating to the establishment of areas in which marine mammals may be protected are complex, and involve biological, legal and political aspects. A number of studies are proposed aimed at clarification of some of these issues and at developing steps toward the creation of further sanctuary areas.

21.   The matters of law and administration dealt with in the Plan relate in general terms to the development of better mechanisms for the effective conservation of marine mammals, both nationally and internationally. Among the matters covered by the Plan are:

(a)   Assistance to individual nations in the improvement of their legal and administrative machinery in this field;

(b)   Relevant articles of the United Nations Convention on the Law of the Sea;

(c)   Management of the Southern Ocean;

(d)   Shared resources;

(e)   Migratory species;

(f)   World Heritage Lists;

(g)   The Biosphere Reserve programme;

(h)   Workshop on legal situation.

22.   The nature of the need for increasing public understanding of marine mammals and their conservation varies greatly among human communities. The Plan considers ways to examine these problems and identify the most important needs for and ways of promoting public understanding under various conditions. It also proposes ways of improving the availability of existing information and materials.

    . . .

Chapter VI

PRIORITIES AND RECOMMENDATIONS

6.1   The recommendations which have been developed in this report in table 1 have been classified according to the general areas with which they are concerned.

6.2   In this table the purposes which the recommendations are intended to serve have been classified in three groups:

A.   **Urgent situations** in which species or populations are known to be in a critical state and steps should be taken to alleviate the most serious threats;

B.   **Information needed** to determine the extent and nature of situations which are believed to be causing threats to marine mammal populations but about which insufficient is known;

C.   **Improve conditions** for the conservation of marine mammals by increasing scientific capability, improving legal and administrative machinery or adding to public understanding.
   . . .

Urgent situations

6.4   The species and populations which are believed to be in the most serious situations are reviewed in detail in appendix 1. The principal source of information on which this is based is the IUCN [International Union for the Conservation of Nature and Natural Resources] Red Data Book, 1978 edition, updated where new information has significantly changed our understanding of the status of species since that time, although other sources of information have also been used.

6.5   It is evident that urgent and specific actions are needed in all the principal areas covered by the plan - scientific, legal, administrative and public awareness. Recommendation 12 proposes immediate actions to be taken by the *ad hoc* planning and co-ordinating committee to identify the particular remedial steps which should be taken to deal with the most urgent situations. On the basis of the recommendations of the *ad hoc* planning and co-ordinating committee the appropriate follow-up actions should be taken by UNEP and associated organizations. Most of these actions would probably be representational or catalytic, but in some cases it might be necessary to arrange for further investigations to be made. Recommendation 12 and the consequent follow-up actions should be given the highest priority. Most of the immediate steps which need to be taken to remedy the identified critical situations are of a legal or administrative nature. There can be no doubt that as studies progress other critical situations or other ways of reducing the risks to stocks known to be threatened will be identified.
   . . .

Means of improving conservation practices

6.7   The proposals falling in this category are numerous and diverse. In the scientific sector they include increasing the supply of scientists, improvement of scientific information systems and, in a rather different category, steps to stimulate independent assessment of the scientific bases for management. The last is of extremely high priority in relation to the development of

Table 1

Summary of the recommendations classified according to the general area of activity to which they relate.

The organizations with primary responsibility, the basis of the need for action and the kind of action required are also shown. The highest priority recommendations are marked with an asterisk.

General area	Subject	Rec. No.	Page	Lead Organizations	Need for action						Kind of action				
					A Urgent situation	B Information needed	C Improved conditions	1 Organi-zation	2 Study	3 Act	4 Repre-	5 Catalyze	6 Meet	7 Finance	8 Plan
Objectives	Optimum level	1	24				X			X					
	Formulate objectives	2	29				X								X
Plan activities	Critical situations	*12	36	SC (SAC)	X										
	Critical situations	*12	36	UNEP, FAO (IUCN)	X				X		X	X		X	
Organize operations	Scientific Advisory Committee	18	42	FAO, UNEP			X	X							
	Standing Committee	36	59	FAO, UNEP			X	X							
	Secretariat	37	60	UNEP, FAO			X	X							
	Review Meeting	38	61	UNEP, FAO, IUCN			X						X		
Review situations	Exploitation not inter-nationally controlled	3	31	FAO		X			X						
	Non-utilizing killing	4	32	FAO		X			X						
	Incidental killing (data)	5	32	FAO		X			X						
	Contaminants	8	34	UNEP (ICES, IOC)						X					
	Effects on breeding areas	9	35	UNEP		X			X						
	Competition for food	*11	36	FAO		X			X						
	Shared resources (P.O.C.)	17	40	UNEP, FAO		X	X				X				
	Shared resources (biological, economic)	17	40	FAO			X					X			
	Incidental killing (legal)	28	51	IUCN			X		X						
Improved informa-tion	Catch statistics	6	33	FAO (UNEP, IUCN, IWC, BIWS)			X								
	Trade statistics	7	33	IUCN (CITES; FAO)						X					
	Scientific information system	19	44	FAO, UNEP (IOC)			X		X						
	Inventory of legislation	27	50	UNEP, FAO, IUCN			X		X						

General area	Subject	Rec. No.	Page	Lead Organizations	Need for action — Urgent situation (A)	Information needed (B)	Improved conditions (C)	Organization (1)	Kind of action — Study (2)	Act (3)	Repr-sent (4)	Catalyze (5)	Meet (6)	Finance (7)	Plan (8)
Increase number of scientists	Provide student fellowships	20	44	UNEP, UNESCO (WWF, CEE)										X	
	Accept fellows	20	44	National bodies			X			X					
	Identify training institutes	20	44	UNEP, UNESCO (FAO)			X			X					
	Identify training needs	20	44	International and regional organizations			X								
	Employ more scientists	20	44	Governments			X			X					
	Provide senior fellows	20	44	Governments and IOC			X			X				X	
Increase scientific activities	Build up observation network	21	45	UNEP, IUCN, NGO			X		X	X					
	Independent monitoring of management research	*22	46	FAO, IUCN			X		X			X		X	
Protected areas	Provision for pinnipeds	13	37	IUCN			X		X						
	Develop concepts and practices	14	38	UNEP (IUCN, IWC, FAO)			X			X					
	Sampling in protected areas	16	39	FAO (UNEP, IWC, IUCN)			X			X					
	Legal issues	29	51	IUCN (UNEP)			X		X		X				
	Follow-up of workshop	15	39	UNEP, IWC, IUCN, UNESCO			X		X	X					

General area	Subject	Rec. No.	Page	Lead Organizations	Need for action						Kind of action				
					Urgent situation A	Information needed B	Improved conditions C	Organization 1	Study 2	Act 3	Represent 4	Catalyze 5	Meet 6	Finance 7	Plan 8
	Management of Southern Ocean	10	35	FAO, UNEP								X			
	Shared resources (Principles of Conduct)	17	40	UNEP			X								
	Law of the Sea	23	48	UNEP, FAO			X				X				
	Renegotiation of agreements	24	49	UN, Specialized Agencies			X				X				
Law and adminis-tration	Actions prior to LOS treaty	25	49	FAO, UNEP			X				X				
	Co-ordination between overlapping bodies	26	50	UNEP			X				X				
	Live capture and harassment	28	51	IUCN			X		X						
	Migratory species	29	51	UNEP			X		X		X				
	World Heritage Lists	30	52	UNEP (UNESCO)			X				X				
	Biosphere Reserves	31	53	UNESCO, UNEP			X		X						
	Legal Workshop	32	54	UNEP, FAO (UNESCO, IUCN)			X		X						
Public informa-tion	Workshop	33	57	UNEP (UNESCO, IUCN)			X						X		
	Production and listing of material	34	57	UNEP, FAO (UNESCO, IUCN, NGOs)			X			X		X			
	Bulletin on Plan progress	35	58	PS			X			X					

satisfactory management techniques particularly for exploited populations. Of the others, the production of additional scientists to work on marine mammals is highly desirable.

6.8   The proposals bearing on legal and administrative problems are very diverse among themselves. As noted above, many of the problems associated with populations which are immediately threatened are of this nature and the sponsoring organizations of the Plan, and its secretariat, should use every effort to assist and encourage the nations concerned in these matters. Highest priority should also be given to steps aimed at adoption of an international convention for the conservation of marine mammals with the widest possible range both of member nations and of species within its ambit.

6.9   Several recommendations are concerned with the improvement of public understanding. Of these, the most fundamental is that proposing an international workshop on ways of increasing world-wide public understanding of questions relating to marine mammals conservation and management. This should be given high priority, with emphasis on means of increasing local understanding in areas where specific problems exist, and on the methods of maintaining accuracy and balance in presentations to the public.

Appendix I

THREATENED MARINE MAMMALS - SYSTEMATIC LIST

A.   This appendix is based largely on the information in the IUCN Red Data Book (1978 Edition), updated where new information has significantly changed our understanding of the status of species since that time.

The IUCN categories "endangered", "vulnerable", "rare" and "indeterminate" are defined as follows:

Endangered   -   In danger of extinction and survival is unlikely if the
                    casual factors continue operating. Included are species
                    which have been reduced to a critical level.

Vulnerable   -   Likely to move into the endangered category in the near
                    future if the causal factors continue operating.
                    Included are species with populations that have been
                    seriously depleted and whose ultimate security has not yet
                    been assured.

Rare   -   With small world populations, not at present endangered or
                    vulnerable but at risk.

Indeterminate -   Suspected of belonging to one of the first three categories
                    but insufficient information is currently available.

The lists do not include forms that were formally threatened, but which were, in 1978, considered by IUCN to be out of danger. The lists are clearly deficient with respect to a number of odontocetes about which little is known but which might be rare. The status of cetaceans has more recently been reviewed by the United Kingdom Nature Conservancy

Council (NCC) for the Parties to CITES [Convention on International Trade in Endangered Species of Wild Fauna and Flora]. In 1983 **all** cetacean species were included in CITES Appendix I. IWC [International Whaling Commission] has listed a number of species and populations of others as Protected Stocks; under the current management procedure these are stocks believed to be 10 per cent or more below MSY [Maximum Sustainable Yield] level. This does not imply that these stocks are necessarily in any danger of extinction.

B.   Species

Certain of the species listed below are "endangered" in terms of the CITES convention. They are identified as "CITES(I)", "CITES(II)" or III as of 1983. The first are "species threatened with extinction which may be affected by trade" and a trade in specimens of which is "subject to particularly strict regulation and only authorized in exceptional circumstances". Appendix II species are species deemed not necessarily to be now threatened with extinction but which may become so unless trade in specimens of them is subject to strict regulation. All cetacean species are included in CITES appendix I. In CITES appendix III are included all species which any Party has "identified as being subject to regulation within its jurisdiction for the purpose of preventing or restricting exploitation, and as needing the co-operation of other Parties in the control of trade".

Some species also are listed in Class A of the Annex to the African Convention on the Conservation of Nature and Natural Resources (AFConA). Species in that Class are "totally protected throughout the entire territory of the Contracting States: hunting, killing, capture and collection being permitted only under licence and when in the national interest or for scientific purpose". Trade in or transport of them or of parts of them is regulated.

Species marked MSC(I) or (II) are respectively listed in Appendix I or Appendix II of the Convention on Conservation of Migratory Species of Wild Animals, which came into force in November 1983. Appendix I lists migratory species which are endangered, meaning they are in danger of extinction throughout all or a significant portion of their range. In Appendix II are listed those which have an unfavourable conservation status and which require international agreements for their conservation and management, as well as those having a conservation status which would significantly benefit from the international co-operation that could be achieved by an international agreement.

1.   **"Possibly or nearly extinct"**

(a)   Japanese sea lion (*Otariidae - Zalophus californianus japonicus*).
One of three races of California sea lion. Now almost extinct, as a result of persecution by fishermen and perhaps also by other human disturbances, on coastal islands of Japan where it was last recorded in the fifties. Continued existence reported on Dokto Island, Sea of Japan and may still exist off the east coast of Korea.

(b)   Caribbean monk seal (*Phocidae - Monachus tropicalis*). Originally off the shores and islands of Caribbean and Gulf of Mexico. Depleted by eighteenth century sealing; survivors persecuted by fishermen. Last authenticated report 1962, a single animal on Isla Mujeres, off Yucatan Peninsula. Possibly still inhabiting Chinchorro Reef, Mexico;

(c)   North Pacific gray whale (*Eschrichtidae - Eschrichtius robustus*). This species as a whole is not endangered, but two of the three known major original stocks are extinct or very nearly so. The surviving eastern North Pacific stock has recovered well from severe depletion due to whaling and is now probably more than 18,000 animals, about its pre-exploitation level. The Atlantic stock has been extinct, possibly due to early whaling, probably for several hundred years. The western North Pacific stock was, until recently, thought to have been exterminated.

However, it has been reported that animals have been sighted there in recent years and that the Republic of Korea and China have caught them. It is possible that these are survivors from the original population or that the eastern region began to be repopulated by an "overflow" from the recovering population in the west. The "subsistence" catch of gray whales - over 100 annually - in the USSR is thought to be derived wholly from the eastern stock. CITES(I).

2.   "Endangered"

(a) Indus dolphin or susu (*CETACEA - Platanistidae - Platanista indi*) (Syn. P. minor). In the mid-nineteenth century inhabited the Indus River and its main tributaries throughout their lengths; a few hundred remain in short stretches of the Indus, between barrages, within Sind and Punjab Provinces of Pakistan, where it is protected by law. Decline caused by restrictions of original habitat, through impoundment and water diversion, but also illegal exploitation as human food continues CITES(I);

(b) Blue whale (*Balaenoptera musculus*). Depleted by whaling in twentieth century. Protected worldwide by IWC since 1960 in North Atlantic, 1965 in Southern Ocean, 1966 in North Pacific, 1967 worldwide. It is known that individuals of this species are still occasionally caught. It is probably increasing but this is not certain. The Southern Hemisphere population is probably about 5,000, with a few thousand in other oceans. There are probably as many again of the pygmy blue whale sub-species which was not seriously exploited until relatively late and has been less depleted than the main stock. CITES(I), MSC(I);

(c) Humpback whale (*Megaptera novaeangliae*). Depleted by whaling in twentieth century. Protected worldwide by IWC since 1966 but no clear evidence of increasing numbers except in northwest Atlantic. A few are still caught regularly in aboriginal subsistence fisheries in the North Atlantic. As this species breeds close to shore and is of interest to the public in some areas it may be affected by disturbance. Present number probably considerably less than 10,000. CITES(I), MSC(I);

(d) Bowhead or Greenland right whale (*Balaena mysticetus*). Depleted throughout its range by nineteenth century whaling. Protected by IWC since 1946, but subject to "aboriginal whaling" for local consumption by IWC members. Probably four distinct populations:

(i)   Eastern North Atlantic - very rare, uncertain evidence of any increase;
(ii) Western North Atlantic - very rare, uncertain evidence of any increase;
(iii) North Pacific (Bering, Chukche and Beaufort Seas) - depleted by commercial whaling in the late nineteenth and early twentieth centuries. Some recovery but now possibly stable under a subsistence catch by Alaskan inuits. Present population about 3,500 about 20 per cent of original. Scientific Committee of IWC has expressed grave concern about the survival of this stock under any exploitation. The current rate of reproduction appears very low;

(iv)   Okhotsk Sea - apparently was increasing up to the sixties but few recent sightings. Was thought exterminated in Sea of Japan but one was caught in the late sixties. CITES(I);

(e)   Black right whale (*Eubalaena glacialis*). Three sub-species were hunted almost to extinction between the fifteenth and nineteenth centuries. Protected by IWC from pelagic whaling since 1946. In western North Atlantic some signs of increase, but in the eastern North Atlantic has not been reported since one was killed about 1959. In the Southern Hemisphere there have been strong indications of increase off South Africa and New Zealand, and possibly off Argentina. Elsewhere no increase is indicated. Sightings suggest a Southern Hemisphere population of about 3,000. No clear sign of recovery of North Pacific population. CITES(I) MSC(I);

(f)   Marine otter (*CARNIVORA - Mustelidae - Lutra felina*) formerly occurred along Pacific coast of South America from Peru south. Gravely reduced, now only in a few areas of Peru where population estimated at 200-300. Still killed by fishermen for alleged damage to prawn fishery. No commercial value. CITES(I);

(g)   Southern river otter (*CARNIVORA - Mustelidae - Lutra provocax*) distributed on west coast of South America from central Chile south. Range not reduced but numbers severely depleted by fur hunting. No population estimates available. No protection in some countries. CITES(I);

(h)   Mediterranean monk seal (*PINNIPEDIA - Phocidae - Monachus monachus*). Off northwest coast of Africa and in Mediterranean basin. A few hundred individuals survive; decline continues as result of persecution by fishermen and by other human disturbances. Legally protected in several countries, but enforcement incomplete. Subject of a specialist meeting convened by IUCN with UNEP support, in Rhodes, Greece, which resulted in a draft Plan of Action for conservation of the species. AfConA: all African States concerned are Party to the convention. CITES(I), MSC(I and II);

(i)   Hawaiian monk seal (*Phocidae - Monachus schauinslandi*). Still occupies its original range, but decreasing in some breeding grounds, although protected and possibly increasing in others. Possibly now fewer than 1,000 individuals. Was nearly exterminated by hunting in the nineteenth century, and now affected by human disturbance wherever this continues, notwithstanding injunctions against "harassment" and molestation under United States and state laws. CITES(I);

(j)   Amazonian manatee (*SIRENIA - Trichechidae - Trichechus inunguis*). Was distributed throughout Amazon system (Brazil, Columbia, Peru) and headwaters of Orinoco (Venezuela), but depleted by hunting; range now restricted but unknown, as is the present population size. Legally protected in Brazil and Peru, but enforcement thought to be incomplete. CITES(I);

3.   "Vulnerable"

(a)   Fin whale (*CETACEA - Balaenopteridae - Balaenoptera physalus*). This species has been heavily exploited in the Southern Hemisphere where the original population of about 400,000 legally takable animals has been reduced to about 80,000, and in the North Pacific where the reduction was from about 43,000 to about 16,000. In both cases this species has been protected by IWC since about 1975. In the North Atlantic a number of local stocks are distinguished by IWC, some are protected, but others are still exploited, notably those off Iceland and Spain. Some catching outside IWC under flags of convenience has also occurred in the North Atlantic in earlier years. CITES(I);

(b)   Northern bottlenose whale (*Ziphiidae - Hyperoodon ampullatus*). In Boreal and Arctic North Atlantic. Depleted by whaling in the nineteenth century. None caught commercially at present and catching prohibited by IWC. Present numbers not known, nor details of present distribution and migration patterns;

(c)   Galapagos fur seal (*Otariidae - Arctocephalus galapagoensis*). Once common throughout the archipelago, nearly exterminated by nineteenth century sealing; thought at beginning of twentieth century to be extinct, but rediscovered on James Island in 1957. Slowly recovering and extending range under protection but now restricted by habitat availability. Now 5 to 10 thousand individuals on ten or more islands. CITES(I);

(d)   Juan Fernandez fur seal (*Otariidae - A. philippii*). Once ranged from Strait of Magellan to Peru. Nearly exterminated by nineteenth century sealing; now slowly recovering under protection on some islands but still only a few hundred individuals on two islands off coast of central Chile. CITES(II);

(e)   Guadalupe fur seal (*Otariidae - A. townsendi*). Originally ranged from southern California to Baja California. Thought to have been exterminated but rediscovered in mid-1950s. Increasing under protection by the United States of America and Mexico and colonies or groups now on several islands, but suitable habitat is limited and may be shrinking. CITES(I);

(f)   West African manatee (*Trichechidae - T. senegalensis*). Formerly distributed from Senegal to Angola, mainly in Senegal, Niger, Benue and Congo Rivers systems. Range now much reduced; reported in Gambia River, eastern shores of Volta Lake, in Benue - Niger systems (including Kainji Lake), possibly Cross River (Nigeria) and Lakes Lere and Trene (Chad). Was depleted by hunting; still declining despite protection by national laws incompletely enforced; vulnerable to incidental capture in fishing nets. AfConA; all States concerned are Party to the convention. CITES(II);

(g)   West Indian (Caribbean) manatee (*Trichechidae - I. manatus*). Range is from Florida (United States of America) to Guyana. Depleted by hunting; apparently secure populations in Belize, Guyana and Suriname, but declining elsewhere. Population in Florida is severely adversely affected by boat traffic and other causes of mortality. Present population possibly in range 5,000-10,000. Vulnerable to incidental catch by fishing nets, to boat propellers and other human disturbances. Protected in most countries by law incompletely enforced. Threatened also by shrinking habitat and herbicide treatment of waterways. CITES(I);

(h)   Dugong (*Dugonidae - Dugong dugon*). Wide range throughout tropical and sub-tropical Indo-Pacific. Depleted by hunting over most of this range but population size unknown. A few large populations (thousands), particularly in the Australian area, but nearly extinct in other areas. Vulnerable to incidental capture in fishing and other nets, to pollution affecting sea-grass beds; and to other human disturbances, as well as continued hunting.

Protected in many countries but law incompletely enforced. AfConA; all African States concerned are Party to the convention. CITES(I and II), MSC(II).

4.   "Rare"

(a)   Saimaa seal (*Phocidae - Phoca hispida saimensis*). Confined to Saimaa Lake system (Finland). Reduced by 1958 to 40 individuals by persecution; now increased under protection to 200-300 animals, but habitat now reduced through pollution, which they avoid. Some licensed shooting following fishermen's complaints;

(b)   Hooker's sea lion (*Otariidae - Phocarctos hookeri*). Confined as a breeding species to a few sub-Antarctic islands off New Zealand and with a population of only circa 6,000. Subject to an unqualified incidental take during squid fishing operations;

(c)   Australian sea lion (*Otariidae - Neophoca cinerea*). Very restricted breeding range on southern Australian coast. Population circa 5,000.

5.   "Indeterminate"

(a)   Whitefin dolphin or Beiji (*Plantanistidae - Lipotes vexillifer*). Originally thought to be confined to streams flowing into Tung Ting Lake (China), now known to exist in the Yangtze River. Numbers unknown but described in Chinese scientific literature as "very rare". CITES(I);

(b)   Kurile harbour seal (*Phocidae - Phoca kurilensis*). Former range unknown and present distribution unsure but occurs in coastal areas of Hokkaido and Kurile, Aleutian Islands, West Alaska (about 5,000 individuals). Protected in United States of America and USSR and partially in Japan, but pups still exploited for local use, and laws incompletely enforced;

(c)   Laptev walrus (*Odobenidae - Odobenus rosmarus laptevi*). Subspecies or race of walrus in Laptev Sea and adjacent parts of Kara and East Siberian Seas. Protected from 1957 under USSR law, but apparently not increasing. Declined from 60,000 to 10,000 individuals in 1930s, for reasons unknown but possibly by hunting, by analogy with decline during 1940s and 1950s of the Atlantic walrus (*O. r. rosmarus*) in the neighbouring region of Novaya Zemlya/Kara Sea.

6.   The sei whale (*Balaenoptera borealis*) was little exploited until about 1960. Heavy catches in the next few years rapidly reduced its numbers in the North Pacific and the southern hemisphere, and it has been protected by IWC of these oceans since 1976 and 1978 respectively. In the North Atlantic the relatively small stocks have been less exploited. It is thus in a somewhat similar situation to the fin whale.

7.   Under the present IWC procedure, baleen whale stocks are placed in the Protection category if they are estimated to be 10 per cent or more below the MSY level, and this is assumed to be 60 per cent of initial stock size. Thus the upper boundary of the Protection Stock category is well above the level at which there is likely to be any risk of moving to extinction in the absence of hunting, and there is probably a substantial margin for errors in the estimates.

8.   During 1978 reviews of the assessments of sperm whales (*Odontoceti - Physeter catodon; syn. P. macrocephalus*) indicated that although still rather abundant and world-wide in distribution, this species has been reduced significantly in some areas by whaling.   In particular, selective hunting for males has reduced their numbers in several areas to well under half of their original values.   In some areas the reproductive rates as shown by the pregnancy rates, appear to have fallen as a result.   In the southern hemisphere and the North Pacific all stocks are now protected except for the western North Pacific coastal stock.   In the North Atlantic catching is continuing but only provisionally.   CITES(I).

9.   Although not listed in the Red Data Book, the Ganges-Bramaputra susu (*Platanistidae - P. gangetica*) is of highly uncertain status.   The ACMRR [Advisory Committee of Experts on Marine Resources Research (FAO)] study reported conflicting opinions as to whether or not it is endangered.   In the view of the vulnerability of freshwater marine mammals in general, especially in river systems with barrages, this species, which occurs in waters of two countries (Bangladesh and India) should be regarded at least as of "indeterminate" status, in IUCN terms, if not "vulnerable".   In particular its status may be affected by the recently completed Farakka Barrage on the Ganges close to the Bangladesh (W. Bengal) frontier, which has separated the "reservoir" population in the relatively less exploited Bramaputra system from that in the Ganges system.   This species is also found in Nepal.   CITES(I).

10.   The sea otter has recovered to a great extent on the western North American coast, both in Alaska and in California.   It has also been established successfully by transplantation at intermediate points.   It is also reported to have recovered under protection in USSR waters to at least 10,000 individuals, and is now to be the subject of a plan for a fur industry.   Its skin provides one of the most valuable of all furs; translocation has been recommended by Soviet scientists.

11.   A number of other cetaceans are, or have been recently, subject to exploitation to a degree which may give cause for concern.   The IWC Scientific Committee noted in 1980 that some stocks of the white whale or beluga (*Delphinapterus leucas*) were being depleted by subsistence hunting.   One stock is believed to be at 10-15 per cent of its initial size, and others are believed to be subject to catches greater than their MSYs.   A catch quota has been imposed on at least one of these stocks, but much wider and more stringent protective measures are needed, and the Committee urged that national and co-operative research programmes should be started by the countries concerned.   There is also rather similar cause for concern for the narwhal (*Monodon monoceros*) in the same area.   Several of the species of porpoises which have been taken in large numbers in the tuna purse-seines have been reproduced below their levels of probable maximum net productivity, although others are still above this level.   However, regulations which have been imposed on much of the industry, preventing setting in tuna schools associated with the most reduced species, have removed most of the present threat.   The striped dolphin is the subject of a fishery off Japan, and preliminary assessments suggest that it may have been reduced to less than 50 per cent of the initial level.   A national research programme is planned.   Dall's porpoise (*Phocornoides dalli*) is taken both directly and in salmon gillnets in the North Pacific.   Preliminary studies suggest that in the salmon fishery an incidental catch of between 9,000 and 25,000 porpoises is taken from a population of 600,000 - 2,300,000.   With this amount of uncertainty in the estimates, and additional uncertainty in the recruitment rate, it is not yet possible to assess the future impact of the fishery upon the population.   Further studies are therefore urgently needed.

12.   The killer whale (*Orcinus orca*) is hunted by Norwegian fishermen on account of reputed damage to the herring fishery; a national catch limit was imposed in 1979 following a recommendation by the IWC Scientific Committee, and catching is now prohibited.   In the 1979-80 season a large catch of killer whales (about 900) was taken for the first time in the Antarctic, from parts of Areas III and IV (0-130°E).   At the 1980 meeting IWC extended the ban on pelagic whaling to include killer whales; it is therefore likely that there will be no further take at least until there are acceptable population estimates.

13.   A considerable number of odontocetes species are not at all well known and may be rare. There are some records of these being occasionally killed by whalers.   Two examples are the pygmy sperm whale (*Kogia breviceps*) and the dwarf sperm whale (*K. simus*).

14.   Other small odontocetes, not especially sought by whalers or cetacean hunters may nevertheless be caught when encountered by them, and sometimes in considerable numbers. Such catches are unregulated.   One such species is the southern bottlenose whale (*Hyperoodon planifrons*).   Others are the false killer whale (*Pseudorca crassidens*), the melon-headed whale (*Preponocephala electra*).   The populations of the bottlenosed dolphin (*Tursiops truncatus*) and the common dolphin (*Delphinus delphis*) in the Black Sea have declined as a result of hunting. The USSR and Bulgaria, have protected them for some years together with Romania and more recently still Turkey is not clear whether these populations are now increasing or not.

15.   One other species of baleen whale, the pygmy right whale (*Caporea marginata*), is of uncertain status, being known only from a few strandings and sightings.

- - - - -

International Whaling Commission   IWC Report 37
Report of 38th Annual Meeting, 1986   Extract

. . .

Chairman's Report of the Thirty-eighth Annual Meeting

6.3   Scientific permits

A Working Group was established last year to study a draft resolution proposed by Sweden and seconded by Switzerland on the subject of scientific permits and any relevant matters.   The Working Group was chaired by Mr. S. Irberger (Sweden) and attended by delegates from Antigua and Barbuda, Australia, People's Republic of China, Iceland, Japan, Republic of Korea, Mexico, New Zealand, Norway, Philippines, St. Lucia, the Seychelles, Sweden, USSR, UK and USA.

The Group was unable to reach consensus in its discussions, and presented a new draft resolution, including a paragraph recommending that the products from special permit catches should not enter international trade, over which divergent opinions were expressed.   Different views were also reported on special permit catches from Protection Stocks.

The UK seconded the resolution, including the trade paragraph. It expressed concern over the permits issued by Iceland and the Republic of Korea in the light of comments on both by the Scientific Committee, and saw no conflict between the proposed resolution and any other legal agreements of Contracting Governments. This position was shared by New Zealand, while the People's Republic of China believed that special permit catches should not be made from Protection Stocks.

Iceland explained its opposition to the trade paragraph, making reference to Articles VIII and VI of the Convention to support its view that research should not be discouraged and that there should be no restrictions on trade. The Republic of Korea also spoke of the importance of scientific research for the Comprehensive Assessment during the pause in commercial whaling, and Japan emphasised the sovereign rights of governments to carry out research and the need to process the whales taken.

Spain pointed out that there was consensus on all the paragraphs of the resolution except one, on international trade, and warned against forcing the issue to a vote. This view was supported by Mexico, France, Norway and the Philippines.

Oman then introduced a new draft resolution, in which the trade paragraph was replaced by one recommending that products from whales taken under scientific permit should not be used for purposes other than scientific research or local consumption as human food; and a second recommending against permits being issued for Protection Stocks unless there is clear scientific evidence that the proposed catch will not further deplete or substantially impede the recovery of the stock.

This proposal was seconded by Sweden, and supported by Switzerland, India and the Seychelles.

Further discussion ensued in which a number of delegations emphasised that scientific permits should not be used to continue commercial whaling under another guise, and Norway and Australia spoke on the freedom of science in this context. Argentina also wished to stop any abuses, but stressed that the Commission is now in a transitional period and care should be taken in establishing any particular line for the future. It therefore suggested that a small Working Group should be set up to try and finalise an agreed form of resolution. The Commission agreed to this suggestion, and Argentina, Iceland, Japan, Norway, Oman, Spain, Sweden, Switzerland and the UK were nominated to the Working Group.

After further protracted discussions in the Working Group, a third draft resolution was developed and presented by the Chairman. The two previous drafts were withdrawn by their sponsors, and the Commission then adopted by consensus the new Resolution . . . [which is shown below].

Sweden declared that it had, in the spirit of consensus, agreed to accept the recommendation on the use of whales taken under special permits for scientific purposes. It hoped that all whaling nations will implement the recommendation conservatively so as not to make the special permit for scientific purposes a cover for continued commercial whaling. Oman associated itself with this statement.

RESOLUTION ON SPECIAL PERMITS FOR SCIENTIFIC RESEARCH (IWC/38/28)

Whereas the purpose of the International Whaling Commission is to provide for the proper conservation of whale stocks and thus make possible the orderly development of the whaling industry; and

Whereas the Commission has decided that catch limits for the killing for commercial purposes of whales from all stocks for the 1986 coastal and the 1985/86 pelagic seasons and thereafter shall be zero, this provision to be kept under review based on the best scientific advice, the Commission being required by 1990 at the latest to undertake a comprehensive assessment of the effects of this decision on whale stocks and consider modification of this provision and the establishment of other catch limits; and

Whereas Article VIII of the International Convention for the Regulation of Whaling provides that notwithstanding anything contained in the Convention any Contracting Government may grant to any of its nationals a special permit authorizing that national to kill, take and treat whales for purposes of scientific research subject to such other conditions as the Contracting Government thinks fit; and

Whereas paragraph 30 of the Schedule of the Convention provides for all proposed permits to be reviewed by the Scientific Committee; and

Whereas the killing, taking and treating of whales for purposes of scientific research should only be undertaken in a manner consistent with the principles and in accordance with the provisions of the Convention.

Now, Therefore, **the Commission,** until the Comprehensive Assessment under Schedule paragraph 10(e) is completed,

Recommends that prior to deciding on the granting of permits for the killing, taking and treating of whales for the purpose of scientific research, Contracting Governments while complying fully with Paragraph 30 of the Schedule, should also take account of guidelines drawn up by the Scientific Committee.

Recommends that the duration of any such permits issued by the Contracting Governments should be strictly limited to the need for completion of the proposed research.

Reaffirms that as stated in Paragraph 30 of the Schedule the preliminary results of the scientific research will be subject to annual review by the Scientific Committee.

Recommends that Contracting Governments when considering proposed research permits and the Scientific Committee when reviewing such permits and when reviewing the results of research from permits previously issued in accordance with the procedures of the Convention should take into account whether:

(1) the objectives of the research are not practically and scientifically feasible through non-lethal research techniques;

(2) the proposed research is intended, and structured accordingly to contribute information essential for rational management of the stock;

(3) the number, age and sex of whales to be taken are necessary to complete the research and will facilitate the conduct of the comprehensive assessment;

(4) whales will be killed in a manner consistent with the provisions of Section III of the Schedule, due regard being had to whether there are compelling scientific reasons to the contrary.

Recommends that Contracting Governments ensure that maximum scientific information be obtained from any whales taken under special permits for scientific research.

Recommends that, taking into account Paragraph 2 of Article VIII of the Convention, following the completion of scientific treatment the meat as well as the other products should be utilised primarily for local consumption.

Recommends that great care should be taken by Contracting Governments when considering issuing special permits for the taking of whales from a Protection Stock. Contracting Governments should take care to ensure that the proposed catch will not further deplete the stock or substantially impede its recovery.

Reiterates that Contracting Governments should grant no permits until the proposals for such permits have been reviewed in accordance with Paragraph 30 of the Schedule and further:

Recommends that Contracting Governments submit proposals for scientific permits and results of research obtained from permits previously issued in accordance with the procedures of the Convention, to the Secretary of the Commission not later than 60 days before the next Annual Meeting of the Scientific Committee.

- - - - -

International Whaling Commission   IWC Report
Report of the 39th Annual Meeting, 1987   Extract

=====

Chairman's Report of the Thirty-ninth Annual Meeting

. . .

8. SCIENTIFIC PERMITS

The USA introduced a proposed Resolution, co-sponsored by Australia, Finland, Netherlands, New Zealand and Sweden. This called upon the Scientific Committee to use four criteria when evaluating research proposed under a special permit, and it would then be within the discretion of the Commission to recommend to member governments whether the proposed research is consistent with the Commission's conservation policy. The USA saw no conflict in such action with the authority reserved to Contracting Governments under Article VIII of the Convention in issuing special permits, stating that its proposal was intended to implement Article VI, that the Commission may from time to time make recommendations to any or all Contracting Governments on any matter which relate to whales or whaling.

Statements of support for this proposal were made by a number of governments. Sweden expressed its concern about the development of whaling for scientific purposes, and saw the resolution as a step forward to avoid abuse. Switzerland emphasised its domestic preoccupations over the use of animals for scientific purposes, and Australia spoke of the need to prevent whaling for scientific research circumventing the effects of the moratorium and affecting the Comprehensive Assessment. The Federal Republic of Germany recognised the two main aspects of the proposal as establishing additional criteria for scientific whaling both for the Comprehensive Assessment and other important research needs, and the right of the Commission to express its view on research programmes of member states which involve the taking of whales.

The Netherlands and the UK were both concerned that commercial whaling may be reintroduced under the guise of scientific study, and believed that the resolution proposed appropriately reflects the Commission's right and responsibility to express its views and the sovereignty of Contracting Governments to issue special permits. The People's Republic of China supported the use of special permits for real research, but opposed their use as an excuse for commercial whaling. It thought permits should be approved by the Scientific Committee and the IWC, and the catches restricted to the needs of the Scientific Committee, to avoid depletion of the whale resources.

Opposition to the proposal was voiced by Iceland, which believed that the issue had been effectively resolved last year. In its view the proposal of the USA was inconsistent with the Convention, and exceeded its authority, so that Iceland would not consider itself bound by such a resolution and would seek remedial methods in accordance with international law. Its further cooperation or participation in the IWC would need to be considered if the resolution were to be adopted. Japan similarly believed that the resolution infringed the sovereign rights of Contracting Governments to issue special permits, and did not think the Commission should make decisions on the scientific soundness of a programme by majority vote. The USSR regarded scientific research on whales as a matter of paramount importance. The decision to terminate whaling has led to a sharp decline in research and loss of biological information. In this situation it believed that research whaling could make a considerable contribution to the collection of biological information and monitoring of the status of stocks. It further considered the proposed resolution to be in contravention with the provisions of Convention Article VIII.

Norway was also dismayed at the re-opening of an issue dealt with last year. It was aware of the concerns, and quoted the World Commission on Environment and Development to this effect, which commented that permissions for such hunting should be stringently applied by IWC members. While Norway was prepared to enter into constructive discussion of the criteria for review of special permits, it had grave misgivings about the preamble, certain operative paragraphs, and the proposed procedure couched in semi-Conventional language in the proposal.

The Republic of Korea also voiced its opposition to the proposed resolution.

The Chairman then adjourned the discussion on this Item until the next session.

Following this adjournment, Norway introduced as an amendment a detailed draft in the same format as the original proposal, but which the Chairman ruled to be a new resolution rather than an amendment of the first. This new draft was based on the two premises that the guidelines established last year should be retained, as in the first proposal, but that any element which raised doubts about conformity with the Convention or the political consequences should be omitted. This was described paragraph by paragraph, seconded by Iceland and supported by Japan.

The UK recognised some useful elements in this proposal, but also some shortcomings, notably the lack of reference to the moratorium on commercial whaling or the Comprehensive Assessment, the need for an annual review and report by the Scientific Committee of research programmes, various details of wording, and the omission of any procedure for the Commission to make a judgement on the matter.

Iceland had some difficulty in participating in the debate on a question of principle, because it believed the USA proposal was unlawful, but nonetheless set out the Icelandic views on the legal situation. This close analysis concerned the relationship between Articles VI and VIII of the Convention. Attention was focused on the terms in Article VIII permitting any Contracting Government to grant its nationals a special permit "notwithstanding anything contained in this Convention", and such killing, taking and treating of whales being "exempt from the operation of this Convention". Iceland believed that the USA's proposal was inconsistent with the Convention because it would infringe the rights of Contracting Governments and impede their ability to fulfill their obligations under Article VIII. It introduced extraneous political and economic considerations by the threat of sanctions under US law and was an attempt to amend Article VIII by unlawful means.

The USSR and Japan supported these views.

The USA emphasised its view that the Commission's position on the moratorium on commercial whaling, which is still not in place, and the Comprehensive Assessment, which is proving difficult to begin, should be strengthened more than by last year's Resolution so that whaling for scientific purposes might not be a way for some to get around the moratorium. It reiterated that the Commission may make recommendations to any Contracting Government under Convention Article VI, and that catches under Article VIII are "for purposes of scientific research". It saw its proposed resolution as an attempt to establish standards following the precedent of last year's Resolution adopted by consensus, and to allow the Commission to express its view as well as the Scientific Committee on proposed special permits.

Australia refuted the Icelandic implication that the resolution it had jointly sponsored was designed primarily to allow the domestic legislation of other countries to bear on IWC members who could be judged to be in contravention of the scientific criteria for special permits. The immediate problem was the duty and responsibility of the Commission to manage and conserve the whale stocks and, given the possibility that some countries may seek to take advantage of the exception in the Convention, make recommendations on scientific permits to interested Governments.

Oman and Netherlands associated themselves with this view.

Norway concurred with the argument put forward by Iceland and supported its conclusions, seeing the USA proposal as an attempt to set up a totally novel procedure using the phraseology that the Commission "agrees" as a more binding relationship than a recommendation.

After a further adjournment to the next session, Japan introduced a series of amendments to the original resolution proposed by the USA and others. These were intended to clarify certain paragraphs and safeguard the position of principle and legal interpretation it held. These amendments were seconded by Iceland.

The Federal Republic of Germany then proposed that the debate should be closed on all the proposals before the meeting, as it believed there was no chance of a compromise because of basic differences of opinion, and the arguments were being repeated.

Norway spoke against the closure, since there had been no opportunity to discuss the amendments recently presented or to consider modifications, and Mexico supported this position.

After clarification of the procedure being followed, the motion to close the debate was adopted by 18 votes in favour, 8 against with 6 abstentions.

The Commission then proceeded to vote separately on each of the nine amendments proposed by Japan to the resolution put forward by the USA and five co-sponsors.

The proposed amendments to preambular paragraphs 1 and 2 were defeated, with 7 votes in favour, 21 against and 4 abstentions; and 5 for, 23 against and 4 abstentions respectively.

The amendment to preambular paragraph 3 was adopted with 24 votes in favour and 8 abstentions.

A proposed new preambular paragraph, amendments to operative paragraphs 1, 2 sub-paragraph 1, 2 sub-paragraph 3, replacing paragraphs 3 and 4 with new wording, and replacing paragraph 6, were all defeated, the voting being 9 for, 19 against, 4 abstentions; 6 for, 18 against, 8 abstentions; 7 for, 19 against, 6 abstentions; 6 for, 21 against, 5 abstentions; 6 for, 19 against, 7 abstentions; and 5 for, 19 against, 8 abstentions respectively.

Turning to the original proposal by the USA and others, now amended by the substitution of the Japanese wording for preambular paragraph 3, Brazil proposed that the third operative paragraph should be voted on separately, and since there was no objection, this was done and the paragraph adopted by 17 votes in favour, 7 against with 8 abstentions. The remainder of the proposed resolution was then voted on as amended, and approved by 19 votes for, 6 against with 7 abstentions. The text as adopted is given in Appendix 1 and the alternative Norwegian proposal was not considered further.

In explaining their votes, Norway, Brazil, Japan, Argentina and Mexico made reference to their legal concerns and rights; Switzerland and Sweden indicated their conservation considerations; and St. Lucia and St. Vincent and the Grenadines spoke of the need for negotiation and consensus.

8.1   Report of the Scientific Committee

Before discussing particular scientific permits, the Scientific Committee reviewed the guidelines established for this procedure, namely the six arising from Schedule paragraph 30, and the four contained in the 1986 Resolution of the Commission. There were some difficulties in interpreting three particular points in the latter, and after discussion the

Commission agreed that it had been intended for the Scientific Committee to report if cold grenade harpoons were used in special permit catches; and that the Resolution just adopted contained new criteria to aid evaluation of whether "proposed catches would facilitate the conduct of the Comprehensive Assessment". No explanation of the term "practically" in the criterion of whether "the objectives of the research are not practically and scientifically feasible through non-lethal research techniques" was forthcoming.

(a) Republic of Korea

The Scientific Committee reviewed the results of an existing scientific permit issued by the Republic of Korea, under which 69 minke whales had been taken last year. Considerable concern was raised by the Committee about the result of research under this permit. Specifically, the Committee agreed that the information collected cannot help with any significant management question, nor is it of any significant value, as only a fraction of the potentially available biological data was collected.

The Scientific Committee requested clarification on the question of whether data reporting requirements/requests in the Schedule were applicable to catches taken under scientific permit. The Chairman of the Commission took the position, without touching on the question of whether or not this information is required, that it would be helpful to the Scientific Committee if Governments did supply these data and they should be encouraged to do so.

A revised permit proposal from the Republic of Korea for a take of 80 minke whales a year from 1987 to 1989, together with independent sightings surveys, in the Sea of Japan-Yellow Sea-East China Sea area, was also reviewed by the Scientific Committee. It expressed concern that there was insufficient precision in both the objectives and methods to be employed (similar to last year's work) to properly evaluate the likely success of either the biological or sightings data gathering, and that the take may further deplete the stock or substantially impede its recovery. It therefore requested that the Commission strongly urges the Government of the Republic of Korea to refrain from issuing the permit until it can fully show that it will materially contribute to the Comprehensive Assessment of this stock.

(b) Iceland

The Scientific Committee reviewed the results obtained from catches taken under special permits by Iceland last year. In 1986 a total of 76 fin whales and 40 sei whales were taken and some 33 studies were underway or proposed. Comments were provided under each of the guidelines for review of special permits. There were differences of opinion on the objectives and contribution of the information, and whether it would facilitate the Comprehensive Assessment. There were excellent arrangements for cooperative investigations and maximum effort was expended to collect and analyse the material. The Scientific Committee was unable to evaluate the effect of the catches of fin and sei whales from these stocks without a better estimate of population abundance.

Work proposed for future years was also discussed. This included a catch of 80 minke whales, which will not be taken until satisfactory arrangements were made regarding the landing of whales at centralised areas and facilities for conducting field research. The fin and sei whale programme will also continue.

(c) Japan

The discussions in the Scientific Committee on a proposed annual research catch of 825 minke whales and 50 sperm whales in the Antarctic as part of a 12 year programme were both lengthy and complicated.

Minke whale samples from Areas IV and V were designed primarily to obtain estimates of age-specific natural mortality, together with information on stock identity, year-to-year variations in biological parameters, feeding ecology and energetics. Some members did not believe the main reason for the Scientific Committee's failure to provide useful advice on replacement yields and the effects of continuing catches from these stocks arose from not having reliable estimates of natural mortality, but rather net recruitment estimates. Concern was also expressed about the feasibility of the methodology proposed to distinguish various effects, and the sampling strategy. Also, the management procedures being developed are robust to imprecision or bias in estimates of population parameters. Other members disputed some or all of these points. The Scientific Committee also considered the Japanese proposal in terms of guidelines for special permits, and presented a range of views.

The proposed take of sperm whales was to investigate the role played by cetaceans in the ecosystem with emphasis on the sperm whale and its food. Secondary objectives include long-term study of reproduction, growth, energetics, stock identity, and pollution. The eight year plan involves a maximum catch of 50 whales in Divisions 4, 5, 6 and 7.

The Scientific Committee agreed that, while important, the role of whales in the ecosystem is not of immediate importance to the Commission's deliberations. Southern sperm whale stocks have not been assessed recently, so no advice could be offered on the effect of the take, but some members noted that the removal of the solitary, large, socially mature bulls in high latitudes may have greater biological significance than the removal of an average sperm whale. The sampling scheme should be carefully considered, and input from cephalopod researchers solicited.

8.2 Action arising

(a) Republic of Korea

In the Commission, the UK and the People's Republic of China expressed their concern on the research carried out by the Republic of Korea.

The Republic of Korea emphasised the difficulties it faced in conducting research, that the proposed research catch is about 10% of the average catch in the last decade, its belief that this will not adversely affect the stock, and its responsibility for conservation in its 200-mile zone. It therefore could not accept any recommendation.

The USA then introduced a proposed resolution recommending that the Republic of Korea refrain from issuing, or revoke, special permits as described in the latter's proposal to the Scientific Committee.

Japan proposed adjournment of the debate on this Agenda Item, to allow time for overnight consultation with its government. Argentina supported this as the Commission's usual practice, and there was no dissent.

On resumption, St. Lucia expressed the view that it would be better to give national institutions an opportunity to improve their methodology or programmes, rather than to ask that governments revoke or refrain from granting permits.

The USA formally proposed its resolution, which was seconded by Switzerland because of the clear and unequivocal advice of the Scientific Committee, and supported by the People's Republic of China. The Republic of Korea then repeated that it could not accept the resolution, and Brazil and Japan while accepting the comments of the Scientific Committee, could not support this action by the Commission on legal grounds.

Argentina requested that the final two paragraphs should be voted on separately, and this was seconded by Brazil but objected to by the USA. On being put to the vote, the proposal was defeated with 12 votes in favour, 13 against and 6 abstentions.

The whole resolution was then adopted by 19 votes for, 3 against with 9 abstentions and appears in Appendix 2.

Brazil explained its position on this and other resolutions to be considered with similar phraseology; it did not object to the substance but only the actions proposed by the Commission. Argentina shared this position.

Norway made a general statement recognising commendable aspects of two other research programmes to be considered, where evaluation of each on its own merits would lead to different conclusions in each case. It was concerned that the Commission was adopting mechanical conclusions, possibly redoing the work of the Scientific Committee, and required a better forum for its discussions.

(b) Iceland

Australia commented on the report of the Scientific Committee, emphasising the points made by those scientists who expressed concerns about allowing this scientific take to continue. It concluded that serious doubts were raised with regard to three of the four criteria established by the 1986 resolution and believed that the Icelandic scientists should submit a revised proposal, and that the Commission should urge the Government of Iceland to refrain from issuing special permits for the taking of fin, sei and minke whales. It therefore tabled a resolution to this effect, which was seconded by New Zealand and supported by Sweden.

Iceland put forward an amendment to this resolution to defer consideration of the report of the Scientific Committee on the research programme of Iceland and any action arising until the 40th Annual Meeting. It argued that the scientific report was not prepared in such a way as to provide all the information necessary for the Commission to take scientific responsibility at this time. Iceland outlined its four-year programme and the North Atlantic sightings survey about to take place. Apart from the legal aspects, it considered the Australian proposal of a destructive nature and with little basis in science.

Norway seconded this amendment, which was defeated with 9 votes in favour, 17 against and 5 abstentions.

Turning to the Australian proposal, Argentina again asked that there be a separate vote on the last two paragraphs, which was agreed.

Before the vote, the UK explained that it was voting solely on the taking of whales and wished to congratulate Iceland on the other parts of the research programme. This position was shared by Denmark, the Federal Republic of Germany, Finland, Switzerland and the Netherlands.

The last two paragraphs of the resolution were then adopted by 16 votes for, 6 against and 9 abstentions.

Brazil expressed its concern over putting a standard paragraph as the conclusion of these resolutions, disregarding elements of merit in the programmes.

The first part of the resolution was then adopted, with 19 votes in favour, 4 against and with 8 abstentions. The full text approved appears in Appendix 3.

(c) Japan

Japan emphasised that its programme has been designed with a genuine scientific aim. A new research institute has been established to implement this long term study. It believed the sample sizes were large enough to give reliable results but would not adversely affect the stocks.

The UK reviewed the comments in the report of the Scientific Committee, and concluded with respect to minke whales that it had not been satisfactorily demonstrated that this large undertaking would produce reliable results, and that sperm whale work was not of essential importance to the Commission at this time. It therefore put forward a resolution recommending the Government of Japan to refrain from issuing the special permit until the uncertainties identified are resolved.

This was seconded by Sweden.

Japan pointed out that a number of the points expounded by the UK were arguable, and the only way to reduce uncertainty in knowledge of the stocks is by carrying out research. It noted that of 16 countries consistently voting for these resolutions, 7 did not attend the Scientific Committee, and another 7 did not submit Progress Reports on research. It appealed for support for scientific advance and on legal grounds.

Japan then put forward an amendment to the UK resolution, deferring consideration and any action until the 40th Annual Meeting.

This was seconded by the Republic of Korea, Norway, Iceland and the USSR, the latter two recognising the serious intent of the research over the future years.

Switzerland asked if the research would also be deferred if the discussion was put off to next year, and Japan responded that as it would lose the funding available now it would proceed. Antigua and Barbuda suggested referring the mathematical problems involved to independent experts for judgement, and Japan stated that it was open to any constructive suggestions, and was already taking such advice. The People's Republic of China believed the sample sizes proposed to be too large; the Scientific Committee should establish the catch size necessary.

The Japanese amendment to defer consideration was defeated by 11 votes for to 16 against, with 4 abstentions.

It was agreed, on the proposal of Argentina, to vote on the last two paragraphs of the UK proposed resolution separately, and these were adopted with 16 votes in favour, 9 against and 6 abstentions. The remainder of the text was then adopted by 18 votes for, 8 against with 5 abstentions. The full text is given in Appendix 4.

St. Lucia and Brazil explained their votes on the grounds of seeking improvements in the research programmes and recognising their merits. Mexico also pointed out its concern with the potential effects on some of the stocks, and appealed for international cooperation. Japan expressed its dismay and disappointment at the decisions being taken.

(d) General

Iceland put forward a proposal designed to be one way out of the legal dispute, by setting up a group of legal experts to consider if the resolutions adopted are consistent with the Convention, and to establish a third-party settlement procedure if there is still disagreement. This was seconded by Norway and Mexico, and supported by Japan.

The USA opposed the proposal, arguing that the legal analysis turns on commonly understood words and is not esoteric. There will always be disagreement among legal experts, so that the Commission would be abdicating responsibility to a third party.

Switzerland and Brazil suggested that this issue could be considered by the Working Group established to examine questions related to the Convention. Following further discussion involving these countries, St. Lucia and Australia, on the question of whether the issue could be referred to the Working Group if the proposal failed at this meeting, the Icelandic proposal was put to the vote and defeated, with 6 votes in favour, 17 against and 6 abstentions.

. . .

Appendix 1

RESOLUTION ON SCIENTIFIC RESEARCH PROGRAMMES

Whereas the International Whaling Commission adopted under Article V of the Convention and incorporated in paragraph 10(e) of the Schedule a regulation providing that catch limits for the killing for commercial purposes of whales from all stocks for the 1986 coastal and the 1985/86 pelagic seasons and thereafter shall be zero, this provision to be kept under review based on the best scientific advice, the Commission being required by 1990 at the latest to undertake a comprehensive assessment of the effects of this decision on whale stocks; and

Whereas Article VI of the Convention provides that the Commission may make recommendations to Contracting Governments on any matters which relate to whales or whaling and in accordance with Article VI of the Commission adopted in 1986 a Resolution on Special Permits for Scientific Research (IWC/38/28) which remains in effect; and

Whereas Article VIII of the Convention provides that a Contracting Government may grant to any of its nationals a special permit authorizing that national to kill, take and treat whales for purposes of scientific research, and that such killing, taking and treating of whales in accordance with the provisions of this Article shall be exempt from the operation of the Convention; and

Whereas paragraph 30 of the Schedule to the Convention provides for the Scientific Committee to review all proposed special permits to be issued by Contracting Governments and research programs under existing special permits that involve the killing, taking, or treating of whales; and

Whereas the Commission recognises that the conduct of the comprehensive assessment as referenced in paragraph 10(e) of the Schedule to the Convention is considered of highest priority for the Commission while such paragraph is applicable;

Now, Therefore, **the Commission,** in order to safeguard and promote its international whale conservation program and in furtherance of the objectives expressed in paragraph 10(e) of the Schedule;

Requests that the Scientific Committee annually review all research programs involving the killing of whales under special permits and report their views on whether the programs under an existing or proposed special permit at least satisfy the following criteria in addition to such guidelines as may be applicable, including the criteria specified in the Resolution adopted in 1986 on Special Permits for Scientific Research (IWC/38/28):

(1) The research addresses a question or questions that should be answered in order to conduct the comprehensive assessment or to meet other critically important research needs;

(2) The research can be conducted without adversely affecting the overall status and trends of the stock in question or the success of the comprehensive assessment of such stock;

(3) The research addresses a question or questions that cannot be answered by analysis of existing data and/or use of non-lethal research techniques; and

(4) The research is likely to yield results leading to reliable answers to the question or questions being addressed.

Agrees to review, annually, beginning with the 39th IWC meeting, the report of the Scientific Committee regarding special permits involving the killing of whales.

Agrees, should an ongoing or proposed research program not satisfy the criteria specified in the Resolution adopted in 1986 on Special Permits for Scientific Research (IWC/38/28) and, additionally, beginning at the 40th IWC meeting, the above criteria in the view of the Commission, to so notify the Contracting Government concerned.

Recommends that Contracting Governments, in providing the Secretary with proposed special permits and in submitting reports on programs under special permits to the Scientific Committee for review, specify how each proposed special permit or program satisfies each of the above criteria in addition to such guidelines as may be applicable.

Recommends that Contracting Governments, in the exercise of their Sovereign rights, refrain from issuing or revoke, permits to its nationals that the Commission, taking into account the comments of the Scientific Committee, considers do not satisfy each of the criteria specified above and therefore are not consistent with the Commission's conservation policy.

Appendix 2

RESOLUTION ON REPUBLIC OF KOREA'S PROPOSAL FOR SPECIAL PERMITS

Whereas the International Whaling Commission adopted in 1986 a Resolution on Special Permits for Scientific Research (IWC/38/28);

Whereas the Commission has considered the Report of the Scientific Committee (IWC/39/4) concerning the research programmes to be conducted under special permits;

Whereas the Commission takes cognizance of Article VIII of the International Convention for the Regulation of Whaling, under which the granting by any Contracting Government to its nationals of a special permit authorising the killing, taking or treatment of whales for purposes of scientific research remains the responsibility of each Contracting Government, exercising its sovereign rights in respect of maritime areas under its jurisdiction and the freedom of the high seas;

Now, Therefore, **the Commission**

Adopts the view that the proposed take of Sea of Japan-Yellow Sea-East China Sea stock of minke whales under scientific permit by the Government of the Republic of Korea, as described in SC/39/O 5, does not satisfy the criteria set forth in the 1986 Resolution on Special Permits for Scientific Research in that it has not contributed information which will answer any significant management questions and the proposed take will not materially facilitate the conduct of the Comprehensive Assessment;

Requests the Secretary to so notify the Government of the Republic of Korea; and

Recommends to the Government of the Republic of Korea that it refrain from issuing, or revoke, special permits to its nationals for the conduct of the research programme described in SC/39/O 5.

Appendix 3

RESOLUTION ON THE ICELANDIC PROPOSAL FOR SCIENTIFIC CATCHES

Whereas the International Whaling Commission adopted in 1986 a Resolution on Special Permits for Scientific Research (IWC/38/28);

Whereas the Commission has considered the Report of the Scientific Committee (IWC/39/4) concerning the research programs to be conducted under special permits; and it is recognised that the sighting survey element of the Icelandic research program is acceptable and commendable.

Whereas the Commission takes cognizance of Article VIII of the International Convention for the Regulation of Whaling, under which the granting by any Contracting Government to its nationals of a special permit authorizing the killing, taking or treatment of whales for purposes of scientific research remains the responsibility of each Contracting Government, exercising its sovereign rights in respect of maritime areas under its jurisdiction and freedom of the high seas;

Now, Therefore, **the Commission**

Adopts the view that the proposed take of fin, sei, and minke whales under special permit as described in SC/37/O 20 and as modified in SC/38/Prog. Rep. Iceland does not fully satisfy the criteria set forth in the 1986 Resolution on Special Permits for Scientific Research.

Recommends that the Government of Iceland revoke and refrain from issuing special permits to its nationals for the conduct of the research program described in SC/37/O 20 and as modified SC/38/Prog. Rep. Iceland until the uncertainties identified in the Scientific Committee Report (IWC/39/4) have been resolved to the satisfaction of the Scientific Committee.

Requests the Secretary to notify the Government of Iceland accordingly.

Appendix 4

RESOLUTION ON JAPANESE PROPOSAL FOR SPECIAL PERMITS

Whereas the International Whaling Commission adopted in 1986 a Resolution on Special Permits for Scientific Research (IWC/38/28);

Whereas the Commission has considered the Report of the Scientific Committee (IWC/39/4) concerning the research programs to be conducted under special permits;

Whereas the Commission takes cognizance of Article VIII of the International Convention for the Regulation of Whaling, under which the granting by any Contracting Government to its nationals of a special permit authorizing the killing, taking or treatment of whales for the purposes of scientific research remains the responsibility of each Contracting Government, exercising its Sovereign rights in respect of maritime areas under its jurisdiction and freedom of the high seas;

Now, Therefore, **the Commission**

Adopts the view that the proposed take of Southern Hemisphere Minke Whales and Sperm Whales under the proposed research program as described in SC/39/O 4 does not satisfy the criteria set out in the 1986 Resolution on Special Permits for Scientific Research in that the proposed research does not appear, on present information, to be structured so as to contribute information essential for rational management of the stock and that the proposed take will not, at least at this stage, materially facilitate the Comprehensive Assessment; and

Requests the Secretary so to notify the Government of Japan; and

Recommends the Government of Japan to refrain from issuing special permits to its nationals for the taking of such whales under the research program described in SC/39/O 4 until such time as the Scientific Committee is able to resolve the serious uncertainties identified in its discussion as to the capability of the research methods proposed to contribute sufficiently reliable results needed for the Comprehensive Assessment or for other critically important research needs.

- - - - -

Additional References

Migratory Species in International Instruments. International Union for the Conservation of Nature (IUCN) Environmental Policy and Law Occasional Paper, No.2.

Compendium of National Legislation on the Conservation of Marine Mammals. FAO Publication, 1986.

- - - - -

XII

MARINE SCIENTIFIC RESEARCH

1

International Co-operation and The Consent Régime

Intergovernmental Oceanographic Commission   IOC/EC-XIX/3
Executive Council
Report of the 19th Session, 1986   Extract

. . .

7.3   Measures to Enhance the Role and Efficiency of the Commission
. . .

321.   . . .The Commission has taken ten years or more to consider amendments to its Statutes to adapt them to the realities of the Commission's role and functions and to the evolution of international marine affairs. Various Articles have been discussed in detail at the Tenth, Eleventh and Thirteenth Sessions of the Assembly and at the Eighth, Eleventh, Twelfth and Fourteenth Sessions of the Executive Council, besides the present one, as well as intensively by two specialized subsidiary bodies: the Working Group on the Future Role and Functions of the Commission, from 1977 to 1978, and the *ad hoc* Task Team to Study the Implications, for the Commission, of the UN Convention on the Law of the Sea, and the New Ocean Régime, from 1980 to 1984.

322.   At the Preparatory Meeting, amendments to the following Articles were agreed by consensus: Article 1, paragraphs 1 and 2; Article 2, paragraph 1, new sub-paragraphs (f), (g), (k), (l) and (m); Article 2, paragraphs 2 and 3; Article 3; Article 4, paragraph 3; Article 5, paragraph 4, and Article 9, paragraph 1; these amendments are given to Annex 1 of Resolution EC-XIX.8.

323.   The Articles on which there was no consensus as to the proposed amendments are given in Annex 2 of Resolution EC-XIX.8. For Article 2, paragraph 1, new sub-paragraph (j), four versions (identified as A, B, C and D) were submitted to the Executive Council for consideration, and for Article 10, paragraph 3, two versions . . . were put forward . . .

324.   **The Executive Council** . . . *decided that* . . . it would . . . consider only amendments (proposed at the Preparatory Meeting) to the Proposed Text for each Article concerned given in Document IOC/EC-XIX/12 . . .
. . .

Article 2, paragraph 3

346.   The Proposed Text was intended to simplify the wording and thus clarify the meaning. The option to restrict it, by limiting it to the Commission, was agreed at the Preparatory Meeting. It constitutes a safeguard to the IOC and to the Member States whose individual position on the nature or extent of the jurisdiction of coastal States, generally or particularly, are not compromised by Article 2 as a whole.

347.   **The Executive Council** *approved* the Proposed Text with the above-mentioned restriction to the Commission.

   . . .

Article 9, paragraph 1

   . . .

358.   **The Executive Council** *recognized* that no agreement on amendments to Article 2, paragraph 1, new sub-paragraph (j), or on Article 10, paragraph 3 could be achieved at the Preparatory Meeting. In the Proposed Text for new sub-paragraph (j) of Article 2, paragraph 1, three new but related ideas are embodied: to include as a function of the IOC the promotion of the "application of the results" of scientific investigation to the benefit of all mankind; then, to achieve this purpose, to facilitate co-operation amongst the Member States; and finally, in carrying out the two aforementioned activities, to take into account the interests and rights of States as far as research in zones under their jurisdiction is concerned. These rights, together with the related duties, are defined in the UN Convention on the Law of the Sea. The main difficulty that arose in the Preparatory Meeting had to do with the implications, of the word "facilitate" (and therefore IOC's role) and the way in which States rights relating thereto should be seen or could be interpreted.

359.   The Delegate of Brazil explained that his opposition to the Proposed Text was based on the idea, implied in this Text, that the IOC could act as an intermediary to facilitate procedures applicable to the authorization of scientific research in zones under national jurisdiction. This authorization is a prerogative of the Member State concerned. He also wished to avoid any text in the Statutes of the Commission that could be construed as attempting to interpret the Articles of the UN Convention on the Law of the Sea. In a spirit of co-operation, he proposed replacing "taking into account" by "subject to". He recognized that, unfortunately, this proposal, although supported by several Delegations, did not produce a consensus. He believed that the Brazilian position is quite compatible with the UN Convention on the Law of the Sea and is inspired by concern to protect the rights of coastal States in respect of marine scientific research. The Delegate thus supported proposal B . . .

360.   The Delegate of Argentina stated that the Articles of the UN Convention on the Law of the Sea on matters of interest to the IOC should prevail and guide any activity in this field, and that any amendments to the Statutes of the IOC should not imply in any way a juridical interpretation of the Articles of that Convention. . . . He was also in favour of incorporating the word "coastal" to qualify the word "States" as in the present text.

361.   This latter proposal was supported by the Delegates of Brazil, Chile, Greece, Peru and Venezuela.

362.   Some Delegates pointed out that the term "coastal" was limiting, since all States had rights and interests in this field. They could consider inclusion of the word "coastal" provided the word "duties", identified in the Convention, was added to the phrase "rights and interests", thus preserving the rights and interests of all States.

363.   The Delegate of Bulgaria reminded the Executive Council that Article 2, paragraph 1, new sub-paragraph (j) was not the place to take up questions of jurisdiction. Nor could the IOC adopt a position on matters of jurisdiction . . . He was ready to support proposals A . . . or C . . . but not B . . . or even D . . .

364.   The Delegate of the USSR supported this view, stressing his firm rejection of proposal B.

365.   The Delegate of the USA declared his preference for proposal D.

366.   The Delegate of Mexico . . . stressed his belief that the Commission's Statutes should be amended in the light of the UN Convention on the Law of the Sea. In particular, he noted that the present Article 2, paragraph 1, new sub-paragraph (j) was quite obviously obsolete and a revised version . . . needs to be negotiated with a view to its adoption by the Assembly.

367.   The Delegate of the Federal Republic of Germany considered the facilitation of international co-operation in marine sciences as one of the key tasks of IOC. He wanted to see this properly reflected in the Statutes.

368.   The Observer of the Netherlands suggested that the second part . . . presents all kinds of problems, for example: ". . . taking into account **all** interests . . ." would seem to be impossible; not only rights and interests of States but also **obligations** should be included; and the rights and interests of States other than coastal States, including geographically disadvantaged States, would have to be mentioned as well.

     . . .

372.   **The Executive Council** *noted* that no agreement could be reached on Article 2, paragraph 2, new sub-paragraph (j) . . .

     . . .

Annex II

Resolution EC-XIX.8

AMENDMENTS TO THE IOC STATUTES

. . .

Annex 2 to Resolution EC-XIX.8

PROPOSED TEXTS FOR ARTICLES FOR WHICH THE PREPARATORY
MEETING COULD NOT REACH CONSENSUS

ARTICLE 2, PARAGRAPH 1, NEW SUB-PARAGRAPH (j)

Four proposals (A, B, C, D) are submitted . . .

A. **Proposed text**	**Present text**
"(j) promote scientific investigation of the oceans **and application of the results thereof** for the benefit of all mankind **and facilitate, to this end, co-operation amongst the Member States,** taking into account all interests and rights of States **in respect of marine** scientific	"(j) promote freedom of scientific investigation of the oceans for the benefits of all mankind taking into account all interests and rights of coastal States concerning

research in zones under their
jurisdiction."

scientific research in the
zones under their jurisdiction."

B.   Proposed text

"(j)   promote scientific investigation of
the oceans **and application of the
results thereof** for the benefit of all mankind **and facilitate, to this end, co-operation amongst
Member States, subject to** all interests and rights
of States **in respect of marine** scientific
research in zones under their jurisdiction."

C.   Proposed text

"(j)   promote scientific investigation of the
oceans **and application of the results
thereof** for the benefit of all mankind **and
facilitate, to this end, co-operation
amongst the Member States, respecting** all
interests and rights of States **in respect
of marine** scientific research in zones
under their jurisdiction."

D.   Proposed text

"(j)   promote scientific investigation of the oceans
and application of the results thereof for the benefit
of all mankind **and facilitate, to this end, co-operation
amongst the Member States.**"

. . .

- - - - -

Intergovernmental Oceanographic Commission   SC/MD/86
Report of the 14th Session of the Assembly, 1987   Extract

. . .

10.   Enhancing the Role of the Commission

10.1   AMENDMENTS TO THE IOC STATUTES

520.   . . . The Council had not, however, been able to agree on revised texts for Article 2,
paragraph 1, new sub-paragraph (j) . . . It had therefore urged the Member States concerned
to consult among themselves during the intersessional period with a view to arriving at agreed
amendments . . .

. . .

528.   **The Assembly** . . . *approved* in principle, without further discussion, all amendments that had been approved by the Executive Council, through Resolution EC-XIX.8 . . . *It noted* that two general questions of style and/or semantics were agreed by the *ad hoc* Sessional Drafting Group: (i) that the term "oceans" should be understood (without being expressed formally in the Statutes) as a generic term including all seas with a marine connection to the oceans (in the geographical sense); and (ii) that any reference to "services" (understood as services provided or promoted by the Commission) should be rendered throughout the Statutes as "ocean services".

   . . .

539.   In view of the difficulty of finding a compromise text to Article 2, paragraph 1, new sub-paragraph (j), yet recognizing that there was a considerable will amongst the Delegates to arrive at a consensus thereon, **the Assembly** *decided* to create another *ad hoc* Sessional Drafting Group on Proposed Amendments to Article 2, paragraph 1, new sub-paragraph (j), . . .

   . . .

541.   In the meeting of the *ad hoc* Sessional Drafting Group, the Delegate of Brazil, on behalf of Mexico and other countries that had worked hard to produce a compromise text, defined three basic elements to the Proposed Text: (i) the function of the IOC to promote scientific research of the oceans and (as a new element relative to the present Statutes) the application of the results thereof; (ii) the modalities - how to assist the Member States; (iii) protection of the rights of coastal States. In his view, the basic text does not contradict the UN Convention on the Law of the Sea.

   . . .

543.   The Delegate of the USA explained the basis of his country's difficulties with the text proposed by Mexico and Brazil. First, the Statutes must be directed to serving the Commission, and should not be amended simply to achieve particular legal objectives. The changes proposed to the Statutes in general at this time are designed to expand the range of functions (e.g. provide ocean services, standards, etc.) or to improve them. The proposed text for Article 2 (1) (j) represents a major change for which there has not been much time for study. . . . He indicated that it is essential to ensure that this amendment is carefully worded so that it does not, when adopted, contradict the UN Convention on the Law of the Sea. The main criteria of amendment should be to make it easier for the Commission to do its work better. His specific objections to the proposed text were: (i) it deletes any reference to freedom of research; (ii) it is not clear what "application of results" means but this change is acceptable if the meaning is clarified in the Summary Report of this Session of the Assembly; (iii) the middle part on modalities could be interpreted restrictively; modalities change and a more rapid mechanism than amendments to the Statutes should be used (e.g., Resolutions); (iv) it is not clear what is to be meant by the term "régime" in the last point of the basic text - it could be interpreted to refer to Law of the Sea rules, customary international law, national definitions or some other definition.

544.   Some Delegates . . . indicated that the rights of all IOC Member States were protected by paragraph 3 of Article 2 and suggested the possibility of transferring the ideas in the last sentence of the basic text of 2 (1)(j) to there. Two Delegates suggested that a reworked Article 2 (3) could be made applicable to all Articles by creating a new final Article out of Article 2(3) as modified. Several Delegates pointed out that the text would be a compromise text and could not satisfy all Member States in every respect. They stressed the importance of not

establishing two régimes ("UNCLOS" and "IOC") for the conduct of marine scientific research in zones under national jurisdiction.

545.   ... The Delegates of Mexico and Brazil drafted an amended text which was accepted by consensus in the Sessional Drafting Group.

546.   **The Assembly** *welcomed* the constructive spirit that had prevailed in the *ad hoc* Sessional Drafting Group *and recognized* that the compromise text proposed could not fully satisfy all the preferences of all Member States.

547.   **The Assembly** *approved* in principle the text proposed . . .

548.   The Delegate of Turkey informed the Assembly that it was his country's considered opinion that the agreed text for Article 2, paragraph 1, new sub-paragraph (j) solely reflects and refers to the rules of customary international law.

549.   The Delegate of the United Kingdom asked to be placed on the record the UK's view that . . . it was not his country's intention to restrict in any way the availability of the oceans for research and other uses. So far as the United Kingdom was concerned, the new text would be considered as being without prejudice to the provisions of other agreements.

   . . .

552.   **The Assembly** *adopted* Resolution XIV-19, with the approved amendments to the Statutes in the Annex to this Resolution.

   . . .

Annex II

Resolution XIV-19

PROPOSED AMENDMENTS OF THE STATUTES OF THE COMMISSION

The Intergovernmental Oceanographic Commission,

Recalling

   (i)   the historic decision of Unesco to establish the Commission in 1960,
   (ii)   the increased use of the oceans and their resources, the great developments in marine science and technology, and particularly international co-operative marine science activities, since 1970, when the present Statutes of the Commission were amended, and then adopted, by the General Conference of Unesco,
   (iii)   the considerable growth in the number of IOC Member States, from 40 in 1961 to 115 in 1987, most of the newer Member States being developing countries,
   (iv)   the emergence of a new ocean régime, inspired by the UN Convention on the Law of the Sea, and reflected widely in national legislation and the practice of States,
   (v)   the increased demands of Member States on the Commission which have enhanced its role in the UN system and moulded its programmes accordingly, leading to the emergence of new areas of marine scientific endeavour, of ocean observing systems and ocean services, and
   (vi)   greatly increased requirements for the relevant training, education and mutual assistance in the marine sciences,

. . .

Approves the amendments contained in the Annex attached hereto;

Requests the General Conference of Unesco to amend the Commission's Statutes (Articles 1, 2, 3, 4, 5, 9 and 10) in accordance with the texts contained in the Annex attached hereto, pursuant to Article 13 of the present Statutes.

Annex

. . .

(The annex to the document contained the text which was subsequently
approved by the Unesco General Conference: see next extract)

- - - - -

UNESCO General Conference   24 C/133
Legal Committee, November 1987   Extract

Amendment to the Statutes of the
Intergovernmental Oceanographic Commission (IOC)

1.   The Legal Committee examined proposed amendments to Articles 1, 2, 3, 4, 5, 9 and 10 of the Statutes of the Intergovernmental Oceanographic Commission submitted by the IOC Assembly, in document 24 C/101.

2.   The proposed amendments were considered admissible by the Legal Committee.
    . . .

General debate

4.   The Chairman of the Legal Committee reminded the Committee that, in view of the fact that the proposed changes had been considered at great length by the Commission, it was not necessary for the Legal Committee to go into the nature of the amendments in detail; rather, it should ensure that the proposed amendments were compatible with the Unesco Constitution.
    . . .

12.   One member suggested that, in Article 2, paragraph 1(j), the words "on request" were not necessary, since the text referred to Member States "wishing to co-operate to these ends"; nor were the words "subject to" required, since activities under this subparagraph need only be "in accordance with international law". One member suggested the term "conventional international law". These suggestions were not supported by others.

13.   Some members pointed out that the proposed text had been arrived at only after long consideration and represented an acceptable compromise on such a complex subject.

14.   At the conclusion of the debate, the Committee, considering that the proposed amendments had been submitted to the General Conference according to the procedures stipulated in Article 13 of the Statutes of the Commission and that there was no legal obstacle to their adoption, decided to submit the following resolution to the General Conference for

adoption in the event of its deciding to endorse the recommendation of the Commission regarding these amendments:

The General Conference,

Having examined the amendments to the Statutes of the Intergovernmental Ocean-ographic Commission (IOC) recommended by the fourteenth session of the IOC Assembly (24 C/101, Part II), and *taken note* of the report of the Legal Committee thereon (document 24 C/133),

Decides to amend the Statutes of the Intergovernmental Oceanographic Commission, as follows:

STATUTES OF THE IOC
(the bold text indicates the amendments)

AMENDED TEXT

ARTICLE 1
Paragraph 1

"(a)   The Intergovernmental Oceanographic Commission, hereafter called the Commission, is established **as a body with functional autonomy** within the United Nations Educational, Scientific and Cultural Organization.

(b)   **It guides the conception and follows the implementation of its programme as approved by the General Conference in the framework of the latter's adopted budget.**"

Paragraph 2

"The purpose of the Commission is to promote marine scientific investigations **and related ocean services**, with a view to learning more about the nature and resources of the oceans through the concerted action of its members."

Paragraph 3
(As in previous Statutes)

ARTICLE 2
Paragraph 1
Sub-paragraph (a)
(As in previous Statutes)

New sub-paragraph (b)

"(b)   Develop, recommend and co-ordinate international programmes for scientific investiga-tion of the oceans and related **ocean** services which call for concerted action by its members;"

New sub-paragraph (c)

"(c)　Develop, recommend and co-ordinate with interested international organizations, international programmes for scientific investigation of the oceans and related **ocean** services which call for concerted action with interested organizations;"

New sub-paragraph (d)
(As in previous Statutes)

New sub-paragraph (e)
(As in previous Statutes)

New sub-paragraph (f)

"(f)　**Promote and co-ordinate the development and transfer of marine science and its technology, particularly to developing countries;"**

New sub-paragraph (g)

"(g)　Make recommendations to strengthen education and training in marine science and its technology, **and promote relevant projects in these fields as components of each of its programmes;"**

New sub-paragraph (h)
(Sub-paragraph (g) of previous Statutes)

New sub-paragraph (i)
(Sub-paragraph (h) of previous Statutes)

New sub-paragraph (j)

"(j)　Promote scientific investigation of the oceans **and application of the results thereof** for the benefit of all mankind, **and assist, on request, Member States wishing to co-operate to these ends. Activities undertaken under this sub-paragraph shall be subject, in accordance with international law, to the régime for marine** scientific research in zones under **national jurisdiction;"**

New sub-paragraph (k)

"(k)　**Promote, plan and co-ordinate observing and monitoring systems, on the properties and quality of the marine environment, as well as the preparation and dissemination of processed oceanographic data and information, and of assessment studies;"**

New sub-paragraph (l)

"(l)　**Promote, recommend and co-ordinate, with international organizations, as appropriate, the development of standards, reference materials and nomenclature for use in marine science and related ocean services;"**

New sub-paragraph (m)

"(m) **Undertake, as appropriate, any other action compatible with its purpose and functions concerning the scientific investigation of the ocean and its interfaces.**"

Paragraph 2

"The Commission, in carrying out its functions, shall **take into account** the special needs and interests of developing countries, including in particular the need to further the capabilities of these countries in marine science and technology."

Paragraph 3

"Nothing in this Article shall **imply** the **adoption** of a position **by the Commission** regarding the nature or extent of the jurisdiction of coastal States in general or of any coastal State in particular."

ARTICLE 3

"1.   The Commission shall give due attention to supporting the objectives of the international organizations with which it collaborates. On the other hand, the Commission may request these organizations to take its requirements into account in planning and executing their own programmes."

"2.   **The Commission may act also as a joint specialized mechanism of the organizations of the United Nations system that have agreed to use the Commission** for discharging certain of their responsibilities in the fields of marine science **and ocean services, and have agreed accordingly to sustain the work of the Commission.**"

ARTICLE 4

(Paragraph 1 and Paragraph 2 of the previous Statutes)

"3.   Any Member **State** of the Commission may withdraw from it by giving notice of its intention to do so to the Director-General of Unesco. **The date of such notice shall be that of its receipt by the Director-General.** The notice shall take effect **on the first day of the next ordinary session of the Assembly following the date of notice of withdrawal if the notice is given more than one year before the first day of said session; if the notice of withdrawal is given less than one year before the first day of the said session, it shall take effect one year after the date of notice of withdrawal.**"

(Paragraph 4 and Paragraph 5 of the previous Statutes)

ARTICLE 5

(Paragraph 1, Paragraph 2, and Paragraph 3 of the previous Statutes)

"4.   During the course of each ordinary session, the Assembly, taking into account the principles of geographical distribution, shall elect:

(a)   A Chairman and four Vice-Chairmen who shall be the officers of the Commission, its Assembly and its Executive Council;

(b)   **A number of Member States to the Executive Council, which number shall not exceed one quarter of the Member States of the Commission; each Member State so elected shall designate its representative on the Executive Council."**

(Paragraph 5 and Paragraph 6 of the previous Statutes)

. . .

ARTICLE 9
Paragraph 1

"1.   With due regard to the applicable Staff Regulations and Rules of the United Nations Educational, Scientific and Cultural Organization, the Secretariat of the Commission shall consist of **a Secretary and such other staff as may be necessary,** provided by the United Nations Educational, Scientific and Cultural Organization, as well as such personnel as may be provided, at their expense, by the United Nations, the Food and Agriculture Organization of the United Nations, the World Meteorological Organization and the **International Maritime** Organization and other organizations of the United Nations system."

Paragraph 2
(As in previous Statutes)

ARTICLE 10
Paragraph 1
(As in previous Statutes)

Paragraph 2

"2.   The expenditure of the Commission shall be financed from funds appropriated for this purpose by the General Conference of Unesco, **from contributions by Member States of the Commission that are not Member States of Unesco,** as well as from such additional resources as may be made available by other organizations of the United Nations system and by Member States, and from other sources."

(Paragraph 3 as in previous Statutes)

- - - - -

Intergovernmental Oceanographic Commission   SC/MD/86
Report of the 14th Session of the Assembly, 1987   Extract

1.   Opening

. . .

21.   [The Special Representative of the Secretary-General of the United Nations for the Law of the Sea] recalled that the United Nations Secretariat has for years maintained a very close

and fruitful working relationship with the Commission. However, it was the first time that he had personally been able to attend a Session of the Assembly. He particularly welcomed this in view of the significant progress in the acceptance by the international community of the new régime of the ocean and the importance of the challenges confronting the organizations and bodies of the United Nations system in assisting States to implement the provisions of the UN Convention on the Law of the Sea. The Convention not only establishes the legal framework for all activities in the marine environment but also represents one of the most important conflict-prevention measures adopted by the international community.

22.   The Convention recognizes that all activities in ocean space are inter-related, since activities of one kind impact on other activities in the marine environment. This calls for an integrated system of ocean management by States.

23.   The Convention calls for co-operation among all States in its implementation; such co-operation contributes not only to their economic development and the enhancement of the quality of life of their people, but also to the maintenance of peace and security among nations.

24.   Knowledge and information derived from marine scientific research play a key role in the successful management of the ocean, and are a prerequisite for rational resource exploitation and control of marine pollution. Since more than 90 per cent of the living resources and all of the presently exploitable non-living resources of the oceans are to be found in the Exclusive Economic Zones of Member States, marine scientific research is of particular importance to the development of these Zones.

25.   The organizations and bodies within the United Nations system have a collective responsibility in matters relating to the oceans and each institution in its own field of competence has to fulfil part of this responsibility.

26.   Beyond its value as a means for increasing mankind's understanding of the global environment, marine scientific research provides the necessary data and information on which the uses of the sea and its resources are based. It is with this awareness that Part XIII of the Convention dealing with Marine Scientific Research stresses the need for the scientific community to obtain authorization from the coastal State whenever research in its Exclusive Economic Zone or its continental shelf is envisaged.

27.   The Under-Secretary-General informed the Assembly that his Office is co-operating closely with the Commission in addressing this subject jointly. This co-operation will lead to the convening of a first workshop to analyse the practice of States and determine the major problems that exist at this time and those that may evolve in the future in this regard. His Office is also co-operating closely in the publication of documents containing a compilation of all national legislation relating to marine scientific research.

28.   Another area where the Law of the Sea Secretariat intends to co-operate closely with the Commission is in the study of the concept and possible modalities of promoting national and regional marine scientific research and technological centres; this is an area where, again, our respective activities can complement each other for the benefit of our Member States.

29.   The Under-Secretary-General recalled that the fundamental objective of the United Nations and the organizations within the system is to ensure a coherent approach to the

implementation of the new régime and to provide assistance to all Member States in order for them to maximize the benefits to be derived from the ocean.

. . .

5.   OCEAN SCIENCES

. . .

5.4   Ocean dynamics and climate

. . .

152.   Funding is a continuing problem, but not the only one; greater progress could be made if a spirit of co-operation could be disseminated through the organizational hierarchies of Member States. Investigators are still stymied in their attempts to obtain data that are known to exist and, for one reason or another, kept from the archives and exchange systems. Scientists planning equipment installation or research cruises continue to run into difficulty in obtaining permission to operate in waters under national jurisdiction, to obtain visas, or to receive or trans-ship equipment and supplies. One step toward solving the problem is the identification of an IOC-WMO TOGA [Tropical Oceans and Global Atmosphere] contact in each Member State for TOGA matters. The Commission may wish to encourage its Member States to adopt internal measures so that the person designated as the TOGA contact would be in a position to assist effectively in solving relevant problems at the national level. Unless resolved, these problems will be multiplied many times over when WOCE [World Ocean Circulation Experiment] moves from the conceptual phase to the operational phase, since WOCE will involve more ships and more nations than those in TOGA, and will require a higher degree of co-ordination of major resources.

153.   The ability of Member States to participate in, and derive benefits from, the WCRP [World Climate Research Programme] is linked directly to their ability to develop a cadre of scientists specially trained in ocean/climate research. Even in the developed nations, the number of scientists with interest in climate modelling needs to be increased substantially. . . .

. . .

155.   The President of SCOR [Scientific Committee on Oceanic Research] also drew attention to the need to ensure that research vessels involved in these international programmes will be able to operate not only in the open ocean, but in coastal areas as well. Access to maritime zones under national jurisdiction will be needed for observational purposes, while access to ports is necessary for the exchange of ship personnel and equipment. SCOR looks to IOC as the most appropriate inter-governmental organization to consider this particular question and to assume the responsibility for ensuring the necessary international co-operation.

. . .

162.   The Delegates of Canada, France, Poland, the Federal Republic of Germany and the USA emphasized the need to strengthen the role of IOC in facilitating access to marine areas under national jurisdiction by research vessels participating in, or contributing to the WCRP, as well as in transfrontier shipment of equipment and in making data from those zones available.

163.   Some other delegations (Argentina, Brazil, Greece and Mexico) expressed their disagreement with the previous view, stressing that it was not within the competence of IOC to

facilitate access to marine areas under national jurisdiction by research vessels. They stressed that these activities should remain subject to the régime for marine scientific research in zones under national jurisdiction.

164.   A large number of Delegates supported the conclusions of the Technical Committee for Ocean Processes and Climate that the present arrangements for international scientific planning and intergovernmental co-ordination for TOGA are satisfactory and provide a good basis for co-ordination between IOC, SCOR and WMO.

. . .

177.   **The Assembly** *agreed* that it is premature to consider a formal intergovernmental mechanism for co-ordination of WOCE and that this matter could be discussed at the time of the International WOCE Scientific Conference in 1988.

. . .

181.   **The Assembly** *decided* to intensify efforts to assist developing countries so that they could not only participate actively in observational components of the WCRP, but also increase the ability of their scientists to contribute to scientific investigations and to applications of the results to national socio-economic development. **It** *called on* the Unesco Division of Marine Sciences to join in this effort.   **It** *requested* the Joint SCOR-IOC Committee on Climatic Changes and the Ocean to prepare a report on new ocean-observing techniques with a view to assisting or enhancing the participation of developing countries in the WCRP.

. . .

8.   CO-OPERATION WITH OTHER ORGANIZATIONS
OF THE UN SYSTEM AND OTHER BODIES

. . .

8.2   Enhancing co-operation between the IOC and the Unesco
Division of Marine Sciences

. . .

455.   One Delegate emphasized that training and education can greatly contribute to facilitating the transfer of knowledge and technology.   Another Delegate described his country's approach to international training for research which, in his view, should have four phases: joint planning of the research, joint collection of the data, joint processing of the data, and joint publication of the research results.

456.   Some Delegates attached considerable importance to strengthening inter-governmental co-operation to enhance marine science capabilities through mutual assistance amongst the Member States. Although bilateral co-operation may be more suitable for industrialized countries, because of their level of development, this form of co-operation may not necessarily be equally suitable for developing countries where multilateral arrangements offer more appropriate opportunities for the development of the required capabilities for marine research, often within the framework of a commonly agreed scientific programme. This is an area where IOC and its regional subsidiary bodies could play a major role.

. . .

463.   Several Delegates drew the attention of the Assembly to some factors that seem to affect present international co-operation in the marine sciences.

464. In particular, the Delegate of the Federal Republic of Germany noted that, in recent years, the consent régime applied to marine scientific research has made the planning of research cruises less simple than in the past. Member States withhold their permission to research vessels from foreign institutions to carry out studies in their respective Exclusive Economic Zones, even when these cruises have been officially announced by the IOC . . . They also prevent such vessels from entering ports of call for the purpose of changing crews, transferring equipment and victualling. This means that the possibilities for co-operation amongst States, including training and transfer of relevant technology to scientists of the developing countries, are decreasing.

465. Delegates stressed that, since many of the regional and global programmes of the Commission require concerted action by States, the IOC should endeavour to assist Member States to co-operate in this domain, through, for example, the formulation of a code of practice for marine scientific research in Exclusive Economic Zones.

- - - - -

Additional References

Promotion of the Oceanographic Components of the World Climate Research Programme (WCRP). IOC Assembly resolution XIV-1. In Report of the 14th session of the Assembly, SC/MD/86.

World Climate Research Programme. In Annual Report of the World Meteorological Organization 1987. WMO - No. 689.

World Climate Programme. Tenth World Meteorological Congress, May 1987. WMO - No. 681.

- - - - -

2

Legal Status of Ocean Data Acquisition Systems

Intergovernmental Oceanographic Commission   IOC/EC-XIX/3
Executive Council
Report of the 19th Session, March 1986   Extract

. . .

5.2.2   Drifting-Buoys
. . .

180.   The Joint WMO-IOC Preparatory Meeting reviewed relevant aspects of past, on-going and planned international drifting-buoy programmes, and listed all aspects of drifting-buoy programmes that might be amenable to co-operative actions, keeping in mind that one of its tasks was to select those aspects of drifting-buoy activities that were most likely to require being taken care of by a workable international co-operative group.

181.   In addressing the question of what form a proposed international co-ordinating mechanism should take, the Preparatory Meeting was faced with a series of partially conflicting requirements and issues:

(i)   whenever international co-operation in the field of drifting buoys has been successfully achieved, it has resulted in an increase in the data available to the major programmes of IOC and WMO, and in generating buoy deployment which would have been impossible without co-operation;

(ii)   however, some activities of the major programmes of IOC and WMO, as many national activities, are organized on programme lines and already have an element of international co-operation within them;

(iii)   opportunities are nevertheless being lost to optimize the availability and use of existing buoy data and to exploit the existing potential to generate additional data from buoys being deployed and to deploy more buoys;

(iv)   if it is therefore essential to generate a form of international and interdisciplinary co-operation in the field of drifting-buoy activities, it is clear that a centralized, executive mechanism charged with implementing drifting-buoy programmes would be costly, probably unworkable and unable to exploit the potential referred to in (iii) above;

(v)   the body to be created, while initially of minimal size, complexity and cost, should be able to evolve and to accommodate the foreseeable growth in drifting-buoy activities;

(vi)   such a body should allow Member States of IOC and Members of WMO to deal with overall co-ordination problems, and provide parentage for future groups needed for the co-operative implementation of drifting-buoy programmes at the regional level;

. . .

182. The Joint WMO-IOC Preparatory Meeting concluded that, to meet the foregoing needs, a Drifting-Buoy Co-operation Panel should be established . . . It felt that the name "consortium" had, for many countries and organizations, formal connotations which were not appropriate to the type of co-operative activities proposed.

    . . .

184. At its Thirty-seventh Session (1985), the WMO Executive Council accepted the recommendation of the Joint Preparatory Meeting to establish a Drifting-Buoy Co-operation Panel and embodied its substance in Resolution 10 (EC-XXXVII). . . .

    . . .

188. . . . The Terms of Reference for the Panel are those given in WMO Executive Council Resolution 10 . . .

    . . .

192. The Delegate of Australia . . . endorsed proposals for continuing meteorological and oceanographic drifting-buoy activities, but pointed out that there may be some degree of incompatibility between meteorological and oceanographic uses of drifting buoys.

    . . .

194. The Delegates of Brazil and Greece, while strongly supporting the proposed mechanism, expressed concern that the important question of the legal status of drifting buoys, and more generally of Ocean Data Acquisition Systems (ODAS), was still pending since the Unesco-IMO Preparatory Conference on the Legal Status of ODAS, in 1972. They felt that it was widely recognized that the use of drifting buoys has substantially increased since that time, so that the findings of the Conference in 1972 cannot be regarded as being up to date. Consequently, they proposed that the legal aspects of the question be examined.

195. Regarding the proposal of the Brazilian and Greek Delegates, **the Executive Council,** recognizing that the legal status of ODAS, including the legal aspects of drifting-buoy operations, had not been reviewed since 1972, *instructed* the Secretary to explore the question with IMO and WMO and to submit his findings to the IOC Assembly at its Fourteenth Session.

    . . .

197. **The Executive Council** *adopted* Resolution EC-XIX.7.

    . . .

Resolution EC-XIX.7

DRIFTING-BUOYS

A

The Executive Council,

    . . .

Recognizing: (i) the increased need for oceanographic and marine meteorological data to meet the objectives of major IOC and WMO programmes, in particular from the many data-sparse areas of the world ocean; (ii) the proved ability of drifting-buoys to provide such data on a routine basis; (iii) the economic benefit that may be gained through international co-ordination of drifting-buoy activities; and (iv) the desirability of providing an appropriate joint IOC-WMO framework for working out this co-ordination;

. . .

Accepts the invitation of WMO to co-sponsor the Drifting-Buoy Co-operation Panel, with the participation of interested Member States of IOC and Members of WMO;

Endorses the Terms of Reference given in Annex 1 to this Resolution;

. . .

B

. . .

Recognizing that the legal aspects related to drifting buoys have not been reviewed since 1972;

Instructs the Secretary to explore the matter, in consultation with IMO and WMO, and to submit his findings to the Assembly at its Fourteenth Session.

Annex 1 to Resolution EC-XIX.7

TERMS OF REFERENCE FOR THE DRIFTING-BUOY CO-OPERATION PANEL

The Drifting-Buoy Co-operation Panel shall:

(i) Consider the expressed needs of the international meteorological and oceano-graphic communities for real-time or archival data from buoys drifting freely in the oceans and request action from its members, technical co-ordinator or action groups to meet these needs;

(ii) Co-ordinate activity on existing programmes so as to optimize the provision and timely receipt of good quality data from them;

(iii) Propose, organize and implement, through the co-ordination of national con-tributions, the expansion of existing programmes or the creation of new ones to supply such data;

(iv) Encourage the initiation of national contributions to drifting-buoy programmes from countries which do not make them;

(v) Promote the insertion of all available and appropriate drifting-buoy data into the Global Telecommunication System;

(vi) Promote the exchange of information on drifting-buoy activities and encourage the development and transfer of appropriate technology;

(vii) Ensure that other bodies actively involved in drifting-buoy use are informed of the workings of the Panel and encourage, as appropriate, their participation in the Panel deliberations;

. . .

(ix) Submit annually to the Executive Councils of the WMO and the IOC a report which shall include summaries of the existing and planned drifting-buoy deployments and data flow.

. . .

- - - - -

Intergovernmental Oceanographic Commission   SC/MD/86
Report of the 14th Session of the Assembly, 1987   Extract

6.2.2   Drifting-Buoy Requirements

. . .

276.   The Executive Council had also instructed (Resolution EC-XIX.7) the Secretary to explore the legal aspects of the operation of drifting-buoy and other Ocean Data Acquisition Systems (ODAS), in consultation with IMO and WMO. As a result of the consultation, . . . it was agreed that a first step would be to make a compilation of existing rules and regulations and other related material. . . .

277.   Some Delegates expressed their concern that action undertaken by the Secretariat pursuant to Resolution EC-XIX.7 was going slowly as far as the legal status of drifting buoys was concerned. They emphasized that this question was of utmost importance in that it addressed matters such as the ownership of the buoys and of the data, drifting-buoy passage in waters under national jurisdiction, liability, responsibility, respect of compulsory security measures with regard to navigation safety, transfer of technology, etc. Countries were already facing such problems which had to be looked into.

278.   Other Delegates stressed that, notwithstanding the importance of legal matters to the operation of drifting buoys, IOC had to take into consideration its limited budget and staffing. Legal problems were highly complex and specialized and would probably be better handled by other organizations such as IMO, with the support of, and input from, the Commission. The latter should mainly focus its efforts on scientific and technical questions.

279.   The Delegate of Brazil recalled that the Executive Council, at its Nineteenth Session, had instructed the Secretary to explore the legal aspects related to drifting buoys and to submit his findings to the Assembly at the present Session. He noted that the Secretary has initiated consultations on the matter with IMO and WMO, but that no conclusive work has been done, and believed that this slow progress was a matter of concern. . . . He believed that the legal implications of the use of such buoys should have already been clarified; for example, responsibilities related to potential damage caused by, or to, the buoys must be thoroughly discussed on the basis of competent advice, so that the Commission's future involvement is clear. The question of access to drifting-buoy data must be clearly defined, especially for those countries to which the data are directly relevant; the quality and completeness of the data to be transmitted to countries concerned must be assured. Also, the use of buoys in jurisdictional waters must be subject to the prior consent of the coastal States, even if the nature of drifting-buoy operations presents difficulties in this respect. The Delegate of Brazil also called for a clear definition of how the technology for manufacturing and deploying drifting buoys should be transferred, so that international co-operation in this field could effectively be enhanced. He also believed that the Commission should examine the allocation of resources to the management and co-ordination of the drifting-buoy programme . . .

. . .

281.   **The Assembly** *agreed* that the legal question relating to drifting buoys was important to Member States and therefore should be given the desired attention within the Commission's

programme of work; it *instructed* the Secretary to proceed step by step in this matter. It *therefore endorsed* the actions already initiated (i.e., that all documentation dealing with the subject should be brought together and a compilation of existing legal material covering also the relevant technical aspects, such as identification markings, prepared for further consideration by Member States). It *stressed* in addition that technical aspects of the use of meteorological and oceanographic drifting buoys were closely linked with the legal aspects thereof. Therefore, there should be close collaboration in this undertaking between IOC, WMO and IMO, the latter playing a key role in dealing with legal aspects.

282. **The Assembly** *reaffirmed* its support for participation in the major drifting-buoy programmes being developed, such as the programme relating to the Southern Ocean. **It** *urged* Member States to make sure that buoy deployers make their data freely accessible by exchanging them in the agreed code forms over the Global Telecommunication System (GTS) of WMO. . . . It *urged* Member States already involved in the development of drifting-buoy technology and deployment to assist other interested countries in developing their own drifting-buoy programmes through appropriate technology transfer, if possible by making use of appropriate existing mechanisms such as the Drifting-Buoy Co-operation Panel.

   . . .

- - - - -

Additional References

Safety Provisions of Ocean Data Acquisition Systems, Aids and Devices (ODAS). UNESCO/IMO 1972.

Third session of the Drifting-Buoy Co-operation Panel, October 1987. Summary Report. IOC/WMO doc.DBCP-III/3.

- - - - -

INDEX

(Text of treaties, conventions and resolutions, etc. is italicized.)